Springer Proceedings in Business and Economics

More information about this series at http://www.springer.com/series/11960

David Procházka
Editor

New Trends in Finance and Accounting

Proceedings of the 17th Annual Conference on Finance and Accounting

 Springer

Editor
David Procházka
Faculty of Finance and Accounting
University of Economics
Prague
Czech Republic

ISSN 2198-7246   ISSN 2198-7254   (electronic)
Springer Proceedings in Business and Economics
ISBN 978-3-319-49558-3   ISBN 978-3-319-49559-0   (eBook)
DOI 10.1007/978-3-319-49559-0

Library of Congress Control Number: 2016958716

This Springer imprint is published by Springer Nature
The registered company is Springer International Publishing AG
The registered company address is: Gewerbestrasse 11, 6330 Cham, Switzerland

Contents

Chapter 1
The Euro Marriage

Aleš Michl

Abstract Is a monetary union advantageous? This analysis proposes an approach to the issue from the vantage point of a small open economy, namely the Czech Republic. Is it sensible for the Czech economy to participate in a monetary union like the EMU? What criteria can we apply to find out? To assess the advantages of joining a monetary union, it is recommended to analyse, instead of the Maastricht criteria, five new criteria that reflect the change in the competitiveness of a country. (1) How do import prices respond to a weaker exchange rate? (2) How do export prices respond to a weaker exchange rate? (3) How does domestic inflation respond to a weaker exchange rate? (4) How do wage costs in firms respond to a weaker exchange rate? (5) How do GDP and employment respond to a weaker exchange rate? Only when a weakening or devaluation of the currency is not beneficial to competitiveness, only then should a country with small open economy consider an entry into a monetary union (like the EMU).

Keywords Real effective exchange rate · Exchange rate · Balancing mechanism · EMU entry criteria · Productivity · Competitiveness · Export · Monetary policy

1.1 Introduction

The sovereign debt crisis inside the European Monetary Union (EMU) as well as competitiveness problems of some EMU members made the members and non-members of the club address one question: Is a monetary union (per se) advantageous? This analysis proposes an approach to the issue from the vantage point of a small open economy—namely the Czech Republic. Is it sensible for the Czech economy to participate in a monetary union like the EMU? What criteria can we apply to find out? To assess the advantages of joining a monetary union, it is

A. Michl (✉)
Department of Monetary Economics, University of Economics,
Prague, Nam. W. Churchilla 4, 130 67 Prague, Czech Republic
e-mail: ales.michl@gmail.com

© Springer International Publishing AG 2017
D. Procházka (ed.), *New Trends in Finance and Accounting*,
Springer Proceedings in Business and Economics,
DOI 10.1007/978-3-319-49559-0_1

recommended to analyse, instead of the Maastricht criteria, five new criteria that reflect the change in the competitiveness of a country.

This analysis starts from the premise that the aim of an economic policymaker should be an internationally competitive (i.e. prosperous) economy. An economic policymaker can only consider entering a monetary union if it boosts the competitiveness of its home country. Now there is price and non-price competition. Firms can compete on international markets with the price of a given quality—let us call this price competition. Or, the authorities can offer them better institutional conditions than elsewhere (e.g. watertight laws, transparent public procurement and smart regulation)—let us call this non-price competition. This analysis addresses the issue of price competition. To those interested in non-price competition, it is recommendable to study, for example, a report from the National Economic Council of the Czech Republic (NERV 2011).

The economic theory of price competition and the theory of the real exchange rate and the effects of currency devaluation on the trade balance of a country have been developed to the greatest extent by Marshall (1923), Lerner (1944), Robinson (1947), Polak and Chang (1950) and Machlup (1955). Some of the empirical case studies on the competitiveness of China or the USA were published recently by Frankel (2004) and Roubini (2010). Concerning European countries, the theory of the real exchange rate and its practical application was developed in the Czech Republic by Capek (1998), Frait and Komarek (1999) and Mandel and Tomsik (2003). The issue in the context of foreign trade of a country emerging from socialism was addressed by Kornai (1992), who had a first-hand experience in Hungary. In Poland, after the year 1989, the Balcerowicz Plan (1997) called for more intense competition. The discourse in Czechoslovakia around the year 1990 was reflected inter alia by Mejstrik (1989) and Klaus (2006). The argumentation of the application to the real economy of Central Europe after the economic recession in 2007–2009 has been summarised by Havlik (2010) and Zamecnik (2010).

1.2 Broad Definition of Price Competition

Price competition of the domestic economy against other countries is measured in this analysis with the real effective exchange rate (REER). Further measurement is possible with the Lafay Index (Lafay 1992). Krugman's specialisation paradigm (Krugman 1991) can be also used, as well as Balassa's revealed comparative advantage (Balassa 1965).

If

'REER' is the index of real effective exchange rate in time t.

'I_{ER}' is the base index of the domestic currency to currency i-th business associate in time t,

'P_{it}' is the ratio between the base index of costs of i-th business associate in time t and the base index of costs of the Czech Republic in time t, where the base year is the same as the base year in the calculation of I_{ER},

'w_i' is the weight of the currency i-th business associate defined according to the shares of the biggest business associates in foreign trade turnover.

Then,

$$\mathrm{REER}_t = 100 \prod_{i=1}^{n} \left(\frac{I_{\mathrm{ER},it}}{P_{it}} \right)^{w_i} \tag{1.1}$$

In this analysis, an indirect quotation of the exchange rate is used. An increase in the index above 100 indicates a real appreciation of the exchange rate against the base period; a fall in the index below 100 means a real depreciation.

1.3   Possibilities and Limitations on Calculating REERs

To have an accurate analysis, it is necessary to discuss the possibilities and limitations on the calculation of REER:

- Possibilities and limitations on the calculation of numerator I_{ER}: The numerator poses no problem. The currencies being analysed are publicly tradable, and their nominal rates can be obtained from databanks such as Bloomberg or Reuters.
- Possibilities and limitations on the calculation of denominator P_{it}: The first problem may be the definition of the costs in the economy which deflate the exchange rate index (numerator).

Supposing we approximate inflation with P_{it}, that is $P_{it} = I_{\mathrm{CPI},it}$, where $I_{\mathrm{CPI},it}$ would be defined as the ratio between the base consumer inflation index of the i-th business associate in time t and the base consumer inflation index of the Czech Republic in time t, then REER could be defined as follows:

$$\mathrm{REER}_t = 100 \prod_{i=1}^{n} \left(\frac{I_{\mathrm{ER},it}}{I_{\mathrm{CPI},it}} \right)^{w_i} \tag{1.2}$$

However, domestic inflation may not reflect the exporter's labour costs in the international competition for a market share. Also, in a given state, there may be trade unions with different powers, and this may decrease/increase the wage indexation ratio to consumer inflation.

Another possibility is to deflate the exchange rate index of industrial enterprise prices—producer price index, i.e. $P_{it} = I_{\mathrm{PPI},it}$, where $I_{\mathrm{PPI},it}$ is defined as the ratio between the base index of industrialists' prices of i-th business associate in time t and the base index of Czech industrial enterprise prices in time t, then

$$\mathrm{REER}_t = 100 \prod_{i=1}^{n} \left(\frac{I_{\mathrm{ER},it}}{I_{\mathrm{PPI},it}} \right)^{w_i} \tag{1.3}$$

The industrialists' prices can better reflect the costs in the economy—as viewed through the eyes of industrialists and exporters. However, a producer price index (PPI) includes the prices of imported raw materials which very much influence the result. There is also the objection that industrial enterprise prices exclude labour costs. Capek (1998) recommends the use of a GDP deflator capturing the pricing dynamic of the final use in the economy.

If $P_{it} = I_{D,it}$ where $I_{D,it}$ is defined as the ratio between the base index GDP deflator of the i-th business associate in time t and the deflator of the Czech GDP in time t, thus

$$REER_t = 100 \prod_{i=1}^{n} \left(\frac{I_{ER,it}}{I_{D,it}} \right)^{w_i} \qquad (1.4)$$

No accurate data for industry are available for this deflator: the price competitiveness of the entire economy could be analysed but not that of industry, which this analysis, as we will see later, requires.

Mandel and Tomsik (2003) focused on industrial enterprises in their broad definition of exporters' costs. Industrial costs C can be defined as follows:

$$C = w_w \times W_{EX} + w_D \times P_D + (1 - w_w - w_D) \times I_{ER} \times P_{F,IM} \qquad (1.5)$$

where

w_w is the weight of the ratio between wages and costs;

W_{EX} are exporters' wage;

w_D is the weight of the ratio between domestic inputs and costs (excluding wages);

P_D is the price index of domestic inputs (excluding wages); and

$P_{F,IM}$ is the price index of imported inputs.

REER is then $P_{it} = I_C$ where I_C is defined as the ratio between the base cost index in industry of the i-th business associate in time t and the costs in industry in time t, then

$$REER_t = 100 \prod_{i=1}^{n} \left(\frac{I_{ER,it}}{I_{C,it}} \right)^{w_i} \qquad (1.6)$$

Another question is: What values would the weights w_w and w_D have in the formula for industrial enterprises' costs C? The OECD monitors advanced countries' multifactor productivity of enterprises in the economy. Thus, we can calculate, for example, that labour costs accounted for 76.1% of the total costs in Germany in 2009, while they amounted to 80% in Austria—the highest percentage. For this reason, a credible REER calculation should include labour costs and this weight should be the greatest, most substantial. The formula could be therefore simplified as follows:

$$REER_t = 100 \prod_{i=1}^{n} \left(\frac{I_{ER,it}}{I_{W,EX,it}} \right)^{w_i} \tag{1.7}$$

where

$I_{W, EX,it}$ is the ratio between the wage costs of the i-th business associate in time t and the base index of wage costs in the home country in time t. However, this indicator would now be oversimplified and static. Wages must be always compared with labour productivity—it is necessary to analyse whether wage rises are justified in terms of labour productivity. Labour costs and labour productivity are best expressed with unit labour costs (ULC).

$$P_{it} = \frac{ULC_{it}}{ULC_{CZt}} = I_{ULC,it} \tag{1.8}$$

Then,

$$REER_t = 100 \prod_{i=1}^{n} \left(\frac{I_{ER,it}}{I_{ULC,it}} \right)^{w_i} \tag{1.9}$$

where ULC are defined as

$$ULC_{it} = \frac{LC_{it}}{LP_{it}} \tag{1.10}$$

where LC is labour costs, and LP is labour productivity.

LC is customarily reported by Eurostat as 'Indicator that covers wages and salaries and employers' social security contributions plus taxes paid minus subsidies received by the employer'. With regard to LP, there are two main calculation methods:

(a) Productivity of the national economy: In the first case, I monitor labour costs for the whole economy. They are the ratio between costs per employee and labour productivity. As I gauge productivity as GDP per employee (EMP),

$$LP_{it} = \frac{GDP_{it}}{EMP_{it}} \tag{1.11}$$

Therefore,

$$ULC_{it} = \frac{LC_{it}}{GDP_{it}/EMP_{it}} \tag{1.12}$$

(b) Industrial productivity: since the Czech Republic is an industrialised country, it is fitting to monitor not only the productivity of the national economy, but also the specific productivity of the industrial sector.

$$\mathrm{IND\,LP}_{it} = \frac{\mathrm{IND\,S}_{it}}{\mathrm{EMP}_{it}} \tag{1.13}$$

where
IND stands for industry;
IND S stands for industrial revenues; and
EMP stands for employment in the economy.

We thus define REER for the entire economy and for the industrial sector (IND REER)—for accuracy, specifically for the Czech Republic (CZ),

$$\begin{aligned}
\mathrm{REER}_t &= 100 \prod_{i=1}^{n} \left(\frac{I_{\mathrm{ER},it}}{P_{it}}\right)^{w_i} = 100 \prod_{i=1}^{n} \left(\frac{I_{\mathrm{ER},it}}{I_{\mathrm{ULC},it}}\right)^{w_i} = 100 \prod_{i=1}^{n} \left(\frac{I_{\mathrm{ER},it}}{\mathrm{ULC}_{it}/\mathrm{ULC}_{\mathrm{CZ}t}}\right)^{w_i} \\
&= 100 \prod_{i=1}^{n} \left(\frac{I_{\mathrm{ER},it}}{(\mathrm{LC}_{it}/\mathrm{LP}_{it})/(\mathrm{LC}_{\mathrm{CZ}t}/\mathrm{LP}_{\mathrm{CZ}t})}\right)^{w_i} \\
&= 100 \prod_{i=1}^{n} \left(\frac{I_{\mathrm{ER},it}}{[\mathrm{LC}_{it}/(\mathrm{GDP}_{it}/\mathrm{EMP}_{it})]/[\mathrm{LC}_{\mathrm{CZ}t}/(\mathrm{GDP}_{\mathrm{CZ}t}/\mathrm{EMP}_{\mathrm{CZ}t})]}\right)^{w_i}
\end{aligned} \tag{1.14}$$

$$\begin{aligned}
\mathrm{IND\,REER}_t &= 100 \prod_{i=1}^{n} \left(\frac{I_{\mathrm{ER},it}}{\mathrm{IND\,P}_{it}}\right)^{w_i} = 100 \prod_{i=1}^{n} \left(\frac{I_{\mathrm{ER},it}}{\mathrm{IND\,I}_{\mathrm{ULC},it}}\right)^{w_i} \\
&= 100 \prod_{i=1}^{n} \left(\frac{I_{\mathrm{ER},it}}{\mathrm{IND\,ULC}_{it}/\mathrm{IND\,ULC}_{\mathrm{CZ}t}}\right)^{w_i} \\
&= 100 \prod_{i=1}^{n} \left(\frac{I_{\mathrm{ER},it}}{(\mathrm{IND\,LC}_{it}/\mathrm{IND\,LP}_{it})/(\mathrm{IND\,LC}_{\mathrm{CZ}t}/\mathrm{IND\,LP}_{\mathrm{CZ}t})}\right)^{w_i} \\
&= 100 \prod_{i=1}^{n} \left(\frac{I_{\mathrm{ER},it}}{[\mathrm{IND\,LC}_{it}/(\mathrm{IND\,SALES}_{it}/\mathrm{IND\,EMP}_{it})]/[\mathrm{IND\,LC}_{\mathrm{CZ}t}/(\mathrm{IND\,SALES}_{\mathrm{CZ}t}/\mathrm{IND\,EMP}_{\mathrm{CZ}t})]}\right)^{w_i}
\end{aligned} \tag{1.15}$$

(c) Possibilities and limitations on the calculation of exponent w_i: now follows a discussion about the last unknown quantity in the calculation of REER—the exponent or weight. The weight has to be deduced from the shares of the individual countries in the total foreign trade turnover. Let use the same weights as those calculated by the Czech National Bank (CNB). The CNB uses the weights derived from the share in the trade turnover of the Czech Republic. The weights can be again defined for the economy as a whole and specifically for industry.[1]

An objection may be raised even to this approach. A case in point is the Czech Republic. The heaviest weight is that of the EMU. But is the Czech Republic really much more dependent on Germany than it is on China? The answer can be found in the

---

[1]For details, see www.cnb.cz/docs/ARADY/MET_LIST/rekulc_en.pdf.

database of the Czech Statistical Office which records exactly what the country exports to Germany: In 2010, parts and accessories for motor vehicles were in first place. Cars ranked only second on the list; third, insulated wires, cables and other conductors of electricity; fourth, computers and data processing equipment displays and keyboards. In fifth place, television sets. At first sight, it is clear that one-third of Czech exports go to Germany. If all the parts, wires, cables, displays and seats were added up, their value would be twice as much as cars are in Czech exports to Germany in 2010. The principal Czech export goods are semi-finished products. The parts are assembled in Germany, labelled 'Made in Germany' and shipped to the USA or China. Therefore, the Czech Republic is dependent on China and USA more than we think—there is the source of demand for Germany and by extension, Czech exports.

However, finding a weighting model, which would reflect the differences in the commodity structure, shares of semi-finished products in the total exports or differences in pricing flexibilities, complicates the REER calculation considerably. One possibility could be the use of MERM—Multilateral Exchange Rate Model. Boughton (2001) writes that the MERM model idea was to derive equilibrium relationships between exchange rates and trade balances by reference to highly disaggregated production functions. Real exchange rate could be derived as a weighted average of bilateral weights, not by the traditional arithmetic based on the value of bilateral trade with each country, but by estimating the elasticity of trade in specific categories of goods to changes in exchange rates. However, there were practical difficulties in the acquisition and calculation of reliable data, Boughton stresses.

1.4   Price Competition in the Economy of the Czech Republic

As data show (Fig. 1.1) in the entire Czech economy, the real exchange rate has risen significantly. The real exchange rate deflated by ULC has risen from 66 in 1998 to 126 in September 2011 (2005 = 100). Why has the real exchange rate appreciated that much in the Czech Republic? The Czech economy as a whole was facing a combination of growth in labour costs and nominal strengthening of the exchange rate of the Czech currency (CZK) against the EUR. The nominal strengthening of the CZK and the wage rises resulted in a rise in the standard of living of citizens of the Czech Republic. On the other hand, this strengthens the motivation of a cost-oriented firm to move production to another state. This entails the risk of higher unemployment with a resulting fall in the standard of living.

However, the loss of competitiveness need not have been as great as the preceding figures show. The key problem in the approach to measuring competitiveness through the real exchange rate is a convergence trend in the economy caused by an increase in labour productivity and technical and utilitarian improvements to products. Mathematics does not take this into account. There is then a reverse causality. It appreciates the real exchange rate thanks to an increase in competitiveness. It

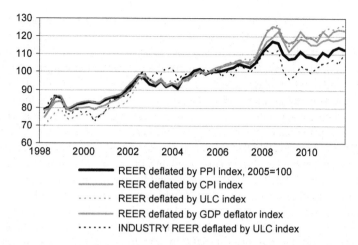

Fig. 1.1 Different models for the construction of the real exchange rate of the Czech Republic. *Source* Czech National Bank. *Note* The author works with an indirect quotation of the exchange rate. An increase in the index above 100 indicates a real appreciation of the exchange rate against the base period. A fall in the index below 100 means a real depreciation

appreciates the real exchange rate because an increase in exports builds up pressures for a nominal appreciation of the currency. A sign of the success of an economy despite real appreciation is then a concurrent improvement to foreign exchange rates. It is therefore necessary to differentiate between a natural convergence trend in the appreciation of the exchange rate and an actual loss of competitiveness. In this analysis, the author advances the thesis that loss of competitiveness is caused by two types of appreciation bubbles in the real exchange rate:

(a) Appreciation bubble in the nominal rate of the crown: Mandel and Tomsik (2003) write that it is necessary to first determine a balanced appreciation trend of the real exchange rate and then monitor divergences from the trend—the bubble. A balanced real exchange rate is an exchange rate, which corresponds to the economy in a state of internal and external equilibrium. Predictions of a balanced real appreciation are, according to Bruha et al. (2010), values around 1.3%. According to a study carried out by Cihak and Holub, they range from 1.6–2.4% (model presented in Cihak and Holub 2005—the outputs are in 'Analysis of economic harmonisation of the Czech Republic and the Eurozone', published by the Czech National Bank in 2008). For more details on the issue of an appreciation bubble in the nominal exchange rate, see also Fig. 1.2.

(b) Increases in labour costs surpassing productivity: a second type of appreciation bubble in the real exchange rate is the increase in labour costs surpassing productivity. The Czech Republic will be competitive when increases in labour costs no longer surpass productivity. This ratio covers unit labour costs as defined above. Their increase signals loss of pricing competitiveness. Labour costs are analysed below.

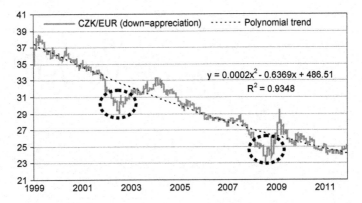

Fig. 1.2 Appreciation bubble in the nominal exchange rate of the Czech Crown (CZK) against the EUR. *Source* Bloomberg. *Note* Downward direction = nominal appreciation

1.5 Price Competitiveness of the Czech Industry

Until now, the economy has been analysed as a whole. The following analysis divides the economy by sectors. Both Figs. 1.1 and 1.3 show that the manufacturing industry in the Czech Republic did not become less competitive between 2007 and 2011. During the recession times, enterprises kept down costs and demanded labour productivity. As the economy as a whole was losing competitiveness, the real exchange rate of the Czech economy rose, and at the same time, the real exchange rate was stagnant in industry, and this points to the non-productive public sphere and services. Graph 3 in the Appendix shows the unit labour costs, the ratio between expenditure in labour and the resulting product, and the difference between the competitiveness of the manufacturing industry and the

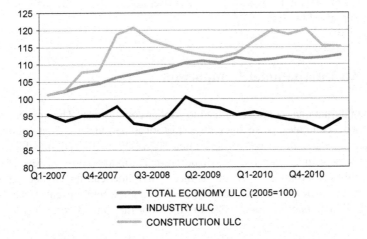

Fig. 1.3 Unit labour costs in by sectors in the Czech Republic (year 2005 = 100). *Source* OECD

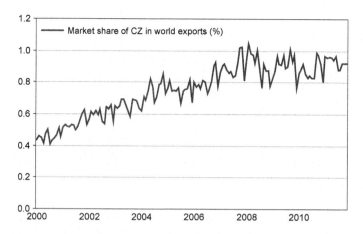

Fig. 1.4 Market share of the Czech Republic in world exports (industry, %). *Source* IMF, Bloomberg

other sectors. The more a sector is exposed to international competition, the more it reacts to world recession (has had to react to the recession). By contrast, the public sphere or, for example, the construction industries, do not have to fight off international competition. If we look at the construction industry, we will see that it did not curb costs as much as the manufacturing industry did. Inadequate competition, local operation and connection to the state finance do not force you to be productive. Politicians have to drive a hard bargain in these sectors and press for more labour productivity. These are sectors that lower our competitiveness (for more details, see Zamecnik 2010).

However, Graph 4 in the Appendix clearly shows, ex ante, that when the competitiveness of the economy as a whole was falling according to the real exchange rate, export-oriented industrial enterprises managed, thanks to productivity, to react to the recession. The Czech Republic only lost a small share in the global exports (Fig. 1.4).

1.6 An International Comparison

Will an international comparison lead to similar conclusions? The greatest debts of developed economies arose over three historical periods: the first followed the Napoleonic wars, the second came after World War II—and the third arrived yesterday is with us today and will be around tomorrow too. A few states can handle this situation. Certainly, this is merely hypothetical, for anyone can still go bankrupt. America now has a public debt somewhere around 100% of its GDP. Eurozone debt is around 88% of GDP. For the sake of comparison, China's public debt is at 17%, thanks to the strength of its economy, while in Brazil and India, it is at 66%, and in Russia at 11%.

At first sight, the problems that Greece ran into in 2009–2011 were caused by debts. But how about Ireland which also hovered on the brink of bankruptcy? Until then, Ireland had been cited as an example of 'sound financial management' (Ireland's government debt was 24.9% of GDP in 2007 according to Eurostat). Incidentally, fiscal discipline is for this reason a condition, which is necessary but not sufficient for greater competitiveness.

A more detailed analysis of unit labour costs in the manufacturing industry (thanks to international competition, this is a productive sector) and in the construction industry (an example of non-productive sector) during the period of recession time presents a paradox: Although the Irish economy as a whole was on the edge of bankruptcy, Irish industrial enterprises pushed for a growth in productivity even harder than the Germans (thanks to imports of cheap labour too). The problem was not therefore in the Irish export sector exposed to international competition, but in the bubble in the property market supported by loans from banks owned predominantly by the Irish. For more details, see Appendix Chart 5.

In solving each specific debt problem, one must distinguish between the problems of solvency and the problems of liquidity. When someone has a liquidity problem, he needs a quick loan to tide him over—in the case of a country, loans keep the economy running. Greece, however, is insolvent. Having the country begin to generate its own revenues—simply to earn the money to pay those debts must solve the problem of insolvency.

1.7 Theory and Recommendations for Economic Policymakers

The paradox in the evolution of unit wage costs in view of international competition in different sectors is a challenge for economic policy. It is advisable to concentrate on unbalanced growth in labour productivity. In theory, this can be inferred from the Balassa–Samuelson Theorem or the Baumol Model. The economy is divided into a productive and a non-productive sector. In the public sphere and services, such as public institutions, state administration, as well as private services, such as restaurants, construction industry or arts, there is as a rule slower labour productivity. By contrast, productivity is higher in industry because firms face direct international competition, there are economies of scale and more use of machines and technologies (although the state can also employ technologies such as e-government).

An improvement in labour productivity is usually followed in the productive sector by an increase in the hourly rate. In this case, unit labour costs will remain constant. But when there are pay rises in the more productive sector, the less performing sector wants to follow suit. This is when what is called in economic terminology wage contagion may occur, when one trade union demands a pay rise at the expense of the others without offering higher productivity or better services. This is a theoretical explanation why the productive sector is able to keep down unit wage costs, whereas they increase in the non-productive sector. Finally, wages are rising and then building up inflation pressures. However, if productivity increases in the public sector less than in the other sectors and if salaries of employees in the public sector are in line with the salaries in other economic sectors, this has a far-reaching consequence for the economic policy: Public expenditure is on the increase. The strength of an economic policy with the ambition to boost competitiveness and at the same time to balance the public budgets is in the prevention of wage contagion, pressing for the highest possible labour productivity in the public sphere and services.

1.8 A Proposal for Rethinking the EMU Entry Criteria

Arguments concerning the advantages/disadvantages of the adoption of a common currency should not be based on the Maastricht criteria but on the philosophy of the real effective exchange rate. The Maastricht criteria do not reflect the competitiveness of a country. Rather, I suggest we test the impacts of the reinforcement of a weaker exchange rate of the national currency on the economy. Only when the exchange rate balancing process of the balance of payments ceases to bear fruit can we consider a monetary union with our business associates. Otherwise let us keep the national currency.

The philosophy of the formula is that export will be profitable after devaluation when earning exceed costs.

$$\text{IND } S > \text{IND } C \tag{1.16}$$

if

$$\text{IND } S = P_{F,EX} \times I_{ER} \tag{1.17}$$

where P_F is the index of foreign prices of exported industrial goods.

We will continue using the Mandel–Tomsik formula (2003). If an exporter is to make profit, it is necessary

$$P_{F,EX} \times I_{ER} > w_w \times W_{EX} + w_D \times P_D + (1 - w_w - w_D) \times I_{ER} \times P_{F,IM} \tag{1.18}$$

A model-testing situation could be: How does the economy react to weakening of the exchange rate I_{ER}? Will weakening of the currency help the economy as a whole or not?

Based on the previous arguments, five criteria can be derived the author recommends to study when thinking about fixing an exchange rate (like in the EMU):

(1) How do import prices $P_{F,IM}$ respond to a weakening of the exchange rate I_{ER}? If the exchange rate weakens, this will help exports, at first sight. The question is, however, whether this will not cause trouble, retrospectively, with dearer imports of raw materials or components (… and how will the USD/CZK rate respond? In imports, we have a good deal of commodities denominated in US dollars).

(2) How do export prices $P_{F,EX}$ respond to a weakening of the exchange rate I_{ER}? A weakening of the currency should allow exporters to cut prices and win over competitors' customers. Will this happen to Czech exports or not? What is the quality of our exports (the so-called unit value ratio), what is our position in respect of the customers? What is the pricing elasticity of exports (this was already addressed by Mejstrik 1989)?

(3) How does domestic inflation P_D respond to a weakening of the exchange rate I_{ER}? What if a weakening of the currency means that the total inflation will rise in the national economy as a result of more expensive imported goods? Although a weaker exchange rate will help exports but the costs will suffer, as a result, for example, of a rise in the cost of electricity or rents, which are usually linked to inflation.

(4) How do wage costs W_{EX} in firms respond to a weakening of the exchange rate I_{ER}? Won't the trade unions demand large pay rises if they recognise inflation?

(5) How do GDP and employment respond to a weakening of the exchange rate I_{ER}?

To sum up, what predominates and will most influence the real GDP and employment with a weakening exchange rate in a short and medium term—more advantageous exports or higher inflation? This amount to how big a role is played in the country by the exchange rate balancing mechanism balance of payments. The country should join the monetary union when the role of the exchange rate mechanism becomes negligible or in the spirit of the criteria when weakening of the currency is no longer an advantage (for instance for the Czech exports). All in all, the author believes that it is advisable to replace the Maastricht criteria with five new criteria, which fit better a small open economy and better realise the necessity of competitiveness for the domestic industry.

1.9 Conclusion

This analysis has shown that appreciation bubbles of the real exchange rate cause a loss of pricing competitiveness in an economy like the Czech Republic. There may be two types of these:

(a) Appreciation bubbles of the nominal rate of the Czech currency; and
(b) Growth in labour costs surpassing growth in productivity.

The best defence of a politician against the two variants is to focus on unbalanced growth in labour productivity. A policymaker should differentiate between productive sectors facing international competition (e.g. the manufacturing industry) and less-productive sectors (public services, the construction sector). Industry sectors and firms facing international competition should be allowed by the government to get on with their work. In the productive sectors of the economy, pressures on labour productivity are not brought to bear by an official but by international competition. On the contrary, the government should press for the highest labour productivity in the public sphere and services to prevent wage contagion. These are the reasons why the Czech Republic loses competitiveness (and this is also the way to a balanced state budget). The author would therefore advise the government to monitor and transparently publish unit labour costs for the whole economy and the different sectors. Their growth may signal the government a loss of price/cost competitiveness, especially if a dwindling market share of the Czech Republic in world exports accompanies this.

Hand in hand with this, the government should focus on non-price competitiveness, i.e. institutional economics, quality of laws, transparent public procurement and smarter rather than bigger regulation, creation of conditions for spontaneous optimisation of the position of enterprises on the value chain towards higher value-added products. In order to do so and in order to assess the advantages of joining a monetary union (like the EMU), it is recommended to analyse, instead of the Maastricht criteria, five criteria which reflect the change in the competitiveness of a given country:

(1) How do import prices respond to a weaker exchange rate?
(2) How do export prices respond to a weaker exchange rate?
(3) How does domestic inflation respond to a weaker exchange rate?
(4) How do wage costs in firms respond to a weaker exchange rate? and
(5) How do GDP and employment respond to a weaker exchange rate?

Only when the exchange rate balancing mechanism ceases to bear fruit, only when a weakening/devaluation of the currency is not beneficial to competitiveness, only then can a country consider (and the Czech Republic is taken as an example here, but this refers to other countries as well) an entry into a monetary union (like the EMU). ⸺

Acknowledgments My thanks for the brainstorming and ideas go to Martin Mandel from the University of Economics in Prague and members of the National Economic Council of the Czech Republic Michal Mejstřík and Miroslav Zámečník. The responsibility for the philosophy, argumentation and the conclusions rests with the author.

References

Balassa B (1965) Trade liberalization and revealed comparative advantage. Manchester Sch Econ Soc Stud 33(2):99–123
Boughton JM (2001) Silent revolution: the international monetary fund, 1979–1989. Stationary Office Books

Bruha J, Podpiera J, Polak S (2010) The convergence dynamics of a transition economy: the case of Czech Republic. Econ Model 27(1):116–124

Capek A (1998) Realny efektivni smenny kurz: Problemy konstrukce. Politicka ekonomie 46 (5):611–631

Cihak M, Holub T (2005) Price convergence in EU accession countries: evidence from the international comparison. Economie Internationale 2(102):59–82

Frait J, Komarek L (1999) Dlouhodoby rovnovazny realny menovy kurz koruny a jeho determinanty. Working Paper No. 9, Czech National Bank

Frankel J (2004) On the Renminbi: the choice between adjustment under a fixed exchange rate and adjustment under a flexible rate. High-level seminar on foreign exchange system, Dalton, China, pp 1–26

Havlik P (2010) Unit labour costs, exchange rates and responses to the crisis in CESEE, WIIW Research Report

Klaus V (2006) Patnact let od zahajeni ekonomicke transformace. Cep. 47:2006

Kornai J (1992) Socialist economy. Princeton University Press, USA

Krugman P (1991) Increasing returns and economic geography. J Polit Econ 99(3):483–499

Lafay G (1992) The measurement of revealed comparative advantages. In: Dagenais MG, Muet P-A (eds) International trade modeling, London

Lerner AP (1944) The economics of control: principles of welfare economics. Macmillan, New York

Machlup F (1955) Relative prices and aggregate spending in the analysis of devaluation. Am Econ Rev 45(3):255–278

Mandel M, Tomsik V (2003) Monetarni ekonomie v male otevrene ekonomice, Management Press

Marshall A (1923) Money, credit & commerce. Macmillan, London, GB

Mejstrik M (1989) Innovation as a quality change: effects of export and export subsidy. Paper presented at 4th annual congress of EEA in Augsburg, 2–4 Sept 1989

NERV (2011) Souhrnna zprava podskupin Narodni ekonomicke rady vlady pro, Prague

Polak JJ, Chang TC (1950) Effect of Exchange Depreciation on a Country's Export Price Level. Int Monetary Fund Staff Pap 1:49–70. http://dx.doi.org/10.2307/3866178

Robinson J (1947) Beggar-My-Neighbour Remediem for unemployment. Essays on the theory of employment. Blackwell, Oxford

Roubini N (2010) Crisis economics: a crash course in the future of finance. Penguin Press HC

Zamecnik M (2010) Kdyz mzdy ujizdeji produktivite, Euro, 13/12

Chapter 2
Does Euro Introduction Ensure Lower Vulnerability of the New Euro Area Members to the External Shocks? The Case of the Central and Eastern European Countries

Vilma Deltuvaitė

Abstract A very intense euro area enlargement during the last two decades rises the question about the impact of the euro introduction on vulnerability of the new euro area members [especially Central and Eastern European Countries (CEECs)] to the external shocks. Since 2007, five CEECs joined the euro area and the euro adoption reduced sovereign bond interest rates, credit default swap (CDS) prices of the new euro area members due to a decrease in foreign exchange risk, and positively affected the CEECs' credit ratings. However, the question about lower vulnerability of the new euro area members to the external shocks is still open. The objective of this study was to assess the impact of euro introduction on vulnerability of the new euro area members to the external shocks. The empirical results show that the announcement of positive convergence report and the euro introduction in the new euro area members did not manifest itself automatically in the short term and last into the long term (except in Latvia and Lithuania). This reaction of the financial market participants could be explained by the fact that most of the new euro area members (Slovenia, Cyprus, Malta, and Slovakia) introduced euro in 2007–2009 during the global financial crisis. The results of generalized impulse response analysis confirm that the new euro area members are still very sensitive to shocks in other CEECs sovereign bond markets. However, new euro area members became less sensitive to the external shocks after the introduction of euro.

Keywords Euro introduction · Euro area · CEECs · Sovereign bond markets

V. Deltuvaitė (✉)
Finance Department, Kaunas University of Technology,
K. Donelaicio g. 73, 44249 Kaunas, Lithuania
e-mail: vilma.deltuvaite@ktu.lt

© Springer International Publishing AG 2017
D. Procházka (ed.), *New Trends in Finance and Accounting*,
Springer Proceedings in Business and Economics,
DOI 10.1007/978-3-319-49559-0_2

2.1 Introduction

Economic and monetary union (EMU) represents a major step in the integration of European Union (EU) economies involving the coordination of fiscal and economic policies as well as a common monetary policy. Despite the fact that all EU Member States are part of EMU and coordinate their economic policy making to support the economic aims of the EU, however, a number of EU Member States have taken a step monetary integration further by replacing their national currencies with the single currency. When the euro was first introduced in 1999, the euro area was made up of 11 of the then 15 EU Member States. Greece joined the euro area in 2001, followed by Slovenia in 2007, Cyprus and Malta in 2008, Slovakia in 2009, Estonia in 2011, Latvia in 2014, and Lithuania in 2015.

The widespread use of the euro in the international financial and monetary system demonstrates its global presence. Firstly, the euro is widely used, alongside the US dollar, as an important reserve currency to hold for monetary emergencies; for example, in 2015, more than 20% of the global foreign exchange holdings were being held in euros. Secondly, the euro is also the second most actively traded currency in foreign exchange markets, and it is a counterpart in around 33% of all daily transactions, globally. Thirdly, the euro is widely used to issue government and corporate debt worldwide; for example, in 2015, the share of euro-denominated debt in the global markets was around 40%, on par with the role of the US dollar in the international debt market. Fourthly, the euro is also gaining momentum as currency used for invoicing and paying in international trade, not only between the euro area and third countries but also between third countries. Fifthly, several countries manage their currencies by linking them to the euro, which acts as an anchor or reference currency. For these reasons, today, the euro is the second most important international currency after the US dollar.

A very intense euro area enlargement during the last two decades rises the question about the impact of the euro introduction on vulnerability of the new euro area members [especially Central and Eastern European Countries (CEECs)] to the external shocks. Since 2007, five CEECs (Slovenia, Slovakia, Estonia, Latvia, and Lithuania) joined the euro area and the euro adoption reduced sovereign bond interest rates, credit default swap (CDS) prices of the new euro area members due to a decrease in foreign exchange risk, and positively affected the CEECs' credit ratings. However, the question about lower vulnerability of the new euro area members to the external shocks is still open. The objective of this study was to assess the impact of euro introduction on vulnerability of the new euro area members to the external shocks. The research object is the CEECs. The research methods are as follows: the systemic, logical, and comparative analysis of the scientific literature and statistical method—generalized impulse response (GIR) analysis.

The organization of the paper is as follows. Section 2.2 overviews the related literature. Section 2.3 describes the research methodology and data. Section 2.4 shows the research results. Section 2.5 discusses the findings and concludes.

2.2   Literature Review

The impact of the euro introduction on the new euro area members' economies can be classified into direct, which will manifest itself automatically in the short term and may also last into the long term, and indirect, which depends on various circumstances and more often manifests itself during a longer time. The direct impact of the euro introduction on the new euro area members can appear in different ways. The substitution of national currency for the euro would reduce interest rates due to a decrease in foreign exchange risk, reducing at the same time foreign exchange and accounting costs, enhancing the balance of the currency structure of the public and private sector's assets and liabilities, and expanding the possibilities for managing liquidity in the banking sector. The indirect impact of the euro adoption on the new euro area members will appear in different ways. The adoption of the euro may positively affect the countries' credit rating (which would reduce interest rates even more), encourage investment and foreign trade, and speed up the growth of the economies and the welfare of the societies.

Scientific literature provides very little evidence on the impact of the euro introduction on the new euro area members' economies. Some authors analyzed the opportunities and challenges of euro adoption in Central and Eastern Europe and carried out a quantitative assessment of the likely impact of the adoption of the euro on the national economy (Lavrač 2007, Bank of Lithuania 2013). The results of the quantitative research suggest that the positive impact of the euro would be long term and would significantly exceed the short-term costs as well as the amount of country's additional financial contributions (Bank of Lithuania 2013). In order for the country to be able to take full advantage of the benefits of being in the euro area to the best possible extent, it is necessary that the economy would effectively use the period of declining interest rates to enhance its competitiveness and that focused economic policy would ensure fiscal sustainability and macroeconomic stability (Bank of Lithuania 2013). Some authors studied the impact of membership in the EU as well as in the euro area on both economic and financial integration. The empirical results show that membership in the EU significantly lowered discount rate and expected earnings growth differentials across countries; however, the adoption of the euro was not associated with increased economic and financial integration (Bekaert et al. 2013). Some authors analyzed the impact of the euro adoption on the level of per capita GDP for a sample of 17 European countries. The empirical results show that in euro, the adoption may have raised the level of per capita GDP as well as the labor productivity by about 4%. However, the impact of the euro adoption has been smaller in countries with a high debt-to-GDP ratio (Conti 2014). Some authors revisited the issue of the appropriate domain of a currency area. The results show that the adoption of a common currency can be beneficial for the members of the monetary union (Forlati 2015). The results also show that the enlargement of the monetary union to another group of small open economies can bring about welfare gains for all countries involved (Forlati 2015). Some economists examined whether the euro introduction had a significant impact on economic integration of EMU. They found that the euro adoption has significantly increased the economic integration of EMU in terms of business cycles synchronization substantially strengthening the conclusion by Frankel and Rose (1997), i.e., a country is more likely to satisfy the criteria for entry into a currency union ex post rather than ex ante (Gächter and Riedl 2014). Some authors investigated the financial liberalization in the context of European monetary and economic integration. They found that after the implementation of financial liberalization, measures of financial openness generate a strongly positive impact on economic growth, capital accumulation, and productivity growth. They also found a positive contribution from the EU membership, while no substantial effect from the euro adoption was identified (Gehringer 2013). Some economists investigated the financial system–growth relationships in the Eurozone and non-Eurozone EU countries as well as the potential impact of the euro adoption on closer and more centralized economic, political, fiscal, and financial cooperation within Eurozone. The empirical results show that the financial sector contributes to economic growth in the Eurozone countries, while a significant negative impact of the banking sector on economic growth was observed in non-Eurozone EU countries (Georgantopoulos et al. 2015). Some economists tested the existence of a break in the macroeconomic dynamics in seven Eurozone countries and three non-Eurozone EU countries. The empirical results revealed very significant breaks for the Eurozone countries in the year of adoption of the Maastricht Treaty and euro. The empirical results also show an increase in the influence of supply shocks on the dynamics of output, unemployment, and the interest rate after the breaks for the Eurozone countries (Legrand 2014). However, some authors examined the impact of entry to the EU and the euro adoption on supply of capital for corporate financing. The empirical results suggest that following membership to EU firms increased equity financing while membership to EU eased access to equity capital. The empirical results suggest that firms also increased debt financing after the euro adoption, while this exogenous event improved access to international debt capital (Muradoğlu et al. 2014). Overall, the scientific literature provides substantial evidence on the positive impact of the euro introduction on the new euro area members' economies.

2.3   Research Methodology and Data

This empirical study focuses on the vulnerability of the sovereign bond markets of the new euro area members to the external shocks. The investigation of the impact of euro introduction on vulnerability of the new euro area members to the external shocks was examined by applying the generalized impulse response (GIR) analysis (Koop et al. 1996; Pesaran and Shin 1998). Impulse response functions measure the time profile of the effect of shocks on the expected future values of variables in a dynamic VAR system (2.1), i.e., the impulse responses outline the reaction of one sovereign bond yield spread to a shock in another (2.2 and 2.3).

$$
\begin{bmatrix} Y_{1,t} \\ Y_{2,t} \\ \vdots \\ Y_{n,t} \end{bmatrix} = \begin{bmatrix} A_{10} \\ A_{20} \\ \vdots \\ A_{n0} \end{bmatrix} + \begin{bmatrix} A_{11,k} & A_{12,k} & \cdots & A_{1n,k} \\ A_{21,k} & A_{22,k} & \cdots & A_{2n,k} \\ \vdots & \vdots & \ddots & \vdots \\ A_{n1,k} & A_{n2,k} & \cdots & A_{nn,k} \end{bmatrix} \begin{bmatrix} Y_{1,t-k} \\ Y_{2,t-k} \\ \vdots \\ Y_{n,t-k} \end{bmatrix} + \begin{bmatrix} \varepsilon_{1,t} \\ \varepsilon_{2,t} \\ \vdots \\ \varepsilon_{n,t} \end{bmatrix},
\tag{2.1}
$$

$$
\varepsilon_{i,t} \sim \mathrm{WN}(0, \Sigma_\varepsilon)
$$

where $Y_{1,t}, \ldots, Y_{n,t}$ is a n-dimensional vector of variables (logarithmic changes in sovereign bond yield spreads) at time t (number of lags—2); $A_{1o}, \ldots, A_{no}$ is a n-dimensional vector of variables' intercept; $A_{11,k}, \ldots, A_{nn,k}$ is a n-dimensional coefficients' matrices; and $\varepsilon_{1,t}, \ldots, \varepsilon_{n,t}$ is an unobservable zero mean white noise vector process with time-invariant covariance matrix.

In order to solve variables' ordering problem, this empirical study applied the generalized approach that is invariant to the ordering of the variables in the VAR system, while the traditional impulse response analysis yields different results depending on the variables ordering.

$$
Y_t = A_1 Y_{t-1} + \cdots + A_p Y_{t-p} + U_t = \Phi(B) U_t = \sum_{i=0}^{\infty} \Phi_i U_{t-i}
\tag{2.2}
$$

$$
\Phi_i = A_1 \Phi_{i-1} + A_2 \Phi_{i-2} + \cdots + A_p \Phi_{t-p}
\tag{2.3}
$$

where Y_t is a n-dimensional vector of variables (logarithmic changes in sovereign bond yield spreads) at time t; Φ_i is the coefficient measuring the impulse response, e.g., $\Phi_{jk,i}$ represents the response of sovereign bond yield spread j to a positive shock of one standard deviation in sovereign bond yield spread k occurring ith period ago.

This empirical study focuses on daily data for EU-28 countries with a special focus on new euro area members: Slovenia, Cyprus, Malta, Slovakia, Estonia, Latvia, and Lithuania. This study also compares the vulnerability of the sovereign bond markets of all CEECs—the group of countries comprising Bulgaria, Croatia, the Czech Republic, Hungary, Poland, Romania, the Slovak Republic, Slovenia, and the three Baltic States: Estonia, Latvia, and Lithuania. Daily sovereign bond yields' (the Maastricht Treaty EMU convergence criterion) data on EU-28 countries for the period of 2005–2015 have been obtained from Eurostat. The Maastricht Treaty EMU convergence criterion series relates to interest rates for the long-term government bonds denominated in national currencies and is based on central government bond yields on the secondary market, gross of tax, with a residual maturity of around 10 years (the bond or the bonds of the basket are replaced regularly to avoid any maturity drift).

2.4 Research Results

The economic theory suggests that participants of financial markets could not only react to the introduction of euro in the new euro area countries but also to the positive convergence assessment. The convergence reports examine whether the EU Member States satisfy the necessary conditions to adopt the single currency— euro. The European Community (EC) Treaty requires the Commission and the European Central Bank (ECB) to issue these reports at least once every two years or at the request of an EU Member State which would like to join the euro area. On the basis of its assessment, the Commission submits a proposal to the ECOFIN Council which decides whether the country fulfills the necessary conditions and may adopt the euro.

In October 2004, the ten countries (Cyprus, the Czech Republic, Estonia, Hungary, Latvia, Lithuania, Malta, Poland, the Slovak Republic, and Slovenia) that joined the EU on May 1, 2004 were assessed for the first time. Although the maximum two-year period referred to by the treaty had not yet elapsed for these countries in 2004, the obligatory reassessment of Sweden was taken as an opportunity to analyze also the state of convergence in the new Member States. The report concluded that none of the 11 assessed countries at that stage fulfilled the necessary conditions for the adoption of the single currency. In 2006, there were two sets of convergence assessments. Lithuania's and Slovenia's state of readiness was examined in convergence reports issued in May 2006 at their own request. While Slovenia was deemed to fulfill all the convergence criteria and ready to adopt the euro in January 2007, the report on Lithuania suggested that there should be no change in its status as a Member State with a derogation. The then remaining nine countries (the Czech Republic, Estonia, Cyprus, Latvia, Hungary, Malta, Poland, Slovakia, and Sweden) were assessed in December 2006. Although the report showed progress with convergence in many countries, none of them was deemed to meet the necessary conditions for adopting the single currency. Aiming to adopt the euro in 2008, Cyprus and Malta submitted requests for re-examination in spring 2007. On the basis of convergence reports issued by the Commission and the ECB in May 2007, the council concluded that both Cyprus and Malta fulfilled the necessary conditions for adoption of the single currency. Consequently, the council decided that the euro would be introduced in the two countries on January 1, 2008. In 2008, the convergence report adopted on May 7 examined progress toward convergence in remaining ten EU Member States with a derogation—Bulgaria, the Czech Republic, Estonia, Latvia, Lithuania, Hungary, Poland, Romania, Slovakia, and Sweden. The report concluded that Slovakia met the conditions to join the euro area in January 2009. In 2010, the Commission concluded on May 12 that Estonia met the requirements for joining the euro, as the result of determined and credible policy efforts and recommend Estonia's membership of the Eurozone from January 1, 2011. In 2012, the Commission concluded on May 30 that none of the countries examined (Bulgaria, the Czech Republic, Latvia, Lithuania, Hungary, Poland, Romania, and Sweden) fulfilled all the conditions for adopting the euro. In 2013,

Table 2.1 Dates of positive convergence report announcement and euro introduction in the new euro area members

Country	Dates of positive convergence report announcements/dates of euro introduction
Slovenia	May 16, 2006/January 1, 2007
Cyprus	May 16, 2007/January 1, 2008
Malta	May 16, 2007/January 1, 2008
Slovakia	May 7, 2008/January 1, 2009
Estonia	May 12, 2010/January 1, 2011
Latvia	June 5, 2013/January 1, 2014
Lithuania	June 4, 2014/January 1, 2015

Source http://ec.europa.eu/economy_finance/euro/adoption/convergence_reports/index_en.htm

the Commission concluded on June 5 that Latvia fulfilled all the conditions for adopting the euro. In 2014, the Commission concluded on June 4 that Lithuania fulfilled all the conditions for adopting the euro. Table 2.1 summarizes the dates of positive convergence report announcements and euro introduction in the new euro area members.

Figure 2.1 demonstrates the dynamics of the sovereign bond yields of the new euro area members during period of 2005–2015.

The statistical data provided by Eurostat show that the announcement of positive convergence report and the euro introduction in the new euro area members did not manifest itself automatically in the short term and last into the long term (except in Latvia and Lithuania). This reaction of the financial market participants could be

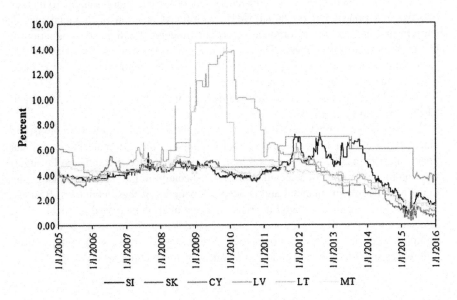

Fig. 2.1 Dynamics of the sovereign bond yields of the new euro area members. *Source* Eurostat

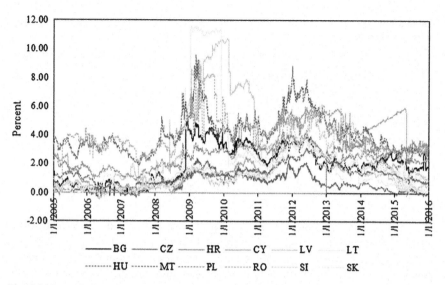

Fig. 2.2 Dynamics of the sovereign bond yield spreads of the new euro area members and CEECs. *Source* Own calculations based on data from Eurostat

explained by the fact that most of the new euro area members (Slovenia, Cyprus, Malta, and Slovakia) introduced euro in 2007–2009 during the global financial crisis. However, the short-term effect of euro introduction was observed in Latvia and Lithuania—countries which introduced euro in more stable time (during 2014–2015). Despite the fact that dynamics of the sovereign bond yields of the new euro area members did not show any short-term effect of the euro adoption, the dynamics of sovereign bond CDS prices showed a significant reaction of financial market participants to positive convergence report announcement and euro introduction in the new euro area members. These differences in reaction of financial market participants can be explained by the fact that sovereign bond CDS market is more liquid compared to sovereign bond market.

Dynamics of the sovereign bond yield spreads of the new euro area members and CEECs are shown in Fig. 2.2.

The sovereign bond yield spreads dynamics of selected countries demonstrate that the reaction of financial market participants to the external shocks (global financial crisis in 2007–2009, sovereign debt crisis in Greece, Ireland, and Portugal) was significant in most of selected countries, especially in Latvia and Lithuania due to the high degree of financial and economic openness of these countries. Besides, some local factors such as banking crisis in Latvia in 2008 increased political risk of selected countries. The reaction of financial market participants shows that this group of countries is very homogeneous in terms of political risk despite existing differences in economic and financial stability of these countries.

Table 2.2 Responses of sovereign bond markets of the new euro area members to generalized one S.D. innovations

Period	Response of LT sovereign bond market to generalized one S.D. innovation									
	Before euro introduction					After euro introduction				
	LT	CZ	CY	SE	MT	LT	ES	MT	CY	BG
1	11.58	2.53	2.46	1.12	0.71	8.66	4.08	2.94	2.87	2.76
2	−3.35	−1.48	−0.92	−0.45	−1.36	1.17	1.98	0.32	1.31	1.41
3	0.18	−0.30	0.59	0.38	0.59	−0.06	1.00	1.12	0.54	0.78
4	0.43	0.05	−0.17	−0.22	−0.24	−0.49	−1.02	−0.93	−0.81	−0.70
5	−0.18	−0.11	0.13	0.06	0.15	−0.58	0.03	0.38	0.38	−0.37

Period	Response of LV sovereign bond market to generalized one S.D. innovation									
	Before euro introduction					After euro introduction				
	LV	ES	IE	FI	CY	LV	ES	MT	AT	CY
1	6.14	0.90	0.71	0.69	0.69	7.59	3.30	3.18	2.80	2.76
2	−1.11	−0.11	0.35	0.28	0.07	−1.31	0.89	−0.97	−2.99	1.52
3	0.98	0.30	0.58	−0.24	0.70	0.50	0.40	0.54	1.20	0.44
4	−0.44	−0.27	−0.80	0.01	0.30	−0.56	−0.67	−0.42	−0.16	−0.77
5	0.34	0.12	0.37	0.01	0.17	0.58	0.24	0.35	0.09	0.48

Period	Response of SK sovereign bond market to generalized one S.D. innovation									
	Before euro introduction					After euro introduction				
	SK	FR	NL	PT	MT	SK	FI	MT	LT	BG
1	10.79	5.23	5.03	4.87	4.78	16.57	3.78	3.24	2.28	2.16
2	−4.66	−4.64	−5.24	−4.00	−4.07	−4.42	−0.98	−2.68	0.05	0.24
3	1.62	2.35	2.35	1.54	1.55	−1.83	−0.23	1.08	0.59	0.83
4	−0.93	−1.13	−0.86	−0.42	−0.66	1.34	−0.27	−0.52	−0.30	−0.44
5	0.33	0.54	0.37	0.06	0.11	0.04	0.48	0.17	−0.14	−0.09

Period	Response of MT sovereign bond market to generalized one S.D. innovation									
	Before euro introduction					After euro introduction				
	MT	NL	SK	FR	PT	MT	FR	NL	PT	SI
1	4.31	2.73	2.60	2.58	2.57	3.68	1.84	1.62	1.55	1.54
2	−2.37	−2.06	−1.30	−1.37	−1.98	−1.98	−1.63	−1.60	−0.59	−0.56
3	0.22	1.31	0.98	0.75	1.01	0.40	0.50	0.40	0.25	0.29
4	0.63	−0.81	−0.49	−0.48	−0.55	−0.10	0.01	0.06	−0.03	−0.11
5	−1.35	0.69	0.15	0.10	0.17	0.00	−0.08	−0.08	−0.01	0.00

Period	Response of CY sovereign bond market to generalized one S.D. innovation									
	Before euro introduction					After euro introduction				
	CY	CZ	HU	PL	MT	CY	BE	BG	SI	PT
1	17.59	8.82	7.52	6.51	5.51	7.69	1.96	1.96	1.92	1.72
2	−0.42	−2.60	2.65	2.24	−7.26	2.24	0.64	0.43	−0.97	−1.60
3	0.35	2.17	5.03	1.20	−0.79	3.14	0.41	0.92	−0.25	0.05
4	−5.00	−1.00	−1.13	−2.72	−0.52	1.67	0.25	0.30	−0.57	−0.65
5	2.55	2.49	3.94	-0.06	2.14	1.57	0.22	0.24	−0.34	−0.32

Period	Response of SI sovereign bond market to generalized one S.D. innovation									
	Before euro introduction					After euro introduction				
	SI	CZ	MT	LV	BG	SI	MT	PT	ES	IT
1	48.70	14.25	12.26	9.72	8.39	13.31	3.42	3.16	3.12	2.71
2	−24.54	−10.70	−9.29	−16.89	−4.62	−4.81	−2.30	−0.93	−0.59	−0.09

(continued)

Table 2.2 (continued)

Period	Response of SI sovereign bond market to generalized one S.D. innovation									
	Before euro introduction					After euro introduction				
	SI	CZ	MT	LV	BG	SI	MT	PT	ES	IT
3	−17.34	−2.14	5.34	15.73	−4.22	−3.79	0.26	1.15	−0.21	0.83
4	14.68	2.82	−10.11	−8.55	3.85	3.57	0.00	−0.86	−0.63	−0.56
5	4.39	0.15	10.08	11.01	−0.01	0.39	0.20	−0.10	0.56	−0.24

Source Own calculations based on data from Eurostat

The generalized impulse response analysis was used to analyze the responses of one sovereign bond market to a shock in another. The responses show short-lasting effects on sovereign bond markets following a shock in other markets (see Table 2.2). After four days, the sovereign bond markets of the new euro area members have in all cases settled back to their pre-shock level. Even though the impact is generally short-lived, all responses are moderate in scale. In order to investigate the impact of euro introduction on vulnerability of the new euro area members to the external shocks, the whole data sample was divided into two subsamples: before euro introduction and after euro introduction. However, the results did not change significantly after the euro introduction except to Malta, Cyprus, and Slovenia. These countries had introduced euro in 2007–2008, and the perception of political risk has changed already. The results of generalized impulse response analysis confirm that the new euro area members are still very sensitive to shocks in other CEECs sovereign bond markets.

2.5 Conclusion

The empirical results provided by this study show that the announcement of positive convergence report and the euro introduction in the new euro area members did not manifest itself automatically in the short term and last into the long term (except in Latvia and Lithuania). This reaction of the financial market participants could be explained by the fact that most of the new euro area members (Slovenia, Cyprus, Malta, and Slovakia) introduced euro in 2007–2009 during the global financial crisis. The results of generalized impulse response analysis confirm that the new euro area members are still very sensitive to shocks in other CEECs sovereign bond markets. However, new euro area members became less sensitive to the external shocks after the introduction of euro (except for Latvia and Lithuania).

Acknowledgments This research was funded by a grant (No. MIP-016/2015) from the Research Council of Lithuania.

References

Bank of Lithuania (2013) Impact of the euro adoption on the national economy: an overview of the quantitative assessment. Occasional papers no. 1/2013

Bekaert G, Harvey CR, Lundblad CT, Siegel S (2013) The European Union, the euro, and equity market integration. J Financ Econ 109:583–603. doi:10.1016/j.jfineco.2013.03.008

Conti M (2014) The introduction of the euro and economic growth: some panel data evidence. J Appl Econ 17:199–211. doi:10.1016/s1514-0326(14)60009-x

Forlati C (2015) On the benefits of a monetary union: does it pay to be bigger? J Int Econ 97: 448–463. doi:10.1016/j.jinteco.2015.07.001

Frankel JA, Rose AK (1997) Is EMU more justifiable ex post than ex ante? Eur Econ Rev 41: 753–760. doi:10.1016/s0014-2921(97)00034-2

Gächter M, Riedl A (2014) One money, one cycle? The EMU experience. J Macroecon 42: 141–155. doi:10.1016/j.jmacro.2014.07.006

Gehringer A (2013) Growth, productivity and capital accumulation: the effects of financial liberalization in the case of European integration. Int Rev Econ Finance 25:291–309. doi:10.1016/j.iref.2012.07.015

Georgantopoulos AG, Tsamis AD, Agoraki MK (2015) The Euro-adoption effect and the bank, market, and growth nexus: new evidence from EU panels. J Econ Asymmetries 12:41–51. doi:10.1016/j.jeca.2015.01.002

Koop G, Pesaran MH, Potter SM (1996) Impulse response analysis in nonlinear multivariate models. J Econometrics 74:119–147. doi:10.1016/0304-4076(95)01753-4

Lavrač V (2007) Euro adoption in central and eastern Europe: opportunities and challenges. Econ Syst 31:225–230. doi:10.1016/j.ecosys.2006.08.004

Legrand R (2014) Euro introduction: has there been a structural change? Study on 10 European Union countries. Econ Model 40:136–151. doi:10.1016/j.econmod.2014.03.020

Muradoğlu YG, Onay C, Phylaktis K (2014) European integration and corporate financing. Int Rev Financ Anal 33:138–157. doi:10.1016/j.irfa.2014.02.002

Pesaran MH, Shi Y (1998) Generalized impulse response analysis in linear multivariate models. Econ Lett 58:17–29. doi:10.1016/s0165-1765(97)00214-0

Chapter 3
Does Strong Employment Support Strong National Currency? An Empirical Analysis for the US Economy

Elvan Akturk Hayat and Ismet Gocer

Abstract Nowadays, the currency wars between the US and China gets accelerated and economic and politic developments in countries' have important effects on the value of national currencies. Employment, manufacturing, and economic growth data of leading countries like the US is closely monitored by the whole world. When non-farm payroll data of the US, announced at first Friday of every month, is above expectations, it is accepted as an indicator that the US economy is getting better, manufacturing and economic growth will be higher in future, and dollar appreciates against other currencies. In this study, the relation between the non-farm payroll employment (NFE) and dollar index (DI) data of the US is analyzed by econometric methods for the period of 1995:M01-2016:M01. The results of the study indicate that there is one-way causality from non-farm payroll employment to dollar index and non-farm payroll employment and dollar index are cointegrated in the long term. Besides, a 1% increases in non-farm payroll data causes dollar index to increase by 2.14%. Error correction mechanism of the model also operates. This study is evaluated to be useful for the policy makers in both developed and developing countries by drawing attention on this issue once again.

Keywords Non-farm payroll employment · The national currency

3.1 Introduction

The banknotes which are in use in present time are called fiat money, and they take credit from the economic power of the country it represents. When the employment and production is high and economic stability is good, the reliability and recog-

E. Akturk Hayat (✉) · I. Gocer
Department of Econometrics, Aydın Faculty of Economics,
Adnan Menderes University, Aydin, Turkey
e-mail: elvanakturk@gmail.com

I. Gocer
e-mail: igocer@adu.edu.tr

© Springer International Publishing AG 2017
D. Procházka (ed.), *New Trends in Finance and Accounting*,
Springer Proceedings in Business and Economics,
DOI 10.1007/978-3-319-49559-0_3

nition of national currency in international markets increase; otherwise, international liquidity of the currency declines. For instance, today, 1 Kuwaiti Dinar corresponds to 3.14 US dollars nearly, and it is globally accepted. On the other hand, 1 Iraqi Dinar corresponds to 0.0009 US dollars, but it is not convertible in the most of the world. Similarly, there is no need to compare the Zimbabwe Dollar and US Dollar and to discuss the validity of them in the world. The reason is the stability and power of the economy behind currencies.

Developments in the US can bring about important consequences not only for itself, but also for the other economies of the world. Non-farm payrolls data in the USA is announced on first Friday of every month, and closely monitored by the whole world market. An increase in this data is perceived as an indicator of the fact that things are getting better in the US economy, and dollar becomes stronger against the other currencies among the world. This case also expands to all of the world economy with domino effect. When the non-farm payrolls data comes lower than expected, the opposite happens. Citigroup, which is the largest foreign exchange trader in terms of transaction volume, has stated that the weak employment in the US economy means a decline in dollar (Bloomberg 2015).

In this context, this study investigates the relationship between non-farm payroll employment and dollar index data of the US by econometric methods for the period of 1995:M01-2016:M01.

The remainder of this paper is organized as follows: Sect. 3.2 gives a brief theoretical framework of the issue and Sect. 3.3 focuses on previous literature. Section 3.4 presents the results of the empirical analysis. The final section gives conclusions and some policy implications. It is evaluated that the study will help both developed and developing countries on managing exchange rate policies by considering employment data and general economic conditions.

3.2 Framework

The exchange rate shows the value of national currency in terms of foreign currencies, and it is an important parameter because of its influence on many variables in the economy. Changes in exchange rate leads to changes in relative domestic/external price structure by changing the relative value of national currency.

On the other hand, exchange rate policies are effective not only on cross-country goods, services, and capital flows. The basic reason for the economic crises in recent years is seemed to be largely the exchange rate policy that is applied (Bilgin 2004). The crisis emerged in certain regions can also affect the relationship between the other countries' exchange rates. Although the reasons are different, all financial crises, Mexico in 1994, Asia in 1997, Brazil in 1998, Argentina in 2000, and Turkey in 2001, have resulted with serious movements in exchange rates.

The real exchange rate is one of the most important determinants of foreign trade in open economies. The fact that domestic and external demand is directed by real exchange rate has an impact on employment levels at the same time (Balaylar 2011). If the real exchange rate falls (national currency loses value), imported goods become more expensive. This leads consumers to substitute domestic goods for imported goods. The employment undoubtedly increase when the demand for domestic goods increase. When the imports become more expensive, the cost of labor becomes relatively cheaper in the sector that used imported inputs. In theory, it leads to increase in employment. However, when the imported inputs become more expensive or devaluation occurs, it could lead to inflation causing a decline in employment by decreasing aggregate demand.

It can be said that, under the assumption of prices are not flexible downward, real exchange rate is negatively related with production and employment and positively related with unemployment. On the other hand, an external impact such as a decline in commodity prices in trading countries can increase unemployment rate under the assumption of wages and prices are not flexible in short term (Carr and Floyd 2001).

Fluctuations in exchange rate increase costs and cause uncertainty in short term. Especially in micro level, it makes difficult for businesses to predict future. This situation naturally makes difficult to have right decisions for economic agents, especially businesses. Therefore, eliminating the fluctuations (uncertainty) in exchange rate positively reflects on the decisions of economic agents. This affects the exports, production, and employment in a positive way. It is clear that employment increase would be more effective in a case that export growth is supported by new investments. Thus, it can be said that there is a linear relationship between exchange rate stability and foreign and between fluctuations in exchange rate and unemployment (Buscher and Mueller 1999).

3.3 Literature Review

Hua (2007), using panel analysis for 29 states of China for 1993–2002 period, determined that increases in the value of real exchange rate has negative impacts on employment. Frenkel and Ros (2006) performed a comparative evaluation of unemployment in 17 Latin American countries and confirmed the effect of real exchange rate on unemployment in Argentina, Brazil, Chile, and Mexico, using panel data over the period 1980–2003. Another study supporting the hypothesis about the real exchange rate has strong effect on unemployment belongs to Damill, Frenkel, and Maurizio (2002). They have examined the effects of real exchange rate value increases on labor market in Argentina.

Bilgin (2004), in the study about the relationship between real exchange rate and unemployment in Turkey in the period of 1991–2004, reaches results supporting the theory. It is reported that a high level of real exchange rate positively affects employment, and it reduces unemployment in period of the analysis. Balaylar (2011) has analyzed the impacts of real exchange rate changes on employment for manufacturing industry in Turkey, and finds that high level of real exchange rates weakens the relationship between the quantity of production and employment in manufacturing industry by rising the import dependence of production and export.

The literature review that relates non-farm payrolls and exchange rates is not extensive. Previous literature on the impact of macroeconomic announcements has mostly focused on bond and currency markets, with fairly clear evidence that macroeconomic news has significant price and volatility effects. Rossi (1998) finds that certain key economic announcements cause U.K government bond yield changes of between 2 and 6 basis points, including beyond the trading day. Fleming and Remolona (1999) find that the arrival of public information has a large effect on prices and subsequent trading activity, particularly during periods in which uncertainty is high. They collected data on 10 macroeconomic announcements: CPI, durable goods orders, gross domestic product (GDP), housing starts, jobless rate, leading indicators, non-farm payrolls, PPI, retail sales, and trade balance. The non-farm payroll, which is released with the jobless rate as part of the monthly employment report, has the largest impact on the market in recent years.

Balduzzi et al. (2001) indicate that a wide variety of economic announcements affect the US Treasury bond prices, with labor market, inflation, and durable goods orders data having the largest impact. Andersen et al. (2003) explore the relationship between macroeconomic news and the US dollar exchange rate against six major currencies. They confirm macroeconomic news generally has a statistically significant correlation with intra-day movements of the US dollar, with "bad" news —for example, data indicating weaker-than-expected growth—having a larger impact than "good" news. Galati and Ho (2003) found similar results using daily data. Ehrmann and Fratzscher (2005) focused on the euro–dollar exchange rate and found that US news tended to have more of an effect on the exchange rate than German news. Roache and Rossi (2009) are investigated which and how macroeconomic announcements affect commodity prices. They focus mainly on announcements about US macroeconomic developments since these have been shown to have the greatest influence on variables such as the US dollar. Roache and Rossi (2010) are also evaluated how commodity prices respond to macroeconomic news and show that commodities have been relatively insensitive to such news over daily frequencies between 1997 and 2009 compared to other financial assets and major exchange rates.

3.4   Empirical Analysis

3.4.1   Data

In this study, we examine the relationship between the exchange rate and employment variable. We use the US non-farm payroll data as a determinant of employment and the US dollar index (DI) data as a determinant of exchange rate. The non-farm payroll data (Nonfarm Payroll Employment: NFE) has been obtained from The Bureau of Labor Statistics of the U.S. Department of Labor. The US dollar index data has also been obtained from The Federal Reserve Bank of St. Louis Web site. All dataset in period of 1995:M01-2016:M01 have been taken logarithm and seasonally adjusted. Time series plots for series are given in Appendix.

3.4.2   Econometric Model

In this study, it has been analyzed the relationships between the US non-farm payroll data and the US dollar index data by following model:

$$LogDI_t = \beta_0 + \beta_1 LogNFE_t + \varepsilon_t \qquad (3.1)$$

3.4.3   Method

Augmented Dickey–Fuller-ADF (1979), the Phillips–Perron-PP (1988), the Kwiatkowski et al. (1992), and the structural break ADF unit root tests are used to determine the stability of the series. It has been tested the causality using Granger (1969) test and has been determined the cointegration relation between series using Johansen and Juselius (1990) method. Long- and short-term analysis has been implemented by Dynamic Ordinary Least Squares (DOLS) method.

3.4.4   Unit Root Tests

The stationarity tests are of great importance to avoid spurious regression problem in time series analysis (Enders 2014). Although ADF (1979) test is the most commonly used method for unit roots, it is considered to be inadequate to test the stationarity of series including trends. In such cases, using PP (1988) test is much better. Hypothesis of KPSS (1992) test is inverse of the ADF and PP tests and can be used to verify the first two tests. Because the tests not considering the structural break are in tendency to find unit root in some stationary series with structural breaks (Perron 1989), the use of the structural break unit root tests in studies would be useful.

Therefore, stationarity of the series has been examined with ADF, PP, and KPSS unit root tests, and ADF test with structural breaks dates method has been used as well. The results of the tests are given in Table 3.1. Results from unit root tests in

Table 3.1 Unit root tests

	ADF	PP	KPSS	ADF test with structural breaks dates	
	ADF test stat.	PP test stat.	LM stat.	ADF test stat.	Structural breaks dates
LogDI	−1.94 [3]	−1.49 [6]	0.26[12]	−2.59 [3]	2003:M08
LogNFE	−2.77 [3]	−1.85 [11]	1.39 [12]	−3.45 [6]	2009:M04
ΔLogDI	−7.51***[2]	−10.16***[0]	0.23***[6]	−11.00***[1]	2008:M10
ΔLogNFE	−2.82*[2]	−5.46***[7]	0.25***[11]	−4.64**[11]	2008:M04

Notes H_0 Unit root process for ADF and PP; in contrast, H_0 stationary process for KPSS
*, **, *** refers to the rejection of H_0 at 0.10, 0.05, 0.01 significance level, respectively
Number of lags in ADF tests is selected according to modified AIC and appear in [ ]
Optimal bandwidth for PP and KPSS appear in [ ]. Structural break dates were determined by
minimizing to Dickey–Fuller t statistics

Table 3.1 show that both series are non-stationary in level values. When the series
in first difference are tested, the null hypothesis of a unit root process is rejected—at
least at a 0.10 significance level. Therefore, the unit root tests conclusively show
that all variables of study are I(1). Considering structural break date, it can be seen
obviously that the US military intervention in Iraq in 2003 and the global economic
crisis in 2008 have a significant effect on the NFE and DI.

3.4.5   Causality Tests

Granger (1969) causality test which is applied to the stationary series is the most
commonly used method and has been used to examine the causality relation
between series. To provide stationary, it has been taken the first differences of the
data. The findings of the Granger causality test have been presented in Table 3.2.
The results of Granger causality test shows that there is one-way causality from
NFE to DI. Accordingly, we could say that the US non-farm payrolls data influences the value of dollar.

Table 3.2 Granger causality test results

Null hypothesis	Optimum Lag.	Criteria	Obs.	F Stat.	Prob.
ΔLogNFE does not Granger Cause ΔLogDI	8	FPE, HQ, AIC	244	1.72	0.09
ΔLogDI does not Granger Cause ΔLogNFE				1.32	0.23

Table 3.3 Cointegration test results

Hypothesized no. of CE(s)	Eigen value	Trace statistic	0.05 Critical value	Prob.	Structural breaks dates
None[*]	0.06	20.21	18.39	0.02	1998:M02, 2001:M10, 2004:
At most 1	0.01	3.46	3.841	0.06	M11, 2009:M05, 2013:M01

Note Optimal lag has been determined via AIC, HQ and FPE
[*] refers to 5%

3.4.6 Cointegration Test

The series which are non-stationary in levels values can bring along the spurious regression problem (Engle and Granger 1987). If the time series are cointegrated in the levels, the analysis of regression would give reliable results (Gujarati and Porter 2008). If the series are integrated at the same order, the cointegration relation between series can be determined using Engle–Granger (1987) or Johansen and Juselius (1990) methods.

In this study, the cointegration relation between the series has been tested with Johansen and Juselius (1990) method. The structural break dates in the cointegration equation have been determined with Bai and Perron (2003) method. Results are presented in Table 3.3.

According to the Table 3.3, we would conclude that there exists one cointegration relation. Namely, the series have a long run relationship and the analysis to be made with this series does not include spurious regression problem. Besides, this means that there is a simultaneous movement both in nonfarm payroll employment and the value of dollar in the US economy. The structural break dates which are determined by Bai and Perron (2003) method have been included in long-term analysis with dummy variables.

The dates are as follows: 1998; Mexico (1997) and Russia crisis (1998), 2001; the monetary expansion that started in the US, 2004; the period in which interest rates begun to rise again, 2009; the last global economic crisis and 2013; and the period when FED announced that expansionary monetary policy to overcome the economic crisis has ended.

3.4.7 Long-Term Analysis

The cointegration coefficients have been estimated by DOLS method. DOLS regression that includes lag and lead terms can produce robust estimates which are resistant to autocorrelation and heteroscedasticity (Esteve and Requena 2006). DOLS estimation results are presented in Table 3.4.

Table 3.4 Long-term analysis results

Variable	Coefficient	t-statistic	p-value
LogNFE	2.14	6.10	0.00
K1998	0.09	0.44	0.65
K2001	0.17	0.82	0.41
K2004	−0.03	−0.14	0.88
K2009	0.04	0.20	0.83
K2013	−0.04	−0.22	0.82
Constant	−20.45	−4.95	0.00
$R^2 = 0.46$	$\bar{R}^2 = 0.43$	$SSR = 1.09$	$JB = 0.07$

Note R^2 Coefficient of determination, $\bar{R}^2$ Adjusted R^2
SSR Sum of Squared Residuals
JB Jarque–Bera normality test

According to Table 3.4, a 1% increase in NFE would cause a 2.14% increase in DI in the relevant period. In other words, increasing employment raises the value of the dollar against other currencies. These findings are consistent with our theoretical expectations.

3.4.8 Short-Term Analysis

The short run analysis has been estimated with DOLS within the framework of error correction model (ECM). It has been used the first difference of series and one lagged values of ECM (ECT_{t-1}) obtained from the long run analysis. The results obtained have been presented in Table 3.5.

According to the Table 3.5, the coefficient of ECM has been found negative and statistically significant, so error correction mechanism of the model operates. It indicates that short-term deviations within series, which move together in long term, will disappear and the series will converge long-term equilibrium value. The results present additional evidence on credibility of long-term analysis.

Table 3.5 Short-term analysis results

Variable	Coefficient	t-statistic	Prob.
ΔLogNFE	1.49	2.23	0.02
ECT_{t-1}	−0.02	−1.44	0.09
Constant	0.00	0.01	0.98
$R^2 = 0.16$	$\bar{R}^2 = 0.11$	$SSR = 0.03$	$JB = 0.00$

Note R^2 Coefficient of determination, $\bar{R}^2$ Adjusted R^2
SSR Sum of Squared Residuals
JB Jarque–Bera normality test

3.5   Conclusion

In today's world, the value of banknotes and coins has taken its power from the country's economy it represents. Many economic and political changes in a country can closely affect the value of national currency. Employment, production, and economic growth are the most commonly used indicators to measure the economic success of the countries. Increasing employment is a precursor of increased production and economic growth in the country. All countries closely follow employment and production data of developing and developed countries, mainly the USA, which have an important role in world economy. Within this scope, the whole world draws attention to the USA's non-farm payrolls data which is released on the first Friday of every month at 8:30. When this data is at expected or higher level in the USA, this implies that the economy evolves in a positive direction in US, and it is perceived as an indicator of an increase in production and economic growth in the future and dollar gains value against other currencies.

In this study, the relationship between the US non-farm payrolls and dollar index data has been investigated by econometric methods for the period of 1995: M01-2016:M01. According to the results, there is a simultaneous movement between the value of dollar and non-farm payrolls data for the USA. It has been revealed that a 1% increases in non-farm payroll causes dollar index to increase by 2.14%. Error correction mechanism of model also operates.

Based on the findings from the study, it can be said that non-farm employment data is also considered to be an important determinant when estimating the international value of the national currency of a country. In today's global economy accelerating currency wars, countries targeting to achieve competitive advantage in foreign trade by trying to reduce the value of the national currency, such as the USA, should pay attention on this issue. It will be quite effective for developing countries, who try to implicate policies by monitoring developed countries, to focus on employment data of other developing countries and take these data into account when making projections.

Appendix

See Fig. 3.1.

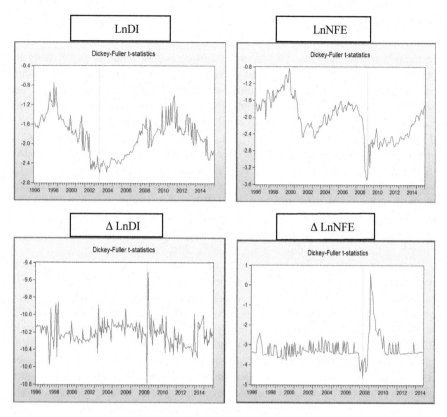

Fig. 3.1 Dataset for the period 1995:M01-2016:M01

References

Andersen TG, Bollerslev T, Diebold FX, Vega C (2003) Micro effects of macro announcements: real-time price discovery in foreign exchange. Am Econ Rev 93:38–62

Bai J, Perron P (2003) Critical values for multiple structural change tests. Econ J 6(1):72–78

Balaylar NA (2011) Reel Döviz Kuru İstihdam İlişkisi: Türkiye İmalat Sanayi Örneği (The Relationship between the Real Exchange Rate and Employment: The Case of Turkey's Manufacturing Industry). Sosyo Ekonomi 2:137–160

Balduzzi P, Elton EJ, Green TC (2001) Economic news and bond prices: evidence from the U.S. treasury market. J Financ Quant Anal 36(4):523–543

Bilgin MH (2004) Döviz Kuru İşsizlik İlişkisi: Türkiye Üzerine Bir İnceleme (Exchange Rate Unemployment Relationship: An Analysis on Turkey). Sosyal Bilimler Enstitüsü Dergisi Kocaeli University 8(2):80–94

Bloomberg HT (2015) Citi: weak employment = weak dollar http://www.bloomberght.com/haberler/haber/1828111-citi-zayif-istihdam-zayif-dolar. Accessed 15 Feb 2016

Buscher HS, Mueller C (1999) Exchange rate volatility effects on the German labour market: a survey of recent results and extensions. IZA Discussion paper no.37, March

Carr JL, Floyd JE (2001) Real and monetary shocks to the Canadian dollar: do Canada and the U. S. form an optimal currency area. Working paper number UT-ECIPA-Floyd–01–02, December

Damill M, Frenkel R, Maurizio R (2002) Argentina: a decade of currency board. An analysis of growth, employment and income distribution. Employment paper no. 42. International Labour Office Geneva

Dickey DA, Fuller WA (1979) Distribution of the estimators for autoregressive time series with a unit root. J Am Stat Assoc 74:427–431

Ehrmann M, Fratzscher M (2005) Exchange rates and fundamentals: new evidence from real-time data. J Int Money Finan 24(2):317–341

Enders W (2014) Applied econometric time series, 4th edn, Wiley, New York

Engle RF, Granger CWJ (1987) Co-integration and error correction: representation, estimation, and testing. Econometrica 55(2):251–276

Esteve V, Requena F (2006) A cointegration analysis of car advertising and sales data in the presence of structural change. Int J Econ Bus 13(1):111–128

Fleming MJ, Remolona EM (1999) Price formation and liquidity in the U.S. treasury market: the response to public information. J Finan 54(5):1901–1915

Frenkel R, Ros J (2006) Unemployment and the real exchange rate in Latin America. World Dev 34(4):631–646

Galati G, Ho C (2003) Macroeconomic news and the euro/dollar exchange rate. Econ Notes 32:371–398. doi:10.1111/1468-0300.00118

Granger CWJ (1969) Investigating causal relations by econometric models and cross-spectral methods. Econometrica 37(3):424–438

Gujarati D, Porter D (2008) Basic econometrics, 5th edn. McGraw-Hill Education, New York

Hua P (2007) Real exchange rate and manufacturing employment in China. China Econ Rev 18:335–353

Johansen S, Juselius K (1990) Maximum likelihood estimation and inference on cointegration—with applications to the demand for money. Oxford Bull Econ Stat 52(2):169–210

Kwiatkowski D, Phillips PCB, Schmidt P, Shin Y (1992) Testing the null hypothesis of stationarity against the alternative of a unit root. J Econ 54:159–178

Perron P (1989) The great crash, the oil price shock, and the unit root hypothesis. Econometrica 57 (6):1361–1401

Phillips PCB, Perron P (1988) Testing for a unit root in time series regression. Biometrika 75 (2):335–346

Roache SK, Rossi M (2009) The effects of economic news on commodity prices: is gold just another commodity? IMF working papers no: 09/140 IMF, Washington, D.C

Roache SK, Rossi M (2010) The effects of economic news on commodity prices. Q Rev Econ Finan 50(3):377–385

Rossi M (1998) Economic announcements and the timing of public debt auctions, IMF working paper 98/44

Chapter 4
The Theory of Debt-Deflation: A Possibility of Incompatibility of Goals of Monetary Policy

Samy Metrah

Abstract This paper provides a detailed exposition of Irving Fisher's debt-deflation theory as well as its proposed "remedies" against the "vicious cycle". We argue, using F. A. Hayek's hypothesis of "dichotomy of rates of interest", that not only may be the main proposed tool of battling debt-deflation, i.e. preventing the price level from falling, considered self-defeating, in the long run at least, but also that goals of the macroprudential policy and the policy of inflation targeting are inherently incompatible if Fisher's and Hayek's theories are taken into account.

Keywords Debt-deflation · Dichotomy of rates of interest · Macroprudential policy · Monetary policy goals

4.1 Introduction

In recent years, two phenomena have had a significant impact both on the world economy and on the economics as a whole. The theoretical foundations of mainstream economics were and continue to be questioned although to some lesser degree lately. The phenomena in question are the profound financial crisis,[1] the consequences of which shook the US financial sector and the entire economy to its core, and the European debt crisis that has almost brought Greece and other heavily indebted members of European Monetary Union to their knees. As it is always the case after crisis having come into existence, the economic theory struggles both to cope with and reflect upon recent developments. The old saying that history has a tendency to repeating itself proved to be correct in a recent case, for especially two theories have come to the fore in recent years—those of Irving Fisher's and Hymen

---

[1] A comprehensive evolution and analysis may be found in Brunnermeier (2009).

S. Metrah (✉)
Department of Monetary Theory and Policy, University of Economics,
Prague, W. Churchill Sq. 4, 130 67 Prague, Czech Republic
e-mail: s.metrah@gmail.com

© Springer International Publishing AG 2017
D. Procházka (ed.), *New Trends in Finance and Accounting*,
Springer Proceedings in Business and Economics,
DOI 10.1007/978-3-319-49559-0_4

Minsky's. Lately, the spectre of deflation has been haunting European economies and European Central Bank along with other central banks have struggled to prevent price levels from falling. The problematic of stability of financial sector stands closely connected with recent deflationary dangers. By the time the crisis hit the US economy, the mainstream economic theory[2] had been caught off-guard completely, for many held the belief of business cycles having finally been eradicated and the so-called "New Financial Architecture" achieved the goal of increasing the resilience of financial sector against risk.[3] Both beliefs turned to be false, as was the case so many times in the past; at least, as far as the phenomenon of business cycles is concerned.

The aim of the paper is to provide a detailed exposition of Irving Fisher's Debt-Deflation theory (DDT) as well as to attempt at formulizing a possible connection between DDT and Hayek's "dichotomy of two rates of interest", and in doing so, show that main tool in fighting deflation may be considered self-defeating. Moreover, we shall argue that this connection may be seen as an "original" representation of incompatibility of the goals of monetary policy—on one hand maintaining the stability of real purchasing power of money, i.e. the stability of the price level of consumers' products, and equalizing savings with investment on the other. We shall also discuss some of possible problems that may arise in the inflation-targeting regime.

The structure of the paper is as follows. The next section contains the exposition of DDT. The third section presents our argument. The final part concludes the paper.

4.2   Theoretical Exposition[4]

In time of its publication, the theory went rather unnoticed, for its author, Irving Fisher, was largely discredited after the Great Depression of 1929. In spite of recent rise in interest, most of the academic discussion focuses mainly on Fisher's paper *The Debt-Deflation Theory of Great Depressions*, which was published in 1933. However, the paper was seen by its author himself "only" as a summary of his primary work (Fisher 1933, p. 337). The core of the theory is to be found in his book *Booms and Depressions: Some First Principles* (1932), which contains knowledge *"both new and important"* (Fisher 1933, p. 337).[5] This way of

---

[2]We are referring to so called "New Consensus", which the monetary theory of inflation targeting is based on, and to the theory of efficient markets.

[3]Possible reflections on the failure of financial institutions and regulators may be found in Kay (2015), Crotty (2009) or Crotty and Epstein (2009).

[4]Due to editorial constrains the exposition in the two following sections will be highly compressed, we welcome interested readers to consult the original works.

[5]Fisher quotes, then, one of the greatest experts in the field of business cycles, however he does not provide the name. It is possible that it was W.C. Mitchell, whom the book is dedicated to.

utilization of the theory might be seen as relatively incorrect from the purely methodological point of view as it omits details and discussions contained within the book. For our present purposes, we shall restrict ourselves with the paper although we shall draw attention to details contained in the book where possible.

Being true to the neoclassical heritage of its author, DDT closely follows the neoclassical dichotomy in distinguishing the real and monetary spheres of economy. What is of utmost importance is the consequence of this distinction—although both spheres may diverge and evolve differently from one another for some time, the monetary sphere must adapt to its real counterpart in a certain moment. It is those "*changes on the part of money*" that do not reflect "*changes on the part of things*" (Keynes 1930, p. 81) that may be identified as the "true" source of business fluctuations.

The point of origin in Fisher's analysis and methodology is to differentiate the facts that are "*[the] historical case[s] of great dis-equilibrium*", i.e. the history of an economy, and tendencies that are influencing an economy in a certain point of time. Thus, every historical case of (great) recession (depression) may be seen as the result of the mix of different tendencies that may reinforce or go against one another (Fisher 1932, pp. 51–53; 1933, pp. 337–338).[6,7] In order to analyse an individual case of economic distress, one must identify particular tendencies that were influencing an economy in a particular time. In other words, each economic crisis is a result of historical culmination of certain tendencies (cycles) (ibid., pp. 58–59). Fisher rejected the idea that the phenomenon of business cycles existed independently of "real" variables. The question whether an economical system may always converge to an equilibrium state is conditional upon exceeding certain limits, beyond which the system does not have power to return to its equilibrium. Although he leans to an idea that economy has a tendency to return to equilibrium state, he rejects the notion of system being in equilibrium for any longer periods of time (Fisher 1933, pp. 388–389).

Two main tendencies are identified as the most destructive—over-indebtedness of economic individuals and falling price level of consumers' products. Other tendencies, nowadays identified as the main causes of fluctuation, such as over-investment or over-production, are not considered to be able to start significant drop in output. For if we take an economy that is characterized by over-investment as a point of origin, then the fall in investment activity would not have been so severe if it had not been financed by loans. The same conclusion is reached in connection with over-optimistic expectations that led to an increase in loans in the past. The common denominator is then identified as over-indebtedness of economic individuals and falling price level of consumers' products that in turn rises the real value of debt.

---

[6]Fisher distinguished "forced" and "free" tendencies; the latter being endogenous and the former exogenous in respect of an economy (1932, pp. 51–53).

[7]In some respect this conception is close to that of Schumpeter's (1911 [2012], 1939 [2005]).

Fisher identifies nine main factors, three of which are the most important in the process of economic crisis. The first three most important are state of over-indebtedness, fluctuations in volume of currency and pressures on falling price level of consumers' products. Other six are the result of workings of the latter, namely state of net worth of businesses; their profits; level of production, trade and employment; velocity of circulation and finally the role of rate of interest. If we take a state of overall over-indebtedness in an economy as our starting point,[8] then the dynamics of the theory is as follows:

1. attempts at debt liquidation lead to distress selling, i.e. *the debt disease*, (Fisher 1932, pp. 8–12)
2. and contraction of deposits (and possibly also the velocity of circulation), i.e. *currency contraction*; (ibid., pp. 14–16)
3. these effects are forcing the price level of consumers' products to fall, i.e. *the dollar disease*, (ibid., pp. 17–26)
4. if not offset, the falling prices (and price level) decrease the net worth of businesses that might, in turn, lead to bankruptcies, i.e. *net worth reduction*; (ibid., p. 29)
5. as a consequence of the latter, the profits tend to fall, i.e. *profit reduction*; (ibid., pp. 29–30)
6. motivating businesses to scale down overall production and thus decreasing the level of employment of factors of production, i.e. *lessened production, trade and employment*; (ibid., pp. 30–32)
7. aforementioned effects will result in spreading pessimism among the public and growing uncertainty, i.e. *pessimism and distrust*, (ibid., pp. 32–34)
8. that leads to hoarding of money, i.e. *retarded circulation*, (ibid., pp. 34–37)
9. the result on the rate of interest being that 'the money rate of interest' lowers, however, the real rate of interest raises. (ibid., pp. 38–39)

It ought to be noted, however, that the above order is not a chronological one (ibid., pp. 40–41).[9] Naturally, individual factors may be at work simultaneously reinforcing one another. The DDT then stands on the premise that only the coexistence of over-indebtedness and falling prices are the true causes for particularly destructive cases of recession. Nevertheless, the common denominator for aforementioned factors are the result of falling price level of consumers' products, with the exception of the first, i.e. debt liquidation, and the last factor, i.e. changes in rate of interest (Fisher 1933, p. 344). Fisher explicitly states that "*[o]f these three*

---

[8]A thorough discussion of the "starters" (of debt-deflation) may be found in Fisher (1932, pp. 44–50).

[9]The outline of possible chronological order is provided in an appendix, see Fisher (ibid., pp. 161–162).

depression tendencies [the first three stated], the second (currency contraction) is important only as a connective process between the other two—which two should be called The Debt Disease (too much debt) and The Dollar Disease (a swelling dollar)" (Fisher 1932, pp. 28–27). It is argued that only one of the two main factors, i.e. either *the debt disease* or *the dollar disease*, should exist, the resulting drop in output (and possibly prices) would be of a relatively lesser magnitude as compared with the case when both factors coexist. The destructive force of the coexistence lies in their reinforcing and "feeding" one another, namely that *"the very effort of individuals to lessen their burden of debts increases it, because of the mass effect of the stampede to liquidate in swelling each dollar owed"* (Fisher 1933, p. 344). The ultimate effect is that *"the more the debtors pay, the more they owe"* (ibid.). In other words, the more debtors try to pay off their debts, the more they force prices to fall and thus the overall price level decreases. The fall in prices is conditional however. One will result in liquidating his or her portfolio only if the profits do not cover either the principal or the interest payments. As Fisher argues that debts are connected to and interconnect individuals in an economy through money (1932, p. 8), it is the state of uncertainty that might force creditors to call in their borrowers' loans—the "domino effect" then begins. If a large part of the public then tries to sell off their assets to meet their liabilities, there may be large drops in prices of sold assets. This "distress selling", or nowadays also called "fire-sales", is the precondition for the aforementioned dynamics.[10]

Insofar as the proposed "remedies" to the debt-deflation are concerned, these are discussed at some length; however, almost all of them are already being utilized by monetary authorities in fighting against the deflation[11]; among proposed countermeasures, we may found recommendations towards control of interest rates through "open market operations" (ibid., pp. 128–132), adjustment of (volume of) credit to business activity (ibid., pp. 124–125), i.e. now identified as "monetarist policy rule". All of these countermeasures have only one goal in their core—to prevent the price level from falling and thus starting the aforementioned vicious cycle, for it is *the dollar disease* that lies in the heart of the explanation of DDT (ibid., p. 39). Moreover, most of these are of monetary nature meaning that mainly monetary variables are used to fight against deflation, one of the other possibilities is to "reflate" businesses' profits through fiscal policies—this provision is heavily rooted into Minsky's hypothesis of financial instability (1977), which is closely connected with DDT.[12]

---

[10]For the original discussion, see Fisher (1933, pp. 8–30).

[11]Consult Fisher (1932, pp. 113–142) for more details.

[12]For a comprehensive and detailed exposition of Financial Instability Hypothesis, see Minsky (1972, 1978, 1980); in spite of being quoted, reference to DDT is scarce in Minsky's works, notable exception being Minsky (1994).

4.3   Hayek's Hypothesis of Two Rates of Interest

In his early work focused on developing what is now known as the Austrian Business Cycle theory, Hayek postulated that monetary authorities, it be a central bank or any other government entity, had to choose the aim of monetary policy—either to stabilize real purchasing power of money, i.e. stability of price level of consumers' products, or to attempt equalizing (real) savings with investment. It is no surprise that this dichotomy draws heavily from Wicksell's theory and it is its critique. Precisely, Hayek highlights serious contradictions to Wicksell's conception, the notion that "*[o]n one hand [...] the price level remains unaltered when the money rate of interest is the same as the natural rate; and, on the other, that the production of capital goods is, at the same time, kept within the limits imposed by the supply of real savings*" is false (1933 [2008], p. 58), for in an expanding economy the money stock must be increasing in order to stabilize the price level; of course, if we presuppose that the velocity of circulation remains the same.[13] But as Fisher also points out, when loans are granted by commercial banks, money stock increases; then, however, "new" (real) purchasing power has been created and investment need not be, and nowadays certainly is not, restrained by supply of (real) savings. As Hayek finally concludes "*the rate of interest at which, in an expanding economy, the amount of new money entering the circulation is just sufficient to keep the [consumers'] price level stable, is always lower than the rate that would keep the amount of available loan capital equal to the amount the amount simultaneously saved by the public*" (ibid., p. 59). In other words, though the price level might remain unchanged, this may not be so in respect to investment activity, i.e. the amount of debts may simultaneously keep raising.

We have reached a sort of a paradox of our own—the main "course of action" to counteract debt-deflation is, at the same time, the underlying process that leads to further accumulation of debts. From this standpoint, DDT may be regarded as a theory explaining workings of economy after the vicious deflationary circle has begun, but with recommendations that, in the long run at least, defeat themselves. Insofar as the monetary policy is concerned, from a purely theoretical point of view, as this paper tried to expose, the main "monetary policy", i.e. inflation targeting, is contradictory to the so-called "macroprudential policy", which aims at stabilizing the financial sector. As most of investments, nowadays, is financed through loans generated by banks, this necessary presupposes that the amount of loans increases; but if the sentiment is rather pessimistic, the banks themselves may be unwilling to grant loans, quite possibly in order to meet regulatory requirements imposed upon them by monetary authorities, i.e. the conduct of macroprudential policy, or the public itself is not willing to pick up more debt. More so, if the policy goals might be viewed as contradictory.

---

[13]It ought to be noted, however, that Hayek's discussion revolves mainly around the problem of maintaining the neutrality of money. Nevertheless, for purposes of this paper, we shall omit this fact as it does not affect our aim.

The workings of the transmission mechanism of inflation targeting itself, i.e. raising the monetary policy tool if the expected inflation is above inflation target and vice versa, may lead to shifts in expectations if accumulated debts are now deemed too high, i.e. state of over-indebtedness. However, in this case the "failures in rates of interest" are not the *result of* over-indebtedness but rather a *consequence of* shifts in monetary policy itself. Analogically, should monetary authority proceed to "tighten" the macroprudential policy, most probably because the accumulated debts, again, in banks' balance sheets are considered too high, or might reach a critical limit in the near future, this, too, might start a debt-deflation process if the public react excessively.[14] Then, the most effective channel of inflation targeting, i.e. channel of expectations, may work against both maintaining inflation target and achieving stability of financial sector.

4.4 Conclusion

In this paper, we tried to provide a more detailed exposition of the debt-deflation theory as well as to illustrate the possible incompatibility of the two main goals of monetary policy—stability of price level, i.e. maintaining the inflation target, and achieving stability of financial sector. Using the Hayek's hypothesis, we endeavored to show that Fisher's main countermeasure in fighting debt-deflation process might be self-defeating, at least in the long run.

Acknowledgments This paper has been prepared under financial support of Internal Grant Agency of the University of Economics, Prague under a research project no. F1/5/2014 "Financial and Economic Cycles", which author gratefully acknowledges.

References

Brunnermeier MK (2009) Deciphering the liquidity and credit crunch 2007–2008. J Econ Perspect 23(1):77–100
Crotty J (2009) Structural causes of the global financial crisis: a critical assessment of the 'new financial architecture'. Cambridge J Econ 33(4):563–580
Crotty J, Epstein G (2009) Avoiding another meltdown. Challenge 52(1):5–26
Fisher I (1932) Booms and depressions: some first principles. Adelphi Company, New York
Fisher I (1933) The debt-deflation theory of great depressions. Econometrica 1(4):337–357
Hayek FA (1933) [2008] Monetary theory and the trade cycle. In: Salerno JT (ed) Prices and production and other works: F. A. Hayek on money, the business cycle, and the gold standard. Alabama: Ludwig von Mises Institute, pp. 1–130
Kay J (2015) Other people's money: the real business of finance. PublicAffairs, Canada

---

[14]The never ending and excessive discussion of Federal Reserve's decision to raise federal-funds rate is an excellent example.

Keynes JM (1930) A treatise on money V1: the pure theory of money. MacMillan and Co., Great Britain (1930)

Minsky HP (1972) Fundamental reappraisal of the discount mechanism: financial instability revisited: the economics of disaster. Bibliogov (2012)

Minsky HP (1977) The financial instability hypothesis: an interpretation of keynes and an alternative to "standard" theory. Challenge 20(1):20–27 (1977)

Minsky HP (1978) The financial instability hypothesis: a restatement. Thames papers in political economy, pp. 1–25

Minsky HP (1980) Capitalist financial processes and the instability of capitalism. J Econ Issues 14 (2):505–523

Minsky HP (1994) The debt deflation theory of great depressions. Hyman P. Minsky archive, paper 159, pp. 1–10

Schumpeter JA (1911) [2012] The theory of economic development an inquiry into profits, capital, credit, interest, and the business cycle. Piscataway, NJ: Transaction Publishers

Schumpeter JA (1939) [2005] Business cycles: a theoretical, historical, and statistical analysis of the capitalist process. New York: Martino Publishing

Chapter 5
Gold Versus Stocks as an Inflationary Hedge: The Case of Spain

Nesrin Ozatac, Mohamad Kaakeh and Bezhan Rustamov

Abstract This study empirically observes two models based on Fisher hypothesis (1930): (1) long-term hedging ability of the stocks and (2) long-term hedging ability of gold against inflation in Spain. Zivot–Andrews (1992) unit root test allowing for one structural break, Maki (2012) cointegration test allowing for five structural breaks, and vector error correction model (VECM) techniques have been applied to monthly data covering the period of January 1994–July 2015. Our results show that stocks and gold are in a long-term equilibrium relationship with inflation. The negative association between inflation and gold with inelastic coefficient and the positive relationship between inflation and stocks with the elastic coefficient are observed. Hence, our findings suggest that only stocks are the hedging instruments against inflation in Spain.

Keywords Inflation · Stocks · Gold · Hedge · Investment

5.1 Introduction

Traditionally, real estate investments served as the main hedging technique (Hamelink and Hoesli 1996; Gyourko and Linneman 1988). However, for the last several decades, investors have preferred commodities and financial assets against inflation. Gold and stocks mainly reshaped the financial markets by offering variety of hedging abilities (Anari and Kolari 2001; Blose 2010). The gold even holds its

N. Ozatac · M. Kaakeh · B. Rustamov (✉)
Department of Banking and Finance, Eastern Mediterranean University,
via Mersin 10, Famagusta, North Cyprus, Turkey
e-mail: bezhan.rustamov@emu.edu.tr

N. Ozatac
e-mail: nesrin.ozatac@emu.edu.tr

M. Kaakeh
e-mail: mohamad.kaakeh@emu.edu.tr

© Springer International Publishing AG 2017
D. Procházka (ed.), *New Trends in Finance and Accounting*,
Springer Proceedings in Business and Economics,
DOI 10.1007/978-3-319-49559-0_5

place in the portfolios as a store of value, because it is durable, universally acceptable, and easily authenticated (Worthington and Pahlavani 2007). The stocks represent claims on real assets. It means that the real returns on stocks and gold are hedged against the changes in consumer prices. These hedging abilities are based on Fisher hypothesis (1930), who first drew the attention on the relationship between assets' rate of return and expected inflation, concluding that the nominal rate of return comprises the expected real rate of return and expected inflation. This hypothesis unfolds the ability of gold and stocks to hedge against inflation.

Researchers investigated the hedging ability of gold and stocks; however, consensus on the nature of the relationships was not obtained. Some of the studies found that this relationship holds (Schotman and Schweitzer 2000; Anari and Kolari 2001; Ciner 2015) and other studies found that stocks or gold could not serve as a hedging tool against inflation (Barnes et al. 1999).

The reason we have chosen Spain for our study is that the country had a volatile inflation rate over the years, reaching levels about 25% in the late 1970s. Spanish inflation rate shows high persistence, especially from the consumer prospective. That means that any external shock on the economy will have a long-standing effect on inflation (Romero-Ávila and Usabiaga 2012). Moreover, the degree of uncertainty of inflation would rise if Spain exits the European Union, as the uncertainty of inflation is decreased when the Euro was introduced. On top of that, since 2007, the inflation uncertainty has been rising internationally; therefore, protection against inflation risk is mandatory (Hartmann and Herwartz 2014). Investors are seeking more diversification to hedge against many risks including inflation risk. This study's aim is to find out whether stock or gold is a better hedge to inflation in the case of Spain.

This study makes several contributions to the literature. We are pioneer in examining the gold's ability to hedge against inflation in the case of Spain, as gold serves as a hedging tool for a number of countries and can be an effective way of reducing inflation risk. We use time series up-to-date monthly data (January 1994 to July 2015) which includes the global financial crisis data and the effects on Spain that no other paper utilized to examine hedging function of gold and stocks in the case of Spain. Additionally, because of the structural breaks occurring in stocks' market, gold's market, and goods' market, we are applying Zivot–Andrews (1992) and Maki (2012) cointegration techniques to examine the association among inflation, gold, and stocks which have the ability to determine the structural breaks that are influencing this long-run association.

5.2 Literature Review

Portfolio optimization and risk reduction are one of the most important topics in the finance literature. Particularly, researchers observe the hedging ability of the instruments in order to reduce a number of risks including inflation. The supporting theory is based on the generalized Fisher (1930) hypothesis implying that there is a one-to-one relation between nominal asset rates of return and inflation. It has found its applicability to examine hedging ability of stocks and gold against inflation.

5.2.1 Stocks and Inflation

Studies on examining hedging ability of stocks against inflation divided researchers on those supporting the Fisher hypothesis (Schotman and Schweitzer 2000; Anari and Kolari 2001; Ciner 2015) and those who found contradictory results (Lintner 1975; Jaffe and Mandelker 1976; Nelson 1976; Fama and Schwert 1977; Fama 1981; Kaul 1987; Barnes et al. 1999).

In Greece (Hondroyiannis and Papapetrou 2006) and six industrial countries including France and Germany (Anari and Kolari 2001), short-term hedging ability of stocks has been observed. Fama (1981) noted that the observed inverse relationship between real stock returns and inflation is spurious, because inflation acts as a proxy for real-activity variables in models that examine stock returns and inflation. Under this "proxy hypothesis," stocks are positively related to expected economic activity, while expected economic activity and inflation have a negative relation, and thus, stocks' prices and inflation have a negative association.

Schotman and Schweitzer (2000) confirmed, however, that when investment horizon changes, negative inflation hedge ability of stocks becomes positive. It is important to observe the way stocks move with inflation in longer periods (Boudoukh and Richardson 1993), because investors hold equities for longtime horizons. Hedging ability of stocks against inflation for long term has been observed in UK (Luintel and Paudyal 2006), USA (Kim and Ryoo 2011), and emerging markets (Spyrou 2004).

The similar results were examined in Spain (Gregoriou and Kontonikas 2010; Omay et al. 2015) but in a cross-country analysis. However, Barnes et al. (1999) examining 25 countries including Spain found a negative association between stocks' returns and inflation. Moreover, Ely and Robinson (1997) could not find a significant long-term relationship between stocks and goods prices and found that the impact of stocks on goods is insignificant. Rapach (2002) found that the series considered for Spain are I (0), and based on that, the author could not investigate the hedging abilities of stocks against inflation in the case of Spain.

5.2.2 Gold and Inflation

Investors have always added gold to their portfolios because of its diversification benefits, hedging abilities against risks such as inflation, currency, political, and oil price fluctuations (Worthington and Pahlavani 2007). Many researchers studied the hedging ability of gold (Jaffe 1989; Aggarwal 1992; Mahdavi and Zhou 1997;

Blose 2010; Mulyadi and Anwar 2012; Bredin et al. 2015) and observed that it is an effective hedge against currency risk (Capie et al. 2005; Ozturk and Acikalin 2008; Joy 2011; Saraç and Zeren 2014), systematic risk with even a zero-beta, and safe haven for stocks (Baur and Lucey 2010; Baur and McDermott 2010; Gurgun and Unalmis 2014), but only it does not hedge against oil price movements (Reboredo 2013).

To confirm the role of the gold as an inflationary hedge in USA, Worthington and Pahlavani (2007) applied Zivot and Andrews (1992) unit root test that allows for one structural break and cointegration test. But in the long term, gold is partially able to hedge future inflation (Beckmann and Czudaj 2013). This result also confirmed better hedging ability of gold in the case of UK and the USA compared to Japan and the Euro by applying the Markov switching vector error correction model.

In a recent study, Shahbaz et al. (2014) stated that investment in gold is a good hedge against inflation not only in the long run but also in the short run. Long et al. (2013) confirmed this short-term association that gold offers hedging inflation and their results align with the Fisher hypothesis in the case of Vietnam.

Gold is an effective hedging tool in a number of countries (among others; USA, Pakistan, Vietnam, UK, and Japan), but the properties of gold against inflation have not been yet studied in the case of Spain. This paper is the first to investigate the hedging abilities of gold against inflation in the case of Spain.

5.3 Data and Methodology

5.3.1 Data

This study investigates the hedging abilities of stocks and gold against inflation by using monthly data of consumer price index (CPI) for the period of January 1994 to July 2015 expressed in terms of index points as a proxy for inflation. IBEX 35 index denominated in Euro with monthly frequency was used as a proxy for stocks. Both series were obtained from DataStream (Thomson Reuters). Monthly data of gold prices denominated in Euro were used in this analysis and were obtained from the World Gold Council. All series are used in their logarithmic form.

In this paper, the following models are estimated:

$$\ln\text{Gold} = \beta_1 + \beta_2 \ln\text{CPI} + \varepsilon_t \tag{5.1}$$

$$\ln\text{Stock} = \beta_1 + \beta_2 \ln\text{CPI} + \varepsilon_t \tag{5.2}$$

where β_1 is the intercept, ε_t is the white noise, β_2 is the long-run coefficient, lnCPI is the logarithmic form of consumer price index, lnGold is the logarithmic form of gold price, and lnStock is the logarithmic form of stock price.

5.3.2   Methodology

This study employed time series econometrics techniques to examine the hedging abilities of gold and stocks against inflation. We tested the stationarity of the series in order to decide on the most appropriate econometrics methods. Zivot and Andrews (1992) unit root test was used to determine whether the series are stationary or not. It is superior to other tests by taking into account structural breaks if any exist in the series. Maki's (2012) cointegration test was applied to examine the existence of long-term relationship even in the existence of structural breaks. Vector error correction models were employed to estimate the long-term coefficients.

5.3.2.1   Unit Root

Traditional unit root tests such as Dickey–Fuller test (1981) and Phillips and Perron (1988) (PP) take serial correlation into account but do not take structural breaks into consideration. Structural breaks occur in many time series as economic conditions change. If these structural breaks are not taken into consideration when testing for unit root in the time series, the results are likely to be misleading. The null hypothesis of unit root existence would not be rejected, but it is likely to be rejected when these structural breaks are considered. In other words, tests such as ADF and PP may falsely show that a series is not stationary, while the opposite is true if the structural break was included in the test.

Zivot and Andrews (1992) developed a test that allows for one structural break and determines the time of the structural break endogenously. The test has three different models: Model A allows for structural break in the intercept; Model B allows for structural break in the slope; and Model C allows for structural break in both the intercept and the slope.

5.3.2.2   Cointegration and Vector Error Correction Models (VECMs)

Maki (2012) developed a new cointegration test that assumes every period to be a possible breaking point. The test calculates t-statistic for each of the periods; after that, the test would compare the t-statistic results and report the periods with the lowest t-values as structural breaks. The test allows up to five structural breaks in the time series. All the series must be integrated of order 1 ($I(1)$) in order to test for cointegration. Maki proposed four models: Model 1—with a break in the intercept and without a trend; Model 2—with a break in the intercept and coefficients, and without a trend; Model 3—with a break in the intercept and coefficients, and with a trend; Model 4—with a break in the intercept, coefficients, and trend.

The test has the null hypothesis of no cointegration against the alternative hypothesis of cointegration with i breaks (maximum five). Critical values for Maki's cointegration test are calculated via Monte Carlo simulations and reported in

Maki (2012). Confirming cointegration between series indicates that there is a long-term relationship between the two variables.

To estimate the short- and long-run coefficients, vector error correction models (VECMs) should be applied. If the sign of the coefficient is positive, we can identify the hedging ability of the instrument.

5.4 Empirical Results

5.4.1 Unit Root Test Results

The result of Zivot and Andrews (1992) unit root test is presented in Table 5.1. Findings reveal that three series are not stationary at their level. But when taking the first difference, the null hypothesis of the existence of the unit root can be rejected. For the lnStock series, the break points are April 1998 and January 2008. It is apparent to have these break dates, because in 1998, Spain was preparing to join the EU and 2008 is a financial crisis period that affected Spain as well. The same break point is present in lnCPI, along with other two significant structural dates: March 2002 and April 2012. In 2002, the euro currency was printed as notes and coins and they began to circulate in the European Union (Silvia 2004). The 2012 is the year when Standard and Poor's Ratings Services downgraded the Spanish government's debt (Davies 2012) and the financial crisis became severe in Spain. It is seen that lnGold has the same break years as lnStock and lnCPI.

Table 5.1 ZA (1992) tests for unit root under a single structural break

	Statistics (level)			Statistics (first difference)			Conclusion
	ZA_B	ZA_T	ZA_I	ZA_B	ZA_T	ZA_I	
lnStock	−3.097	−3.469	−2.838	−7.781[*]	−7.243[*]	−7.486[*]	I (1)
BY	03:2000	06:1997	01:2008	04:1998	09:2011	08:1998	
LL	3	0	3	4	4	4	
lnCPI	−2.402	−2.240	−0.786	−10.05[*]	−9.872[*]	−10.04[*]	I (1)
BY	03:2007	04:2012	03:2002	07:2008	04:2012	07:2008	
LL	4	4	4	3	3	3	
lnGold	−2.689	−2.235	−3.179	−9.320[*]	−8.937[*]	−9.309[*]	I (1)
BY	09:2009	12:1997	09:2005	03:2012	05:2010	12:2011	
LL	3	3	3	2	2	2	

Notes lnStock is price index of Spain's financial market; lnCPI is consumer price index; lnGold is price of gold; BY is break year; and LL is lag length. All of the series are at their natural logarithms. ZA_B represents the model with a break in both the trend and intercept; ZA_T is the model with a break in the trend; and ZA_I is the model with a break in the intercept
[*], [**], and [***] denote the rejection of the null hypothesis at the 1, 5, and 10% levels, respectively
Tests for unit roots were carried out in E-VIEWS 7

5.4.2 Cointegration

5.4.2.1 Maki Cointegration

The Johansen cointegration (1990) test does not consider structural breaks in the series, and it might provide biased results, if there are any structural breaks in the series. Therefore, employing Maki's (2012) method is appropriate. Results of cointegration test for the main effects under multiple structural breaks are given in Tables 5.2 and 5.3.

It is shown in Table 5.2 that the null hypothesis of no cointegration can be rejected with the existence of multiple breaks and through model 3 suggested by Maki (2012) and that confirms the existence of the long-term relationship between stock price and inflation. The most significant break points are July 1998, August 2007, and September 2008, which are consistent with the breaks provided by Zivot and Andrews (1992) unit root test. Table 5.3 shows results that confirm the existence of the long-term relationship between inflation and gold as the null hypothesis of no cointegration can be rejected.

5.4.2.2 Vector Error Correction Model Results

Based on the results from Johansen cointegration, the long-term relationship exists between inflation and stock price and inflation and gold price.

Tables 5.4 and 5.5 present the results of VECM. Both models have a significant speed of adjustment. For the relationship between stock price and inflation, the

Table 5.2 Maki (2012) cointegration test for the main effects under multiple structural breaks

Number of break points	Test statistics [critical values]	Break points
$T_B \leq 4$ Model 3	-7.20 $[-7.009]^{**}$	07:1998; 08:2001; 09:2008; 07:2011
$T_B \leq 5$ Model 3	-7.576 $[-7.414]^{**}$	07:1998; 08:2001; 08:2007; 09:2008; 07:2011

Notes Main Effects Model: lnStock = f (lnCPI). Numbers in corner brackets are critical values at 0.05 level from Table 1 of Maki (2012)
*denotes statistical significance at 0.01 level. **0.05; ***0.1

Table 5.3 Maki (2012) cointegration test for the main effects under multiple structural breaks

Number of break points	Test statistics [critical values]	Break points
$T_B \leq 4$ Model 2	-5.888 $[-6.011]^{***}$	07:1999; 12:2007; 01:2009; 07:2013

Notes Main Effects Model: lnGold = f (lnCPI). Numbers in corner brackets are critical values at 0.05 level from Table 1 of Maki (2012)
*denotes statistical significance at 0.01 level. **0.05; ***0.1

Table 5.4 Results on VECM output (lnStock, lnCPI)

Result	Variable	Coefficient	Standard error	t-statistic	P-value
Speed of adjustment	ΔlnStock	−0.017231	0.00577	−2.98692	0.0031
Long-run relationship	lnCPI (−1)	2.927634	1.31920	2.21924	–

Table 5.5 Results on VECM output (lnGold, lnCPI)

Result	Variable	Coefficient	Standard Error	t-statistic	P-value
Speed of adjustment	Δ lnGold	−0.016148	0.00626	−2.57871	0.0105
Long-run relationship	lnCPI (−1)	−4.363080	0.67467	−6.46702	–

speed of adjustment is 1.72%. It indicates that stock price converges to its long-run equilibrium by the short-run values of inflation at 1.72% speed of adjustment. The long-term coefficient of lnCPI is equal to 2.927, which means that when lnCPI increases by 1%, lnStock increases by 2.927%. It gives an important signal that stocks can hedge inflation.

The relationship between gold price and inflation has the speed of adjustment of 1.61%, which means that gold price converges to its long-run equilibrium by the short-run values of inflation at 1.61% speed of adjustment. The long-term coefficient of lnCPI is equal to −4.363 which mean that when lnCPI increases by 1%, lnGold will decrease by 4.36%. It reveals that gold cannot be utilized to hedge against inflation.

5.5 Conclusion

During times of financial crisis and difficulties, investors often seek to lessen the risk associated with investments, especially the risk of inflation. The hedge properties of stocks and gold against inflation are well covered in the literature. However, studies examining the case of Spain are very limited. This study examined the long-run hedging abilities of stocks and gold against inflation in the case of Spain. Due to the structural changes occurring in the gold's market, stocks' market, and consumer prices, this study used Zivot–Andrews unit root test that allows for one structural break and Maki's cointegration that allows to up to five structural breaks to determine the structural breaks affecting the long-term relationship between gold and inflation and stocks and inflation. We applied data covering the period of January 1994–July 2015 to examine the long-run relationship and investigate the hedging properties of both gold and stocks.

The results confirm the existence of long-term relationship between both stocks and inflation and gold and inflation with several structural breaks. The main structural breaks that affected the hedging ability of gold and stocks are 1999, the global financial crisis years, and 2012. In 1999, Spain joined the EU and started converting its currency to euro, and in 2012, the financial crisis became severe in Spain.

Vector error correction models provided the long-run coefficients that were significant for both models. Gold and inflation model had a negative coefficient of −4.36 which indicates that gold cannot serve as a hedging tool against inflation. On the other hand, stock and inflation model had a positive coefficient of 2.927, which is bigger than one, implying that over the long run, stocks can act as an inflationary hedge. Results are in favor of Fisher's general hypothesis.

References

Aggarwal R (1992) Gold markets. New Palgrave Dictionary Money Finan 2:257–258

Anari A, Kolari J (2001) Stock prices and inflation. J Financ Res 24(4):587–602

Barnes M, Boyd JH, Smith BD (1999) Inflation and asset returns. Eur Econ Rev 43(4):737–754

Baur DG, Lucey BM (2010) Is gold a hedge or a safe haven? an analysis of stocks, bonds and gold. Financ Rev 45(2):217–229

Baur DG, McDermott TK (2010) Is gold a safe haven? international evidence. J Bank Finance 34 (8):1886–1898

Beckmann J, Czudaj R (2013) Gold as an inflation hedge in a time-varying coefficient framework. North Am J Econ Finan 24:208–222

Bredin D, Conlon T, Potì V (2015) Does gold glitter in the long-run? gold as a hedge and safe haven across time and investment horizon. Int Rev Financ Anal 41:320–328

Blose LE (2010) Gold prices, cost of carry, and expected inflation. J Econ Bus 62(1):35–47

Boudoukh J, Richardson M (1993) Stock returns and inflation: a long-horizon perspective. Am Econ Rev 83(5):1346–1355

Capie F, Mills TC, Wood G (2005) Gold as a hedge against the dollar. J Int Financ Markets Inst Money 15(4):343–352

Ciner C (2015) Are equities good inflation hedges? a frequency domain perspective. Rev Financ Econ 24:12–17

Davies N (2012) Spanish economy in "huge crisis" after credit downgrade. Available via Reuters. http://www.reuters.com/article/us-spain-economy-idUSBRE83Q0BQ20120427. Accessed 23 Jan 2016

Dickey DA, Fuller WA (1981) Likelihood ratio statistics for autoregressive time series with a unit root. Econometrica: J Econ Soc 49(4):1057–1072

Ely DP, Robinson KJ (1997) Are stocks a hedge against inflation? international evidence using a long-run approach. J Int Money Finan 16(1):141–167

Fama EF (1981) Stock returns, real activity, inflation, and money. Am Econ Rev 71(4):545–565

Fama EF, Schwert GW (1977) Asset returns and inflation. J Financ Econ 5(2):115–146

Fisher I (1930) The theory of interest. Macmillan, New York

Gregoriou A, Kontonikas A (2010) The long-run relationship between stock prices and goods prices: new evidence from panel cointegration. J Int Financ Markets Inst Money 20(2): 166–176

Gürgün G, Ünalmış İ (2014) Is gold a safe haven against equity market investment in emerging and developing countries? Finan Res Lett 11(4):341–348

Gyourko J, Linneman P (1988) Owner-occupied homes, income-producing properties, and REITs as inflation hedges: empirical findings. J Real Estate Finan Econ 1(4):347–372

Hamelink F, Hoesli M (1996) Swiss real estate as a hedge against inflation: new evidence using hedonic and autoregressive models. J Property Finan 7(1):33–49

Hartmann M, Herwartz H (2014) Did the introduction of the Euro have an impact on inflation uncertainty? - an empirical assessment. Macroecon Dyn 18(06):1313–1325

Hondroyiannis G, Papapetrou E (2006) Stock returns and inflation in Greece: a markov switching approach. Rev Financ Econ 15(1):76–94

Jaffe JF (1989) Gold and gold stocks as investments for institutional portfolios. Financ Anal J 45(2):53–59

Jaffe JF, Mandelker G (1976) The value of the firm under regulation. J Finan 31(2):701–713

Joy M (2011) Gold and the US dollar: hedge or haven? Finan Res Lett 8(3):120–131

Johansen S, Juselius K (1990) Maximum likelihood estimation and inference on cointegration—with applications to the demand for money. Oxford Bull Econ Stat 52(2):169–210

Kaul G (1987) Stock returns and inflation: the role of the monetary sector. J Financ Econ 18(2):253–276

Kim JH, Ryoo HH (2011) Common stocks as a hedge against inflation: evidence from century-long US data. Econ Lett 113(2):168–171

Le Long H, De Ceuster MJ, Annaert J, Amonhaemanon D (2013) Gold as a hedge against inflation: the Vietnamese case. Procedia Econ Finan 5:502–511

Lintner J (1975) Inflation and security returns. J Finan 30(2):259–280

Luintel KB, Paudyal K (2006) Are common stocks a hedge against inflation? J Financ Res 29(1):1–19

Mahdavi S, Zhou S (1997) Gold and commodity prices as leading indicators of inflation: tests of long-run relationship and predictive performance. J Econ Bus 49(5):475–489

Maki D (2012) Tests for cointegration allowing for an unknown number of breaks. Econ Model 29(5):2011–2015

Mulyadi MS, Anwar Y (2012) Gold versus stock investment: an econometric analysis. Int J Dev Sustain 1(1):1–7

Nelson CR (1976) Inflation and rates of return on common stocks. J Finan 31(2):471–483

Omay T, Yuksel A, Yuksel A (2015) An empirical examination of the generalized fisher effect using cross-sectional correlation robust tests for panel cointegration. J Int Financ Markets Inst Money 35:18–29

Ozturk F, Acikalin S (2008) Is gold a hedge against Turkish Lira? S East Eur J Econ Bus 3(1):35–40

Phillips PC, Perron P (1988) Testing for a unit root in time series regression. Biometrika 75(2):335–346

Rapach DE (2002) The long-run relationship between inflation and real stock prices. J Macroecon 24(3):331–351

Reboredo JC (2013) Is gold a hedge or safe haven against oil price movements? Resour Policy 38(2):130–137

Romero-Ávila D, Usabiaga C (2012) Disaggregate evidence on Spanish inflation persistence. Appl Econ 44(23):3029–3046

Saraç M, Zeren F (2014) Is gold investment an effective hedge against inflation and us dollar? Evidence from Turkey. Econ Comput & Econ Cybern Stud & Res 48(4):308

Schotman PC, Schweitzer M (2000) Horizon sensitivity of the inflation hedge of stocks. J Empir Finance 7(3):301–315

Shahbaz M, Tahir MI, Ali I, Rehman IU (2014) Is gold investment a hedge against inflation in Pakistan? a co-integration and causality analysis in the presence of structural breaks. North Am J Econ Finan 28:190–205

Silvia SJ (2004) Is the Euro working? the Euro and European labour markets. J Public Policy 24(02):147–168

Spyrou SI (2004) Are stocks a good hedge against inflation? Evidence from Emerging Markets. Appl Econ 36(1):41–48

Worthington AC, Pahlavani M (2007) Gold investment as an inflationary hedge: cointegration evidence with allowance for endogenous structural breaks. Appl Financ Econ Lett 3(4):259–262

Zivot E, Andrews DW (1992) Further evidence on the great crash, the oil-price shock, and the unit-root. J Bus Econ Stat 10(3):251–270

Chapter 6
Is There a Relation Between HDI and Economic Performances?

Efehan Ulas and Burak Keskin

Abstract The aim of this study is to compare the economic performances of 20 selected countries, in terms of their growth rate, for the period 2010–2014. We include economic performance indicators as growth rate, GDP per capita, youth unemployment, inflation rate, and account balance. Firstly, AHP is used for the determination of the weights for indicators. Then, ranking is carried out with TOPSIS analyses. Results show that the best performance is showed by Germany. In addition, mean HDI (Human Development Index) scores for the period 2010–2014 are calculated and countries are ranked. To understand the effect of HDI on economic performances, we investigated the relationship between these two findings with Spearman's rank correlation coefficient. It is clear that there is a positive correlation between HDI and economic performances.

Keywords TOPSIS · AHP · Economic performance · HDI

6.1 Introduction

In last decades, many countries have achieved varying levels of economic developments. Furthermore, the development rate changes over time. For instance, the rate is decreased if the country is developed. However, other factors are important to understand the economic performance in such countries. Main indicators of improvement play an important role for ranking in economic performance in countries. In many countries, the conduct of a nation's economic policy usually has four goals: unemployment, trade balance, GDP per capita, and inflation. The Organization for Economic Cooperation and Development (OECD) generally used

E. Ulas (✉)
Department of Statistics, Cankiri Karatekin University, Cankiri, Turkey
e-mail: ef_ulas@hotmail.com; efehanulas@karatekin.edu.tr

B. Keskin
Department of Business Administration, Cankiri Karatekin University, Cankiri, Turkey
e-mail: burakkeskiin@gmail.com; burakkeskin@karatekin.edu.tr

© Springer International Publishing AG 2017   61
D. Procházka (ed.), *New Trends in Finance and Accounting*,
Springer Proceedings in Business and Economics,
DOI 10.1007/978-3-319-49559-0_6

these indicators for calculating economic performances of countries. Economic growth has impact on nation's voice on an international scale as well as competes with the other nations in other fields such as military, politics, international treaty, and so on.

The aim of this study is to deliver a report for economic performance in 20 European countries between the years 2010–2014. Our study utilises the Okun's Misery Index, which comprises of unemployment rate and inflation rate. Furthermore, we consider OECD's magic diamond measures which are growth of GDP, inflation rate, unemployment rate, and the GDP-normalized trade balance. Five different indicators are used in this study to evaluate economic performance for each nation. GDP per capita is considered as one of the key indicators which is reflecting a society's welfare and improvement of global competitiveness. Youth unemployment has impact on nation's economic growth. Inflation as measured by the consumer price index reflects the annual percentage change in the cost to the average consumer of acquiring a basket of goods and services that may be fixed or changed at specified intervals, such as yearly. So that it is one of the important factors that affect economic performance. We also consider current account balance and growth rate for economic performance ranking.

In this study, the weights of indicators are determined with analytic hierarchy process (AHP) between the years 2010–2014. Economic performances are calculated and ranked using the method called Technique for Order Preference by Similarity to Ideal Solution (TOPSIS) approach. Furthermore, results will be compared with mean of Human Development Index (HDI) for the years 2010–2014.

6.2 Literature Review

There are many studies in the literature-related economic performances. Some studies had focused on economic growth rates of developing–developed countries, and some of them had focused on region of nations. Literature review on economic performances of different countries is as follows:

Ashourian (2012) used multiple attribute decision making (MADM) method to study the rank of performance of selected Middle East and North Africa (MANA) countries. This approach is a management science technique that is popularly used to rank indicated that the MENA countries achieved higher values of desirable attributes.

Cam et al. (2015) analyzed financial performances of textile firms publicly traded in The Borsa Istanbul via TOPSIS method by using financial rates in 2010–2013. They calculated rates for financial performance and measurements have been converted to one single score through TOPSIS method and firms have been ranked. After, in the next step, the TOPSIS ranking score is compared with the ranking using traditional performance indicators. They found that TOPSIS performance scores show variability in the term and do not match with rankings which are done using traditional performance measurement.

Chattopadhyay and Bose (2015) studied composite indicator design to summarize in a single statistic variety of different facets of macroeconomic performance and assessed relative performances of countries with six different indicators which are the growth rate of real GDP, real per capita GDP, unemployment rate, fiscal balance, rate of inflation, and current account balance. They first calculated the performance scores obtained from TOPSIS method and the country rankings in each year according to those scores. Then, rankings are summarized in terms of measures which together depict the degree of stability or disarray in country-wise rankings over the years. Correspondence analysis (CA) is applied for providing a graphical display of the status of rankings elegantly which summarizes the cross-sectional variability in the relative positions of countries.

Mandic et al. (2014) proposed a multi-criteria fuzzy model that eases financial performance where TOPSIS approach is used to rank the banks and they used the data collected from Serbian banks between the years 2005 and 2010.

Bao et al. (2010) investigated the application of the classical TOPSIS method, for which crisp numerical values replace the linguistic assessments that might face some practical problems because of vague judgment. They use the TOPSIS approach proposed to make a more rational decision.

Gustav (2004) discussed that human development may be a necessary prerequisite for long-term sustainable growth. It may exhibit threshold effects, in the sense that nations must attain a certain HD level before future economic growth becomes sustainable.

6.3   Methodology

Analytic hierarchy process (AHP) and TOPSIS method are applied to the selected indicators to evaluate economic performance of nations between the years 2010 and 2014. The countries are selected from their growth rate. 20 European countries which have the highest GDP rates are included in this study. AHP is used to determine weights of criteria that are subsequently inserted to weighted decision matrix in TOPSIS approach. The implementation is carried out with R statistical software and Excel Solver.

6.3.1   Analytic Hierarchical Process (AHP)

In this study, AHP approach is used to determine weighting of the components of the economic performance. Table 6.1 presents possible classification of the strength of preferences. This nine fundamental scale is introduced by Saaty and Alexander in 1981. The calculation procedure is clearly explained by Wabalickis (1987). Firstly,

Table 6.1 The fundamental AHP scale

Intensity of importance	Definition	Explanation
1	Equal importance	Two activities contribute equally
3	Moderate importance	Experience and judgement slightly favor
5	Strong importance	Experience and judgement strongly favor
7	Very strong importance	An activity is strongly favored
9	Absolute importance	Highest possible order
2, 4, 6, 8	Intermediate values	When compromise is needed
Reciprocals	If activity i has one of the above numbers assigned to it when compared with activity, then j has the reciprocal value when compared with i	
Rationals	Ratios arising from the scale	If consistency were to be forced by obtaining a numerical values to span the matrix

Source Saaty (1987)

each element of the pairwise comparison matrix is divided by the sum of the column. Then, obtained new matrix rows are summed and mean of the rows is taken. Same process is repeated for each column and final matrix is found as weighted matrix. This process is done for countries and indicators separately. Then, final weighted matrix is obtained by multiplying country and indicator matrix.

6.3.2 TOPSIS

After weights are calculated with AHP approach, TOPSIS is used to rank the economic performances of nations. It is a distance-based approach and TOPSIS is a method that is used for multi-attribute decision making by ranking the alternatives according to the closest between the alternative and ideal. TOPSIS has four assumptions (Opricovic and Tzend 2004);

1. A quantitative value, ω_i, can be assigned to each criterion, K_i, representing its importance.
2. For each K_i, a quantitative value, V_{ij}, can be assigned to each alternative, α_j, representing the performance of α_j on the basis of K_i.
3. The performance of each alternative relative to each criterion can be evaluated on the basis of a common scale.
4. The criteria are different and mutually independent.

The computational procedure of TOPSIS method is provided by Mahmoodzadeh et al. (2007) as follows:

1. An $n \times q$ matrix contains the raw consequence data for all alternatives against all criteria.
2. Vector normalization: Each α_j is assigned a quantitative value, each K_i representing the performance of α_j:

$$V_{IJ}^* = \frac{V_{ij}}{\sqrt{\sum_{i=1}^{n} V_{ij}^2}} \tag{6.1}$$

3. Assign weights to criteria:

$$\sum_{i=1}^{n} \omega_i = 1. \tag{6.2}$$

4. Define the ideal and anti-ideal point: Set the ideal point, a^+, and anti-ideal point, a^-. For a benefit criterion c_j, $v_j(a^+) = \max v_j^i$ and $v_j(a^-) = \min v_j^i$; for a cost criterion, c_k, $v_j(a^-) = \max v_j^i$ and $v_j(a^+) = \min v_j^i$.
5. Calculate the separation measures using Euclidean distance, where $U(v_{ij})$ is a weighted value:

$$\delta_j^+ = \sqrt{\sum_{1}^{n} U\big((v_{ij}) - U_i^+\big) \cdot U\big((v_{ij}) - U_i^+\big)} \tag{6.3}$$

$$\delta_j^- = \sqrt{\sum_{1}^{n} U\big((v_{ij}) - U_i^-\big) \cdot U\big((v_{ij}) - U_i^-\big)} \tag{6.4}$$

6. Calculate the relative closeness to the ideal solution. The overall value, $U(a_j)$, of each a_j is calculated using the following:

$$U(a_j) = \frac{\delta_j^+}{\delta_j^+ - \delta_j^-} \tag{6.5}$$

6.4 Implementation and Results

The dataset is obtained directly from World Bank Web site for the period 2010–2014. So that dataset which is used in this study is reliable. Some countries are eliminated from the dataset due to their growth rate because first 20 countries with the highest growth rate are included in this study. The analysis was carried out with the statistical software R and Excel. The weights are calculated with AHP approach.

Then, ranking is done with TOPSIS method. Five important indicators that are affecting the economic performances are selected. The selected indicators are GDP per capita, youth unemployment, inflation, account balance, and growth rate. Indicators were selected based on the survey literature mentioned at the previous section.

The weights and descriptive statistics for indicators can be seen in the Table 6.2.

Table 6.3 gives the mean scores of countries for the years 2010–2014. The analysis was carried out with these mean scores. The first 20 countries with the highest growth rate in Europe are included in this study. Countries included in this paper can be seen in the table below. AHP approach is used to determine weights for indicators. Calculated weights for each indicator are given in Table 6.1. These

Table 6.2 Descriptive statistics

	Growth rate	Youth unemployment	Inflation	GDP per capita	Account balance
Weights	0.2833	0.1806	0.2024	0.1826	0.1511
Mean	0.2	21.88	1.74	47.80	16.51
S.D	1.7278	12.3130	0.7924	19.2604	63.3008
Max	3.16	51.78	4.10	97.09	239
Min	−4.89	8.26	0	21.90	−99.62

Table 6.3 Mean scores of countries between 2010 and 2014

Country	Growth rate	Youth unemployment	Inflation	GDP per capita	Current balance
1. England	1.96	19.62	2.92	41.43	−99.62
2. France	1.01	23.18	1.39	43.51	−32.48
3. Germany	2.01	8.32	1.52	46.57	239.0
4. Luxembourg	3.16	17.00	2.14	75.70	3.30
5. Netherland	0.51	9.58	1.91	52.90	84.53
6. Spain	−0.78	51.78	1.74	30.42	−20.42
7. Italy	−0.54	35.18	1.76	36.21	−18.06
8. Slovenia	0.23	18.92	1.64	23.80	1.37
9. Denmark	0.54	13.58	1.76	61.21	20.51
10. Switzerland	1.91	8.26	0.00	82.34	63.40
11. Norway	1.45	8.80	1.71	97.09	57.81
12. Austria	1.23	8.80	2.23	49.95	6.34
13. Sweden	2.39	23.84	0.96	58.32	38.52
14. Belgium	1.20	21.50	2.00	47.26	1.25
15. Ireland	1.95	28.00	0.80	44.20	7.20
16. Portugal	−0.84	32.90	1.57	21.90	−7.82
17. Finland	0.52	19.18	1.99	49.08	−0.33
18. Greece	−4.89	48.62	1.46	24.80	−12.28
19. Cyprus	0.96	18.32	1.68	19.08	−3.06
20. Iceland	2.97	25.30	2.33	13.22	−19.62
21. World	2.81	13.86	3.45	10.21	15.71

scores are 0.2833, 0.1806, 0.2024, 0.1826, and 0.1511 for growth rate, youth unemployment, inflation, GDP per capita, and account balance, respectively. The mean score for "world" is added to data for the purpose of comparison.

After weights are calculated, the decision matrix is created and normalized decision matrix is obtained from formula (6.1). Then, the normalized values are multiplied by weights and weighted normalized decision matrix is obtained which is shown in Table 6.3. Furthermore, positive ideal and negative ideal scores are calculated. Maximum value in each column of matrix is selected for positive ideal set and minimum value in each column of matrix is selected for negative ideal set.

Positive Ideal: {0.0962, 0.0147, 0.000, 0.0632, 0.1225}
Negative Ideal: {−0.1489, 0.0922, 0.1197, 0.0143, −0.0511} (Table 6.4).

Separation measures from the ideal positive and ideal negative for each country are calculated. Formula (6.5) is used for calculating relative closeness. Ranking of countries in terms of their economic performance can be seen in Table 6.5. Germany is found as the country that shows the best economic performance.

Table 6.4 Weighted normalized decision matrix of countries

Country	Growth rate	Youth unemployment	Inflation	GDP per capita	Current balance
1. England	0.0597	0.0349	0.0853	0.0270	−0.0511
2. France	0.0308	0.0413	0.0406	0.0283	−0.0167
3. Germany	0.0612	0.0148	0.0444	0.0303	0.1225
4. Luxembourg	0.0962	0.0303	0.0625	0.0493	0.0017
5. Netherland	0.0155	0.0171	0.0558	0.0344	0.0433
6. Spain	−0.0238	0.0922	0.0508	0.0198	−0.0105
7. Italy	−0.0164	0.0627	0.0514	0.0236	−0.0095
8. Slovenia	0.0070	0.0337	0.0479	0.0155	0.0007
9. Denmark	0.0164	0.0242	0.0514	0.0398	0.0105
10. Switzerland	0.0582	0.0147	0.0000	0.0536	0.0325
11. Norway	0.0442	0.0157	0.0499	0.0632	0.0296
12. Austria	0.0375	0.0157	0.0651	0.0325	0.0033
13. Sweden	0.0728	0.0425	0.0280	0.0380	0.0197
14. Belgium	0.0365	0.0383	0.0584	0.0308	0.0006
15. Ireland	0.0594	0.0499	0.0234	0.0288	0.0037
16. Portugal	−0.0256	0.0586	0.0458	0.0143	−0.0040
17. Finland	0.0158	0.0342	0.0581	0.0319	−0.0002
18. Greece	−0.1489	0.0866	0.0426	0.0161	−0.0063
19. Cyprus	−0.0509	0.0487	0.0368	0.0189	−0.0007
20. Iceland	0.0323	0.0235	0.1197	0.0262	0.0000
21. World	0.0856	0.0247	0.0604	0.0066	0.0081

Table 6.5 Topsis S+, S−, C*
scores

Country	S+	S-	C*	Ranking
1. England	0.2012	0.2194	0.5217	14
2. France	0.1650	0.2062	0.5555	11
3. Germany	0.0654	0.2936	0.8178	1
4. Luxembourg	0.1376	0.2668	0.6597	5
5. Netherland	0.1293	0.2147	0.6241	7
6. Spain	0.2063	0.1486	0.4188	18
7. Italy	0.1914	0.1578	0.4518	16
8. Slovenia	0.1665	0.1886	0.5311	13
9. Denmark	0.1490	0.2027	0.5764	10
10. Switzerland	0.0982	0.2678	0.7317	2
11. Norway	0.1176	0.2386	0.6698	4
12. Austria	0.1512	0.2165	0.5887	8
13. Sweden	0.1154	0.2561	0.6895	3
14. Belgium	0.1531	0.2098	0.5781	9
15. Ireland	0.1358	0.2401	0.6387	6
16. Portugal	0.1931	0.1550	0.4453	17
17. Finland	0.1620	0.1929	0.5435	12
18. Greece	0.2930	0.0893	0.2336	20
19. Cyprus	0.2032	0.1447	0.4160	19
20. Iceland	0.1868	0.2007	0.5180	15

Switzerland, Sweden, Norway, and Luxembourg are followed, respectively. If we include world as a country in this study, it takes the rank of 4th place. In order to make comparison for economic performances, Human Development Index values are ranked and compared with economic performance ranking which is found in this study.

Human development has important effects on economic growth. More specifically, each of the components of human development is likely to have a distinct impact on economic growth. Thus, to understand its effect on economic performances, we compared mean HDI scores with economic performances found using TOPSIS analysis. Mean scores of HDI values for 2010–2014 can be seen in Table 6.6. The first 20 countries in ranking of economic performances and the first 20 countries which get the highest HDI scores are compared. To see the correlation between HDI and economic performances, Spearman's rank correlation is calculated. Correlation coefficient is found as 0.804 and p-value is 1.09e−05. It is clear that there is a strong correlation between HDI and economic performances. Also, we observed that 8 countries which are Germany, Switzerland, Sweden, Norway, Ireland, Netherland, Belgium, and Denmark appeared in the first 10 countries for both HDI ranking and economic performance ranking.

Table 6.6 Mean HDI values and rankings for 2010–2014

Country	2010	2011	2012	2013	2014	Mean	Ranking
1. England	0.906	0.901	0.901	0.902	0.907	0.903	8
2. France	0.881	0.884	0.886	0.887	0.888	0.885	12
3. Germany	0.906	0.911	0.915	0.915	0.916	0.913	5
4. Luxembourg	0.738	0.751	0.756	0.759	0.761	0.889	11
5. Netherland	0.909	0.919	0.92	0.920	0.922	0.918	4
6. Spain	0.867	0.870	0.874	0.874	0.876	0.8722	16
7. Italy	0.869	0.873	0.872	0.873	0.873	0.872	17
8. Slovenia	0.783	0.79	0.795	0.797	0.798	0.878	15
9. Denmark	0.908	0.920	0.921	0.923	0.923	0.92	3
10. Switzerland	0.924	0.925	0.927	0.928	0.93	0.927	2
11. Norway	0.94	0.941	0.942	0.942	0.944	0.942	1
12. Austria	0.879	0.881	0.884	0.884	0.885	0.882	13
13. Sweden	0.901	0.903	0.904	0.905	0.907	0.904	7
14. Belgium	0.883	0.886	0.899	0.888	0.89	0.889	10
15. Ireland	0.908	0.909	0.91	0.912	0.916	0.911	6
16. Portugal	0.819	0.825	0.827	0.828	0.830	0.826	20
17. Finland	0.878	0.881	0.882	0.882	0.883	0.881	14
18. Greece	0.866	0.864	0.865	0.863	0.865	0.865	18
19. Cyprus	0.863	0.866	0.867	0.868	0.87	0.85	19
20. Iceland	0.829	0.833	0.838	0.84	0.843	0.897	9

6.5 Conclusion

In this study, economic performances of 20 European countries for the period 2010–2014 are analyzed. Indicators used to measure the economic performances of those countries have been identified. Indicators that are included in these analyses are growth rate, youth unemployment, inflation, GDP per capita, and account balance. The weights are determined with the criteria by using AHP. Weights for growth rate, youth unemployment, inflation, GDP per capita, and account balance are found as 0.2833, 0.1806, 0.2024, 0.1826, and 0.1511, respectively. Furthermore, TOPSIS is used to evaluate ranking of 20 European countries. Highest and lowest economic performance rank is highlighted.

After mean HDI scores are calculated and ranked for the years 2010–2014, ranking of economic performances and HDI scores are compared. We found association between HDI and economic performance measured by Spearman's rank correlation coefficient (value of 0.804). Furthermore, 8 countries appeared in the top 10 countries for both HDI ranking and economic performance ranking. For the following studies, different indicators and more countries will be analyzed.

References

Ashourian M (2012) Evaluating the rank of performance of countries of the middle east and north Africa with MADM. J Inf Mathematical Sciences 3:285–292

Bao Q et al (2010) Improved hierarchical fuzzy group decision making for selection of supplier with TOPSIS method. Knowl Based Syst 84–98

Cam AV, Cam H, Ulutas S, Sayin OB (2015) The role of TOPSIS method on determining the financial performance ranking of firms: an application in the Borsa Istanbul. Int J Econ and Res 6(3):29–38

Chattopadhyay S, Bose S et al (2015) Global macroeconomic performance: a comparative study based on composite scores. J Rev Glob Econ 4:51–68

Gustav R (2004) Human development and economic growth. Economic Growth Center discussion paper no. 887

Mahmoodzadeh S, Shahrabi J, Pariazar M, Zaeri MS (2007) Project selection by using fuzzy AHP and TOPSIS technique. In: Proceedings of world academy of science, engineering and technology, 24 Oct 2007. ISSN 1307–6884 (Title of the Paper)

Mandic K, Delibasic B, Knezevic S, Benkovic S (2014) Analysis of the financial parameters of Serbian banks through the application of the fuzzy AHP and TOPSIS methods. Econ Model 43:30–37

Opricovic S, Tzeng GH (2004) Compromise solution by MCDM methods: a comparative analysis of VIKOR and TOPSIS. Eur J Oper Res 156:445–455

Saaty RW (1987) The analytic hierarchy process—what it is and how it is used. Math Model 9 (3):161–176. http://dx.doi.org/10.1016/0270-0255(87)90473-8

Wabalickis RN (1987) Justification of FMS with the analytic hierarchy process. J. Manuf Syst 7:175–182

Chapter 7
Foreign Capital Inflows and Stock Market Development in Turkey

Yilmaz Bayar

Abstract Cross-country capital flows have increased substantially due to accelerating globalization as of 1990s, and these increases have important economic implications for all the countries. This study investigates the causal relationship among foreign capital inflows including foreign direct investment, foreign portfolio flows, remittances, and stock market development in Turkey during the period January 1992–December 2015 using Hacker and Hatemi-J (Appl Econ 38 (13):1489–1500, 2006) bootstrap causality test. We found that there was unidirectional causality from foreign direct investment inflows to stock market development and unidirectional causality from stock market development to foreign portfolio investments.

Keywords Foreign direct investment inflows · Foreign portfolio investments · Remittances, stock market development · Causality analysis

7.1 Introduction

Foreign capital flows generally takes place in two ways direct investments or portfolio investments. On the other hand, remittances also became an important financing source as a result of increasing mobility of the work force and capital together with globalization process. Foreign direct investment (FDI) inflows increased to 1.561 trillion USD (United States dollars) in 2014 from 10.17 billion USD in 1970, and portfolio equity investments increased to 1.086 trillion USD from 1.36 billion USD during the same period (World Bank 2016a, b). On the other hand, remittances reached 510.87 billion USD in 2014 from 1.93 billion USD in 1970 (World Bank 2016c). International capital flows have increased significantly together with the economic and financial globalization, although serious contrac-

Y. Bayar (✉)
Department of Economics, Faculty of Economics and Administrative Sciences,
Usak University, Izmir Yolu 8. Km, Bir Eylul Kampusu B Blok, 64100 Usak, Turkey
e-mail: yilmaz.bayar@usak.edu.tr

© Springer International Publishing AG 2017

D. Procházka (ed.), *New Trends in Finance and Accounting*,
Springer Proceedings in Business and Economics,
DOI 10.1007/978-3-319-49559-0_7

tions sometimes have been seen in the flows of foreign private flows especially during the periods of economic and political crises.

Foreign capital inflows may contribute to the development of stock markets through diverse channels. First, foreign capital inflows to the domestic firms generally cause the increases in the current market values of these firms and in turn increase the stock market capitalization. Secondly, foreign capital inflows foster the development of stock markets through strengthening capital structure and raising institutionalization which also increases the profitability of firms and in turn their market values (Evrim-Mandaci et al. 2013, p. 54). Finally, there has been consensus about positive relationship between FDI, remittances, and economic growth in the literature [see Li and Liu (2005), Gui-Diby (2014) and Iamsiraroja and Ulubaşoğlu (2015)]. Positive economic growth also means the increase in profitability of the firms, this in turn increases the value of firms and contribute to the development of stock markets. Also there has been consensus on the positive relationship between stock market development and economic growth in the literature [see Enisan and Olufisayo (2009), Cooray (2010), Nyasha and Odhiambo (2015) and Pradhan et al. (2015)]. In other words, there is bidirectional causality between stock market development and economic growth, and these two indicators feed each other. On the other hand, foreign capital inflows increase the funds in the economy and in turn contribute to the development of financial intermediation via financial markets. Countries generally improve their institutional quality and try to create a market-friendly environment to attract to foreign capital inflows, these efforts also contribute to the development of stock markets [see Henry (2000), Desai et al. (2006), Soumaré and Tchana (2014)].

Turkey followed a protective policy of import substituting industrialization for a long time during 1960–1980 period, but then shifted from mixed capitalism to free market economy and began to follow the export-oriented growth strategy overcome the prevailing economic problems with 24 January 1980 decisions. In this context, barriers on the movement of capital, goods and services across countries were loosed gradually, and Turkish economy began to integrate with global economy by restructuring the economy. The government let interest rates, foreign exchange rates, and prices of goods and services to be determined by market forces and tax incentives were put into action to attract FDI. Moreover, interbank market was established in 1986, and Borsa Istanbul was established in 1985, and stock trading commenced as of 3 January of 1986 (Bora Istanbul 2016a). But liberalization of economy with inadequate regulations, corruption, and weak economic fundamentals led many financial and political crises during the period 1980–2000. As a consequence, frequent financial crises and political instability have caused significant contractions in foreign portfolio investments and retarded FDI inflows despite the improvements in Turkish economy during this period as seen in Chart 1. But transition to the strong economy program was put into action after February 2001 crisis, and this program created an environment of confidence in a short time by restructuring economy and public administration (CBRT 2016a). Thus, emergent relatively better economic and political stability contributed to the significant increases in FDI net inflows and foreign portfolio net investments as of 2002.

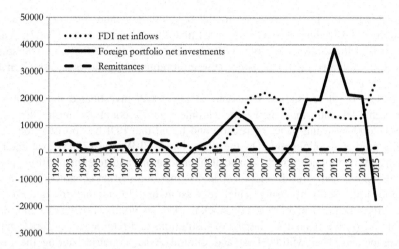

Fig. 7.1 FDI net inflows, foreign portfolio net investments, and remittances (million USD) (1992–2015). *Source* Authors' own elaboration based on data from CBRT (Central Bank of the Republic of Turkey) (2016b)

However, recent crises caused contractions in foreign capital inflows as seen in Fig. 7.1.

This study investigates the causality between foreign net capital inflows and stock market development in Turkey during the period January 1992–December 2015 by using bootstrap Granger causality test developed by Hacker and Hatemi-J (2006). The study is organized as follows: The next section overviews the relevant literature, Sect. 7.3 describes data and econometric methodology and Sect. 7.4 presents empirical analysis and major findings, and Sect. 7.5 concludes the study.

7.2 Literature Review

Extensive empirical studies have been conducted on the nexus between stock market development–economic growth and the macroeconomic and institutional determinants of stock market development. Relatively, few ones from these studies have focused on the impact of foreign capital inflows on stock market development. These studies generally have found that foreign direct investment inflows, foreign portfolio investments, and remittances had positive impact on the development of stock market [see Claessens et al. (2001), El-Wassal (2005), Billmeier and Massa (2007), Adam and Tweneboah (2009), Malik and Amjad (2013), Evrim-Mandaci et al. (2013) and Raza et al. (2015)].

Calderon-Rossell's (1991) study was a pioneer one on the determinants of stock market development and suggested that economic development level and stock market liquidity were major determinants of stock market development. Then many studies have modified this basic model by including more macroeconomic and institutional variables [see Garcia and Liu (1999), Naceur et al. (2007), Yartey (2010)]. In literature review of this study, we focus only on the empirical studies which investigated the relationship between foreign capital flows and stock market development.

In one of these studies, Claessens et al. (2001) investigated the relationship between FDI and stock market development in 77 countries during the period 1990–2000 by using panel regression and found that FDI had positive impact on stock market development. On the other hand, El-Wassal (2005) examined the impact of economic growth, financial liberalization, and foreign portfolio investments on stock market development in 40 emerging market economies during the period 1980–2000 by using panel regression and found that foreign portfolio investments had positive impact on stock market development. Billmeier and Massa (2007) also investigated the impact of institutions and remittances on stock market development in 17 Middle East and Central Asian countries during the period 1995–2005 and found that remittances had positive impact on stock market development.

In another study, Adam and Tweneboah (2009) investigated the relationship between FDI and stock market development in Ghana during the period January 1991–April 2006 by using Johansen cointegration test and impulse-response and variance decomposition and found that FDI had positive impact on stock market development. Kaleem and Shahbaz (2009) examined the nexus between FDI and investment and stock market development in Pakistan during the period 1971–2006 by using ARDL (AutoRegressive Distributed Lag)-bound testing approach and found that FDI had positive impact on stock market development.

Malik and Amjad (2013) also examined the impact of FDI on stock market development in Pakistan during the period 1985–2011 by using Johansen co-integration and Granger causality tests and regression and found that FDI had positive impact on stock market development. On the other hand, Evrim-Mandaci et al. (2013) investigated the impact of FDI, remittances, and credits to the private sector by banks on stock market development in 30 countries during the period 1960–2007 by using panel regression and found that FDI and remittances had positive impact on stock market development.

Ayaydın and Baltacı (2013) examined the impact of corruption, banking sector, and major macroeconomic variables including FDI on stock market development in 42 emerging market economies during 1996–2011 period and found that FDI had positive impact on stock market development. On the other hand, Raza and Jawaid (2014) investigated the impact of FDI, remittances, and economic growth on stock market development in 18 Asian countries during the period 2000–2010 by using ARDL cointegration and Toda and Yamamoto (1995) causality test and found that FDI had negative impact on stock market development and remittances had no significant impact on stock market development. Soumaré and Tchana (2014) also investigated the causality between FDI and stock market development in 29 emerging markets during the period 1994–2006 and found that there was bidirectional causality between FDI and stock market and FDI and stock market development simultaneously affect each other positively.

Zhou et al. (2015) investigated the relationship between major macroeconomic variables including FDI and stock market development in Cameroon during the period 2006–2011 by using dynamic panel regression and found that FDI and private capital flows had positive impact on stock market development. Finally, Raza et al. (2015) investigated the impact of FDI and remittances on stock market development in Pakistan during the period 1976–2011 by using ARDL cointegration and found that FDI had positive impact on stock market development.

7.3   Data and Econometric Methodology

We investigate the casual relationship among foreign direct investment inflows, foreign portfolio investments, remittances, and stock market development in Turkey during the period January 1992–December 2015 by employing bootstrap Granger causality test developed by Hacker and Hatemi-J (2006).

7.3.1   Data

We used the monthly data of stock market capitalization as proxy for stock market development. On the other hand, we used net inflows of foreign direct investment and foreign portfolio investments as proxy for foreign capital inflows. Finally, we included remittances in the model, because it also has become an important financing source especially for developing and emerging market economies. Our study period and sample were determined by data availability. The variables used in the econometric analysis, their symbols, and data sources were presented in Table 7.1.

We benefited from EViews 9.0 and Gauss 11.0 software packages for the econometric analysis. The descriptive statistics and correlation matrix of the variables in the study are presented in Table 7.2.

Table 7.1 Data description

Variables	Symbol	Source
Stock market capitalization (million USD)	SMC	Borsa Istanbul (2016b)
Foreign direct investment, net inflows (million USD)	FDI	CBRT (2016b)
Foreign portfolio investments, net inflows (million USD)	PORTF	
Remittances (million USD)	REM	

Source Authors' own elaboration

Table 7.2 Descriptive statistics and the correlation matrix of the variables in the study

Statistics	SMC	FDI	PORTF	REM
Mean	125,431.0	608.7735	576.3554	183.4007
Median	84,678.63	237.0000	227.0000	125.0000
Maximum	340,580.0	6837.000	9061.000	574.0000
Minimum	9059.920	−697.0000	−4880.000	43.00000
Std. dev.	101,192.6	891.2180	1726.461	124.4208
Skewness	0.530269	3.183693	0.885906	0.986394
Kurtosis	1.768702	18.13659	6.420794	2.922498
Correlation matrix				
SMC	1.000000	0.532486	0.366568	−0.565081
FDI	0.532486	1.000000	0.128010	−0.404381
PORTF	0.366568	0.128010	1.000000	−0.247756
REM	−0.565081	−0.404381	−0.247756	1.000000

7.3.2 Econometric Methodology

In this study, we analyzed the causality between foreign capital inflows and stock market development by Hacker and Hatemi-J (2006) causality test. First, integration level of the variables and optimal lag length of the model should be determined before the causality test. We will test the stationarity of the variables by Augmented Dickey–Fuller (ADF) (1981) and Phillips and Perron (PP) (1988) unit root tests and then investigated the causality among the variables by Hacker and Hatemi-J (2006) causality test.

Hacker and Hatemi-J (2006) causality test is based on Toda and Yamamoto (1995) causality test. VAR $(p + d_{max})$ process of the series is estimated as in the following equation.

$$y_t = v + A_1 y_{t-1} + A_p y_{t-p} + \cdots + A_{p+d} y_{t-(p+d)} + \mu_t \qquad (7.1)$$

In this equation, y_t represents the vector of k independent variables, v represents constant vector, and μ_t represents error term vector, A represents parameter matrix. On the other hand, p is optimal lag length of *VAR* model and d_{max} is maximum integration level among the variables. Therefore, it should not be required that the variables are stationary (Hacker and Hatemi-J 2006). Hacker and Hatemi-J (2006) causality test uses bootstrap distribution instead of chi square distribution unlike from Toda and Yamamoto (1995) causality test and the critical values of the test are obtained by bootstrap simulation. Bootstrap method resamples the dataset to estimate the distribution of test statistics and thus it reduces the deviations by obtaining more accurate critical values. Also this method is not sensitive to normality assumption and regards autoregressive conditional heteroscedasticity (Hacker and Hatemi-J 2006)

7.4 Empirical Analysis

7.4.1 Unit Root Test

We tested the stationarity of the variables by ADF (1981) and PP (1988) unit root tests and the results were presented in Table 7.3. The results showed that FDI, PORTF, and REM were stationary at the level, because the probability values in parentheses were lower than 0.05. However, SMC was not stationary at the level but became stationary after first-differencing. So our maximum integration level was found to be 1. On the other hand, we established a VAR model and found the optimal lag length of the model as 5.

7.4.2 Hacker and Hatemi-J (2006) Bootstrap Causality Test

First, we employed traditional Granger (1969) causality test to investigate the causality among the variables, and the results were given in Table 7.4. The results indicated there was unidirectional causality from stock market capitalization and remittances to foreign portfolio investments and unidirectional causality from remittances to FDI inflows.

We also applied bootstrap Granger causality test developed by Hacker and Hatemi-J (2006) to determine the causality between indicators of foreign capital net

Table 7.3 Results of ADF and PP unit root tests

Variables	ADF (1981)		PP (1988)	
	Constant	Constant+trend	Constant	Constant+trend
SMC	−1.503052 (0.5308)	−2.790872 (0.2019)	−1.497098 (0.5339)	−2.895421 (0.1656)
d (SMC)	−16.29392 (0.0000)***	−16.27061 (0.0000)***	−16.28556 (0.0000)***	−16.26127 (0.0000)***
FDI	−2.434785 (0.1331)	−3.600293 (0.0315)***	−14.52418 (0.0000)***	−16.85096 (0.0000)***
d (FDI)	−17.77982 (0.0000)***	−17.74664 (0.0000)***	−67.42581 (0.0001)***	−67.24238 (0.0001)***
PORTF	−11.76707 (0.0000)***	−12.34802 (0.0000)***	−12.97582 (0.0000)***	−13.09853 (0.0000)***
d (PORTF)	−12.82751 (0.0000)***	−12.81418 (0.0000)***	−104.1309 (0.0001)***	−102.0566 (0.0001)***
REM	−2.033031 (0.2726)	−4.197150 (0.0051)***	−2.781984 (0.0621)*	−4.023333 (0.0090)***
d (REM)	−10.90799 (0.0000)***	−10.88755 (0.0000)***	−27.13171 (0.0000)***	−27.63361 (0.0000)***

***, ** and *, respectively, indicates that it is significant at 1, 5, and 10% significance levels
Source Authors' own elaboration based on the results of ADF and PP unit root tests

Table 7.4 Results of Granger causality test

H_0 hypotheses (no causality)	F-statistic	Prob.
FDI → DSMC	1.86939	0.1561
DSMC → FDI	0.98387	0.3752
PORTF → DSMC	0.36018	0.6979
DSMC → PORTF	**3.99571**	**0.0195****
REM → DSMC	0.26414	0.7681
DSMC → REM	0.13090	0.8774
PORTF → FDI	0.30817	0.7350
FDI → PORTF	0.98794	0.3736
REM → FDI	**8.00039**	**0.0004*****
FDI → REM	1.36419	0.2573
REM → PORTF	**4.17137**	**0.0164****
PORTF → REM	0.27339	0.7610

***, ** and *, respectively, indicates that it is significant at 1, 5, and 10% significance levels
Source Authors' own elaboration based on the results of Granger (1969) causality test

Table 7.5 Results of bootstrap Granger causality test

H_0 hypotheses (no causality)	Test value	Critical values		
		1%	5%	10%
FDI → SMC	**12.452****	**16.972**	**11.692**	**9.661**
SMC → FDI	7.098	16.833	11.922	9.646
PORTF → SMC	7.240	15.319	11.319	9.437
SMC → PORTF	**15.906*****	**15.477**	**11.375**	**9.377**
REM → SMC	2.661	15.512	11.467	9.440
SMC → REM	3.954	15.595	11.297	9.429
PORTF → FDI	**10.397***	**16.380**	**11.847**	**9.627**
FDI → PORTF	5.549	15.673	11.236	9.227
REM → FDI	0.760	16.682	11.576	9.450
FDI → REM	3.904	17.200	11.935	9.747
REM → PORTF	2.443	15.551	11.159	9.241
PORTF → REM	3.202	15.841	11.415	9.448

***, ** and *, respectively, indicates that it is significant at 1, 5, and 10% significance levels
Source Authors' own elaboration based on the results of Hacker and Hatemi-J (2006) bootstrap causality test

inflows and stock market development, and the results were presented in Table 7.5. The results indicated that there was unidirectional causality from FDI inflows to stock market development and unidirectional causality from stock market capitalization to foreign portfolio investments and unidirectional causality from foreign portfolio investments to foreign direct investment inflows. Our findings indicated that FDI inflows are a component of stock market development, and in turn stock market development caused foreign portfolio investments.

7.5 Conclusion

We examined the impact of foreign direct investment inflows, foreign portfolio investments, and remittances on stock market development in Turkey during the period January 1992–December 2015 by employing traditional Granger (1969) causality test and bootstrap Granger causality test developed by Hacker and Hatemi-J (2006). Both causality tests yielded different results. On the one hand, bootstrap causality test indicated that there was unidirectional causality from foreign direct investment inflows to stock market development and unidirectional causality from stock market capitalization to foreign portfolio investments and unidirectional causality from foreign portfolio investments to foreign direct investment inflows. On the other hand, traditional Granger causality test indicated there was unidirectional causality from stock market capitalization and remittances to foreign portfolio investments and unidirectional causality from remittances to FDI inflows.

Our findings are consistent with the findings of empirical studies in the literature and supported that FDI contributed to the stock market development. This study also verified that FDI inflows are very important for the countries, because our findings mean that FDI inflows also affect economic growth through stock market development considering the prevailing consensus about positive relationship between stock market development and economic growth in the literature. Therefore, countries especially with insufficient capital and technology should take measures to attract FDI.

References

Adam AM, Tweneboah G (2009) Foreign direct investment and stock market development: ghana's evidence. Int Res J Finan Econ 26:178–185

Ayaydın H, Baltacı N (2013) Corruption, banking sector, and stock market development: a panel data analysis. Int Assoc Soc Sci Res (Special Issue: Human Resource Management) 94–99

Billmeier A, Massa I (2007) What drives stock market development in the middle east and central Asia—institutions, remittances, or natural resources? International Monetary Fund Working Papers WP/07/157

Borsa Istanbul (2016a) Milestones in Borsa Istanbul History. http://www.borsaistanbul.com/en/corporate/about-borsa-istanbul/milestones-in-borsa-istanbul-history. 13 Jan 2016

Borsa Istanbul (2016b) Consolidated Data. http://www.borsaistanbul.com/en/data/data/consolidated-data. 17 Jan 2016

Calderon-Rossell RJ (1991) The determinants of stock market growth. In: Ghon Rhee S, Chang RP (eds) Pacific basin capital markets research proceeding. Second Annual Pacific Basin Finance Conference, Bangkok-Thailand

CBRT (2016a) Strengthening the Turkish economy-Turkey's transition program. http://www.tcmb.gov.tr/wps/wcm/connect/9d473f48-f02c-4631-94e7-ee64593f250d/strengteningecon.pdf?MOD=AJPERES&CACHEID=ROOTWORKSPACE9d473f48-f02c-4631-94e7-ee64593f250d. 10 Jan 2016

CBRT (2016b) Outstanding external debt and balance of payments. http://evds.tcmb.gov.tr/index_
    en.html. 05 Feb 2016

Claessens S, Klingebiel D, Schmukler SL (2001) FDI and stock market development:
    complements or substitutes? http://www.iadb.org/WMSFiles/products/research/files/pubS-
    FDI-4.pdf. 23 Jan 2015

Cooray A (2010) Do stock markets lead to economic growth? J Policy Model 32(4):448–460

Desai MA, Foley CF, Hines JR Jr (2006) Capital controls, liberalizations, and foreign direct
    investment. Rev Fin Stud 19(4):1433–1464

Dickey DA, Fuller WA (1981) Likelihood ratio statistics for autoregressive time series with a unit
    root. Econometrica 49(4):1057–1072

El-Wassal KA (2005) Understanding the growth in emerging stock markets. J Emerg Mark Finan
    4(3):227–261. doi:10.1177/097265270500400302

Enisan AA, Olufisayo AO (2009) Stock market development and economic growth: evidence from
    seven sub-sahara african countries. J Econ Bus 61:162–171

Evrim-Mandaci P, Aktan B, Kurt-Gumuş G, Tvaronavičienė M (2013) Determinants of stock
    market development: evidence from advanced and emerging markets in a long span. Bus Theor
    Pract 14(1):51–56. doi:10.3846/btp.2013.06

Garcia VF, Liu L (1999) Macroeconomic determinants of stock market development. J Appl Econ
    2(1):29–59

Granger CJ (1969) Investigating causal relationships by econometrics models and cross-spectral
    methods. Econometrica 37(3):424–438

Gui-Diby SL (2014) Impact of foreign direct investments on economic growth in africa: evidence
    from three decades of panel data analyses. Res Econ 68(3):248–256

Hacker RS, Hatemi-J A (2006) Tests for causality between integrated variables using asymptotic
    and bootstrap distributions: theory and application. Appl Econ 38(13):1489–1500. doi:10.
    1080/00036840500405763

Henry PB (2000) Do Stock market liberalizations cause investment booms? J Financ Econ 58(1–
    2):301–334

Iamsiraroja S, Ulubaşoğlu MA (2015) Foreign direct investment and economic growth: a real
    relationship or wishful thinking? Econ Model 51:200–213

Kaleem R, Shahbaz M (2009) Impact of foreign direct investment on stock market development:
    the case of Pakistan. In: 9th global conference on business and economics. Cambridge
    University, Cambridge

Li X, Liu X (2005) Foreign direct investment and economic growth: an increasingly endogenous
    relationship. World Dev 33(3):393–407

Malik IA, Amjad S (2013) Foreign direct investment and stock market development in Pakistan.
    J Int Trade Law Policy 12(3):226–242. doi:10.1108/JITLP-02-2013-0002

Naceur SB, Ghazouani S, Omran M (2007) The determinants of stock market development in the
    middle-eastern and north African region. Manag Finan 33(7):477–489

Nyasha S, Odhiambo NM (2015) Banks, stock market development and economic growth in south
    africa: a multivariate causal linkage. Appl Econ Lett 22(18):1480–1485

Phillips PCB, Perron P (1988) Testing for unit roots in time series regression. Biometrika 75
    (2):335–346

Pradhan RP, Arvin MK, Bahmani S (2015) Causal nexus between economic growth, inflation, and
    stock market development: the case of OECD countries. Glob Finan J 27:98–111

Raza SA, Jawaid ST (2014) Foreign capital inflows, economic growth and stock market
    capitalization in Asian countries: an ARDL bound testing approach. Qual Quant 48(1):375–385.
    doi:10.1007/s11135-012-9774-4

Raza SA, Jawaid ST, Afshan S, Karim MSZ (2015) Is stock market sensitive to foreign capital
    inflows and economic growth? Evidence from Pakistan. J Chin Econ Foreign Trade Stud 8
    (3):142–164

Soumaré I, Tchana FT (2014) Causality between FDI and financial market development: evidence from
    emerging markets. http://papers.ssrn.com/sol3/papers.cfm?abstract_id=1852168. 05 Jan 2016

Toda HY, Yamamoto T (1995) Statistical inference in vector autoregressions with possibly integrated processes. J Econometrics 66(1–2):225–250

World Bank (2016a) Foreign direct investment, net inflows (BoP, Current US$). http://data.worldbank.org/indicator/BX.KLT.DINV.CD.WD. 05 Jan 2016

World Bank (2016b) Portfolio equity, net inflows (BoP, Current US$). http://data.worldbank.org/indicator/BX.PEF.TOTL.CD.WD. 05 Jan 2016

World Bank (2016c) Personal remittances, received (Current US$). http://data.worldbank.org/indicator/BX.TRF.PWKR.CD.DT. 05 Jan 2016

Yartey CA (2010) The institutional and macroeconomic determinants of stock market development in emerging economies. Appl Finan Econ 20(21):1615–1625

Zhou J, Zhao H, Belinga T (2015) Macroeconomic determinants of stock market development in Cameroon. Int J Sci Res Publ 5(1):1–11

Chapter 8
Count Data Modeling About Relationship Between Dubai Housing Sales Transactions and Financial Indicators

Olgun Aydin, Elvan Akturk Hayat and Ali Hepsen

Abstract In this study, illustrating and comparing the performances of count data models such as Poisson, negative binomial (NB), Hurdle and zero-inflated models for the determination of factors affected housing sales in Dubai. Model comparisons are made via Akaike's information criterion (AIC), the Vuong test and examining the residuals. Main purpose of this study is building reliable statistical model for relationship between Dubai housing sales and important financial indicators in Dubai. With this study government, investors and customers would have an idea about housing sales transactions in future according to economic indicators.

Keywords Dubai housing market · Poisson regression · Negative binomial regression · Zero-inflated model · Hurdle model

8.1 Introduction

Over a period of half a century the city state of Dubai has progressed from pre-industrial to industrial to post-industrial status. Change is evident in the economic, social and cultural characteristics of the city and, most visibly, in the scale, pace and nature of real estate development. Dubai has developed into a city of regional importance, with a planned objective of becoming a city of significance within the global urban economic system. Development of the city has been energized by a synergistic relationship between global and local forces embedded

O. Aydin (✉)
Department of Statistics, Mimar Sinan University, Istanbul, Turkey
e-mail: olgun.aydin@ogr.msgsu.edu.tr

E.A. Hayat
Faculty of Economics, Adnan Menderes University, Aydin, Turkey
e-mail: elvanakturk@gmail.com

A. Hepsen
School of Business, Istanbul University, Istanbul, Turkey
e-mail: alihsepsen@yahoo.com

© Springer International Publishing AG 2017
D. Procházka (ed.), *New Trends in Finance and Accounting*,
Springer Proceedings in Business and Economics,
DOI 10.1007/978-3-319-49559-0_8

83

within a particular historical and geographical context. On the other hand, real estate has been a key driver of growth and has been a steady and robust performer over the years for Dubai. Central to the planned urban growth, and as part of the city's strategy to establish itself as the region's hub for commerce, services and leisure, is the construction of a series of, cities within the city, mega-projects. Factors that have been critical to the strong development of this sector include property rights, transaction costs and capital gain taxes. With the opening up of the market to allow freehold ownership of properties to foreigners in Dubai, international investors have driven a huge demand for properties. At that point monitoring the evolution of real estate transactions and the market trend over time is obviously a necessary requirement in Dubai (Hepsen and Vatansever 2011).

The main purpose of this study is to investigate whether there is a relationship between Dubai housing selling transactions and financial indicators by using the count data modeling. Count data modeling is a common task in economics and the social sciences. The Poisson regression model for count data is of often limited use in economic and the social sciences because empirical count data sets typically exhibit over-dispersion and/or excess number of zeros. In recent years, zero-inflated and Hurdle models have gained popularity for modeling count data with excess zeroes. According to Cameron and Trivedi (1998), zero-inflated and Hurdle models can be viewed as finite mixture models with a degenerate distribution whose mass is concentrated at zero. Excess zeroes arise when the event of interest is not experienced by many of the subjects. Zero-inflated and Hurdle models (each assuming either the Poisson or negative binomial distribution of the outcome) have been developed to cope with zero-inflated outcome data with over-dispersion (negative binomial) or without (Poisson distribution). Both models deal with the high occurrence of zeros in the observed data but have one important distinction in how they interpret and analyze zero counts. An overview of count data models in econometrics, including Hurdle and zero-inflated models, is provided in Cameron and Trivedi (1998, 2005).

This paper is organized as follows: Sect. 8.2 provides brief explanation about some count regression models. In Sect. 8.3, we applied count model regression analyses for daily total housing sales in Dubai and the results are reported. In the final section, some concluding remarks are given.

8.2 Methods

The classical Poisson and negative binomial regression models for count data belong to the family of generalized linear models (Zeileis et al. 2008). Poisson model assumes the variance is equal to the mean, an assumption that is often violated. The NB model has a built-in dispersion parameter that can account for variance greater than the mean (over-dispersion) that is due to unobserved heterogeneity and/or temporal dependency (Chin and Quddus 2003). Zero-inflated and Hurdle models are generally used in the setting of excess zeroes. Zero-inflated models are typically used if the data contain excess structural and sampling zeroes, whereas Hurdle models are generally used when there are only excess sampling zeroes.

In this section, we briefly described Poisson regression model, negative binomial regression model, zero-inflated and Hurdle regression models.

8.2.1   Poisson Regression Model

The simplest distribution used for modeling count data is the Poisson distribution (Agresti 2007). The Poisson probability mass function is given by

$$P(Y = y) = \theta^y e^{-\theta}/y!, \quad y = 0, 1, 2, \ldots \tag{8.1}$$

The mean and variance of the Poisson distribution are equal to θ. Thus, for Poisson regression, we have

$$E(Y_i) = \theta = \mu(x_i) = e^{\beta_0 + \beta_1 x_{i1} + \beta_2 x_{i2} + \cdots + \beta_{p-1} x_{i,p-1}}, \tag{8.2}$$

Hence, the Poisson regression model is

$$P(Y = y_i | x_i) = [\mu(x_i)]^{y_i} e^{-\mu(x_i)}/y_i! \quad \text{for } y_i = 0, 1, 2, \ldots \tag{8.3}$$

The mean and variance of the Poisson regression model in Eq. (8.3) are equal to $\mu(x_i)$. Thus, the Poisson regression model is appropriate for data where the mean and variance are about equal. The values of a count response variable y are non-negative. Hence, the mean function $\mu(x_i)$ ensures that the predicted values of y are also nonnegative.

8.2.2   Negative Binomial Regression Model

The negative binomial distribution (NBD) is one commonly used distribution to deal with the over-dispersion problem in count data. The probability mass function for the NBD is given by

$$P(Y = y) = \binom{1/a + y - 1}{y} \theta^y (1 - \theta)^{1/a}, \quad y = 0, 1, 2, \ldots \tag{8.4}$$

The mean and variance of this model are, respectively, given by $\mu = \theta/[a(1 - \theta)]$ and $\sigma^2 = \theta/[a(1 - \theta)^2]$. From the mean and variance, we see that the NBD is over-dispersed, that is the variance exceeds the mean. Suppose the mean of the NBD depends on some predictor variables x_i, then we can write $\mu(x_i) = \theta/[a(1-\theta)]$ and this gives $\theta = a\mu(x_i)/[1+a\mu(x_i)]$. Thus, the negative binomial regression (NBR) model can be written as

$$P(Y = y_i | x_i) = \binom{1/a + y_i - 1}{y_i} \left(\frac{a\mu(x_i)}{1+a\mu(x_i)} \right)^{y_i} \left(\frac{1}{1+a\mu(x_i)} \right)^{1/a}, \qquad (8.5)$$

$$y_i = 0, 1, 2, \ldots$$

The mean and variance of the NBR model are, respectively, given by $E(Y) = \mu(x_i)$ and $V(Y) = \mu(x_i)[1+a\mu(x_i)]$. The NBR model reduces to the Poisson regression model when the dispersion parameter "a" goes to zero.

8.2.3 Zero-Inflated Regression Models

Zero-inflated models (Lambert 1992) take a somewhat different approach: They are mixture models that combine a count component and a point mass at zero. Over-dispersion can also arise as a result of too many occurrences of zeros than would normally be expected from a Poisson model. That is, there could be too many zeros than can be assumed theoretically or expected under such model. In this case, the Poisson model is zero inflated. A zero-inflated model assumes that the zero observations have two different origins: "structural" and "sampling." The sampling zeros are due to the usual Poisson (or negative binomial) distribution, which assumes that those zero observations happened by chance. Zero-inflated models assume that some zeros are observed due to some specific structure in the data.

A zero-inflated discrete model has the probability function of the form

$$P(Y_i = y_i) = \begin{cases} \omega + (1-\omega)f(0), & y_i = 0 \\ (1-\omega)f(y_i), & y_i > 0 \end{cases}, \qquad (8.6)$$

where $f(y_i)$ may be Poisson, negative binomial or generalized Poisson distribution and $0 \leq \omega < 1$.

The zero-truncated regression models can be used in count data regression when the data are truncated at point zero. The probability mass function of zero-truncated Poisson random variable Y_t is

$$P(Y_i = y_i) = \frac{\mu^y e^{-\mu}}{y!(1 - e^{-\mu})}, \qquad y = 1, 2, 3, \ldots \qquad (8.7)$$

The zero-truncated Poisson regression is given by

$$P(Y_t = y_i | x_i) = \frac{\mu(x_i)^{y_i} e^{-\mu(x_i)}}{y_i!(1 - e^{-\mu(x_i)})}, \qquad y = 1, 2, 3, \ldots \qquad (8.8)$$

8.2.4   Hurdle Regression Models

In addition to over-dispersion, many empirical count data sets exhibit more zero observations than would be allowed for by the Poisson model. The Hurdle model, originally proposed by Mullahy (1986) in the econometrics, is capable of capturing both properties (Zeileis et al. 2008). In the Hurdle model, a binomial probability governs the binary outcome that a count response variable is zero or greater than zero (i.e., positive). This is often called the transition stage. If the value of the response variable is positive, the Hurdle is crossed and the conditional distribution of the positives is zero-truncated Poisson distribution. Thus, one distribution governs the zeros, while another distribution governs the nonzero counts. In the zero-inflated model, the same distribution addresses all counts. For the Hurdle Poisson model, we have

$$P(Y_i = y_i) = \begin{cases} (1 - \omega), y_i = 0 \\ \omega f_T(y_i), y_i > 0 \end{cases},$$ (8.9)

where $f_T(y_i)$ is the zero-truncated Poisson model in Eq. (8.8).

8.2.5   Model Comparison

For comparing models, Akaike's information criterion is used commonly. When two models are nested, one can use the likelihood ratio test to compare them. However, for non-nested models, one can apply a test proposed by Vuong (1989). Under the null hypothesis that the models are indistinguishable, the Vuong test statistic is asymptotically distributed standard normal. For more details, see Vuong (1989).

8.3   Application

8.3.1   Data

In this study, the outcome variable is daily total housing sales in Dubai. The explanatory variables are Dubai Federal Market General Index (DFMGI), crude oil price per barrel in USD and gold price per troy ounce in AED data. We also used dummy variables (s1, s2, s3) to determine the seasonal effect on daily total housing sales. The daily total housing sales data are collected from Dubai Statistics Centre. DFMGI, crude oil price, gold price data are collected from Investing.com Web site. According to official records for housing sales in Dubai, we observed transactions in weekends. On the other hand, financial markets are only open in weekdays. Because of that, we used previous weekdays' value of economic indicators for weekends. All data sets are in 2013/10/07–2015/10/5 time range.

8.3.2 Data Analysis

Poisson, negative binomial (NB), zero-inflated negative binomial (ZINB) and Hurdle negative binomial (Hurdle NB) regression models are used to model relationships between macroeconomic indicators and housing sales transaction volume by using "glm" package in R (3.1.3) software packages (http://www.r-project.org/). The descriptive statistics for all variables are given in Table 8.1. The observed mean and standard deviation for the number of housing sales are 34.31 and 817.25, respectively.

The observed variance to mean ratio is 23.81874, clearly indicating over-dispersion. A dispersion test is implemented and the evidence of over-dispersion in data is identified ($z = 16.8002$, p value < 0.000). Hence, we fitted the Poisson model and we test for goodness of fit (GOF) of the model with a Chi-square test based on the residual deviance and degrees of freedom. As expected, the Poisson model does not fit the data ($p < 0.000$). Then, we fitted instead NB model as an alternative to the over-dispersed Poisson model. The GOF test also indicates that the negative binomial model does not fit the data ($p < 0.000$). Possible reason for this situation is having response variable with zeros. Because the response variable has 20.53% zero rate, we also fitted ZINB and Hurdle NB regression models.

Table 8.2 shows the parameter estimates and fit statistics for outcome variable number of daily housing sales and explanatory variables for Poisson and NB models. Table 8.3 shows the parameter estimates and fit statistics for Hurdle NB

Table 8.1 Descriptive statistics

	Min.	Max.	Median	Mean	Std. dev.
Housing sales	0	157	36	34.31	28.5875
FMGI	2993	49868	4103	4271	1877.031
Gold price	3970	5080	4483	4510	245.6791
Oil price	40.47	107.26	74.36	75.58	22.774

Table 8.2 The parameter estimates and fit statistics for the Poisson and NB models

	Poisson			NB		
	Beta	s.e.	p Value	Beta	s.e.	p Value
Intercept	2.64000	0.19660	0.00000	0.00001	0.00000	0.00000
FMGI	0.00000	0.00000	0.70074	0.00008	0.00000	0.00000
Gold price	0.00022	0.00005	0.00001	0.00069	0.00001	0.00000
Oil price	−0.00195	0.00052	0.00020	0.00054	0.00039	0.17104
s1	0.17890	0.02391	0.00000	0.00000	0.00000	0.11679
s2	0.03826	0.02229	0.08606	0.00000	0.00000	0.00437
s3	−0.08281	0.02129	0.00010	0.00000	0.00000	0.01003
AIC	21436.70			20165.76		

Table 8.3 The parameter estimates and fit statistics for the Hurdle NB and ZINB models

| | Hurdle NB | | | | | | ZINB | | | | | |
| | Number of housing sales | | | Probability on having zero housing sales | | | Number of housing sales | | | Probability on having zero housing sales | | |
	Beta (1)	s.e. (1)	p Value	Beta (2)	s.e. (2)	p Value	Beta (1)	s.e. (1)	p Value	Beta (2)	s.e. (2)	p Value
Intercept	3.22	0.1385	0	0.8774	0.2048	0.000018	3.219	0.1376	0	−0.9183	0.3182	0.00391
FMGI	0	0.00007	0.94285	0.000032	0.0004	0.936	−0.00001	0.000068	0.94371	−0.00003	0.000492	0.94785
Gold price	0.00016	0.00006	0.00588	−0.00004	0.000282	0.894	0.000164	0.000059	0.00529	0.000046	0.000379	0.90386
Oil price	−0.0030	0.00198	0.12412	0.007353	0.004955	0.138	−0.00305	0.001989	0.12586	−0.00762	0.005156	0.13938
s1	0.1461	0.1614	0.36533	0.2643	0.3601	0.463	0.1458	0.1623	0.36906	−0.2659	0.3804	0.48461
s2	0.06307	0.1199	0.59876	−0.03878	0.3099	0.9	0.06268	0.1202	0.60195	0.03978	0.3221	0.90171
s3	−0.0143	0.1105	0.89711	−0.2819	0.2914	0.333	−0.01453	0.1105	0.89541	0.2852	0.3009	0.34321
AIC	5487.16						5487.17					

Table 8.4 Vuong statistic

Alternative hypothesis	Vuong test statistics	p Value
Zero-inflated Hurdle is better than zero inf. neg. bin.	−0.42987	0.33364

Table 8.5 Descriptive statistics of residuals

Models	Residuals	
	Mean	Std. dev.
Poisson	−0.936957	5.321947
Negative binom.	0.3859725	4.773163
Hurdle	0.0000111	0.8007759
Zero-inflated neg. binom.	0.0000136	0.8007851

and ZINB models. According to the results, gold prices have significant effect on daily housing sales transaction volume for Dubai (p value < 0.000). According to the Hurdle NB model, when gold prices rise up, daily housing sales transactions volume rises up simultaneously.

To compare models, Akaike's information criterion (AIC; for non-nested models), Vuong statistics (for non-nested models) and summary statistics of residuals are used. According to AIC value shown in Table 8.3, the Hurdle NB model has little bit smaller AIC value than the ZINB model. To decide the best model, Vuong statistics was used and analyzed distributions of residuals of models. With the result of Vuong test, the null hypothesis "Hurdle NB is equal to ZINB" could not be rejected. Best model for these data sets could not have been defined (Table 8.4). Since any model was not defined as the best model, summary statistics of residuals of these models were analyzed. Based on the results in Table 8.3, Hurdle NB model looks better than ZINB model, because Hurdle NB model has smaller mean and standard deviation of residuals than ZINB model (Table 8.5).

8.4 Conclusion

We considered four different models involving either the Poisson or negative binomial distributions for analyzing daily housing sales outcome data. The negative binomial distribution better accommodates over-dispersion in the outcome data compared to Poisson distribution. Zero-inflated and Hurdle models account for over-representation of zero counts in the outcome data.

According to the Hurdle model results, gold prices have significant effect on daily housing sales transaction volume for Dubai. When gold prices rise up, daily housing sales transactions volume rises up simultaneously. With this model, it could be said that when gold prices rise 5% of previous day's value, housing sales transaction volume rises 2.97% of previous day's value.

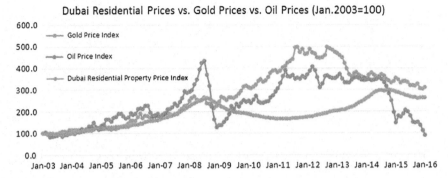

Fig. 8.1 Dubai residential prices versus gold prices versus oil prices

The investors who invest their money in gold sell gold at what time gold prices rise up and put the profit to real estate. For the last years, investors think that real estate is safer than gold for investing, because real estate generates cash flow; otherwise, gold investment does not.

According to Fig. 8.1 obtained from January 2016 report of REIDIN Real Estate Information Platform, gold price has not stable trend; otherwise, REIDIN Dubai Residential Price Index has more stable than gold price. Because of that, investors feel that investing on residential is more properly secured than gold.

References

Agresti A (2007) An introduction to categorical data analysis, 2nd edn. Wiley, New York

Cameron AC, Trivedi PK (1998) Regression analysis of count data. Cambridge University Press, Cambridge

Cameron AC, Trivedi PK (2005) Microeconometrics: methods and applications. Cambridge University Press, Cambridge

Chin HC, Quddus MA (2003) Modeling count data with excess zeroes—an empirical application to traffic accidents. Sociol Methods Res 32(1):90–116

Hepsen A, Vatansever M (2011) Forecasting future trends in Dubai housing market by using Box-Jenkins autoregressive integrated moving average. Int J Housing Markets Anal 4(3): 210–223

Lambert D (1992) Zero-inflated Poisson regression, with an application to defects in manufacturing. Technometrics 34:1–14

Mullahy J (1986) Specification and testing of some modified count data models. J Econometrics 33:341–365

Vuong Q (1989) Likelihood ratio tests for model selection and non-nested hypothesis. Econometrica 57:307–334

Zeileis A, Kleiber C, Jackman S (2008) Regression models for count data. J Stat Softw 27(8):1–25

Chapter 9
Predictive Bankruptcy of European e-Commerce: Credit Underwriters Inexperience and Self-assessment

Karel Janda and David Moreira

Abstract In the current competitive and uncertain e-commerce environment, businesses have the need to predict in advance their likelihood of falling into bankruptcy. The central focus of this paper is to statistically model through different approaches the bankruptcy probability of e-commerce companies in Europe. The authors examine the econometric techniques, two-step cluster, logistic regression, discriminant analysis, data mining tree, and ROC curves, to classify these companies into "bankrupt" and "not bankrupt". This paper finds also evidences about the current credit underwriting inexperience among several financial institutions. The classification approaches included in this paper may be applied in real working practice whether by credit underwriters or by business decision-makers. The research was developed using financial and accounting information available in the Bureau van Dijk database. This paper suggests further analytical developments in the field of predictive bankruptcies and recommends improvements on the credit evaluation scorecards such as the inclusion of advanced online metrics to increase the accuracy of the creditworthiness evaluation of an e-commerce company.

Keywords Europe · Bankruptcy · Econometrics · Prediction

K. Janda (✉) · D. Moreira
Department of Banking and Insurance, University of Economics, Prague,
W. Churchilla 4, 130 67 Praha 3, Czech Republic
e-mail: Karel-Janda@seznam.cz

D. Moreira
e-mail: davidmoreiragaia@gmail.com

K. Janda
Institute of Economic Studies, Charles University, Opletalova 26,
11000 Praha 1, Czech Republic

© Springer International Publishing AG 2017
D. Procházka (ed.), *New Trends in Finance and Accounting*,
Springer Proceedings in Business and Economics,
DOI 10.1007/978-3-319-49559-0_9

9.1   Introduction

In the emergent and fast pace business environment of e-commerce retailers, a predictive analysis about the likelihood of a bankruptcy is crucial for the adoption of the necessary measures to prevent this event. According to Witzany (1991), it is a compromise between the most advanced mathematical modelling techniques and the demand for a practical implementation. From the retail banking perspective, the exposure to financial lending is by far the most important material risk. Teplý and Pečená (2010) state that the credit risk exposure is affected typically by under-performing loans and difficult cash collections especially after the financial crisis period. The financial institutions often rely on credit evaluation models or score-cards to evaluate the credit worthiness of businesses and to predict the likelihood of a bankruptcy event. These credit scorecards are at the core of bank financial activities because they support the underwriter's decisions when evaluating whether the customer is likely to bankrupt or not. Based on this credit underwriting evaluation, the financial institutions decide if it will provide the loan, the related loan interests based on the associated risks, the maturities, and the credit value boundaries.

The aim of this research is to empirically demonstrate with a real case study, evidences about the shortage of experience within credit underwriters when evaluating e-commerce retailers, and recommend improvements on their credit evaluation scorecards. To address this purpose, the authors developed different econometric techniques such as two-step cluster, logistic regression, classification tree, discriminant analysis, and ROC curves, to predict the bankruptcy likelihood of an e-commerce business in Europe. The second purpose of this paper is to compare the accuracy of the econometric classification models and identify which one has the smallest rate of statistical failure and the greatest easiness of practical use. The predictive models included relevant financial accounting ratios of solvability, productivity, and liquidity from e-commerce retailers registered in Europe, and the population in analyses was collected from the Bureau van Dijk database Pagell and Halperin (1999). The choice of the financial ratios is based on the relevant literature and existing credit evaluation scorecards used internally by several financial institutions in Europe. From the perspective of the business decision-makers, there are many important choices that managers have to do with a direct impact on their operations and financial statements, which may lead either to success or to bank-ruptcy (Janda and Rojcek 2014). Profit-orientated shareholders, along with high leverage requirements, fast growth, and uncertain demand, are typical factors that influence the risk management of e-commerce retailers (Pavel and Sičáková 2013). Since the bankruptcy probability is usually the most common risk criteria of the financial decision-makers, the literature developed predictive algorithms that may be applied in real working practice by credit underwriters, and businesses willing to do credit self-assessment to avoid risk, uncertainty and the probability of bankruptcy.

9.2 Literature Review

Statistical research approaches to build an internal corporate bankruptcy evaluation are based on static learning models prepared to process large databases, and able to continuously include other economic variables such as industry behaviour, legal changes or even interest rates (Gama 2010). In this sense, the authors of this paper recommended in the conclusion part the addition of online metrics to better predict a bankruptcy event of an online retailer. The conceptual definition of bankrupt probability is described by the econometrics models used for classification of businesses into "good" and "bad" classes (Hand and Henley 1997). The first-known credit analysts using a consistent framework to evaluate the creditworthiness of businesses were the underwriters sent to the World War II. When these credit analysts left their companies to join the battle, they created tailor-made scorecards and other evaluation requirements to be followed during their absence. In the 1950s, the combination of Bill Fair expertize of business along with Earl Isaac, who was a successful mathematician with forward computing skills, leaded to the creation of the first modern credit score model using advanced predictive statistics. They have used econometric techniques such as logistic regression and multivariate analysis, both applied to predict credit bankruptcy and risk management. When Bill and Earl have created for the first time the credit scorecard in 1958 to predict the credit-worthiness of individuals based on their past behaviour, the bank lending industry had a revolutionary upgrade (Rosenberger and Nash 2009). Further developments have showed that the past track of payment behaviour is a clear factor in the classification between performing and non-performing loans. Durand in 1941 brought this methodology to the credit underwriting evaluation after following-up the first approach of differentiation between the groups developed by Fisher's studies related to the classification problems of varieties of plants in 1936. Many researches made during the last decades were built up from the work contribution of Durand, regarding the selection of relevant risk indicators. The researches made by Witzany (2010a, b, 2011) described in the works about credit scoring functions (2011), and credit risk management modelling (2010a, b), were important contri-butions to the development of the predictive bankruptcy topic developed in this paper. Jakubík and Teplý (2011) constructed a new indicator named the JT index that evaluates the economy's financial stability and is based on a financial scoring model estimated on Czech corporate accounting data.

The financial wealth evaluation of an e-commerce retailer, or the prediction of its financial bankruptcy, is commonly based on the econometric methodologies of discriminant analysis and logistic regression. The methods of discriminant analysis subdivided the dimensions of univariate and multivariate modelling. Beaver (1968) has published a study developing a univariate model using one variable to classify the failure of a company when any of the following situations happened: inexis-tence of funds to pay stock dividends, bank account overdrawn, bond default, and bankruptcy.

9.3   Data, Results, and Discussion

The authors of this paper reviewed several credit scoring reports released by financial institutions and credit insurance companies. The credit reports in review were developed by the following credit financial institutions: HSBC, Dun & Bradstreet, Bisnode, Euler Hermes, Atradius, Credito Y Caucion, Credit Reform, OeKB. The scorecards in review were generally structured by:

- Company historical information—identification, registration, ownership, stock capital, turnover, number of employees, activities, management, board administration.
- Payment behaviour—annually, periodically.
- Financial statements—comparison year-over-year, and ratios of profitability, liquidity, activity, leverage.
- Negative business history—insolvencies, liquidation, executions, debts.
- Observations—press releases, sale of equity participation (among other relevant specific events).

The most typical approach is holistic rather than statistical and quantitative, as it was identified by the authors of this paper when observing the credit reports issued by these financial institutions. The credit evaluation models were in general static and did not adapt when the population in analysis changed, which means that the parameters of credit evaluation did not adjust to the e-commerce industry (Thomas 2010). This misclassification may be responsible for later increasing costs due to potential credit delinquency or to healthy loans not given to costumers.

The credit evaluators generally were relying on out-of-date population that lacked meaningful response, target, or data with quality. This approach led to a lack of confidence when analysing a population sample that should be diverse enough to represent different types of repayment behaviour.

The methodology considered in this research includes different statistical approaches applied in the credit evaluation field such as two-step cluster, logistic regression, discriminant analysis, decision tree, and ROC curve. We also evaluated the best fitting approach that may be more suitable according to each evaluation determinants. The research summarized in this paper gathers a combination of detailed information related to accounting and financial ratios collected from Bureau van Dijk's (Amadeus) database (Klapper et al. 2002). There are existing large number of papers about the credit assessments of brick and mortar retailers; however, just few attempts were made about European e-commerce companies (e.g. addressing the successful billion euro e-commerce businesses such as Asos, Zalando, Vente Privee, among others).

The data used to model the statistical approaches were collected from the last available financial and accounting ratios in the database until the year 2014. To every e-commerce company was assigned a bankruptcy outcome of "0" if not bankrupted, and "1" if bankrupted. The rate of bankruptcy within this sample is 48%, and the number of European companies making part of the data set is 124.

Table 9.1 Predictive variables

X	Variable explanation	Calculation in %
X_1	Solvency ratio asset based	$\text{Solvency asset} = \frac{\text{Shareholders } f}{\text{Total assets}} * 100$
X_2	Return on capital employed	$\text{ROCE (P\&L)} = \frac{\text{P\&L b. tax} + \text{Interest}}{\text{Shareh. } f. + \text{Non-c.l.}} * 100$
X_3	Return on equity using P&L	$\text{ROE (P\&L)} = \frac{\text{P\&L before tax}}{\text{Shareholders funds}} * 100$
X_4	Return on assets using P&L	$\text{ROA (P\&L)} = \frac{\text{P\&L before tax}}{\text{Total assets}} * 100$
X_5	Return on equity using net income	$\text{ROE I.} = \frac{\text{P\&L period (net income)}}{\text{Shareholders funds}} * 100$
X_6	Return on capital employed (income)	$\text{ROCE I.} = \frac{\text{P\&L for period} + \text{Interest paid}}{\text{Shareholders funds} + \text{Non-c.l.}} * 100$
X_7	ROA return on assets using net income	$\text{ROA I.} = \frac{\text{P\&L for period (net income)}}{\text{Total assets}} * 100$
X_8	Profit margin	$\text{Profit M.} = \frac{\text{P\&L before tax}}{\text{Operating revenue (turnover)}} * 100$
X_9	Gross margin	$\text{Gross M.} = \frac{\text{Gross profit}}{\text{Operating revenue (turn.)}} * 100$
X_{10}	EBITDA margin	$\text{EBITDA M.} = \frac{\text{Operating P\&L} + Depr. \& A.}{\text{Operating revenue (turn.)}} * 100$
X_{11}	EBIT earning before interests and taxes	$\text{EBIT M.} = \frac{\text{Operating P\&L (EBIT)}}{\text{Operating revenue (turn.)}} * 100$
X_{12}	Cash flow and operational revenue	$\text{CF O.R.} = \frac{\text{Cash flow}}{\text{Operating revenue (turn.)}} * 100$
X_{13}	Solvency ratio liability based in%	$\text{Solvency L.} = \frac{\text{Shareholders funds}}{(\text{Non-current l.} + \text{Current l.})} * 100$
X_{14}	Cost of employees and operational revenue	$\text{Cost E.} = \frac{\text{Cost of employees}}{\text{Operating revenue (turnover)}} * 100$

Source Amadeus solvency and liquidity ratios

Table 9.1 contains the explanation of each individual variable referring to the accounting ratios of solvency and profitability. The framework of this methodology evolves a unidimensional analysis with a binary output predicting the bankruptcy outlook of e-commerce retailers in Europe. Our approach includes different classification experiments to model and predict this probability. We have considered the statistical classification method named two-step cluster analyses to explore in the data set which were the predictors with more importance and contribution to the model. This method clusters the similarity and statistical power between the predictors supporting the authors in the selection of the independent variables. The other statistical classification approaches included in the paper and also widely accepted in financial credit field were logistic regression, decision tree, discriminant analyses, and ROC curves to measure the accuracy of the models. The following table describes the financial calculation of the predictive variables applied in the statistical methods developed and presented along the paper.

The bankruptcy grouping and segmentation observed in the sample were analysed using the two-step cluster method. The main advantage of this procedure is that it does not require a matrix of distances between all pairs of cases and rather requires only categorical or continuous data. It produces solutions based on a mixture of different variables for different number of clusters. The predictors were also clustered by hierarchical degree of importance (Terziovski 2008). Through this process, the financial ratios (clusters) were compared, and then it was possible to identify which predictor had the higher contribution to the model. Summing up the outcomes, the strongest variables were the financial ratios ROA using P&L before tax, EBIT margin, and profit. The variables that had the least importance to the clustered model were solvency, ROE using P&L, and in the last place ROCE using P&L.

Overall, this approach was fairly successful because it was able to prove statistically the significance of the variables to the binary outcome "Yes bankrupt" and "No bankrupt". Furthermore, the hierarchical clustering of the predictors guided the authors in ranking their significances to the bankruptcy predictions.

9.3.1 Decision Tree

The data mining model decision tree was applied to predict the bankruptcy of internet e-commerce companies, and it led to a bankruptcy classification into groups and predicted outcomes through a ramification of independent values (financial ratios). This decision tree model may have real working practice application to categorize the online companies according to whether or not they represent a financial risk. This model validates tools for confirmatory and exploratory classification analysis. It provides features that allow the identification of homogeneous groups of predictors (variables) with high or low risk of bankruptcy (Janda and Rakicova 2014) and makes easier the prediction of bankruptcies of internet businesses. The method applied to develop the decision tree and to evaluate the credit bankruptcy probability is named chi-squared automatic interaction detection (CHAID). The advantage of using the CHAID approach is that at each step, it chooses the financial ratio (independent variable or predictor) that has the strongest interaction with the bankruptcy probability (dependent variable). In the case the categories of the financial ratios are not significantly different relatively to the probability of bankruptcy (dependent variable), the CHAID method merges them. Although 15 financial ratios (independent variables) were introduced in the model, at the end, only three were included in the final version of the decision tree model. The variables' gross margin, cost of employees/operating revenue, and cash flow/operating revenue were the only ones being included by the model, precisely because they had a significant contribution to the decision tree classification model (Fig. 9.1).

The CHAID process demonstrated that the ratio of gross margin is the best predictor of bankruptcy. Within the range between 14.218 and 25.000% of gross income category, the nodes 3 and 4 had just the node 0 as the only significant predictor of bankruptcy; therefore, they were considered the terminal nodes.

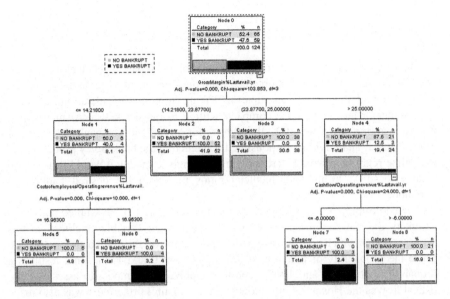

Fig. 9.1 Classification decision tree. *Source* Own calculations based on data from Amadeus

The node 1 corresponds to the lowest gross margin category and its best predictors are the nodes 5 and 6, which are related to the ratio cost of employees/operation revenue. The node 4 is related to the category of e-commerce companies with a gross margin percentage of more than 25.000%. The node 4 classifies the majority of 87.5% businesses that did not bankrupt, and its best predictor of bankruptcy is the category cash flow/operating revenue although representing solely 12.5% of companies bankrupted. Considering that the tree was created with the CHAID method, the chi-square values having the highest significance level are the ones with less than 0.0001% value on all branches in the model. In this respect, only the category cost of employees/operation revenue has a chi-square with a value of 0.006 therefore with a lower significance. Observing the classification results is possible to evaluate that the model works perfectly with the standard error at the value less than 0.0001, and with an overall classification fitting of 100%.

9.3.2 Logistic Model

The logistic model is extensively applied in the financial field to classify subjects based on values of a set of predictor variables, as in the model proposed by Witzany (2009a, b) to estimate the loss given default (LGD) correlation. The predictive probability of bankruptcy using the logistic model is expressed by the formula:

$$P(X) = \frac{1}{1 + e^{-(\alpha + \beta_1 X_1 + \beta_2 X_2 + \beta_3 X_3 + \cdots \beta_\infty X_\infty)}} \tag{9.1}$$

The terms ∞ and β_i in this model represent unknown parameters that the authors estimated based on the data set obtained from the Bureau van Dijk on the X_s and on $P(X)$ (X = probability of bankruptcy). Taking this in consideration, a credit underwriter or an e-commerce company willing to make a self-assessment could use the determined values of X_1 through X_k for a prediction of bankruptcy probability. Thus, if an individual responsible for predicting the bankruptcy probability in the online retail field would start applying this logistic model, it would just have to change these X_i to its own financial ratios to obtain the desired bankruptcy likelihood.

The bankruptcy probability in this model is coded as 1 if bankrupted and 0 if a company did not bankrupt. There are 15 independent variables included in this logistic model which are the estimation predictors of the unknown parameters. Since the probability of bankruptcy must lie within 0 and 1, the final result is a probability between 1 and 100%. The test applied to the model to assess its statistical fit was the Hosmer–Lemeshow goodness-of-fit. Furthermore was also made a diagnostic using a residual plot to observe the change in deviance versus the predictable probabilities, and the Cook's test to observe the distances versus predicted probabilities. The Hosmer–Lemeshow statistical analysis is considered to have a good fit if the significance value is more than 0.05; therefore, as this test had the outcome value of 0.301, the model is considered adequately fitting the data. The statistical test Cox and Snell R^2 based on the log likelihood has a result of 0.538, and the Nagelkerke R^2 test of parameter estimates has the value of 0.718. These two results suggest that the data set included in the model is useful to explain the bankruptcy probability. The Wald statistics identified the following individual parameters, $X_4, X_7, X_8, X_9, X_{10}, X_{11}, X_{12}$, as the most significant to the model. The use of this logistic model to predict the probability of bankruptcy whether by credit underwriters or by e-commerce companies is very accurate and convenient; however, it requires at least an entrance level of accounting, financial, and statistical knowledge to successfully be applied.

9.3.3 Discriminant Analysis

The discriminant analysis is a classification approach that models the value of a dependent categorical variable, based on its relationship with the predictors. It provides a powerful technique for examining differences between two or more groups of objects and several variables simultaneously. In the financial field, credit underwriters may use discriminant analysis to predict or explain which companies will be likely to bankrupt or not. The predictive analysis was made using the IBM SPSS statistical software, and its first step was the assignment of a first function that divided the e-commerce companies into groups. There are several assumptions that have to be met to proceed with the use of a discriminant analysis as following: the predictors cannot be highly correlated; a normal distribution curve; the correlation between the predictors is constant; and the variance and mean of a predictor are also not correlated. The discriminant analysis assigned cases to the two groups, and for each case a classification grading is attributed individually by a hierarchical rank. The e-commerce companies which had the largest solvency ratio are the ones less likely to bankrupt. The tested values of solvency, ROCE (P&L), ROA (P&L), ROE, profit, gross margin, EBITDA, an EBIT, indicate that as higher are these financial ratios as wealthier are likely to be the e-commerce companies, and as less likely are to fall into bankruptcy. In the same fashion, the opposite also holds true. The authors tested the equality of group means to display the outcomes of the unidirectional ANOVA method addressing each financial ratio as the factor. In this test, the maximum threshold of significance is the value of 0.10; therefore, if the independent variable is lower than 0.10, this means that it has contributed to the discriminant model. The Wilks' Lambda test measured the potential contribution of a financial ratio to the model. The smaller results indicate greater discrimination between the groups; moreover, the ratios of solvency, profit and margin were the ones with better performance. The results of the classification model show that 51 out of 59 e-commerce companies that bankrupted were correctly classified, corresponding to a successful percentage of 86.4%. On the other hand, 55 out of 65 companies that did not bankrupt were classified correctly at the level of 84.6%. Considering the overall statistical evaluation, the classification predicted correctly the bankruptcy of e-commerce retailers at the level of 85.5%.

At the end, the ROC curve approach was used to make a comparison of predictive accuracy between the models' logistic regression and discriminant analyses.

The ROC curve is a powerful technique to assess the performance of classification procedures of the two categories (bankrupt and not bankrupt), by which the subjects are classified. A credit underwriter willing to accurately classify e-commerce companies into groups may apply the ROC curve to evaluate the performance of these predictive classifications. Observing the distances from the central reference line, the discriminant analysis and the logistic binomial model are both performing well in terms of bankruptcy prediction. The comparison between these ROC curves shows that the logistic regression slightly performs better than the classification. The area under the curve for both models is significant because they have an asymptotic value of less than 0.05; therefore, they are both correctly predicting the bankruptcy of e-commerce companies. Analysing the confidence test of the asymptotic interval at 95% level is possible to observe that the discriminant analysis is inferior to the logistic regression because the amplitude of its interval has comparatively a lower percentage of lower bound and upper bound. The areas under the curve of this graph provide guidance to the cut-off which determines whether the results are positive or negative. This test is commonly used in finance to test the overall performance of a classifier on training data sets. The best performing models have the curve at the top left corner; therefore, the larger the curve amplitude is, the better the performance is.

9.4 Conclusion

The emergent sector of e-commerce retail is booming all around the world. The new paradigm of retail businesses is shifting from a brick and mortar concept to an online mode denominated as e-commerce. Typically, the online companies are characterized by fast growth rates, large web reach, technologic drive, intangible assets, and strong need of capital to fund the operations. Observing this reality from the financial perspective makes it possible to acknowledge that the access to finance is being constrained by the lack of experience among the credit underwriter's that did not follow the developments in this uprising online field.

The credit evaluation models rely often on out-of-date criteria and basic accounting ratios without taking in consideration the specificities associated with e-commerce businesses such as the online performance metrics. We collected also evidences that several credit scorecards used by large financial institutions do not consider econometric models to evaluate the creditworthiness of these companies. This paper addresses these findings through statistical models and tests such as clustering two-step model, decision tree, logistic regression, discriminant analysis, and ROC curve. These predictive models may be applied in real working practice cases whether by credit underwriters or by business users to predict the likelihood of a bankruptcy event. These classification models in general successfully predicted the e-commerce companies that bankrupted at the level of more than 85%; however, there are differences between the final outcomes and the related easiness of its use. The decision tree can be easier interpreted graphically and thus used in reality. However, it lacks some details regarding the credit risk assessment. The logistic regression performed slightly better than the classification analysis when analysed by the ROC curve test, and in terms of real practice application, the predictive logistic logarithm have showed also high accuracy with the training data set. Although the methods have different fitting characteristics, the logistic regression and the linear discriminant analysis are producing both linear decision thresholds.

The main differences between these two approaches are related to the assumption that in the linear discriminant models, the results are observed through a Gaussian distribution with a similar covariance matrix in each class achieving this way a better performance comparatively to the logistic regression. Notwithstanding in the case that the assumptions of Gaussian distribution are not met, the logistic regression outperforms the other model also because it is applicable to a wider range of financial research situations.

A possibility to extend the studies on this topic is to include a wider population of e-commerce companies and to develop a new credit evaluation scorecard, including the online metrics recommended in this paper.

Recommendations addressed to credit underwriters to improve the financial evaluation of e-commerce companies in Europe:

1. Inclusion of statistical classification analyses to accurately predict the likelihood of a bankruptcy event. The holistic approach is proven to be inefficient.

2. Develop a tailor-made credit evaluation scorecard, including also online metrics such as bounce rate, visitors, conversion rate, page views, time-on-site, returning visitors, average basket value, numbers of orders, online revenue, and number of transactions.

Acknowledgments The research leading to these results received funding from the People Programme (Marie Curie Actions) of the European Union's Seventh Framework Programme FP7/2007–2013 under REA grant agreement number 609642. We also acknowledge support from the Czech Science Foundation (grant 15-00036S). The views expressed in the paper are those of the authors and not necessarily those of our institutions.

References

Beaver WH, Correia M, McNichols M (2011) Financial statement analysis and the prediction of financial distress. Now Publishers Inc

Beaver WH (1968) The information content of annual earnings announcements. J Acconting Res 6 (3):67–92

Bielikova T, Banyiova T, Piterkova A (2014) Prediction techniques of agriculture enterprises failure. Procedia Econ Finan (ECE)

Camp, Filipe, Hammoudi, Piattini (2006) Enterprise information systems. Springer Science & Business Media

Enoch C, Green JH (1997) Banking soundness and monetary policies. IMF Institute International Monetary Fund

Gama J (2010) Knowledge discovery from data streams, London, Chapman & Hall

Gibson C (2010) Financial reporting and analysis: using financial accounting information. Cengage Learning. 6 Apr 2010, pp 469–472

Hand DJ, Henley WE (1997) Statistical classification methods in consumer credit scoring: a review. J Roy Stat Soc A Sta, 160:523–541. doi:10.1111/j.1467-985X.1997.00078.x

Janda K (2009) Bankruptcies with soft budget constraint. Manchester Sch 77(4):430–460

Janda K (2011) Inefficient credit rationing and public support of commercial credit provision. J Inst Theor Econ 167(2):371–391

Janda K, Rojcek J (2014) Bankruptcy triggering asset value: continuous time finance approach. In: Pinto AA, Zilbermand D (eds) Modeling, dynamics, optimization and bioeconomics I. Springer Link, pp 357–382. ISBN:978-3-319-04849-9

Janda K, Rakićová A (2014) Corporate bankruptcies in Czech Republic, Slovakia, Croatia and Serbia. Mnichov

Jakubík P, Teplý P (2011) The JT index as an indicator of financial stability of corporate sector. Prague Econ Pap 20(2):157–176. ISSN 1210-0455

Klapper L, Allende VS, Sulla V (2002) Small- and medium-size enterprise financing in Eastern Europe. World Bank eLibrary

Lucas A (2004) Updating scorecards: removing the mystique. Readings in credit scoring: foundations, developments, and aims. Oxford University, New York, pp 93–109

Pagell RA, Halperin M (1999) International business information: how to find it, how to use it, Global Professional Publishing, p 144

Pavel J, Sičáková E (2013) Do e-auctions really improve the efficiency of public procurement? The case of the Slovak municipalities. Prague Econ Pap: Q J Econ Theor Policy 22(1):111–124. ISSN 1210-0455

Rosenberger LE, Nash J (2009) The deciding factor: the power of analytics to make every decision a winner. Wiley, pp 7–8

Stádník B, Miečienskiené A (2015) Complex model of market price development and its simulation. J Bus Econ Manag 16(4):786–807

Tagarelli A (2012) XML data mining: models, methods, and applications: United States of America. Information Science Reference, pp 471–473

Terziovski M (2008) Energizing management through innovation and entrepreneurship: European research and practice. Routledge

Teplý P, Pečená (2010) Magda credit risk and financial crises. Karolinum Press, Prague. ISBN:978-80-246-1872-2

Teplý P, Tripe D (2015) The TT index as an indicator of macroeconomic vulnerability of EU new member states. Ekonomický časopis (J Econ) 63(1):19–33. ISSN:0013-3035

Thomas LC (2010) Consumer finance: challenges for operational research. J Oper Res Soc 41–52

Thomas LC, Edelman DB, Crook JN (2002) Credit scoring and its applications. SIAM

Witzany J (2009a) Estimating LGD correlation. Financ Risk Manag VII(4):73–83. ISSN:0972-916X

Witzany J (2009b) Loss, default and loss given default modeling. IES Working Paper 9:1. URL: http://ies.fsv.cuni.cz/sci/publication/show/id/3650/lang/en

Witzany J (2010a) Credit risk management and modelling. Oeconomica, Praha. ISBN:978-80-245-1682-0

Witzany J (2010b) On deficiencies and possible improvements of the basel II unexpected loss single-factor model. Czech J Econ Finan 60(3):252–268

Witzany J (2011) Definition of default and quality of scoring functions. Bull Czech Econ Soc 18 (28):33–52. ISSN:1212-074X

Chapter 10
Cost Efficiency of European Cooperative Banks: Are Small Institutions Predestined to Fail?

Matěj Kuc

Abstract Aim of this paper is to make a literature review and also to empirically assess optimal size of cooperative banks in European Union in terms of their cost efficiency. Theoretical explanations for possible efficiency advantages are brought forward and consequently they are compared with existing empirical literature. Furthermore, we created dataset of 283 banks from 15 European countries between years 2006 and 2013 to empirically investigate this problem on recent data. Using descriptive statistics, we found that bigger European cooperative banks are more efficient in terms of cost-to-income ratio than the smaller ones. These results seem to be stable in time and also in individual countries as was shown on analysis of subsamples.

Keywords Cooperative banking · Cost efficiency · Economies of scale

10.1 Introduction

Cooperative banks in nineteenth-century Europe all started similarly: as small institutions created to improve socioeconomic condition and financial services accessibility to its members. Since that time, cooperative banking schemes in Europe diverged: In some countries, cooperative banks grew into big institutions offering broad range of services being practically indistinguishable from commercial banks, some cooperative banks created more or less interconnected networks to enhance cooperation and some other cooperative banks stayed almost the same throughout the ages.

Aim of this paper is to make a literature review and also to empirically assess optimal size of cooperative banks in European Union in terms of their cost efficiency. This assessment will help to answer questions whether we can expect

M. Kuc (✉)
Charles University in Prague, Institute of Economic Studies, IES FSV UK,
Opletalova 26, 110 00 Praha 1, Czech Republic
e-mail: matejkuc@seznam.cz

© Springer International Publishing AG 2017   105
D. Procházka (ed.), *New Trends in Finance and Accounting*,
Springer Proceedings in Business and Economics,
DOI 10.1007/978-3-319-49559-0_10

consolidation of cooperative banks (or credit unions) on current market, how are cooperative banks behaving in relation with too big to fail problem, whether legislation limiting the asset size of cooperative bank (just as in the Czech Republic) is from this point of view economically justifiable, or whether we can expect successful creation of any new credit unions in developed markets. This paper is structured as follows: In Sect. 10.2, we give short overview of history and basic principles of cooperative banking. Section 10.3 describes possible explanation for (dis)economies of scales for cooperative banks. Section 10.4 provides overview on existing empirical literature dealing with cost efficiency of cooperative banks. Section 10.5 provides our own empirical analysis on cost efficiency of European cooperative banks, and finally, Sect. 10.6 concludes the paper and provides ideas for further research connected to this field.

10.2   History and Principles of Cooperative Banking in a Nutshell

Only small share of population took real merits from economic upswing during the time of industrial revolution during the first half of nineteenth century. Petty bourgeoisie was put under pressure by newly emerging big companies. Individual artisans were unable to compete with prices of industrial mass production. Small farmers had problems with saving enough money to buy instruments that would make them competitive. Prices of their products dropped with introducing free trade and thanks to goods imported from colonies. High information asymmetry and cost of enforcement are seen as main obstacles by Guinnane (1993) that hindered access to financial services for broad masses of population.

Individual communities therefore started to create their own financial services in order to escape vicious circle of increasing costs of modernization and insufficient funds. These first cooperative banks were created on the basics introduced by founding fathers of credit cooperatives: Hermann Shulze-Delitzsch and Friedrich Wilhelm Raiffeisen (see, e.g., Schulze-Delitzsch 1855). Important principle of cooperative banks was self-help of involved members and relying only on their own funds and capabilities. Credit unions were able to overcome information asymmetry and enforcement costs by the fact that all members of credit unions were often the members of the same community (Angelini et al. 1998). From these facts, IT is clear that cooperative banks' goal is not to create profit as is the case for shareholder-driven banks but to offer financial services for their members. Because of this fact of not having the single objective, cooperative banks are also called double-bottom-line institutions (see, e.g., Hillman and Keim 2001).

Banks operating on cooperative principles spread quickly across Europe, and their originally similar structure begins to differ in order to assimilate better to local environment and to better satisfy the needs of its members. Cooperative banks have undergone considerable changes since the time of their dawn. Business scope of some of them now spreads out from traditional retail activities to investment banking. Although they are maintaining traditionally strong position on households and SME markets, they tried to enhance their profits by offering new products and services. Cooperative banks therefore become often hardly distinguishable from commercial banks. Cooperatives also grew in size and sometimes even formed extensive international networks. For study on regional differences in European cooperative banks, please see CEPS (2010).

There are around 4000 operating cooperative banks in Europe according to the EACB (2013). Market share of cooperative banks across European states is highly unevenly distributed. Oliver (2012) states that market share of cooperative banks on both customer loans and deposits in the European Union is around 20%. Rabobank (2011) in its study states that market share of cooperative banks on deposit differs from 60% in France, 40% in the Netherlands, 15% in Germany to almost negligible share in some other countries (e.g., in the Czech Republic). We can also spot the difference between new EU member states (Eastern Europe) where cooperative banking market share is often close to zero[1] and Western Europe where cooperative banking tradition was not disrupted by the communist regime.

10.3 Theoretical Explanation of (Dis)Economies of Scale in Cooperative Banks

Cooperative banks are democratically controlled on principle of one member one vote (even though there exist exceptions, see CEPS 2010). Corporate governance model of credit unions (or cooperative banks in general) is created for small organization, and large cooperative banks with millions of members/owners can suffer from problems connected to dispersed ownership. Such organizations have problems with organizational issues and with cooperation among individual members. General meetings attendance may become small, and effective supervision of banks' managers may be lacking. Becht et al. (2002) show that collusion between managers and supervisory board elected to monitor them happens surprisingly often when institution's ownership is highly dispersed. Bad monitoring allows managers to pursue so-called empire building rather than following interests of cooperative banks members.

Cooperative banks will also lose their information advantage of being close to its members as the bank grows bigger. It is hard to imagine that the bank member shares strong common bond if the bank offers wide range of services on vast area.

On the other hand, significant scale economies may be reached using modern technologies (information technology, etc.). There are significant fixed costs

---

[1]For more details on CEE banking sectors we refer to, for example, Černohorská et al. (2012), Janda et al. (2013), Černohorská and Honza (2014), Šútorová and Teplý (2013, 2014) or Vodová (2013).

connected with banking IT systems, but variable costs for every additional client then are only marginal. Therefore, technological progress promotes increasing size of financial institutions. Regulation of financial industry is very complex, and banks have to allocate significant resources to comply with all the rules. There are only minor differences between regulatory burdens laid on shoulders of small and big banks, and therefore, it is relatively more costly for small bank to comply. This problem is further investigated by World Council of Credit Unions (WOCCU 2013).

As can be seen from paragraphs above, there exist theoretical arguments supporting both economies and diseconomies of scale for cooperative banks. In the next section, we will take a look what does the existing empirical literature say regarding this issue.

10.4 Empirical Literature Overview

Given the nature of cooperative bank where profit maximizing is not the ultimate goal of institution, we can assume that profitability of cooperative banks is lower than profitability of shareholder value banks. Altunbas et al. (2001) examined profit inefficiencies of different ownership models on the German banking market. They started discussing the assumption that the lack of capital market discipline, common to mutual and public ownerships, may indicate that management experiences lower intensity of environmental pressure and therefore may operate less efficiently than privately owned institutions (Fama and Jensen 1983). Nevertheless, they thought that this may not be the case in highly competitive banking industry. The study uses data from years 1989 to 1996 and employs stochastic frontier analysis (SFA). Interestingly, they found that cooperative and savings banks can enjoy slight profit and cost advantage over commercial banks. Authors explained the results by lower cost of funds of cooperatives arising from their specialization on retail activities. All the types of banks also seemed to benefit from their size (economies of scale).

Fiorentino et al. (2006) examined consistency of SFA and data envelopment analysis (DEA) on set of German banks in between years 1993 and 2004 showing slight cost advantage of commercial banks over cooperative ones.

Goddard et al. (2004) found weak relationship between banks' size and profitability in selected European countries (namely in: Denmark, France, Germany, Italy, Spain and in the UK) over the 1992–1998 period. They run several cross-sectional, pooled cross-sectional, and dynamic panel data models (system GMM). Goddard and Wilson (2005) examined growth of American credit unions from 1995 to 2001 and concluded that larger credit unions grew on average faster than their smaller counterparts and, moreover, that there is positive persistence of growth effect. Wheelock and Wilson (2012) found that cost efficiency measured by effective frontier of American credit unions during 1989–2006 period fell more for smaller scale institutions and that all but the biggest credit unions became less efficient in time. This result draws similar conclusion as preceding work of Wilcox (2006).

Deelchand and Padgett (2009) are interested in scale economies in cooperative banks in Japan. They use SFA for 2003–2006 panel data and found significant diseconomies of scale for the whole sample of Japanese cooperative banks and also for subsamples divided according to the size of banks.

Barros et al. (2010) used Luenberger indicator approach to assess productivity change of cooperative banks in 10 European countries. They concluded that small scale of some cooperatives may hinder their technological growth.

Kuc and Teplý (2015) showed bad performance of Czech credit unions, which are small-size institutions, in terms of profitability and stability compared to more than 250 cooperative banks from 15 European countries in the 2006–2013 period.

To sum up, the studies in this empirical review often draw conflicting results regarding optimal size of cooperative banks in terms of cost efficiency. The results are highly dependent on selected method, dataset, and time period used for the study. Small Japanese cooperative banks seem to enjoy cost advantage over bigger cooperative banks which is just the opposite to the results of American credit unions. Studies devoted to cost efficiency in Europe often do not distinguish between ownership banking types or the studies that do distinguish are interested in separated countries. Although the evidence is mixed, more studies are showing that bigger cooperative banks perform more cost efficiently than smaller ones.

10.5   Analysis of European Cooperative Banks Cost Efficiency

In our analysis, we will employ cost-to-income ratio as a measure of cooperative banks' efficiency. This measure suffers from several flows: It is an accounting measure, and therefore it may suffer from connected problems such as profit smoothing, and it can be misleading due to some one-off transactions not related directly to bank's effectiveness, etc. We decided not to employ efficient frontier analysis which is popular method to estimate cost efficiency of banking institutions, but we see this as a possible extension to this paper. In his paper, only descriptive statistics of accounting data will be used.

We used BankScope database as main source of accounting data of European cooperatives. To further enrich the dataset, we manually plugged data of Czech credit unions retrieved from their annual reports. To be able to better see shifts in effectiveness of European cooperative banks, we decided to use panel data for 2006–2013 period. We inserted only institutions which had financial statements available throughout the whole period in order to have balanced data set. Altogether, we have 2264 observations from 283 cooperative banks from 15 European states. Geographical distribution of cooperative banks in our data set is given in Table 10.1.

Table 10.1 Geographical
distribution of banks in our
dataset

Country	Banks	Country	Banks
Austria	17	Finland	1
Belgium	1	France	7
Bulgaria	1	Greece	1
Cyprus	1	Croatia	1
Czech Rep.	11	Italy	87
Germany	139	Malta	1
Denmark	2	Slovenia	1
Spain	12	Total	283

Source Own computations based on BankScope and annual
reports

Table 10.2 Cost-to-income
ratio development in time

Year	Cost-to-income ratio		
	1st quartile	Median	3rd quartile
2006	60.0	65.3	71.8
2007	60.1	68.6	75.0
2008	62.1	70.2	76.8
2009	62.9	68.7	74.4
2010	61.2	67.7	76.0
2011	61.4	66.7	73.0
2012	58.4	65.5	72.1
2013	57.7	64.0	71.1
Total	60.3	67.0	74.0

Source Own computations based on BankScope and annual
reports

Large share of German and Italian cooperative banks in our dataset is caused by
size of these countries, strength of local cooperative banking sector, and also
specific nature of cooperative banks in these countries where cooperative banks
operate on small units highly independently and therefore have their financial
statements available. On the other hand, in some countries, cooperative banks are
tightly connected to couple of big institutions and, therefore, we have only small
number of cooperative banks for some other big countries with developed cooperative banking sector. We see this heterogeneity in our data as advantage for our
goal of comparing cost-to-income ratio of cooperative banks with different asset
size (Table 10.2).

Plotting cost-to-income ratio depending on asset size for all our available
observations shows that there is correlation between cooperative banks' size and
given ratio. This relation is represented by linear trendline. The lower
cost-to-income ratio represents higher efficiency of institution, and therefore,
Fig. 10.1 shows that smaller cooperative banks are less efficient. We further plotted
similar graphs for each year from 2006 to 2013, and the picture is similar so it

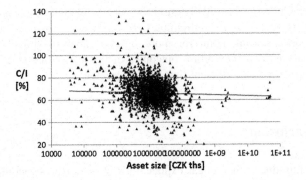

Fig. 10.1 Cost-to-income ratio on whole sample. *Source* Own computations based on BankScope and annual reports

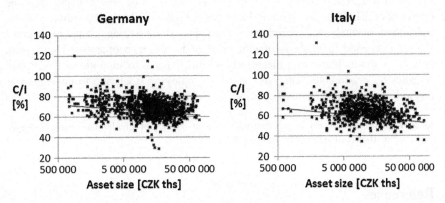

Fig. 10.2 Cost-to-income ratio on German and Italian banks. *Source* Own computations based on BankScope and annual reports

seems that this relation is stable in time. The graphs for individual years are not included in the paper in order to save precious space.

We can further divide our dataset into subsamples according to the countries to work with more homogenous sets of banks. We therefore plot only cooperative banks from Germany and from Italy because we have by far highest number of institutions available from these two countries (Fig. 10.2).

The picture stays the same even in these two subsamples: Bigger cooperative banks enjoy lower cost-to-income ratio, and therefore, they are more efficient than smaller ones. Again, nothing significantly changes if we further divide data by individual years. We also run this analysis on subsamples of Czech, Austrian and Spanish cooperative banks with similar results. For sake of brevity, these graphs are not included in the paper.

From descriptive statistics showed above, we can see that bigger cooperative banks tend to be more efficient than the smaller ones. The results proved to be robust and stable over 2006–2013 period and across different European countries as we showed by analyzing the subsamples. Nevertheless, this descriptive statistics serves just as a starting point for more rigorous analysis (possibly Stochastic Frontier Analysis) that may affirm outcomes of this paper that small cooperative banks in Europe are less efficient than the bigger ones.

10.6   Conclusion

This paper introduced theoretical explanations of scale (dis)economies that may influence optimal asset size of cooperative banks. We used dataset of 283 banks from 15 European countries between years 2006 and 2013 to empirically investigate this problem. We used cost-to-income ratio as efficiency measure and arrived to conclusion that smaller cooperative banks seem to be less efficient than the bigger ones. These results seem to be stable in time and also in individual states as was shown on analysis of individual subsamples. These findings comply with most studies interested in analysis of efficiency of European cooperative banks from previous periods. Interesting idea to extend this paper is to support our descriptive statistics by econometric analysis, possibly employing stochastic frontier analysis method which is heavily used for assessing efficiency of banks.

Acknowledgments   Financial support from the Grant Agency of Charles University in Prague (project No. 105815) is gratefully acknowledged.

References

Altunbas Y, Evans L, Molyneux P (2001) Bank ownership and efficiency. J Money Credit Bank 33(4):926–954
Angelini P, Di Salvo R, Ferri G (1998) Availability and cost of credit for small businesses: customer relationships and credit cooperatives. J Bank Finance 22(6):925–954
Barros AP, Peypoch N, Williams J (2010) A note on productivity change in European cooperative banks: the Luenberger indicator approach. Int Rev Appl Econ
Becht M, Bolton P, Röell A (2002) Corporate Governance and Control. European Corporate Governance Institute - Finance Working Paper No. 02/2002
CEPS (2010) Investigating diversity in the banking sector in Europe—key developments, performance and role of cooperative banks. Brussels
Černohorská L, Honza F (2014) Specifics of the banking sectors in the countries of Former Yugoslavia. In: Stavárek D, Vodová P (eds) Conference: 14th international conference on finance and banking, Ostrava, Czech proceedings of the 14th international conference on finance and banking, pp. 42–50
Černohorská L, Teplý P, Vrábel M (2012) The VT index as an indicator of market liquidity risk in Slovakia. J Econ 60(3):223–238
Deelchand T, Padgett C (2009) Size and scale economies in Japanese cooperative banking. ICMA Centre Discussion Papers in Finance DP2009-02. University of Reading
EACB (2013) Annual report 2012, Brussels

Fama EF, Jensen MC (1983) Separation of ownership and control. J Law Econ 26(2):301–326

Fiorentino E, Karmann A, Koetter M (2006) The cost efficiency of German banks: a comparison of SFA and DEA. Deutsche Bundesbank, Discussion Paper Series 2, Banking No 10/2006

Goddard J, Wilson, JO (2005) US credit unions: an empirical investigation of size, age and growth. Ann Publ Coop Econ 76(3):375–406. Blackwell Publishing Ltd

Goddard J, Molyneux P, Wilson JO (2004) The profitability of European banks: a cross-sectional and dynamic panel data analysis. Manchaster Sch 72(3)

Guinnane TW (1993) Cooperatives as information machines: the lending practices of German agricultural credit cooperatives, 1883–1914. Economic Growth Center Discussion Paper No. 699, Yale University

Hillman AJ, Keim GD (2001) Shareholder value, stakeholder management, and social issues: what's the bottom line? Strateg Manag J 22(2):125–139

Janda K, Michalikova E, Skuhrovec J (2013) Credit support for export: Robust evidence from the Czech Republic. World Econ 36(12):1588–1610

Kuc M, Teply P (2015) A comparison of financial performance of Czech Credit Unions and European Cooperative Banks. IES Working Paper 18/2015. IES FSV. Charles University

Oliver W (2012) Outlook for co-operative banking in Europe 2012. Oliver Wyman's report, lead authors: McCarroll V, Habberfield S

Rabobank (2011) Cooperative banks in the spotlight. Special report 2011/12. Nov 2011

Schulze-Delitzsch H (1855) Vorschuß- Vereine als Volksbanken. Keil, Leipzig

Šútorová B, Teplý P (2013) The Impact of Basel III on lending rates of EU banks. Czech J Finance 23(3):226–243

Šútorová B, Teplý P (2014) The level of capital and the value of EU banks under Basel III. Prague Econ Pap 23(2):143–161

Vodová P (2013) Liquid assets in banking: what matters in the Visegrad countries? E+M Ekonomie Manag 16(3):113–129

Wheelock DC, Wilson PW (2012) The evolution of cost-productivity and efficiency among US credit unions. J Bank Finance 37:75–88

Wilcox JA (2006) Performance divergence of large and small credit unions. FRBS Econ Lett, 2006–19, Federal Reserve Bank of San Francisco

WOCCU (2013) Basel accords. Retrieved 1/3/2016, available online: http://www.woccu.org/memberserv/advocacy/basel

Chapter 11
The Banking Union: A View of the New Regulatory Rules

Luboš Fleischmann

Abstract Amendments to regulatory banking rules come around cyclically depending on financial crises. Thematically, the paper focuses on regulatory rules newly set out in the European Banking Union. Special attention was paid to the part of the Bank Recovery and Resolution Directive (BRRD) dealing with the mechanism of writing off liabilities (called bail-in) and effective reinsurance (Minimum Requirement for own funds and Eligible Liabilities). The author's objective was to address two basic questions concerning the impact on the Czech banking market and the austerity of the adopted regulations.

Keywords Banking Union · Supervision · Regulation · Rules · Banks

11.1 Introduction

Amendments to regulatory banking rules come around cyclically depending on financial crises. They also always bring along heated discussions as to how extensive the changes should be and, above all, how tough or moderate they ought to be. The trend toward stricter regulation also stems from the fact that the banking market has been gradually shifting from free competition toward oligopolistic structure, and furthermore the fact that rapid growth in the productivity of labor in the production sphere releases considerable workforce capacity that finds application, inter alia, in regulatory bodies (Mandel and Tomšík 2011). On the European level, in the regulatory area, particularly interesting was the Banking Union project which alters the rules of supervision over the banking market and problem solving of banks.

The idea of a Banking Union was initially brought up in 2012 by the José Manuel Barroso, then chairman of the European Commission, and has been dis-

L. Fleischmann (✉)
Department of Banking and Insurance, University of Economics, Prague,
Nam. W. Churchilla 4, 130 67 Prague 3, Czech Republic
e-mail: lubos.fleischmann@gmail.com

© Springer International Publishing AG 2017
D. Procházka (ed.), *New Trends in Finance and Accounting*,
Springer Proceedings in Business and Economics,
DOI 10.1007/978-3-319-49559-0_11

cussed on the level of various European institutions about setting up new regulatory rules ever since. While the advocates of change argue on the basis of the fact that concerted supervision, common rules for crisis solving, and a unified fund for securing investments are the best strategic decisions for European banking, the critics of a common Banking Union, predominantly from member countries outside the Eurozone, rely on the supposition that successful and economically healthy banks will bail out the less successful parent companies.

The Banking Union is supplementary to the Economic and Monetary Union (EMU) and the internal market that harmonizes the responsibility for supervision, problem solving of banks, and financing on the EU level, and forces the banks throughout the Eurozone to observe the same rules. This rules make sure, in particular, that banks assume certain risks, so that a bank that makes an error accepts liability for its losses and, if exposed to the danger of closing, the taxpayer's expenses must be minimized (Magnus et al. 2015). The Banking Union consists of three pillars: Single Supervisory Mechanism (SSM), Single Resolution Mechanism (SRM), and the currently incomplete European Deposit Insurance Scheme (EDIS).

On January 1, 2016, yet another part of the European Banking Union began to function—the Single Resolution Fund (SRF) that is part of the SRM. In fact, this first full-fledged project of the Banking Union aimed to remove the implicit linkage between banks and state budgets and reduce the risks of the internal market's fragmentation, thus supporting economic growth in the member countries of the European Union. It is designed primarily for countries that are members of the Eurozone, yet with significant impact even on the countries outside. The regulative measures are felt most strongly by system banks, whereas small and less important banks will hardly feel them.

The above pillars of the Banking Union include individual regulatory rules, some of which will impact significantly on the banking sector in the Czech Republic. In this context, certain issues arise that the author of this paper tries to address. For instance, is the Directive on Crisis Management (BRRD), as it is called, a good idea for the banking market in the Czech Republic? Aren't the newly adopted and proposed regulatory European rules too strict?

11.2 The Banking Union and Regulatory Rules

11.2.1 Status Quo

As mentioned above, the Banking Union consists of two already functioning basic pillars (SSM and SRM) and one under preparation (EDIS) and of basic regulative rules (CRD IV/CRR, BRRD, DGSD[1]). In March 2013, the European Parliament and Council reached an agreement that led to the establishment of a SSM and, by

---

[1]Directive on Deposit Insurance Scheme (DGSD).

extension, to the beginning of a project, whose primary objective is not only to prevent the occurrence of crises in the banking sector, but above all to be able to solve them. The SSM mechanism, which has been functioning since November 4, 2014, operates within the ECB and is responsible for direct supervisions over 123 largest banking groups, while internal national authorities continue to supervise the other banks, whereas the final responsibility is borne by the ECB (Magnus et al. 2015). The SSM's action was to conduct a comprehensive assessment by reviewing the quality of the assets of banks and stress tests. The results revealed that 25 of the 130 tested banks had insufficient capital. Most of the banks rectified the insufficiency quickly or presented remedial plans for their capitalization to the European Central Bank.

A mirror reflection of the SSM is the SRM that was finalized in March 2014. The main objective of the SRM is to ensure that eventual future bankruptcies of the banks in the Banking Union would be resolved effectively, i.e., at minimal costs to the taxpayers and real economy (Magnus et al. 2015). In April 2014, the European Parliament adopted a directive on remedial measures and crisis solving of credit institutions and investment enterprises (BRRD). The directive set forth the procedures for solving the problems of banks in distress. Primarily, it orders that losses are to be covers by the shareholders and creditors, in the first place, so that such banks would not be bailed out from public financial resources. The directive is being implemented as the Banking Union's principal pillar. The Czech Republic integrated it into its legislation by implementing Act No. 374/2015 Coll., on remedial measures and crises solving in the financial market, which came into effect on January 1, 2016, and Act No. 375/2015 Coll., amending certain laws in connection with the adoption of the law on remedial measures and crises solving in the financial market and in connection with the update of the deposit insurance system. The implementation took place, despite the fact that the Czech Republic, as a member of the European Union outside the Eurozone, did not have such an obligation. Thus, the Czech Republic had in joined the Banking Union project.

The third pillar, the European Deposit Insurance Scheme (EDIS), was presented by the European Commission on November 24, 2015. The aim is to improve the protection bank depositors, strengthen financial stability, and restrain the linkage between banks and countries. According to plan, the system is supposed to evolve gradually in three consecutive phases: (1) Reinsurance, (2) Co-insurance, and (3) Full insurance.

For the sake of clarity, the Banking Union may be expressed as an "equation":
BU = SSM + SRM (SRF + SRB) + (BRRD + DGSD) + (CDR IV + CRR), or graphically as shown in Fig. 11.1. Each individual part has its reasons, aims, legislative backup, and mostly also own institutional instruments and classification.

As the above text indicates, common supervision over banking institution is globalizing and goes hand in hand with an inundation of European regulatory rules. In terms of these aspects, the trend of approximation of supervision systems and regulations is quite apparent.

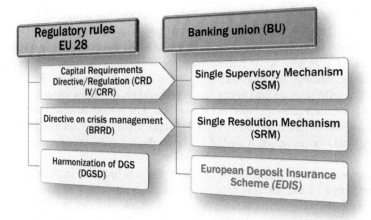

Fig. 11.1 Pillars of the Banking Union, rules and regulations. *Source* Lenka Jurošková, Ministry of Finance, conference development and innovation of financial product, University of Economics, Prague—February 10, 2016, http://www.finance-edu.cz/prezentace/

11.2.2 The Five Chairmen Report

Overshadowed by the migration crisis, the problems of Greece, and last but not the least by considerations of the possible withdrawal of Great Britain from the European Union, the so-called Five Chairmen Report was issued on June 22, 2015, which in essence and as a vision returns to the main motivation that preceded the founding of the Banking Union, namely the expansion and complementation of the Economic and Monetary Union in all contexts. The report was co-authored by the chairman of the European Commission, Jean-Claude Juncker; chairman of the European Council, Donald Tusk; chairman of the Eurogroup, Jeroen Dijsselbloem; chairman of the European Central Bank, Mario Draghi; and chairman of the European Parliament, Martin Schulz.

In the document, the five chairmen describe the procedures of complementing full monetary European integration by means of several objectives:

- aiming at economic union;
- aiming at financial union;
- aiming at fiscal union;
- strengthening of democratic responsibility, legitimacy, and institution: from rules to institutions;
- social dimension of the EMU.

The Five Chairmen Report states that complementation of the Banking Union calls for full implementation of the Directive on Crisis Management (BRRD) by all member countries first. According to the authors, it is of key importance to the sharing of risks by the private sector and the Banking Union is, in essence, a better way of protecting taxpayers from having to bear the costs of bailing out banks. The document returns to the notion of the so-called two-gear Europe, where the dividing line is supposed to run between the countries of the Eurozone and countries that will continue to use their own currency. However, the road leading to this idea is long and thorny, as approving it would require the consent of all member countries of the European Union.

11.3   Bank Recovery and Resolution Directive (BRRD): Bail-In Mechanism and MREL

European Parliament and Council Directive 2014/59/EU on Bank Recovery and Resolution (BRRD) of May 15, 2014, aims to ensure a safer, more reliable, and more transparent functioning of the financial sector. It is yet another of the set of European regulatory norms to stipulate a new, unified regulatory framework for crisis management of credit institution and investment enterprises. The objective is to avoid bankruptcies of financial institutions and, simultaneously, help solve crises without having to bail out banks from public state budgets.

The principal BRRD measure is the so-called bail-in mechanism or, in other words, a mechanism of writing off liabilities and effective reinsurance of funds MREL (Minimum Requirement for own funds and Eligible Liabilities).

This paper will pay considerable attention to the MREL rule, the primary reason being the fact that it is one of the European rules discussed most at the present, especially due to concerns about possible negative impact on the financial market in the Czech Republic.

11.3.1   Bail-In Mechanism

Bail-in mechanisms ensure coverage of the losses of banks in the event of their bankruptcy, whereby the first in the line are the shareholders and major creditors of banks, not minor depositors. The main objective of the bail-in mechanism is to carry over the expenses arising from the bankruptcies of banks from the taxpayers onto the owners and creditors of banks and reduce implicit state guarantees and the possibility of fast recapitalization of banks, while preserving and upholding further functionality of the systemically important parts of the banks.

In the event that a crisis situation is identified, the bank in crisis need not have enough of its own capital to cover its losses. In such cases, the bail-in mechanism makes it possible to create an adequate capacity for absorbing the losses. It would be facilitated by writing off certain of the bank's debt instruments to compensate for all the existing and anticipated losses. The Directive stipulates the formation of strictly instated crisis management authorities ("Resolution Authority," in the Czech Republic, e.g., the Czech National Bank) which are authorized to convert certain debt instruments to own capital for the purposes of the bank's recapitalization, so that it could continue to function. The conversion may be done either in combination with write-offs, or as a separate measure. Absorbing the losses of banks by reducing own liabilities and recapitalization means that the use of public resources may be deferred, reduced, or, ideally, completely avoidable (Avalová and Majdloch 2015).

The BRRD Directive excludes certain liabilities that may not be eligible for the bail-in mechanism, such as liabilities to employees or liabilities to suppliers, secured liabilities (e.g., secured bonds or repo deals), liabilities with initial maturity period shorter than seven days. Completely excluded are insured deposits (Fig. 11.2).

For the banking sector in the Czech Republic, a major problem in the bail-in process appears to be the transfer of losses onto shareholders and subsequently creditors. Due to instability of the political environment on the level of European institutions, where frequent changes of adopted rules are common, the transition from the bail-out process, where problems of banks were compensated from public resources, to the bail-in process in the future against those that are supposed to be protected most—minor depositors. At present, it is impossible to predict whether the limit of €100,000.00 covered by the Deposit Insurance Fund (DIF) would be gradually reduced to a much lower amount.

Moreover, the banking sector will be affected by changes in connection with the DIF due to the implementation of weighed-risk contributions to the Fund.[2] The amount of the annual contribution is to be set by the Czech National Bank (CNB) by May 31 and must be paid by June 30 that year.

11.3.2   MREL

From the perspective of the Czech banking sector, most problematic seems to be the part of the BRRD that sets out minimum capital requirements and eligible liabilities (MREL). The target of criticism is the relevance of the estimated limit of two basic criteria, namely the loss absorption amount (LAA) and subsequent recapitalization

---

[2]The amount of the credit institution's contribution to the Deposit Insurance Fund (henceforth only DIF) depends on the total of covered claims from deposits registered against the credit institution (defined in Sec. 41ca[4] of the Banking Code, as amended; henceforth only "covered claims from deposits") and on its overall risk profile. Pursuant to Directive DGS II, weighed-risk contributions are collected at least once a year, after reaching the minimum required amount of funds in the DIF corresponding to 0.8% covered claims from deposits (no later than July 3, 2024). Pursuant to Sec. 41ca[4] of the Banking Code, as amended, the contribution amount can be set even after reaching the minimum amount of funds in the DIF. In addition to regular contributions, it is possible, if necessary, to request even extraordinary, single-time contributions.

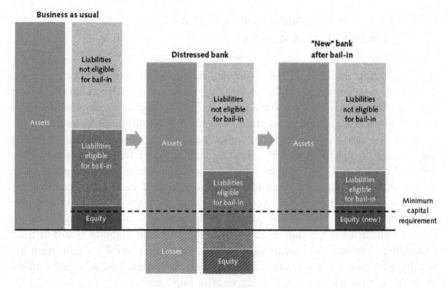

Fig. 11.2 Simplified description of application of the bail-in tool on the balance sheet of a distressed bank. *Source* The bail-in tool from a Swedish perspective. Sveriges Riksbank Economic Review. 2014:2

amount (RCA). The competent authority for crisis solving will be required to evaluate the level of losses that the institution is capable of absorbing, its risk profile, business model, and systemic importance.

The value of the LAA is supposed to be equal to or higher than the summary capital requirement of the given institution, and the value of the RCA is supposed to be set by type of institution.

$$(\alpha + \beta + \gamma)/(\delta + \alpha) \geq x \tag{11.1}$$

where α = own capital, β = unsecured debt instruments with maturity longer than one year, γ = deposits of large corporations with residual maturity longer than one year, δ = total liabilities, x = minimum capital requirements and eligible liabilities.

In the Czech Republic, the proposed MREL limit in the current methodical form may reach 30% RWA (risk-weighted assets). Contrary to most banks in the EMU (Economic and Monetary Union), Czech banks have shareholders, not creditors, and have no need to borrow money. For this reason, the overlap of deposits over credits amounts to approximately 30%.

11.4   The Czech National Bank's Stance
          to Regulatory Changes

The Czech National Bank (CNB) presented its standpoint to regulatory changes at the Annual Conference of the Czech Banking Association (CBA), held on October 21, 2015. The Czech National Bank finds the final version of financial regulation to be hard to predict and presents certain reasons corroborating this statement.

Generally, the ČNB would prefer perfecting supervisions and regulatory caution over constant supplementing and amending the regulatory framework (step-by-step approach), as changes ought to be put into practice only after careful consideration. Moreover, they should not lead to a general easing of cautionary requirements, including capital requirements. Regulations adopted on the level of the European Union should not overtake developments on the international scene, and EU should always wait for final recommendations from the Financial Stability Board or Basel Committee. For healthy business of financial institution, good capitalization and healthy governance are essential, but stable and predictable business environment, including regulatory environment, are equally important.

In the area of the EDIS, the ČNB considers the requirement of 100% insurance of deposits controversial, as part of the Directive on Guarantee Schemes (DGS and DGS II), due to the support of moral hazard. Consequently, this boils down to apprehensions about the disruption of the balance between competences and responsibilities, as insurance encourages risk behavior and expectations—if help was extended in the past, it will come around again (Zamrazilová 2015).

The Czech National Bank is one of the most cautious supervisory bodies in the EU. Using its instruments, it managed to handle the recent crisis, thanks to it well-adjusted system of creating capital reserves in banking institutions.

11.5   Conclusion

Regulation and supervision over the banking sector are indispensable in the field of macroeconomic policy for the attainment of the principal goals of economic development. Some forms of regulation contained in all the main theoretical economic trends—the difference is in the scope and hardness of the regulation. Reoccurring banking crises trigger regularly new schemes for a stricter regulation and criticism from the opponents of regulation greater than necessary. This is logically the case also in the post-Lehman era.

As stated above, the Czech banking sector is in a very good condition and behaves conservatively. Compared to the banks in the EMU, Czech banks have more deposits and fewer credits issued. From this perspective, certain misgivings about the constructiveness of certain regulations in the area of crisis management are quite legitimate, concretely the mode of assessing the minimum requirements on the structure and amount of capital and eligible liabilities (MREL). This provides answers to the issues raised in Introduction of this paper.

Is the Directive on Crisis Management (BRRD) beneficial for the banking market in the Czech Republic?

The BRRD Directive will have a significant effect on the banking sector in the Czech Republic, but its greatest pitfalls cannot be as yet determined analytically. The European regulatory process is not very transparent, as it is very complex, incomprehensive, and above all unpredictable. As stated above, the mode of assessing the minimum requirements on the structure and amount of capital and eligible liabilities (MREL) is problematic. Paradoxically, banking institutions in the Czech Republic may encounter problems due to the high quality of protection based on the ČNB's cautious approach to supervision, which accounts for high capital provisions of the Czech banks. This will consequently make them subject to higher requirements than those imposed on institution in the Eurozone.[3]

In reality, the European banking market might face potential problems arising from the transition of the approach from bail-out to bail-in. For instance, current financial markets signalize problems on the part of the largest German bank—Deutsche Bank. The bank is recording its historic minima—in the third quarter of 2015 alone the DB lost 6 billion EUR. If DB's insolvency were to be announced, a restructuring mechanism in the bail-in system would have to be launched. Its shares and bonds are owed by thousands of institutional investors and footed by a commendable legal apparatus. DB's counsels would, without a doubt, put up a resilient and professionally proficient fight against a declaration of insolvency, claiming that the Bank has to manage its assets with due diligence and would not voluntarily let the financial means of its investors and creditors be nationalized.

The described model example would consequently lead to further disputes over the setup of the mechanism, and EU representative would propose further systemic changes.

Aren't the newly adopted and proposed regulatory European rules too strict?

The current regulatory rules contained in BASEL III are satisfactory and above all adequate for the banks in the Czech environment. This applies especially to the possibility of demanding that banks create higher and better capital reserves to be used eventually for compensating their losses. Burdening the Czech highly regulated market repeatedly with new rules would only jeopardize the stability of the financial market, twice as badly in banking.

In the years to come, the European Union is likely to come up with still more new proposals in the area of regulation and supervision. The point should be, however, to act in response to real problems in financial markets, especially the banking sector, and to do so with a good deal of common sense.

---

[3]Another problem is the circumstance that there exists practically no secured senior financing in the CR with longer maturity eligible for the MREL.

Acknowledgments This is paper has been prepared under financial support of and grant "*Trends in the Banking and Insurance Sectors in Changing Financial Markets*" VŠE IGA F1/21/2016, which authors gratefully acknowledge.

References

Avalová M, Majdloch M (2015) BRRD: Bail-in mechanismus a MREL. Bankovnictví, Praha

Magnus M, Backman J, Power C (2015) Banking union. Available via European Parliament. http://www.europarl.europa.eu/ftu/pdf/en/ftu_4.2.4.pdf. Accessed 20 Jan 2016

Mandel M, Tomšík V (2011) Regulace bankovního sektoru z pohledu ekonomické teorie. Politická ekonomie, Politická ekonomie. doi:10.18267/j.polek.772

Zamrazilová E (2015) Regulace: brzda nebo plyn morálního hazardu? Available CZECH Banking Association.   https://www.czechba.cz/sites/default/files/zlata_koruna_ez_duben_2015.pdf. Accessed 18 Feb 2016

Chapter 12
Forecasting Jumps in the Intraday Foreign Exchange Rate Time Series with Hawkes Processes and Logistic Regression

Milan Fičura

Abstract Methodology for modelling and prediction of jumps in the high-frequency financial time series is presented. The intraday seasonality of jump intensity is modelled through a series of regime-specific dummy variables, while the self-exciting (clustering) behaviour of jumps is modelled with the Hakes process and alternatively with logistic regression. The models are tested on the 15-min-frequency EUR/USD time series with nonparametrically identified jumps via the *L*-estimator. The results indicate strong ability of the models to predict jump occurrences in the 15-min horizon. Most of the predictive accuracy does, however, stem from the intraday seasonality pattern of jump intensity, while the self-exciting component has only a minor effect on the overall performance. The identified self-exciting behaviour of jumps is very strong, but only short-term. Long-term clustering of jumps surprisingly was not identified by the models applied to the intraday frequency. There was also no significant difference in the predictive accuracy of the Hawkes process-based model and the logistic regression-based model.

Keywords High-frequency data · Self-exciting jumps · Hawkes process · Logistic regression

12.1 Introduction

Accurate modelling of jumps in the financial time series plays an important role in many areas of finance such as risk management, derivatives pricing and quantitative trading. One reason for this is that the occurrence of jumps (i.e. discontinuous price changes) increases the size of the tails of the short horizon return distribution, thus increasing the prices of near-maturity out-of-the-money options, increasing the estimates of value at risk, etc. In addition to that, the occurrence of jumps in the

M. Fičura (✉)
Department of Banking and Insurance, University of Economics, Prague,
Nam. W. Churchilla 4, 130 67 Prague, Czech Republic
e-mail: milan.ficura@vse.cz

© Springer International Publishing AG 2017   125
D. Procházka (ed.), *New Trends in Finance and Accounting*,
Springer Proceedings in Business and Economics,
DOI 10.1007/978-3-319-49559-0_12

financial time series decreases the performance of certain hedging strategies used for derivatives pricing, such as delta hedging, based on the assumption of continuously moving prices, as well as certain market-making strategies.

Due to the reasons mentioned above, it would be useful to be able to predict the times of future jump occurrences. This is, however, problematic, as the jumps happen only infrequently on the markets and it is often difficult to distinguish them from the continuous price volatility.

One possible approach of how to identify jumps in the financial time series is through Bayesian methods. When applied to daily prices, the approach has a relatively low accuracy (Fičura and Witzany 2014), while the application to intraday prices is computationally demanding (Stroud and Johannes 2014).

In the recent years, an alternative, nonparametric approach of jump estimation emerged, utilizing high-frequency data and the asymptotic theory of power variations (Andersen et al. 2007). The most well-known jump estimator of this kind is the Z-statistics (Barndorff Nielsen and Shephard 2004), identifying if jumps occurred during a given time period by using the normalized differences between the realized variance and the realized bipower variation. Z-statistics was used in Fičura (2015) to identify jumps in the foreign exchange rate time series on the daily frequency and then model them with self-exciting and cross-exciting processes.

More advanced jump estimators, such as the L-statistics (Lee and Mykland 2008), enable the identification of jumps at the exact times at which they occur during the trading day. This opens a way for more accurate jump prediction models, as well as for models that forecast jumps on the intraday frequency.

In this study, we use the self-exciting Hawkes process and extend it to account for the intraday seasonality of jump intensity, for the purpose of predicting the probabilities of future jump occurrences intra-daily, in the 15-min horizon. We find that the parameters of the Hawkes process applied to the intraday data tend to get fitted primarily to the short-term jump clustering effects, lasting up to several hours at most. These short-term effects are very strong, but they are also entirely different from the effects found when the Hawkes process is applied to the daily frequency, where the self-exciting effects are weaker, but also significantly more persistent, lasting from days, up to several weeks (Fičura 2015).

As to include both of the effects into a Hawkes process model would be difficult, we propose an alternative approach of how to account for jump clustering effects at different frequencies, by using logistic regression, where the numbers of jumps aggregated over past time intervals of different lengths are used as explanatory variables and the future jump occurrences as the target variable.

Both of the models are tested on the EUR/USD exchange rate time series and their out-of-sample predictive accuracy is assessed with the accuracy ratio (i.e. Gini coefficient). The results indicate that the models possess significant power to predict jump occurrences in the 15-min horizon. Most of the explanatory power stems, however, from the intraday seasonality component of the models, while the self-exciting effects increase the explanatory power only slightly.

The rest of the paper is organized as follows. In Chap. 2, the nonparametric method of jump identification is explained. In Chap. 3, the methodology of the two models for jump prediction is presented and in the fourth chapter, the models are applied to the 15-min EUR/USD jump time series. In the last chapter, there is a conclusion of the main results of the research.

12.2   Nonparametric Jump Identification

The jumps in the foreign exchange rate time series are identified nonparametrically with the L-estimator proposed in Lee and Mykland (2008).

In order to explain the logic of the estimator, let us assume that the foreign exchange rate (or any other asset price for that matter) follows the following generally defined stochastic-volatility jump-diffusion process:

$$dp(t) = \mu(t)\,dt + \sigma(t)\,dW(t) + j(t)\,dq(t) \tag{12.1}$$

where $p(t)$ is the logarithm of the asset price, $\mu(t)$ is the instantaneous drift rate, $\sigma(t)$ is the instantaneous volatility, $W(t)$ is a Wiener process, $j(t)$ is a process determining the sizes of the jumps, and $q(t)$ is a counting process whose differential determines the times of jump occurrences.

The total variability of the stochastic process during the period between $t - k$ and t can be expressed with its *quadratic variation*, denoted as $QC(t - k, t)$:

$$QC(t - k, t) = \int_{t-k}^{t} \sigma^2(s)\,ds + \sum_{t-k \leq s < t} \kappa^2(s) \tag{12.2}$$

where $\kappa(s) = j(t)I[q(t) = 1]$ and $I(.)$ is the indicator function. The first term on the right-hand side in Eq. 12.2 represents the continuous component of price variability, called *integrated variance*, while the second term represents the discontinuous component of price variability, called *jump variance*. So it is possible to rewrite the equation as:

$$QC(t - k, t) = IV(t - k, t) + JV(t - k, t) \tag{12.3}$$

where $IV(t - k, t)$ is the integrated variance and $JV(t - k, t)$, the jump variance.

The L-statistics-based jump estimator identifies jumps in the asset returns time series by normalizing the intraday returns with local volatility estimated through the bipower variation, which gives an asymptotically unbiased estimate of the integrated variance over a given period of time. The local volatility estimated via the bipower variation over the last K high-frequency periods is defined as follows:

$$\sigma_{BV}^2(i) = BV(i - K, i - 1) = \frac{1}{K - 2} \sum_{j=i-K+2}^{i-1} |r(j)||r(j - 1)| \tag{12.4}$$

where $\sigma_{BV}^2(i)$ is the local variance estimated for the high-frequency period i, $r(j)$ are the high-frequency returns, defined as $r(j) = p(j) - p(j-1)$, and K is the period used for the local variance estimation. $BV(i-K, i-1)$ is the bipower variation over the period between $i-K$ and $i-1$, which should converge, with increasing frequency of $r(j)$, to the integrated variance $IV(t-k,t)$.

The L-statistics can be defined as follows:

$$L(i) = \frac{r(i)}{\sigma_{BV}(i)} \tag{12.5}$$

where $L(i)$ is the L-statistics, $r(i)$ is the return in the given high-frequency period, and $\sigma_{BV}(i)$ is the local volatility estimated based on the bipower variation.

The method of jump estimation based on the L-statistics utilizes the known distribution of the appropriately normalized maximum value of the L-statistics in a time series A_n of a given length n, under the assumption that the series does not contain jumps. The normalized maximum value is:

$$\xi = \frac{\max_{i \in A_n} |L(i)| - C_n}{S_n} \tag{12.6}$$

where the A_n is the set of the $i \in \{1, 2, \ldots, n\}$ no-jump periods and the constants C_n and S_n are given as follows:

$$C_n = \frac{[2 \log(n)]^{1/2}}{c} - \frac{\log(\pi) + \log[\log(n)]}{2c[2 \log(n)]^{1/2}} \tag{12.7}$$

$$S_n = \frac{1}{c[2 \log(n)]^{1/2}} \tag{12.8}$$

and $c = \sqrt{2}/\sqrt{\pi} \approx 0.7979$.

The jumps in the time series are identified based on the known distribution of ξ in a time series of length n that does not contain jumps. The distribution is:

$$P(\xi \leq x) = \exp(-e^{-x}) \tag{12.9}$$

Jumps are then identified in the time series as the normalized values of $L(i)$, based on Eq. 12.6, that are larger than a given quantile of ξ. So the identified jumps are the normalized values of $L(i)$ that are larger than some conservative quantile α of the maximum ξ in a time series of length n that does not contain jumps.

The jump estimation approach using the L-statistics has two meta-parameters, the period K used for the local volatility calculation and the quantile α used for the jump detection. In our work, we use the value of $K = 156$ recommended by Lee and Mykland (2008) for the 15-min return frequency. For the jump identification, we use the quantile value of $\alpha = 0.95$.

12.3 Forecasting Jumps

Two methods for jump prediction in the intraday foreign exchange rate time series are proposed. The first one utilizes the seasonally adjusted Hawkes process and the second one uses logistic regression. The seasonality pattern is for both of the methods modelled through a series of dummy variables, corresponding to appropriately defined seasons or regimes of the jump intensity during the trading day. The method used to identify these seasons is explained later in the text.

12.3.1 Hawkes Process-Based Model

Hawkes process is a jump process in which the jumps are self-exciting, so that a jump occurrence increases temporarily the intensity of future jumps by a given amount, after which the jump intensity decays exponentially back to its long-term level. This effect allows the process to exhibit the empirically observed jump clustering effects (Ait-Sahalia et al. 2015).

As the constructed model will be applied to the intraday jump time series and the intensity of jumps varies greatly during the trading day, it is necessary to extend the standard Hawkes process to account for the intraday seasonality of jump intensity. For this purpose, the following multiplicative model is used:

$$\lambda(t) = \lambda_{\mathrm{H}}(t)\lambda_{\mathrm{S}}(t) \tag{12.10}$$

where $\lambda(t)$ is the jump intensity at period t, $\lambda_{\mathrm{H}}(t)$ is the self-exciting component of jump intensity, and $\lambda_{\mathrm{S}}(t)$ is a seasonal component of jump intensity.

The self-exciting component of jump intensity is modelled with a discretized Hawkes process:

$$\lambda_{\mathrm{H}}(t) = \alpha_J + \beta_J \lambda_{\mathrm{H}}(t-1) + \gamma_J Q(t-1) \tag{12.11}$$

where $\lambda_{\mathrm{H}}(t)$ is the self-exciting component of jump intensity at time period t, $Q(t-1)$ is an indicator of jump occurrence in the period $t-1$, α_J is a constant, β_J is the decay parameter determining how fast does the elevated jump intensity return back to its long-term level, and γ_J is the self-exciting parameter determining how much does the jump intensity increase in the period following a jump occurrence. The equilibrium level of jump intensity can approximately be calculated as $\lambda_{\mathrm{LT}} = \alpha_J / (1 - \beta_J - \gamma_J \lambda_{\mathrm{S,average}})$, where $\lambda_{\mathrm{S,average}}$ is the average value of the seasonality adjustment $\lambda_{\mathrm{S}}(t)$ (defined in Eq. 12.12).

The seasonality component of jump intensity $\lambda_S(t)$ is modelled as:

$$\lambda_S(t) = \sum_{j=1}^{k} \lambda_{S,j} d_j(t) \tag{12.12}$$

where $\lambda_{S,j}$ denotes the multiplicative adjustment of the jump intensity at season j, $d_j(t)$ denotes the dummy variable corresponding to the season j, and k denotes the number of seasons. Note that due to the multiplicative formulation of the model, the number of dummy variables $d_j(t)$ will be equal to the number of the seasons; one of the parameters has, however, to be fixed to one and will not be optimized in the estimation procedure.

12.3.2 Using Logistic Regression to Model Jumps

Logistic regression is one of the most commonly used statistical techniques to forecast the value of a binary target variable based on a series of explanatory variables. The underlying assumption of the logistic regression is a linear relationship between the covariates and the log-odds ratio (i.e. the logarithm of the ratio of the probability that the target variable will be one to the probability that it will be zero). By using the log-odds ratio, logistic regression can be expressed as follows:

$$\ln\left(\frac{\lambda_t}{1-\lambda_t}\right) = \beta^{\mathrm{T}}[1;X_t] + \varepsilon_t \tag{12.13}$$

where λ_t is the jump intensity at time t, X_t is a vector of explanatory variables used to forecast λ_t, β is a vector of model parameters and ε_t is a Gaussian white noise. The left-hand side of the equation represents the log-odds ratio of the jump occurrence probability, i.e. the logarithm of the ratio between the probability of jump occurrence at period t to the probability of jump nonoccurrence at period t.

In our case, the value of 1 corresponds to the occurrence of a jump in the given 15-min time period t and the value of 0 corresponds to no-jump.

As for the explanatory variables in the matrix X, the number of past jumps in the last hour, 4 h, day, week, month (20 days), 3 months (60 days) and one year (252 days) is used, together with the dummy variables corresponding to the different seasons of the jump intensity pattern during the day. If needed, other explanatory variables may easily be added into the model, but we will not do this in order to keep the model more comparable with the Hawkes process model.

12.4   Predicting Jumps in the EUR/USD Exchange Rate

The analysis is performed on the 15-min frequency of the EUR/USD exchange rate time series ranging from 1.11.1999 to 15.6.2015, provided by forexhistorydatabase. com, containing overall 385,988 records. The jumps in the time series were identified using the L-statistics, with the local volatility calculated based on 156 intraday (15-min) periods and the confidence level set to 95%.

Currencies on the foreign exchange market are traded for 24 h a day on all of the work days. There is no trading during the weekends and some of the international holidays. The price changes (gaps) during the weekends will look as jumps in the time series, but as they are caused by a different phenomenon, we exclude them from the analysis (i.e. replacing such jumps by zero).

The goal of the study is to forecast jump occurrences in the 15-min horizon, by using the information from the past history of the jump time series only. The metric used for the comparison of the predictive accuracy of the models is the accuracy ratio, also known as the Gini coefficient.

All of the models use intraday seasonality dummy variables in order to account for the intraday seasonality of jump intensity. As has been found, the intraday seasonality pattern plays a crucial role in predicting the probabilities of future jump occurrences during the day. Therefore, the two proposed jump clustering models are compared with a benchmark model utilizing only the seasonality pattern.

In all of the models, the in-sample period (first 200,000 records, covering approximately 50% of the data, ranging from 1.11.1999 to 12.12.2007) is used to estimate the model parameters, while an out-sample period (ranging from 13.12.2007 to 15.6.2015) is used to assess the predictive power of the models.

12.4.1   Model of the Intraday Jump Seasonality

In order to model the intraday seasonality pattern of jump intensity, the empirical jump intensity for every 15-min period during the day was computed. As shown in Fig. 12.1 (left), the jump intensity varies erratically during the trading day (the highest being at the time of the opening of the US session). It would therefore be difficult to fit it with some smooth parametric function.

An approach utilizing a set of dummy variables was applied instead. As there are 96 15-min periods during the trading day, 96 dummy variables would fully account for any possible jump intensity seasonality pattern. Using such a large number of dummy variables would, however, most probably lead to overfitting. In order to reduce the number of dummy variables, k-means clustering algorithm was applied

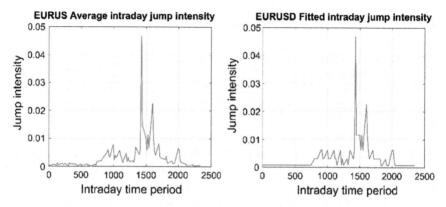

Fig. 12.1 Intraday average and fitted jump intensity (with 6 clusters). *Source* Authorial computation

to divide the empirical jump intensities in the 96 periods during the day into k clusters representing different intensity regimes. These will be incorporated into the jump models by using k dummy variables.

In order to estimate a reasonable value of k, a simple seasonality model is constructed, in which the jump intensity for every 15-min period is replaced by the centroid intensity for the given cluster as computed by the k-means clustering algorithm. The in-sample accuracy ratio for $k \in \{1, 2, ..., 20\}$ is plotted in Fig. 12.2. As shown in Fig. 12.2, the in-sample accuracy ratio increases rapidly until $k = 6$, but not so much afterwards. Based on this behaviour, we decided to use $k = 6$ in all of the following models. In second line of Fig. 12.2, it is apparent that the choice of $k = 6$ is close to optimal also for the out-sample period.

Fig. 12.2 Accuracy ratio of the k-means seasonality model based on the number clusters. *Source* Authorial computation

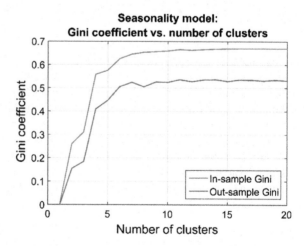

12.4.2   Modelling Jump Intensity with Hawkes Process Models

The model based on the self-exciting Hawkes process was applied to the EUR/USD jump time series. The parameters of the model were estimated through a numerical maximization of the likelihood function in the in-sample period. In order to achieve good convergence, it was necessary to choose initial values of the parameters sufficiently close to the optimal ones; otherwise, the optimization tended to converge to statistically inferior local optima. As the problem of local optima seems to be caused mainly by the intraday seasonality adjustment parameters, the initial values of these parameters were set based on the centroid jump intensity of the k-means clusters, as described in the previous section. The cluster with the highest jump intensity was chosen as the one with parameter value set to 1 (i.e. the one that is not estimated), while the initial values of the other parameters were calculated as the ratio between the centroid intensity in the respective clusters and the centroid intensity in the cluster with the highest jump intensity.

The parameters of the Hawkes process model can be shown in Table 12.1. The estimates of the standard errors were derived from the Hessian.

We can see from Table 12.1 that the parameters β_J and γ_J, modelling the self-exciting behaviour of the Hawkes process, are both statistically significant. This confirms our hypothesis that the jumps in the time series are self-exciting. Interestingly, the values of the parameters significantly differ from the values usually seen when the Hawkes process is applied to the jumps aggregated on the daily frequency (Fičura 2015). Most importantly, the β_J parameter, which tends to be close to one, is in the intraday case significantly smaller, indicating that the self-exciting behaviour of the intraday jumps is only short term. At the same time, the value of γ_J is extremely large compared to the long-term jump intensity λ_{LT}. This indicates that the jump intensity increases greatly during the first 15 min following a jump occurrence; it does, however, decay quickly to its long-term level.

The results indicate that there exist two different components of the jump self-exciting behaviour. One that is very strong, but short term, and another one, much weaker, that is long lasting (identified in the previous studies). The intraday Hawkes model has, however, been able to identify only the shot-term effect.

Table 12.1 Maximum likelihood estimates of the Hawkes process model parameters

	λ_{LT}	β_J	γ_J	$\lambda_{S,1}$	$\lambda_{S,2}$	$\lambda_{S,3}$	$\lambda_{S,4}$	$\lambda_{S,5}$
Parameter	0.0541	0.4172	0.3899	0.0105	0.0519	0.1190	0.2254	0.4882
Std. error	0.0048	0.1109	0.0701	0.0017	0.0061	0.0136	0.0420	0.0752

Source Authorial computation

12.4.3 Modelling Jump Intensity with Logistic Regression

As it appears from the results in the previous section, the intraday Hawkes process cannot account for all of the effects of the past jumps on the future jump intensity. Therefore, we propose an alternative approach based on logistic regression.

The target variable in the logistic regression model is the jump occurrence over a given 15-min time period (1 corresponds to jump occurrence, while 0 corresponds to no-jump). The explanatory variables are the numbers of realized jumps over different past-time horizons (last 15 min, 1 h, 4 h, 1 day, 1 week, 1 month, 3 months and 1 year), together with the dummy variables used for the intraday seasonality of jump intensity modelling.

A key assumption of the logistic regression is that the relationship between the log-odds ratio and the explanatory variables is linear. If it is not, then the explanatory variables have to be transformed via some function, or to categorical ones. In order to find, if it is suitable to directly use the aggregated past numbers of jumps as explanatory variables, we plotted the empirical log-odds ratios against the numbers of jumps in the past time periods. Results, the one-year (i.e. 252 days) case is shown in Fig. 12.3.

We can see that the log-odds ratio does increase approximately linearly with the numbers of jumps aggregated over the last 252 days, as it shows the weighted linear regression line in Fig. 12.3 (left). In Fig. 12.3 (right), it is apparent that the several outliers on the left figure were probably caused just by low number of observations for the given counts of jumps.

For the other aggregation periods (hour, 4 h, day, week, month and 3 months), the linear relationship between the number of jumps and the log-odds ratio seems to

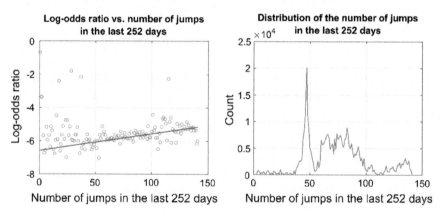

Fig. 12.3 Log-odds ratio vs. the number of jumps in the last 252 days. *Source* Authorial computation

Table 12.2 Parameters of the logistic regression model

	Constant	15 min	4 h	1 day	Seas1	Seas2	Seas3	Seas4	Seas5
Parameter	−2.82	2.02	0.55	−0.26	−4.63	−3.08	−2.31	−1.82	−0.76
St. dev	0.10	0.21	0.14	0.09	0.16	0.12	0.13	0.14	0.16

Source Authorial computation

hold as well. Therefore, the untransformed numbers of jumps will be used as explanatory variables in the logistic regression model.

In order to determine whether all of the explanatory variables are truly needed in the model, stepwise selection procedure with 5% confidence levels was used. The procedure surprisingly dropped most of the proposed explanatory variables, so that the final model contains only the aggregated jumps over the last 15 min, 4 h and 1 day, together with the seasonality adjustment dummy variables.

The values of the estimated parameters of the model are shown in Table 12.2.

The results indicate a strong co-jump effect; i.e. a jump in the last 15-min period greatly increases the probability of an additional jump. Similarly, the number of jumps in the last 4 h increases the probability of future jumps occurring, but surprisingly, the number of jumps over the last 1 day (24 h) decreases the future jump intensity. The values of the seasonality dummy variables correspond to the pattern where the seasons are defined with a rising jump intensity. As the jump intensity in season 6 corresponds to the constant of the model, all of the dummy variables have to be negative, i.e. decrease the jump intensity.

12.4.4   Assessing the Predictive Accuracy of the Models

In order to quantify the predictive accuracy of the proposed models, the accuracy ratio (i.e. the Gini coefficient) is used. The in-sample and out-sample values of the accuracy ratio for the 3 models (Seasonality model, Hawkes model and Logistic model) are shown in Table 12.3.

It is shown in Table 12.3 that the discriminatory power of the proposed models is relatively high. The vast share of this power comes, however, from the intraday seasonality of the jump intensity modelling. The self-exciting effects, added in the

Table 12.3 In-sample and out-sample accuracy ratios of the proposed models

Accuracy ratios	Seasonality model	Hawkes model	Logistic regression
In-sample	0.6257	0.6569	0.6688
Out-sample	0.5058	0.5377	0.5434

Source Authorial computation

Hawkes process model and the logistic regression model, increase the discriminatory power only slightly. We can also see that the logistic regression model is only negligibly better (in the out-sample period) than the Hawkes process model.

12.5 Conclusion

Methodology of how to model and predict jumps in the intraday time series of the EUR/USD exchange rate was presented. In comparison with similar studies performed on the daily frequency, it was necessary to account for the strong intraday seasonality of jump intensity, which was done by utilizing a series of regime-specific dummy variables in the analysed models. Two models were proposed with the task of predicting the future jump occurrences in the 15-min time horizon. The first is based on the Hawkes process and the second uses logistic regression. The results show that the proposed models possess relatively high accuracy in distinguishing between future jump and no-jump periods. Most of the predictive power does, however, stem from the seasonality component of the jump intensity, with only minor increase being caused by the self-exciting component.

The parameters of the models tended to get fitted to the strong short-term jump self-excitation and to the co-jump behaviour, while ignoring the weaker but longer lasting effects that were discovered in similar studies performed on the daily frequency. Extended models would be needed to account for both of the effects.

An interesting area of future research would be to quantify the economic benefits of the proposed models, for example, by analysing the effects of the intraday seasonality of the jump intensity and the self-exciting effects of the jumps on the out-of-the-money option prices.

Acknowledgments This paper has been prepared under financial support of a grant "Advanced methods of financial asset returns and risks modelling" IGA VŠE F1/23/2015 which the author gratefully acknowledges.

References

Ait-Sahalia Y, Cachio-Diaz J, Leaven R (2015) Modeling financial contagion using mutually exciting jump processes. J Financ Econ 117(3):585–606

Andersen TG, Bollerslev T, Diebold FX (2007) Roughing it up: including jump components in the measurement, modeling and forecasting of return volatility. Rev Econ Stat 89(4):701–720

Barndorff-Nielsen OE, Shephard N (2004) Power and bipower variation with stochastic volatility and jumps. J Financ Econometrics 2(1):1–37

Fičura M (2015) Modelling jump clustering in the four major foreign exchange rates using high-frequency returns and cross-exciting jump processes. In: Procházka J (ed) Procedia economics and finance. 16th annual conference on finance and accounting, vol 25. Elsevier, Prague, pp 208–219

Fičura M, Witzany J (2014) Estimating stochastic volatility and jumps using high-frequency data and Bayesian methods. In: Málek J (ed) Risk management 2014. Oeconomica, University of Economics, Prague, pp 9–33

Lee SS, Mykland PA (2008) Jumps in financial markets: a new nonparametric test and jump dynamics. Rev Financial Stud 21(6):2535–2563

Stroud JR, Johannes MS (2014) Bayesian modeling and forecasting of 24-hour high-frequency volatility. J Am Stat Assoc 109(508):1368–1384

Chapter 13
Influence of Selected Factors on Hedge Fund Return

Stanislav Hába

Abstract This paper deals with a unique form of an alternative investment: hedge funds. Specifically, the paper researches the influence of certain factors on hedge fund returns. Specifically, four factors are tested: (1) inclusion of funds into market hedge fund index, (2) possibility to close to new investors, (3) type and level of charged fees and (4) reporting delay/concealment. The data are compiled for more than 4000 funds for 23 years and cover all types and statuses of hedge funds. The most important results found no significant additional yield for increased remuneration for fund administration. Additionally, the regression confirmed the hypothesis of the time return decay in most hedge funds (so-called backfill bias). The other two hypotheses of market inclusion and openness to new capital have not been validated on a significant level. Throughout the whole text, the paper describes typical problems that are connected with hedge funds and their respective data.

Keywords Hedge fund · Investment management · Portfolio return

13.1 Introduction

Hedge funds surely belong to the most interesting phenomena of today's financial world. Their infamous popularity is caused besides other thing by two factors. Firstly, hedge funds fill first pages of financial newspaper with sensational releases such as astronomic remuneration of hedge fund management, illegal practises and large leverage on economics. Secondly, hedge fund tends to stay in information and regulatory shadows that foster speculation, inaccuracies and certain mystification of the whole hedge fund industry.

In connection with the boom of alternative investments, hedge funds aroused interest also from academia, and the research of hedge funds appears more often

S. Hába (✉)
Department of Monetary Theory and Policy, University of Economics, Prague, Nam.
W. Churchilla 4, 130 67 Prague, Czech Republic
e-mail: xhabs01@vse.cz

© Springer International Publishing AG 2017
D. Procházka (ed.), *New Trends in Finance and Accounting*,
Springer Proceedings in Business and Economics,
DOI 10.1007/978-3-319-49559-0_13

than any time before. This trend is supported by stepwise regulation of hedge funds in large financial centres and to some extent by decline of information secretiveness.

In this text, I decided to test four factors whether they influence performance of hedge funds. To be specific, the factors include: (1) membership of fund in market index, (2) openness to new investors, (3) fee structure and (4) length of reporting.

The paper is structured as follows: The first part introduces hedge funds in general, their specifics and basic literature. The second part describes data about hedge funds and connected problems. The third part tests each hypothesis with similar steps: hypothesis explanation, method, result and commentary. The last part only concludes the overall findings.

13.2   Hedge Funds

The first natural step in research suggests describing a hedge fund. Unfortunately, the primary problems arise even in definition of a hedge fund as a form of collective investment. Thus, most literature omits an exact definition and settles for a list of characteristics and inclusion of hedge funds into a larger category of alternative investments (together with private equity and real estate). Another literature sources substitute this approach with very broad-based outline such as investment structure for asset management that invests into securities and derivatives, and employs leverage, and its mandate is absolute return (Travers 2012).

Hedge funds can be characterized by specific features that distinguish it from other alternative investments and other collective investment instruments. However, this list must be taken as demonstrative and not all hedge funds fulfil all the criteria.

- Absolute return as the main goal: This aim differentiates hedge funds from other types of collective investment instruments that usually link their performance to a benchmark. Opposite to this, hedge funds strive to achieve uncorrelated yield to traditional assets.
- Flexible investment strategy: Whereas most forms of collective investment must proceed according to the explicitly formulated investment strategy and legal requirements, hedge funds enjoy a large leeway in this area. Hedge funds define their investment strategy very vaguely with a large opportunity for discretion and some hedge funds do not develop their external investment strategy at all.
- Leverage: Most hedge funds actively employ financial leverage in the form of both debt and derivatives.
- Management engagement: As a general rule, top management of hedge fund put their own funds in the fund managed by them, and their money makes a significant part of the fund's capital.

- Fee structure: Apart from standard management fee that is based on assets under management, hedge funds charge their clients rather complicated fee structures with additional clauses such as hurdle rate, watermark and other.
- Capital in- and outflow limitation: Some hedge funds can be closed for additional investors in order to keep the invested capital with its optimum strategy and no to dilute the most efficient portfolio. The other way around, hedge fund can block an exit of any investor by gate provision clause activation that limits the amount of withdrawals from the fund during the redemption period.
- Accessibility to a small number of qualified investors: Minimum invested amount into a hedge fund lies considerably higher than in most other collective instruments. In more specific terms, the minimum investment does not usually lie below 1 mil. USD and even the smallest funds do not accept investments under 100 thousand USD.

Furthermore, hedge funds are distinguished by their very limited transparency towards public. This problem is related to their low level of regulation, which can be described in simple terms as not regulated at all (especially in comparison with typical collective investment vehicles). Although there is a certain trend in the tightening of hedge fund regulation, generally we can assume that all the information coming from hedge funds is published exclusively on voluntary basis. [For further information see Nelken (2007: Chap. 8.2).]

Overall, the literature about hedge fund can be divided into three broad categories. First group is based on the description of history, structure and fundamental principles of hedge funds with the accent on practical aspects (e.g. Travers 2012; Mirabile 2013 or Wilson 2010). Second group consists of relatively new critique of hedge funds and emphasis on their shortcomings, which are generally marginalized in the first group (e.g. Lack 2012 or Johnson 2010). The third group investigated performance of hedge funds (Sharpe ratio, alfa, etc.) and additionally risks and termination aspects (Chan et al. 2005 or Yasuaki 2010).

It is noteworthy to mention also the literature researching fee structures of hedge funds and backfill bias. While some authors proved positive relationship between fees and performance (e.g. Elton et al. 2003), other sources deny the idea of higher fees–higher profit link (e.g. Brown 1998). The latter idea of backfill bias is mirrored in studies that almost without exception proved strong negative yield influence and significant delay between fund inception date and first performance number release. The negative influence varies from 1.4% (Fung and Hsieh 1997) to up to 5% (Posthuma and van der Sluisz 2003), while reporting is delayed by 343 days in median (Fung and Hsieh 1997), and half of information is backfilled (Posthuma and van der Sluisz 2003). For further reading, see Baquero et al. (2005) or Ibbotson et al. (2011).

13.3 Data

The primary input data are provided by the financial data vendor Bloomberg. This system monitors dozens of thousands of funds (not only hedge funds) and shows data for individual funds, which is the main advantage to other databases (Credit Suisse, Barclays or Lipper) that provide only summary data for segments preventing us from deeper statistical inquiry and customized selection.

Unfortunately, even Bloomberg does not remove other classic problems of hedge funds—information distortion. It is again important to remark that all the hedge funds report everything voluntarily and solely on their own discretion. Thus, there is a reasonable assumption that most hedge fund managers wait a few periods until the first performance data are published. If a hedge fund does not bring good yield, then the hedge is silently closed and data are not posted anywhere. But in the opposite case where a hedge fund performs well, the fund's management reveals information to public. This discloses not only current data, but also history data. These two distortions are described as backfill bias and self-selection bias. For further reading, see Dichev and Yu (2011), Pool (2009) or Lack (2012).

To be specific, I searched for all the hedge funds that reported any performance data and additionally that posted net asset value in at least two consecutive years in order to calculate year-over-year performance. Furthermore, one fund was removed due to dubiously positive performance in one year (+15 mil.%), which would twist all the results. Regarding the status of funds, I included all the statuses (active, acquired, delisted, liquidated, etc.) After this narrowing down, I obtained a basic dataset for 4032 hedge funds.

In this dataset, I downloaded (if possible) net asset value (NAV) for the each year from 1994 to 2016. The annual performance is calculated accordingly as a year-over-year percentual change of NAV. It is necessary to point out the problem of reporting periods of hedge funds, as opposed for example to mutual funds that report usually daily. In the hedge fund world, data are released mostly monthly, with some funds reporting varying from weekly to quarterly basis. In the monthly set-up, data are released first Friday in calendar month. However, if the first Friday would be the 5th or higher day of month, the results are published preceding Friday, i.e. the last Friday of the previous month.

13.4 Hypotheses

In the next part, I will be testing the individual hypotheses: specifically, if selected factors (index membership, openness to new investors, fee level and length of history) have effect on the most important goal for investors: return. Within each factor, I introduce the hypothesis, method, results and comments.

13.4.1 Does Hedge Fund Inclusion into Index Bring Enhanced Yield?

Hypothesis: Hedge fund indexes draw a clear analogy to other market indexes, whose essential role is to replicate a portfolio with certain composition. For this purpose, I chose the Bloomberg Hedge Fund Index (BAIF). This broad index of hedge funds covers all types of hedge funds regardless of their strategy. My hypothesis concerns the motivation of hedge fund management. Generally, it is reasonable to assume that inclusion of fund into index mirrors the most attractive funds and funds included in the index should outperform the omitted ones. If a fund included in the index shows low results, the management would face temptation to stop public reporting, after that be removed from the index and do not point out the poor yield. By contrast, high-performing funds pursue the index inclusion as a mean of marketing and positive visibility.

Method and Results: The database includes 4032 funds with description of BAIF index membership yes or no. In the subselection, I calculate the arithmetic average of annual yield for the whole group of index included/not-included funds. Naturally, an alternative suggests that we calculate the total performance of the funds and decompose it into annualized result. However, this method would smooth the volatility that is a part of my research. The data are not weighted by fund's asset volume in order to maintain equal representation of each fund in time (Table 13.1).

Interpretation: The general overview of results suggests that funds included in index bring increased yield of 5.99% p.a. opposed to not-included ones of 4.34% and that this yield is outweighed by larger risk (measured in volatility) of 45.20% in comparison with non-member volatility of 21.30%. However, these statistical results are merely insignificant, because the difference between these two groups is too small in relationship to their respective standard error and group standard deviation. Therefore, we can reject the hypothesis that fund membership in index brings additional profit to their investors.

Table 13.1 Results

	Number of funds	Average yield (%)	Standard deviation (%)
Total	4032	4.64	27.20
Included in index	604	5.99	45.20
Not included in index	3428	4.34	21.30

Source Own calculations

13.4.2 Does Optimum Hedge Fund Size Bring Additional Yield?

Hypothesis: Hedge funds employ undoubtedly very unconventional strategy. A part of this tactics seeks arbitrage opportunity or very large deviations from "correct" valuation. Hence, it is clear that these opportunities do not arise very often and their distribution is not equal through time. By contrast, most compensation schemes for hedge fund managers are based on (among other criteria) assets under management and their growth. Therefore, managers are strongly motivated to acquire new capital despite lack of investment opportunities. In these conditions, the fund must inevitably invest into less profitable instruments that would be not conducted if the fund was closed for new investors. For more information, see Lack (2012, Chap. 9). Ergo, a question suggests itself whether the hedge funds that can activate a clause to close for new investors after reaching optimum size bring investors additional yield.

Method and Results: Bloomberg provides 3664 funds with available attribute whether the fund is open or closed to new investors. It is necessary to point out the difference between closed-end funds and funds closed to new investors. Whereas closed-end funds are generally closed to new capital due to limited shares number, the latter type of funds is open to new capital up to the moment when management closes to new stockholder to keep the ideal volume. (This clause poses an option for management and is not the object of research whether the clause has been activated or not). The further method is analogical to previous section (Table 13.2).

Interpretation: The brief look at numbers reveals that closed funds bring on average more-than-double yield with almost the same volatility in comparison with open funds. Nonetheless, the statistical affirmation still lacks its validity and we can reject the hypothesis of relationship between the option to close the fund and yield booster. As in the previous case, the stumbling block is represented by a relatively very large volatility of year-over-year results of funds that makes any statistically judgement difficult.

Table 13.2 Results

	Number of funds	Average yield (%)	Standard deviation (%)
Total	3664	4.49	27.45
Closed to new investors	184	9.59	27.33
Open new investors	3480	4.17	27.42

Source Own calculations

13.4.3 Does Higher Fee Bring Higher Return?

Hypothesis: Hedge fund management belongs to the best paid financial sector representatives and hedge funds employ special techniques how the fund's management is remunerated. Generally, there are three types of fees. Firstly, front-end load is charged at the time of the initial purchase for an investment (% of the investment amount). Secondly, management fee is paid every year as a fixed percentual payment for asset management of the fund. Thirdly, a part of positive yield is transferred from clients/shareholders to the fund's management each year, which is called performance fee. It is worth mentioning that the fee structure can be much more complicated (with complex computations such as hurdle rate or watermark) and can include some other fees.

Naturally, it is a justified question to investigate whether higher fees bring additional performance to fund's clients or simply drag down net yield. Therefore, I will be looking for a relationship between the three main types of fees and value added for investors (return enhancement).

Method and Results: The database provides fee information for almost all funds. These data were removed for nonsense fee structures (triple zero fee), which would not be economically viable. The remaining 3910 funds are burdened with these three types of fees. In statistic terms, I will be testing the significance of the following regression:

$$\text{Yield} = \beta_0 + \beta_1 \times \text{Front} + \beta_2 \times \text{Mgmt} + \beta_3 \times \text{Perf} \tag{13.1}$$

where Yield stands for arithmetic average annual yield (in %), Front for front-end load fee (in %), Mgmt for management fee (in %), Perf for performance fee (in % share on return), β_0 for constant, and β_1–β_3 for regression coefficients (Table 13.3).

Interpretation: The regression brought very interesting results. Not surprisingly, the constant came out as insignificant which can be presumably attributed to very large embedded volatility of hedge fund performance. Front-end load fee proved to be insignificant to performance too. This suggests that funds should be chosen with lower front-end load fees as they do not have any added value. Management fee coefficient can be (with very large tolerance) accepted on the 10% level of significance. However, the sign of coefficient is negative; therefore, we proved a negative relationship between asset management remuneration and return.

Table 13.3 Results

	Coefficient	SD	p-value	
β_0	1.46976	0.980991	0.13416	–
β_1	0.226357	0.17217	0.18869	–
β_2	−0.724791	0.452582	0.10937	–
β_3	0.108454	0.0425523	0.01085	**

Source Own calculations

** 5 %

In other words, every 1% paid on management fee even decreases clients' return by 0.72%. Lastly, the performance fee proved to be significant even on very high level of significance, and its value is 0.11. Otherwise stated, every 10% of the return passed to the fund management produces additional 1.1% return for fund's clients.

13.4.4 Does Hedge Fund Returns Diminish in Time?

Hypothesis: As described in the previous parts, the phenomenon of backfill bias often appears in the hedge fund universe, which largely distorts the real performance data of hedge funds. If this turns out to be true, there should be a proper trend where yields of a hedge fund decrease in time. This return attrition is caused by simple non-obligatory reporting of hedge funds. The simple rationale behind this tells us that hedge fund managers wait a few periods until the return crosses attractive rate or if it does not then they do not start reporting at all. In this case, it should be observable that after the effect of hidden reports wears out, the return should decrease.

Method and Results: Similarly like in third hypothesis, I will be testing statistical significance of the regression coefficient. This time the regression equation is as following:

$$\text{Yield}_{y,x} = \beta_0 + \beta_1 \times \text{Year}_y \tag{13.2}$$

where $\text{Yield}_{y,x}$ stands for annualized return of the x-th hedge fund in the y-th year, Year_y for y-th year of reporting, β_0 for constant and β_1 for regression coefficient.

To prove the backfill bias, the β_1 coefficient should be significant and negative. Note: the data were limited only to years where number of reporting funds exceeded 50, which was fulfilled in years 1–13 (Table 13.4).

Interpretation: The result showed undoubtedly that the returns diminish in time. With strong statistical confidence, we can assert that the following pattern can be observed within hedge fund performance. The typical hedge fund starts with return of 5.58% (6.02–0.44) in the first reported year, and this yield decreases each year by 0.44% (in observed years up to the 13th year). Thus, the hypothesis of backfill bias (in other words diminishing returns) is fully confirmed and the hedge fund clients can expect ongoing reductions of their returns, most likely caused by non-disclosure of first unsuccessful results of failure funds.

Table 13.4 Results

	Coefficient	SD	p-value	
β_0	0.0602	0.0043	0.0000	***
β_1	−0.0044	0.0010	0.0001	***

Source Own calculations
*** 1 %

13.5 Conclusion

The text researched non-traditional factors and their influence on hedge fund performance. With the help of various statistical methods, these influences were quantified or disproved.

Firstly, the inclusion of a fund into market index brings minor additional yield, but this result can be attributed to normal deviation and volatility. A quite similar conclusion can be drawn about the second factor of openness/closeness to new investors where potentially closeable funds reported more-than-double return than open ones. However, again this figure must be regarded within volatility tolerance and statistically speaking the fund status do not implicate any different yield.

Thirdly, an influence has been proved for fee structures on fund return. None of three charged fees brings investor adequate countervalue. Front-end fee does not influence return at all, management fees even decrease the projected yield (though on low level of significance), and profit-sharing-based performance fee increases on side return but every 10% of profit give-up to fund management raise fund return by only 1.1%.

Fourth, probably the most important finding of this text is confirmation of backfill bias and hypothesis of selective reporting of hedge funds. The regression proved a very strong relationship between time and fund returns, where each year means lessening of return by average 0.44%. This observation of diminishing returns can be credited to self-selection in first years where hedge funds start reporting just as on only when return seems attractive, but must keep publicizing even results do not turn well afterwards.

Nonetheless, all the findings should be taken with great caution regarding two difficulties. The former is represented by data, which will always be self-selected by hedge funds and even when made public do not necessarily comply with standard performance measurement and audit standards. The latter obstacle consists of various statistical methods where different models with various assumptions produce heterogeneous results.

References

Baquero G, Ter Horst J, Verbeek M (2005) Survival, look-ahead bias, and persistence in hedge fund performance. J Financ Quant Anal 40(03):493–517

Brown SJ et al (1998) offshore hedge funds: survival & performance 1989–1995 (No. w5909). National Bureau of Economic Research

Chan N et al (2005) Systemic risk and hedge funds. NBER Working Paper No. 11200

Dichev ID, Yu G (2011) Higher risk, lower returns: what hedge fund investors really earn. J Financ Econ 100:248–263

Elton EJ, Gruber MJ, Blake CR (2003) Incentive fees and mutual funds. J Finance 58(2):779–804

Fung W, Hsieh DA (1997) Empirical characteristics of dynamic trading strategies: the case of hedge funds. Rev Financ Stud 10(2):275–302

Ibbotson RG, Chen P, Zhu KX (2011) The ABCs of hedge funds: alphas, betas, and costs. Financ Analy J 67(1):15–25

Johnson B (2010) The hedge fund fraud casebook. Wiley, Hoboken (NJ)

Lack S (2012) The hedge fund mirage the illusion of big money and why it's too good to be true. Wiley, Hoboken (NJ)

Mirabile K (2013) Hedge fund investing: a practical approach to understanding investor motivation, manager profits, and fund performance. Wiley, Hoboken (NJ)

Nelken I (ed) (2007) Hedge fund investment management. Elsevier/Butterworth-Heinemann, Amsterdam

Pool V, Bollen N (2009) Do Hedge fund managers misreport returns? Evidence from the pooled distribution. J Finance 64(5):2257–2288

Posthuma N, van der Sluisz PJ (2003) A reality check on hedge fund returns. Serie Research Memoranda, VU University, Amsterdam (No 0017). http://www.hedgefundmarketing.org/wp-content/uploads/2010/05/hf_reality_check_2003.pdf. Accessed 01 Mar 2016

Travers FJ (2012) Hedge fund analysis: an in-depth guide to evaluating return potential and assessing risks. Wiley, Hoboken (NJ)

Wilson RC (2010) The hedge fund book: a training manual for professionals and capital-raising executives. Wiley, Hoboken (NJ)

Yasuaki W (ed) (2010) The recent trend of hedge fund strategies. Nova Science Publishers, New York

Chapter 14
Interest Rate Sensitivity of Non-maturing Bank Products

Martina Hejdová, Hana Džmuráňová and Petr Teplý

Abstract This paper focuses on interest rate sensitivity of volumes of non-maturing bank products in the Czech Republic. First, we theoretically discuss economic reasons why non-contractual liabilities are expected to be interest rate sensitive, while non-maturing assets are not. Second, we test our hypotheses on time series of dynamics of volumes and client rates of non-maturing products in the Czech Republic in the 1993–2015 period. We conclude that non-maturing liabilities exhibit interest rate sensitivity of volumes, while non-maturing assets are largely insensitive.

Keywords Non-maturing products · Interest rate sensitivity · Time series analysis · Cointegration · Finance

14.1 Introduction

Banks are financial intermediaries with principal purpose to gather deposits from subjects with excess liquidity and to grant loans to subjects with lack of liquidity (Mejstřík et al. 2014). Both deposits and loans are products that can be divided into two major groups—maturing and non-maturing products. Maturing products are products that have defined cash flows and interest rate behaviour in the contract. Typical examples of such products are term deposits on liability side and term loans

M. Hejdová (✉) · P. Teplý
Faculty of Finance and Accounting, Department of Banking and Insurance, University of Economics in Prague, Prague, Czech Republic
e-mail: mhejdova@gmail.com

P. Teplý
e-mail: petr.teply@vse.cz

H. Džmuráňová
Faculty of Social Sciences, Institute of Economic Studies, Charles University in Prague, Prague, Czech Republic
e-mail: hanadzmuranova@gmail.com

© Springer International Publishing AG 2017
D. Procházka (ed.), *New Trends in Finance and Accounting*,
Springer Proceedings in Business and Economics,
DOI 10.1007/978-3-319-49559-0_14

like consumer loans on the asset side. Non-maturing products do not have cash flows and interest rate behaviour defined by the contract. Typical examples of non-maturing products are current accounts on the liability side and credit cards on the asset side.

In this paper, we deal with interest rate sensitivity of non-maturing bank products. We discuss theoretically how liquidity and interest rate behaviour of non-maturing products depend on interest rate environment, with focus on the Czech Republic banking sector. First, we define why non-maturing deposits' volumes and deposit interest rate are expected to be interest dependent and how. Second, we define why non-maturing assets' volumes and client rates are not interest rate dependent and why. Third, we test these hypotheses by time series analysis and we discuss conclusions.

The rest of the paper is structured as follows: Sect. 14.2 discusses interest rate sensitivity of non-maturing products (volumes and client rates) in theory, and Sect. 14.3 provides empirical analysis and drives conclusions. Finally, Sect. 14.4 concludes the paper.

14.2   Interest Rate Sensitivity of Non-maturing Products—Motivation

The description of liquidity and interest rate risk management of non-maturing liabilities is broadly discussed in Džmuráňová and Teplý (2015a, b). In this paper, we focus only on the description of dynamics of volumes of non-maturing products in relation to market rates development and we study whether deposit rates and loan client rates of non-maturing products are interest dependent. The analysis presented here is a step one analysis in estimation of interest rate risk and liquidity risk of non-maturing products, which is one of the principal concerns of all banks in terms of interest rate risk management of the banking book (IRRBB).[1]

14.2.1   Interest Rate Sensitivity of Non-maturing Liabilities

First, we focus on interest rate sensitivity of non-maturing liabilities. If market interest rate environment changes, the client's reaction may be either keeping or leaving the deposit in a bank and bank's reaction may be repricing or keeping the client rate unchanged. Therefore, we can define two types of interest rate sensitivity—interest rate sensitivity of volumes and/or of client rate.

---

[1]Besides the IRRBB, market risk management in financial institutions is discussed by, among others, Resti and Sironi (2007), Černohorská et al. (2012), Horváth and Teplý (2013), Janda and Zetek (2014) or Stádník (2014, 2015).

The first type, interest rate sensitivity of volume, comes from a decision-making process based on yield maximization and risk minimization. Generally, non-maturing liabilities like demand deposits are assumed as stable funding source by banks. However, this stability depends on market rate environment and type of demand deposits.

If the market yield of alternative opportunity possibility is not high enough (mainly during low rates environment), some clients may prefer less risky liquid demand deposit to riskier investments. Due to this, some volumes, that are relatively unstable in terms of interest rate sensitivity, are left on demand deposits. This volume is likely to be withdrawn when market rates increase and reinvested into more profitable products. Thus, we define such volume as rate-sensitive demand deposits or non-core demand deposits which are in accordance with regulatory definition (BCBS 2015). For example, savings accounts are typical example of non-maturing liabilities with interest-rate-sensitive volumes; see also Džmuráňová and Teplý (2014).

On the other hand, large portion of demand deposits are transactional accounts. By definition, such account is not dedicated to savings, but for transactions. Second, transactional accounts bear extremely low deposit rates, usually 0.01%. Due to these characteristics, transactional accounts are more stable than savings accounts and their volumes should be less sensitive to market rates. However, this may not be true in case of a long-term period of low or negative market rates and government bond yields. Under such interest rate environment, alternative opportunity of reinvestment may not even be available and spare client funds simply end up at transactional accounts as clients have nowhere else where to place them. Therefore, we can say that under low rates environment in an economy with excess liquidity as in the Czech Republic, there is high probability that significant portion of volumes currently placed on transactional accounts cannot be considered as core volume, i.e. a volume that is not expected to be repriced (BCBS 2015) and shall be seen as interest-rate-sensitive (non-core) demand deposits by banks.

The second type of interest rate sensitivity discussed in this paper is the client rate sensitivity to market rates. The client rate sensitivity is assumed to be a reaction of client rate to development of market interest rate. Banks increase the client rate to protect demand deposits portfolio from volume outflows while keeping the net interest income stable. Usually, banks' adjustment of deposit rate to market rates tends to be asymmetric; see, for example, Paraschiv (2011) who provides nice model and evidence for asymmetric adjustment features of deposit rates. Banks usually react more quickly with repricing downward than upward. On the other hand, competition and liquidity pressures also play a role.

Again, as well as with interest rate sensitivity of volumes, we can distinguish between non-maturing liabilities for which we expect higher interest rate sensitivity of client rate and non-maturing liabilities for which we rather do not expect high sensitivity of client rate to market rates. For savings accounts, we expect that client rate should be interest rate sensitive given that banks will need to keep stable savings accounts deposit base in a long term to be competitive. If a bank would not keep up with competition pricing in a long term, it could lead to diminishing portfolio of savings accounts, which in turn might lead to liquidity pressures. On the other hand, it depends on many factors as banks do not decide only to keep deposits, but also net interest rate income development plays a role on the one side and client relationship on the other side.

Regarding interest rate sensitivity of client rate on transactional accounts, we expect practically no interest rate sensitivity of client rate in case of transactional accounts as these accounts are by definition not designed for savings. On the contrary, in case of savings accounts, we would expect interest rate sensitivity of client rates as savings products are expected to have more competitive pricing as banks aim to attain client–bank relationship. However, as transactional accounts form 60% of all retail demand deposits in the Czech Republic, in this paper, we focus only on interest rate sensitivity of demand deposits as total, and hence, we assume that demand deposits in the Czech Republic should have deposit rates largely independent from market rate development.

Last but not least, we have to bear in mind that both effects of interest rate sensitivity are simultaneous. When market rates increase, sensitive part of volume is shifted to a more profitable product and the remaining part is partially repriced according to the market rate development.

14.2.2 Interest Rate Sensitivity of Non-maturing Assets

Interest rate sensitivity of non-maturing assets is largely dependent on usage and pricing of such loans in the analysed economy. In the Czech Republic, there are two main representatives of non-maturing assets—credit cards and overdrafts.

The interest rate sensitivity of volumes and client rates of credit cards and overdrafts would be relevant assumption for a market where large amount of loans is formed by non-maturing assets. In such market, banks would compete for non-maturing assets by competitive pricing of such products. However, as we show later, this is not the case in the Czech Republic. Due to this, we expect that non-maturing assets in the Czech Republic will be largely interest rate non-sensitive in terms of volumes as well as in terms of deposit rates.

14.3 Interest Rate Sensitivity of Non-maturing Products—Empirical Analysis

In this chapter, we analyse interest rate sensitivity of non-maturing bank products in the Czech Republic.

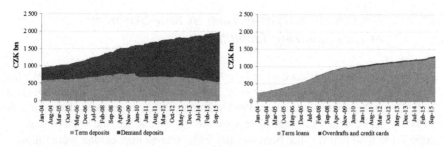

Fig. 14.1 Maturing and non-maturing liabilities and assets in the Czech banks. *Source* Authors based on data from CNB (2016)

Table 14.1 Single-equation Engle–Granger cointegration test

Variable	Description	Stationarity	Cointegrated with 1M PRIBOR
M1	1M PRIBOR—market rate representative	I(1)	x
DD_share	Share of demand deposits on total deposits	I(1)	No
DD_rate	Client rate of demand deposits	I(1)	No
OVD_share	Share of overdrafts on consumer loans (OVD incl.)	I(1)	No
CC_share	Share of credit cards on consumer loans (OVD and CC incl.)	I(1)	No
OVD_rate	Client rate of overdrafts	I(1)	No
CC_rate	Client rate of credit cards	I(1)	No

Source Authors' own calculations using data provided by CNB (2016)

As we can see in Fig. 14.1, on the liability side, non-maturing products amount to more than 60% of all clients' deposits. This makes them the main source of interest rate risk on the liability side in the Czech Republic. On the contrary, on the asset side, overdrafts and credit cards form only small portion (up to 10%) of clients' assets.

In our analysis, we analyse volumes and client rates and their dependence on market rates. Basics statistics of analysed time series are summarized in Table 14.1 where the denotation of used variables is in the first column and the short description of the variable is in the second column. The order of integration based on augmented Dickey–Fuller test (Dickey and Fuller 1979) is in the third column. Last, the fourth, column shows the results of pairwise Engle–Granger single-equation cointegration test (Engle and Granger 1987) and signalizes whether the particular variable is cointegrated with market rate 1M PRIBOR that is used as representative market rate in our analysis. We thereby refer to 1M PRIBOR as market rate in the following text.

14.3.1 Empirical Analysis of Interest Rate Sensitivity of Non-maturing Liabilities

First, we analyse dependence of volumes on interest rates. Figure 14.2 shows the share of demand deposits on total deposits, deposit rate and market rates development in the Czech Republic from January 1993 to January 2015, respectively, from January 2004 to December 2015 in case of deposit rate. As we can see, the share of demand deposits on total deposits has been steadily increasing as market rates were falling.

In this paper, the volume sensitivity of demand deposits to changes in market rates is understood as percentage points response to market rate changes. The causality, i.e. the dependence of the share on market rates, is verified by the Granger causality approach. Granger causality approach is based on the assumption that if a variable X Granger causes variable Y, then we are able to predict X_t using all available information apart from Y_t, i.e.

$$\sigma^2(X|U) < \sigma^2\left(\overline{X/U - Y}\right),$$

which means that if the variance of X is predicted using the universe of information, U, then it is less than the variance of X predicted using all information except variable Y (Granger 1969).

Based on Table 14.2, we can conclude that the market rate influences the share of demand deposits on total deposits in a Granger way. Hence, market rate can explain the dynamics of share of demand deposits on total deposits.

As both share of demand deposits and market rate time series are trend stationary, we can simplify the analysis and analyse deterministic trends development. Figure 14.3 shows the development of share of demand deposits and market rate and of their deterministic trends from January 1992 to December 2015. We observe two types of deterministic trends, depending on the overall direction of market rates. When market rate environment was increasing, we can see that share of demand deposits on total deposits was decreasing and vice versa. This is consistent with assumption we described in theoretical part, where we discussed that demand deposits' volumes increase during low market rates due to the lack of investment opportunities.

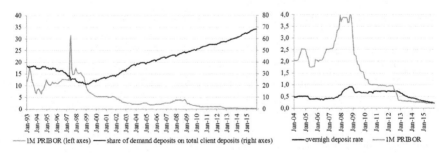

Fig. 14.2 Dynamics of share of demand deposits on total deposits and client coupon. *Source* Authors based on data from CNB (2016)

Table 14.2 Pairwise Granger causality tests—market rate and share

Null hypothesis	Obs	F-statistic	Prob.
Lags: 1, 2, 3			
M1 does not Granger cause DD_share	275	39.9189	1.E-09
M1 does not Granger cause DD_share	274	25.8462	5.E-11
M1 does not Granger cause DD_share	273	19.9269	5.E-11

Source Authors' own calculations using data provided by CNB (2016)

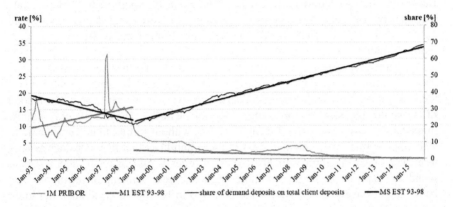

Fig. 14.3 Trend dynamics of demand deposits and 1M PRIBOR in the Czech Republic. *Source* Authors' own calculations using data provided by CNB (2016)

Table 14.3 Estimated deterministic trends

Period	Parameter	DD share	M1	Response
01/93–12/98	Slope	−0.23	0.08	−2.69
	Intercept	39.21	9.57	–
01/99–12/15	Slope	0.22	−0.03	−7.69
	Intercept	22.61	5.35	–

Source Authors' own calculations using data provided by CNB (2016)

Deterministic trend is represented by the trend line in a form

$$\widehat{Y}_t = \alpha + \beta t,$$

where α (intercept) and β (slope) are estimated parameters. As the slope is interpreted as a change in variable Y between two time periods, we can derive the resulting proportional impact by the comparison of estimated slopes for both demand deposit share and market rate. Estimated parameters are shown in Table 14.3.

As we can see in Table 14.3, opposite signs of slopes of trend lines prove that the dependence of share of demand deposits on total deposits and market rate is indirect. This is consistent with our theoretical assumption, i.e. the share of demand deposits on total deposits is influenced by the level of market rates in a Granger way. As a response in the share, or market rate, respectively, to unit change in time is represented by the slope of the deterministic trend, we can estimate the change in share of demand deposit by the simple one-reaction movement on these trend lines.

Therefore, to calculate the change of demand deposits on total deposits in case of increasing market rates, we forecast it based on increasing trend in market rate, and from that, we derive decreasing trend in share of demand deposits on total deposits. Based on this procedure, we can conclude that if representative market rate increases by 1% point, then the estimated impact into demand deposits is shift of CZK 150bn (11% of all total demand deposits) from demand deposits to other, more profitable, products.

As demand deposits are assumed to be stable liabilities, especially current accounts, which are assumed to form stable core balances, banks usually invest them into long-term investment products. However, as we can see, when market rates would increase sharply, app. 11% of demand deposits would outflow immediately (assuming one-off change impact, without further trend continuation). This implies that banks might currently invest liabilities that they consider as long term into long-term reinvestments, but when rates would increase, clients would withdraw deposits in favour of more profitable reinvestment opportunities and banks might have to sell a part of the portfolio to be able to stand such outflows. This would be mainly an issue of banks that do not have high excess of deposits over loans and investments.

A client interest rate of demand deposits is usually given by the price list of the bank that can be changed anytime by a bank's discretion. If bank wants to reach stable net interest income in long-term horizon, it should change the price of demand deposits when market rates level tends to be different. This is mainly true in case of savings accounts, as we discussed in the theoretical part of this article. The interest rate sensitivity of coupon is an expression of a reaction function of the bank's discretion (i.e. client rate) to market rate environment. Again, we test whether market rate in any way influences deposit rate on demand deposits by Granger causality test. Time series of market rate and deposit rate from January 2004 to December 2015 can be seen in Fig. 14.2.

If market rate influences client coupon rate in a Granger way, the long-term relationship should be further analysed. As we can see in Table 14.3, there is evidence that market rate influences deposit rate in terms of Granger causality, and hence, we should test our hypothesis that deposit rates are market rate dependent.

According to augmented Dickey–Fuller test, both market rate and client interest rate are considered to be non-stationary, integrated of order one.[2] Therefore, the error correction model is the appropriate way for analysing the long-term

---

[2]M1 is I(1) for time series spanning from January 2004 to December 2015, while from January 1993 to December 1999 and from January 2000 to December 2015, it is trend stationary.

relationship between market (MR) and client rate (CR) (Curcio and Gianfrancesco 2010), i.e. under assumption of market rate exogeneity:

$$\Delta CR_t = \beta_0 \Delta MR_t + \gamma(\alpha + CR_{t-1} - \beta MR_{t-1}) + \varepsilon_t,$$

where α is a stable, independent margin (i.e. spread between client and market rate), β is a long-run multiplier, γ represents the speed of adjustment back to equilibrium, and β_0 shows the short-term relationship between client and market rate (Charemza and Deadman 1997).

In order to avoid spurious regression, both time series have to be cointegrated. As we assume market rate exogeneity, the single-equation Engle–Granger cointegration test (Granger 1987) may be used.

The results presented in Table 14.4 indicate that no long-term relationship (cointegrating) between market and client rate exists. Therefore, the error correction model cannot be constructed and individual stationarity transformation should be a base for a model of short-term reaction of client rate to market rate. However, the short-term reaction is not of our interest as we rather focus on long-term directions in deposit rate development. Generally, it can be concluded that there is no stable spread between market rate and average client rate of demand deposits. We can say that deposit rates on demand deposits are not derived from market rates. This is in accordance with our expectations described in the theoretical part of this article given that transactional accounts form a major part of analysed time series (Table 14.5).

However, this result has some limitations. First, we cannot observe more interest rate cycles in the Czech economy. Second, banks react differently on various market rates changes during observed history.

Table 14.4 Pairwise Granger causality tests

Null hypothesis	Obs.	F-statistic	Prob.
Lags: 1, 2, 3			
M1 does not Granger cause DD_rate	143	16.0455	0.0001
M1 does not Granger cause DD_rate	142	9.91883	9.E-05
M1 does not Granger cause DD_rate	141	8.91221	2.E-05

Source Authors' own calculations using data provided by CNB (2016)

Table 14.5 Single-equation Engle–Granger cointegration test

Dependent	Tau-statistic	Prob.*	Z-statistic	Prob.*
M1	−0.843449	0.9267	−1.490321	0.9520
ON_DEPOS_RATE	−0.647749	0.9497	−1.466331	0.9528

Source Authors' own calculations using data provided by CNB (2016)

14.3.2 Empirical Analysis of Interest Rate Sensitivity of Non-maturing Assets

Analysis of interest rate sensitivity is done in the same way as for non-maturing liabilities. Figure 14.4 (left) shows the development of share of overdrafts and credit cards to total consumer loans (overdrafts and credit cards including) and client coupon dynamics (right) from January 2004 to December 2015.

First, we analyse dependencies with the Granger causality. Based on the results shown in Table 14.6, we can conclude that there is no explanatory power of market rate. Hence, we conclude that there is no dependency between market rate and share of overdrafts, or credit cards, respectively, to total consumer loans overdrafts, or overdrafts and credit cards including.

We also briefly analysed client rates as well using similar procedures as described for demand deposits. We can conclude that there is no interest rate

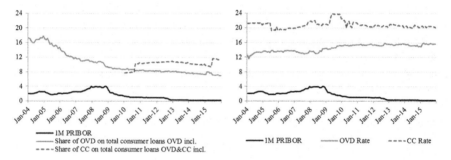

Fig. 14.4 Dynamics of share of non-maturity assets on total loans and client coupon. *Source* Authors' own calculations using data provided by CNB (2016)

Table 14.6 Granger causality—summary of results for overdrafts and credit cards

Null hypothesis	Obs	F-statistic	Prob.	Obs	F-statistic	Prob.
Lags: 1, 2, 3		Share			Rate	
M1 does not Granger cause OVD share/rate	143	0.06341	0.8016	143	1.30278	0.2557
M1 does not Granger cause OVD_share/rate	142	0.17829	0.8369	142	1.8996	0.1535
M1 does not Granger cause OVD_share/rate	141	0.49515	0.6863	141	2.43134	0.0679
M1 does not Granger cause CC share/rate	71	0.18604	0.6676	143	1.35666	0.2461
M1 does not Granger cause CC_share/rate	70	0.04989	0.9514	142	0.80902	0.4474
M1 does not granger cause CC_share/rate	69	0.18280	0.9077	141	1.11327	0.3461

Source Authors' own calculations using data provided by CNB (2016)

sensitivity of both volumes and client coupon rates. The decreasing share of non-maturing assets to total consumer loans is more likely to be the result of improving financial skills of clients.

14.4 Conclusion

In this paper, we analysed dynamics of volumes and client rates of non-maturing bank products in the Czech Republic. We divided non-maturing products into two main classes—demand deposits and overdrafts/credit cards.

In the theoretical part, we discussed characteristics of demand deposits that imply that demand deposits should exhibit interest rate sensitivity in terms of volumes and that demand deposits might exhibit interest rate sensitivity in terms of client rates. Concerning credit cards and overdrafts, we assumed neither interest rate sensitivity of volumes nor client rates.

In the empirical part, we showed that demand deposits are indeed interest rate sensitive in terms of volumes, but that interest rate sensitivity of client rates was not verified. We also showed that volumes and client rates of credit cards and overdraft are largely interest rate non-sensitive.

Our analysis contributes to research of non-maturing bank products with embedded options in the Czech Republic. Our findings are similar to findings in other studies (Maes and Timmermans 2005; Kalbrener and Willing 2004; Frauendorfer and Schuerle 2006; Dewachter et al. 2006; Brůna 2007; Horváth and Podpiera 2009), with exception of dynamics of deposit rates, that are usually modelled as market rate dependent by many authors. This interest rate non-sensitivity of client rates of demand deposits in the Czech Republic stems from the fact that major part of demand deposits are transactional accounts, while other authors mostly analyse savings deposits only or savings deposits have higher share on demand deposits in analysed economics than in the Czech Republic. Therefore, the next step in our analysis would be to divide demand deposits into transactional deposits and savings deposits (savings accounts) and then analyse their volume and client rate sensitivity separately.

Acknowledgments This paper has been prepared under financial support of the Grant Agency of Charles University in Prague (project No. 165215), the Czech Science Foundation (Project No. 16-21506S) and University of Economics in Prague (project No.VŠE IGA F1/21/2016), which authors gratefully acknowledge.

References

BCBS (2015) Interest rate risk in the banking book. Consultative Document. Basel Committee for Banking Supervision, Basel
Brůna K (2007) Úrokový transmisní mechanismus a řízení úrokové marže bank v kontextu dezinflační politiky České národní banky. Politická ekonomie 6:829–851

Černohorská L, Teplý P, Vrábel M (2012) The VT index as an indicator of market liquidity risk in Slovakia. J Econ 60(3):223–238

Charemza WW, Deadman PF (1997) New directions in econometric practice. Edward Elgar Pub, Lyme, N.H

CNB (2016). ARAD time series database. ČNB, 2016. Available online at: http://www.cnb.cz/docs/ARADY/HTML/index.htm

Curcio D, Gianfrancesco I (2010) Modelling Italian bank retail interest rates under an error correction framework: implications for banking risk management. Rivista Bancaria. Minerva Bancaria 66(5–6):5–29

Dewachter et al (2006) A multi-factor model for the valuation and risk management of demand deposits. National Bank of Belgium working paper research No. 83

Dickey DA, Fuller WA (1979) Distribution of the estimators for autoregressive time series with a unit root. J Am Stat Assoc 74:427–431

Džmuráňová H, Teplý P (2014) Risk management of savings accounts. IES Working Paper 2014-09. Institute of Economic Studies, Prague

Džmuráňová H, Teplý P (2015a) Duration of demand deposits in theory. Procedia economics and finance. 16th annual conference on finance and accounting, ACFA, vol 25, pp 278–284

Džmuráňová H, Teplý P (2015b) Liquidity characteristics of demand deposits in the Czech Republic—implications for bank liability management in a low interest rate environment. International conference on finance and accounting

Engle RF, Granger CWJ (1987) Co-integration and error correction: representation, estimation, and testing. Econometrica 55(2):251–276

Frauendorfer K, Schurle M (2006) Dynamic modeling and optimization of non-maturing accounts. University of St. Gallen, Institute for Operational research and Computational Finance

Granger CWJ (1969) Investigation causal relations by econometric models and cross-spectral methods. Econometrica 37(3):424–438

Horváth R, Podpiera A (2009) Heterogeneity in bank pricing policies: the Czech evidence. IES Working Paper 2009-08. Institute of Economic Studies, Prague

Horváth R, Teplý P (2013) Risk management of building societies in the Czech Republic. Ekonomicky Casopis 61(1):24–46

Janda K, Zetek P (2014) Macroeconomic factors influencing interest rates of microfinance institutions in Latin America and the Caribbean. Agric Econ 4(60):159–173

Kalkberener M, Willing W (2004) Risk management of non-maturing liabilities. J Bank Finance 28(7):1547–1568

Meas K, Timmermans T (2005) Measuring the interest rate risk of Belgian regulated savings deposits. National Bank of Belgium Financial Stability Review 2005. National Bank of Belgium, Brussel, pp 137–151

Mejstřík M, Pečená M, Teplý P (2014) Banking in theory and practice. Karolinum Press, Prague

Paraschiv F (2011) Modeling deposit rate and volumes of non-maturing savings accounts. University of St. Gallen Dissertation No. 3924

Resti A, Sironi A (2007) Risk managements and shareholders' value in banking: from risk measurements models to capital allocation policies. Wiley, West Sussex

Stádník B (2014) The puzzle of financial market distributions. Ekonomický Časopis (J Econ) 62 (7):709–727

Stádník BM (2015) Complex model of market price development and its simulation. J Bus Econ Manage 16(4):786–807

Chapter 15
Examining the Interdependencies Between Leverage and Capital Ratios in the Banking Sector of the Czech Republic

Karel Janda and Oleg Kravtsov

Abstract In this paper, we discuss the implications of the Basel III requirements on the leverage ratio for the banking sector in the Czech Republic. We identify the potential binding constraints from regulatory limits and analyze the interactions among leverage and capital ratios over the country's economic cycle (2007–2014). By analyzing the components of ratios, we conclude that the banks are focusing more on the optimization of risk-weighted assets. Strong co-movement patterns between leverage and assets point to the active management of leverage as a means of expanding and contracting the size of balance sheets and maximizing the utility of the capital. The analysis of correlation patterns among the variables indicates that the total assets (and exposure) in contrast to Tier 1 capital are the main contributors to the cyclical movements in the leverage. The leverage and the total assets also demonstrate a weak correlation with GDP, but a strong co-movement with loans to the private sector.

Keywords Leverage ratio · Capital ratio · Basel III · Czech republic

K. Janda (✉) · O. Kravtsov
Department of Banking and Insurance, University of Economics,
W. Churchilla 4, 13067 Praha 3, Czech Republic
e-mail: Karel-Janda@seznam.cz

O. Kravtsov
e-mail: krao02@vse.cz

K. Janda
Institute of Economic Studies, Charles University, Opletalova 26,
11000 Praha 1, Czech Republic

© Springer International Publishing AG 2017   161
D. Procházka (ed.), *New Trends in Finance and Accounting*,
Springer Proceedings in Business and Economics,
DOI 10.1007/978-3-319-49559-0_15

15.1   Introduction

It is widely believed that one of the causes of the latest financial crisis was the excessive build-up of the on- and off-balance sheet leverage in the banking system. In some cases, the banks accumulated excessive leverage while evidently maintaining strong risk-based capital ratios (BCBS 2014). To address this issue and enhance the banks' resilience to crisis, the Basel Committee in 2010 introduced a minimum leverage ratio as an additional prudential tool to complement minimum capital adequacy requirements. The leverage ratio is defined as a Tier 1 capital divided by on- and off-balance sheet exposure. The leverage ratio should be disclosed in the public reports of financial institutions from January 1, 2015, onwards and fully implemented at the start of 2018 after appropriate review and calibration.

In our paper, we discuss the implications of leverage and capital requirements for the banking sector in the Czech Republic. We identify the potential binding constraints from regulatory limits and analyze the interactions among ratios over the country's economic cycle (during the period 2007–2014). The following questions are of primary focus of our analysis. Which regulatory ratio in the Basel III regime (i.e., Tier 1 capital ratio, capital adequacy or leverage ratio) represents a main binding constraint in the country's banking sector during the crisis and recovery periods (over the years 2007–2014)? What degree of correlation exists between leverage and capital ratio, and their variables over the economic cycle (2007–2014)? What leverage and capital ratios can say about the behavior and strategy of the banks in the Czech Republic?

15.2   Literature Review

In the debate about financial market regulations and their impact on the economies Musílek (2011) and Černohorský et al. (2011) in their works are dealing with the challenges of the Basel III guidelines for the EU and Czech banking sector. The banking regulations and systematic risk in financial market systems are investigated by Klinger and Teply (2016) with special focus on the capital regulations in studies of Avery and Berger (1991), Gropp and Heider (2009), and Estrella et al. (2006). Notably few studies are focusing on the implications caused by interactions among regulatory ratios, for example, between capital and leverage ratios as risk- and non-risk-based measures. In the studies by Adrian and Shin (2010, 2011), Kalemli-Ozcan et al. (2011), and Brei and Gambacorta (2014), the cyclical properties of the ratios are tested taking into account structural shifts in banks' behavior during the global financial crisis and its aftermath. They suggest that in normal times the new leverage ratio based on the exposure measure is always more countercyclical than the other ratios. In contrast to capital ratios, it is a tighter constraint for banks in economy upturn and a looser constraint in recession. Nuno and Thomas (2013) argue that bank's leverage is endogenously determined by market forces. They found that leverage contributes at least as much as equity to the cyclical movements in total assets and leverage is negatively correlated with equity. Apparently it is positively correlated with assets growth and to a lesser extent with GDP. The impact of capital on bank survival during financial crises and normal times is examined by Berger and Bouwman (2013). Mainly focusing on the economic roles of capital depending on bank size and time period, they indicate that the capital helps to enhance the survival probabilities of small banks at all times and for medium/large banks primarily during the banking crises and with limited government support. They note similarly that the off-balance sheet activities of banks are impacting the capital and consequently survivability of banks over the crisis.

The effectiveness of the Basel Accords as a regulatory framework and its implications on the Czech banking sector were investigated by Šútorová and Teplý (2013, 2014), Teply and Vejdovec (2012). In country-specific case study, Kellermann and Schlag (2013) examine the binding constraint factors of ratios on the Swiss banking sector. From their analysis, it is evident that the minimum leverage ratio shows a strong tendency to undermine the risk-based requirements. Since at least during the period 2009–2011, the minimum leverage ratio requirement became a binding rule for the major Swiss bank UBS. Furthermore, they pointed out that this fact might adversely encourage banks to take greater risks. Cathcart et al. (2013) investigate the interdependencies and procyclical nature of capital and leverage ratios of the US banking institutions prior to the first 1990 to 1991 and the second credit crunch of 2007–2009. Their results demonstrate that unlike during the first credit crunch, the leverage ratio during the crisis of 2007–2009 was a binding constraint and generally more to blame for triggering the subprime crisis. Furthermore, they argue that the reversal in correlation patterns between the two ratios was a main reason of the change in binding constraint. The correlation patterns of the ratios are seemingly related to loan growth and GDP market signals.

15.3 Data, Results, and Discussion

The data sample in Table 15.1 comprises of data of the main banking institutions and subsidiaries of international banks which operate in the Czech Republic on standalone basis and provide a standard range of banking services, i.e., units in the sample are comparable. It consists of 15 main Czech banks and covers the period of 8 years from 2007 to 2014 that refers to the full economic cycle with financial crisis, aftermath, and recovery. The financial data have been extracted directly from the annual reports of the financial institutions to provide the best possible estimates of banks' exposure measures for the leverage ratio calculation according to the Basel III definition.

The Basel III leverage ratio (LR) is defined as the capital measure (the numerator) divided by the exposure measure (the denominator), with this ratio expressed as a percentage:

Table 15.1 Statistics summary

Variable	Obs	Mean	Std. dev.	Min	Max
Leverage ratio (%)	111	8.3	6.2	1.9	43.6
Capital ratio Tier 1 (%)	110	18.6	22.6	7.4	211.6
Exposure (CZKm)	113	279,041	360,007	331	1,167,064
Tier 1 capital (CZKm)	112	17,814	20,713	80	76,164
Risk-weighted assets (CZKm)	110	133,386	151,282	284.2	503,360
Total assets (CZKm)	115	245,222	323,855	331	968,723

Source Annual financial reports and own calculations

$$LR = \frac{K_t}{Exp_t} \tag{15.1}$$

where K_t denotes a Tier 1 capital and Exp_t—the exposure measure, at the end of reporting period t. The capital measure represents the numerator of the leverage ratio and is based on the new definition of Tier 1 class of capital as set out by Basel Committee (BCBS 2010). The exposure represents the denominator of the leverage ratio. The exposure measure in definition of the Basel Committee on Banking Supervision (BCBS 2014, 2015) is the sum of the on-balance sheet exposures, derivative, and securities financing transactions and off-balance sheet items.

By introducing a leverage ratio, the Basel Committee pursued several goals. The minimum leverage provides a simple and transparent accounting measure that serves as a non-risk-based "backstop" which ultimately serves to protect against model risk, and the reduction of capital requirements and generally it reinforces risk-based requirements (BCBS 2014). It captures both the on- and off-balance sheet exposure which in fact could bear significant risks due to the complex and not fully transparent derivative and guarantees exposures. Finally, the primary goal of leverage is to constraint a build-up of excessive leverage in banking system during the times of credit boom and help to soften the deleveraging processes in downturn economy cycle. These cyclical qualities of the leverage and capital ratios have been indicated in several studies. The evidences by Adrian and Shin (2010, 2011) and Nuno and Thomas (2013) are based on the empirical analysis of the US financial intermediaries that operate primarily through the highly liquid and dynamic capital markets. They suggest that these financial institutions are adjusting their balance sheets actively in such way that leverage tends to be higher during the economy booms and lower during the slowdown and recession. In normal times, however, leverage is less cyclical. The capital ratios reveal opposite countercyclical qualities and seem to be more stable and less procyclical in the crisis times (Brei and Gambacorta 2014; Kellermann and Schlag 2013). According to this logic, both leverage and capital measures might represent a binding constraint for the banks in various economy cycles. Depending on which one of the two ratios is the stricter binding constraint, the incentive for the bank strategies might have different approach according to Blundell-Wignall and Atkinson (2010), Cathcart et al.

(2013). It implies that the management of bank capital and leverage ratios over the course of the business cycle might be as important as the risk-based capital requirements particularly by determining the cyclical impact of capital regulation.

In Fig. 15.1, we summarize the historical evolution and potential regulatory constraints on the capital and leverage ratios for the largest Czech banks over the economic cycles. The period 2007–2009 refers to crisis period and years of 2010–2014 as a recovery and normal times. The following ratios are evaluated: (a) the new Basel III leverage ratio (as Tier 1/Exposure measure); (b) the accounting leverage ratio (Tier 1/Total assets); (c) the capital-to-risk-weighted-assets ratio (Tier 1/risk-weighted assets); and (d) the capital adequacy (total capital/risk-weighted assets). The first three ratios (a), (b), and (c) have different denominators but relate to each other with the same numerator—Tier 1 capital. The capital ratio (d) has been added to estimate the development of the banks' capital adequacy over the period. The regulatory guidelines on minimum requirements under the Basel III regime are the following: minimum leverage requirement ≥3.0% during the testing period from January 1, 2013, to January 1, 2017, with disclosure requirement starting from January 1, 2015 (BCBS 2014, 2015, 2010); minimum requirement for Tier 1 capital (including Tier 1 additional capital) ≥6.0% of risk-weighted assets (RWA) with minimum Tier 1 capital ratio in Basel III phase-in arrangements in 2013 ≥4.5%, in 2014 ≥5.5% and starting from 2015 ≥6.0%; minimum total capital requirement (sum of total Tier 1 and Tier 2 capital) ≥8.0% of RWA.

The weighted median of all risk- and non-risk-based ratios reveal an upward trend during the various economic cycles, newly analyzed by Stádník and Miečinskienė (2015). Between the crisis period of 2007–09 and recovery years 2010–14, the median of the risk-weighted Tier 1 capital ratio increased from 11.3 to 14.9%, while the leverage ratio in the Basel III regime increased very moderately from 5.6 to 6.8%. The total capital ratio (capital adequacy) increased even at larger extent from 12.3 to 15.8%. Černohorský et al. (2011) and Matejašák (2015) similarly noted that Basel III requirements on capital are not presenting a larger

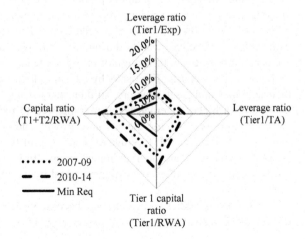

Fig. 15.1 Average leverage and capital ratios in crisis (2007–09) and recovery period (2010–14). *Source* Annual reports and own calculation (*Note* All ratios are weighted average by respective denominator)

Leverage ratio (Tier1/Exp)

20.0%
15.0%
10.0%
5.0%
0.0%

Capital ratio (T1+T2/RWA)

Leverage ratio (Tier1/TA)

•••••• 2007-09
— — 2010-14
——— Min Req

Tier 1 capital ratio (Tier1/RWA)

constraint because of the historically high capital ratios of the Czech banks. The data show that contrary to the capital ratios, the leverage of the Czech banks might represent potentially larger constraint in terms of meeting the transitional minimum regulatory limits. We observe that in 5% of cases from total sample the leverage of few banks has happened to be lower than the regulatory guidelines at some point of time. The mean of the leverage ratio across the sample is around 8.3% that is overall higher than recommended guidelines $\geq 3.0\%$.

In order to assess the strategies of banking sector toward adjustments in capital and leverage ratios, we take a closer look into interdependencies between the components of the leverage ratio and the Tier 1 capital ratio. Since both of them have the same numerator (Tier 1 Capital), it allows us to relate and analyze changes in their denominators—risk-weighted assets versus exposure or total assets (Berger and Bouwman 2013; Cathcart et al. 2013). We rearrange the relation of Tier 1 capital ratio to leverage ratios (both ratios with exposure based and accounting measure of total assets) as follows:

$$\frac{\text{LR}}{\text{CR}} = \frac{\frac{K_t}{\text{Exp}_t}}{\frac{K_t}{\text{RWA}_t}} = \frac{\text{RWA}_t}{\text{Exp}_t} \tag{15.2}$$

where K_t denotes a Tier 1 capital, RWA_t stands for risk-weighted assets, and Exp_t denotes the exposure measure (or total assets on the balance sheet), at the end of reporting period t.

The relationship of risk-weighted assets to exposure (or total assets) captures also the riskiness of the business model of the banks. The higher ratio of risk-weighted assets to total assets suggests that the portfolio contains more risky assets. For example, the sovereign bonds portfolio has usually the lowest risk, depending significantly on the level of interest rates—(Stádník 2014), weight up to 0.0% (in standardized approach of credit risk measurements under the Basel II capital adequacy guidelines), since this asset class is considered to be the safest and on opposite, traded securitization products have the highest up to 1250% risk weight. In Fig. 15.2, we exhibit the historical evolution of risk weights over the period of 2007–2014 of the largest Czech banks. The notable trend is that both risk weights tend to decline steadily during the entire period. Apparently the banks are focusing more on the optimization of risk-weighted assets and structuring portfolios with lower risk weights. The banks by adjusting their business model are changing their activities and asset structure, so their income might be impacted too. For the banks with a higher leverage level, it could lead to reduction in lending volumes and hence poses risks for the income growth and profitability. As a result of inclusion into the Basel III leverage exposure the off-balance sheet items with 100% credit conversion factor, the trade finance transactions and hedging activities of the Czech banks will be affected by higher capital requirements noted by Černohorský et al. (2011).

The cyclical qualities of the leverage become visible by comparing the leverage toward the annual growth of total assets (Fig. 15.3). The annual changes in the

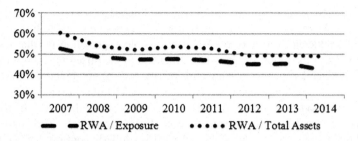

Fig. 15.2 Average leverage and capital ratios in crisis (2007–09) and recovery period (2010–14). *Source* Annual reports and own calculation

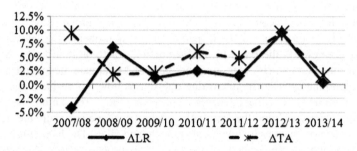

Fig. 15.3 Annual growth in total assets versus annual change in leverage for the top 10 Czech banks 2007–2014. *Source* Annual reports and own calculation

balance sheets over the observed period seemingly follow the economic cycle with "reverse" movement of leverage toward the assets characteristic for the crisis years 2008–2009. In overall, the adjustments in the leverage (co-movement with total assets) reveal similar pattern described by Brei and Gambacorta (2014), Adrian and Shin (2010). As explained by these authors, such a strong co-movement signifies an active management of leverage as a means of expanding and contracting the size of balance sheets. They suggest that the largest banks might be able to use the increased equity as basis for further lending which will increase assets (and lia-bilities) relative to equity with the outcome that asset and leverage is no longer inversely related. In other words, the banks are attempting to maximize the capital utility and by doing so they increase their assets, respectively. The potential risk is that this way the banks could be incentivized to increase their risk appetite. Given the actual level of capital and confronted with the choice between low risk and low margin, and higher risk but higher margin, most banks will likely opt for the second option according to EBA (2015)

Building on the study and using similar methodological approach of Cathcart et al. (2013), Estrella et al. (2006), and Nuno and Thomas (2013), we try to capture any patterns of co-movements of both ratios and interdependencies among their variables. For the purpose of analysis, we use the Pearson correlation measure between leverage and capital ratio. The results depicted on Fig. 15.4 demonstrate that a high degree of positive correlation indeed exists between both ratios (with a range of coefficient from 0.6 to 0.9). The possible explanation for that lies in the components of the ratios and mostly attributable to the offsetting effect of increase in capital (Tier 1 capital is a numerator of both ratios) combined with the adjustments in the assets (described in previous section). The time horizon of our analysis covers the period of constantly increasing capitalization of the Czech banks driven by stricter regulatory requirements and business model. The findings by Černohorský et al. (2011) and Matejašák (2015) similarly confirm that capital basis of the Czech banks increased substantially over the period 2009–2013 and consequently improving on average regulatory capital ratios.

The interactions between macroeconomic conditions, bank regulations, and governmental policies are relevant for all advanced economies and especially for newly EU integrated economies of Central and Eastern Europe (Cevik et al. 2016; Janda 2011; Janda et al. 2013). In particular, by introducing the leverage in the Basel III framework, the Basel Committee aimed exactly at reinforcing the capital requirements with non-risk measures and this way to mitigate the magnifying effect of the economic cycles. The interesting question is how the business cycles in the Czech Republic affect the interactions of both ratios. To exhibit the effect of business cycles, we plot the correlation patterns altogether with the economic cycles' indicators such as loan volumes growth, and GDP. The loan volume growth in the economy is represented by the "Loans to private sector—Annual growth rates" from the official statistics of the CNB. The annual changes in gross domestic product relate to economy conditions and cycles (Fungáčová and Jakubík 2013; Izák 2011). To capture a lagged effect of macroeconomic factors on the microeconomic level of banking sector, we use a half-year-delayed GDP figures. The results in Fig. 15.4 underline the fact that leverage and capital ratios have a tendency to co-movement in normal times and a slightly countermovement in the time of downturn or upswing. However, it does not reveal at all the negative correlation between leverage and capital ratio in crisis period, which was described by Cathcart

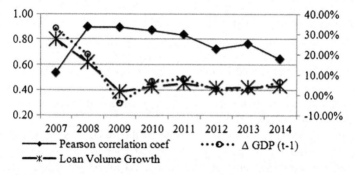

Fig. 15.4 Correlation pattern changes in leverage/capital ratio versus loan volume and GDP growth during 2007–2014. *Source* Annual reports and own calculation

et al. (2013). It implies that the change in the binding constraint from one to another ratio does not explicitly occur during the period of our observation.

In order to understand the contribution of the single factors to the fluctuations in the leverage ratio, we analyze and compare the cyclical qualities of the variables that we discussed earlier. We extract the cyclical components of the variables by applying the cycle band-pass filter for economic time series of Baxter and King (1999). Based on the statistics of previous US business cycles, they developed a set of approximate filters to measure the business cycles of macroeconomic activity. The procedure enables to isolate business cycle component transforming the macroeconomic data by applying the particular moving averages. The filter allows extracting a cyclical component which persists for the periods of two to eight years, and leaves the characteristics of this component undistorted. The cyclical (de-trended) components of the variables were used to compare the volatility of the variables and plot their correlation patterns.

First of all, we try to assess the contribution of the total assets and Tier 1 capital to the cyclical fluctuations in the leverage ratio. Secondly, it is of interest for us to estimate how leverage and capital correlate with each other, and how each component correlates with total assets. A related question is how the leverage ratio and the assets of banks correlate with aggregate economic activity, as represented by annual GDP in constant prices and loan to private sector volumes from the official statistics of the CNB. Furthermore, the certain degree of volatility in leverage, assets, and Tier 1 capital relative to those in real economic activity is itself a matter of empirical interest.

The aggregated results are exhibited in Table 15.2 and can be summarized in the following points. The leverage in the sample is less volatile than assets and equity capital, but it fluctuates stronger than economic indicators GDP and loan volumes growth. The standard deviation of leverage is more than twice of the capital and total assets. The higher volatility in a variable might suggest a larger possible error in evaluating the cyclical co-movement patterns with other variables. The total assets and exposure, in contrast to Tier 1 capital show the largest contribution to the cyclical movement of the leverage. The strong negative correlation with leverage (coefficient -0.540) reiterates the observations by Adrian and Shin (2010) and Brei and Gambacorta (2014) and points out that the leverage ratio represents a tighter constraint in the upturn cycle by expanding balance sheet and a looser one in the recession period when assets are shrinking.

Moreover, our findings suggest that the capital Tier 1 indicates a weak correlation with negative vector to the leverage ratio. That fact contradicts to the mathematical logic of ratio that implies a positive correlation. The explanation is that the data in our sample covers the period when the capital increase was accompanied mostly by growth in assets. A larger data sample or a comparison with other countries banking sectors would be useful to investigate further on this issue. The leverage and total assets show a strong correlation with economic cycle indicator "loans to private sector" (coefficients -0.271 and 0.645, respectively) that is

Table 15.2 Business cycles and leverage components

Standard deviations		Correlations		
Coefficient			Coefficient	P values
Leverage	0.5066	Leverage − total assets	−0.540**	0.000
Tier 1	0.9559	Leverage − exposure	−0.552**	0.000
TA	1.1831	Leverage − capital Tier 1	−0.122	0.200
Exp	1.1511	Leverage − GDP	0.056	0.556
GDP	0.0038	Leverage − loan volumes	−0.271	0.004
Loan	0.0102	Assets − loan volumes	0.645**	0.000
		Assets − GDP	0.084	0.382

Note All variables are natural logarithms. Excel-based add-in of the Baxter-King band-pass filter employed with the standard settings Burns-Mitchell for annual data, i.e., min 2 and max 8 years, $k = 3$ low-pass filters. *Asterisks* denote statistical significance of nonzero correlation at the 5% (**) confidence level. Significance two-tailed tests are reported in parenthesis
Source Own calculation, data from Czech National Bank, annual reports

quiet self-explanatory. However, we observe weak correlation of leverage and total assets with GDP (coefficients 0.056 and 0.084). The degree of correlation is low possibly due to the delayed macroeffect on the banking sector; however, the positive vector points out the co-movement tendencies.

15.4 Conclusion

In our empirical study, we used a data sample of 15 major banks operating in the Czech Republic over the period 2007–2014. The historical data confirm stronger capital ratios of the banks and an overall solid leverage level. By analyzing the components of ratios, we were able to learn more about the strategies of the Czech banks. Evidently, the banks are focusing more on the optimization of risk-weighted assets and structuring portfolios with lower risks. Strong co-movement patterns between leverage and assets also suggest the active management of leverage in terms of expanding and contracting the size of balance sheets and maximizing the utility of the capital.

The correlation patterns between leverage and capital ratios reveal mild procyclical qualities. The economic cycle indicators such as a loan volume growth and GDP change point to the countercyclical movements of the leverage versus capital ratio during the downward cycle in 2007–2008. The analysis of correlation patterns among the variables indicates that the total assets (and exposure) in contrast to Tier 1 capital are indeed the main contributors to the cyclical movements in the leverage. The leverage and the total assets also demonstrate a weak relation to GDP, but a stronger correlation with loan volumes to the private sector.

The introduction of the Basel III regulations on leverage is another incentive for the Czech banks to strengthen more their capital position and reduce indebtedness.

It is a major improvement over Basel II treatment of indebtedness and credit risk (Witzany 2010). On the other hand, it has certain implications. For the banks with a higher leverage level, it could lead to reduction in lending volumes and hence poses risks for the income growth and profitability. The risk appetite of the banks might increase, since the banks may be forced to choose how to optimize their capital usage. It could lead to adjustments in their business models and consequently affect their earnings.

Acknowledgments The research leading to these results received funding from the People Programme (Marie Curie Actions) of the European Union's Seventh Framework Programme FP7/2007-2013 under REA Grant Agreement Number 609642. We also acknowledge support from the Czech Science Foundation (Grant 15-00036S). The views expressed in the paper are those of the authors and not necessarily those of our institutions.

References

Adrian T, Shin HS (2010) Liquidity and leverage. J Financ Intermediat 19:418–437
Adrian T, Shin HS (2011) Procyclical leverage and value-at-risk. Social Science Research Network. Rochester
Avery RB, Berger A (1991) Risk-based capital and deposit insurance reform. J Bank Finance 15:847–874
Baxter M, King R (1999) Measuring business cycles: approximate band-pass filters for economic time series. Rev Econ Stat 81:575–593
BCBS (2010) Basel III: a global regulatory framework for more resilient banks and banking systems. Bank for International Settlements, Basel
BCBS (2014) Basel III leverage ratio framework and disclosure requirements, Jan. 2014. Bank for International Settlements, Basel
BCBS (2015) Frequently asked questions on the Basel III leverage ratio framework. Bank for International Settlements, Basel
Berger AN, Bouwman C (2013) How does capital affect bank performance during financial crises? J Financ Econ 109:146–176
Blundell-Wignall A, Atkinson P (2010) Thinking beyond Basel III: necessary Solutions for Capital and Liquidity. OECD J: Financ Mark Trends 2010:9–33
Brei M, Gambacorta L (2014) The leverage ratio over the cycle. Bank for International Settlements, Basel
Cathcart L, El-Jahel L, Jabbour R (2013) The Basel capital requirement puzzle: a study of changing interconnections between Leverage and risk-based capital ratios. In: European Financial Management Association Meeting
Černohorský J, Šobotníková P, Teplý P (2011) The challenges of Basel III for the Czech banking sector. In: International conference on finance and banking—proceedings. Silesian University, School of Business Administration, Ostrava, Czech Republic, pp 84–99
Cevik RnK, Dibooglu S, Kutan A (2016) Real and financial sector studies in Central and Eastern Europe: a review. Czech J Econ Finance (Finance a uver) 66:2–31
EBA (2015) EBA report on potential implications for banks' business models from regulatory measures
Estrella A, Park S, Peristiani S (2006) Capital ratios as predictors of bank failure. Social Science Research Network, Rochester
Fungáčová Z, Jakubík P (2013) Bank stress tests as an information device for emerging markets: the case of Russia. Czech J Econ Finance (Finance a uver) 63:87–105

Gropp R, Heider F (2009) The determinants of bank capital structure. European Central Bank

Izák V (2011) The Welfare state and economic growth. Prague Econ Pap 2011:291–308

Janda K (2011) Inefficient credit rationing and public support of commercial credit provision. J Inst Theor Econ (JITE) 167:371–391

Janda K, Michalikova E, Skuhrovec J (2013) Credit support for export: robust evidence from the Czech Republic. World Econ 36:1588–1610. doi:10.1111/twec.12061

Kalemli-Ozcan S, Sorensen B, Yesiltas S (2011) Leverage across firms, banks, and countries. National Bureau of Economic Research

Kellermann K, Schlag C (2013) Occupy risk weighting: how the minimum leverage ratio dominates capital requirements: A Swiss example. J Financ Reg Compliance 21:353–372. doi:10.1108/JFRC-06-2012-0019

Klinger T, Teply P (2016) The nexus between systemic risk and Sovereign crises. Czech J Econ Finance (Finance a uver) 66:50–69

Matejašák M (2015) Did the Czech and Slovak Banks increase their capital ratios by decreasing risk, increasing capital or both? Procedia Econ Finance 25:256–263. doi:10.1016/S2212-5671 (15)00736-4

Musílek P (2011) European system of financial supervision. Český finanční a účetní časopis 2011:7–17

Nuno G, Thomas T (2013) Bank leverage cyles. Society for Economic Dynamics

Stádník B (2014) The volatility puzzle of bonds. Vilnius, Lithuania, pp 313–319

Stádník B, Miečinskienė A (2015) Complex model of market price development and its simulation. J Bus Econ Manag 16:786–807. doi:10.3846/16111699.2015.1076028

Šútorová B, Teplý P (2013) The impact of Basel III on lending rates of EU Banks. Czech J Econ Finance (Finance a uver) 63:226–243

Šútorová B, Teplý P (2014) The Level of capital and the value of EU Banks under Basel III. Prague Econ Pap 23:143–161. doi:10.18267/j.pep.477

Teply P, Vejdovec O (2012) An analysis of economic capital allocation of global banks. Int J Soc Behav Educ Econ Bus Ind Eng 6:953–956

Witzany J (2010) On deficiencies and possible improvements of the Basel II unexpected loss single-factor model. Czech J Econ Finance (Finance a uver) 60:252–268

Chapter 16
Alternative Approaches to Insurance of Extreme Flood Risk

Hana Bártová

Abstract Extreme flood risk belongs to actual issues of insurance industry. Flood risk is higher than in the past due to extreme events caused also by climate changes. This risk influences negatively the role of commercial insurance. Insurers make exceptions in cover of extreme flood claims. Risk of excessive floods becomes uninsurable and insurers look for alternative approaches to cover extreme impacts of flood risk realization. An effective solution is offered by cooperation among insurers, state and supervisor based on insurance pool. Reserves are concentrated within common flood fund. In case of extreme floods, fund covers excessive claims. Uninsurable flood risk is mitigated through pool system. Other approaches are provided by alternative risk transfer methods. Cover of extreme flood risk is provided by selected financial instruments and divided among different financial market participants. Extreme flood risk is also significant in conditions of foreign insurance markets. Alternative approaches have been introduced in the USA, Great Britain, Norway, etc. Common features of mentioned approaches are a system based on cooperation of related participants and a need to cover extreme flood risk.

Keywords Uninsurable risk · Flood · Alternative risk transfer · Czech insurance market

16.1 Introduction

Extreme flood risk is a part of current issues of insurance industry. This risk weakens the role of commercial insurance. Insurers make exceptions in cover of extreme flood claims. Flood risk is higher than in the past due to extreme events caused also by effects of climate change.

H. Bártová (✉)
Department of Banking and Insurance, University of Economics, Prague, Nam.
W. Churchilla 4, 130 67 Prague, Czech Republic
e-mail: hana.bartova@vse.cz

© Springer International Publishing AG 2017   173
D. Procházka (ed.), *New Trends in Finance and Accounting*,
Springer Proceedings in Business and Economics,
DOI 10.1007/978-3-319-49559-0_16

Reflecting the changing conditions, commercial insurance still belongs to significant means of extreme flood risk cover. However, there are alternative approaches to deal with extreme losses. New trends in flood risk development offer pool systems based on mutual cooperation among different members of insurance market and innovative risk transfer methods.

Extreme flood risk is the most significant non-life risk in the Czech insurance market. Floods in 1997 and 2002 had significant impacts on whole economy and have changed general approach of insurers. A system of flood zones was established including the fourth-riskiest flood zone, which is practically uninsurable through standard insurance products. New ways of effective solution of uninsurable flood risk have been developed. A possibility of protection based on flood pool is introduced within the chapter focused on alternatives in uninsurable flood risk cover.

Foreign insurers solve the same problem with dealing of extreme consequences of flood risk. Non-life flood risk becomes continuously uninsurable. A cover of flood risk is non-profitable from a view of commercial insurers. Nevertheless, a cover of flood risk is seriously important to maintain availability of effective commercial insurance and to protect threatened individuals, property and sustainable development in insurance industry, respectively, in economy. Selected foreign approaches to extreme flood risk are described in the last chapter.

16.2   Extreme Flood Risk

Extreme flood events influence negatively lives, health and property in different economies in the world. These events are enormous and unpredictable and have wide range of consequences and serious negative impacts connected with uncertainty and risk assessment. Extreme floods, such as results of extreme events, are often repeating events. In conditions of the Czech insurance market, we assume that extreme flood risk is each flood, which has wider impact than local flood and extends into the riskiest fourth flood zone, which is uninsurable through standard insurance products. We highlight floods in 1997 and 2002 in the Czech Republic such as extreme floods. The fourth flood zone is a subject of uninsurable risk as a result of extreme flood risk realization in the past.

Risk of floods has negative impact on insurance industry. Random events cause enormous and unexpected losses. Individual insurers cover flood consequences, which exceed risk calculations. Despite improvement in forecasting methods, extreme flood risk has changed existing insurance business. Prudential approach and technical reserves could be insufficient. Reserves are almost continuously increased. New regulatory requirements on appropriate risk management have limited possibility to influence negative development of extreme flood risk. Risk mitigation actions of insurers are ongoing. Commercial insurance looks for effective ways of solution to deal with negative impacts of floods.

The role of commercial insurance protection is weakened by risk realization of excessive losses, which occurs more often. Risk realization has negative impact on decreasing value of property in flood-affected areas and also has impact on urban development. Repetitive claims meet a need to build anti-flood barriers and to implement preventive measures. In order to protect property, health and lives against consequences of floods, governments of affected countries look for an effective solution. Existing methods fail.

An issue of loss solution of extreme flood risk has two points of view—national level and regional level. The Czech landscape is typical for its density of rivers and streams. The worst claims development was dated in 1997 and in 2002, which were caused by floods at the national level. In 1997, natural catastrophe of flood requested 62.6 billion CZK, which has meant 3.3% GDP. Vast losses almost stopped life in hundreds of municipalities, infrastructure collapsed, and countryside was changed. After a wave of solidarity and government interventions, the Czech authorities have financed modern rescue system and recovery of flood-affected areas and have organized prevention process. Subsequently widespread floods in 2002 displayed unpreparedness of systems mentioned above, which were in progress and losses exceeded the last enormous flood in 1997. Total flood costs in 2002 were 73.14 billion CZK. It equals to 2.8% GDP. Reinsurers had covered more than 87% of insured costs (28.7 billion CZK). Totally the Czech insurance companies paid 32.9 billion CZK to insured clients (Czech Insurance Association 2016). In a half of the year 2016, there were announced more than 5 thousand of flood insurance events (i.e., 438% growth in comparison with previous year). Overall losses have exceeded a level of 215 million CZK (i.e., nearly 800% year-on-year growth in losses for the same time period).

The state has started a process of improved rescue system implementation, early warning system and process including recover of flood remains. The state authorities have determined a strategic target—to reduce costs of claims removed and to increase expenditure on prevention. Nevertheless, partial modifications of anti-flood barriers, aquatic constructions and other arrangements have not solved negative impacts on property of inhabitants affected by twenty-year, thirty-year and also hundred-year floods (Camrová and Jílková 2006). Flood risks have not been removed. We can distinguish four flood zones including the riskiest uninsurable flood zone.

Foreign situation is not different from the Czech case. Extreme flood events result in inability of commercial insurers to cover extreme flood losses. New approaches to cover extreme flood risk are developed. Changing relations within different members of insurance market appear. Some of them benefit from alternative risk transfer, or from new cooperation performing in insurance market. Both of these effects are described in the following chapters.

16.3   Alternatives in Uninsurable Flood Risk Cover

Changes in claims development are closely related to climate changes and to interventions in landscape as a human decision (Daňhel et al. 2008). Nevertheless, there are alternative approaches to cover extreme flood risk. Alternative ways, mentioned in this paper, are based on cooperation within participants of insurance market and on alternative risk transfer methods.

16.3.1   Pool System of Cooperation

An alternative system based on cooperation benefits from positive effects of insurance pool system. This model consists of three main components: state, insurance companies and insurance intermediaries. An insurance pool constitutes a core of the model. The pool is designed as a fund serving to save membership payments and fees. Insurance companies are members of the pool. Membership in the insurance pool is compulsory for predetermined group of insurance companies, which provide non-life insurance of property and household contents. Participation in the pool is based on compulsory entry fee and regular payments based on contribution to the pool according insurers' share to the pool. In case of extreme flood, payments from the pool cover losses of insurers' clients. Pool resources have a special purpose and are strictly determined to cover extreme flood costs.

Pool approach includes four key features—compulsory participation of insurers, profitability of the pool, pool contribution of insurers based on equal principles and the state supervision to control of pool activity. Contribution to the pool, insurance payments, accumulation of reserves and net premium calculation are described in detail (Bártová and Hanzlík 2013).

16.3.2   Alternative Risk Transfer Methods

Next to the pool, extreme flood risk can be covered by alternative risk transfer (ART). Methods of ART are known since 1960s in the USA. Insurance goals are fulfilled by instruments, which do not have primary insurance features. Such reasons to apply ART are listed customization, flexibility, cross-sector integration, costs reduction and exceptions of insurance cover formed in insurance market in comparison with standard insurance products (Banks 2004).

Insurers are perceived as traditional credit investors. Due to implementation of ART methods, there are convergence movements within general insurance and other financial market participants. Risk products are provided by insurers (reinsurers) or banks (investment banks, funds, etc.). Institutions offer ART products, which increase risk capacity of financial market. Financial risk is transferred to end users through ART products. End users are represented by insurers, reinsurers, banks or corporations.

Advantages of ART are mentioned such as increasing insurance (reinsurance) capacity, elimination of insurance (reinsurance) premium rates volatility, cheaper insurance (reinsurance) protection, use of capital markets capacity, reduction in credit risk and tax optimization (Banks 2004).

ART is usually known such as multi-year contracts, which cover broad range of risks. Contracts are customized according to consumers' needs. ART increases limits of insurability in comparison with only standard insurance products. ART offers self-insurance and reduce moral hazard of insured subjects. Insurance risks are also secured by provided securities or derivatives.

Risk is transferred to risk bearer. Risk is usually taken by captive insurance (reinsurance) company, risk retention group, capital market including special-purpose vehicles, pool, or is mitigated within self-insurance. Risk takers provide risk transfer through portfolio of ART instruments such as finite reinsurance, insurance-linked bonds (securities), insurance option, insurance swap, contingent capital or multi-products. ART instruments support the meaning of convergence of insurance and other segments of financial market. ART methods are not so widespread in conditions of the Czech insurance market. However, ART methods in general offer an alternative way to deal with extreme uninsurable flood risk.

16.4   Foreign Approaches to Extreme Flood Risk

Excessive losses caused by floods are common features of several economies in the world. Changes in global climate affect loss development. Insurance cover of the most of commercial insurance products is insufficient. Insurance companies change insurance conditions and make exceptions of insurance protection. Risk realization has negative impact on decreasing value of property in flood-affected areas and also has impact on urban development. Repetitive claims meet a need to build anti-flood barriers and to implement preventive measures.

In order to protect property, health and lives against consequences of floods, foreign governments look for an effective solution. Some foreign solutions are also applicable in conditions of the Czech Republic. A few examples of developed systems are summarized below:

- National Flood Insurance Program (the USA)
- Flood Re (UK of Great Britain and Northern Ireland)
- Natural Catastrophe Compensation System (the Kingdom of Norway)

Mentioned approaches are existing systems of flood loss solutions. The approaches are different, but have similar aim. Some features could be a starting point in case of extreme flood risk solution in conditions of the Czech insurance market (Bártová and Hanzlík 2015).

16.4.1 National Flood Insurance Program

National Flood Insurance Program (NFIP) is a system established in the USA. The Program is a substitute for insurance products in cases of poor commercial insurance protection. NFIP covers only risks of floods.

NFIP was set up to solve consequences of flood risk realization, which include following:

- insurance exclusions
- flood risk areas founding
- increasing costs of commercial insurance protection

The Program was introduced by the Congress of the USA in 1968. NFIP was implemented by the National Flood Insurance Act. Insurance protection is guaranteed by the state and provided by insurance companies. In 2010, nearly 5.5 million of American households were members of the Program. Repetitive and excessive claims had negative impacts on results of the Program, which has reported financial losses (loss of 24 billion USD in 2014).

Insurance companies are members of Federal Emergency Management Agency (FEMA), which provides insurance protection according to risk profile of insured objects and distinguishes types of protected objects. The Program also differentiates the two groups of protected areas:

- high-risk area
- medium- and low-risk area

Insurance is offered by insurance agents. Losses are settled by value of costs paid for loss removal and by value of property at the moment of risk realization. Minimum annual premium costs 129 USD.

The state also supports building of anti-flood barriers, which can decrease costs of losses (respectively, costs of insurance protection). Attendance in the Program is compulsory for objects located in high-risk areas. The main advantages of the NFIP are following:

- simple differentiation of risks (high and medium/low)
- two risk profiles of risk areas
- compulsory attendance

Significant disadvantage of the Program is unprofitable development. However, the NFIP provides cover of uninsurable flood risks and cooperates with commercial insurance companies.

16.4.2   Flood Re

Flood Re is an approach focused on solution of uninsurable excessive flood risk in Great Britain. Flood Re is a part of Flood Re Scheme, which has been implemented into the Water Act legislation since 2014. Governmental organization DEFRA (Department for Environment, Food and Rural Affairs) prepares and provides regulation. Experts, insurance specialists, the British association of insurance companies, representatives of banks and brokers, members of the Parliament and other interest and lobby groups took attendance in a process of approach definition.

The main aim of the British government was to reduce occurrence of uninsurable objects in risk areas and to influence trend of increasing costs of commercial insurance protection. The approach should be an effective solution offering protection for 350 thousand British households. Costs of insurance protection were calculated on the level of 210 GBP annually.

Flood Re Scheme distinguishes roles of system participants:

- DEFRA
- the state (the Parliament)
- National Audit Office
- supervisor

DEFRA is responsible for legislation and for ensuring of the main aim (i.e., an effective cover of uninsurable flood risks). DEFRA screens risk profile and provides risk assessment of floods. Flood Re subsequently participates in financial management and provides information to DEFRA, which analysis impacts on public finance and defines objects of insurance protection. DEFRA reports information to the British Parliament, which is connected with the National Audit Office (NAO). NAO controls compliance with rules of economy, effectiveness and efficiency. Authority of supervision takes care about legislation and prepares rules binding for insurance companies and analysis compliance with capital requirements of commercial insurance companies.

The main advantages of the Flood Re are following:

- strengthened role of commercial insurance industry
- unified legislation
- clear definition of reserves establishment and administration
- changing reserves in case of negative risk development
- compatibility of risk assessment and calculation of premium
- prevention of increasing costs of insurance protection

Flood Re benefits from results of wide discussion with experts. Flood Re is a non-profitable entity. Management of Flood Re has also introduced a system of issuing flood bonds. Disadvantages of Flood Re are difficult legislation and high number of administrative participants. Intermediary of insurance protection has not been defined clearly.

16.4.3   Natural Catastrophe Compensation System

Natural Catastrophe Compensation System (NCCS) of Norway was set up as a reaction to the most frequent non-life losses caused by floods. NCCS covers negative impacts of excessive flood risk realization. NCCS also supports research focused on prevention and reduction in risks, which are connected with climate changes. The system includes the Norwegian Natural Disaster Fund and the Norwegian Natural Perils Pool.

Norway suffers from natural catastrophes especially due to its unsuitable location. In 1929, the Natural Disaster Fund was established in order to help in dealing with consequences of natural damages. According results of NCCS research, the most significant natural damage in Norway is caused by flood, which is followed by landslide and storm. Compensation for flood losses paid from the fund reached the level of 128 thousand NOK in 2014. Nevertheless, payments from the fund also cover measures for improving safety measures after natural disasters. Compensation of flood risk realization equaled to 73% of overall fund compensations in 2014. Over 2000 of claims were settled in 2014. The highest claims were recognized in 2012, i.e., nearly 3500 of claims (Consorcio Seguros 2016).

Respecting recent development, the fund has focused on safety functions in crisis situations to reduce major accidents and amount of claims. The highest compensation in 2014 was dedicated to destroyed roads and bridges and to recovery of agriculture land.

Reserves of the fund are also considered as appropriate to ensure efficient and qualitative protection of risk exposed area. The fund has to be responded to changing climate conditions. However, the whole society and public sector tend to cooperate and reflect a complex of given tasks—operational measures in case of risk realization, land use planning, emergency procedures, compensation and safety measures. These tasks are solved in cooperation within public matters. Individual plans are considered as not so effective with respect to extreme claims and excessive losses.

The system focuses on risk mapping, which leads to contingency planning and improvement in crises management. This includes an extended cooperation among governmental and private entities. The cooperation constitutes one of the features, which are similar to the model of extreme flood risk cover in conditions of the Czech Republic mentioned above. Other similar features are pool-based approach and fund system. Resources are concentrated in pool and drawn in case of claims. Participation of the state, respectively, of the government is another example of similar characteristic. The main difference is a weak inclusion of commercial insurance companies, which play major role in the system described within the Czech conditions. However, both systems are focused on the same need of an effective tool, which is able to cover extreme flood risks.

16.5 Conclusion

Uninsurable risks belong to actual issues of insurance industry. These risks cause enormous losses and significantly weaken the role of commercial insurance. Insurance companies make exceptions in cover of extreme claims development. Selected risks are uninsurable through the way of commercial insurance products.

Extreme flood risk influences negatively millions of people all around the world. Property, health and lives are exposed to flood risk, which is not covered by common insurance products. Increasing losses lead to a need of an effective solution, which is able to cover realization of extreme flood risk. In specific conditions of the Czech insurance market, a solution is based on insurance pool including fund system. Cooperation among commercial insurance companies, intermediaries, state and supervisor is an integral part of the system. Reserves are accumulated within the fund and distributed in case of negative claims development to cover consequences of extreme floods.

Different approach is provided by alternative risk transfer (ART) methods. Negative impacts of floods are covered by selected portfolio of financial instruments. ART increases capacity of insurance market and availability of insurance protection. Insurance companies represent significant risk takers. Although ART methods are not widespread in conditions of the Czech insurance market, this solution offers an alternative way to deal with extreme uninsurable flood risk.

Extreme flood risk is considerable also in conditions of foreign insurance markets. Some economies have established own systems in order to influence negative effect of insurance exceptions within commercial insurance products. Similar systems (to mentioned solution of the Czech insurance market) have been developed in the USA, Great Britain or Norway. These systems are based on similar assumptions such as the Czech system. Despite some differences, foreign approaches are focused on the same need of an effective tool, which is able to cover extreme flood risks.

Current claims development of extreme floods influences negatively insurance industry. Nevertheless, commercial insurance still plays major role in cover of extreme flood risk.

Acknowledgments This paper has been prepared within the research project "Trends in Banking and Insurance within changing financial markets" (supported by the Internal Grant Competition of the University of Economics in Prague, No. IG102046).

References

Banks E (2004) Alternative risk transfer: integrated risk management through insurance, reinsurance, and the capital markets. John Wiley & Sons

Bártová H, Hanzlík K (2013) Uninsurable Risks of floods, deluges, overflows and the system of solution. Eur Financ Acc J, Prague

Bártová H, Hanzlík K (2015) Foreign approaches to cover uninsurable risks offering opportunities for the Czech insurance market. In: Procházka D (ed) The 16th annual conference on finance and accounting. Vysoká škola ekonomická, Praha, pp 615–621

Čamrová L, Jílková J (2006) Flood losses and instruments to loss minimization. Institut pro ekonomickou a ekologickou politiku při FNH VŠE v Praze, Prague

Česká asociace pojišťoven (2013) Mimořádné živelní škody. Statistické údaje, 2007–2013. http:// cap.cz/statisticke-udaje/ostatni

Česká asociace pojišťoven (2016) Živelní škody. Statistické údaje, 2007–2016. http://cap.cz/ statisticke-udaje/zivly

Consorcio de Compensacion de Seguros (2016) The Norwegian natural catastrophe compensation system in the past and the future. http://www.consorsegurosdigital.com/en/numero-02/front-page-02/the-norwegian-natural-catastrophe-compensation-system-in-the-past-and-the-future

Daňhel J, Ducháčková E, Radová J (2008) Hlavní globální vývojové trendy ve světovém komerčním pojišťovnictví. Ekonomický časopis 56(6):598–606

Department for Environment, Food & Rural Affairs (2014) The flood reinsurance scheme—regulations. Department for Environment, Food & Rural Affairs, VB: DEFRA. https://consult. defra.gov.uk/flooding/floodreinsurancescheme/supporting_documents/Consultation%20on% 20Flood%20Re%20Regulations.pdf

Chapter 17
Non-life Insurance Purchases of Polish Households: A Study of Leading Trends

Monika Wieczorek-Kosmala, Daniel Szewieczek, Helena Ogrodnik and Maria Gorczyńska

Abstract The studies on the households' performance on non-life insurance market remain scarce. In order to fill in this gap, the aim of this paper was to provide an insight into the identification of the leading trends of the purchases of non-life insurance by households in Poland. The study has asked several questions on the contribution of households to the non-life market and on the changes of the products' structure of their purchases. It was found that the contribution of households (as the share in total non-life gross premiums written) was growing since 2002. The motor insurance-related products (with compulsory third-party liability in particular) remained most important, with the share of c.a. 70% of total non-life premiums paid by households. There were no critical changes in the insurance purchases by households, broken by products (as measured by volatility of the premiums paid).

Keywords Non-life insurance · Households · Insurance decisions · Poland

17.1 Introduction

Poland, as one of transition countries, was implementing the regulation enhancing the functioning of financial sector since the 1990s (Schipke et al. 2004). Since then, the Polish insurance market developed significantly, mainly due to the growing

M. Wieczorek-Kosmala (✉) · D. Szewieczek · H. Ogrodnik · M. Gorczyńska
Department of Corporate Finance and Insurance, Faculty of Finance and Insurance,
University of Economics in Katowice, Katowice, Poland
e-mail: m.wieczorek-kosmala@ue.katowice.pl

D. Szewieczek
e-mail: daniel.szewieczek@ue.katowice.pl

H. Ogrodnik
e-mail: helenao@ue.katowice.pl

M. Gorczyńska
e-mail: mgorczynska@ue.katowice.pl

© Springer International Publishing AG 2017   183
D. Procházka (ed.), *New Trends in Finance and Accounting*,
Springer Proceedings in Business and Economics,
DOI 10.1007/978-3-319-49559-0_17

competition. The harmonization with European Union regulations was followed by deep structural changes of the legal framework of insurance market, with the set of legal acts implemented in 2003. Further development of insurance market was observed since the Polish EU accession in May 2004, with some disturbances in the period of the global financial crisis. As reported by Swiss Re, non-life insurance markets in the CEE region (in this Poland) grew significantly till 2007, as noted by Lorenzo and Lauff (2005), Enz (2006), Baez and Staib (2007), Staib and Bevere (2008). However, after the crisis this growth was significantly slowed down due to both the economic downturn and the number of natural hazards (Staib and Bevere 2009, 2010, 2011; Fan et al. 2012; Seiler et al. 2013). However, there is a virtual lack of research related exclusively to non-life market performance in Poland. The existing research debate often focuses on the performance of the insurance sector as a whole and its contribution to financial sector (Wieczorkiewicz and Dąbrowska 2002; Wartini 2009; Handschke 2009), which is consistent with the leading worldwide research interests in insurance (e.g., Scholtens 2000; Hermes and Lensink 2000; Bonin and Wachtel 2003; Reininger et al. 2002).

The insurance demand of households remains relatively well explored in the context of life insurance (e.g., Li et al. 2007). However, the studies related to the non-life insurance decisions of households remain scarce. Probably, the reason is that the determinants of the demand for non-life insurance from households perspective are highly diversified and complex. The nature of household indicates that the demand for protection is driven by financial and psychological stimulators. A strong correlation of non-life insurance purchases with the level of households' wealth was found by Dragos (2014).

Similar cognitive gap is observed in Polish studies, as there are virtually no studies related to the performance of households on the Polish non-life insurance market. Accordingly, the purpose of this paper was to identify the leading trends of the purchases of non-life insurance by households in Poland. The time frame of this study covers the period since the beginning of the new millennium. Accordingly, it reflects the changes followed by the process of transition, then the changes in the period of European Union accession, and the possible fluctuations observed in the aftermath of the global financial crisis. In particular, the study asks several research questions: (1) Is the contribution of households to the non-life insurance market increasing? (2) In which segment of the market the contribution of households is most relevant, considering the products' structure? (3) Are there any critical changes in the products' structure of households' insurance purchases?

In order to answer these questions, the study revises several variables based on the volume of gross premiums written. For the closer look on the Polish non-life market, it relies on the data provided by national statistics office (GUS 2014) and in supervisory body databases (KNUiFE 2002, 2003), in the period of 2002–2014. However, the study is preceded by a more general outlook on the non-life insurance market in Poland, in cross-country comparative basis. For these purposes, the data accessible in OECD database (insurance statistics) were used for the years 2000–2013.

The paper is organized as follows. The first section offers a general insight into the developments of Polish non-life insurance market. The second section provides the analysis and discussion on the general contribution of the households to the non-life insurance market in Poland, with regard to the gross premiums written paid by households, broken by insurance products. The third section revises more in-depth the structure of non-life gross premiums written paid by households in the context of the changes in the products structure. The fourth section concludes the study.

17.2   Polish Non-life Insurance Market—Introductory Considerations

The outlook of the general performance of the non-life market, in cross-country comparative perspective, allows understanding the specifics of the given domestic market. This supports more in-depth studies, such as the contribution of households, which is developed further in this study. The performance of insurance market is usually analyzed by the application of three core parameters: (1) volume of premiums written, (2) insurance penetration ratio (gross premiums written to GDP), and (3) insurance density ratio (gross premiums written per capita). The detailed data for the period 2000–2013 for Poland, as compared to Czech Republic, Hungary, and Slovak Republic (as the countries which overcame transition and accessed European Union at the same time), are provided in Annex. The comparison includes additionally the data on average for the 15 "old member" European Union countries (hereafter EU-15: Belgium, France, Italy, Luxembourg, Netherlands, Germany, Denmark, Ireland, UK, Greece, Spain, Portugal, Austria, Sweden, and Finland).

The data in Fig. 17.1 indicate the similar trends of the overall changes in the non-life insurance market between the compared countries. The dynamics of the gross premiums written was similar, with the visible decline after the crisis 2008+.

However, the data in Fig. 17.2 indicate that the insurance penetration ratio strongly differed between the UE-15 and emerging new EU countries. The insurance penetration in Czech Republic was significantly higher than in Poland, Hungary, and Slovak Republic. Trend analysis indicated that the insurance premium remained stable over time and the variance of the ratio was driven mainly by the changes of GDP. The observable distance of the penetration ratio between the EU-15 and the other compared countries was not narrowing. It signalizes that the growing GDP was not bringing substantial growth in insurance coverage demand. The differences in the non-life insurance market development between the EU-15 and the other countries were confirmed by the data in Fig. 17.3.

The differences of the insurance density are partially explainable by the historical and cultural conditions, in this the impact of transition (the lack of commercial insurance). The insurance density index in Poland, the Czech Republic, Slovak

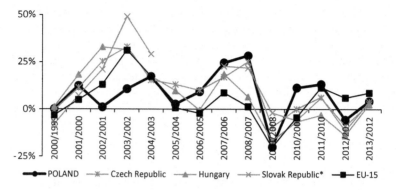

Fig. 17.1 Dynamics of gross premiums written on non-life markets. *Asterisk* data on gross premiums written in 2005 not available. *Source* Authorial computation based on OECD.Stat (2016)

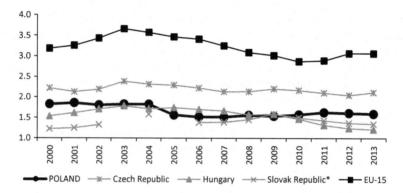

Fig. 17.2 Insurance penetration ratio of non-life insurance markets (as a percentage). *Asterisk* data for 2003 and 2005 not available. *Source* OECD.Stat (2016)

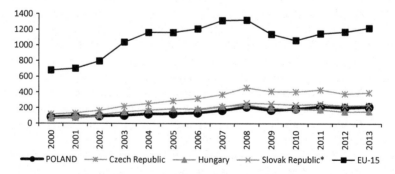

Fig. 17.3 Insurance density ratio of non-life insurance markets (in USD per capita). *Asterisk* data for 2003 and 2005 not available. *Source* OECD.Stat (2016)

Republic, and Hungary was associated with a significantly lower value of assets that can be insured in the commercial entities and households, as well as property insurance distant priority in the hierarchy of needs.

Generally, the insurance density and penetration ratios indicate that the observed differences between the EU-15 and the analyzed post-transition countries are not diminishing over time. The persistence of such a trend will cause that the assets of entities in the growing post-transition countries will be less protected against the effects of random events, as compared to assets of the entities in the EU-15.

17.3   Contribution of Households to the Non-life Market in Poland

The importance of non-life insurance for households in relation to the entire property insurance market in Poland is changing over time, as presented in Fig. 17.4. There was a visible increase of the share of premiums paid by households, in total premiums paid by all entities purchasing insurance on the non-life market. This trend may indicate that the interest in insurance (and the insurance awareness of households) has increased. The increase goes along with the economic development of Poland and with the increase of household's wealth subject to insurance coverage.

Figure 17.5 shows the contribution of households to the non-life market, broken by the insurance products. Households remain the greatest contributors to the compulsory third-party liability insurance for the owners of motor vehicles. This contribution is steadily declining; however, it was still of c.a. 75% in 2014. Households contribute also significantly to the Casco insurance of land vehicles. In general, the contribution of households to Polish motor insurance sector shall be still regarded as relevant. Similar trend (the decrease of contribution) is observed in the case of accident and sickness insurance, which is quite obvious—on the Polish

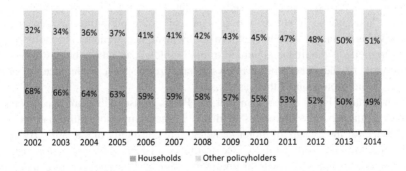

Fig. 17.4 Contribution of Polish households to non-life insurance market (by the share in gross premiums written). *Source* Authorial computation based on GUS (2014), KNUiFE (2002, 2003)

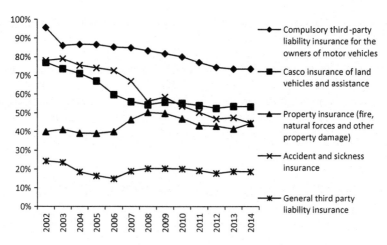

Fig. 17.5 Contribution of Polish households in the non-life insurance market by insurance products. *Source* Authorial computation based on GUS (2014), KNUiFE (2002, 2003)

non-life market this insurance is mainly sold as a component of motor insurance package. The contribution to property insurance (such as fire, theft) remains relatively stable, similarly as the contribution to the general third-party liability insurance. In addition, in the case of third-party liability insurance this contribution is rather low, which indicates that the individual cognition of the need of liability coverage shall be judged as low.

17.4 The Products' Structure of Non-life Purchases by Polish Households

17.4.1 General Preferences

Figure 17.6 provides another insight into the insurance products' preferences of Polish households. It shows the structure of gross premiums written paid by households on the non-life market, broken by insurance products. Accordingly, this measure reflects the financial burden of households incurred by the cost of non-life insurance. At the same time, it allows to analyze the basic preferences of households in the protection of their assets.

The data in Fig. 17.6 confirm that the Polish households purchase mainly the motor insurance. The premiums paid due to the compulsory third-party liability insurance for the owners of motor vehicles were constantly of c.a. 50%. By adding the premiums paid due to the Casco insurance of land vehicles, motor insurance represented of c.a. 70% of total premiums paid by households in Poland on the non-life market. It is a significant contribution. The sickness and accident insurance,

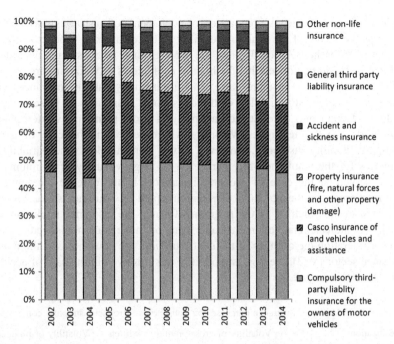

Fig. 17.6 Structure of non-life gross premiums written by households in Poland, broken by insurance products. *Source* Authorial computation based on GUS (2014), KNUiFE (2002, 2003)

as a relevant element of motor insurance packages, remained relatively stable, with c.a. 7% share in total non-life gross premiums paid by households.

Property insurance purchases remained relatively constant over the analyzed period and currently represent of c.a. 20% of premiums paid by the households. There was a significant upward trend, which is explainable by the rapid development of Polish real estate market, accompanied by the growth of the mortgage market (where property insurance of real estate is required as a collateral of mortgage loans). The share of the purchases of general third-party liability insurance (non-compulsory) remained low. However, in the post-crisis period there was a slight growing trend. Other types of non-life insurance (e.g., business interruption and other financial insurance) did not constitute a significant impact on the structure and value of total premiums written in this class of insurance.

17.4.2   Volatility of the Products' Structure

The analysis of products structure of non-life insurance purchases by households has shown some identifiable changes. In order to answer the question about the possible critical changes of this product structure, the analysis was deepened by the computation of coefficients of variation for the defined variables (as specified in

Table 17.1). In this case, a comparison of coefficients of variations may be interpreted as the signal of the scale of volatility of the changes in product's structure purchases of the households. If high, the changes shall be considered as critical.

First, it should be noticed that the highest coefficients of variations are observed in the case of property insurance and general third-party liability insurance, which signalizes the greatest variability of the households' purchases of these insurance products. Taking into account the variability of gross premiums written paid by households (V_2), the highest volatility was observed in the case of general third-party liability insurance. However, it was comparable to the variability of premiums for the whole non-life market (V_1). High volatility of premiums was also observed in the case of property insurance. In the case of the remainder insurance products, the volatility of premiums paid by households was lower, as compared to the volatility of the premiums for non-life insurance market in total, which may indicate relatively more stable situation in the households sector. Taking into consideration the changes of the contribution of the households to the non-life insurance sector (V_3), the highest volatility was observed in the case of accidents and sickness insurance.

Table 17.1 Volatility of insurance purchases by households—products' structure context

Specification	Volatility of gross premiums written (%)			Volatility of products' structure ratios (%)	
	Market in total (V_1)	Households (V_2)	Households to market in total (V_3)	Market in total (V_4)	Households (V_5)
All non-life insurance products	24.11	14.89	10.01	n.a.	n.a.
Motor insurance (in total)	19.62	12.09	8.84	5.44	3.96
In this					
Casco insurance of land vehicles and assistance	14.60	6.12	13.86	10.67	14.34
Compulsory third-party liability insurance for the owners of motor vehicles	23.75	17.63	7.54	4.43	5.80
Property insurance (fire, natural forces and other property damage)	29.32	31.14	8.64	6.83	17.67
General third-party liability insurance	44.16	42.30	12.67	21.92	29.50
Accident and sickness insurance	32.87	14.74	20.05	11.17	5.32

Source Authorial computation based on GUS (2014), KNUiFE (2002, 2003)
Notes Table presents coefficients of variations for the following variables: V_1—non-life gross premiums written in total (for all policyholders); V_2—non-life gross premiums written paid by households; V_3—the percentage share of non-life gross premiums written paid by households in non-life gross premiums written in total (V_2 relative to V_1); V_4—the products' structure of non-life gross premiums written in total (for all policyholders); V_5—the products' structure of non-life gross premiums written paid by households

Similar conclusions can be drawn if taking into account the volatility of products' structure ratios. In the case of households (V_5), the highest volatility was observed for the share of general third-party liability, and it was visibly higher as compared to the market as a whole (V_4). The more stable share in the products structure of the households segment of the non-life market was observed in the case of motor insurance (and in compulsory third-party liability insurance in particular), then in the case of accident and sickness insurance. In general, the coefficients of variation do not signalize critical changes in the products' structure of non-life purchases by households in Poland in the analyzed time frame.

17.5 Conclusion

The Polish non-life insurance market develops similarly as the remainder post-transition countries, if taking into account the premiums written, insurance density and insurance penetration ratios. This study aimed at extending the perception of the general contribution of households to the Polish non-life market, as such studies remain scarce. It confirmed that the contribution of households to the total non-life insurance market in Poland was growing since 2002. The data indicated that the share of premiums paid by households has increased in the total premiums paid by all types of policyholders. However, taking into account the contribution broken by types of insurance products, this contribution diminished in the case of motor insurance-related products and extended in the case of property and liability insurance. Taking account the products structure of Polish non-life insurance market in the context of premiums paid by households, the study has shown a significant contribution of motor insurance package, with c.a. 70% of total premiums paid by households on non-life market. There was an observable upward trend in the case of property insurance, which was related to the growth of real estate market in Poland. Addressing the third research question, concerning the identification of critical changes of the products structure purchases of households on non-life market, the study did not found any significant variations in the analyzed period.

Although this study provides rather general comments on the non-life insurance purchases of Polish households, it offers a starting point for further, more in-depth studies. In particular, it may be extended by the cross-country comparisons, as well as by the extended studies within a given type of insurance products. Such approach may finally lead to a more complex study, revealing the drivers of households demand on non-life products, in this the influence of macro- and microeconomic factors.

Annex

Main characteristics of non-life insurance markets in Poland (PL), as compared to Czech Republic (CZ), Hungary (HU), Slovak Republic (SLO), and the EU-15 countries

Country	2000	2001	2002	2003	2004	2005	2006	2007	2008	2009	2010	2011	2012	2013
Gross premiums written on non-life insurance markets (in billions of USD)														
PL	3.19	3.58	3.62	4.02	4.71	4.84	5.29	6.59	8.46	6.77	7.54	8.54	8.07	8.42
CZ	1.24	1.38	1.73	2.30	2.66	3.01	3.32	3.88	4.86	4.41	4.42	4.70	4.17	4.34
HU	0.72	0.86	1.14	1.50	1.76	1.94	1.93	2.29	2.44	2.03	1.90	1.84	1.59	1.63
SLO	0.35	0.38	0.46	0.69	0.89	n.a.	0.95	1.17	1.43	1.40	1.32	1.40	1.28	1.32
EU-15	309.56	325.04	367.47	482.04	565.60	570.05	558.09	606.82	615.41	491.76	470.55	524.59	556.60	605.13
The share of non-life market in total insurance market (gross premiums written on non-life insurance markets as a percentage of gross premiums written in total)														
PL (%)	66.4	65.6	64.9	62.6	62.2	50.5	43.8	41.7	34.3	41.1	42.0	44.3	41.9	46.0
CZ (%)	67.8	65.0	62.5	61.2	60.7	61.6	61.3	59.3	59.3	58.2	54.0	53.6	53.1	54.3
HU (%)	54.1	58.2	58.9	59.9	59.4	56.0	49.6	45.1	47.5	49.7	46.8	45.4	47.0	45.5
SLO (%)	59.3	57.1	56.9	59.1	59.7	n.a.	52.7	50.3	47.7	48.5	47.0	46.8	46.2	44.5
EU-15 (%)	39.2	42.3	44.6	45.2	44.8	42.1	35.7	34.3	38.1	35.6	35.2	37.9	40.0	42.3
Insurance penetration of non-life insurance markets														
PL	1.8	1.9	1.8	1.8	1.8	1.6	1.5	1.5	1.6	1.5	1.6	1.6	1.6	1.6
CZ	2.2	2.1	2.2	2.4	2.3	2.3	2.2	2.1	2.1	2.2	2.2	2.1	2.0	2.1
HU	1.5	1.6	1.7	1.8	1.7	1.7	1.7	1.7	1.6	1.6	1.5	1.3	1.2	1.2
SLO	1.2	1.3	1.3	n.a.	1.6	n.a.	1.4	1.4	1.5	1.6	1.5	1.4	1.4	1.3
EU-15	3.2	3.3	3.4	3.7	3.6	3.5	3.4	3.2	3.1	3.0	2.9	2.9	3.1	3.1

(continued)

(continued)

Country	2000	2001	2002	2003	2004	2005	2006	2007	2008	2009	2010	2011	2012	2013
Insurance density of non-life insurance markets (in USD per capita)														
PL	81.7	92.2	93.4	103.5	120.9	124.3	135.7	168.7	216.3	173.4	191.5	217.4	204.7	215.6
CZ	120.3	133.9	168.2	223.3	257.9	291.5	320.5	372.8	460.9	413.5	408.8	433.7	383.2	399.1
HU	70.7	83.6	111.6	147.2	173.3	190.8	189.8	225.5	240.2	200.4	187.6	182.2	156.7	160.2
SLO	65.4	70.5	85.6	n.a.	165.2	n.a.	177.3	217.8	263.8	256.9	242.1	255.0	231.5	238.0
EU-15	678.9	702.2	795.5	1037.1	1162.5	1162.4	1209.1	1315.5	1321.6	1141.3	1061.6	1149.8	1172.3	1221.4

Source OECD.Stat (2016)

References

Baez M, Staib D (2007) World insurance in 2006: premiums came back to "life". Sigma, No. 4/2007. Swiss Re, Zurich

Bonin J, Wachtel P (2003) Financial sector development in transition economies: lessons from the first decade. In: Financial markets, institutions and instruments, vol 12(1). New York University, Salomon Center

Dragos S (2014) Life and non-life insurance demand: the different effects of influence factors in emerging countries from Europe and Asia. Economic Research—Ekonomska Istraživanja 27 (1):169–180

Enz R (2006) World insurance in 2005: moderate premium growth, attractive profitability. Sigma, No. 5/2006. Swiss Re, Zurich

Fan I, Seiler T, Staib D (2012) World insurance in 2011: non-life ready for take-off. Sigma, No. 3/2012. Swiss Re, Zurich

GUS (2014) Polski Rynek Ubezpieczeniowy. Główny Urząd Statystyczny, Warszawa. http://stat. gov.pl/obszary-tematyczne/podmioty-gospodarcze-wyniki-finansowe/przedsiebiorstwa-finansowe/polski-rynek-ubezpieczeniowy-2014,11,4.html. Accessed 15 Jan 2016

Handschke J (2009) Polskie doświadczenie w formowaniu i rozwoju rynku ubezpieczeń—wybrane aspekty, vol 3. Wiadomości Ubezpieczeniowe, pp 56–69

Hermes N, Lensink R (2000) Financial system development in transition economies. J Bank Finance 24(4):507–524

KNUiFE (2002) Biuletyn Roczny. Rynek ubezpieczeń. Komisja Nadzoru Ubezpieczeń i Funduszy Emerytalnych, Warszawa. http://www.knf.gov.pl/opracowania/rynek_ubezpieczen/Dane_o_rynku/Dane_roczne/rocznik10.html. Accessed 15 Jan 2016

KNUiFE (2003) Biuletyn Roczny. Rynek ubezpieczeń. Komisja Nadzoru Ubezpieczeń i Funduszy Emerytalnych, Warszawa. http://www.knf.gov.pl/opracowania/rynek_ubezpieczen/Dane_o_rynku/Dane_roczne/rocznik8.html. Accessed 15 Jan 2016

Li D, Moshirian F, Nguyen P, Wee T (2007) The demand for life insurance in OECD countries. J Risk Insur 74(3):637–652

Lorenzo A, Lauff V (2005) World insurance in 2004: growing premiums and stronger balance sheets. Sigma 2/2005. Swiss Re, Zurich

OECD.Stat (2016) http://stats.oecd.org. Accessed 08 Feb 2016

Reininger T, Schardax F, Summer M (2002) Financial system transition in Central Europe: the first decade. Oesterreichische Nationalbank, Vienna

Schipke A, Beddies C, George SM, Sheridan N (2004) Capital markets and financial intermediation in the Baltics. International Monetary Fund Occasional Paper No. 228. International Monetary Fund, Washington. http://www.imf.org/external/pubs/nft/op/228/. Accessed 10 Jan 2016

Scholtens B (2000) Financial regulation and financial system architecture in Central Europe. J Bank Finance 24(4):525–553

Seiler T, Staib D, Puttaiah M (2013) World insurance in 2012: progressing on the long and winding road to recovery. Sigma, No. 3/2013. Swiss Re, Zurich

Staib D, Bevere L (2008) World insurance in 2007: emerging markets leading the way. Sigma, No. 3/2008. Swiss Re, Zurich

Staib D, Bevere L (2009) World insurance in 2008: life premiums fall in the industrialised countries—strong growth in the emerging economies. Sigma, No. 3/2009. Swiss Re, Zurich

Staib D, Bevere L (2010) World insurance in 2009: premiums dipped, but industry capital improved. Sigma, No. 2/2010. Swiss Re, Zurich

Staib D, Bevere L (2011) World insurance in 2010: premiums back to growth—capital increases. Sigma, No. 2/2011. Swiss Re, Zurich

Wartini J (2009) Wybrane wyniki działalności lokacyjnej i finansowej sektora ubezpieczeń w Polsce w warunkach globalnego kryzysu gospodarczego, vol 4. Wiadomości Ubezpieczeniowe, pp 17–28

Wieczorkiewicz A, Dąbrowska K (2002) Poziom rozwoju sektora ubezpieczeniowego w Polsce na tle instytucji ubezpieczeniowych z obszaru UE oraz Czech i Węgier, vol 3. Studia Europejskie, pp 103–120. http://www.ce.uw.edu.pl/pliki/pw/3-2002_Wieczorkiewicz.pdf. Accessed 10 Jan 2016

Chapter 18
Ukrainian Exchange Returns: The Day-of-the-Week Effect

Zoriana Matsuk and Fitim Deari

Abstract The day-of-the-week and weekend effect are examined by different authors and different evidences are found. There is no unique evidence as results of many studied factors. For example, the sample selected and methodology used is very important in results providing. This article tried to contribute also in this line brining evidence for case of Ukrainian Exchange Market. Authors believed that this study can be viewed as a pioneering work in this case. Even the study has own limitations, its evidence can be helpful for next studies and decision makers. The article contains empirical evidence that refute the day-of-the-week effect, one of the most recognized anomalies in stock markets. Evidence is generated using data from UX. Data were selected for the period January 2008–December 2015. Data were analyzed using Stata and Excel program. Data were corrected for observations belonging in Saturday. Hence, analyses were performed for trading days from Monday to Friday. Results were obtained using discretely compounded rate of return. Average return was analyzed per day and year, and then per day and month. Hence, Tuesday, Wednesday and Friday experienced a positive trend, whereas Monday and Thursday a negative trend of average return. Approaches based on the use of descriptive statistics, F-statistics and regression analysis allow refuting the weekend effect on the Ukrainian Exchange Market. Results denoted that index return in each day was negative, except Friday which was lower but non-negative. The study indicated that differences of returns between five days were insignificant. Thus, the study proved that the day-of-the-week effect wasn't found in this case. The conclusions demonstrated effectiveness of the provisions of the efficient market hypothesis with respect to Ukraine's stock market due to existence of the statistically refuted the "day-of-the-week effect". Finally, authors believe that dividing the

Z. Matsuk (✉)
Department of Finance, Ivano-Frankivsk National Technical University of Oil and Gas, 15 Karpatska St., Ivano-Frankivsk 76000, Ukraine
e-mail: zoriana_01@yahoo.com

F. Deari
Department of Finance and Accounting, South East European University, Bul. "Ilindenska" number 335, 1200 Tetovo, Republic of Macedonia
e-mail: f.deari@seeu.edu.mk

© Springer International Publishing AG 2017
D. Procházka (ed.), *New Trends in Finance and Accounting*,
Springer Proceedings in Business and Economics,
DOI 10.1007/978-3-319-49559-0_18

197

analyzed period into sub periods and using an advanced methodology is welcomed. Hence, this study remains an open window for next studies in the case of Ukrainian Stock Exchange toward examining the day-of-the-week and weekend effect.

Keywords Anomaly · Day-of-the-week effect · Efficient market hypothesis

18.1 Introduction

A characteristic feature of the present stage of transformation of the domestic stock market is a dynamic development process of trading due to the impact of globalization, financial crises, and the expansion of trading tools. The innovative nature of the stock market contributed to the improvement of securities accounting, reducing transaction costs on financial transactions, possibilities to trade structured derivatives and, accordingly, attracting individual investors for independent exchange trading.

Today the process of infrastructural changes in the stock market of Ukraine is increasing due to globalization, increased competition between exchanges, and rapid growth of on-line trading systems. In recent years not only the access speed increased, but also the rate of turnover of capital. Ukrainian exchanges become more dynamic, structured and more liquid. The change in investors' structure has led to the emergence of new models of business and the market in general.

Just a decade ago, an individual investor has been separated from the stock marketplace, and only a member of the stock exchange—broker—had the best access to information, his main clients were institutional investors, industrial and commercial multinationals. Today, Internet technologies set all investors in roughly equal conditions. The Ukrainian stock market quotes, reports and analytical studies become available to all interested in it, margin trading system decreased price level access to trading, communications become widespread, the process of attracting investment of individual investors to exchange trading develops rapidly.

It is difficult to surprise anyone in Ukraine by receiving information from Exchange webpages in online mode by any internet user. In particular at the Ukrainian Stock Exchange (http://www.ux.ua), the First Stock Trading System (http://www.pfts.ua/) anyone can get necessary information on prices and exchange rates on financial assets, get acquainted with the rules of these exchanges, receive informational messages about the risks and the main participants of exchange trade, analytical materials on financial assets that are traded on exchanges.

Moreover, through Internet exchange participants are offered round the clock access to online services—a stream of quotes in real time, visualization and technical analysis of data, news and reports of the company, tracking the status of the investment portfolio, advice on buying and selling, researching the stock market as a whole and its individual segments, debating with other investors, the possibility of mandated transactions educational training for credit, and more. In addition to receiving information on current stock prices and exchange and political and economic events that affect them, exchange participant has the opportunity to be virtually present at the exchange auctions, see their orders execution by the stockbrokers.

Another point that should be noted is lower prices for the Internet services and personal computers in Ukraine, which led to the growth of a new service offered by national exchange—possibility of investment portfolio management via the Internet.

Revolutionary changes in national stock exchanges enabled through synchronizing trades combine stock markets that operate in different parts of the world at a certain time of day into one global stock market, which operates around the clock. The development of Internet has led to the transformation of the national stock exchanges: the stock—exchanges became electronic, e-trading is much cheaper than the standard exchange for both—founders of electronic trading systems, and for their users. At present Ukrainian stock exchanges make evolutionary reorientation to individual investors.

Information is the primary source for decision making in the process of trading and gives us an idea about the causes of stock indices movement, changes in sectors, industries and stock prices of individual companies. There are a lot of information in Internet, and the trader doesn't have time to analyze it, so it's important to know how to use information. There is no doubt that for the investigation of information flows the modern methods of analysis of financial information are necessary. Even the information flow by itself is transformed; the amount of data that need to be processed is not possible without the involvement of new technologies. Exchange trade participant must have a serious analytical training, because today is not enough to have the "piece of chalk and blackboard to post quotes" as it was 10 years ago. It is obvious that one of the mechanisms of the stock exchange in the world today is the interaction of three components: market participants, information systems and technological environment, and for the choice of efficiency technological environment plays an important role.

Analyzing the information about stock market researchers claim the presence of cycles in the movement of indices that promotes the predictability of stock indexes behavior and contradicts the efficient market hypothesis. Observation of the fact of the "week effects" on the stock market is the subject of research on the part of traders seeking opportunities for profit, and by the researchers, which aims to search for evidence that the efficient market hypothesis is not implemented.

In scientific studies, the negative yield on Monday has many different and inconsistent explanations. In particular, the "Monday effect" observed on the markets of USA, Europe and Asia, suggests that this cycle recurrence is a universal phenomenon. However, Chang et al. (1993) and Yu et al. (2008) reported that the Monday effect completely disappeared from the US stock market, despite the fact that it still observed in foreign markets. On contrary, Brusa et al. (2003) showed that the "Monday effect" on the US market exists since 1990, and in foreign markets, this "traditional effect" persists. Because of different conclusions by researchers made in different countries and different periods, the question whether there is the "Monday effect" on Ukrainian stock exchange is very fascinating subject of study.

18.2   The Day-of-the-Week Effect: Theoretical Analysis

The stock market can be imagined as an information system that accumulates data of companies' financial reports, information of rating agencies and analytics of macro and microeconomic nature, political news, reports of natural disasters, etc. The reaction of the stock market on incoming information appears in the form of price changes of related securities.

In scientific sources the "Monday effect" was first introduced by French (1980), claiming that market tends to generate positive return on assets before weekend and negative—on Monday, and the "weekend effect" means that prices of financial assets are significantly higher on Friday if compared with Monday. The various theoretical hypotheses trying to explain this trend have different explanations. In particular, behavioral finance examine the interdependence of negative expectations of market participants on Monday instead of Friday due to the psychological perception of it as the worst day of the week. An alternative hypothesis asserts the existence of a boom in buying assets on Friday, which in turn inflates their prices, by deferred payment over the weekend, which is effectively an interest-free loan. Hypothesis of implementation information says that during the week the information is positive, and on weekends—negative, which leads to a positive return on assets on Friday and negative—on Monday. Variety of concepts determines the magnitude of approaches to understanding and modeling of "weekend effect" in the stock market.

18.3   Literature Review

In the works of foreign scholars the issue of modeling market "weekend effect" is widely covered.

Cross (1973) analyzing the movement of Standard and Poor's Composite Stock Index from Friday to Monday (from January 1953 to December 1970), paid attention to preferential growth of this index on Friday, compared with Monday. French (1980) studied the daily yield of Standard and Poor's Composite portfolio for the 1953–1977 period and found the existence of the negative yield on Monday compared to other days of the week.

The results of the study by Keim and Stambaugh (1984) show a negative return on Monday for 55 years, since 1928. Jaffe and Westerfield (1985) examined stock market returns in four countries: in UK, Japan, Canada and Australia. Their study confirmed "weekend effect" in all four countries, they also found that the lowest return in Australia and Japan occurred not on Monday, but on Tuesday. Rogalski (1984) discovered that all negative returns from Friday close to Monday close occurred during the nontrading period from Friday close to Monday open. He also concluded that the January effect was interrelated with the weekend effect.

Smirlock and Starks (1986) research using hourly data of the Dow Jones Industrial Average confirm the existence of gains for the equities on Friday. They verified the results found by Rogalski (1984) which indicated that the weekend effect was due to the negative average returns from Friday close to Monday open. Penman (1987) speculates that because of companies tend to publish bad news earning reports on Mondays is coincident with the negative effect in stock returns.

Works of Rystrom and Benson (1989) explain the fact of existence of "weekend effect" because Friday is accepted better by traders psychologically than Monday. The investigation of 19 stock markets made by Agrawal and Tandon (1994), suggests evidence of "weekend effect" for stock exchanges of USA, Great Britain, Canada, Germany and Brazil. Sias and Starks (1995) explain the appearance of "weekend effect" by the movement of shares in institutional investors' portfolio. On the other hand Kazemi (2013), Chen and Singal (2003) see the reason of weekend effect in closing speculative positions by traders on Friday.

The scientists Olson et al. (2011) tried to improve the modeling methodology of "weekend effect" based on stability test and Racicot test (Racicot) (2011). At the same time the "weekday effect" denied in the works of Ariel (1990), Connolly (1989), Christophe et al. (2009). Disagreement of scientific statements concerning identification, confirmation of the existence of a "weekend effect" and its modeling from the perspective of stock market operations necessitate own scientific research in this direction.

The efficient market hypothesis states that it is impossible to "beat the market" because stock market efficiency causes existing share prices to always incorporate and reflect all relevant information. It should be emphasized that the hypothesis of the existence of absolutely efficient stock markets sounds ideal from a theoretical point of view but cannot be applied in practice. This fact is confirmed by a number of empirical regularities of behavior of ordinary shares that is shown every year.

For Ukrainian Exchange (UX) the research concerning calendar anomalies was conducted by Plastun and Makarenko (2015). The authors analyzed data on index futures UX for the period from 2010 to 2015, calculating the average yield of indices by days of the week. The authors concluded that the daily dynamics of prices for futures UX during Monday–Thursday were not showing abnormal behavior. However, Friday was different from other days and showed stable and relatively significant positive movements that do not fit into the normal pattern of behavior of prices for the analyzed instrument. The presence of statistical anomalies on Friday was confirmed by Student's *t*-test. The trading strategy developed on the basis of this statistical anomaly is able to generate profits (up 15% excluding transaction costs).

Despite the presence of a number of studies dedicated to "weekend effect", the analysis for the Ukrainian Stock Exchange was not conducted, so we decided to fill this gap.

18.4   Analysis of the Ukrainian Stock Exchange Index

18.4.1   The Methodology

Data used in this study are downloaded from http://www.ux.ua/ accessed on February 12, 2016. The analyzed period is from January 8, 2008 to December 30, 2015. Rest two months of 2016, i.e. January and February are not included due to "distortion" of data because 2016 will not be completed as a full year. Analyses are performed using program Stata and Excel. In first sample selection are observed few cases which belonged to Saturday as a trading day. These observations are dropped. Thus, trading days are from Monday to Friday. Hence, finally totally 1971 observations are examined for further analyzes.

Different authors used different measures for the rate of return. For example, the price returns of the stock following Benninga (1997, p. 68) is calculated as:

$$\ln\left(\frac{P_t + D_t}{P_{t-1}}\right) \tag{18.1}$$

where

P_t is the closing price of the stock at the end of time t,
D_t is the stock paid dividend in the period $(t - 1, t)$.

Moreover, Benninga (1997) explained the discretely compounded rate of return calculation as

$$R_t = \frac{P_t}{P_{t-1}} - 1 \tag{18.2}$$

and the continuously compounded rate of return calculated as:

$$R_t = \frac{P_t}{P_{t-1}} \tag{18.3}$$

The last calculation following Benninga (1997, p. 80) assumes that "$P_t = P_{t-1}e^{r_t}$, where r_t is the rate of return during the period $(t - 1, t)$ and where p_t is the price at time t."

In this study, three measures of the index returns (index values) are calculated. The first calculation presents discretely compounded rate of return as:

$$R_t = \left(\frac{V_t}{V_{t-1}} - 1\right) \times 100 \tag{18.4}$$

where

V_t is value of index at the end of day t and
V_{t-1} is value of index at the end of previous day t.

The second calculation presents continuously compounded rate of return as:

$$R_t = \left(\frac{V_t}{V_{t-1}}\right) \times 100 \qquad (18.5)$$

The third calculation presents again continuously compounded rate of return, but here returns try to be more normalized due to up-downs values:

$$R_t = \ln\left(\frac{V_t}{V_{t-1}}\right) \times 100 \qquad (18.6)$$

All three returns calculations are expressed in percentages rather in values. Differences in calculations are given in Table 18.3. However, further analyzes are based on discretely compounded rate of return, following hence authors as Keim and Stambaugh (1984), Nasir et al. (1988).

Data related with returns are checked whether they satisfied the condition of normality. For this reason Shapiro-Wilk W and Shapiro-Francia W' tests for normal data are performed based on trading days. Neither day passed these two tests for normality (Prob > z, 0.00000 respectively 0.00001). Hence, we conclude that data used in this study don't have normal distributions.

18.5   Results

Data are organized in the form of time-series. Returns are expressed on daily terms (time difference is one day). The distribution of data is presented as following in Table 18.1. As Table 18.2 presents, there is a less or more a balanced distribution between five analyzed days. Monday as a day participated with 18% in overall sample. Hence, it is the day with lower observations number. Whereas, is evidenced that Wednesday and Thursday have higher observations number compared with rest days.

Table 18.1 Frequencies per day

Day	Freq.	Percent	Day	Freq.	Percent
Fri	395	20	Tue	403	20
Mon	364	18	Wed	405	21
Thu	404	21	Total	1971	100

Source Authors' calculations

Table 18.2 Summary statistics (mean and standard deviation) per day

Day	$R_t = \left(\frac{V_t}{V_{t-1}} - 1\right) \times 100$	$R_t = \left(\frac{V_t}{V_{t-1}}\right) \times 100$	$R_t = \ln\left(\frac{V_t}{V_{t-1}}\right) \times 100$
Fri	0.0349	100.0349	0.0158
	1.9618	1.9618	1.9575
Mon	−0.0007	99.9993	−0.0368
	2.6873	2.6873	2.6936
Thu	−0.0724	99.9276	−0.0966
	2.2018	2.2018	2.2001
Tue	−0.1320	99.8680	−0.1649
	2.5587	2.5587	2.5716
Wed	−0.0482	99.9518	−0.0705
	2.1212	2.1212	2.1138
Total	−0.0449	99.9552	−0.0716
	2.3139	2.3139	2.3158

Source Authors' calculations

Table 18.2 presents mean and standard deviation per day according to three returns' calculations (measurements) as above presented in Eqs. (18.3), (18.4) and (18.5).

Since rates of returns are already in percentages, then means and standard deviations are too. Results denoted that overall mean of returns is negative for five days. All days, except Friday, have experienced negative means of returns. Hereafter, analyzes are focused on rate of return according to Eq. (18.3). View from the calculation in first equation, Monday experienced a lower negative mean of return (−0.0007%), whereas Tuesday with higher negative return (−0.1320%). Monday experienced higher standard deviation of return with 2.6873%, whereas Friday with lower (1.9618%). Results are slightly contradictory in this sense. Friday has experienced higher return and lower risk.

Moreover, the mean of return is analyzed per day and year, and than per day and month as presented in Tables 18.3 and 18.4. Based on calculation in Table 18.3, is sketched in Fig. 18.1.

Table 18.3 Return's mean per day and year

Year	Day				
	Fri	Mon	Thu	Tue	Wed
2008	−0.2847	−0.2131	−0.4735	−0.9585	−0.4645
2009	0.3702	0.1858	0.7825	0.0332	0.1027
2010	−0.0631	0.5101	0.0495	0.3479	0.3935
2011	−0.0454	−0.3279	−0.2225	−0.3553	0.0056
2012	0.0943	0.1851	−0.5952	0.0398	−0.4439
2013	0.0822	−0.2130	0.1528	0.0239	−0.0912
2014	0.3078	0.2012	−0.1300	−0.0001	0.0203
2015	−0.1795	−0.3189	−0.1693	−0.2020	0.0689

Source Authors' calculations

Table 18.4 Return's mean per day and month

Month	Day				
	Fri	Mon	Thu	Tue	Wed
Apr	1.0077	−0.3728	0.7265	−0.4522	0.3447
Aug	−0.1705	0.2195	−0.7503	−0.3481	−0.7781
Dec	−0.2432	−0.0756	0.5873	0.1423	0.2386
Feb	0.3187	0.5102	−0.3095	−0.2108	0.4572
Jan	−0.3732	0.3209	0.1788	0.3348	−0.2650
Jul	−0.0321	0.5252	0.3652	−0.0723	−0.3264
Jun	−0.2469	0.3046	−0.4257	−0.1844	−0.4436
Mar	0.2630	−0.6987	−0.2513	0.0787	0.0724
May	−0.0432	−0.1559	−0.3410	−0.0096	0.1303
Nov	0.0925	0.4740	−0.2263	0.0298	0.2079
Oct	−0.3523	−0.2433	−0.0033	−0.3509	−0.3487
Sep	0.1481	−0.7604	−0.5432	−0.4650	0.1318

Source Authors' calculations

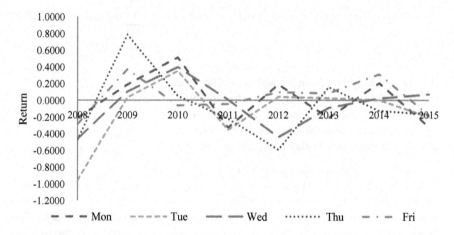

Fig. 18.1 Return's mean. *Source* Authors' calculations

As Table 18.3 presents, Tuesday, Wednesday and Friday experienced a positive trend, whereas Monday and Thursday a negative trend. Respectively trends according to week days are presented as:

- Monday: $y = -0.0276x + 0.1254$;
- Tuesday: $y = 0.0542x - 0.3777$;
- Wednesday: $y = 0.0169x - 0.127$;
- Thursday: $y = -0.0297x + 0.0581$; and
- Friday: $y = 0.0119x - 0.0184$.

Table 18.5 Regression results

$R_t = \left(\frac{V_t}{V_{t-1}} - 1\right) \times 100$	Coef. (mean)	t	$P > t$
MonD	−0.0006665	−0.01	0.996
TueD	−0.131964	−1.14	0.253
WedD	−0.0481877	−0.42	0.675
ThuD	−0.0724253	−0.63	0.53
FriD	0.0349235	0.3	0.764

Number of obs = 1971; F (5, 1966) = 0.39; Prob > F = 0.8533

Source Authors' calculations

Testing whether there is a weekend effect in our data selected, we run the regression model following Smilrock and Starks (1986). In fact, authors examined three return measures as: daily close to close, close to open and open to close. Thus, the model that should be estimated is:

$$R_t = a_1 D_{1t} + a_2 D_{2t} + a_3 D_{3t} + a_4 D_{4t} + a_5 D_{5t} + \tilde{\varepsilon}_t = \sum_{k=1}^{5} a_k D_{kt} + \tilde{\varepsilon}_t \qquad (18.7)$$

where

D_{1t} is 1 if day t is a Monday and zero otherwise,
D_{2t} is 1 if day t is a Tuesday and zero otherwise,
D_{3t} is 1 if day t is a Wednesday and zero otherwise,
D_{4t} is 1 if day t is a Thursday and zero otherwise,
D_{5t} is 1 if day t is a Friday and zero otherwise.

Results of regression and are presented in Table 18.5.

Results denote that neither mean (coefficient) is statistically significant. Using the F statistic (same results are obtained from Anova analysis) we test the null hypothesis that there is no difference between five days mean against alternative hypothesis that there is difference. Since p-value is higher than 0.05 we fail to reject the null hypothesis. Hence, we come to conclusion that the day-of-the-week effect is not present in our study.

18.6   Conclusion

The purpose of this study was testing the day-of-the-week effect for Ukrainian Stock Exchange Index. The study was motivated by previous researches in line of day-of-the-week or weekend effects. Data were selected and analysed for the period from January 8, 2008 to December 30, 2015. Results denoted that index return in each day was negative, except Friday which was lower but non-negative. Study indicated that differences of returns between five days weren't significant. With other words, the day-of-the-week effect is not found in our study. For further studies, is recommended to analyze selected index furthermore and comparing with other indexes. Moreover, is recommended to divide the period into sub-periods and using more an advanced methodology.

Acknowledgments This is paper has been prepared under financial support of Ukrainian Stock Exchange, which authors gratefully acknowledge.

References

Agrawal A, Tandon K (1994) Anomalies or illusions? Evidence from stock markets in eighteen countries. J Int Money Finance 13:83–106

Ariel RA (1990) High stock returns before holidays: existence and evidence on possible causes. J Financ 45(5):1611–1626

Benninga S (1997) Financial modeling, uses excel. Massachusetts Institute of Technology Press, Cambridge

Brusa J, Liu P, Schulman C (2003) The "reverse" weekend effect: the U.S. market versus international markets. Int Rev Financ Anal 12:267–286

Chang E, Pinegar M, Ravichandran R (1993) International evidence on the robustness of the day-of-the week effect. J Financ Quant Anal 28:497–513

Chen H, Singal V (2003) Role of speculative short sales in price formation: the case of the weekend effect. J Finance 58:685–706

Christophe M, Ferri S, Angel J (2009) Short-selling and the weekend effect in stock returns. J Financ Rev 1:31–57

Connolly R (1989) An examination of the robustness of the weekend effect. J Financ Quant Anal 24(2):133–169

Cross F (1973) The behavior of stock prices on fridays and mondays. Financ Anal J: 67–69

French K (1980) Stock returns and the weekend effect. J Financ Econ 8(1):55–69

Jaffe J, Westerfield R (1985) Pattern in the Japanese common stock returns: day of the week and turn of the year effect. J Finance Quant Anal 20(2):261–272

Kazemi H (2013) Stock market volatility, speculative short sellers and weekend effect: international evidence. J Financ Risk Manage 3:47–54

Keim DB, Stambaugh RF (1984) A further investigation of the weekend effect in stock returns. J Finance 39(3):819–835

Nasir A, Mohamad Sh, Hamid M (1988) Stock returns and the weekend effect: the Malaysian experience. Pertanika 11:107–114. [Online]. Retrieved 7 Feb 2016. http://psasir.upm.edu.my/2690/1/Stock_Returns_and_the_Weekend_Effect.pdf

Olson D (2011) Stages in the life of the weekend effect. D. Olson et al.—2011//http://louisville.edu/research/for-faculty-staff/reference-search/1999-references/2011-business/olson-et-al-2011-stages-in-the-life-ofthe-weekend-effect

Penman SH (1987) The distribution of earning news over time and seasonalities in aggregate stock return. J Finance Account 18:199–228

Plastun O, Makarenko I (2015) Analysis of the weekend effect in the stock market of Ukraine. Visnyk NBU 2:48–52

Racicot F-É (2011) Low-frequency components and the weekend effect revisited: evidence from spectral analysis. Int J Finance 2:2–19

Rogalski RJ (1984) New findings regarding day-of-the-week returns over trading and non-trading periods: a note. J Finance 39(December):1603–1614

Rystrom DS, Benson E (1989) Investor psychology and the day of-the-week effect. Financ Anal J: 75–78

Sias RW, Starks LT (1995) The day-of-the week anomaly: the role of institutional investors. Financ Anal J: 58–67

Smirlock M, Starks L (1986) Day-of-the-week and intraday effects in stock returns. J Financ Econ 17:197–210. North-Holland. [Online]. Retrieved 7 Feb 2016. http://citeseerx.ist.psu.edu/viewdoc/download?doi=10.1.1.517.6341&rep=rep1&type=pdf

Yu HC, Chiou I, Jordan-Wagner J (2008) Does the weekday effect of the yen/dollar spot rates exist in Tokyo, London, and New York? An analysis of panel probability distribution. Appl Econ 40 (20):2631–2643

Chapter 19
Selected Passages from the Development History of Hungarian Banking Supervision in the Turn of Twentieth Century's Period

Bence Varga

Abstract In this paper we attempt to present the early stage of Hungarian banking supervision's history, with respect to the proposals of the organisation of different supervisory bodies from the second half of the nineteenth century until the establishment of the Financial Institution's Centre (1916), inclusive. We present the opinions connected with the shaping of banking supervision, the related arguments for and against, the proposals and initiatives for the establishment of specific supervisory bodies and operational frameworks thereof.

Keywords Banking system · Supervisory organisation · Financial oversight

19.1 Introduction

As a result of the peculiar development of the Hungarian financial institutional system, the establishment of the banks was preceded in time by the emergence of other types of institutions (e.g. savings banks, cooperative financial institutions), thus naturally the demand for the oversight of the banks also appeared later. Namely, in the eighteenth century in Hungary, the Royal Credit Fund was established (1772) and the primary purpose of which was to satisfy the state's credit demands and the collection of deposits. Although from 1776 it was also permitted to place loans, it was not available for the general public. The wide-ranging development of the financial institution system was hindered by several factors, such as the monetary shortfall experienced in certain areas and by the fact, that the banks—due to their location and structure—typically preferred lending of high amounts, and upon lending they primarily focused on profit-oriented considerations (financial creditworthiness), contrary to the cooperative institutions which also

B. Varga (✉)
Division of Finance, Faculty of Economics and Business Administration,
University of Szeged, Törökvész lejtő 10/B., 1026 Budapest, Hungary
e-mail: varga.caius@gmail.com

© Springer International Publishing AG 2017
D. Procházka (ed.), *New Trends in Finance and Accounting*,
Springer Proceedings in Business and Economics,
DOI 10.1007/978-3-319-49559-0_19

considered decent borrower morals, i.e. moral creditworthiness (Schandl 1938). The cooperative financial institutions could gain ground in the areas were the earnings potential of the economic agents was relatively lower and their borrowing and credit demand was not high either (Pólya 1894). Since the members of the cooperative society operating in a given settlement typically all came from the same settlement, the cooperative society was in the position to expand its activity with non-profit services like the development of the local infrastructure or facilitating the economic development of the given settlement (Botos 1996), which contributed to the increase of the population's trust in the cooperative societies. This kind of trust also manifested itself in the case of the savings banks, which is also attributable to the core function thereof, like in the case of General Savings Bank of Brasov, namely that the Savings Bank was established for philanthropic considerations and used its profit for aids and the support of the Brasov hospital; furthermore, it also created a charity fund for the needy households (Soós 1993).

We can mention reasons why the oversight requirement related to the banks was not so urging compared to the oversight need pressed for in the case of the cooperative societies and savings banks, because Austro-Hungarian Bank could exercise some oversight of the banks' operation through its refinancing policy from the second half of the 1870s (Kövér 1993). However, at the same time, in the second half of the nineteenth century, some sort of concentration process started with regard to the banks, which as a contrary effect pressed for the organisation of the oversight. By 1913 as a result of the concentration process, the largest industrial, mining, commercial and transport companies belonged to the sphere of interest of a few domestic large banks; therefore, the Hungarian banking sector significantly increased its influence in the control of the domestic economy (Tomka 1999), and furthermore by 1901, already 987 banks and savings banks operated in Hungary and it is further increased to 1183 by 1905 (Müller et al. 2014), which also had pressing effect for the oversight.

Thus, in Hungary the emergence of the cooperative financial institutions and savings banks preceded in time the creation of banks, and as such the requirements related to the oversight of banks also appeared later, e.g. in connection with the oversight of the savings banks, the Central Mortgage Bank of the Hungarian Savings Banks was established in 1892 at the initiative of the contemporary prime minister István Tisza, the primary objective of which was to facilitate the access of the rural smallholder society to credits. In the course of this, it liaised only with such savings banks that agreed that the Mortgage Bank could review its balance sheet and entire business administration annually (Domány 1926; Botos 2002). Nevertheless, the controversies related to the financial supervision and the need for that also effected the development of the banking supervision as well.

The term of "oversight" in this age did not solely mean the state's role in today's sense, but it rather included internal, intra-organisational oversight (self-regulation by the supervisory board) and the exercise of oversight by the non-state councils and business federations. In this paper we also present the professional debates and views related to the various oversight approaches.

19.2 Initiatives for the Establishment of Supervisory Bodies

It was widely well-known in the second half of the nineteenth century that the supervisory board due to the conflicts of interests within the organisation of the financial institutions did not fulfil its role properly (Lengyel 1917), and the judicial system was not able to ensure the prudent conduct either. In respect of the operation of the supervisory board, it became a widespread view that their operation thereof is generally unsatisfactory and it is only a "pictus masculus" (Sugár 1899), a "quantité négligeable" (Éber 1911) and the existence thereof is completely unnecessary. This rather superficial inspection practice was substantiated by Section 195 of Act XXXVII of 1875 (Commercial Code), which prescribed the inspection of the management by the supervisory board not as an obligation, but merely as a possibility, there were different views in place on the relation of the supervisory board and the oversight (e.g. "Anglo-Saxon" approach: supervisory board is necessary only when the state control is not implemented, but in this case, the increase of supervisory board's controlling role and to expand its competences are necessary).

Of the initiatives to establish an institutionalised supervisory body and supervisory control, it is worth highlighting the initiative submitted in the 1870s to the Miskolc Chamber of Commerce and Industry, which raised the idea of the need for mandatory inspection to be implemented in the form of an autonomous association independent from the government (Jirkovsky 1945). This form was supported by a major part of the professional public opinion, e.g. by László Lukács, minister of finance between 1895 and 1905 and later prime minister, as well as Henrik Trautmann, university professor and later director of the Commercial Academy and Antal Éber, politician, subsequent chairman of the Budapest Chamber of Commerce and Industry and of the Hungarian Economic Association also deemed a similar idea feasible for the inspection of the financial institutions. Éber wanted to conduct the inspections by establishing a central inspection council in a way that the council member financial institutions in Budapest and in the provinces could apply to the council to submit the given financial institution to inspection (Éber 1911; 1912a). In the event when the inspection council did not find the continued operation of the financial institution "sound", the situation of the financial institution could be made unsustainable by the gradual deprival of lending, thereby preventing the systemic consequences of an abrupt shock.

In 1889 the Miskolc Chamber of Commerce and Industry invited the financial institutions in its catchment area to a conference. Several proposals related to the reform of financial institutions—such as the need to review the capital position (e.g. subscribed capital, capital reserves), the board of directors and the supervisory board of the financial institutions—as well certain accounting issues (e.g. balance sheet compilation) were discussed at the conference. The establishment of an independent inspection body, as well as the nationwide extension of the Miskolc conference, which was essentially a regional level conference, was also on the agenda. However, all proposals were unanimously rejected at the conference; the participants regarded the operation of the provincial financial institutions as adequate and the risk arising from their operation as low. Although in terms of its outcome the Miskolc conference was not a breakthrough in oversight, the financial institution participants recognised several facts that were determinant with regard to their later development, thus indirectly also in terms of the oversight history. Namely, several participants of the conference openly voiced a number of problems that they blamed for the failures of mostly the savings banks, but from time to time also of the banks (e.g. maturity mismatch, their operation differed from their original purpose etc.). In connection with the need of state intervention, the typical approach was that of the "invisible hand" by Adam Smith, as the conference regarded any kind of state intervention not only unnecessary, but even harmful (Jirkovsky 1945). The participating financial institutions only found acceptable to establish an autonomously organised central institution that would elaborate and review certain transaction management and accounting rules, which expels the financial institution members that do not comply with the proposals.

19.3   Debates Concerning the Organisation of Supervisory Bodies

No full agreement was reached in respect of the autonomous or state nature and the scope of the inspection in Hungary at that time. In the opinion of Miksa Havas, academy professor and chamber inspector, substantial control may only be achieved if it is performed with regard to all institutions by a state agency or any other independent agency appointed by it (Éber 1912a); therefore, Havas regarded the Austrian normative provisions related to savings banks as the guiding principle. His opinion was also supported by Lengyel (1917), who was of the view that the inspection can attain its goal only if it is mandatory. The opinion of Havas and Lengyel was opposed by Lipót Horváth influential banker, and Manó Zsengery, member of the supervisory board of National Hungarian Mutual Insurance Cooperative Society also highlighted certain risks of the mandatory inspection, as they believed that a mandatory inspection, with its opinion of subjective nature, could have a negative impact on the given institution's assessment and operation, and by "ousting" the creditors, it may also plunge it in a crisis situation. Zsengery was of the opinion that it could also have a negative impact on the public, as the public—trusting in the institution of mandatory inspection—presumably would not scrutinise the institution's public accounts and even excessive, unsubstantiated trust may develop with regard to the institutions inspected by the public authority. Whereas the optional inspection—apart from being easier to implement—also provides wider room for manoeuvre in respect of the inspection theme, the appointed inspectors and the principles along which the inspection should be conducted. However, Zsengery—also recognising the shortcomings of the mandatory inspection—came to the conclusion that the inspection must be implemented on a mandatory basis, irrespective of the size of the institution, also covering the evaluation of corporate governance, but without intervening in the business policy. Sándor Matlekovits, lawyer and university professor, and later member of the Board of MTA (Hungarian Academy of Sciences), for example, regarded the review of specific credit transactions, and in fact any other review that goes beyond the assessment of the balance sheet with regard to its correctness is perfectly harmful and dangerous from a business perspective (Éber 1912b). In connection with the rotation enforced during the inspections, Zsengery proposed to implement it over several years, in order to eliminate the extra time and difficulties related to the obtaining of the same information on several occasions, which would be inevitable upon the appearance of a new inspector as a result of the frequent rotation (Éber 1912a). However, with regard to the arguments against the mandatory inspection, we should note that the risk attached to the opinions of subjective nature cannot be eliminated in the case of optional inspection either; this risk can be mitigated by duly substantiated findings and the conduct of detailed inspection, and—in the light of the subsequent economic events—the disciplinary power of publicity and its ability to scrutinise account is rather limited. However, based on the foregoing, two main schools should be differentiated even within the autonomous inspection, where according to the first one the given financial institution may apply for the inspection at its discretion, and in the absence thereof it is exempted from the inspection; the other school represented the establishment of a unit that has the necessary competences and may decide on the inspection of a given financial institution based on necessity and practicability criteria.

Hantos (1916) warned already in 1911 about a phenomenon that unfortunately did occur later, albeit for a short period, where in the case of the operation of a financial inspection organisation with relatively weak ability to enforce interest, the conduct of the inspections will presumably depend on the member institutions' own decision, and as such exactly those institutions will evade the inspection that would need to be inspected the most. Consequently, Hantos considered the operational framework of the inspection of the financial institutions feasible on a so-called self-government basis in an autonomous form (e.g. as a chamber or business federation). In connection with the inspection, Hantos pressed for a gradual expansion of the range of inspected institutions and the scope of the inspection, starting primarily with the smaller—in terms of the balance sheet total—institutions, and within these institutions, he regarded particularly the assessment of the adequacy of the corporate governance as an area to be reviewed. Within this framework, the inspector's duties would have been fulfilled by an external member of the supervisory board belonging to the autonomous organisation, elected for 3 years. The Hungarian Association of Inspectors established in 1911, initially chaired by the then Minister of Commerce, József Szterényi, could be regarded as such an—already existing—autonomous organisation, which qualified as an organisation in charge of performing the professional rating and intermediation of the inspectors (Jenei 1970). Admission to the Association was subject to minimum 8 years of professional practical experience and to successfully graduating from a 2-year inspectors' course covering both academic and practical subjects (Éber 1912b).

Under this approach, only those financial institutions would have been subjected to inspection that have a deposit business[1] with share capital not exceeding 10 million crowns (in order to strengthen the inspection willingness in the relations of the financial institutions the "inspection subject status" could have been a benefit in view of the fact that during the interbank lending the financial institutions already subject to inspection presumably would have been more willing to lend). The condition mentioned first was substantiated by the protection of the households' interests, while the latter one was justified by the assumption (no longer valid in the present financial and economic environment) according to which there is less need for the "external" inspection of the financial institutions that are larger in terms of their size and typically pursuing complex financial activity. An additional argument for determining an upper limit of the share capital for inspection purposes was that the inspection required an extremely large administration. The proposal of Hantos with regard to enhancing the professional quality of the supervisory board— according to which the supervisory board must have at least one expert, the required professional skills of whom should be specified in a separate decree—could be worth considering (Hantos 1916). Miksa Havas took a different position on the proposal that the inspection should depend on the upper limit of the share capital, as he believed that it would be much more important to conduct the inspection of the institutions, the deposit portfolio of which substantially exceeds their share capital (thereby having higher capital leverage) and that pursue complex business activity (Éber 1912a).

Despite all these—often sharp—polemics and professional consultations, in the second half of the nineteenth century, the idea of institutionalised supervisory control at the banks found no response in terms of the practical implementation, although in 1876 Kálmán Széll, the contemporary finance minister, also emphasised the need for financial institution supervision and regulation (Hantos 1916). At the same time, the bust of the Vienna stock exchange in 1873—as a result of which 26 banks and savings banks went bankrupt or were liquidated in Hungary, and of the five large banks established after the Austro-Hungarian Compromise of 1867 only the Hungarian General Credit Bank survived the crisis with a substantial capital injection—could have given cause for the development of the institutionalised supervision. The fact that despite the crisis the inspection of credit institutions did not gain weight was probably attributable to the fact that part of the professional actors who proposed the organisation of supervision were not hit too hard by the fall in the number of credit institutions—the number of which substantially increased in the period of the "Gründerzeit"—in the wake of the crisis. These actors followed a so-called free-market economic philosophy approach, according to which contrary to the bureaucratic coordination the market automatisms provide sufficient efficiency for the adequate market operation, thus—in the opinion of the

---

[1]The importance of the protection of depositors had been laid by János Galgóczy in 1878; i.e. in respect of the banks both for the purpose of regulation and oversight the primary consideration was the protection of the interests of the household sector, and particularly that of the deposit holders (Galgóczy 1878).

followers of this economic philosophy—the organisation of the supervision could no longer contribute substantially to increase its efficiency.

19.4   Conclusion

In respect of the oversight of financial institutions, the operational frameworks of the so-called expert institution were elaborated in detail; according to the plans, within the structure of expert organisation, the experts—as independent, responsible "functionaries"—would have reviewed the functioning of the financial institutions annually. In practice the expert institution would have operated in a way that the official expert qualification could have been obtained at a so-called review committee. The idea was that (similarly to the presently operating financial supervisory system in Hungary) the expert institution should be operated by two types of experts, i.e. internal and external members; the external member of the institution was in charge of conducting the inspections, while the internal member performed the background, support and analytical tasks. The on-site inspectors, if they found the institution's accounting records in order, issued a certificate to this effect; otherwise, they prepared a report to the central government, which also had powers to take action. Under this doctrine, it was proposed to perform the inspection unexpectedly, without prior notice. It was also important for the operation of the expert institution that during the on-site inspection, the individual inspectors should become the specialists of a specific area in accordance with their skills and they would summarise their inspection findings in open publications, thereby contributing—in addition to the practical skills—to the expansion of the academic expertise and supporting the actors of the financial system in the implementation of prudent operation. The open publication could be relevant at present as well, because—apart from the previously listed arguments—it could considerable contribute to the increase of transparency and also simplify future inspections due to the fact that the institutions would have the opportunity to remedy the problems existing at them prior to the inspection, bearing in mind the content of the report on the frequent errors and shortcomings.

The expert institution would have operated independently of politics, subordinated solely to the administrative court. It was proposed that the administrative court should also include economists and mathematicians to support the expert institution (Havas 1901). Based on the proposals, the intention was to organise the expert institution, in several respects, based on the activity of the Institute of Chartered Accountants in England and Wales, adjusted to the domestic conditions; namely, it was also proposed that the inspectors should be members in the supervisory board of the individual financial institutions, thereby also ensuring a certain level of continuous on-site presence. However, the expert institution has not been elaborated that time; there were several elements of the concept (rotation, independent operation, examination report etc.) which highly influenced the latter organised supervisory scheme.

In the beginning of the twentieth century, the idea of developing the supervision was supplemented with the idea of implementing it in the form of a business federation, which was widely supported. Of the established business federations, we should highlight the MPOSZ (National Association of Hungarian Financial Institutions) established in 1903, the activity of which is also worth mentioning in terms of the subsequently institutionalised supervision, as its tasks included the provision of professional guidance (determining the correct business principles), financial and moral support of the provincial financial institutions in crisis situation, if any (Botos 1994; Jakabb et al. 1941). Apart from MPOSZ, we should also mention POE (National Association of Financial Institutions), established around the same time, the activities of which included the studying of the issues related to the domestic credit conditions and financial life, the formulation of opinions, the identification of the factors hindering the development of the financial institutions, as well as the introduction of a standardised bookkeeping and balance sheet compilation practice (Müller et al. 2014). Both organisations had supervisory duties as well, but the rather wide scope of activities, overly diverse tasks, the rivalry between the organisations and the voluntary accession by the financial institutions (and thereby the voluntary submission to audit) all contributed to the fact that they could not function as efficient supervisory bodies (Hantos 1916).

Although an efficient supervisory body was not established in the turn of twentieth century's period, the studying of the different examples and the domestic conditions, the professional debates at various forums, and also the bankruptcies, as natural phenomena, all contributed to the establishment of the first supervisory "super body", i.e. the Financial Institution's Centre on 1 June 1916.

Acknowledgments The author owes thanks to Pallas Athena Domus Scientiae Foundation for supporting the elaboration of this paper.

References

Botos J (1994) A magyarországi pénzintézetek együttműködésének formái és keretei (forms and frameworks of the Hungarian financial institutions' cooperation). Közgazdasági és Jogi Könyvkiadó, Budapest

Botos K (1996) Elvesz(t)ett illúziók (lost illusions). A magyar bankrendszer helyzete és távlatai (the situation and prospects of the Hungarian banking system). Közgazdasági és Jogi Könyvkiadó, Budapest

Botos J (2002) A magyarországi jelzálog-hitelezés másfél évszázada (one and a half century of mortgage lending in Hungary). Szaktudás Kiadó Ház Rt., Budapest

Domány G (1926) Bankpolitika, különös tekintettel a hitelpolitikára (banking policy, with special regard to the lending policy), vol 50. Közgazdasági Szemle (Economic Review), Budapest, pp 432–457

Éber A (1911) A pénzintézetek revisiójáról (on the inspection of financial institutions), vol 35. Közgazdasági Szemle (Economic Review), Budapest, pp 795–805

Éber A (1912a) Közlemények és ismertetések (notices and reviews): a pénzintézetek revisiója (inspection of the financial institutions). Vita (debate), vol 36. Közgazdasági Szemle (Economic Review), Budapest, pp 55–65

Éber A (1912b) Közlemények és ismertetések (notices and reviews): vita a pénzintézetek revisiójáról (debate on the inspection of financial institutions), vol 36. Közgazdasági Szemle (Economic Review), Budapest, pp 209–216

Galgóczy J (1878) Hitelügyeink szabályozásának kérdéséhez (to the regulation of our credit affairs), vol 2. Nemzetgazdasági Szemle (National Economic Review), Budapest, pp 1–30

Hantos E (1916) A pénzintézeti reform (the financial institution reform): a Pénzintézeti Központ törvényének és alapszabályainak jegyzetes szövegével (with the distinctive wording of the Act on and the Statutes of the Pénzintézeti Központ), 2nd enlarged edn. Pénzintézetek Országos Egyesülése (National Association of Financial Institutions), Budapest

Havas M (1901) A pénzintézetek ellenőrzése tekintettel a biztosító társaságokra (inspection of the financial institutions in view of the insurance companies), vol 25. Közgazdasági Szemle (Economic Review), Budapest, pp 212–222

Jakabb O, Reményi-Schneller L, Szabó I (1941) A Pénzintézeti Központ első huszonöt éve (the first twenty-five years of the Pénzintézeti Központ) (1916–1941). Királyi Magyar Egyetemi Nyomda, Budapest

Jenei K (1970) A Pénzintézeti Központ szerepe a Magyar Tanácsköztársaság bankrendszerében (role of the Pénzintézeti Központ in the banking system of the Hungarian Soviet Republic). Publication of the Section of Works History of the Hungarian Historical Society (Magyar Történelmi Társulat Üzemtörténeti Szekciója). Special imprint from vol 40 of the National Archives Publications, pp 37–55

Jirkovsky S (1945) A magyarországi pénzintézetek története az első világháború végéig (history of the Hungarian financial institutions until the end of World War I). Athenaeum Kiadó, Budapest

Kövér G (1993) Az Osztrák-Magyar Bank (the Austro-Hungarian Bank), 1878–1914. In: Bácskai T (ed) A Magyar Nemzeti Bank története I (history of the Magyar Nemzeti Bank I): Az Osztrák Nemzeti Banktól a Magyar Nemzeti Bankig (from the Austrian National Bank to Magyar Nemzeti Bank) (1816–1924). Közgazdasági és Jogi Könyvkiadó, Budapest, pp 259–342

Lengyel S (1917) Könyvrevizorok képzése (education of accounting auditors), vol 41. Közgazdasági Szemle (Economic Review), Budapest, pp 244–261

Müller J, Kovács T, Kovács L (2014) A Magyar Bankszövetség története (history of the Hungarian Banking Association). Tarsoly Kiadó, Budapest

Pólya J (1894) A magyar szövetkezeti ügy (the cause of Hungarian cooperative societies), vol 18. Közgazdasági és Közigazgatási Szemle (Economics and Public Administration Review), Budapest, pp 625–647

Schandl K (ed) (1938) A magyar szövetkezés negyven éve (Az Országos Központi Hitelszövetkezet munkája és eredményei) (forty years of the Hungarian confederation) (the work and achievements of the National Central Credit Association). "Pátria" Irodalmi Vállalat és Nyomdai Rt., Budapest

Soós L (1993) Az Osztrák Nemzeti Bank (the Austrian National Bank), 1816–1851. In: Bácskai T (ed) A Magyar Nemzeti Bank története I (history of the Magyar Nemzeti Bank I): Az Osztrák Nemzeti Banktól a Magyar Nemzeti Bankig (from the Austrian National Bank to Magyar Nemzeti Bank) (1816–1924). Közgazdasági és Jogi Könyvkiadó, Budapest, pp 81–154

Sugár I (1899) Pénzintézetek reformja (reform of financial institutions), vol 23. Közgazdasági Szemle (Economic Review), Budapest, pp 403–425

Tomka B (1999) Érdek és érdektelenség (interest and uninterest). A bank-ipar viszony a századforduló Magyarországán (the bank-industry relation in Hungary at the turn of the century, 1892–1913. Multiplex Media—Debrecen U.P., Debrecen

Chapter 20
State Aid for Rescuing and Restructuring Firms in Difficulty and Its Impact on the State of Public Finances in the European Union in the Years 1999–2014

Piotr Podsiadło

Abstract The subject of the article is an analysis of the rules of state aid admissibility on the basis of the implementing regulations, adopted by the European Commission on rescue and restructuring aid. This should lead to verify the hypothesis of the influence of state aid on the size of the *general government* sector debt in the EU member states, which have provided state aid for undertakings in difficulty in the years 1999–2014. This analysis was carried out based on the linear regression model. The response variable (dependent variable Y) is the size of the *general government* sector debt, and explanatory variable (independent variable X) is the expenditure on state aid.

Keywords European union · State aid · Legal regulation · Rescue and restructuring · General government sector debt

20.1 Introduction

In all member states, there is a more or less pronounced tradition of using state resources to help undertakings in financial difficulties. In particular, if a large number of direct or indirect jobs are and risk and an intervention appear necessary to those politically responsible, state aid is used to keep firms threatened with insolvency afloat. The crisis in the financial markets, which began in 2007, in a short time began to significantly affect the real economy. This effect could be observed by a strong downward turn in the overall economy, which affected directly both households and undertakings. The result of the financial crisis in the

P. Podsiadło (✉)
Department of Local Government Finance, Faculty of Finance and Law,
Cracow University of Economics, Rakowicka 27, 31-510 Cracow, Poland
e-mail: piotr.podsiadlo@uek.krakow.pl

© Springer International Publishing AG 2017
D. Procházka (ed.), *New Trends in Finance and Accounting*,
Springer Proceedings in Business and Economics,
DOI 10.1007/978-3-319-49559-0_20

banking sector in the member states of the European Union was the process carried out by banks of reducing own debt relation to equity capital (Bringmann 2015). Banks have therefore become less willing to take risk comparing to the previous years, which in turn led to reduced availability of credits as a source of financing for undertakings and reduce the number of credits in general. This trend had negative consequences not only for enterprises that did not have adequate financial security in case of insolvency, but even for enterprises with good and stable financial condition, which were suddenly reduced the credit line or denied the credit. Taking into account that affordable and sufficient access to finance is a prerequisite for undertakings in making investments and creating new jobs, it should be noted that a restrictive credit policy affected mainly small- and medium-sized enterprises, which access to financing is more difficult compared with large enterprises. Hence, in this economic situation, state aid granted by the member states started to be an important complement of efforts to unblock credits for enterprises. But we have to also take into consideration that the consequence of the financial crisis affecting the restriction of access to finance and the crisis in the real economy which leads mainly to a decline in production is a crisis of excessive public debt and budget deficit resulting from the slowdown in the various fields of economy.

The purpose of this article is to analyze the conditions of admissibility of state aid for rescuing and restructuring undertakings in difficulty. This should lead to verify the hypothesis of the influence of state aid on the size of the *general government* sector debt in the member states, which have provided aid to enterprises in difficulty in the years 1999–2014, i.e., since the adoption by the European Commission of harmonized rules on rescue and restructuring aid. It is possible—with a certain simplification—to accept that since the premise of granting such aid is prosperity and increase of the competitiveness of the European Union, such aid should have a positive impact on public finances, as the expenditure on this aid will be offset by a strong reduction of operational aid granted to cover current cost of the enterprise activities as well as budget revenues from taxes and other public levies paid by effectively functioning, restructured enterprises. Thereby, it will be possible to say that the amount of expenditure on state aid to undertakings in difficulty for the particular member states should be negatively correlated with the size of the *general government* sector debt. The negative correlation of the size of the *general government* sector debt with the amount of expenditure on state aid for rescuing and restructuring undertakings would mean that with increasing amount of state aid to enterprises in economic difficulty, the *general government* sector debt of member states providing such aid should decrease.

20.2   Methodology of the Research

A feature of applied research method is the analysis of the intervention instruments used by the state from the point of view of concepts of state aid within the meaning of art. 107 par. 1 of the Treaty on the functioning of the European Union

(TFEU 2012). The adoption of such a method provided an opportunity to: firstly—determining the semantic scope of admissibility and the rules of providing aid as interpreted by the Court and the Court of Justice of the European Union, and secondly—capturing the specific characteristics of state aid for enterprises in difficulty (Biondi 2013). Another feature of the method used in the paper is the analysis of the relation between the member states expenditure on state aid designed for rescuing and restructuring undertakings in difficulty and the size of the *general government* sector debt of these countries. This analysis was carried out in accordance with the linear regression model. The response variable (dependent variable Y) is the size of the debt of the *general government* sector, and the explanatory variable (independent variable X) is the expenditure on state aid.

Statistical analysis was carried out based on three source tables. The first and second tables show the calculations for the linear regression model concerning, respectively, the intersection parameter (free term α) and slope parameter (directional factor β). The factors a and b of the regression function II are the estimators of the parameters α and β of regression function I (Bielecka 2011). The standard error Sa is the standard error of the estimator a of the parameter α, whereas the standard error Sb is the standard error of the estimator b of the parameter β. The designations "Lower 95%" and "Upper 95%" concern lower and upper limits of so-called confidence interval of numerical values for parameters α and β, where these parameters are with a probability of 95%.

The t Stat is a test of linear relationship occurrence between expenditure on state aid to enterprises in difficulty and the size of the *general government* sector debt. This statistical test allows to verify the authenticity of the so-called null hypothesis that the parameters of the regression function I type α and β are equal to zero, with the alternative hypothesis that they are not equal to zero (H_0: $\alpha = 0$; H_A: $\alpha \neq 0$ and H_0: $\beta = 0$; H_A: $\beta \neq 0$). The acceptance of the null hypothesis that the parameter $\alpha = 0$ would mean that if the expenditure on state aid is zero (state aid does not exist), then the value of the *general government* sector debt will also decrease to zero. In turn, the acceptance of the null hypothesis that the parameter $\beta = 0$ would mean that the increase in the value of expenditure on state aid by 1 million will not cause any changes in the size of the *general government* sector debt which means the lack of any relationship between expenditure on state aid and the size of the *general government* sector debt. In other words, the acceptance of the null hypothesis means the lack of the influence of the state aid for rescuing and restructuring undertakings provided by the member states of the European Union on the size of their *general government* sector debt. From the perspective taken in this paper, it will be essential to reject the null hypothesis in favor of the alternative hypothesis which states that between the studied phenomena—expenditure on state aid and the size of the *general government* sector debt—there is a significant statistical relationship. From the tables of critical values of Student's t test, it is seen that $\pm t_{\frac{\alpha}{2}} = \pm 2.1448$ for $\alpha = 0.05$ and $n - 2 = 14$ degrees of freedom. The null hypothesis can be rejected in favor of the alternative hypothesis only when $t_b < t_{\frac{\alpha}{2}}$ or $t_b > t_{\frac{\alpha}{2}}$, that is when—$t_b < -2.1448$ or $+t_b > +2.1448$.

The p value is the probability of making so-called type I error, involving the rejection, based on the results of the test, of the hypothesis that assumes the values of the parameters α and β are equal to zero, when in fact they are equal to zero in the whole population. In other words, type I error is a rejection of a real null hypothesis. The higher the value of the t test means the lower the probability of type I error. In general, it is assumed that if the p value is less than 0.05, the null hypothesis can be rejected in favor of the alternative hypothesis and thus claim that there is a statistically significant relationship between the expenditure of EU member states on state aid directed at enterprises in difficulty and the size of the *general government* sector debt of these countries.

The third table contains regression statistics. Among the regression statistics are the correlation coefficient, determination coefficient, standard error, and the parameters of F test, that is the value of F test and the probability of making type I error, when the hypothesis is verified concerning the lack of impact of expenditure on state aid on the size of the *general government* sector debt (irrelevance of state aid expenditure in the regression model). F test, similarly as described above t test, is used for testing the significance of linear regression coefficient β evaluation. The checking of this test is a statistic F having F-Snedecor distribution of k_1 and k_2 freedom degrees. When rejecting the null hypothesis $F > F_\alpha$ of no relation between expenditure on state aid and the size of the debt of the *general government* sector and accepting the alternative hypothesis of the existence of a statistically significant relationship between the variables. From the table of critical values of the F-Snedecor for $k_1 = 1$ (1 independent variable) and $k_2 = n - 2 = 14$ degrees of freedom and $\alpha = 0.05$ we read $F_{0.05} = 4.600$. Thus, the alternative hypothesis can be adopted only when $F > 4.600$.

20.3 Admissibility of State Aid for Rescuing and Restructuring Undertakings in Difficulty

The granting of rescue and restructuring aid has significant effects on competition, especially in the case of saturated markets. In particular, such aid may unfairly burden a competitor that might have been able to survive in the market, if the firm in difficulty received no aid and would be forced to withdraw from the market. In general, with the granting of state aid to undertakings in difficulty, there lurks a danger that other, previously competitive firms will experience difficulties as a result (Valle and Van de Casteele 2004a). The rescue and restructuring of firms with the help of state aid can, however, in exceptional cases, have a positive impact on competition—particularly where it helps to open up new markets or prevents remaining competitors from acquiring a monopolistic or oligopolistic market position.

The existing rules for granting aid to undertakings in difficult economic situation were largely based on the practice of supporting the steel sector in Europe in recent decades. In article 4 point c of the Treaty establishing the European Coal and Steel Community, it was specified that any state aid is incompatible with the common market of coal and steel (ECSC 1951). In practice, such a provision would mean that state aid is prohibited within the Community. This provision, however, proved to be too far-reaching and, consequently, granting of certain types of aid was allowed, recognizing them as the Community aid—it mainly concerned state aid for the mining sector in order to secure energy supplies in the Community. The first report on Competition Policy of 1971 stated that the European Commission will not, as a rule, oppose granting aid by the member states to enterprises in difficulty, if such aid will be used in exceptional circumstances and on the basis of clearly specific program of reorganization, so that it becomes a real contribution to the reorganization of their respective enterprises or regions (Anestis et al. 2004). Based on the experience gained, the European Commission announced in subsequent reports on competition policy more detailed rules for granting aid to undertakings in difficulty (Borghetto 2014). As a result, the conditions of admissibility of state aid directed at rescuing and restructuring of enterprises in difficulty were determined in the appropriate Community guidelines adopted in the form of communications from the European Commission (Valle and Van de Casteele 2004b; Pesaresi and Mamdani 2012; Schütte 2012; Petzold 2014).

The Commission adopted its original Guidelines on state aid for rescuing and restructuring undertakings in difficulty in 1994 (European Commission 1994). In 1997, the Commission added specific rules for agriculture (European Commission 1997). A modified version of the guidelines was adopted in 1999 (European Commission 1999). In 2004, the Commission adopted new guidelines (European Commission 2004), the validity of which was first extended until October 9, 2012 (European Commission 2009) and subsequently until their replacement by new rules (European Commission 2012) in line with the reform program set out in the Commission Communication of May 8, 2012 on EU state aid modernization (SAM 2012). From August 1, 2014, the provisions entered into force of the new guidelines on state aid for rescuing and restructuring non-financial undertakings in a difficult situation (European Commission 2014), which introduces some changes, most favorable to the beneficiaries—e.g., temporary restructuring support.

20.4   Does the Provision of State Aid by the EU Member States for Rescuing and Restructuring Enterprises in Difficulty Affect Their *General Government* Sector Debt?

Taking into account the rules of admissibility of aid for rescuing and restructuring undertakings in difficulty, the enterprise interested in receiving aid must comply with a number of conditions. While the rescue aid is a one-off operation, the aim of which is a temporary improving finances of the enterprise for the time needed to prepare a restructuring or liquidation plan, the restructuring aid is based on the specified plan to restore long-term profitability of the enterprise. Hence, in the latter case, to get the support of the public authorities, the undertaking must provide a detailed recovery plan that describes how to return to financial liquidity and reduce the production, which is a form of compensation for other enterprises in the sector of the economy that did not receive state aid.

In the period 1999–2006, state aid for rescue and restructuring firms in difficulty was granted mainly by the Czech Republic, Germany, Romania, France, Italy, and Poland. Among the nine member states, there can be noted a significant growth in the rescue and restructuring aid in 2008–2010, when the most intense anti-crisis measures were taken. These were the Czech Republic, Greece, Spain, France, Italy, Hungary, Austria, Poland, and Portugal. However, as in the case of the EU level, the increase in the absolute value of this kind of aid did not translate into a significant increase in relation to the total state aid, which resulted from an increase of the expenditures at the same time by the member states on regional and horizontal aid.

In the so-called group of countries of "old fifteen," which have provided this kind of support to domestic entrepreneurs in the greatest amount there should be indication on Austria, Germany, the UK, and Italy. In the period 2009–2014, these countries provided aid for rescuing and restructuring primarily to large enterprises of iron and steel sector (ThyssenKrupp—Germany and Arcelor—France) and air transport (Alitalia—Italy and Olympic Airlines—Greece) and the automotive sector (Opel—Germany and Peugeot Citroen—France). However, in the group of 13 countries that joined the European Union since 2004, the support provided in this direction is characteristic mainly for Poland, and in most cases, it is also sectoral aid.

Does the aid provided by member states to enterprises in difficulty have an adverse effect on the condition of their public finances, leading to an increase in the *general government* sector debt? Or does such aid not have any impact on the *general government* sector debt? Answers to these questions will be provided by the regression analysis. Table 20.1 shows the test result for the sought relationship between the state aid for rescuing and restructuring undertakings in difficulty and the size of the *general government* sector debt, whether the intersection of the regression line with the axis of ordinates (free term) is equal to zero.

The formulated hypothesis concerning the size of the *general government* sector debt in the member states of the European Union, according to which lack of state aid to enterprises in difficulty will reduce the *general government* sector debt to zero, must be rejected. The test for individual member states exceeds a critical value $t_{\frac{\alpha}{2}} = \pm 2.1448$ for $\alpha = 0.05$ and $n - 2 = 14$ degrees of freedom. The probability of making type I error is smaller than the accepted significance level of 0.05, and thus, it is very unlikely that the wrong conclusion will be drawn that not granting state aid by a member state for rescuing and restructuring undertakings cannot lead to a total decrease of the *general government* debt in the European Union. With a probability of 0.95, it can be concluded that in the absence of state aid for rescuing

Table 20.1 Size of state aid for rescuing and restructuring undertakings in difficulty and the size of the *general government* sector debt—analysis of variance: the line "intersection"

EU member states	Free term a	Standard error Sa	t Stat ta	p value	Lower 95%	Upper 95%
Austria	196,172.6	13,922.93	14.08989	1.16E−09	166,310.9	226,034.3
Bulgaria	7,455.44	566.4969	13.1606	2.84E−09	6,240.425	8,670.455
Czech Republic	46,176.2	5,139.433	8.984686	3.46E−07	35,153.21	57,199.18
France	1,436,722	109,804.1	13.08441	3.06E−09	1,201,216	1,672,229
Germany	1,726,884	93,488.71	18.47158	3.15E−11	1,526,370	1,927,397
Greece	251,356.8	24,140.4	10.41229	5.65E−08	199,580.8	303,132.8
Italy	1,749,552	69,985.68	24.99871	5.13E−13	1,599,447	1,899,656
Lithuania	7,970.508	1,174.161	6.788255	8.76E−06	5,452.182	10,488.83
Malta	4,112.359	303.6962	13.54103	1.95E−09	3,460.996	4,763.723
Poland	146,026.5	15,370.81	9.500248	1.76E−07	113,059.4	178,993.6
Portugal	148,701.5	15,754.58	9.438621	1.9E−07	114,911.3	182,491.8
Romania	28,079.75	5,041.697	5.569504	6.91E−05	17266.39	38,893.12
Slovenia	12,085.48	2,425.25	4.983191	0.000201	6883.84	17,287.13
Spain	584,793.5	64,098.35	9.123379	2.87E−07	447316.2	722,270.8
United Kingdom	852,010.1	205,451.6	4.147011	0.000987	411360.2	1,292,660
UE-28	9,326,145	650,789.9	14.3305	9.3E−10	7930340	10,721,951

Source Own calculations

and restructuring in the EU the *general government* sector debt of all 28 member states should adopt a value between (€7930.34 billion, €10721.95 billion). In the case of Czech Republic and Poland, this range would form (€35.15 billion, €57.20 billion) and (€113.10 billion, €178.99 billion).

The most essential statistical test in a simple regression analysis is a test of whether the regression coefficient equals zero. If in a particular case a conclusion can be drawn that the slope coefficient of the true regression line in the population equals zero, it will mean that between expenditures on state aid to enterprises in difficulty and the size of the *general government* sector debt there is no linear relationship, or expenditures on aid and the size of the *general government* sector debt are not linearly dependent. Therefore, it is needed to test the occurrence of linear relationship between expenditures on state aid for rescuing and restructuring undertakings in difficulty in the member states and the size of the *general government* sector debt. The statistics on this test are shown in Table 20.2.

On the basis of the calculations set out in Table 20.2, it should be distinguished that the statistical basis for the recognition of the occurrence of a linear relation between expenditure on state aid and the size of the *general government* sector debt exist only in the case of 2 member states, i.e., Czech Republic and Italy. This relation also occurs at the level of the European Union (EU-28). In these three cases, there is a negative relation between the variables analyzed. For Czech

Table 20.2 Size of state aid for rescuing and restructuring undertakings in difficulty and the size of the *general government* sector debt—analysis of variance: the line "variable X"

EU member states	Regression coefficient b	Standard error Sb	t Stat tb	p value	Lower 95%	Upper 95%
Austria	−1.84261	54.37692	−0.03389	0.973446	−118.469	114.7843
Bulgaria	7.566578	18.53039	0.408333	0.689206	−32.1772	47.31032
Czech Republic	*−9.36975*	*3.844532*	*−2.43716*	*0.028745*	*−17.6155*	*−1.12405*
France	−360.658	217.1862	−1.66059	0.119018	−826.476	105.1604
Germany	−73.3311	49.22386	−1.48975	0.158472	−178.906	32.24363
Greece	−311.38	510.5564	−0.60988	0.55171	−1406.41	783.6545
Italy	*−556.032*	*199.3188*	*−2.78966*	*0.014472*	*−983.528*	*−128.535*
Lithuania	−76.1226	36.63646	−2.07778	0.056609	−154.7	2.454837
Malta	−8.87073	6.442975	−1.37681	0.190191	−22.6895	4.948073
Poland	−35.6374	34.45996	−1.03417	0.318592	−109.547	38.27188
Portugal	−1853.25	934.9139	−1.98226	0.06743	−3858.44	151.9455
Romania	−12.7227	8.158654	−1.55941	0.141212	−30.2213	4.775849
Slovenia	−18.4137	77.83106	−0.23659	0.816405	−185.345	148.5173
Spain	−339.791	248.9674	−1.3648	0.19385	−873.773	194.1911
United Kingdom	770.7115	620.1104	1.242862	0.234333	−559.293	2100.716
EU-28	*−370.813*	*143.9951*	*−2.57518*	*0.022015*	*−679.652*	*−61.9743*

Source Own calculations

Republic, Italy, and Eu-28 level, regression coefficients are negative, which means that expenditure on state aid for rescuing and restructuring undertakings in difficulty has a negative impact on the size of the *general government* sector debt in these countries. The increase in expenditure on public aid by €1 million comes together with a fall in *general government* sector debt, respectively, with an average of €9.37 million, €556.03 million, and €370.81 million. Estimation errors are, respectively, €3.84 million, €199.32 million, and €144.00 million. Taking into account, however, the confidence interval for the regression coefficient, it can be said with a probability of 95% that the increase of granted guarantees for banks with €1 billion will cause fall in *general government* sector debt by the value of the interval (€1.12 million; €17.62 million) for Czech Republic; (€128.54 million; €983.52 million) for Italy; and (€61.97 million; €679.65 million) for Eu-28 level. It should also be noted that the probability of type I error (*p* value), involving the rejection of a true null hypothesis that, in the case of Czech Republic and Italy providing state aid in the form of guarantees for banks, do not significantly affect the size of the GDP *per capita* of the countries, is below the accepted level of significance, i.e., 0.05. The consequence is that the result of the study in relation to these countries, may be considered important, and thus, the null hypothesis can be rejected in favor of the alternative hypothesis. Such a conclusion also applies to the EU-28 level.

Occurrence of the linear relationship between expenditure on state aid for rescuing and restructuring undertakings in difficulty in the above-mentioned member states, and the size of the *general government* sector debt is also confirmed by the *F* test parameters, i.e., the value of *F* test and the probability of type I error when the hypothesis is verified on the lack of impact of expenditure on state aid to the size of the *general government* sector debt (irrelevance of state aid expenditure in the regression model). For all the indicated countries and EU-28 level, *F* test values are higher than the applied critical value of 4.600, and the probability of type I error is less than 0.05. The calculations in this regard are presented in Table 20.3.

While analyzing the value of the correlation coefficient, it should be noted that in the case of countries for which there is a linear relationship between expenditure on state aid and the size of the *general government* sector debt, they are included in the interval (0.55; 0.60) and at the level of the EU-28: 0.57. Countries, such as Czech Republic and Italy, are characterized by very weak negative relationship occurring between the amount of provided state aid and the level of their *general government* sector debt. Moreover, in the case of Czech Republic, Italy, and EU-28 level, there can be no satisfactory adjustment of the regression line to the empirical data. The determination coefficients for these countries equal 0.2978; 0.3573; and for EU-28: 0.3214. So, in the case:

(a) Czech Republic: the variability of size of the *general government* sector debt was explained in 29.78% by variability of expenditure on state aid for rescuing and restructuring undertakings in difficulty. The remaining 70.22% is the effect of random and non-random factors (other non-aid variables, imprecise fit of a straight line to the empirical data, etc.).

Table 20.3 Size of state aid for rescuing and restructuring undertakings in difficulty and the size of the *general government* sector debt—regression statistics and *F* test

EU member states	Regression statistics			F test	
	Correlation indicator	Determination coefficient	Standard error	F	Significance F
Austria	0.009056	8.2E−05	51609.83	0.001148	0.973446
Bulgaria	0.108488	0.01177	2128.818	0.166736	0.689206
Czech Republic	*0.545789*	*0.297885*	*17974.35*	*5.939763*	*0.028745*
France	0.405656	0.164556	380109.3	2.757566	0.119018
Germany	0.36991	0.136833	351272.7	2.219343	0.158472
Greece	0.160875	0.025881	73850.49	0.371958	0.55171
Italy	*0.597723*	*0.357273*	*233755.4*	*7.782199*	*0.014472*
Lithuania	0.485479	0.23569	4009.749	4.317176	0.056609
Malta	0.34533	0.119253	890.0071	1.895598	0.190191
Poland	0.266405	0.070971	54555.99	1.069503	0.318592
Portugal	0.468143	0.219158	52490.32	3.929367	0.06743
Romania	0.384697	0.147992	17647.94	2.431774	0.141212
Slovenia	0.063104	0.003982	7813.422	0.055973	0.816405
Spain	0.342674	0.117425	229595.5	1.862681	0.19385
United Kingdom	0.315233	0.099372	480480.1	1.544705	0.234333
EU-28	*0.566946*	*0.321427*	*1984161*	*6.631544*	*0.022015*

Source Own calculations

(b) Italy: the variability of size of the *general government* sector debt was explained in 35.73% by variability of expenditure on state aid. The remaining 64.27% is the effect of random and non-random factors.

(c) EU-28: the variability of size of the *general government* sector debt was explained in 32.14% by variability of expenditure on state aid. The remaining 67.86% is the effect of random and non-random factors.

If the determination coefficient takes less than 0.5, the regression explains only less than 50% of the variation of the size of the *general government* sector debt and predictions based on such a regression model may be unsuccessful because the regression model explains then very little.

20.5   Conclusion

The question that now arises is whether: Is the (potential) lack of impact of state aid for rescuing and restructuring undertakings on the size of the *general government* sector debt the sufficient justification for its granting? It should be noticed that the principle of compatibility of state aid to the mechanisms of the Single European Market is to provide state aid for the "positive" purposes that is in order to encourage beneficiaries of this aid to the activities that are considered desirable from the point of view of common European interest. Taking into account that the purpose of the "common interest" may be of a social or economic nature, state aid granted by member states is to be directed at targets, such as environmental protection, job creation, investment in research and innovation; or the development of small- and medium-sized enterprises. State aid in accordance with the provisions of the Treaty is to encourage activities to a greater extent than the market would be willing to provide. Therefore, what is the purpose of the state aid for rescuing and restructuring enterprises in difficulty? The aim of this seems not to support a particular activity, but to support the activities "as such." State aid for rescuing and restructuring undertakings in difficulty, that is, enterprises often already standing on the brink of bankruptcy, is concerned to protect existing business activities from the disappearance, which seems to be inevitable without state intervention. The conclusion can be drawn that such aid is not so to encourage specific actions as to prevent the liquidation of its business activities, which would be a natural consequence of the action of the market mechanism. This is especially seen in the case when the state aid is not for the actual restructuring of the enterprise, but it is spent to pay debts or maintain overcapacity. Such activities are often the result of the resistance of the public authorities from the introduction of the necessary, but difficult from the social perspective, changes. But this phenomenon can lead to favoring specific social groups, which can be seen in the case of big enterprises threatened with bankruptcy which operate in sensitive sectors, e.g., the mining industry, shipbuilding, rail, and automotive. And does this kind of aid only delay necessary from economical point of view, but unacceptable for political reasons, certain restructuring actions, in particular the reduction of employment? The answer to this question is essential primarily from the perspective of the notification procedure under which the European Commission assesses the compatibility with the internal market of the plans of aid notified by the member states. As far as in the case of any other state aid, the notification procedures which are to determine the admissibility of aid occur between the authorities of the member state and the European Commission whereas the beneficiary is not formally a party to these proceedings, in the case of aid for rescuing and restructuring, the role of the beneficiary is principally important. In this case, the beneficiary, which is often enterprise standing at the brink of bankruptcy, must develop a restructuring plan, and then implement it and consistently realize. Member state should have in this regard extra responsibility that comes from the fact that when reporting to the European Commission a restructuring plan, the member state confirms the legitimacy and rationality of the destination of public funds for the project, thereby confirming its credibility.

References

Anestis P, Mavroghenis S, Drakakakis S (2004) Rescue and restructuring aid. A brief assessment of the principal provisions of the guidelines. Eur State Aid Law Q 3(1):27–34

Bielecka A (2011) Statystyka dla menedżerów: Teoria i praktyka. Wolters Kluwer Polska, Warszawa

Biondi A (2013) State aid is falling down, falling down: an analysis of the case law on the notion of aid. Common Mark Law Rev 50:1719–1743

Borghetto E (2014) EU law revisions and legislative drift. Eur Union Politics 15:171–191. doi:10. 1177/1465116513513345

Bringmann C (2015) Bankenbeihilfen im Zuge der Finanzkrise. Duncker & Humblot, Berlin

ESCS (1951) Treaty establishing the European Coal and Steel Community. Retrieved from: http://polskawue.go.pl/files/polska_w_ue/prawo/traktaty/Traktat_EWWiS.pdf. 25 Feb 2016

European Commission (1994) Community guidelines on state aid for rescuing and restructuring firms in difficulty, OJ C 368/12. 23 Dec 1994

European Commission (1997) Community guidelines on state aid for rescuing and restructuring firms in difficulty. OJ C 283/2, 19 Sept 1997

European Commission (1999) Community guidelines on state aid for rescuing and restructuring firms in difficulty. OJ C 288/2, 9 Oct 1999

European Commission (2004) Community guidelines on state aid for rescuing and restructuring firms in difficulty. OJ C 244/2, 1 Oct 2004

European Commission (2009) Commission communication concerning the prolongation of the community guidelines on state aid for rescuing and restructuring firms in difficulty. OJ C 156/3, 9 July 2009

European Commission (2012) Commission communication concerning the prolongation of the application of the community guidelines on State aid for rescuing and restructuring firms in difficulty of 1 Oct 2004. OJ C 296, 2 Oct 2012

European Commission (2014) Communication from the commission: guidelines on state aid for rescuing and restructuring non-financial undertakings in a difficulty. OJ C 249/1, 31.7.2014

Pesaresi N, Mamdani G (2012) Latest developments in the rules on state aid for the rescue and restructuring of financial institutions in difficulty. Eur State Aid Law Q 11(4):767–776

Petzold HA (2014) Rescue and restructuring (R&R) guidelines—thoughts and comments on the commission's draft. Eur State Aid Law Q 13(2):289–294

SAM (2012) Communication from the commission to the European parliament, the council, the European economic and social committee and the committee of the regions on EU state aid modernisation. COM/2012/209 final

Schütte M (2012) Revising the rescue and restructuring aid guidelines for the real economy—a practitioner's wishlist. Eur. State Aid Law Q. 11(4):813–819

TFEU (2012) Treaty on the Functioning of the European Union, Consolidated version 2012, OJ C 326, 26 Oct 2012

Valle E, Van de Casteele K (2004a) Revision of the state aid rescue and restructuring guidelines. Competition policy Newsletter No. 3

Valle E, Van de Casteele K (2004b) Revision of rescue and restructuring guidelines: a crack down? Eur State Aid Law Q 3(1):9–16

Chapter 21
Dependence of VAT Revenues on Other Macroeconomic Indicators

Jana Morávková

Abstract The article concerns with the macroeconomic factors affecting VAT revenues in European countries. GDP, GDP per capita, households' consumptions costs, consumptions costs, government's consumption costs, export and the size of the shadow economy are used as the explanatory factors. First of all, we computed correlation coefficient by using yearly differences in order to avoid illusory correlation. We found out that in 13 countries, the VAT revenues are dependent on at least 4 out of 7 factors. Then, we performed multilinear regression thanks to which we were able to stipulate formula for estimation of VAT revenues. We did control the functionality of the formula by computing VAT revenues for 2014 which was not included in our primary calculation. Thanks to this, we could conclude that the formula worked and can be used for the estimation of VAT revenues in future years. The analysis works with Eurostat data on the size and development of shadow economy extended by Schneider (2015).

Keywords VAT revenues · GDP · Consumption costs · Correlation coefficient · Multilinear regression

21.1 Introduction

Taxes constitute a major part of country revenues. Considering the case of the Czech Republic, the state revenue reached CZK 908,536,294 thousands in 2015. With CZK 735,831,821 thousands, the tax-related part of the revenue comprised nearly 81% of the whole income. In particular, the collected value added tax

J. Morávková (✉)
Department of Public Finance, Faculty of Finance and Accounting,
University of Economics, Prague, Nám. W. Churchilla 4,
130 67 Praha 3, Žizkov, Czech Republic
e-mail: janet.moravkova@gmail.com

© Springer International Publishing AG 2017   231
D. Procházka (ed.), *New Trends in Finance and Accounting*,
Springer Proceedings in Business and Economics,
DOI 10.1007/978-3-319-49559-0_21

(VAT) amounted to CZK 166,708,821 thousands in the same year[1] which means that VAT revenues compounded more than 22% of the overall tax revenues. Moreover, with the recently introduced concept of VAT control statement, the VAT share in the tax mix is supposed to increase. According to the tax authority, the revenue will increase for approximately CZK 10,000,000 thousands.[2] Therefore, a study on the relationship between VAT revenue and standard macroeconomic indicators is of practical importance as VAT plays a significant role in state income.

VAT plays an extremely important role in state budget. The aim of this article is to stipulate the dependence of VAT revenues on several selected factors and which of these factors possess the biggest influence. These factors were chosen according to already published articles which concern with VAT. Furthermore, we added the size of shadow economy as a factor influencing VAT revenues as it could have interesting impact on results.

We assume that the gross domestic product, gross domestic product per capita, export, overall consumption costs, households' and government's consumption costs should positively influence VAT revenues. On the other hand, the size of the shadow economy should have negative impact on VAT revenues.

The article is divided into four chapters. In the first one, the basic features of VAT are presented. The second part sums up the literature overview which concerns VAT. The third part contains analysis of factors affecting VAT revenues where we used different functions in Excel. The last part is conclusion.

21.2   Features of VAT

VAT shows several positive properties. First of all, it is one of the largest parts of countries' tax revenues. Secondly, the VAT is able to stabilize state budget during economic recession (Bikas and Andruskaite 2013). This feature member states of European Union (furthermore only EU) represent very well. Fig. 21.1 shows how the tax rates changed between years 2007 and 2012.

Figure 21.1 shows that 17 out of 28 European countries raised VAT rate during or shortly after recent financial crisis. The VAT rate in the rest 11 countries remained the same. Average increase reached 1.55 p.p. We could observe the highest growth of the rate in Hungary where the government increased VAT rate by 7 p.p. Thanks to higher VAT rate, the VAT revenues did not dropped so significantly and in spite of economic crisis they even increased in some countries.

Another convenient characteristic of VAT is that almost all individuals and active companies, institutions and organizations are obliged to pay this tax (Bikas and Rashkauskas 2011). Moreover, indirect taxes including VAT are less visible

---

[1]According to the http://monitor.statnipokladna.cz/2015/statni-rozpocet/.

[2]According to the Czech tax authority; available: http://www.financnisprava.cz/assets/cs/prilohy/d-seznam-dani/KH_caste_omyly_20151112.pdf.

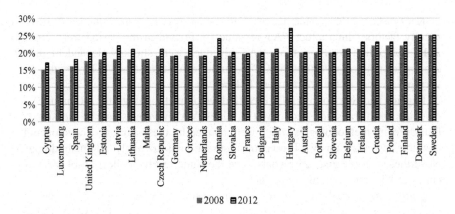

Fig. 21.1 VAT rates in 2008 and 2012 in European countries. *Source* Eurostat (2014): Taxation trends in the European Union

than direct taxes. Therefore, the government will support increase in indirect tax rates instead of increasing direct tax rates (Fasora 2009). We can observe this fact in the Czech Republic. VAT rates were increasing steadily since 2005. In contrary, the corporate income tax rates were decreasing continuously (or remained the same) in the same period of time (VAT Act and the Income Tax Act).

21.3 Literature Review

As stated above, VAT revenues are extremely important for every country in European Union; therefore, many authors and European institutions concern with this issue. Development of VAT (revenues, tax rates) is regularly observed by European Union. Every year taxation trends in the European Union (Data for the EU Member States, Iceland and Norway) are published. This publication includes, for example, the VAT rates and revenues of European countries.

Factors affecting VAT revenues were researched by Bikas and Andruskaite (2013). These authors calculated correlation coefficient of VAT revenues and factors influencing them in EU. Concretely, they investigated a relationship between VAT revenues and GDP, GDP per capita, consumption costs, households' consumption costs, export, import, unemployment. Their concluded that VAT income is more influenced by the households' consumption than the government's one.

Bikas and Rashkauskas (2011) examined VAT dimension in the case of Lithuania. Authors concluded that the greater difference between the standard and reduced tariff had significant positive influence on VAT revenues. Their article also points out that unemployment during 1995–2009 affected VAT revenues in Lithuania too.

Kaczyńska (2015) concerned with the VAT revenues in Poland and tried to specify factors which affect VAT revenues in Poland in the period from 2000 to 2013. According to the author, VAT revenues were strongly dependent on the economic situation measured by GDP. Author also stated that VAT revenues were very procyclical in the short run in Poland.

Legeida and Sologoub (2003) tried to develop methodology for estimating VAT revenues for a transition economy (Ukraine). VAT revenues can be measured by four different methodologies which were applied by these authors. They concluded that the best way for VAT revenues estimation is to apply all methodologies. Nevertheless at the end, all models gave the same result—collection of VAT revenues in Ukraine is highly imperfect.

Studies performed by researchers far outside European borders support the importance of VAT not only for European Union but all over the world. Karagöz (2013) is concerned with the determinants of tax revenues including VAT. According to the author, the agricultural and industrial sectors' share on GDP has a major effect on tax revenues in Turkey. Wawire (2011) researches determinants of VAT revenues in Kenya and states that GDP, institutional, demographic, and structural characteristics of the economy determine VAT revenues.

21.4 Analysis of Factors Affecting Value Added Tax Revenues

VAT revenues are affected by several factors. According to Legeida and Sologoub (2003), VAT revenues depend on structural aspects of the tax (tax rates, bases), then on the scale of taxable activities and tax compliance. Bikas and Andruskaite (2013) add that VAT revenues are affected by lots of factors including gross domestic product which describes the economic situation of the country. Furthermore, VAT revenues are influenced by consumption level in the country. Other factors, which can influence VAT revenues, could be export and import (Bikas and Andruskaite 2013).

For the purpose of this article, we have chosen several factors, which are supposed to influence VAT revenues. Concretely we assume that GDP, GPD per capita, households' consumption costs, overall and government's consumption costs, export and size of shadow economy should influence VAT revenues. First of all, we calculated correlation coefficient in European countries by using data from Eurostat and data presented by Schneider (2015). Data from Eurostat are in million euros, and it can be expected that the method of its collection is the same in all European countries. Nevertheless, there were some data missing. As an example, VAT revenues for Greece in 2005 can be stated. Schneider (2015) presented size of the shadow economy in % of GDP. We applied statistical functions CORREL in Excel.

Table 21.1 Correlation coefficient based on yearly differences in European countries

Country	GDP	GDP per capita	Household's consumption costs	Consumption costs	Government's consumption costs	Export	Size of shadow economy % of GDP
Austria	0.50	0.49	0.44	0.47	0.24	0.43	−0.43
Belgium	0.87	0.85	0.66	0.49	−0.62	0.84	−0.61
Bulgaria	0.76	0.73	0.62	0.85	0.80	0.66	−0.66
Croatia	0.81	0.81	–	0.79	0.51	0.86	−0.85
Cyprus	0.83	0.89	0.83	0.84	0.23	0.78	−0.69
Czech Republic	0.87	0.85	0.90	0.88	0.76	0.64	−0.46
Denmark	0.76	0.78	0.78	0.69	−0.31	0.72	−0.67
Estonia	0.78	0.78	0.72	0.66	0.16	0.38	−0.32
Finland	0.70	0.70	0.67	0.63	0.09	0.66	−0.41
France	0.94	0.93	0.86	0.75	−0.57	0.97	−0.66
Germany	0.45	0.46	0.01	−0.29	−0.56	0.31	−0.11
Great Britain	0.92	0.93	0.92	0.90	0.81	0.87	−0.47
Greece	0.64	0.60	0.98	0.46	0.10	0.36	−0.55
Hungary	0.62	0.63	0.76	0.67	0.33	0.38	−0.60
Ireland	0.93	0.95	0.86	0.02	−0.04	−0.05	−0.84
Italy	0.78	0.81	0.75	0.68	0.05	0.80	−0.50
Latvia	0.84	0.85	0.82	0.80	0.58	0.76	−0.57
Lithuania	0.97	0.97	0.89	0.87	0.64	0.77	−0.83
Luxemburg	0.31	0.23	0.27	0.67	0.37	0.21	−0.22
Malta	0.44	0.40	0.56	0.47	0.45	0.12	−0.48
Netherlands	0.83	0.82	0.82	0.61	0.09	0.74	−0.85
Poland	0.93	0.93	0.90	0.90	0.87	0.93	−0.73
Portugal	0.58	0.56	0.77	0.44	−0.38	0.95	−0.66
Romania	0.90	0.89	0.97	0.89	0.49	0.93	−0.34
Slovakia	0.65	0.65	0.65	0.53	0.30	0.39	−0.55
Slovenia	0.89	0.90	0.70	0.55	0.16	0.83	−0.82
Spain	0.21	0.32	0.46	0.17	−0.36	0.76	−0.35
Sweden	0.98	0.98	0.96	0.95	0.93	0.94	−0.45
Arith. mean	0.74	0.74	0.72	0.62	0.22	0.64	−0.56

Source of data Eurostat, Schneider (2015), own calculation

The correlation coefficient was calculated by using differences between individual years. Thanks to this calculation, we avoided illusory correlation which could be observed if the correlation coefficient was calculated by using values of individual years. Correlation coefficient of each European country is presented in Table 21.1.

As we applied the difference between individual years, the correlation coefficient is not so strong. Nevertheless, we can observe that relationship between VAT revenues and GDP, GDP per capita and household's consumption costs is quite strong (see the line with arithmetic mean).

Dependence (correlation coefficient exceeding 0.80) of VAT revenues on GDP was confirmed in 14 countries, on GDP per capita in 15 countries, on household's consumption costs in 12 countries and on export in 10 countries. The dependence of VAT revenues on overall consumption costs was confirmed only in 9 countries and on government's consumption costs in only 3 countries. In the case of the size of shadow economy, the correlation coefficient shows various results. The value dropped under −0.80 in only 4 countries. It means that the size of shadow economy influences VAT revenues only in 4 countries.

In 8 countries (Germany, Hungary, Luxembourg, Malta, Slovakia, Finland, Spain and Austria), it seems that VAT revenues are rather not dependent on tested macroeconomic factors.

On the other hand, in 13 countries the VAT revenues are dependent on at least 4 out of 7 tested macroeconomic factors. Concretely these countries are Croatia, the Netherlands, France, Romania, Slovenia, Sweden, Great Britain, Cyprus, Latvia, Poland, Lithuania, Czech Republic, and Ireland.

As a next step, we performed multilinear regression by using tools for data analysis, exactly regression in Excel. We used data from 2005 to 2013. We did not include data of the year 2014 as it is supposed to work as a control mechanism whether the calculated formula functioned or not. We worked on significance level of 5%. Based on P value GDP per capita, export and size of shadow economy are not statistically significant. Therefore, these indicators were excluded and the formula is as follows:

$$y = -1237.64 + 0.076x_1 - 0.018x_2 - 0.026x_3 + 0.055x_4 \qquad (21.1)$$

where,

x_1 gross domestic product;
x_2 households' consumption costs;
x_3 consumption costs; and
x_4 government's consumption costs.

As a next step, we computed VAT revenues for the period 2005–2014 by using formula Eq. 21.1. We calculated and compared the results with actual VAT revenues in relevant period of time. Our results are shown in Fig. 21.2 (VAT revenues are in millions of EUR). As stated above, we did not include the year 2014 for the computation of the formula. Even though that the results slightly differ, they offer quite solid estimation of VAT revenues. We can conclude that our formula can be used for the computation of VAT revenues in future years in spite of they were not included in multilinear regression computation. In Fig. 21.2 is visible a gap in 2013. This was caused by several missing data in 2013 (e.g., consumption costs).

As it was discussed above, even though the data in 2014 slightly differ, our formula can be used for an approximate estimation of VAT revenues for the next year.

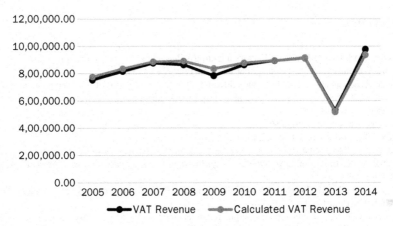

Fig. 21.2 Comparison of computed VAT revenues with the actual ones

21.5 Conclusion

The aim of this article was to stipulate which factors affect VAT revenues and how do they affect them. We expected that VAT revenues depend on GDP, GDP per capita, households' consumptions costs, consumptions costs, government's consumption costs, export and the size of the shadow economy. We assumed that all of the factors except the shadow economy should have positive influence on VAT revenues. First of all, we computed correlation coefficient to find out whether there exist some relationship between VAT revenues and other macroeconomic factors. We did use yearly differences in order to avoid illusory correlation. Due to that the correlation coefficient was much lower. Nevertheless, in 13 European countries the dependence of VAT revenues on at least 4 macroeconomic factors was confirmed. Nevertheless, in some countries (for example, Germany) it seems that VAT revenues are not dependent on any of used macroeconomic factors.

Then, we performed multilinear regression in order to obtain formula which can estimate the amount of VAT revenues only according to the macroeconomic data. We did not include the year 2014 for the computation of the formula as we wanted to compare results based on our formula with actual revenues which were reached in 2014. The results did not differ significantly, and the formula can be used for future years.

VAT revenues represent one of the most important elements of tax system and for countries' budget are crucial. There exist plenty of possible future fields of research in this area which can bring interesting results.

Acknowledgments This paper has been prepared within the research project IG108016 Veřejné finance v ČR a v EU.

References

Bikas E, Andruskaite E (2013) Factors affecting value added tax revenue. Eur. Sci. J. Available: http://eujournal.org/index.php/esj/article/viewFile/1230/1239

Bikas E, Rashkauskas J (2011) Value added tax dimension: the case of Lithuania, Ekonomika, 90 (1):22–38. ISSN 1392-1258. Avaiable: http://www.zurnalai.vu.lt/files/journals/37/articles/958/public/22-38.pdf

Czech income tax act (No. 586/1992)

Czech value added tax act (No. 235/2004)

Fasora O (2009) Fiskální iluze a daňové kánony Adama Smithe. Ekonomická fakulta VŠB-TU Ostrava [online]. Avaiable: http://www.ekf.vsb.cz/shared/uploadedfiles/cul33/Fasora. Ondrej.pdf

Kaczyńska A (2015) The analysis of VAT revenue in Poland—the size and determinants. The 3rd Global Virtual Conference

Karagöz, K. (2013) Determinants of tax revenue: does sectorial composition matter? J. Finan. Account. Manage. 4(2). Available: http://www.gsmi-ijgb.com/Documents/JFAM%20V4% 20N2%20P04%20-Kadir%20Karag%C3%B6z%20-Determinants%20of%20Tax%20Revenue. pdf

Legeida N, Sologoub D (2003) Modeling Value Added Tax (VAT) Revenues in a transition economy: case of Ukraine, Institute for economic research and policy consulting working paper No. 22

Schneider F (2015) Size and development of the shadow economy of 31 European and 5 other OECD countries from 2003 to 2015: different developments. Available: http://www.econ.jku. at/members/Schneider/files/publications/2015/ShadEcEurope31.pdf

Taxation trends in the European Union. Data for the EU Member States, Iceland and Norway (Eurostat). http://ec.europa.eu/taxation_customs/resources/documents/taxation/gen_info/ economic_analysis/tax_structures/2014/report.pdf

Wawire, NHW (2011) Determinants of value added tax revenue in Kenya. CSAE conference paper

Chapter 22
Shares in Central Government Income Taxes as a Revenues Source of Urban Municipalities in Poland

Jarosław Olejniczak

Abstract In Poland, local government shares in personal income tax (PIT) and corporate income tax (CIT) are included in their own revenues. Along with the increasing scope of own tasks implemented by the municipalities, which was the effect of advancing decentralization, the legislator granted to municipalities' larger part of PIT and CIT taxes collected on their territory by the budget. This analysis is aimed at examining the significance of shares in PIT and CIT constituting the revenues in all Polish urban municipalities in the years 1996–2014. The conducted analysis of data from the years 1996–2014 shows the existence of significant differences between the urban municipalities in Poland in the scope of acquired shares in PIT and CIT. This diversity has its basis both in different tax bases of the urban municipalities in PIT tax and CIT tax. However, while the CIT tax plays a small role in the budget revenues of most municipalities, in the case of PIT its share in general revenues can be recognized as relatively significant. By examining changes in the scope of scale of funding the urban municipalities with above-mentioned revenues, it can be noted that despite the increase in the percentage rate of share in the case of PIT, the share of this type of revenue in the budgets of municipalities did not increase in significant manner.

Keywords Municipality · Share in central government income taxes

22.1 Introduction

Providing budget revenues to municipalities, which are adequate to their needs, is still a significant problem in Poland. Since the early nineties of twentieth century, the Polish municipalities have been financed based on three main sources of rev-

J. Olejniczak (✉)
Department of Finance, Wroclaw University of Economics,
Komandorska 118/120, 53-341 Wrocław, Poland
e-mail: jaroole@ue.wroc.pl

© Springer International Publishing AG 2017
D. Procházka (ed.), *New Trends in Finance and Accounting*,
Springer Proceedings in Business and Economics,
DOI 10.1007/978-3-319-49559-0_22

enues—own revenues, general grants, and purpose grants. Such solution was supposed to level out the differences in the revenue base, resulting from geographical location and economic conditions. Own revenues can be divided into (local) taxes, charges, shares in central government taxes personal income tax (PIT) and corporate income tax (CIT), revenues from municipal property, and other revenues (Olejniczak 2015). Taxes consist of two subgroups—first, real estate tax, agriculture tax, forest tax, and means of transportation (vehicle) tax, where the local self-government councils have taxing powers (negative), and second, flat rate income tax, inheritance and donation tax, and tax on civil law entities, where local government have no taxing power. Next group includes stamp duty, market (sell) charge, local charge, administrative charge, dog charge, or charge from premises for selling alcoholic beverages (rates are usually set by local self-government councils).

Due to high diversity of income in communes, there is an advanced compensatory system aimed at protecting local government units that have a low-income potential. The differences in income are subject to the compensatory mechanism that is progressive in nature. The compensatory part of the overall grant for communes is composed of the basic amount and the supplementary amount. With respect to the basic amount, it is significant to determine the amount of the basic taxable income (BTI) per resident. In general, the basic amount is received by the communes where taxable income per resident is lower than 92% of the average taxable income per resident of the country (Olejniczak 2013). It is a kind of horizontal equalization—called "Robin Hood tax" because the compensatory part is determined as the total amount of the payments made by the communes whose BTI ratio exceeds 150% of the BTI per capita in the country. This system is supported by educational general grant. The algorithm used for it takes into consideration different weights significant for most of the local governments. The main idea is to distribute money from central budget to self-governments according to "weighted number of pupils" (not necessary according to real costs of delivering educational services) (Olejniczak 2016). Along with the increasing scope of own tasks implemented by the municipalities, which was the effect of advancing decentralization, the legislator granted to municipalities larger part of PIT and CIT taxes collected on their territory by the budget. This analysis is aimed at examining the significance of shares in PIT and CIT constituting the revenues in Polish urban municipalities in the years 1996–2014. Its purpose is to answer the question concerning the existence of differences in the level and share of revenues of the urban municipalities in individual regions of Poland, which will form the basis for consideration of the legitimacy of adopted direction of revenue distribution between the state and the municipalities.

22.2   Research Methods, Scope, and Purpose of Work

This chapter will include the presentation of research results concerning the structure of budget revenues of 308 out of approx. 314 Polish urban municipalities (only those municipalities were omitted for which the data from minimum 2 studied years were not available). The research covered urban municipalities, which due to their specificity are characterized by relatively similar possibilities of tax base creation in the long term. Unlike the urban municipalities and urban–rural municipalities, these municipalities are characterized by a large number of residents who are the taxpayers of PIT tax and usually a larger number of entities covered by CIT taxation. As a result, the structure and the significance of revenues from shares in these taxes to the budgets of municipalities should be similar in the urban municipalities.

The first part of the chapter will describe the reasons for selection of the systems of shares in central taxes as one of the sources for funding the municipalities in Poland. Then, a short analysis of the evolution of scale and form of funding the budgets of municipalities by shares in PIT and CIT, throughout the studied period, will be conducted. This analysis will be conducted based on the legal sources and the literature research.

The second part of the chapter will be devoted to the analysis of data obtained from the Local Data Bank of the Central Statistical Office concerning individual revenues of municipalities in the studied period.

22.3   Literature Review

The problem of revenue division between the state budget and the local government units in the unitary countries is usually associated with the degree of decentralization of public finances in the individual countries. Poland as a signatory of the European Charter of Local Self-Government, before its ratification, had based the funding system of newly created municipalities on the patterns contained therein. This means that Poland tried to respect both the principle of giving the municipalities their own revenues—article 9, item 3 ECLSG (by granting them the taxing power and by introducing shares in taxes, which are included in Poland to own revenues, constituting the central government revenues—PIT and CIT)—and the principle of adequate financial resources for tasks (among others) by the increase in the subsequent years, along with the growth of the scope of tasks transferred to municipalities, the scale of transferred shares in income taxes—article 9, item 2 and 4 ECLSG.

In the subject literature, there is a dispute about the placement of shares in PIT and CIT in the structure of revenues of municipalities. Until the end of the nineties, theses revenues, in accordance with Polish legal regulations, constituted a revenue category that was separated from the own revenues. Such placement of these revenues was in line with the views of many national authors (Kosek-Wojnar and Surówka 2007, pp. 71–72; Ruśkowski and Salachna 2007, p. 107; Swianiewicz 2004, p. 31), which seem to reflect the position of the Council of Europe recognizing the shares in central taxes, in regard to which the municipalities do not have direct impact on their shaping, as equivalent to grants and not to own revenues (Wojtowicz 2013). From a legal point of view in Poland, these shares currently constitute own revenues under the Act of 2003 on revenues of local government units. This solution is criticized as ostensible increasing in the revenue independence of municipalities, due to the above-mentioned lack of taxing powers of municipalities in relation to the mentioned shares (Surówka 2004, pp. 21–27).

The premise for granting shares to municipalities in PIT and CIT generated in their territory was mainly the supplementation of limited revenues from local taxes and charges, as well as the desire to mobilize local communities to increase the tax base of municipality. The specificity of PIT taxation in Poland seems to consider such assumption to be doubtful. This tax still is not a general tax—because a significant number of people are statutorily exempted from its regulation—i.e., people conducting agricultural activity. However, in the studied urban municipalities, this assumption seems to be correct.

It should be also noted that the size of municipality revenues from shares in PIT and CIT was affected by numerous changes in tax regulations, mainly associated with the changes in tax rates and changes in the structure of allowances. For example, in 2005, the share rate in PIT was lower than in 2004, but some part of allowances in PIT was eliminated, which raised the revenues of the part of municipalities, while in 2008, due to the introduction of pro-family allowance, the municipalities reported a loss of revenues despite the increased share.

In the early years, these shares represented from 15% in the period 1992–1996 to 17% in 1998 and 27.6% of tax revenues from PIT collected within the territory of given municipality and 5% of revenues from CIT. After 2003, the target share in PIT for municipalities was supposed to amount to 39.34%; however, the reaching of this level was started from 35.72% in 2004 and currently amounts to 37.53% (Table 22.1). For example, the calculation of share in PIT in the given year (t) is based on the determination of the share of given municipality in total PIT incomes from $t - 2$ year and the use of this rate to calculate the current amount attributable to the municipality. Therefore, it is a rolling mechanism that only after two years reflects the changes in the activity of taxpayers of the given municipality in comparison with other municipalities.

Table 22.1 Percentage shares of municipalities in PIT and CIT in 1996–2014 years (%)

	1996	1997	1998	1999–2003	2004	2005	2006	2007	2008	2009	2010	2011	2012	2013	2014
PIT	15	16	17	27.6	35.72	35.61	35.95	36.22	36.49	36.72	36.94	37.12	37.26	37.42	37.53
CIT	5	5	5	5	6.71	6.71	6.71	6.71	6.71	6.71	6.71	6.71	6.71	6.71	6.71

Source Own work

22.4   Data Analysis Results

The importance of funds from the shares in revenue taxes for the budgets of municipalities can be illustrated by its relation to the entirety of revenues. It should be noted that in the studied period, in the case of average value, as well as the median of this type of revenues, there were slight changes oscillating around the level of 20% of total revenues (Fig. 22.1). While comparing the above-mentioned changes with the course of business cycle in Poland, it should be noted that these fluctuations are consistent with the periods of prosperity and downturn in Poland. This demonstrates the vulnerability of the mentioned revenue categories in regard to the impact of business cycle (more about business cycle in Poland, e.g., Gradzewicz et al. 2010, p. 50). At the same time, while examining the differences in significance of the discussed budget revenues in the regional aspect, it is worth noting that the lowest percentage share of incomes from PIT and CIT was noted by municipalities with specific revenue base—municipalities of tourist nature from the Pomerania Voivodeship (e.g., Łeba, Krynica Morska) and Lower Silesia Voivodeship (Duszniki Zdrój, Polanica Zdrój, Świeradów Zdrój). On the other hand, since the beginning of 2000, the highest shares of revenues from PIT and CIT have been reported by municipalities of Silesia Voivodeship, which was the result of existence of strong tax base on their territory associated with mining and industry. However, in the subsequent years, the highest incomes from the studied sources of revenues were achieved (in relation to the revenues in general) by city municipalities of Mazovia Voivodeship, which can be associated with their functioning on the outskirts of Warsaw.

The analysis of the share of own revenues in the general revenues indicates the existence of significant difference between the cities. While the average share of own revenues in the general revenues oscillates around 60% in the studied period, it is still possible to note cities, in which it is by 30 percentage points higher or lower (Fig. 22.2). In the second half of the nineties, among municipalities with the lowest

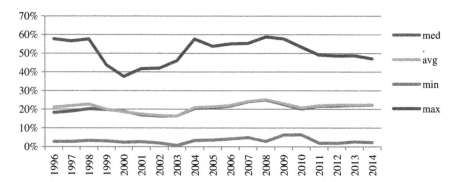

Fig. 22.1 PIT and CIT shares as a part of total revenues in surveyed municipalities in 1996–2014. *Source* Authorial calculation based on BDL data

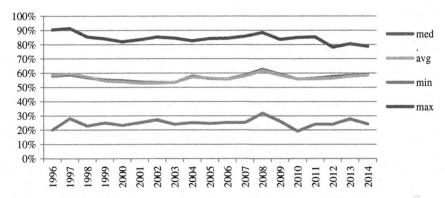

Fig. 22.2 Own revenues as a part of total revenues in surveyed municipalities in 1996–2014.
Source authorial calculation based on BDL data

revenue potential, there were usually the municipalities from voivodeships of central Poland (Kujawy–Pomerania Voivodeship, Łódź Voivodeship) and eastern Poland—Podlaskie Voivodeship and Lublin Voivodeship, while the most numerous representation had Kujawy–Pomerania Voivodeship. After 2000, the most numerous representations had municipalities located in such voivodeships as: Kujawy–Pomerania Voivodeship, Podlaskie Voivodeship, Lublin Voivodeship, Podkarpackie Voivodeship, and Małopolskie Voivodeship. After the amendments to regulations in 2003, the structure of regions that included municipalities with the lowest percentage of own revenues in relation to general revenues changed— among the municipalities with the lowest share of own revenues, the municipalities from Lower Silesia Voivodeship and Wielkopolska Voivodeship appeared. However, after 2010, it has been visible that mainly municipalities from three voivodeships—Kujawy–Pomerania Voivodeship, Lublin Voivodeship and Podkarpackie Voivodeship—have been included to the municipalities with the lowest percentage of own revenues. On the other hand, in the entire studied period, among municipalities with the highest percentage of own revenues in relation to general revenues, the municipalities of Wielkopolska Voivodeship, Mazovia Voivodeship, Silesia Voivodeship, and Lower Silesia Voivodeship were dominating.

Therefore, it is necessary to ask whether in these municipalities, the revenues from shares in PIT and CIT are significant. While comparing data concerning municipalities with low share of own revenues and with level of shares in PIT and CIT in relation to own revenues, it should be indicated that in less than 40% share of own revenues in relation to general revenues, only from 20 to 35% of own revenues are the funds from PIT and CIT. At the same time, among municipalities with low share of own revenues in relation to general revenues, there are no tourist municipalities that were mentioned before. This means that in the case of part of urban municipalities, the low level of shares in PIT and CIT can be replaced by other own revenues.

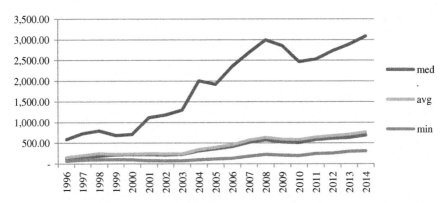

Fig. 22.3 Total revenues per capita in surveyed municipalities in 1996–2014 period. *Source* Authorial calculation based on BDL data

While analyzing the situation of urban municipalities in the years 1996–2014, it should be noted that total nominal revenues per capita are characterized in most units by stable growth and only few municipalities—with the highest tax base showed a large variation in revenues. The analysis of revenues of individual municipalities showed that the decreases in revenues from income taxes collected within the given municipality were compensated in some part by other grants from the state budget (Fig. 22.3).

When undertaking the analysis of changes in the level of nominal tax revenues per capita, the attention must be mainly paid to these revenues that are associated with the shares in PIT tax. The reason for this is the fact that these revenues in most municipalities constitute main part of the funds obtained by municipalities from the shares in tax revenues of the state. In the years 1996–2002, with a relatively low 15–16 % share of municipalities in PIT, these units did not show large difference in the level of revenues (Fig. 22.4). In accordance with the presented data, in the years 1996–2000, the disparity of revenues from share in PIT per capita of urban municipalities was not significant, because there was nearly double difference between the poorest municipality and the median, and less than triple difference

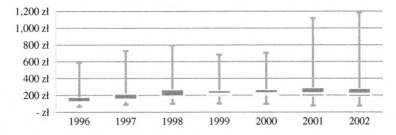

Fig. 22.4 PIT share per capita in surveyed municipalities in 1996–2002 period. *Source* Authorial calculation based on BDL data

between the poorest municipality and revenues of the municipality designating the third quartile. After 2001, and especially since 2003, after the changes of shares of municipalities in PIT, these disproportions have started to grow, which resulted in the fact that the median exceeded it three times at minimum and the value of third quartile more than four times (minimum). Only the period of economic slowdown after 2008 has brought a reversal of this trend and the consolidation of relation of the median at level of 2.2 times (minimum) and in the case of third quartile—nearly the three times level at minimum (Fig. 22.5).

In turn, when analyzing the focus of tax shares from PIT per capita by the quotient of the value of third and first quartiles, it must be indicated that since 1996, there has been a slow decline in regard to this relation—because in 1996, it constituted twice the amount, while in the last period this relations amounts only to the level of 1.5 times. Other trend may be noted, when analyzing the direction of changes in the relation of minimal and maximum values. Changes in the scale of share as well as economic changes had a significant impact on the revenues of some municipalities. While in the initial period, the relation of maximum amount in regard to minimum amount of shares per capita oscillated around 8, then in 2004, it reached the maximum level of 20 times. However, in the subsequent years, it has declined by approx. 10, which was partially caused by changes in the tax legislation and partially by economic downturn.

The analysis of median distribution of PIT revenues per capita in regional aspect (Fig. 22.6) also indicates, as in the case of analysis of individual urban municipalities, significantly larger revenue potential of the municipalities of Mazovia Voivodeship (14), Silesia Voivodeship (24), and Wielkopolska Voivodeship (30). On the other hand, the lowest revenue potential per one resident, from perspective of the median, is exhibited by the municipalities of following voivodeships: Podlaskie Voivodeship (20), Świętokrzyskie Voivodeship (26), West Pomerania Voivodeship (32), and Łódź Voivodeship (10).

The lowest tax revenues per one resident in the late nineties were generated in Lublin Voivodeship (6) and Podlaskie Voivodeship (20)—they did not exceed 100 PLN/person (1997). However, after 2000, a group of municipalities was revealed,

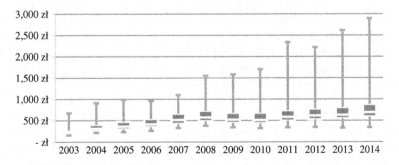

Fig. 22.5 PIT share per capita in surveyed municipalities in 2003–2014 period. *Source* Authorial calculation based on BDL data

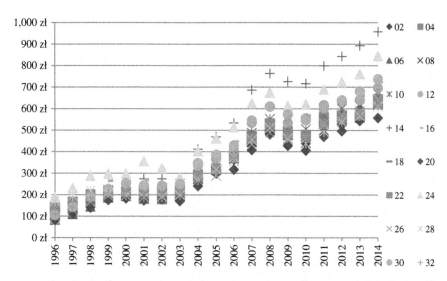

Fig. 22.6 PIT share per capita in surveyed municipalities aggregated to NUTS 2 level (voivodeship) in 1996–2014 period, where *02* dolnośląskie, *04* kujwskopomorskie, *06* lubelskie, *08* lubuskie, *10* łódzkie, *12* małopolskie, *14* mazowieckie, *16* opolskie, *18* podkarpackie, *20* podlaskie, *22* pomorskie, *24* śląskie, *26* świętokrzyskie, *28* warmińsko-mazurskie, *30* wielkopolskie, *32* zachodniopomorskie. *Source* Authorial calculation based on BDL data

which annually recorded the lowest tax shares per capita. These municipalities included the following: Piława, Górna, Pieszyce, Wojcieszów from Lower Silesia Voivodeship, Łęknica and Gozdnica from the Lubuskie Voivodeship, Dynów and Radymno from Podkarpackie Voivodeship (18), and individual municipalities from other voivodeships. The highest revenues from PIT per capita were achieved by large cities, such as Warsaw, Gdynia, Poznań and cities of Warsaw agglomeration—among others, Podkowa Leśna, Piastów.

When analyzing the spread of the revenues of municipalities that determine the median in individual voivodeships, it can be observed that these values (in the entire studied period) do not show any significant differences and they tend to get similar. The relation of maximum and minimum values recorded in sixteen voivodeships, in the initial years, exceeded 2.2 times, while from 1999, it fell below 2 and after 2007, it stabilized at the level of 1.7 times. It can be demonstrated that relation of the revenue value from PIT per capita for the median of revenues, calculated for the voivodeship determining third and first quartiles, is only 1.15, and therefore, it is a highly flattened structure.

When examining scale of disparity between the median of shares in CIT per capita obtained by municipalities in individual voivodeships (Fig. 22.7), it should be noted that the major differences in medians between the urban municipalities are mainly determined by the number of cities in the given voivodeship and business entities operating in their area. For example, in the Opole Voivodeship, only three cities are included in examination—two of them achieve shares in CIT at the level

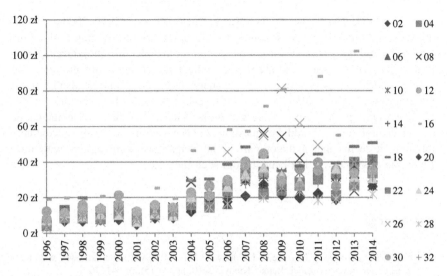

Fig. 22.7 CIT share per capita in surveyed municipalities aggregated to NUTS 2 level (voivodeship) in 1996–2014 period, where see Fig. 22.6. *Source* Authorial calculation based on BDL data

above 100 PLN per capita (large business entities are located within their area), and this results in their high median. However, the average value for these cities is much lower, because it oscillated around 60 PLN per capita. Similar situation applies to municipalities of Lubuskie Voivodeship and Świętokrzyskie Voivodeship. As can be seen in the case of share in CIT, the largest disparities occur in the urban municipalities—because these municipalities obtain very small incomes from this tax (excluding adjustments) and these are also the municipalities that have shares in CIT oscillating between 400 and 600 PLN per capita.

22.5   Conclusion

The conducted analysis of data from the years 1996–2014 shows the existence of significant differences between the urban municipalities in Poland in the scope of acquired shares in PIT and CIT. This diversity has its basis both in different tax bases of the urban municipalities in PIT tax and CIT tax. However, while the CIT tax plays a small role in the budget revenues of most municipalities, in the case of PIT its share in general revenues can be recognized as relatively significant. By examining the changes in the scope of scale of funding the urban municipalities with the above-mentioned revenues, it can be noted that despite the increase in the percentage rate of share in the case of PIT, the share of this type of revenue in the budgets of municipalities did not increase in significant manner. It should be also noted that such structure of the revenues of municipalities was susceptible to the fluctuations of business cycle, which was visible in the years 1999–2003 and 2008–2011. At the same time, the structure of share in the tax, functioning in the Polish legislation, did not guarantee the compensation for the effects of introduced changes in the system of tax rates and allowances, which caused numerous protests of the municipalities' authorities. In the case of shares in PIT, it should be also noted that there are visible fixed differences in the levels of revenues between the voivodeships. To sum up, the purposefulness of further increase in shares of municipalities in the central taxes should be questioned, because on the basis of conducted research, it seems that a major part of municipalities from regions with lower economic potential will not benefit from such increase.

References

Gradzewicz M, Growiec J, Hagemejer J, Popowski P (2010) Cykl koniunkturalny w Polsce – wnioski z analizy spektralnej. Bank i Kredyt, 2010, no. 41 (5), pp. 41–76

Kosek-Wojnar M, Surówka K (2007) Podstawy finansów samorządu terytorialnego. PWN, Warszawa 2007

Olejniczak J (2013) Compensatory grant in polish rural communes: modification concept and its impact on finance and communes. In: Klimova V, Zitek V (ed) 16th international colloquium on regional sciences. Conference proceedings, pp 541–548, Masaryk University. http://doi.org/10.5817/CZ.MUNI.P210-6257-2013-68

Olejniczak J (2015) Fiscal efficiency and stability of own revenues in urban local self-governments' budgets before, during and after crisis—example from Lower Silesian voivodeship. In: Klimova V, Zitek V (ed) 18th international colloquium on regional sciences. Conference proceedings, pp 440–446. Masaryk University. http://doi.org/10.5817/CZ.MUNI.P210-7861-2015-59

Olejniczak J (2016) Część oświatowa subwencji ogólnej a poziom wydatków w gminach województwa dolnośląskiego w latach 2011–2014. In: Jedlicka P (ed) The international conference Hradec economic days 2016. Economic development and management of regions. Peer-reviewed conference proceedings, Hradec Kralove 2016, pp 153–164

Ruśkowski E, Salachna JM (2007) Finanse lokalne po akcesji. Wolters Kluwer SA, Warszawa 2007

Surówka K (2004) Kierunki zmian systemu zasilania budżetów jednostek samorządu terytorialnego. Zeszyty Naukowe Wyższej Szkoły Ekonomicznej w Bochni 2004(2):21–27

Swianiewicz P (2004) Finanse lokalne teoria i praktyka. Municipium, Warszawa

Wójtowicz K (2013) Udziały samorządów w podatkach państwowych - własne czy obce źródło dochodów JST? Dylematy teorii a praktyka budżetowa wybranych państw. Prace Naukowe Uniwersytetu Ekonomicznego we Wrocławiu 2013(306):501–512

Chapter 23
Can the Charitable Tax Deduction Stimulate Corporate Giving? Evidence from the Russian Banking System

Anna Kireenko and Sofia Golovan

Abstract The advantages and disadvantages of indirect subsidization of public goods and services through the mechanism of preferential tax treatment are analyzed. The current level of participation of banks in corporate philanthropy is evaluated in view of preferential taxation as a mechanism to reduce the cost of charitable services for the company. The study attempts to construct a theoretical model describing the effect of tax incentives for the financing of the charitable sector. The study has used a sample of 49 banks operating in Irkutsk Oblast as a constituent member of the Russian Federation in the years 2011–2014. As the study has shown, the majority of banks do not go beyond posting information about their activities on their official Web sites. Nearly half the banks have shown a sustainable strategy for charity understood as having charitable aid beneficiaries over several time periods or in the area of a prioritized activity. It has also been found that, regardless of the charitable expenditure limit set as part of total expenses, the majority of credit organizations could exploit a maximum potential growth of donations (from 49.5 to 74% of the studied credit institutions, depending). It is concluded that introduction of preferential tax treatment might mean a possible rise in charitable expenditures, and the optimal level of charitable expenditure accounts as an expense in terms of budget efficiency is substantiated.

Keywords Charitable deduction · Charity · Tax deduction · Corporate philanthropy · Social responsibility of banks

A. Kireenko (✉) · S. Golovan
Department of Taxation and Customs, Baikal State University,
Lenina Str. 11, 664003 Irkutsk, Russian Federation
e-mail: kireenko-ap@bgu.ru

S. Golovan
e-mail: free9sonjas@gmail.com

D. Procházka (ed.), *New Trends in Finance and Accounting*,
Springer Proceedings in Business and Economics,
DOI 10.1007/978-3-319-49559-0_23

23.1 Introduction

Charitable deduction is generally determined as the preferential tax treatment of expenditures or gifts to organizations that the law qualifies as having a socially beneficial characteristic and for which the donor is not motivated by direct benefit when making the contribution. The most widespread form of this preferential tax treatment is charitable deduction when taxpayers have been allowed to deduct gifts to charitable and certain other nonprofit organizations. Hereafter, such organizations will be called "charitable" (Mulgan 1995). A charitable deduction extends the benefits of exemption to taxpayers, so that income donated to charitable organizations is exempted from all levels of income taxation. The deduction is intended to subsidize the activities of private organizations that provide viable alternatives to direct government programs.

The development and support of nonprofit organizations with a social orientation stands out at the moment as one of the key objectives for the federal and regional authorities in the Russian Federation. The proper state regulation of charitable activities of commercial organizations could provide additional inflow of funds in socially significant directions. Development and support of nonprofit organizations with a social orientation is an important element of social support during a growing crisis. Directions of charitable support provided by commercial organizations have the same purpose as the financial support of the state. Charitable donations in this case are funneled to the same end-recipients of public services and public funding. This allows for an analysis of benefits for the benefactors as a replacement tool by private donations of the budget funds allocated on financing social spending.

The deduction subsidizes giving by lowering the price that donors must pay privately to support charitable organizations. This price reduction affects giving in two ways, which economists refer to as income and substitution effects. The income effect is due to the reduced price that effectively makes more income available for all consumption (Bakija 1999). If people normally give more as income rises, the income effect of price reduction will induce people to increase giving. The substitution effect arises because the reduced price makes giving cheaper relative to other commodities, which will induce people to give more.

The awareness of charitable tax deduction influence on the amount of giving has grown in recent years, but still remains incomplete. The empirical evidence shows that the amount of giving is at least partly sensitive to the cost of giving. The evidence also suggests that giving is fairly responsive to temporary changes in the cost of giving, though few researchers agree on how sensitive it is to more permanent price changes. But much remains to be learned, especially about charitable giving in the Russian Federation, where charity is not as extensive as in OECD countries (Bennett 1998). The ability to deduct the costs of charitable donations from taxable income existed in Russian tax law before 2002, but today, there are no tax benefits available to corporate donors in Russia.

The main objectives of this paper are to study the degree of current participation of commercial entities in the support of charitable activity, on the one hand, and the socioeconomic benefits of preferential tax treatment and feasibility of its introduction, on the other. Assessment of the socioeconomic benefits of preferential tax treatment of charitable activity is expressed in the social consequences of the tax incentives, reflecting the importance of the benefits of using a supported activity—in this case, the charitable activities of commercial organizations taking place due to reduced tax payments organization. In this paper, we estimate the socioeconomic impact of tax benefits by comparing the existing charitable contributions and the contributions that could be expected if the tax benefit was introduced (Auten et al. 2000). This value is called the "potential for larger donations," that is, the amount by which a particular organization could increase their welfare costs by compensating the effect of the introduction of tax exemptions.

23.2   Literature Review

There is an abundant literature on the analysis of charity and the study of economic and noneconomic factors affecting its output. For example, in a study conducted by C. Clotfelter on the data for the period of 1936–1980, an undoubted positive effect of preferential taxation in the USA in respect of corporate charity was noted. He also noted the strong role played by private donations in funding the nonprofit sector (Clotfelter 1997). Regarding the differences in the value of corporate philanthropy that depend on the area of "activity," there was a link between communications with consumers of goods and services of the organization and the work in the field of charity (Clotfelter and Steuerle 1981). So the largest share in the profit value of charitable contributions was held by the banking sector and trade in foods and other essential commodities. According to C. Clotfelter, this can be explained in terms of the value that the management and owners of the company attribute to the formation of a positive image. The effect of preferential tax treatment on increasing the volume of charitable activities has been studied by Fack and Landais (2010). According to their findings, the response of a donor to preferential tax treatment depends largely on the volume of donations made earlier. So in their research, they came to the conclusion that the more generous donors have tended to respond more rapidly to the increase in the tax credit rate for donations in France after the reform. Therefore, they note that high tax credit rate in France can be economically justified, based on the premise that private foundations are able to perform many tasks more efficiently than the state.

Carroll and Joulfaian (2005) have shown in their article on the role of taxation in the behavior of commercial organizations in the field of charitable activities that the applicable taxes are an important factor in determining the amount of charitable donations. So they came to a conclusion, on the basis of a large amount of surveyed companies, that the value of charitable donations is reduced with an increase in prices for the company's contributions after tax and growing together with the company's income and the amount of advertising costs. It should also be noted that according to Carroll and Joulfaian, companies with foreign owners donate more. J.R. Boatsman and S. Gupta's research (1996) based on the data from 212 donor firms, over the period of 1984–1988, suggests a negative correlation between corporate charitable donations and the amount of income tax rate. Wallace and Fisher (1977) express a concern that higher tax rates would discourage private charity. In other words, high tax rates hinder the development of charity. Tax incentives for philanthropists as a means of state support for nonprofit organizations have also been considered by the Russian authors Makarenko and Rudnik (1997).

Another direction of charitable tax deduction investigation is the price elasticity of giving. Price elasticity of giving is a measure of how responsive giving is to a change in its cost. It assesses the degree to which donors give more or less depending on how expensive the donations are (Feenberg 1987).

As has become obvious from the literature review, there is much uncertainty about how much the cost of giving affects charitable contributions (Steinberg 1990).

The first generation of statistical studies of private giving, conducted in the 1970s, generally found that the price elasticity of giving was equal to or greater than 1 (in absolute value), in some cases significantly so. The implication was that giving was fairly sensitive to the after-tax cost of giving and that changes in tax rates that raised or lowered the cost of giving could significantly affect the amount of charitable contributions.

There were concerns that if private giving were as sensitive to cost as implied by the existing research, lower tax rates would cause private giving to fall by an appreciable amount. The predicted drop in giving, however, did not materialize. With the exception of taxpayers in the highest income tax brackets, charitable giving remained quite stable. The implication was that giving may not be as sensitive to price incentives as indicated by some econometric models.

In the 1980s and 1990s, improved data made it possible to better distinguish between temporary and permanent changes in the cost of giving. As expected, researchers using these data generally find that annual giving is less responsive to permanent than to temporary tax changes. Indeed, the results of several recent studies suggest that the price elasticity of giving may be less than 1, perhaps closer to −0.40 (Johnson 1981).

23.3 Modeling of Corporate Giving in Russian Banking System

In the Russian Federation, there are no tax benefits available to corporate donors. An individual can claim a charitable deduction up to 25% of their taxable income.

The ability to deduct the costs of charitable donations from taxable income existed in the Russian tax law before 2002. In accordance with the law "On taxes on profits of enterprises and organizations," passed on December 27, 1991, corporate taxpayers were allowed to deduct the costs of charitable donations up to 5% (for banks and insurance companies up to 3%) of the taxable income for the year. The tax incentives for businesses involved in charitable activities were canceled in 2002, after Chap. 25 of the tax code came in effect. According to the Letter of the Russian Ministry of Finance, if the firm provided free services or donated its products, the costs which arose at the same time did not reduce the firm's payments to the budget. In the literature of that period tax, incentives for charity were described as an example of negative, inefficient use of tax mechanism. There was an opinion that commercial organizations were rarely motivated to make donations due to the low level of confidence of the tax system.

In our study, tax relief means a reduction in the tax base profit in a certain percentage of the profit. To assess the hypothetical value of increased costs due to charity benefits the following method was used:

Step 1:   At this stage, were unloaded banks represented in the Irkutsk Oblast, excluding from the sample those banks that have received comments from the Central Bank in connection with some doubts in their reporting. This sample was grouped according to the amount of capital in accordance with the proposed principle of 2011. At the same time, we received initial empirical data for the period of 2011–2014 about the income, the value of charitable expenses, and the current income tax.

Step 2:   Calculation of the hypothetical limits accounting for charitable expenditure as an expense on the study sample for the respective years.

Step 3:   Comparison of actual costs to the value of hypothetical limits.

Step 4:   For the banks whose actual costs do not exceed the prescribed limits, calculation of the increase in charitable expenditure to be compensated through the mechanism of preferential tax treatment, the so-called potential to increase donations.

Step 5:   Summation of actual costs and the potential to increase in each test organization for the respective years.

Step 6:   Comparison of the amount received with the value of the hypothetical limits.

Step 7:   For the banks where the amount exceeds the limit, the full potential of an increase will be equal to the difference between the amount of the limit and the amount of the actual costs and will be considered as fixed at a sub-maximal level.

Step 8:   For the banks where the amount does not exceed a predetermined limit, the full potential will be considered as fixed at the maximum level.

The study has been based on a sample of banks operating in one region of the Russian Federation, Irkutsk Oblast, in 2011–2014 years. In order to improve the quality of the study, the banks which the Central Bank had expressed concerns about or suspected of dubious performance reports were not taken into account. Thus, the survey covered 49 banks represented in Irkutsk Oblast. The study sample was divided into three groups according to the principle proposed for the evaluation of social responsibility of banks in the USA. According to this principle, the first group included banks with the volume of own funds of less than 10 billion rubles (small banks). The second group included organizations with the volume of capital more than 10 billion but less than 100 billion rubles (medium-size banks), and the third group—with a volume of more than 100 billion rubles (large banks) (Cornett 2013).

To obtain data on the degree of involvement of the investigated banks in corporate philanthropy, we used the information provided on the official Web sites of credit institutions and the information provided in annual reports.

The calculated data on the value of committed expenditures and the net profit of researched credit institutions broken down by size are presented in Table 23.1. As shown in the table, the average value of charity spending committed by credit institutions grew steadily throughout the study period.

To assess the quality parameters of the banks' participation in charitable activities, the criteria have been used developed by the Czech researchers on the basis of the banking system of the Czech Republic (Burianová and Paulík 2014). These options were designed to assess the level of corporate social responsibility at the level of banks. In order to evaluate the participation of the banking system in supporting charity, these parameters have been adapted to meet the needs of our study. Thus, the main elements of the existing involvement of credit institutions in support of socially important areas for today, according to the authors, will be as follows:

Table 23.1 Dynamics of charitable expenses and net income of investigated credit institutions broken down by the size of capital for the years 2011–2014

Indicator/year	2011	2012	2013	2014	Growth 2014/2011, %
Average value of costs, thousand rubles	128,026.4	164,213.2	185,299.8	230,439.3	79.9
Group of small banks	485.8	408.4	451.9	527.9	8.7
Group of medium-sized banks	68,904	69,694.2	42,081.8	25,430.5	−63.1
Group of large banks	474,914.6	650,623	758,332.5	1,061,551.5	123.5
Average value of net profit, thousand rubles	10,549,761	12,175,842	13,204,975	10,700,570	1.4
Group of small banks	266,823.9	435,023	371,551	353,106	32.3
Group of medium-sized banks	2,475,960	3,267,787	2,364,711	1,343,119	−45.8
Group of large banks	45,793,115	51,732,955.8	55,677,373.9	47,462,622	3.6

- Publication of social reports on the results of the work done;
- Provision of open and full information on the types and forms of charitable activities and support for the recipient on the company's official Web site;
- Involvement of employees in the exercise of charity, support, and encouragement of voluntary initiatives in the team of the company;
- Creation and active introduction of banking products at the service of charity; and
- Availability of long-term sustainable strategy for charitable activities in the framework of corporate social responsibility.

Based on the totality of the credit organizations represented in Irkutsk Oblast, we can conclude that the actual amount of own contributions exceeds the limit of 10% of taxable profit at the few of banks. Therefore, the proposed model does not make sense to consider options in the amount of more than 10%. Thus, in this study, variations in the amount of 1, 3, 5, and 10% of the taxable income have been reviewed. We can determine the maximum amount of charitable donations of each bank basing on the following assumptions:

- Since tax relief in the model is considered from the point of view of the company's charitable resource cost reduction mechanism, the existence of a stable system of charitable activities, namely the actual donations in the absence of economic reinforcement, is a necessary condition for predicting the impact of benefits. If the organization did not use the tools of charitable donations in its social policy, we should not expect an introduction of incentives to motivate commitment to expenditure.
- If, at the end of the period, the company recorded a loss and charitable donations had been made, the amount of the hypothetical donation within the model could not be increased, because there would be no basis for the calculation of income tax; therefore, there is no point speaking about the volume that could be compensated with the privilege.
- If the amount of the organization's actual donation exceeds the volume of hypothetical donations, it should not be increased within the model. As a privilege in this case will not cover the entire amount of committed expenditure, it makes no sense to speak about affirmative action benefits.
- If an increase in the amount of the organization's own actual contributions compensated the benefits above the specified limit of taxable income, the amount of hypothetical donation could be increased to a size which would be covered by incentives. Since a further increase in this case would occur at the expense of net profit, it would not be possible to ascertain the degree of influence of preferential tax treatment. Such volume of donations in the model can be considered submaximal.
- In an increase in the amount of contributions does not exceed the maximum allowable for tax purposes, this size can be taken as the maximum amount of donations for the organization in the framework of the model.

23.4 Results

The study provided data on the prevalence of charitable activities of credit institutions on the basis of selected quality indicators (Fig. 23.1).

Information on the forms and directions of support of charitable activities in the organization can be found on the official Web sites of 67.3% of credit institutions. Based on the 95% confidence intervals, we can speak of 53.8–80.2% in the total population of banks in the Russian Federation. Reference to long-term partnerships with a particular recipient of donations or prioritized charitable activities was found in 46.9% of the banks [95% CI 32, 9–60, 8]. Promotion of volunteer initiatives in the team, as well as organization of volunteer projects, featured in 28.5% of the studied organizations [95% CI 15, 8–41, 1], and the development of banking products oriented to charity 38.7% [95% CI 25, 1–52, 3].

Regarding the differences investigated involvement of credit institutions, depending on the size of the capital, we can say that most of the indicators significantly hire in the group of large credit institutions than for the others banks involved in philanthropy ($p < 0.05$). Thus, information about the organization's philanthropy could be found on the official Web sites of 44% of small banks [95% CI 21, 2–66, 9], 71.4% of medium-sized banks [95% CI 52, 1–90, 7], and all the large banks without any exception. Volunteer work in the organization is encouraged by 5.5% of small banks [95% CI 5–16, 03] and 23.8% of medium-sized banks [95% CI 5, 6–42, 01], while 80% of the large banks in the study group [95% CI 55, 2–104, 8] mention projects that involve employees. It should be noted that the study has revealed an interesting trend: While the big banks are much more involved in charitable activities than small banks on all evaluated parameters ($p < 0.05$), the

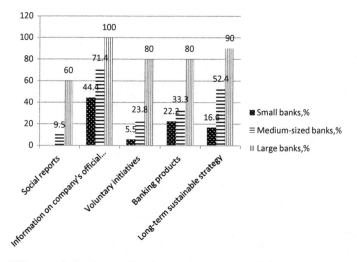

Fig. 23.1 Differences in the degree of involvement in support of charity, depending on the size of the bank's capital

differences between the involvement of medium and large banks have been identified only in terms of reflecting a significant own contribution.

Because of the lack of information about the forms and types of charitable
activities on the banks sites, it is difficult to draw conclusions about the differences
in the group strategy of charity. However, other indicators for large credit institutions differ from the small- and medium-sized bank indicators. While some indicators are already close to those of the larger banks, in terms of requiring a
significant own contribution, medium-sized banks still differ from the large banks.
This may explain the limited available financial and human resources of
medium-sized banks. So they are ready to commit spending, but do not have more
opportunities to adequately inform the public about their activities and to support
the charity in many forms, not just in the form of direct cash donations.

Figure 23.2 shows the mechanism of action of the preferential taxation,
depending on the limit donations account as an expense.

Based on Fig. 23.2, we can conclude that setting any level of charitable donations account for the majority of banks benefit can form the potential to increase
charitable expenditure. In addition, the overwhelming majority of banks have the
potential to form the maximum size to be increased in the model. Thus, taking into
account contributions as an expense for tax purposes at a rate of up to 1% of the
taxable profit, the number of banks that could increase their donations to the
maximum volume amounted to 49.5% of all the banks operating in Irkutsk Oblast.
On the basis of confidence intervals, it can be assumed, with a 95% probability, that
in the Russian Federation with the introduction of preferential taxation and setting
limits on the size of the accounting of donations amounting to 1%, the share of
banks in which the benefit would form the potential to maximize would be in the
interval from 42.5 to 56% of the entire population. In the transition from the lowest
level for each subsequent average, the share of banks in this group is gradually
increased from 61.9 to 80% of the population.

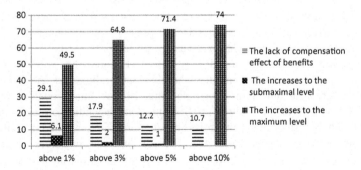

Fig. 23.2 Impact of preferential profits tax depending on the limit of charitable donations account
as an expense

At the same time, the share of credit institutions, which have not shown an increased spending through the compensation effect of the benefit, is relatively high at 1% level accounting for tax purposes, ranging from 22.7 to 35.5% of all the banks. Changing the number of credit institutions that are attributable to this group is the opposite of the change in the group with the potential to maximize and would have fallen to a relatively small number of 10.7% at the maximum limit. The share of banks that did not make donations and, consequently, for their benefit tax profits could not be a motivating factor to an increase in donations, ranged from 3.8 to 22.8% and was independent of the level of spending in charity account expenses. There are banks in the considered sample (2%) that made charitable spending but ended the year with a negative financial result, and consequently, it was not possible to determine the potential to increase, caused by the action of the benefits due to the lack of base of income tax. The share of banks whose potential to increase charitable donations to a set maximum size limit was close to the limit and, therefore, stopped at submaximal level, ranging from 1 to 6.1% depending on the set limit, with no bank reaching the limit of 10% for this group.

23.5 Conclusion

As the review of the literature has shown, over the recent decades, the importance of searching for alternative sources of financing for nonprofit organizations as providers of public goods and services in relation to the direct subsidies has been growing. One such source that has several advantages over direct financing is a mechanism for preferential tax treatment of charitable activities used in the Western countries.

In conclusion, with regard to the quality indicators expressing support for charity, the study has shown that in terms of opening up, the majority of banks post information about their activities on their official Web sites. Nearly a half had a sustainable charity strategy, which is understood to work with partners of charitable aid over several time periods or selected priority. At the same time, taking advantage of corporate philanthropy by using special forms of charity, it is inherent in the banking sector but developed fairly weakly. The study has also found that for every limit, taking into account the charitable expenditure as an expense, the majority of credit organizations have a potential for maximum growth of donations (from 49.5 to 74% of the study of credit institutions depending on the limit of the account). These results suggest that the introduction of preferential tax treatment of charitable activities could boost the flow of financial resources for socially important areas of commercial organizations, in this case, the banking sector.

Acknowledgments This work was financially supported by the State Task № 26.1348.2014/K to do work in the field of research activities in the project part, the project № 1348 "Influence of the shadow economy on the quality of life in Russia and the Ukraine: A comparative analysis" (State Registration Number in FGASI CITaS 114091140015).

References

Auten GE, Clotfelter CT, Schmalbeck RL (2000) Taxes and philanthropy among the wealthy. In: Slemrod J (ed) Does Atlas Shrug: the economic consequences of taxing the rich. Russell Sage and Harvard University Press, New York, pp 392–424

Bakija J (1999) Consistent estimation of permanent and transitory tax-price and income elasticities: the case of charitable giving. Working paper, Department of Economics, University of Michigan

Bennett R (1998) Corporate philanthropy in France, Germany and the UK: international comparisons of commercial orientation towards company giving in European nations. Int Mark Rev 15(6):458–475

Boatsman JR, Gupta S (1996) Taxes and corporate charity: empirical evidence from microlevel panel data. Natl Tax J, 193–213

Burianová L, Paulík J (2014) Corporate social responsibility in commercial banking—a case study from the Czech Republic. J Compet 6(1):50–70

Burlingame DF (1993) Altruism and philanthropy: definitional issues. Indiana University Center on Philanthropy, Indianapolis

Carroll R, Joulfaian D (2005) Taxes and corporate giving to charity. Public Financ Rev 33(3): 300–317

Clotfelter CT (1997) The economics of giving. In: Barry JW, Manno BV (eds) Giving better, giving smarter. National Commission on Philanthropy and Civic Renewal, Washington, DC, pp 31–55

Clotfelter CT, Steuerle CE (1981) Charitable contributions. In: Aaron HJ, Pechman JA (eds) How taxes affect economic behavior. Brookings Institution, Washington, DC, pp 20–23

Cornett M (2013) Corporate social responsibility and its impact on financial performance: investigation of the U.S. Commercial Banks. Presentation at the Bentley University Council's Research Colloquium on the topic of responsible innovation: environmental sustainability, financial accountability, and information and communication technology (ICT) ethics, Bentley University

Fack G, Landais C (2010) Are tax incentives for charitable giving efficient? Evidence from France. Am Econ J Econ Policy 2:117–141

Feenberg D (1987) Are tax price models really identified: the case of charitable giving. Natl Tax J 40(4):629–633

Johnson JA (1981) Determinants of charitable giving with special emphasis on the income deduction under the income tax-A survey of the empirical literature. Can Tax 3:258–263

Makarenko OV, Rudnik BL, Shishkin SV, Yakobson LI (1997) State and non-state non-profit organizations: forms of support and cooperation. Signal, Moscow (in Russian)

Mulgan G, Landry C (1995) The other invisible hand: remaking charity for the 21st century. Demos, London

Steinberg R (1990) Taxes and giving: new findings. Int J Volunt Nonprofit Organ 34:61–79
Wallace JA, Fisher RW (1977) The charitable deduction under section 170 of the Internal Revenue
    Code. Research Papers Sponsored by the Commission on Private Philanthropy and Public
    Needs. U.S. Department of the Treasury 4:2131–61

Chapter 24
The Impact of Taxation on Unemployment of University Absolvents

Ladislav Bušovský

Abstract The aim of this paper was to estimate the impact of tax quota and tax revenues on unemployment rate of public university absolvents. This paper is focused on the negative impact of tax revenues on absolvent's unemployment rate. Afterwards, found variables will be able to be used in more complex econometrical model. This paper is based on econometric analysis of examined impacts based on already reached statistical significant explanatory variables. Results are summarized in tables and graphs, and they are commented as a tool of unemployment optimization. This paper works with regression models of standardized unemployment rate of university absolvents, tax quota, tax revenue, personal income tax, social security contributions, expenditure on university institutions, numbers of university students and number of officials. The results show tax quota, tax revenues and personal income taxation as the most important variables.

Keywords Standardized absolvent's unemployment rate · Taxation · Tax quota · Tax revenues · Overeducation

24.1 Introduction

The system of tertiary education was huge reformed in last two decades in Czech Republic, and it is still evolving since the new political and cultural trends change every year. These changes could be seen in the whole system of the tertiary education sector. The most noticeable are changes in system of financing universities and in the following situation on labour market. The situation on labour market could be considered as a partly result of education sector settings (Urbánek and Maršíková 2013). The tertiary education sector settings affected by latest political

L. Bušovský (✉)
Department of Public Finance, Faculty of Finance and Accounting,
University of Economics, Prague, Nám. W. Churchilla 4,
130 67 Praha 3, Žizkov, Czech Republic
e-mail: xbusl01@vse.cz

© Springer International Publishing AG 2017
D. Procházka (ed.), *New Trends in Finance and Accounting*,
Springer Proceedings in Business and Economics,
DOI 10.1007/978-3-319-49559-0_24

and culture trends in connection with situation of unemployment of university absolvents on labour market were my primary point of inspiration to this paper.

The unemployment of university absolvents becomes very topical issue throughout the world nowadays. As it was quite unique for common citizens to reach tertiary education in the Czech Republic in past, it is possible to perceive it common nowadays. The OECD published its Education at glance 2015 project (hereinafter "EaG") which has been focus on mapping the tertiary education situation in countries around the world. Based on EaG results, from 30 to 70 % of all 25- to 35-year-olds have already attained tertiary education (Fig. 24.1).

As result of "education boom", universities produce enormous counts of absolvents every year. However, the lack of just primary educated citizens is noticeable. The first issue of this change could be noticeable in labour market. The labour market needs have not been changed so dramatically as structure of education in population. Craftsmen are still needed, and there are still limited jobs for financial managers. The distortion between labour market demand and supply curves is obvious, and it results in unemployment of university absolvents. This effect is examined by theory called over-education (overeducation) (Sang and Levin (1985); Psacharopoulos (1987); Leuven and Oosterbeek (2011)). Overeducation theory (as its name points) tries to point on huge "education boom" in recent years over the world. More closely about this theory and its factors refers Barr and Crawford (2005) from UK. A lot of different opinions about solution of this overeducation effect have been done by many authors, but none has been chosen as a correct one yet. The most of authors seems the solution in regulation of university students, but there are also alternatives solutions (Becker 1993). Some alternative solutions summarize Urbánek (2007).

This paper builds on my latest papers focused on unemployment of university absolvents with aim to figure out a possible impact of taxation on the issue of

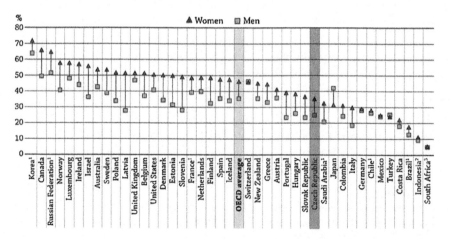

Fig. 24.1 Percentage of 25- to 34-year-olds who have attained tertiary education, by gender (2014). *Source* OECD 2015, Education at Glance 2015, custom processing

overeducation in Czech Republic (Urbánek et al. 2009). As my latest topics about examining tax quota and tax revenues (Bušovský 2015a) impact on absolvent's unemployment rate showed opposite impacts that was not presumed, this paper focuses on merging both examined results together and reveals the reason why tax quota and tax revenues cause an opposite impact on absolvent's unemployment rate.

24.2   Data and Methodology

24.2.1   Selected Data

This paper works with several data sources. The base consists of the number of university students from the Czech Statistical Office, number of officials from Czech Statistical Office, tax, quota and tax revenue data from the OECD database, personal income tax data from the OECD database, social security contributions data from the OECD database and the survey REFLEX 2013 as a project focusing on employment/unemployment graduates and their impact on labour market.

Data are structuralized to time series. Due to limited time series I work with the period from 2002 to 2012. This period shows constant and still current structure of tertiary education. It also contains all necessary data of all considered variables (Fig. 24.2).

The regression model works primarily with the number of university students (public and private), tax quota, tax revenue, personal income tax, social security contributions, number of officials and the standardized unemployment rate of university graduates. The standardized unemployment rate acts as a regionally adjusted unemployment rate of university graduates obtained on the basis of survey REFLEX 2013. The tracking data were considered in the months of April for each year. I chose the tracking data to the first April of each due to the higher number of

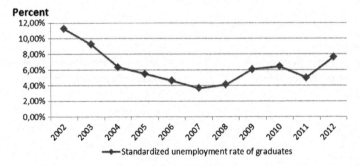

Fig. 24.2 Standardized unemployment rate of graduates. *Source* OECD 2015, Education at Glance 2015, custom processing

observations in the time series. The April data also contain form of adjustment in unemployment since most of the graduates have more time to find a place on labour market during free months after graduation.

24.2.2 Analysis Methodology

Researched dependencies between variables were performed using regression analysis. For estimates, compiled models used the least squares method using econometric software EViews 8.

All reached (or modified) time series exhibit non-stationarity in its course. Therefore, to overcome any apparent effect regression, which could skew the results statistically insignificant variables to statistically significant once, I chose the generation of the first differences (annual) for all non-stationary time series (Arlt 1997, 2007). In some cases, it was necessary to generate also logarithms of time series and then the difference between them to gain relevant time series. The modified time series exhibit non-stationarity and prepared to be used in model. It is also cleansed from other relevant problems (heteroskedasticity, autocorrelation), and therefore there are no problems in continuing the analysis (Table 24.1).

The analysis focuses on analysing the impact of public expenditure and taxation (tax quota and tax revenues) and numbers of students of universities on standardized unemployment rate of absolvents. Only selected variables has been chosen based on the results of my latest papers. Only the number of public university students was taken into account, excluding the number of private university absolvents due to not confirmed impact on unemployment. This analysis considers the standardized unemployment rate of university absolvents (d1_unemprate) as the response variable. The explanatory variables are tax quota (d1_log_taxquota), tax revenue (d1_log_rev), personal income tax including social security contribution (d1_log_pitsoc), expenditure on education institutions (d1_inst), number of officials (d1_offi) and numbers of students of public universities (d1_studpub).

Table 24.1 Tested variables in regression model

Name of variable	Variable label
Standardized unemployment rate	Standardized unemployment rate
Students of public universities	Students of public universities
Tax quota	Tax quota
Tax revenue	Tax revenue
Expenditure on education institutions	Expenditure on education institutions
Personal income tax and social security contribution	Personal income tax and social security contribution
Personal income tax and social security contribution	Personal income tax and social security contribution

Source Custom processing

24.3   Analysis Results

This chapter briefly capture the results estimated using econometric software EViews 8. The results are summarized in Table 24.2. Subsequently, the estimated results are used to structure the mathematical equation and lately commented in terms of their usefulness and meaning.

As the model works with already tested variables in previous papers, it was presumed that there will not be any statistical insignificant variables. The only variable newly tested is the number of officials in the Czech Republic which has been chosen based on presumption that tax revenues are used by government to employ part of the absolvents in public sector. Moreover, employing the university absolvents in public sector is considered just for official job which usually (in the Czech Republic) requires tertiary education level.

All of the examined variables were considered as statistically significant on standard significance rate of 5 %, so no variable was excluded from model.

Table 24.2 summarizes statistics of the estimated model. Based on a comparison of the coefficients of determination and Durbin-Watson statistic, it is possible to deduce the apparent absence regression (coefficient of determination is greater than DW statistics). It is also possible to notice that coefficient of determination value reaches 99 % that could highlight the quality of model or point on some issues in connection with examined time series (link between tax quota and tax revenues could be marked as a potential issue for next model estimations). Moreover, it is presumed that effect of tax revenues is not fully explained just by the change in number of officials, so more explanatory variables for tax revenues effect could be considered in next models also. However, based on statistics, the model could be considered as quality one.

Also, it is necessary to remind that model is working with relatively short time series which could also be explaining option of high determination coefficient. Longer time series could be more effective to show the model quality.

Table 24.2 Tested variables in regression model

Explanatory variables	Coefficient	Standard deviation	p-value
Constant	−0.038793	0.0020	0.0003
d1_log_taxquota	0.427689	0.0387	0.0016
d1_log_revenues	−0.337880	0.0737	0.0195
d1_log_pitsoc	0.226589	0.0719	0.0513
d1_inst	−0.027127	0.0014	0.0003
d1_studpub	0.004723	0.0000	0.0003
d1_offic	−0.000384	0.0008	0.0181
Model statistics		Value	
Determination coefficient		0.9962	
Durbin–Watson statistic		2.4317	

Source ČSÚ, MŠMT, OECD, own estimate by using econometric software EViews8

Unfortunately, the verification by long time series is not possible at this time due to the novelty of tertiary education system in Czech Republic.

As mentioned, final regression equation has been structured based on estimated model results:

$$\text{Unemployment} = -0.0387 + 0.4276 * \text{TQ} - 0.3378 * \text{TR} + 0.2265 * \text{PitSoc}$$
$$- 0.0271 * \text{InstExp} + 0.004723 * \text{Stu} - 0.00038 * \text{Offi}$$

$$(24.1)$$

where

Unemployment	Standardized unemployment rate,
TQ	Tax quota,
TR	Tax revenues,
PitSoc	Personal income taxation with social security contribution,
InstExp	Expenditures on institutions,
Stu	Number of public university students, and
Offi	Number of officials.

For purposes of describing the impact of all explanatory variables on standardized absolvent's unemployment rate, it should be reminded that all variables are considered in form of their first difference modification. Consequently variables will be no longer explicitly mentioned as in first differences or logarithm forms; however, they were considered in model as such.

As results, the standardized absolvent's unemployment rate is decreasing constantly by 0.0387% every year. The rest impacts could be described as follows:

- the increase in the tax quota (d1_log_taxquota) by 1% causes an increase in standardized absolvent's unemployment rate by 0.4276%,
- the increase in the tax revenues (d1_log_revenues) by 1% causes a decrease in standardized absolvent's unemployment rate by 0.3378%,
- the increase in the personal income taxation including social security contributions (d1_log_pitsoc) by 1% causes an increase in standardized absolvent's unemployment rate by 0.2265%,
- the increase in the expenditures on university institutions (d1_inst) by 1 billion CZK causes a decrease in standardized absolvent's unemployment rate by 0.0271%,
- the increase in the number of public university student (d1_studpub) by 1 thousand causes an increase in standardized absolvent's unemployment rate by 0.0047%, and
- the increase in the number of officials (d1_offic) by 1 causes a decrease in standardized absolvent's unemployment rate by 0.00038%.

24.4   Conclusion

Based on the model results, it is obvious that all latest reached results (Bušovský 2015b) have been confirmed. Moreover, the rate of impact is very similar, and there are not huge differences. All the explanatory variables have also proved as statistically significant in estimated model.

It is possible to observe the opposite effect of tax quota and tax revenues variables in the model. Based on deeper examination, this effect could be explained by using tax revenues as a salary for absolvents employed in state jobs. This theory has been partly confirmed by using number of officials in the model. As more officials are being employed in last years in the Czech Republic, the absolvent's unemployment rate is decreasing. However, it could be handful to focus on employing absolvents to other state jobs than officials in next models.

The impacts of the rest of variables have been already explained in my latest papers. However, it would be appropriate to point on personal income taxation with social security contributions. Personal income taxation with social security contribution has logically meaning. Absolvents do not prefer working when the rate of taxation is high that could be explained by basic taxation mechanism and theory of preference between free time capacity and working.

This paper and its results support the finding of alternative way to solve the problem of overeducation by making changes on the side of state while opposite way is usually chosen—paying tuition by university students. Based on the results, it is obvious that there is another way which could be chosen to stop distortions on labour market of university absolvents without forcing them to pay tuitions and other payments. Also it is important to remind that results are based on short time series which means that results could differ from the long time series results.

Acknowledgments This is paper has been prepared under financial support of IG108023 project, which author gratefully acknowledges.

References

Arlt J (1997) Regresní analýza nestacionárních ekonomických časových řad. [online]. VŠE, Praha, [cit.2014-05-04]. ISBN 0032-3233

Arlt J (2007) Ekonomické časové řady: [vlastnosti, metody modelování, příklady a aplikace]. 1. vyd. Grada, Praha, 285 s. ISBN 978-80-247-1319-9

Barr N, Crawford I (2005) Financing higher education: answers from the UK. Routledge, Abingdon, UK, ISBN 0-415-34620-7

Becker GS (1993) Human capital: a theoretical and empirical analysis, with special reference to education, 3rd ed. The University of Chicago Press, Chicago, c1993, xxii, 390 p. ISBN 02-260-4120-4

Bušovský L (2015a) The impact of tax revenue on graduate's standardized unemployment rate in the Czech Republic. In: Theoretical and practical aspects of public finance 2015: proceedings of the 20th international conference. Oeconomica, Praha, s. 31–34. ISBN 978-80-245-2094-0

Bušovský L (2015b) The impact of public finance on tertiary education. Procedia Econ Finance 25:530–534

Leuven E, Oosterbeek H (2011) Overeducation and mismatch in the labor market. In: IZA DP: No. 5523. [online]. [cit. 2014-05-04]. Available on: http://ftp.iza.org/dp5523.pdf

Psacharopoulos G (1987) Economics of education: research and studies, vol xvi, 1st ed. Pergamon Press, New York, 482 p. ISBN 00-803-3379-6

Sang MC, Levin HM (1985) The economics of overeducation. Econ Educ Rev. [online] 4(2): 93–104 [cit. 2014-05-04]. Available on: http://www.tc.columbia.edu/faculty/tsang/Files/29.pdf

Urbánek V (2007) Financování vysokého školství. Oeconomica, Praha. ISBN 978-80-245-1313-3

Urbánek V, Maršíková K (2013) Investment in education: earnings and returns, 1st ed. Technická univerzita v Liberci, Liberec, 20132014, 124 s. ISBN 978-80-7494-018-7

Urbánek V, Maršíková K, Řehořová P (2009) Návratnost investice do vysokoškolského vzdělání: komparace očekávaných a reálných výdělků I. monografie. Vyd. 1. V Liberci: Technická univerzita, 171 s. ISBN 978-80-7372-556-3

Chapter 25
Analysis of Tax Burden in the Slovak Republic with Emphasis on Depreciation

Miroslava Vašeková and Martina Mateášová

Abstract One of the most important sources of funding for state and state institutions is clearly the income tax. The final amount of the income to the state budget, obtained by the state collection of the tax, depends not only on its rate. The key role played the rules that must be followed by taxpayers when quantifying the tax base. One of the key areas of the depreciation rules directly affects the amount of tax-deductible expense for depreciation of fixed assets. The trend of recent years in the tax legislation of the Slovak Republic is stricter rules for applying tax-deductible expense to maximize tax collection. This fact confirms also the amendment of the law on income tax, which came into force on January 1, 2015. In this paper, we analyzed the impact of certain changes in depreciation rules and we came to the conclusion that their introduction causes an increase in the tax burden for business entities.

Keywords Tax burden · Tax depreciation 2015

25.1 Introduction

Income tax is one of the most important sources for the state and state institutions funding. The final amount of the state budget income, which state receives by collecting the income tax, is not dependant only on the income tax rate. An essential role also has the rules, which the subjects must obey when quantifying the tax base. The rules for application of tax-deductible expense have become stricter in Slovak tax legislation in recent years in order to maximize state income from taxation

M. Vašeková · M. Mateášová (✉)
Department of Accounting and Auditing, Faculty of Informatics,
University of Economics in Bratislava, Dolnozemská cesta 1/b,
852 35 Bratislava, Slovakia
e-mail: martina.mateasova@euba.sk

M. Vašeková
e-mail: miroslava.vasekova@euba.sk

© Springer International Publishing AG 2017
D. Procházka (ed.), *New Trends in Finance and Accounting*,
Springer Proceedings in Business and Economics,
DOI 10.1007/978-3-319-49559-0_25

(Mateášová and Vašeková 2015; Vašeková and Mateášová 2015). By means of these stricter rules, the Slovak Ministry of Finance aims to lead a systematic and conceptual fight against the tax frauds as well as to consolidate public finances. As a part of this effort, the Slovak Parliament adopted an amendment to Law no. 333/2014 Z.z., amending and supplementing Law no. 595/2003 Z.z. on income tax, as amended, and which amends certain laws. The law introduces a number of significant changes in the taxation of individuals and legal entities. An important change, which we analyze in this paper, is the change in the system of the depreciation of tangible assets. Some of the changes that the amendment to the Law on income tax introduced are: The number of depreciation groups changed from four to six, the possibility of applying the accelerated depreciation method was limited, the specific procedure for the depreciation of assets leased under finance lease was canceled, and the possibility of suspending depreciation was limited.

Apart from that, in this paper, we focus on quantifying the difference in the amount of tax before and after the introduction of the changes regarding the depreciation. As input data, we used specific data of two business entities. These two entities were selected from a group of 47 business entities, which were used in the analysis of the impact of the changes in depreciation rules to their tax burden.

25.2   Literature Review

On January 1, 2015, in the Slovak Republic came into force Law no. 333/2014 Z.z., which amended Law no. 595/2003 Z.z. on income tax, as amended (henceforth "the Law on income tax"). The Law on income tax is the latest amendment of the basic legal standard in the Slovak Republic, which governs the taxation of income tax in the Slovak Republic. Among other things the Law on income tax defines the options for application of tax-deductible expense when determining the tax base for taxpayers, i.e., legal entities as well as individuals.

One of the areas, which are legally regulated by the Law on income tax, is the depreciation of tangible assets. The Law on income tax defines the depreciation as "the progressive inclusion of depreciation of tangible assets and intangible assets in tax expense, which is accounted or registered according to § 6. 11 and is used to acquire taxable income." As we see, the Law on income tax emphasizes that it is always only that long-term tangible assets that are accounted for in the assets of the taxpayer or are registered in the records of an individual—entrepreneur. In the definition of depreciation, we also find a reference to accounting. That means that for the start of depreciation for tax purposes, it is required that all the conditions which are required by the accounting rules are also fulfilled. Tangible assets which are subject to depreciation include independent movable objects or movable objects that have an independent technical-economic purpose, whose entry price is higher than the statutory amount and the operating-technical functions longer than one year, buildings and other constructions, cultivation areas of permanent undergrowth with fertility period longer than three years, animals and other assets, e.g., opening of new quarries, sand pits, clay pits, technical recultivation, technical improvement of realty of cultural sites, technical improvement of leased property (Máziková 2013; Baštincová 2014). Basic general principle is that the tangible assets are depreciated by the taxpayer who has that property ownership from the input price. As the input price, the most frequently used values are: the acquisition price, the amount of the assets' costs, general price according to the Civil Procedure Code (for the tangible assets acquired through inheritance), the price according to Low No. 382/2004 Z.z. on experts, interpreters and translators, as amended (for tangible assets acquired through donation).

In the first year of depreciation, the taxpayer assigns the tangible assets classified by the classification of production and classification of constructions into one of the depreciation groups pursuant to Annex no. 1 set out in the Law on Income Tax and chooses a depreciation method. The depreciation method can be either a uniform depreciation method or an accelerated depreciation method. Assets can be depreciated only up to the amount of input price. The amount can possibly be increased by the amount of technical improvements made to the assets or by the amount of increased residual value (in the case of accelerated depreciation method). When applying depreciation of assets, an annual depreciation in the same percentage, in which the taxpayer claims expenses (costs) pursuant to § 19 par. 2 font. t) is included into expenses (costs) for achievement, provision and maintenance of the taxable income. The percentage is therefore either 80% or a relative provable percentage (§ 24 par. 8). In case of usage of assets that may have the character of personal usage and related costs, the tax-deductible sum is admitted only in relative proportion in which the assets are used for achievement, provision and maintenance of the taxable income, unless the Law on income tax states otherwise.

25.3 Data, Results and Discussion

The above mentioned amendment to the Income Tax Law brought significant changes in depreciation. The most important changes in this area include the change of the number of depreciation groups, from original four to current six. Depreciation group 3 (depreciation period of 8 years) is created by transferring selected types of assets from the original depreciation group 3 (depreciation period 12 years). Subsequently, from the original depreciation group 3 originated the depreciation group 4 which keeps the depreciation period of 12 years. The remaining two depreciation groups 5 and 6 were created by redistribution of the assets from original depreciation group 4, resulting redistribution of wealth from the initial depreciation group 4. Group 5 keeps the original depreciation period of 20 years, while the newly created depreciation group 6 has the depreciation period of 40 years, which is double the original period.

As the most significant change, we consider the assignment of buildings and constructions into two depreciation groups based on their intended use. Depreciation group 5 includes buildings and constructions with exception of: residential buildings, hotels and similar buildings, office buildings, buildings for culture events and public entertainment, education and health, civil engineering and non-residential buildings except for non-residential agricultural buildings and barracks for firefighters. All the buildings and constructions which are not included in depreciation group 5 are included, according to the new classification, in depreciation group 6. Given that the new situation can present a problem when one building or construction is simultaneously used for multiple purposes, it was necessary to establish the rules for such multi-purpose buildings. The Law on Income Tax states that the assignment of such buildings or construction into a depreciation group depends on its main usage. The main usage is determined by the ratio of the total utility area.

Next change, which we will take into account in the analysis of the tax burden on business entity in this paper, is tightening of the application of depreciation on tangible assets whose purpose of usage is lease. The amended regulation of § 19 (3) letter a) of the Law on Income Tax allows the owner of the leased property to include the depreciation into his expenses maximally up to the amount of time-resolved expense (income) from the leasing of the property in the relevant tax period. Part of the annual depreciation of leased tangible assets which was not claimed shall be claimed from the year which follows after the end the period of depreciation of the relevant asset up to the amount of rental income.

In this paper, we focus on quantifying the difference in the amount of tax before and after the introduction of the above described changes. As input data, we used specific data of two business entities. The first entity (ALFA) uses a property for its own administrative activities. The second entity (BETA) leases a property for educational purposes. These two entities are selected from a group of 47 business entities which we used in the analysis of the impact of the changes in depreciation rules to their tax burden. Our analysis showed that some entities are not affected by the change in the depreciation rules neither in a positive nor in a negative way. This is caused by the fact that the impact of these changes is related to the structure of the depreciated assets, purpose of its use, the chosen depreciation method and, more broadly, it even depends on other factors (e.g., payment ability, intensity of use of the assets). These factors are not discussed here in detail due to the limited extent of the article. Just for completeness, a neutral impact of the changes in depreciation rules is, for example, on those business entities which have assets only from the depreciation group 1 and use the uniform depreciation method. The changes in depreciation rules as tax expenditure from January 1, 2015, may, under certain circumstances, also have a positive impact on the tax burden. However, this can only happen in such case, if the business entity had had assets included in depreciation group no. 3 (initial depreciation period of 12 years), and these assets would after reclassification pursuant to Annex no. 1 to the Law on Income Tax, effective from January 1, 2015, remained in depreciation group no. 3 (new depreciation period of 8 years). In this case, the depreciation period is shortened, resulting in an increase in annual depreciation, i.e., the tax-deductible expense arising from the depreciation, thus reducing the tax base and subsequently the tax. However, in the group of business entities used in our analysis, we have not identified such positive impact on the tax burden.

The amendment to the Law on Income Tax, effective from January 1, 2015, imposed on the taxpayers an obligation to review the assignment of the assets to the new depreciation groups, including the assets acquired and put into use before that date, while previously applied depreciations will not be adjusted retrospectively (Table 25.1).

The tax burden for ALFA company in the tax year 2015 is increased by €427.02 in comparison with the tax period of 2014 (assuming that the other expenses and income are the same in both tax periods). Another question that arose after intro-duction of the depreciation group 6, more accurate after setting its depreciation period to 40 years, is the life span of the business entities. We tried to obtain official statistics on the average life span of companies in Slovakia, but we failed to acquire this number. The former Shell's head Arie de Geus estimates an average life span of European companies to be 12.5 years.[1] There is another study of American scientists from the Yale School of Management led by the professor of economics Richard Foster. In their study, they reviewed the Standard & Poor's 500 New York Stock Exchange, which contains shares of 500 largest companies in the USA. The results of the study show that "a hundred years ago the average life span of the companies from the index was 67 years, while now the average life span has dropped to 15 years."[2] According to the website of the Austrian daily paper Die Presse: "The economists investigated, how many years can a company operate in the USA economy and concluded that the average life span of a company in the USA is 10 years."[3] Based on the above mentioned studies, it is possible to assume that the average life span of Slovak companies is similar to this level, if not even shorter. This, in context of the depreciation period of 40 years, has a demotivating effect rather than a stimulating effect when making decisions about investing into realties that should be used for business purposes. While doing research for this paper we even met with managers who were considering the disposal of property from business assets, even if it could possibly cause a negative impact on the business entity at present (e.g., limitation of application of the residual value as an expenditure affecting the tax base, the obligation to pay VAT on the residual value) (Table 25.2).

The tax burden for BETA Company is increased by 4011.04 EUR in the tax year 2015 in comparison with the tax period of 2014 (assuming that the other expenses and income are the same in both tax periods). In this case, the increase in the tax burden may even be higher, since the assets are intended for lease. As was already mentioned, from January 1, 2015, a new rule applies which allows the owner of the

---

[1]http://www.etrend.sk/podnikanie/preco-aj-uspesne-firmy-krachuju.html.

[2]http://www.etrend.sk/podnikanie/preco-aj-uspesne-firmy-krachuju.html.

[3]http://ekonomika.sme.sk/c/7772952/americke-firmy-na-trhu-posobia-v-priemere-iba-desat-rokov.html.

Table 25.1 ALFA—non-residential property used as an office

Name: non-residential property ID: DHM1201					B
				Date of purchase: 10.07.2012	
				Date of recognition: 02.08.2012	
				Date of disposal:	
Year	Method	Depreciation group	Entry price	Depreciation rate (%)	Annual charge
2012	Straight-line	4	77,640.95	2.08	1618.00
2013	Straight-line	4	77,640.95	5.00	3883.00
2014	Straight-line	4	77,640.95	5.00	3883.00
2015	Straight-line	6	77,640.95	2.50	1942.00
↓	↓				↓
2049	Straight-line	6	77,640.95	2.50	1942.00
2050	Straight-line	6	77,640.95	0.42	286.95
Total					77,640.95
Name: non-residential property ID: DHM1201					A
				Date of purchase: 10.07.2012	
				Date of recognition: 02.08.2012	
				Date of disposal:	
Year	Method	Depreciation group	Entry price	Depreciation rate (%)	Annual charge
2012	Straight-line	4	77,640.95	2.08	1618.00
2013	Straight-line	4	77,640.95	5.00	3883.00
2014	Straight-line	4	77,640.95	5.00	3883.00
2015	Straight-line	4	77,640.95	5.00	3883.00
↓	↓				↓
2031	Straight-line	4	77,640.95	5.00	3883.00
2032	Straight-line	4	77,640.95	2.92	2245.95
Total					77,640.95

A—initial calculation of depreciation under the Law on Income Tax, which was in force until December 31, 2014, depreciation group 4, depreciation period 20 years (2012–2032)

B—new calculation of depreciation according to the legislation in force since January 1, 2015: VC (entry price)/n (number of years of depreciation in the depreciation groups) = RO (annual depreciation ceiling-rounded to whole euros) | ZC (residual price as at 31.12.2014)/RO = ZDO (remaining depreciation period in years) (in the last year, an aliquot part of the period which has not been applied in the first year of depreciation and amount is calculated as the difference already applied depreciation and entry price.) | Calculation: 77640.95/40 = 1942.00 |(77640.95 − 1618.00 − 3883.00 − 3883.00) = 68256.95/1942.00 = 35.14| 35 years (2015 − 2049) × 1942.00| 2050 (7 months) depreciation 286.95 (77640.95 − (1618.00 + (2 × 3883.00) + (35 × 1942.00))) = 286.95

Table 25.2 BETA—non-residential property intended for lease

Name: non-residential property ID: DHM1201					**B**
				Date of purchase: 01.12.2012	
				Date of recognition: 01.12.2012	
				Date of disposal:	
Year	Method	Depreciation group	Entry price	Depreciation rate (%)	Annual charge
2012	Straight-line	4	729,291.18	0.42	3039.00
2013	Straight-line	–	729,291.18	0.00	0.00
2014	Straight-line	4	729,291.18	5.00	36,465.00
2015	Straight-line	6	729,291.18	2.50	18,233.00
↓	↓				↓
2051	Straight-line	6	729,291.18	2.50	18,233.00
2052	Straight-line	6	729,291.18	2.50	15,166.18
Celkom					729,291.18
Name: non-residential property ID: DHM1201					**A**
				Date of purchase: 01.12.2012	
				Date of recognition: 01.12.2012	
				Date of disposal:	
Year	Method	Depreciation group	Entry price	Depreciation rate (%)	Annual charge
2012	Straight-line	4	729,291.18	0.42	3039.00
2013	Straight-line	–	729,291.18	0.00	0.00
2014	Straight-line	4	729,291.18	5.00	36,465.00
2015	Straight-line	4	729,291.18	5.00	36,465.00
↓	↓				↓
2032	Straight-line	4	729,291.18	5.00	36,465.00
2033	Straight-line	4	729,291.18	4.58	33,417.18
Celkom					729,291.18

The procedure for calculation of the depreciation is the same as in the case of ALFA

leased property to include the depreciation into his expenses maximally up to the amount of time-resolved expense (income) from the leasing of the property in the relevant tax period. In the case of BETA Company, the monthly rent is set at 2000.00 EUR, which means that depreciation of 18,233.00 EUR can be applied in full amount, since the income from rent is higher. However, if it was a production hall (depreciation group 5, with a depreciation period of 20 years), i.e., the annual depreciation would be the same as the annual depreciation in the initial depreciation plan, calculated to be 36,465.00 EUR, a limiting condition would have to be applied. In such case it would have been possible to apply the depreciation only in the amount of 24,000.00 EUR, which would cause an even greater increase in the tax burden on company BETA.

25.4   Conclusion

In this paper, we presented only two selected situations, but individually, we also analyzed the situations in a number of entities with various structures of long-term assets and various business focuses, because, in our opinion, these factors have an essential influence on whether the new depreciation rules will have a negative, a neutral or even a positive impact on a particular business entity. Primarily, we have focused on the analysis of the tax burden on business entities, which is associated with changes in depreciation rules, namely the introduction of new depreciation groups. This, for certain types of assets, resulted in an increase in the number of depreciation periods and limitation of the amount of depreciation in relation to earnings (income) from the leasing of a property. Based on the calculations we performed in this study, we can conclude that the introduction of the above mentioned changes in the depreciation rules, which came into force on January 1, 2015, the tax burden on business entities will certainly increase. At this point, it should be noted that there are significantly more changes regarding the depreciation and all of them will eventually increase the tax burden on business entities in the Slovak Republic. As examples of further changes in depreciation rules, we could mention: specific limitation as expenses influencing the tax base introduced for a specific group of tangible assets, which includes passenger cars (Classification products code 29.10.2) with an entry price of more than 48,000 EUR; the possibility of using the accelerated depreciation method only for assets that are included in depreciation groups 2 and 3 according to the Annex. 1 of the Law on Income Tax; the limitation of the application of the residual price on the sale of selected types of property; the obligation to suspend depreciation of tangible assets in the tax period in which the tangible assets are not used for business purposes (except for specified exceptions) and so on.

Acknowledgments The contribution is the result of grant project: the importance of valuation of transactions between related parties and their impact on entity profit, registration number 1/0486/14.

References

Baštincová A (2014) Účtovníctvo a dane fyzických osôb. Wolters Kluwer, Bratislava. ISBN 978-80-8168-132-5
Máziková K a kol (2013) Účtovníctvo podnikateľských subjektov I. Bratislava: Iura Edition, 2013. 297 s. ISBN 978-80-8078-563

Mateášová M, Vašeková M (2015) Odpisovanie dlhodobého hmotného majetku z daňového hľadiska - zmeny od 1. januára 2015. In Účtovníctvo - audítorstvo - daňovníctvo: v teórii a praxi - Bratislava: SÚVAHA, 2015. ISSN 1335-2024. Roč. 23, mimoriadne číslo (2015), s. 25–30

Vašeková M, Mateášová M (2015) Zákon o dani z príjmov - zmeny od 1. januára 2015. In Účtovníctvo - audítorstvo - daňovníctvo: v teórii a praxi - Bratislava: SÚVAHA, 2015. ISSN 1335-2024. Roč. 23, mimoriadne číslo (2015), s. 14–24

Zákon č. 595/2003 Z. z. o dani z príjmov v znení neskorších predpisov

Chapter 26
Fees or Taxes? The Question for the Czech Municipality

Pavlína Brabcová

Abstract This paper is focused on the analysis of the basic patterns of the municipal revenue in the Czech Republic, especially the trade-off between the tax and fee financing. Data reveal that the Czech municipalities often introduced local coefficient of 2 which doubled the basic property tax revenue. This is the mean value applied for more than one half of the surveyed units. Local fee is often introduced at the level of 500 CZK per capita. It seems that the municipality rather prefers such values, which are used by the vast majority of municipalities. We can hypothesise it is due to a competitive effect, when citizens move from one municipality to another to reach lower taxes or fees, ceteris paribus. In this paper was also analysed the relationship between tax and non-tax revenues. Moreover, it seems there is not a trade-off between the tax and fee financing. It also seems that both larger and "richer" municipalities prefer lower level of fees. It is in accordance with the hypothesis that the revenue needs of the larger municipalities are sufficiently financed by the taxes or by other sources.

Keywords Tax · Fee · Local coefficient · Fee for the municipal waste

26.1 Introduction

Fees for municipal waste ("fees") together with tax for buildings and land tax ("property tax") represent a significant source of income for municipalities which amount is under the control of municipality.

The purpose of this paper is to examine the basic factors of decision whether to use taxes or fees for financing of municipal services. The basic premise was that there is a trade-off between taxes and fees in the Czech municipalities. In our analysis, we control the set of factors as the industry level in the municipality, the

P. Brabcová (✉)
Department of Public Finance, University of Economics in Prague,
Nam. W. Churchilla 4, 130 67 Prague, Czech Republic
e-mail: xbrap23@vse.cz

© Springer International Publishing AG 2017
D. Procházka (ed.), *New Trends in Finance and Accounting*,
Springer Proceedings in Business and Economics,
DOI 10.1007/978-3-319-49559-0_26

size of the municipality, the number of inhabitants and the electoral preferences. We have also analysed a set of 160 municipalities from the South Bohemian region. We have analysed tax revenues, non-tax revenues ("fees"), the size of municipality and the number of inhabitant.

26.2 Financing Municipal Services—Theoretical Background

The trade-off between "tax on" and "fee for" was addressed for example by Stiglitz (2012), Jackson and Brown (2003), Kurtis and Janeba (2011), Semerád and Sobotková (2012), Lambe and Farber (2012) or recently Houdek and Koblovský (2015). Semerád and Sobotková (2012) focused on the impact of higher education on economic performance. The result of this investigation was that it is better to finance education from taxes, rather than through fees. Lambe and Farber (2012) studied how we can be taxes and fees used to deal with the greenhouse effect and to reduce its overall impact on the environment. They focus on the difference between "tax" and "fee" effects. Similar areas, applied to China, were analysed in MAZuo (2002), which examined how public support of industry and agriculture by fees and tax credits influenced their economic performance. The study concluded that it is better to support these sectors through taxes than through fees. Sedmihradská and Bakoš (2015) describe the process of creating the municipal budget. They also describe the application of the fiscal competence in respect tax on immovable property and using local coefficients.

For excellent summary of this phenomenon see Kurtis and Janeba (2011). They state that both taxes and fees funding have advantages and disadvantages. Fees correspond to the principle of benefit and equivalence. The taxpayers pay for what they actually (genuinely) want. We can eliminate "free riders", and this principle is quite fair and supports desirable behaviour. Taxes, on the contrary, guarantee a certain degree of solidarity and represent the advance guaranteed income for the local administration.

In this paper, we focus on the municipal level, and the basic hypothesis is that the municipality will introduce higher "taxes on" (additional charge to property tax) rather than "fees for". There are three factors supporting this hypothesis.

1. Fees are more "visible" and thus less tolerated by payers. Moreover, taxes are generally set up on the state level rather than municipality level. Thus, the higher level of taxes is less harmful to voters' preferences of municipality officers. To sum up, municipality officers would prefer taxes.
2. Smaller municipalities will prefer increasing of both fees and taxes. They do not have access to other kinds of public support.
3. Larger municipalities will prefer to decrease both fees (and partly taxes too). They do have access to other supplementary kinds of public support. These

other sources are "more friendly for citizens" because they (citizens) "do not bear the burden" directly.

On the contrary, the reason for fees (and not for uniform taxes) can be the occurrence of negative externalities. So-called Pigouvian taxes (fees) can reduce their impact (Sandmo 2006). "In the case of negative externalities, Pigouvian taxes are one way to correct this market failure, where the optimal tax leads agents to internalize the true cost of their actions. ... We show that a uniform tax performs very poorly in eliminating a deadweight loss..." (Knittel and Sandler 2013).

In our contribution, we decided to examine the factors of decision whether to use taxes or fees. The basic premise was that there is a trade-off between taxes and fees in Czech municipalities. In our analysis, we control the set of factors as the industry level in municipality, the area of the municipality, the number of inhabitants and the electoral preferences. These are the factors that could play their role in the decision. The municipality, which is located in the industrial zone, will prefer to use taxes because of a higher tax yield from industrial enterprises. Generally, the taxation of industrial objects and areas is substantially higher.

The article is treated as one of the outputs under the IGA: F1/2/2013 "Public finance in developed countries".

26.2.1 Financing Municipal Services—Legislative Perspective

In this chapter, we briefly discuss the potential ways of municipality budget inflow in the Czech Republic. The first part is devoted to the "property tax", which is significantly affected by the local coefficient. The second is focused on "fees for" municipal waste, tax and non-tax revenues.

Property tax is the "property tax" according to the Law No. 338/1992 Collections amended. Municipalities can generally introduce (1) the so-called correction coefficient, (2) the so-called coefficient of 1.5 or/and (3) the so-called local coefficient. The correction coefficient is determined by the number of inhabitants of the municipality, other coefficients are fully under the control of municipality. The tax is multiplied by these coefficients; therefore, they significantly influence the final tax revenue.

The most important is the local coefficient which takes the value 2, 3, 4, or 5 and is fully under the control of municipality. They can be used to multiply tax duty on all types of real estate, with the exception of arable land, vineyards, gardens, plantations and permanent grassland.

The second kind of municipality revenue focused on in our study is municipal fee for waste. Municipalities introduce fee for municipal waste according to Act No. 185/2001 Coll., on waste and amending certain other acts, as amended, according to law No. 280/2009 Coll., the tax code, as amended.

There is the fixed fee for the "container" and "periodicity of collection" under section §10b of the Act on local fees. The payers of these fees are individuals specified as follows:

- individual having a permanent residence in the municipality,
- foreign individual having temporary stay for a period longer than 90 days,
- individual having been granted international protection in accordance with the law governing asylum or temporary protection in accordance with the law governing foreigners' temporary protection,
- having in their ownership a building intended for individual recreation, flat or family house.

The other important part of this research is tax and non-tax revenues and also expenditures. In this paper were analysed the expenditures on agriculture, industry, services, security, and public administration. These variables were studied from web pages of municipalities.

26.3 Methodology and Data

The correlation analysis method was chosen as an appropriate method to measure mutual statistical relations. The correlation analysis examines the mutual dependency of one variable to another one. Variables are correlated to each other if both variables occur together. The correlation coefficient has values from <−1 to 1>. In the case of it being zero, it means that the variables are not correlated. The Pearson correlation coefficient was used for the calculation. We also test the significance (Gujarati 1995) of the correlation coefficient using following formula:

$$t = r\sqrt{\frac{n-2}{1-r^2}} \tag{26.1}$$

where "r" is Pearson correlation coefficient and t value follows the t—distribution with $(n-2)$ degree of freedom.

As the explanatory variables, we choose set of factors including the industry level in municipality, the size (area) of the municipality, the number of inhabitants and the electoral preferences. There is a list of variables (and basic statistics) below that were used in our analysis (Table 26.1).

The local coefficient has implemented 484 municipalities. From the amount of municipalities which applied the local Coefficient 2 (which means the tax was doubled in comparison with its basic level) was used by 84%, coefficient 3 was used by 11%, coefficient 4 was used by 1%, and coefficient 5 was used by 4%. The link between the size of the municipality and the local coefficient values is generally ambiguous.

If we focus on "fee" financing, the total of 50% of the municipalities applied the value of the fee at the level of CZK 500, 30% in the amount of CZK 500 and the remaining 20% of municipalities apply a higher rate of fee.

Table 26.1 Input data for analysed subset of municipalities

Variables	Definition	Source
Local coefficient (later indicated as "tax")	Coefficient used to adjust property tax. The measure of preference of tax financing	The Ministry of Finance
Local fee (later indicated as "fee")	Local fee for municipal waste according to Act No. 185/2001 Coll.	Municipality web pages
Number of inhabitants	Number of inhabitants according to the latest census	Municipality web pages
Tax Revenue	In CZK/year	Municipality web pages
Non-tax revenue	In CZK/year	Municipality web pages
Capital revenue	In CZK/year	Municipality web pages
Subsidy	In CZK/year	Municipality web pages
Expenditures on agriculture	In CZK/year	Municipality web pages
Expenditures on industry	In CZK/year	Municipality web pages
Expenditures on services	In CZK/year	Municipality web pages
Expenditures on security (police)	In CZK/year	Municipality web pages
Expenditures on public administration	In CZK/year	Municipality web pages
Deficit/Surplus	In CZK/year	Municipality web pages

Source Own research

To sum up, in most cases the amount of the "fee" is set up at the level of CZK 500 and the value of the coefficient on the local level 2. From the above mentioned, it could be concluded that the municipality rather prefers such values, which uses the vast majority of municipalities. We can hypothesise it is due to a competitive effect, when citizens move from one municipality to another to maximise their personal utility (lower taxes or fees, ceteris paribus; the so-called Tiebout effect).

We also use in our analysis the set of 160 municipalities. We have analysed multiple regression.

We also analysed all variables and studied the changes in two years—2011 and 2012. These years were selected because of availability of data on variables.

26.4 Results and Discussion

The results of correlating analysis for all dependent and independent variables are summarised in appendix.

At the beginning, we focus on the trade-off between "tax" and "fee" financing. We measured the correlation between the amount of the "fee" and the value of the local coefficient ("tax"). In this case, the correlation coefficient of +0.11 came out slightly positive. One could infer from this that the municipalities, which have a higher value for the local coefficient, at the same time introduce even higher fees for municipal waste. But it is necessary to take into account the fact that this is a very low positive value and it is not statistically significant on the standard levels. It seems there is not a trade-off between tax and fee financing and the choice between tax and fee financing seems to be independent.

Let us focus on the factors influencing the degree of the tax financing. The background information is expressed in Table 26.2.

We measured the dependency between the value of the local coefficient and the number of inhabitants. In this case, the correlation value of +0.11 came out, slightly positive, thus a higher coefficient was used by a larger municipalities, once again with a very low statistical significance.

In the case of measuring the correlation between an established amount of local coefficient (tax) and area of municipality, correlation coefficient was 0.0, thus these data does not reveal any relationships. Again, it is in accordance with our knowledge of structure of the Czech municipality budget. The Czech budgetary allocation law does not take into account the municipality area directly. On the other side, the level of industrialisation is the inherent part of the Czech budgetary regulation, thus we can suppose the high level of correlation. The Czech municipalities receive resources not only by raising taxes from its residents, but also from any businesses that are located in their vicinity. The correlation coefficient is large and positive and statistically significant, it reaches almost 0.9.

Let us focus on the factors influencing the degree of "fee" financing. The correlation coefficients between "fee" and other explanatory variables were all negative; see table below. It seems that the higher rate of the "fee" is introduced in the smaller municipalities. It is in accordance with our preliminary hypothesis that smaller municipalities will prefer increasing both the fees and taxes. Only large municipalities are able to reach other supplementary kinds of public support, which are "friendlier for citizens", thus also preferred by municipality representatives.

It also seems that both larger and more industrialised municipalities prefer lower level of fee. It is in accordance with our preliminary hypothesis that their financial needs are sufficiently covered by taxes or by other sources.

Table 26.2 Pearson correlation coefficients for the tax financing	Variables	Correlation coefficient
	Tax and number of inhabitants	0.11
	Tax and area	0.02
	Tax and industry	0.89*

Source Own research
*10%

The analysis also revealed some interesting correlations between explanatory variables. When assessing the industry of municipalities and tax revenues that could be divided into three sections:

Tax revenues

- Non-tax revenues
- Capital revenues
- Subsidy.

The other variables are expenditures; they could be also divided in other basic sections:

- Expenditures on agriculture
- Expenditures on industry
- Expenditures on services
- Expenditures on security
- Expenditures on public administration.

There is also much to do in the case of the future analysis. Our sample was rather small, it should be enlarged and some our implications could not be generalised yet. We also believe the multiple regressions would be a better tool for future attempt in uncovering some other factors of tax/fee financing.

We have also analysed 160 municipalities of Czech bohemian region. We have analysed relation between these variables:

- area
- population (popul)
- industry
- tax revenue (tax)
- no-tax revenue (fee)
- other no-tax revenue (fee1)
- tax/all.

Area represents the area of municipality. Population represents the number of inhabitants. Tax revenue represents revenue from taxes; no-tax revenue represents revenue from fees. No-tax revenues included other no-tax revenues, which include fees for municipal waste.

According to the multiple regressions, there is no significant relation between variables. There is only relation between area of municipality and the tax revenue. Bigger municipalities have higher tax revenues than smaller. Tax/all represents divided of tax revenue on summary of tax and no-tax revenue. Fee1/all represents revenue from fee for municipal waste and similar fees divided all revenues (tax and no-tax). Fee/all represents revenue from fee divided summary of fee and tax revenue.

According to the research (Table 26.3), there is a relation between tax revenue divided all revenues and tax and fee. The higher tax revenue related with the higher fee revenue. Table 26.4 shows relation between other fee revenue divided all revenue and other variables.

Table 26.3 Model OLS using observations 1–160, dependent variable: TAX/all

	Coefficient	Std. error	t-ratio	p value
Const	0.867958	0.0224222	38.7097	<0.0001***
Industry	−3.09316e−05	0.000131958	−0.2344	0.8150
Popul	−4.79872e−06	−4.79872e−06	−0.7865	0.4328
Tax	1.24613e−09	5.14391e−010	2.4225	0.0166**
Fee	−2.86841e−09	8.63883e−010	−3.3204	0.0011***
Fee1	−1.58149e−08	8.6792e−09	−1.8222	0.0704*
Industry/popul	0.066041	0.683713	0.0966	0.9232
Mean dependent var	0.867958		S.D. dependent var	0.097946
Sum squared resid	−3.09316e−05		S.E. of regression	0.090531
R-squared	−4.79872e−06		Adjusted R-squared	0.145676
$F(6, 153)$	1.24613e−09		P value (F)	0.028873
Log-likelihood	−2.86841e−09		Akaike criterion	−307.7576
Schwarz criterion	−1.58149e−08		Hannan-Quinn	−299.0166

Source Own research (gretl)
*10%
**5%
***1%

Table 26.4 Model OLS using observations 1–160, dependent variable: Fee1/all

	Coefficient	Std. error	t-ratio	p value
Const	0.0145723	0.0203027	0.7178	0.4740
Industry	−3.78459e−05	3.63498e−05	−1.0412	0.2994
Popul	4.25898e−06	1.88678e−06	2.2573	0.0254**
Tax	−3.26233e−010	1.50978e−010	−2.1608	0.0323**
Fee	1.36111e−010	1.17801e−010	1.1554	0.2497
Industry/popul	0.380181	0.710404	0.5352	0.5933
Mean dependent var	0.024288		S.D. dependent var	0.049229
Sum squared resid	0.380218		S.E. of regression	0.049689
R-squared	0.013268		Adjusted R-squared	−0.018769
$F(5, 154)$	1.228329		P value(F)	0.298456
Log-likelihood	256.3446		Akaike criterion	−500.6891
Schwarz criterion	−482.2381		Hannan-Quinn	−493.1968

Source Own research (gretl)
**5%

According to the research, there is a relation between other fees population and tax revenue. The higher municipalities (in context of inhabitants) have higher tax and no-tax income. The same relation is in the case of fees and these variables (Table 26.5).

Table 26.5 Model OLS using observations 1–160, dependent variable: Fee/all

	Coefficient	Std. error	t-ratio	p value
Const	0.132042	0.0224222	5.8889	<0.0001***
Industry	3.09316e−05	0.000131958	0.2344	0.8150
Popul	4.79872e−06	6.1014e−06	0.7865	0.4328
Tax	−1.24613e−09	5.14391e−010	−2.4225	0.0166**
fee	2.86841e−09	8.63883e−010	3.3204	0.0011***
Industry/popul	−0.066041	0.683713	−0.0966	0.9232
Fee1	1.58149e−08	8.6792e−09	1.8222	0.0704*
Mean dependent var	0.133932	S.D. dependent var	0.097946	
Sum squared resid	1.253966	S.E. of regression	0.090531	
R-squared	0.177915	Adjusted R-squared	0.145676	
$F(5, 154)$	2.423296	P value (F)	0.028873	
Log-likelihood	160.8788	Akaike criterion	−307.7576	
Schwarz criterion	−286.2314	Hannan-Quinn	−299.0166	

Source Own research (gretl)
*10%
**5%
***1%

26.5 Conclusions

The analysis of municipal revenue in the Czech Republic reveals that the local coefficient of 2 is often introduced, which doubled the basic property tax revenue. This is the mean value applied for more than one half of the surveyed units. Local fee is most often introduced at the level of 500 CZK per capita. From the above, it could be concluded that the municipality rather prefers such values, which uses the vast majority of municipalities. We can hypothesise it is due to a competitive effect, when citizens move from one municipality to another to reach lower taxes or fees ceteris paribus.

Moreover, it seems there is not a trade-off between the tax and/or fee financing and the choice seems to be independent.

On the other side, the analysis revealed that the level of industrialisation is a relevant factor of the financing of the municipality. The Czech municipalities receive resources not only by raising taxes from its residents, but also from any businesses that are located in their vicinity. The correlation coefficient is large and positive and statistically significant.

It also seems that both larger and more industrialised municipalities prefer lower level of fees. It is in accordance with the hypothesis that the revenue needs of larger municipalities are sufficiently financed by the taxes or by other sources.

The analysis also revealed some interesting relations between chosen explanatory variables. It seems that both larger and industry-oriented municipalities vote for the right-wing parties.

According to the research of 160 municipalities there is also a relation between population, tax, and fees. Bigger municipalities (in context of number of inhabitant) have more revenues (tax and fees).

Acknowledgments The contribution is processed as an output of a research project Public Finance in developed countries registered by the IGA under the registration number F1/2/2013.

References

Gujarati DN (1995) Basic Econometrics. McGraw-Hill, New York, p 838

Houdek P, Koblovský P (2015) Where is my money? New findings in fiscal psychology. Society 52/2:155–158. ISSN 0147-2011

Jackson PM, Brown CV (2003) Ekonomie veřejného sektoru. Imprint: EPOLEX BOHEMIA, Praha. ISBN 80-86432-09-2

Knittel R, Sandler R (2013) The welfare impact of indirect Pigouvian taxation: Evidence from Transportation. 2011. Munich Germany. ISSN 1617-9595

Kurtis SJ, Janeba E (2011) California's Cap-and-trade auction proceeds: taxes, fees or something else? Berkeley Law's Center for Law, Energy & the Environment, University of California

Lambe D, Farber D (2012) Climate vulnerability and adaptation study for California, California energy commission, Publication number: CEC-500-2012-019.

MaZuo (2002) Studies on reform of rural taxes and fees. Human Agricultural University, London

MOS—Městská a obecní statistika: Public database. Cited 2015-04-25. Online http://www.rozpocetobce.cz/seznam-obci

Sandmo A (2006) Optimal taxation in the presence of externalities. Norwegian School of Economics and Business Administration, Bergen, Norway

Semerád P, Sobotková V (2012) Tax justice of the reform of higher education: tution fees or tax relief? Acta univ. agric. et silvic. Mendel. Brun, LX. No. 7, pp 259–264

Sedmihradská L, Bakoš E (2015) Who applies the real estate tax's local coefficient? In: Sedmihradská L (ed) Proceedings of the 20th international conference theoretical and practical aspects of public finance 2015 [CD ROM], Praha. 17.04.2015–18.04.2015. Nakladatelství Oeconomica, Praha, s. 206–210. ISBN 978-80-245-2094-0

Stiglitz JE (2012) The price of inequality: How today's divided society endangers our future, 1st edn. WW Norton & Company, New York, pp 560

Chapter 27
Game-Theoretic Model of Principal–Agent Relationship Application in Corporate Tax Policy Design

Vladimir Kirillov

Abstract The paper considers game-theoretic model of principal–agent relationship application in corporate tax policy design and emphasizes the corporate tax policy issues because modern economics is built on corporations and it is essential to manage the whole corporate structure as a whole unit. This research is dedicated to the choice of a set of optimal strategies, which compose corporative tax policy, with the use of coalition model to decision-making process. In daily routine, every enterprise faces the problem of effective allocation of assets. The solution of this problem is usually related to the complexity of stated plan (project) and a set of condition in which the plan can be accomplished. It is obvious that the results of each project (or even variety or type of action) differ and depend on condition (either internal or external). Every organization is challenged with uncountable impacts. And the degree of influence of each impact is depended on strategy organization chosen. We analyze tax impact, and solve the problem of effective tax policy design within principal–agent theory.

Keywords Corporate tax policy design · Game theory · Agent relationships

27.1 Introduction

This study is concentrated around a math explanation of rational corporate tax policy design. There is a great deal of various attempts undertaken to explain principal–agent intermediation based on game-theoretic model in order to give an answer to question what kind of strategy is supposed to be optimal for corporate tax system design (Gailmard 2012). The questions of effective corporate tax policy have been investigated by researchers as well as practitioners (Allingham and

V. Kirillov (✉)
Department of Managerial Accounting and Controlling, Kazan State University,
Butlerov St 4, Kazan, Russia
e-mail: vladimir_kirillov_kzn@mail.ru

© Springer International Publishing AG 2017
D. Procházka (ed.), *New Trends in Finance and Accounting*,
Springer Proceedings in Business and Economics,
DOI 10.1007/978-3-319-49559-0_27

Sandmo (1972); Shigaev et al (2014)). Despite possible divergences in their private points of view, both of them converge in one crucial issue.

Comprehensive investigation of all feasible modes and parameters, their choice and implementation in corporate tax policy have significant impact on valuation of any company. In this case, game-theoretic model serve as a universal tool not only for tax burden reduction but also for strategic planning.

In modern conditions of highly competitive and unstable global economic system, every wrong decision produces certain consequences and could impose additional expenses on business (in the context of corporate tax system design, there is a wide range of penalties, which could be implemented for tax evasion) or even lead to bankruptcy. This is why it is important to give rational explanation to corporate tax policy design and use math modeling for these purposes.

This study is a part of the research dedicated to the system of accounting and analysis for corporate tax policy design, on which the author has been working currently.

The aim of this paper is to present math model useful to corporate tax activity planning. The paper discusses such aspects as core concepts, model description, application and calculations.

27.2 Problem Statement

Before we start to analyze the subject of our research, it is essential to consider some basic elements in order to present the conceptual foundation of our research.

An organization is considered as a system with its hierarchical multi-level structure, internal elements, intermediate channels. Moreover, we take into account that this system is permanently under the influence of external conditions, created during the interaction with other systems and organizations. One of such so-called mega systems is government with its tax policy. In accordance with the statement about the nature of entropy and its initial characteristics, we can note that organization as any other system tends to move toward stable condition. Conditions, in which an obligation to pay taxes exists, might be represented with a set of elements (external characteristics $q_j \in Q$). System tries to adopt the external influence and get to the state of an optimal order which provides stability. All of those processes proceed within corporate tax policy based on optimal strategy oriented to reduce the pressure of external influence.

Corporate tax policy that comprised a set of strategies S_j is aimed at the restriction of the number of external elements q_j. So we closely get to the core of general purpose—optimization of tax structure and tax burden. Obviously tax structure goes together with tax burden, but how it is possible to reduce taxation impact?

We investigate this question under principal–agent theory, which helps to find appropriate conditions for both sides. This type of relationships between two systems (either collaboration or competition) might be depicted with game-theoretic model of inspection (or principal–agent model) where the first part is represented by inspector (principal) and the second one is inspected (agent). Each of them tends to maximize his/her own utility function $U_{PR}(u_j)$ and $U_{Ag}(u_i)$. These functions can be characterized with interrelation (27.1)

$$U_{PR}(u_j) = \frac{1}{U_{Ag}(u_j)} \qquad (27.1)$$

From this point of view, in order to define the optimal level of tax reduction and its limit, we need to find out the intersection point of these two functions in equilibrium. This point is called Pareto efficiency when marginal utility equals to marginal cost. Before searching for a solution, we need to consider many other aspects in order to develop the comprehensive understanding of core concepts.

27.2.1 Concept Core

The framework of our model is based on some assumptions:

1. The level of revenue neither rises nor goes down;
2. Every action is supposed to be considered within a certain period, which is called relevant period;
3. Taxpayer tends to optimize his/her own tax burden without breaking the law and/or criminal code;
4. Every taxpayer action is oriented to the maximization of his/her function of utility;
5. Every decision (action) is associated with expenditure;
6. When making decisions, taxpayer compares expenditures for any decision (rational choice);
7. The existence of environmental characteristics. Each of these characteristics is defined in parameter μ, is dependent on any player's (principal or agent) decision and does not constitute the part of anyone's strategy. For example, no one of players could impact on precedential court statement but this statement explicitly impacts on probability.

27.2.2 Model Framework

As mentioned before, our model has some assumptions and restrictions or limitations. In accordance with these aspects, the rules of the game are described below.

1. Sum of i taxes payable in relevant period (absolute value of tax burden) $T\{i\}$.

$$F(Ti) = \sum_{i=1}^{n} Ti \qquad (27.2)$$

$$F(Ti) \begin{cases} \sum_{i=1}^{n} Ti > 0 \\ n \to \min \\ \sum_{i=1}^{n} Ti \to 0 \end{cases} \qquad (27.3)$$

2. Basic amount for calculation taxable in monetary term of ith tax $(B_i, B_i > 0, B_i \to \min)$.
3. Tax rate for ith tax $(r_i, r_i > 0)$
4. Numerical characteristics of penalty in case of ith tax evasion $E_i, E_i > 0$

$$F(E_i) = \left[\left(T_i^0 - T_i^1 \right) * e_i \right] + \alpha_i^j - \beta_i^k \qquad (27.4)$$

where $T_i^0 - T_i^1$—Payable arrear of ith tax. In a particular case if $\sum T_i^1 \to 0$, then $\sum T_i^1 \to Ti$;

$\quad e_i$ amount of penalty rate;
$\quad \alpha_i^j$ amount of jth aggravating circumstance for ith tax evasion;
$\quad \beta_i^k$ amount of kth extenuating circumstance for ith tax evasion

5. a_m activity of tax payer aimed at tax burden optimization;
6. Cost of activity to draft any action aimed at tax burden reduction C_i^{am} where j is the number of activity oriented to ith tax;
7. Probability of recognition that the mth action is invalid and aimed to tax evasion $P(a_{im})$, $0 < P(a_{im}) < 1$;
8. Probability of tax inspection initiation $P(Q_i)$, $0 < P(Q_i) < 1$, depended on different parameters such as the average level of tax burden in branch divergence, the amount of tax deduction, etc.
9. Economical effect ε_i, $\varepsilon > 0$;
   Probability to become sentenced for kth strategy implementation $P(\alpha_i)$, $0 < P(\alpha_i) < 1$, $P(\alpha_i) = P(Q_i) * P(a_{im})$
11. Probability of success for kth strategy implementation $P(\beta_i)$, $0 < P(\beta_i) < 1$, $P(\beta_i) = 1 - P(\alpha_i)$

So, keeping in mind all abovementioned notifications and assumptions, we transfer described interaction between taxpayer and government to the principal–agent model pattern. Let there be the game:

$$\Gamma(\text{PR,AG,G(PR,AG)}, D(\text{PR,AG})) \tag{27.5}$$

with the following matrix:

$$\text{PR} = \begin{pmatrix} \text{pr}_0 \\ \text{pr}_1 \end{pmatrix} \tag{27.6}$$

where PR is set of government's strategies, pr_0—recognize decision as an evasion and pr_1—deny decision as an evasion;

$$\text{AG} = (\text{ag}_0 \ \text{ag}_1) \tag{27.7}$$

where AG is set of taxpayer's strategies, ag_0—confirm a decision and ag_1—deny a decision.

$$G(\text{PR, AG}) = (g_{ij})$$
$$= \begin{pmatrix} 0 & B_i * r_i \\ P(a_{im}) * (B_i * r_i + F(E)) - \varepsilon & B_i * r_i + P(Q_i) * (B_i * r_i + F(E)) - \varepsilon \end{pmatrix} \tag{27.8}$$

$$D(\text{PR, AG}) = (d_{ij})$$
$$= \begin{pmatrix} T_i^0 - T_i^1 & B_i * (1 - r_i) \\ T_i^0 - T_i^1 - P(a_{im}) * (B_i * r_i + F(E)) - \varepsilon & B_i - B_i * r_i - P(Q_i) * (B_i * r_i + F(E)) - \varepsilon \end{pmatrix} \tag{27.9}$$

In accordance with feasible strategies (27.5) and (27.6), we have got the following payoff matrices represented with principal's (government) (27.7) and agent (27.8). Thus, the game Γ (27.4) characterizes competition between government and corporation. Obviously everyone possessed two pure strategies. Every strategy is built in regards to assumptions and restrictions mentioned above.

Eventually, the game Γ (27.4) solution hided in pure strategy.

$$\text{NE}_{00} : \begin{cases} B_i r_i > \{C_i^{a_{im}}\} \\ B_i r_i < \frac{\varepsilon}{P(Q_i)*F(E)} \end{cases} \tag{27.10}$$

$$\text{NE}_{01} : \begin{cases} B_i r_i > \min\{C_i^{a_{im}}\} \\ B_i r_i < \min\left\{\frac{\varepsilon}{P(Q_i)*F(E)}\right\} \end{cases} \tag{27.11}$$

$$\text{NE}_{10} : \begin{cases} B_i r_i > \max\left\{\frac{\varepsilon}{P(a_{im})*F(E)}\right\} \\ B_i r_i < \max\left\{\frac{C_i^{a_{im}}}{1-(P(a_i m)-P(Q_i)*F(E))}\right\} \end{cases} \tag{27.12}$$

$$NE_{11} : \begin{cases} B_i r_i > \left\{ \frac{\varepsilon}{P(a_{im})*F(E)} \right\} \\ B_i r_i < \left\{ \frac{C_i^{a_{im}}}{1-(P(a_{im})-P(Q_i)*F(E))} \right\} \end{cases} \tag{27.13}$$

Every represented strategy of each competitor depends on its own effectiveness. According to this postulate, an organization tends to maximize utility function (27.2) and (27.3) depended on tax burden $T\{i\}$. Considering equilibriums NE_{00} (27.10), NE_{01} (27.11), NE_{10} (27.12), NE_{11} (27.13), the basic item used for effectiveness estimation is $B_i r_i$. It is important to note the next Eqs. (27.14), (27.15), which say that effectiveness of each participant is inverse.

$$C_i^{a_{im}} = \frac{P(a_{im}) * F(E)}{\varepsilon} \tag{27.14}$$

$$\frac{C_i^{a_{im}}}{1 - (P(a_{im}) - P(Q_i) * F(E))} = \frac{P(Q_i) * F(E)}{\varepsilon} \tag{27.15}$$

Equations NE_{00} (27.10) and NE_{11} (27.13) are mutually inversed. In some order their functions curves $F(NE_{00})$ and $F(NE_{11})$ intersects in multi-dimension. For our general question of what kind of tools and what is the level of tax burden optimization ought to be preferred, the answer will be the vector W $(C_i^{am}, \varepsilon, (Q_i), P(a_{im}))$. It is followed with another question: what are the numeral characteristics of vector W $(C_i^{am}, \varepsilon, (Q_i), P(a_{im}))$?

27.3 Computation

We have already stated all assumptions and restrictions of our model and found the appropriate equilibrium in particular conditions which provides the best solution. Any theory possesses as much benefit as it is useful to practice. In the next step of our study, we are going to show how the model described above can be applied by practitioners. In this part of the paper, we focus on computations under our model.

Let's suppose that all aforementioned assumptions and restrictions exist. Principal is represented by controlling officials (PR) and agent is represented by company (AG). Agent (AG) has an intention to optimize his function of utility with only factor—tax burden $T\{I\}$.

The initial economic data are presented in Table 27.1.

Using the data from Table 27.1, we conclude that $\sum_{i=1}^{4} T_i = 477{,}663$, $N = 4$. This shows that we could reduce a count of taxes (n) and therefore total tax burden to level which closely gets to the minimum. And thus we have challenged with the first question: what is the level of tax optimization? In this example, indirect tax amount is the restriction line or limit of optimization (27.16).

Table 27.1 Economic data report

Item	Amount (€)
Total revenue	3,352,417
Value added tax	359,520
Gross margin	2,992,897
Expenses	2,654,179
Amortization and depreciation	150,000
Maintenance fees	20,000
Rental	0
Property tax	50,000
Vehicle tax	1000
Taxable profit	275,718
Income tax	55,144
Net profit (bottom line)	220,575
Total amount of taxes (including indirect tax)	477,663
Amount of direct taxes	118,144
Tax burden	15.96%

Source Own computation

$$\text{Lim of tax optimization}$$
$$= \text{Total amount of taxes(including indirect tax)} - \text{direct taxes} \qquad (27.16)$$

Thus, the limit of tax burden optimization amount equals to 359,520 € (an amount of indirect tax).

For tax rate reduction, we consider four different varieties (types) represented in Fig. 27.1.

The company expects to restrict its payoffs related to taxation. An organization tries to cut the amount and quantity of taxes. On basic scenario, enterprise pays four different types of taxes and the total amount of taxation payoff gets to 477,663 €. By the way, the company is able to get lower level of tax burden by getting rid of objects of taxation. It is suitable only for two types of taxes—property tax and vehicle tax. Technically it is possible to outsource transport and properties to rent them back.

Other scenarios are supposed to lead to the same decision but provide companies with tax incentives (a company can apply special tax regime to obtain lower level of taxation and use cash basis method of accounting). In this way, corporation is able to manage tax burden by accepting receivables payable at incorporated affiliated enterprises. The amount depends on the rental fees. Setting high rental prices for transport and properties, incorporated companies inflate tax expenditures and consequently tax burden. But excessive increase of rent price (which surpasses annual amount more than threshold) might be stated under transfer pricing. In this case, the probability to recognize the decision is invalid and aimed at tax evasion.

All scenarios represented in Fig. 27.1 possess numerical characteristics presented in Table 27.2.

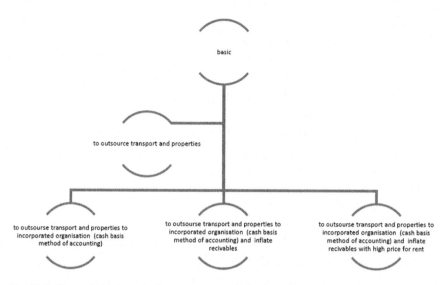

Fig. 27.1 The varieties (types) of tax structure optimization. *Source* Author

Table 27.2 Strategy types estimation, thousands €

Item	Type 2				Type 3			
	A	B	C	Σ	A	B	C	Σ
Tax burden (%)	14.95	6%	6%	13.2	13.7	6%	6%	11.6
Income (€)	2992.9	10	20		2992.8	360	20	
Expenses (€)	2433.1	0	20		2433.1	0	20	
Maintenance		0	20			0	20	
Amortization	0	0	0		0	0	0	
Rent	0				0			
Tax expenses	447.5	0.6	1.2	449.2	411.4	21.6	1.2	434.3
Retrenchment				211				247
Taxation	51	0	0	51	87	0	0	87
Vehicle tax	1				1			
Property tax	50				50			
Income tax	0				36			
Other associated exp.	160	0	0	160	160	0	0	160

Item	Type 4			
	A	B	C	Σ
Tax burden (%)	12.4	0%	0%	11.1
Income (€)	2992.9	0	0	
Expenses (€)	2433.1	0	20	
Maintenance	0	0	20	
Amortization	0	0	0	

(continued)

Table 27.2 (continued)

Item	Type 4			
	A	B	C	Σ
Rent	0			
Tax expenses	371.5	0	0	371.5
Retrenchment				273.7
Taxation	90	21.6	1.2	113.7
Vehicle tax	1			
Property tax	50			
Income tax	39.9			
Other associated exp.	160	0	0	160

Source Own computation

Table 27.3 Parameters of strategies

Variety no.	$\sum T\{i\}$	N	C_i^{am}	Tax burden (%)	P (a_{im})	P (Q_i)	ε
Basic	477,663	4	0.00	15.96	0.0	0.0	0
1st	483,463	2	180,000	16.15	0.0	0.0	−129,000
2nd	447,463	2	20,000	14.95	0.1	0.1	211,000
3rd	411,463	2	20,000	13.75	0.3	0.1	247,000
4th	359,520	2	20,000	12.41	0.7	1.0	273,774

Source Own computation

The results summarized below demonstrate how aforementioned issues change in every variety (type) of strategy.

Analyzing data, represented for each feasible strategy in Tables 27.3 and 27.4 Applying this data to our model we get the following:

As we note optimal strategy achieves from equilibrium (27.17).

$$\begin{cases} NE_{11} < NE_{00} \\ NE_{00} < NE_{11} \end{cases} \tag{27.17}$$

Table 27.4 Assessment data dynamic analysis

Variety	$\sum T\{i\}$	C_i^{am}	Tax burden (%)	P (a_{im})	P (Q_i)	ε_i (€)	P (α_i)	P (β_i)
Basic	477,663	0	15.96	0.0	0.0	0	0.0	1.0
1st	483,463	180,000	16.15	0.0	0.0	−129,000	0.0	1.0
2nd	447,463	20,000	14.95	0.1	0.1	211,000	0.01	0.99
3rd	411,463	20,000	13.75	0.3	0.1	247,000	0.03	0.97
4th	359,520	20,000	12.41	0.7	1.0	273,774	0.7	0.3

Source Own computation

Obviously the success of any chosen strategy depends of $W\left(C_i^{am}, \varepsilon, (Q_i), P(a_{im})\right)$ rates.

Using Eqs. (27.14) and (27.15), we find the most apt set of decision composed our strategy.

To assess our strategy, we use the following Eq. (27.18).

$$\begin{cases} \{C_i^{a_{im}}\} < \sum_{i=1}^{n} B_i r_i < \{\varepsilon_i\} \\ \{P(a_{im}) * P(Q_i)\} < \{[1 - P(a_{im})] * [1 - P(Q_i)]\} \end{cases} \qquad (27.18)$$

Explore dynamic of rate

$$\begin{cases} \left\{\dfrac{\partial C_i^{a_{im}}}{\partial C_{i-1}^{a_{im}}}\right\} < \dfrac{\partial \sum B_i r_i}{\partial \sum B_{i-1} r_{i-1}} < \dfrac{\partial\{\varepsilon_i\}}{\partial\{\varepsilon_{i-1}\}} \\ \dfrac{\partial\{P(a_{im}) * P(Q_i)\}}{\partial\{P(a_{i-1m-1}) * P(Q_{i-1})\}} < \dfrac{\partial\{[1 - P(a_{im})] * [1 - P(Q_{i-1})]\}}{\partial\{[1 - P(a_{i-1m-1})] * [1 - P(Q_{i-1})]\}} \end{cases} \qquad (27.19)$$

Using information from Table 27.4, we are about to conclude that the most rational strategy of all is number 3. This strategy guarantees the corporation 247,000 € marginal economy with minimal probability to be sentenced for tax evasion.

Thus, within some assertions and restrictions, economic data from accounting report provided us with exact parameters to choose the most rational decision.

27.4 Conclusion

This paper presented math model based on principal–agent theory, explained parametric characteristics of the model and demonstrated how exactly it applies.

References

Allingham M, Sandmo A (1972) Income tax evasion: a theoretical analysis. J Public Econ 1 (3/4):323–338

Gailmard S (2012) Accountability and principal-agent models. Oxford handbook of public accountability. Oxford University Press, Oxford, p 2012

Shigaev AI, Needles BE, Powers M, Frigo ML (2014) Operating characteristics of high performance companies: strategic direction for management. In: Antonio D, Epstein MJ, Manzoni J-F (ed) Performance measurement and management control: behavioral implications and human actions (studies in managerial and financial accounting), vol 28. Emerald Group Publishing Limited, pp 25–51

Chapter 28
Shadow Economy in the Regions of the Russian Federation and the Ukraine

**Anna Kireenko, Yuriy Ivanov, Ekaterina Nevzorova
and Olga Polyakova**

Abstract The aim of this paper is to determine shadow economy on regional level in connection with quality of life. The paper focuses on shadow economy's regional differences in two countries: the Russian Federation and the Ukraine. The research methods are factor analysis and MIMIC modeling. Using these methods, we conducted a factor analysis of the relationships of quality and standard of living in regions of Russian Federation for the years 2002–2013 and in Ukraine for the years 2004–2013 in the same indices of 17 sections. The factors most common for the two countries are the demographic factor and the criminogenic factor, but the significant differences are in the standard of living monetary support factor. In Russia, monetary income and formal employment have shown a weak correlation, while in the Ukraine they are closely related. The demographic indices for the quality of life are significantly affected by the ethno-socio-cultural factors; therefore, their application in the analysis of correlations between the various manifestations of shadow economy is quite limited. Finally, the fact that the indices for the standard and quality of living can be regularly explained by the influence of various factors shows that there is a gap between the economic and societal components in

A. Kireenko (✉)
Department of Taxation and Customs, Baikal State University, Irkutsk,
Lenina Str. 11, 664003 Irkutsk, Russian Federation
e-mail: kireenko-ap@bgu.ru

Y. Ivanov · O. Polyakova
Research Center of Industrial Problems of Development,
National Academy of Sciences of Ukraine, Kharkiv, Ukraine
e-mail: yuriy.ivanov.ua@gmail.com

O. Polyakova
e-mail: polya_o@ukr.net

E. Nevzorova
Department of World Economy and Public Administration, Baikal State University,
Irkutsk, Lenina Str. 11, 664003 Irkutsk, Russian Federation
e-mail: nevzorova_kat@mail.ru

© Springer International Publishing AG 2017
D. Procházka (ed.), *New Trends in Finance and Accounting*,
Springer Proceedings in Business and Economics,
DOI 10.1007/978-3-319-49559-0_28

the functioning of the two states. Using results of factor analysis, the MIMIC model was developed. The results point out that the level of shadow economy in Russian Federation varies from 48 to 62% from GRP at considered regions during the years 2000–2013.

Keywords Shadow economy · Quality of life · MIMIC model

28.1 Introduction

Shadow economy becomes a very popular object of study now, but as will be discussed in more detail later, shadow economy is difficult to measure. Still, there is sufficient evidence that it is extensive and commonplace in nearly all countries. For the Russian Federation, the most reliable estimates suggest that shadow economy constitutes 35–40% of GDP. Evidence from other post-socialist countries (e.g., Ukraine) clearly indicates that the Russian experience is not a unique.

A lot of research is focused on the effects of shadow economy on allocation, distribution, stabilization, and fiscal policy. The impact of shadow economy on the quality of life has not been sufficiently investigated.

In this paper, we undertake a study of the relationship between shadow economy and various socio-economic indicators that reflect the quality of life. Different models allow the size of the shadow economy. Some of the models show links to specific indicators of life quality. However, in more thorough models quality of life is the casual variable; changes in this variable lead to changes in the latent variable (the shadow economy). Our task is to determine the reverse effect of shadow economy on the quality of life. The aim of this paper is to identify what factors determine shadow economy on the regional level and to group these factors using shadow economy and quality-of-life factors as variables.

We also discuss the current research on shadow economy measurement. Over the past years the literature has grown, providing many important insights. Shadow economy exists in a regional framework which has a significant role in explaining its dimensions. There is a lot of research on shadow economy in different countries and its influence on economic growth. The area of regional estimation of shadow economy is narrow, and it is this area that we examine. We focus on the regional differences in the level of shadow economy in two countries: the Russian Federation and the Ukraine. How extensive is the influence of shadow economy on the quality of life in these countries? What factors indicate the influence of shadow economy on the quality of life? Can we estimate the danger of shadow economy using the quality-of-life indicators? These are the questions we will try to answer.

28.2 Measurement of Shadow Economy in Regions: Literature Review

Various methods of measuring the size of shadow economy on a regional level can be divided into three approaches:

- Direct approach includes tax auditing, surveys, and other researches based on voluntary replies. We can find some examples of measuring the shadow economy in regions by this method: a micro-survey of the informal sector in eight geographical regions of Romania (Albu et al. 2008) and a micro-survey of the regions in Estonia, Latvia, and Lithuania (Putniņš 2011).
- Indirect approach includes: the method using differences between income and expenditure statistics; the method using differences between officially measured and actual participation rates; the transactions method; the monetary methods; the physical input method (based on the data of electricity consumption), including the Kaufmann–Kaliberda method and the Lackó method. An example of monetary measures (based on the denomination of banknotes) is the estimation of 19 municipalities of the Brussels-Capital Region (Dotti et al. 2015). On the basis of the currency ratio/demand method estimations have been made for the Spanish regions (González-Fernández and González-Velasco 2015) and Italian provinces (Ardizzi et al. 2011). Income and expenditure measures have been used by Alderslade et al. (2006) to measure shadow economy in the USA and by Fortin et al. (2010) for the Province of Quebec (Canada). Indirect non-monetary measures based on electricity consumption in different states of the USA have been used by Heath and Jones (2013), and the method of spatial patterns of nighttime imagery has been used for the states of Mexico (Ghosh et al. 2009) and for the states and union territories of India (Ghosh et al. 2010).
- Model approach. This approach is implemented by compiling econometric models using statistical tools to assess shadow economy as an 'unobservable' variable. Structural equation modeling (SEM) examines statistical links between unobservable and observable variables. Special cases are SEM—MIMIC (multiple-indicator multiple-cause model) and DYMIMIC (dynamic multiple-indicator multiple-cause model). Shadow economy is investigated as a 'latent' variable, which is connected, on the one hand, with a set of observable indicators (reflecting changes in the size of the shadow economy) and, on the other hand, with a set of observed independent variables, which are considered as most significant factors determining unrecorded economic activity. There is also a large and growing literature on the MIMIC model on the regional level: for the federal states of Germany (Schneider 2003; Mummert and Schneider 2001), major states of India (Chaudhuri et al. 2006), EU regions (Tafenau et al. 2010), districts in Germany (Buehn 2012), states of the USA (Wiseman 2013). MIMIC modeling in estimating shadow economy in the Russian regions has been used in a number of studies (Komarova 2003; Bilonizhko 2006; Vorobyev 2015).

28.3 The Model of Shadow Economy in the Regions

28.3.1 Selection of Model Indicators on the Basis of Factor Analysis

The use of factor analysis is based on the assumption that, with a low level of shadow economy, the income and expenses of a population should be mostly defined by formal employment. Meanwhile, the low correlation between employment, unemployment, and income indicates the existence of an outside source of income. The use of factor analysis in assessing the level of shadow economy has been mentioned in some research, but mostly as a specific case of a more general approach to SEM.

This research has used an exploratory factor analysis based on the assumption that it is not known from the start which set of factors makes a description of the correlational matrix possible. Thus, the number of factors and the relationships between them are not fixed by default.

Thus, the factors most common for the two countries are the demographic factor and the criminogenic factor. There are significant differences in the structure of the standard of living monetary support factor. In Russia, monetary income and formal employment have shown a weak correlation, while in the Ukraine they are closely related. The demographic indices for the quality of life are significantly affected by the ethno-socio-cultural factors; therefore, their application in the analysis of correlations between the various manifestations of shadow economy is quite limited. Finally, the fact that the indices for the standard and quality of living can be regularly explained by the influence of various factors shows that there is a gap between the economic and societal components in the functioning of the two states.

Using this method, we conducted a factor analysis of the relationships of quality and standard of living in the regions of the Russian Federation for the period for the years 2002–2013 and in the Ukraine for the period for the years 2004–2013 in the same indices of 17 sections. The results of calculations of factor loadings, obtained by main component analysis and refined using varimax rotation are presented in Table 28.1. Significant factor loadings are highlighted in bold type. Calculations were done using the Statistica 8.0 software application. Comparative results of the factor analysis according to the most indicative year 2012 for the two countries are given in Table 28.1.

The most significant factor in Russia turned out to be the demographic factor, which explains also the variation of unemployment and the provision of preschool institutions. In general, this factor explains 26–31% of the dispersion parameters. Unemployment, birth rate, and natural growth rate in the whole time interval are co-directional factors, and mortality rate—the opposite of them (in the matrix of factor loadings these figures correspond to the number of different signs). This, apparently, is explained by the socio-ethno-geographical reasons.

For the Ukraine, the demographic factor turned out to be the second largest for the entire period except the year 2004, when it was the most significant. However, it

Table 28.1 The most significant factors for the Russian Federation and the Ukraine in 2012

Indicators	Russian Federation		Ukraine	
	1—Socio-demographic	3—Cash security	2—Socio-demographic	1—Cash security
Average monthly cash income per capita	0.001	**0.946**	0.090	**0.915**
Average consumption expenditure per capita	−0.107	**0.912**	−0.122	**0.903**
Share of food consumption expenditure in total consumption expenditure	0.457	−0.389	−0.488	0.219
Quantity of passenger cars (per 1000 inhabitants)	−0.399	0.274	0.280	0.431
Bank deposits of individuals at credit institutions per capita	−0.077	**0.889**	−0.208	**0.946**
Birthrate	**0.880**	−0.164	**−0.912**	−0.082
Mortality rate	**−0.873**	−0.208	**0.829**	−0.360
Rate of natural increase	**0.955**	0.011	**−0.945**	0.165
Infant mortality	0.478	−0.078	0.102	0.121
Unemployment rate	**0.790**	−0.386	0.146	−0.387
Employment rate	−0.649	0.640	0.116	0.645
Coverage of children by preschool institutions	**−0.704**	0.431	**0.710**	0.324
Population per one hospital bed	0.437	−0.188	−0.172	−0.485
Criminality (number of registered crimes)	−0.070	0.130	0.213	0.298
Serious crimes	0.299	−0.063	0.235	0.128
Juvenile delinquency	0.015	0.017	0.212	−0.240
Life expectancy at birth	0.210	0.038	−0.353	0.293
Explained dispersion	4.931	3.621	3.643	4.115
The share of the total explained dispersion	0.290	0.213	0.214	0.242

Source Authors' calculation

is not connected with any employment or unemployment. There is the same slightly transparent alignment of availability of preschool institutions and mortality rate. It can be assumed that a similar relationship in the Ukraine is a side effect of agglomeration—the need for preschool institutions in the cities is higher, and opportunities for provisions from the city budget are also higher. Thus, from the point of view of the purpose of our study, demographic indicators cannot be considered as a unique quality of life and require further study.

The second most important factor for the Russian Federation, and the third for the Ukraine, reflects the criminal situation in the regions. It is remarkable that the level of criminality (all types included in this factor) is closely related to the negative connection to the life expectancy at birth (mostly demographic indicators). It implicitly supports the idea that the criminal situation is a socio-economic problem, but not exclusively moral. A special feature of the Ukraine is that in the years 2006–2008 this factor was closely (greater than 0.7) associated with a specific gravity of food expenses. In the Russian Federation we also observe a similar relationship, but significantly weaker (at the level of 0.4–0.5). While in the Ukraine these were not the crisis years, a slight increase in stratification of the population by income can be observed.

Therefore, we can assume that criminality rates can be a reflection on the quality of life and the level of social tension in the region. It is more typical for the Russian Federation, where the national average crime rate since 2006 has been going down, and life expectancy growing. In the Ukraine, the criminality rate dynamics is unstable, so it is impossible to make definitive conclusions; however, in the context of regions the situation is similar. It should also be noted that the criminality rate significantly depends on the effectiveness of law enforcement and, therefore, requires a more in-depth study to clarify the relationship with the living level.

28.3.2   MIMIC Model

We develop our model basing on the results of the preliminary factor analysis, which revealed some significant factors explaining dispersion of all variables included in the sample.

Casual variables for life quality are as follows:

- Coverage of children by preschool institutions (as a particular measure of public goods' provision);
- Population per one hospital bed (as a particular measure of public goods' provision);
- Number of registered crimes (literature review also confirms their appropriateness for MIMIC model);
- Rate of natural increase (as a result of our factor analysis);
- Life expectancy at birth;
- Ratio between bank deposits of individuals at credit institutions per capita and cash income per capita (measure of purchasing power but eliminating inflation impact);
- Ratio between consumption expenditure per capita and cash income per capita (measure of purchasing power but eliminating inflation impact);
- Quantity of passenger cars (a partly similar approach has been developed by Braguinsky et al. (2014). Their estimation is based on the direct method using the data on discrepancy between the data on car registries and employers' records of paid earnings).

Indicator variables demonstrate some dimensions of productive activity:

- Employment rate (this variable is frequently using in MIMIC models, including models for the regional level);
- Electricity intensity: Ratio between electricity consumption in the region and the gross regional product [this measure is rather popular in estimation of shadow economy both as an indicator in electricity consumption method (cf., e.g., Vorobyev 2015) and as a possible indicator in MIMIC models at the regional level (cf., e.g., Wiseman 2013)].

Our variable definitions and their explanations are given in Table 28.2.

Table 28.2 MIMIC model estimation results

Variables	Explanation	Theoretically expected signs	Values
Causal variables			
Coverage of children by preschool institutions	CHILDCARE	−	−0.621
Population per one hospital bed	HOSPITAL	+	0.087
Number of registered crimes	CRIME	+	0.144
Rate of natural increase	NAT_INCR	Indefinite	−0.071
Life expectancy at birth	LIFE_EXP	Indefinite	−0.234
Ratio between bank deposits of individuals at credit institutions per capita and cash income per capita	DEP_TO_I	+	−0.093
Ratio between consumption expenditure per capita and cash income per capita	CONS_TO_I	−	0.073
Quantity of passenger cars	CARS	−	−0.122
Indicator variables			
Employment rate	EMPLOYMENT	Normalizing variable, with its coefficient fixed to −1	−1
Electricity intensity	ELECTRIC	+	0.107
Statistical tests			
Root mean square error of approximation (RMSEA) P value for test of close fit (RMSEA <0.05)			0.000 0.827
Chi-square for independence model (45 df)			119.120
Adjusted goodness-of-fit index (AGFI)			0.900
Degrees of freedom			18
Number of observations			790

Source Authors' calculation

It doesn't seem possible to make a single model for two countries (Russia and Ukraine) for now, since the statistical analysis of the data revealed a discrepancy. There are no data in the following Ukraine statistical surveys:

- Consumption expenditure (no data for 2003–2004);
- Quantity of passenger cars (per 1000 inhabitants) (no data for 2003–2004 and 2012);
- Unemployment rate (no data for 2001–2003);
- Coverage of children by preschool institutions (no data for 2004);
- Life expectancy at birth (indicator on regions of Ukraine began to be published in 2012);
- Lack of correct data on energy consumption for all period.

The main difficulty is the absence of correct data about energy consumption for the considered period. Electricity statistics is a key indicator for the shadow economy estimation. We could reject to take into account the regions where electricity intensity is very deviates from the average value, i.e., extreme southern and northern regions. However, we fused such approach for the purpose of maximal possible coverage of our evaluation, and chose variable "Employment rate" as key indicator based on the literature review.

We use data from 79 regions, including Moscow and St. Petersburg, but excluding the Chechen Republic (for lack of data in the considered period). The period considered is from 2002 to 2013. Normalizing variable is employment rate. All variables are calculated as average growth rate of initial statistical data during the considered period. Estimation of our MIMIC model has been done by means of a special software application for the analysis of covariance structures, LISREL. The results of our MIMIC model estimations are presented in Table 28.2 and Fig. 28.1.

The estimated MIMIC coefficients allow us to determine only relatively estimated sizes of shadow economy, which describe the pattern of the shadow economy in a particular country over time. In order to calculate the size and trend of the shadow, we must convert the MIMIC index into 'real-world' figures measured as percentage of the official GRP. This final step requires an additional benchmarking or calibration procedure.

As a first step, the MIMIC model index of the shadow economies is calculated using the structural equation, i.e., by multiplying the coefficients of the significant causal variables with the respective time series. The structural equation is:

$$SHADOW = -0.621 * CHILDCARE + 0.087 * HOSPITAL$$
$$+ 0.144 * CRIMES - 0.071 * NAT\_INCR - 0.234 * LIFE\_EXP$$
$$- 0.093 * DEP\_TO\_I + 0.073 * CONS\_TO\_I - 0.122 * CARS$$

$$(28.1)$$

This index can be converted into absolute values of the shadow economies, which take up a base value in a particular base year. For example, we could use the

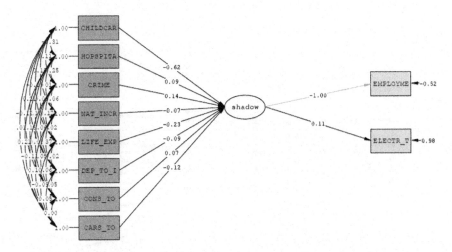

Fig. 28.1 Results of MIMIC model estimation

base value from Bilonizhko (2006), where estimates of the shadow economies in the years 2001–2003 are given.

Thus, the size of the shadow economy Shadow$_t$ value at time t is given as:

$$\text{Shadow}_t = \frac{\text{Shadow}_{\text{Index } t}}{\text{Shadow}_{\text{Index base}}} * \text{Shadow}_{\text{base}} \qquad (28.2)$$

where

Shadow$_{\text{index } t}$ denotes the value of the MIMIC index at t according to equation,
Shadow$_{\text{index base}}$ is the value of this index in the base year 2002, and
Shadow$_{\text{base}}$ is the exogenous estimate (base value) of the shadow economies in 2002.

Applying this benchmarking procedure, the final estimates of the shadow economies can be calculated for each region. Estimation of the model requires the normalization of the calculated index to an a priori value in order to convert the MIMIC index into "real-world" figures. In this research, calculated indices of shadow economy are not calibrated, as all potential calibration estimates have substantial variation across regions. Thus, none of the estimators can be considered as reliable.

28.4 Results

According to the average value of estimated index of shadow economy during the investigated period, the St. Petersburg has the lowest hidden economy, while Ingushetia has a higher rank; the other leaders are Tyva Republic, Republic of

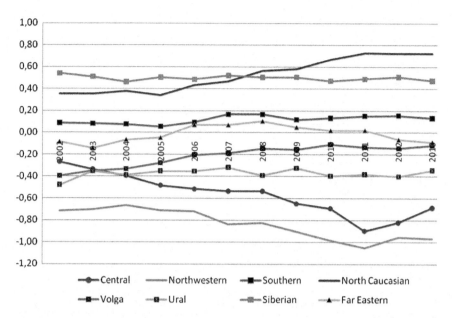

Fig. 28.2 The weighted average index of the shadow economy in Federal Districts of Russian Federation (weight—official GRP)

Dagestan, Altai Republic, and Republic of Buryatia; the lowest positions are occupied by Murmansk region, Kamchatka Krai, Magadan region, and Chukotka Krai. In whole, index of shadow economy varies from −1.736 to 2.047 at considered regions during investigated period. A summary of results is shown in Fig. 28.2.

28.5 Conclusion

The results support our hypothesis concerning the impact of shadow economy on quality of life.

Signs of coefficients in Eq. (28.1) indicate that the shadow economy is the larger,

- the less the coverage of children by preschool institutions,
- the more population per one hospital bed,
- the more number of registered crimes,
- the less rate of natural increase,
- the less life expectancy at birth,
- the less the ratio between bank deposits of individuals at credit institutions per capita and cash income per capita,

- the more the ratio between consumption expenditure per capita (per month, rubles) and cash income per capita,
- the less quantity of passenger cars (per 1000 inhabitants).

Thus, 7 out of 7 theoretically expected signs have been confirmed.

We believe that the proposed approach to evaluation of shadow economy at the regional level can be used to justify decisions on the allocation of funds from the federal budget in the form of transfers to regional budgets, which are aimed at improving the quality of life. Assessing the contribution of causal variables in the value of the shadow economy index indicates the key role of life quality variables in explaining the size of the shadow economy in Russia over considered period.

Acknowledgments This work was financially supported by the State Task № 26.1348.2014/K to fulfill research work as part of Project 1348 "Influence of shadow economy on the quality of life in Russia and Ukraine: a comparative analysis" (State registration number in FGASI CITaS: 114091140015).

References

Albu LL, Ghizdeanu I, Stanica CA (2008) Model to estimate spatial distribution of informal economy: theoretical and empirical investigation. 48th Congress of the European Regional Science Association, Liverpool, UK

Alderslade J, Talmadge J, Freeman Y (2006) Measuring the informal economy: one neighborhood at a time. A discussion paper prepared for the Brookings Institution Metropolitan Policy Program, Washington, DC, USA

Ardizzi G, Petraglia C, Piacenza M, Turati G (2011) Measuring the underground economy with the currency demand approach: a reinterpretation of the methodology, with an application to Italy. Department of Economics and Public Finance "G. Prato", Working paper series, no. 22

Bilonizhko O (2006) Measurement and determinants of the hidden economy in regions of Ukraine and Russia: MIMIC approach. EERC Master's thesis, NaUKMA, Ukraine

Braguinsky S, Mityakov S, Liscovich A (2014) Direct estimation of hidden earnings: evidence from Russian administrative data. J Law Econ 57(2):281–319

Buehn A (2012) The shadow economy in German regions: an empirical assessment. Ger Econ Rev 13(3):275–290

Chaudhuri K, Schneider F, Chattopadhyay S (2006) The size and development of the shadow economy: an empirical investigation from states of India. J Dev Econ 80(2):428–443

Dotti NF, van Heur B, Williams CC (2015) Mapping the shadow economy: spatial variations in the use of high denomination bank notes in Brussels. Eur Spat Res Policy 22(1):5–21

Fortin B, Lacroix G, Pinard D (2010) Evaluation of the underground economy in Quebec: a microeconomic approach. Int Econ J 24(4):463–479

Ghosh T, Sutton P, Powell R, Anderson S, Elvidge CD (2009) Estimation of Mexico's informal economy using DMSP nighttime lights data. Urban Remote Sensing Event, IEEE

Ghosh T, Powell R, Anderson S, Sutton PC, Elvidge CD (2010) Informal economy and remittance estimates of India using nighttime imagery. Int J Ecol Econ Stat 17(P10):16–50

González-Fernández M, González-Velasco C (2015) Analysis of the shadow economy in the Spanish regions. J Policy Model 37(6):1049–1064

Heath EB, Jones LR (2013) Using electricity demand to estimate state-level underground economic activity in the US. Int J Bus Soc Sci 4(8):272–280

Komarova T (2003) Hidden economy in Russian regions. MA thesis, New Economic School

Model of evaluation and prediction the shadow economy of Donetsk region. [Electronic source]. The National Academy of Sciences of Ukraine, Institute of Industrial Economics. URL: http:// iep.donetsk.ua/projects/shadow/shadow2.html. Accessed 26 Apr 2016

Mummert A, Schneider F (2001) The German shadow economy: parted in a united Germany? Discussion paper, Department of Economics, University of Linz, Austria

Putniņš TJ (2011) Size and determinants of shadow economies in the Baltic States. Baltic J Econ 2:5–25

Schneider F (2003) The size and development of the shadow economies and shadow economy labor force of 22 transition and 21 OECD countries: what do we really know? In: Belev B (ed) The informal economy in the EU accession countries: size, scope, trends and challenges to the process of EU enlargement. Center for the Study of Democracy, Sofia, pp 23–61

Social Compact. URL: http://socialcompact.org. Accessed 26 Apr 2016

Tafenau E, Herwartz H, Schneider F (2010) Regional estimates of the shadow economy in Europe. Int Econ J 24(4):629–636

Vorobyev P (2015) Estimating informal economy share in Russian regions. EERC working paper, no. E15/02

Wiseman T (2013) US shadow economies: a state-level study. Const Polit Econ 24(4):310–335

Chapter 29
Availability of Healthcare Services in Rural Areas: The Analysis of Spatial Differentiation

Paulina Ucieklak-Jeż, Agnieszka Bem and Rafał Siedlecki

Abstract The aim of this research is an analysis of the spatial differentiation in access to health benefits in rural areas in Poland and its consequences for the state of health of the population. We have tested three hypotheses: (H1) the accessibility to healthcare benefits in rural areas is regionally diversified; (H2) the availability of health services has not improved in the analysed period; (H3) the availability of healthcare services affects the population's state of health. Basing on Perkal's method, we have proved that access to health care is regionally diversified and this differentiation is stable in the period of analysis. We have also found weak relationship between the state of health of the population and the level of access to healthcare services. Regardless of the existing regional diversity, particular concern has arisen by the fact that most of the regions have not applied effective health policy, which would lead to the improvement in access to benefits for rural residents.

Keywords Rural areas · Access to health care · Geographical accessibility · Perkal's method

P. Ucieklak-Jeż (✉)
Faculty of Social Sciences, Jan Długosz University, Waszyngtona 4/8,
42-200 Częstochowa, Poland
e-mail: p.ucieklak@o2.pl

A. Bem · R. Siedlecki
Faculty of Management, Informatics and Finance, Wrocław University
of Economics, Komandorska 118/120, 53-345 Wrocław, Poland
e-mail: bemagnieszka@gmail.com

R. Siedlecki
e-mail: rafal.siedlecki@ue.wroc.pl

© Springer International Publishing AG 2017
D. Procházka (ed.), *New Trends in Finance and Accounting*,
Springer Proceedings in Business and Economics,
DOI 10.1007/978-3-319-49559-0_29

29.1 Introduction

A process of "health production" describes relationships between the combination of non-medical and medical inputs and obtained results, which could be measured both as a quantity of the provided services and using healthcare state's indicators. This process is strongly affected by healthcare system's construction and the volume of resources involved, as well as social, economic and physical conditions (Or 2000; Łyszczarz-Wyszkowska 2010). The healthcare system should ensure good and equal access to healthcare services of accepted quality, which is accompanied by the desire to build an efficient, comprehensive, cost-effective and fair institutional system (White 2000; Williams and Torrens 1988; Ucieklak-Jeż and Bem 2014a, b).

A fair healthcare system should provide equal access to healthcare services, regardless of a place of residence—in both urban and rural areas. It is important, because WHO studies indicate existence of a number of differences between urban and rural areas, which stimulate important differences in access to health care, which include: lack of skilled health professionals, distance from major hospitals, access to specialised health services, access to prevention and health promotion, presence of pharmacies and essential drugs, financial barriers in access to benefits— related to lower income and additional costs (like costs of transport), effectiveness of the emergency system and quality of infrastructure and equipment in the health units (WHO 2010). Others risk factors related to poorer access to health care are numerous and confirmed by several studies (Casey et al. 2000; Bennett et al. 2012). The villagers are less likely to benefit from regular visits to the doctor (Arcury et al. 2005), including prevention services (Valet et al. 2009). Residents of rural areas have, usually, weaker access to emergency services (Watts et al. 1999; Fan et al. 2011), which are generally located in urban areas. It is also important that inhabitants of rural areas are also exposed to specific risks related to the agricultural production processes, including exposure to pathogens of animal origin, chemical substances used in plant protection, less efficient waste management system and environmental monitoring (WHO 2010).

A factor that has a significant impact on access to benefits is the population's mobility, especially in the case of people under 18 years of age and the elderly, who have a significantly reduced mobility (Field 2000; Jarczewska and Jarczewski 2015; Fan et al. 2011; Arcury et al. 2005). Lack of mobility is important in view of the generally weaker or dispersed medical infrastructure (Casey et al. 2000; Valet et al. 2009; Arcury et al. 2005; Bennett et al. 2012), in relation to a poorer road network, or lack of public transport (Berkowska et al. 2010; Goins et al. 2005; Arcury et al. 2005). Financial constraints constitute additional barriers (Goins et al. 2005; Rosenthal and Fox 2000; Szczygiel et al. 2015; Ciura 2010; Gavurova and Soltes 2016; Bartak and Gavurova 2015). These factors (longer distance to healthcare providers, lack or poor public transport, lower socioeconomic status) constitute usually a profile of rural areas.

What is important is that accessibility can be analysed in many ways or dimensions—as the identification of healthcare needs or as the delivery of health-care benefits (Wilson and Rosenberg 2004; Harding 1999). Research on spatial accessibility employs a wide variety of methods—from population-to-provider ratios to gravity-type metrics (Fransen et al. 2015; Guagliardo 2004; McGrail and Humphreys 2009). Studies based on population-to-provider ratio are relatively common, due to good access to the data—analysed ratios can cover a quantity of providers or medical professionals per capita (Rosenthal et al. 2005), as well as a quantity of the services provided to the population.

The study on inequalities in health in Poland has been carried out for many years; however, they are characterised by a large dispersion (Sowa 2010). Previous studies carried out in the year 2000 or earlier (1994 and 1996) showed that only 14.7% of the villages in the year 2000 have a health centre and only 5.3% a pharmacy. Nearly half of the villages had a health centre further than 5 km away. The percentage of villages having a health centre decreased by approximately 10% —it was the result of a concentration process taking place in medical industry, which undoubtedly worsened spatial availability in rural areas (Sikorska 2001; Wrzochalska 2005).

Regardless of the health policy, rural–urban healthcare disparities are still visible. In terms of the health infrastructure, and hence the possibility of the provision of health services, a village still gives way to the city (Krawczyk-Soltys 2014; Ruszkowska 2011). Rural areas, however, do not form a homogeneous set. There are some characterised by a considerable diversity, on the basis of the fulfilled functions. Diversification of rural areas has its consequences in varying levels of accessibility of healthcare services. Different access to benefits in rural areas situated in different regions can result from many causes, including the level of socio-economic development or the policy implemented by local authorities. In Poland, local authorities, at the level of regions (NUTS 2) and counties (NUTS 3), are responsible for ensuring equal access to ambulatory and stationary health care (Bem 2013).

The aim of this research is the analysis of the spatial differentiation in access to health benefits in rural areas of Poland and its consequences for the population's state of health. Methodology, employed in this study, allows also to identify the regions, which provide good or even very good access to healthcare services for rural area residents and regions, which are characterised by poor or very poor access.

We have formulated the following research hypotheses:

H1: the accessibility to healthcare benefits in rural areas is regionally diversified;

H2: the availability of health services has not improved in the analysed period;

H3: the availability of healthcare services affects the state of health of the population.

The H1 hypothesis assumes that rural areas in Poland offer different levels of access to healthcare services, as a consequence of flawed mechanism of allocation of resources, resulting in lower volume of services available for rural residents. The

H2 hypothesis is an amplification of H1 hypothesis—we have formulated an assumption that those differences are rooted, which also means that in the analysed period no corrective action has been taken. In the construction of the H3 hypothesis, we have presumed that there is a statistically significant relationship between the availability of healthcare services in the voivodeships and the state of health of the populations measured by LE (life expectancy).

The data were analysed at the level of regions, corresponding to the NUTS2 level. In the case of Poland, it means an analysis at the level of 16 regions (voivodeships). We have adopted the definition of rural areas based on territorial division, accepted by the Central Statistical Office in Poland (Wilkin 2007).

The data were obtained from the Central Statistical Office and the Centre for Healthcare Information Systems (public institution which collects public data concerning health care in Poland) and covered the years 2005–2013.

29.2   Data and Methods

The aim of the research is the analysis of regional differentiation of the availability of healthcare services in rural areas. We have decided to employ Perkal's indicator, which is a synthetic measure of regional development. The construction of a synthetic indicator, which is the sum of standardised indicators, consists of several stages: [1] selection of variables, [2] standardization, [3] conversion of de-stimulants into stimulants and [4] constructing a synthetic indicator.

Variables used in this study have different weights and denominations, so they must be standardised, which leads to elimination of units of measurement and adjustment of the values of the variables, in accordance with the model (Malkowski 2007):

$$z_{ik} = \frac{x_{ik} - \bar{x}}{S_k} \tag{29.1}$$

where $\bar{x}$ denotes the k-variable and S_k denotes the standard deviation of the k-variable given by the formula:

$$S_k = \sqrt{\frac{\sum (x_{ik} - \bar{x_k})^2}{n}} \tag{29.2}$$

whereas the following formula is used for de-stimulants:

$$z_{ik} = \frac{\bar{x} - x_{ik}}{S_k} \tag{29.3}$$

Basing on previous research, we have pointed out several indicators characterising access to healthcare services (Bem and Ucieklak-Jeż 2015; Ucieklak-Jeż and

Table 29.1 Selected healthcare resources' indicators

Variable	Definition
X_1	The number of healthcare facilities in rural areas per 10,000 inhabitants by regions
X_2	The number of medical practices in rural areas per 10,000 inhabitants by regions
X_3	The number of pharmacies per 1000 inhabitants by regions
X_4	The number of pharmacy's points per 1000 inhabitants by regions
X_5	The number of medical consultations per capita

Source Own study

Bem, 2015; Bem et al. 2013, 2014, 2015; Ucieklak-Jeż et al. 2015). Initially, we have analysed 25 variables, which generally reflect provider-to-population approach, accompanied by several indicators of healthcare services' utilisation. Based on the discrimination analyses, we have selected five variables, character-ising healthcare resources and services, important from the point of view of the rural population of the elderly. Data have been transformed into relative value in relation to the number of inhabitants in the administrative village (Table 29.1). The observation matrix has been created by describing each of the voivodeships with five selected indicators.

On the basis of the value of the selected indicators, the synthetic Perkal's indicator for the accessibility to health services in rural areas has been calculated. We have also specified five classes of availability (Table 29.2).

The state of health of the population has been measured by LE (life expectancy) indicator, respectively, for male and female population at the age of 60, due to the fact that the state of health of the people at this age is, to a larger extent, dependent on access to health services.

Then, for the statistical population, characterised by Perkal's indicators and LE for men and women of the age of 60, the strength and direction of relationship have been estimated, using Pearson's correlation coefficient, according to the following formula:

$$r_{xy} = \frac{\frac{1}{n} \cdot \sum_{i=1}^{n} (x_i - \bar{x}) \cdot (y_i - \bar{y})}{s_x \cdot s_y} \tag{29.4}$$

Table 29.2 Classes of availability

Class	Definition
A	The highest access to healthcare services: $z_{ik} > \bar{x} + s$
B	Larger-than-average access to healthcare services: $\bar{x} < z_{ik} < \bar{x} + s$
C	Average access to healthcare services: $\bar{x} = z_{ik}$
D	Low access to healthcare services: $\bar{x} - s < z_{ik} < \bar{x}$
E	The lowest access to healthcare services: $z_{ik} < \bar{x} + s$

Source Own study based on Małkowski (2007)

29.3   Results and Discussion

In order to verify the H1 hypothesis, we have estimated Perkal's indicators for Polish regions, and a class of availability of healthcare services, according to interpretation presented in Table 29.2.

We can observe a significant differentiation in the level of access to healthcare services in rural areas—only three regions (Małopolskie, Śląskie and Podkarpackie) are characterised by very good access and three regions by very low access (Zachodniopomorskie, Warmińsko-Mazurskie and Pomorskie). Four regions offer larger-than-average access to healthcare services (Podlaskie, Opolskie, Lubelskie and Lubuskie), while six regions (Wielkopolskie, Świętokrzyskie, Mazowieckie, Łódzkie, Kujawsko-Pomorskie and Dolnośląskie) low access to healthcare services (Table 29.3). *Generally, we can conclude that in seven regions the rural population has good or very good access to healthcare system, while in nine regions this access is, to a greater or lesser extent, limited. These findings have entitled us to adopt the H1 hypothesis.*

Our study has confirmed the existence of interregional differences in access to health care. In the construction of the H2 hypothesis, we have assumed that those

Table 29.3 Indicators and classes of availability of health care in rural areas of Poland, in 2013, by regions

Voivodeships	Standardised values				Z_{2005}	Class
	Z_{2013X1}	Z_{2013X2}	Z_{2013X3}	Z_{2013X4}		
Dolnośląskie	−0.33	−0.51	−0.42	−0.11	−1.36	D
Kujawsko-Pomorskie	−0.72	−0.30	−0.35	0.50	−0.88	D
Lubelskie	−0.16	1.69	2.08	−1.91	1.69	B
Lubuskie	−0.23	0.52	−1.71	1.57	0.16	B
Łódzkie	−0.01	−1.18	0.73	0.05	−0.41	D
Małopolskie	3.44	−1.52	0.80	−0.30	2.41	A
Mazowieckie	−0.29	−0.79	0.26	−0.29	−1.11	D
Opolskie	−0.14	1.27	−0.23	0.48	1.38	B
Podkarpackie	0.38	1.78	−0.01	0.47	2.63	A
Podlaskie	0.22	0.11	−1.08	2.06	1.31	B
Pomorskie	−0.64	−0.66	0.40	−1.48	−2.38	E
Śląskie	1.02	0.54	1.46	1.06	4.08	A
Świętokrzyskie	−0.37	−0.47	0.32	−0.12	−0.65	D
Warmińsko-Mazurskie	−0.59	0.03	−1.26	−0.47	−2.29	E
Wielkopolskie	−0.85	0.82	0.39	−0.60	−0.24	D
Zachodniopomorskie	−0.74	−1.33	−1.38	−0.90	−4.34	E

Interpretation: A—WP > 2.09; B—WP ϵ (0.0; 2.09]; C—WP ϵ [0.00]; D—WP ϵ (−2.09; 0.0); E—WP $\leq$ −2.09

Source Own study

differences are of stable character. We have investigated whether classes of availability changed in the analysed period of time—from 2005 to 2013.

We found that the class of availability did not change in seven regions, regardless of the starting point (A, B, D, E)—that pertain also to the regions characterised (in 2005) by low or very low availability (Dolnośląskie, Mazowieckie, Warmińsko-Mazurskie, Zachodniopomorskie). We can also observe that access to health care actually worsened in six regions—especially in the case of Łódzkie voivodeship, which went down from the class A to class D. Only three regions improved their access to health care for rural residents—Lubuskie, Małopolskie and Wielkopolskie (Table 29.4).

Basing on the analysis presented above, we can adopt the H2 hypothesis. We can conclude that during the 8-year period, the availability to healthcare services in rural areas generally did not improve.

In order to prove the H3 hypothesis, we have analysed the relationships between access to healthcare services and the population's state of health. We have calculated the Pearson correlation coefficient between values of Perkal's synthetic indicator of healthcare availability (in the years 2005, 2010, 2012 and 2013) and expected life expectancy for women and men at the age of 60 (in the year 2013).

We have observed that there is a weak positive relationship between LE for women and men at the age of 60, in the year 2013, and the level of access to health

Table 29.4 Indicators and classes of availability of health care in rural areas of Poland, in 2005, by regions

Voivodeships	Standardised values				Z_{2005}	Class
	Z_{2005X1}	Z_{2005X2}	Z_{2005X3}	Z_{2005X4}		
Dolnośląskie	−0.02	−0.46	−0.30	−0.51	−1.28	D
Kujawsko-Pomorskie	0.35	−1.28	−0.23	1.19	0.02	B
Lubelskie	0.81	0.67	2.34	−0.97	2.86	A
Lubuskie	−0.91	−0.66	−1.63	1.62	−1.58	D
Łódzkie	1.20	−0.35	1.32	0.56	2.73	A
Małopolskie	0.76	−0.65	0.49	−0.40	0.20	B
Mazowieckie	0.10	−1.50	−0.08	−0.62	−2.10	D
Opolskie	0.07	2.19	−0.21	−0.44	1.62	B
Podkarpackie	0.85	−0.37	0.23	0.80	1.51	B
Podlaskie	−0.36	1.21	−0.75	2.01	2.11	B
Pomorskie	−0.67	1.09	0.47	−1.92	−1.03	D
Śląskie	1.30	1.01	1.19	0.36	3.85	A
Świętokrzyskie	1.29	−0.93	−0.01	0.19	0.54	B
Warmińsko-Mazurskie	−1.34	−0.16	−1.33	−0.58	−3.41	E
Wielkopolskie	−1.78	−0.60	−0.24	−0.68	−3.30	E
Zachodniopomorskie	−1.66	0.79	−1.27	−0.62	−2.77	E

Interpretation: A—$W_P > 2.24$; B—$W_P \in (0.0; 2.24]$; C—$W_P \in [0.00]$; D—$W_P \in (−2.24; 0.0)$; E—$W_P \leq −2.24$

Source Own study

Table 29.5 Correlation matrix

	Z_{2005}	Z_{2010}	Z_{2012}	Z_{2013}	LE_{f60}	LE_{m60}
Z_{2005}	1	0.68	0.72	0.7	0.08	0.15
Z_{2010}	0.68	1	0.73	0.7	0.05	0.11
Z_{2012}	0.72	0.73	1	0.94	**0.36**	**0.27**
Z_{2013}	0.7	0.7	0.94	1	**0.34**	**0.22**
LE_{k60}	0.08	0.05	0.36	0.34	1	0.73
LE_{m60}	0.15	0.11	0.27	0.22	0.73	1

Source Own study

care in the years 2012 and 2013. This relationship is slightly stronger for women than for men. This difference might be rooted in the fact that women in rural areas, although, on average, they live longer, are more heavily burdened by disability (Bem and Ucieklak-Jeż 2014). We can also observe some time-lag in the analysed relationship—the correlation coefficient is higher for the year 2012 than for 2013 (Table 29.5).

Although the strength of the analysed relationship is weak, it has entitled us to, at least partial, adoption of the H3 hypothesis.

29.4   Conclusions

Equal access to health benefits is one of the objectives of the healthcare system. This means that the allocation mechanisms should promote equal access by increasing the allocation of financial and non-financial resources in regions, where health needs are greater—due to the socio-economic situation or demographic structure.

Many studies confirmed the differences in access to health care between rural and urban areas. Our research has confirmed that access to health care in rural areas is also highly diversified—in Poland there are areas, where availability of benefits is poor and regions, which offer better access to health services. Among regions with poor access, there are both regions considered as more economically developed and those that are considered to be poorer. The same applies to the regions which ensure a very good access to benefits. Regardless of the existing regional diversity, particular concern has arisen by the fact that most of the regions have not applied effective health policy, which would lead to the improvement in access to benefits for rural residents.

Our study has certain weaknesses and limitations. First of all, you should take into account that health depends on many other factors, not just potential access to health. Future research should take into account several improvements, for example a larger number of variables characterising revealed, not only potential access to benefits or health status's assessment based on the other indicators, including morbidity. The other direction is to incorporate into the analysis of variables characterising the socio-economic and demographic situation in the regions.

References

Arcury TA, Gesler WM, Preisser JS, Sherman J, Spencer J, Perin J (2005) The effects of geography and spatial behaviour on health care utilization among the residents of a rural region. Health Serv Res 40(1):135–155

Bartak M, Gavurova B (2015) Economics and social aspects of long-term care in the context of the Czech Republic and the Slovak Republic EU membership. In: Proceedings of 12th international scientific conference: Economic policy in the European Union member countries, p 35–44

Bem A (2013) Public financing of health care services. E-Finanse 2:1–23

Bem A, Ucieklak-Jeż P (2014) Health status of the rural population in Poland. Manage Theor Stud Rural Bus Infrastruct Dev 36(2):235–243

Bem A, Ucieklak-Jeż P (2015) Nierówności w zdrowiu na terenach wiejskich. In: Andrzejak R (ed) Zdrowie dla regionu. Wydawnictwo Uczelniane Państwowej Wyższej Szkoły Zawodowej im. Angelusa Silesiusa, Wałbrzych, p 59–66

Bem A, Ucieklak-Jeż P, Prędkiewicz P (2013) Effects of inequalities in access to health services in rural areas in Poland. Manage Theor Stud Rural Bus Infrastruct Dev 35(4):491–497

Bem A, Prędkiewicz K, Prędkiewicz P, Ucieklak-Jeż P (2014) Health System's Financing Inequalities in Selected European Countries. Eur Financ Syst 34–40

Bem A, Prędkiewicz P, Ucieklak-Jeż P (2015) Effectiveness of allocation of health system non-financial resources. In: Brătianu C, Zbuchea A, Pînzaru F, Vătămănescu EM, Leon RD (eds) Strategica. Local versus global. Faculty of Management, Bucharest, pp 647–656

Bennett KJ, Probst JC, Vyavaharkar M, Glover SH (2012) Lower rehospitalization rates among rural medicare beneficiaries with diabetes. J Rural Health 3:227–234

Berkowska E, Rasz H, Stankiewicz D (2010) Infrastruktura techniczna wsi. In: Kłos C, Stankiewicz D (eds) Rozwój obszarów wiejskich w Polsce. Studia BAS 24(4):184–224

Casey MM, Thiede Call K, Klingner JM (2010) Are rural residents less likely to obtain recommended preventive healthcare services? Am J Prev Med 3:182–188

Ciura G (2010) Warunki życia ludności wiejskiej. In: Kłos C, Stankiewicz D (eds) Rozwój obszarów wiejskich w Polsce. Studia BAS 24(4):165–186

Fan L, Shah M, Veazie PF (2011) Factors associated with emergency department use among the rural elderly. J Rural Health 27:39–49

Field K (2000) Measuring the need for primary health care: an index of relative disadvantage. App Geogr 4:305–332

Fransen K, Netens T, De Maeyer P, Deruyter G (2015) A commuter-based two-step floating catchment area method fo measuring spatial accesibility of daycare centers. Health & Place (32):65–73

Gavurova B, Soltes M (2016) System of day surgery in Slovakia: analysis of pediatric day surgery discrepancies in the regions and their importance in strategy of its development. E & M Ekonomie Manage 19(1):74–92

Goins RT, Williams KA, Carter MW, Spencer M, Solovieva T (2005) Perceived barriers to health care access among rural older adults: a qualitative study. J Rural Health 3:206–213

Guagliardo MF (2004) Spatial accessibility of primary care: concepts, methods and challenges. Int J Health Geogr 3(3). http://doi.org/10.1186/1476-072X-3-3

Harding O (1999) What is access? What are 'whole systems'? Br Med J 319

Jarczewska D, Jarczewski W (2015) Dostępność geograficzna ośrodków podstawowej opieki zdrowotnej w Krakowskim Obszarze Metropolitalnym. Problemy Rozwoju Miast 1:7–13

Krawczyk-Soltys A (2014) Dostępność do ambulatoryjnej opieki zdrowotnej na wsi w Polsce. Ujęcie przestrzenno-czasowe. J Agribusiness Rural Dev 2:79–86

Łyszczarz B, Wyszkowska Z (2010) Socjoekonomiczne determinanty stanu zdrowia - perspektywa regionalna. Nierówności Społeczne a Wzrost Gospodarczy 16:303–313

Malkowski A (2007) Wielowymiarowa analiza przestrzennego zróżnicowania rozwoju społeczno-gospodarczego województw w latach 1999–2004

McGrail MR, Humphreys JS (2009) The index of rural access: an innovative integrated approach for measuring primary care access. BMC Health Serv Res 9(1):1

Or Z (2000) Determinants of health outcomes in industrialised countries: a pooled, cross-country, time-series analysis. OECD Econ Stud 30:55

Rosenthal M, Zaslavski A, Newhouse J (2005) The geographic distribution of physicians revisited. Health Serv Res (40):1931–1952

Rosenthal TC, Fox C (2000) Access to health care for the rural elderly. JAMA 16:2034–2036

Ruszkowska J (2011) Likwidowanie nierówności społecznych nowym priorytetem dla europejskiej i światowej promocji zdrowia. Polityka Społeczna 38(10(451)):8–11

Sikorska A (ed) (2001) Przemiany strukturalne we wsiach objętych badaniem IERiGŻ w latach 1996–2000. Warszawa

Sowa A (2010) O nierównościach w korzystaniu z usług ochrony zdrowia ze względu na wykształcenie. Polityka Społeczna 9:33–36

Szczygieł N, Rutkowska-Podolska M, Michalski G (2015) Information and communication technologies in healthcare: still innovation or reality? innovative and entrepreneurial value—creating approach in healthcare management. In: Nijkamp WP, Kourtit K, Buček M, Hudec O (eds) 5th Central European conference in regional science conference proceedings, Technical University of Košice, pp 1020–1029

Ucieklak-Jeż P, Bem A (2014a) System ochrony zdrowia – finansowanie, efektywność, restrukturyzacja. Wydawnictwo im. Stanisława Podobińskiego Akademii im. Jana Długosza w Częstochowie

Ucieklak-Jeż P, Bem A (2014b) Opieka zdrowotna – wybrane zagadnienia. Wydawnictwo im. Stanisława Podobińskiego Akademii im. Jana Długosza w Częstochowie

Ucieklak-Jeż P, Bem A (2015) Wpływ niefinansowych zasobów systemu ochrony zdrowia na stan zdrowia kobiet i mężczyzn w Polsce. In: Ucieklak-Jeż P (ed) Prace naukowe Akademii im. Jana Długosza w Częstochowie. Pragmata tes Oikonomias, Wydawnictwo im. Stanisława Podobińskiego Akademii im. Jana Długosza w Częstochowie, Częstochowa (9):8–20

Ucieklak-Jeż P, Bem A, Prędkiewicz P (2015) Relationships between health care services and health system, outcomes—empirical study on health system efficiency. In: Kajurová V, Krajíček J (eds) European financial systems 2015. Proceedings of the 12th international scientific conference, Masaryk University, Brno, p 633–640

Valet RS, Perry TT, Hartert TV (2009) Rural health disparities in asthma care and outcomes. Am Acad Allergy Asthma Immunol 6:1220–1225

Watts PR, Dinger MK, Baldwin KA, Sisk RJ, Brockschmidt BA, McCubbin JE (1999) Accessibility and perceived value of health services in five western Illinois rural communities. J Community Health 2:147–157

White D (2000) Consumer and community participation: a reassessment of process, impact, and value. In: Albrecht G, Fitzpatrick R, Scrimshaw S (eds) Handbook of social studies in health and medicine, Sage Publication, London, Thousand Oaks, New Delhi, p 465–480

Wiliams S, Torrens P (1988) Introduction to health services. Delmar Publishers Inc, New York

Wilkin J (2007) Obszary wiejskie w warunkach dynamizacji zmian strukturalnych. Ekspertyzy do strategii Rozwoju Społeczno-Gospodarczego Polski Wschodniej do roku 2020, vol 1

Wilson K, Rosenberg MW (2004) Accessibility and the Canadian health care system: squaring perceptions and realities. Health Policy 67:137–148

World Health Organization (2010) The world health report: health system financing. World Health Organization, Geneva, p 4

Wrzochalska A (2005) Wybrane cechy społeczno-ekonomiczne ludności wiejskiej a rozwój wsi i rolnictwa. Warszawa: Instytut Ekonomiki Rolnictwa i Gospodarki Żywnościowej - Państwowy Instytut Badawczy

Chapter 30
Spatial Analysis of Turkish Voter Behaviours: Does Regional Distribution of Public Expenditures Affect Voting Rate?

Guner Tuncer and Ersin Nail Sagdic

Abstract The aim of this study is to determine what kind of a spatial distribution and disparity is seen in 7 June and 1 November 2015 elections and to drop hints for the ruling and opposition parties by associating these determinations with public expenditures. The spatial distribution and disparities of the elections in terms of the relevant parties were determined with Exploratory Spatial Data Analysis (ESDA). Besides, as the political choices are important economic indicators and important reflections in the economic field, the regional distribution of the public expenditures and the vote rates of the ruling and opposition parties were compared in terms of spatial distribution in this study. As a result of this study, some important signs showed that the public expenditures were used to manipulate the voter preferences in Turkey.

Keywords Voter behaviors · Spatial analysis · Public expenditures · ESDA

30.1 Introduction

The actualization of extensive liberalization practices in economic field and the social and political reforms began in 1980s in Turkey. Twenty governments have come into power in the process beginning from 1983 to our day. Among these governments, only two parties which are the Motherland Party and Justice and Development Party (AKP) managed to get enough seats to form a single party government. Since coming into power in 2002, the AKP has remained the largest single party in power in the multi-party political history of Turkey. When post-2002 is evaluated, voter profile and the regional distribution of the votes of AKP are quite

G. Tuncer (✉) · E.N. Sagdic
Department of Public Finance, Dumlupınar University, Kutahya, Turkey
e-mail: guner.tuncer@dpu.edu.tr

E.N. Sagdic
e-mail: ersinnailsagdic@dpu.edu.tr

© Springer International Publishing AG 2017
D. Procházka (ed.), *New Trends in Finance and Accounting*,
Springer Proceedings in Business and Economics,
DOI 10.1007/978-3-319-49559-0_30

remarkable compared to other parties. AKP, as a center party, has a quite high-class interaction with its median voter. The main reason of this interaction is the way AKP effectively uses economic and social tools on the median voters.

Turkey has undergone an important general election on 7 June 2015. In this election, the ruling party in Turkey for 13 years, AKP was unable to reach 276 seats required to form a majority in Parliament. When the efforts to form a government within the constitutional process proved to be unsuccessful, the President used his constitutional right and decided to go to an early election. The early election was carried out on 1 November 2015. Although it was only 5 months later, a very different election result was reached compared to 7 June elections. AKP, which lost the majority on 7 June, managed to get 317 seats and to form a government in 1 November elections.

Although it was only nearly 5 months between the two elections, it is also possible that spatial disparities were also effective in the different election results. The aim of this research is to determine what kind of a spatial distribution and disparity is seen in 7 June and 1 November elections and to drop hints for the ruling and opposition parties by associating these determinations with public expenditures. Based on this, the spatial distribution and disparities of the parties in the last two elections were determined with Exploratory Spatial Data Analysis (ESDA) which has an importance place in spatial analysis. Many economic, social and political policies are behind the obtained spatial distribution and spatial disparities. In this study, the public expenditure variable was chosen as it was an important economic indicator reflecting the political choices in the economic field. From this point of view, some hints were developed out of spatial distribution through disparities and similarities of the ruling and main opposition parties. Distribution maps and ESDA analysis were made with GeoDa software. We review some of the key studies in the literature. O'Loughlin (2002) uses ESDA for Protestant Support for the Nazi Party period of Weimar Germany. He finds that the Weimar German electoral map does not show much evidence of a nationalized electorate, but is better characterized as a mosaic of support for milieu parties, mixed across class and other social lines, and defined by a strong attachment to local traditions, beliefs, and practices. Broner and Delicado (2006) work The Exploratory Analysis technique to the results of the 2004 General Elections in the city of Barcelona at level of Small Research Zones. Tomaselli and D'Agata (2010) analyze the role of spatial contiguity. They measure spatial autocorrelation and estimate autoregressive spatial models in order to explain the pattern of relationship among territorial units and they investigate the electoral performance of Lega Party, comparing two northern Italian regions Lombardia and Veneto.

The studies specific to Turkey are as below. Carkoglu (2000) focuses on the geographical distribution of electoral support across Turkish provinces in the April 1999 elections. He analyses provincial election returns divided into seven clusters. He finds that party system characteristics as well as socioeconomic development levels exhibit striking disparities across clusters and the least developed eastern and southeastern provinces, where Kurdish separatist activities have been most effective, show a high degree of fractionalization and sizeable electoral volatility.

Additionally, Central Anatolian provinces that once heavily voted for Islamists shifted toward the ultra-nationalists. The fact that all provinces other than the most developed western group predominantly support either anti-systemic or ultra-nationalist parties is posited as the central puzzle of Turkish electoral politics.

Carkoglu (2002) reviews the main characteristics of the Turkish party system, presents a historical evaluation of the context of the most recent November 2002 elections and analyses in depth the nature of the patterns that emerge from the provincial election returns. The account underlines the challenges awaiting the newly elected Justice and Development Party on the domestic social and economic fronts as well as potentially dangerous events in foreign relations with the EU and the Cyprus and the Iraqi conflicts.

West (2005) examines the overlapping cultural and economic constitution of Turkey provinces for 1999 and 2002 national parliamentary elections with the techniques of electoral geography. He finds that religion, ethnicity, regional economic prosperity, and previous state association are four major divisions shaping the electoral geography.

Carkoglu (2009) researches a descriptive geographic account of the March 2009 local elections in Turkey. Cluster analysis is employed to investigate the results and changing voting patterns compared with the 2004 local government elections. According to the author, Justice and Development Party has stalled but remains the dominant party in the system. He finds that the electoral map indicates three main regions: the coastal western and most developed provinces where the opposition is strong, the east and south-eastern provinces with rising Kurdish ethnic electoral support, and the more conservative provinces in between where the governing Justice and Development Party remains dominant with the Nationalist Action Party (MHP) trailing behind. He implies economic developments and the potential reshaping of ethnic Kurdish support will shape the next general election outcome.

Luca and Pose (2015) research geographical allocation of public investment across the 81 provinces of Turkey between 2005 and 2012. They find that although the Turkish government has indeed channeled public expenditures to reward its core constituencies, socioeconomic factors remained the most relevant predictors of investment. Moreover, in contrast to official regional development policy principles, authors uncover the concentration of public investment in areas with comparatively higher levels of development. Authors interpret this as the state bureaucracy's intentional strategy of focusing on efficiency by concentrating resources on the better off among the most in need.

30.2   Data and Methodology

According to Waldo Tobler (1979), the basic law of geography is as follows; everything is related to everything else, but near things are more related than distant things. Therefore, similar values belonging to a variable usually appear in close locations, and this causes spatial clustering. For instance, the crime rates in cities surrounding a city with a high crime rate may be high or, the income levels in cities surrounding a city with a low income level may be low (Anselin 1992).

Spatial dependence or autocorrelation is defined as overlapping value similarities with regional similarities (Anselin 1988, 1999). Therefore positive spatial auto-correlation is formed when a random variable's high or low values are in a tendency of clustering in space. Negative spatial autocorrelation, on the other hand, is formed when geographical regions are in tendency of being (turnover) surrounded by neighbors with many unlike values. Another spatial effect is spatial heterogeneity. Spatial heterogeneity means economic variables are not stable along the space and polarization or stratification models can be related under the form of spatial patterns: the situation in which a cluster of poor regions contradicts a cluster of rich regions (Ertur and Koch 2006).

Spatial interactions among regions can be analyzed using ESDA method. ESDA is a method used for explaining and visualizing spatial distributions, defining atypical locations or spatial contradictions, discover spatial partnership, clustering or models of the active points, and reveal spatial patterns or other forms of spatial heterogeneity (Anselin 1988, 1999; Dall'erba 2005; Ertur and Koch 2006). ESDA present the opportunity of comparing inter-regional disparities (Celebioglu and Dalll'erba 2010).

30.2.1 Spatial Analysis

According to Waldo Tobler (1979), the basic law of geography is as follows; everything is related to everything else, but near things are more related than distant things. Therefore, similar values belonging to a variable usually appear in close locations, and this causes spatial clustering. For instance, the crime rates in cities surrounding a city with a high crime rate may be high or, the income levels in cities surrounding a city with a low income level may be low (Anselin 1992).

Spatial dependence or autocorrelation is defined as overlapping value similarities with regional similarities (Anselin 1988, 1999). Therefore positive spatial auto-correlation is formed when a random variable's high or low values are in a tendency of clustering in space. Negative spatial autocorrelation, on the other hand, is formed when geographical regions are in tendency of being (turnover) surrounded by neighbors with many unlike values. Another spatial effect is spatial heterogeneity. Spatial heterogeneity means economic variables are not stable along the space and polarization or stratification models can be related under the form of spatial patterns: the situation in which a cluster of poor regions contradicts a cluster of rich regions (Ertur and Koch 2006).

Spatial interactions among regions can be analyzed using ESDA method. ESDA is a method used for explaining and visualizing spatial distributions, defining atypical locations or spatial contradictions, discover spatial partnership, clustering or models of the active points, and reveal spatial patterns or other forms of spatial heterogeneity (Anselin 1988, 1999; Dall'erba 2005; Ertur and Koch 2006). ESDA present the opportunity of comparing inter-regional disparities (Celebioglu and Dalll'erba 2010).

30.2.2 Spatial Weight Matrix

The spatial weight matrix is a tool that is necessary for determining the effect of the neighborhood relation on the spatial data set. In general spatial statistics literature neighbors are studied in binary terms (0-non-neighbour, 1-neighbour). In this study one basic method was used to account for neighborhood relations, namely proximity (border sharing). Proximity based weight matrix was constructed on rook and queen neighborhood definition. If the regions share a border that has no corners, they are rook neighbors. The queen neighborhood determines neighboring units as those that have any point in common, including both common boundaries and common corners (Anselin 2005). Since Turkey's general structure of province borders form from queen neighborhood, in this study queen weight matrices were built as per these concepts.

30.2.3 Moran's I for Global Spatial Autocorrelation

The correlation of a variable with itself in the given space expresses spatial autocorrelation. This value might be positive (high values are in correlation with high neighborhood values or low values are in correlation with low neighborhood values) or negative (the existence of spatial outliers for high-low or low-high values). It must be considered that the positive spatial autocorrelation might be related to a low negative value (e.g. -0.01) as the average of finite samplings does not centralize over 1 (one). The spatial autocorrelation analysis includes the tests and visualizations of both global (testing for clustering) and local (testing for sets) Moran's I statistics (Anselin et al. 2006). Global spatial autocorrelation is a measure of total clustering and it is measured using Moran's I. It expresses the size of total clustering in a given data set. It is assessed by means of a test of a null hypothesis of random location. The rejection of this null hypothesis which is represented in a scatter map or box diagram suggests a spatial structure or spatial order that facilitates our understanding of the data distribution. It measures the degree of linear association, for each and every variable, between the value it gets at a given location and the average of spatially weighed neighborhood value and it is shown as follows (Anselin 1995; Anselin et al. 2007):

$$I_t = \frac{\sum_{i=1}^{n} \sum_{j=1}^{n} \overset{*}{w}_{ij}(k) x_{it} x_{jt}}{\sum_{i=1}^{n} \sum_{j=1}^{n} x_{it} x_{jt}} \tag{30.1}$$

In this equation w_{ij}^* represents the level of relationship between the spatial variables i and j (standardized series) and x_{ij} stand for the variable of the numerator in region i in year t (it is calculated as the deviation from the mean value for the related year). Higher (lower) I values from the expected $E(I) = -1/(n-1)$ value denote positive (negative) autocorrelation. In this study 999 permutations were used for making deductions. 999 permutations means resampling the data set 999 times and the I statistics is automatically calculated. The values obtained for the real data set are compared to the empirical distribution obtained from the resampled data sets.

30.3   Findings and Regional Comparisons

In this study, distribution maps were created first, in order to put forward the spatial distributions. In the distribution maps, there is an eight-color category. As the colors get darker, they indicate an increase in values. Four parties entered parliament following the last two elections: AKP, Republican People's Party (CHP), Nationalist Action Party (MHP) and Peoples' Democratic Party (HDP). The distribution maps drawn with the votes of these parties are shown in Figs. 30.1, 30.2, 30.3 and 30.4 (7J represents 7 June election and 1N represents 1 November election).

Evaluating the distribution maps of the votes of AKP for both electoral periods, it is concluded that similar spatial patterns are seen. AKP has particularly low vote rates in the Thrace region, coastal Aegean region, coastal Mediterranean region, Eastern Anatolia and some parts of South-eastern Anatolia region compared to other regions.

According to the spatial pattern of the votes of CHP, it is seen that the vote rates are particularly quite low in the Eastern Anatolia and South-eastern Anatolia regions. CHP were more successful in the Thracian, coastal Aegean and coastal Mediterranean regions.

According to the spatial pattern of the votes of MHP, it was unsuccessful with low vote rates in the Eastern Anatolia and South-eastern Anatolia regions. MHP was more successful in some parts of the central Anatolia region.

According to the spatial pattern of the votes of HDP, it is seen that the vote rates are particularly quite high in the Eastern Anatolia and South-eastern Anatolia regions. However, especially in central and eastern black sea region, it was unsuccessful.

It can be said according to the distribution maps that these four parties got similar spatial disintegration results in both electoral periods. Although the regional disintegration of variables is visually expressed over the map, they do not represent spatial inequality. In order to conduct the analysis the Moran's I values were calculated.

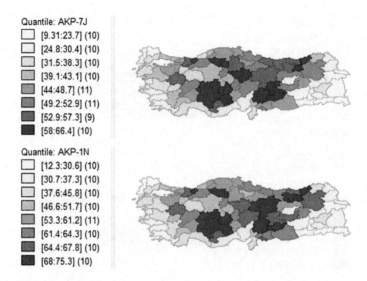

Fig. 30.1 Quantile maps of AKP

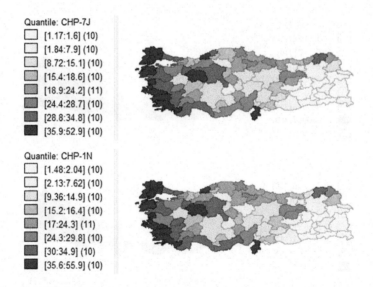

Fig. 30.2 Quantile maps of CHP

The Moran's I values of the four parties for both electoral periods are shown in Table 30.1. The Moran's I value of AKP which was 0.533938 in 7 June election dropped down to 0.474892 in 1 November elections. This statistic shows that the spatial inequality in the vote rates of AKP decreased. The Moran's I value of CHP which was 0.650847 in 7 June election dropped down to 0.619161 in 1 November

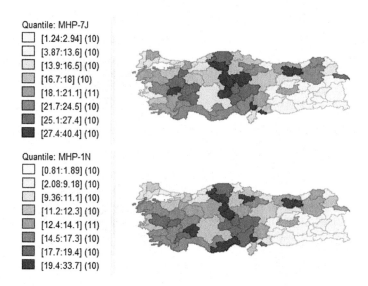

Fig. 30.3 Quantile maps of MHP

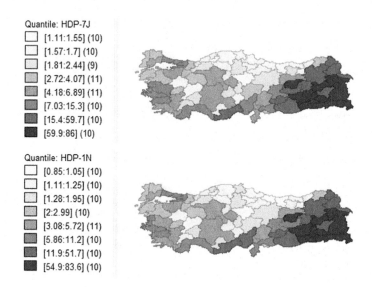

Fig. 30.4 Quantile maps of HDP

elections. HDP also got a similar spatial inequality decrease. However, MHP got a result which increased its spatial inequality as opposed to the other three parties. The Moran's I value of MHP which was 0.512209 in 7 June election raised to 0.541934 in 1 November elections.

Table 30.1 Moran's I and
p-value

Variables	7 June 2015 election		1 November 2015 election	
	Moran's I	*p*-value	Moran's I	*p*-value
AKP	0.533938	0.001	0.474892	0.001
CHP	0.650847	0.001	0.619161	0.001
MHP	0.512209	0.001	0.541934	0.001
HDP	0.846585	0.001	0.82614	0.001

Over the past decade, AKP managed to increase its vote share both arithmetically and regionally. The main reasons behind this increase are economic, social and political strategies considering on the median voter. AKP has become a central party especially after 2007 general elections and created a significant dominance on the median voter. AKP came to power after November 2000 and February 2001 economic crises and ensured significant economic growth by taking sound steps in financial discipline.

In addition to being a central party, AKP increased its share of votes with a strategy that increased public expenditures especially in Eastern Anatolia and South-eastern Anatolia regions where it was less successful. We visualize this situation in Fig. 30.5.

The geographical distribution of public expenditures during 2002–2014 is visualized in Fig. 30.5.[1] It can be stated that AKP preferred to increase the public expenditures in Eastern Anatolia and South-eastern Anatolia region where it has performed poorly during the past decade compared to other regions. One of the main hints in this map is that the per capita public expenditures is lower in Coastal Aegean and Coastal Mediterranean region where vote rates of AKP is lower. In these regions, CHP which is the main opposition party has a high potential to get votes.

Despite the increasing public expenditures in Eastern Anatolia and South-eastern Anatolia regions, AKP was unable to gain dominance in getting votes in these regions. Without a doubt, the influence of HDP on Kurdish voters is behind this result. The unclear political atmosphere in between 7 June 2015 and 1 November 2015 caused the voters to think that economic problems could get worse. The voters who passed from AKP to MHP and HDP in the 7 June 2015 election returned to AKP in 1 November 2015 election because of the instabilities before 2002.

It is necessary to show the statistical relationship between the public expenditures and AKP's vote rates. It is conducted a simple regression analysis and the results are given in Table 30.2.

---

[1] As population density is at high rates in Turkey's metropoles such as Istanbul, Ankara and Izmir and in the main industry cities, the public expenditures are also at high rates. It is necessary to create spatial equality criterion for spatial analysis. For this reason, the public expenditure variable is used per capita in the analysis.

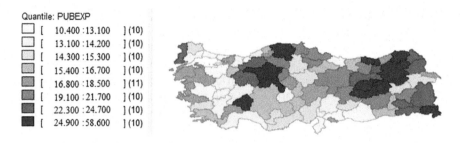

Quantile: PUBEXP

[	10.400 : 13.100	] (10)
[	13.100 : 14.200	] (10)
[	14.300 : 15.300	] (10)
[	15.400 : 16.700	] (10)
[	16.800 : 18.500	] (11)
[	19.100 : 21.700	] (10)
[	22.300 : 24.700	] (10)
[	24.900 : 58.600	] (10)

Fig. 30.5 Quantile map of total public expenditures (per capita Turkish Lira) 2002–2014

Table 30.2 Regression results

Dependent variable	R-squared	Prob (F-statistic)	Dependent variable	R-squared	Prob (F-statistic)
AKP-7J	0.0462040	0.0539698	AKP-1N	0.0529730	0.0387271
Variable	Coefficient	Probability	Variable	Coefficient	Probability
CONSTANT	49.22596	0.0000000	CONSTANT	59.99965	0.0000000
PUBEXP	−0.0004033	0.0539700	PUBEXP	−0.0004805	0.0387300

According to the regression results, it is determined a negative relationship between AKP' vote shares and public expenditures both 7 June 2015 and 1 November 2015. This result shows parallelism with spatial similarities at Figs. 30.1 and 30.5.

30.4   Conclusion

In this study, spatial disparities of the ruling and opposition parties were determined with ESDA analysis by taking the last two elections in Turkey into account. AKP which lost the majority on 7 June elections regained the majority on 1 November election and its spatial disintegration decreased in the vote distribution according to provinces. It can be said that the main reasons why the voters changed their votes significantly, although the duration between the two elections were short, are that there was a substantial propaganda after 7 June about the political and economic instabilities caused by the coalition governments in previous periods and that the number of terrorist incident rose significantly up and the rapid changes[2] seen in important macroeconomic factors such as the exchange rate and the inflation. The

---

[2]1 dollar was 2.7515 TL on 8 June 2015, 3.0583 TL on 14 September 2015 and 2.8245 TL on 1 November 2015. As for the Euro, 1 Euro was 3.1080 TL on 8 June 2014, 3.4545 on 14 September 2015 and 3.1115 on 1 November 2015. In addition, while the annual inflation rate was 7.20% in June 2015, it was 8.10% in November 2015.

vote rates of the ruling and opposition parties and the relationships between public expenditures were evaluated in the study within the context of the distribution maps. According to the evaluation results; it was determined that AKP tended to increase public expenditures in Eastern Anatolia and South-eastern Anatolia region in order to increase its votes in these regions. In addition to this, it was determined that the per capita public expenditures was lower in Coastal Aegean and Coastal Mediterranean regions where the main opposition was stronger and the vote rates of AKP was lower. As a result of the regional evaluations and analysis, it is concluded that AKP has a significant vote distribution on a regional level and that it used the public expenditures to manipulate the votes. Besides it is determined a statistically negative relationship between AKP's vote share and public expenditures. This result shows parallelism with spatial similarities and the results given in this study.

Acknowledgments This is paper has been prepared under financial support of Dumlupınar University Committee of Scientific Research Projects (Project number: 2016-30), which authors gratefully acknowledge.

References

Anselin L (1988) Spatial econometrics methods and models. Kluwer Academic Publishers, Dordrecht

Anselin L (1992) Spatial data analysis with GIS: an introduction to application in the social sciences. National Center for Geographic Information and Analysis, University of California, Santa Barbara

Anselin L (1995) Local indicator of spatial association—LISA. Geogr Anal 27:93–115

Anselin L (1999) Interactive techniques and exploratory spatial data analysis. In: Longley PA, Goodchild MF, Maguire DJ, Rhind DW (eds) Geographical information systems: principles, techniques, management and applications. Wiley, New York, pp 251–264

Anselin L (2005) Exploring spatial data with GeoDaTM: a workbook. Spatial Analysis Laboratory, Department of Geography University of Illinois, Center for Spatially Integrated Social Science

Anselin L, Syabri I, Kho Y (2006) GeoDa: an introduction to spatial data analysis. Geogr Anal 38 (1):5–22

Anselin L, Sridharan S, Gholston S (2007) Using exploratory spatial data analysis to leverage social indicator database: the discovery of interesting patterns. Sos Indic Res 82(2):287–309

Broner S, Delicado P (2006) Spatial data analysis for 2004 electoral data in Barcelona, International Workshop on Spatio-Temporal Modelling. In: Proceedings of the international workshop on spatio-temporal modelling (METMA3), pp 93–94

Celebioglu F, Dalll'erba S (2010) Spatial disparities across the regions of Turkey: an exploratory spatial data analysis. Ann Reg Sci 45(2):379–400

Carkoglu A (2000) The geography of the April 1999 Turkish elections. Turk Stud 1(1):149–171

Carkoglu A (2002) The rise of the new generation pro-islamists in Turkey: the justice and development party phenomenon in the November 2002 elections in Turkey. S Eur Soc Polit 7 (3):123–156

Carkoglu A (2009) The March 2009 local elections in Turkey: a signal for takers or the inevitable beginning of the end for AKP? S Eur Soc Polit 14(3):295–316

Dall'erba S (2005) Distribution of regional income and regional funds in Europe 1989–1999: an exploratory spatial data analysis. Ann Reg Sci 39(1):121–148

Ertur C, Koch W (2006) Regional disparities in the European Union and the enlargement process: an exploratory spatial data analysis 1995–2000. Ann Reg Sci 40(4):723–765

Luca D, Pose AR (2015) Distributive politics and regional development: assessing the territorial distribution of Turkey's public investment. J Dev Stud 51(11):1518–1540

O'Loughlin J (2002) The electoral geography of Weimar Germany: exploratory spatial data analysis (ESDA) of protestant support for the Nazi Party. Polit Anal 10(3):217–243

Tobler W (1979) Cellular geography. In: Gale S, Olsson G (ed) Philosophy in geography, pp 519–536

Tomaselli VM, D'Agata R (2010) Spatial analysis for electoral data: the spread of territorial parties in Italy. In: 45th Scientific Meeting of the Italian Statistical Society

West WJ (2005) Regional cleavages in Turkish politics: an electoral geography of the 1999 and 2002 national elections. Polit Geogr 24(4):499–523

Chapter 31
Does Privatization Affect Airports Performance? A Comparative Analysis with AHP-TOPSIS and DEA

Burak Keskin and Efehan Ulas

Abstract This paper investigates the effect of privatization and deregulation strategies on performance of European busiest twenty airports using TOPSIS multi-criteria decision-making method and data envelopment analysis (DEA) with panel data for 2010–2014. Firstly, annual passenger number, operational revenue, number of runway, cargo traffic and aircraft movements have been determined as performance evaluation criteria. Secondly, TOPSIS method has been applied to decision-making units (DMUs) and performance ranking has been acquired. In this stage, criteria weights were calculated by using analytic hierarchy process (AHP). Later, airports have been divided into two groups as private owned and public owned to compare their performance. Finally, DEA was employed to the data. From this point of view, number of runways, cargo traffic and aircraft movements are determined as input parameters; annual passenger numbers and financial revenue are determined as output parameters.

Keywords Airport performance analysis · Privatization · AHP-TOPSIS · DEA

31.1 Introduction

Since 1970s, the aviation industry has been undergoing a process of deregulation and privatization. This deregulation has stimulated demands for faster and more efficient processing of aircrafts, passengers, cargo transportation and airports (Lin and Hong 2006). Therefore, additional to airlines, airports should be performed well to survive in market.

B. Keskin (✉)
Department of Business Administration, Cankiri Karatekin University, Cankiri, Turkey
e-mail: burakkeskiin@gmail.com; burakkeskin@karatekin.edu.tr

E. Ulas
Department of Statistics, Cankiri Karatekin University, Cankiri, Turkey
e-mail: ef_ulas@hotmail.com; efehanulas@karatekin.edu.tr

© Springer International Publishing AG 2017
D. Procházka (ed.), *New Trends in Finance and Accounting*,
Springer Proceedings in Business and Economics,
DOI 10.1007/978-3-319-49559-0_31

335

Airports performance evaluation has been a burgeoning area of recent years. These analyses are important for a variety of stakeholders, including airports, governments, passengers and airlines. Motivations for investigating airport performance include evaluating financial and operational performance, assessing alternative investment strategies and monitoring airport activity (Lai et al. 2015).

The deregulation of the aviation market over the past decades has induced the need for developing reliable performance measurement in the airport industry. Airports nowadays operate in competitive markets and have to evaluate critically the performance of them. Furthermore, many airports are operated as semiprivate enterprises or full-private enterprises. Airport operators and stakeholders need, therefore, quantitative information on the relative performance of airports in terms of passengers, cargo, revenues or market share. Comparative analysis of airports' performance indicators using benchmarking principles has become a useful method for performance improvement (Suzuki et al. 2014).

An airport is a multi-product firm with complicated business, where disparate elements and activities are brought together to facilitate, for passenger and freight, an interchange between air and surface transport. Government interventions and industry structure can affect the performance of airports (Curi et al. 2010).

The importance of airports has been of interest in contemporary economics, given airports' increasingly strategic importance in the movement of people and cargo transportation in the globalized world (Barros and Dieke 2007). Additionally, airports have been strategically important for countries economic development. From this point of view, an airport's financial and operational performance is so important for economy policy makers.

The trend towards airport privatization began in UK 25 years ago. The consequences provide an important case study for policy makers worldwide to evaluate privatize or retain ownership of their airports. Privatization policy has been referred to as the "… most significant economic development of modern times" (Pirie 1995). The UK has led the way with its privatization program, which has influenced economic policy throughout the world.

Privatization can be defined as the transfer by governments to private sector investors of the assets of public-owned enterprises, so that the new entity gains a legal status that enables it to act as a private company (Humphreys 1999).

Airport privatization is a controversial, yet increasingly important, theme in government policy throughout the world. The first major privatization occurred in UK in 1987, and since then a number of other countries, both in developed and in developing regions, have seen it become a significant political force. In a global study of 459 airports in 2007, it was found that 24% of them had full or partial private ownership. Moreover, these partial or fully privately owned airports handled proportionally more European passenger traffic (48%), since private operators are predominantly found at larger airports (Graham 2011).

31.2   Methodology

Hwang and Yoon (1981) originally proposed the order performance technique based on similarity to ideal solution (TOPSIS), in which the chosen alternative should not only have the shortest distance from the positive ideal reference point, but also have the longest distance from the negative ideal reference point, to solve multi-criteria decision method (MCDM) problems. There have been lots of studies in the literature using TOPSIS for the solution of MCDM problems. Lai et al. (1994) extended TOPSIS to solve a multiple objective decision problem (Rostamzadeh and Sofian 2011). Since TOPSIS is a well-known method for classical MCDM problems, many researchers have applied TOPSIS to solve MCDM problems in the past.

The positive ideal solution is a solution that maximizes the benefit criteria and minimizes the cost criteria, whereas the negative ideal solution maximizes the cost criteria and minimizes the benefit criteria. In short, the positive ideal solution is composed of all best values attainable of criteria, whereas the negative ideal solution consists of all worst values attainable of criteria. In this paper, TOPSIS method is used for determining the final ranking of the airports. Main steps of TOPSIS method can be seen below:

Step 1:   Creating decision matrix (A_{ij}) using decision-making units (DMUs) and performance criteria (where m is the number of DMU, n is the number of criteria),

$$A_{ij} = \begin{bmatrix} a_{11} & a_{12} & \cdots & a_{1n} \\ a_{21} & a_{22} & \cdots & a_{2n} \\ \cdot & & & \cdot \\ \cdot & & & \cdot \\ \cdot & & & \cdot \\ a_{m1} & a_{m2} & \cdots & a_{mn} \end{bmatrix} \qquad (31.1)$$

Step 2:   Calculate the normalized decision matrix. The normalized value r_{ij} is calculated as follows. And normalized decision matrix (R_{ij}) can be seen below.

$$r_{ij} = x_{ij} \sqrt{\sum_{i-1}^{m} x_{ij}^2} \quad i = 1, 2, \ldots, m \text{ and } j = 1, 2, \ldots, n \qquad (31.2)$$

$$R_{ij} = \begin{bmatrix} r_{11} & r_{12} & \cdots & r_{1n} \\ r_{21} & r_{22} & \cdots & r_{2n} \\ \cdot & & & \cdot \\ \cdot & & & \cdot \\ \cdot & & & \cdot \\ r_{m1} & r_{m2} & \cdots & r_{mn} \end{bmatrix} \qquad (31.3)$$

Step 3: Calculate the weighted normalized decision matrix. The weighted normalized value v_{ij} is calculated as follows:

$$v_{ij} = r_{ij} \times w_j \quad i = 1, 2, \ldots, m \text{ and } j = 1, 2, \ldots, n.$$

(where w_j is the weight of the jth criterion or attribute and $\sum_{j=1}^{n} w_j = 1$.)

Step 4: Determine the ideal (A^*) and negative ideal (A^-) solutions.

$$A^* = \left\{ \left(\max_i v_{ij} \,|\, j \in C_b \right), \left(\min_i v_{ij} \,|\, j \in C_c \right) \right\} = \left\{ v_j^* \,|\, j = 1, 2, \ldots, m \right\} \tag{31.4}$$

$$A^- = \left\{ \left(\min_i v_{ij} \,|\, j \in C_b \right), \left(\max_i v_{ij} \,|\, j \in C_c \right) \right\} = \left\{ v_j^- \,|\, j = 1, 2, \ldots, m \right\} \tag{31.5}$$

Step 5: Calculate the separation measures using the m-dimensional Euclidean distance. The separation measures of each alternative from the positive ideal solution and the negative ideal solution, respectively, are as follows:

$$S_i^* = \sqrt{\sum_{j=1}^{m} \left(v_{ij} - v_j^* \right)^2}, j = 1, 2, \ldots, m \tag{31.6}$$

$$S_i^- = \sqrt{\sum_{j=1}^{m} \left(v_{ij} - v_j^- \right)^2}, j = 1, 2, \ldots, m \tag{31.7}$$

Step 6: Calculate the relative closeness to the ideal solution. The relative closeness of the alternative A_i with respect to A^* is defined as follows:

$$C_i^* = \frac{S_i^-}{S_i^* + S_i^-}, \quad i = 1, 2, \ldots, m \tag{31.8}$$

Step 7: Rank the preference order from highest score of C_i^* to the lowest (Wu and Chuang 2013).

Additionally, to compare the results of TOPSIS, data envelopment analysis (DEA) was employed to the data. The idea of efficiency measurement was developed by Farrel during mid-twentieth century when he used the nonparametric efficiency limit approach to measure relative distances from border efficiency. This measurement, which is well known as empirical or relative efficiency, was later expanded on by researchers, especially Charnes et al. (1978). They called the technique DEA

Developed by Charnes, Cooper and Rhodes (CCR) in 1978 and further developed by Banker, Charnes and Cooper (BCC) in 1984, DEA is a nonparametric method that does not require the specification of the functional form relating inputs to outputs or the setting of weight for the various factors.

In this paper were used the original BCC models of DEA. CCR model is suitable for industries that show a constant return to scale (CRS). BCC model is suitable for industries that show a variable return to scale (VRS) such as aviation industry. For that reason, in this study only BCC model was employed.

Using DEA model, researchers are required to formulate the problem into mathematical expression. The mathematical formulation of DEA consists in the solution of a set of linear programming models (Charnes et al. 1978) aimed at maximizing the efficiency of each DMU. The DEA mathematical model is as follows:

$$\text{Max} h_j = \frac{\sum_{r=1}^{n} u_r y_r}{\sum_{i=1}^{m} v_i x_i} \tag{31.9}$$

where h_j is effectiveness of j decision-making unit. The goal should be maximization of h_j. Constrains can be shown as follows:

$$\frac{\sum_{r=1}^{n} u_r y_r}{\sum_{i=1}^{m} v_i x_i} \leq 1$$

$$u_r \geq 0 \tag{31.10}$$

$$v_i \geq 0$$

where n, m, u_n, y_n, v_m, x_m show output number, input number, weight of n output, amount of n output, weight of m input and amount of m input, respectively, for $j = 1, 2,\ldots, S$, and S is the number of DMUs (Ulas and Keskin 2015).

31.3 Implementation

31.3.1 TOPSIS

In this study, it is aimed to measure the operational performance of busiest twenty airports—according to their passenger numbers in 2014—between the years 2010 and 2014 by using TOPSIS multi-criteria decision-making method. From that point of view, first step is to determine the performance criteria. After review of the literature and face-to-face interview with experts in aviation industry, annual passenger numbers, financial revenue, runways, cargo traffic and aircraft movement were determined as performance criteria. Secondly, one of the most widely known multi-criteria decision-making methods—TOPSIS method—was chosen to measure the operational performance of airports. As mentioned in methodology section,

TOPSIS method has seven steps. Before starting to analyse stage, the data were collected from airports' annual reports and financial statements for the years 2010, 2011, 2012, 2013 and 2014. The data list used in this study is listed in Table 31.1.

Table 31.1 Data list used in study

Countries	Airports	Ownership category
1. England	Heathrow	Private
2. France	CDG	Private
3. Germany	Frankfurt	Private
4. Turkey	Ataturk	Private
5. Netherland	Schiphol	Private
6. Spain	Barajas	Public
7. Italy	Da Vinci	Private
8. Russia	Sheremetyevo	Public
9. Denmark	Copenhagen	Public
10. Switzer	Zurich	Private
11. Norway	Oslo	Public
12. Austria	Vienna	Private
13. Sweden	Arlanda	Public
14. Belgium	Brussels	Public
15. Ireland	Dublin	Public
16. Portugal	Lisbon	Public
17. Finland	Helsinki	Public
18. Greece	Athens	Public
19. Czech R	Vaclav Havel	Public
20. Poland	Chopin	Public

Airports	Annual passenger	Total revenue	Runway number	Cargo traffic	Aircraft movements
Heathrow	70.18	3.01	2	1.47	471
CDG	67.58	2.63	t4	2.17	492
Frankfurt	56.92	2.39	4	2.09	476
Ataturk	44.50	1.11	3	1.05	364
Schiphol	50.70	1.33	6	1.54	434
Barajas	45.26	1.09	4	0.35	382
Da Vinci	37.10	0.65	4	0.16	358
Sheremetyevo	25.16	0.15	1	0.27	253
Copenhagen	23.44	0.47	3	0.37	249
Zurich	24.46	0.84	3	0.42	269
Oslo	22.04	0.45	2	0.11	238
Vienna	21.48	0.59	2	0.28	240
Arlanda	19.76	0.55	3	0.20	177
Brussels	19.16	0.34	3	0.46	226
Dublin	19.62	0.45	2	0.07	205
Lisbon	15.66	0.41	4	0.12	140
Helsinki	14.78	0.15	3	0.18	174
Athens	14.08	0.31	2	0.08	163
Vaclav Havel	11.26	0.65	3	0.06	121
Chopin	9.78	0.32	2	0.04	120

After computed the mean of 5-year data, weighted and normalized decision matrix values were acquired by utilizing Eq. (2) for each airport as given in Table 31.2. The criteria weights are calculated by using AHP and as shown below:

$$W1 = 0.2902; W2 = 0.3627; W3 = 0.0551; W4 = 0.1033; W5 = 0.1884$$

The AHP is a theory of measurement through pairwise comparisons and relies on the judgements of experts to derive priority scales. These scales measure intangibles in relative terms. The comparisons are made using a scale of absolute judgements that represent how much more one element dominates another with respect to a given attribute. The judgements may be inconsistent, and how to measure inconsistency and improve the judgements, when possible to obtain better consistency, is a concern of the AHP (Saaty 2008).

As listed in Table 31.2, all values have been converted between 0 and 1. Later, positive (A^*) and negative ideal (A^-) solutions were computed for each column by utilizing Eqs. (4) and (5), respectively. Positive and negative ideal solutions are shown as follows:

Table 31.2 Weighted and normalized decision matrix

Airports	Annual passenger	Total revenue	Runway number	Cargo traffic	Aircraft movements
Heathrow	0.1276	00.2029	0.0077	0.0383	0.0656
CDG	0.1229	0.1775	0.0154	0.0568	0.0686
Frankfurt	0.1035	0.1612	0.0154	0.0545	0.0664
Ataturk	0.0809	0.0746	0.0116	0.0275	0.0507
Schiphol	0.0922	0.0899	0.0231	0.0402	0.0605
Barajas	0.0823	0.0731	0.0154	0.0092	0.0532
Da Vinci	0.0675	0.0437	0.0154	0.0041	0.0499
Sheremetyevo	0.0458	0.0098	0.0039	0.0070	0.0353
Copenhagen	0.0426	0.0318	0.0116	0.0097	0.0347
Zurich	0.0445	0.0566	0.0116	0.0110	0.0375
Oslo	0.0401	0.0305	0.0077	0.0029	0.0332
Vienna	0.0391	0.0400	0.0077	0.0072	0.0334
Arlanda	0.0359	0.0369	0.0116	0.0052	0.0246
Brussels	0.0348	0.0227	0.0116	0.0121	0.0315
Dublin	0.0357	0.0305	0.0077	0.0018	0.0285
Lisbon	0.0285	0.0275	0.0154	0.0032	0.0196
Helsinki	0.0269	0.0103	0.0116	0.0047	0.0243
Athens	0.0256	0.0210	0.0077	0.0021	0.0227
Vaclav Havel	0.0205	0.0238	0.0116	0.0014	0.0168
Chopin	0.0178	0.0213	0.0077	0.0010	0.0168

$$A* : \{0.1276, 0.2029, 0.231, 0.0600, 0.0686\}$$
$$A- : \{0.0178, 0.0098, 0.0039, 0.0000, 0.0168\}$$

In the process of determination of positive ideal solutions, the highest value chooses each column; in the process of determination of negative ideal solutions, the lowest value chooses each column. After this process, to rank operational performance of each airport, it is required to calculate $S*$, S^- and $C*$ values separately by utilizing Eqs. (6), (7) and (8), respectively. These values are listed in Table 31.3.

The ranking of DMU carries out according to their $C*$ values in TOPSIS method. As listed in Table 31.3, the results show that the best operational performance was carried out by Heathrow Airport. And the ranking goes Paris CDG, Frankfurt, Schiphol and Ataturk from the best to the poor, respectively. Additionally, the lowest performance was carried out by Chopin, Vaclav Havel and Athens Airports, respectively.

After ranking, a question arises in mind: "Do private-owned airports perform well than public-owned airports?" To answer this question, airports have been divided into two groups as public owned and private owned. The data used in this study comprise eight private-owned airports and twelve public-owned airports. As given in Table 31.3, it can be seen clearly that the best operational performances are

Table 31.3 S^+, S^- and C^* values

Airports	S^+	S^-	C^*	Ranking
Heathrow	0.0242	0.2306	0.9049	1
CDG	0.0270	0.2123	0.8871	2
Frankfurt	0.0489	0.1890	0.7945	3
Ataturk	0.1413	0.1005	0.4155	5
Schiphol	0.1199	0.1255	0.5114	4
Barajas	0.1465	0.0985	0.4020	6
Da Vinci	0.1793	0.0697	0.2799	7
Sheremetyevo	0.2190	0.0341	0.1346	13
Copenhagen	0.2001	0.0394	0.1647	10
Zurich	0.1776	0.0590	0.2494	8
Oslo	0.2045	0.0348	0.1454	12
Vienna	0.1957	0.0412	0.1738	9
Arlanda	0.2017	0.0347	0.1467	11
Brussels	0.2112	0.0293	0.1218	15
Dublin	0.2075	0.0301	0.1265	14
Lisbon	0.2144	0.0239	0.1004	16
Helsinki	0.2282	0.0146	0.0601	19
Athens	0.2210	0.0154	0.0651	18
Vaclav Havel	0.2224	0.0162	0.0679	17
Chopin	0.2261	0.0121	0.0507	20

carried out by private-owned airports. Additionally, to compare operational performance and operational efficiency, DEA is applied to the data.

31.3.2 Data Envelopment Analysis

To employ DEA, firstly it is required to determine input and output parameters. From this point of view, number of runways, cargo traffic and aircraft movement are determined as input parameters; annual passenger numbers and financial revenue are determined as output parameters.

Because VRS is suitable for aviation industry, only BCC model was employed to the data. For that purpose, firstly, technical and pure technical efficiency scores were computed. Later, scale efficiency scores were computed by using technical and pure technical efficiency scores for each year. These efficiency scores of airlines are given in Table 31.4, and referral of clustering analysis of airlines is given in Table 31.5.

In Table 31.4, the first column represents the numbers of airports that are given in Table 31.1 previously. Second column indicates overall technical efficiency scores under CRS assumption. Third column shows pure technical efficiency score

Table 31.4 Results of DEA

FIRM	CRSTE	VRSTE	SCALE	
1	1.000	1.000	1.000	–
2	0.871	0.871	1.000	–
3	0.817	0.817	1.000	–
4	0.980	1.000	0.980	Drs
5	0.779	0.781	0.998	Irs
6	0.933	0.967	0.964	Drs
7	1.000	1.000	1.000	–
8	1.000	1.000	1.000	–
9	0.731	0.732	0.999	Irs
10	0.703	0.710	0.990	Drs
11	1.000	1.000	1.000	–
12	0.765	0.767	0.997	Drs
13	1.000	1.000	1.000	–
14	0.650	0.651	0.999	Drs
15	1.000	1.000	1.000	–
16	0.908	0.969	0.937	Irs
17	0.687	0.694	0.990	Irs
18	0.794	0.999	0.794	Irs
19	1.000	1.000	1.000	–
20	1.000	1.000	1.000	–
Mean	0.881	0.898	0.982	

Table 31.5 Referral of clustering analysis

No.	Referral clustering	Referral frequency	No.	Referral clustering	Referral frequency
1	1	8	11	11	2
2	1, 13	–	12	1, 7, 8, 11, 15	–
3	1, 13	–	13	13	7
4	4	–	14	7, 1, 13	–
5	1, 13	–	15	15	6
6	7, 1	–	16	20, 15, 13	–
7	7	6	17	7, 15, 13	–
8	8	1	18	15, 20, 11	–
9	15, 7, 1, 13	–	19	19	1
10	7, 1, 19, 15	–	20	20	2

under VRS. In last column, scale efficiency scores are given. As listed in Table 31.4, pure technical efficiency contributes more compared to technical efficiency scores. This is because of that aviation industry is more suitable for VRS characteristics. The lowest scale efficiency score is observed by Brussels Airport. Deciding to the most efficient airport, it is required to look referral of clustering analysis in Table 31.5. When the efficiency score is equal to 1, it means that DMU is efficient. The DMU that has the most referral frequency is labelled as the most efficient DMU.

Table 31.5 shows the referral frequency for every airport in the BCC model. The results show that Heathrow Airport has the highest referral frequency (8 times referred). The airports referred the Heathrow Airport are CDG, Frankfurt, Schiphol, Da Vinci, Copenhagen, Oslo, Arlanda and Brussels Airports. Arlanda and Dublin Airports have the second and third referral frequency with 7 and 6 times, respectively. Furthermore, 8 relatively efficient airlines were also referred. Among 9 efficient airports, Heathrow that operated by private sector enterprises is found as the most relatively efficient airport. When comparing private-owned airports with public-owned airports, Mann–Whitney U test was employed to the data, and it was found that there is no statistically significant difference between their efficiency scores.

31.4 Conclusion

In this study, AHP-TOPSIS and DEA methods were applied to busiest European airports—according to 2014 passenger traffic—for the years of 2010, 2011, 2012, 2013 and 2014. First, TOPSIS method was applied to the data to measure those airports operational performances. According to TOPSIS results, best performances were carried out by Heathrow, CDG and Frankfurt airports that operated by private sector enterprises. Moreover, it is found that the best public-owned airport performance was carried out by Barajas Airport. And the lowest public-owned airport performance was carried out by Frederic Chopin Airport as given in Table 31.3.

Additionally, DEA was employed to the data to measure airports' efficiencies. As a result, Heathrow Airport was found to be the most efficient airport in the data as given in Table 31.5. Not only TOPSIS results, but also DEA results show that private-owned airports have higher performance values. But especially in DEA, statistically significant results between the private-owned and public-owned airports could not be acquired according to Mann–Whitney U test results.

References

Barros CP, Dieke PU (2007) Performance evaluation of Italian airports: a data envelopment analysis. J Air Transp Manag 13(4):184–191

Charnes A et al (1978) Measuring the efficiency of decision making units. Eur J Oper Res, 429–444

Curi C, Gitto S, Mancuso P (2010) The Italian airport industry in transition: a performance analysis. J Air Transp Manag 16(4):218–221

Graham A (2011) The objectives and outcomes of airport privatisation. Res Transp Bus Manag 1(1):3–14

Humphreys I (1999) Privatisation and commercialisation: changes in UK airport ownership patterns. J Transp Geogr 7(2):121–134

Hwang CL, Yoon K (1981) Multiple attribute decision making methods and applications, a state-of-the-art survey. Springer-Verlag, New York

Lai YJ, Liu TY, Hwang CL (1994) TOPSIS for MODM. Euro J Oper Res 76:486–500

Lai PL, Potter A, Beynon M, Beresford A (2015) Evaluating the efficiency performance of airports using an integrated AHP/DEA-AR technique. Transp Policy 42:75–85

Lin LC, Hong CH (2006) Operational performance evaluation of international major airports: An application of data envelopment analysis. J Air Transp Manag 12(6):342–351

Pirie M (1995) Reasons for privatisation, In: Morgan P (ed) Privatisation and the welfare state: implications for consumers and the workforce. Dartmouth, Aldershot, pp 21–28

Rostamzadeh R, Sofian S (2011) Prioritizing effective 7Ms to improve production systems performance using fuzzy AHP and fuzzy TOPSIS (case study). Expert Syst Appl 38(5): 5166–5177

Saaty TL (2008) Decision making with the analytic hierarchy process. Int J Serv Sci 1(1):83–98

Suzuki S, Nijkamp P, Pels E, Rietveld P (2014) Comparative performance analysis of European airports by means of extended data envelopment analysis. J Adv Transp 48(3):185–202

Ulas E, Keskin B (2015) Performance evaluation and ranking of Turkish banking sector. Procedia Econ Financ 25:297–307

Wu F, Chuang C (2013) The optimal relationship between buyer and seller obtained using TOPSIS method. J Adv Manag Sci 1(1):133–135

Chapter 32
An Empirical Analysis of Post-contractual Behaviour Regarding Public Contracts for Construction Work in the Czech Republic

Michal Plaček, František Ochrana, Martin Schmidt and Milan Půček

Abstract The article analyses the post-contractual behaviour of actors dealing with public tenders on a sample of 200 randomly selected public works contracts. In this sample, we examined public contracts awarded in 2013, for which it was possible to trace information regarding the final price. Using an econometric model, we have tried to find the factors which have a statistically significant effect on the ratio between the final price paid and the tendered price. The results were compared with similar studies compiled from the conditions in Slovakia. The model shows that the number of offers constitutes a statistically significant indicator of the price. Conversely, factors with negative impact were identified as being the difference between the estimated price and the real tendered price, as well as the use of subcontractors.

Keywords Public procurement · Post-contractual behaviour · Construction work

M. Plaček (✉) · F. Ochrana · M. Schmidt
Faculty of Social Sciences, Charles University, Smetanovo Nábřeží 995/6,
Prague, Czech Republic
e-mail: michalplacek@seznam.cz

F. Ochrana
e-mail: frantisek.ochrana@fsv.cuni.cz

M. Schmidt
e-mail: m.schmidt@email.cz

M. Půček
The College of Regional Development in Prague, Želanského 68/54,
Prague, Czech Republic
e-mail: milan.pucek@seznam.cz

© Springer International Publishing AG 2017
D. Procházka (ed.), *New Trends in Finance and Accounting*,
Springer Proceedings in Business and Economics,
DOI 10.1007/978-3-319-49559-0_32

32.1   Introduction

The institute of public procurement in the Czech Republic and in the Slovak Republic is an important tool for the allocation of public resources as well as being an instrument of fiscal policy. In 2015, the total volume of public procurement expenditures was 13.7% of GDP (see the Annual Report of Public Procurement 2014, MMR, May 2015). In the EU-28, the total share amounted to 13.67% of GDP in 2013 [percentage of total expenditure on works, goods and services excluding utilities as a % of GDP 13.67% (EC 2015)]. Public contracts exhibit a high risk of corruption in the Czech Republic and Slovakia, which among other things has been shown in the rankings of the Czech Republic and Slovakia in terms of Corruption Perception Index. Corruption risk in public procurement can be influenced by a number of factors such as the openness of competition (Ochrana and Maaytová 2012), the competitive effect (Strand et al. 2011; Nemec et al. 2015; Pavel 2010), transparency in public procurement procedures (Burguet and Che 2004; Pavel and Sičáková-Beblavá 2008) and the quality of regulations (Jurčík 2012). Scientific studies dealing with the problem of corruption are strongly focused on identifying corruption risks in the preparatory phase (pre-bidding) and the bidding phase (evaluation, selection and procurement). Any analysis of the post-contractual phase (post-bidding) has been largely ignored. In the scientific literature, we found only one study (Pavel and Sičáková-Beblavá 2012), which deals with research on the post-contractual behaviour of actors regarding public procurements and the potential risk of corruption. This study, based on a sample of data for public contracts awarded in the Slovak Republic, examines the role of amendments to contracts as a symptom of the risk of corrupt behaviour. Pavel and Sičáková-Beblavá work with the hypothesis that the authority agrees with a particular tenderer for a corrupt gain, where "the authorities struggle to maintain control over a low number of bids". Subsequently, an open tender procedure is announced. As a result of the competitive effect, the applicants then offer low prices. The applicant, who negotiated the agreed bid (corrupt offer) with the contracting authorities, must offer the lowest price. In this situation, it can be expected that the tenderer and the contracting authority will want to obtain a "corrupt gain" by concluding an amendment to the contract for additional works. Pavel and Sičáková-Beblavá tested for this based on the factor of openness, the likelihood of an amendment being added to the contract based on the number of offers, and the difference between the final price and the tendered price.

The aim of this article is to use an econometric model to identify statistically significant factors that influence the relationship between total price paid and the tendered value of public contracts, and to compare these results with secondary data for the Slovak Republic.

32.2 Basis of the Analysis

Public contracts have three basic phases (EU 2013): a pre-bidding phase, a bidding phase and a post-bidding phase. In terms of the efficiency of public procurement, e.g. the efficiency of the allocation of public resources through this institution, the phase following the signing of the contract with the successful tenderer for the implementation of public procurement (i.e. the post-bidding phase, post-contractual phase) is no less equally important. It is in this phase of the life cycle of the public procurement, where it is actually implemented and where the payment of the price to the contracting authority for the services rendered. The price actually paid, however, often differs from the price at which the contract was tendered. These differences may be both an increase in and a decrease in the final price. This is mainly connected with public works contracts (due to their complexity and pro-longed implementation process).

Generally, in the case of construction contracts, it is reasonable to assume that there may be some changes regarding the final price. This is due to us not living in a perfect world in which construction projects are implemented according to plan. In the real world, one cannot accurately determine the volume of some work or materials ex-ante, or make such determinations effectively regarding the associated costs. Additionally, the implementation of public procurements may lead to unforeseen circumstances or a project may contain certain inaccuracies or errors. Outside the outlined objective reasons for changes to the public contract, tenderers may calculate contract prices (a consequent increase in the price after contract conclusion) with a view to the existence of asymmetric information.

Generally, a public works contract is defined as a so-called measured contract where the tendered unit price and the final price depend on a number of completed units, or the contract may be defined as a contract for a fixed price, where the risk of possible changes is borne mainly by the supplier, or it may be a combination of both.

The Public Procurement Act counts on the possibility for changes to a public contract after the contract has been signed and it sets out the conditions under which it is possible to carry out any such change, e.g. concluding a contract amendment. In particular, the conditions for using the "negotiated procedure without publica-tion" are specified in § 23 par. 7 letter a) of the Public Procurement Act.

According to that provision, the same suppliers may apply for additional con-struction work if the need arose due to unforeseen circumstances, or when such works cannot be reasonably implemented separately, and if the scope of the additional work does not exceed 30% of the initial public contract.

32.3 Data and Methods

For our analysis, we have used classical linear regression. We utilized 200 randomly selected works contracts for the inputs in our model, which, according to the Bulletin of public contracts, were awarded in 2013 (orders this year were chosen because it can be assumed that these contracts have already been completed, while in the case of public contracts started since April 2012, they were paid by the transparency amendment no. 55/2015 Coll., where the obligation to disclose the price actually paid was on the profile of the contracting authority). The actual prices paid or these contracts were tracked on the individual profiles of the contracting authorities, and due to some missing records as well as some incomplete information on others, 137 full records of the relevant public contracts were obtained.

32.3.1 Response Variables

In our analysis, we focus on the relative changes in prices, and as the response variable, we therefore choose the ratio of "actual paid price" and "the tendered price" (the price paid/tendered price). In this variable, the average value and the median move to 1. On average, the changes in the actual paid prices arise in a fairly neutral way, but they may be affected by some orders which were not completely implemented on the scale envisaged, just partially. Figure 32.1 presents a more detailed frequency distribution.

The histogram shows that the most common example is when the order is realized at a price close to the tendered price (approximately 44% of cases) and relatively common are price increases up to 10 and 20%.

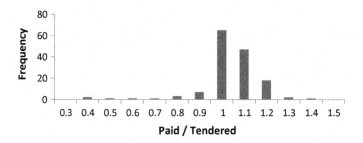

Fig. 32.1 Histogram of price changes. *Source* Authors

32.3.2   Explanatory Variables

As the main explanatory variables, we have considered the following:

1. Tendered/expected price—this variable indicates an increase in the tendered price against the estimated value of public contracts by the contracting authority (mean 0.71, median 0.70).
2. Type of contracting authority—in this variable, we utilized the divisions according to Journal of Public Procurement (Table 32.1).
3. Type of procurement—for this variable we utilized the divisions of types of procurement procedures under the Public Procurement Act (Table 32.2).

For other variables, we chose the following:

- The number of bids submitted,
- Variables characterizing the region (GDP per inhabitant, the number of registered economic entities in the district, headquarters of contracting authority, the number of entities operating in the construction sector),
- Use of electronic auctions,
- Central procurement,
- Use of subcontractors,
- Evaluations according to the lowest prices,
- Funding from EU subsidies.

Individual explanatory variables have been chosen based on the results of previous studies that examined the influence of individual variables on the standard

Table 32.1 Characteristics of the variable: type of contracting authority

Type of contracting authority	Frequency
Regional or local authority	78
National or federal agency/office	16
Public institutions	10
Regional or local agency/office	12
Ministry or any other national or federal authority, including their components	7
Other	25

Source Authors

Table 32.2 Characteristics of the variable: type of award procedure

Type of procurement procedure	Frequency
Open	74
Limited	5
Negotiated procedure without publication	7
Simplified below-threshold	62

Source Authors

price, and also on the basis of the study (Pavel and Sičáková-Beblavá 2012), and to ensure at least partial comparability.

32.4 Results

Table 32.3 presents the results of a regression model.

White's test did not reject the hypothesis of homoscedasticity. Variance inflation factors do not indicate a problem with collinearity between the response variables.

The model shows that of the considered explanatory variables, the number of tenders, e.g. a higher number of bids, is an important variable. Competition reduces potential increases in prices after the signing of the contract. Another important variable is the use of a subcontractor, which, according to the model, increases the actual paid price during implementation of the contract versus the tendered price by a projection of 5.6%. The reason can seemingly be the reality that the contractor, when engaging a subcontractor, does not have enough control over the costs and volume of work actually carried out, but this depends to a certain extent on another subject—the subcontractors (Table 32.4).

The model further shows that there are some public contracts with a lower tender price compared to the anticipated price which are more vulnerable to increases in

Table 32.3 Results of a regression model

	Coefficient	Std. error	t-ratio	p-value	
Const	1.15639	0.049805	23.2184	<0.00001	***
Number of bids	−0.00410278	0.00171279	−2.3954	0.01801	**
Tendered/expected price	−0.183007	0.0526566	−3.4755	0.00069	***
Central procurement	−0.279293	0.056416	−4.9506	<0.00001	***
Subcontractor	0.0564156	0.0216754	2.6027	0.01031	**

Model: OLS, using observations 1–148 ($n = 137$), missing or incomplete observations dropped: 11, dependent variable: paid tendered
Source Authors
** 5%
*** 1%

Table 32.4 Characteristics of a regression model

Mean dependent var	0.995787	SD dependent var	0.137350
Sum squared resid	1.972246	SE of regression	0.122234
R-squared	0.231290	Adjusted R-squared	0.207996
$F(4, 132)$	9.929082	p-value(F)	4.69e−07
Log-likelihood	96.10075	Akaike criterion	−182.2015
Schwarz criterion	−167.6016	Hannan–Quinn	−176.2685

Source Authors

the price after the contract has been signed, which may to some extent confirm the hypothesis that in the event of the presence of pressure on having a low bid price (and tendered contracts at a price considerably lower than the price estimated) additional pressures on a price increase exist via additional changes to the agreement; this subsequent rise in prices is relatively low—the model indicates that a decline in the tendered price versus the anticipated price of about 1% results in a subsequent rise in the price after the signing of the contract by an average of 0.2%.

The model also indicates that the contracts awarded centrally account on average for a smaller increase in the bid price, but this factor does not seem to be too strong due to the fact that the sample contained just a few contracts awarded centrally.

In contrast to this, other parameters have not demonstrated statistical significance—the type of authority or procurement procedure, the size of the contract, regional characteristics or the method for evaluating bids; the anticipated value also was not statistically significant—i.e. the parameter indicating the size of the public contract; a price increase is equally likely among smaller and larger public contracts.

32.5   Discussion

Given the very limited number of studies on this topic, we are comparing our results with the studies of Pavel and Sičáková-Beblavá (2012). Like the aforementioned authors, we have managed to identify the relationship between the competitive effect of the response variable regarding the actual paid price/tendered price utilizing the example of the Czech Republic. In our case, this effect reduces the price increase after the contract has been signed. Regarding Pavel and Sičáková-Beblavá (2012), it was the opposite. Explanations can be found in the correlation of the variables dealing with the number of bids and the tendered price/estimated value. Since the variable tendered price/estimated value has a positive effect in our model, the resulting price increases after the contract has been signed. On the contrary, the effect of transparency was proved.

We can consider the role of subcontractors, whose use increases the final price paid, to be statistically significant.

Unlike Pavel and Sičáková-Beblavá (2012), who state that there is a lower increase in the final price paid by the municipalities rather than the state, our model did not demonstrate a statistically significant effect based on the type of authority.

Regarding the main findings, the fact that the low value of the variable tendered price/estimated price leads to an additional increase in the price paid should be considered. We did not encounter the contrary findings (Pavel and Sičáková-Beblavá 2012), regarding the possibility of limiting concluding amendments for extra work, but we did in the pre-contractual stage, via the use of the economic advantage criteria over the criterion of the lowest price. However, this solution may work only in response to a change in approach of the control authorities and the regulator. As notes Nemec et al. (2014), the current administrative framework can be characterized by the over-legislation of words, it should lead to the simplification of legislation and supervisory authorities, and the regulator should take into account not only the procedural and formal point of view, but also achieving efficiency.

32.6 Conclusion

The article analyses the post-contractual conduct on a random sample of public works contracts in the Czech Republic. Due to the difficulty of accessing these data, so far there have been no relevant empirical investigations. The main contribution of the paper can be considered to be the confirmation of the impact of the competitive effect on the final price paid, whereas the impact of the effect of transparency was not found. These results are compared with secondary data for the Slovak Republic. Finally, several recommendations for public policy in the field of public procurement are raised in "Discussion" section.

References

Burguet R, Che YK (2004) Competitive procurement with corruption. RAND J Econ 35(1):50–68
European Commission (2015) Public procurement indicators 2013. DG GROW G4—Innovative and e-Procurement, Brussel
European Union (2013) Identifying and reducing corruption in public procurement in the EU, Brussel
Jurčík R (2012) Discussion about the economic and legal aspects of the transparency and anti-corruption amendment forced from April, 1st, 2012 and Proposals of new EC procurement directives. Ekonomický časopis 60(7):766–768
Ministerstvo pro místní rozvoj (2015) Výroční zpráva o stavu veřejných zakázek za rok 2014, 2015. MMR, Praha
Nemec J, Pavel J, Grega M (2015) Competitiveness in public procurement and its impact on results: evidence from the Czech and Slovak Republic. IRSPM, Birmingham
Nemec J, Šumpíková M, Klazar S, Grega M (2014) Efficiency versus economy in public procurement. In: Löster T, Pavelka T (ed) Conference proceedings: the 8th international days of statistics and economics. 1. vyd. Melandrium, Praha, pp 1054–1063
Ochrana F, Maaytová A (2012) Východiska pro utváření transparentního a nekorupčního systému zadávání veřejných zakázek. Ekonomický časopis 60(7):732–745
Pavel J, Sičáková-Beblavá E (2012) Postkontraktační chování veřejných zadavatelů na Slovensku. Politická ekonomie : teorie modelování, aplikace. 60(5):635–648
Pavel J (2010) Analýza vlivu míry konkurence na cenu rozsáhlých staveb dopravní infrastruktury. Politická ekonomie 58(3):343–356
Pavel J, Sičáková-Beblavá E (2008) Transparentnosť trhu verejného obstarávania. Ekonomický časopis 56(2):168–181
Strand I, Ramada P, Canton E et al (2011) Public procurement in Europe. Cost and effectiveness. European Commission, Brussel

Chapter 33
Reasons for Differences in European Financial Reporting

Marcela Žárová

Abstract Despite the fact that European-listed companies adopted IFRS since 2005 for their consolidated accounts at least, European countries have all retained their national accounting systems. This paper brings comparison of two approaches in financial reporting based on legal systems. Facts that come from the comparison of British approach against Continental European one not necessarily bring a clear view which approach is better. Therefore, there should be considered the question of whether the state or the accountancy profession should be the strongest influence in determining the rules and practice of financial reporting.

Keywords Legal system · Accounting differences · Continental European approach · British approach

33.1 Introduction

Despite the fact that IFRS became mandatory rules for a decade, European countries have all retained their national accounting systems. As accounting systems were developed under different political, economic and social conditions, systems produce differences in financial reporting. Differences in financial reporting are norm (Nobes and Parker 2008). Despite the fact that accountants have to follow a set of rules, no set covers every eventuality and therefore there is a space for professional judgement and consequently for differences too. Reasons why even introduction of IFRS has not eliminated differences in financial reporting are evident.

Firstly, IFRS became mandatory accounting rules for companies listed on European stock exchanges; secondly, IFRS are mostly used for consolidated financial statements only, because majority of EU member states has not enlarged the obligation to use IFRS. Moreover, according to Commission Communication

M. Žárová (✉)
Department of Financial Accounting and Auditing, University of Economics, Prague, Nam. W. Churchilla 4, 130 67 Prague, Czech Republic
e-mail: zarova@vse.cz

© Springer International Publishing AG 2017   355
D. Procházka (ed.), *New Trends in Finance and Accounting*,
Springer Proceedings in Business and Economics,
DOI 10.1007/978-3-319-49559-0_33

and proposal for Directive,[1] more than 75% of European enterprises are defined as micro-undertakings and there are about 23% of small- and medium-sized undertakings. IFRS are used by large undertakings, which represent only around 2%. The EU's Fourth and Seventh Directives remain in force for the consolidated accounts of non-listed companies and for the individual accounts of both listed and non-listed companies, unless a member state avails itself of the option to extend the IFRS to these accounts. The number of undertakings using IFRS was dependent on how the member states implement the option to enlarge the obligation to use IFRS. That was the reason why most European companies remained subject to the directives. Regulation of accounting by EU directives brings options into member states' legislations. Member States may permit or require. They are member state options which a member state may implement as a company option.

The European Commission was investigating for several years conditions under which small and smaller entities run their businesses. Commission continued its efforts to review those Directives. Review of directives recognises the central role played by small- and medium-sized enterprises in the Union economy and aims to improve the overall approach to entrepreneurship and to anchor the "think small first" principle in policy-making from regulation to public service.

Directive 2013/34/EU[2] on the annual financial statements, consolidated financial statements and related reports of certain types of undertakings, amending Directive 2006/43/EC of the European Parliament and of the Council and repealing the EU's Fourth and Seventh Directives was issued in June 2013. This Directive takes into account the Commission's better regulation programme, and the Commission Communication entitled "Smart Regulation in the European Union" (see Footnote 2), which aims at designing and delivering regulation of the highest quality while respecting the principles of subsidiarity and proportionality and ensuring that the administrative burdens are proportionate to the benefits they bring. The Commission Communication entitled "Think Small First—Small Business Act for Europe".

33.2 Literature Review

Accounting research on differences in financial reporting tried to answer on question why differences in financial reporting exist. There is also opinion that differences will not been eliminated in future. Research provided by Choi and Meek

---

[1] Communication from the Commission to the Council, the European Parliament, the European Economic and Social Committee and the Committee of the Regions—"Think Small First"—A "Small Business Act" for Europe {SEC(2008) 2101} {SEC(2008) 2102}; Proposal for a Directive of the European Parliament and of the Council on the annual financial statements, consolidated financial statements and related reports of certain types of undertakings {SEC(2011) 1289 final} {SEC(2011) 1290 final}.

[2] Directive 2013/34/EU of the European Parliament and of the Council of 26 June 2013.

(2008), Radebaugh et al. (2006) brings a list of possible causes of international differences. Other researchers studied whether perceived differences in accounting practices correlate with causal factors (Frank 1979; Doupnik and Salter 1995). Jaafar and McLeay (2007) examine whether accounting differences between companies are mainly influenced by country where company operates, size, sector or number of stock exchange listings.

There is another widespread approach that differences are coming from a list of factors: legal system, corporate financing and tax system. This approach is represented by Nobes and Parker (2012). Nobes identifies legal system as the fundamental cause of international differences. Legal systems fall into two categories. Legal system that relies upon a limited amount of statute law, which is then interpreted by courts and which build up large amounts of case law to supplement the statutes, is known case law or as common law. This law system was formed in England and was extended into countries influenced by England like Ireland, USA (Federal law), Canada, Australia and New Zealand. This law influences commercial law which traditionally does not prescribe detailed rules for accounting which may be in the form of standard or recommendation and accountants themselves establish rules for accounting practice. On the contrary, there are countries, where system of law is based on codified Roman law system like in France, Italy, Germany, Spain, Netherlands and Portugal. Classification of legal systems is discussed by David and Brierley (1985). Nobes (2011) and Flower (2002) described and examined opinion that there exists British approach against Continental one.

33.3 Results and Discussion

As European countries operate within two different legal systems, it is evident that there is not any special European approach to financial reporting. Comparison of characteristics for financial reporting under British and Continental approaches is in the following text. In order to receive a clear picture of differences, a method of comparison was used. Undisputable characteristics have been selected. For the purpose of comparison only, selected characteristics for each individual aspect were considered. As for this simplification, British and Continental European approach are called "simplified British approach" and "simplified Continental European approach". From the perspective of simplification, comparison has been prepared.

1. What is a principle driving force for financial reporting?

    (a) In simplified British approach, the principle driving force is accountancy profession.
    (b) In simplified Continental European approach, the principle driving force is state.

This should be understood that in Britain, the accountancy profession has stronger influence than the State. In Continental Europe, the situation is vice versa.

2. What are primary and secondary objectives of financial statements in Europe?

   (a) Primary objective in simplified British approach is to provide information for capital market.
   (b) Primary objective in simplified Continental European approach is to regulate distributions to stakeholders.
   (c) Secondary objective in simplified British approach is to assist shareholders in controlling the enterprises' management.
   (d) Secondary objective in simplified Continental European approach is to constraints the enterprises's management in interest of stakeholders.

Here under primary objective, stakeholders cover not only the shareholders but all groups with an interest in the enterprise such as creditors, employees and the government. The financial statements enable the division of the enterprise's wealth and income among these groups. If the enterprise's funds are consumed through the payment of excessive dividends to shareholders, this will increase the danger of the enterprise being unable to repay its debts to creditors. Important function of financial statements is to limit the amount that may be distributed as dividend so as to protect the position of creditors. Another partner in the enterprise, the government, is entitled to receive about a part of the profits by way of tax in most European countries. The proper division of the profits between the shareholders and the government is clearly a matter importance to both parties and the financial statements assist for this division.

Under secondary objective, the British give priority to the shareholders while the Continental Europeans to the wider group of stakeholders. The second difference is rather finer. In Britain, the role of the financial statements is to provide information that assists shareholders in controlling management; if the income statement reveals that profits are unsatisfactory, shareholders may decide to dismiss the present management. In Continental approach, financial statements provide information that is useful for control purposes, but in addition the financial statements in themselves act as a constraint on management, preventing it from acting in ways that would be contrary to the interests of particular stakeholders.

3. What should be measured by financial statements?

   (a) The profitability and solvency of the enterprise
   (b) "Efficiency" of the enterprise from the viewpoint of society

Profitability is the prime measure in British approach, but it needs to be backed up by a measure of solvency since it is possible for a profitable enterprise to become bankrupt. Profitability is measured from the viewpoint of the shareholder. In Continental Europe, there is sometimes a wider view taken.

4. Which qualitative characteristic of financial statements is considered as the most important under simplified British approach and Continental European one?

   (a) Relevance
   (b) Reliability

Each approach emphasises on different qualitative characteristics of financial statements. The capital market requires information that is relevant for investment decisions. On the other hand, to regulate distributions to stakeholders, it is absolutely essential that all parties accept that profit and other elements of the accounts are measured in an objective way and priority is given to preventing the management manipulating the figures to the advantage or disadvantage of a particular party. The emphasis of relevance or reliability can lead to misapplication. Financial statements preparers use their freedom to draw up accounts that present an unjustifiably favourable picture that could lead to "creative" accounting.

In accordance with simplified British approach and Continental European approach, there are various consequences of the decision if priority to relevance or to reliability is given. British approach emphasises on substance over form principle, while in some Continental countries accounting systems do not respect priority of economic reality against legal ownership.

In Britain, preparers may use their professional judgement in drawing up the financial statements. In certain circumstances, accountants can ignore the rules in order to present the most relevant information. Accountants on the Continent must follow the rules. This is also an aspect of difference in the relative importance of the accountancy profession and the state under the both approaches.

"True and fair view" is overriding principle in Britain. Financial statements preparers may adapt the general rules to the specific requirements of the individual enterprise, so that, for each enterprise, the most relevant information is provided. Flexibility (adaptation to the needs of the individual enterprise). The specific rule should be disregarded when this is necessary to present a true and fair view of the individual enterprise. On the Continent, such flexibility is not permitted. In Continental approach, the same rules should be applied by everyone.

Alexander and Archer (2000) suggested that it is a myth that there is a coherent group of countries that was using Anglo-Saxon accounting. But as Nobes (2011) argues, much of their discussion concerned not accounting practices but regulatory systems which are indeed different in the UK and the USA.

It would be wrong to portray all Continental European countries as having the same homogeneous approach to financial reporting. The Netherlands, to a lesser extent, and the Scandinavian countries are in some respects more similar to Britain than to the other European countries. The EU's decision that European-listed companies adopted IFRS from 2005 is a further manifestation of a weakening of the Continental approach.

On the other hand, even if diversity of accounting rule-making bodies within the EU has decreased in recent decades (Nobes 2011) there are differences in accounting rules mostly for all other undertakings than large ones.

33.4 Conclusion

Despite the fact that European-listed companies adopted IFRS since 2005 for their consolidated accounts at least, European countries have all retained their national accounting systems. The impact of the EU's efforts at harmonisation through its directives has been very limited. Differences in financial reporting within the EU are still significant. As European countries operate within two different legal systems, it is evident that there is not unified European approach to financial reporting. In financial reporting, two different legal systems are represented by British approach against Continental European one.

This paper brings comparison of two approaches in financial reporting based on legal systems. Based on the results from the comparison, the paper recommends to introduce terms "simplified British approach" and "simplified Continental European approach" instead of terms "British approach" and "Continental European approach". Facts that come from the comparison of British approach against Continental European one not necessarily bring a clear view which approach is better. The EU's decision that European-listed companies adopt IFRS since 2005 is a manifestation of a weakening of the Continental approach. Each approach has some advantages and disadvantages. Therefore, there should be considered the question of whether the state or the accountancy profession should be the strongest influence in determining the rules and practice of financial reporting.

Acknowledgments This paper has been prepared under financial support of research projects IP100040, which author gratefully acknowledges.

References

Alexander D, Archer S (2000) On the myth of "Anglo-Saxon" financial accounting. Int J Acc 35:539–557

Choi F, Meek G (2008) International accounting. Prentice Hall, New Jersey

David R, Brierly J (1985) Major legal systems in the world today. Stevens and Sons, London

Doupnik TS, Salter SB (1995) External environment, culture, and accounting practices: a preliminary test of a general model of international accounting development. Int J Acc 30:189–207

Flower J (2002) Global financial reporting. Palgrave, UK

Frank WG (1979) An empirical analysis of international accounting principles. J Acc Res 17: 593–605

Jaafar A, McLeay S (2007) Country effects and sector effects on the harmonization of accounting policy choice. Abacus 43:156–189

Nobes C (2011) IFRS practices and the persistence of accounting system classification. Abacus 47:267–283. doi:10.1111/j.1467-6281.2011.00341.x

Nobes C, Parker RH (2008) Comparative international accounting, 10th edn. Pearson Education, Harlow

Nobes C, Parker RH (2012) Comparative international accounting, 12th edn. Pearson Education, Harlow

Radebaugh LH, Gray SJ, Black EL (2006) International accounting and multinational enterprises. Wiley, New York, NY

Chapter 34
Forced IFRS Adoption: Direction of the "EU-15 Parents—CEE Subsidiaries" Links

David Procházka

Abstract The paper adopts a view of business research on the positive effects of the parent–subsidiary links on the performance of subsidiaries. The paper focuses on the Central and Eastern European subsidiaries and surmises that a high-quality IFRS adoption in a chain "foreign parent—local subsidiary" may positively affect an undeveloped accounting practice in a transition country, if the number of such subsidiaries is significant. Similarly, if subsidiaries from transition countries, experiencing a lower quality of financial reporting, form a significant share of consolidated groups, the expected increase in accounting quality after the IFRS adoption is endangered. This may hold even for parents domiciled in countries with a traditionally transparent capital markets and well-working financial reporting. The paper aims at identifying the subsidiaries of EU listed companies, with a special focus on the assessment of the links between "EU-15 parents and their CEE subsidiaries".

Keywords IFRS adoption · Forced adopters · Parent–subsidiary links · Central and Eastern Europe

34.1 Introduction

Recent accounting research has documented various economic consequences of worldwide accounting harmonisation through the IFRS adoption (Soderstrom and Sun 2007; Brüggemann et al. 2013), including conditions, under which companies/countries may expect positive net benefits from joining the harmonisation. The results of empirical studies show that both country- and company-specific prerequisites have to be met to benefit from comparable financial statements under harmonised accounting standards. The reporting incentives of companies and the

D. Procházka (✉)
Department of Financial Accounting and Auditing, University of Economics, Prague, Nam. W. Churchilla 4, 130 67 Prague, Czech Republic
e-mail: prochazd@vse.cz

© Springer International Publishing AG 2017
D. Procházka (ed.), *New Trends in Finance and Accounting*,
Springer Proceedings in Business and Economics,
DOI 10.1007/978-3-319-49559-0_34

functioning enforcement regime are crucial factors of the success. Because of institutional deficiencies, the IFRS adoption faces many obstacles to improve the quality of financial reporting in majority of transition countries of the Central and Eastern European region.

As the IFRS are developed primarily to satisfy the informational needs of investors in capital markets, the accounting research addresses mainly the impact of IFRS adoption on listed companies. However, other types of entities cope with the usage of IFRS, but the data (un)availability is a limiting factor for research. The most prominent group of IFRS adopters are subsidiaries of parent companies reporting under IFRS regime. As these subsidiaries are not usually listed, the IFRS figures are available only if their local regulatory framework allows them to adopt the IFRS voluntarily in statutory accounts and they do that. There is some limited research in this area, e.g. Guerreiro et al. (2012). Following the model of Oliver (1991), the reaction of a subsidiary to the parent's commands may range from a passive acceptation to an active resistance. A successful implementation of the group's policies boosts the performance of a subsidiary (Kostova and Roth 2002) and promotes thus economic development of emerging or transition countries (Albu et al. 2014).

The paper adopts this view and surmises that a high-quality IFRS adoption in a chain "foreign parent—local subsidiary" may positively affect a country's accounting practice, if the number of such subsidiaries is significant. Similarly, if subsidiaries from transition countries (with a low quality of financial reporting) form a significant share of consolidated groups, the expected increase in accounting quality after the IFRS adoption is endangered. This may hold even for parents domiciled in countries with traditionally transparent capital markets and well-working financial reporting. As the first step of the research, the paper aims at identifying the subsidiaries of EU listed companies, with a special focus on the assessment of the links between "the EU-15 parents and their CEE subsidiaries".

The paper is organised as follows. After the introduction, literature review is finalised. Chapter 3 presents data and discusses the results. Final chapter concludes the exposition, outlines its limitations, and suggests the way of future research in the area.

34.2   Literature Review

Accounting research evidences mixed results on the economic consequences of the IFRS adoption around the world. Despite the general goal of promoting smoothly operating capital markets, many listed companies decided to go private after the announcement of planned mandatory IFRS adoption. There are two possible explanations of delisting—expected higher pressure on accounting and disclosure quality induced by the IFRS adoption or expected higher costs than benefits from the changeover (Christensen 2012). The first factor refers to the reporting incentives of companies to provide users with useful information for decision-making. From a global perspective, the delisting of companies not possessing enough incentives can be regarded positively. However, the latter reason for going private may impair functioning of capital markets. Whatever reason is behind the decision, there is some evidence that issuers had left stock exchanges following the announcement of mandatory IFRS adoption (Vulcheva 2011), resulting thus in a significant decrease in the number of listed companies in particular countries (Procházka and Pelák 2015a).

Despite shrinkage in number of issuers, an increase in accounting quality following the IFRS adoption is not automatic. Empirical studies stress once again the importance of individual reporting incentives and the quality of enforcement (Christensen et al. 2015; Jeanjean and Stolowy 2008; Houqe et al. 2012; Glaum et al. 2013). Studies usually conclude that the impact of IFRS adoption on accounting quality is questionable, especially in countries with undeveloped institutions and insufficient quality of reporting environment. This is also the case of the new EU members from the Central and Eastern Europe (CEE). As listed companies in the region are owned predominantly by domestic investors as a result of privatisation (Estrin et al. 2009), the possibilities of international transfer of best practices (Gray et al. 1995) are restricted. Furthermore, informing through private channels (Holland 1998) seems to play a more important role than public transparency, which negatively impacts the accounting quality (Florou and Kosi 2015).

A not improved quality of financial reporting together with a massive delisting (except for Poland) may lead to a conclusion that the IFRS adoption has not brought any significant benefits for the CEE countries. However, the assertion on low benefits may be relevant for capital markets only. Although stock exchanges do not play an important role in the CEE economies, the adoption of IFRS can have substantial consequences, but on another group of companies than listed. As the economic development of these countries depends crucially on foreign direct investments flows, the biggest group of IFRS adopters are subsidiaries of foreign companies, which consolidate the group's accounts in compliance with the IFRS. The IFRS adoption by subsidiaries is surrounded by specific effects compared to the mandatory adoption by listed companies and the link "parent-subsidiary" creates a unique background. In particular, the subsidiary (a) is a forced IFRS adopter by the parent's command (without possibility to avoid this duty) and (b) may benefit from the transfers of resources, knowledge, technology, staff, organisational structures (Birkinshaw and Hood 1998; Delios and Beamish 2001; Fang et al. 2007; Gaur et al. 2007; Fang et al. 2010). The transfers help in mitigating of defects in economic, legal, social institutions of transition countries (Fey and Björkman 2001; Luo 2003).

To reveal the economic consequence of IFRS adoption by forced adopters, the population of relevant subsidiaries has to be identified. This will be made in the remainder of the paper.

34.3   Data, Results, and Discussion

To assess the paper's goal, we employ data from the Amadeus Bureau Van Dijk database, which contains comprehensive information on around 21 million companies across Europe with principal focus on private companies. Except for financial information, Amadeus encompasses also information on ownership and subsidiaries. Furthermore, the database shows the accounting standards used for the preparation of financial statements.

Due to the nature of data and selection criteria in the Amadeus database, the top-down approach is a quicker method for the determination of subsidiaries under control of a parent reporting under IFRS regime. However, as data on the reporting regime are not always consistent (the reporting system is displayed for consolidated financial statements in some instances, in other cases for stand-alone financial statements), the sample is restricted only to the EU listed companies, which shall pursuant the Article 4 of the Regulation (EC) 1606/2002 prepare their consolidated accounts in conformity with the international accounting standards. This restriction sets the minimum number of entities preparing the IFRS consolidated statements. The final sample consists of 7851 EU listed companies. Table 34.1 summarises the sample selection.

For each parent company, following data are extracted:

- country code;
- number of all subsidiaries;
- country code for each subsidiary (Table 34.2).

In total, 7851 EU public companies have control over 285,565 subsidiaries all around the world, out of which 128,878 have jurisdiction in EU-28 countries. Furthermore, 15,529 of subsidiaries are located in new member countries from the CEE region. As absolute numbers do not enable identifying the national-specific patterns, averages per one listed company are calculated as well as relative shares for each country; the results are presented in Table 34.3.

Irish companies build up the most complicated structures, as parents domiciled in this country control 112 subsidiaries on average. A quite considerable gap arises between Ireland and the second group of companies from the Netherlands, Austria, France, Germany, or Luxembourg—these having over 60 subsidiaries per one listed company. On the other hand, Romania experiences the simplest composition of economic groups, as a Romanian listed company executes control over less than

Table 34.1 Sample composition

Criterion	No. of companies
All active companies	19,855,554
Listed companies	12,410
EU 28 region	7851

Source Amadeus

Table 34.2 Distribution of subsidiaries of the EU listed companies: absolute

Country	No of listed companies	Subsidiaries total	Subsidiaries in the EU	Subsidiaries in the CEE region
Austria (AT)	79	5287	2961	584
Belgium (BE)	145	6246	2954	211
Bulgaria (BG)	320	1395	1114	1105
Cyprus (CY)	101	661	361	46
Czech Rep. (CZ)	17	239	178	175
Germany (DE)	725	45,423	24,401	1973
Denmark (DK)	134	4210	1815	263
Estonia (EE)	16	242	172	137
Spain (ES)	392	16,854	7764	398
Finland (FI)	134	6583	3213	402
France (FR)	784	49,401	17,851	921
G. Britain (GB)	1571	84,186	35,419	833
Greece (GR)	207	2687	1926	141
Croatia (HR)	133	800	490	459
Hungary (HU)	39	639	421	377
Ireland (IE)	74	8286	2405	156
Italy (IT)	269	10,355	5864	251
Lithuania (LT)	29	397	355	350
Luxembourg (LU)	44	2826	1039	351
Latvia (LV)	28	134	85	81
Malta (MT)	19	161	126	4
Netherlands (NL)	159	11,538	4486	348
Poland (PL)	851	6660	5128	4476
Portugal (PT)	53	2481	1453	154
Romania (RO)	813	647	518	508
Sweden (SE)	581	16,489	5898	384
Slovenia (SI)	44	545	315	290
Slovakia (SK)	90	193	166	151
Totals	7851	285,565	128,878	15,529

Source Own calculations based on data from Amadeus

one subsidiary on average. Uncomplicated structures (with less than 10 subsidiaries per a parent) are also typical in Slovakia, Bulgaria, Latvia, Croatia, Cyprus, Poland, Malta, i.e. for the public companies under the jurisdiction of the new EU countries. In terms of geographical dispersion, the highest number of EU-placed subsidiaries is achieved by Austrian parents, followed by German and Irish listed companies. A big group of countries (exclusively from "old EU-members") have between 20 and 30 subsidiaries per a parent.

Taking into account the relative shares, we get although opposite results. Except for Slovenia (but only just), the listed companies from the new EU countries have more than 60% of subsidiaries located within the EU. This limit is reached in case of the old EU members by Greece only. The lowest relative share can be identified

Table 34.3 Distribution of subsidiaries of the EU listed companies: averages and relative shares

Totals	Total (average per company)	EU (average per company)	CEE (average per company)	EU (share on total) (%)	CEE (share on total) (%)
AT	66.9	37.5	7.4	56.0	11.0
BE	43.1	20.4	1.5	47.3	3.4
BG	4.4	3.5	3.5	79.9	79.2
CY	6.5	3.6	0.5	54.6	7.0
CZ	14.1	10.5	10.3	74.5	73.2
DE	62.7	33.7	2.7	53.7	4.3
DK	31.4	13.5	2.0	43.1	6.2
EE	15.1	10.8	8.6	71.1	56.6
ES	43.0	19.8	1.0	46.1	2.4
FI	49.1	24.0	3.0	48.8	6.1
FR	63.0	22.8	1.2	36.1	1.9
GB	53.6	22.5	0.5	42.1	1.0
GR	13.0	9.3	0.7	71.7	5.2
HR	6.0	3.7	3.5	61.3	57.4
HU	16.4	10.8	9.7	65.9	59.0
IE	112.0	32.5	2.1	29.0	1.9
IT	38.5	21.8	0.9	56.6	2.4
LT	13.7	12.2	12.1	89.4	88.2
LU	64.2	23.6	8.0	36.8	12.4
LV	4.8	3.0	2.9	63.4	60.4
MT	8.5	6.6	0.2	78.3	2.5
NL	72.6	28.2	2.2	38.9	3.0
PL	7.8	6.0	5.3	77.0	67.2
PT	46.8	27.4	2.9	58.6	6.2
RO	0.8	0.6	0.6	80.1	78.5
SE	28.4	10.2	0.7	35.8	2.3
SI	12.4	7.2	6.6	57.8	53.2
SK	2.1	1.8	1.7	86.0	78.2
Totals	36.4	16.4	2.0	45.1	5.4

Source Own calculations based on data from Table 34.2

for Ireland, confirming thus a previous assertion on complicated structures of Irish groups (motivated, for example, by tax purposes, for which subsidiaries are set up outside the EU area).

Table 34.4 presents a further breakdown of geographical distribution of subsidiaries across the CEE countries. The particular cells capture an average number of subsidiaries per one listed company from a given country. The row and the column labelled "Total" express the absolute number of subsidiaries. The most subsidiaries are located in Poland, followed by the Czech Republic, Bulgaria,

Table 34.4 Geographical location of subsidiaries of the EU listed companies

Country	BG	CZ	EE	HR	HU	LT
AT	0.405	1.354	0.013	0.468	1.835	0.051
BE	0.090	0.310	0.014	0.021	0.207	0.028
BG	3.416	0.003	0.000	0.000	0.003	0.000
CY	0.040	0.040	0.030	0.020	0.040	0.010
CZ	0.471	6.765	0.000	0.000	0.118	0.000
DE	0.109	0.581	0.025	0.097	0.477	0.036
DK	0.075	0.328	0.149	0.052	0.134	0.157
EE	0.375	0.000	6.125	0.000	0.000	0.813
ES	0.071	0.184	0.008	0.033	0.153	0.003
FI	0.052	0.366	0.679	0.052	0.216	0.403
FR	0.055	0.235	0.015	0.026	0.166	0.020
GB	0.022	0.086	0.015	0.015	0.081	0.011
GR	0.295	0.019	0.000	0.000	0.024	0.000
HR	0.030	0.008	0.000	3.158	0.038	0.000
HU	0.103	0.154	0.000	0.359	7.897	0.000
IE	0.122	0.324	0.014	0.041	0.284	0.027
IT	0.037	0.123	0.007	0.033	0.112	0.000
LT	0.000	0.000	1.552	0.000	0.000	9.862
LU	0.045	4.545	0.000	0.205	1.591	0.045
LV	0.000	0.000	0.071	0.000	0.000	0.000
MT	0.000	0.053	0.000	0.053	0.053	0.000
NL	0.082	0.264	0.044	0.019	0.283	0.031
PL	0.016	0.058	0.002	0.009	0.021	0.019
PT	0.057	0.113	0.000	0.000	0.434	0.000
RO	0.002	0.000	0.000	0.000	0.002	0.000
SE	0.036	0.107	0.067	0.022	0.072	0.036
SI	0.114	0.136	0.000	0.568	0.068	0.023
SK	0.000	0.200	0.000	0.000	0.078	0.000
Total	1506	1629	369	687	1473	491
Foreign (%)	27	93	73	39	79	42
Index-abs	92	38	116	118	51	114
Index-rel	109	46	83	119	49	115
Country	LV	PL	RO	SI	SK	Total
AT	0.013	1.342	0.785	0.405	0.722	584
BE	0.007	0.497	0.179	0.014	0.090	211
BG	0.003	0.003	0.019	0.003	0.003	1,105
CY	0.020	0.040	0.119	0.010	0.089	46
CZ	0.000	1.353	0.471	0.000	1.118	175
DE	0.029	0.852	0.218	0.092	0.206	1,973
DK	0.112	0.687	0.127	0.037	0.104	263
EE	0.813	0.250	0.000	0.000	0.188	137
ES	0.003	0.327	0.163	0.008	0.064	398
FI	0.291	0.649	0.090	0.075	0.127	402
FR	0.017	0.375	0.145	0.033	0.088	921

(continued)

Table 34.4 (continued)

Country	LV	PL	RO	SI	SK	Total
GB	0.009	0.150	0.085	0.011	0.045	833
GR	0.000	0.077	0.261	0.005	0.000	141
HR	0.000	0.015	0.023	0.173	0.008	459
HU	0.000	0.231	0.462	0.077	0.385	377
IE	0.027	0.797	0.311	0.041	0.122	156
IT	0.004	0.301	0.164	0.074	0.078	251
LT	0.483	0.172	0.000	0.000	0.000	350
LU	0.023	0.750	0.295	0.000	0.477	351
LV	2.786	0.000	0.000	0.000	0.036	81
MT	0.053	0.000	0.000	0.000	0.000	4
NL	0.031	1.044	0.182	0.019	0.189	348
PL	0.006	5.065	0.038	0.004	0.022	4,476
PT	0.000	1.415	0.792	0.000	0.094	154
RO	0.000	0.002	0.617	0.000	0.000	508
SE	0.067	0.167	0.034	0.015	0.036	384
SI	0.023	0.091	0.091	5.432	0.045	290
SK	0.000	0.033	0.000	0.000	1.367	151
Total	268	6527	1396	468	715	15,529
Foreign (%)	71	34	64	49	83	51
Index-abs	128	22	64	126	82	xxx
Index-rel	106	90	114	82	56	xxx

Source Own calculations based on data from Amadeus

Hungary, and Romania. The domestic control (i.e. both parent and subsidiary from the same country) is usually the most frequent type of the link in each country, including the most numerous observations in the case of Poland and Bulgaria. Five CEE countries have over 50% share of control over the subsidiaries in the sample by domestic listed companies. On the other hand, the Czech Republic, Hungary, and Slovakia experience a different pattern of ownership, as German listed companies have command over the biggest number of subsidiaries in given countries. These countries also evidence the lowest share of domestic control (or the highest share of foreign control, respectively).

Regarding average figures, all CEE countries display the biggest number of home subsidiaries per one domestic listed company, except for Romania (where Austrian and Portuguese parents are more influential). If horizontally read, Table 34.4 reveals that Poland, the Czech Republic, and Hungary are the most attractive countries from the CEE region for the companies from EU-15, when deciding where to place a subsidiary. This can be shown by an index measuring a rank among the CEE countries based on an average number of subsidiaries per parent from the EU-15, when individual ranks for each pair "EU-15 parent—CEE subsidiary" are aggregated. Poland reaches a value of the Index = 22 (11 times first place, one time second place, and three times third position); the Czech Republic has the index of 38. On the other side, the least favourable country is Latvia (having

Index = 138). As this approach favours big "receiving" countries, the index is also recalculated for the average number of subsidiaries per parent from the EU-15 and per one million inhabitants from the CEE. Based on this alternative measure, the most attractive CEE country for incoming business investments is the Czech Republic, with Hungary being the second by a margin and Slovakia the third. The biggest CEE country Poland drops down to the sixth place, if the relative share is preferred. The most subsidiaries (in absolute terms—the row "Total") are located in Poland, followed by the Czech Republic, Bulgaria, Hungary, and Romania. The domestic control (i.e. both parent and subsidiary from the same country) is usually the most frequent type of the link in each country, including the most numerous observations in the case of Poland and Bulgaria. Five CEE countries have over 50% share of control over the subsidiaries in the sample by domestic listed companies. On the other hand, the Czech Republic, Hungary, and Slovakia experience a different pattern of ownership, as German listed companies have command over the biggest number of subsidiaries in given countries. These countries also evidence the lowest share of domestic control (or the highest share of foreign control, respectively).

34.4 Conclusion

The paper presents summary statistics on the subsidiaries of the EU listed companies, with a special focus on the CEE region. As all EU listed companies are mandatory adopters of IFRS for the preparation of consolidated financial statements, the parents require their subsidiaries to provide with the IFRS figures for the consolidation purposes as well as for the managing the group. The subsidiaries cannot avoid the command to adopt the IFRS. Furthermore, the subsidiaries in many countries are prohibited by local law to adopt the IFRS voluntarily in their statutory accounting. We denote this specific hidden IFRS adoption as forced to distinguish it from both mandatory and voluntary adoption. A distinct denotation is used to highlight a crucial factor that the forced IFRS adopters face to a completely different mix of regulatory framework, institutional environment, and degree of freedom to decide, whether to adopt the IFRS.

Using data on all listed EU companies from Amadeus Bureau Van Dijk database, we find out that about 12% of all EU-based subsidiaries of the EU listed companies are located in the CEE region (with the leading Poland, followed by the Czech Republic, Bulgaria, Hungary, and Romania). The domestic control is usually the most frequent type of the link in each CEE country. On average, foreign companies have control over 51% of domestic companies with the highest share in the case of the Czech Republic, Slovakia, and Hungary. Finally, the Poland, Czech Republic, and Hungary are the most attractive countries from the CEE region for the companies from EU-15, when deciding where to place a subsidiary. This can be shown by an index measuring a rank among the CEE countries based on an average number of subsidiaries per parent from the EU-15.

The relevance of the paper's findings is subject to several limits, which are simultaneously the suggestions for future research. Firstly, the paper focuses on subsidiaries of listed companies only. However, many EU countries require/allow other companies to employ the IFRS in the preparation of consolidated statements. The exact identification of all relevant parent companies reporting under IFRS regime requires a detailed analysis of regulatory framework, as noted by Nobes (2010). A possible practical approach is suggested by Procházka and Pelák (2015b). Secondly, the paper investigates the number of subsidiaries, but not their economic importance in the group. The additional analysis should take into account the share of subsidiaries' revenue, total assets, gross profit, or net profit on the consolidated figures of the group. Finally, these individualised relative shares may be used as an explanatory variable in the models attempting to assess the impact of IFRS adoption on accounting quality. The suggested approach might be helpful in removing the source of contradicting results on this research question as evidenced by Barth et al. (2008) compared to Callao and Jarne (2010) or Ahmed et al. (2013).

Acknowledgments This paper has been prepared within the research project "Economic Impacts of the IFRS Adoption in Selected Transition Countries" (supported by the Czech Science Foundation, No. 15-01280S).

References

Ahmed AS, Neel M, Wang D (2013) Does mandatory adoption of IFRS improve accounting quality? Preliminary evidence. Contemp Acc Res 30:1344–1372

Albu N, Lupu I, Sandu R (2014) Multinationals as vectors of corporate governance improvement in emerging economies in Eastern Europe: a case study. In: Boubaker S, Nguyen DK (eds) Corporate governance in emerging markets. Springer, Berlin, pp 331–349

Barth ME, Landsman WR, Lang MH (2008) International accounting standards and accounting quality. J Acc Res 46:467–498. doi:10.1111/j.1475-679X.2008.00287.x

Birkinshaw J, Hood N (1998) Multinational subsidiary evolution: capability and charter change in foreign-owned subsidiary companies. Acad Manag Rev 23:773–795. doi:10.5465/AMR.1998. 1255638

Brüggemann U, Hitz J-M, Sellhorn T (2013) Intended and unintended consequences of mandatory IFRS adoption: a review of extant evidence and suggestions for future research. Eur Acc Rev 22:1–37. doi:10.1080/09638180.2012.718487

Callao S, Jarne JI (2010) Have IFRS affected earnings management in the European union? Acc Eur 7:159–189

Christensen HB (2012) Why do firms rarely adopt IFRS voluntarily? Academics find significant benefits and the costs appear to be low. Rev Acc Stud 17:518–525. doi:10.1007/s11142-012-9202-y

Christensen HB, Lee E, Walker M, Zeng C (2015) Incentives or standards: what determines accounting quality changes around IFRS adoption? Euro Account Rev 24:31–61. doi:10.1080/09638180.2015.1009144

Delios A, Beamish PW (2001) Survival and profitability: the roles of experience and intangible assets in foreign subsidiary performance. Acad Manag J 44:1028–1038. doi:10.2307/3069446

Estrin S, Hanousek J, Kočenda E, Svejnar J (2009) The effects of privatization and ownership in transition economies. J Econ Lit 47:699–728. doi:10.1257/jel.47.3.699

Fang Y, Jiang G-LF, Makino S, Beamish PW (2010) Multinational firm knowledge, use of expatriates, and foreign subsidiary performance. J Manag Stud 47:27–54. doi:10.1111/j.1467-6486.2009.00850.x

Fang Y, Wade M, Delios A, Beamish PW (2007) International diversification, subsidiary performance, and the mobility of knowledge resources. Strateg Manag J 28:1053–1064. doi:10.1002/smj.619

Fey CF, Björkman I (2001) The effect of human resource management practices on MNC subsidiary performance in Russia. J Int Bus Stud 32:59–75. doi:10.1057/palgrave.jibs.8490938

Florou A, Kosi U (2015) Does mandatory IFRS adoption facilitate debt financing? Rev Account Stud 20:1407–1456. doi:10.1007/s11142-015-9325-z

Gaur AS, Delios A, Singh K (2007) Institutional environments, staffing strategies, and subsidiary performance. J Manag 33:611–636. doi:10.1177/0149206307302551

Glaum M, Schmidt P, Street DL, Vogel S (2013) Compliance with IFRS 3- and IAS 36-required disclosures across 17 European countries: company- and country-level determinants. Acc Bus Res 43:163–204

Gray SJ, Meek GK, Roberts CB (1995) International capital market pressures and voluntary annual report disclosures by US and UK multinationals. J Int Financ Manag Acc 6:43–68

Guerreiro MS, Rodrigues LL, Craig R (2012) Voluntary adoption of international financial reporting standards by large unlisted companies in Portugal—institutional logics and strategic responses. Acc Organ Soc 37:482–499. doi:10.1016/j.aos.2012.05.003

Holland JB (1998) Private disclosure and financial reporting. Acc Bus Res 28:255–269. doi:10.1080/00014788.1998.9728914

Houqe MN, van Zijl T, Dunstan K, Karim AKMW (2012) The effect of IFRS adoption and investor protection on earnings quality around the world. Int J Acc 47:333–355

Jeanjean T, Stolowy H (2008) Do accounting standards matter? An exploratory analysis of earnings management before and after IFRS adoption. J Account Public Policy 27:480–494

Kostova T, Roth K (2002) Adoption of an organizational practice by subsidiaries of multinational corporations: institutional and relational effects. Acad Manag J 45:215–233. doi:10.2307/3069293

Luo Y (2003) Market-seeking MNEs in an emerging market: how parent subsidiary links shape overseas success. J Int Bus Stud 34:290–309

Nobes C (2010) On researching into the use of IFRS by private entities in Europe. Acc Eur 7:213–226. doi:10.1080/17449480.2010.511889

Oliver C (1991) Strategic responses to institutional processes. Acad Manag Rev 16:145–179. doi:10.5465/AMR.1991.4279002

Procházka D, Pelák J (2015a) The development of capital markets of new EU countries in the IFRS Era. Procedia Econ Finance 25:116–126. doi:10.1016/S2212-5671(15)00720-0

Procházka D, Pelák J (2015b) How to measure the extent of accounting harmonisation? A case for the IFRS adoption index. In: Kapunek S (ed) 18th annual international conference, enterprise and competitive environment. Mendel University, Brno, pp 737–746

Soderstrom NS, Sun KJ (2007) IFRS adoption and accounting quality: a review. Eur Account Rev 16:675–702. doi:10.1080/09638180701706732

Vulcheva MI (2011) International accounting standardization across countries with unequal enforcement-questionable benefits at a high price? Thesis, Emory University, Atlanta

Chapter 35
The IFRS Adoption by BRICS Countries: A Comparative Analysis

Tatiana Dolgikh

Abstract This article presents the modern trends of IFRS adoption by some of BRICS countries: Russia, India, and Brazil. The paper is focused on the difficult convergence process and modern trends of accounting development of these countries. At modern stage, each of these countries is in a position of adaption of IFRS in accounting practices. This process is a consequence of the users' demand of high-quality financial statements comparable across all entities. It is observing the changes in all areas of economic activities, as a result of the world globalization process. However, it should be noted that the conceptual basis of IFRS and the accounting methodology are fundamentally different from Russian, Brazilian and Indian systems of accounting and financial reporting. The article introduces recommendations and measures, how to improve the convergence of financial reporting of these three BRICS countries with IFRS.

Keywords IFRS adoption · Brazil · India · Russia

35.1 Introduction

In the modern market economy, accounting is considered to be the language of business, and data of the financial reporting are the basis for the most important managerial decisions. Effective construction of accounting and financial reporting systems ensures transparency and openness of an organization, which increases its investment attractiveness and competitive position, reduces the cost of borrowed funds, and improves the country's financial market condition. For example, Lambert et al. (2007) studied in their article question of importance of accounting information and its influence on the cost of capital. They proved mathematically that increasing

T. Dolgikh (✉)
Department of Financial Accounting and Auditing,
University of Economics, Prague,
Nam. W. Churchilla 4, 130 67 Prague, Czech Republic
e-mail: midday88@gmail.com

© Springer International Publishing AG 2017   373
D. Procházka (ed.), *New Trends in Finance and Accounting*,
Springer Proceedings in Business and Economics,
DOI 10.1007/978-3-319-49559-0_35

quality of accounting reduces the cost of capital for each firm in the economy. A modern process of accounting harmonization allows countries with different economic, political, and judicial systems to find a common language in the different areas of economic relations. The cooperation of the BRICS group is the example.

Fifteen years ago, Jim O'Neill, the Goldman Sachs economist, suggested the acronym "BRIC countries," which allowed grouping of the countries with the different levels of economic development, such as Brazil, Russia, India, and China into a common economic system. O'Neill predicted that the size of these economies will exceed the size of the six largest developed economies by 2040. He also suggested that the main potential of world economic growth is connected to the largest emerging markets. The BRIC countries have since gone on to meet and seek out opportunities for cooperation in trade, investment, infrastructure development, and other areas. China invited South Africa to join the group of BRIC nations in December, 2010, and hosted the third annual BRIC Summit in April, 2011. Thus, the BRICS group was transformed from the theoretical term into the real union.

The objective of this article is to analyze different issues connected to the modern trends of accounting and financial reporting development in three of five BRICS member states mentioned above: Russia, India, and Brazil. It will help to draw conclusions about the level of accounting development in each country and also to evaluate the possibilities of economic communication between them. Such methods as information searching for a certain subject, classification, analysis, synthesis of observation and also comparing were used in this article.

The paper is organized as follows. After the introduction, literature review is finalized. Chapter 3 presents data and discusses the results. Final chapter concludes the exposition, outlines its limitations, and suggests the way of future research in the area.

The article is divided into four sections. The introduction outlines the paper's goal, and literature review describes basic literature. Section 35.3 provides data, discusses the results, and concludes the final section.

35.2 Literature Review

This article is based on the analyses of different papers, books, and journals. According to Sokolov (2007), evolution of Russian accounting is a complicated and complex process that needs to be comprehensively studied. Kozhevnikova (2015) described the stages of modern accounting development in Russia, process of convergence of Russian Accounting Standards (hereinafter RAS) and International Financial Reporting Standards (hereinafter IFRS) in her monography. She also specified differences between the standards in detail. Evolution of modern accounting in Brazil is a continuous process, which is studied by Szuster (2015) in his article. Steinbach and Tang (2014) studied the question of completed IFRS convergence in Brazil and described this process in their article. The question of modern accounting in India, its principles, differences between Indian Accounting

Standards and IFRS, and also the possibility of their full convergence is outlined in CMC Senior Theses Paper of Pal (2015). Borker (2012) in his article studied questions of different accounting systems of BRIC states and also their cultural differences. Thus, the modern development of accounting is a very popular topic for scientific articles in the contemporary world.

Also, there are many empirical studies focusing on motivations and purposes of IFRS adoption in different countries. Special attention in such articles is given to emerging economies. Hope et al. (2006) describe positive and negative aspects of the IFRS adoption and suggest, on the basis of empirical research, that "countries with weaker investor protection mechanisms are more likely to adopt IFRS." Also, the research shows that "IFRS represent a vehicle through which countries can improve investor protection and make their capital markets more Accessible to foreign investors." Ramanna and Sletten (2014) show in their research that "countries with low bargaining power are more susceptible to adopting IFRS because others are doing so, consistent with such countries being less distinctive in their approach to IFRS harmonization." Also they assumed that "low-bargaining-power countries (countries with lower GDP), also tend to have weak market institutions, implying IFRS adoption in these countries is less likely to be effective." Alon and Dwyer (2014) draw conclusions that "countries with greater resource dependency, as evidenced by weak governance structures and weak economies, were the early adopters who were more likely to require the use of IFRS." Also they mentioned that "required adoption may not always be accompanied by an appropriately supportive infrastructure; thus, there are implications not only for adoption of IFRS, but also for the diffusion of other transnational regulation that influences global business environment."

35.3   Data, Results, and Discussion

Due to the fact that this article describes contemporary aspects of modern accounting in three of five BRICS states, the section will introduce several economic characteristics of these three BRICS states (Brazil, India, and Russia). The data will focus on the development of basic economic indicators since 2001.

As Table 35.1 shows, Brazil, India, and Russia are large countries with a high level of population. For example, the total number of the population of these countries by the end of 2014 is approximately 1.6 billion people. The level of GDP in the countries is constantly growing (except GDP of Russia, which has fallen almost 4% in 2015), and they are among the top ten on the list of countries by absolute GDP. However, the level of GDP per capita of the countries presented in this article is quite low, and they cannot compete on the global scale. Inflation in all three countries was approximately on the same level of 6–8% in 2014. The level of foreign direct investment in the economies of these three states is fairly high, although it reaches a small percentage of GDP in each country. The largest number of listed domestic companies is registered in India—5541 companies by the end of

Table 35.1 Development indicators

Indicator	Years			
	2001	2005	2010	2014
Brazil				
Population, total (millions)	178.4	188.5	198.6	206.1
GDP at market prices (millions of US dollars)	559,611.9	892,103.2	2,209,433.3	2,346,076.3
GDP per capita (US dollars)	3136.5	4733.2	11,124.2	11,384.4
Inflation, consumer prices (annual %)	6.8	6.9	5.0	6.3
Foreign direct investment, net inflows (BoP, millions of US dollars)	22,457.3	15,460.0	53,344.6	96,895.2
Foreign direct investment, net inflows (% of GDP)	4.0	1.7	2.4	4.1
Listed domestic companies, total	426	342	373	351
Market capitalization of listed domestic companies (millions of US dollars)	186,237.6	474,646.9	1,545,565.7	843,894.2
Market capitalization of listed domestic companies (% of GDP)	33.3	53.2	70.0	36.0
India				
Population, total (millions)	1071.9	1144.3	1231.0	1295.3
GDP at market prices (millions of US dollars)	493,954.2	834,214.7	1,708,458.9	2,048,517.4
GDP per capita (US dollars)	460.8	729.0	1387.9	1581.5
Inflation, consumer prices (annual %)	3.7	4.2	12.0	6.4
Foreign direct investment, net inflows (BoP, millions of US dollars)	5471.9	7269.4	27,396.9	33,871.4
Foreign direct investment, net inflows (% of GDP)	1.1	0.9	1.6	1.7
Listed domestic companies, total	5795	4763	5034	5541
Market capitalization of listed domestic companies (millions of US dollars)	–	553,073.7	1,613,829.5	1,558,299.7
Market capitalization of listed domestic companies (% of GDP)	–	66.3	95.5	76.1
Russia				
Population, total (millions)	146.0	143.5	142.8	143.8
GDP at market prices (millions of US dollars)	306,602.7	764,017.1	1,524,917.5	1,860,597.9
GDP per capita (US dollars)	2100.4	5323.5	10,675.0	12,736.0
Inflation, consumer prices (annual %)	21.5	12.7	6.9	7.8
Foreign direct investment, net inflows (BoP, millions of US dollars)	2748.3	15,508.1	43,167.8	22,890.5
Foreign direct investment, net inflows (% of GDP)	0.9	2.0	2.8	1.2
Listed domestic companies, total	–	253	249	254
Market capitalization of listed domestic companies (millions of US dollars)	–	–	954,573.4	385,926.7
Market capitalization of listed domestic companies (% of GDP)	–	–	62.6	20.7

Source www.worldbank.org

2014, although their market capitalization is low. The crucial economic indicators of those countries are volatile and not always satisfying comparing to developed countries, but nevertheless, these countries play a big role in the world economy.

35.3.1   Modern Accounting in Russia

The main regulator of the accounting system in Russia is the state. Methodology of accounting system is issued by Russian government with the help of the Ministry of Finance and the Central Bank of the Russian Federation. It means that accounting system in Russia is under strict control of legislature. The modern stage of Russian accounting development began in 1991 in connection with the transition to the market economy. In the early years of reforming, the Ministry of Finance implemented the continental model of accounting. During this period, tax base for corporate income tax was calculated through a series of adjustments to the accounting base. Changes to the initially chosen policy were made by the tax code of Russia approved in 1998, that is, when the transition to the Anglo-American accounting model began. This policy has been secured by the adoption of tax accounting in 2001. So, the current legislation requires at least two types of accounting—financial accounting and tax accounting, each of them has its own purpose.

In the mid-1990s, International Financial Reporting Standards (hereinafter IFRS) begin to play an important role in the world economy. International Organization of Securities Commissions (IOSCO) encourages the use of IFRS for international listing. Basel Committee on Banking Supervision has also actively supported the introduction of these standards (Getman 2009). In this connection, the Russian government chose a policy of convergence of Russian Accounting Standards (hereinafter RAS) and IFRS in 1998. The first step to implement this policy was the Resolution of the Government of Russia in March 1998, which claimed that "the purpose of the accounting system reform was to adjust the national accounting system to the requirements of market economy and IFRS." The next step in the reforming was the adoption of the "Concept of development of accounting and reporting in the Russian Federation in the medium term," which was approved by the Ministry of Finance in July 2004. The text of the concept included the description of stages of reforming for the period from 2004 to 2010. The main points of convergence had primarily dealt with the shift of consolidated financial statements of business entities to the IFRS and the possibility of preparation and presentation of consolidated financial statements in accordance with IFRS. The crucial point of this process was the adoption of the Federal Law No 208-FZ "On Joint-Stock Companies" in July, 2010.

In March 2011, the government resolution which endorsed the use of IFRS in Russia was signed. According to paragraph 7 of the resolution, IFRS should be implemented on the territory of Russia by stages. The first stage introduces the use of IFRS on the voluntary basis, and at the second stage, its use is obligatory. There were no specific dates in the resolution that would set the limit on IFRS implementation process duration in Russia, which means that it is a long process that could be prolonged indefinitely. In December 2011, 37 IFRS and 26 interpretations to them entered into force on the territory of Russia. A new law on accounting then entered into force on January 2013.

Next step was the plan for the years 2012–2015 for the development of accounting and accountability in the Russian Federation on the basis of IFRS that was approved by the Ministry of Finance and issued under Order no. 440 of November, 30 2011. It provides that the system of Russian Accounting Standards has been brought into line with IFRS by the end of 2015. And according to the requirements of the Federal Law No 208-FZ, all credit and insurance organizations and other organizations whose securities are traded on the stock exchanges and other security markets have to provide consolidated financial statements in compliance with IFRS since January 2012 along with the reports prepared according to national financial reporting standards. The list of the organizations that have to comply will be extended with the private pension funds, investment funds, mutual funds, and clearing organizations starting with the reports for the year 2015. At the moment, 41 IAS and 13 IFRS are translated and adopted in Russia.

However, despite the work done, there are still fundamental differences between the Russian accounting system and IFRS. The essence of the difference is that the RAS, which currently regulate the process of accounting and reporting in the Russia, are based on rules, and IFRS are based on principles. Another fundamental difference between these standards is the fact that IFRS regulates the financial reporting and does not resolve every detail of the accounting transactions, and RAS regulates very strictly. There are also other differences: IFRS prioritize the information needs of investors and owners, whereas the financial statements that have been prepared in accordance with RAS are aimed at information needs of tax authorities and other government agencies; the balance sheet asset value according to RAS is based on the historical cost basis it results in an overestimation of the assets value on the balance sheet—RAS are not focused on the presentation of true and objective view of the financial position and results of the organization activities. Often organizations do not fully disclose relevant information in the notes to the financial statements; RAS do not take into account changes in purchasing power of ruble, which makes it impossible to compare the results of the companies' activities in time under the current inflation rate; tradition of a professional accountant judgment in Russia is just arising. At the present time, Russian accountants only play a role of the executives of different laws, decrees, and instructions.

Also, as was noted in articles by Alon (2013, 2014), the process of harmonization with the IFRS in Russia is very specific because of some reasons. In Russia exists so-called dual institutionality. It means that companies use RAS and IFRS at once, even in case of mandatory use of IFRS. This leads to the use of two different logics of accounting process. Thus, Russian companies are insufficiently motivated to apply the IFRS and sometimes do not understand the usefulness of international practices and views. At the same time, politicians and state authorities do not always understand the purpose of international practices and set the application of IFRS by force. However, voluntary adoption of IFRS and their correct understanding have more positive influence on the IFRS adoption.

Thus, modern Russian system of accounting and financial reporting is in the process of harmonization with the IFRS. The basic elements of infrastructure for their application are created. The essence of further development of accounting and financial reporting is based on using the IFRS to fulfill the function of generating information that would be useful for internal and external users in economic decision-making process by creating an appropriate infrastructure and building an effective accounting process.

35.3.2 Modern Accounting in Brazil

Accounting in Brazil was under control of the state. All accounting rules were issued by the central government or by different agencies responsible for specific areas, such as Central Bank of Brazil (Banco Central do Brasil—BC) and the Brazilian Securities Commission (Comissão de Valores Mobiliários—CVM). Before modification, accounting standards were under the direct influence of legal directives—tax laws and government regulations. The Brazilian Company Law (Law no. 6.404 of December 15, 1976) provided fundamentals of the accounting for firms listed on the Sao Paulo Stock Exchange. Although this company law was inspired by US-GAAP, Brazil adopted a continental model accounting structure.

US-GAAP was very popular in the middle 1990s in connection with the macroeconomic stabilization program and huge importance of the American capital market as a source of funds for the largest Brazilian corporations. At the beginning of the twenty-first century, Brazil was classified as "investment grade" by the major rating agencies and Brazilian companies started to find important opportunities in the local markets both for equity and debt capital. This new direction has increased the demand for informative accounting reports. Brazil started the process of issuing norms in accordance with IFRS. First step was made by the Central bank of Brazil in 2006 according to which all major financial institutions have to present IFRS consolidated financial statements by the end of 2010. The same direction was chosen for public companies by CVM in 2007. So, in December 2007, Brazil adopted the Law 11638/07, which announced its intention to converge from Brazilian GAAP to IFRS by the end of 2010. This process was divided into two phases of minor and major convergences. Modifications were to be issued by the Brazilian Accounting Standards Board (CPC) and must be valid for individual and consolidated financial statements. The first phase involved publically owned and all financial institutions. They were required to follow 15 new standards and interpretations prior to 2009. This phase was completed by the end of 2008. These standards only harmonized insignificant differences between Brazilian GAAP and IFRS, but major convergences were taken in 2009 and 2010. Additional 40 standards and interpretations were adopted by the end of 2010. Also, this process was expanded by the including all Brazilian firms into the convergence. Small- and medium-sized enterprises were obliged to use the IFRS for SMEs. The law, which was adopted in 2007, was also important for another reason—it separated financial and tax accounting. Companies started to prepare financial statements according to CPC rules and then make some adjustments in their records to calculate taxable profits. Tax rules were separated from accounting rules.

Brazilian companies are still preparing financial statements under IFRS and BR GAAP. This is complicated because regulatory authority requires IFRS for external reporting purposes, while the Brazilian tax authority determines taxable income in accordance with Brazilian GAAP. Currently, Brazil is working on this: In 2013, provisional measure (MP) no. 627/13 was enacted by the Brazilian government. MP introduced new tax rules related to IFRS with some exceptions in specific topics. This MP was converted into the Law no. 12,973 in 2014. Szuster (2015) states "Brazil is already recognized worldwide for expertise in the Accounting field. Many scholars and professionals have contributed and keep working on this process. However, it is crucial to extend this excellence to a larger number of Brazilian entities, including the government sector. The importance of accounting information as an element that generates trust within the economic system and a basis for reducing the risk of equity losses should be highlighted. The need of Accounting for society as a whole is undeniable and the appreciation of professionals will grow by improving the work quality."

Thus, Brazil is now working on the qualitative component of the accounting system and improving it more and more in accordance with IFRS rules.

35.3.3   Modern Accounting in India

All accounting standards in India are issued by the Institute of Chartered Accountants of India (ICAI). The ICAI is the national professional accounting organization of India, which was established on July, 1 1949. The ICAI works in conjunction with the Ministry of Corporate Affairs (MCA) in case of adoption and implementation of accounting standards in the country. In 1977, the ICAI established the Accounting Standards Board (ASB) that formulated the first set of the Indian Accounting Standards (IAS) in the 1980s. Currently, there are 35 accounting standards issued by the ICAI. First, IAS were based on the international standards issued by the International Accounting Standards Committee (IASC), the immediate predecessor of the International Accounting Standards Board (IASB) responsible for developing IFRS. But later, during the process of convergence of IAS and IFRS, the Indian standards lost the pace of its development and began to keep up with international trends. Currently, two separate sets of accounting standards exist in India: Indian Accounting Standards converged with the IFRS (known as Ind AS) and the Existing Accounting Standards.

European Union adopted IFRS in 2005. In this connection, the ICAI decided to focus on the convergence of Indian GAAP and IFRS (rather than adopt them) and announced a concept paper in 2007. Also, the ICAI made a public commitment to put into practice the convergence before the end of 2011. Later, the MCA set a road map of implementation of Indian GAAP for companies, which do not belong to banking and insurance sector. After that, the same was made for banking and insurance companies on March 2010. It was a three-phased road map for Indian companies with deadlines, which were set for certain companies to conform to new Indian Accounting Standards by April, 1 2011, 2013, or 2014. Different insurance companies in India had to start using new standards by 2012, whereas banks in India had to accept these changes in either 2013 or 2014, and it depended on the volume and character of their activities. The MCA released all 35 Indian Accounting Standards converged with IFRS (they were named Ind AS) on their Web site by the end of February 2011 (there were some standards, which were not included such as IFRS 9—Financial Instruments, IAS 26—Accounting and Reporting by Retirement Benefit Plans, and IAS 41—Agriculture). But at that time, these standards were in breach of the Companies Act of 1956 and with the tax framework. So, the MCA decided to scrap the earlier plan and made a new one.

Since 2012, the Indian government has made different measures for improving the process of harmonization. New Companies Act was issued by The Indian government in 2013. Also, the Indian Ministry of Finance drafted Tax Accounting Standards to resolve conflicts between accounting and taxation. "There is an urgent need to converge the current Indian accounting standards with the International Financial Reporting Standards (IFRS). I propose for adoption of the new Indian Accounting Standards (Ind AS) by the Indian companies from the financial year 2015–16 voluntarily and from the financial year 2016–17 on a mandatory basis. Based on the international consensus, the regulators will separately notify the date of implementation of AS Ind for the Banks, Insurance companies, etc. Standards for the computation of tax would be notified separately," said Finance Minister, Arun Jaitley in his Budget speech in July 2014 (India Budget 2014). As the reaction on Jaitley's words, ICAI developed a new road map with new terms. For the better adoption of the IFRS, new financial statements were created. The Companies Act of 2013 defines five forms of financial statements: "a balance sheet, a profit or loss account (equivalent to the income statement in the US), cash flow statement, a statement of changes in equity (equivalent to the statement of retained earnings in the US) and any explanatory notes" (MCA 2013). In February 2015, the MCA set the criteria of applying Ind AS to the accounting period beginning on or after April, 1 2016, for the following company types:

- entities listed or in the process of listing on any stock exchange in India or abroad, containing a net worth of Rs. 500 crores or more (equivalent to 80.25 million USD),
- unlisted companies having a net worth in excess of Rs. 500 crore,
- holding companies, subsidiaries, joint venture or associated of the companies attested to be in (1) or (2).

Thus, currently, India is in the process of harmonization with IFRS, and it is the initial stage of implementation these standards in the accounting practice.

35.4 Conclusion

The paper complements the huge area of comparative international accounting by focusing on three selected BRICS countries, which focuses on regulatory framework for and specifics of the adaption of International Financial Reporting Standards. By analyzing the contemporary stage of accounting development in Russia, India, and Brazil, it should be noted that each of these countries has its own unique way. At modern stage, each of these countries is in a position of adaption of IFRS in accounting practices. This process is a consequence of the users' demand of high-quality financial statements comparable across all entities. It is observing the changes in all areas of economic activities, as a result of the world globalization process. This leads to the growth of capital mobility, the creation of standard form of financial statements, and the emergence of the need to provide useful and clear information to all interested users at the international level. It also helps to establish economic relations between different countries such as India, Brazil, and Russia, which have different political, juridical, and cultural system.

However, it should be noted that the conceptual basis of IFRS—a system of theoretical requirements for accounting and reporting—is fundamentally different from Russian, Brazilian, and Indian systems of accounting and financial reporting. Also, IFRS practice differs significantly from the traditional Brazilian, Russian, and Indian views on the accounting methodology.

Some recommendations, how to improve the convergence of financial reporting of these three BRICS countries with IFRS, can be made:

- harmonization of the key terms and concepts used in IFRS with national accounting and financial reporting systems of BRICS countries will align the conceptual frameworks of these both systems,
- it should be noted that at the present stage of public relations, development in the budget sphere increases role of finance in the process of renewal of the main funds for the production of public goods in various forms (health protection and medical care assistance, education, defense, stabilization of the financial sector, creation of material base for the development of scientific, and innovation potential of the country). Introduction of IFRS in all spheres of public life, including budget, provides openness, transparency, and clarity of financial information to investors, establishing effective financial control at the state level and the prevention of financial offenses,
- to solve the problem of specialist and auditor shortage, it is necessary to organize effective and full system of training of specialists in the area of IFRS on a state level. Specialists and auditors will be able to compile accounting statements and check them correctness.

Acknowledgments This paper has been prepared within the research project "Economic Impacts of the IFRS Adoption in Selected Transition Countries" (supported by the Czech Science Foundation, No. 15-01280S).

References

Alon A (2013) Complexity and dual institutionality: the case of IFRS adoption in Russia. Corp Gov Int Rev 21:42–57. doi:10.1111/j.1467-8683.2012.00927.x

Alon A, Dwyer P (2014) Early adoption of IFRS as a strategic response to transitional and local influences. Int J Account 49:348–370

Borker D (2012) Accounting, culture, and emerging economies: IFRS in the BRIC Countries. J Bus Econ Res 10:313–324. doi:http://dx.doi.org/10.19030/jber.v10i5.6983

Getman V (2009) International accounting standards. Finance and statistics, Moscow

Hope O, Jin U, Kang T (2006) Empirical evidence on jurisdictions that adopt IFRS. J Int Account Res 5:1–20. doi:10.2139/ssrn.751264

India Budget (2014) The union budget for 2014–15 from 10 July, 2014. http://indiabudget.nic.in/ub2014-15/bs/bs.pdf

Kozhevnikova S (2015) International Financial Reporting Standards as a condition of effective implementation of the financial activities in Russian Federation. Dissertation, University of Moscow

Lambert R, Leuz C, Verrechia R (2007) Accounting information, disclosure, and the cost of capital. J Account Res 45:385–420. doi:10.1111/j.1475-679X.2007.00238.x

MCA (2013) The companies Act from 30 August, 2013. http://www.mca.gov.in/Ministry/pdf/CompaniesAct2013.pdf

Pal S (2015) Differences between Ind AS and IFRS: can full convergence ever occur between the two? CMC Senior theses, Claremont McKenna College

Ramana K, Sletten E (2014) Network effects in countries' adoption of IFRS. Account Rev 89:1517–1543

Sokolov J (2007) IFRS in Russia: their present and future. Accounting 8:6–10

Steinbach K, Tang R (2014) IFRS convergence: learning from Mexico, Brazil, and Argentina. J Corp Account Finan 25:31–41. doi:10.1002/jcaf.21937

Szuster N (2015) We have some reasons to be proud of accounting in Brazil. Revista Contabilidade & Finanças. 26:121–125. doi:10.1590/1808-057x201590050

Chapter 36
Intangibles Disclosure: Evidence from Annual Reports of the Jordanian Industrial Public Listed Companies

Radhi Al-Hamadeen, Malek Alsharairi and Haya Qaqish

Abstract This study investigates the disclosure practices pertaining the intangible assets (IA), given the limited attention given to intangibles reporting in the developing countries. Specifically, this paper documents the disclosure practices, both mandatory and voluntary, related to intangibles by the industrial Jordanian firms, and to what extent they do report information about IA. This study contributes to the literature by providing empirical evidence from a developing country's business environment. Based on relevant literature and the requirements of accounting standards (namely, IAS38), we apply a research index that consists of 24 'general and technical' items on 69 publicly listed companies classified under the industrial sector at Amman Stock Exchange (ASE) for the year 2012. Our findings suggest that most of the investigated firms either disclose a minimal amount of information about IA or not at all, which indicates that the concept of IA remains ambiguous and is neglected. The overall percentage of intangibles' disclosure as per the research index is only 9.7%. Consistent with the extant literature (such as Kumar 2013), our results indicate that intangibles' technical disclosure is associated with the market capitalization, whereas the intangibles' general disclosure (non-technical) is linked to the firm's sub-sector. The findings of this research raise concerns about the firms' reporting efficiency in communicating their ability to maintain, create and sustain innovation within their business environment on the long run.

Keywords Intangible assets · IAS38 · Disclosure · Industrial PLCs · Jordan

R. Al-Hamadeen (✉) · H. Qaqish
Department of Accounting, King Talal Faculty of Business and Technology,
Princess Sumaya University for Technology, Amman 11941, Jordan
e-mail: r.hamadeen@psut.edu.jo

M. Alsharairi
Department of International Accounting, School of Management and Logistics Sciences,
German Jordanian University, Amman 11180, Jordan
e-mail: malek.alsharairi@gju.edu.jo

© Springer International Publishing AG 2017   385
D. Procházka (ed.), *New Trends in Finance and Accounting*,
Springer Proceedings in Business and Economics,
DOI 10.1007/978-3-319-49559-0_36

36.1 Introduction

One of the today's challenges concerning financial accounting is to cope with a world that is becoming more immaterial than material (Grojer 2001). The creation and deployment of the intangible assets (IA) is becoming greater in the modern economies. As a result, the accounting profession has to respond to the rising issues of IA related to expensing versus capitalization (Knivsfla and Hùegh-Krohn 2000).

Most companies in the developing countries, such as in Jordan, provide detailed information on their tangible assets, but they neglect reporting detailed information about their IA (Al-Hamadeen and Suwaidan 2014). This study contributes to the literature by focusing on the magnitude of disclosure as well as the level of compliance with IAS38 in the annual reports of the industrial publicly listed firms in Jordan.

Indeed, information about intangibles is value-relevant. For the majority of the modern corporations, intangibles are essential for operations, competition and corporate value (Duizabo and Guillaume 1996; Goldfinger 1997). Therefore, firms realize how important it is to disclose their IA and related activities in order to grow in value (Canibano et al. 2000).

The disclosure of IA has naturally evolved as a response to the rapid growth and development of firms and their need to attract capital (Kampanje 2012). Accordingly, the disclosure of IA is outlined by the International Accounting Standards Board (IASB) at IAS38, which helps the capital providers to learn about the firms' intangibles when they make economic decisions (Healy and Palepu 2001; Graham 2005; Lambert et al. 2007). IA empower companies and sustain competitiveness given the fact that they are relatively unique among firms and they are hard to be imitated (Kaplan and Norton 2004).

The overwhelming European companies have at least one type of intangible asset other than goodwill (Tsalavoutas et al. 2014). Hence, a priori is that these companies reveal more details about these assets. In the same context, the Global Intangible Tracker (GIT) confirms that the developed countries are focusing more and more on disclosing information about intangibles. As a consequence of the mismeasurement and poor reporting of IA, there is a considerable deterioration in the informational content of key financial statement items. A second consequence is the reportedly undervaluation of intangibles by companies that are intensive in intangibles (Lev 2001).

Since the literature gives limited attention to the intangibles in the developing countries, this study focuses on IA disclosures in Jordan, where international accounting standards are mandated for all public corporations since the fiscal year 1990 (Alsharairi and Al-Abdullah 2008). Specifically, this study examines to what extent do the industrial publicly listed companies in Jordan disclose information about intangibles in their annual audited reports. Our investigation emphasizes the reporting companies' compliance with IAS38 disclosure's requirements. Therefore, the current research addresses two main questions: (1) to what extent do the Jordanian public listed industries disclose information about IA? and (2) what factors are associated with the disclosure of IA?

36.2 Literature Review

Several studies in the different fields of accounting and other business disciplines investigate the reporting patterns and the influencing factors of intangibles' disclosure, mostly in North American and European samples (see for example, Choi et al. 2000; Stolowy et al. 2001; Rowbottom 2002; Busacca and Maccarrone 2007; Dahmash et al. 2009; Sahut et al. 2011; Jerman 2013; Kumar 2013; Devalle and Rizzato 2014; Frey and Oehler 2014). However, we know little about the special corporate disclosure practices (such as those of intangibles) within the emerging countries (Leventis and Weetman 2004). A limited number of studies in the developing countries seem to focus on intellectual capital (IC) in addition to intangibles' disclosure (see, for example, Abeysekera 2007; Sharabati et al. 2010; Kang and Gray 2011; Al-Hamadeen and Suwaidan 2014).

Among the main concerns of the researchers in the area of IA is valuation. Choi et al. (2000) present empirical evidence that reveals that the reported financial assets are positively valued by the financial market and that the market's valuation of a dollar of IA is lower than its valuation of other reported assets. Farther, Stolowy et al. (2001) and Busacca and Maccarrone (2007) question the quality of intangible-related information under IFRS since that there is a difficulty in the international harmonization process of accounting for intangibles since there is a link between 'relevance' and Anglo-American accounting philosophy as well as between 'reliability' and Continental–European accounting.

In UK, Striukova et al. (2008) find that the reporting companies use a wide range of different corporate intellectual capital information reported for communication, richer than the firms' annual reports themselves. Another European evidence obtained by Sahut et al. (2011) indicates that the capitalized goodwill, when disclosed by local GAAP, is more relevant than goodwill under IFRS, according to the perceptions of the European investors. Thus, European companies' balance sheets provide more value-relevant information for shareholders on the identifiable IA. In an attempt to investigate the Eastern Europe case, Jerman (2013) explores the importance of intangibles reported in the annual reports of the Slovenian companies and their impact on the economy. Jerman (2013) concludes that intangibles are more important in the traditionally advanced economies. Interestingly, voluntary disclosures are customary by the Slovenian companies, given the negligible amount of disclosures reported. In another study, Kumar (2013) finds that larger firms, more dispersed in their ownership, lower in leverage and those from more individualistic countries disclose more voluntary information about intangibles. In a US-based research, Whitehouse (2013) attempts to set criteria for measuring goodwill levels and impairments among companies and sectors. The results indicate that 10.5% of the companies with a reported goodwill in 2012 have actually recorded impairment. In addition, companies in the industrial sector, health care and information technology accounted for 67% of the total goodwill 'write-down' in 2012.

In a Jordanian study, Al-Hamadeen and Suwaidan (2014) investigate the intellectual capital (IC) voluntary disclosures reported by the Jordanian industrial PLCs.

Based on the previous literature (namely, Edvinsson and Malone 1997; and Johnson 1999), the researchers use a research index on 60 industrial companies listed on Amman Stock Exchange (ASE) for the year 2012. The results indicate that information about the intellectual capital is extensively disclosed by the large industrial companies in Jordan. Up to 59% of the hypothesized IC disclosure items are reportedly found in the annual reports of the study sample. Al-Hamadeen and Suwaidan's (2014) evidence reveals that human capital is the most disclosed aspect among all three investigated components of IC (i.e. human, internal and external capital). Moreover, size and ownership concentration have the highest explanatory power since the larger companies with greater concentration in their ownership tend to disclose more information about their intellectual capital.

It could be argued that an increasing trend in disclosure of IA in annual reports is anticipated in the foreseeable future. Moreover, it could be noticed how rare research endeavors are on the developing countries, especially those of MENA region. Therefore, this study aims at investigating the extant practices of intangibles' disclosure in Jordan. In the same vein, previous literature provides several implications for the current research (namely, Kang and Gray 2011; Kumar 2013; Whitehouse 2013; Al-Hamadeen and Suwaidan 2014). These implications include considering influential factors on intangibles' disclosure (e.g. size of market capitalization, sub-sector and age of the reporting company), as well as considering the methodological implications (i.e. components of the research index applied in the current study).

36.3   Research Design, Sample and Data

According to the reviewed literature, we consider the hypothesized relationships between the level of IA disclosure and three suggested factors: size, age and sub-sector of the reporting companies. Hence, we posit the following null hypotheses:

H_{01}: *There is no significant positive relationship between the age of the company and the level of intangible assets disclosure.*
H_{02}: *There is no significant positive relationship between the market capitalization of the company and the level of intangible assets disclosure.*
H_{03}: *There is no significant relationship between the sub-sector of the company and the disclosure of intangible assets.*

The current study adopts an analytical methodology for the annual reports of the study sample in order to achieve the research objectives. The research data are collected by a research index informed by prior studies and based on the standards' requirements (namely, KPMG Checklist 2013 and IAS38). Therefore, content analysis is used to gather information related to IA and their related disclosures in the firms' annual reports. The research index employed in this study consists of 25 items related to the general characteristics of the reporting companies and the technical disclosures related to intangibles.

The sample of the study includes the annual reports of all the 69 industrial companies that are listed on ASE and active during 2012. Two-stage reliability check of the developed research index is performed. First, the content of the research index is reviewed by two referees, who are academics and specialized in financial accounting, and second by performing stability tests (intra-rater) and 'reproducibility test'. Therefore, Cohen's kappa coefficient is used to test the reliability of the research index and the coefficient result is ($K = 92\%$), which confirms the validity of the research index.

36.4 Results and Discussion

Table 36.1 presents the results of the descriptive analysis related to the characteristics of the reporting companies. In fact, the industrial sector in Jordan includes 28.4% of the total companies listed on ASE during the year 2012. The industrial sector consists of 8 sub-sectors, as presented in Table 36.1, noting that 'Mining and Extraction' sub-sector makes the highest weight in the industrial sector with a number of firms representing (23.2%), followed by 'Others' (18.8%) and 'Food and Beverages' sub-sectors (15.9%).

A number of prior studies argue that the company's age is among the most important factors that affect the level of disclosure (Delaney and Huselid 1996; Xianbing and Anbumozhi 2009). In this study, age is divided into six different categories (see Table 36.1). The majority of the companies (26.1%) are located within the (1–10 years) age category, while companies aged between (11–20 years) represent 17.4%, companies between the age of (21–30 years) represent 17.4%, companies between the age (31–40 years) represent 17.4%, and companies between the age (41-50 years) represent 7.2%, and only 14.5% of the investigated companies have been actively operating in the market for more than 50 years.

Further, size is expected to impact the level of intangibles' disclosure. Larger firms usually have adequate resources to collect, process and communicate an extensive amount of information at a minimal cost (Firth 1979). In this study, size is measured by the firm's market capitalization. We divide the research sample in terms of size into three categories: small, medium and large, as presented in Table 36.1.

The results presented in this section are related to the technical disclosure of the IA. These results are obtained from the quantitative information disclosed in the main body of the financial statements of the Jordanian industrial companies.

The information presented in Table 36.2 reveals that the disclosure items vary in terms of being reported by the sampled companies as their existence ranges between 5.8 and 17.4% in the overall industrial sector. Regarding the disclosure of the 'gross carrying amount', the detailed results indicate that there are 'unsystematic' approaches of disclosure. Two companies disclose the gross carrying amount

Table 36.1 Information of the reporting companies

Sector/sub-sector of the reporting company (Industrial)	Frequency	(%)
Pharmaceuticals and medical	6	8.7
Chemicals	10	14.5
Paper and cardboard	3	4.3
Food and beverage	11	15.9
Tobacco and cigarettes	2	2.9
Mining and extraction industries	16	23.2
Engineering and construction	8	11.6
Others	13	18.8
Age of the company (in years)		
From 01 to 10	18	26.1
From 10 to 20	12	17.4
From 20 to 30	12	17.4
From 30 to 40	12	17.4
From 40 to 50	5	7.2
More than 50	10	14.5
Size of the market capital		
Small (1)	64	92.8
Medium (2)	2	2.9
Large (3)	3	4.3

Source Own calculations based on data from Amman Stock Exchange (ASE)

Table 36.2 Technical disclosure of intangible assets

Disclosed intangible item(s)	Frequency	(%)
Useful life or amortization rate	9	13.0
Amortization method	9	13.0
Gross carrying amount	12	17.4
Accumulated amortization and impairment losses	11	15.9
Intangible's amortization is disclosed within line items in the income statement	6	8.7
Information disclosed about reconciliation of the carrying amount of goodwill at the beginning and the end of the period	9	13.0
Basis for determining that the intangibles have an indefinite life	4	5.8
Disclosure of intangibles in general	12	17.4

Source Own calculations based on data from annual reports of the targeted companies

of goodwill and other IA, while only one company discloses the gross carrying amount of patents and other IA. In the same vein, four companies only disclose the gross carrying amount of goodwill, whereas five companies disclose the gross carrying amount of other intangibles. The least disclosed item is the one related to the 'basis of determining the indefinite/definite life of intangible asset' which is reported only by 5.8% of the sample (4 companies out of 69).

Table 36.3 Factors affecting the value of intangibles

Information disclosed about reconciliation of the carrying amount at the beginning and the end of the period—details in this regard show:	Frequency	(%)
Additions (business combinations disclosed separately)	7	10.1
Retirements and other disposals	0	0.0
Revaluations	1	1.4
Impairments (include carrying out the impairment test)	2	2.9
Reversals of impairments	0	0.0
Amortization	6	8.7
Foreign exchange differences	0	0.0

Source Own calculations based on data from annual reports of the targeted companies

Table 36.3 illustrates the detailed factors tested under the reconciliation item. According to the disclosure requirements of IAS 8, IA are normally affected by several transactions including: Additions (from business combinations), Revaluations, Impairment and Amortization. The effect of these transactions is usually mentioned in the reconciliation of the carrying amount of intangibles at the beginning and the end of the period (IAS38). Table 36.3 presents the transactions that affect intangibles' value as disclosed by the investigated companies.

The findings show that the industrial companies provide information about the intangibles' additions due to business combinations or in buying new intangibles. In this regard, 7 companies out of the 69 disclose additions of intangibles which represent the highest percentage (10.1%). The results of the disclosure of the 'useful life or amortization rate' item indicate that 13.0% (9 cases) disclose related information, two of them disclose the useful life or amortization rate of goodwill, while one company disclose the useful life or amortization rate of patents and other IA. The remaining 6 companies disclose information about the useful life or amortization in general. Furthermore, the results indicate that limited information is disclosed about the amortization methods of different intangibles. In terms of the 'accumulated amortization and impairment losses', only 15.9% (11 cases) of the targeted companies disclosed information in these issues.

Table 36.4 presents the descriptive results related to the non-technical disclosures of intangibles (items C.1–C.6 in the research index). The results show that the information disclosed about the amount of research and development expenditure recognized as an expense in the current year has the highest percentage of companies (26.1%). Two of the companies disclose about IA developed internally, and two companies disclose information about individually material IA (description and carrying amount). None of the sampled companies disclose information about assets acquired by way of government grants, information about IA whose title is restricted and contractual commitments to acquire IA.

Table 36.4 Non-technical disclosure of intangible assets

Disclosed intangible item(s)	Frequency	(%)
Information disclosed about individually material intangible assets (description and carrying amount)	2	1.4
Information disclosed about intangible assets developed internally	2	1.4
Information disclosed about intangible assets acquired by way of government grants	0	0.0
Information about intangible assets whose title is restricted is disclosed	0	0.0
Contractual commitments to acquire intangible assets (if any) are disclosed	0	0.0
Information disclosed about the amount of research and development expenditure recognized as an expense in the current year	18	26.1

Source Own calculations based on data from annual reports of the targeted companies

Overall, it could be argued that the average of intangibles' disclosure reported by the Jordanian industrial businesses is very modest when compared with similar studies from the developed countries (see, for example, Ragini 2012). The overall percentage of the intangibles' disclosure revealed in the current study is 9.7%.[1]

The results related to the technical disclosure show that 4 tests are statistically significant at the 0.05 sig. level, and hence, the null hypotheses are accepted with p value < 0.05. As for the other results, 20 of the tests (83.3%) are rejected with p value > 0.05. Two of the tests (8.3%) are found invalid (p value $= 1.00$). Table 36.5 summarizes the results of the tests for the technical disclosure. In contrast to Whitehouse (2013), the overall results show that there is no association between each of age and sub-sector of the reporting company and the technical disclosure of IA. However, there is a significant association between reporting company's size of market capitalization and the level of technical disclosures of the IA. This result is consistent with Kumar (2013).

The results of the technical disclosure reveal that 4 of the tests are accepted (22.2%) at p value < 0.05, 9 of the tests are invalid (50%) which are C.3, C.4 and C.5, and 5 of the tests are rejected (27.8%) as p value > 0.05. Table 36.6 summarizes the results of the tests for the non-technical intangibles' disclosure. The overall findings indicate that there is no relationship between each of the age and the size of the market capitalization of the reporting companies and the level of the non-technical disclosure of IA. However, we document a significant relationship between the firm's sub-sector and the general (non-technical) disclosures of IA.

---

[1]This percentage was calculated based on the following formula:

$$\frac{\text{Total Frequency of the key investigated items}}{\text{Items of the index} * \text{No. of total companies}} = \frac{94}{14 * 69} = 9.7\%.$$

Table 36.5 Pearson's Chi-square, Fisher's exact tests—independent variables versus technical items of intangibles' disclosure

Item	Description
B.1	Useful life or amortization rate
B.2	Amortization method
B.3	Gross carrying amount
B.4	Accumulated amortization and impairment losses
B.5	Intangible's amortization is disclosed within line items in the income statement
B.6	Information disclosed about reconciliation of the carrying amount of goodwill at the beginning and the end of the period
B.7	Basis for determining that the intangibles have an indefinite life
B.8	Disclosure of intangibles in general

Independent variables	Dependent variables							
	B.1	B.2	B.3	B.4	B.5	B.6	B.7	B.8
Sub-sector	0.602	0.762	0.471	0.608	0.481	0.312	0.239	0.106
Age	0.261	0.728	0.735	0.133	0.734	0.710	1.000	0.735
Market capital size	0.124	0.025	0.015	0.002	0.184	0.014	1.000	0.051

Source Own calculations based on data from annual reports of the targeted companies

Table 36.6 Pearson's Chi-square, Fisher exact tests—independent variables versus non-technical items of intangibles' disclosure

Item	Description
C.1	Information disclosed about individually material intangible assets (description and carrying amount)
C.2	Information disclosed about intangible assets developed internally
C.3	Information disclosed about intangible assets acquired by way of government grants
C.4	Information about intangible assets whose title is restricted is disclosed
C.5	Contractual commitments to acquire intangible assets (if any) are disclosed
C.6	Information disclosed about the amount of research and development expenditure recognized as an expense in the current year

Independent variables	Dependent variables					
	C.1	C.2	C.3	C.4	C.5	C.6
Sub-sector	0.016	0.016	n/a	n/a	n/a	0.014
Age	0.647	0.647	n/a	n/a	n/a	0.895
Market capital size	1.000	1.000	n/a	n/a	n/a	0.024

Source Own calculations based on data from annual reports of the targeted companies

36.5 Conclusion

This study investigates the disclosure of IA in a developing country by evaluating both mandatory and voluntary disclosures reported by the publicly listed industrial companies in Jordan. Using an index developed based on both the relevant literature and the relevant accounting standards, data are collected from the annual reports of the fiscal year 2012 of all industrial companies listed on ASE in Jordan. The findings reveal that disclosure about IA is little or none at all, indicating that the concept of IA is of negligible importance.

This paper documents that only a quarter of the industrial companies in Jordan disclose at least one technical and non-technical information item about intangibles, respectively. The implications of such findings are not favorable, indeed. It could be argued that the industrial sector in Jordan does not lend significant importance to intangibles, which raises concerns about the sector's long-term ability to maintain, create and sustain an innovative working environment within the organizations and to compete in the dynamic markets.

The nonparametric statistical tests provide that the relationships between each of the proposed factors (i.e. age, market capitalization and sub-sector) and the overall intangibles' disclosure (in both parts technical vs. non-technical) vary. Consistent with the literature (for example, Kumar 2013), we report that company's market capitalization is positively associated with intangibles' disclosure in its technical part. Further, the firm's sub-sector is correlated with non-technical (general) disclosure of intangibles. No other relations in this research are found affecting the level of IA disclosure.

Compared to conventional tangible assets, it could be concluded that intangibles are relatively neglected in the industrial sector in Jordan. This may be detrimental to the Jordanian industrial sector in terms of creating and promoting innovation within the organizations. Moreover, it is observed that research and development (R&D) activities are almost absent. Hence, it is not surprising that companies in Jordan do not have access to an active market for intangibles. Eventually, this results in a weak and unreliable valuation of intangibles in general and goodwill in specific.

Given the importance of the IA to the economic growth, the implications of this research are of importance to the regulators in Jordan, as they could provide tax incentives to support successful R&D activities. Future research can investigate the association between other factors and the level of disclosure of IA such as corporate governance and board characteristics, organizational culture and ownership structure including foreign investment.

Acknowledgments The paper benefited from the comments received from anonymous reviewers and participants at the 17th Annual Conference on Finance and Accounting, University of Economics, Prague.

References

Abeysekera I (2007) Intellectual capital reporting between a developing and developed nation. J Intellect Capital 8(2):329–345

Al-Hamadeen R, Suwaidan M (2014) Content and determinants of intellectual capital disclosure: evidence from annual reports of the Jordanian industrial public listed companies. Int J Bus Soc Sci 5(8):165–175

Alsharairi MA, Al-Abdullah RJ (2008) The impact of adopting IASs on the Jordanian environment: the perspective of accountants, auditors and academicians, an exploratory study. In: International conference on business globalization: challenges and opportunities in the 21st century, University of Bahrain

Busacca G, Maccarrone P (2007) IFRSs and accounting for intangible assets: the Telecom Italia case. J Intellect Cap 8(2):306–328

Canibano L, Garcia-Ayuso H, Sanchez P (2000) Accounting for intangibles: a literature review. J Account Lit 19:102–130

Choi W, Kwon S, Lobo G (2000) Market valuation of intangible assets. J Bus Res 49(1):35–45

Dahmash F, Durand R, Watson J (2009) The value relevance and reliability of reported goodwill and identifiable intangible assets. Br Account Rev 41(2):120–137

Delaney J, Huselid M (1996) The impact of human resource management on perceptions of organizational performance. Acad Manag J 39(4):949–969

Devalle A, Rizzato F (2014) IAS 38-intangible assets and Italian listed companies: the determinants of the quality of mandatory disclosure. In: Annual international conference on accounting and finance, University of Turin, School of Management and Economics, pp 42–45

Duizabo S, Guillaume N (1996) Approche d'une nouvelle typologie des actifs immateriels. Echanges 119:34–39

Edvinsson L, Malone M (1997) Intellectual capital: realizing your company's true value by finding its hidden brainpower, 1st edn. HarperCollins Publisher Inc., New York

Firth M (1979) The impact of size, stock market listing, and auditors on voluntary disclosure in corporate annual reports. Account Bus Res 9(36):273–280

Frey H, Oehler A (2014) Intangible assets in Germany: analysis of the German stock market index DAX and a survey among the German certified public accountants. J Appl Account Res 15 (2):235–248

Goldfinger C (1997) Understanding and measuring the intangible economy: current status and suggestions for future research. CIRET seminar, Helsinki

Grojer J (2001) Intangibles and accounting classifications. in search of a classification strategy. Acc Organ Soc 26(7–8):695–713

Healy PM, Palepu KG (2001) Information asymmetry, corporate disclosure and the capital market: a review of the empirical disclosure literature. J Account Econ 31(1–2):405–440

Jerman M (2013) Intangible assets and their reporting practices: evidence from Slovenia. In: Albu CN, Mustață RV (ed) Account Cent East Eur (Res Account Emerg Econ) 13:187–2042

Johnson WHA (1999) An integrative taxonomy of intellectual capital: measuring the stock and flow of intellectual capital components in the firm. Int J Technol Manage 18:562–575

Kampanje B (2012) Accounting for intangible assets in public limited companies in Malawi. Available at SSRN: http://ssrn.com/abstract=2027713. Date of retrieval 10 Nov 2014

Kang HH, Gray SJ (2011) Reporting intangible assets: voluntary disclosure practices of top emerging market companies. Int J Account 46(4):402–423

Kaplan R, Norton D (2004) Measuring the strategic readiness of intangible assets. Harv Bus Rev, 1–14

Knivsfla KH, Hùegh-Krohn NE (2000) Accounting for intangible assets in Scandinavia, the UK, the US, and by the IASC: challenges and a solution. Int J Account 35(2):243–265

KPMG (2013) IFRS guide to annual financial statements—disclosure checklist. KPMG IFRG Limited, Sept 2013, UK

Kumar G (2013) Voluntary disclosures of intangibles information by U.S.-listed Asian companies. J Int Account Audit Tax 22(2):109–118

Lambert R, Leuz C, Verrecchia R (2007) Accounting information disclosure, and the cost of capital. J Account Res 45(2):385–420

Lev B (2001) Intangibles: management, measurement, and reporting. Brookings Institution Press, Washington, DC

Leventis S, Weetman P (2004) Voluntary disclosures in an emerging capital market: some evidence from the Athens stock exchange. Adv Int Account 17:227–250

Ragini (2012) Corporate disclosure of intangibles: a comparative study of practices among Indian, US, Japanese companies. J Decis Makers 37(3):51–72

Rowbottom N (2002) The application of intangible asset accounting and discretionary policy choices in the UK football industries. Br Account Rev 34(4):335–355

Sahut J, Boulerne S, Teulon F (2011) Do IFRS provide better information about intangibles in Europe? Rev Account Financ 10(3):267–290

Sharabati AA, Jawad SN, Bontis N (2010) Intellectual capital and business performance in the pharmaceutical sector of Jordan. Manag Decis 48(1):105–131

Stolowy H, Hallerb A, Klockhaus V (2001) Accounting for brands in France and Germany compared with IAS 38 (intangible assets): an illustration of the difficulty of international harmonization. Int J Account 36(2):147–167

Striukova L, Unerman J, Guthrie J (2008) Corporate reporting of intellectual capital: evidence from UK companies. Br Account Rev 40(4):297–313

Tsalavoutas I, André P, Dionysiou D (2014) Worldwide application of IFRS 3, IAS 38 and IAS 36, related disclosures, and determinants of non-compliance, Certified Accountants Educational Trust, ACCA Research Report 134, London, UK

Whitehouse T (2013) Goodwill impairments jumped to $51 billion in 2012. Compliance Week 10 (119):9–10

Xianbing L, Anbumozhi V (2009) Determinant factors of corporate environmental information disclosure: an empirical study of Chinese listed companies. J Clean Prod 17(6):593–600

Chapter 37
Specifics of Accounting in the Agricultural Sector

Irena Honková

Abstract The subject of this article is in the area of accounting for private companies—legal entities operating in the agricultural sector. A questionnaire survey was carried out covering four areas of accounting—forms of accounting, workers in accounting, the function of accounting and the individual areas of accounting. The data obtained were analysed and processed in the software Statistica using methods of statistical analysis. Two hypotheses were tested and confirmed. H1: The number of accountants is not dependent on the legal form of business. H2: The companies studied conduct their bookkeeping in the same accounting areas. Other information was also acquired: the form of bookkeeping most often used is separate accounting software. Accountants are mostly persons with secondary school education. Companies also to a large extent use the services of external accountants and tax advisors. Conversely, audit services are used mainly because of obligations imposed by law. Two final areas are somewhat in disagreement, as the main function of accounting has been reported as the obligation to keep accounts under the Accounting Act, while the analysis of various areas of accounting (such as the method of inventory accounting, the use of Analytic accounts, departmental and order accounting) has shown that companies use accounting as a basis for decision-making.

Keywords Accounting forms of bookkeeping · Accountant · Tax advisor · Audit · Accounting functions · Analytic accounts · Departments · Orders

I. Honková (✉)
Faculty of Economics and Administration, Institute of Business Economics and Management, University of Pardubice, Studentská 95, Pardubice, Czech Republic
e-mail: irena.honkova@upce.cz

© Springer International Publishing AG 2017
D. Procházka (ed.), *New Trends in Finance and Accounting*,
Springer Proceedings in Business and Economics,
DOI 10.1007/978-3-319-49559-0_37

37.1 Introduction

The term accounting can be understood in three distinct and to some extent close meanings. It can be understood as the name of a type of mathematical science, the practical implementation of business (accounting) or as the name of a file of results of practically implemented business activities, in the form of entries in accounting books (Janhuba 2005).

This article focuses on accounting as the practical implementation of an activity which is charged, or accounted. The aim is to analyse the current situation and to test possible dependencies of accounting areas for the purpose of drawing general conclusions and final recommendations.

Historically, three basic accounting systems have developed: simple accounting, cameral accounting and double-entry bookkeeping (Strouhal et al. 2012).

This article deals with the double-entry accounting system, which is based on collecting accounting information using a double-entry method. Property is viewed both in terms of form and in terms of the sources of its coverage, and the financial results are the difference between revenues and costs.

The subject of the research was forms of accounting, accountants, and tax advisors and auditors, as well as individual accounting areas: a method of inventory accounting and also accounting for exports, imports, VAT, accounting for Analytic accounts, departmental and order accounting and, last but not least, the function of accounting, as perceived by the respondents.

37.2 Literature Review

The article is divided into four areas, namely forms of accounting, accounting workers, individual areas of billing and the function of accounting.

37.2.1 Forms of Accounting

Transactions or accounting events are always recorded as an accounting entry in two different accounts, on opposite sides. The initial account balance is written on the side on which the relevant item appears on the balance sheet with a positive value. Increases are written on the side of the initial balance and decreases on the opposite side (Janhuba 2005).

The accounting record of the event is generally given on the basis of a financial document.

The form of an accounting record is a specific way of recording content, while an accounting record may have (Strouhal et al. 2012):

- paper form,
- technical (i.e., digital) form,
- mixed form.

All forms of accounting records are viewed the same; i.e., the forms are equal. The content and its changes in the accounting records have in both cases the same results. In proceedings in accounting matters or arising from the accounting, conclusive accounting records can be used as evidence regardless of whether they are in paper or technical form (Ryneš 2013).

Janhuba (2005) distinguishes the paper form of the elementary entries, accounting in bound books of accounts and accounting on loose pages.

The research tested bookkeeping manually in books, in separate accounting software and an accounting program which was part of a company's information system.

37.2.2 Workers in Accounting

Professional accountants, i.e., accountants, auditors, internal auditors, financial managers, tax advisors and management consultants, play an important role in a company-wide context, as the accounting users (see below) rely on the principle that professional accountants will provide accurate financial accounting and reporting statements, effective financial management and competent advice for the entire spectrum of business and tax matters. The attitude and behaviour of professional accountants in the provision of such services has an impact on a company's economic well-being (Strouhal et al. 2012).

Professional accountants should meet the following requirements: credibility, professionalism, quality of service and confidence in accounting.

Professional accountants should therefore be honest, objective, respectful to the confidentiality of information, and, last but not least, competent.

Any accountant who is an employee of a company is caught between two disparate constraints, namely, loyalty to his/her employer and ethics in relation to the profession. From an ethical point of view, an employer does not have the right to force an employee to violate the law or professional regulations, lie to or mislead the person conducting a company audit or sign his/her name to a statement which may significantly distort the facts.

The objective of the research in this area was to determine how the companies monitored use internal accounting employees and to what extent they prefer to use external accountants. In connection with the requirements mentioned above, educational background in accounting was also examined as well as the means of their further education.

Hypothesis H1 was tested: the number of accountants is not dependent on the legal form of business.

As well, the research also focused on the use of tax consultants and auditors, whereby an audit was checked to determine whether the company conducted the audit compulsorily or voluntarily.

The requirement for ordinary and extraordinary audits of financial statements applies to joint stock companies if, as of the balance sheet date of the reporting period for which the financial statements are verified and the accounting period immediately preceding, at least one of the following three criteria has been reached or exceeded (Ryneš 2013):

- Balance sheet total exceeds 40 million CZK (gross assets),
- Net turnover is greater than 80 million CZK,
- The average number of employees during the reporting period is more than 50.

For other commercial companies, cooperatives and business owners, an audit is mandatory if, as of the balance sheet date of the reporting period for which the financial statements are verified and the accounting period immediately preceding, at least two of the three given criteria have been met.

"Gross assets" refers to the total assets ascertained from the balance sheet in a valuation unadjusted for correction (Strouhal et al. 2012).

"Annual net turnover" refers to the amount of revenue less any sales discounts and done by the number of months commenced, for which the accounting period lasted, multiplied by twelve.

"Average number of employees" refers to the state identified by the methods laid down by special legislation (for statistical purposes).

The objective of an audit of financial statements is to provide a statement from an independent, qualified person (auditor) as to whether the financial statements published by an accounting entity accurately present a true and fair view of a company's assets and liabilities, financial position and results of operations in accordance with applicable accounting legislation.

37.2.3   Functions of Accounting

Every accounting system performs the following basic functions: it provides a means of fixing the events in the life of a company, evidence in court proceedings, a written overview for the owner, the basis for tax assessment, and information on the company's fitness and management (Janhuba 2005).

The primary objective of financial reporting is to faithfully present the economic reality of the company such that external users of the financial information may establish a proper view of the current financial position of the company and be able to correctly estimate its future development. But accounting is not only for the related environment. It is also to serve the managers of the company and provide them with ready, quality information regarding the financial management of the company and the needs of internal management. This requires that the accounting provides data for both short-term decision-making tasks as well as for strategic management and forecasting (Kovanicová 2008).

A company is not only described by a given accounting system, but is also evaluated on the basis of the accounting results, i.e., data from financial statements (Ryneš 2013).

Accounting users (Strouhal et al. 2012) are: the company management, owners (shareholders, partners), employees, banks, commercial creditors (suppliers), competitors, holders of debt securities and potential investors, and government authorities.

The research identified the main reason why the monitored companies keep accounts, namely what function in their business the accounting serves.

37.2.4 Individual Areas of Accounting

Czech accounting standards offer two methods of inventory accounting. A company may choose either regardless of the need for an audit (Ryneš 2013).

A company may keep track of acquisitions and disposals of inventory by one of two methods: continuous—method A (with the common use of accounts in accounting class 1 Inventory), or periodically—method B. In this way, the accounting class 1 is accounted at the end of the balance sheet date on the basis of the inventory conclusively determined from the records kept (Kovanicová 2008).

The accounting units have the ability to independently define Analytic accounts (Ryneš 2013). Analytic accounts are the decomposition of some synthetic accounts according to the needs of management (Kovanicová 2008).

Value added tax is imposed by a company on the completed deliveries of goods, provision of services, and imports of goods. A business owner is subject to this tax regime by being legally required to meet certain set requirements (see below) or voluntarily filing for registration (Křemen 2014). A payer is a taxable person established within the country whose turnover for the immediately preceding maximum of 12 consecutive calendar months exceeds 1,000,000 CZK, with the exception of a person who carries out only tax-exempt transactions without the right to tax deductions (Ryneš 2013).

In relation to the VAT tax return, a taxpayer is required to keep in his/her records all information needed to correctly determine tax liability. Detailed records must also be kept for the delivery of "goods" transacted with other EU countries (see below) in order to be able to prepare a "summary report" (Kovanicová 2008). Since the time that the Czech Republic entered the EU, for the purposes of VAT, a distinction must be made between purchases/sales made with EU Member States and those made with any other third country, whereby the terms import/export refer only to trade with "outside" third countries. Deliveries between the Czech Republic and other EU countries are considered to be "intra-community trade" (Kovanicová

2008). For the purpose of this article, it is not important whether a transaction took place and thus whether it was accounted as for a third country or whether it is intra-community trade.

Accounting by departmental centre is used by companies which apply the system of "line management of responsibility centres". Responsibility accounting primarily deals with questions such as how the individual responsibility centres contribute to the financial results of the company or how to manage the responsibility centres so that their activities aim towards the optimum fulfilment of the company's objectives as a whole (Strouhal et al. 2012). In some companies, process-oriented accounting plays a significant role. The significance of process accounting is based on the response to the question "what is the cost effectiveness or the value added by the company's activities, operations and processes (or more simply the "order"—author), which the company engages in (Strouhal et al. 2012).

This article aims to analyse the accounting in these selected areas to explore and examine the proposed dependencies. We also tested hypothesis H2: the companies studied conduct their bookkeeping in the same accounting areas.

37.3   Methods

37.3.1   Determining the Basic and Sample Sets

The obligation of bookkeeping applies to (Ryneš 2013):

- Legal entities based in the Czech Republic,
- Foreign legal entities if they conduct business in the Czech Republic,
- Organisational units of the State under special legislation,
- Natural persons,

    - who are recorded in the commercial registry,
    - whose turnover for the previous calendar year exceeded 25 million CZK,
    - who conduct their bookkeeping on the basis of their sole discretion,
    - who are members of an association, if at least one of the members of this association is a person or entity who is obligated to keep accounts,
    - who keep their accounting under special legislation.

The basic set was defined as a legal person based in the Czech Republic. Then, there was the requirement for uniformity in the accounting; thus, a selection was made in one field of operation. Farming companies were selected.

The basic set was modified to the sample set (Kozel et al. 2011) with the number of respondents at 262.

37.3.2   Data Collection Methods

A questionnaire was chosen as the data collection method. The reason for this was that it allowed the simultaneous collection of data from a large number of respondents across the country.

To verify the normality of the probability distribution, a Chi-square was used (Kubanová 2004). The determination index and the Spearman test were used for detecting dependencies (Kubanová 2004). The Friedman test was used to test the compliance of variances (Kubanová 2004). Statistical analysis was done using the Statistica software.

37.4   Results and Discussion

Results from the area of forms of accounting show that most companies use a separate accounting program (58.8%). In contrast, manual bookkeeping is negligible at 2%.

Hypothesis H1: "There is no dependence of the number of accountants on a company's turnover" has been confirmed. Determination index R has a value of 0.017. 24% of the companies monitored have an external accountant. Most businesses (37%) have 2 internal accountants. 5% of the companies have more than 10 internal accountants. Regarding the education of accountants, secondary education is dominant (category 3 -...). 4% of accountants have a Master's level of post-secondary education. For further education, internal accountants primarily make use of training (92%).

55% of the companies monitored use the services of a tax consultant. While more than half of the companies use the services of a tax consultant, companies generally do not conduct voluntary financial audits (13%). In connection with what was written above concerning the functions of accounting, practice has verified that businesses do their accounting (theoretically quite incorrectly) mainly in order to meet their legal obligations (68.7%).

The companies make more use of inventory accounting method "A" (77%), which is more demanding but allows the current state of the inventory to be determined directly from the accounting. The agricultural companies which took part in our survey are not primarily focused on foreign trade. This is attested by the fact that only 38% of the companies deal with exports. 43% of the companies deal with imports.

The vast majority of the companies monitored (96%) are registered for VAT. Most of them primarily due to exceeding the annual turnover; see Act No. 235/2004 Coll., as amended, § 6, paragraph 1. Analytic accounts are used by 83% of the companies surveyed in their accounting. Centres are used quite a bit by agricultural companies, as evidenced by the fact that 71% of the companies use them in their accounting. 63% of companies surveyed account on orders.

Variable	Inventories, Method "A"	Export	Import	VAT	Analytic Accounts	Units	Orders
Inventories, Method "A"	1,000000	-0,057949	-0,034685	0,270695	0,241139	0,372214	-0,225938
Export	-0,057949	1,000000	0,863507	0,074499	0,058722	-0,017181	0,173518
Import	-0,034685	0,863507	1,000000	0,094471	0,064772	0,085991	0,124167
VAT	0,270695	0,074499	0,094471	1,000000	0,230246	0,223843	0,013886
Analytic Accounts	0,241139	0,058722	0,064772	0,230246	1,000000	0,387825	0,082177
Units	0,372214	-0,017181	0,085991	0,223843	0,387825	1,000000	0,177227
Orders	-0,225938	0,173518	0,124167	0,013886	0,082177	0,177227	1,000000

Spearman correlation (database.sta)

Marked correlations are significant. p <,05000

Fig. 37.1 The largest correlation. *Source* Author

Friedman test and Kendall coefficient (database.sta)
chí-kv. (N = 262, sv = 6) = 345,4818 p =0,00000
Coefficient of concordance = ,21977 r = ,21678

Variable	Average order	Sum of order	Average	Standard deviation
Inventories, Method "A"	3,664122	960,000	0,229008	0,420998
Export	5,026718	1317,000	0,618321	0,486728
Import	4,839695	1268,000	0,564885	0,496721
VAT	2,996183	785,000	0,038168	0,191968
Analytic Accounts	3,450382	904,000	0,167939	0,374527
Units	3,877863	1016,000	0,290076	0,454666
Orders	4,145038	1086,000	0,366412	0,482746

Fig. 37.2 Testing hypothesis H2. *Source* Author

The largest correlation can be observed in the mutual dependence of accounting of imports and exports (value of 0.86). Significant correlations also appear for centres and Analytic accounts (value of 0.39) and the correlation of inventory accounting and centres (value 0.37) (Fig. 37.1)

In testing hypothesis H2 on the uniformity of accounting among companies in the monitored sector, it was found that most companies account with VAT, Analytic accounts and inventory accounting as per method "A". The least number account with imports and exports. The ambivalence, however, is low.

The Friedman test then confirmed hypothesis H2 that: the companies monitored keep their books in the same areas of accounting (Fig. 37.2).

37.5 Conclusion

The companies should connect their accounting programs more with their company-wide software in order to be able to connect items such as orders issued and received with the accounting. This would greatly improve, accelerate and reduce the costs of internal communication. Company-wide software streamlines communications.

When deciding on the number of accountants, company managers must take into consideration the number of accounting entries (records) rather than the volume of turnover.

Many people still remember the time when large companies had three floors of offices filled with accountants. The development of computer technology reduced the complexity of accounting and decreased the number of accountants in the companies. Almost a quarter of the companies even do without their own accounts.

With the progressive computerisation of documentary accounting (Strouhal et al. 2012; Ryneš 2013), the complexity of accounting will continue to decrease.

The low percentage of university-educated accountants is most likely associated with an accounting routine. Manual accounting requiring a large number of accountants has been replaced by accounting software. Accounting, however, remains routine, even though computer technology has changed the character of the original routines. Accounting programs today watching certain control numbers have set mechanisms for checking, etc.

Companies prefer to employ accountants with secondary education, as it means lower labour costs for them.

It is also likely that accountants with post-secondary education work as external accountants or tax advisors and auditors. Many companies have economists with college or university education, who have merely an advisory function for the accountants.

Starting from the idea that the majority of accountants have secondary school education, and the work for them is routine, it is likely that these accounts will give priority to training, where they learn practical and fresh information. The literature intended for accounting practices should be up-to-date and clear. An interesting fact is that the Internet was not listed at all as an additional source of accounting information.

While companies most likely employ accountants with secondary school education in an effort to save money, they do not hesitate to invest money into tax consultants. The reason for this is to optimise the tax obligations, unclear tax legislation or delaying tax returns and thereby also the income tax from legal entities by 3 months.

On the contrary, companies do not generally use the services of auditors, unless the law specifies that they must. The reason is that they likely do not bring (relative to their cost) any real benefits. Penalties imposed because of incorrectly assessed tax or optimising their tax obligation is more important than the accuracy of the accounting.

The question is how businesses perceive the importance of accounting. The main reason for bookkeeping was given as being the fulfilment of their legal obligations, but the great popularity of the accounting centres or order accounting indicates that businesses use accounting as a basis for decision-making. More often they conduct their accounting in more detail than necessary by law, such as using Analytic accounts or inventory accounting according to method A.

The survey found interesting correlations in inventory accounting using method "A", the use of Analytic accounts and simultaneous accounting through departmental centres. These areas of accounting require a higher level of detail, but they also have higher information value.

The Friedman test testing hypothesis H2 confirmed that the companies in this sector behave similarly when accounting in detail, which is optimistic. Thus in reality, accounting is not perceived only as a compulsory evil, but also as a management tool.

References

Janhuba M (2005) Základy teorie účetnictví. Oeconomica, Praha

Kovanicová D (2008) Abeceda účetních znalostí pro každého. Bova Polygon, Praha

Kozel R, Mynářová L, Svobodová H (2011) Moderní metody a techniky marketingového výzkumu. Grada Publishing, a. s., Praha

Křemen B (2014) 100 legálních daňových triků 2014. Grada Publishing, a. s., Praha

Kubanová J (2004) Statistické metody pro ekonomickou a technickou praxi. Statis, Bratislava

Ryneš P (2013) Podvojné účetnictví a účetní závěrka, průvodce podvojným účetnictví k 1.1.2013. Anag, Olomouc

Strouhal J, Židlická R, Knapová B et al (2012) Účetnictví 2012: Velká kniha příkladů. BizBooks, Brno

Chapter 38
New Legislation Concerning Cash Accounting in the Czech Republic and Comments on the Application of the Cash Flow Principle

Jan Molín

Abstract This paper analyses the new Czech legislation of cash accounting, particularly in the context of the application of cash flow principle. The paper starts by discussing basic premises, i.e. general theoretic thoughts about the accrual principle and cash flow principle. This is followed by a part which analyses the new legislation concerning cash accounting, adopted with effect of 1 January 2016 together with other amendments to Czech accounting regulations. The principal part is dedicated to the analysis of the new legislation in light of the application of the cash flow principle.

Keywords Cash accounting · Single-entry accounting · Cash flow principle · Accrual principle

38.1 Introduction

As of 1 January 2016, there have been rather extensive amendments to the Czech accounting standards, which is due particularly to the obligatory transposition of new EU Regulation. However, there have been some other changes brought about by these amendments.

These changes include reintroduction of legislation concerning cash accounting. The aim of this paper is to analyse this legislation, particularly in relation to the application of the cash flow principle, on which the cash accounting legislation is based. The aim of my research is an analysis of some other theoretic issues, especially the relation between cash accounting and the so-called single-entry accounting.

J. Molín (✉)
Department of Financial Accounting and Auditing, University of Economics,
Prague, Czech Republic
e-mail: jan.molin@vse.cz

© Springer International Publishing AG 2017   407
D. Procházka (ed.), *New Trends in Finance and Accounting*,
Springer Proceedings in Business and Economics,
DOI 10.1007/978-3-319-49559-0_38

The paper is organized in the following manner: Chapter 2 deals with basic background and literature review. Chapter 3 discusses the new legislation concerning cash accounting by putting it in the historic context and analyses it thoroughly. Chapter 4 is the crucial part of the paper analysing the new legislation in relation to the application of the cash flow principle. At the end of the paper, I present a conclusion summarizing my findings.

For the purpose of writing this paper, I used qualitative methodology. I have studied literature and other sources, and I discuss them in the context of my own research. I have also used a comparative analysis.

38.2 Basic Premises and Literature Review

It is a well-known fact that there are two principles applied in accounting. The more popular and preferred one is the accrual principle, explained by, for example, Kovanicová (2003, pp. 46–47), and its consequences are discussed by, inter alia, Skálová (p. 102 et seq.), which is complemented by the alternative cash flow principle. As, for example, Luminita (2014, p. 671) explained, in the cash method of accounting, transactions are recorded only when cash is received or paid.

At the same time, it is apparent that accounting based on the cash flow principle is alternative (in comparison with the accrual accounting that recognizes also revenues and expenses), it is simplified, and its output, especially in short term, may be misleading. Cotter (1996, 149) concluded that on average, disaggregated earnings are better able to reflect value-relevant events than disaggregated cash flows over return intervals of one to ten years. She went on to add that, however, it is clear that the accrual measure is better able to reflect market value changes associated with these activities than the cash flow measure when long return intervals are considered. Conclusions on the difference between the two principles are substantial, and they have broad consequences interfering with, for example, statistics, as Fischer (2003, p. 46) suggested.

For these reasons, accounting based on the cash flow principle is usually intended for rather small entities. As Reider (2007, pp. 33–34) concluded, these entities have one advantage after all: they do not need to distinguish between profitability and liquidity: "The main reason profitability does not always ensure liquidity is the system of accruals used by most businesses in accounting for profit and loss. Small businesses that maintain their financial records on a cash basis do not have these concerns". Therefore, some authors analyse the application of cash accounting in small and medium-sized entities, e.g. Ristea (2010, pp. 211–219). For example, Kovanicová (2006) tangentially commented on this subject.

In the context of the legislation concerning cash accounting in the Czech Republic and particularly with respect to the term used by the Czech law: "single-entry accounting" (in Czech: "jednoduché účetnictví"), it is necessary to discuss also some theoretic background. As Janhuba (2010, p. 17) pointed out, "single-entry accounting is a system of records of partial economic facts concerning the company providing the user with a limited amount of value indicators about the balance and flow of the components of its assets, particularly about money, receivables and liabilities, and enabling—on condition that inventory and debt taking is regularly conducted—to determine the annual economic results by comparing the net assets balance (i.e. the difference between the assets and debts) at the end of the previous period and at the end of the current period". For these and other reasons, we need to conclude—see Janhuba (2010, p. 18)—that the terms cash accounting and single-entry accounting differ with their meaning in the Czech Republic. The concept of this accounting corresponds with the principle of cash flows, which is why I refer to it in this paper as cash accounting, although the formal legal term is—as stated above—"single-entry accounting".

38.3   Legislation Concerning Cash Accounting in the Czech Republic

38.3.1   Historic Context[1]

Cash accounting was a part of Czech accounting regulations for quite some time. Until 2003, accounting entities used either double-entry accounting or cash accounting. Act No. 563/1991 Coll., on Accounting, as amended (hereinafter referred to as the "Act on Accounting") thus defined two accounting systems—see also Müllerová (2010, p. 22), while single-entry accounting could be used by specified accounting entities such as some "non-profit" accounting entities (e.g. citizen associations, churches—provided their total income did not exceed CZK 6 million) and natural persons (entrepreneurs) who did not claim a percentage of their income as deductible expenses for the purpose of income taxation.

A significant milestone in legislation concerning cash accounting dates back to 2004. With effect as of 1 January 2004, the cash accounting system was left out of the Act on Accounting and the legislation concerning cash accounting was abolished. This fact had two fundamental consequences:

(a) a different system for record keeping of economic transactions for entrepreneurs had to be created—this resulted in the so-called tax evidence system regulated by the Act on Income Taxes,[2]
(b) other accounting entities that could use cash-basis accounting until 31 December 2003 had to (according to the initial intention) switch to double-entry accounting as of 1 January 2005.

---

[1]This paper discusses only the legislation which was in force after November 1989, for previous situation see, for example, Plachá and Hrdý (2007).
[2]Schematically on accounting system in the Czech Republic, see Mejzlík (2006, p. 86).

However, later on it proved that the defined deadline was not definite for "non-profit" accounting entities, as other amendments to the Act on Accounting were adopted which postponed the obligatory commencement of keeping accounts on double-entry basis and eventually a provision of Art. 38(a) was adopted according to which certain entities were granted a permanent exception to use cash-basis accounting. The fact is that the accounting of these organizations was actually regulated by abolished legal standards. This fact, together with some other aspects, was the main reason for introducing new legislation.

38.3.2   Basic Principles of Legislation Concerning Cash Accounting as of 1 January 2016

If we take a look at the new legislation concerning cash accounting and compare it with the legislation which was in force until 31 December 2003, we may observe it was conceived in a rather different manner. Primarily, the Act on Accounting does not consider cash accounting to be an (independent) accounting system. When we take into consideration the systematic structure of the legislation concerning cash accounting (and the text of the statement of reasons), we may infer that the intention of the lawmaker was to define cash accounting in the extent of a system for keeping accounts sui generis. Legislation concerning the factual aspects of cash accounting is thus included in Art. 13(b) of the Act on Accounting (in the passage following the legislation concerning accounting in a simplified extent).

We may also infer from the legislation the above-discussed basic principle of cash accounting: the principle of cash flows. In comparison with double-entry accounting, which is based on the accrual basis,[3] the items recorded in cash accounting are cash inflows, cash outflows, assets and liabilities. Unlike in double-entry accounting, where an organization's results are determined by comparing revenues and expenses, in cash accounting results are "measured" by how much cash inflow exceeds cash outflow (revenues and expenses are not recorded in cash accounting). This concept is in line with the arrangement of statements of cash accounting—in the terminology of the Act on Accounting referred to as "overviews". The outcome of cash accounting is two overviews: statement of receipts and expenditures and statement of assets and liabilities. In this context, I am of the opinion that the main positive aspect of the new legislation is the explicitly expressed objective for the compilation of these two statements (and actually also the objective of cash accounting), which is that the two above-specified statements "provide comprehensive information on cash inflows, cash outflows, assets and liabilities of an accounting entity".[4]

---

[3]Naturally, the cash is important and relevant also in accrual-basis accounting. That is why the cash flow statement has to be compiled—for detailed information, see, for example, Vašek (2006, pp. 39–58).

[4]See provision of Art. 13(b) of the Act on Accounting.

Concerning the form of legislation—as it has become a matter of habit in Czech accounting regulations—a part of legal standards concerning cash accounting is included in the Act on Accounting, which is followed by Decree of the Ministry of Finance of the Czech Republic No. 325/2015 Coll. (hereinafter referred to as the "Decree").[5]

38.3.2.1 Accounting Entities that May Use Cash-Basis Accounting

The Act on Accounting defines in the provision of Art. 1(f)(1) the accounting entities that may use cash-basis accounting. There are four cumulative conditions (i.e. each of them has to be met), while the last of them is alternative:

(a) the entity is not a value-added tax payer,
(b) total income[6] in the previous (closed) period did not exceed CZK 3 million,
(c) the value of assets[7] does not exceed CZK 3 million and
(d) the entity is:

1. an association,
2. a labour union, a labour union subsidiary, an international labour union and an international labour union subsidiary,
3. an employer association, an employer organization subsidiary, an international employer organization subsidiary,
4. church and a religious society or a religious institution that is a legal entity registered in accordance with the act regulating the status of churches and religious societies, or
5. hunting society.

It should be added that the proposed amendment originally defined that the maximum value of entities that would be entitled to use cash-basis accounting would be CZK 1.5 million, presuming this asset value generates a twofold income value (the assumption was thus similar to other analogous provisions in the Act on Accounting, e.g. criteria for obligatory audit of financial statements). However, during the legislative procedure the maximum amount was changed to CZK 3 million.

---

[5]For a wider context of accounting regulation, please see, for example, Procházka (2006, pp. 30–48) or Lewis and Pendrill (2004, pp. 8–21).

[6]In accordance with the provision of Art. 1(4) of the Act on Accounting, the total income is the total of income as indicated in the statement of receipts and expenditures for the relevant accounting period. The total of income does not include interim items and cash inflows from the sale of fixed assets and random and extraordinary cash inflows.

[7]In accordance with the provision of Art. 1(5), the total of assets indicated the statement of assets and liabilities at the balance sheet day. The total of assets does not include receivables resulting from the sale of fixed assets and the relevant expenditures as well as random and exceptional receivables and the relevant expenditures.

At the same time, the Act on Accounting defines that the above-mentioned entities may use cash-basis accounting when they are established or start operating; if there is a reasonable assumption, they will meet the above-specified conditions at the balance sheet day for the first accounting period.

At the same time, if an accounting entity using cash-basis accounting no longer meets the conditions for using cash-basis accounting, it has to switch to double-entry accounting, i.e. according to the definition of the law: to accounting in full extent or in a simplified extent as of the first day following the accounting period in which the accounting entity became aware of this fact. There is also the so-called consistency principle stipulating that an accounting entity may (with the exception of termination of its activity) stop keeping accounts on double-entry basis only after five consecutive accounting periods.

38.3.2.2 Accounting Books, Accounting Methods and Statements

The Act on Accounting defines three groups of accounting books for cash accounting:

(a) cash book,
(b) book of receivables and liabilities, and
(c) auxiliary books on other assets.

The cash book is an accounting book where accounting records are arranged chronologically and which includes at least information about:

(a) money in cash and on banking accounts, especially in banks, savings and credit cooperatives,
(b) actual cash inflows and outflows received and paid in the relevant accounting period,
(c) interim items, i.e. cash flows that are not final revenue or expense as defined above in (b).

With respect to the fact that accounting entities using cash-basis accounting have to revaluate money denominated in a foreign currency as of the day balance sheet day, a cash book has to, in accordance with the legal provisions in the Decree, include also exchange rate differences resulting from the revaluation. It should be added that other assets and debts (in a foreign currency) are not to be revaluated as of the balance sheet day.

Records from a cash book are then used for the compilation of the statement of receipts and expenditures mentioned above: its structure (arrangement and designation of items) is defined in Annex No. 1 to the Decree. The basic prism of the statement of receipts and expenditures arrangement is the division into the main and economic activity of the accounting entity, which is why this aspect is also applied to the classification of cash inflows and cash outflows in the cash book.

Receivables and liabilities are recorded in another accounting book: the book of receivables and the book of liabilities (in the terminology of the Decree referred to as the book of receivables and liabilities). The Decree explicitly stipulates that records in this book include provisions defined by special legal (tax) regulations: the so-called legal provisions.

Other components of the assets and liabilities are recorded in auxiliary book on other assets. In these books, accounting entities keep records particularly of the following:

(a) fixed (intangible and tangible) assets,
(b) financial assets,
(c) inventory and
(d) stamps and vouchers.[8]

Figures of the assets and liabilities recorded in the above-defined books are then used as a basis for the compilation of statement of assets and liabilities, whose structure (arrangement and designation of items) is included in Annex No. 2 to the Decree. It should be added that the Act on Accounting presumes—even in the case of cash accounting—that inventory is taken in accordance with the provision of Art. 29(1).

In both cases, the items are reported in thousands of CZK. The reports are to be compiled within 6 month after the end of each accounting period at the latest, while they have to follow the provision of Art. 18(3) of the Act on Accounting, i.e. the statements have to include the following:

(a) name and registered office of the accounting entity,
(b) ID No. of the entity (if any) and in accordance with the act on public registers of legal entities and natural persons also information on registration in a public registry stated in business papers,
(c) legal form of the accounting entity and information indicating that the accounting entity is in liquidation (if relevant),
(d) type of activity, or the purpose for which the accounting entity was established,
(e) the balance sheet day,
(f) the day when statements are compiled,
(g) signature of the statutory body of the accounting entity.

Also statements shall be (this is rather unfortunate from the perspective of terminology) compiled at the balance sheet day, which is the day when accounting books are closed. They are compiled either as regular (as of the last day of the accounting period) or extraordinary. Statement of assets and liabilities is now subject to disclosure duty in accordance with the provision of Art. 21(a)(1) of the

---

[8]For exact definition of the items, see Decree No. 504/2002 Coll., implementing regulations of Act No. 563/1991 Coll., on Accounting, as amended, for accounting entities whose main activity is not business and they keep accounts on double-entry basis.

Act on Accounting, both statements have to be archived for ten years (as the case is with final accounts).

With respect to the fact that cash accounting is based on different principles than double-entry accounting, as we discussed above, some provisions of the Act on Accounting are excluded for the application of legislation on cash accounting:

(a) provisions concerning only double-entry accounting (e.g. provisions concerning guide chart of accounts, some provisions concerning final accounts) are explicitly excluded,
(b) provisions concerning write-offs, adjustments, provisions and fair value are excluded,
(c) accounting entities using cash-basis accounting cannot use a fiscal year as an accounting period, whereas they are not prohibited from having an accounting period 3 months longer or shorter when establishing or cancelling an accounting entity (see provisions of Art. 3(4) of the Act on Accounting),
(d) other provisions shall be used by accounting entities using cash-basis accounting so that they are in accordance with the sense, purpose and methods defined for cash accounting and so that the statements disclose comprehensive information on cash inflows, cash outflows, assets and liabilities of an accounting entity.

With respect to the above-specified exclusion of certain methods, in order to ensure legal certitude of accounting entities using cash-basis accounting, it is explicitly defined that using cash-basis accounting is not considered by the rules and methods stipulated by the Act on Accounting a breach of the true and fair representation of the subject of accounting and financial situation of a given accounting entity.

38.4 Assessment of the New Legislation Concerning Cash Accounting in Relation to the Principle of Cash Flows

As I have mentioned above at several places in this paper, the new legislation is based on the application of the cash flow principle. Therefore, the "performance" of an accounting entity is measured by how much the cash inflows exceed cash outflows in a given accounting period. This is one of the reasons why cash accounting cannot be referred to as single-entry accounting, as it, according to the theoretic approach—see Janhuba (2010, pp. 17–18), does not measure the difference between cash inflows and cash outflows, but profit or loss by comparing the net assets at the beginning and at the end of an accounting period.

The book where records of the inflows and outflows are kept is—as we stated above—a cash book. We may then infer from the legislation that a cash book includes entries by which an accounting entity evidences records of the following:

(a) cash inflows and cash outflows,
(b) cash inflows and cash outflows on accounts in banks or saving and credit cooperatives,
(c) interim items of mutual cash transfers to banking accounts and between banking accounts and
(d) exchange rate differences resulting from revaluating of cash and banking account balance in a foreign currency at the balance sheet day or another moment when the cash book is closed.[9]

Records of cash inflows and outflows in a cash book are linked to the above-mentioned statement of receipts and expenditures, which has the following structure:

A. Receipts

01 Sale of goods
02 Sale of products and services
03 Income from public collections
04 Cash donations received from other sources than public collections
05 Member fees received
06 Grants and contributions received from public budgets
07 Others
08 Interim items
09 Exchange rate differences
10 Total inflows

B. Expenditures

01 Fixed intangible and tangible assets
02 Material
03 Goods
04 Services
05 Wages
06 Insurance paid for employees and employer
07 Other personal expenses
08 Others
09 Interim items
10 Exchange rate differences
11 Total outflows
99 Difference between receipts and expenditures

Through the linguistic interpretation of the above-quoted provisions, we may infer that the subject of records kept in a cash book and thus also the content of the statement of receipts and expenditures are cash inflows and cash outflows.

---

[9]See, inter alia, provisions of Art. 2(1) of Decree No. 325/2015 Coll.

However, in this context it is necessary to ask the question whether such an approach (i.e. recording only cash transactions) is in line with the cash flow principle. From the name of the principle, we may infer it is so; however, in my opinion, such an approach would be too narrow.

What is actually the content of this principle? As we may indirectly infer from, for example, Pelák (2015), the difference between the accrual principle and the cash flow principle lies in the moment when (i.e. how soon) transactions are reflected in a company's performance. We may infer that the intention of the accrual principle is that it tries to reflect transactions during the period when they occur without having to wait for their completion. We may use as an example a sale of service and how it is recorded in when we issue an invoice that is recorded at the moment when we provide the service, not when the invoice is settled and the transaction is completed by receiving an actual payment. By contrast, the cash flow principle reflects transactions at the moment when a payment is actually received.

On the other hand, we cannot infer whether the subject of keeping records on a cash flow basis is only cash inflows—as required by the Czech legislation concerning cash accounting. Actually, non-monetary inflows are equivalent to non-monetary inflows, since these inflows result in an increase in the net assets value of an accounting entity. In the example mentioned in the previous paragraph, this would be, for example, a revenue from a service sold through a barter—that is for a compensation not in a monetary form. In this case, there will be no cash inflow, but I am of the opinion that this should not imply such a transaction will not be put down in accounts.

Therefore, I hereby present the fundamental critics of the cash flow principle in cash accounting under the Czech legislation. This legislation requires keeping records only of monetary inflows, not non-monetary inflows. This may lead to elementary conceptual errors when disclosing the difference between receipts and expenditures (or their structure), which may concern non-profit organizations, for which cash accounting is intended.

These subjects usually receive money (in the form of donations or grants), which they then use for funding their activities, but quite often they receive non-monetary donations. When keeping records of only cash inflows, conceptual discrepancies may arise when keeping records of two similar economic transactions. We may use as an example a situation when an organization receives money (as a gift) later used for purchasing fixed assets and compare it with a situation when these fixed assets are donated (i.e. in a non-monetary form). While the former will be recorded in accounts by including the cash inflow in the cash book together with the subsequent purchase (expense) of the fixed asset, a contrario, the latter will not be recorded at all under Czech regulation of cash accounting. Factually identical operations (i.e. receiving an inflow which increases the assets value—whether in monetary or non-monetary form) will be recorded differently.

38.5 Conclusion

Amendments to accounting standards effective of 1 January 2016 resulted in the reintroduction of legislation concerning cash accounting. This legislation was a part of Czech accounting regulations before, later it was released, and accounting regulations governed only double-entry accounting based on accrual basis. Nevertheless, some entities (mostly smaller non-profit organizations) were allowed to use cash-basis accounting in accordance with the abolished legislation. This was one of the reasons for reintroducing legislation concerning cash accounting into Czech accounting regulations.

We may conclude that the new legislation is based on the application of the cash flow principle, which—unlike the accrual principle—measures "performance" of an accounting entity by comparing cash inflows and cash outflows, i.e. by profit or loss. In this context, it is necessary to distinguish cash accounting from single-entry accounting, for which it is often, particularly in a company's every day routine, mistaken. In principle, single-entry accounting does not measure performance by comparing inflows with outflows, but detects profit or loss by comparing the net assets at the end and at the beginning of an accounting period.

However, the new legislation should be subjected to critique when it comes to the cash flow principle, since only (monetary) cash inflows and (monetary) cash outflows are to be recorded in Czech cash accounting. It is thus necessary to observe that this is the principal drawback of the new legislation. The critique is aimed at the fact that non-monetary inflows (and outflows) are not to be recorded in cash accounting. This may then result into non-conceptual deficiencies, when economically similar transaction (in the form of receiving an inflow—whether monetary or non-monetary) is to be disclosed differently.

Acknowledgments This paper has been prepared under the financial support (intended as the institutional support of long-term conceptual development of research, development and innovations) of the Faculty of Finance and Accounting, University of Economics, Prague, which the author gratefully acknowledges.

References

Cotter J (1996) Accrual and cash flow accounting models: a comparison of the value relevance and timeliness of their components. Account Financ 36(2):127–150
Fischer J (2003) K využití dat podnikového účetnictví pro statistické účely (in English: To the use of business accounting data for statistical purposes). Statistika 40(3):44–46
Janhuba M (2010) Teorie účetnictví (výběr z problematiky) (in English: Accounting theory). Nakladatelství Oeconomica, Praha
Kovanicová D (2006) Harmonizace účetního výkaznictví malých a středních podniků: projekt Spojených národů (in English: Financial reporting harmonization of small and medium-sized enterprises: United National Project). Český finanční a účetní časopis 1(3):9–21
Kovanicová D, a kol (2003): Finanční účetnictví. Světový koncept (in English: Financial accounting. A global approach). Polygon, Praha

Lewis L, Pendrill D (2004) Advanced financial accounting. Prentice Hall, London, p 2004

Luminita R (2014) Is it important the accounting model used by the economic entity in making decisions by the users of the information? points of view. Ann Univ Oradea Econ Sci Ser 23(1):669–677

Mejzlík L (2006) Možnosti a rizika technologického řešení převodu českých účetních závěrek do IFRS (in English: Possibilities and risks of the translation of the Czech financial statements to IFRS by accounting informations systems). Český finanční a účetní časopis, 1(1):84–98

Müllerová L, a kol (2010) Analýza vývoje účetnictví a výkaznictví malých a středních podniků (in English: Analysis of development of the accounting and reporting for small and medium enterprises). Český finanční a účetní časopis 5(1):20–36

Pelák J (2015) Vztah mezi účetnictvím a daní z příjmů: styčné body, limity a omezení (in English: Relationship between accounting and income tax: contact points, limits and restraints). Bulletin Komory daňových poradců České republiky 3(3)

Plachá D, Hrdý M (2007) Analýza historického vývoje účetnictví v českých zemích v letech 1918–2006 (in English: Analysis of accounting historical development in bohemian countries in years 1918–2006). E + M Ekonomie a management 10(2):65–73

Procházka D (2006) Approaches to the regulation of the accounting. Eur Financ Account J 1(2):30–48

Reider B (2007) Operating your business on a cash basis. J Corp Account Financ 19(1):29–38

Ristea M, a kol (2010) Small and medium-sized entities between the accrual basis of accounting and cash accounting. Roman Econ Bus Rev 5(4):208–220

Vašek L (2006) Výkaz peněžních toků – Mezinárodní standardy účetního výkaznictví a jejich srovnání s českou účetní legislativou (in English: Cash flow statement—International financial reporting standards and their comparison with Czech accounting standards). Český finanční a účetní časopis 1(2):39–58

Chapter 39
Comparison of Accounting for Mergers in the Czech Republic and Poland

Jiří Pospíšil and Marzena Strojek-Filus

Abstract The aim of this article was to examine the bond of the national regulation of accounting for mergers in the Czech Republic and Poland to the theoretical methods of accounting for business combinations and to compare the national regulations assuming finding potential clashes. Our assumption was that since Poland's capital market is more advanced than Czech's capital market, the regulation for mergers and the accounting for this type of transactions will also be more advanced; but at the same time, since both national regulations arose from the same geopolitical background and embodies the same directives of the European Union, therefore, we assumed that the basic concepts of accounting for mergers will be very much alike. Both assumptions proved to be correct. We found that the differences between Czech national regulation and Polish national regulations are many, but the similarities are greater. Both regulations aspire to some extent to the IAS/IFRS regulation of merger accounting as well as to the theoretical concepts of merger accounting and its methods. We found that Czech national regulation is a bit behind with its convergence to the IAS/IFRS which is in our opinion cause by the reluctance of the Czech national legislation to embrace the comprehensive and coherent method-based approach over the strict legal regulation.

Keywords Accounting for mergers · Business combinations · Goodwill

J. Pospíšil (✉)
Department of Financial Accounting and Auditing, University of Economics,
Nam. W. Churchilla 4, 130 67 Prague, Czech Republic
e-mail: Jiri.Pospisil@vse.cz

M. Strojek-Filus
Department of Accounting, University of Economics in Katowice, Katowice, Poland
e-mail: mstrojek@ue.katowice.pl

© Springer International Publishing AG 2017   419
D. Procházka (ed.), *New Trends in Finance and Accounting*,
Springer Proceedings in Business and Economics,
DOI 10.1007/978-3-319-49559-0_39

39.1   Introduction and Literature Review

The aim of this article was to examine the bond of the national regulation of accounting for mergers in the Czech Republic and Poland to the theoretical methods of accounting for business combinations and to compare the national regulations assuming finding potential clashes, which might provide valuable matter for further research as both countries enter several cross-border mergers and other business combinations every year (see for example, Žárová and Skálová 2014). The examination of the matter will be performed using the comparison method—a comparison of the relevant legal acts.

The methodology of accounting for mergers and other business combinations has been undergoing a significant development in both countries and at the level of IAS/IFRS, US GAAP (see for example, Aghimien et al. 2014) and general theoretical level (see for example, Nurnberg and Sweeney 1998 or Ayers et al. 2000). The evolution of the Czech national regulation of merger accounting has been a subject to great discussions (Vomáčková 2012) and the difficulties of implementation of the theoretical concepts of accounting for mergers to the Czech regulation (Vomáčková 2006).

Our assumption is that since Poland's capital market is more advanced than Czech's capital market, the regulation for mergers and the accounting for this type of transactions will also be more advanced. At the same time, both national regulations arise from the same geopolitical background and embodies the same directives of the European Union; therefore, we assume that the basic concepts of accounting for mergers will be very much alike.

39.2   Accounting for Mergers in the Czech Republic

In the Czech Republic, the accounting for mergers is regulated by the Act No. 563/1991 Coll. on accounting, its implementing decrees, and the Czech accounting standards. The accounting for mergers is greatly influenced by the regulation of mergers in the Act No. 128/2005 on the transformation of companies and cooperatives which regulates the process of mergers, spin-offs, and other business combinations. Similarly to Poland, Czech Republic implemented the Regulation EC No. 1606/2002 on the application of international accounting standards, which allowed the application of the IAS/IFRS for companies listed on stock markets of European Union, or companies having their securities traded on public markets in the EU. Also, companies in holdings which parent company makes its consolidated financial statements in accordance to IAS/IFRS may apply IAS/IFRS for their individual financial statements. These companies follow the regulation for merger accounting set out in the IAS/IFRS.

39.2.1 Accounting Methods for Mergers Based on Czech Regulation

Unlike the IAS/IFRS, the accounting for mergers in the Czech Republic according to the Act No. 563/1991 Coll. is not based on coherent methodology; thus, there are no explicitly formulated methods for merger accounting. Even so, upon close examination of the applicable regulation, we find that the regulation of merger accounting according to the Act No. 563/1991 Coll. is quite similar to the three major methods of accounting for mergers: the acquisition method, the new entity method, and the pooling of interests method. The similarities are many, while the differences are numerous too. We will discuss these similarities and differences in the following text which will allow us to describe the accounting for mergers in Czech Republic at the same time.

The **acquisition method** puts an emphasis on the fact that one of the companies can be identified as an acquirer who acquires another company or business. This method is applicable in the case of a capital acquisition (i.e., the acquirer purchases majority of shares) or business acquisition (i.e., the acquirer purchases the business of the other company) or a merger (i.e., the acquirer assimilates the business of the other company and this company cease to exist). The acquisition method stipulates the revaluation of assets and liabilities acquired to their fair value during the consolidation process and the goodwill calculation. In the case of the acquisition method, the "acquisition difference" needs to be calculated as a difference between the acquisition price (a sum of purchase price and acquisition-related costs) and the value of the net assets acquired. The acquisition difference is usually referred to as the "goodwill", if the difference has a positive value, or as the "bargain purchase", if the acquisition difference has a negative value. Generally speaking, the acquisition difference (whether negative or positive value) can be reported as an asset (usually long-term intangible asset) or as a gain/loss in the equity.

The acquisition method is applied on most of the capital acquisitions and business combinations in the Czech Republic even though its usage is limited to certain types of companies: "společnost s ručením omezeným" (limited liability company) and "akciová společnost" (joint-stock company/public limited company). The modifications the national regulation made to this generally accepted method lie in several important aspects of this method: revaluation, acquisition price determination and the treatment of the acquisition difference. While the generally accepted acquisition method assumes all the transferred assets and liabilities to be revalued at their fair value, the Czech legislation allows to revaluate the assets only. Even more so, the acquirer may choose not to revaluate at all and adopt the book prices from the company acquired. Another difference is the determination of the acquisition price. Czech regulation excludes the merger-related costs to be included in the acquisition price for the purposes of acquisition difference calculation. Apart from the modified acquisition difference calculation, there are some specific provisions for the treatment for the acquisition difference. In the case the acquirer decides to revaluate the acquired assets at their fair value, the acquisition difference will be either a "goodwill"—an intangible long-term asset with a given period of amortization of 5 years, or a profit of the transaction and therefore accounted as a profit to the equity of the acquirer. In the case the acquirer decides no to revaluate the acquitted assets and keep their value at their historical prices level, the acquisition difference will be either "valuation difference from business combination"—a tangible long-term asset with given period of amortization of 15 years, or a profit of the transaction and therefore accounted as a profit to the equity of the acquirer.

The pooling of interests method assume the merger of equals, i.e., unlike in the situations where the acquisition method is applied, in the case of transactions using the pooling of interests method, none of the merging companies can be identified as an acquirer. This is a very important assumption which also limits the usage of this method to a great extent. The transactions where the merging companies could be considered as "equals" are rather rare. From the accounting point of view, the specific characteristic of this method is that unlike the acquisition method or the new entity method, pooling of interests method does not assume the revaluation of the assets and liabilities of any participating companies. The reason behind is the fact that none of the participating companies could be identified as an acquirer and there is no purchase transaction, therefore the basis for revaluation is missing. This fact constitutes the reasons for other characteristics of pooling of interest method: There is no acquisition difference, and the merger-related costs are accounted as expenses.

The **pooling of interest method** is—similarly to the acquisition method—not defined in any Czech legal document. Even though some aspects of the pooling of interest method can be identified in the mergers of specific types of companies in Czech Republic: "veřejná obchodní společnost" ("partnership"), "komanditní společnost" (limited partnership), and "družstvo" (cooperative). The first similarity lies in the valuation used in the consolidated financial statements (i.e., the first statement after the merger). Regardless of the actual characteristics of the transaction, the current legislation does not allow the revaluation of assets and liabilities for mergers of these types of companies. This means that even in transactions where the acquirer can be identified, the revaluation is not allowed. Another similarity to the pooling of interest method lies in the fact that "veřejná obchodní společnost" and at some extent also "komanditní společnost" usually do not form the registered capital. Registered capital represents the investments of the investors and also represents their ownership. In the typical scenario of the mergers of "společnost s ručením omezením" or "akciová společnost," the acquirer takes over the net assets and issues new set of shares to the owners of the acquired company. This is not applicable in the case of "veřejná obchodní společnost" and "komanditní společnost" since there is no or very limited registered capital.

The method of a **new entity**, also known as the method of a **fresh start,** is the third of generally accepted methods for merger accounting. This method assumes establishing new company which poses as an acquirer of the other companies entering the merger. This method like the acquisition method requires to identify acquirer, which in this case is always the new established company. The acquirer in this case comes to existence at the point where the companies entering the merger cease to exist—the continuum is essential here. The newly created company issue shares which are distributed to the owners of the merging companies in the proportion that would respect the fair value of their former ownership in the merging companies. The valuation of the merging companies and the revaluation of their assets and liabilities are necessary for this method. The successor company assimilates the net assets of the merging companies at their fair value and calculates the "acquisition difference" which is usually interpreted as a goodwill (positive or negative) and dealt with in the manner similar to what is applied in the case of acquisition method. An important difference between the acquisition method and the new entity method is that using the new entity method ensure, the successor company will not take over the equity items from its predecessors. This is particularly important in the case of the retained earnings which might have been distributed through dividends in the predecessor companies but cannot be distributed from the successor.

The new entity method is used with some modifications in Czech Republic for mergers of "společnost s ručením omezeným" and "akciová společnost." The major specification of the Czech application of this method from its core concept is the valuation of the assets and liabilities transferred to the successor company. National legislation does not allow the revaluation of liabilities transferred and the successor company to take over the assets at their historical prices (i.e., the book values of the predecessor company). These modifications have got a significant impact to the calculation of the acquisition difference, which in Czech Republic is either goodwill or "valuation difference from business combination" depending on the decision of the successor company to take over the assets at their fair value or the historical prices. The treatment of these two types of acquisition difference according to the Czech legislation is the same as for the acquisition differences emanating from the application of the acquisition method (see above).

39.2.2 Treatment of the Acquisition Difference and Merger Date in Czech Republic

Czech legislation stipulates two types of acquisition difference: Goodwill and "Oceňovací rozdíl k nabytému majetku" (also referred to as the "valuation difference from business combinations"). Both acquisition differences can be reported at positive or negative amount. Amortization of the acquisition difference is accounted to the profit and loss account. The amortization method is the same for positive and negative values; the only difference is that while the amortization of the positive values are accounted as an expense, the amortization of the negative value is accounted as a gain.

Goodwill is recognized to the balance sheet as a long-term intangible asset. Goodwill is the difference between the value of the acquired company (based on the valuation report by the expert) and the difference between assets at their fair value (also based on the valuation report by the expert) and liabilities at their book value. Czech regulation stipulates linear amortization method and the amortization period of goodwill of 5 years. The amortization period might be longer or shorter based on the decision of the company, but the reasons for a different amortization period need to be properly explained in the notes to the financial statements.

Valuation difference from business combinations is recognized to the balance sheet as a long-term tangible asset. Valuation difference from business combinations is a difference between the value of the acquired business (based on the valuation report by the appointed expert) and the net assets acquired (valued at their book prices). Czech legislation stipulates linear amortization method and the amortization period of the valuation difference from business combinations of 15 years. The amortization period might be shorter than 15 years only in the situation when all transferred assets have got their depreciation period shorter than 15 years. Also in the moment when the last part of the assets transferred is written-off, the valuation difference from the business combinations must be written-off as well.

The deployment of the merger date, i.e., the date from which the merger is effective and all the transactions are accounted on behalf of the successor company. From 1992 to 2000, the merger date was fixed at the day of the registration of the merger by the Corporate Register. From 2001 to mid-2008, the law required the merger date not to precede the day of filling at the Corporate Register more than 9 months, which was later extended to 12 months. This regulation created an obstacle for cross-border mergers, since many of the European Union states kept their merger date at the day of registration of the transaction by the Corporate Register. As discussed in Pospíšil (2015), the respective law was then amended and effective from January 1, 2012; companies were allowed to choose the effective day of the merger almost any day in the 365-day period prior to the date of application for registration of transformation in the Corporate Register; moreover, it allows to set the day of the registration in the Corporate Register as an effective date. After the amendment, it is also possible to separate so-called balance sheet date, i.e., the date on which the regular or interim financial statements will be drawn up which the valuation expert will use to perform the valuation of the company and which also becomes the source data of the project of the transformation.

39.3 Accounting for Mergers in Poland

In Poland, the issue of accounting for mergers was regulated for the first time by the Accounting Act (in force from January 1, 1995) which is currently the main legal act on accounting in Poland (the Accounting Act of 29 September 1994, last consolidated text in the Journal of Laws 2013, item 330 as amended, hereinafter as the Acc. Act).

The original Acc. Act text did not sufficiently delineate legal business combinations of entities and capital mergers in the form of capital groups. The accounting methods presented in Acc. Act also referred to the preparation of consolidated statements. Only subsequent amendments to Acc. Act brought a clear separation of accounting methods for business combinations and methods of drawing up consolidated financial statements of capital groups.

Since the implementation of the Regulation of the European Parliament and of the Council (Regulation EC No. 1606/2002 on the application of international accounting standards), the use of IAS/IFRS is obligatory for a specified group of companies. Since January 1, 2005, all companies listed on stock markets and banks preparing consolidated financial statements are required to follow IAS/IFRS. Security issuers whose securities are admitted for trading or intend to apply for trading on one of the regulated markets of countries of the European Economic Area can draw up financial statements according to IAS/IFRS too. Moreover, entities in a capital group, in which a parent draws up consolidated financial statements according to IAS/IFRS, may adopt these standards as a legal basis for drawing up their individual statements. Polish companies following the IAS/IFRS either mandatory or by their choice apply the IAS/IFRS accounting methods for merger accounting. Other Polish companies keep their accounting books to the provisions of Acc. Act, and this legal act lays down the rules of accounting for their mergers as well.

Polish Commercial Law takes a significant part in conducting mergers and accounting for them. From this point of view, business combinations are regulated by the Code of Commercial Companies (Act of 15 September 2000; Code of Commercial Companies; Journal of Laws No. 94, item 1037, further referred to as CoCC). According to CoCC, a business combination comes down to two cases:

- a transfer of all assets and liabilities of one company being acquired to another acquiring company (the company being acquires ceases to exist). Referred to as incorporation,
- a formation of a new company by merging companies, which cease to exist; the assets and liabilities are transferred to in exchange for shares in a new company.

CoCC strictly specifies the permitted legal forms for acquiring, being acquired, and newly formed companies as well as a merger plan.

There is substantial difference between the definition of a merger in CoCC and IAS/IFRS. In terms of CoCC, the mergers takes place on business and legal level, and the outcome of this process is supposed to be one legal entity: an acquiring company or a new established company. The IAS/IFRS concept is broader as it includes the business combinations on the capital acquisition level too which means maintaining legally separated entities (although economically interconnected) and separate reporting.

According to the Polish regulation, the merger date of companies is assumed to be the date when the merger is entered in the Business register.

39.3.1 Accounting Methods for Mergers Based on Acc. Act

The methods used for accounting for mergers in Poland depend on the adopted legal basis for drawing up financial statements:

- the acquisition method according to IAS/IFRS regulations,
- the acquisition method according to Acc. Act regulations,
- the pooling of interest method according to Acc. Act regulations.

We will not analyze the accounting methods according to the IAS/IFRS, as there are plenty other papers dealing with this IAS/IFRS methodology (see for example, Aghimien et al. 2014). The following articles will focus on national regulation of accounting for mergers in Poland. Acc. Act allows two accounting methods for mergers: the acquisition method and the pooling of interests method.

The acquisition method has been recognized as the main method of accounting for mergers. The accounting takes place in the account books of the company to which the assets of the merging companies are transferred (acquiring company) or of a newly formed company. This method is characterized by a clear recognition of the company gaining control.

According to Article 44b. 1 of Acc. Act, accounting for merger by acquisition method is based on totaling particular items of financial statements of the acquiring company and the company being acquired, whereas assets and liabilities of the latter should be valued at their fair value determined as at the date of their merger. The equity of the acquired company is excluded from the items of the aggregated report. While accounting the merger, it is also necessary to take into consideration the assets and liabilities of the company being acquired, which have not yet been recognized in the books of the acquired company, but have been identified during the merger. Acc. Act stipulates the permitted ways of determining the fair value of individual groups of assets and liabilities.

The second method defined by the Acc. Act is the pooling of interests method. The pooling of interest method can be used exclusively for the transactions when the existing shareholders do not lose control over the merging companies and none of the merging companies can be identified as the acquirer. A special case of such transaction is the merger of subsidiaries (direct and indirect) of the same parent entity.

Contrary to the acquisition method, the assets and liabilities are not revalued to their fair value. The individual items of corresponding assets and liabilities of the merging companies are merely summed up at their book values. Thus, the recognition of the merger in the financial statements is based on the historical cost concept rather than fair value concept.

The value that is excluded is the initial capital of the company whose assets were transferred to another company, or companies removed from the register as a result of the merger. The difference between total assets and liabilities is accounted to the equity of the company to which assets of the consolidated companies or the newly formed company are transferred. As a result, neither goodwill nor negative goodwill is recognized. When using this method, costs incurred in relation to merger need to be recognized as financial costs.

39.3.2 Goodwill

In the case of the acquisition method, it is particularly important to compare the acquisition price with the fair value of net assets of the company being acquired.

The acquisition price is:

- in the case of new shares issue—the market price of these shares or their fair value determined otherwise, whereas the excess of this value is to be included in the capital reserve; this price is determined as of the date on which all material conditions of merger were satisfied,
- in the case of acquiring own shares—their acquisition price,
- in the case of acquiring shares of the acquired company—their acquisition price,
- in the case of making payment in other form—fair value of item being paid for (e.g., certain assets), and
- in the case of making payment in various forms—sum total of the relevant values described above.

The acquisition price is increased by the costs directly incurred in connection with the merger of companies.

If the acquisition price is higher than the fair value of net assets of the acquired company, then the surplus is recognized in the acquiring company or in the newly established company as goodwill. This value may have a powerful impact on the evaluation of financial situation of the company after the merger, in particular when its share in total assets is significant. Goodwill as an asset represents future economic benefits arising from the merger of companies. It represents a current value of additional benefits which the acquiring company expects to achieve (Lycklama á Nijeholt 2010, p. 20).

The rules of accounting for goodwill have been changed several times. According to the last amendment of the Acc. Act, a company makes amortization charges on goodwill through the whole period of its economic useful life. If it is impossible to estimate the period of economic useful life in a reliable manner, the period used should be no longer than 5 years. Acc. Act allows for writing-off goodwill by the linear method recognized as other operating costs.

If the merger price is lower, then negative goodwill is written down. Negative goodwill up to the amount not exceeding fair value of the acquired fixed assets (except for long-term financial assets listed on regulated markets) is recognized by the entity in a separate entry of the consolidated balance sheet. The possible excess of this value is recognized as an income. Negative goodwill recognized in the balance sheet is amortized. The amortization is carried out through the period which is calculated as a weighted average of the economic useful life of the acquired amortizable assets. This is very different from the provisions of the IAS/IFRS according to which negative goodwill cannot be recognized, rather total difference should be accounted for as a gain/income of the period when the merger took place. Negative goodwill has been a controversial item and interpreted in different ways in the literature for many years (Strojek-Filus 2013, pp. 26–28). It quite often indicates mistakes in the net asset valuation and overestimation of their value.

39.4   Conclusion

The concept of regulation of the accounting for mergers is quite alike in Poland and Czech Republic. Both countries regulate the accounting for mergers through the accounting acts with a close linkage to their commercial law. Unlike Poland, Czech Republic has earmarked the regulation of the mergers from the commercial code and created a dedicated law on transformation of companies which enumerate the possible transactions for existing forms of corporations. A strict regulation of this area is another common denominator of the mergers in both Poland and Czech Republic—both laws strictly specify the permitted legal forms for acquiring, being acquired, and newly formed companies as well as a merger plan. Both Czech Republic and Poland were required to implement the Regulation EC No. 1606/2002 on the application of international accounting standards which means that those companies, who are required (or allowed) to follow IAS/IFRS regulation, will account for the mergers in the same manner. Adoption of Regulation EC No. 1606/2002 created an alternative to national regulation, which will probably persist in both countries parallel to the national regulation for years to come.

Concerning the accounting methods applied, there is a substantial difference between the Czech and Polish concept. While Poland chose to follow a theoretical concept, which is used to define the accounting method explicitly, the Czech concept of accounting for mergers prefers a detailed regulation lacking any underlying theoretical design. While Polish accountant specialists may rely on the theoretically well-developed concepts, Czech accountant specialist need to rely on their interpretation of the relevant provisions of the related legislation, which unfortunately is scattered among several legal documents and a concise and coherent methodology is missing.

The acquisition method used in Poland is very similar to the one prescribed by the IFRS 3 and represents the main accounting method for mergers in Poland. Czech version of the acquisition method is a bit different and resembles the former purchase method of IAS 22 rather than the current methodology of IFRS 3. Both countries apply their own modifications to the acquisition method, especially in the terms of revaluation of net assets and acquisition difference treatment which we will compare in the following paragraphs. Apart from the commonly used acquisition method, both countries apply the pooling of interest method for specific transactions and in the case of Czech Republic, with several modifications to the original theoretical concept. The same applies for the new entity method.

We found that most differences in the methodology used in Poland and Czech Republic lie in the application of the acquisition method. While Poland respects the IFRS 3 concept in terms of revaluation of the transferred assets and liabilities to its fair value, in the Czech Republic companies may choose between keeping the book values from the predecessor option and revaluation of the transferred assets (not liabilities) option. Another substantial difference lies in the identification and fair value valuation of all the transferred assets and liabilities including those assets and liabilities which were not recognized in the balance sheet of the predecessor. This step is inevitable part of IFRS 3 acquisition method and Polish national regulation respects it. In contrast, Czech national regulation does not allow recognizing any new assets or liabilities. Lastly, the constitution of the acquisition price (therefore the calculation of goodwill) in Poland includes the costs induced by the merger process (as stipulated by IFRS 3) unlike in Czech Republic, where the merger-induced costs must be included in the acquisition price.

Goodwill treatment is another issue where the differences are significant. Czech Republic distinguish between two types of "acquisition difference" in relation to the decision of the acquirer to revaluate transferred assets to the fair value (then "goodwill" is recognized as a intangible asset) or to take over the assets at their book value from the acquiree (then "Oceňovací rozdíl k nabytému majetku" is recognized as a tangible asset). Polish regulation assumes only one type of acquisition difference in the form of goodwill, respecting the provisions of IFRS 3 about the revaluation of both assets and liabilities and the purchase price allocation to newly recognized assets (usually intangible assets). Significant differences were found in the amortization of these acquisition differences, nevertheless we can conclude, that both national regulations stipulate recognition of positive and negative acquisition differences in the asset section of the balance sheet, rather than accounting the negative acquisition difference to the equity as a gain (as stipulated by IFRS 3), although Polish national regulation allows under certain circumstances to move some part of the negative goodwill to the equity as a gain.

There are other differences between Czech and Polish regulations which are common to all merger accounting methods mentioned above. These differences include the deployment of the merger date and the distribution of the accounting tasks between the participating companies. The merger date in Poland is set to the day of the registration of the merger by the Corporate Register, while in the Czech Republic the merger day may be placed freely in the time span of twelve months prior the filling for the registration at the Corporate Register or alternatively the day of the registration at the Corporate Register. The distribution of the accounting tasks related to merger is different in Poland compared to the Czech Republic. In Czech Republic, all the transactions steaming from the revaluation of assets and other merger-related transactions need to be accounted to the books of acquired company contrary to Poland, where all these transactions are done in the books of the successor company.

We can conclude that the differences between Czech national regulation and Polish national regulations are many, but the similarities are greater which confirms our first assumption. Both regulations aspire to some extent to the IAS/IFRS regulation of merger accounting as well as to the theoretical concepts of merger accounting and its methods. Our initial assumption was confirmed as we found that Czech national regulation is a bit behind with its convergence to the IAS/IFRS which is in our opinion caused by the reluctance of the Czech national legislation to embrace the comprehensive and coherent method-based approach over the strict legal regulation.

The primary limitation of this paper lies in the fact that this paper deals with the matter on the theoretical level only. The following research should focus on the empirical research—an empirical study performed on financial statements of the companies that underwent a business combination in order to find out/verify, what effect the different concepts of accounting for business combinations might have on the users of the financial statements. In this regard, detailed case studies should be performed tracking the steps of the business combination and analyzing the outcomes and potential pitfalls of the accounting methods applied. The research might continue on the theoretical level too as this paper does not pay much attention to the business combinations under the common control.

Acknowledgments This paper has been prepared under financial support of Vysoká škola ekonomická v Praze: FFU, project no. 47/2015 (IG105055) "Relevance of accounting information on the consolidated basis in business and public sector," which authors gratefully acknowledge.

References

Aghimien P, Asiri AA, Yamani AG (2014) Accounting for business combinations: application of rules from IFRS, Saudi Arabia, and USA. Int J Bus Acc Finance 8(1):63–78

Ayers BC, Lefanowicz CE, Robinson JR (2000) The financial statement effects of eliminating the pooling-of-interests method of acquisition accounting. Acc Horiz 14(1):1–19

Lycklama á Nijeholt MP (2010) Goodwill and value creation of acquisition, Doctoral thesis, E.M. Meljers Institute for Legal Studies, Faculty of Law, Leiden Universit

Numberg H, Sweeney J (1998) Comparative effects of alternative methods of accounting for business combinations. J Fin Statement Anal 4(1):16–38

Pospíšil J (2015) Valuation date in the process of M&A. In: Procházka D (ed) 16th Annual Conference on Finance and Accounting, ACFA. Elsevier, Amsterdam, pp 106–115

Strojek-Filus M (2013) Determinanty oraz skutki wynikowo-bilansowe identyfikacji i rozliczania wartości firmy w grupie kapitałowej. Wydawnictwo Uniwersytetu Ekonomicznego w Katowicach, Katowice

Vomáčková H (2006) Obecné koncepce pro účetnictví fúzí. Český finanční a účetní časopis 1 (2):95–115

Vomáčková H (2012) Vývoj účetního řešení přeměn obchodních společností a družstev za posledních dvacet let. Český finanční a účetní časopis 7(1):33–51

Žárová M, Skálová J (2014) Tax aspects of mergers and cross-border mergers. Eur Fin Acc J 9 (3):25–49

Chapter 40
The Revised Control Concept in the Consolidated Financial Statements of Czech Companies

Tereza Gluzová

Abstract Consolidated financial statements present information for a group of companies formed by a parent company and subsidiary companies, which are controlled by the parent. The existence of control is the most important factor to determine whether a company is included in the scope of consolidation. The paper focuses on the revision of the control concept introduced by IFRS 10 Consolidated Financial Statements and its impact on the companies quoted on Prague Stock Exchange (PSE). It investigates the materiality of changes in the scope of consolidation which were recorded in response to the IFRS 10 adoption. Secondary focus of the paper is on the adjustments of the related accounting policies. The findings suggest that IFRS 10 had only a very limited impact on the consolidated financial statements of the analysed companies. Paper's findings also reveal the definitions of control in the accounting policies are inconsistently applied by the companies.

Keywords Consolidated financial statements · Control concept · Disclosure · IFRS

40.1 Introduction

The main purpose of consolidated financial statements is to present financial information for a group of companies acting as a single economic unit. The group consists of the parent company and the subsidiary companies, which are controlled

T. Gluzová (✉)
Department of Financial Accounting and Auditing, University of Economics, Prague, Nam. W. Churchilla 4, 130 67 Prague, Czech Republic
e-mail: xglut00@vse.cz

© Springer International Publishing AG 2017   433
D. Procházka (ed.), *New Trends in Finance and Accounting*,
Springer Proceedings in Business and Economics,
DOI 10.1007/978-3-319-49559-0_40

by the parent. Consolidated financial statements of the companies with equity or debt securities listed on a regulated market are obligatorily prepared according to International Financial Reporting Standards (IFRS). This rule is applicable for both companies in the Czech Republic and remaining member countries of the European Union.[1]

For a period of more than 20 years, international standard IAS 27 Consolidated and Separate Financial Statements was applied for preparation of consolidated financial statements. For accounting periods beginning 1 January 2014 and later, rules for consolidated statements have relocated to IFRS 10 Consolidated Financial Statements. Adoption of the new consolidation standard has changed neither the aim of consolidated statements nor principles of consolidation. The most substantial impact of IFRS 10 is the introduction of a revised control concept used in deciding which companies are included in the consolidated statements.

Identification of control and, as a consequence, formation of the scope of consolidation influence the value relevance of consolidated financial statements. Should the consolidated statements be relevant and reliable, scope of consolidation must meet two important criteria. Each company under control is included in the financial statements by applying full method of consolidation. As opposed, when relationship of control is not indicated, interest in such company is accounted for using alternative methods.[2]

The main aim of the paper is to investigate how reporting practices and accounting policies of selected companies changed after IFRS 10 have been adopted. The study focuses on the companies listed on Prague Stock Exchange (PSE), and the research sample consists of companies quoted therein. To answer the research question, we conducted an analysis based on the comparison of financial statements in a year IFRS 10 was adopted by the company and a year immediately preceding. Following the analysis, we assess the materiality of changes in response to the novelized control concept and examine how accounting policies defining control were updated. The outputs are subsequently compared with expected impact of IFRS 10, which were described in the preliminary effect analyses.

The remaining of the paper is organized as follows. The second chapter compares definitions of control under IAS 27 and IFRS 10 and detects the most substantial differences. The third chapter reviews the relevant literature. The research methodology and results are included in the fourth chapter. Final chapter summarizes the conclusions, presents limitations of the study and possibilities of a further research.

---

[1]In the Czech Republic, the adoption of IFRS is voluntary also for non-listed companies preparing consolidated financial statements and subsidiary companies subject to consolidation. In such situation, both consolidated and individual financial statements may be prepared in compliance with IFRS instead of Czech accounting standards (Žárová 2013).

[2]Alternative methods include equity method, accounting for financial instrument at fair value through profit or loss or through other comprehensive income.

40.2   Revised Control Concept

IAS 27 defined control as the power to govern the financial and operating policies of an entity so as to obtain benefits from its activities. Control was deemed to exist when the parent company owned more than 50% of the voting rights in another company. Alternatively in a limited situations control could exist without the majority of voting rights. The standard explicitly mentioned contractual agreements, ability to appoint the majority of the members of the governing body or to cast majority of votes at the meeting of the governing body. However, it were voting rights that were primarily the indicator of control and other indicators were rarely considered.

At the same time, there was interpretation SIC-12 Special Purpose Entities applied to decide whether a Special Purpose Entity (SPE) should be consolidated by the parent.[3] As the interpretation stated, company consolidated SPE when it was exposed to majority of risks and rewards from its activities.

Two existing approaches to principles of control resulted in non-uniform application and caused numerous inconsistencies when deciding on control over an entity. International Accounting Standards Board (IASB, the standard-setting body of IFRS) therefore commenced to work on a project to unify the control principles and reduce the area for the possible dual approach. After almost a decade of preparation, in 2011 IASB issued a set of new or amended standards on consolidation and related issues. Date of application for companies in European Union was for accounting periods beginning on or after 1 January 2014.[4]

From the set of standards, IFRS 10 Consolidated Financial Statements affected the view on the scope of consolidation. IFRS 10 amended the definition of control, which is currently based on three conditions. The investor controls an investee when, at the same time, it meets the following:

- power over an investee;
- exposure to variable returns from an investee; and
- ability to use power to affect returns.

Revised definition of control is more general than were those in IAS 27 and SIC-12. Although voting rights remain to be mentioned as an indicator of power over an investee, the standard clearly states that the majority of voting rights in itself may not be sufficient to have control. What is more important, IASB devoted to situations when power (and possibly control) exists despite the investor owns less than 50% of the voting rights.

---

[3]SIC-12 defined SPE as an entity created to accomplish a narrow and well-defined objective, often created with legal arrangements that impose strict limits on the decision-making powers of the governing body over the operations of the SPE.

[4]A year later than the official IASB application date, because all standards need to pass an endorsement process to become a part of the European legislation.

Mainly in case of structured entities (formerly special purpose entities), power often arises from other than voting rights.[5] Consequently, chapters on power and control when voting rights are not the dominant factor to affect investee's returns have been added.

The effects of the application of new or amended standards are presented within the notes to the financial statements. Newly adopted or amended accounting policy is applied retrospectively, unless otherwise stated by the standard. The financial statements need to be amended as if the accounting policy has always been applied. This leads to the adjustments of both opening balances and the statements presented for comparative period(s). IFRS 10 contains guidance on the transition from IAS 27/SIC-12 and allows limited reliefs from retrospective application.[6] In general, adoption of IFRS 10 could result in the following:

- the consolidation of a new subsidiary;
- the deconsolidation of a former subsidiary; or
- no impact on the scope of consolidation.

40.3   Literature Review

Value relevance of consolidated financial statement, when compared to separate (parent-only) financial statement, has been subject to a great deal of studies. Srinivasan and Narasimhan (2012) confirmed value relevance of consolidated statements published on a quarterly basis on the emerging market of India. Müller (2011) investigated financial statements of companies listed on stock exchanges in London, Paris and Frankfurt and proved the superior role of consolidated statements to the investors. Similar results were proven by other researchers (Abad et al. 2000 or Niskanen et al. 1998) for Spanish and Finnish markets, respectively.

A thorough overview of the development of the control concept and the shift from ownership to control as a basis of consolidation has recently been described by Nobes (2014). IFRS credits control concept a major role in determining the scope of consolidation according to Müller et al. (2010). In their study, authors discussed the future development of more rigorous guidance that later resulted in the revision of control concept in IFRS 10. Wen-hsin Hsu et al. (2012) compared consolidated statements under control-based approach with those under ownership-based approach on the sample of Taiwan companies. Their results showed that broader definition of control could provide more useful accounting information.

---

[5]Structured entity is equivalent to SPE; the latter of these terms is no longer applied in IFRS. Structured entity is defined as designed so that voting or similar rights are not the dominant factor in deciding who controls the entity.

[6]A parent does not retrospectively consolidate a former investee, which would be controlled under IFRS 10, when the control was lost before the date of initial application of IFRS 10. Next relief is in the situation when the retrospective application is impracticable.

In recent years, many studies were devoted to revised consolidation requirements presented by IFRS 10 (i.e. Gornik-Tomaszewski and Larson 2014; Van Noordwyk et al. 2014; Zelenková 2014; Büdy-Rósza 2012). Prior to obligatory IFRS 10 application, Vašek and Gluzová (2014) analysed expected the impact of the revised control concept on companies listed on PSE. The outputs suggested only one of the analysed thirteen companies expected changes in the scope of consolidation as a result of the IFRS 10 adoption.

However, there has been no study to assess the impact in the years after IFRS 10 was adopted. Since 2014 was the year of adoption of IFRS 10 by the majority of the European companies, the appropriate data for a thorough analysis were not available until 2015. After the financial statements for the year 2014 have been issued, the paper focuses on the impact of the revised control concept on the consolidated financial statements.

40.4   Data, Results and Discussion

The research sample includes companies with shares listed on the regulated market of PSE as at 1 February 2016. The presumption was that listed companies must present financial statements according to IFRS and meet the most demanding requirements with regard to financial reporting. In the next step, companies presenting financial statements with reporting framework different from IFRS were excluded.[7] Companies whose financial statements for one of the years (initial application of IFRS 10 and a year before) were not available were excluded in the next step. A total of five companies were excluded due to the above described reasons.

The final sample comprises 19 companies. Financial statements of the companies were further analysed with an emphasis on:

- the year of the initial application of IFRS 10;
- the definition of control in accounting policies; and
- the impact of IFRS 10 on the scope of consolidation.

The results of the analysis show that the majority of companies opted for IFRS 10 adoption consistent with the EU effective date. There was only one company who chose an early adoption. With regard to impact of IFRS 10 on the scope of consolidation, two out of the nineteen companies stated it had influence on their financial statements. At the same time, two companies did not describe the impact explicitly. Table 40.1 provides details of the conducted analysis:

---

[7]The case of company CME, that is primarily listed on NASDAQ in the USA and dual-listed on PSE. Therefore, the company is allowed to present financial statements under US Generally Accepted Accounting Principles.

Table 40.1 IFRS 10 adoption and its impact on the financial statements

Company	Initial application of IFRS 10	Impact of IFRS 10
Borealis Exploration Limited	2014	No impact
ČEZ, a.s.	2014	No impact
E4U, a.s.	2014	No impact
Energoaqua, a.s.	2014	No impact
Energochemica SA	2014	No impact
Erste Group Bank AG	2014	With impact
Fortuna Entertainment Group N.V.	2013	No impact
Komerční banka, a.s.	2014	No impact
New World Resources Plc.	2014	No impact
O2 Czech Republic, a.s.	2014	Impact not stated
Pegas Nonwovens SA	2014	No impact
Phillip Morris ČR, a.s.	2014	No impact
Pivovary Lobkowicz Group, a.s.	2014	Impact not stated
RMS Mezzanine, a.s.	2014	No impact
Stock Spirits Group Plc.	2014	No impact
Toma, a.s.	2014	No impact
Unipetrol, a.s.	2014	No impact
VGP NV	2014	No impact
Vienna Insurance Group	2014	With impact

Source Author's compilation based on the financial statements of the selected companies

The summary of the effects is provided in Table 40.2. The assessment of control under the revised rules led to the consolidation of 19 new subsidiaries. On the contrary, no former subsidiary had to be deconsolidated. Not surprisingly, the affected companies were the largest two (measured by total assets). Furthermore, these two companies consolidated greatest amount of subsidiaries.

Both Erste Group Bank AG (Erste) and Vienna Insurance Group (VIG) restated their financial statements at the date immediately preceding the day of initial application of IFRS 10 (i.e. 31 December 2013). Total assets of Erste increased by 0.12% as a result of IFRS 10 application, whereas VIG recorded a 0.16% decrease.

The transition to IFRS 10 should affect also the accounting policies of the companies with regard to the definition of control and the policies applied to determine control over an investee. Although it is not explicitly required by the standards, Fig. 40.1 reveals that the majority of 84% of the companies disclosed the definition of a subsidiary in their accounting policies. In a year of first application of IFRS 10, seven companies (i.e. 37% from the research sample) remained to focus on obtaining benefits through power over financial and operating policies. This suggests their accounting policy has not been updated. Only 47% of the companies defined control based on the revised control concept and highlight power, variable returns and linkage between those.

Table 40.2 Effect of IFRS 10 on the scope of consolidation

Company	Impact of IFRS 10	Impact on total assets (CZK thousand)	Total assets after restatement (CZK thousand)
Erste Group Bank AG	Retrospective consolidation of 18 investment funds	Increase by 6,773,975	5,870,897,175
Vienna Insurance Group	Retrospective consolidation of 1 subsidiary	Decrease by 1,798,230	1,149,418,006

Source Author's compilation based on the financial statements of the selected companies

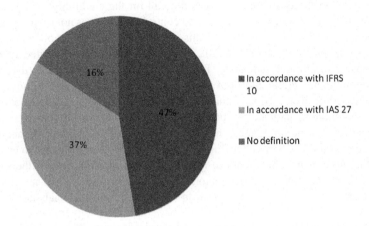

Fig. 40.1 Definition of control. *Source* Author's calculation

40.5   Conclusion

When the revised control concept was introduced by IFRS 10, companies were required to review the composition of their scope of consolidation. The objective of the revision was to reassess whether they consolidate each investee they control and conversely whether each consolidated company is under actual control. This paper examined the impact of this revision on the companies quoted on PSE. The results of the analysis reveal that only two out of the nineteen companies identified changes to their scope of consolidation. After the restatement following the IFRS 10 adoption, total assets increased by 0.07%. Nineteen investees who had not been consolidated before met the revised definition of control. As a result, they were retrospectively consolidated. The affected companies include one bank and one insurance company. This is consistent with the effect analysis by EFRAG (2012), where the banks and insurers were expected to record the most significant impact.

Revision of the control concept was not expected to cause revolutionary changes to the conclusions whether control over an investee exists. As IASB (2013)

presented in their effect analysis: "…IFRS 10 does not introduce new concepts. Instead, it builds on the control guidance that existed in IAS 27 and SIC-12 but adds additional context, explanation and application guidance that is consistent with the definition of control". Findings of the article confirmed such expectations. A slight increase in both the number of consolidated companies and total assets may be evaluated as insignificant.

Interesting results were revealed from the analysis of the accounting policies of the companies. All the companies proclaimed they revised judgements applied when assessing control over an investee. However, 37% of the companies from the research sample remain to define control in accordance with IAS 27. Such an inconsistency may be caused by a lack of attention of the preparers of the financial statements. On the other hand, it casts a doubt on the credibility of the financial statements as it is possible that the revised control concept was not properly applied.

There are two main limitations of this study. The research sample consists only of the companies quoted on the PSE. Thus, it analyses only a limited sample of companies from limited industries. The next possible limitation is that the analysis focuses on the numerical impact of the revised control concept. It does not evaluate the increased or decreased usefulness to the users of the financial statements. Both of these limitations indicate potential of a further research in this field.

Regardless of the limitations, the study contributes by providing the analysis of the revised control concept after IFRS 10 was adopted. The results, when compared with the preliminary effect studies, may be of particular interests to the standard setters, EFRAG and other regulators. They could also be of advantage to researchers who focus in their studies on the consolidated financial statements.

Acknowledgments This is paper has been prepared under financial support of a research project Relevance of Accounting Information on a Consolidated Basis in Business and Public Sector registered by the Internal Grant Agency of University of Economics in Prague under the registration number F1/47/2015.

References

Abad C, Laffarga J, García-Borbolla A, Larran M, Piñero JM, Garrod N (2000) An evaluation of the value relevance of consolidated versus unconsolidated accounting information: evidence from quoted Spanish firms. J Int Financ Manage Account 11:156–177. doi:10.1111/1467-646X.00060

Büdy-Rósza I (2012) New trends in consolidation—challenging the changes of new IFRS rules. Periodica Polytech Soc Manage Sci 20:11–22. doi:10.3311/pp.so.2012-1.02

EFRAG (2012) Feedback report on field-tests on IFRS 10, IFRS 11 and IFRS 12. http://www.efrag.org/files/EFRAG%20public%20letters/Consolidation/Feedback_report_on_field_tests_on_IFRS_10_IFRS_11_and_IFRS_12.pdf. Accessed 31 Jan 2016

Gornik-Tomaszewski S, Larson RK (2014) New consolidation requirements under IFRS. Rev Bus 35:47–58

IASB (2013) Effect analysis. IFRS 10 consolidated financial statements and IFRS 12 disclosure of interest in other entities. http://www.ifrs.org/Current-Projects/IASB-Projects/Consolidation/Consol-disclosure/Documents/Effect-Analysis-IFRS%2010-and-IFRS-12-Updated-July-2013.pdf. Accessed 31 Jan 2016

Müller V (2011) Value relevance of consolidated versus parent company financial statements: evidence from the largest three European capital markets. Account Manage Inf Syst 10:326–350

Müller V, Cardos IR, Ienciu AI (2010) Consolidation policy: past, present and future approaches to the concept of control. Ann Univ Oradea Econ Sci Ser 19:541–547

Niskanen J, Kinnunen J, Kasanen E (1998) A note on the information content of parent company versus consolidated earnings in Finland. Eur Account Rev 7:31–40. doi:10.1080/096381898336565

Nobes C (2014) The development of national and transnational regulation on the scope of consolidation. Account Audit Accountability J 27:995–1025. doi:10.1108/AAAJ-03-2013-1287

Srinivasan P, Narasimhan MS (2012) The value relevance of consolidated financial statements in an emerging market. Asian Rev Account 20:58–73. doi:10.1108/13217341211224727

Van Noordwyk R, Wise H, Ludolph S (2014) New consolidation standard lessons learned so far. Accountancy SA 5:24–25

Vašek L, Gluzová T (2014) Can a new concept of control under IFRS have an impact on a CCCTB? Eur Financ Account J 9:110–127. doi:10.18267/j.efaj.133

Wen-hsin Hsu A, Duh R, Cheng K (2012) Does the control-based approach to consolidated statements better reflect market value than the ownership-based approach? Int J Account 47:198–225. doi:10.1016/j.intacc.2012.03.003

Žárová M (2013) Changes in EC directives and impact on presentation of financial statements in the Czech Republic. Eur Financ Account J 8:21–45

Zelenková M (2014) Změny v pojetí ovládání a spoluovládání. Český finanční a účetní časopis 9:18–30. doi:10.18267/j.cfuc.391

Chapter 41
Audit Market Concentration Analysis Focusing on Auditors of Public Interest Entities

Michal Šindelář and Libuše Müllerová

Abstract The aim of this paper is to analyze the market concentration of audit services in the Czech Republic and compare its results with the international research. The analysis is based on transparency reports, which cover the year 2014. Among other information, auditors are required to present their total remuneration split into remuneration of audit services and remuneration of non-audit services in the transparency report. Globally recognized Herfindahl–Hirschman index is selected as an appropriate analytical tool for measurement of the market concentration. Herfindahl–Hirschman index is complemented by indicator of market share (current ratio). In the year 2014, the Big4 firms occupied 80% of total remuneration and 84% of audit remuneration. The analysis indicates a high level of market concentration of audit services in the Czech Republic, but the international comparison shows slightly lower market concentration in the Czech Republic than in the Germany and in the UK.

Keywords Audit market concentration · Audit fees · Herfindahl–Hirschman index · Auditor's independence

41.1 Introduction

The fall of Enron in the year 2002 was the impulse for the US government to become more interested in the market of audit services in the USA. Several scientific articles dealt with analyzing the causes of the bankruptcy of Enron. As one of mentioned reasons was also failures and deception of audit firm Arthur Andersen. Healy and Palepu (2003) argued that the possibility of loss of remu-

M. Šindelář (✉) · L. Müllerová
Department of Financial Accounting and Auditing, University of Economics, Prague,
Nam. W. Churchilla 4, 130 67 Prague, Czech Republic
e-mail: xsinm00@vse.cz

L. Müllerová
e-mail: libuse.mullerova@vse.cz

© Springer International Publishing AG 2017   443
D. Procházka (ed.), *New Trends in Finance and Accounting*,
Springer Proceedings in Business and Economics,
DOI 10.1007/978-3-319-49559-0_41

neration for other services led the audit firm Arthur Andersen to adopt aggressive or even fraudulent accounting policies of Enron, because Arthur Andersen earned in 2000 from Enron $25 million for auditing services and $27 million for other non-audit services. Even Europe was not spared of similar fraudulent conduct in case of the Italian food company Parmalat. One of problems of the audit market, which began the US and European regulators to deal with, is the risk of the independence of auditors due to simultaneous providing both auditing and other services. European Commission (2002) in this regard stated that the remuneration for other services may jeopardize the independence of the auditor. To be unified the audit approach across the European Union, the European Commission issued a Directive 2006/43/EC (European Commission 2006) that governing the requirements and rules of statutory audit. This Directive is implemented to the Czech legal system by the act no. 93/2009 Coll., on auditors. The aim of the Directive is, i.a., to minimize the negative impacts of oligopolistic structure, which was confirmed in international surveys (Beattie et al. 2003; Bigus and Zimmermann 2008) in countries with more developed and globally significant capital market.

In the economic theory is the most emphasized role of audit in agency theory—"Principal-agent theory" (Hayes et al. 2014). During separate management and ownership of companies arises the information asymmetry to the detriment of owners and those faces the question, how to minimize the conduct of managers, which would lead to a decrease in the market value of the company. One option is to set an appropriate remuneration system (Lambert 2001), and another option is expending the monitoring costs, such as on verification of financial statements by an independent person. The existence of agency costs and trying to minimize them create a demand for verification (audit) services by an independent body. As a necessary condition for achieving the main purpose of the audit, i.e., the reduction in opportunistic behavior of management is to ensure the independence of the auditor from the audited entity. Then, the auditor will be able to truthfully announce the possible breach of contractual agreements between owners and managers (Watts and Zimmerman 1983). Although Watts and Zimmerman (1983) provided the evidence that audit has begun to promote on an individual voluntary basis, the current situation is characterized by a preference of approach consisting of public regulation. This approach, on the one hand, reduces the explicit costs on concluding contracts (Leuz 2010); on the other hand, it precludes the individual terms settings (Ray 2011). As stated by (Myddelton 2004), "An unified approach for all" allows to justify a bad practice just for compliance with regulatory requirements without companies have faced the sanctions that would face them in case of an unregulated market. Regulation itself can be a source of market failure that could result in opportunistic behavior of subjects. Nevertheless, regulators are trying to prevent market failure and therefore they are looking for possible failure indicators. In case of audit market, it is especially the oligopolistic structure (Pong 1999). Oligopolistic structure among audit firms has an impact on the choice of audit firm and therefore penalizes the customers. Simultaneously, it could be threatened the independence of the auditor, if the customer generates a substantial portion of his revenue.

The paper analyzes the market concentration of audit services in the Czech Republic and compares the results with an international research. The paper examines the audit market concentration for the year 2014. The results are also compared with an international research. The paper is structured as follows. After the introduction, identifying the key objective of the article follows the analysis of international research, on which the hypotheses are formulated. Next section presents data that are used for research and statistical tool, by which the market concentration is measured. This part is followed by the audit market analysis in the Czech Republic. The paper analyzes the actual market concentration in the year 2014. Then, the market concentration of audit services in the Czech Republic is compared with the audit market concentration of selected countries. Conclusion of the paper summarizes the major findings and presents options for further research in this area.

41.2 Literature Review and Research Hypotheses Formulation

Concentration on the audit market services is in the international context quite often analyzed problem. But in the Czech Republic we wouldn't find many articles that deal with an analysis of the local audit market. Concentration on the Czech audit market was analyzed by Heß and Stefani (2012), who presented an analysis of audit services provided to 14 companies that are listed on the Prague Stock Exchange. The audit market concentration analyses can be divided into two periods—the period, in which the company had no obligation to indicate the auditor's remuneration in their financial statements, and the period, when this obligation is already compulsory for the companies. In the first period, there was used a suitable criterion for measuring the concentration, for example, the number of clients, total clients sales or their total assets. Current research considers as the most appropriate measure of audit market concentration the total audit remuneration that the companies have to indicate in their financial statements divided into auditing fees and fees for other services.

Beattie et al. (2003) presented the analysis of market concentration of audit services for listed companies in the UK at the time of the merger of Arthur Andersen with Ernst and Young (EY). It concludes that 96% of the market is controlled by four firms (Big4—KPMG, PricewaterhouseCoopers (PwC), Deloitte, EY). The strongest (PwC) has achieved a market share of 37%. In the same period in the USA was conducted a detailed analysis of the audit market (US-GAO 2003). The study is based on data obtained directly from the individual audit firms. The study was prepared due to the need to evaluate and analyze the evolution of market concentration of audit services after the mergers among audit firms that have occurred in the 1980s and 1990s of the twentieth century, after the fall of the consulting firm Arthur Andersen. One of the reasons for the high market concentration is presented the high barriers to entry the market of auditors of listed companies. High barriers to entry are in microeconomics considered as one of the prerequisites for the creation of oligopolistic structures (Hořejší et al. 2010). Due to different fundamentals of financial reporting in the Anglo-Saxon countries, there is the need to evaluate research in the area of concentration on the audit market in continental Europe. Audit market concentration in the field of German companies listed on the stock market DAX30, MDAX, SDAX, TecDAX and GEX is analyzed by Bigus and Zimmermann (2008). The study concludes that 87% of the audit fees and 90% of total fees accrue to Big4 companies. Further research in the area of market concentration of audit services was done, for example, in Switzerland (Stefani 2006) and Denmark (Thinggaard and Kiertzner 2004). In all cases, the international research confirms that there exists a concentration on the audit market. Audit market for companies belonging to public interest entities (defined in § 1a of Act no. 563/1991 Coll., on accounting, as amended from January 1, 2016, but by the end of 2015 defined in § 2a of Act no. 93/2009 Coll., on auditors and amending certain laws, as amended) in the Czech Republic should fulfill all the requirements for the creation of high market concentration, which leads me to hypothesis:

H1:   We expect a higher concentration on the market for audit services in the Czech Republic in 2014 measured by the Herfindahl–Hirschman index (HHI) based on the actually received remuneration of audit firms, compared with a HHI used by regulators in the European Union and in the USA.

The above-mentioned research (e.g., Bigus and Zimmermann 2008; Beattie et al. 2003; US-GAO 2003) also concludes that a significant market share is held by companies forming Big4. This conclusion can be demonstrated, for example, by the fact that these companies operate globally, and audited companies forming the group, including companies from several countries, have in the most cases the same audit firm, which is determined for the whole group by the parent company. This leads us to the second hypothesis:

H2:   We expect the market share of the Big4 companies in the Czech Republic in 2014 more than 65%, which represents the limit for the high market concentration (see Table 41.2).

41.3   Data and Methodology

41.3.1   Data

The international research is based on an analysis of remuneration paid to audit firm that are included in the financial statements of listed companies (Bigus and Zimmermann 2008; Thinggaard and Kiertzner 2004). In the Czech Republic, there is a complication of a small number of listed companies. Therefore, the analysis

Table 41.1 Structure of the turnover of the remuneration to the auditors in 2014, remuneration in mil. CZK

Number of analyzed firms = 41	Total remuneration	Audit services	Non-audit services
Mean value	85.37	70.01	15.37
Error of the mean	32.97	28.35	5.37
Median	9.87	6.50	2.37
Minimum	0.47	0.07	0.00
Maximum	867.97	709.00	190.69
The share of total turnover (in %)		82.00	18.00

Source Own analysis of data from the transparency reports of relevant audit firms

presented here is based on data obtained from publicly available transparency reports of individual audit firms that conducted an audit of public interest entities in the year 2014. Due to the fact that the Chamber of Auditors of the Czech Republic, the Public Audit Oversight Board or other institution don't have a list of auditors of public interest entities, data were obtained by analyzing the Web sites of audit firms. Auditor of public interest entity is obliged to compile a transparency report (§ 43 of the Act no. 93/2009 Coll.) stating the financial information, from which it can determined the position of the audit firm on the audit market. Audit firms reported the amount of their turnover divided into remuneration for audit services and other non-audit services. In the transparency report, audit firms reported the remuneration earned from all audits and all other services provided, not only remuneration received from audit of public interest entity. This fact allows in terms of the scope of the tested sample comparison with the results of international research. In the international research, data are drawn directly from audit firms in the US study (US-GAO 2003). Table 41.1 provides descriptive statistics of the analyzed sample. The table shows the remuneration of auditors ranging from 70 thousand CZK to 709,000 thousand CZK. Already a significant difference in the mean value of the remuneration (70 mil. CZK) and median (6.5 mil. CZK) anticipates the existence of several strong players in the audit market.

41.3.2 Methodology

In the literature, different analytical tools are used for concentration measurement, of which are widely used the concentration ratio (CR (g)) and the HHI. Concentration ratio (CR (g)) is used to measure the concentration of a market in a way that shows the ratio between the chosen value of g-largest companies and the total sum of the selected values in the industry. The paper applied concentration factor in accordance with international research (Beattie et al. 2003; Bigus and Zimmermann 2008; US-GAO 2003). The literature indicates the concentration

Table 41.2 Interpretation of concentration ratio

Concentration ratio	Low market concentration	Medium market concentration	High market concentration
For 3 largest companies	CR(3) < 10%	10% < CR(3) < 25%	25% < CR(3)
For 4 largest companies	35% < CR(4) < 50%	50% < CR(4) < 65%	65% < CR(4)

Source Bigus and Zimmermann (2008)

Table 41.3 Interpretation of Herfindahl–Hirschman index

Herfindahl–Hirschman index	Low market concentration	Medium market concentration	High market concentration
EU[a]	HHI < 0.10	0.10 < HHI < 0.20	0.20 < HHI
US	HHI < 0.10	0.10 < HHI < 0.18	0.18 < HHI

[a]In the European Union, in the context of assessing the impacts of mergers, the HHI between 0.10 and 0.20 is not assessed as problematic if as a result of the merger the value of HHI increases of less than 0.025 and the value of HHI greater than 0.20 is not assessed as problematic if as a result of the merger its value increases by less than 0.015
Source Bigus and Zimmermann (2008) and European Commission (2004)

factor for a variety of companies. This research will work with a concentration factor for three or four biggest companies. Interpretation of this indicator is shown in Table 41.2.

The second applied analytical tool is the HHI—a tool for measuring market concentration based on more comprehensive view on the market than the concentration ratio. In contrast to the concentration ratio, HHI takes into account the market shares of all companies operating in the relevant market. For the purposes of this research, HHI serves very well because its characteristics are able to assess whether the market concentration exists or not. In this analysis, HHI is applied on the basis of its general validity and is used in accordance with international research (Beattie et al. 2003; Bigus and Zimmermann 2008). Method of interpretation HHI in relation to the measurement of the market concentration is shown in Table 41.3 and is different for the European Union and the USA.

41.4   Discussion

Table 41.4 shows the indicators for the Czech audit market in 2014.

For concentration ratio (CR(3)) and (CR(4)) of the total remuneration for the services provided by audit firms and for remuneration of audit services, the data show that the critical value indicating a high concentration of the market was exceeded. The analysis also shows the values for the area of total remuneration are not very different from remuneration for audit services. The four largest companies

Table 41.4 Indicators of audit market concentration in the Czech Republic for year 2014

	Total remuneration	Audit services	Non-audit services
CR(2)	0.47	0.48	0.44
CR(3)	0.67	0.70	0.54
CR(4)	0.80	0.84	0.64
Herfindahl–Hirschman index	0.18	0.19	0.14

Source Own analysis of data from the transparency reports of relevant audit firms

occupy 84% of the market of audit services in the Czech Republic, which leads to the confirmation of hypothesis H2. At first glance, it is also relatively high share of the two largest companies in the total remuneration.

Interpretation of HHI compared with the critical values is not clear. In case of remuneration of auditing services, it could be concluded under the rules applicable in the USA that a high concentration exists in the Czech audit market, because HHI exceeds the critical value and in case of total remuneration HHI is equal to the critical value. Under the rules adopted by the European Union, it couldn't be concluded the high market concentration of audit services. The analysis confirmed the medium market concentration with the value of HHI 0.19 (resp. 0.18), which is close to the upper limit of the medium range. In case of EU rules, the existence of concentration could be established at a possible merger between audit firms depending on a change in the value of HHI prior-merger and post-merger. The performed analysis thus offers different solutions for the hypothesis H1. If we apply the US rules for the HHI, we can confirm the hypothesis H1, because the value of HHI in 2014 for the Czech audit market falls in the high concentration range. The hypothesis H1 can't be confirmed within the rules applicable in the European Union, since the value of HHI falls into the medium concentration range rather than into the high concentration range. The area of other remuneration paid to audit firms shows the lowest concentration of the analyzed variables of Czech audit market. It reaches the medium concentration in terms of both US and EU rules.

Table 41.5 provides comparison of values of concentration on the Czech audit market with studies carried out in Germany and the UK. This table shows that the Czech audit market shows the similar values as markets in Germany (Bigus and Zimmermann 2008) and the UK (Beattie et al. 2003). In the measurement of concentration by the concentration ratio, the analysis indicates that the Czech audit market shows a slightly lower market concentration than the German and British markets. This could be caused, for example, by the fact that this research is based on transparency report, which contains the remuneration for all performed audits, while the German and British research is based on the financial statements of listed companies, where, due to the higher difficulty and complexity of audit, it could be expected higher concentration. HHI is in the Czech Republic lower than in Germany and the same in comparison with the UK.

Table 41.5 Comparison of the Czech audit market concentration with international research

	This study	Bigus and Zimmermann (2008)	Beattie et al. (2003)
Database	2014 Audit services remuneration	2005 Audit services remuneration	2002 Audit services remuneration
CR(2)	0.48	0.66	0.62
CR(3)	0.70	–	–
CR(4)	0.84	–	–
CR(6)	0.89	0.96	0.98
Herfindahl–Hirschman index	0.19	0.29	0.19[a]
Number of analyzed firms	41	175	1168

[a]This indicator is in the study based on total assets, not on remuneration for auditing services
Source Own analysis of data from the transparency reports of relevant audit firms, Bigus and Zimmermann (2008), Beattie et al. (2003)

41.5   Conclusion

The paper analyzes the market concentration in the Czech Republic on the audit market and compares the values of selected indicators with an international research, especially from Germany and the UK. As the database is chosen from transparency reports of audit firms in which these firms are required to disclose their total remuneration from services, they are divided into remuneration for audit services and other services. Czech market for audit services doesn't show significant deviations in comparison with other audit markets. The most important findings, which could help to highlight the problems that concentrated market in the Czech Republic arises, are:

- The value of concentration ratio for three or four biggest companies is 0.70, respectively, 0.84 and significantly exceeds the critical values;
- The value of the HHI of 0.19 for the remuneration for audit services shows a high market concentration (if using US rules) and approaches the critical value for determining high concentrations within the rules applied in the European Union;
- In the international comparison, the audit market in the Czech Republic shows no significant differences in the analysis of its concentration.

Czech audit market shows elements of the oligopolistic structure just as it was confirmed by international research in developed countries, including Germany, the UK or the USA. This concentration may cause problems in practical operation of the market, such as the use of an oligopolistic position by Big4 companies for audit pricing and others. The existence of oligopolistic structures should lead supervisory authorities, the Chamber of Auditors of the Czech Republic and the Public Audit Oversight Board to pay attention to the relationship between the quality of audit and the cost of this audit.

As the oligopolistic structure of the audit market still represents a big problem and current legislation can't effectively deal with this issue, the European Commission adopted a new regulation no. 537/2014 (European Commission 2014a) governing the statutory audit of public interest entities. Furthermore, the European Commission decided to adopt an amendment of the directive on statutory audit of annual accounts and consolidated accounts (European Commission 2014b). All these changes should lead to reducing the threat of violation of auditor independence and thus should help eliminate the issue of oligopoly on the audit market.

At the end, we consider appropriate to mention the fact that the article is a basic overview of the audit market in the Czech Republic and should represent an initial analysis of the audit market, which will be followed by further research. One of possible direction should be the individual analysis of the structure of the remuneration of the auditors according the financial statements of clients (e.g., financial statements of individual subjects of public interest). This type of research is typical for the international research (e.g., Bigus and Zimmermann 2008; Beattie et al. 2003). Future research shall also address the impact of oligopoly on the Czech audit market on the audit quality.

Acknowledgments This paper is processed as an output of the research project "Empirical rationalization of fundamental changes in the European audit legislation from the perspective of the auditing profession in the Czech Republic (with a focus on training in audit, quality audit and issue the audit market oligopoly)" (IGA VSE F1/33/2015).

References

Act. no. 563/1991 Coll. on accounting, as amended
Act no. 93/2009 Coll. on auditors and amending certain acts, as amended
Beattie V, Goodacre A, Fearnley S (2003) And then there were four: a study of UK audit market concentration—causes, consequences and the scope for market adjustment null. J Financ Regul Compliance 11:250–265. doi:10.1108/13581980310810561
Bigus J, Zimmermann R-C (2008) Non-audit fees, market leaders and concentration in the German audit market: a descriptive analysis. Int J Audit 12:159–179. doi:10.1111/j.1099-1123.2008.00378.x
European Commission (2002) Recommendation 2002/590/EC statutory auditors' independence in the EU: a set of fundamental principles. Official Journal L 191. http://eur-lex.europa.eu/legal-content/EN/TXT/HTML/?uri=CELEX:32002H0590&from=EN. Accessed 12 Jul 2015
European Commission (2004) Guidelines on the assessment of horizontal mergers under the Council Regulation on the control of concentrations between undertakings (2004/C31/03). Official Journal C 031. http://eur-lex.europa.eu/legal-content/EN/TXT/HTML/?uri=CELEX:52004XC0205(02)&from=EN. Accessed 12 Jul 2015
European Commission (2006) Directive on statutory audits of annual accounts and consolidated accounts, amending Council Directives 78/660/EEC and 83/349/EEC and repealing Council

Directive 84/253/EEC. Official Journal L 157. http://eur-lex.europa.eu/legal-content/EN/TXT/HTML/?uri=CELEX:32006L0043&qid=1430085923680&from=EN. Accessed 12 Jul 2015

European Commission (2014a) Regulation No 537/2014 on specific requirements regarding statutory audit of public-interest entities and repealing Commission Decision 2005/909/EC. Official Journal L 158. http://eur-lex.europa.eu/legal-content/EN/TXT/HTML/?uri=CELEX:32014R0537&qid=1430086316932&from=EN. Accessed 20 Mar 2015

European Commission (2014b) Directive 2014/56/EU amending Directive 2006/43/EC on statutory audits of annual accounts and consolidated accounts. Official Journal L 158. http://eur-lex.europa.eu/legal-content/EN/TXT/HTML/?uri=CELEX:32014L0056&qid=1430086474798&from=EN. Accessed 20 Mar 2015

Hayes R, Gortemaker H, Wallage P (2014) Principles of auditing: an introduction to international standards on auditing, 3rd edn. Financial Times, Prentice Hall, Harlow

Healy PM, Palepu KG (2003) The fall of enron. J Econ Perspect 17:3–26. doi:10.1257/089533003765888403

Heß B, Stefani U (2012) Audit market regulation and supplier concentration around the world: empirical evidence. Working paper series no. 2012-33, University of Konstanz. http://www.uni-konstanz.de/FuF/wiwi/workingpaperseries/WP_Hess-Stefani_33-12.pdf. Accessed 12 Jul 2015

Hořejší B, Soukupová J, Macáková L, Soukup J (2010) Mikroekonomie (Microeconomics). Management Press, Praha

Lambert RA (2001) Contracting theory and accounting. SSRN Electron J. doi:10.2139/ssrn.235800

Leuz C (2010) Different approaches to corporate reporting regulation: how jurisdictions differ and why. SSRN Electron J. doi:10.2139/ssrn.1581472

Myddelton DR (2004) Unshackling accountants. Institute of Economic Affairs, London

Pong CKM (1999) Auditor concentration: a replication and extension for the UK audit market 1991–1995. J Bus Finance Acc 26:451–475. doi:10.1111/1468-5957.00263

Ray K (2011) One size fits all? costs and benefits of uniform accounting standards. SSRN Electron J. doi:10.2139/ssrn.1940696

Stefani U (2006) Anbieterkonzentration bei Prüfungsmandaten börsennotierter Schweizer Aktiengesellschaften. Betriebswirtschaft 66:121–145

Thinggaard F, Kiertzner L (2004) The effect of two auditors and non-audit services on audit fees: evidence from a small capital market. Working paper no. 04-02. Aalborg University

US-GAO (United States General Accounting Office) (2003) Public accounting firms, mandated study on consolidation and competition. Report to the Senate Committee on banking, housing, and urban affairs and the House Committee on financial services. http://www.gao.gov/assets/240/239226.pdf. Accessed 20 Mar 2016

Watts RL, Zimmerman JL (1983) Agency problems, auditing, and the theory of the firm: some evidence. J Law Econ 26:613–633

Chapter 42
Audit Committees in Corporate Governance: Selected Issues in the Czech Environment

Jaroslava Roubíčková and Robert Jurka

Abstract This paper deals with the selected issues of the audit committee in corporate governance and with tax aspects of remunerations received by member of audit committee. Audit committees and regulation of their activities have in the past few years undergone a number of significant changes. The legislation in the Czech Republic is subject to the obligation to incorporate the relevant European Union legislation within the framework of local laws.

Keywords Audit committee · Public interest entities · Taxation of remuneration for member of audit committee

42.1 Introduction

The issue of corporate governance or the implementation of the rules of good governance of a company has for a long time been subject of interest in the world. Changes in the management of a company, which occurred mainly in the nineties, were one of the reasons why the importance of corporate governance has increased in the world. In the Czech Republic, the topic of corporate governance is not given sufficient attention, which motivated us to prepare this article, in which we have focused on the audit committee. The article will deal with the selected issues of the audit committee in the Czech Republic.

The aim of this article is to draw attention to the gradual implementation of the European Union legislation, to the prominent role of the audit committee as a part of corporate governance, and the current tax aspects of the remuneration of the members of the audit committee.

J. Roubíčková (✉) · R. Jurka
Department of Financial Accounting and Auditing, University of Economics, Prague,
Nam. W. Churchilla 4, 130 67 Prague, Czech Republic
e-mail: jaroslava.roubickova@vse.cz

R. Jurka
e-mail: xjurr01@vse.cz

© Springer International Publishing AG 2017
D. Procházka (ed.), *New Trends in Finance and Accounting*,
Springer Proceedings in Business and Economics,
DOI 10.1007/978-3-319-49559-0_42

42.2   Literature Review

The issue of corporate governance initially focused only on selected fields such as, for example, legal regulation related to the functioning of companies, mutual relations between bodies in the companies, independence of members in individual bodies of the companies (Shleifer and Vishny 1997) or how to resolve conflicts arising due to different interests of shareholders of the companies (Post-Preston-Sachs 2002).

The modern concept of corporate governance is an interdisciplinary field that combines corporate governance in terms of law, economics, accounting, management accounting, internal audit and external audit, taxation and other areas. It is due to the interdisciplinary nature that we can find different interpretations of the concept of corporate governance.

Cadbury Report (1992) defines corporate governance as follows:

> Corporate governance is the system, by which companies are directed and controlled. Boards of directors are responsible for the governance of their companies. The shareholders' role in governance is to appoint the directors and the auditors and to satisfy themselves that an appropriate governance structure is in place. The responsibilities of the board include setting the company's strategic aims, providing the leadership to put them into effect, supervising the management of the business and reporting to shareholders on their stewardship. The board's actions are subject to laws, regulations and the shareholders in general meeting.

OECD (2005), for example, understands the following under the term corporate governance:

> Procedures and processes according to which an organisation is directed and controlled. The corporate governance structure specifies the distribution of rights and responsibilities among the different participants in the organisation – such as the board, managers, shareholders and other stakeholders – and lays down the rules and procedures for decision-making.

In the Czech Republic, the concept of corporate governance is defined by the Ministry of Finance of the Czech Republic as follows:

> Corporate governance represents legal and executive methods and procedures that bind primarily publicly traded companies to maintain a balanced relationship between the company and those it comprises, i.e. the shareholders, statutory bodies, executive management, employees and customers, or possibly other stakeholders.

The past economic crisis has impacted, among others, corporate governance in domestic companies. Cost savings in the companies have affected, among others, voluntary bodies (committees) of a company, in which the Corporate Governance Code recommends introducing, in addition to the mandatory bodies, as a part of good corporate governance. These include, for example:

- Audit committee,
- Internal audit,
- Committee for the appointment of members of statutory and supervisory bodies,

- Committee for remuneration of those members.

These committees, if they are independent of the company management, greatly help in setting and monitoring compliance with the statutory conditions in the company, prevent corruption, money laundering or any other form of economic and other crimes.

42.3 Audit Committee

As previously stated, various committees with their focus play an important role in corporate governance. In the following text, we deal with the role of audit committees.

Audit committees and regulation of their activities have in the last few years undergone a number of significant changes. Even legislation in the Czech Republic is subject to the obligation to incorporate the relevant European Union legislation in local laws and regulations.[1]

Audit committees are established only by certain entities, i.e. those falling into the category of "public interest entities" (further referred to as PIE). Essential incentives regarding these entities and their responsibilities are embedded in the directives of the European Union. PIE are more visible and more significant in terms of economic performance and, therefore, stricter requirements should be placed on statutory audit of their annual accounts and consolidated accounts.

Audit committees and an effective internal control system help to minimize financial and operational risk and compliance risk and improve the quality of financial reporting.

We will focus on this issue in terms of legal regulation in the Czech Republic. The original and relatively broad definition of PIE included in Article 2 of the Act No. 93/2009 Coll., on Auditors, effective until the end of 2015, can be called specific to the Czech Republic. The European directive requires that this concept includes all publicly traded companies, banks and insurance companies and allows Member States to include other entities. Extension to savings and credit cooperatives, pension funds and investment funds, securities traders, depository and settlement system operators, as well as business corporations and consolidating units with an average number of employees for the immediately preceding period above 4000 was particular for the Czech regulation.

---

[1]Directive 2006/43/EC of the European Parliament and of the Council of 17 May 2006 on statutory audits of annual accounts and consolidated accounts, amending Council Directives 78/660/EEC and 83/349/EEC and repealing Council Directive 84/253/EEC, as amended by Council Directive 2008/30/ES.

Directive 2013/34/EU of the European Parliament and of the Council of 26 June 2013 on the annual financial statements, consolidated financial statements and related reports of certain types of undertakings, amending Directive 2006/43/EC of the European Parliament and of the Council and repealing Council Directives 78/660/EEC and 83/349/EEC.

Table 42.1 Public interest
entities in the Czech Republic
since 2016

Type of public interest entity	No. in 2016
Securities issuers	52
Banks, savings and credit cooperatives	48
Insurance and reinsurance companies	43
Health insurance companies	12
Pension companies	5

Source Prepared according to the contribution of Jiří Nekovář,
president of the Public Audit Oversight Committee in the Czech
Republic (RVDA), during the roundtable discussion of RVDA
with auditors organized in December 2015; see also magazine
Auditor no. 1/2016; authors' own table

According to the definition we find, as of 2016, in the Act No. 563/1991 Coll.,
on Accounting (Article 1a), this category does not any longer include investment
companies, securities traders, central depository and business corporations with
more than 4000 employees.[2] According to the original definition of public interest
entities with 370 entities, there are about 160 entities remaining in this category; see
Table 42.1 Public interest entities in the Czech Republic since 2016.

The focus of the audit committee activities has also been extended since 2016.
The audit committee monitors: the effectiveness of internal control, risk management system; effectiveness of internal audit and ensures its functional independence, if the internal audit function is established; internal audit is in this case
functionally subordinate to the audit committee; the process of compiling the
financial statements and consolidated financial statements; statutory audit process.

The audit committee recommends an auditor to the inspection authority, whereas
it duly justifies this recommendation.

The audit committee assesses the independence of statutory auditors and audit
firms and the provision of additional services of the public interest entity by the
statutory auditor and audit firm.

In case of section of internal audit, this concerns changes, in particular, in the
actual functional subordination to the audit committee and not to the Board of
Directors; it concerns changes in the organizational structure. As regards a particular public interest entity, it also means adjustment of procedures, methodologies
and the way of communication with senior management.

Other responsibilities of PIE include publication of the list of members of the
audit committee on its website;[3] in selected cases[4] when the PIE have not established an audit committee, it includes publication on its website, which body performs the functions of the audit committee and the names of persons who are its
members, stating the reasons for the establishment of the audit committee.

---

[2]Exceptions from the obligation to establish audit committee in PIE are further governed by Article
44b of the Act No. 93/2009 Coll., on Auditors.

[3]Act No. 93/2009 Coll. Article 44 (6).

[4]Act No. 93/2009 Coll. Article 44b.

Table 42.2 Published data with regard to PIE in the Czech Republic in 2014

Type of public interest entity	No. in 2014
Securities issuers	13
Banks	24
Insurance companies	7
Health insurance companies	7
Reinsurance companies	1

Source Prepared according to the published annual statement in the Commercial Register; author's own table

In relation to the above obligations of PIE, analysis of the published data for the year 2014 was conducted to verify compliance with the legal obligations to disclose the requested information. From a total of 370 PIE (according to the legal provisions valid until the end of 2015), 52 entities were selected in the structure as shown in Table 42.2.

The analysis resulted in the following findings:

- From the total of 52 entities (PIE), 38 entities (i.e. 73%) stated in the published data that they have established audit committees,
- Of these 38 entities (PIE), 7 entities (i.e. 18.4%) did not publish a list of names of audit committee members,
- In other published information on the activities of the audit committee with regard to these 38 entities (PIE), 19 had no data (i.e. 50%),
- With regard to the remaining 19 entities (i.e. 50%) out of the total of 38 entities (PIE), legal obligations were cited in the scope of business; with regard to 5 entities, it was stated who replaces activities of audit committee (exercised by supervisory board or audit committee).

42.4   Tax Aspects of Remuneration of the Members of Audit Committees

Taxation of remuneration of a member of audit committee is based on the opinion of the General Tax Directorate from 2015, which with regard to this issue was discussed within the Coordination Committee in relation to the proposed contribution from Trezziova (2016).[5]

On 20 January 2016, the General Directorate of Finance assessed the tax regime of remuneration of a member of the committee as follows.

---

[5]Contribution of JUDr. Ing. Dana Trezziová, tax advisor no. 7, no. 459/16.09.15 *Taxation of remuneration of a member of audit committee*, coordination committee dated 20 January 2016, contribution concluded with reservation.

42.4.1 Taxation of Remuneration of a Member of Audit Committee

According to Article 6 (10) (b) of the Act No. 586/1992 Coll., on Income Taxes, as amended (further referred to as "ZDP"), the following are considered functional benefits: remuneration for the performance of functions and services provided in connection with current or former duties in

1. The bodies of municipalities and other local government body,
2. The state authorities,
3. Associations and interest groups,
4. Trade unions,
5. Chambers,
6. Other bodies and institutions.

The following is also considered income from employment (functional benefit): remuneration for performance of functions in unspecified bodies, i.e. also performance of a function in the audit committee. The performance in the form of functional benefit is taxed according to Article 6 (1) (a) point 2 of the Income Tax Act, regardless of:

- Legislation that regulates the mutual rights and obligations as a member of the audit committee and the public interest entity,
- Type of contract that establishes mutual rights and obligations as a member of the audit committee and public interest entity,
- Method of work and payment of remuneration for it,
- The fact that a member of the audit committee is a non-executive member of the supervisory authority of the public interest entity or third party.

For the purposes of tax assessment, it is not important that with regard to the stated function the audit committee members may conclude mandate contract with the public interest entity governing the exercise of their functions.

42.4.2 Assessment of Tax Deductibility of the Remuneration of a Member of the Audit Committee

The remuneration of a member of the audit committee is, providing all the conditions set by ZDP are met, a tax-deductible expense for public interest entity according to Article 24 (1) of ZDP that pays the said remuneration to a committee member.

In case of the tax regime of premium for liability for damage caused by a member of the audit committee in the performance of functions, it holds true that when the following are subject to the insurance relationship bound to pay premium:

- Member of the statutory body, it is from the perspective of legal entity a voluntary payment of expenses—premium by legal entity on behalf of another entity (audit committee member), and therefore, this expense is not tax deductible under Article 25 (1) (d) of ZDP.
- Legal entity and the premium are paid on the basis of its contractual obligation to insure damage, thus, not payment; "on behalf of" a member of the audit committee, the premium can be claimed as a tax-deductible expense under Article 24 (1) of ZDP. Legal entity must demonstrate a causal link between the conclusion of the insurance contract in question and achieving, securing and maintaining income.

42.5 Conclusion

Audit committees and regulation of their activities have in the past few years undergone a number of significant changes. The legislation in the Czech Republic is subject to the obligation to incorporate the relevant European Union legislation within the framework of local laws. Essential incentives regarding these entities and their responsibilities are embedded in the directives of the European Union. Audit committees are established only by certain entities, i.e. those falling into the category of "public interest entities".

To conclude, we can state that the disclosure obligations are with regard to the public interest entities and in case of internal audit fulfilled in some cases only partially; in aggregate, we can say that the breadth of information is provided to the extent necessary according to legal requirements.

The performance in the form of functional benefit for membership in the audit committee is taxed with regard to a committee member according to Article 6 (1) (a) section 2 of the ZDP. Provided the conditions stipulated by law are fulfilled, this remuneration is a tax-deductible expense for public interest entities, which provided remuneration to a committee member.

Acknowledgments This paper has been prepared under financial support of research projects IP100040, which author gratefully acknowledges.

References

Auditor (1/2016): Discussion paper - Jiří Nekovář, president of the Council for Public Audit Oversight in the Czech Republic (RVDA), at a meeting Roundtable RVDA with auditors, held in December 2015
Cadbury A (1992). Report of the committee on the financial aspects of corporate governance (Vol. 1). Gee.
Deloitte [online], corporate governance page. http://www2.deloitte.com/cz/cs/pages/risk/topics/czech-center-for-corporate-governance.html

Directive 2006/43/EC of the European Parliament and of the Council of 17 May 2006 on statutory audits of annual accounts and consolidated accounts, amending Council Directives 78/660/EEC and 83/349/EEC and repealing Council Directive 84/253/EEC, as amended by Council Directive 2008/30/ES

Directive 2013/34/EU of the European Parliament and of the Council of 26 June 2013 on the annual financial statements, consolidated financial statements and related reports of certain types of undertakings, amending Directive 2006/43/EC of the European Parliament and of the Council and repealing Council Directives 78/660/EEC and 83/349/EEC

OECD (2005) Glossary of statistical terms. Corporate governance. [online], Organization for Economic Corporation and Development, Paris. http://stats.oecd.org/glossary/detail.asp?ID= 6778

OECD: OECD Guidelines on corporate governance of state-owned enterprises. [online], Organization for Economic Corporation and Development, Paris. http://www.oecd.org/ corporate/

Post JE, Preston LE, Sachs S (2002) Redefining the corporation: stakeholder management and organizational wealth. Stanford University Press, Redwood 2002

Shleifer A, Vishny RW (1997) A survey of corporate governance. J FINANC 52(2):737–783

Trezziová D (2016) Taxation of remuneration of a member of audit committee, coordination committee dated 20 January 2016, contribution concluded with reservation. http://www. financnisprava.cz/assets/cs/prilohy/d-prispevky-kv-kdp/Zapis_KV-KDP_2016-01-20.pdf

Chapter 43
The Municipality Economic Review by Auditor or by Regional Authority?

Petra Baranová

Abstract This paper is focused on economic review carried by an auditor or by a regional authority in the Czech Republic. The first part of paper summarizes basic terms, legislation and procedures. The second part contains statistics provided by Ministry of Finance in the Czech Republic. The proportion between auditor and regional authority is analysed according to the various aspects.

Keywords Municipality audit · Municipality economic review · Public sector entities · Accounting · Czech auditing standard no. 52

43.1 Introduction

The issue of an economic review is still relevant. The professional public is divided into two groups—auditors and regional authority. One way or another, the self-governing territorial units (also municipalities) must have an economic review done—this obligation is by law. It is obvious that an economic review carried out by a regional authority is free of charge, while economic review from an auditor/audit firm is not. The fact that a review is carried out by employees who deal with economic reviews only speaks in favour of the regional authorities, while auditors are more specialized in entrepreneurs and less in the public sector. Auditors only expand their portfolio of provided services by carrying out an economic review of municipalities.

An economic review should be a public matter because the municipalities are managed by public funds. Besides the reviewed areas, controllers/auditors should examine whether e.g. one kilometre of highway is overpriced. Before that, we need to know how much one kilometre of a standard highway costs.

P. Baranová (✉)
Department of Financial Accounting and Auditing, University of Economics,
Prague, Nam. W. Churchilla 4, 130 67 Prague, Czech Republic
e-mail: xbarp47@vse.cz

© Springer International Publishing AG 2017
D. Procházka (ed.), *New Trends in Finance and Accounting*,
Springer Proceedings in Business and Economics,
DOI 10.1007/978-3-319-49559-0_43

43.2 Literature Review

Municipality economic review is regulated by following acts, regulation and audit directive: act no. 320/2001 Coll., act no. 128/2000 Coll., act no. 563/1991 Coll., act no. 250/2000 Coll., act no. 137/2006 Coll., regulation no. 410/2009 Coll., act no. 420/2004 Coll. and the Czech auditing standard no. 52.

According to the act no. 137/2006 Coll. (on public procurements), public procurement is a procurement based on a contract where object of this contract is related to paid providing of supplies or services or construction works. When provided supplies, services or construction works exceed the limit determined by this act, municipality must proceed with public procurement according the act on public procurement.

Accounting is only one area which is reviewed. Accounting is carried out in accordance with the act no. 563/1991 Coll. and regulation no. 410/2009 Coll. Municipalities are entities which must carry out accounting and we call them selected entities. Other selected entities are contributory organisations, state funds, health insurance companies, state organisational units etc.

The basic terms are defined (bodies in municipalities, individual and delegated competences of municipalities, management of municipalities' property, etc.) in the act no. 128/2000 Coll.

The act no. 320/2001 Coll. is focused on public administrative control and internal control system. A budgetary process of municipalities (budget revenues and expenditures) and establishments of municipalities are defined in the act no. 250/2000 Coll.

The last mentioned act is the act no. 420/2004 Coll. on self-governing territorial units and Voluntary association of municipalities economic review. As the title implies, this is one of the most important acts for review.

All mentioned acts and regulations are obligatory for municipalities (and other selected entities). These obligations are verified by controllers and auditors/audit firms. The Czech auditing standard no. 52 is important only for auditors.

There are not many monographs on this topic. The reason is obvious—just laws would be quoted. One of those books is Peterová (2008). This book was published in 2005 and in 2008. But municipality economic review is just only one chapter in this book and this chapter has about 15 pages. In other chapters we can read about municipalities' money management, state budget, state funds and about tax revenues. Urbancová and Hakalová (2012) deal with an economic review and audit of financial statements. Authors write about state accounting reform and most important legislation or about financial statements. In this paper we can learn about economic review and audit of FS in epitome. Authors summarize the basic terms, legislation and the procedures.

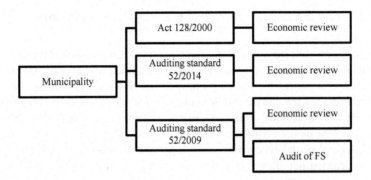

Fig. 43.1 Economic review versus audit of FS. *Source* Based on the Act no. 128/2000 Coll. and Auditing standard no. 52, author's visualization

43.3   Economic Review

43.3.1   Term

A term "economic review" is used in relation to auditors/audit firms as well as regional authority. Previous auditing standard was focused on audit of financial statements (FS). The new one only incorporates an economic review. Municipalities could have an audit of financial statements done. Audit of financial statements is not obligatory unlike to economic review and audit can be carried out by auditors/audit firms. Voluntary audit of FS is not, although, regular in the Czech Republic (Fig. 43.1).

43.3.2   Legislation

According to the act no. 128/2000 Coll., all municipalities have an economic review done. Municipalities can choose between an auditor and a regional authority. By the end of June of the calendar year, municipalities are required to notify on how they had decided to secure its economic review (Act 420/2004).

As soon as a municipality signs a contract with an auditor, the regional authority must be informed about this contract. The deadline for providing this information is January 31st of the following year. If a municipality does not ask for an economic review, the economic review is carried out by a regional authority.

A final account and a report from economic review must be discussed by the municipal council by the end of June of the following year, and all errors and deficiencies must be corrected.

43.3.3 The Economic Review by a Regional Authority

Regional authority prepares a plan of economic reviews based on the information from municipalities until the end of June of the following year. The size of a municipality is critical for carrying out a partial or one-time review. Two partial economic reviews are carried out in municipalities with more than 800 inhabitants, and a one-time economic review is carried out in municipalities up to 800 inhabitants. The first partial economic review is carried out in fall of the calendar year, and the second partial economic review is carried out after year end. The one-time review is carried out after year end.

Employees of regional authority ("controllers") carry out an economic review according to act no. 420/2004 Coll. The subject of economic review is, e.g.

- budget revenues and expenditures,
- financial transactions relating to creation and use of monetary funds,
- costs and revenues of municipality business activity,
- billing and settlement of financial transactions to the state budget, regional authority budget and municipal budgets, other budgets, state funds.
- handling and management of property owned by municipality
- handling and management of state assets which were entrusted to municipality
- execution of tenders,
- liability for obligations of individuals and private companies
- pledging of tangible and intangible assets in favour of third parties,
- accounting carried out by municipality.

All previous points are verified in terms of compliance with the obligations under special regulations (regulations on financial management of self-governing territorial units, on management of its assets, on accounting and remuneration); whether a financial management is in conformity with the budget; if a received grand or refundable financial assistance were used according to the conditions; the formal and substantive correctness of documents submitted.

According to the information from municipalities, the regional authority draws up a plan for economic reviews.

Controller receives documents (mostly in binders) and goes through them. Then all the information is entered into the Information system for planning and reviewing "IS MPP". IS MPP (also called "Aktovka") allows to generate a final report. A special mode (called "aktovka") is used during review of a municipality. We can see the unofficial name for information system came from this special mode. The time spent in a municipality depends on its size.

A report from economic review includes place, period and reviewed year, description of detected errors and a review conclusion. All documents which were used during a review must be properly marked.

Three basic types of conclusion are: 1. No errors and deficiencies found, 2. Controllers identified errors and deficiencies which are not serious and 3. Controllers identified errors and deficiencies which are serious (e.g. accounting is incomplete, incorrect or insubstantial; municipality did not meet the requirements for a review; municipality did not remove errors and deficiencies identified before; a municipality breached budgetary discipline).

43.3.4   Economic Review by an Auditor

Auditors/audit firms work with auditing standard no. 52 (issued by the Czech Chamber of Auditors) during economic review. The auditing standard no. 52 (effective from 23. 11. 2013) was divided into 5 parts—introduction, economic review, audit of FS, other auditor's responsibilities in providing audit services to self-governing territorial units and annexes.

The latest auditing standard no. 52 is longer and more detailed and it contains 5 parts too—introduction, objective, requirements, application and explaining part and annexes. This standard considers an economic review as an assurance engagement according to International Standard on Assurance Engagements (ISAE) 3000. The report from economic review must be in line with act no. 420/2004 Coll. and with ISAE 3000 and must be debated with a municipality mayor.

43.4   Statistics

Every year, the Ministry of Finance of the Czech Republic publishes the annual statistics on its website based on the results of the economic review carried out in the period from July 1 to June 30.

Please note that from the 1st of January 2010, the reform of the municipalities' accounting is valid. This reform had an impact mainly on accounting more than on the economic review process. Accountants in municipalities and regional controllers had to learn more about the new regulation and accounting practices that were common only for entrepreneurs, but not for municipalities (e.g. depreciation, creation of bad debt provision, accruals). The beginning of the reform was very hard. New Czech accounting standards for selected units were issued in addition to the new regulation.

43.4.1   Frequency of the Economic Review

We can observe that the basic ratio of the economic review has been carried out more by regional authorities. Almost 86% of municipalities were reviewed by regional authorities (+Prague), and only 14% were reviewed by auditors/audit firms (Fig. 43.2).

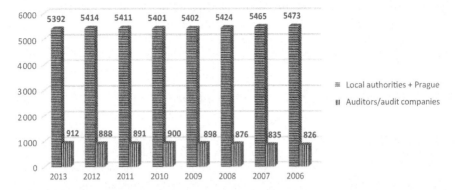

Fig. 43.2 conomic reviews during 2006–2013. *Source* Ministry of Finance of the Czech Republic (2013), http://www.mfcr.cz/cs/verejny-sektor/uzemni-rozpocty/prezkoumani-hospodareni-uzemnich-celku/vysledky-prezkoumani-hospodareni/2013/vysledky-prezkoumani-hospodareni-a-dozor-20564

We can see that total number of municipalities is stable during the years 2006–2013. The reason is obvious: establishment, termination or separation of municipalities is not so common.

We can see municipality distribution according to the size in the next table. In municipalities with population up to 4999, the economic review is carried out by regional authorities. Economic review is carried out by auditors/audit firms in municipalities over 5000 of inhabitants.

Regional authorities have only limited number of controllers so it is impossible to carry out an economic review in all required municipalities. That is why large municipalities are rejected by regional authorities. Large municipalities have only last option—ask an auditor/audit firm. Other reason why municipalities up to 4999 of inhabitants have the economic review done by regional authorities is money. Economic review carried out by regional authorities is free of charge, and those municipalities cannot afford an auditors/audit firm (Table 43.1).

43.4.2 Number of Errors

This part deals with the number of errors found out by regional authorities and by auditors/audit firms. It is evident that auditors/audit companies are more strict based on comparison of following two tables.

Trend in regional municipalities is in favour of the increasing number of result "no errors". One of the reasons can be the fact controllers cooperate with a municipality for a long time and during this time, most of errors or deficiencies were identified and corrected (Fig. 43.3).

Table 43.1 Economic reviews in municipalities according to the size

Population	2013		2012		2011	
	RA+P (%)	Auditors (%)	RA+P (%)	Auditors (%)	RA+P (%)	Auditors (%)
0–199	94	6	95	5	95	5
200–999	90	10	91	9	91	9
1000–4999	75	25	75	25	75	25
5000–19,999	35	65	36	64	35	65
Over 20,000	19	81	19	81	17	83

Note RA+P … Regional authorities + City of Prague
Source Ministry of Finance of the Czech Republic, section "Economic review results". Please refer http://www.
mfcr.cz/cs/verejny-sektor/uzemni-rozpocty/prezkoumani-hospodareni-uzemnich-celku/vysledky-prezkoumani-
hospodareni

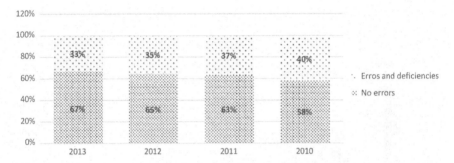

Fig. 43.3 Errors and deficiencies found out by regional authorities. *Source* Ministry of Finance of
the Czech Republic, section "Economic review results". Please refer http://www.mfcr.cz/cs/
verejny-sektor/uzemni-rozpocty/prezkoumani-hospodareni-uzemnich-celku/vysledky-prezkoumani-
hospodareni

We can see that auditors/audit firms had problems with delivery of reports. In
2010, 9% of reports were not delivered back to auditors. Small auditors could have
a problem to be in line with ethic codex, because those auditors are sometimes
absolutely depended on their clients. It is absolutely unacceptable to be a dependent
on any client (Fig. 43.4).

43.4.3   Imperfections by Acts (Regularity Audit)

During the regular audit, the controllers check whether the activities are in accordance with a specific legislation. An examination of a substantive and formal
correctness is one of the elements. One advantage of a regularity audit is minimizing of law infringements. The Fig. 43.5 demonstrates that the most breached are

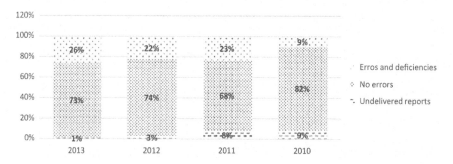

Fig. 43.4 Errors and deficiencies found out by auditors/audit firms. *Source* Ministry of Finance of the Czech Republic, section "Economic review results". Please refer http://www.mfcr.cz/cs/verejny-sektor/uzemni-rozpocty/prezkoumani-hospodareni-uzemnich-celku/vysledky-prezkoumani-hospodareni

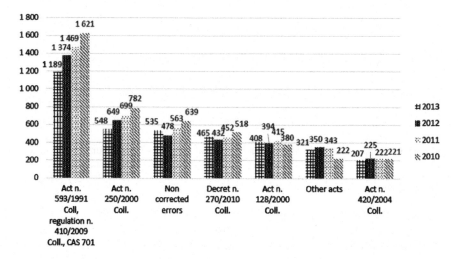

Fig. 43.5 The breaches of legal acts during 2010–2013. *Source* Ministry of Finance of the Czech Republic, section "Economic review results". Please refer http://www.mfcr.cz/cs/verejny-sektor/uzemni-rozpocty/prezkoumani-hospodareni-uzemnich-celku/vysledky-prezkoumani-hospodareni

accounting laws, then the act no. 250/2000 Coll. (budgetary rules). The third place belongs to non-corrected errors. A decreasing trend in years 2010–2013 is evident for all types of breaches.

The most often breaches of legislation include, e.g.:

- Accounting laws:

    - A municipality did not carry out a stock take.
    - An accounting entry was insubstantial.

Table 43.2 Economic review conclusions types

	Auditors			Regional authorities		
	No errors	Less severe	Severe	No errors	Less severe	Severe
2013						
City of Prague	4	7	4	25	4	7
South Bohemia	47	19	2	228	46	34
South Moravia	111	6	4	48	64	75
Karlovy Vary Region	8	1	0	15	2	12
Vysočina Region	79	16	6	44	84	74
Hradec Králové Region	48	8	2	81	30	29
Liberec Region	16	9	0	19	16	12
Moravia-Silesia	45	19	8	12	8	18
Olomouc Region	37	4	0	30	10	6
Pardubice Region	5	3	3	40	22	16
Plzeň Region	78	13	2	31	43	32
Central Bohemia	120	38	12	136	110	139
Ústí Region	53	19	10	24	24	6
Zlín Region	14	19	0	71	23	23
Czech Republic total	665	181	53	804	486	483
2012						
City of Prague	2	9	4	7	13	22
South Bohemia	39	21	1	273	200	88
South Moravia	105	11	2	334	48	169
Karlovy Vary Region	6	1	1	97	11	15
Vysočina Region	72	18	10	447	42	113
Hradec Králové Region	52	1	3	290	61	41
Liberec Region	20	2	1	143	17	32
Moravia-Silesia	47	20	6	193	14	19
Olomouc Region	34	3	1	275	71	14
Pardubice Region	6	5	0	338	72	30
Plzeň Region	69	8	1	282	33	86
Central Bohemia	125	30	8	469	180	328
Ústí Region	69	3	6	208	31	37
Zlín Region	12	22	0	149	60	62
Czech Republic total	658	154	44	3505	853	1056
2011						
City of Prague	16	0	0	8	26	7
South Bohemia	39	16	3	191	185	188
South Moravia	100	0	0	206	62	286
Karlovy Vary Region	7	1	0	74	26	23
Vysočina Region	102	0	0	377	82	143
Hradec Králové Region	46	8	2	224	87	81
Liberec Region	0	0	0	144	15	33
Moravia-Silesia	57	17	1	142	35	48
Olomouc Region	39	0	0	248	69	42
Pardubice Region	13	0	0	302	89	47

(continued)

Table 43.2 (continued)

	Auditors			Regional authorities		
	No errors	Less severe	Severe	No errors	Less severe	Severe
Plzeň Region	13	0	0	285	32	84
Central Bohemia	173	0	0	338	250	383
Ústí Region	64	3	9	198	33	47
Zlín Region	0	0	0	125	80	66
Czech Republic total	669	45	15	2862	1071	1478

Source Ministry of Finance of the Czech Republic, section "Economic review results". Please refer http://www.mfcr.cz/cs/verejny-sektor/uzemni-rozpocty/prezkoumani-hospodareni-uzemnich-celku/vysledky-prezkoumani-hospodareni

- – A municipality did not follow accounting procedures.
- – A municipality booked on short-term liabilities and short-term receivables.
- – A municipality did not booked correctly in connection with transfers.

- • Act no. 250/2000 Coll.:

  - – Draft of a final account was not publicized appropriately.
  - – Approval of a final account was not carried out in accordance with the law.
  - – A budget forecast was not draw up or a municipality did not manage according to the budget.

- • Act no. 128/2000 Coll.:

  - – The intention of a municipality was not published on the official notice board for at least 15 days prior to the decision.
  - – The municipal council did not approve the budget and final account (Table 43.2).

43.5   Conclusion

Once a year, municipalities have an economic review done. Municipality can choose between a regional authority or auditor/audit firm. Review which is carried out regional authority is free of charge. If the municipality chooses an auditor, they have to sign a contract. Legislation for economic review is the same for auditor as well as regional authority, except for auditing standard, which is used only by auditors. All requirements in relation with carrying out audit are written in laws. The conclusion from economic review must be debated with municipality mayor. There are three types of conclusion: 1. No errors and deficiencies found, 2. Controllers identified errors and deficiencies which are not serious and 3. Controllers identified errors and deficiencies which are serious.

Regional authorities have only small capacity of employees. Due to it, regional authority must reject bigger municipalities. We can see in statistics provided by Ministry of Finance of the Czech Republic that municipalities over population of 5000 are reviewed mainly by auditors. Approximately 86% of all municipalities are reviewed by local authority, and only 14% of municipalities are reviewed by auditor/auditors firm. During economic review a regularity audit is performed. Regularity audit is related to a breach of legislation. From year 2010 to 2013, we can see the most breaches in accounting legislation.

Acknowledgments This is paper has been prepared under financial support of research projects IP100040, which author gratefully acknowledge.

References

CSFR. Zákon č. 563/1991 ze dne 12. prosince 1991 o účetnictví. In: Sbírka zákonů České a Slovenské federativní republiky. 1991, částka 107, [s 2802-2809]. [ISSN 1210-0005]. Dostupné také z: https://portal.gov.cz/app/zakony/zakon.jsp?page=0&nr=563 ~ 2F1991&rpp= 15#seznam

Czech Republic. Zákon č. 128/2000 ze dne 12. dubna 2000 o obcích (obecním zřízení). In: Sbírka zákonů České republiky. 2000, částka 38. ISSN 1211-1244. Dostupné také z http://www.zakonyprolidi.cz/cs/sbirka

Czech Republic. Zákon č. 250/2000 o rozpočtových pravidlech územních rozpočtů. In: Sbírka zákonů České republiky. 2000, částka 73. ISSN 1211-1244. Dostupné také z http://www.zakonyprolidi.cz/cs/2000-250

Czech Republic. Zákon č. 320/2001 ze dne 9. srpna 2001 o finanční kontrole ve veřejné správě a o změně některých zákonů (zákon o finanční kontrole). In: Sbírka zákonů České republiky. 2001, částka 122. ISSN 1211-1244. Dostupné také z http://www.zakonyprolidi.cz/cs/2001-320

Czech Republic. Zákon č. 420/2004 ze dne 10. června 2004 o přezkoumávání hospodaření územních samosprávných celků a dobrovolných svazků obcí. In: Sbírka zákonů České republiky. 2004, částka 138. ISSN 1211-1244. Dostupné také z http://www.zakonyprolidi.cz/cs/sbirka

Czech Republic. Zákon č. 137/2006 ze dne 14. března 2006 o veřejných zakázkách. In: Sbírka zákonů České republiky. 2006, částka 47. ISSN 1211-1244. Dostupné také z http://www.portal-vz.cz/getmedia/85b22a3c-a510-4487-bc9e-1225323f625c/137-2006-od-1-1-2016.pdf

Czech Republic. Vyhláška 410/2009 ze dne 11. listopadu 2009. In: Sbírka zákonů České republiky. částka 133. ISSN 1211-1244. Dostupné také z http://www.zakonyprolidi.cz/cs/2009-410

Czech Republic. Auditorský standard č. 52 Přezkoumání hospodaření územních samosprávných celků. Dostupné také z http://www.kacr.cz/auditorske-standardy-2014

HAKALOVÁ, Jana. URBANCOVÁ, Alžběta. Účetní reforma veřejných financí v 010Ceské republice a její vliv na účetnictví, účetní závěrku, přezkoumání hospodaření a audit účetní závěrky některých vybraných účetních jednotek [příspěvek] © 2012. Dostupné z https://www.ekf.vsb.cz/export/sites/ekf/k117/.content/galerie-dokumentu/clanky/clanek-5.pdf

PETEROVÁ. Helena. Finanční hospodaření územních samosprávných celků a jeho přezkum. Vyd. 2., dopl. Praha: Institut pro místní správu, 2008. ISBN: 80-86976-13-6

Chapter 44
All for One and One for All: A Cross-Sector Analysis of Reporting Standards

Tudor Oprisor and Andrei-Razvan Crisan

Abstract This paper aims to provide a comparative view between the private and the public sectors through the "lens" of reporting standards and question whether the differences are so pronounced to provide the necessity for distinct sets of regulations and guidelines. To achieve this, we analyze the two sectors in comparison with the use of the literature and official documents. On this ground, we give an insight on the current status of the specific sets of regulations and guidelines (on each level of information). Our findings show that the current reporting practice (taking integrated reporting into account) leads toward a diminishing in the different treatment of the two sectors (from a reporting point of view). All the constituting elements and principles of reporting standards (as well as initiatives from major standard setters) are driven toward one concise communication (the integrated report), thus reducing the gap. Also, the conceptual framework does not purposely discriminate between sectors; it treats them equally and offers implementation perspectives for all entities (by providing principles, fundamental concepts, and theoretical model).

Keywords Private sector · Public sector · Standards · Financial reporting · Integrated reporting

44.1 Introduction

The underlying assumption of the recent dynamics in reporting standardization and practice is that the governing bodies (or standard setters) are trying to instate a balance between financial and non-financial information—and for a fair reason

T. Oprisor (✉) · A.-R. Crisan
Department of Accounting and Auditing, Faculty of Economics
and Business Administration, Babes-Bolyai University of Cluj-Napoca,
Cluj-Napoca, Romania
e-mail: tudor.oprisor@econ.ubbcluj.ro

A.-R. Crisan
e-mail: andrei.crisan@econ.ubbcluj.ro

© Springer International Publishing AG 2017
D. Procházka (ed.), *New Trends in Finance and Accounting*,
Springer Proceedings in Business and Economics,
DOI 10.1007/978-3-319-49559-0_44

because not all focus should be solely on the financial capital, which is just one component of a functional model embedding an organization's activity.

The emergence of new reporting trends—complementary to financial reporting (such as sustainability reporting and integrated reporting) and the creation of new reporting standards setters (such as the International Integrated Reporting Council) have given the prerequisite for this shift in balance between informational components of the reports, but at this point there is still a certain level of disproportion (mainly because there is no unifying set of standards for the majority of reporting entities). Although we understand the differences between sectors (and we even emphasize them within one chapter of this paper), we put a question mark on whether they are so pronounced to require different sets for different sectors (most of all, in the context of a holistic reporting setting, such as integrated reporting).

Hence, we structure the core of our paper into three main parts. First of all, we emphasize the essential differences between the public and private sectors, by developing a comparison of certain indicators, such as the purposes of the two sectors, the efficiency, the financial control, the leadership style, or motivation style. Second of all, we present the major sets of reporting standards (for both sectors), basically by reviewing the academic literature and official regulatory documents. Afterward, we synthesize the main aspects regarding the regulations and guidelines and we postulate the idea that there is a discrepancy between the standardization on specific reporting components (e.g., financial and non-financial information) and the standardization of integrated reporting as a whole. Last, but not least, we issue some concluding remarks and we present the limitations and development perspectives for future research.

44.2 Research Methodology

In the past decades, the international accounting bodies and practitioners have been increasingly concerned about the particular features of the public sector in relation to the private sector. In order to achieve the accounting harmonization process in the two sectors, IASB and International Public Sector Accounting Standards Board (IPSASB) developed international accounting standards applicable in the private sector [International Accounting Standard (IAS)/International Financial Reporting Standards (IFRS)] and public sector International Public Sector Accounting Standards (IPSAS). This split represents the basic element from which we start our analysis, with the specification that we take into consideration a certain degree of overlapping between the standards.

Therefore, our main research question is the following:

To what extent are different sets of reporting standards necessary for the public and the private sectors?

Although it sets the case for a broader, much more complex research, we consider this question relevant to the context of an intense debate regarding the evolution (both retrospective and prospective) of the standardization process in the two sectors.

To achieve our goal, we employ several methods within our conceptual paper. First of all, to present the basic characteristics in line for both sectors we use comparative analysis. This gives us a head-to-head matching of the core attributes for both sectors and the fundamental level of differentiation between reporting entities and (ultimately) regulations and guidelines.

Also, we acknowledge the work from the academic literature and practice by constructing a review of the relevant research from the field (with focus on the evolution of standards and the way in which they can be analyzed in parallel). This review is relevant because it gives us a picture of the current level of knowledge regarding reporting standardization (with the positioning of important front-runner researchers on this topic) and allows us to perform a development direction spotting.

Ultimately, we discuss the conceptual findings and provide insights on the particularities (and peculiarities) of the major regulations and guidelines, which we frame (even graphically, using an encompassing model) within recent developments and trends in reporting (more specifically, integrated reporting).

44.3 A Conceptual Comparison Between Sectors

Regarding the private sector, it has some particular features. Firstly, the primary objective of the private sector is the maximization of the profit. Related to performance and financial position of the private sector organizations, the focus is on the financial result (profit or loss), vulnerability, solvency, and adaptation ability (Guthrie 1998). Another main feature is that within the private sector the companies have the ownership of the goods used to produce and supply goods. Also, regarding financing, the private sector entities raise capital from investors to finance the assets purchases and working capital needs (Barton 1999).

Chan (2009) identifies the main characteristics of the private sector accounting: There is an unambiguous distinction between financial accounting and management accounting, double-entry bookkeeping is typically used in the financial accounting, the accrual accounting is always required in the financial accounting, and the consolidated financial statements are published annually to meet the needs of external users.

The public sector includes that part of the national economy whose activities, both economic and noneconomic, are controlled by the government. Also, the public sector produces goods and services to maximize the well-being of the population (Ibanichuka and Aca 2014).

The literature identifies also the three predominant criteria for distinguishing the private and public sectors (Meier and O'Toole 2009): the ownership, the source of financial resources, and the model of social control (polyarchy vs. market).

Regarding the parallel between the public and private sector, the academic literature identifies the following main differences between the two sectors: (Table 44.1).

Moreover, in the case of the public sector accounting, the specialists consider that the budgetary deficit for a financial year is the most important indicator of fiscal performance of the administration; therefore, the budget execution is the expression of the financial performance of the entity (Chan 2009). Also, Rainey et al. (1976), cited by Boyne (2002), states that the main conventional distinction between the private and the public organizations is the ownership.

On the other hand, the time perspectives of public organizations have a tendency to be relatively short time horizons (maximum 18 months) due to the political calendar and political needs. The private organizations have long time perspectives and incline to have investments, market developments, and technological novelty (Allison 1983). In the private sector, measuring the performance of the entity is much easier. The objective of the private organization is to make profit (Van Thiel and Leeuw 2002; Propper and Wilson 2003). Moreover, in the private entities there are numerous techniques of testing the performance. Therefore, in the public organization we cannot talk about the profit. The purpose of public organizations is to produce goods and services (which serve social needs) (Van Thiel and

Table 44.1 The essential differences between public and private sectors

The considered variable	Private sector	Public sector
Mandate	The maximization of profit, considering corporate interests only	The welfare maximization, taking into consideration the interests of community
Goal	Generally clear	Often vague to meet the needs of different stakeholders
Efficiency	Technical efficiency requirements	Economic efficiency is often at cost of technical efficiency
Costs	The costs of firm for the decision making	Community costs
Prices	Determined by the market	Determined by the policy
Revenue	From sales	Also from some natural monopolies
Financial control	Cash flow is crucial to survive	The government has a macro monetary role, so the cash is not an operating constraint
Product choice	Established by the corporation	Mandated by the government
Ownership	Partly owned entities	Relation to assets remain complex
Other stakeholders	Communities, creditors, suppliers, employees	The stakeholders are the same, but the communities weight much higher
Governance	Managers and directors	Ministers, the parliament, agency heads

Source Madhani 2014

Leeuw 2002). The tests for measuring the performance are fewer than in the private sector. The role of the press and media for public entities take place with constancy. In the private organization, this is exactly the contrary process.

There are dissimilarities also concerning the leadership style. In the public organizations, leadership style is change-oriented. This style means plans for the future, different manners of doing things, new ideas, and projects due to the prompt change of the managers (Arvonen and Ekvall 1999 cited by Andresen 2010). The private organization has a relationship style of leadership. The managers show concern for colleagues and making decisions process made together (Arvonen and Ekvall 1999 cited by Andresen 2010).

Motivation style is similarly different between the private and public sectors. Motivation style used in the public sector is achievement. The managers' aspiration is to do something unique, exceed the set standards, and achieve better results than someone else. In the private sector, managers use power motivation. They want to make influential actions to impress the others (McClelland 1972 cited by Andresen 2010).

44.4 Reporting Standardization for Both Sectors: A Never-Ending Story?

The transformation of the public institutions in the entrepreneurial entities generates numerous controversies in the literature related to the introduction of private sector management techniques in the public sector (Roje et al. 2012). One solution to this debate may be the reform of financial reporting system, a key element of New Public Management (Guthrie et al. 1999).

The process of adopting a uniform set of accounting standards, as a part of the universal convergence of financial reporting systems, is obvious a fundamental feature of the globalization of the world economy (Herz 2007). The tendency of international convergence and harmonization strategy of private sector accounting and IFRS has also made the sway on the process of whole public sector restructuring that made progress worldwide. Additionally, the changes the in public sector accounting were central to the public sector reform (Roje et al. 2012).

IFRS cannot be literally applied in the public sector, because they do not cover all transactions of public institutions. There are some areas specific to the public institutions such as revenues from taxes, transfers, social benefits, budget issues, and national accounts (Ristea et al. 2010). Also, the aim of profit maximization, specific to the private sector, does not apply to the public sector. Plus, the users of the public sector financial statements do not have needs similar to the users of the financial statements issued by the private sector entities. Also, the accounts of public accounting are significantly different from the accounts used in the private sector accounting (Bellanca and Vandernoot 2013). Another critical difference between IAS/IFRS and IPSAS is that former are based heavily on the concepts derived from the fair value accounting and balance sheet approach. These issues generate problems in the measurement and assessment of the liabilities and assets within the public sector (Oulasvirta 2014).

IPSAS represent a set of standards based on accrual and cash accounting (one standard). These standards are designed and developed by the IPSASB, whose main activity is to develop and publish these standards. One of the most important issue is that IPSAS are published in English, and most of them have a correspondent IAS or IFRS. IPSAS are designed to be applied only by the public institutions, not the government business enterprises (GBE) (Aggestam 2010). The strategy of IPSASB for the development of a set of some high-quality public sector accounting standards used IAS/IFRS to save time and resources (Lombrano and Zanin 2013).

The essential objectives of IPSAS are the improvement of comparability, as well as the reliability and transparency of the public accounts, and the achievement of the public sector accounting harmonization process. Therefore, the European Union member states are very interested in the implementation of IPSAS and the relevance of these standards (Bellanca and Vandernoot 2014).

Several authors (Chan 2003; Jones 2007; Bergmann 2009) support the idea that IPSAS represents one of the most relevant examples of the influence of the private sector on the public sector, given that these standards are based largely on standards available for private sector accounting standards (IAS/IFRS).

Although many of the IPSAS are relatively aligned to IFRS, there are numerous significant deviations. Without them, IPSAS would not account effectively for specific issues of the public sector. Also, IPSAS provide extra guidance, a terminology specific to public sector and some transition clauses more generous than IFRS (Sanderson and Van Schaik 2008). Moreover, some countries such as Spain have a tradition to base the public sector accounting standards on private sector accounting standards (Brusca et al. 2013).

An essential difference between the IPSAS and IFRS is that the implementation of IPSAS is not mandatory, but recommended. The governments and regulatory bodies have the right to establish the national accounting rules available in their jurisdictions. Moreover, IPSASB suggests that IPSAS could be a helpful tool for regulators in developing new rules for increasing comparability (Biondi and Sierra 2015). On the other hand, it is very well known that the European Commission required adoption of the IAS/IFRS for all listed corporate groups in the European Union member states (Biondi and Soverchia 2014).

In the literature, there are some authors and international bodies (Christiaens et al. 2013; Eurostat 2012) who consider that the significant similarity between IFRS and IPSAS makes latter not feasible for implementation at the European Union level. Newberry (2014) considers that the differences between IFRS and IPSAS should not be considered as substantial, given that both are designed to produce information useful for capital markets: stock markets and bond markets, incorporating government bond markets.

Based also on some previous research (Pina et al. 2009 cited by Christiaens et al. 2013), we consider important to mention that the Anglo-Saxon municipalities stipulate in the annual reports they publish on their Web sites that they use IFRS as a basis for the financial reporting process. Regarding the UK that country has taken no action to implement IPSAS, but the central and local governments use the accounting in compliance with IFRS. That fact makes the transition to IPSAS easier than in other European countries (Bellanca and Vandernoot 2014).

However, the most of the member states have a problem with the governance and due process of IPSASB. In this case, the European Union sets up its own governance with the necessary powers to legislate its own accounting standards, namely the European Public Sector Accounting Standards (generically abbreviated EPSAS) (Jones and Caruana 2015).

Regarding the EPSAS governance structures, the EPSAS project should decide to what extent EPSAS should approach the IPSAS, considering the fact that the latter transpose the IFRS in the public sector. The EPSAS project is viewed as very important because it should establish the accounting referential for the European Union member states. IPSAS tend to have a clear preference for an approach based on "balance sheet" and an alignment between standards for the public and private sector. However, both choices could have some fundamental implications on the work of the European Union, since both accounting and public finances are some significant elements of the institutional framework of the European Union (Biondi 2014).

In terms of content analysis, on the regulations and social reporting practices, we have noticed that there are studies conducted on local public administrations from Italy, which compare their practices with the GRI guidelines, with the main purpose of determining similarities and discrepancies between them. Also, there is a focus on social reports generated by municipalities and provinces, with the key content elements, as opposed to GRI guidelines (Farneti and Siboni 2011).

Integrated reporting has recently become a very popular subject, with most of the discussions being focused on regulatory perspectives and reporting performance improvement. The IIRC—as the main governing body—has been putting intense efforts to promote and issue guidelines for integrated reporting. The first brick was set in April 2013; the Council issued a Consultation Draft for the Integrated Reporting Framework (IIRC 2013a), thus inviting companies, organizations, and various stakeholders from all over the world to consult the document and provide comments for the <IR> construct. After considering improvements and feedback from stakeholders, the IIRC issued its final version of the Framework (IIRC 2013b).

Regarding the perspective of implementation for <IR> in the public sector, one of the front-runner studies is conducted by Bartocci and Picciaia (2013). Based on the literature and following a content analysis method (similar to our approach), they manage to provide an insight of the grounds for shifting to new trends of reporting (with clear mentioning of public accountability), as well as an outline of the main trends in reporting in the public sector (with emphasis on various forms of non-financial reporting). Ultimately, the authors analyze the <IR> Consultation Draft and provide assertions on which aspects need adjusting in order to provide the opportunity for <IR> to be implemented in public sector entities. Most of the conclusions are in line with the comments provided by the respondents in the consultation process conducted by the IIRC.

44.5   Connecting the Dots: Insights and Discussion on Reporting Standards and Principles

As we notice from the previous section, the debate on the requirement for different standards is ongoing in the literature (with advocates on both sides, all having valid reasons). The analysis reveals some significant differences between the private and public sectors, and that could be considered a prerequisite for the existence of multiple standards sets. However, an important "catalyst" of these developments is the political dimension (referring to the stance taken by governing bodies and the standard setters). It is in the interest of these organizations to use these differences as a justification for their initiatives (and ultimately, their existence). The fact that the IPSAS are largely based on IAS/IFRS (with adjustments for the public sector), emphasized by several sources from the literature cited in the previous chapter, shows the motif for these developments: the desire to differentiate coming from the governing bodies (and not necessarily from practice).

Also, the prevalence of the financial capital is (and will be) evident in the economic environment, in any functioning entity. Although the integrated reporting model proposes a six-capital model, not all capitals are weighted equally. As we can observe a background paper developed solely to delineate the capitals (ACCA and NBA 2013), the financial capital and manufactured capital are considered the most important when assessing and reporting the use of resources and effects obtained from an activity. As we might assume, all the capitals are interconnected (on different extensions, encompassing one another); if one of them is not managed properly, all the others are impacted. Yet, the interesting fact is that the two mentioned capitals are in the spotlight.

At this point, it is important to emphasize the fact that the [integrated reporting] *"Framework is written primarily **in the context of the private sector**, for-profit companies of any size but it can also be applied, adapted as necessary, by public sector and not-for-profit organizations"* (IIRC 2013a; paragraph 1.4). For a privately owned entity, the deliverables are the most important (quantifiable) indicators needed to measure efficiency (in terms of inputs, outputs, and outcomes). The rest of the capitals are supporting elements in the "business model."

In the public sector, things are not fundamentally different, only marginally. Entities also have a set of target deliverables and have to ensure efficient allocation and use of resources (only that the products and services are addressed to a broader range of users and performance is quantified by another set of indicators).

As implementation of integrated reporting is supported for all sectors of activity, the Conceptual Framework does not differentiate its fundamental concepts (the capitals and value creation) and content elements for different sectors. Thus, we have a contradiction between the parts and the whole, respectively:

- When we address the capitals (with emphasis on the financial one) as elements of a holistic form of reporting (like integrated reporting), the private and public sectors are treated equally and construct their reports by the same principles.

- When we address the capitals (with emphasis on the financial one) as elements of financial reporting, the private and public sectors are treated separately and report by their own specific sets of standards and principles.

This segmentation between sectors (and even within the sector—see the IPSAS/EPSAS debate) has emerged on a historic basis. The initial focus on financial information in the decision-making process provided the ground for the split in standard sets. In time, the focus has slowly shifted by taking account of the need to ensure intergenerational use of resources (else said—sustainable development) and the role of stakeholders. Curiously enough, these principles apply to both sectors. Moreover, the principles and guidelines driving non-financial reporting (especially when referring to sustainability reporting) are essentially the same: GRI (regardless of the sector).

Within Fig. 44.1, we synthesize the findings we spotted by analyzing the differences between sectors and standards into an encompassing model which has the purpose of signaling that, even though we start from separate sets of standards for exhaustive financial information and one major set of guidelines for non-financial information, ultimately the sectors are treated equally in a holistic form of reporting. The information is blended and restructured on a six-capital model. We consider that this is a logical course of action leading toward efficient communication (else called "the conciseness principle"), coming from accounting governing bodies and standard setters and given the level of complexity which exists in financial reporting.

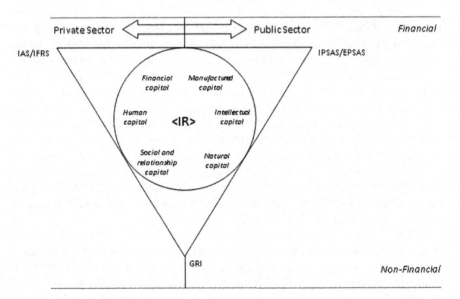

Fig. 44.1 The encompassing model for reporting standardization. *Source* Authors' projection (based on the findings)

44.6 Conclusion, Limits and Perspectives

Both private and public sectors have some particular features, a fact that leads to the need for different reporting frameworks. The two sectors have different purposes, financing sources, leadership style, ownership, stakeholders, and governance structures. The influence of private sector on the public sector is substantial. The literature indicates some significant controversies toward introducing some management techniques in the public sector, and that creates a bridge between the two sectors and reduces the gap between them. For that purpose, accrual accounting is implemented within the financial reporting and budgeting.

Also, it is essential to mention that the globalization phenomenon has a significant influence on the economy world, including the field of accounting. That fact leads to the existence of the need for creating and developing a uniform set of accounting standards, to promote reliability, transparency, and credibility of the accounting information for all the users. However, it is not feasible to create one set of accounting standards for both private and public sectors. The significant differences between the private and public sectors is a prerequisite for the existence of multiple standards sets. Although IPSAS are significantly inspired from IAS/IFRS, the public sector has some specific issues that former cannot meet. Also, the implementation of IPSAS is only recommended, instead of the application of IFRS that is mandatory for the listed companies. On the other hand, the review of the literature finds that the disparities between IFRS and IPSAS should not be viewed as important, given that both are planned to produce information beneficial for capital markets: stock exchanges and bond markets.

Regarding the implementation of integrated reporting, the fact that the Conceptual Framework does not differentiate its essential concepts among the private and public sectors generates a significant contradiction between the whole and its constituent parts. Thus, addressing the capitals emphasizing the financial one as elements of a holistic form of reporting, the private and public sectors are seen similarly and construct the reports using the same principles. On the other hand, addressing the capitals with emphasis on the financial one as elements of financial reporting, the public and private sectors are treated in different manners and report by their particular sets of standards and rules.

The main limitations of the study regard the fact that it targets only a conceptual level. The integrated reporting shows a high degree of novelty and, at least in the public institutions, there is a scarcity of data. On the other hand, EPSAS are at the moment only in a draft form, and there are still numerous controversies related to the necessity of the EPSAS existence.

Concerning the research perspectives, we intend to make an analysis of standards, regulations, and guidelines for both sectors and determine the information overlapping between the necessities for the two sectors, taking as a benchmark the disclosure requirements specified in the specific standards and guidelines.

Acknowledgments This work was supported by a grant of the Romanian National Authority for Scientific Research and Innovation, CNCS–UEFISCDI, project number PN-II-RU-TE-2014-4-0265.

References

ACCA, NBA (2013) Capitals. In: Background paper for <IR>. Available online: http://www.theiirc.org/wp-content/uploads/2013/03/IR-Background-Paper-Capitals.pdf. Accessed: 20 Feb 2015

Aggestam C (2010) A project management perspective on the adoption of accrual-based IPSAS. Int J Gov Financ Manage 10(2):49–66

Allison TG (1983) Public and private management: are they fundamentally alike in all unimportant respects? In Perry JL, Kraemer KL (eds) Public Management: Public and Private Perspectives: Mountain View, CA: Mayfield 72–92

Andresen JA (2010) Public versus private managers: how public and private managers differ in leadership behaviour. Public Administration Review 70(1):131–141

Arvonen J, Ekvall G (1999) Effective leadership style-both universal and contingent? Creativity and Innovation Management (4):242–250

Bartocci L, Picciaia F (2013) Towards integrated reporting in the public sector. In Busco C et al. (eds) Integrated reporting: concepts and cases that redefine corporate accountability. Springer International Publishing, Switzerland, p. 191–207

Barton A (1999) Public and private sector accounting—the non-identical twins. Aust Acc Rev 9(2):22–31

Bellanca S, Vandernoot J (2013) Analysis of Belgian public accounting and its compliance with International Public Sector Accounting Standards (IPSAS) 1, 6 and 22. Int J Bus Manage 8(9):122–133

Bellanca S, Vandernoot J (2014) International Public Sector Accounting Standards (IPSAS). Implementation in the European Union (EU) member states. J Mod Acc Auditing 10(3):257–269

Bergmann A (2009) Public sector financial management. Pearson Education, New Jersey

Biondi Y (2014) Harmonising European Public Sector Accounting Standards (EPSAS): issues and perspectives for Europe's economy and society. Acc Econ Law 4(3):165–178

Biondi Y, Soverchia M (2014) Accounting rules for the European communities: a theoretical analysis. Acc Econ Law 4(3):179–214

Biondi Y, Sierra M (2015) Accounting for pension flows and funds: a case study for accounting, economics and public finances. EGPA XII permanent study group public sector financial management workshop, Zurich-Winterthur

Boyne GA (2002) Public and Private Management: What's the Difference? J MANAG STUD 39(1):97–122

Brusca I, Montesinos V, Chow DSL (2013) Legitimating International Public Sector Accounting Standards (IPSAS): the case of Spain. Public Money Manage 33(6):437–444

Chan JL (2003) Government accounting: an assessment of theory, purposes and standards. Public Money Manage 23(1):13–20

Chan JL (2009) A comparison of government accounting and business accounting. Int J Gov Financ Manage 1(3):29–38

Christiaens J, Vanhee C, Manes-Rossi F, Aversano N (2013) The Effect of IPSAS on reforming governmental financial reporting: an international comparison. Working Paper; University of Ghent, Belgium

Eurostat (2012) Public consultation—assessment of the suitability of the international public sector accounting standards for the member states. Available at http://epp.eurostat.ec.europa.eu/cache/ITY_PUBLIC/D4_2012/EN/D4_2012-EN.PDF

Farneti F, Siboni B (2011) An analysis of Italian governmental guidelines and of local governments' practices for social reports. Sustain Acc Manage Policy J 2(1):101–125

Guthrie J (1998) Application of accrual accounting in the Australian public sector—rhetoric or reality? Financ Acc Manage 14(1)

Guthrie J, Olson O, Humphrey C (1999) Debating developments in new public financial management: the limit of the global theorising and some new ways forward. Financ Acc Manage 15(3–4):209–228

Herz RH (2007) Towards a global reporting system: where are we and where are we going? Paper presented at the AICPA national conference on SEC&PCAOB reporting developments, December 2007

Ibanichucka EAL, Aca OKJ (2014) A critique on cash basis of accounting and budget implementation in Nigeria. Eur J Acc Auditing Financ Res 2(3):69–83

IIRC (2013a) The consultation draft of the international <IR> framework. Available online at: http://www.theiirc.org/wp-content/uploads/Consultation-Draft/Consultation-Draft-of-the-InternationalIRFramework.pdf. Accessed 06 Mar 2014

IIRC (2013b) The international <IR> framework. Available online at: http://www.theiirc.org/wp-content/uploads/2013/12/13-12-08-THE-INTERNATIONAL-IR-FRAMEWORK-2-1.pdf. Accessed on 06 Mar 2014

Jones R (2007) The functions of government accounting in Europe. Revista de Estudos Politecnicos Polytechnical Stud Rev 5(1):89–110

Jones RH, Caruana J (2015) EPSAS—worrying the wrong end of the stick? Int J Public Adm 38 (4):240–252

Lombrano A, Zanin L (2013) IPSAS and local government consolidated financial statements—proposal for a territorial consolidation method. Public Money Manage 33(6):429–436

Madhani PM (2014) Corporate governance and disclosure public sector vs. private sector. SCSM J IND MANAGE 11(1):5–20

McClelland D (1972) To know why men do what they do. Psychology Today. January, 35–75

Meier KJ, O'Toole LJ Jr. (2009) Comparing public and private management: theoretical expectations. Prepared for presentation at the public management research conference, The Ohio State University, Columbus, 3 October 2009

Newberry S (2014) The use of accrual accounting in New Zealand's central government: second thoughts. Acc Econ Law 4(3):283–297

Oulasvirta L (2014) The reluctance of a developed country to choose international public sector accounting standards of the IFAC. A critical case study. Crit Perspect Acc 25(3):272–285

Pina V, Torres L, Yetano A (2009) Accrual accounting in EU local governments: one method, several approaches. Eur Acc Rev 18(4):765–807

Propper C, Wilson D (2003) The use and usefulness of performance measures in the public sector. Oxford Review of Economic Policy 19(2):250–267

Rainey HG, Backoff RW, Levine CH (1976) Comparing Public and Private Organizations. Public Administration Review 36(2):233–244

Ristea M, Jianu I, Jianu I (2010) Experiența României în aplicarea Standardelor Internaționale de Raportare Financiară și a Standardelor Internaționale de Contabilitate pentru Sectorul Public. Revista Transilvană de Științe Administrative 1(25):179–192

Roje G, Vašiček D, Hladika M (2012) The perspectives of IPSASs introduction in Croatian public sector. Int J Public Sect Perform Manage 2(1):25–43

Sanderson I, Van Schaik F (2008) Public sector accounting standards: strengthening accountability and improving governance. Accountancy Ireland 40(5):22–24

Van Thiel S, Leeuw F (2002) The performance paradox in the public sector. Public Performance & Management Review 25(3):267–281

Chapter 45
Disclosure of Financial Information About the General Government Sector by IPSAS

Marianna Kršeková

Abstract International Public Sector Accounting Standards are the basis for international harmonization of public sector accounting and financial reporting around the world, including European countries. The application on the IPSAS supports consistency and comparability of the public sector financial reporting with the aim of achieving the objectives of financial reporting, which is to provide transparent information to users that is useful for accountability and decision-making purposes. Disclosure of financial information about the general government sector belongs to the specific problems of public sector financial reporting. The paper deals with requirements related to disclosure of financial information about the general government sector in the consolidated financial statements of a government. The general government sector comprises all organizational entities of the general government as defined in statistical bases of financial reporting. The disclosure of financial information about the general government sector in the consolidated financial statements of the government can support the transparency of financial reports and provide for a better understanding of the relationship between financial statements and statistical bases of financial reporting.

Keywords Public sector · Financial reporting · Accounting · General government sector · International public sector accounting standards

45.1 Introduction

Public sector accounting and financial reporting is a separate specific area of international harmonization of accounting. The main objective of public sector accounting and financial reporting is to provide comparable, relevant and understandable financial information to the users of such information. It is important to

M. Kršeková (✉)
Department of Accounting and Auditing, University of Economics in Bratislava,
Dolnozemská cesta 1/b, 852 35 Bratislava, Slovakia
e-mail: marianna.krsekova@euba.sk

© Springer International Publishing AG 2017   485
D. Procházka (ed.), *New Trends in Finance and Accounting*,
Springer Proceedings in Business and Economics,
DOI 10.1007/978-3-319-49559-0_45

harmonize the information provided by the public sector entities by IPSAS. International Public Sector Accounting Standards (IPSAS) form the basis for the harmonization of accounting and financial reporting by public sector entities. The harmonization of public sector accounting and financial reporting is a continuing process, which gradually leads to amendments of existing IPSAS and to the issuance of new IPSAS. IPSAS requirements are gradually taken into public sector accounting legislation of each state around the world, including European countries.

Disclosure of financial information about the general government sector belongs to the specific problems of public sector accounting and financial reporting. That problem is specified in IPSAS 22—Disclosure of Financial Information about the General Government Sector. Information about the general government sector from the financial statements provides a uniform basis for the consolidation of the data in the public sector, which is the basis for compiling financial reports for statistical purposes in accordance with the statistical bases of financial reporting. These bases reflect requirements derived form the System of National Accounts 1993 (SNA 1993), Government Finance Statistics Manual 2001 (GFSM 2001) and European System of Accounts 2010 (ESA 2010). In connection with the solution of this problem, it is important to define the public sector and general government sector in accordance with IPSAS and the statistical bases of financial reporting.

The public sector according to IPSAS includes:

- National governments;
- Regional governments—state, provincial, territorial;
- Local governments—city, town; and
- Related governmental entities—agencies, boards, commissions, enterprises.

The public sector according to the statistical bases of financial reporting includes:

- General government sector (GGS);
- Public financial corporations sector (PFC sector); and
- Public non-financial corporations sector (PNFC sector).

The general government sector (GGS) comprises all organizational entities of the general government as defined in the statistical bases of financial reporting. It consists of all resident central, state and local government units, social security funds at each level of government and non-market nonprofit institutions controlled by government units.

The PFC sector comprises resident government-controlled financial corporations,[1] quasi-corporations[2] and nonprofit institutions[3] which primarily engage in

---

[1]Corporations are the legal entities created for the purpose of producing goods and services for the market.

[2]Quasi-corporations are the enterprises that are not incorporated or otherwise legally established, but function as if they were corporations.

[3]Non-profit institutions are the legal or other entities that produce or distribute goods and services, but which do not generate financial gain for their controlling entity.

financial intermediation and the provision of financial services for the market. The PFC sector also comprises government-controlled banks, including central banks, and other government financial institutions that operate on a market basis (IFAC 2015a, p. 750).

The PNFC sector comprises resident government-controlled non-financial corporations, quasi-corporations and nonprofit institutions that produce goods or non-financial services for the market. The PNFC sector also comprises entities such as publicly owned utilities and other entities that trade in goods and services (IFAC 2015a, p. 751).

45.2 Literature Review

The researched object that is disclosure of information about the general government sector in the consolidated financial statements of the public sector was chosen because of its timeliness and dynamic development. This topic is a comprehensive solution in International Public Sector Accounting Standards. We got information about the researched object from book and magazine sources, conference proceedings and from our own previous knowledge of the research activities. We have worked with the current literature published in 2015, which was mainly in English. This literature is listed in the References section. The above issue deals mainly with provisions of relevant International Public Sector Accounting Standards that are listed in the Handbook of International Public Sector Accounting Pronouncements, which was published in 2015 on the IFAC Web site and was divided into two volumes (IFAC 2015a, b). We also used our knowledge of our research activities that is listed in monograph related to international harmonization of financial reporting in the financial statements of the public sector (Kršeková 2011) and articles in scientific journals and conference proceedings related to international harmonization of public sector accounting and financial reporting by IPSAS (Kicová 2006, 2007, 2008; Kovalčíková and Kordošová 2004, 2005). The knowledge gained forms the basis for the processing of Results and Discussion.

45.3 Data and Methodology

The aim of this paper is to describe and analyze knowledge about the specific problems of financial reporting by public sector, in particular results of the analysis of requirements for the disclosure of the information about the general government sector in the consolidated financial statements of public sector in accordance with International Public Sector Accounting Standards and the statistical bases of accounting. We applied epistemology as a basic method for researching this problem. Standard research methods, such as selection, analysis and synthesis, presenting basic methodical approach to paper processing are applied. We combined the obtained knowledge to form new, higher level of knowledge of research problems. In particular, ways of understanding and explaining requirements for the disclosure of the information about the general government sector in the consolidated financial statements of public sector, the inductive-deductive and analytic-synthetic logical scientific methods are used. In the conclusion, we stated opinions, in which we highlighted the importance of the disclosure of the information about the general government sector in the consolidated financial statements of public sector in a way that meets the objectives of financial reporting to provide information that is useful for accountability and decision-making purposes. The disclosure of information about the general government sector in the consolidated financial statements of public sector is useful to government to enhance the transparency of financial reports and provide for a better understanding of the relationship between the market and non-market activities of the government and between financial statements and statistical bases of financial reporting.

45.4   Results and Discussion

A government discloses financial information about the general government sector in the consolidated financial statements under the requirements of the System of National Accounts 1993 (SNA 1993), Government Finance Statistics Manual 2001 (GFSM 2001) and European System of Accounts 2010 (ESA 2010), if it decides to. The general government sector comprises entities controlled by government that primarily undertake non-market activities and rely primarily on allocations from the government budget to fund their service delivery activities. These entities make key functions of government as their primary activity. The government also provides information about the public financial corporations sector that primarily engages in market activities and the public non-financial corporations sector and the public sector as a whole in accordance with statistical bases of financial reporting.

The government increases its resources from taxes, transfers and a range of market and non-market activities in order to finance their activities related to service delivery activities. They operate through a large number of entities that provide goods and services to the constituents. These entities rely primarily on appropriations or allocations from taxes or other government revenues to fund their service delivery activities. Other entities called government business enterprises (GBE) may generate their funds primarily from commercial activities.

Government business enterprise is an entity with the power to contract in its own name; it has been assigned the financial and operational authority to carry on a business; it sells goods and services, in the normal course of its business, to other entities at a profit or full cost recovery; it is not reliant on continuing government funding to be a going concern; and it is controlled by a public sector entity (IFAC 2015a, p. 164).

Financial statements prepared by government in accordance with IPSAS provide an overview of:

- The assets controlled by the government;
- The liabilities incurred by the governments;
- The cost of services provided by the government;
- The taxations; and
- The other revenues intended for financing service delivery activities.

IPSAS 22 prescribes disclosure requirements for governments that elect to present information about the general government sector in their consolidated financial statements and prepare consolidated financial statements under the accrual basis of accounting in accordance with IPSAS. Disclosures required by this standard provide a useful springboard for statistical bases of financial reporting. IPSAS 22 applies only to the consolidated financial statements of the government. Information about the general government sector in the consolidated financial statements is separated by sector in accordance with the statistical bases of financial reporting. Reporting entity does not include information on entities that are not under its control in the consolidated financial statements, although statistical information about government finances may include information on these entities.

Consolidated financial statements comprise only controlled entities. This requirement is not made in statistical bases of financial reporting. Some national governments control state and local government entities, and its financial statements consolidate those levels of government, but some national governments do not. IPSAS currently in force, with the exception of IPSAS 22, do not require to present and disclose information about the general government sector in financial statements of public sector, but they required to prepare financial statements which contains information about all the resources controlled by the reporting entity and prescribe rules for consolidation of the data for all controlled entities. Under statistical bases of financial reporting, the general government sector of all levels of government is combined and includes entities that financial statements do not consolidate.

The objectives of financial statements prepared in accordance with IPSAS and the statistical bases of financial reporting are different in some aspects. The objective of financial statements prepared under the IPSAS is to provide information useful for decision making and to demonstrate the accountability of the entity for the resources entrusted to it and which it controls. The objective of financial statements prepared under the statistical bases of financial reporting is to provide information useful for analyzing and evaluating fiscal policy.

Financial information about the general government sector should be presented and disclosed in accordance with the accounting policies adopted in the preparation and presentation of consolidated financial statements of the government. In accordance with the provisions of IPSAS 22, the entities should apply the requirements of IPSAS 3—Accounting Policies, Changes in Accounting Estimates and Errors for the preparation and presentation of financial statements.

Statistical bases of financial reporting and IPSAS have many similarities and differences in their treatment of particular transactions and events, for example:

- Statistical bases of financial reporting require all assets and liabilities (except loans) to be revalued to market value at each reporting date. IPSAS require or permit cost and current values for certain classes of assets and liabilities;
- Statistical bases of financial reporting treat dividends as expenses. IPSAS treat dividends as distributions;
- Statistical bases of financial reporting make a distinction between transactions and other economic flows for presentation of financial information, but IPSAS do not currently make a similar distinction; and
- Statistical bases of financial reporting focus on the presentation of financial information about the general government sector and the other sectors of the public sector as separate components and adopt the same rules for recognition and measurement as are adopted for presentation of the rest of the economy to ensure consistency of the macroeconomic totals. IPSAS focus on consolidated financial statements that present financial information about all the assets, liabilities, revenues, expenses and cash flows controlled by the entity.

The disclosure of information about the general government sector in financial statements can support and enhance the decision making of users of those statements. It means that disclosure of information about the general government sector is consistent with enhanced transparency of financial reporting and assists users of the financial statements to better understand the resources allocated to support the service delivery activities by the general government sector and the government's financial performance in delivering those services and the relationship between the general government sector and the corporations sectors and the impact each has on overall financial performance.

The disclosure of information about the general government sector provides useful information from the financial statements for the users of such information, particularly in those jurisdictions where financial information is presented in the financial statements prepared both in accordance with IPSAS and with statistical bases of financial reporting. Users of this information better understand the relationship between market and non-market activities of the government. Benefits of this information may not be significantly greater than the costs of obtaining and disclosure of that information, so disclosure of that information is not required.

The disclosure of financial information about the general government sector by IPSAS 22 should include at least the following items (IFAC 2015a, p. 753):

- Assets by major class, showing separately the investment in other sectors;
- Liabilities by major class;
- Net assets/equity;
- Total revaluation increments and decrements and other items of revenue and expense recognized directly in net assets/equity;
- Revenue by major class;
- Expenses by major class;
- Surplus or deficit;
- Cash flows from operating activities by major class;

Table 45.1 Statement of financial position for the general government sector at December 31, 20X2 (illustrative example)

	General government sector (GGS)		PFC and PNFC		Eliminations		Total W-of-G	
	20X2	20X1	20X2	20X1	20X2	20X1	20X2	20X1
Assets								
Current assets								
Cash and cash equivalents	X	X	X	X	(X)	(X)	X	X
Receivables	X	X	X	X	(X)	(X)	X	X
Inventories	X	X	X	X			X	X
Prepayments	X	X	X	X	(X)	(X)	X	X
Investment	X	X	X	X			X	X
Other current assets	X	X	X	X			X	X
	X	X	X	X	(X)	(X)	X	X
Non-current assets								
Receivables	X	X	X	X	(X)	(X)	X	X
Investments	X	X	X	X	(X)	(X)	X	X
Investments in other sectors	X	X			(X)	(X)		
Other financial assets	X	X	X	X	(X)	(X)	X	X
Infrastructure, plant and equipment	X	X	X	X			X	X
Land and buildings	X	X	X	X			X	X
Intangible assets	X	X	X	X			X	X
Other non-financial assets	X	X	X	X			X	X
	X	X	X	X	(X)	(X)	X	X
Total assets	X	X	X	X	(X)	(X)	X	X
Liabilities								
Current liabilities								
Payables	X	X	X	X	(X)	(X)	X	X
Short-term borrowings	X	X	X	X			X	X
Current portion of borrowings	X	X	X	X			X	X
Provisions	X	X	X	X			X	X
Employee benefits	X	X	X	X			X	X
Other current liabilities	X	X	X	X	(X)	(X)	X	X
	X	X	X	X	(X)	(X)	X	X
Non-current liabilities								
Payables	X	X	X	X	(X)	(X)	X	X
Borrowings	X	X	X	X			X	X
Provisions	X	X	X	X			X	X
Employee benefits	X	X	X	X			X	X
Other liabilities	X	X	X	X			X	X
	X	X	X	X	(X)	(X)	X	X

(continued)

Table 45.1 (continued)

	General government sector (GGS)		PFC and PNFC		Eliminations		Total W-of-G	
	20X2	20X1	20X2	20X1	20X2	20X1	20X2	20X1
Total liabilities	X	X	X	X	(X)	(X)	X	X
Net assets	X	X	X	X	(X)	(X)	X	X
Net assets/equity								
Reserves	X	X	X	X	(X)	(X)	X	X
Accumulated surpluses/ (deficits)	X	X	X	X	(X)	(X)	X	X
	X	X	X	X	(X)	(X)	X	X
Total net assets/equity	X	X	X	X	(X)	(X)	X	X

Source Appendix of IPSAS 22—Disclosure of Financial Information about the General Government Sector

Table 45.2 Statement of financial performance for the general government sector for the year ended December 31, 20X2—classification of function of the government (illustrative example)

	General government sector (GGS)		PFC and PNFC		Eliminations		Total W-of-G	
	20X2	20X1	20X2	20X1	20X2	20X1	20X2	20X1
Revenue								
Taxes	X	X			(X)	(X)	X	X
Fees, fines, penalties	X	X	X	X	(X)	(X)	X	X
Revenue from other sectors	X	X	X	X	(X)	(X)		
Transfers from other governments	X	X	X	X			X	X
Other operating revenue	X	X	X	X	(X)	(X)	X	X
Total revenue	X	X	X	X	(X)	(X)	X	X
Expenses								
General public services	X	X					X	X
Defense	X	X					X	X
Public order and safety	X	X	X	X			X	X
Economic affairs	X	X					X	X
Environmental protection	X	X	X	X	(X)	(X)	X	X
Housing and community amenities	X	X	X	X	(X)	(X)	X	X
Health	X	X	X	X			X	X
Recreational, cultural and religious	X	X					X	X
Education	X	X	X	X	(X)	(X)	X	X
Social protection	X	X	X	X	(X)	(X)	X	X
Total expenses	X	X	X	X	(X)	(X)	X	X
Surplus/(deficit) for the period	X	X	X	X	(X)	(X)	X	X

Source Appendix of IPSAS 22—Disclosure of Financial Information about the General Government Sector

- Cash flows from investing activities; and
- Cash flows from financing activities.

IPSAS 22 specifies the components of the financial statements in accordance with the provisions of IPSAS 1—Presentation of Financial Statements, which identifies the components of the financial statements under the accrual basis of accounting. In accordance with IPSAS 1, financial statements comprise:

- Statement of Financial Position;
- Statement of Financial Performance;
- Statement of Changes in Net Assets/Equity;

Table 45.3 Statement of financial performance for the general government sector for the year ended December 31, 20X2—economic classification of expense (illustrative example)

	General government sector (GGS)		PFC and PNFC		Eliminations		Total W-of-G	
	20X2	20X1	20X2	20X1	20X2	20X1	20X2	20X1
Revenue								
Taxes	X	X			(X)	(X)	X	X
Fees, fines, penalties	X	X	X	X	(X)	(X)	X	X
Revenue from other sectors	X	X	X	X	(X)	(X)		
Transfers from other governments	X	X	X	X			X	X
Other operating revenue	X	X	X	X	(X)	(X)	X	X
Total revenue	X	X	X	X	(X)	(X)	X	X
Expenses								
Compensation of employees	X	X	X	X	(X)	(X)	X	X
Use of goods and services	X	X	X	X	(X)	(X)	X	X
Consumption of fixed capital	X	X	X	X	(X)	(X)	X	X
Interest	X	X	X	X	(X)	(X)	X	X
Subsidies	X	X	X	X	(X)	(X)	X	X
Social benefits	X	X	X	X	(X)	(X)	X	X
Other expenses	X	X	X	X			X	X
Total expenses	X	X	X	X	(X)	(X)	X	X
Surplus/(deficit) for the period	X	X	X	X	(X)	(X)	X	X

Source Appendix of IPSAS 22—Disclosure of Financial Information about the General Government Sector

- Cash Flow Statement;
- When the entity makes publicly available its approved budget, a comparison of budget and actual amounts either as a separate additional financial statement (Statement of Comparison of Budget and Actual Amounts) or as a budget column in the financial statements; and
- Notes, comprising a summary of significant accounting policies and other explanatory notes.

The disclosure of information about the general governments sector in accordance with IPSAS 22 and statistical bases of accounting may vary in its content and nature. IPSAS 22 requires disclosure of the major classes of assets, liabilities, revenues, expenses and cash flows reflected in the financial statements, but it does not specify the manner in which the general government sector disclosures shall be made. Governments that make the disclosures of information about the general government sector in accordance with IPSAS 22 may make such disclosures by way of note disclosure, or separate columns in the primary financial statements, or otherwise. Entity may also make additional disclosures of information about the general government sector that are necessary for users to better understand the nature and character of the information presented. Entity shall disclose a list of the significant controlled entities that are included in the general government sector. It shall also disclose the changes in the controlled entities included in the general government sector that enable users to control the relationship between the consolidated financial statements and the information about the general government sector over the time (Tables 45.1, 45.2 and 45.3).

45.5 Conclusion

The aim of this paper was to describe and analyze knowledge about the specific problems of public sector financial reporting, in particular results of the analysis of requirements for the disclosure of the information about the general government sector in the consolidated financial statements of public sector in accordance with International Public Sector Accounting Standards and the statistical bases of financial reporting. This issue is covered by the relevant International Public Sector Accounting Standards which develops and publishes by International Federation of Accountants in the context of international harmonization and regulation of public sector accounting and financial reporting, namely IPSAS 22—Disclosure of Financial Information about the General Government Sector. The result of examination of that topic is a comprehensive set of knowledge about the disclosure of the information about the general government sector in the consolidated financial statements of public sector in a way that is useful for preparers of financial statements to meet the objectives of financial reporting to provide information that is useful for accountability and decision-making purposes. This comprehensive set of knowledge is useful to government to enhance the transparency of financial reports and provide for a better understanding of the relationship between the market and non-market activities of the government and between financial statements and statistical bases of financial reporting. International Federation of Accountants (IFAC) and International Public Sector Accounting Standards Board (IPSASB) support the convergence of IPSAS and the statistical bases of financial reporting in cases where it is appropriate. The statistical community encouraged the IPSASB to develop IPSAS dealing with the disclosure of the information about the general government sector as part of the consolidated financial statements of the government, which should support the convergence of IPSAS and the statistical bases of financial reporting.

Acknowledgments This article is an output of the project of the Scientific Grant Agency of the Ministry of Culture of the Slovak Republic and Slovak Academy of Sciences (VEGA) no. 1/0512/16 (2016–2018) "Retention and Development of Business Property of Company as a Relevant Tool for Sustainable Development."

References

International Federation of Accountants (2015a) Handbook of international public sector accounting pronouncements, vol I. [online]. IFAC: International Public Sector Accounting Standards Board, 2015. https://www.ifac.org/system/files/publications/files/IPSASB-2015-Handbook-Vol-I-v2.pdf

International Federation of Accountants (2015b) Handbook of international public sector accounting pronouncements, vol II. [online]. IFAC: International Public Sector Accounting Standards Board, 2015. https://www.ifac.org/system/files/publications/files/IPSASB-2015-Handbook-Vol-II-v2.pdf

Kicová M (2006) Medzinárodné účtovné štandardy pre verejný sektor (IPSAS) ako základ medzinárodnej harmonizácie účtovníctva vo verejnom sektore. In: AIESA 2006. EKONÓM, Bratislava, pp 1–7

Kicová M (2007) Medzinárodná harmonizácia účtovníctva verejného sektora. In: Mezinárodní Baťova doktorandská konference. Univerzita Tomáše Bati ve Zlíně, Zlín, pp 1–14

Kicová M (2008) Prezentovanie informácií o ústrednom vládnom sektore v účtovnej závierke subjektov verejného sektora. Ekonomika a informatika: scientific journal of FHI EU in Bratislava a SSHI 6(1):21–36

Kovalčíková A, Kordošová A (2004) Medzinárodné účtovné štandardy pre verejný sektor v procese medzinárodnej harmonizácie účtovníctva. Ekonomické rozhľady: scientific journal of University of Economics in Bratislava 33(1):61–67

Kovalčíková A, Kordošová A (2005) Medzinárodná harmonizácia a regulácia účtovníctva vo verejnom sektore. Účtovníctvo - audítorstvo - daňovníctvo: v teórii a praxi, vol 13(10), pp 345–348

Kršeková M (2011) Medzinárodné účtovné štandardy pre verejný sektor – IPSAS. IURA EDITION, Bratislava

Chapter 46
The Comparative Analysis of CAS and IPSAS Requirements on Tangible Fixed Assets

Martin Dvořák and Lukáš Poutník

Abstract The paper deals with the differences in accounting concepts, accounting treatments and disclosure requirements related to tangible fixed assets between IPSAS and CAS. The analysis is based on the comparison of current version of IPSAS 17 and CAS. The wording of both accounting frameworks is examined in detail for the purpose of finding the similarities or dissimilarities between them with the aim to give an answer whether the CAS rules get closer to IPSAS approach after the conceptual reform of public sector accounting in the Czech Republic.

Keywords IPSAS · CAS · Tangible fixed assets

46.1 Introduction

The process of public sector reporting convergence contributing to comparability of financial information presented in financial statements has influenced most of national accounting rules including the Czech Republic. To achieve the goal of convergence, the high competence and transparency should be ensured during the creation of national accounting legislation. The International Public Sector Accounting Standards (hereinafter referred to as "standards" or "IPSAS") as an instrument directly linked to convergence process represent these crucial characteristics currently. The issued standards can be found as an appropriate information basis for creation of comprehensive national accounting rules. The standards as a whole are based on International Financial Reporting Standards (hereinafter referred to as "IFRS") and therefore cover widespread accounting issues.

M. Dvořák (✉) · L. Poutník
Department of Financial Accounting and Auditing,
University of Economics, Prague, Nam. W. Churchilla 4,
130 67 Prague, Czech Republic
e-mail: xdvom63@vse.cz

L. Poutník
e-mail: xpoul4@vse.cz

© Springer International Publishing AG 2017   497
D. Procházka (ed.), *New Trends in Finance and Accounting*,
Springer Proceedings in Business and Economics,
DOI 10.1007/978-3-319-49559-0_46

It is typical for public sector bodies that the items of tangible fixed assets represent a major share of total assets, and thus, it is logical this element of financial statements is the subject of strong interest. Therefore, the aim of this paper is to make the differential analysis of Czech Accounting Standards (hereinafter referred to as "CAS") and IPSAS requirements on tangible fixed assets, especially their accounting concepts, treatments and disclosures, and bring the clear answer how much these rules are similar or not and whether the CAS represent high-quality set of public sector accounting standards.

46.2   Review of Literature and Background of the Paper

Despite the rare use of IPSAS throughout the world, there is an apparent trend of implementing the high-quality set of accounting rules for public sector bodies to be able to provide the useful information for managing the public finance. This trend has an impact for EU member states including the Czech Republic as well. Besides, Bergmann (2009) explains how contemporary financial management techniques can be applied specifically to the public sector. To make the qualified decision, the accrual-based accounting is necessary. IPSAS meet these characteristics. Berger (2012) provides the comprehensive view of them.

There are relatively many foreign sources about the implementing process in individual countries around the world and about the analysis of particular IPSAS. For example, Biancone and Secinaro (2015) bring the analysis about the issues of consolidation of public sector bodies in Italy in accordance with Italian accounting standards and IPSAS and try to assess which ones are more convenient in perspective of information needs of stakeholders. Similar sources can be found in Austria for example as well. Tudor (2010) talks about the similarities and deficiencies between IPSAS and Romanian accounting standards with the conclusion that high degree of correspondence exists. Lutilsky and Percevic (2011) emphasize the need of fair value concept in Croatian public sector and examine what alternatives (including the IPSAS implementation) can be taken into account. Bellanca and Vandernoot (2013) discuss the Belgian public sector accounting reform in 2003 and analyse its compliance with IPSAS. Some papers are concerned with specific public sector accounting issues, e.g. emphasizing the issue of certain balance sheet items (Turlea et al. 2011).

On the other hand, there are not many papers analysing the particular IPSAS being compared to CAS in the Czech Republic, albeit several theoretical papers about the need to determine the elements of financial statements (such as assets, liabilities, equity, expenses and revenues) referring to IPSAS were published (Zelenka 2014). For example, Svoboda (2011) mentions the problems of IPSAS implementation process in Czech environment. In respect of pervasive discussion on implementation of high-quality public sector accounting standards in EU, it is necessary to stress the need of publishing the papers on IPSAS. The Czech Republic as an EU member state is no exception. Potential IPSAS implementation in the Czech Republic has been discussed since 2005. Therefore, the contribution of this paper can be considered as substantial.

Table 46.1 Methodology of comparative analysis

The level of correspondence	Definition of the level
Absolute	Analysed accounting principle/treatment/disclosure in accordance with IPSAS and CAS is identical. There is no deviation between these two accounting frameworks
Partial	It contains the following: (i) the formal differences between IPSAS and CAS exist (e.g. Another terms used that can move the meaning of seemingly same accounting areas); (ii) the analysed area of certain accounting framework does not cover the same scope of requirements (e.g. a framework lets some specifics unregulated); (iii) some substance issues that are not significant exist (e.g. certain terms move closer to the term of more precise accounting framework but cannot be considered as the same)
No correspondence	It contains the following: (i) no match can be found because of undefined accounting area of some framework; (ii) the significant substance issues exist (e.g. The same area is solved by a different way)

As it said, fixed assets of public sector entities in the Czech Republic represent the main share on total assets in balance sheet (58% approximately). Thus, it is clear that possible implementation of IPSAS as an accounting framework for public sector entities should have significant impact into the financial statements structure and total assets amount. Our approach can be described as a comparative analysis that examines current version of CAS and IPSAS 17—Property, Plant and Equipment. The text of IPSAS 17 was segmented into three basic groups in perspective of definitions, accounting treatments and disclosure requirements. Every basic group was divided into many detailed parts which were confronted with the analogous requirements/rules in accordance with CAS. Every analysed part was assessed by one of three levels of correspondence (Table 46.1).

We consider that the contribution of this paper resides in precise answering the question whether the CAS are similar to IPSAS in context of tangible fixed assets, because many definition were newly implemented or specified after the radical reform of public sector accounting in 2010. Mentioned reform has improved the quality of reporting and emphasized the aim to transform the public sector accounting into the fully accrual base.

H: The CAS requirements in context of tangible fixed assets correspond generally with the IPSAS 17 after the conceptual reform of public sector accounting in the Czech Republic.

The hypothesis will be confirmed even if the most of analysed areas (in Tables 46.2, 46.3 and 46.4) are assessed by the "absolute" level of correspondence.

Table 46.2 Conceptual differences between IPSAS 17 and CAS

Analysed area	IPSAS 17	CAS	Level of correspondence
Name	Property, plant and equipment (PPE)	Tangible fixed assets	Partial
Definition	Tangible items, that: Are held for use in the production or supply of goods or services, for rental to others, or for administrative purposes Are expected to be used during more than one reporting period	General definition does not exist, only The list of concrete individual items	Partial
		Lands regardless of value level; building regardless of value level and useful life; individual movable assets with the useful life longer that 1 year and value higher than 40,000 CZK, etc.	
Heritage assets	Assets of cultural, environmental or historical significance	Undefined	No correspondence
	Characteristics: Their value is unlikely to be fully reflected in a financial value based purely on a market price Legal and/or statutory obligations may impose prohibitions or severe restrictions on disposal by sale They are often irreplaceable and their value may increase over time, even if their physical condition deteriorates It may be difficult to estimate their useful lives, which in some cases could be several hundred years	Regulation mentions only namely "immovable cultural heritage" or "cultural objects"	
		Cultural object represent movable cultural heritage, museum collections, objects with cultural value, works of art	
		If the historical costs are unknown, the value will be determined at 1 CZK	
Measurement at recognition	Cost/fair value	Historical cost/reproduction cost	Partial
Book value	Initial measurement after deduction of accumulated depreciation and impairment	Initial measurement after deduction of accumulated depreciation and impairment	Absolute

(continued)

Table 46.2 (continued)

Analysed area	IPSAS 17	CAS	Level of correspondence
Elements of cost	Purchase price + directly attributable costs + initial estimate of the costs of removing the item and restoring the site on which it is located	Price of acquired assets including the directly attributable costs	Partial
Entity-specific value	Present value of the cash flows an entity expects to arise from the continuing use of an asset and from its disposal at the end of its useful life	Undefined	No correspondence
Depreciable amount	Cost of an asset, or other amount substituted for cost, less its residual value	Historical cost of asset less its (possibly set) residual value	Absolute
Recoverable amount	The higher of a cash-generating asset's fair value less costs to sell and its value in use	Undefined	No correspondence
Recoverable service amount	The higher of a non-cash-generating asset's fair value less costs to sell and its value in use	Undefined	No correspondence
Residual value	Estimated amount that an entity would currently obtain from disposal of the asset, after deducting the estimated costs of disposal	Provable positive estimated amount which could be acquired at expected date of disposal	Absolute
Useful life	The period over which an asset is expected to be available for use by an entity; or The number of production or similar units expected to be obtained from the asset by an entity	Undefined explicitly; the term used indirectly only	Partial
		Used for need of fixed/current assets classification and for depreciation	

(continued)

Table 46.2 (continued)

Analysed area	IPSAS 17	CAS	Level of correspondence
Impairment loss of a cash-generating asset	The amount by which the carrying amount of an asset exceeds its recoverable amount	Undefined	No correspondence
Impairment loss of a non-cash-generating asset	The amount by which the carrying amount of an asset exceeds its recoverable service amount	Undefined	No correspondence
Infrastructure assets	(a) They are part of a system or network (b) They are specialized in nature and do not have alternative uses (c) They are immovable (d) They may be subject to constraints on disposal	Undefined	No correspondence

Source Authors

Table 46.3 The differences of accounting treatments between IPSAS 17 and CAS

Analysed areas	IPSAS 17	CAS	Level of correspondence
Recognition of assets	The cost of an item of property, plant and equipment shall be recognized as an asset if: (a) It is probable that future economic benefits or service potential associated with the item will flow to the entity (b) The cost or fair value of the item can be measured reliably	Fixed asset are recognized in case of: Its purchase, other cash transition or transfer, donation or internal production; gratuitous changes of competence to disposition of state property or transfer of property into the administration or gratuitous transition or transfer of property	No correspondence

(continued)

Table 46.3 (continued)

Analysed areas	IPSAS 17	CAS	Level of correspondence
Other possibility of asset recognition	IPSAS 17 referring to IPSAS 13-Leases requires to report PPE acquired under the finance lease. The same thing is required with IPSAS 32-Service concession arrangements: grantor	Undefined	No correspondence
Subsequent costs	IPSAS 17 does not permit the recognition of expenditures described as repairs and maintenance into the carrying amount of PPE. But it permits replacement of certain components which are considered as necessary (e.g. replacement of asphalt surface of the road) or decreasing the periodicity of future replacement. The carrying amount of original component must be derecognized if any. Executed inspection must increase the carrying amount of PPE, if this execution represents the precondition of future using	CAS recognize so-called technical evaluation. The Regulation No. 410/2009 Coll. Defines the technical evaluation as intervention to fixed assets resulted in change of its purpose or technical parameters, or expansion of facilities or applicability of property including superstructure, extension and construction works. The amount of that technical evaluation must exceed certain limit contained in Regulation	Partial
Depreciation methods	The chosen depreciation method shall reflect the development of future economic benefit or service potential. The entity must reassess the used depreciation method every year whether it is appropriate. The basic methods are straight-line method, diminishing balance method and the units of production method	The entity shall update the depreciation plans with respect to expected using of property. These plans may be changed only when the new accounting period begins. Used depreciation methods are straight-line method, units of production method and component depreciation	Partial

(continued)

Table 46.3 (continued)

Analysed areas	IPSAS 17	CAS	Level of correspondence
Measurement after recognition	The entity can choose between the cost model and revaluation model. The cost model represents the acquisition price (historical cost) after the accumulated depreciation and impairment. Choice of revaluation model is conditioned by reliable fair value measurement. Then, the carrying amount of this asset is measured as fair value less any subsequent accumulated depreciation and subsequent accumulated impairment losses. If the carrying amount of a class of assets is increased as a result of a revaluation, the increase shall be credited directly to revaluation surplus. However, the increase shall be recognized in surplus or deficit to the extent that it reverses a revaluation decrease in the same class of assets previously recognized in surplus or deficit. The opposite scenario is analogous. IPSAS 17 deems necessary 3- to 5-year revaluation period	CAS strictly keep the concept of historical costs but one exception. Fixed assets held for sale have to be revalued at fair value/market value. At the same time the depreciation of that asset have to be interrupted and existing accumulated depreciation and impairment losses have to be derecognized	Partial
Derecognition	The item of PPE shall be derecognized: (a) on disposal, (b) When no future economic benefits or service potential is expected from its use or disposal. The gain or loss arising from derecognition of an item of PPE shall be included in surplus or deficit	Derecognition of fixed assets is not defined precisely. Czech accounting norms characterize the various possibility of disposal by exhaustive way only. Potential economic benefit from disposal is recognized as revenue, and the related expense is reported separately	Partial

Source Authors

Table 46.4 Differences between IPSAS and CAS disclosure requirements for fixed assets

Analysed areas	IPSAS 17	CAS	Level of correspondence
The extent and structure of presented financial information in financial statements	The following financial information must be presented for each class of PPE: (a) used measurement bases, (b) used depreciation methods, (c) used useful life or depreciation rate, (d) gross carrying amount and the accumulated depreciation including the accumulated impairment losses at the beginning and the end of the period, (e) reconciliation of the carrying amount at the beginning and the end of period showing additions, disposals, acquisitions through the entity combinations, etc.	The notes to financial statements shall contain more detailed information explaining the financial information in financial statements. The tangible fixed assets shall be divided into two groups—the constructions and lands. The notes must provide the information relating to revaluation of fixed assets held for sale or about the received transfers for acquisition of fixed assets. The CAS talk indirectly about other disclosure requirements (such as accounting methods used)	Partial

Source Authors

46.3 The Development of Public Sector Accounting Standards

Accounting rules represent generally the comprehensive set of methods and instruments with the aim of providing the financial information towards to the user of financial statements. Many concepts of these rules are characterized in professional paper. Nobes (1999) distinguishes two fundamental concepts—concept specified by legislative way and concept built on stable business practices. While the first conception is based on the role of the state as a subject determining "the rules of game", the second conception is symbolized by a consistence of accounting methods. However, both of conceptions should be used permanently and transparently. In accordance with the concept of Feleagă and Malciu (2002), the accounting rules should be patterned from the true and fair view concept when each accounting transaction should be reported in compliance with the "substance over form" concept.

No uniform accounting rules have existed among the government and international organization financial reporting for a long time which would contribute to harmonization or standardization of financial reporting with respect to many differences in public sector. From this point of view, IPSAS should raise the accountability and transparency of accounting as an information base which results in better level of management and financial planning as well.

If we look at the Czech environment, Act No. 563/1991 Coll. on Accounting is the fundamental legislative document related to the accounting which has to be followed by the public sector entities as well. The Accounting Law defines them as "selected entities". Definition "selected entities" comprises the organizational, state funds under the budget rules, local authorities, voluntary associations of municipalities, the Regional Council, organizations and health insurance companies. The Regulation No. 410/2009 Coll. is another but crucial legislative document for public sector entities. This Regulation provides more detailed information (than Law) which is specific for the public sector, such as the definition of fixed assets, their acquisition, depreciation/amortization or reporting and valuation of assets held for sale. The extent and way of financial statements preparation is another very important area that the Regulation solves. Relevant articles deal with structure, designation and content definition of every part of financial statements including the off-balance sheet items. The appendix of Regulation contains chart of accounts and structure of financial statements which are obligatory for selected entities.

To achieve the conformity of accounting methods and higher level of comparability of financial statements, the Accounting Law requires issuing particular accounting standards (hereinafter referred to as "AS"). Up to this day, ten AS were published (AS No. 701-710). AS No. 706—Adjustments and receivables write-off, AS No. 708—Depreciation of fixed assets and AS No. 710—Intangible and tangible fixed assets are the subjects of our analysis.

46.4   Differential Analysis

Our analysis is inspired by Turlea et al. (2011). It focuses on the identification of differences between IPSAS and CAS. Particularly, it is divided into three main groups: (i) similarity/dissimilarity regarding the concepts related to tangible fixed assets, (ii) similarity/dissimilarity regarding the accounting treatments related to the tangible fixed assets and (iii) similarity/dissimilarity of disclosure requirements related to the fixed assets.

Both accounting concepts (Table 46.2) clearly show how public sector accounting tries to move closer to accounting of private sector. After all, the IPSAS have been patterned on International Financial Reporting Standards (IFRS) which serve for corporations. At present, CAS for public sector are directed to profit sector as well. In last decade, public sector CAS were moving forward significantly by strengthening the accrual principle. On the other side, it is necessary to emphasize permanently the specificity of public sector where certain characteristics are diametrically different from the private sector, for example the matching principle and taxes reported as revenues.

Table 46.2 obviously shows that the level of full correspondence was identified only in three parts—book value, depreciable amount and residual value. Other terms of CAS can be classified as partly corresponding or absolutely not. Moreover when it is not possible to make reference to another legal norm (e.g. the Civil Code or budgetary rules), considerable legal uncertainty emerges during the explanation of these terms. Several problematic issues can be found in the Czech environment where the budgetary definition of individual items of tangible fixed assets is in direct conflict with their view in accounting. Czech accounting approach for recognition of tangible fixed assets is very specific. They determine through the Regulation the concrete levels of amount for classification into two groups: (i) tangible fixed assets with the level of 40,000 CZK and (ii) low-value tangible fixed assets with the level of 3000 CZK. Besides the lack of definition of assets in CAS, the heritage assets do not have logically their definition too. The issue of heritage assets is very questionable because they can be relatively complicatedly assessed and the estimate of useful life represents the same problem. Given this fact, the reporting of heritage assets according to IPSAS is permitted on voluntary basis.

It is apparent from the previous table (and following ones as well) that the characteristic "undefined" stated in "CAS column" is quite extended. It is linked to the absence of accounting framework or precise definition list. This fact has its consequences. The selected entities are forced to use the individual approaches. Accounting Law (article no. 7) requires to apply accounting methods guaranteeing the true and fair value. The chosen and used accounting solution must be disclosed in the notes subsequently.

Table 46.3 shows that no absolute consensus was found in monitored areas. In our opinion, this fact is caused mainly by the coexistence of non-accounting legal sources in Czech legislation, in particular, the Act No. 218/2000 Coll., on budgetary rules, as well as the Act No. 219/2000 Coll., on property of the Czech Republic, and the Act No. 320/2001 Coll., on financial control in public administration. From the theoretical point of view, the broader accounting framework in Czech accounting legislation is missing historically which would offer general solution in a number of areas. For example, the recognition of asset is based on the list of standardized accounting transaction that could occur, but there is need of subsequent amendment of that list if some undefined transaction happens. By contrast, IPSAS have already offered general solutions which can be applied to current and future accounting situations without any amendments.

Capitalization of subsequent expenses in CAS is allowed through the so-called technical evaluation. The technical evaluation is defined in Regulation as finished intervention into the fixed assets resulted in change of its purpose or technical parameters, or expansion of facilities or applicability of property. The IPSAS does not define the technical evaluation specifically but distinguishes routine repairs or maintenance (with no impact into the carrying amount) and replacement of the old component for a new one with subsequent increasing in carrying amount of fixed asset and derecognition of carrying amount of old component at the same time.

The IPSAS view of depreciation methods is clear. The selected method always should correspond to the development of future economic benefits or service potential. In any case, entity should revise chosen depreciation method annually. According to Czech accounting legislation, the selected entities have depreciated fixed assets since 2011 after the radical reform of public sector accounting. The selected entities were forced to determine the carrying amounts of fixed assets which had already been used (and never depreciated) for a long time, at the date of 12 December 2011 (the computed value of accumulated depreciation was recognized as an equity item "Valuation differences caused by the changes of accounting methods"). At present, the selected entities have the possibility to depreciate through the straight-line method, unit of production method and component depreciation method. The CAS permit to apply the diminishing balance method. The Czech concept also implies the need of updating the depreciation policy with the option of retrospective computation of accumulated depreciation and reassessment of remaining useful life of the asset by means of qualified estimate. The institute of residual value is not forgotten as well. It is often determined implicitly into the depreciation policy mostly at the start of useful life of assets, for example, by a fixed amount of 5% of acquisition price which is being applied for all depreciated fixed assets strictly. The Annex no. 1 to AS No. 708—Depreciation of fixed assets categorizes the fixed assets into the depreciation groups. This fact reflects the clear intention of the legislators to typify the fixed assets for the purpose of useful life classification.

In the case of subsequent measurement, IPSAS offer the cost model and the revaluation model where revaluation model application is conditioned by the reliability of fair value assessment. On the other hand, the CAS generally permit the cost model only. But there is one situation when the revaluation model is applied—the (redundant) fixed assets held for sale. If the moment of decision about the redundancy of fixed asset with the goal of its sale happens, such asset must be revalued on the basis of fair value.

The area of tangible fixed assets disposal in CAS is not sufficiently specified. CAS bring only the list of standardized cases illustrating the alternatives of fixed asset disposal. On the contrary, IPSAS mention the general proposition about derecognition of fixed asset at the date of its disposal or at the date when loses the future economic benefits or service potential completely.

Table 46.4 illustrates the fundamental differences in disclosure requirements. It can be found a certain approximation of CAS to IPSAS because selected entities must determine their own level of materiality for the purpose of financial statements preparation in accordance with CAS at present. The balance sheet items "Constructions" and "Lands" must provide detailed information about depreciation methods used, acquisition or disposal of such assets and so on. The separate area of disclosure in the notes is represented by the fixed assets held for sale comprising the list of such assets and their values, the quantities, the revaluation differences and, if necessary, the reasons for their sale. As it can be seen, CAS bring relatively detailed requirements what the selected entities have to present or disclose in their financial statements (they have binding structure). On the other side, the IPSAS 17 provide clear instructions forming the comprehensive disclosure requirements (without the binding structure of financial statements).

Table 46.5 Summary of levels of correspondence between CAS and IPSAS 17

Analysed groups	Level of correspondence			Total
	Absolute	Partial	No correspondence	
Accounting concepts	3	5	7	15
Accounting treatments	0	4	2	6
Disclosures	0	1	0	1
Total	3	10	9	22

Source Authors

46.5   Conclusion

The paper dealt with the issue of accounting concepts, treatments and disclosures of tangible fixed assets in accordance with IPSAS 17 and CAS. The analysis was based on detailed comparison of individual parts both of accounting frameworks. As it can be seen despite the fact that the conceptual reform of public sector accounting in the Czech Republic was made, certain significant differences of CAS compared to IPSAS 17 still exist.

Table 46.5 shows that only 3 of 22 analysed areas correspond absolutely. It is only 14%. The rests can be classified as an area with partial or no correspondence. Therefore, the stated hypothesis has been rejected. In perspective of current pervasive discussion about the IPSAS/EPSAS implementation in EU, it will be very important to monitor the development of public sector CAS and demonstrate the possible move forward to IPSAS.

Acknowledgments This paper has been prepared under financial support of the research project "Relevance of accounting information on the consolidated basis in business and public sector" (IGA VSE F1/47/2015), in which authors gratefully acknowledge.

References

Bellanca S, Vandernoot J (2013) Analysis of Belgian public accounting and its compliance with international public sector accounting standards (IPSAS) 1, 6 and 22. Int J Bus Manag 8:122–133. doi:10.5539/ijbm.v8n9p122

Berger M-MT (2012) IPSAS explained: a summary of international public sector accounting standards, vol 2. Wiley, Somerset, GB, p 257

Bergmann A (2009) Public sector financial management. Pearson Education, Harlow, p 186

Biancone P, Secinaro S (2015) Public Local Group: the financial statement effects of adopting the international public sector accounting standards (The Case of Italy). Int Bus Manag 10:1–5. doi:10.3968/6739

Feleagă N, Malciu L (2002) Accounting policies and options. Economica Publishing House, Bucharest

Lutilsky ID, Percevic H (2011) The possibilities of the appliance of fair value concept in Croatian public sector. In: The 9th international conference: challenges of Europe: growth and competitiveness—reversing trend, p 311

Nobes Ch (1999) Pocked accounting. Profile Books, London

Svoboda M (2011) Accounting for accountability—Czech or IPSAS way? In: Mezinárodní Baťova konference pro doktorandy a mladé vědecké pracovníky-7. ročník. Univerzita Tomáše Bati, Zlín

Tudor AT (2010) Romanian public institutions financial statements on the way of harmonization with IPSAS. Account Manag Inf Syst 9:422–447

Turlea E, Stefanescu A, Nicolae F (2011) Interferences and limits of the accounting policies specific to fixed tangible assets into the public sector entities in Romania. Ann Univ Apulensis: Series Oeconomica 13(2):325–335

Zelenka V (2014) Vymezení prvků účetních výkazů účetních jednotek veřejného sektoru. Český finanční a účetní časopis 9(3):34–45

Chapter 47
Sustainability Reporting Versus Integrated Reporting: BIST Sustainability Index

Gülşah Atağan

Abstract Sustainability accounting and reporting can be considered as a complement to financial accounting. When used together, financial information and sustainability information can provide a complete view of the performance and value creation of a corporation. Sustainability consists of three dimensions: economic, environmental and social. Sustainability approach requires the integration of these dimensions into business strategies and reporting the performance of business activities related to these three dimensions. An integrated report is a concise communication about how an organization's strategy, governance, performance and prospects, in the context of its external environment, lead to the creation of value over the short, medium and long term. The aim of this study is to evaluate the interaction between integrated reporting and sustainability accounting in theoretical framework. The research has been done by literature review and analyzing the firms which are listed in BIST Sustainability Index.

Keywords Social responsibility accounting · Sustainability reports · Integrated reports · BIST Sustainability Index

47.1 Introduction

Businesses are appearing as not only profit-oriented organizations but also an element that ought to fulfill responsibilities toward society and environment. Businesses are social entities that have social responsibilities. As a necessity of social responsibility principle, voluntarily or as a legal necessity, businesses which have interactions with current economic and social surroundings provide and render reports associated with corporate social responsibility and environment. These reports are gaining significance day by day due to expansions of traditional per-

G. Atağan (✉)
Faculty of Economics and Administrative Sciences, Business Administration Department,
Dokuz Eylul University, Dokuzçeşmeler Campus, 35160 Buca-İzmir, Turkey
e-mail: gulsah.ugurluel@deu.edu.tr

© Springer International Publishing AG 2017   511
D. Procházka (ed.), *New Trends in Finance and Accounting*,
Springer Proceedings in Business and Economics,
DOI 10.1007/978-3-319-49559-0_47

formance standards focusing on social and environmental performance indicators in addition to corporate net profit that causes more investors to advocate environmental and social factors effectiveness of corporate value of businesses. In preparation of these reports, accounting has significant duty. Accounting information system gains important role on measuring, evaluation and reporting of every kind of information in businesses.

Corporate sustainability can be defined as enterprises' undertaking of social, economic and environmental as well as financial responsibilities. The information related to new responsibilities placed on companies must be presented to stakeholders just like the financial information. Inadequacy of financial reporting, in providing information related to new responsibilities of companies to large numbers of stakeholders spread all over the globalized world, has led to emergence of a new vehicle. This new tool, used by companies to communicate their activities with internal and external stakeholders, is called sustainability reporting.

Corporate sustainability had become popular with the publication Brundtland Report entitled "Our Common Future" and had defined as to ensure that it meets the needs of the present without compromising the ability of future generations to meet their own needs.

In 1990s, Triple Bottom Line reporting method which is put forward by Elkington provides economic, social and environmental components together. Contrary to traditional reporting that takes into account net income as an indicator of performance, it includes a much further concept multidimensional reporting model comprising of social and environmental performance (Fleischman and Schuele 2006: 43)

Social responsibility reports can be defined as the provision of financial and non-financial information relating to an organization's interaction with its physical and social environment, as stated in corporate annual reports or separate social reports. Sustainability concept brings in the question that all corporate activities have social, economic and environmental results and it is necessary to report all of them as a whole.

Giving place to this type of information in companies' sustainability reports can cause sustainability reports and integrated reports to be perceived as the same. However, integrated reporting is the kind of reporting that covers much wider and more sustainable reports. In this study, the terms of integrated reporting and sustainability reporting have been examined in a detailed way. Although there is not any company making integrated reporting in Turkey, there are still 29 companies registered under BIST Sustainability Index publishing their sustainability reports. Two registered companies under BIST enrolled in the pilot program of IIRC, and a vast number of companies announced that they will make integrated reports in the upcoming days. The basic principles of BIST Sustainability Index are considered in detail in this study, and a proposal for integrated reporting is made.

47.2 Sustainability Reporting

Sustainability is an old concept; developments in the business world and increased competition have caused the business entities to refocus on this concept in order to safeguard their continuity. Sustainability consists of three dimensions: economic, environmental and social. Sustainability approach requires the integration of these dimensions into business strategies and reporting the performance of business activities related to these three dimensions. Sustainability accounting and reporting can be considered as a complement to financial accounting. When used together, financial information and sustainability information can provide a complete view of the performance and value creation of a corporation.

Sustainability Reports provide "information relating to a corporation's activities, aspirations and public image with regard to environmental, community, employee and consumer issues. Within these headings will be subsumed other, more detailed, matters such as energy usage, equal opportunities, fair trade, corporate governance and the like" (Gray et al. 2001: 329).

Elkington (1988) suggested that financial reporting should expand beyond traditional bottom line as net income and success indicators such as social and environmental performance should be also taken into account.

Statistics from GRI also reflect a growing uptrend in the world that more and more companies start using the Global Reporting Initiative (GRI)—modern and comprehensive Sustainability Reporting Framework enabling organizations to measure and report their economic, environmental, social and governance performance—the four cornerstones of sustainability. Every year, an increasing number of reporters adopt GRI's Guidelines (Gurvitsh and Sidorova 2012: 28).

47.3 Integrated Reporting

The International Integrated Reporting Council (IIRC) defines integrated reporting as "a process that results in communication by an organization, most visibly a periodic integrated report, about how an organization's strategy, governance, performance, and prospects lead to the creation of value over the short, medium and long-term" (http://integratedreporting.org/ 06.02.2016).

Integrated reporting is more than creating a comprehensive annual report. It can be used as an effective governance tool for performance-oriented management.

According to the PWC report (August 2013), integrated report is a way to respond to the evolving needs of stakeholders in the capital markets.

- Capital market stakeholders are finding it valuable when companies provide information on environmental, social and governance issues impacting their businesses. Stakeholders are increasingly considering internal and external non-financial factors, such as resource scarcity or demographic shifts, when assessing companies' long-term prospects.

- Integrated reporting builds on the existing financial reporting model to incorporate non-financial information that can help stakeholders understand how a company creates and sustains value over the long term. This is in line with the continued growth of sustainability rating systems and investment policy disclosure requirements. The trend toward reporting non-financial information is increasing and will likely continue.
- Globalization of and interdependencies in supply chains, rapid population growth and increasing global consumption are impacting the quality, availability and price of resources. Integrated reporting has the potential to make the impact of these and other factors on companies' strategies and business models more transparent to stakeholders.
- Companies that have embarked on the integrated reporting journey view it as a change process that has enabled them to think differently about their businesses. Among the benefits they have realized are strengthened financial reporting across business activities, enhanced internal collaboration and increased internal and external communications. Some have also used the process to develop key performance indicators to provide clarity regarding their business models.

There is no standard format for an Integrated Report and no specific disclosure requirements. Instead, the Discussion Paper issued by the IIRC sets out five Guiding Principles and six Content Elements for an Integrated Report:

- Guiding Principles
- Strategic Focus
- Future Orientation
- Connectivity of Information
- Responsiveness and Stakeholder Inclusiveness
- Conciseness, Reliability and Materiality

Content Elements

- Organizational overview and business model
- Operating context, including risks and opportunities
- Strategic objectives
- Governance and remuneration
- Performance
- Future outlook

The IIRC also contrasts eight differences between current and integrated reporting in Table 47.1.

Integrated reporting is based on two fundamental and interconnected concepts: value creation and the capitals. Value creation emphasizes that value is not created by or within the organization alone, but is influenced by the external environment, the organization's relationships with others and the resources used and affected. Value creation can best be understood as the change in value of the capitals over time (Integrated Reporting Committee (IRC) of South Africa 2014).

Table 47.1 Current reporting and integrated reporting

Feature	Current reporting	Integrated reporting
Trust	Narrow disclosures	Greater transparency
Stewardship	Past, financial	Past and future; connected; strategic
Thinking	Isolated	Integrated
Focus	Past, financial	Past and future; connected; strategic
Time frame	Short term	Short, medium and long term
Adaptive	Rule bound	Responsive to individual circumstances
Concise	Long and complex	Concise and material
Technology enabled	Paper based	Technology enabled

Source (KPMG April 2013)

The concept of capitals seeks to assist an organization in identifying all the resources and relationships it uses and affects to report in a comprehensive manner. The six capitals are:

- Financial capital, such as shareholder equity and funds raised by issuing bonds
- Manufactured capital, such as equipment and public infrastructure
- Intellectual capital, such as technology, patents, research and development, and the organization's internal systems, procedures and protocols
- Human capital, such as people's skills and experience
- Social and relationship capital, such as key stakeholder relationships, brands and reputation, as well as community involvement
- Natural capital, such as water, land and minerals

According to the IIRC, an integrated report is a concise communication about how an organization's strategy, governance, performance and prospects, in the context of its external environment, lead to the creation of value over the short, medium and long term (IIRC). Although providers of financial capital are the primary intended IR users, an integrated report should be designed to benefit all stakeholders—including employees, customers, suppliers, business partners, local communities, regulators and policy makers—interested in an organization's ability to create value over time. The key objective of integrated reporting (IR) is to enhance accountability and stewardship with respect to the broad base of six types of capital, or "capitals" (financial, manufactured, intellectual, human, social and relationship, and natural), and promote understanding of their interdependencies. Through this approach, IR is designed to support integrated thinking, decision making and actions that focus on sustainable value creation for stakeholders (Di Donato et al. 2013, 208).

The comparison made by Fasan (2013) related to the application reports can be found in the table below. It can be clearly seen that sustainability reports and integrated reports do resemble each other in many aspects. For this reason, these two reports can be perceived as the same. But integrated reporting goes a long way, including sustainability reports also in Table 47.2.

Table 47.2 Sustainability and integrated reports main features

	Annual reports	Sustainability reports	Integrated
Target	Specific stakeholders (shareholders and investors)	Several stakeholders (social and environmental perspective)	Primary providers of financial capital
Mandatory/voluntary	Mandatory	Voluntary (with some exceptions: Denmark, Sweden, France)	Voluntary (with some exceptions: South Africa)
Regulation or guidelines	National and international laws and GAAP (or IAS/IFRS)	Global reporting initiative (GRI)	IIRC framework
Comparability	High	Medium	Low
Industry customization	Low	Medium (sector supplements)	High
Assurance level	High	Low	Low
Scope	Financial reporting entity (company or group of companies)	Broader than financial reporting entity (supply chain, LCA approach)	Broader than financial reporting entity (supply chain, LCA approach)

Source (Fasan 2013; 50)

47.4   BIST Sustainability Index

BIST Sustainability Index aims to provide a benchmark for İstanbul Stock Exchange companies with high performance on corporate sustainability and to increase the awareness, knowledge and practice on sustainability in Turkey. Moreover, the index is a platform for institutional investors to demonstrate their commitment to companies managing environmental, social and governance (ESG) issues with high performance. İstanbul Stock Exchange has signed a cooperation agreement with Ethical Investment Research Services Limited (EIRIS) to create BIST Sustainability Index. In accordance with this agreement, EIRIS assesses İstanbul Stock Exchange listed companies based on the international sustainability criteria. The assessment is based upon only publicly available information, and assessment costs of companies are covered by İstanbul Stock Exchange.

EIRIS is an independent London-based research organization, specialized on environmental, social and governance issues for more than 30 years and serving asset owners, asset managers and index providers globally. Johannesburg and Mexico Stock Exchanges are the other exchanges that EIRIS provides sustainability research service.

BIST Sustainability Index has been launched on November 4, 2014, with the code XUSRD. The initial value of the index is 98.020,09 based upon the second session closing value of BIST 30 index on November 3, 2014. The relative weight of each constituent is capped at 15%.

Table 47.3 Environmental criteria

Panel A: Environment policy

Environmental policy	**High-impact companies**	**Medium-impact companies**	**Low-impact companies**
	The company meets the following: –Four core indicators (at 2 pts or above) –Three core indicators (at 2 pts or above) and one desirable indicator—Three core indicators with one at a higher level of quality (3 pts) –Membership of one listed initiatives	The company meets one of the following: –Four core indicators (at 2 pts or above) –Three core indicators (at 2 pts or above) and one desirable indicator—Three core indicators with one at a higher level of quality (3 pts) –Membership of one listed initiatives	No requirements
	Core indicators: – Reference to all key issues* – Level of senior responsibility** – Commitment to use of objectives and targets ** – Commitment to monitoring/auditing – Commitment to public reporting *This indicator is scored on a scale of 0 pt, 1 pt and 2 pts **These indicators are scored on a scale of 0 pt, 1 pt, 2 pts and 3 pts	**Desirable indicators:** – Globally applicable corporate operating standards – Commitment to stakeholder involvement – Commitment to address product or service impact – Strategic moves toward sustainability **Initiatives:** – ICC (International Chamber of Commerce) membership – CERES membership	

Panel B: Environmental management system

Environmental management system	**High-impact companies**	**Medium-impact companies**	**Low-impact companies**
	The company meets one of the following: – Coverage is less than 33%, and the company meets four (or more) indicators – Coverage is 33% or greater, and the company meets three (or more) core indicators – Any evidence of ISO14001/EMAS certified systems – Any "other" indicator	The company meets one of the following: – Coverage is less than 33%, and the company meets four (or more) core indicators – Coverage is 33% or greater, and the company meets three (or more) core indicators – Any evidence of ISO14001/EMAS certified systems—any "other" indicator	No requirements

(continued)

Table 47.3 (continued)

Panel B: Environmental management system

	Core indicators:	**Other indicators:**
	– Evidence of environmental policy – Identification of significant impacts – Setting objectives and targets – Outline of processes and responsibilities, manuals, action plans, procedures – Internal system audits – Internal reporting and management review	– Commitment to obtain ISO14001 or EMAS —EIA undertaken for all projects – Supplier audits certified systems—ISO14001 certification – EMAS (Eco-management and audit scheme) registration

Panel C: Biodiversity

Biodiversity policy	**High-impact companies**	**Medium-impact companies**	**Low-impact companies**
	The company meets at least one indicator	No requirements	Not assessed

Panel D: Climate change

Climate change management response	**Very-high-impact companies**	**High-impact companies**	**Medium-impact companies**	**Low-impact companies**
	The company meets at least one indicator	No requirements	No requirements	Not assessed

Table 47.4 Governance criteria

Panel A: Board practice

Board practice	**All companies**
	The company meets at least two indicators

Panel B: Countering bribery

Countering bribery policy	**All companies**
	The company meets at least one indicator
Countering bribery system	The company meets at least one indicator

47.4.1 BIST Sustainability Index Ground Rules

The purpose of BIST Sustainability Index (the index hereafter) is to create an index whose constituents are selected by the companies whose corporate sustainability performance is at high level among the listed companies in İstanbul Stock Exchange and in extent to increase awareness, know-how and hands-on practice of the companies about sustainability in Turkey, especially the ones listed in İstanbul Stock Exchange. The index will provide companies to compare their corporate sustainability performance in local and global basis. With the index, İstanbul Stock Exchange provides companies an instrument for evaluating their performance and consequently adopting new targets or furthering their performance while allowing them to develop their risk management abilities for corporate transparency, accountability and sustainability. The index also aims to create an instrument which will allow investors to select and invest in companies that adopt principles of sustainability and corporate governance.

47.5 BIST Sustainability Index Inclusion Rules

BIST Sustainability Index Inclusion Rules are broadly explained below. There are 3 main criteria in the index: environmental criteria, governance criteria and social criteria, which are given in Tables 47.3, 47.4 and 47.5, respectively.

Table 47.5 Social criteria

Panel A: Human rights policy			
Human rights policy	**Companies involved in oil and gas or mining activities with large presence in high-risk countries**	**Companies involved in oil and gas or mining activities with smaller presence in high-risk countries**	**Companies in other sectors with large presence in high-risk countries**	**Companies in other sectors with smaller presence in high-risk countries**
	The company has policy which explicitly mentions 2 ILO core labor or has a statement on fundamental human rights	The company has policy which explicitly mentions 2 ILO core labor or has a statement on fundamental human rights	The company has policy which explicitly mentions 2 ILO core labor or has a statement on fundamental human rights	No requirements
	Alternatively, the company meets one of the following: • The company has published human rights policies which include explicit support for the OECD Guidelines for Multinational Enterprises (this is a proxy for having a policy on all the ILO core labor areas) • The company is a signatory to the UN Global Compact (this is a proxy for having a policy on all the ILO core labor areas) • SA8000 for its owned operations (this is a proxy for having a policy on all the ILO core labor areas)			No requirements
Panel B: Human rights system			
Human rights system	**Companies involved in oil and gas or mining activities with large presence in high-risk countries**	**Companies involved in oil and gas or mining activities with smaller presence in high-risk countries**	**Companies in other sectors with large presence in high-risk countries**	**Companies in other sectors with smaller presence in high-risk countries**
	The company meets at least one indicator	No requirements	No requirements	No requirements
Panel C: Human rights system			
Health and safety system	**All companies**		
	The company meets at least one indicator (except senior responsibility)		

47.5.1 Expected Contribution from Index

The index provides competitive advantage to Turkish companies managing their corporate risks and opportunities effectively. An investible index on which new instruments can be developed is in place to attract capital for companies. The Index reflects companies' approach to important sustainability issues including global warming, draining of natural resources, health, security and employment, while allowing an independent assessment of their operations and decisions regarding these issues and, in a sense, their registration.

The Index offers companies the opportunity to compare their sustainability performance on both local and global level. With the Index, İstanbul Stock Exchange provides companies an instrument for evaluating their performance and consequently adopting new targets or furthering their performance while allowing them to develop their risk management abilities for corporate transparency, accountability and sustainability. This, in turn, allows companies to gain a competitive edge. Inclusion in the Index adds to their visibility and prestige.

The index facilitates for companies the access to global clients, capital and lower-cost finance. The project aims to create an instrument which allows investors to select and invest in companies that adopt principles of sustainability and corporate governance. Today, responsible investment is preferred mainly by institutional investors. BIST Sustainability Index encourages founding such funds, while facilitating for index constituent companies to get a larger share from such funds. At the same time, the index offers a new financial asset category for all investors shown in Table 47.6.

Table 47.6 Sustainability index constituents for the period between November 2015 and October 2016

1	AKBNK	AKBANK	16	PETKM	PETKİM
2	AKSEN	AKSA ENERJİ	17	SAHOL	SABANCI HOLDİNG
3	AEFES	ANADOLU EFES	18	SAFGY	SAF GMYO
4	ARCLK	ARÇELİK	19	TSKB	T.S.K.B.
5	ASELS	ASELSAN	20	TAHVL	TAV HAVALİMANLARI
6	BRISA	BRİSA	21	TOASO	TOFAŞ OTO. FAB.
7	CCOLA	COCA COLA İÇECEK	22	TCELL	TURKCELL
8	DOAS	DOĞUŞ OTOMOTİV	23	TUPRS	TÜPRAŞ
9	ERGL	EREĞLİ DEMİR ÇELİK	24	THYAO	TÜRK HAVA YOLLARI
10	FROTO	FORD OTOSAN	25	TTKOM	TÜRK TELEKOM
11	GARAN	GARANTİ BANKASI	26	ULKER	ÜLKER BİSKÜVİ
12	ISCTR	İŞ BANKASI (C)	27	VAKBN	VAKIFLAR BANKASI
13	KCHOL	KOÇ HOLDİNG	28	VESTL	VESTEL
14	MGROS	MİGROS TİCARET	29	YKBNK	YAPI VE KREDİ BANKASI
15	OTKAR	OTOKAR			

47.6   Conclusion

This paper reviews the relatively short history of sustainability and integrated reporting. The quality of the reports is as important as their numbers in their related countries. Although the USA, Canada, Denmark, Japan and some other countries have many reports by number, it is stated in KPMG's study in 2013 that when suppliers, value chain, governance, risk, opportunities and strategy criteria are considered, they seem to come after Italy and Spain who have less number of reports.

As a result of literature review, a great majority of the reports are identified as GRI reports both in Turkey and other countries. This can be considered as a result of GRI guidebooks' being prepared according to all the qualities of company criteria and prepared in many different languages, and although there is no consensus about integrated reports formatting, it is still thought to construct a new report format that can shape this report related to 6 capital elements constituted by IIRC and IRC. The GRI Sustainability Reporting Guidelines (the Guidelines) offer Reporting Principles, Standard Disclosures and an Implementation Manual for the preparation of sustainability reports by organizations, regardless of their size, sector or location.

References

Di Donato D, Bordogna R, Busco C (2013) The case of Eni, integrated reporting concepts and cases that Redefi ne corporate accountability. ISBN 978-3-319-02167-6, ISBN 978-3-319-02168-3 (eBook). doi:10.1007/978-3-319-02168-3. Springer International Publishing, Switzerland, pp 207–225

Elkington J (1998) Cannibals with forks: the triple bottom line of 21st century business. New Society Publishers, Gabriola Island, BC

Fasan M (2013) Annual reports, sustainability reports and integrated reports: trends in corporate disclosure, integrated reporting concepts and cases that redefine corporate accountability, ISBN 978-3-319-02167-6, ISBN 978-3-319-02168-3 (eBook). doi:10.1007/978-3-319-02168-3. Springer International Publishing, Switzerland, pp 41–59

Fleischman RK, ve Schuele K (2006) Green accounting: a primer. J Acc Educ 24:35–66

G4 Sustainability Reporting Guidelines. http://www.globalreporting.org, (23.02.2016)

Gray R, Javad M, Power DM, Sinclair CD (2001) Social and environmental disclosure and corporate characteristics: a research note and extension. J Bus Finance Account 28(3):327–356

Gurvitsh N, Sidorova I (2012) Survey of sustainability reporting integrated into annual reports of Estonian companies for the years 2007–2010: based on companies listed on tallinn stock exchange as of october 2011. Procedia Econ Finance 2:26–34

International Integrated Reporting Council, http://integratedreporting.org/, 06.02.2016

Integrated Reporting Committee (IRC) of South Africa (2014) Preparing an integrated report a starter's guide. ISBN 0-86983-391-X

İstanbul Stock Exchange Sustainability Index, http://www.borsaistanbul.com/endeksler, 10.02.2016

KPMG International (2013) Introducing Integrated Reporting, 2013

PWC sustainability report (2013)

Chapter 48
Management Control Systems Through the Lens of the Agency Theory

Hana Vimrová

Abstract The article focuses on the analysis and development of the agency theory framework and seeks to define the conditions and functions which management control systems (MCSs) should meet according to the agency theory. The aim is to assess to what extent, under what conditions, and whether at all the validity of the agency theory assumptions can be ensured and the functions of MCS realistically achievable. More specifically, the article discusses the theoretical foundations of the agency theory, but also pays attention to the stewardship theory, assesses current knowledge in the area of different approaches to MCSs through the lens of the agency theory, and suggests conditions and functions of MCS reflecting the principles of the agency theory and the stewardship theory, including their critical evaluation.

Keywords Agency theory · Agency costs · Management control systems · Stewardship theory · Strategic performance measurement systems

48.1 Introduction

Management control systems (MCSs) represent an interconnected system of tools and techniques used by managers with the intention of ensuring the achievement of corporate goals (Král 2010). Their conception goes beyond the content of management accounting, including its strategic version, and enriches it with the element of control (Chenhall 2003; Drury 2012). In Chenhall's (2003) view, they not only ensure the implementation of corporate strategy, but they also represent an effective instrument that can help with its formulation by providing managers with feedback regarding the scope of the existing strategy implementation.

H. Vimrová (✉)
Department of Management Accounting, University of Economics,
Prague, Nam. W. Churchilla 4, 13067 Prague, Czech Republic
e-mail: xvimh01@vse.cz

© Springer International Publishing AG 2017   523
D. Procházka (ed.), *New Trends in Finance and Accounting*,
Springer Proceedings in Business and Economics,
DOI 10.1007/978-3-319-49559-0_48

Strategic performance measurement systems (SPMSs) perform a similar function. Simons (1995) and Drury (2012) defined them as a subset of MCSs focusing on performance measurement and management based on outputs (Král 2010), while Bititci et al. (2012) did not see any significant differences between these systems, and Šiška (2015) even considered them to be a synonym for MCSs.

There is a wide range of differentiated approaches to the concept of management control systems. Some of these are based on the agency theory (Parporato 2011; Franco-Santos et al. 2012), or the coalition theory, also known as the stakeholder theory (Sundin et al. 2008), others are based on institutional theories (Sundin et al. 2008), management theories (Chenhall 2003), behavioural theories (Parporato 2011), (Chenhall 2003) or include psychological, ecological, and social aspects (Chenhall 2003) in MCSs. Scholars dealing with management accounting, which is a key component of MCS (Chenhall 2003; Drury 2012), include also political- and power-related elements in the concept of MCS (Baxter-Chua 2003). In their view, MCS is not seen only as a mechanism helping managers to achieve the optimal allocation of resources and as a system supporting corporate performance, but also as a political system supporting the power position of particular interest groups within a company (Chenhall 2003).

Probably the most widely recognized concept of MCSs is based on the contextual factors and contingency theory based on the organizational theory (Parporato 2011). The contingency approach explores the influence of contingency factors on MCS as such (Chenhall 2003), how MCS is used, i.e., whether the company prefers to apply it in a diagnostic or interactive manner, and its outputs in the form of organizational performance of the company, risk management, and financial performance.

Different theoretical approaches to MCS have a direct influence on its design and functions. Some scholars reject the idea of integrating the different approaches, more specifically the contingency theory and its alternatives, and claim that the alternative approaches to MCSs should remain separated from the concept based on contingency factors and remain an alternative to the contingency theory because they believe that attempts at their integration are doomed to failure and the synthesis is very difficult if not impossible to reach (Covaleski et al. 1996; Dirsmith et al. 1985). Other authors attempt to view MCS through a combination of several approaches. Jönsson and Macintosh (1997), for example, tried to imply new conclusions in the area of MCSs by assimilating the ideas brought forward by alternative approaches. Chenhall (2003), who researched various contextual factors, even believed that including alternative approaches into the concept of MCSs based on the contingency theory will be the driving force of further development of this approach, and he prefers integrating the different approaches to MCSs with the contingency approach.

In common business practice, it is not only the owner, who sacrifices his scarce resources, which he owns and invests them in the form of capital, time, effort, reputation, and clean record in the business activities of the company with the expectation of their future appreciation and who enters into relations described by the agency theory with company management. Other stakeholders also sacrifice their scarce resources in different forms and with different intensity, willingly or less willingly, with the hope in their appreciation, or at least expecting that they will not be depreciated. They are also in the position of agents or principals in relation to the company.

The aim of the paper is to analyse and develop the agency theory framework, define the conditions and functions which MCS should perform within the agency theory and assess to what extent, under what conditions, and whether at all these conditions can be met and the functions of MCS are realistic.

The research methods used include analytical description and comparison based on a critical review of domestic and foreign literature.

The paper is divided into four chapters. The first chapter discusses the theoretical background of the agency theory, the second chapter assesses current knowledge in the area of different approaches to MCSs from the perspective of the agency theory, the third chapter suggests the conditions and functions of MCS reflecting the principles of the agency theory, and the final chapter summarizes the research results and includes suggestions for future research.

48.2   The Agency Theory

The relationship between agents and principals is defined by Jensen (2000) as a contractual relationship in which one or more persons called "principals" hire another person or people called "agents" to perform certain activities in their interest. The decision-making power is at the same time transferred to agents.

The agency theory is based on the new institutional economic theories (Marek 2007). Its important characteristics include the existence of information asymmetry (Akerlof 1970), i.e., a situation in which one party is more informed than the other, and a specific way in which one or both of these parties behave referred to either as adverse selection (Akerlof 1970), in case that the less-informed party is unable to make an optimal selection, or moral hazard (Akerlof 1970), in case that one party intentionally acts for their own benefit at the expense of the other party, which results in ineffective solutions. Mackintosh (1994) adds that the agency theory is associated with the agent's self-interest, a system of incentives and contracts between the two parties and signalling behaviour, which means the effort of the more-informed party to pass information to the less-informed party.

The relationship between principals and agents is not limited only to owners and managers, in which case the agency theory focuses on the decision-making of the owners in accordance with the principles of this theory (Jensen and Meckling 1976) or on the decision-making of the managers in the context of the managerial models of the firm (Williamson 1964). The same specific relationship also occurs between companies, between the company represented by managers and employees, the company and customers, between the majority and minority shareholders, creditors and debtors (Marek 2007), between senior management and lower-level management, the company and the state.

In practice, it may happen that each person gets into the position of principal or agent in different relationships or will play the role of a principal and an agent simultaneously in the same relationship (Marek 2007).

Research in the area of the agency theory was recently broadened to include the existence of multiple agents as well as the objectives of the individual participants involved the mutual relationships. The basic principles of the agency theory have been the subject of research in various cultures (Davis 1997; Namazi 2013; Paporato 2011), and the role of the agency theory was also examined with regard to the implementation of management control (Namazi 2013). Namazi (2013) saw the company as a nexus of contractual agreements among different individuals that provide an appropriate means for resource allocation and reveal the scope of the firm's activities and as a powerful framework for effective management control.

When applying the agency theory, the key factors include the organizational and ownership structure of the company, access to information, ineffective behaviour, and attitude to risk, the number of subjects among which the risk can be spread and other characteristics of the parties which participate in closing explicit or implicit contracts. These factors influence the agency costs, including the costs of monitoring the agent (whether these costs relate to the implementation, running and innovation of the performance measurement and management systems or, e.g., the audit) and their impact on business performance.

Agency costs include all costs arising from the existence of the agency relationship (Jensen and Meckling 1976), and the resulting value can be obtained by summarizing the monitoring, motivation, or bonding costs and residual loss (Marek 2007; Boučková 2015), where residual loss is caused by random influences. Despite the efforts of the principal to spend a sufficient amount on monitoring and bonding costs, which should ensure an adequate behaviour of the agent and acceptable benefit for the principal, this benefit is reduced by random elements causing additional residual costs. Agency costs are not fixed, and the relationships between various principals and agents may be characterized by different classifications of agency costs.

Principals' objectives are focused on maximizing or achieving an acceptable level of benefits (in the case of owners these include, for example, maximum revenue, profit, or market value of the company). These correspond with the distribution and diversification of risk or its transfer to agents. Principals strive to minimize one-off contractual costs, reduce the costs of monitoring agents, achieve an acceptable level of bonding costs representing a share on principals' benefits (e.g. managers' bonuses or profit sharing for employees) provided that these steps will not compromise the level of principal's benefit. Principals may also make an effort to implement strategically oriented performance measurement and management systems in order to monitor the efforts and activities of agents if adequate systems of performance control are available. Rising agency costs have a negative impact on the principals' utility function, but the benefit of principals influences it positively.

Applying the agency theory will depend on the type of benefit, because principals usually prefer a different form of benefit than the one that suits agents, and therefore, require that their benefits are transformed to the agents' benefits with minimal costs. Principals also look for possibilities to minimize random factors which are part of the agent's utility function and which the agent is unable to influence. These factors deform the agents' efforts and reduce the usefulness of their activities, and consequently, the random factors contribute to reducing the final value of the benefit, agent's share on it and thus limit the benefit for both parties. The question is whether it is the principal, the agent or a third party who should be responsible for eliminating the random factors and to what extent elimination or at least minimizing these factors is achievable.

It is in the interest of agents to maximize their own utility, which is a partly decreasing and a partly increasing function of their efforts. The work they do for principals, on the one hand, reduces the benefit of agents, but, on the other hand, leads to its growth due to the higher share on the principal's benefit. The agent also selects the most reasonable combination between his own efforts and free time. Under these circumstances, it is desirable to determine whether the agent's reward for the owner is conscious or whether the principal is not completely aware of it (or some part of it), ignores it or does not even include it in his utility function (e.g. subordinates' salaries decided on by the manager or other employee benefits included in the Williamson's managerial model). Agents will also seek to reduce their own risk arising from their activities and the existence of random factors (e.g. managers will want to transfer these risks to the company owners or creditors).

If the agent is at the same time in the position of a principal or vice versa (e.g. one of the owners starts to participate in the management of the company), his objectives will combine those of both parties, and he will search for the best combination of objectives in order to increase his benefit.

Agency costs presented so far in this article can be described as secondary agency costs or costs incurred by trying to solve complications resulting from the agency. Marek (2007) also listed costs in the narrower sense, the primary costs that are caused by fraud, excessive consumption, the inability, or indifference of the agent.

Assuming that the primary form of agency costs, which can be significant, quite dangerous, and difficult to influence, is replaced by the agency costs intended to find a solution, while the consequences of random factors are part of both forms of costs, this transformation will be effective if the growth of secondary agency costs (SAC) causes a proportionately higher decrease in the agency costs in the narrower sense (PAC), i.e., the costs change form, but the decline in the original "narrowly defined" agency costs is replaced only to some extent, as shown by the flat curve in Fig. 48.1. This condition seems to be essential in incurring secondary agency costs, because otherwise expending these costs would not make sense.

Management control systems should not only respect the basic principles of the agency theory, but also ensure the transformation of various forms of benefits between individual principals and agents with the lowest possible costs of benefit redistribution. In addition, they should outline the interdependence between the two forms of agency costs and the relation of their replacement. The costs related to the

Fig. 48.1 Agency costs
transformation. *Source*
Author

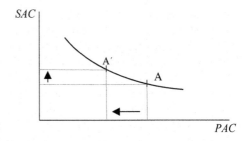

implementation, innovation, and application of MCSs and their tools should cause
multiple decrease in agency costs in the narrow sense and contribute to the elimination of random influences.

48.3 MCSs Through the Lens of the Agency Theory

In the 1970s and 1980s, the agency theory started to be applied also in the area of
management accounting, as a fundamental instrument of the MCSs. It contributed
to the creation of adequate accounting controls to monitor agents' behaviour
(Baiman 1990; Namazi 2013; Parporato 2011).

The agency theory framework was used to explore the individual components of
the management accounting system, i.e., budgets (Shields and Young 1993), fixed
costs allocation procedures (Parporato 2011), performance measurement tools,
where, for example, the construction of optimal performance measures is determined by the utility functions of the agent and the principal (Shields 1997), and
models used primarily in strategic management accounting, and the contribution of
the agency theory to further development and improvement in management
accounting was certainly not negligible (Parporato 2011). The agency theory has
also shown potential in the area of management control development (Namazi
2013).

Baiman (1990) also addressed the agency theory and its application when
designing MCSs, particularly in the area of modelling management accounting. He
recognized three branches of the agency theory which can be applied in the context
of management accounting research: the principal–agent, the transaction costs and
the Rochester school. The principal–agent model typically takes the organization of
the firm as given and concentrates on the choice of ex ante employment contracts
and information systems (Parporato 2011). The objective of the Rochester model is
to understand how agency problems arise and how they can be mitigated by contractual and more generally by organizational design (Parporato 2011; Boučková
2015).

Shields (1997) summarized and analysed the research carried out in North
America in the 1990s which was related to cost accounting, cost management,
management accounting, and MCSs. He found that the agency theory was the

economic theory applied most frequently in management accounting and MCSs research.

The agency theory principles also served as strong arguments explaining the consequences of the contemporary performance measurement systems that include organizational capabilities, behaviour, and performance (Franco-Santos et al. 2012). In this context, the agency theory focused on explaining especially two phenomena. Firstly, it was used to justify how multi-criteria performance measures enhance organizational performance by helping to reduce the information asymmetry. Secondly, the lessons learned using the agency theory were applied when searching for meaningful answers to the question of why the use of performance measures for individual performance evaluation and compensation is required in order to increase agents' motivation and focus on principals' goals (Franco-Santos et al. 2012).

The approach to MCSs in the agency theory context was not only praised but also became the subject of criticism. One of the weaknesses of the agency theory proved to be the negligence of the principle of contract creation between agents and principals. The theory also fails to address the trade-offs connected to other elements of MCS (Chenhall 2003), as research has so far focused primarily on the issue of incentives.

The main task of management accounting, and MCS such as, is to monitor and detect the unwanted behaviour of agents (especially managers) and regulate their behaviour in the desired manner through a system of incentives (Boučková 2015), which is linked to the tools of management accounting or performance measurement and management systems.

It is, however, necessary to consider whether MCS is really a suitable candidate for a monitoring system in terms of the agency theory. There are, indeed, doubts about who is actually able to control MCS or even manipulate it for his own benefit. In other words, it is problematic that in the relationship between the management and the owner, it is in most cases the management (the agent) who chooses the form of the monitoring system, which can support the information asymmetry. In contrast to that, the principal is usually the one who finances the monitoring system and monitoring costs may become secondary agency costs characterized by low efficiency, not to mention the final impact on the overall business performance.

In theory, more situations may occur. The agent either selects a monitoring system in order to ensure his own interests and successfully hide his opportunistic behaviour, and the principal should then strive to minimize the costs associated with the running of MCS. Another scenario involves agents and principals, selecting the monitoring system together. In rare situations, the agent selects a monitoring system which closely monitors his behaviour in order to inform the principal about his effort. This is a certain form of signalling behaviour.

The agent and the principal can fully or partially cooperate when selecting MCS or SPMS, or the agent and the principal can decide about the selection independently. The agent and the principal use their superiority or their position of power when deciding about the fundamental issues relating to the implementation or innovation of MCS. In addition, more agents or more principals with different power positions can participate in deciding about the selection of MCS. They may or may not be inclined to cooperate. Agents can, moreover, involve other agents in the selection and implementation, in relation to whom they are in the position of principals, often against the wishes of their own principals. For example, managers can collaborate with subordinates against owners (the employees are in the position of an agent in relation to the managers and owners and the manager as the principal is more important for them than the owner). It can be concluded that the type of agent and principal has an impact on the efficiency and effectiveness of MCS because there is a difference between who decides about MCS, who pays the cost of its operation, and who actually uses it.

No other theory is as rich as the agency theory in explaining the reasons for developing management control systems, considering their elements, and how they can be effectively established in various organizations (Namazi 2013).

Namazi (2013) looked at ways of using the agency theory to monitor the manager (agent). The agent can be monitored either only based on the results of his activity, or it is possible to additionally monitor his efforts, or it is also possible to include the influence of other factors. Namazi (2013) found that the implementation of a control mechanism depends on how accessible the information associated with the control is for the agent and the principal. He also proposed the fundamental roles played by the agency theory in the implementation of MCS. The agency theory provides an accurate quantitative, mathematically based model which explains why monitoring is important, why it should be reflected in the organizational structure of the company and why it creates the need to seek and construct performance indicators. The answer is so that the efforts and outputs of the agent or other stakeholder groups can be monitored, and this monitoring role is associated with the development of management accounting or MCS directly. The agency theory also fulfils the allocation role and thus provides an efficient mechanism for the allocation of resources in the company. Finally, the agency theory provides a mathematical demonstration of the importance of MCS in an environment of uncertainty and changing conditions. It also takes into account other (behavioural) aspects of management control implementation and enables counterparties to close optimal contracts in various situations, including the offer of the control mechanism and adherence to them (Namazi 2013).

The main weakness of the roles outlined above is that they are more agent-oriented and do not allow for an alternative to agents' automatic cooperative approach. In other words, they do not take into account the contribution and activity of principals, nor the agent's need to also see principals' effort and the way in which they participate in the resulting benefit.

Atkinson et al. (1997) believed that the owners' wealth can be generated by achieving stakeholders' secondary goals. Although these authors base their article on the relationship between the company and its stakeholders, the results of their research can be reflected in the concept of MCSs viewed through the lens of the agency theory. Secondary objectives of the company are measured by various performance measures which provide information on the extent to which stakeholders' requirements are satisfied. According to Atkinson et al. (1997), SPMS thus fulfils a diagnostic, monitoring, and coordinating role. In other words, SPMS is used to monitor the mutual contracts between the company representatives and stakeholders, in which expectations of all parties are specified, and mutual benefits are balanced in such a way that neither party has any desire to end the relationship. This means that the company is actually attempting to show signalling behaviour that will not only allow it to find out what is done for stakeholders, but this information may also be indirectly provided to stakeholders. Stakeholders can act as both principals and agents. As agents, stakeholders can learn about their share on the common benefit and what was the effort necessary to achieve it. As principals, stakeholders acquire information on whether the company acts in accordance with their own interests and about the costs incurred in order to obtain such information, taking into account the fact that the monitoring costs are taken over by the company. SPMS thus fulfils the function of a monitoring system for both sides, i.e., both for the company represented by management and for other stakeholders. SPMS fulfils this function for both sides in keeping with the agency theory, and both parties also enter into the position of a principal and an agent, often at the same time.

Atkinson et al. (1997) further defined the conditions under which individual stakeholders break contact with the company and lose interest in long-term contracts and cooperation. Atkinson et al. (1997) also listed the reasons for ending the relationship, claiming that SPMS should ensure that does not happen and that stakeholders' requirements are satisfied, and they have no reason to leave the company.

In the classical concept of the agency theory, the company would be in the position of an agent, monitored in some way by the principals (stakeholders). But here the company in fact monitors itself as the agent in order to eliminate the risk that principals will leave it. It is not the principal, but the agent himself who in this case tries to prevent his own opportunistic behaviour, because he is afraid that the outcome of his opportunistic behaviour would be smaller than if he acts also in the interest of the principal. The agent himself, unfortunately, is not capable of sufficiently controlling his behaviour (e.g. due to the lack of morale or his own incompetence), and therefore, voluntarily uses an external control instrument, which is represented by SPMS, or MCS.

A somewhat different situation can occur if we assume the validity of the so-called stewardship theory. According to this theory, the agent's behaviour is not opportunistic but cooperative and characterized by a collective approach. Agents (mainly managers) are called stewards and prefer mutual trust and cooperative behaviour because it leads to increased organizational performance, thereby fulfilling their own needs. Stewards thus have greater benefit from cooperative approach than from self-interest approach (Davis 1997). It is difficult for principals to estimate in advance whether agents will remain opportunistic agents, or whether they will tend to cooperate, and which of them will. Davis (1997) defined the factors that determine the process of selecting an agent, some of which are the same as the contingency factors of MCSs (e.g. culture). On this basis, he formulates four possible combinations of agents and principals, who prefer self-interest or cooperation, when the principal's and agent's decision to enter into a stewardship relationship together leads to minimizing monitoring costs and maximizing business performance. If one party decides to join the stewardship relationship and the other does not, the first party feels frustrated and betrayed (Davis 1997).

It is worth considering whether MCS has the potential to help in distinguishing stewards from opportunistic agents, and if the agent decides not to prefer self-interest, the effect it has on MCS and on the agency costs. Should the principal respond to this inverse situation? If monitoring costs have already been incurred, does he not undergo an unnecessary risk? Is it not easier to assume that all counterparties remain selfish agents and expect opportunistic behaviour from them in advance (ex ante)? On the other hand, there is a certain likelihood that secondary agency costs (mainly the costs of control) will not substitute the primary agency costs to such an extent since the primary costs will not be so high due to the non-standard approach of the agent and the trade-off between the primary and secondary costs will suddenly be the opposite of what is desirable, which means that the secondary agency costs will actually be expended in vain.

48.4 MCS Functions Derived from the Agency Theory

The use of MCS in a company should ensure a balance between principals' and agents' utility which will be acceptable to both parties, i.e., neither party will need to raise its benefit at the expense of the other party. In other words, the benefits for both sides will be optimized. There are a number of pairs of principals and agents in the company. Their position in a certain role is not stable since their position changes with the membership of the counterparties in various, but also the same, coalitions with different interests. A coalition can thus be formed across the company, often bearing no relation to the traditional roles in the company. In addition, the company is also affected by its surroundings, and this influence is mutual.

An appropriate MCS should support signalling behaviour which bridges the differences between the more-informed and the less-informed parties on the market or in a mutual relationship. As a result, the risk of adverse selection will be reduced. The MCS should also facilitate the redistribution of risk between principals and agents in order to eliminate the possibility of moral hazard, but also make it possible to distribute utility between the counterparties in a proportion corresponding to the risk distribution.

Another function of MCS should focus on distributing the benefits between principals and agents in such a way that the positive effect of reward for the agent exceeds the negative effect resulting from his own efforts. The agent's benefit resulting from his own efforts should therefore have a stronger impact on his utility than the negative effect of his efforts. At the same time, the principal's benefit reduced by the agent's reward and monitoring costs (costs associated with the implementation, running, and innovation of MCS) must still remain acceptable for the principal.

MCS should contribute at least partially to reducing the random factors that influence negatively the final effect of agents' activity and tend to reduce agents' utility. Random factors are reflected in the increasing difficulty and at the same time limit the range of benefits that can be generated by agents' activities for both agents and the principal. In this case, it is not entirely clear whether MCS is even able to fulfil this function. This function could probably be achieved by an appropriate combination of two approaches to the concept of MCSs, i.e., the agency theory and the contingency approach. Contextual factors, which are presented, for example, by Chenhall (2003), and which determine the final form and applied methods in MCS, in fact include random effects such as the company's external environment, company growth, and technological influences.

MCSs should also maintain an acceptable ratio between the primary and secondary agency costs and transformation of various forms of benefits between principals and agents with the lowest possible costs of benefit redistribution. There is, however, the problem of measurability and verifiability of both types of agency costs, including their development, i.e., there is a question whether the assumption of the slower growth of the secondary costs with the rapid decline of primary agency costs will hold indefinitely or only until a certain level of primary costs is reached. It is simplest to consider a convex curve showing the evolution of these costs in graphic terms, where the proportion of mutual cost transformation is high at the beginning (when PAC is high) but later declines with the decreasing volume of primary costs.

Within the stewardship theory, MCS can function in three ways. MCS will make it easier to differentiate between agents and stewards and will provide this information to principals. This means that the secondary agency costs will be spent more effectively. Another two functions are based on the fact that MCS will facilitate the selection for agents and motivate them to the change from the agent to the steward, or MCS will contribute to the growth of organizational performance of the company, leading to a voluntary transition from the position of an agent to the position of a steward. While the first function seems somewhat controversial, the other two functions seem feasible in practical terms. Despite that, these functions may be counterproductive since the relations between agents and principals are subject to dynamic changes, and usually are neither their first nor last relations of this type. If either of the counterparties has already voluntarily decided to participate in a stewardship relationship and was deceived by the other party which decided to maintain an agency relationship, then the first party will automatically reject a bond based on cooperation and trust in every relationship that follows.

The likelihood that the above-mentioned functions will be realized will grow on condition that the basic principles and theoretical assumptions of the agency theory or the stewardship theory (if free choice on the part of agents and principals to enter into a stewardship relationship is possible) are fulfilled.

MCS should be associated with the lowest possible costs of monitoring agents' activities, the costs of detecting secret activities, and the costs to bridge the lack of information on the part of principals, but also agents, in the event that informational disadvantage occurs on their side. MCS should also make it possible to reduce these costs in the future.

It is also necessary to ensure the validity of the assumption of mutual cooperation during the selection, implementation and running of MCS, at least for those groups of agents and principals, who can significantly interfere with the running of the company. Unfortunately, there are a number of agents and principals who have the opportunity to contribute to the company's prosperity and are at the same time able to seriously threaten the future development and prosperity of the company. It may not be acceptable to allow that all agents contribute to the design and implementation of MCS. In addition, there is still the unresolved issue of the costs of MCS, i.e., to what extent the right to participate on the decision-making and implementation of MCS should be compensated by the obligation to participate also on covering the costs associated with MCS. Combining the agency theory with the stakeholder theory (Mitchell et al. 1997) of the company could reduce the instability of this requirement by assigning attributes of importance, closeness, or danger to individual principals and agents, which will make it possible to organize them into a hierarchy in relation to the question of their involvement in the implementation and funding of MCS.

Finally, it should be clearly and unequivocally defined who finances MCS, who uses the information provided by MCS, who works with it and who has benefit from its application in the company. At the same time, it should be clear whether the person or group is in the position of a principal, an agent, or a steward to the company and other parties or whether he is a member of any company coalitions.

48.5 Conclusion

The analysis which was conducted does not show that the agency theory is the best theoretical basis when formulating and applying MCSs or SPMSs. However, it does not indicate or insist that the theory is absolutely inappropriate or outdated either. It only looks for new ways in which it could be possible to apply it within MCSs, especially when detecting and formulating functions that MCS should be more or less able to ensure in order for its output to be adequate in terms of both the company and other groups of agents and principals connected to the company. Such groups may be part of the company's internal or external environment, and the company itself is in the position of a principal, an agent, or a steward in relation to them.

Future research could continue to focus on verifying the functions of MCSs in the context of the agency theory in practical terms. It could extend or modify the set of potential functions of MCSs or identify other conditions for the effective functioning of MCSs and the successful achievement of its desired functions. The conditions which will be reflected in the design, innovation, structure, and final application of MCSs, including the assessment of the degree of probability of the assumptions mentioned in this paper or new assumptions in business practice, could also be subject to further investigation.

In addition, this research attempted to outline other alternatives of applying the agency theory in combination with the contingency approach and other theoretical bases (psychological, stakeholder theory). These approaches implemented (considered) together can provide a broadened view of the ever-evolving and improving concept of MCSs.

On the other hand, as Parporato (2011) claims, the agency theory—as well as the popular contingency approach to MCSs—falls under the functionalist paradigm. The functionalist perspective is, however, criticized because it assumes that a company responds in a stable way to conditions (contextual factors) changing over time. Therefore, if the integration of approaches to MCSs or a combination of the approaches of the agency and contingency approach does not overcome this functionalist paradigm, then the contribution of future research in this area will be highly questionable.

Acknowledgments This paper has been prepared under financial support of the Internal Grant Agency of the University of Economics, Prague, Grant No. F1/13/2015, which author gratefully acknowledges.

References

Akerlof GA (1970) The market for "lemons": quality uncertainty and the market mechanism. Q J Econ 84(3):488–500. doi:10.1007/978-1-349-24002-9_9

Atkinson AA, Waterhouse JH, Robert BW (1997) A Stakeholder Approach to Strategic Performance Measurement. Sloan Manag Rev 28(3):25–37

Baiman S (1990) Agency research in managerial accounting: a second look. Acc Organ Soc 15 (4):341–371. doi:10.1016/0361-3682(90)90023-N

Baxter JA, Chua WF (2003) Alternative management accounting research—whence and whither. Acc Organ Soc 28(2–3):97–126. doi:10.1016/S0361-3682(02)00022-3

Bititci U, Garengo P, Dörfler V, Nudurupati S (2012) Performance measurement: challenges for tomorrow. Int J Manage Rev 14(3):305–327. doi:10.1111/j.1468-2370.2011.00318.x

Boučková M (2015) Management accounting and agency theory. Procedia Econ Finan 25:5–13. doi:10.1016/S2212-5671(15)00707-8

Chenhall RH (2003) Management control systems design within its organizational context: findings from contingency-based research and directions for the future. Acc Organ Soc 28:127–168. doi:10.1016/S0361-3682(01)00027-7

Covaleski MA, Dirsmith MW, Samuel S (1996) Managerial accounting research: the contributions of organizational and sociological theories. J Manage Acc Res 8:1–35

Davis JH (1997) Toward a stewardship theory of management. Acad Manag Rev 22(1):20–47. doi:10.5465/AMR.1997.9707180258

Dirsmith MW, Covaleski MA, McAllister JP (1985) Of paradigms and metaphors in auditing thought. Contemp Acc Res 2(1):46–68. doi:10.1111/j.1911-3846.1985.tb00606.x

Drury C (2012) Management and cost accounting. Cengage Learning EMEA, Andover (Hampshire)

Franco-Santos M, Lucianetti L, Bourne M (2012) Contemporary performance measurement systems: a review of their consequences and a framework for research: challenges for Tomorrow. Manage Acc Res 23(2):79–119. doi:10.1016/j.mar.2012.04.001

Jensen MC (2000) A theory of the firm: governance, residual claims, and organizational forms. Harvard University Press, Cambridge

Jensen MC, Meckling WH (1976) Theory of the firm: managerial behavior, agency costs, and ownership structure. J Financ Econ 3(4):305–360. doi:10.1016/0304-405X(76)90026-X

Jönsson S, Macintosh NB (1997) Cats, rats, and ears: making the case for ethnographic accounting research. Acc Organ Soc 22(3/4):367–386. doi:10.1016/S0361-3682(96)00040-2

Král B (2010) Manažerské účetnictví. Management Press, Praha

Macintosh NB (1994) Management accounting and control systems: an organizational and behavioral approach. Wiley, New York

Marek P (2007) Vliv teorie zastoupení na teorii podnikových financí. Český finanční a účetní časopis 2(2):6–16

Mitchell RK, Agle BR, Wood DJ (1997) Toward a theory of stakeholder identification and salience: defining the principle of who and what really counts. Acad Manag Rev 22(4):853–886. doi:10.5465/AMR.1997.9711022105

Namazi M (2013) Role of the agency theory in implementing management's control. J Acc Taxation 5(3):38–47. doi:10.5897/JAT11.032

Parporato M (2011) Management control systems' literature development: theoretical approaches and critiques within the functionalist paradigm. Rev Universo Contábil 7(2):146–173. doi:10.4270/ruc.2011218

Shields MD (1997) Research in management accounting by North Americans in the 1990s. J Manage Acc Res 9:3–61

Shields MD, Young SM (1993) Antecedents and consequences of participative budgeting: evidence on the effects of asymmetrical information. J Manage Acc Res 5:265–280

Simons RL (1995) Levers of control: how managers use innovative control systems to drive strategic renewal. Harvard Business School Press Book, Boston

Sundin HJ, Brown DP, Booth PJ (2008) Perspectives on multiple stakeholders and management control systems institutional and stakeholder theory: friend or foe? In: 31st Annual congress european accounting association conference website papers. European Accounting Association (EAA), pp 1–20

Šiška L (2015) The concept of management control system and its relation to performance measurement. Procedia Econ Finan 25:141–147. doi:10.1016/S2212-5671(15)00722-4

Williamson OE (1964) The economics of discretionary behavior: managerial objectives in a theory of the firm. Prentice-Hall, Englewood Cliffs

Chapter 49
Sustainable Controlling: Measuring Method Based on the Catalogue of Controller Tasks

Michał Chalastra, Anna Siemionek and Roman Kotapski

Abstract The process of financial controlling implementation is a very complex project. It requires coordination of many activities from various spheres. Following works should be conducted within different areas such as financial and management accounting, organization management, informatics and education. During its implementation, one should involve people representing key areas of the company from many departments. Not only employees of the company but also external consultants should be engaged in that process. The aim of the article is to identify methods of measuring the correctness of financial controlling according to the concept of sustainable development. One of the ways to perform the implementation correctly is to obey the rule of sustainable development. The concept is based on the rule of sustainable balanced scorecard. In that situation, perspectives aiming goals and implemented actions should be adapted to the requirements of the specific nature of this type of project. These perspectives should be relevant to the category of their activities. It is not correct to carry out the process in an unsustainable way. This situation reveals in failure to perform certain tasks or insufficient implementation. Therefore, it is worth to develop methods measuring balanced implementation of such projects. This measurement can be done by analyzing the amount of time of specific tasks and their costs. The concomitant usage of these two categories

M. Chalastra
Department of Accounting, University of Gdansk, ul. Armii Krajowej 101,
81-824 Sopot, Poland
e-mail: michal.ch@nord-controlling.com.pl

A. Siemionek (✉)
Department of Corporate Finance, University of Gdansk,
ul. Armii Krajowej 101, 81-824 Sopot, Poland
e-mail: anna.siemionek@wzr.ug.edu.pl

R. Kotapski
Department of Management Accouning, Wrocław University of Economics,
Komandorska 118/120, 53-345 Wrocław, Poland
e-mail: roman.kotapski@ue.wroc.pl

© Springer International Publishing AG 2017
D. Procházka (ed.), *New Trends in Finance and Accounting*,
Springer Proceedings in Business and Economics,
DOI 10.1007/978-3-319-49559-0_49

537

of measures is due to the fact that the cost parameters are often difficult to determine. Some of the tasks are carried out by the company's employees who implement controlling system. Valuation of the costs is not free from subjective
assumptions. Determination of the time performing specific tasks does not also
provide clear information. This is due to the fact that there is a possibility to find
significant deviations between planned and actual data. It is moreover worth to
measure the degree of sustainable controlling system implementation using two
categories of measures at the same time. It is also determined by the fact weather
the measurement will be conducted on the basis of the data available with the
planned budget and actual one.

Keywords Controlling · Sustainable development · Management accounting

49.1 Introduction

The aim of the article is to present methods of examining the condition of functioning financial controlling within sustainable development. Measurement of
sustainable development is taken by tasks which are dedicated to that system. The
article has been written on the basis of the data obtained during interviews conducted among employees of companies which use financial controlling system and
companies that can pride themselves on using good practices in that system.

49.2 Tasks of Modern Controlling

At the beginning of the twentieth century, financial controllers were already hired in
American enterprises. It does not mean that those specialists were absent in companies before, but it was not that popular. It was quite rare to hire them before that
time. Controlling as a professional specialization has the history of more than a
hundred years. Thus, we can come to conclusion that it is a mature field of management. It is therefore important to specify which tasks should be realized by
contemporary financial controller. Identification of these tasks is not a new issue.
Controller's Institute of America which was founded in 1931 was the first one who
developed the list of controller tasks (Nesterak 2013, p. 37–54, 2015, p. 29–41;
Drury 1996, p. 14–15; Weber 2001, p. 2–18).

According to this catalogue, financial controller should be responsible for the
following tasks such as

- planning,
- internal reporting,
- external reporting,
- process optimization,

- internal consulting,
- strategic analysis,
- economic education.

Due to the development of controlling, since the time when the catalogue of controlling was defined, last additional task such as economic education should be introduced.

Planning—Activities related to the operation of the whole planning system should be the part of that task. It relates both to strategic and operational planning. These tasks should not only include plans performed periodically such as the annual budget but also occasional types of projects such as budgets of projects and investments.

Controllers should be, however, responsible for the development of a planning system and then supervising the correctness of its functioning.

Internal reporting—This task consists of activities related to forwarding the management information to managers of various organizational units. These activities can be divided into regular and occasional. Cyclical are those which are carried out regularly. The most important is the analysis of budget implementation. The tasks which are carried out occasionally are reporting on the special requests of the manager.

External reporting—Within this task, activities related to the creation and transmission of economic information about the company toward external organizations are included. This information is mainly the part of management accounting system. This part of reports is not created for statistical office or tax authorities.

Process optimization—The tasks and activities of financial controller are based on continuous analysis of economic parameters defining the processes implemented in the company and the available resources. Numerical parameters defining these processes, such as indicators of the level of unit costs, productivity, profitability and potential, are analyzed. The size of these indicators should be comparable to the so-called good practice.

The task of controlling is to observe constantly these indicators in terms of value achieved in the company and the standard size. In case of detection of adverse conditions, the role of financial controller is to initiate optimization measures.

Internal consulting—Controlling department plays a consultative role for the managers of responsibility centers. Implementation of tasks from this area is complementary to the activities related with internal reporting.

Strategic analysis—Within this task, it is important to create a comprehensive system of strategic analysis and then implementation of tasks related to its practical functioning.

These tasks are associated with the existence of strategic planning systems. Department of controlling is responsible for the functioning of the planning area. It is also responsible for well-organized functioning of the strategic planning system.

Controlling should not deal with strategic planning. The plans are developed by managers responsible for each specific strategy.

Economic education—It is a new task for controllers which is not included originally in the US directory. The need for it has occurred due to the following factors:

- high decentralization of management,
- center managers use more and more advanced management tools,
- controlling the usage of tools by specialists from other organizational units than the control department.

Today's requirements for controlling require the use of sophisticated tools mainly in the field of management accounting. Controllers should also systematically improve their knowledge. So, it becomes necessary to undertake educational activities (Kotapski 2014, p. 333–335).

49.3 Sustainable Controlling

Controlling tasks presented above can be divided into two following categories:

- administrative,
- developmental.

The administrative tasks are characterized by carrying out activities concerning creating various types of reports. This could be planned budgets and reports with analysis of their conduction. The purpose of their implementation is mainly to present the data. These actions may present a lack of creative development. The preparation of the report does not always cause the realization of companies' objectives focused on its development.

Developmental tasks tend to have a completely different character. Their aim is not only technical data reporting but also improving active eager to improve results. Thus, the controllers should analyze available information in order to correct the results. The values appearing in the company are compared with so-called good practices. This can be internal data of the company. This allows functioning of good practices within the company. Another source of reference data are external ones. This can be competitive units or leaders recognized in a particular field of activity. In this case, the aim is to reach best practices. Controlling actions to optimize the result should be implemented in both strategic and operational perspectives. Therefore, data regarding the entire enterprise such as financial statement should be analyzed. This may be also information about individual processes or even the resources and the activities. When the controllers detect that they have still potential left, they should actively improve their results using optimization measures. All these activities should be carried out in a well-organized and continuous way (Dobroszek and Szychta 2009, p. 38–40).

Table 49.1 Division of controlling tasks divided into administrative and developmental

Controlling tasks	Category of controlling tasks
Planning	Administrative
Internal reporting	
External reporting	
Process optimization	Developmental
Internal consulting	
Strategic analysis	
Economic education	

Source Own work

In Table 49.1, the division of controlling tasks divided into two categories in which the dominate ones are administrative and developmental has been presented. There should be highlighted that this classification is not at all clear. In practice, due to the allocation of specific activities, there are tasks which may have a different classification. If a group of controller tasks has been designated into administrative category, it does not mean that it does not pursue development tasks as well. That is why the presented division should therefore be considered as an indicative analysis.

One of the signs of a sustainable functioning of controlling is the implementation of all above-mentioned tasks. One activity should not be developed more significantly at expense of other activities. This situation should be considered as a lack of sustainable controlling. In practice, in many Polish companies, controllers very often realize mainly administrative tasks, whereas they realize development activities to a limited extent. This mentioned situation is caused by the following factors:

- limitation of mainly personal resources,
- lack of knowledge about the developmental tasks,
- lack of good practices controllers' patterns.

The consequence of such a situation can be a negative assessment of the effectiveness of the entire controlling system. It generates significantly both direct and indirect costs. Direct costs are as follows:

- employees maintenance,
- department maintenance,
- costs of information systems dedicated to controlling,
- costs of special activities undertaken by controlling for other organizational units.

Indirect costs are also important for functioning of the controlling system. The most important one of them should include the time spent by managers of centers of responsibility for carrying out the tasks imposed on them due to operating of the controlling system. When the costs are extremely high, controlling may not give expected results. Due to this reason, in many Polish and not only companies, there is a conviction that the controlling system is inefficient. Expenses carried out for its implementation and operation are disproportionate to the expected benefits. There can even occur the desire to liquidate it. One of the important reasons of this situation is that there is a predominance of administrative tasks which causes the lack of sustainability of the controlling system.

49.4 Sustainable Controlling Measures

Income and expenses for the audited activity should be defined for this purpose. For measurement of the effects of the controlling, it is theoretically possible to identify both types of parameters. Revenues generated by the controlling can still determine the revenue growth of the company as a result of this system. The company's costs due to the controlling actions can be also reduced. The costs will, however, be determined as direct and indirect costs generated by the actions of controlling system. Precise identification of these items for controlling is, however, impossible in practice. It is therefore impossible to determine to what extent the income or expenses changed the company's result. This is due to the fact that too many factors influence on that. To sum up, the lack of possibility to establish as indisputable revenues and costs which have arisen as a result of the operation of controlling means that simple parameters determining the profitability should not be used to evaluate the activity of this system. Another category of measurement parameters used in the economy is costs. It is possible to determine the total costs generated by the controlling system. They are therefore direct and indirect costs of this management system. In order to determine the direct costs, it is sufficient to establish an independent cost center and record all incurred costs. Techniques activity-based costing (ABC) enable the determination of the indirect costs of the system controlling. Determined in this way costs relate to maintenance of the whole system. This method does not identify, however, the costs related to the execution of individual tasks. Analysis of costs for these tasks will only to determine the degree of balance controlling. However, the activity-based costing method (ABC) allows dividing these costs. In this case, the direct costs are usually calculated by the settlement costs which are performed by department controlling. The allocation of costs should be implemented using individual work time tasks for its implementation what is presented in Table 49.2.

At the level of the controlling department, the analysis of the results should therefore be held on the basis of synthetic data from the main items presented according to the catalogue of controller tasks. The data recorded for individual tasks should be added up to a synthetic position according to its catalogue. The research should consist of determining the structure of working time percentage spent on the specific tasks of controlling. In theory, the ideal situation would be when there would be the same amount of working hours for each task. Such a situation would be considered as ideal one. Unfortunately, in practice, such a situation is very rare to happen. In particular periods, when the analysis is formed, the intensity of actions would be different. Therefore, the conclusions should be done based on the data for a longer period. It is particularly worth to analyze dynamics of various

Table 49.2 Process of costs allocating for the tasks realized by the controlling department

The annual costs of maintaining the controlling department	The potential cost of 1 man-work in controlling department	Number of working hours	Individual tasks realized by controllers	Synthetic category tasks in accordance with the catalog of controller tasks	Total number of working hours	Structure %
		→	A-1	→		
		→	A-2	→ A		
		→	A..	→		
		→	B-1	→		
		→	B-2	→ B		
		→	B..	→		
		→	C..	→ C		
				Total		

Source Own work

positions. During interpreting the results, in addition, supplementary information about qualitative measures should be considered. As they can even change the assessment done on the basis of quantitative data, such an example might be a situation when the reduction of development activities in relation to administration ones is observed. This situation theoretically should be considered as undesirable. On the other hand, it can be caused by a very large range of development activities in previous periods. This could happen due to the fact of implementation of such tools in the company so there is no longer justification for continuing to devote so much time for such operations (Table 49.3).

As it was already mentioned, all the costs of controlling system are regarded costs for other organizational units of the execution of controlling tasks. These are usually cost related to working staff time which is involved. In this case, it is also important to determine the costs of controlling system dividing them into individual tasks. Determination of costs should be performed according to the rules described by activity-based costing (ABC). The process of cost allocation should be made on the basis of the same rules as for the controlling department. Summing up those two categories of costs would only give the total cost of controlling system. The identification of those costs is presented in Table 49.4.

The process of determining the degree of sustainability of the controlling should take place not only on the basis of cost parameters but also according to the time. The costs are determined by applying different rates per hour of operation in particular departments. In order to determine controlling costs correctly, it is necessary to identify cost centers according to the rules of management accounting. Items related to the staff maintenance must be included in a separate cost center.

Table 49.3 Table measuring the degree of sustainability of controlling system at the level of the controlling department based on the analysis of working time related to the execution of standard tasks

Controlling tasks	Number of working hours	Previous period		Current period		Dynamics of changes in %
		Number of working hours	Structure %	Number of working hours	Structure %	
Administrative	Planning					
	Internal reporting					
	External reporting					
	Total (administrative tasks)					
Developmental	Process optimization					
	Internal consulting					
	Strategic analysis					
	Economic education					
	Total (development tasks)					
Total						

Source Own work

Table 49.4 Identification of costs of controlling system divided into realized tasks

Controlling tasks	Costs of controlling department	Costs of other departments related to controlling tasks	Total costs of controlling system	Structure %
Planning				
Internal reporting				
External reporting				
Process optimization				
Internal consulting				
Strategic analysis				
Economic education				
Total				

Source Own work

These are the so-called personal cost centers. They include all the items related to the maintenance of a specific group of employees such as labor costs, office supplies, training and information technology. One should not include such costs as maintaining the technical potential of production equipment or real estates (Chalastra 2014, p. 173–188). However, the analysis of working time may benefit with important information. One should bear in mind that one hour of working time of expensive specialists is not equivalent to an hour of work of less skilled workers.

49.5 Conclusion

The proposed process of cost accounting method activity-based costing (ABC) is based on the generally applicable rules. The key issue is, however, to determine the details of making the settlement. Due to the lack of standardization, it is necessary to measure the amount of hours spent on various tasks. This measurement can be taken regularly every month. This method is, however, not applicable in practice due to following disadvantages:

- large commitment of work time of many people,
- high costs,
- lack of reliability.

Analysis of the degree of sustainability of financial controlling activities on a monthly basis does not bring practical benefits. It can even provide with misleading information. It is because of the fact that there are periods when the activities are mostly homogeneous as it is for example during budget planning. To sum up, this expensive and laborious measurement can lead to unreliable conclusions. For this reason, it is worth to propose costing for longer period of time. A good solution would be also six months or a year. Distribution of hours worked on each task should be done by expert method. In this case, the employees basing on their own experience would determine their working time. The account be characterized by a lack of precision. The actual situation may differ from the one reported in the research. The results, however, seem to be reliable enough to be a base to make adjustments to the rules of controlling system. Another important issue is the period for which the analysis is performed. According to the proposal, this analysis should be performed for a longer period of time. The aim of measurement of sustainability controlling is to optimize its functioning. These are strategic activities, and there is a high need of investment and time. To sum up, today's controlling system must perform different tasks. It is important that the degree of involvement of the potential of their performance is balanced. This condition can be called sustainable controlling system. It is one of the reasons why that system is considered to be effective. Measurement of controlling balance is not an easy task, and the results obtained are accurate. Today's economic reality requires, however, to carry out this kind of researches and investigations.

References

Chalastra M (2014) Identyfikacja centrów kosztów w rachunkowości finansowej a zarządczej. Zarządzanie i finanse rok 12 nr 2, czerwiec 2014, Wydział Zarządzania Uniwersytetu Gdańskiego Sopot

Dobroszek J, Szychta A. (2009) Koncepcyjny i ewolucyjny wymiar controllingu, Zeszyty teoretyczne rachunkowości, tom 52(108), Warszawa

Drury C (1996) Management and cost accounting. Thomson Business Press, wydanie 4, London

Kotapski R (2014) Budżetowanie w zarządzaniu przedsiębiorstwem budowlano-montażowym. Wydawnictwo MARINA, Wrocław

Nesterak J (2013) Ewolucja controllingu w Polsce i na świecie, Zeszyty Naukowe Uniwersytet Ekonomiczny w Krakowie Zarządzanie 905, Kraków

Nesterak J (2015) Controlling zarządczy. Projektowanie i wdrażanie, Wyd. Oficyna a Wolter Kluwer business, Warszawa

Weber J (2001) Wprowadzenie do controlling, Wyd. Oficyna Controllingu Profit, Katowice

Chapter 50
Empirical Study of Approach to Sustainability Management and Reporting in the Czech and Slovak Republic

Petr Petera, Jaroslav Wagner and Renáta Pakšiová

Abstract The paper examines an approach to the sustainability management and reporting of the large companies established in the Czech or Slovak Republic from selected industrial sectors. Investigated is also correlation between selected factors and relevance of sustainability for companies. Data were collected via web-based questionnaire, and we obtained 63 answers from Czech companies and 41 answers from Slovak companies. Slovak companies outperform Czech companies in most researched areas. Possible explanation of this difference is the fact that companies in the sample from the Slovak Republic are more multinational.

Keywords Sustainability management · Sustainability reporting · Understanding sustainability · GRI

50.1 Introduction

Sustainable development is usually defined as "development that meets the needs of the present without compromising the ability of future generations to meet their own needs" (WCED 1987), and according to numerous scholars and surveys (e.g. KPMG 2013), importance of addressing sustainability is increasing.

P. Petera (✉) · J. Wagner
Department of Management Accounting, University of Economics, Prague,
W. Churchill Sq. 1938/4, 130 67 Prague 3, Czech Republic
e-mail: petr.petera@vse.cz

J. Wagner
e-mail: wagner@vse.cz

R. Pakšiová
Department of Accountancy and Auditing, University of Economics in Bratislava,
Dolnozemská Cesta 1, 852 35 Bratislava, Slovak Republic
e-mail: renata.paksiova@euba.sk

© Springer International Publishing AG 2017
D. Procházka (ed.), *New Trends in Finance and Accounting*,
Springer Proceedings in Business and Economics,
DOI 10.1007/978-3-319-49559-0_50

Rising importance of sustainability is accompanied with the continuous growth of literature on this topic. For example, Linnenluecke and Griffiths (2013, p. 382) mentioned that quantity of academic publications on corporate responsibility has been growing exponentially in recent years. In spite of large amount of both theoretically and empirically oriented literature, there is a research gap, which consists of relatively small amount of research aimed at sustainability understanding, management and reporting in Central-Eastern Europe (hereinafter abbreviated as CEE) countries. Moreover, for both Western European (hereinafter abbreviated as WE) and CEE countries, there is a lack of questionnaire-based empirical surveys into sustainability-related issues.

The main goal of this paper is to address this research gap by presenting and interpreting key results of original empirical research (questionnaire survey) aimed at understanding of sustainability, management of sustainability, sustainability accounting and reporting on sustainability in CEE countries. Specifically, we analyse answers of businesses from the Czech Republic (hereinafter abbreviated as CR) and the Slovak Republic (hereinafter abbreviated as SR). The second goal consists of presenting the preliminary results of investigation into factors influencing relevance of sustainability for businesses.

50.2 Literature Review

Although sustainability may be understood narrowly, such approach is scarce today. Both researchers and practitioners usually define corporate sustainability at least in terms of economic, environmental and social responsibility (traditional dimensions of sustainability). The importance of integrating of these traditional dimensions as well as the need for their balance is often mentioned in the contemporary literature (e.g. Hahn et al. 2015). Moreover, some authors (e.g. Epstein 2008, pp. 36–41) advocate yet broader understanding of sustainability and explicitly mention ethics, governance, transparency (i.e. disclosure of information on sustainability-related issues), business relationships, financial return, community involvement, value of products and services, employment practices and protection of the environment as important parts of sustainability. Another issue, which is often emphasized in both theory and practice, is the importance of promoting sustainability over and beyond the borders of an individual organization, i.e. spreading sustainable practices over the whole supply chain. Last but not least, the crucial role of integration of sustainability into corporate strategy is also discussed in the recent literature (Engert et al. 2016).

Fifka (2012, p. 45) mentioned that first reports on social and environmental activities of companies were published in the early 1970s. From the chronological viewpoint, Fifka (2012, pp. 62–63) summarized that focus of social and environmental reporting moved from social area (which was prevailing in 1970s) to environmental issues (during decade from 1990) and finally, after the turn of the millennium, to a broader reporting about both social and environmental issues (this kind of reports is often called "sustainability reports" or "corporate responsibility reports"). KPMG (2013, pp. 11–12) mentioned the following global trends in reporting: first, corporate responsibility reporting sees exceptional growth in emerging economies; second, there is a narrowing gap between leading and lagging industry sectors; third, 51% of companies worldwide include information about corporate responsibility into their annual financial reports; fourth, the use of the Global Reporting Initiative Guidelines is growing; fifth, 59% of the world's largest companies invest in external assurance of corporate responsibility reports. Sustainability reporting can be realized through various communication channels, e.g. press releases, regular annual reports, standalone sustainability reports, integrated reports, web pages. The most comprehensive reports are usually the sustainability standalone reports and the integrated reports. Although some companies disclose relatively comprehensive sustainability-related information also in their annual reports, research in the CR (Petera et al. 2014) showed that the published information often does not exceed legal requirements.

A specific research issue are key factors, which may influence approach of organizations to the area of sustainability management and reporting. In the literature (e.g. Athanasios et al. 2013), there are identified numerous such factors, for example, company size (measured, e.g. by sales or by average number of full-time employees), industry, type of ownership and multinational nature of a company. For the extent of sustainability reporting are crucial also mandatory requirements.

Last but not least, it is important to highlight that there are regional differences in sustainability management/reporting and in the amount of existing research on this topic. Specifically, numerous scholars highlight the existence of substantial differences between businesses from WE and CEE countries (especially due to the long-time attention paid to sustainability in WE in contrast to CEE countries, where sustainability is a relatively new topic). Fifka (2012, pp. 63–65) advocated that in WE countries are plentiful both social/environmental reporting per se and the research on this reporting. On the contrary, reporting in CEE countries is not so advanced and also research in this area is incomplete. Steurer and Konrad (2009, p. 24) proposed that the concept of corporate responsibility is not so well known among average businesses in new CEE countries and that the businesses that are most familiar with this concept are multinational ones. From the viewpoint of sustainability management and reporting, it is possible to suppose that CEE countries are relatively similar to each other and we therefore hypothesize that approach to the corporate responsibility should be similar in the CR and SR.

50.3 Methodology

Methodology is to a large extent determined by the fact that the presented research is a part of international project (managed by International Performance Research Institute), which is aimed at sustainability reporting and management in 10 CEE countries. The presented research has a quantitative character, and data were collected via a web survey and processed in IBM SPSS Statistics 23.

The analysis in this paper includes only businesses domiciled in the CR or in the SR, which met the following criteria: (more than 250 employees) and (turnover over EUR 50 Mio or balance sheet total over EUR 43 Mio) and (belonging to industries [NACE Rev. 2] under sections C—manufacturing, D—Electricity, gas, steam and air conditioning supply, F—Construction, G—Wholesale and retail trade; repair of motor vehicles and motor-cycles and J—Information). In the CR was utilized database Albertina and in the SR was utilized database Finstat. In the CR the dataset included 648 businesses, and in the SR the dataset included 261 businesses.

The survey started in June, 2015 and continued till November, 2015. To maximize the response rate, all respondents were reminded twice by email and if possible also by a phone.

The main features of the questionnaire were first designed by coordinator of the whole international project, and after comments and recommendations from researchers from individual participating countries was prepared the final version of the questionnaire in English and in individual national languages.

The final questionnaire contained 27 questions of various types (classifying questions as well as meritory questions; questions measured on nominal and ordinal scale; multiple choice questions with both single answer and multiple answers as well as open-ended questions); nevertheless, respondents were asked only the questions relevant to them thanks to the flow control, which was built into the questionnaire. These questions were divided into several groups, and in chapter "Results" are presented key outcomes of the survey.

50.4 Results

In total, we obtained 63 responses in the CR (response rate 9.72%) and 41 responses in the SR (response rate 15.71%). From the description of the process of data collection in the previous chapter, it is evident that our sample can be hardly classified as a random sample, because of the self-selection of our respondents. It is therefore necessary to be extremely cautious with any inferences from our sample to the whole population, and our sample can be understood as containing mainly large businesses with relatively high-quality approach to sustainability management and reporting. Results can be therefore interpreted as a comparison of "best practice" in the CR and SR. Basic characteristics of our respondents can be found in Table 50.1.

It is possible to summarize that the SR has higher percentage of respondents who operate in more than 5 countries than the CR and similar pattern can be found in the case of turnover and FTE (respondents from the SR are accumulated in higher categories). In our sample can be found 11 Czech respondents with turnover under EUR 50 Mio. This situation occurred probably because of the fact that the latest

Table 50.1 Basic characteristics of respondents

Value	CR+SR			CR			SR		
	FRQ	%	Cumulative %	FRQ	%	Cumulative %	FRQ	%	Cumulative %
Number of full-time employees in 2014									
1–249	0	0.0	0.0	0	0.0	0.0	0	0.0	0.0
250–499	20	19.2	19.2	12	19.0	19.0	8	19.5	19.5
500–999	43	41.3	60.6	30	47.6	66.7	13	31.7	51.2
1000–4999	33	31.7	92.3	17	27.0	93.7	16	39.0	90.2
Over 5000	8	7.7	100.0	4	6.3	100.0	4	9.8	100.0
Total	104	100.0		63	100.0		41	100.0	
Turnover in 2014 (Mio EUR)									
1–49	11	10.6	10.6	11	17.5	17.5	0	0.0	0.0
50–99	34	32.7	43.3	19	30.2	47.6	15	36.6	36.6
100–499	38	36.5	79.8	25	39.7	87.3	13	31.7	68.3
Over 500	21	20.2	100.0	8	12.7	100.0	13	31.7	100.0
Total	104	100.0		63	100.0		41	100.0	
Number of countries, where company operates									
Local	18	17.3	17.3	9	14.3	14.3	9	22.0	22.0
<5	17	16.3	33.7	15	23.8	38.1	2	4.9	26.8
≥5	69	66.3	100.0	39	61.9	100.0	30	73.2	100.0
Total	104	100.0		63	100.0		41	100.0	

Source Own data

available turnover for these respondents in Albertina database was over EUR 50 Mio, but decreased under this value in the year 2014.

In the rest of this chapter are consequently addressed the following issues: relevance of sustainability and inclusion of sustainability into corporate strategy; aspects of sustainability management; collecting information on sustainability above legal requirements; spectrum of collected information; involvement in sustainability accounting; organization of sustainability accounting; channels used for sustainability reporting. The chapter is closed by discussion of selected factors with potential to influence understanding and approach to sustainability.

First, we asked our respondents about relevance of sustainability and answers are summarized in Table 50.2.

For the CR the mean value of the answers is equal to 2.78, std. deviation 0.302, median 3.00, mode 3.00, minimum 1 and maximum 4. For the SR is the mean value of the answers equal to 3.17, std. deviation 0.543, median 3.00, mode 3.00, minimum 2 and maximum 4. Results suggest that proportion of respondents from the

Table 50.2 Relevance of sustainability [(1) sustainability is not relevant, (2) sustainability is mainly a PR/marketing concept, (3) sustainability is a strategic management responsibility and task, (4) sustainability is implemented as an organization principle and is involved in the whole corporate management]

Answer	CR+SR			CR			SR		
	FRQ	%	Cumulative %	FRQ	%	Cumulative %	FRQ	%	Cumulative %
1	3	2.9	2.9	3	4.8	4.8	0	0.0	0.0
2	12	11.5	14.4	8	12.7	17.5	4	9.8	9.8
3	27	26.0	40.4	22	34.9	52.4	5	12.2	22.0
4	62	59.6	100.0	30	47.6	100.0	32	78.0	100.0
Total	104	100.0		63	100.0		41	100.0	

Source Own data

SR, who consider sustainability highly relevant (categories 3 and 4), is higher than in the CR and especially significant difference is in the fourth category. Concretely, in the CR belong to categories three and four 82.5% of respondents and in the SR 90.2% of respondents. Moreover, 78.0% of respondents from the SR indicated that their company belongs to the category 4, while in the CR only 47.6% of respondents belong to this category.

Second, we asked our respondents about inclusion of sustainability into corporate strategy. Answers are summarized in Table 50.3.

For the CR is the mean value of the answers equal to 3.25, std. deviation 0.861, median 3.00, mode 4.00, minimum 1 and maximum 4. For the SR is the mean value of the answers equal to 3.68, std. deviation 0.650, median 4.00, mode 4.00, minimum 2 and maximum 4. It is possible to summarize that data in Table 50.3 suggest relatively more comprehensive inclusion of sustainability into corporate strategy among the respondents from the SR.

Third, we examined selected aspects of sustainability management and results related to stakeholder communication, implementation of sustainable activities/practices and broadening sustainability over supply chain can be found in Table 50.4.

Table 50.3 Inclusion of sustainability into corporate strategy [(1) there is no sustainability strategy, (2) there is a sustainability strategy but it is not related to the corporate strategy, (3) sustainability strategy is part of the corporate strategy, (4) sustainability strategy is the main content of the corporate strategy]

Answer	CR+SR			CR			SR		
	FRQ	%	Cumulative %	FRQ	%	Cumulative %	FRQ	%	Cumulative %
1	9	8.7	8.7	9	14.3	14.3	0	0.0	0.0
2	8	7.7	16.3	5	7.9	22.2	3	7.3	7.3
3	68	65.4	81.7	40	63.5	85.7	28	68.3	75.6
4	19	18.3	100.0	9	14.3	100.0	10	24.4	100.0
Total	104	100.0		63	100.0		41	100.0	

Source Own data

Table 50.4 Selected aspects of sustainability management

Answer	CR+SR			CR			SR		
	FRQ	%	Cumulative %	FRQ	%	Cumulative %	FRQ	%	Cumulative %
Stakeholder communication [(1) there is no stakeholder communication/dialogue, (2) irregular and incident-driven stakeholder communication/dialogue, (3) regular top-down stakeholder dialogue, (4) regular bottom-up and top-down stakeholder dialogue]									
1	7	6.7	6.7	7	11.1	11.1	0	0.0	0.0
2	11	10.6	17.3	8	12.7	23.8	3	7.3	7.3
3	36	34.6	51.9	22	34.9	58.7	14	34.1	41.5
4	50	48.1	100.0	26	41.3	100.0	24	58.5	100.0
Total	104	100.0		63	100.0		41	100.0	
Implementation of sustainable activities/practices [(1) there are no sustainable activities/practices, (2) sustainable activities/practices are unsystematic and isolated, (3) sustainable activities/practices are systematic and refer to our strategy, (4) sustainable activities/practices are involved in (almost) every part of the value chain]									
1	2	1.9	1.9	2	3.2	3.2	0	0.0	0.0
2	12	11.5	13.5	11	17.5	20.6	1	2.4	2.4
3	67	64.4	77.9	44	69.8	90.5	23	56.1	58.5
4	23	22.1	100.0	6	9.5	100.0	17	41.5	100.0
Total	104	100.0		63	100.0		41	100.0	
Broadening sustainability over supply chain [(1) there are no specific requirements, (2) acting social and environmental responsible along the supply chain is partially required, (3) acting social and environmental responsible along the entire supply chain is expected and required, but there is no own standard, (4) acting social and environmental responsible along the entire supply chain is required. Own standards often exceed the normal requirements]									
1	6	5.8	5.8	6	9.5	9.5	0	0.0	0.0
2	17	16.3	22.1	12	19.0	28.6	5	12.2	12.2
3	28	26.9	49.0	18	28.6	57.1	10	24.4	36.6
4	53	51.0	100.0	27	42.9	100.0	26	63.4	100.0
Total	104	100.0		63	100.0		41	100.0	

Source Own data

Mean values of answers about all three aspects are higher in the SR. Median value of answers is also higher for the SR except the question about implementation of sustainable activities/practices, where median value is equal to three in both the CR and SR. It is therefore possible to conclude that the companies from the SR declared higher quality of their approach to sustainability management than respondents from the CR. It is necessary to point out high concentration of answers by respondents from SR into the fourth (best) category.

Fourth, we asked our respondents about their approach to collecting information on sustainability-related issues above legal requirements, see Table 50.5.

Findings are quite surprising because there is a significant difference between Czech and Slovak companies. It is possible to interpret the results so that 60.3% of the Czech respondents utilize sub-par approach to collecting information on sustainability. This is also true for some Slovak respondents, but only for 22.0%.

Table 50.5 Collecting information on sustainability-related issues [(1) sustainable outcomes above legal requirements are not collected, (2) outcomes are single and isolated collected and analysed, (3) outcomes are collected and analysed by a sustainability accounting system that is linked with strategic objectives, (4) outcomes are collected and analysed by a sophisticated sustainability accounting system as the basis for all corporate decisions]

Answer	CR+SR			CR			SR		
	FRQ	%	Cumulative %	FRQ	%	Cumulative %	FRQ	%	Cumulative %
1	25	24.0	24.0	20	31.7	31.7	5	12.2	12.2
2	22	21.2	45.2	18	28.6	60.3	4	9.8	22.0
3	34	32.7	77.9	15	23.8	84.1	19	46.3	68.3
4	23	22.1	100.0	10	15.9	100.0	13	31.7	100.0
Total	104	100.0		63	100.0		41	100.0	

Source Own data

Table 50.6 Spectrum of collected information

Answer	CR+SR		CR		SR	
	FRQ	Valid %	FRQ	Valid %	FRQ	Valid %
Balance of information regarding environmental and social issues						
Only on environmental issues	0	0.0	0	0.0	0	0.0
Mainly on environmental issues	10	12.7	5	11.6	5	13.9
Balanced	67	84.8	38	88.4	29	80.6
Mainly on social issues	2	2.5	0	0.0	2	5.6
Only on social issues	0	0.0	0	0.0	0	0.0
Total	79	100.0	43	100.0	36	100.0
Balance of information regarding engineering themes and softer aspects						
Only on engineering themes	2	2.5	1	2.3	1	2.8
Mainly on engineering themes	14	17.7	10	23.3	4	11.1
Balanced	61	77.2	30	69.8	31	86.1
Mainly on softer aspects	2	2.5	2	4.7	0	0.0
Only on softer aspects	0	0.0	0	0.0	0	0.0
Total	79	100.0	43	100.0	36	100.0

Source Own data

Fifth, our respondents were asked whether collected information is balanced between environmental and social issues and between engineering themes and non-technical (softer) aspects. Results can be found in Table 50.6.

It is possible to draw a conclusion that both in the CR and in the SR the modal answer indicated balanced approach to collecting information on environmental and social issues as well as engineering themes and softer aspects.

Table 50.7 Summary of answers related to organization of sustainability accounting [answers on scale (1) not at all, (2) to a slight extent, (3) to a moderate extent, (4) to a great extent, (5) to a very great extent]

Answer	To which extent are reporting guidelines (e.g. GRI) relevant for sustainability accounting?			To which extent are sustainability data routinely generated?			To which extent is the information generation process formalized?		
	CR + SR	CR	SR	CR + SR	CR	SR	CR + SR	CR	SR
Mean	3.27	2.98	3.61	3.52	3.30	3.78	3.72	3.49	4.00
Median	3.00	3.00	4.00	4.00	3.00	4.00	4.00	3.00	4.00
Mode	3	3	4	4	3	4	4	3	4
Std. dev.	0.98	0.94	0.93	0.92	0.91	0.87	1.06	1.06	1.01
Minimum	1	1	1	1	1	1	1	1	1
Maximum	5	5	5	5	5	5	5	5	5
N valid	79	43	36	79	43	36	79	43	36
N missing	25	20	5	25	20	5	25	20	5

Source Own data

Sixth, we examined who decides what aspects are covered within sustainability accounting. There are substantial differences between Czech and Slovak businesses in this area—while in the CR only 60.5% of respondents agreed with the claim that decision making in this area is in hand of senior management, in the SR it was 86.1%. It is possible to propose that in the SR are sustainability issues addressed by higher management levels than in the CR.

Seventh, various aspects of organization of sustainability accounting were examined and results are summarized in Table 50.7.

It is possible to conclude that the businesses from SR declared better performance (expressed by higher mean, median and mode) in all three surveyed areas.

Eighth, we asked respondents to indicate, which channels they use for sustainability reporting (see Table 50.8).

It is possible to sum up that in both the CR and SR is the most common reporting channel annual report, which is followed by internal reports. The largest difference in the percentage of respondents using a given reporting tool is in standalone sustainability reports, which are used by 50.0% respondents from the SR, but only by 23.3% respondents from the CR. In comparison with respondents from the SR respondents from the CR also use less intranet (by 11.4%) and interned-based interactive reports (by 9.7%). On the contrary, respondents from the CR use significantly more "other" reporting channels than respondents from the SR (by 22.3%).

Last but not least, we addressed the key factors with influence on approach to sustainability by analysing correlations between various variables (size of the company measured by full-time employees, size of the company measured by turnover and multinational character of the company measured by the number of countries where it operates) and other ordinal variables (e.g. relevance of

Table 50.8 Channels used for sustainability reporting

Type of report	CR + SR (N = 79)		CR (N = 43)		SR (N = 36)	
	N	Valid % of cases	N	Valid % of cases	N	Valid % of cases
Annual	52	65.8	30	69.8	22	61.1
Internal	46	58.2	25	58.1	21	58.3
Intranet	39	49.4	19	44.2	20	55.6
Web-based (e.g. homepage)	38	48.1	20	46.5	18	50.0
Stand alone sustainability	28	35.4	10	23.3	18	50.0
Internet-based (interactive)	20	25.3	9	20.9	11	30.6
Other	14	17.7	12	27.9	2	5.6
Integrated	10	12.7	6	14.0	4	11.1
Total	247		131		116	

Source Own data

sustainability, integration of sustainability into strategy). This analysis was conducted within merged dataset from the CR and SR. We can summarize that the strongest correlation was found between relevance of sustainability and multinational character of a company, for details see Table 50.9.

This claim is supported by values of correlation coefficients (Kendall's tau-b, Kendall's tau-c, Gamma, Spearman Correlation), which are all positive. For example, coefficient gamma is equal to 0.295 (asymptotic standardized error not assuming the null hypothesis is 0.142; approx. T using the asymptotic standard error assuming the null hypothesis is 1.902 and approx. sig. is 0.057).

Table 50.9 Cross-tabulation of relevance of sustainability and multinational character of the company

Relevance of corporate sustainability		Number of countries, where company operates			
		Local	Less than 5	5 or more	Total
1. Not relevant	Count	0	0	3	3
	Row %	0.0	0.0	100.0	100.0
2. Mainly a PR/marketing concept	Count	3	4	5	12
	Row %	25.0	33.3	41.7	100.0
3. Strategic management responsibility and task	Count	7	5	15	27
	Row %	25.9	18.5	55.6	100.0
4. Implemented as an organization principle and is involved in the whole corporate mgmt	Count	8	8	46	62
	Row %	12.9	12.9	74.2	100.0
Total	Count	18	17	69	104
	Row %	17.3	16.3	66.3	100.0

Source Own data

50.5   Conclusion

The main goal of this paper was to provide information on the differences and similarities of the Czech and Slovak companies in the area of understanding, managing and reporting sustainability-related issues. Additional research aim was examination of correlation between relevance of sustainability and selected factors.

The first goal was fulfilled by statistical analysis of data obtained via our original empirical research (web-based survey), which was simultaneously realized and harmonized in several CEE countries, including the CR and SR. Responses from the CR and SR were mutually compared in several areas. It can be hypothesized that the CR and SR should be in the area of sustainability relatively homogenous. Contrary to this hypothesis, we found interesting differences, which are reported in this paper. It is possible to summarize that on average respondents from the SR outperformed Czech respondents in areas of perceived relevance of sustainability, inclusion of sustainability into corporate strategy, management of sustainability, as well as sustainability accounting and reporting systematically. Another interesting finding was that 86.1% of Slovak respondents (and only 60.5% of Czech respondents) declared that senior management decides what aspects are covered within sustainability accounting. It is possible to hypothesize that among Slovak respondents sustainability is on the agenda of higher managerial level than among Czech respondents and further research is needed.

The second goal was fulfilled by correlation analysis. Strongest correlation exists between relevance of sustainability and multinational character of a company.

We can sum up that in the CEE countries there is a lack of research in the area of sustainability-related themes and findings presented in our paper indicate possible agendas for future research. For example, it would be interesting to analyse contingency factors influencing sustainability relevance, management, accounting and reporting with help of structural equation modelling (Siska 2015, p. 344); nevertheless, this approach requires the sample size of hundreds of respondents.

Acknowledgments   This paper is an outcome of project supported by the Grant No. F1/37/2016—Internal Grant Agency of the University of Economics, Prague and of project of the Scientific Grant Agency of the Ministry of Culture of the Slovak Republic and Slovak Academy of Sciences (VEGA) No. 1/0512/16 (2016–2018) "Retention and Development of Business Property of Company as a Relevant Tool for Sustainable Development."

References

Athanasios V, Antonios S, Despina G (2013) Company characteristics and human resource disclosure in Greece. In: 6th international conference on information and communication technologies in agriculture, food and environment (Haicta 2013), vol 8, pp 112–121. doi:10.1016/j.protcy.2013.11.016

Engert S, Rauter R, Baumgartner RJ (2016) Exploring the integration of corporate sustainability into strategic management: a literature review. J Clean Prod 112:2833–2850. doi:10.1016/j.jclepro.2015.08.031

Epstein MJ (2008) Making sustainability work: best practices in managing and measuring corporate social, environmental, and economic impacts. Greenleaf Publishing, United Kingdom

Fifka M (2012) The development and state of research on social and environmental reporting in global comparison. J Betriebswirtsch 62(1):45–84. doi:10.1007/s11301-012-0083-8

Hahn T, Pinkse J, Preuss L, Figge F (2015) Tensions in corporate sustainability: towards an integrative framework. J Bus Ethics 127(2):297–316. doi:10.1007/s10551-014-2047-5

KPMG (2013) The KPMG survey of corporate responsibility reporting 2013. Available via https://assets.kpmg.com/content/dam/kpmg/pdf/2015/08/kpmg-survey-of-corporate-responsibility-reporting-2013.pdf. Accessed 27 Feb 2016

Linnenluecke MK, Griffiths A (2013) Firms and sustainability: mapping the intellectual origins and structure of the corporate sustainability field. Glob Environ Change 23(1):382–391. doi:10.1016/j.gloenvcha.2012.07.007

Petera P, Wagner J, Bouckova M (2014) An empirical investigation into CSR reporting by the largest companies with their seat in the Czech Republic. In: Doucek P, Chroust V, Oskrdal V (eds) IDIMT-2014: networking societies—cooperation and conflict. 22nd interdisciplinary information management talks, vol 43. Podebrady, Czech Republic, Sept 2014. Schriftenreihe Informatik, Trauner, pp 321–329

Siska L (2015) Factors influencing design and outcomes of performance management systems. In: Doucek P, Chroust V, Oskrdal V (eds) IDIMT-2015: information technology and society interaction and interdependence. 23rd interdisciplinary information management talks, vol 44. Podebrady, Sept 2015. Schriftenreihe Informatik, Trauner, pp 337–347

Steurer R, Konrad A (2009) Business-society relations in Central-Eastern and Western Europe: how those who lead in sustainability reporting bridge the gap in corporate (social) responsibility. Scand J Manag 25(1):23–36. doi:10.1016/j.scaman.2008.11.001

WCED (1987) Report of the world commission on environment and development: our common future. Oxford University Press, Oxford

Chapter 51
Adoption of Strategic Management Accounting Techniques in Czech and Slovak Companies

Markéta Boučková and Ladislav Šiška

Abstract The purpose of this paper is to classify strategic management accounting (SMA) techniques. More specifically, two objectives were stated: (1) to derive a classification of SMA theoretically and then (2) to verify such classification empirically. To achieve these objectives, our study deploys literature review and empirical survey. Convenience sample of 99 profit-seeking companies domiciled in the Czech Republic and Slovak Republic was analyzed by means of descriptive statistics and principal component analysis. The latter method identified three broader categories of SMA techniques: Internally focused; Competitor focused; Stakeholder focused SMA techniques. Such findings only partly correspond to the theoretically derived classification that enumerates five broader categories, which were identified in SMA literature: product accounting; process accounting; customer accounting; competitor accounting; and performance measurement. The comparison of both classifications reveals that respondents perceived internally focused groups of SMA techniques similarly and did not differentiate among them. Further detailed analysis also shows influence of some control variables such as industry, size of the respondent's company or differences between independent enterprises and subsidiaries/parent companies.

Keywords Strategic management accounting · Management accounting techniques · Customer focus · Competitor focus

M. Boučková (✉)
Department of Management Accounting, University of Economics, Prague,
W. Churchill Sq. 4, 130 67 Prague, Czech Republic
e-mail: marketa.bouckova@vse.cz

L. Šiška
Department of Corporate Economy, Faculty of Economics and Administration,
Masaryk University, Lipova 41A, 602 00 Brno, Czech Republic
e-mail: ladislav.siska@econ.muni.cz

D. Procházka (ed.), *New Trends in Finance and Accounting*,
Springer Proceedings in Business and Economics,
DOI 10.1007/978-3-319-49559-0_51

51.1 Introduction

The first use of the term "strategic management accounting" (SMA) is ascribed to Simmonds (1981). He defined SMA as information provided by managerial accounting about the company and its competitors. Using such information, managers can better formulate and above all successfully execute the business strategies. Well formulated and implemented strategies are considered by many authors (Kaplan and Norton 1996) to be the main source of company's sustainable competitive advantage and in turn the source of its long-lasting high performance. These facts give reasons why to pay attention to SMA.

Shank (1989) presents SMA as the next development phase of management accounting. He sees SMA as the application of methods that control costs, which ultimately lead to the consolidation of the strategic position of the company and to cost reduction. Kremin-Buch (2007) brought another notion of SMA. He understands SMA rather as an integration of strategy, measures and instruments that can be used for the appropriate handling of costs. According to Bhimani and Langfield-Smith (2007), SMA provides informational support to managers for their strategic decision making and other strategic processes. Dixon (1998) also sees SMA as accounting for strategic management, when accounting information is interpreted for the purposes of strategic management.

Contrary to the presented notion, SMA can be alternatively viewed as linkage between strategy and management accounting, therefore as the use of managerial accounting techniques with strategic orientation. However, the field of SMA still lacks a comprehensive and compact list of its typical techniques. SMA is enriched by research in areas such as management, marketing, strategic management, performance measurement, management accounting and control. Multidisciplinary research led to the development of different approaches along with a variety of characteristics of SMA. Lord (1996) identified the following features associated with the strategic management accounting—gathering information about competitors; use of accounting for strategic decision making; reducing cost in relation to strategic decisions and obtaining a competitive advantage. The shift from insider viewpoint of management accounting to SMA is documented by reporting about the external environment of the company. Bromwich (1990) argues that companies should focus on the external environment and direct their attention to the market, product selling proposition and customer satisfaction. Shank (1989) even integrates external environment into the broader value chain model as external suppliers and customers.

Following the briefly outlined evolution of SMA, the first objective of this article is to derive a classification of SMA techniques and their groups, which is based on the current literature search; next objective aims to verify the SMA techniques classification by means of pilot empirical study among companies domiciled in Czechia and Slovakia.

The remainder of the paper is organized as follows. In the next section, the SMA techniques are classified. Then, the methodology of empirical study is described and the findings are presented. Finally, the conclusion section summarizes the identified state of art in the field of SMA techniques in the countries in question and describes the possible limitation of our study.

51.2   Strategic Management Accounting (SMA) Techniques

There are various proposals of lists of SMA techniques, e.g., classification by Guilding et al. (2000), Cinquini and Tenucci (2006), Cadez and Guilding (2008) or Shah et al. (2011), which are more or less substantiated in various theories. There are even more empirically derived lists and taxonomies of SMA techniques, like the survey of the CIMA (Chartered Institute of Management Accountants), whose researchers Ross and Kovachev (2009) collected 439 of responses about current and intended usage of more than 100 management accounting tools. Similarly, Pavlatos and Kostakis (2015) grouped management accounting practices based on the empirical evidence they collected. In our attempt to classify SMA techniques, we preferred the theoretical studies to empirical despite the fact that empirical survey served as the source of our inspiration as well.

Cadez and Guilding (2008) enhanced the former classification of Guilding et al. (2000). It consists of five categories of SMA techniques—strategic costing; strategic planning, control and performance management; strategic decision making; competitor accounting; customer accounting. We found some weaknesses in the classification. Above all, some typical SMA techniques like ABC/M, BSC or JIT are completely left out.

Cinquini and Tenucci (2006) present four areas of SMA techniques: the customer area; the competitor-oriented area; the long-term-oriented area; activity-oriented techniques. This categorization is rather an attempt to divide the techniques into groups based on influential factors. Besides limitations in selected SMA techniques, this approach fails to incorporate some techniques, namely integrated performance measurement or benchmarking. Criticism is not only directed at missing techniques but at content too. Soljakova (2012) points out that some included techniques might be described as a mere extension of the original traditional concepts of ABC, quality costing, etc.

Based on comparison of the scientific articles, we proposed general classification of SMA techniques, which is presented in Table 51.1. The categories of the classification mirror the information needs of strategic managers.

The first category of our SMA techniques classification focuses on product cost control. Products should not be too costly, but still need to meet the customer expectations and the quality requirements. This category includes SMA techniques with main focus on the relation between strategic thinking and cost accounting.

The second category of our SMA techniques classification maps value creation in a company. That encompasses the process view of the company (Shank 1989).

Table 51.1 Classification of SMA techniques

SMA category	SMA techniques	Questionnaire
Product accounting	Quality costing	q27b
	Life cycle costing	q27a
	Target costing	q27a
Process accounting	Activity based costing/management	q27c
	Value chain costing	q27c
	Benchmarking	q27d
Customer accounting	Customer profitability analysis	q27i
	Valuation of customers as assets	q27j
Competitor accounting	Competitor position monitoring	q27g
	Competitor performance appraisal	q27g
	Competitor cost assessment	q27f
Performance measurement	Integrated performance measurement	q27e
	Balanced scorecard	q27e
	Shareholder value	q27h

Source Authors

Process category informs about the cost-effectiveness of company activities and analyzes the necessity of individual processes and activities in the value creation.

The third and fourth categories of our SMA techniques classification consider the external orientation of SMA. Competitor accounting provides information about the performance of competitors and monitors competitor sales, unit costs and market share. SMA also includes information on customers such as determination of the current customer profitability and on future expected profits from the relations with him. Basically, we look at customers as an added value for the company.

The last category of our SMA techniques classification takes into account performance of the company and its contribution to increasing shareholder value it creates for its owners. Performance measurement should connect all management levels and areas of company's activity including monitoring critical factors of company's future success. Current performance measurement systems are expected to integrate both financial and non-financial indicators (Bhimani and Langfield-Smith 2007).

51.3 Methodology of Empirical Study

The second objective of this article, verification of the proposed classification of SMA techniques, was conducted through empirical survey. It targeted at answering the following research questions:

- (RQ1) Do companies residing in the Czech Republic and Slovak Republic apply SMA techniques and how intensively?

- (RQ2) To which extant is an adoption of SMA techniques influenced by context variables such as size of the company, industry it operates in or membership of the responding company in the group of companies?
- (RQ3) Are there some patterns in using particular SMA techniques at the same time and do they overlap with the SMA category from the introduced classification?

Based on findings of the previous studies, we hypothesized the following answers:

- (H1) Customer profitability analysis, benchmarking with outside organizations and Balanced Scorecard are the most popular SMA techniques [based on Ross and Kovachev (2009), Pavlatos and Kostakis (2015)].
- (H2) The size of the company is the dominant contingency factor for selection of SMA technique, in which case the bigger the organization the broader spectrum of SMA techniques it uses (Ross and Kovachev 2009; Chenhall 2003).
- (H3) There are five latent components hidden behind the SMA techniques adoption, and these correspond to the SMA categories from Table 51.1 [introduced classification derived especially from Cadez and Guilding (2008), Cinquini and Tenucci (2006)].

51.3.1 Data Collection and Sample of Responses

A web-based questionnaire using Google Docs technology served as the tool for data collection. Each questionnaire started with a covering letter explaining the study's purpose and a glossary of terms used. The questionnaire operationalized the SMA categories from Table 51.1. The exact wording of the particular 27th question of the questionnaire and its subquestions are presented in Table 51.2 in the Findings section. It also shows that the 11-point Likert scale was used, ranging from 0 to 10.

Students of Masaryk University helped with distribution of the questionnaire and randomly contacted managers from the profit-seeking companies. The preferred targeted recipients were top managers, especially financial managers.

Total of 99 answers was gathered within the period from December 2015 to February 2016. The count of top managers or owners amounted to 45, middle managers to 43 and 11 respondents were without managerial rank. Subsequent Kruskal–Wallis test did not identify statistically significant differences among answers of top, middle and non-managers.

As far as the functional structure is concerned, the sample of respondents consisted of 27 general managers (CEOs) or owners, 23 people from finance departments, 16 from marketing and selling department, 14 from technical or operations department, 5 from procurement and 14 from other departments of profit-seeking companies.

Table 51.2 Ranking of SMA techniques

To which extent are the following techniques/methods applied in your company for the purposes of strategic management? (0-not at all…10-dominant technique)	N	Mean	Std. deviation	Percentiles		
				25th	50th (median)	75th
q27g. Competitive position monitoring	98	6.378	2.9058	5	7	9
q27d. Benchmarking to other competitors	98	5.949	3.1765	3	7	8
q27j. Long-range value of customers and theirs portfolios (customer equity)	98	5.806	3.2001	4	7	8.25
q27i. Customer profitability analysis	97	5.515	3.5093	3	6	8
q27h. Shareholder value generation (incl. economic value added)	97	5.485	3.2279	3	6	8
q27b. Quality costs collection	98	5.041	3.2930	2	6	8
q27f. Competitor cost assessment	98	4.551	3.0193	2	5	7
q27a. Strategic costs of products/services (e.g., target costing, life cycle costing)	99	4.283	3.5284	0	5	7
q27e. Integrated financial and non-financial metrics (e.g., balanced scorecard)	98	3.796	3.6382	0	3	7
q27c. Value chain analysis (including activity based management)	98	3.143	3.1295	0	3	5

From the sectoral point of view, 53 out of 99 responding companies were industrial ones. Trade organizations amount to 19 and 27 provided services as their main activity.

Regarding the size of the companies in the sample, 25 of them were classified as "large" with more than 250 full-time employees (FTE), 33 as "medium" with FTEs in interval from 50 to 250 and finally 41 companies were "small" businesses with FTEs ranging from 10 to 50.

All data processing was done in IBM SPSS 22. Since the majority of data had ordinal character, in addition with non-normal distribution, the following non-parametric tests were applied:

- Kruskal–Wallis test for testing differences between more than 2 categories of control variables like "Size" or "Sector."
- Mann–Whitney U test comparing 2 classes–variables—e.g., independent enterprise versus member of the group of companies.

Relatively long scale of the variables of adopted SMA techniques was the reason why we decided to treat them as continuous variables (despite their ordinal character) and applied exploratory factor analysis (EFA) so that we get the latent common factors behind the observed SMA techniques adoption variables. Prior EFA application, the Kaiser–Meyer–Olkin (KMO) measure verified the sampling adequacy. The result KMO = 0.781 can be interpreted as "middling" and therefore acceptable according to Hutcheson and Sofroniou (1999). All KMO values for individual SMA techniques were greater than the acceptable limit of 0.5 based on Field (2013). The Bartlett's test of sphericity was significant ($p = 0.000$) with Chi-square criterion 334.365 and 45 degrees of freedom.

For extracting factors, the method of principal component analysis (PCA) was applied. Three components evolved with eigenvalues over the Kaiser's criterion of 1 (the particular eigenvalues were 4.076, 1.301 and 1.285). These components in combination explained 66.619% of the total variance. In order to achieve easier interpretation, the identified components were rotated orthogonally through Varimax method with Kaiser Normalization. The resulting components and their affiliation to the original questions about SMA techniques are depicted in Fig. 51.2 in graphic terms.

51.4 Findings

This section concentrates only on the main findings of the pilot study concerning SMA techniques and their adoption (question 27 in the questionnaire used). The presentation follows three hypothesized answers to the research questions addressed above.

Table 51.2 presents the SMA techniques in ranking (H1) from the most dominantly adopted SMA techniques down to the least used ones. The "N" column shows the number of responses. Despite the ordinal character of answers, information about mean is presented and complemented with standard deviation so that the level of variation could be assessed, both assuming that respondents perceived the steps in the scale as the same increases and similarly to each other. Then, the last three columns give the more complex picture of the distribution of responses showing all quartiles.

We further investigated impact of control variables (H2). The variable of "Sector" (with categories industry, trade, services) statistically significantly influenced only "q27b Quality costs collection." With Chi-square value of 9.028 with 2 degrees of freedom, the significance level achieved 0.011. The reason reveals Fig. 51.1. Quality control involving cost collection prevails as SMA technique among industrial companies while service providers and trading companies adopt quality management significantly less often.

Size was identified as the most influential control variable as expected. Table 51.3 presents the results of Kruskal–Wallis tests. Statistically significant differences were found among large, medium and small companies in adopting the following SMA techniques: "27a. Strategic costing of products/services"; "27b. Quality costs collection"; "27e. Integrated financial and non-financial metrics"; "27h. Shareholder value generation (EVA)"; "27i. Customer profitability analysis"; "27j. Customer equity."

Fig. 51.1 Boxplot of
"Quality cost collection" in
different sectors. *Source*
Authors

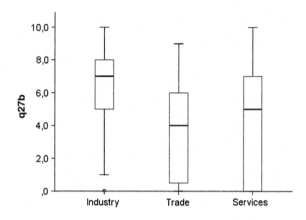

Table 51.3 Kruskal–Wallis
tests for the impact of the
control variable of "Size"

	Chi-square	df	Asymp. sig.
q27a	28.311	2	0.000
q27b	13.706	2	0.001
q27c	5.258	2	0.072
q27d	3.682	2	0.159
q27e	16.661	2	0.000
q27f	4.846	2	0.089
q27g	0.300	2	0.861
q27h	16.476	2	0.000
q27i	18.942	2	0.000
q27j	9.342	2	0.009

Source Authors

Detailed analysis of the boxplots revealed that the level of adoption SMA techniques asked in q27b, q27e and q27h increases with the size of the company. Questions q27i and q27j indicate higher adoption by large and medium companies. Strategic costing (q27a) techniques are used predominantly by large companies only.

Table 51.4 reveals that the comparison of answers from independent companies and from members of the group shows similar findings to the size as the independent companies tend to be smaller (55.6% of independent companies were small, 37% medium and 74% large).

We also examined components of SMA and the classification of its techniques (H3). EFA identified only 3 latent components instead of expected 5. Figure 51.2 depicts which SMA techniques loaded on which component. Component 1 consists especially of q27a, q27b, q27c and q27e. Questions q27d, q27f and q27g form the second component. Finally, the third component is saturated through q27i, q27j and from a lower portion through q27h.

Table 51.4 Tests of differences between independent companies and companies in groups

	Mann–Whitney U test	Sig. (2-tailed)
q27a	747.0	0.001
q27b	934.0	0.062
q27c	929.5	0.052
q27d	1022.5	0.221
q27e	760.5	0.002
q27f	1133.0	0.669
q27g	1137.0	0.690
q27h	915.5	0.064
q27i	1079.0	0.506
q27j	1083.0	0.432

Source Authors

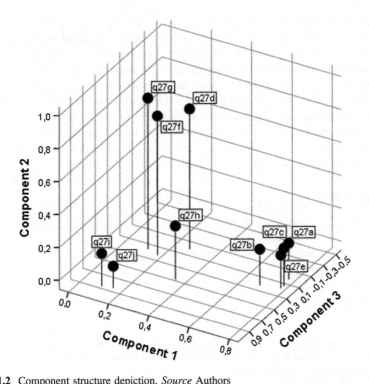

Fig. 51.2 Component structure depiction. *Source* Authors

51.5 Conclusions

In accordance with the stated objectives, we outlined above the classification of SMA techniques and their grouping. Five distinct categories were identified: product accounting; process accounting; customer accounting; competitor accounting;

and performance measurement. Subsequently, we carried out the verification of the classification. For that reason, we used data from empirical study among companies domiciled in the Czech Republic and in the Slovak Republic.

Our empirical study verified the list of the SMA techniques. In contrast to our third hypothesis, the PCA identified only three (instead of 5) components representing the broader categories of SMA techniques.

The first component (i.e., empirically derived category) can be characterized as "Internally focused SMA techniques." The rate of their adoption is the lowest in comparison to the other categories. It comprises the strategic costing techniques, value chain analysis, cost of quality control, integrated financial and non-financial performance measurement. The latter two techniques are typical especially for industrial companies. In addition, larger companies are keener adopter of the techniques from this category.

The label of "Competitor focused SMA techniques" can be introduced for the second empirically derived category. These techniques prevailed in strategic management of the majority of responding companies. The category involves SMA techniques such monitoring of competitors' position and benchmarking to them. Less common seems to be the competitors' cost assessment.

The third identified category was not as coherent as the previous ones. The label for it might sound "Stakeholder focused SMA techniques." It consists of customer oriented techniques such as customer profitability in the shorter and in the longer term. These two techniques are intensively used by the majority of medium-sized and large companies. The techniques concerning shareholder value represent the third member of the category. Its importance gradually increases with the size of organization and possibly higher degree of separation between ownership and management.

Acknowledgments This paper was prepared under financial support of the Internal Grant Agency of the University of Economics, Prague, Grant No. F1/13/2015 and institutional research subsidy of Masaryk University, Brno, which authors gratefully acknowledge.

References

Bhimani A, Langfield-Smith K (2007) Structure, formality and the importance of financial and non-financial information in strategy development and implementation. Manag Acc Res 18:3–31. doi:10.1016/j.mar.2006.06.005

Bromwich M (1990) The case for strategic management accounting: the role of accounting information for strategy in competitive markets. Acc Organ Soc 15:27–46. doi:10.1016/0361-3682(90)90011-I

Cadez S, Guilding C (2008) An exploratory investigation of an integrated contingency model of strategic management accounting. Acc Organ Soc 33:836–863. doi:10.1016/j.aos.2008.01.003

Chenhall RH (2003) Management control systems design within its organizational context: findings from contingency-based research and directions for the future. Acc Organ Soc 28:127–168. doi:10.1016/S0361-3682(01)00027-7

Cinquini L, Tenucci A (2006) Is the adoption of strategic management accounting techniques really 'strategy driven'? Evidence from a survey. In: Munich personal RePEc archive, MPRA paper No. 11819, conference paper, cost and performance in services and operations, Trento, Italy

Dixon R (1998) Accounting for strategic management: a practical application. Long Range Plan 31:272–279

Field A (2013) Discovering statistics using IBM SPSS statistics. Sage, London

Guilding C, Cravens KS, Tayles M (2000) An international comparison of strategic management accounting practices. Manag Acc Res 11:113–135. doi:10.1006/mare.1999.0120

Hutcheson G, Sofroniou N (1999) The multivariate social scientist. Sage, London

Kaplan RS, Norton DP (1996) The balanced scorecard: translating strategy into action. Harvard Business School Press, Boston

Kremin-Buch B (2007) Strategisches Kostenmanagement. Gabler Verlag, Wiesbaden

Lord B (1996) Strategic management accounting: the emperor's new clothes? Manag Acc Res 7:347–366. doi:10.1006/mare.1996.0020

Pavlatos O, Paggios I (2015) Management accounting practices in the Greek hospitality industry. Adv Acc 31:150–164

Ross L, Kovachev I (2009) Management accounting tools for today and tomorrow. Chartered Institute of Management Accountants, London

Shah H, Malik A, Malik MS (2011) Strategic management accounting—a messiah for management accounting? Aust J Bus Manag Res 1:1–7

Shank J (1989) Strategic cost management: new wine, or just new bottles? J Manag Acc Res 1:47–65

Simmonds K (1981) Strategic management accounting. Manag Acc 59:26–29

Soljakova L (2012) Strategic management accounting development during last 30 years. Eur Fin Acc J 2:24–35

Chapter 52
The Use of Assessment of Work Performance of Human Resources as a Tool of Management Accounting to Result Controls in Slovak Companies

Pavol Ďurana

Abstract Human resources mean for companies the biggest wealth and potential to obtain profit. It is very important to know, how human resources contribute to whole company performance. Finding out this fact is made by a tool assessment of work performance of human resources. The article discusses current situation of assessment of human resources in Slovak companies on the base of questionnaire survey. It was analysed if Slovak companies use formal system of assessment, what category of employees is assessed and actions after assessment.

Keywords Assessment · Work performance · Human resources · Management accounting · Personnel management

52.1 Introduction

Human resources have been, are and will be the base of prosperity of every company, but not all entities of human resources represent the source of competitive advantage, so companies have been trying to find from their point of view the right human resources that will have as far as possible positive influence to their total profit. Assessment of work performance of employees as a cross-cutting tool of management accounting and personnel management becomes the main instrument of recruitment and selection of employees with appropriate characteristics and compatibility for companies. Assessment helps as an indicator of use of existing staff potential in current work positions or in the projects in which they participate and also assists to create the processes of reverse remuneration, education and development of employees. Assessment of human resources in companies that have already established formal systems is carried out mainly with the intention to find

P. Ďurana (✉)
Department of Economics, The Faculty of Operation and Economics of Transport and Communications, University of Žilina, Univerzitná 1, 010 26 Žilina, Slovakia
e-mail: pavol.durana@fpedas.uniza.sk

© Springer International Publishing AG 2017
D. Procházka (ed.), *New Trends in Finance and Accounting*,
Springer Proceedings in Business and Economics,
DOI 10.1007/978-3-319-49559-0_52

571

out the quality and productivity of employees and their individual contribution into company plans. It is important to analyse work performance of all categories of employees from management to workers and after carrying out assessment to allow employees their feedback on the results and then make a future deal what and how will be done for every side's satisfaction. Understanding and managing the implementation of assessment of work performance can be a key factor for company in their business success. Consequences of assessment of human resources are so large that is why the present article tries to analyse the current status of the use of this tool in Slovak companies.

52.2 Theoretical Background

Nowadays, many strong forces affect the development of management accounting (Kral 2010). We insert one of the most impacting—broader content shot. It is possible to see the growth amount of information that is monitored, measured and assessed. Along noted situation pushes to the foreground, the work performance of human resources so here creates a place to intersection between tools of management accounting and personnel management. Following sections will be dealt step by step the way from management control system over management accounting to assessment of work performance of human resources.

52.2.1 Management Control System

Management control system is comprehensive view of issue of managing company. It connects knowledge of management accounting, management, company theory and personnel management (Kral 2010). Managers and other users of various kinds of managerial and control tools do not need to know from what discipline knowledge is, but they need to know how effective use gained knowledge (Cisko and Kliestik 2013). It follows that management control system integrates a lot of tools to achieve the targets of company through proper work performance of all employees.

Table 52.1 shows classification of tools management control system according to Ouchi (1977) that divided all tools to 3 main groups—action controls, personnel and cultural controls and result control. For our purposes, we look in detail only to result controls.

Table 52.1 Tools of management control system

Tools of management control system		
Action controls	Personnel and cultural controls	Result controls

Source Author on the base of Ouchi (1977)

52.2.2   Result (Output) Controls Versus Management Accounting Versus Personnel Management

Result controls are the most used tools form in management control system and in one breath the most used tools are tools of management accounting, so result controls are parallel to tools of management accounting (Ponisciakova et al. 2015). In our case, when we are focused on result controls of human resources, results are synonym of work performance of human resources. Here is uprising next parallel between management accounting and personnel management, because management accounting takes over well-established system of assessment of work performance from personnel management and do not have to generate new ways how to do that.

52.2.3   Assessment of Work Performance of Human Resources

The assessment of human resources is personnel activity that deals with:

- detecting how employees perform their work, how employees satisfy their work tasks and requirements of their work place and how employees behave on their work place,
- notifying of employees of their work results and discussing with them these results,
- looking for of way to correct under average results.

The process of assessment of work performance of human resources

- Phase of gaining information

  - Determining of responsible person for gaining information and performing of assessment. The assessor can be: supervisor of employee, senior manager, employee, colleagues, personnel section, assessment commission or team assessment, assessment centre, independent external assessor, other public, assessment of 360 or 540° feedback (Mateides 2006).
  - Continuing of assessment to the documentation of gained information.

- Phase of assessment of information about work performance

  - Comparing actual results with target results, given or average standards.
  - Discussion with assessment employee.
  - Subsequent observation of work performance of employee, providing assistance for improvement, examining the effectiveness of assessment.

52.2.4   The Methods of Assessment

The level of assessment surely depends on used method of assessment. In this time, a lot of helpful methods of assessment of human resources in companies are described in detail. Here are placed the most frequently used methods: assessment according to performance, assessment according to scale, assessment according to the report, assessment according to the standard, assessment according to the key cases, assessment survey, assessment according to the benchmarking, assessment interview, self-assessment and managerial audit (Kachanakova et al. 2013).

The periodicity of assessment

- Informal assessment is ongoing assessment of employees of their supervisors during work time. This assessment belongs to everyday relationship between supervisor and subordinate, part of check. Mostly this type of assessment is not noticed and occasionally is the cause for some personnel decision.
- Formal (systematic) assessment creates standardised, periodic system and its typical aspects are planned nature and systematic method (Mihalcova 2007).

52.3   Paper Objective and Methodology

As Merchant and Stege (2003) write, there is something to measure in every work situation, so the question related to this statement "What is the right and the effective to measure?" Every company should answer this question for its own conditions. The work performance of human resource is absolutely the proper area to measure.

The management accounting has been trying to overcome its narrow disciplinary orientation with focusing on expanding its management systems. The expand leads to often use of management accounting tools to carry out management mechanisms, because the majority of companies manage its core activities to result controls and results depends on human resources. It cannot be possible to detect the quality of human resources, if management accounting does not have useful platform of extended tools to assessment of work performance.

The target of paper is to analyse current situation of assessment of work performance of human resources in Slovak companies. There were four key issues of finding out:

- an existence of formal systems of assessment,
- an existence of dividing of assessment systems according to category of employees,
- an existence of option of employees to react to assessment results,
- following use of gained information from assessment of work performance.

The information used in the article was gained from the secondary sources:

- Questionnaire survey. The survey was made by Kachanakova, Stachova and Stacho in the years 2010–2012. The survey sample of companies was randomly addressed. There were 239 respondents in the 1 stage, and there were 340 respondents in 2 and 3 stages of survey. The questions had form of an open, close and scale questions. The main objective of annual survey was to detect the way of human resources management in Slovak companies,
- Foreign and domestic literature search linked to presented issue. The key areas of interest were management accounting and personnel management.

Some else methods that were used as well: the analysis of results and gained information, synthesis and the method of deduction, the first as a tool for overall review of level of assessment of work performance of human resource in Slovak companies, its use and its impact and as a tool of connecting of findings between personnel management and management accounting, and the second in order to support the conclusions, the method of induction when the theories of development were discussed.

52.4   Results and Discussion

Assessment of work performance is good starting point in process of increasing efficiency of human resources. It helps to set up current level of human resources and shows the gaps in managing human resources and possible ways of improving. Optimal system of assessment makes conditions for aim education of human resources, aim motivation and of course causes the base to fair, clear and addressed remuneration.

52.4.1   Formal Systems of Assessment

Firstly, the questionnaire survey detected percentage of companies that had established the formal system of assessment of human resources. Underlying figure demonstrates the answers of Slovak companies. Percentage spread of companies that have formal system of assessment was from 65 to 85%. There can be seen positive rising trend—an increase in 15% and there is premise of increasing yet (Fig. 52.1).

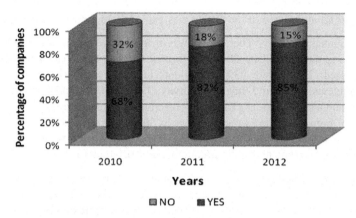

Fig. 52.1 Result of survey task—have you had a formal system of assessment of work performance in your company? *Source* Author on the base of Kachanakova et al. (2013)

52.4.2 Dividing of Systems of Assessment According to Categories of Employees

When companies had have the system of assessment, the survey found out the scale of complexity of assessment, it meant if company assessment covered every category of employee or only the chosen one. There was annual improvement in every category. In 2012, the assessments of all categories of employees reached minimally 80% level, except for the category of workers. Well, the survey showed that the category of employees—management, specialist, technical workers and administrative employees—is more often subject of assessment than the workers. This fact offers a great chance for companies to obtain a competitive advance through understanding work performance of their workers, because workers are the part of the company that creates value and quality (Chlebikova and Bielikova 2015) (Fig. 52.2).

52.4.3 An Option to React to Results of Assessment

After every assessment should have employees an opportunity to react to the results, to discuss with their assessor. It was very remarkable to compare the expected situation to actual course in Slovak companies. The reality was so striking, less than 50% of assessed human resources had an option to react to reached results. This means great lack of process of assessment, and it is necessary to change this state. Assessment loses the target, is ineffective if there is no conversation about the results, about causes influenced results and last but not least deals about future results, requirements and ways to do things better (Chlebikova and Ponisciakova 2014). This area belongs in Slovak companies to the areas where it is needed to improve satisfaction of all participate sides (Fig. 52.3).

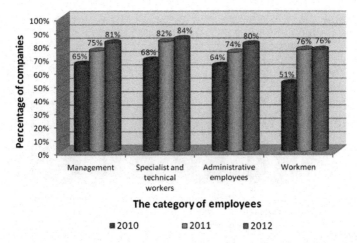

Fig. 52.2 Result of survey task—have you had a formal system of assessment of work performance divided according to categories of employees in your company? *Source* Author on the base of Kachanakova et al. (2013)

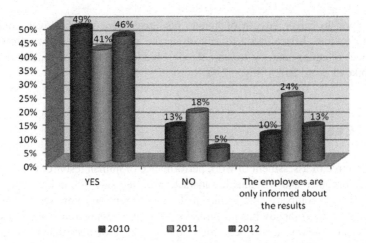

Fig. 52.3 Result of survey task—have the employees had an option to react to the results of their assessment of work performance? *Source* Author on the base of Kachanakova et al. (2013)

52.4.4   Use of Gained Information from Assessment

Use of gained information has two basic tasks—reverse remuneration of work performance and career growth and development. The aim of this survey questions was to determine whether both of tasks are fulfilled. On the one hand, the percentages of companies that use gained information to remuneration were quite high between 73 and 84%, and on the other the percentages of companies that use gained

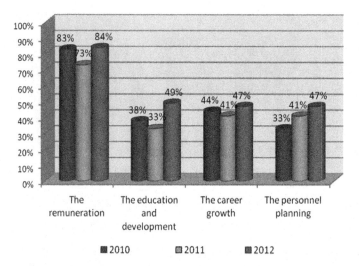

Fig. 52.4 Result of survey task—how has been gained information about work performance used? *Source* Author on the base of Kachanakova et al. (2013)

information to career growth of human resources were weak. Slovak companies have to review their attitude to education and development, career growth and personnel planning and try to start flowing hidden potential of human resources (Chlebikova et al. 2015) (Fig. 52.4).

52.5 Conclusion

The objective of assessment of work performance of human resources is to increase their performance and sustainable satisfaction on the side of employees as well as on the side of company. We cannot make assessment and improve of work performance, if the company has no formal system of assessment. On the basis of the questionnaire survey, it has been found out that 85% of questioned Slovak companies have implemented system of assessment, although it is a positive trend that the tool assessment is used increasingly, but there is still a place for a change. Subject to next questioning could be what kind of barrier hinder companies to implement the system, whether it is an obstacle in the financial field or companies do not consider assessment on relevant indicator.

Slovak companies which actively use assessment have been expressed, if they have a comprehensive system of assessment for all categories of employees. More than 60% of companies have a system of assessment for all categories of employees and an interesting fact resulted that most are assessed managers and at least workers, what is another subject for future discussion, why workers are not assessed sufficiently when their daily activity largely affects to company running and subsequent customer satisfaction.

A surprising fact was showed in Slovak companies in communication after assessment, only less than half of the assessed employees got an opportunity to express their opinion to reached results. It would be interesting to find out the reason of the fact whether it deals with work occupancy or unwillingness of assessor to communicate with employees. In future, it is necessary to increase significantly the proportion of employees in Slovak enterprises which have an option to comment assessment.

We can talk about effective use of assessment information when they are used to reverse remuneration of human resources and development of employees. The Slovak companies have placed in the foreground rather than remuneration development, which is big shame. Professional community should put pressure on companies not to forget the long-term development and education of human resources.

Slovak companies use the tool assessment of work performance of human resources, but in their systems there are still some gaps, so these systems stay in front of a long way of development and improvement.

Acknowledgments This paper has been prepared under financial support of VEGA 1/0244/16 personnel marketing as a new approach of the ensuring and maintaining the skilled workforce in Slovak companies, in which author gratefully acknowledges.

References

Chlebikova D, Ponisciakova O (2014) Key performance indicators and their exploitation in decision-making process. In: 18th international conference on transport means, Kaunas, pp 372–375

Chlebikova D, Bielikova A (2015) Business environment and measurement of competitiveness of Slovak Republic. In: 10th international scientific conference financial management of firms and financial institutions, Ostrava, pp 422–428

Chlebikova D, Misankova M, Kramarova K (2015) Planning of personal development and succession. Procedia Econ Fin 26:249–253

Cisko S, Kliestik T (2013) Financny manazment II. Edis Publishing, Zilina

Kachanakova A, Stachova K, Stacho Z (2013) Riadenie ludskych zdrojov v organizaciach posobiacich na Slovensku. Iura Edition, Bratislava

Kral B (2010) Manazerske ucetnictvi. Management Press, Praha

Mateides A (2006) Manazerstvo kvality. Epos, Bratislava

Merchant KA, der Stege WA (2003) Management control systems. Performance measurement, evaluation and incentives. Prentice Hall/Pearson Education, Harlow

Mihalcova B (2007) Riadenie ludskych zdrojov. Ekonom, Bratislava

Ouchi WG (1977) The relationship between organizational structures and organizational control. Adm Sci Q 22(1):95–113

Ponisciakova O, Gogolova M, Ivankova K (2015) Calculations in managerial accounting. Procedia Econ Fin 26:431–437

Chapter 53
Use of Management Accounting Information for the Formation of the Business Model of a Public Company

Rosa Grigoryevna Kaspina and Lyudmila Sergeevna Khapugina

Abstract The article is dedicated to the matter of dependency between the structure of public organization's business model and the information disclosed in the management reporting. To prove this connection, the authors generalized various definitions of the business model; analyzed its structure; demonstrated the necessity to use management accounting methods in the description of individual elements of the business model. The authors recommended method of activity-based costing to describe the business model elements representing information on costs and results of public company as this method allows the company to allocate overhead costs more precisely and develop an efficient pricing policy, which is the key factor in the company's value chain.

Keywords Business model · Management accounting · Reporting · Activity-based management · Activity-based costing

53.1 Introduction

The analysis of world experience shows that market participants in conditions of market economy struggle both for possession of capital resources and for ability to develop and implement effective innovations of organizational and economic nature. Researchers associate modern sources of economic growth more with technology (39%) rather than with capital (34%) and labor force (27%) (Korshunov 2008). One of the priority directions of development for entities is a goal-oriented

R.G. Kaspina (✉) · L.S. Khapugina
Department of Management Accounting and Controlling, Institute of Management,
Economics and Finance, Kazan Federal University, 18 Kremlyovskaya Street,
Kazan 420008, Russia Federation
e-mail: rosakaspina@yandex.ru

L.S. Khapugina
e-mail: 19196886553@outlook.com

© Springer International Publishing AG 2017   581
D. Procházka (ed.), *New Trends in Finance and Accounting*,
Springer Proceedings in Business and Economics,
DOI 10.1007/978-3-319-49559-0_53

system of arrangements for design, implementation, and development of various tools and techniques of management accounting in the united corporate information system of organization management (Shneidman 2012).

Each organization in order to succeed in a competitive environment needs to develop a business model that would allow the company to understand the processes that raise its value (Boyeva and Nazarova 2013). A study conducted in 2010 by a group of Economist Intelligence Unit showed that according to 50% of managers the innovative business models are more important for the company prosperity than innovative products or services. A poll among Corporate Heads conducted in 2011 by IBM showed similar results. Almost all respondents expressed the need for business models adjustment with consideration of new conditions. In tough economic times, companies are considering the business models as one of the most important factors of stability in a volatile environment. However, according to a study by the American Management Association, global companies allocate for the development of new business models even less than 10% of the total investment in innovation (Markova 2010).

53.2 Methods

The study is based upon a method of comparison and synthesis of different approaches to the definition of business model. Unfortunately, the science has not worked out the most precise definition of "business model" yet. Although this term is found in works of many specialists and scientists engaged in research on the strategic management and strategic management accounting. We have considered the main approaches to the definition of the business model and its components in Table 53.1.

Approaches to the business model definition considered in Table 53.1 treat this concept as logic and method of doing business, on the one hand, and as a way of adding value for customers and increment in the company's market value, on the other.

53.3 Data, Results, and Discussion

Analysis and synthesis of various definitions of "business model" have allowed us to formulate, in our view, a more accurate and comprehensive definition: business model is a structured description of financial and economic activity of the company that reflects the way of its value increment. Let us distinguish the main components of each business model:

- structure and management system in the company;
- markets and proposed values (products, services);

Table 53.1 Comparative characteristics of different approaches to the definition of "business model"

Country	Researcher	Definition of the term "business model"	Structural element of a business model
Russia	V. Gusakov	Business model is how and at what expense the company makes money (Gusakov 2009)	(a) Goals and vision of the company's prospects (b) Structure and management system in the company (c) Company's markets and products (d) Corporate culture (e) Value chain within the company
Russia	V. Kotelnikov	Business model is a method of sustainable performance which converts the base values (resources, company's capabilities, and innovation— in economic results) (Kotelnikov 2007)	Components of business: (a) Business strategy (b) Economics and Finance (c) Marketing and competition (d) Entrepreneurship
USA	Larry Bossidy and Ram Charan	Business model is a robust, reality-based process for thinking about the specifics of your business in a holistic way (Bossidy and Charan 2001)	Business model is effective if the external realities and the company's financial goals are in harmony with its internal capacities, resources
USA, Germany	Mark Johnson, Clayton Christensen, Henning Kagermann	Determine the business model as a set of the following four elements (Johnson et al. 2009)	(a) Customer value proposition (b) Profit formula (c) Key resources (d) Key processes
	D. Hambrick and J. Friedrickson	Business model is a definition of a business model give a list of five questions, the answers to them form the business model definition and structure (Hambrick and Friedrickson 2001)	(a) Questions that develop the definition of a business model (b) Arenas: where will we be active? (c) Vehicles: how will we get there? (d) Differentiators: how will we win in the marketplace? (e) Economic logic: how will we obtain our returns? (f) Staging: what will be our speed and sequence of moves?

- value chain: financial component of the value chain (cost structure, income structure, cash flow structure); economic component of the value chain (mechanisms of interaction with suppliers and contractors, other partners);

- clients: vehicles of sales and promotion of the product in market; targeted group of buyers; mechanisms of interaction with customers;
- corporate culture.

It is a well-known fact that the effective management decisions are usually made by virtue of information provided in the management reporting of the enterprise. The term and the concept of management reporting are studied in works by many American and European researchers in the field of economic sciences, such as Ray Garisson, Eric Noreen, Peter Bruay, Anthony A. Atkinson, Rajiv D. Banker, Robert S. Kaplan, and others (Porter 1985; Brugemann et al. 2005; Kaplan and Anderson 2004; Armstrong 2002). Analyzing and summarizing the authors' definitions, we can say that management reporting is one or several documents in which financial and nonfinancial information about the company for a certain period of time is organized and generalized. One of the management reporting features is that it contains the very information required to make effective management decisions in the company. Management reporting is a trade secret of the company, on the one hand, and is unique for each organization on the other.

Quality and success of management reporting is directly dependent on management accounting techniques. In our opinion, methods of management accounting, and techniques for classification and grouping of accounting information may also be a means to describe the financial component of business model. The role of management accounting within the proposed structure of business model is shown in Fig. 53.1.

How, then, can the formed business model as a whole and its elements affect the disclosure of information in the management reporting? To explain Fig. 53.1, let us note that the goal of business model of any company is to demonstrate the value chain process. The company value raise, in turn, is one of the goals of the business entity.

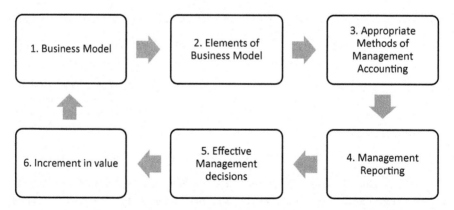

Fig. 53.1 The logical interrelation of the business model and methods of management accounting

53.4   Conclusion

Effectiveness of the company activities is conditioned by accurate choice of managerial accounting methods and efficiency of the management reporting that must meet the needs of the company's management by disclosing business information. In this case, by effectiveness of the company we mean the net financial result and the increment in value.

Thus, we can conclude that the structure of the business model affects information disclosed in management reporting. The company can describe such an element of the business model as a financial component using selected management accounting methods. We recommend, among others, the activity-based costing method, since in comparison with the traditional methods of management accounting it allows to determine the cost of production more accurately and to develop an effective pricing policy.

References

Armstrong P (2002) The costs of activity-based management. Acc Organ Soc 27:99–120

Bossidy L, Charan R (2001) Confronting reality. Doing what matters to get things right; Translation into Russian. Williams, Moscow, p 92

Boyeva NA, Nazarova AI (2013) Generation of business models by means of conduct of an innovative audit for small and medium-sized enterprises. Educ Res 2:10–21

Brugemann W, Everaert P, Steven SR et al (2005) Modeling logistic costs using TDABC: a case in a distribution company. University Ghent, Faculty of Economics and Business Administration http://www.ideas.repec.org/p/rug/rugwps/05-332.html. Accessed 13 Feb 2005

Gusakov VA (2009) Clear business strategy. Vershina, Moscow, p 115

Hambrick DC, Friedrickson JW (2001) Are you sure you have a strategy? Acad Manag Executive 4:48

Johnson M, Christensen C, Kagermann H (2009) Reinventing your business model. Harvard Bus Rev 63–72

Kaplan RS, Anderson SR (2004) Time-driven activity-based costing. Harvard Bus Rev 45

Korshunov IA, Trifilova AA (2008) Modern innovation management. Innovations 2:85

Kotelnikov YV (2007) New business models for era of swift changes moved by innovations. Eksmo, Moscow, p 84

Markova VD (2010) Business model: essence and innovative component. In: Eurasian international scientific and analytical magazine Problems of Modern Economy. http://www.m-economy.ru/art.php?nArtId=3072#ftn1. Accessed 08 Feb 2010

Porter ME (1985) Competitive advantage: creating and sustaining superior performance. Free Press, New York, p 67

Shneidman LZ (2012) Review of consolidated reporting structure in Russia. Accounting 11:6–9

Chapter 54
How Demands of Donors Influence the Design of the Management Control System of Not-for-Profit Nongovernmental Organizations

Ondřej H. Matyáš

Abstract Main goal of the paper is to present the review of main characteristics that differentiate various types of financial sources of not-for-profit organizations. The emphasis is placed mainly on the contractual framework of these sources, as it is the keystone for proper design of management control system used in financial management of projects financed by the above-mentioned sources. Based on the research conducted in the largest CEE not-for-profit nongovernmental organization, analysing ca 400 different projects, the paper provides the basic typology and corresponding characteristics of various types of donors which can be used with the advantage by the not-for-profit organizations in setting up their management control system effectively.

Keywords Not-for-profit nongovernmental organization · Management control system design · Donors

54.1 Introduction

Almost all not-for-profit nongovernmental organizations are at least partly financed through project financing. This way of financing the operations of the organizations means that the organizations raise funds by letting the donor to finance a specific project or activity, following the donor's requirements on financial management controls that are supposed to be used by the organization in order to carry out the project outcomes effectively (Lewis 2009; Král 2010).

For most not-for-profit organizations, the project financing is even prevailing in terms of their structure of financial sources (Skovajsa et al. 2010). Therefore, the paper identifies huge potential in helping the organizations with setting up their

O.H. Matyáš (✉)
Department of Management Accounting, University of Economics, Prague,
Nam. W. Churchilla 4, 130 67 Prague, Czech Republic
e-mail: ondrej.matyas@vse.cz

© Springer International Publishing AG 2017
D. Procházka (ed.), *New Trends in Finance and Accounting*,
Springer Proceedings in Business and Economics,
DOI 10.1007/978-3-319-49559-0_54

management control systems according to typical donors' demands on the design of management control tools that should be applied by the not-for-profit organizations receiving the funds from donors (Anthony and Govindarajan 2003; Anthony and Young 2003).

Main goal of the paper is to present the review of main characteristics that differentiate various types of financial sources of not-for-profit nongovernmental organizations (Holland and Ritvo 2008). The emphasis is placed mainly on the contractual framework of the funding, as it is the keystone for proper design of management control system used in financial management of projects financed by the above-mentioned sources.

The review is based on the research that processed the data from the organization called People in need (Člověk v tísni, o.p.s.). People in need is the largest CEE not-for-profit nongovernmental organization. It operates in 29 countries worldwide and employs circa 600 FTEs (local employees included). Its turnover totalled 1500 mil. CZK in 2015.

The research was based on the analysis of almost 400 projects, which were fully or partially implemented and administrated by the organization in previous years. Based on this analysis, the paper provides the basic typology and corresponding characteristics of various types of donors which can be used with the advantage by the not-for-profit organizations in setting up their management control system effectively.

54.2   Typology of Donors

The most influential factor governing the demands of a donor seems to be:

(a) the fact whether the donor is a Czech-based entity or a foreign one
(b) whether the donor provides public funds (i.e. state funds, the European Union or other international organizations and agencies), or it is a private entity (Table 54.1).

Key financial and administrative features of the projects can be analysed with regard to these groups of donors as every group represents specific demands and/or limits when the not-for-profit organization is carrying out the projects financed by these groups.

(1) State budget of the Czech Republic

These are the resources obtained from the state budget through central government authorities (usually ministries). Allocation of funds is in the form of the decision to grant subsidies from the state budget, and regardless what authority provides the funds, basic procedures and conditions remain similar all the time as they are regulated by specific acts governing the way the organizations can treat with the property of the Czech Republic in general.

Table 54.1 Classification of donors

	Country of origin		
	Czech Republic	Combinations	Foreign country
Public sources	(1) State budget of the Czech Republic (2) The budgets of local authorities	(9) The European Union funds administered by the Czech governing bodies	(7) State and local budgets of other states (8) of the EU budget is administered by the European Commission (10) Other foreign donors (UN agencies, etc.)
Private sources	(3) Endowments provided by foundations (4) Public collections (5) Gifts (6) Partnerships		

Source Authorial representation

(2) Budgets of Czech local authorities

Nonprofit organizations can raise funds from local authorities. Compared with subsidies from the central authorities, these are typically lower-scale projects representing also smaller budgets. In terms of reporting requirements, this is a heterogeneous group, as local authorities (regions, municipalities) developed in the past diverse practices and ideas about what to require from the beneficiaries.

(3) Endowments provided by foundations

The endowment provided by the foundations is legally performed as a grant contract, in which the foundation defines, among other things, its requirements, especially how the beneficiary can treat with the endowment, what processes organizations must adhere. Given that most foundations distribute funds received by their own efforts (and not the public funds raised by taxes), it is understandable that foundations can be more flexible and responsive to the needs of not-for-profit organizations, at least compared to state institutions, region or municipal authorities.

(4) Public collections

Public collections represent own resources for not-for-profit organizations, however still (at least partially) regulated by the law. Public collection is a form of financing resources standing between sources from institutional donors and donations. If an organization decides to open a public collection to raise funds from individual donors, it must follow various obligations in a way the public collection is documented and reported to local municipal authorities.

(5) **Donations**

Donations represent own resources of the organization with quite a high level of freedom to handle acquired funds. To some extent, it depends on the amount and the method of obtaining the donation: the donation may be the result of long-term and donor-tailored fundraising activity. In this case, during the fundraising process the donor also formulates, for which purpose the donation is provided and the way the use of donation should be used and documented. On the other hand, in case of rather small, periodically recurring or one-time support from sympathizers of the organization, the organization itself set the rules how the donation is used.

(6) **Partnership**

Numerous institutional donors motivate nonprofit organization to form collaborative networks, partner alliances, etc. The goal of this effort is to promote cooperation between organizations, as well as mutual exchange of information and know-how, usually in the form of spreading the best practice models in the not-for-profit industry.

When the donor requires the partnership financing model, the organizations form the partnership structure which consists of lead organization [also referred as the main or principal organization (or partner or beneficiary)] and partnership organizations. The funds are distributed among the members of the partnership according to the preapproved budget for each organization which participates in the project. The funds which the organization gains in the partnership model from the main partner are usually restricted according to the requirements of the donor. It means that they are handled in the same way as any other public sources and could be classified like this. On the other hand, the only entity which has any legal relationship with the donor is the main partner, which also faces the main risks.

Typical risks in case of partnership financing models are:

- the rules for mutual cooperation of partners are not clear and/or predefined before the project starts; therefore,
- it requires time-consuming and demanding communication among partners, and, as a result of above-mentioned risks
- defining financial and administrative parameters of cooperation between the partners fall behind the actual implementation works performed within the project and represents a burden for administration and financial management capacities of organizations involved in the project, as well as quite a frustrating experience for everyone who participates in administration management of this kind of project.

(7) **State or local budgets of foreign national authorities and agencies**

Especially in funding for humanitarian and development assistance, we can observe that the organization raise funds applying to other (foreign) national institutions and development agencies. The purpose of such cooperation is usually aggregation and consolidation of resources and operations worldwide.

The administration and financial management of projects financed from foreign donors is usually quite demanding, because national specifics of accounting systems and other legislation and donor-specific requirements are mixing all together. Furthermore, the process is complicated by a great geographic distance between the seat of the donor, the place where the project is implemented and the headquarters of a not-for-profit organization, which manages and administrates the project.

(8) **Funding related to the European Union budget and funding related to off-budgetary funds administrated by the European Commission authorities**

Individual European Commission's Directorates announced, as part of their thematic programs, calls, in which not-for-profit organizations submit proposals, competing among others for obtaining the grant. When an organization receives funding from the European Union budget provided directly by the European Commission and the Directorates, the donors' requirements are challenging, but more or less clear, logical and accomplishable. The European Commission as well as other EC-related supranational authorities represents the donor with clearly formulated demands respecting the unity, consistency and standard form for all funds from the EC budget across various directorates and/or thematic programs.

(9) **European Union funds administered by Czech authorities**

A similar situation should—at least theoretically—apply for structural funds administered by the European Union through various operational programs of the Czech managing authorities (governing bodies). However, organizations receiving this kind of funds should be prepared for the fact that Czech authorities in the position of managing authorities sometimes interpret the EU guidelines extensively and/or not in a qualified way. In recent years, the qualification of staff, as well as general administration practice of Czech managing authorities, improved and standardized. Still, management control of this type of funding can be to some extent quite frustrating experience for the organizations' management and financial staff.

(10) **Other foreign donors (UN agencies, etc.)**

Besides the EU-based entities, also other international organizations play important role in financing the operations of not-for-profit organizations. The United Nations and its various agencies take the key part among them, e.g. United Nations High Commissioner for Refugees (UNHCR), UN Office for the Coordination of Humanitarian Affairs (OCHA) and others share a lot in financing the operations of Czech-based not-for profit organizations.

From the perspective of setting up adequate management control measures, the organizations should be prepared for huge diversity of procedures, requirements and conditions defined by various UN agencies. Moreover, the diversity can be observed even in case of two delegacies of the same agency which have different opinions on interpretations of the same rules, guidelines, etc., as well as in connection with personnel changes on a certain managerial position within the agency, which also can lead to the change in demands or interpretation of rules, etc. For an organization receiving a grant from such a donor, it is crucial to be prepared for such a situation especially in terms of the need of personnel capacities because of time-consuming process of revealing and/or redefining the requirements of the donor.

Unlike the resources of the European Union, which are under the standard control mechanisms not just by the donating agency themselves, but also the control of the European Court of Auditors and the European Anti-Fraud Office, the UN are not supervised by any other entity that could provide the harmonization and standardization efforts and accents into the area of rules and regulations connected to the way the UN agencies distribute their financial support.

54.3 Key Management Control Parameters of Projects

After establishing basic categories, which could provide the not-for-profit organizations with the framework for fundamental identification of the character of donors' demands on management control of the project, the research focused on defining the key management control parameters which should enable the organizations to orient themselves quickly and to design their management control systems effectively.

Therefore, the research offers following lists of these parameters:

1. Donor's contractual framework
2. Eligibility of costs
3. Cash flow
4. Exchange rate risks
5. Flexibility of the budget, possibility of budgetary amendments
6. Co-financing
7. Form of financial reports and audit
8. Other risks

The list is pragmatic and, of course, not the only possible one. It would certainly be possible to develop it further, or, vice versa, to aggregate it to fewer parameters. On the other hand, based on the research conducted, this list covers the vast majority general topics and especially pitfalls in the management control of projects, as the experience of numerous not-for-profit organizations shows. Furthermore, not all of the parameters are applicable for every project, of course. For example, in case the organization provides its services in the Czech Republic and the income from its donor is also in Czech crowns, the exchange rate risks are out of topic for them. Similarly, for a project where the donor does not require co-financing and therefore the project is not co-financed, the whole parameter can be ignored then.

However, the organization should use this as a check list all the time when starting the implementation of a new project and setting up their systems according to the needs of this new project, respectively, according to the requirements of the donor financing this project.

54.4 Donor's Contractual Framework

As declared in the introduction, the paper focuses mainly on the donor's contractual framework, as the contractual framework represents the groundwork for all other parameters.

Surprisingly, it does not have to be so easy for the organization to grasp the whole framework. Of course, the organization usually signs the contract with the donor, the contract usually contains annexes and/or references to other legal documents that help to define both the content and the context of the relationship between the organization and the donor, but still, it can be quite hard to find especially relevant control findings and/or interpretation of various documents that have been already passed and will be applied especially in case of audits and other inspections examining whether the rules defined by the donor have been followed.

Therefore, the research identified typical risks and/or pitfalls in the organization's effort to map the whole contractual framework for the above-defined types of donors.

1. State budget of the Czech Republic and budgets of Czech local authorities

In this case, the decision of the authority to grant the subsidy (referred as the Decision, later on in this paper) represents the key legal document here. The Decision determines the basic conditions of the project, i.e. what is going to be delivered in the project, the amount of funds provided, payment schedule, co-financing requirements, and conditions for eligibility and sanctions for breaching various types of conditions.

Even the fact that this is the Decision, i.e. not the contract between two parties, is quite a symptomatic fact that describes the mindset of this type of donors. Compared to this, EC-based authorities use grant agreements, and however a lot of the content of this kind of agreement is preset and not negotiable by the organization, still their approach is more likely to be peer to peer.

Besides the Decision that is issued individually for every project, common legislative rules specifying the way of handling state funds in general are applied here. These are especially:

* Law no. 218/2000 Coll. on budgetary rules (usually referred as "big" budgetary guidelines by not-for-profit staff in practice) and

- Guidelines for granting subsidies from the state budget of the Czech Republic, nongovernmental organizations by central government authorities, the Government Resolution no. 1333/2008 Coll. (usually referred as "small" budgetary guidelines by not-for-profit staff in practice)

2. Endowments provided by foundations

In the case of funds provided by the foundations, the basic document governing the relationship between the organization and the donor is usually the agreement on providing the grant. The key factor in this case, and the information that the organization should find out in its best interest, is whether the foundation distributes "own" funds, usually raised from public or from private donor, or whether the foundation acts "only" as a hired administrator, mediator between another back-funding institution and the nonprofit organization (typical situation for so-called Norway funds, for example). Then, the conditions of this back-funding institution are applied.

3. Public collections

In case the organization raises voluntary monetary contributions from previously undefined segments of contributors, it fulfils the key features of a public collection and is therefore obliged to follow the law no. 177/2001 Coll. on public collections.

Key responsibilities from the financial and administrative point of view are, in particular:

- the obligation to announce the launch of the collection to the responsible department of the local authority, where the organization has its registered seat.
- to collect funds according to the procedures defined by the law, namely (and solely) through the collection account and petty cash boxes, fundraising events, selling charity goods, subscription lists and leased phone lines. As can be observed, this list is to some extent obsolete and also with lack of flexibility which is demanded by the practice, mainly in terms of the technological development. For example, the list still does not reflect the fact that donor text messages (DMS) have been already used for couple of years. Another example is payments using the alternative payment systems such as Paysec/Paypal. As a result of this, these forms of fundraising stand in a legal vacuum, and from the puristical legal point of view, they are not legal as they are not allowed by the respective law. Anyway, it must be admitted that this vacuum has not been misused by state authorities against the interests of NGOs and their donors yet, fortunately.
- the obligation to submit ongoing report annually and the final report when the collection is terminated
- the obligation of transferring of unused funds to the local authority which allowed the public collection; the authority is obliged to spend the funds on similar projects which the collection promoted.

The reporting stands more on a cash basis rather than the concept of revenues and expenses. This may be not so easy to process, especially for larger organizations administrating more public collections, as well as other types of funding, as they have to overcome the usual way of reporting on the income statement basis and use other kind of accounting information to report right according to the requirements defined by the law.

4. Donations

The most common legal title, under which the organization obtains the gifts, is the gift agreement which pursues § 2055 of the Civil Code. Purely from the legal point of view, it is quite hard—at least according to the Czech legal order—to bind the gift with certain level of compliance with any conditions defined by the donor, and the fact of binding cannot be formalized. Therefore, in case the donor requires to bind the organization contractually, the donor should consider innominate contract which pursues § 1746 of the Civil Code to define the relationship between the donor and the organization.

The key aspect of donations is whether the donor and the done declare the gift in the same tax regime. While legally the status of the gift, and the exact form of relation between the donor and the organization can be to some extent blurry, from the tax point of view the gift is subject to the gift tax or the income tax and should be identified in the same way by both parties.

5. Partnership

As mentioned in the section describing the nature of partnership of two or more organization in project implementation, from the perspective of management control the partnership tends to be a demanding and often frustrating experience.

The basic contractual document is the partnership agreement, usually in the form of innominate contract which pursues § 1746 of the Civil Code. Regardless how solid and well prepared the partnership agreement is, the lead organization still has to accept the main risk that it guarantees the work of all partners in the project and it also guarantees meeting all financial constraints and guidelines posed on project implementation process by the donor, while taking into consideration that this kind of risk is almost impossible to eliminate. The lead organization can, of course, transfer by the contract the risk of penalties resulting from breaching the donor's guidelines and other regulations, but the experience of many organizations shows that while the partner organization has not enough skills and/or capacities to meet the donor's requirements, they also do not have enough financial capacity (i.e. the funds, in other words) to cover the penalties and/or to pay the project expenses that became ineligible due to not meeting the donor's requirements, etc. Therefore, the enforceability of such compensation by the lead organization is extremely low in the not-for-profit industry.

6. State or local budgets of foreign national authorities and agencies

In case of a contractual relationship with foreign national authorities and agencies, it is essential to define precisely the risks that the organization undertakes towards the donor. It is obvious that the not-for-profit organization is typically in the weaker party in the negotiation process with the donor. For example, while trying to set the applicable law for the agreement is essential, on the other hand it is quite hard to renegotiate the default set-up used by the donor.

The usual characteristic, especially in case the organization and this type of donor work together for the first time, is a late detection of expectations of both parties. Rather high differences in rules, conventions and industry culture in general of the donors and not-for-profit organizations cause this kind of dissension in expectations of both parties.

Unfortunately, there is no better advice than to focus on the process of contracting and to keep it as transparent and manageable as possible in order to use it to achieve maximal congruence of both parties. To consult management control system set (especially budgeting and reporting practice ups) in detail with relevant employees of the donor brings a lot of clearness and efficiency for everyone involved.

7. Funding related to the European Union budget and funding related to off-budgetary funds administrated by the European Commission authorities

Unlike some of the previous donors, whose requirements were sometimes blurry (to say at least), EU-based funding administrated by the European Commission authorities represents challenging, but also transparent, stable guidelines which are, on the top of that, managed by professional staff.

The most frequent donors providing the Czech NGOs with funds from the European Commission are mainly Directorate General (DG) for International Cooperation and Development (DG DEVCO/EuropeAid), Humanitarian aid and Civil Protection department (ECHO), DG Employment, Social Affairs & Inclusion, DG Education and Culture and DG Justice and Consumers.

The contractual relationship between the European Commission and/or its authorities and the organizations is represented by a grant agreement. The structure of related documents is always similar and the key annexes defining the demands on the management control system of the organization are: Annex II (general conditions defining mainly eligibility of costs), Annex IV (tender procedures and general demands on transparency in spending) and Annex VII defining the structure and the content of the report of factual findings (a report describing the findings of the auditor who conducts the project audits).

This structure should be, at least in theory, the same as for European Union funding administered by the Czech governing bodies. In spite of this, there is a huge difference—see below. Therefore, the funding distributed directly by the European Commission authorities can serve as a best practice benchmark which enables to observe how Czech political-bureaucratic "creativity" affected formerly logical and usually sound EC requirements.

8. European Union funds administered by Czech authorities

As already stated before, EU funding is an extremely important source for Czech nonprofit sector. Management of such projects, however, puts high demands on the management control system of the organization, mainly because of sometimes not fully functional guidance from the governing bodies and also not completely logical and consistent donor requirements, resulting from the "creativity" of Czech authorities which are supposed to govern the operational programmes financed from two—for the Czech not-for-profit sector—most important structural funds, the European Regional Development Fund (ERDF) aimed at financing investment projects, as well as the European Social Fund (ESF), focused on noninvestment projects.

9. Other foreign donors (UN agencies, etc.)

Contracts with other foreign donors vary a lot, and this variance is the underlying principle that helps to understand the characteristic of the contractual framework. As stated above, when describing this kind of donors in general, the level to which these donors themselves are audited and made accountable for their performance is lower than in case of other private or public donors, mainly due to less intensive public control compared to public donors at the European or national level.

On the other hand, due to the lack of standardization, many contractual parameters are negotiable, such as payment schedule, the possibility of budget changes, the method of reporting, subsequent approvals that can be obtained from the donor, etc.

The most demanding issue, which is also a result of low standardization, is how to categorize the nature of the relationship with the donor from the income tax point of view, especially because for the donors the distinction between donating and paying for delivery of predefined service is not so clear.

54.5 Conclusion

The paper complies with real needs of not-for-profit nongovernmental organizations, for which the project financing is often prevailing form of financing. Based on the research described above, the paper delivered the typology of donors that enables the organizations to find general characteristics for every type of donor. Based on this, the organization can consider in advance, how demanding and costly can be to adapt its management control system, as they have to be designed according to the requirements of donors.

The typology distinguishes two basic factors that helps to understand the nature of demands of donors (the country of origin of the donor: Czech-based donor/foreign donor/combination) and whether the donor is of an institutional character, providing the organizations with funds obtained from taxpayers previously, or a private donor who does not have to follow general political and social requirements on transparency and/or unbiased approach. Based on these two factors and employing other, mostly organization-based culture contexts, the paper delivers ten main categories of donors.

Furthermore, the paper outlines eight basic parameters which influence the concrete set-up of management control for a particular project and argues that the contractual framework is the key one, as it determines most of other issues for effective project management control.

Therefore, typical traits of every type of donor, i.e. the donors' advantages and/or strengths, as well as pitfalls and/or weaknesses of them, are presented. Based on this, the nature of contractual framework as the key factor for every project-based management control process is outlined and discussed for every type of donor.

Acknowledgments This paper has been prepared under the financial support of FFU VSE IP 100040 research project which author gratefully acknowledges.

References

Anthony R, Govindarajan V (2003) Management control systems, 11th edn. McGrawHill, New York

Anthony RN, Young DW (2003) Management control in nonprofit organizations. McGraw-Hill/Irwin, Boston

Holland TP, Ritvo RA (2008) Nonprofit organizations: principles and practices. Columbia University Press, New York

Král B (2010) aj. (2010): Manažerské účetnictví. Praha, Management Press

Lewis T (2009) Practical financial management for NGOs—getting the basics right: course handbook [on-line]. Oxford, Management Accounting for Non-governmental Organizations, c2009, Quated 29 Oct 2013. http://www.mango.org.uk/Guide/FreeDownloads

Skovajsa M et al (2010) Občanský sektor. Organizovaná občanská společnost v České republice, Praha, Portál

Chapter 55
Actual Problems of Accounting Ensuring Asset Management at the Enterprises of Ukraine

Yuliya Timoshchenko

Abstract At this stage of development of Ukraine, a task of management of assets of the enterprises working in the conditions of an unstable social and economic environment, it is necessary to solve in system approach. The conducted research confirms opinion that traditional balance theories cannot always be base for formation of actual information at different adoption of decisions, both internal and external users. The assessment of assets at historical cost has a shortcoming which, under certain conditions, can become very essential. This type of an assessment will lead to distortion of financial position, as fixed assets which have identical characteristics, but have been acquired at different times, will have also different cost. The principle of an assessment at prime cost protects interests of the state represented by tax authorities better: providing more exact calculation of profit, it promotes increase in the income of the state budget at the expense of taxes. Use of this or that cost has to be reasonable and has system character. For this purpose, it is necessary to develop scientific justification of the applied methods of estimation of cost of assets of the enterprises depending on a stage of their development.

Keywords International financial report standards · Assets · Valuation of assets · Fair value

55.1 Introduction

At this stage of development of Ukraine, a task of management of assets of the enterprises working in the conditions of an unstable social and economic environment, it is necessary to solve in system approach. Such situation causes need of

Y. Timoshchenko (✉)
Accounting Economic Department, Odessa National Economic University, Shyshkarivska Str. 7, 4/1, Sumy 40000, Ukraine
e-mail: ulkattt@gmail.com

© Springer International Publishing AG 2017   599
D. Procházka (ed.), *New Trends in Finance and Accounting*,
Springer Proceedings in Business and Economics,
DOI 10.1007/978-3-319-49559-0_55

ensuring high dynamism for a control system of assets which would take into account the changes in the above factors, potential of formation of financial resources, rates of economic growth, form of the organization of production and financial activity, financial state and other parameters of functioning of the enterprise.

Control system of the enterprise in general is responsible for timely and effective response to changes in internal and environment. Part of a control system is accounting which forms information and analytical providing. According to the current legislation, it is defined as process of identification, measurement, registration, accumulation, generalization, storage and information transfer about activity of the enterprise to external and internal users for decision-making. Thus, the main source of information is data which are created by a management subsystem—the accounting obligatory for all enterprises and the organizations.

Management of assets of the enterprise represents system of the principles and methods of development and implementation of administrative decisions on formation, effective use, and also on the organization of their turn. Realization specified it is impossible without carrying out the reliable cost assessment of assets corresponding to the basic principles of management at the enterprise.

It should be noted that assets are the most difficult of objects of an assessment that it is connected with influence of a large number of factors. These objects depending on their belonging to classification groups (floating assets, fixed assets, cash assets, concealed assets, tangible and intangible assets, financial, etc.) can be used or keep at the enterprise a long time, and their assessment will be influenced by inflation, moral and physical ageing and so forth.

Allocation in the independent control unit of assets as separate direction, from the general system it is connected with the need of addition and development of methods of the analysis, planning, justification of operational administrative decisions and control of assets. In recent years, great attention is paid in the foreign and domestic scientific, educational, professional literature for these problems. Among the scientists dealing with this problem have also made the significant contribution to this development, they are I. Blanc, Zvi Bodi, M. Bondar, F. Butynets, S. Golov, V. Kovalev, G. Leman, L. Lovinska, N. Malyuga, R. Merton, V. Paliy, M. Pyshkar, Y. Sokolov, I. Suprunova, G. Titarenko, N. Urban. At the same time, there are a number of problems of methodological and practical character. In particular, it is aspect of management of non-financial assets considering information opportunities accounting evaluations.

Research objective is definition of topical issues of accounting estimation of cost of assets of the enterprises which work in the conditions of the unstable environment, for the purpose of realization of problems of management in the general strategy of business management.

55.2 The Place of Assets in an Enterprise Management System

Assets of the enterprise are one of the major economic categories and represent the economic resources created at the expense of the capital invested in them which are controlled by the enterprise and are characterized by the cost, productivity, ability to generate the income. Their constant turn in the course of use is connected with risk factors, time and liquidity.

The specified characteristics which reflect essence of assets of the enterprise cause system of the main objectives of their management for achievement of a main goal—ensuring maximizing welfare of owners of the enterprise in the current and perspective periods. In turn, this objective is realized through maximizing market value of the enterprise.

Scientific researches on problems of management of assets, in connection with carrying out in economy of Ukraine of the market principles, have gained development; however, a number of the directions remain insufficiently studied. One of them—methods of estimation of cost of assets of the operating enterprises, their influence on financial results of activity, on indicators of the financial analysis, on an assessment of market value of the enterprise.

It is necessary to notice that the purpose of management of assets is inseparably linked with a main objective of activity of the enterprises. For achievement of the purpose, it is necessary to provide realization of the basic principles: integration with the general control system, complex nature of formation of administrative decisions, high dynamism of management, variability of approaches when developing separate administrative decisions, focus on strategic objectives of development of the enterprise.

At the same time, the end results of financial activity directly or indirectly depend on administrative decisions on formation and use of assets. In this regard, management of assets has to be considered as the complex functional operating system which provides development of the interconnected administrative decisions to be identified. This will be made in the remainder of the paper.

55.3 The Accounting Valuation of Assets in the Theory and Normative Regulation

Adoption of many financial decisions leans on what actual cost of the available assets. According to Zvi Bodi and R. Merton, determination of actual cost of an asset possesses the second place on a number of three analytical "columns" on which the financial theory leans. Valuation of assets—is the most important factor in making many financial decisions (Bodie and Merton 2000).

A significant role in system of theoretical bases of management of assets of the enterprises is played by the concept of their cost. The purpose of this article is

research of the existing theories and justification of the applied methods of estimation of cost of assets in modern financial management.

55.4 Theoretical Aspects of Estimation of Cost of Assets

In modern economic literature, it is possible to select three existing theories of
estimates in which basis approaches to determination of cost are: objective, subjective, book (Malyuga 1998).

So, the theory of objective estimates is based on the principle of sale prices
which could be received at realization of assets at the moment on which the balance
is made. These prices are objective as are established in the market irrespective of
who exactly and why realizes the assets. Users of external financial statements are
interested in objective estimates of the balance sheet subtotals, separate articles of
assets and obligations of the enterprise, forced to make the current business decisions on investment and financing only after they estimate stability of a financial
condition of the enterprise, and define quality of its available assets. However, to
get economically sound estimates of actual costs, the perspective of market participants upon realization of assets shall be followed.

It is considered that the objective theory of an assessment is repaid better and it
is authentically realized only in case of liquidation (sale) of the enterprise.
Application of this theory to continuously functioning enterprise sharply underes-
timates its efficiency as a monetary assessment perhaps only at predictable, probable, to the hypothetical prices. These estimates especially prove in the conditions
of quickly changing economic environment. They will constantly change in time
and depending on structure of buyers.

The theory of value judgment is based on a reasoning that the cost of assets
depends on those individual conditions in which they are at this economic entity:
the same subject can have various values in various enterprises and also in the same
economy during the different periods of his work. Therefore, each balance reflects
the subjective assessment of which have assets in the enterprise at a time.

Modern financial management is almost based on value judgment of assets and
obligations. The interested users of information on the income and expenses, assets
and obligations are persons who exercise the right of operational management and
control of activity of the enterprise. Internal assessment of the enterprise it is
accented on the fact that the same thing in hands of different owners has different
value. Accordingly, the owner's perspective on assets' measurement in balance
sheet will apply value the asset is expected to bring to the owner. Distinctions of an
assessment can follow to destination this or that subject: some things have consumer appointment, others—exchange. The theory of value judgment focuses
attention on income-generating character of property of the enterprise, expert definition of a condition of economic resources which are intended for achievement of
the purpose of business. The types of such assessments often perform estimates of

operational suitability, which the capitalizations of the income received by method, it is expected (future economic benefits).

The theory of book estimates recognizes correct only such estimates by which assets or obligations are considered in books (registers of the account), that is estimates of receipt of values in economy; for property and other material values it expenses, for obligations—their nominal assessment will be incurred.

55.5 Standard Regulation of Estimation of Cost of Assets

In economic practice, various methods of an assessment and types of estimates are applied. Assessment methods—methods of definition of a project cost of an assessment in which sequence of estimated procedures gives the chance to realize a certain methodical approach.

According to the Ukrainian legislation, property which can be estimated objects in a material form, buildings and constructions (including their integral parts), cars, the equipment, vehicles and so forth is considered; shares, securities; intangible assets, including objects of intellectual property right; complete property complexes of all forms of ownership.

Methodical regulation of an assessment of property is carried out in the relevant normative legal acts, provisions (national standards) of a property assessment which are approved by the Cabinet of Ministers of Ukraine, techniques and other normative legal acts which are developed taking into account requirements of provisions (national standards) and are approved by the Cabinet of Ministers of Ukraine or fund of the state property of Ukraine.

Development of normative legal acts according to property is carried out on the principles of the international standards of an assessment.

The international standards of an assessment define that cost is economic concept, establishes connection between the goods and services available to acquisition, on the one hand, and those who buy them, with another. It is specified in standards that professional appraisers avoid the use not specified the term "cost", replacing his adjective with the message that concretizes what cost means. Cost—not the fact, but an assessment of values of concrete goods and services in a concrete timepoint according to established determination of cost. The economic concept of cost expresses a market view of benefits, the owner of goods or the one who receives service, at the time of an assessment receives (International Valuation Standards).

National provisions as well as the international standards of accounting do not contain separate definition of concept of cost and give his contents combining with a type of cost. In turn, the national standard according to property and property rights determines the cost as the equivalent of value of object of an assessment expressed in the probable sum of money (National Standard number 1).

National provisions of accounting in Ukraine have provided a possibility of application of the specified assessment methods depending on a type of an asset and a situation which has developed at the enterprise at the time of preparation of information (Table 55.1).

National accounting standards were harmonized with IFRS procedures on fair value (IFRS 13) in July 2012.

These IFRS determine fair value as the sum for which it is possible to exchange an asset or to extinguish debt in operation between the informed, interested and independent parties. With entry into force of IFRS 13, fair value is the price which would be received for sale of an asset or is paid for transfer of the obligation in usual operation between participants of the market for date of an assessment (IFRS 13 Fair Value Measurement).

This standard describes an order of determination of fair value at initial recognition. It is noted that when it is acquired an asset in operation of an exchange of

Table 55.1 Types of estimation of cost of assets according to national standards of Ukraine

Type of a cost assessment	Definition	Source
Initial cost	Historical (actual) prime cost of non-turnaround assets in the sum of money or fair value of other assets, the paid non-turnaround assets (transferred), spent for acquisition (creation)	National provision (standards) of accounting 7
Salvage value	Estimated value, which the enterprise expects to receive at the end of useful life	
The cost, which is amortized	The initial or overestimated cost of non-turnaround assets minus their liquidating cost	
Revaluated value	The cost of non-turnaround assets after their revaluation	
Net value of realization of stocks	The expected price of realization of stocks in the conditions of usual activity minus the expected expenses on completion of their production and realization	National provision (standards) of accounting 9
Fair value	The sum on which the asset exchange, or payment of the obligation as a result of operation between the informed, interested and independent parties can be carried out	National provision (standards) of accounting 19
Finished goods	The realization price minus expenses on realization and the sums of an extra charge (profit), proceeding from an extra charge (profit) for similar finished goods	
Work in progress	The price of realization of finished goods minus expenses on end, realization and extra charges (profit) calculated by the size of profit of similar finished goods	
Intangible assets	Current market value. In the absence of such cost—the estimated cost in which the enterprise would pay for an asset in case of operation between the informed, interested and independent parties, proceeding from the available information	
Fixed assets	Market value. In case of lack of data on market value—the recovery cost (cost of acquisition) minus the wear sum for date of an assessment. The recovery cost (cost of acquisition) minus the wear sum for date of an assessment	

Source authorial computation

such asset, the price of the transaction is the price paid for acquisition of an asset (that is the occurrence price). From the opposite side, fair value of an asset is the price which would be received for sale of an asset (that is the exit price).

The enterprises not necessarily sell assets at the prices, paid at their acquisition. The price of the transaction is equal in many cases to fair value. For example, it can be in case for date of operation of acquisition of an asset happens in the market in which the asset would be sold.

Whether defining it is equal to fair value at initial recognition of the transaction price, according to IFRS 13, the enterprise has to consider all factors characteristic of this operation and an asset. For example, there is no operation under pressure, and/or not compelled seller to agree to the price in operation, experiencing financial difficulties.

It is necessary to remember that if other IFRS demands or allows the enterprise to estimate an asset at fair value and the price of the transaction differs from fair value, then the enterprise recognizes profit or the loss received as a result as a part of profit or a loss, except for cases when such IFRS provide other.

Thus, fair value becomes a type of the cost applied at acquisition, realization and further is used when forming information on assets for reporting date. In our opinion, the superior preference of usage of historical cost is justifiable only at a production phase.

So, entry into force of IFRS 13 "Fair value measurement" has to influence not only practice of activity of subjects of managing when forming information on the cost of assets at all stages of their circulation, but also induces scientific community to researches concerning a ratio of historical and fair value, and also acquisition of broad consumption in accounting of new terms at fair value—"the occurrence price" and "the exit price".

55.6 Current State of Display of Information on Assets in the Report on a Financial State

It is well known that the financial statements, including the report on a financial state, represent a source of important information, both for internal and for external users. The main administrative decisions are made by owners and potential investors, financial institutions, contractors, and in certain cases managers of the enterprise, proceeding from the analysis of reporting data.

Argumentation of the fact that the possibility of adoption of effective administrative decisions depends on quality of information prepared and provided in the financial statement does not demand detailed justification as it is conventional. Therefore, it is possible to claim with confidence that types, methods and ways of estimation of cost of the assets used by drawing up are important.

The Ukrainian legislation has formalized the principle of historical (actual) prime cost according to which the assessment of assets of the enterprises proceeding from costs of their production and acquisition is recognized priority. Under the law, one of the principles of drawing up and submission of financial statements—the principle of historical (actual) prime cost—means that "... the assessment of assets of the enterprise, proceeding from costs of their production and acquisition is priority" (Law "On accounting and financial reporting in Ukraine" 1999).

The assessment of assets at historical cost has a shortcoming which, under certain conditions, can become very essential. Value, for example, of fixed assets changes over time. Even if the prices are left without changes, the potential of fixed assets does not remain invariable as the term of their service is reduced, fixed assets become morally and physically outdated. This type of an assessment will lead to distortion of financial position, fixed assets which have identical characteristics, but have been acquired at different times, will have also different cost. The principle of an assessment at prime cost protects interests of the state represented by tax authorities better: providing more exact calculation of profit, it promotes increase in the income of the state budget at the expense of taxes.

Besides, in Ukraine at the present stage there is a process of privatization of the state property. And in most cases, privatization is followed by frauds in which considerable part is carried out by manipulations with estimation of cost of fixed assets.

We conducted research of statistical data for the purpose of determination of level of reliability of financial statements of the historical cost made with observance of the principle.

The cost indexes characterizing process of reforming of property—the comparative size of cost of property determined by professional appraisers (expert, market), with the residual cost of the same property on regions, by types of economic activity and countrywide have been for this purpose analysed.

Results of research have allowed to formulate conclusions about impossibility of adoption of effective decisions on the basis of the data created at the book value as she is significantly lower than estimated. So, during active privatization in Ukraine (2001–2006) the market value of assets exceeded balance several times—in the range from 1.2 to 8.6 times in different branches of a national economy.

Besides, it is noted that in the large cities, the industrial and port centres representing the region, attractive to development of the industry and business, the difference between market and residual value is higher, than in the cities with low development of transport infrastructure, the industry and with insignificant population. This results from the fact that similar factors are considered by experts at the determination of estimated cost of property. In our opinion, detection of dependence of a deviation of a difference in estimates by types of economic activity has characteristics:

- the cost of incomplete construction reflected in balance is ten times lower than market;
- the most attractive were trade enterprises—the market value of their property more than by 3 times has exceeded balance;

- the enterprises of the industry had the market value nearly 50% higher than balance;
- the slightest deviations are noted in agriculture.

The conducted research confirms opinion that traditional balance theories cannot always be base for formation of actual information at different adoption of decisions, both internal and external users. Similar conclusions were drawn also by other authors.

For example, Lovinska L. G. points out the defects of the information base created on the basis of historical cost. In her opinion, they are connected with the "ageing" of historical cost caused by currency changes, of course, dynamics of market conditions, scientific and technical progress. She claims that inadequacy of an assessment of assets at initial cost even in the conditions of a stable economic situation in the country becomes obvious within several years from the moment of recognition of assets (Lovinska 2006).

This opinion in the works was expressed also by Sokolov Y.: "The so-called paradox of Burnisyen works—then is longer a firm, the less her real reporting data" (Sokolov 2000). According to professional appraisers, the revaluation of assets are commonly required for enterprises with average assets' useful life over 10 years.

Assessment method at fair value as indicated by the study of possible ways of revaluation most corresponds to requirements of market economy. At the same time, the frequency of revaluations depends on fluctuations of fair value of assets.

55.7   Conclusion

We consider fair to opinion of scientists that historical prime cost is not able to satisfy modern information requirements; therefore, it is necessary to apply more widely other types of cost which are provided by regulatory base: initial cost, production prime cost, cost of sales, fair value, liquidating cost, book value, residual cost, net value of realization, present cost. In our opinion, for an assessment of assets, there has to be an establishment of financial balance in structure of economic enterprise assets and sources of their education, definition of the optimum directions of development.

In our opinion, it is not enough to determine the asset cost by fair, liquidating or real value, etc., use of this or that cost has to be reasonable and has system character. For this purpose, it is necessary to develop scientific justification of the applied methods of estimation of cost of assets of the enterprises depending on a stage of their development.

References

International Valuation Standards (1999) Principles, standards and regulations—Kyiv: UKRels

IFRS 13 Fair Value Measurement (2012)

National Standard number 1 "General Principles of valuation of property and property rights" of 10 September 2003 r. № 1440

National provision (standards) of accounting 7

National provision (standards) of accounting 9

National provision (standards) of accounting 19

On accounting and financial reporting in Ukraine: The law of Ukraine (1999)

Bodie Z, Merton R (2000) Finance: studies allowance—M.; St. Petersburg; K: Williams

Lovinska L (2006) Evaluation in accounting: monograph. K.: KNEU

Malyuga N (1998) Ways to improve assessment of accounting: theory, practice and perspectives: institute of content and teaching methods Zhytomyr Engineering—Institute of Technology—Exactly

Sokolov Y (2000) Fundamentals of accounting theory. Moscow: Finance and Statistics

Chapter 56
Direct and Indirect Influence of Information and Communication Technology on Corporate Performance

David Špičák

Abstract The relation between ICT, its use in the business context and corporate performance is addressed by several authors. However, the number of works published on this topic is relatively small. Despite differences in the areas of focus, methods, definitions and performance measures used in the works that were presented in this paper, it seems that various authors come to the conclusion that ICT in general probably has positive impact on corporate performance. The impact of ICT on performance seems to be indirect, as the adoption of ICT-related solutions allows for ICT-driven changes, which in turn bring positive impact on non-financial and financial performance. Nevertheless, the matter of the mutual relation between ICT in general and corporate performance is relatively complex and involves many specifics. Caution should be used when assessing whether or not the adoption of ICT-related solutions within specific conditions will be beneficial to an organization or not as the conclusions may differ based on a number of factors. Further research in this area may be needed in order to help us gain better understanding of the influence of ICT on corporate performance.

Keywords Corporate performance · Information and communication technology · Performance measurement and management

56.1 Introduction

Information and Communication Technology (ICT) permeates all aspect of human activities and plays an ever increasing role in more and more everyday aspects of our lives. Both ordinary people and numerous companies realized various means from the realm of ICT can be utilized to their advantage. This intuitive notion, quite frequently strongly encouraged by sales and marketing activities of companies

D. Špičák (✉)
Department of Management Accounting, University of Economics, Prague,
Prague, Czech Republic
e-mail: xspid05@vse.cz

© Springer International Publishing AG 2017
D. Procházka (ed.), *New Trends in Finance and Accounting*,
Springer Proceedings in Business and Economics,
DOI 10.1007/978-3-319-49559-0_56

dealing in the ICT industry, leads not only ordinary people to purchase the newest gadgets, but also numerous companies to invest heavily into ICT. In the case of companies, this decision is often driven by the hope of improving their performance, performance measurement and management—be it on the operative, tactical or strategic level.

In my paper, I focus on the analysis of research and studies dealing with both direct and indirect influence of utilizing ICT on corporate performance. The aim is to gain a better insight into this matter and to establish whether any generally applicable conclusions can be drawn, or whether the mutual relation between ICT and corporate performance is more complex.

56.2   Methods

The original intention was to search for, review and analyze existing reports, studies and papers dealing with empirical findings related to the possible relation between utilizing specific types of transactional or analytical ICT and both financial and non-financial corporate performance.

The search and review were primarily aimed at scholarly articles and papers written on this matter. At the same time—for the purposes of conducting relatively unbiased analysis—I refrained from using any information published by dealers, resellers and producers of ICT solutions, which in my opinion may often have the character of materials supporting marketing goals rather than serious and scientifically conducted research.

The search for relevant sources to be analyzed was initially intended to be conducted in accordance with the following steps:

- search for sources in Czech or English language,
- search in electronic databases of scholarly articles, namely Web of Science and Scopus, using relatively broadly defined search phrases, such as *ICT AND performance*,
- if possible, narrow down the search results using relatively specific search phrases, such as *"performance management" AND ((IT OR ICT) AND (contribution OR role OR influence OR impact)* in order to break down the search results into smaller categories,
- narrow down the search to only closely related fields, such as *"computer science," "finance and accounting"* and *"management,"*
- narrow down the search results by limiting the search only to contributions published between the years 2010 and 2015,
- use only the most relevant works by choosing contributions published by the most frequently cited authors.

The research conducted in accordance with the above stated steps yielded very few relevant results. Even after using less limiting criteria—i.e., using more broadly defined search phrases, such as *"ICT and performance,"* not limiting the year of publishing and not filtering the results by the most frequently cited authors—the search was not very fruitful.

As a result, I refrained from limiting the search results, expanded the search to publicly accessible Internet sites, namely Google Scholar, and subsequently even to the general Web using Google search engine.

The works found as the result of the described search are introduced in more detail further on in this paper.

56.3 Results

The relation between ICT, its use in the business context and corporate performance is addressed by several authors. General conclusion that can be drawn upon analyzing their works is that the approaches, definitions of ICT and corporate performance that are used by them, and the conclusions they draw, differ vastly from one author to another.

Carr (2007) asserts in his article, in which he ponders on the role of ICT in relation to business that the role of ICT is overrated. Carr states that ICT managed to progress from being seen as a curiosity at the edge of companies' attention, where it was being perceived with skepticism or outright disregarded, to a powerful tool that found its way to the offices of top managers where it started to enable strategic planning and decision-making. During this transition, many managers started to view ICT as a means of gaining competitive advantage. According to Carr, they started to incorrectly assume that better accessibility and growing potential of ICT also lead to the growth of its strategic value; in fact, it is the other way round—as strategic value is brought only by scarce and inimitable resources. In his article, Carr states ICT should be regarded as infrastructural technology, which can bring strategic value to organizations in early stages after being discovered, as it is still relatively rare (scarce) and has rather proprietary character. The use of proprietary technologies enables organizations to gain competitive advantage because they are able to perform their activities faster, using fewer resources and within shorter time. Once ICT tools become more common, the competition starts catching up, the strategic value for a limited number of their owners (companies) starts disappearing, and they start becoming beneficial to the human race as a whole.

Although Carr's skeptical view of ICT's value is often being brought up, and in general the point he makes is a valid one, it should be pointed out that Carr treated ICT "as a whole" and did not focus closely on the potential role of specific parts of ICT (individual applications or their types) and on specific conditions (influence of observed external and internal factors). ICT is a heterogeneous group of tools, techniques and technologies that are continuously developing. The purpose, context and conditions of using ICT, as well as the characteristics of each individual ICT component, may differ from one company to another. Thus, as demonstrated further in this paper on the findings of works that will be introduced, the role ICT plays in relation to corporate performance should not be dismissed so easily.

Kallunki et al. (2011) focused in their study on the relation between the adoption of Enterprise Resource Planning Systems (ERPS), formal and informal Management Control Systems (MCS) and financial and non-financial performance. Kallunki's team mentions a number of researches and studies dealing with this matter and points out that conclusions various teams drew differ. According to Kallunki's team, a direct link between ERPS implementation and non-financial performance can be expected. This relation may show results at different levels: operative (e.g., process automation), managerial (e.g., better resource planning and management), strategic (e.g., growth and competitive advantage), ICT infrastructure (e.g., ICT savings) and organizational (in the sense of "learning organization") (Kallunki et al. 2011).

As far as financial performance is concerned, no clear conclusions can be reached whether a direct or indirect link with ICT exists. It also seems likely that the link between ICT and financial performance is influenced by numerous company-specific factors (Kallunki et al. 2011). There is also no clear answer to the relation between ICT and MCS, because conclusions of studies dealing with this matter differ as well (Kallunki et al. 2011).

After conducting empirical study among 70 Finnish business units, Kallunki's team also concludes that formal types of MCS mediate positive effect of ERPS adoption and non-financial performance, but the manifestations of this effect come with some delay; in the case of informal types of MCS no such relation was identified. Another conclusion Kallunki's team draws is that there is a significant relation between non-financial and financial performance.

The role of ICT in relation to business was also researched by Muhammad et al. (2013). In their study, they explored the impact of ICT on the performance of Nigerian commercial banks.

Muhammad's team states that the Nigerian banking sector, especially electronic banking, faces challenges that could be categorized into 5 groups: human factor (e.g., health restrictions, population aging, illiteracy), operative (e.g., insufficient security of transferred financial funds, frauds), technical (e.g., insufficient technological infrastructure), psychological and behavioral (e.g., aversion to change, preference of personal contact) and financial (e.g., investments required for introducing technologies) (Muhammad et al. 2013).

Muhammad and his colleagues conclude that utilization of ICT in Nigerian banks has positive impact on Return on Equity (ROE). They also conclude that there is an inverse relation between additional investments into ICT and performance and suggest organizations to find ways of utilizing ICT more effectively instead of investing additional resources into it.

The categories of factors introduced by Muhammad that should be considered in relation to electronic banking might be generalized, modified and subsequently applied to assessing factors that should be considered in other sectors and geographies.

Another look at ICT and its role in relation to business is offered by Koellinger (2006). The author focuses on the relation between ICT and corporate performance, productivity and employment dynamics. With regard to employment dynamics, Koellinger asserts that based on specific conditions or the level on which the relation is explored, ICT may bring either the increase or decrease of employment, based on which of two contradicting factors prevails. On the one hand, the use of ICT may lead to innovations, which in turn lead to growing outputs and a bigger number of work opportunities. On the other hand, ICT may lead to more efficient processes, which in turn may lead to lower need of human resources and cause the decrease of work opportunities. Conclusions may vary also depending on what level the situation is being analyzed at—if the influence of ICT is being analyzed at the level of individual organization, the whole sector or at the macroeconomic level (Koellinger 2006).

As for the relation between ICT and corporate performance, Koellinger holds the same view as Kallunki's team and postulates that opinions on this matter differ. Koellinger recons one of the causes may be the chosen way of measuring and analyzing performance and the impact of ICT on it (Koellinger 2006).

Koellinger concludes his report by stating that there is no direct relation between ICT and economic variables such as profitability, productivity or employment dynamics; ICT only has an indirect effect which manifests itself through innovations enabled by the adoption of new ICT (Koellinger 2006).

Choy et al. (2013) focused their attention on the impact of ICT on performance in logistics and distribution segment. Unlike the above-mentioned works, they introduced a complex model of influences, their relations and possible impacts they may have on the mutual relation between ICT and performance; this model was subsequently tested using a sample of 210 logistics companies operating in the region of Hong Kong and Pearl River delta.

In relation to corporate performance, Choy's team considers service quality and competitive advantage to be interlinked and crucial. They observed changes of these two variables in relation to using ICT in three different forms—broadly defined ICT in general; the use of Logistics Information Systems (LIS) and the use of Business Intelligence (BI).

Choy and his team conclude that no direct link between using ICT and service quality or competitive advantage can be found. At the same time, they come up with a finding that LIS and BI mediate achieving higher levels of service quality; a more important role in this context is played by LIS (Choy et al. 2013).

Choy's team strongly suggests logistics companies to invest more into the adoption of LIS and BI as both types of applications can contribute to improving logistics processes and service level, thus contributing also to gaining competitive advantage in the long run (Choy et al. 2013).

I consider the model introduced by this team to be very inspirational. I believe the model can be modified in such a way that it will enable to cover even other factors, their mutual relations and influence on individual components. The proposed model could be used as a foundation for a more general model that could in turn be applied to even other segments and geographies.

Lee et al. (2011) focused on the relation between adopting ICT, business process reengineering and performance. The authors postulate that studies undertaken to date they were dealing with did not help identify any generally applicable conclusions (Lee et al. 2011). They work with the premise that there are numerous internal and external factors that influence the adoption of ICT; the adoption of ICT influences the change of business processes; changed business processes subsequently influence performance. This premise was captured by Lee and team in a model (Lee et al. 2011) which they tested empirically using data gathered through a questionnaire that was sent to Taiwanese organizations in 2007. They concluded that the adoption of ICT really is influenced by both internal and external factors. Thanks to the adoption of ICT, it is consequently possible to optimize processes and achieve better financial performance (Lee et al. 2011). Lee's team also found out that the relation between the adoption of ICT, better outputs of internal processes and customer satisfaction is only indirect and possible thanks to improved internal processes supported by adopting ICT (Lee et al. 2011).

Steinfield (2010) focuses in their study on the relation between ICT, social capital and performance in a cluster of companies, whose activities require a broad knowledge base. The study Steinfield's team conducted was done on a sample of Danish and Swedish companies dealing in the biotechnology sector. According to Steinfield's team, the results they got indicate that when ICT was used as a means to access human and intellectual capital, alternatively to aid collaboration, it led to better performance (Steinfield 2010).

German Institute for Economic Research (DIW) conducted a study (2008) between the years 2007 and 2008 that was focused on the economic assessment of ICT adoption and its impact on innovation and performance in selected sectors in EU. The study was done on subjects in 6 different sectors—Chemicals, rubbers and plastics; Furniture; Steel; Banking; Transport and Logistics services; and Retailing (DIW Berlin 2008). The authors postulate that ICT and the added value it generates form an ICT value chain which consists of three phases: ICT adoption and use; ICT-enabled innovation; the impact of ICT-enabled innovation and organizational change on economic performance (DIW Berlin 2008). When testing their hypotheses, assessing whether certain factors play a role in various stages of the ICT value chain, they got different results for different economic sectors (DIW Berlin 2008).

Kouki (2015) focuses in his study on the joint impact of Enterprise Resource Planning Systems (ERPS) and non-financial performance indicators (NFPI) on corporate financial performance. In his study, Kouki used a comparative analysis on data gathered between the years 2001 and 2006 from French listed companies that used only ERPS, only NFPI and the combination of both of them. The author postulates that the use of NFPI is important for financial performance. On the operative level, the use of ERPS and NFPI reflects the long-term strategy aimed at improving business processes. To reach strategic targets, the alignment of business processes, ICT and Key Performance Indicators (KPI) is important. The study concludes that the combination of ERPS and NFPI leads to significantly higher Return on Assets (ROA) than when only one of these "tools" is used in isolation.

Kossaï and Piget (2014) explore in their study the relation between the adoption of ICT and profitability of Tunisian companies from electrical and electronic industries falling into SME category. The authors postulate that ICT plays an important role in relation to corporate performance in developed countries and assess whether the same conclusion can be drawn about companies in Tunisia using Net Profit Margin as the financial indicator. Based on the data, the authors gathered they conclude that there exists strong statistical evidence supporting the notion that the use of ICT has impact on performance of the Tunisian companies whose performance they analyzed.

A current attempt at mapping the intertwined net of mutual relations—in this case not limited to only ICT and performance, but understood in a broader context and dealing with factors influencing design and outcomes of performance management systems, where ICT plays a part—was made by Šiška (2015). Empirical research, in which the assumed existence of a Web consisting of direct and indirect relationships among ICT, performance and various factors will be tested, is currently being prepared by Šiška's research team.

The outcomes of this research, as well as further research conducted by other authors, may help understand the direct and indirect influence of ICT on corporate performance better.

56.4 Discussion

Based on the presented studies and works, the following general conclusions related to the role or importance of ICT in relation to corporate performance may be drawn:

- By offering companies a vast array of tools that can be utilized, ICT probably has positive impact on corporate performance. To quantify specific benefits may prove to be problematic as the tools and technologies chosen by each company, as well as the conditions each company finds itself in, will always depend on very specific circumstances, needs and requirements—and therefore lead to achieving different results.
- The impact of ICT on performance is probably indirect. By adopting specific ICT-related solutions, companies gain certain advantage (such as improved or more efficient processes and better information base supporting more accurate decision-making). These ICT-driven changes in turn lead to improvements in the execution of internal processes and activities the company is involved in, which may in turn have positive impact on non-financial and financial performance.

Nevertheless, it is very important to keep in mind that there are several possible pitfalls to forming such general conclusions based on the review of identified research and studies. The reasons supporting cautious approach can be summarized as follows:

- Relatively few works were written on the topic. To find current, relevant and credible resources dealing with this matter is relatively challenging. Not only the general Web, but also prestigious scientific and scholarly databases include only relatively few records on this topic. This may indicate that although the role and contribution of ICT may instinctively be viewed as beneficial by many people—be it everyday users or managers deciding about investments into ICT in their companies—little consistent research has been done in order to assess the correctness of this assumption.
- The published studies are generally based on findings from very narrowly defined industries (logistics, banking sector, manufacturing). It is therefore possible that the results may not be applicable to other sectors of economy as they may be governed by different rules and principles.
- The studies were done in relatively heterogeneous geographies, quite often relatively distant from each other (e.g., Nigeria, Hong Kong, Northern Europe and USA). This may mean that each geography has so different characteristics (given by different historical and cultural context, different level of development, state of infrastructure, etc.) that the results and conclusions may be distorted by factors applicable only to these geographies.
- There are differences in when the data were collected and how long that were being collected (some data were gathered over several years, some over shorter periods; each study was undertaken during different period). Thus, it may be possible that both the changes in microeconomic and macroeconomic characteristics, as well as advancements in ICT, may be so significant that they influenced and distorted the results.
- Each study takes into consideration different area of ICT (different groups of technologies that are to be used either in specific industries (e.g., banking, logistics) or for supporting different types of tasks [e.g., transactional applications or decision support applications]). Thus, quite unrelated technologies with oftentimes very different characteristics, intended for varying purposes, are all "put next to each other" and compared. This may lead to generalizing assumptions, which may prove to be problematic.
- Performance is understood, defined and measured differently in each study. Some authors deal with non-financial performance, some with financial, some with both of them. Even when talking about for example financial performance, different financial measures and indicators are used to quantify it. It may well be possible that positive development of one measure may be accompanied by negative development in another. Thus, two studies using different financial measures may not be comparable.

56.5   Conclusion

The above stated reasons lead me to believe that in order to avoid any misleading conclusions and generalizations, future research needs to take into consideration the following assumptions:

- External factors influence corporate performance

A company always performs its activities in a particular context and within given external conditions or factors that influence the parameters of its functioning. The influences a company is exposed to may be, for example, geographical (remote location, densely populated location), geopolitical (stability of the region, security threats), political (regime, legislation, attitude to corruption), demographical (average age and structure of population), economic (economy growth and strength, exchange rates, inflation, trade restrictions), social and cultural (customs, traditions, opinions, preferences, openness to innovations, willingness to take risks, education), religious (taboos, restrictions), historical (development, relationships with neighboring countries), infrastructural (transportation network, communication network, logistics network) and climatic (prevailing climate, temperatures).

Some of these factors influence the business environment as a whole, and the possibility to influence them is very limited. However, companies are able to influence part of these factors by what choices they make and how they act. Each company may therefore find itself conducting its activities in very unique conditions that may influence its ability to achieve the desired results either positively or negatively.

- External factors influence internal factors

The characteristics of external factors determine the characteristics of internal factors. For example, the behavior, habits and values of employees from certain social groups or cultural backgrounds will also influence how a given employee will behave and act in the work context, etc.

- External factors influence organization's ICT

External factors, whose examples were mentioned in the text above, influence not only corporate performance, but also the ICT of an organization. For example, poor mobile signal reception may lead to using land lines; unreliable Wi-Fi signal may lead to preference of Ethernet connection; security threats in a geographical region may lead to the transition of data center to another location; customers and users demanding the option to purchase goods over the Internet will "force" the company to open an e-shop, etc. In this way, external factors may influence the characteristics of the ICT a company uses.

- Internal factors influence corporate performance

Corporate performance is influenced by internal factors, such as business factors (size, number of branches, contracts with suppliers and customers, payment terms, delivery terms, business model), employees' qualification (education, experience, skills), management style (democratic, authoritative) and corporate culture (customs, values). Similar to external factors, internal factors also help form very unique conditions under which a company realizes its activities.

- Internal factors influence organization's ICT

Internal factors influence the characteristics of the organization's ICT. For example, the core business and business model determine what ICT the organization will most likely need and use. Similarly, the maturity of the organization will influence whether or not the organization will use analytical tools (younger and forming organizations will likely focus primarily on mastering processes and transactions— and will probably rely on transactional applications more; better established and stable organizations will probably want to understand their processes better and will start considering the acquisition of analytical applications). Abilities, skills and experience of employees may influence what technologies, tools and functionality they will be able and willing to use and in what extent—it may therefore happen that an organization may have certain ICT tools, but they will not be used in the extent and for the purposes they were intended for.

- Organization's ICT influences its performance

ICT offers a wide range of technologies, applications, tools, etc. Each of these components has its characteristics. The same is true about their combination. Characteristics like the number of devices, performance, speed, data throughput, degree of integration, scalability, durability, age of the components, life-cycle phase, number of relations, version, functionality, provider (internal ICT department, external vendor), Service Level Agreement conditions and many others determine how ICT "functions," with what costs and benefits and how it contributes to the organization's performance.

- Organization's performance influences its ICT

Organization's performance influences the characteristics of its ICT. For example, an organization that finds the implementation of automated manufacturing control system and a related analytical module beneficial (because they help save production costs and generate higher revenues through decreased costs and higher volumes of goods sold) may be motivated to invest more into ICT. Also, for example the inability of the organization to achieve desired results may lead to investments into ICT, which may in turn help reveal possible causes of the organization's problems. Similarly, the availability of disposable financial means or access to convenient financing options could be the grounds for investing into ICT.

Acknowledgments This is paper has been prepared under financial support of the Internal Grant Agency of the University of Economics, Prague, Grant No. F1/13/2015, which author gratefully acknowledges.

References

Carr N (2007) IT doesn't matter: part 1. In: Rough Type. http://www.roughtype.com/?p=644. Accessed 14 Apr 2015

Choy KL et al (2013) Impact of information technology on the performance of logistics industry: the case of Hong Kong and Pearl Delta region. J Oper Res Soc. doi:10.5353/th_b3195351

DIW Berlin (2008) An economic assessment of ICT adoption and its impact on innovation and performance: Impact Study No. 10/2008. http://ec.europa.eu/enterprise/archives/e-business-watch/studies/special_topics/2007/documents/Study_10-2008_ICT-Impact.pdf. Accessed 14 Apr 2015

Kallunki JP et al (2011) Impact of enterprise resource planning systems on management control systems and firm performance. Int J Acc Inf Syst. doi:10.1016/j.accinf.2010.02.001

Koellinger P (2006) The European e-business Market Watch. Impact of ICT on Corporate Performance, Productivity and Employment Dynamics: Special Report No. 01/2006. http://www.empirica.com/themen/ebusiness/documents/TR_2006_ICT-Impact_I.pdf. Accessed 14 Apr 2015

Kossaï M, Piget P (2014) Adoption of information and communication technology and firm profitability: empirical evidence from Tunisian SMEs. J High Tech Manage Res. doi:10.1016/j.hitech.2013.12.003

Kouki A (2015) Joint impact of ERP systems and non financial performance indicators on corporate financial performance: evidence from French listed companies. Manage Sci Lett. doi:10.5267/j.msl.2014.12.004

Lee YC et al (2011) Corporate performance of ICT-enabled business process re-engineering. Ind Manage. doi:10.1108/02635571111137287

Muhammad A et al (2013) Impact of information and communication technology on bank performance: a study of selected commercial banks in Nigeria (2001–2011). Eur Sci J. http://eujournal.org/index.php/esj/article/view/866. Accessed 14 Apr 2015

Steinfield C (2010) Social capital, ICT use and company performance: findings from the medicon valley biotech cluster. Tech FS Change. doi:10.1016/j.techfore.2010.03.004

Šiška L (2015) Factor influencing design and outcomes of performance management systems. In: Doucek P, Chroust G, Oškrdal V (eds) IDIMT-2015 (Information Technology and Society Interaction and Interdependence). Poděbrady: Trauner Verlag Universität, pp 337–347

Chapter 57
Facility Management as a Partner of Cost Controlling at Costs Optimization in the Selected Enterprise

Ladislav Vagner

Abstract Facility management implementation trend tends to bring reactions that it is only a useless luxury. This article will point out one of the few practical benefits in which the implementation of facility management into the businesses brings. Together with cost controlling, whose monitoring of the cost structure revealed a relatively high proportion of heating costs, we defined a suitable area for optimization. The project, in which facility management brings in, refers to the possibility of energy cost reduction using appropriately invested capital. Savings are significant and returns of the entire investment are likely to be approximately 9 years. Together with a cost reduction, this would also prolong the lifetime of the whole building and also increase its intrinsic value.

Keywords Cost controlling · Facility management · Operating costs · Thermal transmittance

57.1 Introduction

Controlling has its own steady place in majority of companies. The most frequently used form is just the cost controlling, whose main task is monitoring and subsequent cost optimization. For the cost optimization, also other company departments are important. The root cause of costs creation is best known by departments for which those cost are assigned. Therefore, by revealing increased costs in some areas of a company, it is needful to integrate also those concerned departments into the optimization process.

In this article, we would point out just on the cooperation of facility management and cost controlling. Controlling registers increased amount of costs for energy

L. Vagner (✉)
The Faculty of Operation and Economics of Transport and Communications,
Department of Economics, University of Zilina, Univerzitna 1,
010 26 Zilina, Slovak Republic
e-mail: ladislav.vagner@fpedas.uniza.sk

© Springer International Publishing AG 2017
D. Procházka (ed.), *New Trends in Finance and Accounting*,
Springer Proceedings in Business and Economics,
DOI 10.1007/978-3-319-49559-0_57

consumption and starts the whole process of optimization. In this stage arrives the facility management, by which the investment project is introduced, in order to decrease costs for energy consumption. The project has to fulfill all required standards and at the same time, it has to prove the adequate investment return. The appropriateness of a project is reviewed by investment and cost controlling, and however, the last word for decision-making belongs to manager or managing department of the company.

57.2 Theoretical Background

The cost controlling term refers to a procedure in which company makes its processes of documentation, billing, scheduling, calculations, budgeting and cost controlling. The basic objective of cost controlling is to make profits and prosperity in a company (Ponisciakova 2014). It also monitors the origin of costs and allows its transparency, its streams throughout the enterprise, improves costs planning and improves decision-making. Based on acquired cost information, it is constantly trying to improve the cost and calculation system of the company.

Every work-related activity includes actions, which do not necessarily cohere in achieving goals; however, without their contribution we would hardly accomplish important results. No institution would be able to meet its business objectives without buildings, furniture, computer networks' security, technology equipment and other supporting subsistence activities. Here comes the facility management on stage.

The aim of facility management is to streamline support processes in companies and to reduce their operating costs using the appropriate settings. It is a method of mutual harmonization of employees, work activities and working environment, which incorporates principles of business administration, architecture, humanities and science technology (Cotts et al. 2010).

Facility management is an interdisciplinary field primarily focused on operating, maintenance and care of objects (Rondeau et al. 2006). It should be performed not only during the phase of the operation, but throughout building's life cycle, which usually lasts several decades. Apart from buildings such as hospitals, hotels, office "business" complexes, arenas, educational and congress centers, it also includes sport facilities, traffic centers and highways and parts of towns with the individual housing and multipurpose buildings.

According to the International Association of Facility Management (IFMA), it is "a profession that involves multiple disciplines to ensure the functionality of built and adjacent environment by integrating people, place, processes and technology."

The definition of facility management according to EN 15221-1 says it is the integration of processes within an organization in order to ensure and develop the agreed services which support and enhance the efficiency of its illegal work.

57.3 Paper Aim and Methodology

These days are characterized by optimizing business processes—leading to costs lowering. The prosperity of companies in such a highly competitive environment brought in the global market is largely dependent on company's ability to effectively deal with available funding.

This article aims to point out the possibility of a systematic reduction in operating costs in the majority of companies, using the examples of cooperation between cost control and facility management in the selected operating facility—transport company in the County of Martin. The aim is to optimize the selected operating expenses, which are beneficial for the company especially from the long-term perspective. To achieve desired goal, we would use a method of applying the knowledge of facility management from the technological state of buildings into controlling and then comparing the expected benefits of proposed measures to the initial state of the company.

Correlation analysis, with two or three variables based on recalculating indicators, would be the main method for determining appropriate techniques to reduce the costs. For example—when determining the technological process in reconstruction of the building's circumference covering, we would make a ratio from the isolation thickness, costs per square meter of isolation and the expected savings from the completed reconstruction. From such a correlation, we will choose the best option with taking into account the standards which are to be followed during the reconstruction.

57.4 Process of Reducing Heating Costs

Total costs for energy consumption in the company were 149,336.64 € in 2014. Cost controlling revealed the fact that in 2014, there were heating costs of 36,557.18 € for a building. This implies that costs for heating represent up to 24.48% of total costs for energy consumption. Therefore, the facility management proposal for renewal of exterior building coat appeared to be in place.

The building, in which a retirement home is running by the company, is 52 years old and is built of reinforced concrete panels. Except of the standard maintenance and partial reconstruction of a leaking roof, there was no work done on the building. At the present, the building would require reconstruction of joining seams between concrete panels, through which the water is getting into the building during the rainy seasons. Facility management proposed complex exterior building coat renewal, because of advanced age, and breach of energy standards of a building (Fig. 57.1).

The best and the most accurate picture of reconstruction needs for facility management was brought by shots created via thermal imaging camera. Based on this analysis, several parts of the building construction, which require higher

Fig. 57.1 Places from where
the heat escapes. *Source*
http://www.
termoviznemeranie.com/

attention, can be determined. Majority of them are so-called thermal bridges, i.e., places where the greatest loss of heat is. Risk-bearing places, with occurrence of fungoid growth and energy loss represent by heat leaking, led to the building insulation project. The most accurate solution is insulation of the whole building and following hydraulic regulation of a heating system. Building insulation involves replacement of windows, glazed walls and doors, insulation of external walls, roof, possibly the ceiling above not heated ground floor or entrance floor. Such a complex solution can decrease the energy consumption by more than 50%. Partial insulation cannot ensure such a massive saving (Fig. 57.2).

Fig. 57.2 Illustrative pictures created via thermal imaging camera. *Source* http://www.
termoviznemeranie.com/

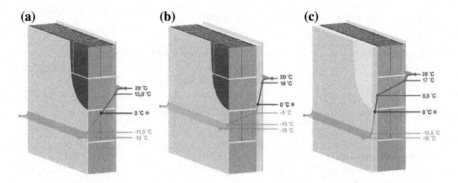

Fig. 57.3 Heat transfer scheme. *Source* https://www.siea.sk

Contribution of external wall to heat accumulation is limited. Freezing point (0 °C) is located in walling. Temperature changing and water vapor pressure can be the cause of condensation, which freezes in the winter. Changes in volume can result in cracks and progressive disruption of a walling solidity.

In case of insulation from the internal part, the external walls do not contribute to heat accumulation of the building. The freezing point is shifted to the thermal isolation layer, behind the border of inner part of a walling (Fig. 57.3a).

Although the thermal isolation inhibits escaping of the heat from the interior, it does not protect the walling against freezing. Under certain circumstances, there can be still generated fungi in the inner part (Fig. 57.3b).

By external wall insulation, the accumulation capacity of the walling is increased. Thermal insulation layer prevents the interior from loss of heat and also protects walls against freezing, because the freezing point is located in the thermal insulation layer in front of the external part of walling (Fig. 57.3c).

While planning the complex reconstruction, mandatory requirement for thermal properties of specific constructions cannot remain unnoticed. Those requirements, described in the technical standard STN 73 0540-2: 2012 Thermal protection of buildings, have to be respected at the design of building reconstruction. Whereas the sufficient minimal requirement for fulfilling the standard STN 75 0540-2: 2002 was just insulation of walls by expanded polystyrene thick from 6 to 8 cm, nowadays it is from 10 to 12 cm and after the year 2021 it can grow to 15 and more centimeters. Likewise, it is in case of windows (Table 57.1).

Project was designed so the mandatory standards would be taken into account. It also was looking for a solution, which would be economically acceptable. Expenses incurred for insulation of a building coat are not in the linear dependence with the energy savings effect. Current building standards are already reflecting that thermal properties will be gradually and fundamentally toughen. Also economical calculations indicates that one or two centimeters more will not be as much reflected in the price, because the thermal isolation is not the most greatest item on the list of

Table 57.1 Thermal transmittance of a construction

Thermal transmittance of a construction				
Type of a building structure	Maximal value For buildings reconstructed in the past	Normalized value For renewed and new buildings	Recommended value From 1.1.2016	Final recommended value From 1.1.2021
	(W/(m² K))			
	U_{max}	U_N	U_{r1}	U_{r2}
Exterior wall and sloping wall above the living area with the angle >45°	0.46	0.32	0.22	0.15
<Flat wall and sloping roof above the living area with the angle <45°	0.3	0.2	0.1	0.1
The ceiling above external area	0.3	0.2	0.1	0.1
The ceiling under not heated area	0.35	0.25	0.15	0.1
Window, doors, glazed roof in circuit wall, internal dormer	1.7	1.4	1	0.8
Doors to other areas	4.3	3	2.5	<2

Source https://www.siea.sk

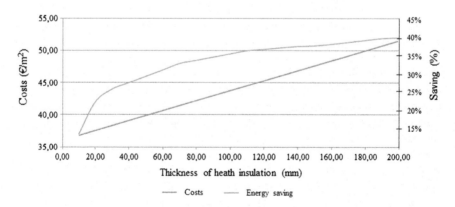

Fig. 57.4 Ratio from the isolation thickness, costs per square meter of isolation and the expected savings. *Source* Produced by author

contact insulation system. Still, the work has to be paid, which is usually the most expensive item in the budget, but also scaffold, plasters, glues, spatulas and other building chemicals (Fig. 57.4).

Constructing literature defines heat transfer coefficient by following formula: (Garimella et al. 2016)

$$U = 1/(R_N + R_K + r_N)$$

where:

U is heat transfer coefficient in W/(m^2 K),
R_K is thermal resistance of a construction in m^2 K/W,
R_N 0.13 m^{2}K/W is common and also normed resistance for heat transmission on the internal surface of the construction,
r_N 0.04 m^{2}K/W is common and also normed resistance for heat transmission on the external surface of the construction.

In the project which for a reconstruction would prepare the facility management, the use of thermal isolation material is considered with a thickness of 120 mm on the outer wall. That would provide a reduction in heat transfer coefficient (U) to a level 0.2 W/(m^2 K) from original levels 0.98 W/(m^2 K) which would represent 79.59% decrease. When replacing original windows, the replacement by 6-chamber PVC windows with double isolation glass would be taken into consideration. The heat transfer coefficient (U), in this case, would drop after the windows' replacement from the original 2.78 to 1.00 W/(m^2 K). The third step of the complex reconstruction would be the roof isolation. The roof at its original state does not meet the standards at $U = 0.63$ W/(m^2 K). After the reconstruction, we should get to the level of $U = 0.98$ W/(m^2 K).

The building should comply with all the necessary technical standards after the reconstruction. However, it is necessary to make calculations to see whether the applied measures would bring the economic savings. Costs for the complete reconstruction are captured in calculations of total isolation. As per the calculations, the total costs would be €230,049.86.

We need to know the amount of estimated heating costs after the complete reconstruction, in order to evaluate the suitability of investment. Having the floor area of the building 3427.02 m^2 and price of the heat €27.690/GJ, we can calculate the amount of the estimated annual cost to be €12,199.39. Then, we deduct the estimated costs from the original heating costs, which were 36,557.18 € in 2014, and thus, we get the amount of the annual savings. Expected heating costs saving after the reconstruction is €24,357.79 pa (Table 57.2).

From annual savings and the overall costs needed for reconstruction, we can easily calculate the return making a ratio of €230,049.86/€24,357.79/pa = 9.44/pa. That means that the investment into the reconstruction of the company would return like heating savings—9.44 pa. However, if we want to include factors of rising energy prices and interests into the calculation, we must use the formula of a dynamic recovery to calculate the payback (Table 57.3).

When calculating the dynamic recovery, we will count on the interest percentage $p_1 = 5\%$ ($q_1 = 1.05$) and an average annual growth of energy prices 3% ($q_2 = 1.03$). Calculation is made using the following formula: Nd = ln

Table 57.2 Total calculation of building insulation

Total calculation of building insulation

	Work item	Price €/m without VAT	Price €/m^2 with VAT	Price € without VAT	Price € with VAT
1	Reconstruction of a building facade	35.74	54.88	79006.84	121,317.73
2	Reconstruction of a roof construction	18.35	22.02	7826.83	9392.19
3	Insulation of a ground floor	28.9	34.68	12,326.72	14,792.06
4	Windows construction	–	–	68,037.32	81,644.78
			Total	16,7197.71	227,146.76
5	Accessories for insulation systems	–	–	2322.48	2903.1
			Total	16,9520.19	230,049.86

Source Produced by author

Table 57.3 Specific heat energy demand for heating

Specific heat energy demand for heating

	Initial status (before reconstruction)	Estimated status (after reconstruction)
$Q_{H,nd1}$ [kWh/ (m^2 a)]	107.01	35.71
Q_p[GJ/year]	1,320,211	440,564
C (€/year)	36,557.18	12,199.39
RU (€)	–	24,357.79
$Q_{H,nd1}$	Specific heat energy demand for healing per m^2	
Q_p	Presupposed heat energy demand for heating	
C	Estimated heat price for heating per year	
RU	Annual cost savings for heating	

Source Produced by author

[Ni. $(qx - 1) + 1$]/ln (qx), when $qx = q_1/q_2 = 1.05/1.03 = 1.019417$. The dynamic recovery after the complex reconstruction is 8,76 years. It is the dynamic recovery which can be considered as an indicator needed when deciding whether to perform the planned reconstruction.

From operating costs point of view, this step should reduce heating costs and thus reduce their portion in energy consumption costs from 24.48 to 9.76 [12,199.39/(149,336.64 − 24,357.79)]. Energy costs would then get to €124,978.85. Yet, this number may not be the final one; in case that the company would decide to continue the trend of so-called socially responsible enterprises, it could invest into other so-called green actions that would lead to a further energy costs reduction.

57.5 Conclusion

Project, which was developed by facility management for the reconstruction of the building, proved to be beneficial for cost controlling. The need for cost optimization is a present topic in every company. Prepared reconstruction project capturing all technical standards, costs level and expected savings of planned reconstruction is an ideal input for cost controlling.

From these calculations, we can deduct that we managed to reach a target and proposed solution would lead to costs reduction associated with energy consumption. That is why even the company's management likes the reconstruction project. It is still necessary to figure out the financing of entire project. As soon as there are funds, the company plans to implement the project.

Such a move may cause that other companies, which also use older buildings, would apply similar steps. Nowadays, the road to a success goes through the system of cost optimization. Companies, which can effectively manage its property, have a significant advantage.

Acknowledgments This paper has been prepared under financial support of VEGA No. 1/0870/16 Application of facility management in managing the transport companies in the Slovak Republic, which authors gratefully acknowledge.

References

Cotts DG, Roper KO, Payant RP (2010) The facility management handbook, 3rd edn. Amacom, New York, xiv, 661s. ISBN 978-0-8144-1380-7

Garimella S, Fronk BM, Thome JR (2016) Encyclopedia of two-phase heat transfer and: condensation heat transfer method. World Scientific Pub. Co. Pte. Ltd., New Jersey, 342s. ISBN 978-981-4623-24-7

https://www.siea.sk/aktuality/c-8910/odporucania-na-spracovanie-energetickeho-auditu-verejnej-budovy/

http://www.termoviznemeranie.com/

Ponisciakova O (2014) Controlling reporting in transport companies. In: 18th international conference on transport means, transport means—proceedings of the international conference, Kaunas, LITHUANIA, pp 206–210. ISSN: 1822-296X

Rondeau EP, Brown RK, Lapides PD (2006) Facility management, 2nd edn. Wiley, Hoboken, 589s. ISBN 978-0-471-70059-3

Chapter 58
Pecking Order Theory and Innovativeness of Companies

Katarzyna Prędkiewicz and Paweł Prędkiewicz

Abstract The purpose of this paper is to explore whether the "pecking order hypothesis" applies to the capital finance preferences of innovative companies. The research is based on a survey of 409 companies. We asked them about attitude towards innovation—three answers were possible (neutral, innovation "on occasion" and pro-innovative attitude) and to indicate the financing hierarchy for five sources of capital (retained earnings, bank credit or loan, additional capital from the current owners, loan from the owners and new external equity capital). We found that in general, the hierarchy is consistent with the pecking order theory. On the first place with the higher frequency, retained earnings were pointed out, on the second place—bank credit or loan, and on the last (fifth)—new external equity. Innovativeness of companies changes the hierarchy of financing in the third and fourth place. Innovative companies after retained earnings and bank loans prefer loans from the owners, whereas companies with neutral attitude towards innovation, additional capital from the current owners. Moreover, the group that describes their attitude towards innovations as "innovation on occasion" is the most diverse in their preferences, whereas the group with "pro-innovative" strategy has consistent preferences.

Keywords Capital structure · Innovation · Pecking order theory

K. Prędkiewicz (✉)
Department of Corporate Finance Management, Wrocław University
of Economics, ul. Komandorska 118-120, 53-345 Wrocław, Poland
e-mail: katarzyna.predkiewicz@ue.wroc.pl

P. Prędkiewicz
Department of Finance, Wrocław University of Economics,
ul. Komandorska 118-120, 53-345 Wrocław, Poland
e-mail: pawel.predkiewicz@ue.wroc.pl

© Springer International Publishing AG 2017
D. Procházka (ed.), *New Trends in Finance and Accounting*,
Springer Proceedings in Business and Economics,
DOI 10.1007/978-3-319-49559-0_58

58.1 Introduction

There are several main concepts in finance that try to determine the factors influencing the choice and proportion of primary sources of funding in companies. One of them is the pecking order theory (Myers 1984; Myers and Majluf 1984) which assumes that companies follow a hierarchy of financing sources and prefer internal financing when available, and then, if external financing is required, debt is preferred over equity.

Some papers empirically verified the pecking order theory (POT), but also modified it, by adding additional sources of capital or changing the hierarchy. The latter appeared especially in studies based on a sample of small- and medium-sized enterprises or subsamples which are separated basing on uniform features, such as the speed of growth or stage of the development of, for example, start-up companies (Paul et al. 2007). Among these features, there is also innovativeness of firms measured by R&D intensity (Aghion et al. 2004). The explanation of POT is based not only on the asymmetry of information, but also on other factors, such as the agency theory, taxes, behavioural factors or in case of SME—the problem with access to capital and owner mentality (Kubiak 2013).

Based on literature review, it can be said that the area of study which concerns the impact of company innovativeness on their capital structure, especially in SME, is still not enough addressed; then, the aim of this paper is to verify empirically the selection order of different sources of capital in innovative companies compared to those with neutral attitude towards innovation. We intend to investigate how innovativeness of companies impacts the preferences for five sources of capital and whether those preferences are in line with the pecking order theory principles, especially in small- and medium-sized enterprises. Better understanding of innovative companies in terms of their financial preferences could help in designing financial instruments by policy makers which can support those firms in access to capital. The paper shall follow a standard structure, i.e. Introduction, Literature review, Research Design, Results and discussion, Conclusion and References. The structure can be adjusted to reflect a specific research method applied in the paper, e.g. if the paper reviews recent literature in a particular field.

58.2 Literature Review

Initially, the POT mainly explained the observed financing hierarchy of large and publicly traded companies. However, it was soon empirically confirmed that this theory may also be applied to clarify the financing choices of non-publicly traded SMEs that might not have the additional financing alternative of issuing external equity finance (Hall et al. 2000; Lopez-Gracia and Aybar-Arias 2000; Zoppa and McMahon 2002; Cassar and Holmes 2003; Van Caneghem and Van Campenhout 2012).

The foundation of POT is the assumption that entrepreneurs do not seek an optimal capital structure and that internal managers are better informed than external capital providers. Generally, companies follow a hierarchy of financing sources and prefer internal financing when available, and then, if external financing is required, debt is preferred over equity.

Ang (1991) had proposed a modified pecking order of financing preferences for SMEs which involves new capital contributions from owners ranking behind internal finance, but in front of debt finance, however, this proposal was not supported by empirical research.

The extended list of preferences was verified by Zoppa and McMahon (2002) based on studies of 871 manufacturing Australian SMEs. They have provided further substantial empirical evidence broadly suggesting the pecking order for financing behaviour among SMEs. "On the basis of this and prior empirical research in the field, a full specification for a modified POT of financing for SMEs could appear as follows (from the most preferred source of finance to the least preferred):

1. Reinvestment of profits (fully reflecting 'in-kind' contributions of existing owner-managers such as long working hours and below market salaries).
2. Short-term debt financing (beginning with major reliance upon trade credit and including the use of personal credit card financing).
3. Long-term debt financing (possibly beginning with longer-term loans from existing owners and owner-managers (that is, quasi-equity), and perhaps from their families and friends).
4. New equity capital injections from existing owners and owner-managers (perhaps including their families and friends, and fully reflecting acceptance by existing owners and owner-managers of low or zero dividends).
5. New equity capital from hitherto uninvolved parties (including new owners and owner-managers, venture capitalists, business angels and Second Board listing)".

Stream of research concerning the financial hierarchy in innovative companies focuses mainly on start-up companies (Schäfer et al. 2004; Hogan and Hutson 2005; Paul et al. 2007) or larger publicity traded corporations (Aghion et al. 2004).

Using a sample of 117 Irish software companies, Hogan and Huston (2005) had proved that when a country has well-developed venture capital and an informal equity market, the pecking order theory could not be used to explain the financial choices of companies that focus on new technology. Based on analysis of capital structure, it was found that internal funds are the most important source in financing hierarchy, which is consistent with most research undertaken so far on SME financing. However, then, the financing hierarchy differs and equity financing is the prime source of external finance, whereas the use of debt is occasional.

Similar result was obtained by Paul et al. (2007) through in-depth interviews with 20 Scotland-based start-ups. They confirmed that entrepreneurs in start-ups choose internal sources first, that is, their own funds, what is consistent with POT.

The second choice is not debt, but external equity. The changed order is explained by two reasons: "First, entrepreneurs consider debt to be a personal liability as it invariably requires to be underwritten by personal guarantees". and "Second, entrepreneurs deliberately seek out equity investment as a means of obtaining added value over and above the finance invested". It means that even if external equity capital is expensive, it is worth employing this source of financing because "well-chosen investor can add business skills and social capital in the form of commercial contacts and access to relevant networks".

Aghion et al. (2004) conducted the study based on large and publicly traded UK companies. The conclusions are as follows: "firms that report positive but low R&D use more debt finance than firms that report no R&D, but the use of debt finance falls with R&D intensity among those firms that report R&D"; moreover "firms that report R&D are more likely to raise funds by issuing shares than firms that report no R&D, and this probability increases with R&D intensity". These results confirm that large and innovative corporations perform differently to non-innovative ones in term of capital preferences.

The above-presented prior research indicates that the pecking order theory should be modified by adding a new source of capital in relation to small- and medium-sized enterprises or the selection order may change when taking into account the innovativeness of the company.

We intend to test the pecking order theory in relation to innovative enterprises, which are in our sample mostly SMEs, so the list of potential sources of capital is extended to loans from existing owners and new equity capital injections also from them.

Based on literature review, we hypothesize that selection order may differ in innovative enterprises compared to non-innovative.

Verification of POT in the literature is based on three main approaches: observation of relations between different variables and the capital structure, observation of changes in the capital structure that are caused by different events and a survey (Kubiak 2013), and we used the last technique—a survey.

The advantage of testing financial decisions by surveys is that data directly reveal how managers claim to behave, but also has some weaknesses, e.g. number of observation is reduced compared to methods based on financial data, and it is also not clear whether the survey participants may think that they should indicate a "correct" financing hierarchy.

58.3 Data and Methodology

The results presented in the paper are a part of broader study on financing innovation. The survey aimed to diagnose the level of innovation of companies on the one hand and the patterns of financing activities, especially innovative ones, on the other hand.

The study was conducted on a non-probability sample of 409 companies operating in Poland from various industries. There were 162 companies up to 49 employees (40%), 199 with number of employees between 50 and 249 (49%) and 48 large entities with number of employees more than 250 (11%).

The interviews were conducted in the period from September to November 2015. Survey respondents were recruited from the board members, management, financial departments, accountants and CFOs. The questionnaire was divided into three main parts: the first concerned the innovative activity in last 36 months, the second concerned financing decisions, and the third part collected other important characteristics of company (the market, number and status of shareholders, family character, etc.).

We asked in first part of questionnaire inter alia about type and number of innovations introduced over the last 36 months, whether the company conducts research and development activities, whether it has strategy of intellectual property protection and how the company cooperates with research institutions, other companies when developing the innovations, etc.

In the second part, the sources of capital that are preferred by companies and application success rate in obtaining different kinds of capital were recognized. Also the factors that impact access to different types of capital were examined.

Hence, the questions often concerned people from different departments, depending on whether the survey related to innovation or financial strategy.

The questions that correspond with hypotheses are connected with the preference for capital sources. The interviewees were asked to indicate the order of employing five sources of capital. The options were as follows:

- retained earnings,
- bank credit or loan,
- additional capital from the current owners,
- loan from the owners,
- new equity capital from outside (new owners, new issue of shares).

We added to traditional POT two sources: additional capital from the current owners and loan from the owners, because it could be an important source of capital before obtaining equity capital from external sources, especially in small- and medium-sized companies, which are the main object of the study (however, we examined also a sample of large companies to compare whether the behaviour of SME differs from that of large firms significantly).

Another question concerned the attitude towards innovation, and the companies were able to declare three different strategies:

1. Neutral—when the company is not inclined to launch innovation.
2. Occasional—when innovation is not priority of company, the company does not run continuous action to bring innovation to market and it is rather introduced "by the way" of the various projects, or they are a necessity.

Table 58.1 Structure of sample

Company size	Innovation—neutral (%)	Occasional innovation (%)	Pro-innovative (%)
Micro-companies	50	38	13
Small companies	31	48	21
Medium companies	14	52	34
Large companies	13	38	50

Source Original research

3. Pro-innovative—when the company is constantly looking for innovation, does research and innovation are priority for and important part of the company's strategy.

The number of companies that declared neutral attitude towards innovation was 84, strategy called "innovation on occasion" was indicated by 199 firms, and "pro-innovative strategy" was claimed by 126 companies. A more detailed structure of the sample that takes into account the size of a company an innovation strategy exposes that the neutral strategy dominates in smaller companies (Table 58.1). The bigger the company is, the more often "pro-innovative" strategy is declared. Strategy "innovation on occasion" was adopted almost by half of sample in group of small and medium enterprises.

To test the hypothesis, we compared the structure of answers (preferences) for each source of capital and for each group of innovation strategies using Chi-square test. The tests were also made for two groups: pro-innovative companies compared to others—with neutral attitude and "innovation on occasion" strategy. We also compared the average and standard deviation to evaluate the distribution of preferences within the group.

58.4 Results

Preferences for selection order for five indicated sources of capital do not differ significantly from the pecking order theory, in general, in the whole sample (Table 58.2), but there were also companies in the sample that indicated a changed order in relation to POT. Retained earnings were pointed out as the first source of capital by 61% of the sample (250 companies), as the second source by 15% (61 companies), the third source 10% (39), the fourth source only 2%, and last, the fifth potential way of financing by 13% (52). Most of the companies indicated bank credits and loans as a second source of financing (51%—209 companies) and then loan from the owners (42%). As the fourth way of financing, additional capital from the current owners was chosen (44% of the sample), and then, on the last place, new outside equity capital—from new owners or new issue of shares—with 63% of display.

Table 58.2 Selection order—the whole sample

The selection order	Retained earnings (%)	Additional capital from the current owners (%)	New equity capital from outside (new owners, new issue of shares) (%)	Loan from the owners (%)	Bank credit and loan (%)
1	61	4	3	8	24
2	15	11	13	10	51
3	10	33	11	42	5
4	2	44	11	28	16
5	13	8	63	12	4

Source Original research

When we compared the average and standard deviation of the preferences from the answers in the whole sample and each group with different innovation strategies, it seems that the group describing their attitude towards innovations as "innovation on occasion" is the most diverse in its preferences, whereas the group with "pro-innovative" strategy has consistent preferences. For example, the average preference for "retained earnings" is 1.61 in case of neutral innovators and 1.34 for pro-innovative companies, which clearly indicated that retained profits are the most important source of capital. In the group with "innovation on occasion" strategy, the average for retained earnings is 2.38, which does not confirm that there is a clear preference to choose this source of capital in the first place, especially that for bank credit and loan, the average is 2.21. Additionally, standard deviation is the lowest for pro-innovative companies (0.88) and the highest for the entities which implement innovation irregularly (1.58). This first analysis confirmed that groups of companies with different innovation strategies are not similar in terms of preferences for choosing the source of capital and the most homogeneous is group of companies with "pro-innovative strategy" (Table 58.3).

Supplementary to the analysis of the arithmetic mean and standard deviation, which completes the picture of selection hierarchy, is the analysis of the sample structure. For each innovation strategy and each source of capital, we have analysed the selection order based on the share of answers in the subsample separated on the attitude towards innovation (Fig. 1, 2, 3).

An analysis of selection preferences for retained earning confirms, what was noticed above, that this source of financing is the first choice in hierarchy, but the three separated groups based on innovativeness strategy differ. Even 82% of pro-innovative companies indicated the retained earnings as the first source of financing, whereas in neutral to innovation entities, it was 67% and in the last group ("innovation on occasion") 46% (Fig. 58.1). The "pro-innovative" group is definitely more consistent in their preferences for source of capital.

Similar situation occurs in case of bank credit and loan. Seventy-five percentages of companies with pro-innovative strategy indicated this source of capital on the second place, whereas in neutral towards innovation entities, it was 50% and in firm with "innovation on occasion" 36%.

Table 58.3 Average and standard deviation

	Retained earnings	Additional capital from the current owners	New equity capital from outside (new owners, new issue of shares)	Loan from the owners	Bank credit and loan
	Average				
Whole sample	1.90	3.40	4.17	3.27	2.26
Innovation—neutral	1.61	3.14	4.13	3.49	2.63
Innovation on occasion	2.38	3.37	3.90	3.15	2.21
Pro-innovative	1.34	3.62	4.61	3.33	2.10
	Standard deviation				
Whole sample	1.38	0.94	1.22	1.06	1.12
Innovation—neutral	1.07	0.93	1.33	1.06	1.21
Innovation on occasion	1.58	0.99	1.29	1.18	1.22
Pro-innovative	0.88	0.80	0.85	0.79	0.77

Source Original research

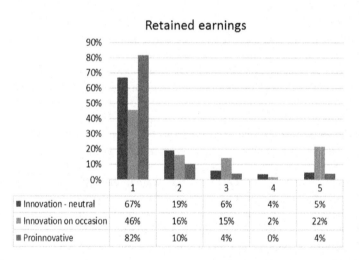

Fig. 58.1 The selection order in case of retained earnings. *Source* Original research

We recognized different selection ordered preferences about the third place and the fourth place. For the group of companies with neutral innovation strategy on the third place has located additional capital from the current owners (with indication rate 48%), whereas for two other groups—loan from owners (with share 59% for pro-innovative companies and 34% for firms with occasional strategy on innovation) (Fig. 58.2).

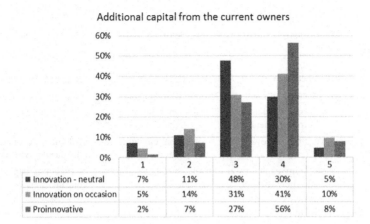

Fig. 58.2 The selection order in case of additional capital from the current owners. *Source* Original research

As a last, fifth source of capital, new outside equity from new owners or new issue of shares, was indicated more frequently by all three groups of companies. Again the most consistent in preferences are enterprises that declared pro-innovative strategy. About 79% of this subsample positioned this source of capital on the last place, whereas in group with neutral strategy 65%, and "innovation on occasion" strategy 51%.

Verification of hypothesis is based on Chi-square test. We compared whether the structure of answers (preferences) for each source of capital and for each group of innovation strategies differ statistically significantly. The tests were also made for two groups: pro-innovative companies compared to others—with neutral attitude and "innovation on occasion" strategy.

All *p*-values are less than 1% (and in most cases below 0.01%) so the conducted series of Chi-square testes confirmed that there is a significant difference in preferences structure between all groups (Table 58.4).

As the result of above-described studies, we sum up the outcomes—the selection order for five sources of capital in three groups with different innovation strategies in Table 58.5.

Table 58.4 Selection order distribution Chi-square test results

Source of capital	Retained earnings (%)	Additional capital from the current owners (%)	New equity capital from outside (new owners, new issue of shares) (%)	Loan from the owners (%)	Bank credit and loan (%)
P-value	<0.01	0.58	<0.01	<0.01	<0.01

Source Original research

Table 58.5 Pecking order theory versus different attitudes towards innovation—summary

The selection order	Innovation—neutral	Innovation on occasion	Pro-innovative
1	Retained earnings	Retained earnings	Retained earnings
2	Bank credit or loan	Bank credit or loan	Bank credit or loan
3	Additional capital from the current owners	Loan from the owners	Loan from the owners
4	Loan from the owners	Additional capital from the current owners	Additional capital from the current owners
5	New equity capital from outside (new owners, new issue of shares)	New equity capital from outside (new owners, new issue of shares)	New equity capital from outside (new owners, new issue of shares)

Source Original research

58.5 Conclusion

We tested how the innovation strategy of companies impacts the selection order for different sources of capital. Generally, for the whole sample the hierarchy is consistent with the pecking order theory. On the first place with the higher frequency, retained earnings were pointed out, on the second place—bank credits or loans, and on the last—new external equity.

The above results confirmed that innovativeness of companies changes the hierarchy of financing in the third and fourth place. Innovative companies prefer loans from the owners after retained earnings and bank loans, whereas companies with neutral attitude towards innovation prefer additional capital from the current owners. It could be explained that innovative activity raises the risk of enterprises—choosing the loan from the owners instead of increase in equity through additional financing from existing owners or managers of innovative companies protects the owners—the loan is repaid even if the innovative project fails. Another explanation is that managers are aware that the owners would not risk their own funds in additional innovative project and prefer a loan, which will be repaid regardless of the outcome of the project, because the owners are worse informed than managers. So, to raise the chance of financing an innovative project, the managers prefer a loan from owners instead of additional equity. The influence on this selection order has also other factors that are not examined under this study, such as the size of companies and what is connected with this, separation of ownership and management. If the owner manages the company, he/she is better informed than the manager who acts like the owner in bigger companies. In another case, when there is a separation of ownership and management, there is a asymmetry of information between manager and owner(s), and the managers are better informed. When we analysed the sample structure, it occurs that the pro-innovative companies are rather bigger ones, so it could be also the factor that affect the conclusions, and the loan from owners is preferred before equity. Neutral to innovation companies are smaller with better-informed owners, so they put additional equity capital from current owners (themselves) before loans from the owner. They count on receiving the additional profits that are higher than the interest rates and expect the increase in company value.

Moreover, group that describes their attitude towards innovations as "innovation on occasion" is the most diverse in their preferences, whereas the group with "pro-innovative" strategy has consistent preferences.

In this paper, companies' innovativeness is based on declared attitudes towards innovation, so the measure is subjective. The authors are conscious that the innovativeness of companies may be measured in the more sophisticated ways, and there are plans to develop such objective indicator based on the different aspects of innovation activity, for example numbers of implemented products, process and organizational innovation, existence of R&D department, R&D expenditure (these data were also collected during the survey). We have also access to financial statement of sample group, so we could also verify the financial preferences of the companies with different innovative strategies based on objective financial data. The outcomes of further research steps will be presented in forthcoming papers.

Acknowledgments The project was funded by the National Science Centre allocated on the basis of the decision number DEC-2013/11/D/HS4/03941.

References

Aghion P, Bond S, Klemm A, Marinescu I (2004) Technology and financial structure: are innovative firms different? J Eur Econ Assoc 2:277–288. doi:10.1162/154247604323067989

Ang JS (1991) Small business uniqueness and the theory of financial management. J Entrep Finance 1:1–13

Cassar G, Holmes S (2003) Capital structure and financing of SMEs: Australian evidence. Account Finance 43:123–147

Hall G, Hutchinson P, Michaelas N (2000) Industry effects on the determinants of unquoted SMEs' capital structure. Int J Econ Bus 7:297–312. doi:10.1080/13571510050197203

Hogan T, Hutson E (2005) Capital structure in new technology-based firms: evidence from the Irish software sector. Glob Finance J 15:369–387. doi:10.1016/j.gfj.2004.12.001

Kubiak J (2013) Zjawisko asymetrii informacji a struktura kapitału przedsiębiorstw w Polsce. Wydawnictwo Uniwersytetu Ekonomicznego w Poznaniu, Poznań

Lopez-Gracia J, Aybar-Arias C (2000) An empirical approach to the financial behaviour of small and medium sized companies. Small Bus Econ 14:55–63. doi:10.1023/A:1008139518709

Myers SC (1984) The capital structure puzzle. J Finance 39:574–592

Myers SC, Majluf NS (1984) Corporate financing and investment decisions when firms have information that investors do not have. J Financ Econ 13:187–221

Paul Stuart, Whittam Geoff, Wyper Janette (2007) The pecking order hypothesis: does it apply to start-up firms? J Small Bus Enterp Dev 14:8–21. doi:10.1108/14626000710727854

Schäfer D, Werwatz A, Zimmermann V (2004) The determinants of debt and (private) equity financing: the case of young, innovative SMEs from Germany. Ind Innov 11:225–248. doi:10.1080/1366271042000265393

Van Caneghem T, Van Campenhout G (2012) Quantity and quality of information and SME financial structure. Small Bus Econ 39:341–358

Zoppa A, McMahon RG (2002) Pecking order theory and the financial structure of manufacturing SMEs from Australia's business longitudinal survey. Small Enterp Res 10:23–42

Chapter 59
A Compulsory Corporate Finance: Reflections on the Scope and Method

Artur Walasik

Abstract The importance of social norms and legal regulation for organizing contemporary economy impacts on theoretical discussion of the scope and method of corporate finance. The term of "a compulsory corporate finance" is coined to pay more attention to novel approach to both financing and investment decision taken by firms. This paper identifies the scope and the method of compulsory corporate finance based on discovering territories of the confluence of social norms and the economics of corporate finance. The scope of compulsory corporate finance should embrace the influence of social norms on financial decisions made by firms and complement the well-investigated relations between legal regulations and corporate finance. The methodology of compulsory corporate finance finds the cooperation but not competition as the essence of the theory of financial decisions. The promotion of Buchan symbiotics should be provided to make the theory of corporate finance closer to contemporary economy and society.

Keywords Compulsory corporate finance · Welfare economics of corporate finance · Corporate social responsibility · Social norms · Legal regulation

59.1 Introduction

The contemporary economic and social background of corporate activity influences the inevitability of detailed discussion of the relation between corporate finance and both social norms and legal regulations. The more modern the society, the more important the social and legal norms are for organizing economy. The term "compulsory corporate finance" is coined to pay more attention to novel approach to both financing and investment decision taken by firms. The aim of this paper was to identify the scope and the method of compulsory corporate finance. This paper

A. Walasik (✉)
Department of Corporate Finance and Insurance, University of Economics in Katowice,
ul. 1 Maja 50, 40-287 Katowice, Poland
e-mail: artur.walasik@ue.katowice.pl

© Springer International Publishing AG 2017   643
D. Procházka (ed.), *New Trends in Finance and Accounting*,
Springer Proceedings in Business and Economics,
DOI 10.1007/978-3-319-49559-0_59

attempts to discuss the area of the confluence of social norms and the economics of corporate finance. This paper takes into consideration the method of compulsory corporate finance but in a manner of very preliminary draft. This paper starts from discussion of the contribution of Coase (1937) to study limitation of corporate finance. The subsequent part is the mainstay for the exploration of problem in question, that is the delimitation of the scope of compulsory corporate finance within the field of corporate finance. The last paragraph identifies the method-ological aspects of compulsory corporate finance, exploring the symbiotics of Buchanan (1964).

59.2 The Origin of the Economics of Corporate Finance Within Limits

Social norms, very probably, and legal regulation, out of discussion, could be found as the determinants of human action. The part of human activity is economic one, and consequently, the ethics and the law should be found as the source of critical limitations to business operations.

The very origin of the economics of firm which operates under limits could be drawn from the essence of seminal paper written by Nobel awarded Coase (1937). Being one of most influential in the field of economics, The Nature of Firm indi-cates corporation as the reflex of increasing costs of market transaction. The fresh approach to organization of market economy proposed in 1937 by R.H. Coase was founded on an obvious observation that there are two accessible mechanisms of coordination: market and entrepreneurship. Each of them incurs the costs: firstly, the cost of market transactions placed out of firm; secondly, the costs of organizing and managing the process within firm. A very simple results of coordination could be everything but costless.

The occurrence of firm is the consequences of costs soared by transaction taken place in the market. Following the suggested idea and asking himself what deter-mines the size of firm when it has been established, R.H. Coase implied the law of diminishing returns to management. The law in question could be treated as the fundamental rule of the economics of firm. In detail, two crucial assumptions should be made in advance, and there preceded the law of diminishing returns to man-agement. From the perspective of the idea of compulsory corporate finance, these assumptions allow to draw the limits of corporate finance, as well.

The first assumption of Coasian approach reflects that enlargement of firm induces decreasing returns to the entrepreneurship, what equals to the simple observation: the incorporation of additional transaction within the firm will drive up the cost of coordination provided by managers. The second assumption manifests the competition within firm (e.g., among departments or branches) to use the scarce means; import of market transaction to organize them within the firm implies the managers' failures more possible; in particular, the greater the firm, the worser the use of the scare means. Twofold important fruits of transfer from above assumptions to the theory of corporate finance could be discovered. The lower the costs of financial intermediation, the lesser the size of corporate finance is efficient. Other words, if efficiency of financial market decreases, it could be expected that the size of corporate finance will expand. The greater the firm (more transactions are annihilated by firm), the stronger the competition for limited funds is open to managers within firm. Equally, the cost of agency grows when the size of firm (the number of transactions coordinated by managers) broadens. To sum up, thanks to Coase wide-inspiring reflections exhibited in The Nature of Firm, a very curious observation could be done: the limits of firm, and in the consequence, the boundaries of corporate finance are the products of the plausibility of diminishing the cost of market transactions. The easier to lower the costs of transaction taken place on market, the lesser the propensity to make the size of firm greater.

Two distinguishable coordination mechanisms—market and firm—enable to split the field of corporate finance into two areas, when one complements another. The first one investigates the coordination of processes within the firm and it is an economics of inner corporate finance; the other studies the bridge between firm and processes taken place out of firm and it is an economics of outer corporate finance. Hence, it will be convenient to distinguish the issues being the product of the design of infrastructure of corporate finance from the problems arisen from the design of market where firm operates. Both agency theory and leverage seem to be the best example of the first, the asymmetry of information by Akerlof (1970) as well as Fama (1970), and efficient market hypothesis of Fama (1991) the second.

59.3   The Roots and Fruits: The Scope of Compulsory Corporate Finance

Let start form the meanings of corporate finance. Easy said: Corporate finance teaches us how corporations make financial decisions, in particulars how they purchase real assets—investment decisions and how they sale of financial assets—financing decisions (Brealey et al. 2011). Similarly, Vernimmen et al. (2009, 1) read the role of financial managers and find their responsibility in conjunction with the real economy (industries and services) and the world of finance (financial markets and structures). A different view can be found in Brealey et al. (2001), who consider the corporate finance and the role of financial managers as the bridge between real firm's assets and financial markets. On the scope of corporate finance for educational purpose, there is a balance sheet model of firm provided by Ross et al. (2006). Another dimension of corporate finance could be extracted, if it adheres to Watson and Head (2007) meaning of corporate finance. Corporate finance is concerned with the efficient and effective management of the finance of an organization in order to achieve the objectives of that organization. The stance of modern theory of finance is reviewed by Baskin and Miranti (1997), and there could be found a very profound discussion on the scope of the economics of corporate finance. And last but not least, recently Nobel Prize awarded Tirole (2006) draws the paths of contemporary theory of corporate finance since 1950s.

To make a success the definition of the economics of corporate finance, let me import definition of economics by Robbins (1945): Economics is the science which studies human behavior as a relationship between ends and scarce means which have alternative uses. The economics of firm is the science which studies corporate behavior as a relationship between ends and scarce means which have alternative uses. And truncated it to finance, the economics of corporate finance is the field of art which investigates financial decisions of firm as a relationship between ends and scarce funds which have alternative uses.

Soaring significance of complex interactions between firm and social and legal circumstances has forced economist to ask what changes the economics of corporate finance in the contemporary economy. I suggest to coin a juxtaposed field of economics as "a compulsory corporate finance." The scope of compulsory corporate finance is parallel to the subject we can read contents of corporate finance handbooks, but the perspective is novel. The novelty of approach is thanks to engagement with sociological aspects of corporate finance. Nevertheless, compulsory corporate finance would be the part of microeconomics, because it studies of firms and their relations with other economic agents. At macroeconomic level, several congruences between economy and society, and then between economics and sociology were presented by Parsons and Smelser (1984) in their influential monograph originated economic sociology as the field of art where economists and sociologists could meet each other. But, such a field of economics is beyond the scope of this paper.

Legal factors of corporate finance are solid within the theory of corporate finance. The story of modern theory of corporate finance started with the problem of tax regulation influence on the capital structure and value of firm. Nonetheless, first comments of Modigliani and Miller (1958) milestone paper failed to capture tax premium. Neither Rose (1959) nor Durand (1959) investigated tax regulation in their detailed discussion of Modigliani–Miller original model. But for a few years later, the correction of the model proposed by their authors was dedicated to repair wrong statement found in their 1958 paper; that is, the market values of firms in each class must be proportional in equilibrium to their expected returns of net taxes (i.e., to the sum of the interest paid and expected net stockholder income). Thanks to meticulous attention hold by Modigliani and Miller (1963), the economics of taxation was invited into the theory of corporate finance, dedicated to the lack of taxation in their previously built model of corporate finance.

If norms provide either ethical or social approach to academic manner discussion of human behavior, the emblematic paragraph of interference of corporate finance and ethics and sociology could be excerpted from Welch (2009) who starts from inspiring idea: There is one principal theme that carries through all finance. It is value. Hence, in my opinion, the crucial reason for studying compulsory corporate finance is emerged from strong conviction that it is impossible to fully and adequately elucidate financial decision of firm that not taken into consideration of social norms which govern behavior of stakeholders. Social norms interfere relation between agent–principal. A very slightly and preliminary approach to relation between corporate finance and social background is discussed by Viswanath (2007), who finds obvious observation that managers do not live in an ethical vacuum. The executives being agent for shareholders as principals, hence, the investigation of conditions when social welfare reflects social utility could be or should be the alternative goal for the maximization of shareholders utility.

Compulsory corporate finance would investigate corporate finance paying much attention to the influence of social norms as well as legal regulation on financial decision made by firms. Compulsory corporate finance discusses the reflection of social norms in both financing and investment decisions of firm. Compulsory corporate finance investigates also the impact of regulations on the structure of assets and the influence of legal rules on capital structure. Compulsory corporate finance should be focused on the review of both objective and criteria of management in the context of social norms and legal requirements. The societal aspects of corporate finance are cornerstone of compulsory corporate finance. Hence, welfare economics of corporate finance could be an intriguing aspect of compulsory corporate finance. For a very preliminary example, the fruits of welfare economics of corporate finance are harvested by Ehrhardt and Brigham (2011) who ask if firm attempts to maximize its stock price, is this good or bad for society? They show three reasons for positive answer: (a) To a large extent, the owners of stock are society; (b) consumer benefit thanks to low-cost business forced by approaching to maximize stock price by managers; (c) employees benefit. There allows to condense that the same actions that maximize stock prices also benefit society.

Compulsory approach to study corporate finance provides another intriguing question: Does being open-to-publicity benefit corporate? In particular, the demand for corporate social responsibility forces managers to reveal information for a wide range of interest groups, not restricted to shareholders. Many years ago, MacKie-Mason (1990) asks do firms care who provides their financing and answer that hidden information problems predict firm preferences over providers of funds but not security types; hence, it run entirely contrary to the optimal leverage factors affect choice of security types but not of provider funds. In detail, determinants that depend on type of securities are as follows: tax shield, asset composition, bankruptcy probability, and also maybe forecast variance. Choice determinants predict to have effect on types of provider that are attributed to paying dividends, forecast variance, and public regulation and also may effect on bankruptcy likelihood.

The compulsory corporate finance is rooted in the Coasian transaction costs model of economic coordination and supplemented by numerous works of G.S. Becker. He pictured the model of pressure groups competing for political influence (Becker 1983) and found the reason for set up cooperation to rise profits thanks to out-of-market transactions. I consider it could be auspicious path to bridge the gap between the economics of corporate finance and social welfare, and could be the methodology of the welfare economics of corporate finance. To shift the essence of

Beckerian model to corporate finance theory, it could be assumed that the pressure group will be formed, if the cost of out-of-market pressure on financial decisions taken by corporation (e.g., by legal implementation of social norms) is below the cost of market pressure (e.g., thanks to decreasing of demand). The size of the pressure group depends on the tendency to free ridership (the higher, the lower size) as well as the differences in expectations (the more homogeneously interests, the greater size).

59.4 Many Questions but One Answer: The Method of Compulsory Corporate Finance

To compete or not to compete but to cooperate, the semantics matters. The economics of corporate finance comes back to 1950s and Modigliani–Miller model of corporation. One decade later, the founder of public choice theory, Buchanan (1964), asked what should economists do? Strictly, he did nothing but conferred the method of economics with the most quoted definition of economics provided by Robbins (1945) in his influential An Essay on the Nature and Significance of Economic Science. The Buchanan's idea of markets as coordinators of human interaction and mechanisms of exchange increase utility was inspired by attending Frank H. Knight's classes at the University of Chicago (Breit 2002).

Nevertheless, J.M. Buchanan suggested the methods of coined by himself symbiotics. There could be the basis for the scientific projects on examined compulsory approach to corporate finance. J.M. Buchanan enhanced the axiological and methodological essence of symbiotics in several papers. Both Buchanan (1975) and Buchanan (1988) could be examples of crucial ones. Many parallels could be recommended as well: Kirzner (1965), Carden (2014), Boettke (2014), and Shughart II and Thomas (2014).

The complex interpretations of Buchanian approach to economic methods are contents of papers by Marciano (2009), Rubin (2014a), and Rubin (2014b), where the first of Rubin is the leader. The comments of Rubin (2014a) is based on the assumption that approaches of mainstream economics as well as Buchanian symbiotics are regular core of the field of economic analysis: An economic agents aimed to maximize utility are engaged in certain economic activity. The crucial cause for the differentiation between economics and symbiotics is the method of explanation of this kind of activity. The ontology is the same, but the epistemology matters. Rubin (2014a) reads Buchanan (1964) and finds that economic activity could be investigated as either competition or cooperation. The lexicography matters, even if both competition and cooperation could be interpret as nothing, but the labels imposed and depend on observer (economist) lexicography. The language reveals the axiological dimension of economist's approach to study economy and drivers of economic agents' behavior. Marciano (2009) interprets Buchanan (1964) and notes his idea of the aim of economics should be at analyzing exchange. Hence, catallactic perspective (called symbiotics) would dominate maximizing principle as the essence of economic analysis.

Rubin (2014b) traces the path of symbiotics and suggests three main assumptions of symbiotics. The first one places the transaction as the fundamental unit of economics; hence, if the attribute of transaction is cooperativeness, it will be sufficient to assume the sequence:

the bit of economy is the transaction laid on the cooperation,

and hence, to state that the essence of economy is cooperation, not competition. It follows to second assumption of symbiotics. There is both sufficient and necessary to juxtapose the cooperation as the aim of economy, and the competition as the means for cooperation:

competition is important,
but it is nothing but a tool to improve cooperation.

Twist to corporate affairs, the third assumption elucidates the essential relations of contemporary economy, that is:

economy is the sum of markets
and market is the sum of firms compete for the right to cooperate.

To sum up, well-known and aesthetically designed Modigliani–Miller model of corporate finance flows along the axiology and methodology (paradigm) of the mainstream economics (the aim of corporate finance is to maximize the value of firm); on the contrary, discussed compulsory approach to corporate finance examines Buchanan model of economics, which is based on the idea of symbiotics. It allows defining the aim of corporate finance as the exchange of the value by firm and its cooperatives.

Transfer from Modigliani and Miller to Buchanan explicates the desire for compulsory approach to corporate finance. The discussion of the details of ontology, axiology, and epistemology could find prolegomena of compulsory corporate finance. Ontologically, the firm could be study as either the sum of stakeholders (Buchanan symbiotics) or the sum of shareholders (Modigliani–Miller economics). For a very example, Sacconi (2000) hypothesizes that for the success and stability of the firm (investigated as an institution, which is able to regulate and organize economic transactions), the constitutional social contract among stakeholders is incumbent and indispensable.

Axiological approach to firm attributes the maximization principle for Modigliani–Miller, and the exchange paradigm for Buchanan approach. The critical readings of the maximization principle of firm, ranged from economics through management science to ethics, are made by Koslowski (2001). The essence of paper is to discuss when "shareholder value" should be instrumental or teleological for the firm.

And finally, epistemology of corporate finance could be the analysis of choice (Modigliani–Miller) or the analysis of exchange (Buchanan). When Modigliani–

Table 59.1 Paradigm of Modigliani–Miller and Buchanan models of corporate finance

Subfield of the art of corporate finance	Variable 1	Variable 2
Ontology	Firm is the sum of shareholders	Firm is the sum of stakeholders
Axiology	The aim of corporate finance is to maximize value of the firm	The aim of corporate finance is to exchange value within the firm
Epistemology	To analyze choice	To study of exchange

Source Own elaboration

Miller model tends to stress competition, Buchanan model of corporate finance will promote cooperation. The main differences between two approaches to corporate finance are resolved at Table 59.1. Remarkably, Rubin (2014a) finds the arguments against the metaphor of competition and makes intriguing observations in favor of the metaphor of cooperation. Corporations transact business when several market failures occur: Asymmetry of information and public goods are prime examples. Rubin points clearly that both of them are examples of the failure of cooperation. Hence, market interventions claim for restoring cooperation (making its occurrence valuable thanks to Pigovian benefits) or forcing cooperation (making its deficiency valueless thanks Pigovian taxes). The more market failures occurred, the more explainable compulsory approach to corporate finance seems to be.

59.5　Conclusion

The study of correlation between corporate finance and social norms as well as legal regulations plays very undisputable role in contemporary economy. It is because of the crucial significance of both ethics and law as the source of principles of organizing modern society. The need for a field of new corporate finance is caused by theory as well as practice. The economics of corporate finance should investigate deeper than to date the interaction between financial decision taken by corporations and moral and ethical aspects of behavior of economic agents (households, other firms, government, etc.). The reveal of the exchange as the mainstay of the compulsory approach to corporate finance, as well as the description of the structure of the intersect of corporate finance and household, public, or other corporate finance on the base of cooperation, would be the cause for a refreshment of the epistemology of corporate finance. The symbiotics of corporate finance, as the method of compulsory corporate finance, allows to push theory of corporate finance to the study of cooperation instead of competition.

The ontology of compulsory corporate finance reflects the crucial processes, which has taken place for decades, when redrawing boundaries of firm has emerged. In classical theory of corporate finance, the firm is just about the shareholders. A moder corporate finance theory expands the view of a firm beyond the shareholders' perspective. The axiology of compulsory corporate finance finds exchange of value as the very aim of firm and studies the maximization of market value of firm as means instead of goal of firm. The epistemology of compulsory corporate finance arises from the inspirations extracted from The Nature of Firm by R.H. Coase and cornerstone paper, The Cost of Capital, Corporation Finance and the Theory of Investment by F. Modigliani and M. Miller, and approached to What Economist Should Do? by J.M. Buchanan, each of fourth Nobel awarded. The method of corporate finance should favor the inquisition of exchange (transactional approach to corporate finance) rather than the investigation of choice (allocative approach to corporate finance).

Acknowledgments This paper has been advanced under financial support of University of Economics in Katowice, Faculty of Finance and Insurance, which author gratefully acknowledges. The scope of scientific project *Oddziaływanie sytuacji finansowej przedsiębiorstw na równowagę budżetową jednostek samorządu terytorialnego* (*The Influence of the Stance of Corporate Finance on the Budgetary Equilibria of Sub-Central Governments*) incorporates the subject of this paper.

References

Akerlof GA (1970) The market for "Lemons": quality uncertainty and the market mechanism. Quart J Econ 84:488–500

Baskin JB, Miranti PJ (1997) A history of corporate finance. Cambridge University Press, Cambridge

Becker GS (1983) A theory of competition among pressure groups for political influence. Quart J Econ 98:371–400

Boetke PJ (2014) What should classical liberal political economists do? Const Polit Econ 25:110–124

Brealey RA, Myers SC, Allen F (2011) Principles of corporate finance. McGraw-Hill Irwin, New York

Brealey RA, Myers SC, Marcus AJ (2001) Fundamentals of corporate finance. McGraw-Hill, Boston

Breit W (2002) Buchanan-as-Artist. A retrospective. In: Brennan G, Kleimt H, Tollison RD (eds.) Method and morals in constitutional economics. Essays in honor of James M. Buchanan. Springer, Berlin, pp 44–50

Buchanan JM (1964) What should economists do? South Econ J 30:213–222

Buchanan JM (1975) A contractarian paradigm for applying economic theory. Am Econ Rev 65:225–230

Buchanan JM (1988) Contractarian political economy and constitutional interpretation. Am Econ Rev 78:135–139

Carden A (2014) What should Austrian economists do? On dolan on the Austrian paradigm in environmental economics. Q J Austrian Econ 17:218–223

Coase RH (1937) The Nature of the Firm. Economica 4:386–405

Duncan D (1959) The cost of capital, corporation finance and the theory of investment: comment. Am Econ Rev 49:639–655

Ehrhardt MC, Brigham EF (2011) Corporate finance. A focused approach. South-Western Cengage Learning, Mason

Fama EF (1970) Efficient capital markets: a review of theory and empirical work. J Finance 25:383–417

Fama EF (1991) Efficient capital markets: II. J Finance 46:1575–1617

Kirzner IM (1965) What economists do? South Econ J 31:257–261

Koslowski P (2001) The shareholder value principle and the purpose of the firm. In: Shionoya Y, Yagi K (eds) Competition, trust, and cooperation. A Comparative Study. Springer, Berlin, pp 179–209

MacKie-Mason JK (1990) Do firms care who provides their financing? In: Hubbard RG (ed) Asymmetric information, corporate finance, and investment. University of Chicago Press, Chicago, pp 63–104

Marciano A (2009) Buchanan's constitutional political economy: exchange versus choice in economics and in politics. Const Polit Econ 20:42–56

Modigliani F, Miller MH (1958) The cost of capital, corporation finance and the theory of investment. Am Econ Rev 48:261–297

Modigliani F, Miller MH (1963) Corporate income taxes and the cost of capital: a correction. Am Econ Rev 53:432–443

Parsons T, Smelser NJ (1984) Economy and society. A study in the integration of economic and social theory. Routledge and Kegan Paul, London

Robbins L (1945) An essay on the nature and significance of economic science. Macmillan, London

Rose JR (1959) The cost of capital, corporation finance and the theory of investment: comment. Am Econ Rev 49:638–639

Ross SA, Westerfield RW, Jaffe JF (2006) Corporate finance. McGraw-Hill Irwin, New York

Rubin PH (2014a) Emporiophobia (fear of markets): cooperation or competition? South Econ J 80:875–889

Rubin PH (2014b) Buchanan, economics, and politics. South Econ J 80:912–917

Sacconi L (2000) The social contract of the firm. Economics, ethics and organisation. Springer, Berlin

Shughart WF II, Thomas DW (2014) What did economists do? Euvoluntary, voluntary, and coercive institutions for collective action. South Econ J 80:926–937

Tirole J (2006) The theory of corporate finance. Princeton University Press, Princeton

Vernimmen P, Quiry P, Dallocchio M, LeFur Y, Salvi A (2009) Corporate finance. Theory and Practice. Wiley, Chichester

Vishwanath SR (2007) Corporate finance. Theory and practice. Response Books, New Delhi

Watson D, Head A (2007) Corporate finance. Principles and practice. Financial Times Prentice Hall, Harlow

Welch I (2009) Corporate finance. An introduction. Prentice Hall, New York

Chapter 60
Socially Responsible Investment Market Size in Poland: The Content Analysis

Anna Doś and Monika Foltyn-Zarychta

Abstract This study attempts to examine socially responsible market size in Poland by exploiting content analysis as a method. Analyzed documents of institutional investors include documents, whose preparation is guided by legislation and industry standards. The selection criteria reduce self-reporting biases. The study revealed that Polish institutional investors very rarely report on embedding ESG criterions in their financial policies. This is interpreted as a lack of actual following SRI practices by Polish institutional investors. This conclusion, however, still can be challenged under agency-relationship assumptions. The SRI market size estimated through the content analysis accounts for 1.9 bln PLN. This number is much smaller than Polish SRI market size estimated by EUROSIF report. SRI disclosure requires further investigation.

Keywords Socially responsible reporting · Corporate social responsibility · Content analysis · Financial market · Investment

60.1 Introduction

EUROSIF report (2014) refers to sustainable and responsible investments (SRI) defining them as "any type of investment process that combines investors' financial objectives with their concerns about environmental, social and governance (ESG) issues." This innovative way of investing has a potential to change financial markets landscape diverting it from purely financial gain-seeking. Thus, it is crucial

A. Doś (✉)
Department of Corporate Finance and Insurance, University of Economics
in Katowice, ul Bogucicka 14, 40-287 Katowice, Poland
e-mail: anna.dos@ue.katowice.pl

M. Foltyn-Zarychta
Department of Investment and Real Estate, University of Economics in Katowice,
ul Bogucicka 3a, 40-287 Katowice, Poland
e-mail: monika.foltyn-zarychta@ue.katowice.pl

© Springer International Publishing AG 2017
D. Procházka (ed.), *New Trends in Finance and Accounting*,
Springer Proceedings in Business and Economics,
DOI 10.1007/978-3-319-49559-0_60

to understand how big is the market size for SRI (SRI market size is understood as the value of assets under management following SRI criterions). This issue is significantly under-investigated in Central and Eastern Europe Countries. The only report on SRI market size in Poland, which is the biggest financial market among CEEs, is EUROSIF report (2014). EUROSIF report is based on a survey among institutional investors and may suffer from self-reporting biases. This paper attempts to examine SRI market size in Poland by exploiting alternative method—a content analysis, where estimation of SRI market size is based on analysis of documents, whose preparation is guided by legislation and industry standards, which reduces self-reporting biases.

60.2 Socially Responsible Investment Market Size—Literature Review

Socially responsible investing (SRI), also known as ethical investing, refers to the integration of environmental, social and corporate governance considerations (ESG) into the investment process. Pasewark and Riley (2010) put forward that terms "socially responsible investing" and "ethical investing" became popular in the 1990s. Since the financial collapse is caused by the subprime turmoil, SRI is sometimes even considered as an answer to the crisis of capitalism (Capelle-Blancard and Monjon 2012; Nofsinger and Varma 2014). The observed increase in SRI share in the financial market and the potential impact of SRI decisions on firms' non-financial policies and performance is believed to become a very powerful mechanism to influence business practices (Crifo and Mottis 2013), i.e., it is argued that companies who attract financial resources from socially responsible investors face less capital constrains (Cheng et al. 2014). Thereof, the role of institutional investors creating SRI market appears as crucial.

Literature sources analysis shows a widespread conviction that the change in the business landscape is actually possible. Many scholars are impressed by the fact that SRI from a niche phenomenon turned into a financial market feature (Berry and Junkus 2013), and a claim SRI has to became a market reality, if not a force (Park and Kowal 2013). Most of studies, which contribute to this belief (e.g., Lean et al. 2015; Sandberg 2013; Escrig-Olmedo et al. 2013), are based on SRI market size estimation provided by EUROSIF report as Europe is the largest SRI market in the world.

Poland, which is the biggest financial market in Central and Eastern Europe (CEE), seems to be a pioneer of SRI among CEE countries. The first sustainable index was launched in Warsaw in 2009 (GPW Respect). Thereof, knowledge on SRI market size in Poland can contribute to predicting on how SRI may develop in CEE countries. However, information on the size and types of investments on Polish SRI market can be found rarely in the literature. There are two recent studies investigating the issue that are most commonly used as a source of such data.

The first, most often quoted study, is EUROSIF report (2014). The report is a joint product between Eurosif and its national member SIFs, and it is based on a survey among all European professional investors (the study covers 13 national markets—including Poland). The respondents were asked to report on data from December 2013. The report does not inform on how many respondents actually filled in the questionnaire, and it only states that some major players did not respond. Missing data were supplemented by secondary information sources, including data from 2011. The report informs that SRI market size in Poland is 12.6 bln PLN.

The second study is a much less known report of Pracodawcy RP (2011). This report presents, among others, the results of a survey conducted among Polish institutional investors. The method was a telephone interview. From among 87 institutions selected for the interview, only 10 agreed to answer all 18 questions. The study revealed that institutions make their investment decisions on the basis of financial criterions. Little attention is paid to environmental and social issues. The report does not inform which institutions revealed their practices; thereof, it is not possible to investigate their capital investment market share.

Since mentioned SRI studies are both based on surveys, they both may suffer from a number of biases. The first is self-reporting bias anchoring respondents who might be susceptible to respond in socially desirable way (Donaldson and Grant-Vallone 2002). The second is the white-hat effect biasing the participants' answers to disregard facts and distort the truth to serve righteous ends (Cope and Allison 2010) (e.g., promoting SRI). These biases impair the validity of research.

Concerning a significant knowledge gap, it is important to provide a new insight into the problem of SRI market size in Poland.

60.3 Research Design

In search for reliable source of information on SRI, it is inevitable to pay particular attention to documents issued by institutional investors. Annual reports, statutes, prospectuses, corporate social responsibility (CSR) reports, mission statements and Web sites are all under strong regulatory, industrial and social screen. Thereof, it is highly probable that they provide reliable information on investment strategies and policies, including ESG criterions embedded in investment decisions. Formal and informal rules guiding non-financial information reporting in the area of CSR and sustainable reporting practices will be presented in this part of the paper.

Directive 2013/34/EU on the annual financial statements as well as Polish legal acts on accounting (Ustawa o Rachunkowości 2013; Krajowy Standard Rachunkowości Nr 9 2014) regulate that reports should include, apart from financial information, information about impact on the natural environment, employment and other information. National Accounting Standards No. 9 devoted to the Activity Report suggest including information about social responsibility, environmental protection activities, policies and activities in those areas. It states that any reports on environmental impacts, intellectual capital and corporate responsibility should be an integral part of the Activity Report. However, not all non-financial is formally required. The companies that are characterized by the highest transparency in reporting non-financial data related to all ESG areas are banks mainly (Czerwińska 2013).

The reasons for banks outperforming other sectors are numerous. Prevailing part of financial institutions which operate on Polish market, belong to multinational financial groups—from among many follow UNEP Finance Initiative principles. UNEP Finance Initiative indicates rules that institutional investors should follow to act in the best long-term interests of their beneficiaries and to respect environmental, social and corporate governance issues affecting the performance of investment portfolios. One of this principles states that institutional investors should report on activities and progress toward implementing the principles.

UN also formulated the Global Compact Initiative, which was joined by ten financial institutions in Poland. CSR reporting is also strongly enhanced and systemized by international standards, whose best examples is Global Reporting Initiative.

Other sources of ESG and SRI rules, i.e., Guidelines for Multinational Enterprises (OECD 2011) indicate that enterprises should apply high quality standards for non-financial information including environmental and social reporting where they also disclose information on relationships with employees and other stakeholders.

Mentioned principles have been operationalized in audit and certification systems such as the Social Accountability 8000 system or International Standard Organization (Berry and Junkus 2013).

Apart from legal regulations indicated by worldwide organizations, ESG reporting may be enhanced by accompanying economic performance of companies following ESG, due to the fact that benefits resulting from reporting on commitment to social responsibility are multiple and significant (Hahn and Kühnen 2013; Hess 2014). Companies are aware of this benefits, which is confirmed by numerous studies that identify an abundance of positive information in corporate sustainability reports and a lack of negative voluntary disclosures (e.g., Calace et al. 2014; Lougee and Wallace 2008; Holder-Webb et al. 2009). This notice is supported by the observation that at the Web sites of all Polish banks and insurance companies there is easily detectable information of this institutions' contribution to solving diverse social and environmental problems.

Following the above reasoning, it is assumed that institutional investors, who commit to sustainability by embedding ESG criterions in investment decisions, face numerous formal and informal incentives to report on it. Thereof, it is argued that it is very probable that institutional investors, who follow non-financial criterions in their investment practices, communicate it to their stakeholders using their main communication tools: published documents and Web sites.

The qualitative content analysis is a widely used qualitative research technique for systematic text analysis. As a research method, it is a systematic and objective mean of describing and quantifying phenomena (Krippendorff 2012). It is often exploited as a method of analyzing documents. Text data might be in verbal, print or electronic form (Kondracki et al. 2002). Qualitative content analysis is based on explicit rules of coding. Coding can be a priori or data-derived (Sandelowski 2000). It is oriented at detecting words used in communication of phenomena, which are under research. The coding allows for systemic word-frequency counting; however, it has to be verified through checking the context, because some words can have more than one meaning (Vaismoradi et al. 2013).

For the purpose of the study, the documents issued by Polish institutional investors, including banks, insurance companies, mutual funds and pension funds, were analyzed. Final set of documents included: annual reports (banks, insurance companies), prospectuses and Web sites (pension funds, mutual funds), CSR reports (banks, insurance companies) and statutes (banks, insurance companies), thereby all documents, where institution's investment strategy, can be communicated to investors (Table 60.1). The documents were obtained via institutions Web sites or the Web site of Polish Financial Supervision Authority. The documents were gathered in October 2015.

The coding was partially prepared a priori and partially derived in the study. The a priori coding resulted from the review of the literature on SRI. It allowed for preparing of a list of words, which describe socially responsible motives of investment decisions (e.g., ethics, moral, good, sustainable, society, common good, environment, protection, nature, contribution, non-financial, noneconomic and green). Then, the material was reviewed to prepare the list of words used to describe investment practices and investment strategy (e.g., investment strategy, practices, portfolio, choice, locate, buy and acquire). The coding was done in Polish, because the documents analyzed are in Polish.

The content of above-mentioned documents was analyzed twice, following two approaches. Under the first approach, all information about institutions attitude toward social responsibility was scanned to find, if there is any reference to investment strategy or investment practices. Under second approach, all information on investments strategy and practices was scanned to find, if institutional investors declare to follow motives other than economic ones (return, risk, time-scope, branch and geographical area). Since SRI includes investing in "ethical" or "green" sectors (e.g., renewable energy), it was checked if any declared sectorial specialization can be attributed to as SRI.

Table 60.1 Documents published by Polish institutional investors screened under the content analysis scheme

Type of investor/type of the document	Web site (including mission statements)	Statutes	Annual report	CSR report	Prospectus
Investment funds	x				
Pension funds	x				x
Banks	x	x	x	x	
Insurance companies	x	x	x	x	

Source Authorial computation

60.4 Results and Discussion

The content analysis revealed that there are institutional investors, who inform on embedding ESG criterions in their investment practices. Such investors can be acknowledged as SRI investors. However, such practices are rare. Detailed results are presented in Table 60.2.

The number of Polish SRI institutional investors is very small; however, to provide a proper insight into the SRI market the value of assets allocated following ESG criterions should be examined as well.

The first segment of institutional investors analyzed in respect to the value of SRI assets constitutes of investment fund management companies and investment funds. There are 61 investment fund management companies and investment funds authorized by Polish Financial Supervision Authority. In October 2015, they offered 1232 funds. Their asset value accounted for 1,838,825,000 PLN. The names of 1232 funds were scanned to find out, if they inform about the profile of a fund. In case of doubts, the fund management company Web site was scanned in order to find information about such fund. It was discovered that some funds are named as "sustainable"; however, the context of this word does not refer to SRI. This word is used to inform about the risk–return profile of a fund. Thereof, the coding context approach resulted in excluding such funds from the list of socially responsible investment products.

It was discovered that only 20 out of 1232 funds (1.5% of funds offered) be identified as a broadly defined SRI products. However, only 11 out of these 20 invest in Poland (EUROSIF report investigates only investment located at domestic market). These funds are presented in Table 60.3.

In case of only 6 out of 11 of SRI products offered by mutual funds, it was possible to gain information about their assets value. Assets value exceeds 1,931,941 thousands of PLN. It accounts for 1.1% of all investment funds' assets value. Five funds listed in Table 60.2 do not publish information on their assets value. In case of two of them, it is debatable if the fund can be acknowledged as

Table 60.2 Polish institutional investors communicating embedding ESG criterions in their investment decisions

Type of investor	Total number of investors in Poland	Number of SRI investors according to results of content analysis	% share of SRI investors
Investment funds	1232	11	0.9
Pension funds	12	0	0
Banks	37	2	5.4
Insurance companies	59	0	0
Total	1340	13	0.1

Source Authorial computation

Table 60.3 Socially responsible investment funds in Poland, 2015

No	Funds name	Assets value (PLN)
1	PZU Subfundusz Energia Medycyna Ekologia	1,300,410 000
2	SKARBIEC Skarbiec—Zdrowia Fundusz Inwestycyjny Zamknięty Aktywów Niepublicznych	417,000,000
3	SKOK Etyczny 2	155,830,000
4	FINCREA TFI WI Lasy Polskie Fundusz Inwestycyjny Zamknięty Aktywów Niepublicznych	46,682,364
5	Conerga green ENERGY Fundusz Inwestycyjny Zamknięty Aktywów Niepublicznych	6,592,000
6	SKOK Etyczny 1	5,427,000
7	ALTUS Kompleksowe Rewitalizacje i Odbudowa Polskich Kamienic Fundusz Inwestycyjny Zamknięty Aktywów Niepublicznych 2015	n.a.
8	BPS TFI Uzdrowiska Polskie Fundusz Inwestycyjny Zamknięty Aktywów Niepublicznych	n.a.
9	BPS TFI Zielony Fundusz Inwestycyjny Zamknięty Aktywów Niepublicznych	n.a.
10	OPOKA TFI Opoka Ecowipes	n.a.
11	OPOKA TFI Opoka Energia Odnawialna	n.a.

Source Authorial computation

SRI or not. This first case is ALTUS Kompleksowe Rewitalizacje i Odbudowa Polskich Kamienic. The fund focuses on revitalization and reconstruction of Polish tenement houses. This can be regarded as protection of the national heritage (and thus seen as SRI); however, at the same moment this can be no more than conventional profit-aimed investment in the real estate. In the second case—BPS TFI Uzdrowiska Polskie Fundusz Inwestycyjny Zamknięty, the investment fund locates capital in Polish baths (spas). Financing health is definitely socially desirable; however, it is possible that the fund invests only in cosmetic services, which does not distinct from other ways of allocating capital. Another three funds, which do not publish data, are ecological funds.

The next analyzed group of institutional investors was pension funds. There are 12 open pension funds, and their long-term and short-term financial assets value in October 2015 was more 2,161,242 thousand of PLN. The analysis of prospectuses of pension funds revealed that none of them embed ESG criterions in their investment decisions. Thereof, pension funds do not contribute to SRI sector in Poland at all.

Another group of institutional investors are banks. There are 37 banks in the form of joint-stock companies in Poland. Bank sector in Poland in September 2015 held financial assets (excluding credits) worth 1,521,613,318 thousand of PLN. Banks statuses, annual reports and reports on social responsibility were reviewed under the scheme described above. The analysis revealed that only two banks inform about embedding ESG criterions in their investment decisions: Bank Zachodni WBK and Deutsche Bank Polska. However, they do not inform neither about the share of their investment, which is guided by non-financial criterions, nor about socially responsible strategy they follow. Additionally, Deutsche Bank Polska (2014a) informs about its commitment to SRI not on the Polish Web site, but on the Web site of the Deutsche Group. It is thereof not clear, if the ESG guided investment strategy is applied in Poland. The value of corporate bonds and shares owned by Bank Zachodni WBK in October 2015 was accounted for 4,533,000 PLN (Bank Zachodni 2015). The value of corporate bonds and shares owned by Deutsche Bank Polska in this period was accounted for 9,512,000 PLN (Deutsche Bank Polska 2014b). It can be assumed that at least part of this value is SRI.

The last group of institutional investors are insurance companies. In Poland, there are 49 insurance companies operating as joint-stock companies (including 25 life insurance and 24 non-life insurance companies). There are also 10 mutual insurance companies. Their financial assets value in September 2015 accounted for 102,409,496 thousand of PLN. The review of their statutes, annual reports and social responsibility reports revealed that none of them informs about including ESG criterions in making investment decisions.

The content analysis oriented at exploring the market size of SRI in Poland demonstrated that only two banks and eleven investment funds report on embedding ESG criterions in their investment decisions. Data on assets value are available in case of 6 out of 11 mentioned funds. The sum of assets allocated with regard to ESG criterions in the 3rd quarter of 2015 was about 1,945,986 thousand of PLN and accounted for about 0.13% of institutional investors financial assets (excluding credits and remittances from the insured).

The content analysis of documents published by Polish institutional investors revealed that they publish very few information confirming embedding ESG criterions in their investment decision. Taking into consideration the fact that institutional investors are formally and informally encouraged to report on their commitment to social responsibility, we argue that lack of information on investing in socially responsible way is connected with actual lack of following SRI practices by the predominating part of Polish institutional investors.

This conclusion, however, still can be challenged by pointing at the possibility that institutional investors may embed ESG criterions in their decision making and at the same time may not report on this. Such situation is possible if institutional investors strive for achieving environmental and social goals when their stakeholders (certificate owners, shareholders, depositors, etc.) are not willing to follow goals other than financial ones. This, however, should be acknowledged as manifestation of agency conflict, where agent—institutional investor—pursues its goals at the cost of a principal (depositor, investor). Cheng et al. (2013) find support for SRI as overspending on social and environmental goals being in fact a failure to comply fiduciary duties (doing good with other people's money). Answering to this type of challenge on the basis of conclusions from the content analysis requires further studies.

The most striking finding is a huge discrepancy of the SRI market size in Poland reported by EUROSIF, and the value of SRI according to the content analysis of documents issued by Polish institutional investors. EUROSIF report states that SRI in Poland in 2014 accounted for more than 12.6 bln PLN while the content analysis performed by the authors indicates much smaller amount: 1.9 bln PLN. This huge difference cannot be explained by missing data about assets value of 5 investment funds (cf. Table 60.3).

60.5   Conclusion

The content analysis revealed that Polish institutional investors very rarely report on embedding ESG criterions in their financial policies. Assuming that informing stakeholders on commitment to sustainable development is beneficial, we argue that lack of information on investing in socially responsible way is related to actual lack of following SRI practices by Polish institutional investors. This conclusion, however, still can be challenged under agency-relationship assumptions. The problem of SRI market size in Poland thus requires further research, exploiting other research methods and exploring the problem of communication of investment strategy and practices. This conclusion is in accordance with notices that the area of SRI disclosure is still relatively under-researched (cf. Banasik et al. 2010).

References

Banasik E, Barut M, Kloot L (2010) Socially responsible investment: labour standards and environmental, social and ethical disclosures within the SRI industry. Aust Account Rev 20:387–399. doi:10.1111/j.1835-2561.2010.00102
Bank Zachodni WBK SA (2015) Raport Grupy Kapitałowej Banku Zachodniego WBK S.A. za III kwartał 2015 r. http://static3.bzwbk.pl/asset/G/r/u/Grupa-BZ-WBK-3Q-2015_58959.pdf
Berry T, Junkus J (2013) Socially responsible investing: an investor perspective. J Bus Ethics 112:707–720. doi:10.1007/s10551-012-1567-0
Calace D, Morrone D, Russo A (2014) Corporate sustainability, green marketing and reporting: where are we going. Ann Univ Oradea 2014:59–68
Capelle-Blancard G, Monjon S (2012) Trends in the literature on socially responsible investment: looking for the keys under the lamppost. Bus Ethics Eur Rev 21:239–250. doi:10.1111/j.1467-8608.2012.01658.x
Cheng I, Hong H, Shue K (2013) Do managers do good with other people's money? Natl Bur Econ Res (No. w19432). doi:10.3386/w19432
Cheng B, Ioannou I, Serafeim G (2014) Corporate social responsibility and access to finance. Strateg Manage J 35:1–23. doi:10.1002/smj.2131

Cope B, Allison D (2010) White hat bias: examples of its presence in obesity research and a call for renewed commitment to faithfulness in research reporting. Int J Obes 2010:84–88. doi:10.1038/ijo.2009.239

Crifo P, Mottis N (2013) Socially responsible investment in France. Bus Soc. doi:10.1177/0007650313500216

Czerwińska T (2013) Evaluation of ESG risk in listed companies. In: Sroka R (ed) ESG analysis of companies in Poland. Polish Association of Listed Companies (SEG), Warszawa

Deutsche Bank Polska (2014a) Corporate responsibility report 2014, Deutsche Group. https://cr-report.db.com/2014/en/servicepages/downloads/files/dbcr2014_entire.pdf

Deutsche Bank Polska (2014b) Skonsolidowane Sprawozdanie Finansowe Grupy Kapitałowej Deutsche Bank Polska S.A. za 2014 rok. https://www.deutschebank.pl/file-9273344.bdoc

Directive 2013/34/EU of The European Parliament and of The Council of 26 June 2013 on the annual financial statements, consolidated financial statements and related reports of certain types of undertakings, amending Directive 2006/43/EC of the European Parliament and of the Council and repealing Council Directives 78/660/EEC and 83/349/EEC

Donaldson S, Grant-Vallone E (2002) Understanding self-report bias in organizational behavior research. J Bus Psychol 17:245–260. doi:10.1.1.365.6592

Escrig-Olmedo E, Muñoz-Torres M, Fernández-Izquierdo M (2013) Sustainable development and the financial system: society's perceptions about socially responsible investing. Bus Strategy Environ 22:410–428. doi:10.1002/bse.1755

EuroSIF (2014) European SRI study. http://www.eurosif.org/wp-content/uploads/2014/09/Eurosif-SRI-Study-20142.pdf

Hahn R, Kühnen M (2013) Determinants of sustainability reporting: a review of results, trends, theory, and opportunities in an expanding field of research. J Clean Prod 59:5–21. doi:10.1016/j.jclepro.2013.07.005

Hess D (2014) The framework for CSR assessment, measurement, and reporting. In: Okonkwo B (ed) Christian ethics and corporate culture. Springer International Publishing, New York, pp 177–192. doi:10.1007/978-3-319-00939-1_13

Holder-Webb L, Cohen J, Nath L, Wood D (2009) The supply of corporate social responsibility disclosures among US firms. J Bus Ethics 84:497–527. doi:10.1007/s10551-008-9721-4

Kondracki N, Wellman N, Amundson D (2002) Content analysis: review of methods and their applications in nutrition education. J Nutr Educ Behav 34:224–230. doi:10.1016/S1499-4046(06)60097-3

Krajowy Standard Rachunkowości Nr 9 "Sprawozdanie z działalności", Dz. U., 2014, poz. 17

Krippendorff K (2012) Content analysis: an introduction to its methodology. Sage, Los Angeles. doi:10.1111/j.1468-4446.2007.00153_10.x

Lean H, Ang W, Smyth R (2015) Performance and performance persistence of socially responsible investment funds in Europe and North America. North Am J Econ Finance 34:254–266. doi:10.1016/j.najef.2015.09.011

Lougee B, Wallace J (2008) The corporate social responsibility (CSR) trend. J Appl Corp Finance 20:96–108. doi:10.1111/j.1745-6622.2008.00172.x

Nofsinger J, Varma A (2014) Socially responsible funds and market crises. J Bank Finance 48:180–193. doi:10.2139/ssrn

Odpowiedzialne Inwestycje Kapitałowe (2011) Warszawa file:///C:/Users/HP/Downloads/odpowiedzialne_inwestycje_kapitalowe_pracodawcyrp.pdf

OECD (2011) Guidelines for multinational enterprises. OECD Publishing. http://dx.doi.org/10.1787/9789264115415-en

Park J, Kowal S (2013) Socially responsible investing 3.0. Georgetown Pub Policy Rev 18:17–18

Pasewark W, Riley M (2010) It's a matter of principle: the role of personal values in investment decisions. J Bus Ethics 93:237–253. doi:10.1007/s10551-009-0218-6

Sandberg J (2013) (Re-) interpreting fiduciary duty to justify socially responsible investment for pension funds? Corp Gov Int Rev 21:436–446. doi:10.1111/corg.12028

Sandelowski M (2000) Focus on research methods-whatever happened to qualitative description? Res Nurs Health 23:334–340. doi:10.1002/1098-240X(200008)23:4<334:AID-NUR9>3.0

UNEP Finance Initiative, http://www.unpri.org/about-pri/the-six-principles/

Ustawa o rachunkowości, Dz.U. 2013 poz. 330, art 49, ust. 3

Vaismoradi M, Turunen H, Bondas T (2013) Content analysis and thematic analysis: implications for conducting a qualitative descriptive study. Nurs Health Sci 15:398–405. doi:10.1111/nhs.12048 Epub 2013 Mar 11

Chapter 61
The Role of Convertible Bonds in the Corporate Financing: Polish Experience

Joanna Błach and Gariela Łukasik

Abstract The role of bonds in the corporate financial strategy is considered from the point of view of the issuer and investors. This results from the interactions of investment and financing decisions with regard to the level of acceptable risk. The issuer should consider the expectations of investors in order to define properly the terms and conditions of the issue. While investors will evaluate the elements that determine the profitability, risk and liquidity of this form of investment with regard to the structural changes in the company. This paper discusses the importance and potential application of the convertible bonds in the corporate financing decisions. The main aim of this paper is to analyze and evaluate the most important reasons and consequences of the issuance of convertible bonds and their role in the corporate financial strategy. This paper is based on the critical literature review on corporate bonds supported by the analysis of normative regulations and selected empirical data from the Polish financial market.

Keywords Capital structure · Corporate financing decisions · Debt securities · Bond market in Poland

61.1 Introduction

The role and importance of bonds (debt securities) in the corporate financial strategy is considered from the point of view of the issuer (as deficit unit) and investors (capital providers as surplus units). This is due to the interactions of investment and financing decisions with regard to the level of acceptable risk. The issuer should anticipate and take into account the expectations of investors in order

J. Błach (✉) · G. Łukasik
Department of Corporate Finance and Insurance, University of Economics
in Katowice, ul. 1 Maja 50, 40-287 Katowice, Poland
e-mail: jblach@ue.katowice.pl

G. Łukasik
e-mail: gabriela.lukasik@ue.katowice.pl

© Springer International Publishing AG 2017   665
D. Procházka (ed.), *New Trends in Finance and Accounting*,
Springer Proceedings in Business and Economics,
DOI 10.1007/978-3-319-49559-0_61

to define properly the terms and conditions of the offering. While investors will evaluate the elements that determine the profitability, risk and liquidity of this form of investment with regard to the structural changes taking place in the company and the associated risks. The decisions of each of the parties involved (both investors and issuer) require the assessment of trends in the financial market mainly related to the level and term structure of interest rates, their diversity and volatility, the difference between the interest on public debt and corporate debt and the normative solutions for the corporate bond issuance.

The development of financial markets, including the bond market, results in the introduction of the new securities—hybrid instruments—that allow issuers to combine the advantages of debt and equity financing. These new instruments may be also regarded as the response to the volatility of the market parameters and the increased risk of investment projects realized by the companies, which results in the difficulties in forecasting future cash flows.

This paper discusses the importance and potential application of the convertible bonds (as the examples of hybrid securities) in the corporate financing decisions. The main aim of this paper is to analyze and evaluate the most important reasons and consequences of the issuance of convertible bonds and their role in the corporate financial strategy. This conceptual paper is based on the critical literature review on corporate bonds supported by the analysis of normative regulations and selected empirical data obtained from the Polish financial market institutions.

The paper is organized as follows. After the introduction, Chap. 2 presents the theoretical framework for the convertible bonds issuance from the issuer's point of view with regard to the potential opportunities and threats. Chapter 3 analyzes the market for corporate bonds in Poland and discusses the exemplary convertible bonds placed in the Polish market illustrating their role in the corporate financing strategy. Final conclusion is presented in Chap. 4.

61.2 Convertible Bonds as a Corporate Financing Instrument (Opportunities and Threats)

Traditionally, the corporate capital structure decisions focus on the debt-equity choice (Myers 2001). However, the development of financial markets, together with the advanced financial engineering, enables the issuers to create the new classes of securities, such as hybrid instruments. A convertible bond is a type of a hybrid security that can be converted into preferred or common stock of the bond issuer (Culp 2006; Rose and Marquis 2009).

The decisions to apply the convertible bonds in the corporate financing strategy fall into the more general problem of the optimal capital structure (Leland 1994). For the investors convertible bonds, as hybrid securities, give a chance to adopt a safer position in the financial market. This is particularly important in the face of difficulties in assessing the investment risk and the uncertainty as to the direction of the market changes. The decision to issue convertible bonds is of great importance not only for the potential buyers, but also for the existing shareholders. A positive market assessment of the company's strategy and the efficient allocation of the acquired capital may cause an increase in the market value of the company and create benefits not only for the bondholders but also for the current shareholders and potential future investors. The bond issuer assesses the chances of raising capital and its cost, while the investor assesses the risk-return profile of the potential investment in the particular convertible bonds. Each of them should conduct an assessment of the potential impact of the convertible bonds issuance for the future market valuation of the company.

The choice and range of hybrid instruments is related to the stage of development of the company, which is characterized by the limited access to both the debt capital and equity capital. Convertible bonds allow the company to cross the boundaries of the traditional debt taking into account all payments associated with it and the current and future available cash flow (Węcławski 2006). These instruments can be designed for companies:

- with good growth prospects, but significant investment risk (often companies in the early stages of development),
- engaged in the restructuring processes that allow to undertake the new growth projects,
- with limited access to capital in the financial market.

The greatest benefits from the issuance of convertible bonds may gain a company characterized by a relatively high investment risk, a weaker market position but with a high rate of growth and increasing creditworthiness. The nature of the product development cycle is also important as it allows to predict an increase in the share price with the rising market position of the company. At the same time, the investors are offered with the opportunity to participate in the growth of the company. These instruments allow the issuers to reduce the capital gap in the situation of the limited access to external sources of financing. This is of particular importance for the innovative companies, especially in the early stages of development (Łukasik 2010).

Hybrid instruments, including convertible bonds, can be regarded as a risk management tool. They allow both investors and issuers to take advantage of the market volatility and the future market valuation of a company. At the same time, these instruments allow to transfer part of the market risk to creditors and give the access to the markets and new sources of funds. Convertible bonds may increase market liquidity and offer new investment opportunities for investors. For the issuer, they may create a risk of the unfavorable changes in the ownership structure and as a consequence the dilution of the future free cash flows.

Hybrid instruments are often used by the existing owners to protect against the loss of control over the company and to reduce the risk of dilution of the decision-making centers. They allow the issuer to exceed acceptable (safe) level of debt, creating the possibility to postpone the repayment of liabilities depending on the increase in the company's value. However, this may create additional risk connected with the risky investment projects and excessive usage of debt (leverage). Part of this risk may be transferred to the creditors (by risk shifting), and the usage of additional rights for bondholders may allow the company to offer lower interest rate. Another advantage is that convertible bonds enable the issuer to match the cash outflows (for the bondholders) with the cash inflows generated by the realized investment projects. As to the disadvantages: there is a risk of unfavorable changes in capital structure and the ownership structure, the undesired time of conversion and the participation of bondholders in future profits earned by the existing owners.

Unlike straight bonds, convertible bonds combine traditional economic functions related to raising capital with the function of stimulating the specific direction of structural changes (in terms of the company's capital structure and organization structure). This allows issuers to simultaneously reduce the adverse effect of the "dilution of earnings", especially for companies with high growth potential and substantial capital needs. In comparison with the classical form of debt instrument, company may offer a lower interest rate in exchange for a commitment to the non-cash benefits (conversion rights). This allows to accept and finance investment projects with lower expected rate of return.

An important element related to the issuance of convertible bonds is to determine the conversion ratio, which defines the relationship between the nominal value of the bonds and the number of shares to which the bonds can be converted (Culp 2006). The basis for determining this ratio is the accepted conversion price (for shares), which is not only important for the success of the issue and the attractiveness of the security but also for the position of the existing shareholders comparing to the future owners. The conversion price is the effective price that the company obtains for one ordinary share at the time of conversion.

Setting the conversion price may be an area of the conflict of interest. Bondholder will be interested in the lowest possible conversion price, because it will determine the chances of obtaining capital gains in the future. The issuer will be interested in the highest possible conversion price in relation to the current market price of shares at the time of issuance. Current shareholders will try to adopt the conversion price at the minimum level corresponding to the book value per share.

The conversion price may be determined by (Damodaran 2001):

- the current market price of shares,
- the expected increase in the share price resulting from the development of the company after the bond issuance,
- the business risk resulting from the issuer's current financial situation and the potential credit rating illustrating the expected future structural changes in the company.

Convertible bonds allow issuers to raise hybrid capital at lower cost of capital comparing to equity and with lower financial (bankruptcy) risk as compared to debt capital. They offer investors the safety of bonds and the growth potential of shares (Groppelli and Nikbakht 2006). The convertible bond issuer acquires a commitment to the bondholder, which may be implemented as one of the two alternative benefits: (1) cash payments, including the principal repayment and coupon payments for creditors (bondholders) (2) non-cash benefit involving the conversion of bonds into shares.

The right to choose the type of benefit belongs usually to the bondholder (unless it is specified in the terms and conditions of the bonds' issuance). By purchasing convertible bonds, investors are expected to benefit from a potential increase in the market price of the shares received in exchange for bonds over the level of conversion price. There is certain risk linked to this, as the market price of shares at the conversion moment can be at a lower level, at which the conversion will be unprofitable. The possibility of conversion of bonds into shares is therefore a right not an obligation. If it would be unprofitable, the bondholder may decide not to convert the bonds and receive a cash benefit (interest with principal repayment).

The issue of convertible bonds gives the company possibility to improve its financial liquidity (as debt is self-liquidating), increase its net asset value, reduce borrowing costs and speed up the procedure for obtaining funds (Bender and Ward 2009). Convertible bonds give the possibility to transfer the risk from the issuer to the bondholders and company's existing and potential owners. Convertible bonds offer the opportunity to raise capital at a lower cost for companies that have high growth potential but limited creditworthiness. They can reduce the weighted average cost of capital and increase the value of the company. The main threat associated with the issuance of convertible bonds is the potential dilution of ownership, loss of control over the company and unfavorable relation of the conversion price to the market price of share. There may appear new shareholders in the ownership structure, whose expectations may be contrary to the interests of the company, which may lead to an increase in the agency costs and decrease in company's efficiency. The company can reduce this risk by including call option in the convertible bond construction giving the issuer the right to call for early redemption, which allows the company to force conversion or refinance debt depending on the relationship between the conversion price and the market price at early redemption.

Analysis of hybrid instruments should be complemented with other types of bonds, which can be effectively used by the company in the financing strategy. These instruments may include exchangeable bonds and reverse convertible bonds.

Exchangeable bonds entitle the investor to convert the bond into shares of another company than the bond issuer (Parker and Dunton 2001). Such an instrument consists of the traditional bond combined with the option to purchase the shares of another company. Exchangeable bonds can be used by affiliated companies. This is due to the fact that the parent company may undertake the issue of bonds exchangeable for shares of its subsidiary on more favorable terms compared to the possibility of the issuance of convertible bonds by a subsidiary itself.

Reverse convertible bonds (reverse convertibles) give the issuer the right to complete the conversion of bonds into shares at a specified date in the future at predetermined conditions (Culp 2002). The security of this type is a combination of the straight bond and option to sale the new shares issued by the issuer of the bonds. If at the maturity date the market price of shares is below the strike price of the put option, the issuer has the option to choose between paying the nominal value of the bonds and call for their conversion into shares of the new issue. An investor deciding to purchase reverse convertible bonds has to accept the risk associated with the obligation to convert bonds into shares even if the conversion will not be beneficial for him/her. In exchange for the increased risk, reverse convertible bonds provide investors with interest rates higher than the average level of market interest rates. The difference in interest rates on reverse convertible bonds and ordinary bonds is the premium paid by the issuer to the investor for the right to choose how to redeem the bonds.

61.3 The Issuance of Convertible Debt: The Experience of Polish Companies

The development of the financial market in Poland offers the companies greater possibilities to issue debt securities. The legal basis for the issue of corporate bonds in Poland has evolved over a period of time, taking into account not only the expectations of the investors but also the needs of the issuers. New law regulations have given the opportunity to invest in the securities characterized by the higher level of risk and to liberalize the rules of trading and issuing bonds. The most important changes include the resignation of mandatory objective and collateral of the issue and the establishment of the bank representative (Act on Bonds 2015).

A special function in the corporate bond market is fulfilled by the intermediaries responsible for the organization of trading platforms, including the Catalyst market, which consists of the regulated market and the alternative trading systems (both retail and wholesale markets).

Bonds placed in the market should be dematerialized and registered in KDPW (Central Securities Depository of Poland). It is also required for the issuer to prepare the information document that includes data important for the investors as they may affect the price of a financial instrument and its investment attractiveness. New legal regulations and organizational changes increased the interest of the Polish companies in issuance of corporate bonds.

Since the launch of the Catalyst market in 2009, systematic development of this platform can be observed, taking into account both the number of bond issuers and the value of bonds issued each year. In 2015 there were listed 535 series of debt securities issued by 194 issuers with a total nominal value of PLN 613.1 billion. This represents quite significant increase comparing to the first year of the Catalyst market, when there were listed 47 series of debt securities with a total nominal value of PLN 10.6 billion (Catalyst Report 2014).

However, the degree of development of the bond market in Poland measured by the ratio of outstanding debt to GDP is still quite low, as it equals only to 15% and

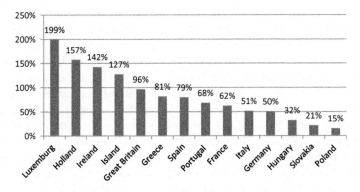

Fig. 61.1 Outstanding debt securities expressed as GDP%. *Source* PwC Report (2015)

is the lowest one comparing even to other CEE countries (compare Fig. 61.1). This demonstrates the high potential for the development of the debt market in Poland, including the market for corporate bonds. This potential for the development is illustrated by the increasing value of the debt instruments issued by both the public (State Treasury and municipal authorities) and private entities (financial institutions and non-financial companies).

The share of corporate bonds according to the total value of debt securities listed in the Catalyst market (excluding Treasury bonds) at the end of 2014 amounted to 87.6%. The share of the remaining debt securities was as follows: mortgage bonds (covered bonds)—6.3%, municipal bonds—5%, co-operative bonds—1% (Catalyst Report 2014) (Table 61.1).

In the early years of the Catalyst market, the decision to introduce the bonds to the organized trading system has been taken by 10 companies, offering bonds with a nominal value of PLN 6.8 billion. In the following years, it was observed a significant increase in the number of issuers and the value of the acquired capital. In 2015, there were traded bonds of 148 issuers and the total value of the capital raised amounted to over PLN 60 billion.

Companies from different sectors acquire capital in the Catalyst market by offering bonds. The most important group of issuers represents following sectors:

Table 61.1 Corporate bonds in the Catalyst market

Year	Number of issuers	Number of series	Issue value (PLN million)
2015	148	360	60,358
2014	148	357	56,139
2013	133	291	55,820
2012	119	239	46,366
2011	66	140	34,522
2010	40	53	17,345
2009	10	10	6819

Source Catalyst Fact book (2009–2015)

financial services, developers, construction, IT, retails and food, wood, chemicals, energy, oil & gas, pharmaceutical, technology and transportation.

The average nominal value of the issued corporate bonds in the 2009–2014 period amounted to PLN 40.3 million. The average value of the municipal bonds was PLN 45.6 million, the co-operative bonds—PLN 11.2 million and the bonds of commercial banks—PLN 169 million. Given the size of funds raised—the issues of corporate bonds were very diverse—ranging from offerings below PLN 500 thousand—up till PLN 2 billion. The most common size of the corporate bonds offerings in the 2009–2014 period was up to PLN 10 million.

A part of the issuers does not stop at a single bond issue. There are companies that regularly raise funds in the Catalyst market, considering issuance of bonds as a permanent part of their financing strategy (compare Table 61.2).

Corporate bonds offer the highest interest rate comparing to the bonds of other issuers. The average interest rate on corporate bonds in the period 2009–2014 amounted to 9.41%, compared to the municipal bonds—5.48%, the bonds of commercial banks—6.52% and the bonds of co-operative banks—7.45%, while the average interest rate on the bonds with regard to the market of shares listing was as follows:

- Entities listed in the New Connect market (ALM operating in Poland since 2007)—11.8% (representing 18% of bond issuers)
- Unlisted entities—9.73% (representing 32.7% of bond issuers)
- Entities listed on the WSE Main List—8.04% (representing 49.3% of bond issuers).

Interest rates on individual corporate bonds were also very diverse—ranging from 3.5 to 18%. Changes in the level of interest rates over a period of time follow the changes in the global financial system in 2009–2014. This level of interest rate on corporate bonds, in comparison with the interest rate on bank deposits (on average 1.2–1.6% in 2015) and government bonds (2.2% on average in 2015) as an alternative form of investment, indicates the possibility of obtaining relatively higher rate of return, which can be regarded as a premium for additional risk taken by investors. This additional risk arises also from the fact that more than 60% of corporate bonds were issued without any collateral (Pawłowski 2015).

For the issuers, it is possible to offer convertible bonds in the Catalyst market; however, these instruments are not very often used. In the 2009–2014 period, only

Table 61.2 Most active issuers of the corporate bonds in the 2009–2014 period

Issuer	Number of series	Total nominal value of series (PLN million)
Kruk S.A.	26	681
E-Kancelaria	20	48.2
Ghelamco invest	15	837.6
Gant development	15	245.9
RoBYG	14	407.8

Source Catalyst Report (2014)

13 series of convertible bonds were placed by 8 issuers in the Catalyst market. Out of this, 6 companies were listed in the WSE Main Market and 2 were listed in the New Connect market (compare Table 61.3). The interest rate on the convertible bonds ranged between 13.94 (for bonds offered by Miraculum) and 3.90% (in the case of bonds of Warimpex). One company—Warimpex (developers) offered 4 series of convertible bonds acquiring hybrid capital with a total value of PLN 115.75 million and a weighted average interest rate of 7.11%.

Convertible bonds are also placed outside the Catalyst market by means of a private placement. In 2000–2013, altogether 22 companies successfully placed 25 series of convertible bonds (Regucki et al. 2014).

In January 2014, it took place the first issuance of exchangeable bonds. The Czech company CEZ listed in the Warsaw Stock Exchange issued bonds exchangeable for the shares of its subsidiary—the Hungarian MOL. The bonds were without interest rate with a conversion price set at EUR 61.25 per share including a 35% premium over the weighted average market price of MOL shares listed in the Budapest Stock Exchange. Interestingly, the right to exchange the bonds belongs to the issuer.

Table 61.3 Corporate convertible bonds placed in the Catalyst market in 2009–2014

Issuer	Sector	Market of shares listing	Date of issuance	Nominal value (PLN)	Interest rate on the issuing day (%)	Conversion price
MCI Management	Financial services	WSE Main Market	11.09.2011 21.03.2014	50,000,000 50,000,000	8.39 6.59	9 zł 17.54zł
Marvipol	Developers	WSE Main Market	29.06.2010 16.09.2011	39,400,000 30,791,000	6.84 9.42	11zł, 12zł, 13zł 12.8zł
Gant Development	Developers	WSE Main Market	29.09.2010	26,000,000	8.16	5zł
Mera	Building materials	New Connect	23.04.2010	758,500	12.33	5zł
Rubicon Partners NFI	Financial services	WSE Main Market	26.04.2011	32,000,000	10.69	1.60zł
Warimpex	Developers	WSE Main Market	25.05.2011 28.03.2013 29.10.2013 29.10.2013	66,250,000 26,500,000 15,000,000 8,000,000	8.5 4.88 3.90 9.12	7.06zł
Mew	Energy	New Connect	15.06.2011	5,060,000	12	5.5zł
Miraculum	Pharmaceutics	WSE Main Market	09.11.2011	4,775,000	13.94	0.09zł, 0.16zł, 0.18zł, 0.20zł

Source Catalyst Report (2014)

The detailed analysis of the particular cases of the convertible bonds offerings (offered both in a regulated and OTC market) indicates that the acquired funds were spent not only on the investment and development of the company but also to finance current operations and the restructurization of debt. The most common form of issue was addressed to qualified investors by means of a private placement. In most cases, the issuers have determined only the upper limit of the offer or the minimum and maximum size of the capital increase. The nominal value of the bonds was different and ranged from PLN 1 to PLN 250,000. In most cases, the issuing price was equal to the nominal value of bonds. In some cases, the issuing price was settled in order to reflect the market price of the shares, the market trends, the consolidated profit or the capital needs of the company. In one company, the bonds were offered without interest (Regucki et al. 2014).

One should also note the role of investment funds interested in investing in convertible bonds. Since November 2014 one of such funds operates in Poland. This is Aviva Investors Convertible Bonds, whose investment strategy focuses only on investing directly in convertible bonds or in investment certificates (shares) of funds investing in convertible bonds. Its asset portfolio includes, among others shares in: Aviva Investors Global Convertibles, Morgan Stanley Global Convertible Bond and Deutsche Invest I Convertibles.

The analysis of the sample convertible bonds offerings indicated different motives of the issue, mainly related to:

- the need to diversify the sources of finance
- the possibility to determine flexible conditions of the acquired capital
- the limited access to the bank financing
- the unfavorable situation in the stock market at the moment of acquiring capital.

The issuers also stressed the speed of the procedure, the marketing effect and the possibility of acquiring significant funds, despite the disclosure requirements and strict legal regulations.

61.4 Conclusion

The analysis of the current development of the corporate bond market in Poland indicates the wide possibilities of growing interest in the corporate debt securities issuance, including convertible bonds.

This is connected not only with the need to raise corporate funds for investments, but also with the limited access to the banking finance due to the creditworthiness and safety requirements imposed by the banking sector on the corporate debtors. New, innovative companies may have limited access to bank capital, and thus, the issuance of bonds can provide them a chance to develop. Large fluctuations in share prices in the capital market and the associated uncertainty of achieving capital gains directs investors' interest on convertible bonds. Higher rate of return on such investments is also important for investors (including institutional ones). Convertible bonds can be a chance to increase the safety of transactions in the financial market, to balance the benefits of shareholders and bondholders and for the companies to guarantee higher share prices in case of the conversion. However, this requires further legislative work expanding catalog of financial instruments, including not only hybrid, but also structured instruments, allowing for greater financial risk management of the issuer and the investor.

References

Act on Bonds (2015) (Dz.U. 2015 poz. 238, z dnia 15.01.2015)

Bender R, Ward K (2009) Corporate financial strategy. Routledge, London

Catalyst Factbooks (2009–2015) Warszawa Stock Exchange. Available online https://www.gpw.pl/Fact_book_2015

Catalyst Report (2014) Grant Thornton, Warszawa. Available online http://www.gpwcatalyst.pl/publications

Culp ChL (2002) Contingent capital integrating corporate financing and risk management decisions. J Appl Corp Finance 15(1):46–56

Culp ChL (2006) Structured finance and insurance. The ART. Of managing capital and risk. Wiley, Hoboken

Damodaran A (2001) Corporate finance. Theory and practice. Wiley, Hoboken

Groppelli AA, Nikbakht E (2006) Finance. Barron's, New York

Leland HE (1994) Corporate debt value, bond covenants, and optimal capital structure. J Finance 49(4):1213–1252

Łukasik G (2010) Strategie finansowaia rozwoju współczesnych przedsiębiorstw. Uniwersytet Ekonomiczny w Katowicach, Katowice

Myers SC (2001) Capital structure. J Econ Perspect 15(2):81–102

Parker Ch, Dunton M (2001) How convertibles can help in tough times. Int Financ Law Rev: 43–46

Pawłowski M (2015) Rynek obligacji korporacyjnych w Polsce. Uwarunkowania i perspektywy rozwoju. CeDeWu, Warszawa

PwC Report (2015) Rynek kapitałowy jako narzędzie finansowania regionów. PwC, Warszawa

Regucki T, Stępniewska-Janowska M, Zygucki J (2014) Warunkowe podwyższenie kapitału zakładowego w spółkach giełdowych. Analiza empiryczna. Working paper 10, Instytut Allerhanda, Kraków

Rose PS, Marquis MH (2009) Money and capital markets. McGraw Hill, New York

Węcławski J (2006) Hybrydowe instrument finansowania przedsiębiorstw. In: Karpuś P (ed) Finanse przedsiębiorstwa. Uniwersytet Marii Curie-Skłodowskiej, Lublin

Chapter 62
Evaluation of Investment Attractiveness of Commonwealth of Independent States

Victoria Chobanyan

Abstract The paper covers evaluation of parameters influencing investment attractiveness of the countries of the Commonwealth of Independent states (CIS) by correlation analyses of regional competitiveness factors and foreign direct investments (FDIs) inward stock levels on the territory for the period of 1992–2014. Based on the correlation matrix, we can conclude that the highest impact on investment attractiveness for FDI in CIS is coming from the size of the markets, both domestic and foreign. Institutional characteristics that include legal and political environment in the region also show high correlation levels. High impact on investment attractiveness of CIS comes also from the parameter "strength of auditing and reporting standards." On the other hand, administrative, infrastructure, economic and social characteristics of the territory, such as inflation, taxation, procedures of starting business, trade tariffs and barriers, government budget balance, gross national savings, access to loans, labor market efficiency, life expectancy, health, educational system, do not have significant impact on FDI inward stock levels in CIS.

Keywords FDI · Investment attractiveness · Investment climate · CIS · IFRS

62.1 Introduction

Topic of country's investment attractiveness is relevant nowadays because fast changing economic reality influences redistribution of resources. It gets even more important in the era of globalization with unexpected crises and political events and emergence of new trends in social life and business.

Creation of environment favorable to investments is a standard tool of economic policy of each country. Financial resources within countries' territories are often

V. Chobanyan (✉)
Department of Financial Accounting and Auditing, University of Economics,
Prague, Nam. W. Churchilla 4, 130 67 Prague, Czech Republic
e-mail: vchobanyan@gmail.com

© Springer International Publishing AG 2017   677
D. Procházka (ed.), *New Trends in Finance and Accounting*,
Springer Proceedings in Business and Economics,
DOI 10.1007/978-3-319-49559-0_62

limited. Therefore, governments seek ways to create beneficial conditions for businesses and increase investment attractiveness of their countries. Level of inflowing foreign direct investments (FDIs) is often used as an indicator showing investment attractiveness of a territory.

Before taking investment decisions, enterprises perform business analyses of investment opportunities in different countries to identify ways of increasing their market share and companies' profits.

Furthermore, various aspects of investment process are the subject of scientific research.

The goal of the paper is to evaluate parameters influencing investment attractiveness in Commonwealth of Independent States (CIS).[1] CIS has been selected because few analyses of investment attractiveness have been found for the region despite the facts that these former soviet countries represent 16% of world territory, 4% of world population (281 mln. of inhabitants), 3% of global GDP (2,502,907 mln. US dollars). At the same time, recent growth of investment activity in the area and development of trade relations with other countries is increasing importance of CIS: For example, exports and imports of CIS states toward European Union (EU) have increased by 234% from 2002 to 2013 (based on Eurostat data). Evaluation of parameters forming investment climate and attracting FDI to the CIS states will allow us to better understand current reality and conclude on determinants of FDI in transition economies.

The paper is organized as follows. After this introduction, next chapter reviews the literature. Chapter 3 contains correlation analyses of parameters of countries' competitiveness with inward FDI stocks.

62.2 Literature Review

Investment attractiveness of a territory reflects the business environment in the area: the more favorable business environment is, the more investors are interested in investing into the region. The main characteristic of regional investment attractiveness is regional business climate. Regional investment climate consists of regional potentials and regional risks.

The level of regional investment potential depends on the following characteristics: consumption potential of the region, production potential of the region, resource potential (minerals, climate, etc.), human potential of the region (population characteristics, like education level, working-age population), innovation potential, infrastructure potential, economical potential (taxes, conditions for doing business, such as adoption of IFRS).

---

[1]The Commonwealth of Independent States (CIS) consists of eleven countries: Armenia, Azerbaijan, Belarus, Kazakhstan, Moldova, Russian Federation, Turkmenistan, Ukraine and Uzbekistan.

The level of regional risks comes from the following risk factors: economical risks, political risks, social risks, criminal risks, ecological risks.

It is important to mention separately the role of economic risks and potentials in the decision making for company investments. These risks and potentials comprise financial and legal factors that have a significant influence on company costs. Economic risks have a probability to influence company expenses, while economic potentials bring possibilities for companies to increase the income part of investment projects.

The common questions are: "What are the determinants stimulating investment flows in countries and regions? And how to identify and reach the needed level of these determinants to enable payback investments?"

In recent years, the subject of investment determinants and factors was investigated by a range of researchers for different countries. Agarwal (1980), Schneider and Frey (1985), Biswas (2002), Demirhan and Masca (2008), Walsh and Yu (2010), Resmini and Casi (2011), Chan et al. (2014) analyze factors influencing attractivity of regions investments.

Based on the econometric analyses of FDI in 80 less developed countries, Schneider and Frey (1985) discover that country attractiveness for FDI depends on political–economical factors, such as real GNP per capita, level of payments deficit, political stability. Demirhan and Masca (2008) consolidate the research materials on determinants of FDI and by using cross-sectional econometric model evaluate factors of FDI inflows in 38 developing countries for the period of 2000–2004. The finding of the investigation is that different scientists came to different conclusions about the impact of the same parameters on FDI flows. As about results of cross-sectional econometric model, significant impact on FDI flow comes from growth rate of GDP per capita, telephone main lines and degree of openness having direct relationship, inflation rate and tax rate showing inverse relationship. Walsh and Yu (2010) divide investments into three sector types—primary, secondary and tertiary—and find dependence for each of them on set of indicators in developing and developed countries. The outcome is that FDI flows into primary sector have low dependence on any of variables, while investments into secondary and tertiary sectors are differently affected by parameters and the effect is often different in advanced and emerging countries. Resmini and Casi (2011) look into investments distribution on both country level and regions inside countries trying to identify national and regional components of attractiveness for FDI. Valentey (2012) present the results of their research of investment attractiveness of Russian regions based on innovative and social and economic characteristics. Liargovas and Skandalis (2012) evaluate trade openness and FDI inflows in 36 developing economies (in Latin America, Asia, Africa, CIS and Eastern Europe) for the period 1990–2008 and came to conclusion that in long-term perspective trade openness has a positive impact on FDI attraction in developing countries. Chan et al. (2014) find out that GDP growth has a direct influence on FDI flows in short and long terms, and at the same time growth in local infrastructure has indirect impact.

Today, more and more companies try to enlarge the coverage of world markets by investing into foreign countries. Very often, they are penetrating new markets by FDI. Such investments are often connected to larger projects with higher investment values and are intended to bring high level of ROI. In such conditions, company management is focusing on finding investment possibilities where they could decrease expenses and save money on taxes and transactional costs. Therefore, financial aspect is getting higher attention by investors. To stimulate cross-country investments, governments try to create conditions supporting capital integration in between regions by accounting standardization, for example by adopting IFRS.

Several researches were looking into this topic trying to find correlation between IFRS adoption and FDI flows. Marquéz-Ramos (2011) concludes that there is a connection between FDI level and the accounting harmonization in the country. Gordon et al. (2012) after having analyzed data for the periods of 1996–2009 state that adoption of IFRS leads to increased FDI inflows by countries with developing economies. Chen et al. (2014) based on the research of 30 OECD countries between 2000 and 2005 confirm the hypotheses that the convergence of local accounting standards with the globally harmonized ones (such as IFRS) supports growth of FDI in the receiving countries that is caused by decreasing costs for information processing by investing companies.

In other words, when company decides about investment needs and starts to identify investment alternatives, it is important to choose a project that is believed to bring acceptable for investor level of ROI and a region where the implementation of the investment project will secure the best results because of certain regional characteristics. In general, when choosing a region to invest companies pay attention both on the possibilities for a stable and high growth and possibilities to minimize costs. Based on the analyses of a vast literature base connected to this topic, Procházka and Procházková Ilinitchi (2011) summarize that there are a lot of evidences of correlation between regional attractiveness for FDI and the adoption of the IFRS standards on the territory, although it is not the only influencing factor.

As an example, we see a lot of multinational companies investing into production on the territory of special economic zones in China—they give advantages both in tax conditions and general conditions for organizing and running business, 90–95% alignment with IFRS and low-cost working force that allows companies to have a major decrease in costs for running business.

As summarized in Table 62.1, variety of economic, political, social, innovative and administrative characteristics of doing business in countries have an impact on FDI inflows, but each of them has a different level of influence. Stemming from the paper's goal and the literature review, following hypothesis will be tested: Biggest impact on investment attractiveness for FDI in CIS countries is coming from political factors as well as economic potential, while infrastructure parameters and level of accounting harmonization do not play crucial role.

Table 62.1 FDI determinants, identified by different authors

Determinant	Authors
Political stability	Schneider and Frey (1985)
GDP, GNP	Schneider and Frey (1985), Demirhan and Masca (2008), Chan et al. (2014)
Payments deficit	Schneider and Frey (1985)
Openness of country economy	Demirhan and Masca (2008), Liargovas and Skandalis (2012)
Innovative potential	Valentey (2012)
Social characteristics	Procházka and Procházková Ilinitchi (2011), Valentey (2012)
Telephone main lines	Demirhan and Masca (2008)
Accounting harmonization	Procházka and Procházková Ilinitchi (2011), Marquéz-Ramos (2011), Gordon et al. (2012), Chen et al. (2014)

Source Created by author

62.3   Methodology, Data and Results

Nowadays, a lot of international researches are made to understand drivers and identify recent trends in development of world economies. In this paper, The Global Competitiveness Report prepared by World Economic Forum will be used to find out factors influencing FDI inflows in CIS countries. As the indicator showing the investment attractiveness of the territory, we will use the FDI inflow levels (Fig. 62.1). The trend that from the first year of CIS functioning FDI inward stocks is growing. During this period (1992–2014), there were also two big drops that could be explained by the two events that happened in the CIS area—financial crisis of 2008 (that had an impact on most of the CIS economies) and Ukrainian events of 2014 (that strongly influenced Russian and Ukrainian economies).

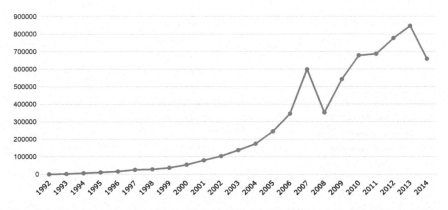

Fig. 62.1 FDI inward stocks development in CIS in 1992–2014, mln. US dollars. *Source* Prepared by author based on The Global Competitiveness Index Historical Dataset © 2005–2015 World Economic Forum, UNCTAD FDI/TNC database

As determinants we will use the parameters of countries' competitiveness from the Global Competitiveness Index that comprises a variety of factors that are divided into three main categories—subindexes: basic requirements (that are key for factor-driven economies); efficiency enhancers (key for efficiency-driven economies) and innovation and sophistication factors (key for innovation-driven economies). Each of these three subindexes consists of several groups of parameters.

Table 62.2 Correlation between FDI inflow stock and parameters of countries' competitiveness in CIS countries

Competitiveness parameter	Parameter type	Correlation coefficient
Property rights	Institutions	0.8
Intellectual property protection	Institutions	0.8
Diversion of public funds	Institutions	−0.8
Public trust in politicians	Institutions	0.8
Irregular payments and bribes	Institutions	0.7
Judicial independence	Institutions	0.8
Favoritism in decisions of government officials	Institutions	0.8
Wastefulness of government spending	Institutions	0.8
Burden of government regulation	Institutions	0.8
Efficiency of legal framework in settling disputes	Institutions	0.8
Efficiency of legal framework in challenging regs	Institutions	0.3
Transparency of government policymaking	Institutions	0.8
Business costs of terrorism	Institutions	0.8
Business costs of crime and violence	Institutions	0
Organized crime	Institutions	0.8
Reliability of police services	Institutions	−0.8
Ethical behavior of firms	Institutions	0.8
Strength of auditing and reporting standards	Institutions	0.8
Efficacy of corporate boards	Institutions	0.8
Protection of minority shareholders' interests	Institutions	−0.6
Strength of investor protection, 0–10 (best)	Institutions	−0.4
Quality of overall infrastructure	Infrastructure	0.2
Quality of roads	Infrastructure	−0.3
Quality of port infrastructure	Infrastructure	0.6
Quality of air transport infrastructure	Infrastructure	0.1
Available airline seat km/week, millions	Infrastructure	0.5
Quality of electricity supply	Infrastructure	0.4
Fixed telephone lines/100 pop	Infrastructure	0.2
Mobile telephone subscriptions/100 pop	Infrastructure	0.4
Government budget balance, % GDP	Macroeconomic environment	0
Gross national savings, % GDP	Macroeconomic environment	0.1
Inflation, annual % change	Macroeconomic environment	0.1

(continued)

Table 62.2 (continued)

Competitiveness parameter	Parameter type	Correlation coefficient
General government debt, % GDP	Macroeconomic environment	−0.2
Business impact of tuberculosis	Health and primary education	0.3
Tuberculosis cases/100,000 pop	Health and primary education	−0.1
Business impact of HIV/AIDS	Health and primary education	0.2
Infant mortality, deaths/1000 live births	Health and primary education	−0.3
Life expectancy, years	Health and primary education	0.1
Quality of primary education	Health and primary education	0.4
Primary education enrollment, net %	Health and primary education	0.2
Secondary education enrollment, gross %	Higher education and training	0.2
Tertiary education enrollment, gross %	Higher education and training	0.3
Quality of the education system	Higher education and training	0.1
Quality of math and science education	Higher education and training	0.3
Quality of management schools	Higher education and training	0.3
Internet access in schools	Higher education and training	0.8
Availability of research and training services	Higher education and training	0.7
Extent of staff training	Higher education and training	0.4
Intensity of local competition	Goods market efficiency	0.7
Extent of market dominance	Goods market efficiency	0.4
Effectiveness of anti-monopoly policy	Goods market efficiency	0.4
Effect of taxation on incentives to invest	Goods market efficiency	−0.1
No. of procedures to start a business	Goods market efficiency	0.1
No. of days to start a business	Goods market efficiency	−0.1
Agricultural policy costs	Goods market efficiency	−0.3
Total tax rate, % profits	Goods market efficiency	0
Prevalence of trade barriers	Goods market efficiency	−0.3
Prevalence of foreign ownership	Goods market efficiency	−0.3
Business impact of rules on FDI	Goods market efficiency	−0.3
Burden of customs procedures	Goods market efficiency	0.1
Imports as a percentage of GDP	Goods market efficiency	−0.3
Trade tariffs, % duty	Goods market efficiency	−0.1
Degree of customer orientation	Goods market efficiency	−0.1
Buyer sophistication	Goods market efficiency	0.3
Cooperation in labor–employer relations	Labor market efficiency	−0.4
Hiring and firing practices	Labor market efficiency	0.1
Flexibility of wage determination	Labor market efficiency	0.3
Effect of taxation on incentives to work	Labor market efficiency	−0.3
Redundancy costs, weeks of salary	Labor market efficiency	−0.1
Pay and productivity	Labor market efficiency	0.4
Reliance on professional management	Labor market efficiency	0.5
Country capacity to retain talent	Labor market efficiency	0.1
Country capacity to attract talent	Labor market efficiency	0.2

(continued)

Table 62.2 (continued)

Competitiveness parameter	Parameter type	Correlation coefficient
Women in labor force, ratio to men	Labor market efficiency	0.1
Affordability of financial services	Financial market development	0.4
Availability of financial services	Financial market development	0.6
Financing through local equity market	Financial market development	0.5
Ease of access to loans	Financial market development	0.3
Venture capital availability	Financial market development	0.1
Soundness of banks	Financial market development	0
Regulation of securities exchanges	Financial market development	0.4
Legal rights index, 0–10 (best)	Financial market development	−0.2
Availability of latest technologies	Technological readiness	−0.1
Firm-level technology absorption	Technological readiness	0.2
FDI and technology transfer	Technological readiness	−0.4
Individuals using Internet, %	Technological readiness	0.4
Fixed broadband Internet subscriptions/100 pop	Technological readiness	0.3
Int'l Internet bandwidth, kb/s per user	Technological readiness	−0.1
Mobile broadband subscriptions/100 pop	Technological readiness	0.2
GDP (PPP$ billions)	Market size	0.5
Exports as a percentage of GDP	Market size	0
Domestic market size index	Market size	0.9
Foreign market size index	Market size	0.8
Local supplier quantity	Business sophistication	0.1
Local supplier quality	Business sophistication	0.2
State of cluster development	Business sophistication	0.2
Nature of competitive advantage	Business sophistication	0.2
Production process sophistication	Business sophistication	0.1
Willingness to delegate authority	Business sophistication	0.2
Control of international distribution	Business sophistication	0.5
Extent of marketing	Business sophistication	0.6
Value chain breadth	Business sophistication	0
Capacity for innovation	Innovation	0
Quality of scientific research institutions	Innovation	0.5
Company spending on R&D	Innovation	0.4
University–industry collaboration in R&D	Innovation	0.7
Government procurement of advanced tech products	Innovation	0.1
Availability of scientists and engineers	Innovation	0.3
PCT patents, applications/million pop	Innovation	0.5

Source Created by author based on The Global Competitiveness Index Historical Dataset © 2005–2015 World Economic Forum, UNCTAD FDI/TNC database

To identify the parameters of countries' competitiveness influencing FDI inward stock levels in CIS countries, correlation coefficients were calculated (Table 62.2).

Based on the correlation matrix, the following indicators have high level of direct correlation with FDI inward stock (coefficient value ≥ 0.8): property rights, intellectual property protection, public trust in politicians, judicial independence, favoritism in decisions of government officials, wastefulness of government spending, burden of government regulation, efficiency of legal framework in settling disputes, transparency of government policymaking, business costs of terrorism, organized crime, ethical behavior of firms, strength of auditing and reporting standards, efficacy of corporate boards, Internet access in schools, foreign market size index, where the highest is domestic market size index (with the 0.9 correlation index). The above-mentioned parameters having high correlation with FDI inward stock levels represent three areas of countries' characteristics: institutions, higher education and training and market size. Group of parameters "higher education and training" is represented only by one indicator out of eight that from our opinion is not sufficient to conclude that this group of factors has significant impact on investment attractiveness of territory. At the same time, two parameters from the group of institutional characteristics (diversion of public funds and reliability of police services) show high level of negative correlation with FDI inward stock. Administrative characteristics, such as number of procedures or days to start a business, business impact of rules on FDI, burden of customs procedures, show low level of correlation, both positive and negative. On the other hand, being an administrative factor, parameter "strength of auditing and reporting standards" has high correlation with the FDI inwards stock level in CIS. It is also important to mention that some of the parameters have high pair correlation, meaning that they depend from each other.

62.4 Conclusion

FDI are very important for the regional economy being a "motor" in countries' development as they positively contribute to different areas of life on the territory: economic, social, innovative, etc. They increase countries' revenues, support improvement of infrastructure, stimulate population development and their involvement in regional economic activities, introduce innovative methods of working and bring know-how.

To secure high FDI inward stock, governments need to understand the factors influencing the decision making of investors that is very often connected to the level of development of the investment climate in the area. It is important to keep in mind that investment process is characterized by a certain level of risks, depending on the macro- and micro-characteristics, or in other words, on the regional and project parameters. Investors are taking decision to go for an investment project when the level of ROI is reasonable compared to the level of risks. Risks are often evaluated and reflected in the ROI calculations as possible costs to be able to preview the different scenarios of projects development. Regional market opportunities have an influence on the income part of investment projects. Therefore, while identifying factors that influence investment attractiveness of the area, government representatives should take care both of the enlarging market opportunities and minimizing regional risks.

Based on the above analyses of the FDI inward stock levels in CIS, we can conclude about how different parameters of countries' competitiveness influence the level of investment attractiveness of a territory. The strongest correlation levels are shown for the two groups of parameters: market size and institutions. Institutional characteristics include legal and political environment that was expected in the hypothesis. Infrastructure and business sophistication, as well as administrative procedures and level of bureaucracy, do not show high correlation levels that also support the hypothesis. On the other hand, macroeconomic indicators do not reflect high correlation levels with investment attractiveness as paper hypothesis proposed.

The main limitation of the paper is connected to the level of details that are taken into account, as well as the fact that CIS is taken as a region, differences between countries within the association and the impact levels of separate economies are not considered. Future research shall deeper assess different parameters of business environment and its correlation with regional investment attractiveness and evaluate it on country level within the CIS.

Acknowledgments This paper has been prepared within the research project "Economic Impacts of the IFRS Adoption in Selected Transition Countries" (supported by the Czech Science Foundation, No. 15-01280S).

References

Agarwal JP (1980) Determinants of foreign direct investment: a survey. Weltwirtschaftliches Archiv 116(4):739–773

Biswas R (2002) Determinants of foreign direct investment. Rev Dev Econ 6:492–504

Chan MW, Luke Hou, Keqiang Li, Xing Mountain, Dean C (2014) Foreign direct investment and its determinants: a regional panel causality analysis. Q Rev Econ Finance 54(4):579–589

Chen CJP, Ding Y, Xu B (2014) Convergence of accounting standards and foreign direct investment. Int J Account 49(1):53–86

Demirhan E, Masca M (2008) Determinants of foreign direct investment flows to developing countries: a cross-sectional analysis. Prague Econ Papers 17(4):356–369

Gordon LA, Loeb MP, Zhu W (2012) The impact of IFRS adoption on foreign direct investment. J Account Public Policy 31(4):374–398

Liargovas PG, Skandalis KS (2012) Foreign direct investment and trade openness: the case of developing economies. Soc Indic Res 106(2):323–331

Márquez-Ramos L (2011) European accounting harmonization: consequences of IFRS adoption on trade in goods and foreign direct investments. Emerg Mark Finance Trade 47(4):42–57

Procházka D, Procházková Ilinitchi C (2011) The theoretical relationships among foreign direct investments, migration and IFRS adoption. Eur Fin Account J 6(4):85–100

Resmini L, Casi L (2011) The determinants of foreign direct investments: regional vs. national characteristics. European Regional Science Association. ERSA conference papers 10:466

Schneider F, Frey BS (1985) Economic and political determinants of foreign direct investment. World Dev 13(2):161–175. doi:10.1016/0305-750X(85)90002-6. Accessed 20 Jan 2016

Valentey S (2012) Russian regions and innovative development. In: Kommersant–online. http://www.kommersant.ru/doc/2035347. Accessed 20 Jan 2016

Walsh JP, Yu J (2010) Determinants of foreign direct investment: a sectoral and institutional approach. IMF Working Papers: 1–27

Chapter 63
Using Rating for Credit Risk Measurement

Anna Siekelová

Abstract Credit risk is the risk of loss of principal or loss of a financial reward stemming from a borrower's failure to repay a loan or otherwise meet a contractual obligation. The rating can be a relatively simple and quality tool for investors. It is an independent evaluation of the entity's ability and willingness to meet its future obligations. Rating is a standard product of the financial and capital markets, whereby it is possible to determine the risk of the entity. Risk rating analysis consists in evaluating financial ("hard factors") and non-financial factors ("soft factors"). Hard facts are calculated from the financial statements of the company through the implementation of financial-economic analysis to provide a reliable statement about the financial stability of the company and its financial health. The values of indicators which are achieved are combined according to their significance, and then they are transferred to the internal rating scale. Then, this value is used to express quantitative rating of entity. This contribution deals with calculation of quantitative criteria. The aim of the paper is determining the rating of selected companies through quantitative indicators compared to the values of these indicators that are reached in the industry. Based on the practical implementation, we show how we can use rating for credit risk measurement.

Keywords Rating · Rating agency · Risk · Credit risk · Credit risk measurement

63.1 Introduction

The issue of rating and credit risk is interconnected. There are two types of dependences between the probability of default and rating: negative (the probability of default is lower, and thereby rating is higher) and also positive correlation (the probability of default is higher when the time from rating is higher)

A. Siekelová (✉)
FPEDAS, Department of Economics, University of Žilina, Univerzitná 1,
010 26 Žilina, Slovakia
e-mail: anna.siekelova@fpedas.uniza.sk

© Springer International Publishing AG 2017   689
D. Procházka (ed.), *New Trends in Finance and Accounting*,
Springer Proceedings in Business and Economics,
DOI 10.1007/978-3-319-49559-0_63

(Adamko et al. 2014). Credit risk can be defined as a risk of borrower's failure to repay a loan or otherwise meet a contractual obligation. Rating is an independent assessment of the entity's ability and willingness to meet its future obligations (Cisko and Kliestik 2013). In general, the higher rating, the higher probability a company meets its obligations properly and on time. So we can say that the rating is one of the tools for the assessment of credit risk that is associated with a specific client (Frajtova-Michalikova et al. 2014).

63.2 Literature Review

According to Regulation (EC) No 1060/2009 of the European Parliament and of the Council of 16 September 2009 on credit rating agencies, the credit rating is defined as an opinion regarding the creditworthiness of an entity, a debt or financial obligation, debt security, preferred share or other financial instrument, issued using an established and defined ranking system of rating categories. (Regulation 1060/2009 of The European Parliament and of The Council on credit rating agencies).

Rating historical development is related mainly to financial markets development in the USA. John Moody was the first person who started with evaluation of obligations of railway undertakings in 1909 (Kliestik et al. 2015). Less than a year, he focused his activities on public and industrial companies. Moody's Investors Services was established by John Moody in 1914. It was the first credit rating agency. The others were established a few years later. Currently, there are three major rating agencies on the market, namely Moody's Investors Services with a market share approximately 40%. Standard and Poor's with the same market share and Fitch Rating with the market share approximately 16%.

Rating is a product of nearly a hundred-year tradition in the world. Rating in Slovakia has begun to develop from the late 1990s. Local rating agency in Slovakia was established in 2001. Slovak Rating Agency, Inc., has become an integral part of the European Rating Agency, Inc. (ERA). This integration is a natural process of integration of local companies into European collaboration. ERA has begun to transform to the credit rating agency in 2009 according to regulations of The European Parliament and The Council. It is the first credit rating agency with a focus on Central, Eastern Europe and the Balkans (available on http://www.euroratings.co.uk/index.php?option=com_content&view=category&layout=blog&id=44&Itemid=48&lang=sk).

The ways of determining rating have changed. The methodology of calculating the rating has been modified in relation to changes in the market in which the rated entities operate. Currently, credit rating agencies use highly developed analytical models, whose role describes rated entity and the environment in which it operates, including its activities, to establish a rating correctly (Frajtova-Michalikova et al. 2015).

Table 63.1 Rating scale in relation to the probability of default

Fitch	S&P	Moody's	The probability of default to 20 years
AAA	AAA	Aaa	To 1%
AA	AA	Aa	Approximately 2%
A	A	A	Approximately 5%
BBB	BBB	Baa	To 13%
BB	BB	Ba	To 36%
B	B	B	To 63%
CCC	CCC	Caa	Entity against the default or in default
CC	CC	Ca	There is 80% probability that the receivable will not be paid
C	C	C	
DDD	D		
DD			
D			

Source Own processing based on Compel' (2006)

Table 63.2 Slovakia credit rating

	Fitch	S&P	Moody's
Slovakia credit rating	A+	A	A3

Source Available on http://www.fxstreet.cz/rating-sp-moodys-a-fitch.html

Rating evaluation is calculated by the banks themselves based on their own models, but there are also companies whose services are used by clients themselves. The higher rating client achieves the higher probability of cheaper finance (Levich et al. 2002). Table 63.1 shows the rating scale in relation to the probability of default, which is used by three major rating agencies in the world.

The effort by companies is to get the highest possible credit rating mark. It increases their credibility. The highest investment level is Aaa. Its acquisition is very difficult. It is usually given to states or supranational institutions. There are only about 15 commercial entities that have been granted such a high rating in the world. In addition to the rating mark, it is necessary to monitor also supplement to it. The first rating mark on which the supplement is added is Aa. Supplement determines creditworthiness of the risk degree. Table 63.2 shows information about Slovakia's ability to meet obligations, according to Moody's, S&P and Fitch the date of 25.02.2016.

The highest rating is permanently awarded to the developed countries whose economy is characterized by stable economic growth, low inflation, low unemployment, a high level of education and quality infrastructure. Most credit rating agencies see the position of Slovakia as a stable.

63.3 Data, Results and Discussion

The rating analysis uses two types of factors, qualitative (so-called soft factors) and quantitative (so-called hard factors). The quantitative factors can include financial or quantitative client characteristics like ratio of revenue to the long-term liabilities and current liabilities, ability to pay commitments, revenue development, cash flow, current ratio, quick ratio, net working capital. (Kollar and Bartosova 2014) The qualitative factors can include quality of accounting, ownership structure and management, market range, comparison with competitors or diversification of customers or suppliers, etc.

The aim of the paper is determining the rating of selected companies through quantitative indicators compared to the values of these indicators that are reached in the industry. There may be five different situations:

1. If the value of financial indicator is higher than the upper quartile (upper quartile represents 75% level which was achieved in this sectorial indicator), the company receives 20 points.
2. If the value of financial indicator is lower than the upper quartile, but it is closer to the upper quartile than to the median (median represents 50% level which was achieved in this sectorial indicator), the company receives 15 points.
3. If the value of financial indicator is closer to the median than the upper quartile or the lower quartile (lower quartile represents 25% level which was achieved in this sectorial indicator), the company receives 10 points.
4. If the value of financial indicator is higher than the lower quartile, but it is closer to the lower quartile than to the median, the company receives 5 points.
5. If the value of financial indicator is lower than the lower quartile, the company does not receive any points.

We chose 15 indicators values of which are calculated. The maximum number of points that can be achieved is 300. Rating is assigned based on the number of points according to Table 63.3.

Table 63.3 Slovakia credit rating

300–240	A	Excellent client
240–180	B	Very good client
180–120	C	Above-average client
120–60	D	Below-average client
60–0	E	Client with high probability of default

Source Own processing

Table 63.4   Financial indicators

Financial indicators	2009	2010	2011	2012	2013
EBIT	8,704,342	2,843,777	2,682,924	4,317,641	3,661,319
Upper quartile	14,017	14,855	111,668	13,431	11,464
Median	342	505	316	392	295
Lower quartile	−3962	−3369	−3072	−3830	−3027
Score	20	20	20	20	20
Total costs	59,234,088	58,837,610	61,458,471	61,400,766	57,594,080
Upper quartile	499,037	488,905	438,009	52,5772	370,219
Median	115,562	112,339	95,497	113,268	87,223
Lower quartile	18,425	19,076	15,338	21,325	14,742
Score	0	0	0	0	0
Total revenues	67,527,914	61,280,805	63,678,944	65,462,722	61,071,336
Upper quartile	471,972	479,778	423,408	497,861	359,938
Median	106,001	101,351	84,819	101,399	77,429
Lower quartile	13,698	14,937	11,273	167,66	12,255
Score	20	20	20	20	20

Source Own processing

Within the next sections, we will focus on direct calculation of selected financial indicators in a particular company, comparing them with the upper, lower quartile and median of the values that these indicators achieved within the industry. Finally, based on the results we assign rating mark for the selected company.

We chose Slovak company from food industry to assign rating. The data were taken from the published financial statements for the years 2009–2013. The following tables show an overview of selected indicators and their comparison with the values of these indicators achieved in the industry. It is important to point out one fact that before rating itself, we have to consider whether we want selected financial indicator maximize or minimize. In case when we evaluate financial indicator which we want to minimize, we have to look at the scoring scale from the opposite side. (Misankova and Weissova 2015) Based on the data mentioned above, we defined score for chosen company. Due to the sum of scores, we assign a rating for selected company (Tables 63.4, 63.5, 63.6 and 63.7).

Table 63.8 shows the sum of points for the period under review with a rating mark.

Realized rating based on quantitative indicators allocated to selected companies a rating C. On that basis selected, the company can be described as above-average client.

Table 63.5 Debt management and liquidity ratios

Debt management	2009	2010	2011	2012	2013
Debt ratios	69.90	69.35	67.89	63.99	60.79
Upper quartile	101.26	100.42	99.60	99.09	96.28
Median	71.08	70.53	69.63	69.01	64.56
Lower quartile	30.57	30.33	26.33	28.57	22.90
Score	10	10	10	10	10
Equity ratio	30.10	30.65	32.11	36.01	39.21
Upper quartile	62.86	57.15	58.68	67.35	72.47
Median	24.16	24.82	22.48	26.88	31.89
Lower quartile	−1.50	−2.83	−0.82	0.76	0.89
Score	10	10	10	10	10
Financial leverage	3.32	3.26	3.11	2.78	2.55
Upper quartile	2.46	2.44	2.44	3.62	3.28
Median	0.41	0.43	0.39	1.46	1.41
Lower quartile	−1.01	−1.00	−1.00	0.68	1.00
Score	20	20	20	15	15
Liquidity ratio	2009	2010	2011	2012	2013
Net working capital	−5,516,695	−3,531,829	−7,771,912	−5,173,748	−6,238,171
Upper quartile	20,491	22,227	20,789	23,075	22,984
Median	2783	3079	3434	3949	4715
Lower quartile	−33.599	−30.407	−25.618	−29.883	−18.914
Score	0	0	0	0	0
Cash ratio	0.02	0.02	0.005	0.01	0.01
Upper quartile	0.67	0.69	0.74	0.74	0.97
Median	0.13	0.13	0.14	0.14	0.17
Lower quartile	0.01	0.01	0.01	0.01	0.02
Score	5	5	0	0	0
Quick ratio	0.56	0.59	0.44	0.48	0.44
Upper quartile	1.53	1.57	1.64	1.68	2.04
Median	0.67	0.71	0.72	0.78	0.87
Lower quartile	0.19	0.19	0.18	0.21	0.24
Score	10	10	5	5	5
Current ratio	0.74	0.81	0.63	0.70	0.63
Upper quartile	1.86	1.95	2.04	2.15	2.48
Median	0.96	0.98	0.98	1.01	1.08
Lower quartile	0.34	0.36	0.35	0.43	0.47
Score	10	10	5	5	5

Source Own processing

Table 63.6 Assets
management

Assets management	2009	2010	2011	2012	2013
Creditors payment period	69.01	63.43	52.64	43.48	41.81
Upper quartile	82.02	78.21	79.89	85.36	89.93
Median	32.33	32.14	32.28	37.61	35.78
Lower quartile	1.79	2.95	2.91	1.49	1.20
Score	15	15	10	10	10
Average collection period	68.15	67.94	67.22	71.85	78.82
Upper quartile	81.84	76.85	76.34	82.05	80.21
Median	25.84	23.57	23.98	27.57	25.55
Lower quartile	1.38	1.31	1.19	2.54	1.43
Score	5	5	5	5	5

Source Own processing

Table 63.7 Profitability
ratios

Profitability ratios	2009	2010	2011	2012	2013
ROA	13%	4%	4%	7%	7%
Upper quartile	9%	9%	8%	9%	9%
Median	1%	1%	1%	1%	1%
Lower quartile	−8%	−7%	−7%	−7%	−8%
Score	20	15	10	15	15
ROE	42%	13%	12%	21%	18%
Upper quartile	42%	42%	36%	34%	32%
Median	7%	7%	5%	5%	5%
Lower quartile	−1%	−1%	−1%	−2%	−3%
Score	15	10	10	15	10
ROS	11%	3%	3%	5%	4%
Upper quartile	4%	5%	4%	4%	4%
Median	1%	1%	1%	1%	1%
Lower quartile	−5%	−4%	−4%	−5%	−6%
Score	20	10	15	20	15

Source Own processing

Table 63.8 Rating for
selected company

	The amount of points	Rating
2009	180	C
2010	160	C
2011	140	C
2012	150	C
2013	140	C

Source Own processing

63.4 Conclusion

The rating as a tool for credit risk measurement has been talked about quite often. Credit rating agencies have become the subject of criticism since the crisis in 2008, mainly because it was wrongly estimated systemic risk of excessive growth of the mortgage market in the USA and other developed countries, and therefore that the credit rating of debt securities was overvalued (Misankova et al. 2014). Trust in credit rating agencies falling. But they are still significant because they have strong know-how. Numbers of investors still rely on their ratings. In our paper, we set out rating for selected Slovak company in a simplified manner (only based on quantitative factors), but if we want to get a complete view of the company rating, we would have to take qualitative criteria, too. Sometimes, it is very useful to add the rating by complex financial and economic analysis.

Acknowledgments This is paper is an output of the science project VEGA 1/0656/14—Research of Possibilities of Credit Default Models Application in Conditions of the SR as a Tool for Objective Quantification of Businesses Credit Risks.

References

Adamko P, Kliestik T, Misankova M (2014) Applied comparison of selected credit risk models. In: Advances in social and behavioral sciences. 2nd International conference on social sciences research (SSR 2014), pp 155–159
Balance sheet of the selected company 2009–2013
Cisko S, Kliestik T (2013) Financny manazment podniku II. EDIS Publishing, University of Zilina
Compeľ P (2006) Stanovení ratingu spolenosti J&T BANKA, a. s, Vysoká škola ekonomická v Praze, p 93
Frajtova-Michalikova K, Spuchalakova E, Cug J (2014) A comparative anatomy of credit risk models. In: Advances in education research. 2nd International conference on economics and social science (ICESS), pp 69–74
Frajtova-Michalikova K, Kliestik T, Musa H (2015) Comparison of nonparametric methods for estimating the level of risk in finance. Procedia Econ Finance 24:228–236
http://www.euroratings.co.uk/index.php?option=com_content&view=category&layout=blog&id=44&Itemid=48&lang=sk
http://www.fxstreet.cz/rating-sp-moodys-a-fitch.html
Kliestik T, Musa H, Frajtova-Michalikova K (2015) Parametric methods for estimating the level of risk in finance. Procedia Econ Finance 24:322–330
Kollar B, Bartosova V (2014) Comparison of credit risk measures as an alternative to VaR. In: Advances in social and behavioral sciences. 2nd International conference on social sciences research (SSR 2014). pp 167–171
Levich RM, Majnoni G, Reinhart MC (2002) Rating, rating agencies and the global financial system. Kluwer Academic Publisher, Boston
Misankova M, Weissova I (2015) Derivatives and their use for credit risk management. In: 10th International scientific conference financial management of firms and financial institutions, Ostrava, pp 815–824

Misankova M, Kocisova K, Frajtova-Michalikova K, Adamko P (2014) CreditMetrics and its use for the calculation of credit risk. In: Advances in education research. 2nd International conference on economics and social science (ICESS 2014), pp 124–129

Profit and loss statement of the selected company 2009–2013

Regulation 1060/2009 of The European Parliament and of The Council on credit rating agencies

Chapter 64
Applicability of Selected Predictive Models in the Slovak Companies

Ivana Weissová

Abstract Nowadays, the issue of companies' bankruptcy is very actual topic not only in Slovakia but also in abroad. Many companies have problem with the question of their probability of default or bankruptcy and also with their financial health as a whole. In this paper, we will try to show the importance of predictive models in the area of possibility to predict company's default. It means in this paper we will choose several predictive models and we will calculate these models in the selected companies from Slovak Republic. Furthermore, we will choose one method for the determination of the value of company and we will calculate this method in all of the selected companies. Thanks to the comparison between the results of predictive models and the results of method for the determination of the value of company we will try to show the applicability and successfulness of the selected predictive models in the Slovak companies. This will be the main aim of this paper.

Keywords Predictive models · Economic value added · Default of company · Bankrupt of company · Financial health

64.1 Introduction

Nowadays, the issue of companies' bankruptcy is very actual topic not only in Slovakia but also in abroad. Many companies have problem with the question of their probability of default or bankruptcy and also with their financial health as a whole. Works dealing with this issue have already appeared in the 30s of the last century. Bankruptcy of company directly affects all subjects entering into a relationship with that company. The failure of the company has diverse forms, manifestations, and consequences. Fear from possibility of default forces companies to

I. Weissová (✉)
FPEDAS, Department of Economics, University of Žilina,
Univerzitná 1, 010 26 Žilina, Slovak Republic
e-mail: ivana.weissova@fpedas.uniza.sk

© Springer International Publishing AG 2017   699
D. Procházka (ed.), *New Trends in Finance and Accounting*,
Springer Proceedings in Business and Economics,
DOI 10.1007/978-3-319-49559-0_64

obtain necessary information which could warn them of their negative development (Knapkova and Pavelkova 2010). Financial analysts are looking ways by which we will be able to predict companies default. One of the useful tools for measuring probability of default is predictive model from financial analysis ex ante (Kralovic and Vlachynsky 2002). In this paper, we will try to show the importance of predictive models in the area of possibility to predict company's default. It means in this paper we will choose several predictive models and we will calculate these models in the selected companies from Slovak Republic. Furthermore, we will choose one method for the determination of the value of company and we will calculate this method in all of the selected companies. Thanks to the comparison between the results from predictive models and the results from the method for the determination of the value of company we will try to show the applicability and successfulness of selected predictive models in the Slovak companies. This will be the main idea of this paper (Misankova et al. 2015).

64.2 Theoretical Background and Methodology

Predictive models belong to ex ante analysis. It means that their primary function is the prediction of company's financial health. They are based on the financial indicator of company's previous and current status (Altman 2006). Predictive models contain a combination of these indicators and their weights suitable for evaluating the efficiency and credibility of the company. Traditionally, we can divide predictive models into the several main categories, namely bankruptcy models, creditworthy models, logit and probit models, and structural predictive models. In this paper, we chose eight predictive models from different categories and based on the various criteria. Except for predictive models in this chapter, we also provide methods which were used in this paper (Cisko and Kliestik 2013; Altman 1968).

First of all, we had to choose some suitable companies from Slovak Republic. We decided for five companies which are situated in Slovakia. Our selection was random. We chose companies from different regions, with different numbers of employees and with different types of business. In addition, it is necessary to mention that these are not public traded companies. For the purposes of our article, we had to obtain their financial statements. For better and more credible results, we used financial statements for last four years (2014–2011). In this paper, these companies are called Company 1, Company 2, Company 3, Company 4, and Company 5.

As the second point, it was necessary to choose suitable predictive models. We did random selection again. Finally, we chose five bankruptcy predictive models, namely Altman Z-score, Taffler Z-score, IN05, Poznanski model, and Sprintage model which are based on the multidimensional discriminant analysis (Kliestik et al. 2015). We also chose CH-index which is from the category of creditworthy models. We also chose Ohlson model and Zmijewski model which are from the category of logit and probit models, which are based on the logistic regression (Zmijewski 1984). Our selection of appropriate model is based on the affinity conditions, upon which the model was developed. This is the reason why we chose model IN05 because this model was created in Czech Republic, we chose Poznanski model because this model was created in Poland and Ch-index because this model was created in Slovak Republic. Ch-index has one disadvantage it was mainly created for agricultural companies. In this second point, we calculated these models in each of five selected companies (Kliestik and Majerova 2015). We calculated these predictive models for last four years in each of the companies based

Model	State	Year	Category
Altman model	USA	1968	Bankruptcy
Formula			
$Z^{'} = 0{,}717x_1 + 0{,}847x_2 + 3{,}107x_3 + 0{,}420x_4 + 0{,}998x_5$			
Taffler model	UK	1972	Bankruptcy
Formula			
$T = 0{,}53x_1 + 0{,}13x_2 + 0{,}18x_3 + 0{,}16x_4$			
IN05	CZ	2005	Bankruptcy
Formula			
$IN05 = 0{,}13x_1 + 0{,}04x_2 + 3{,}97x_3 + 0{,}21x_4 + 0{,}09x_5$			
Poznanski model	PL	2002	Bankruptcy
Formula			
$FD = 3{,}562x_1 + 1{,}588x_2 + 4{,}288x_3 + 6{,}719x_4 - 2{,}368$			
Springate model	CAN	1978	Bankruptcy
Formula			
$S = 1{,}03x_1 + 3{,}07x_2 + 0{,}66x_3 + 0{,}4x_4$			
Ohlson model	USA	1980	Logit and probit
Formula			
$O = -1{,}32 - 0{,}407x_1 + 6{,}03x_2 - 1{,}43x_3 + 0{,}0757x_4 - 2{,}37x_5 - 1{,}83x_6 + 0{,}285x_7 - 1{,}72x_8$ $- 0{,}521x_9$			
Zmijewski model	USA	1984	Logit and Probit
Formula			
$ZM = -4{,}336 - 4{,}413x_1 + 5{,}679x_2 + 0{,}004x_3$			
CH-index	SVK	1998	Creditworthy
Formula			
$CH = 0{,}37x_1 + 0{,}25x_2 + 0{,}21x_3 - 0{,}1x_4 - 0{,}07x_5$			

Fig. 64.1 Theoretical aspects of selected predictive models. *Source* Own processing based on the Chrastinova (1998), Altman (2006), Taffler (1982)

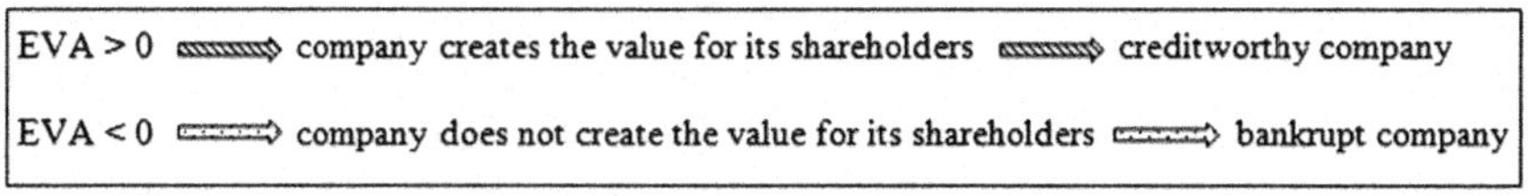

EVA > 0 ⟹ company creates the value for its shareholders ⟹ creditworthy company

EVA < 0 ⟹ company does not create the value for its shareholders ⟹ bankrupt company

Fig. 64.2 Theoretical aspects of selected predictive models. *Source* Own processing based on the Sedlacek (2011)

on their financial statements. In this place of the paper, we provide short theoretical aspects of selected predictive models. We can find more information about these models (financial indicators, limits, and so on) in the literature from the area of corporate finance (Bellovary et al. 2007; Altman and Narayanan 1997) (Fig. 64.1).

In the third point, we chose the method by which we are able to measure the value of company and we decided for Economic Value Added (hereinafter referred to as "EVA"). However, our aim of the paper is to compare the results of predictive models with the results of EVA. Furthermore, the idea of this paper is to estimate the success of these predictive models in the selected Slovak companies based on this comparison. It means that we had to calculate EVA in each of selected company for last four years based on the financial statements of these selected companies. For our calculation and comparison, several basic rules of EVA were important. These rules are provided in Fig. 64.2 (Marik et al. 2011).

64.3 Data Analysis and Results

In this chapter of the paper, we show the results of our calculation. As we say above, first of all it was necessary to calculate selected predictive models in Slovak companies for last four years. In the second step, we calculated EVA so we can compare the results of predictive models and results of EVA each other. This chapter is divided into the three parts. The first part shows the results of predictive models, the second part captures the results of EVA, and the third part contains the comparison of predictive models with results of EVA.

64.3.1 Results of Predictive Models

We captured the results of predictive models in tables. Each of the tables contains eight predictive models and their results. These results of models are shown during four years from 2011 to 2014. And we determined the area of results for predictive models in every of reporting years; it means that we included our results in the bankrupt zone, grey zone, or creditworthy zone. The bankrupt zone indicates a bad financial situation of the company with a significant probability of bankruptcy. For grey zone is interesting that in this zone the situation is not clear. It means that company in this zone can go bankrupt but also can go into the creditworthy zone (Kocisova and Misankova 2014). In this case is better to wait or calculate predictive models in the several other periods. When the result is situated in the creditworthy zone, the situation for company is well. And the probability of its bankrupt is low (Zalai et al. 2013). Each of the following five tables captures only one company, eight predictive models which are calculated in this company, and results of predictive models in last four years.

Table 64.1 shows the results of selected predictive models in the Company 1 for last four years. In this first table, we can see that the majority (75%) of predictive models for Company 1 are grouped into the bankrupt zone. This situation is balanced in every of reporting years. It means that probability of company's bankrupt is high.

In Table 64.2, we can see the results of predictive models for the Company 2. In 2014, the majority of predictive models (50%) are grouped into the creditworthy zone vice versa in 2011 the majority of predictive models (63%) are grouped into the bankrupt zone. In 2012 and 2013, the situation was almost balanced.

Table 64.3 captures the results of predictive models for the Company 3. This table shows that the majority of predictive models are grouped into the creditworthy zone in every of reporting years. However, a substantial portion of the models classifies the Company 3 rather into the grey zone.

Table 64.4 captures the results of predictive models for Company 4. In 2014, the majority of predictive models (63%) are grouped into the creditworthy zone vice versa in 2011 the majority of predictive models are grouped into the bankrupt zone. In 2012 and 2013, the situation among creditworthy, grey zone, and bankrupt zone is almost balanced.

Table 64.1 Results of predictive models in the Company 1

| | Company 1 | | | |
	2014	2013	2012	2011
Altman Z-score	Bankrupt	Bankrupt	Bankrupt	Bankrupt
Taffler Z-score	Creditworthy	Bankrupt	Creditworthy	Creditworthy
IN05	Bankrupt	Bankrupt	Bankrupt	Bankrupt
CH-index	Bankrupt	Bankrupt	Bankrupt	Bankrupt
Springate model	Bankrupt	Bankrupt	Bankrupt	Bankrupt
Poznanski model	Creditworthy	Creditworthy	Creditworthy	Creditworthy
Ohlson model	Bankrupt	Bankrupt	Bankrupt	Bankrupt
Zmijewski model	Bankrupt	Bankrupt	Bankrupt	Bankrupt
Creditworthy	25.00%	25.00%	25.00%	25.00%
Grey zone	0.00%	0.00%	0.00%	0.00%
Bankrupt	75.00%	75.00%	75.00%	75.00%

Source Own processing based on the information from company's financial statements

Table 64.2 Results of predictive models in the Company 2

	Company 2			
	2014	2013	2012	2011
Altman Z-score	Grey zone	Grey zone	Grey zone	Grey zone
Taffler Z-score	Creditworthy	Creditworthy	Creditworthy	Creditworthy
IN05	Creditworthy	Grey zone	Grey zone	Bankrupt
CH-index	Bankrupt	Bankrupt	Bankrupt	Bankrupt
Springate model	Grey zone	Grey zone	Grey zone	Bankrupt
Poznanski model	Creditworthy	Creditworthy	Bankrupt	Creditworthy
Ohlson model	Creditworthy	Creditworthy	Creditworthy	Bankrupt
Zmijewski model	Creditworthy	Creditworthy	Bankrupt	Bankrupt
Creditworthy	50.00%	37.00%	37.00%	24.00%
Grey zone	25.00%	38.00%	38.00%	13.00%
Bankrupt	25.00%	25.00%	25.00%	63.00%

Source Own processing based on the information from company's financial statements

Table 64.3 Results of predictive models in the Company 3

	Company 3			
	2014	2013	2012	2011
Altman Z-score	Creditworthy	Creditworthy	Creditworthy	Creditworthy
Taffler Z-score	Creditworthy	Creditworthy	Creditworthy	Creditworthy
IN05	Grey zone	Bankrupt	Grey zone	Grey zone
CH-index	Grey zone	Grey zone	Grey zone	Grey zone
Springate model	Creditworthy	Creditworthy	Creditworthy	Creditworthy
Poznanski model	Creditworthy	Creditworthy	Bankrupt	Creditworthy
Ohlson model	Creditworthy	Creditworthy	Creditworthy	Creditworthy
Zmijewski model	Grey zone	Grey zone	Grey zone	Grey zone
Creditworthy	63.00%	63.00%	63.00%	63.00%
Grey zone	37.00%	25.00%	37.00%	37.00%
Bankrupt	0.00%	12.00%	0.00%	0.00%

Source Own processing based on the information from company's financial statements

Table 64.5 captures the results of predictive models for Company 5. This table shows that the situation is balanced in every year; it means that the results are identical over the complete period of four years. Specifically, 63% of predictive models are grouped into the creditworthy zone, 25% of predictive models are grouped into the grey zone, and 12% of predictive models are grouped into the bankrupt zone. Predictive models assume that company is in the good situation and its bankrupt is unlikely.

Table 64.4 Results of predictive models in the Company 4

	Company 4			
	2014	2013	2012	2011
Altman Z-score	Creditworthy	Grey zone	Bankrupt	Grey zone
Taffler Z-score	Creditworthy	Creditworthy	Creditworthy	Creditworthy
IN05	Creditworthy	Grey zone	Grey zone	Bankrupt
CH-index	Grey zone	Grey zone	Grey zone	Bankrupt
Springate model	Bankrupt	Bankrupt	Bankrupt	Bankrupt
Poznanski model	Creditworthy	Creditworthy	Creditworthy	Creditworthy
Ohlson model	Creditworthy	Creditworthy	Creditworthy	Creditworthy
Zmijewski model	Bankrupt	Bankrupt	Bankrupt	Bankrupt
Creditworthy	63.00%	38.00%	38.00%	38.00%
Grey zone	13.00%	38.00%	24.00%	12.00%
Bankrupt	24.00%	24.00%	38.00%	50.00%

Source Own processing based on the information from company's financial statements

Table 64.5 Results of predictive models in the Company 5

	Company 5			
	2014	2013	2012	2011
Altman Z-score	Creditworthy	Creditworthy	Creditworthy	Creditworthy
Taffler Z-score	Creditworthy	Creditworthy	Creditworthy	Creditworthy
IN05	Grey zone	Grey zone	Grey zone	Grey zone
CH-index	Grey zone	Grey zone	Grey zone	Grey zone
Springate model	Creditworthy	Creditworthy	Creditworthy	Creditworthy
Poznanski model	Creditworthy	Creditworthy	Creditworthy	Creditworthy
Ohlson model	Creditworthy	Creditworthy	Creditworthy	Creditworthy
Zmijewski model	Bankrupt	Bankrupt	Bankrupt	Bankrupt
Creditworthy	63.00%	63.00%	63.00%	63.00%
Grey zone	25.00%	25.00%	25.00%	25.00%
Bankrupt	12.00%	12.00%	12.00%	12.00%

Source Own processing based on the information from company's financial statements

64.3.2   Results of Economic Value Added

In the last section, we calculated selected predictive models in five Slovak companies. Next chapter was necessary to calculate EVA like a method by which we are able to determine the value of company. The aim of this calculation was to compare results of predictive models with results of EVA. Based on this comparison, we tried to determine the predictive ability of individual models.

We calculated EVA in five selected companies in the last four years. This calculation was based on financial statements of these companies. Results of EVA are captured in Table 64.6.

Table 64.6 Results of EVA in selected companies

EVA	2014	2013	2012	2011
Company 1	Bankrupt	Bankrupt	Bankrupt	Bankrupt
Company 2	Creditworthy	Bankrupt	Bankrupt	Bankrupt
Company 3	Creditworthy	Creditworthy	Creditworthy	Creditworthy
Company 4	Creditworthy	Bankrupt	Bankrupt	Creditworthy
Company 5	Creditworthy	Creditworthy	Creditworthy	Creditworthy

Source Own processing based on information from the financial statements of companies

In this table, we can see the results of EVA for five companies during the last four years. In 2014, only Company 1 was in the bankrupt zone, other companies were in the creditworthy zone (it means that their value of EVA was higher than 0). In 2013 and 2012, the results were same. Companies 1, 2, and 4 were in the bankrupt zone, and Companies 3 and 5 were in the creditworthy zone. In 2011, Companies 1 and 2 were in the bankrupt zone, other companies were in the creditworthy zone.

64.3.3 Verification of Predictive Models with EVA

In the last step, we compared the results of predictive models and results of EVA. We tried to capture predictive ability of selected predictive models. The main idea of this comparison was to show the applicability and successfulness of these models in Slovak companies.

In Fig. 64.3, we can see that the Ohlson model achieved the best results each year. Specifically in 2014, the success rate was 100%, and in the years 2011, 2012, and 2013, the success rate was 80%. Springate and Poznanski model also achieved

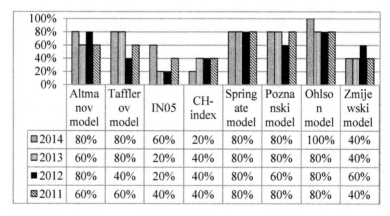

	Altmanov model	Tafflerov model	IN05	CH-index	Springate model	Poznanski model	Ohlson model	Zmijewski model
2014	80%	80%	60%	20%	80%	80%	100%	40%
2013	60%	80%	20%	40%	80%	80%	80%	40%
2012	80%	40%	20%	40%	80%	60%	80%	60%
2011	60%	60%	40%	40%	80%	80%	80%	40%

Fig. 64.3 Verification of predictive models with EVA. *Source* Own processing based on previous calculations

very good and balanced results each year. Specifically, Springate model which was created in Canada achieved 80% success rate in each of the reporting years. Furthermore, Poznanski model from Poland achieved 80% success rate in 2014, 2013, and 2011, and in 2012, this model achieved 60% success rate. But interesting is that CH-index from Slovak Republic and IN05 from Czech Republic achieved the worst results. CH-index only achieved 40% success rate in years 2011–2013 and just 20% success rate in 2014. Interesting is the fact that as we mention above, this is the predictive model which was created in Slovak Republic and this model achieved the worst results. But in this place, we have to say this model was created mainly for companies from agriculture sector.

64.4 Conclusion

The aim of this contribution was to compare the results of selected predictive models with results of economic value added in the five real Slovak companies. In this paper, we choose eight predictive models. And based on this calculation, the ability of the selected predictive models that predict bankrupt of the company was determined. The better results regarding the ability to predict a company's default are identified for Springate and Ohlson models. The worst results and ability of predict company's default achieved IN05 and CH-index. In addition, we choose EVA and calculated the value of the company. Finally, we compare results of predictive models and results of EVA. The complex analysis of the results produced by potential predictive models enables the assessment of their applicability in the Slovak companies.

Acknowledgments This research was financially supported by the Slovak Research and Development Agency—Grant NO. APVV-14-0841: Comprehensive Prediction Model of the Financial Health of Slovak Companies.

References

Altman EI (1968) Financial ratios, discriminant analysis and the prediction of corporate bankruptcy. J Finance 23:589–609
Altman EI (2006) Corporate financial distress and bankruptcy. Wiley, New York
Altman EI, Narayanan P (1997) Business failure classification models: an international survey. Financ Markets, Inst Instrum 6:1–57
Bellovary J, Giacomino D, Akers M (2007) A review of bankruptcy prediction studies: 1930—present. J Financ Educ 33:1–42
Chrastinova Z (1998) Metódy hodnotenia ekonomickej bonity a predikcie finančnej situácie poľnohospodárskych podnikov. Bratislava: VÚEPP
Cisko S, Kliestik T (2013) Finančný manažment. Žilina: Edis Publishing, University of Žilina

Kliestik T, Majerova J (2015) Selected issues of selection of significant variables in the prediction models. In: Ostrava: 10th international scientific conference financial management of firms and financial institutions, pp 537–543

Kliestik T, Majerova J, Lyakin NA (2015) Metamorphoses and semantics of corporate failures as a basal assumption of a well-founded prediction of a corporate financial health. In: 3rd International conference on economics and social science (ICESS 2015), advances in education research, vol 86, pp 150–154

Knapkova A, Pavelkova D (2010) Finanční analýza. Komplexní průvodce s příklady. Praha: Grada Publishing, a.s.

Kocisova K, Misankova M (2014) Prediction of default by the use of Merton's model and black and cox model. In: Singapore: 4th international conference on applied social science (ICASS 2014), advances in education research, vol 51, pp 563–568

Kralovic J, Vlachynsky K (2002) Finančný manažment. Bratislava: Iura Edition, spol. s r.o.

Marik M et al (2011) Metody oceňování podniku. Praha: Ekopress, s.r.o.

Misankova M, Spuchlakova E, Frajtova-Michalikova K (2015) Determination of default probability by loss given default. Procedia Econs Finance 26:411–417

Sedlacek J (2011) Finanční analýza podniku. Brno: Computer Press, a.s.

Taffler RJ (1982) Forecasting company failure in the UK using discriminant analysis and financial ratio data. J Roy Stat Soc 145:342–358

Zalai K et al (2013) Finančno-ekonomická analýza podniku. Bratislava: Sprint 2 s.r.o.

Zmijewski M (1984) Methodological issues related to the estimation of financial distress prediction models. Journal of Accounting Research, 1984, Vol. 22, pp. 59–82

Chapter 65
Model of Hospitals' Financial Distress Forecasting: Comparative Study

Agnieszka Bem, Rafał Siedlecki, Paulina Ucieklak-Jeż
and Tatana Hajdikova

Abstract Bankruptcy forecasting models represent a higher level of financial analysis—bankruptcy models can predict impending danger of bankruptcy. The importance of bankruptcy models lies in the detection of approaching financial problems and what gives a chance of adopting appropriate management actions. The aim of research was to compare different bankruptcy forecasting models and their results for 133 hospitals from Poland, The Czech Republic and Slovakia. We have posed the following hypotheses: (H1) different bankruptcy forecasting models may give different signals and (H2) bankruptcy forecasting model elaborated for hospital industry gives more similar signals. We have found that employed model provide different results and that FSI' results are much closer to results obtained from models elaborated for commercial companies (IN05, G INE PAN), rather than M-Model constructed on a basis of Czech, Polish and Slovak hospitals. What is more, we have found that FSI gives far more consistent results in models developed for the business sector—IN05 and G INE PAN. Our results also suggest that models dedicated to commercial businesses activity should not be directly applied to hospitals.

Keywords Hospital · Financial distress · Forecasting · M-Model

A. Bem (✉) · R. Siedlecki
Faculty of Management, Informatics and Finance, Wroclaw University
of Economics, Komandorska 118/120, 53-345 Wroclaw, Poland
e-mail: bemagnieszka@gmail.com

R. Siedlecki
e-mail: rafal.siedlecki@ue.wroc.pl

P. Ucieklak-Jeż
Faculty of Social Sciences, Jan Dlugosz University in Czestochowa,
Waszyngtona 4/8, 42-200 Częstochowa, Poland
e-mail: p.ucieklak@o2.pl

T. Hajdikova
Department of Management, University of Economics in Prague,
Jarošovská 1117/II, 377-01 Jindřichův, Hradec, Czech Republic
e-mail: hajdikova@fm.vse.cz

© Springer International Publishing AG 2017
D. Procházka (ed.), *New Trends in Finance and Accounting*,
Springer Proceedings in Business and Economics,
DOI 10.1007/978-3-319-49559-0_65

65.1 Introduction

Financial distress forecasting has been a subject of scientific research since the 1960s. However, from the point of view of dynamic changes, which characterize modern economy, nowadays the ability to predict the occurrence of financial difficulties is still of particular importance for all stakeholders. A synthetic, universal indicator, which, as far as possible, would describe company's financial condition, is still a subject of research.

First studies, originated by Beaver (1966) and Altman (1968, 1983, 1999) led to creation of well-known bankruptcy's predictor—Altman's Z-score. The effectiveness of this model and its popularity encouraged other researchers to launch further studies in this area (comp.: M. Tamari, R.J. Taffler, M. Blum, S. Appetiti, R. Edminster, E.B. Deakin or M. Zmijewski).

Generally, bankruptcy forecasting models represent a higher level of financial analysis and, with regard to their explanatory power, they can be divided into creditworthiness and bankruptcy models. The first ones, which determine whether the financial management is good or bad, are based on the analyses of financial ratios. On the other hand, bankruptcy models can predict impending danger of bankruptcy. The first bankruptcy forecasting models were constructed using real data from companies in financial distress—there were based on the assumption that a company, prior to entering bankruptcy, would show typical characteristics that could be generalized. The importance of bankruptcy models lies in the detection of approaching financial problems and what gives a chance of adopting appropriate management actions (Beaver 1966; Michalski 2016; Brozyna et al. 2015; Bartak and Gavurova 2015; Gurčík 2002; Neumaierová and Neumaier 2002; Tamari 1966).

From the point of view of financial distress forecasting, hospitals are uncharacteristic entities. This specificity arises from different, and difficult, interpenetration of economic and medical processes. The healthcare market is strictly regulated by the state, and, at the same time, it is characterized by an increasing competitive pressure. Despite this, very few studies in this area suggest that tools of financial distress forecasting, after certain adjustment, can also be employed in hospitals, regardless of its special character. An occurrence of financial difficulties, in case of a hospital, has, usually, serious consequences for local communities, going far beyond effects of bankruptcy of an average company. Inability to continue operational activities (providing of healthcare services) leads to limitation of access to healthcare benefits or can be a source of lower quality—in extreme cases, it leads not only to foregoing of scheduled treatments (medical procedures), but it can also lower the potential to treat patients in life-threatening condition (Bazzoli and Andes 1995; Chen et al. 2009; Michalski 2015a; Gavurova and Soltes 2016; Harkey and Vraciu 1992; Holmes and Pink 2013; Kim 2010; Landry 2009; Langabeer 2005; Jervis et al. 2011; McCue et al. 2003; Noh et al. 2006; Pink et al. 2006; Price et al. 2005; Price 2005; Richards 2014; Michalski 2015b; Michalski et al. 2015; Michalski 2010; Alexander et al. 2006). We can also observe a tendency to assess hospitals like commercial enterprises. That suggests the importance of financial management processes, related to, for example, investments or working capital management (Michalski et al. 2015; Michalski 2016; Raisova et al. 2014). In this context, a warning signal may be treated as an opportunity to carry out remedial actions, which, under normal conditions, would not be accepted by stakeholders (comp.: Michalski 2015b; Szczygiel et al. 2015).

Literature's review indicates that there are no universal models, which can be used, without any limitations, in different sectors. Only very few studies concern hospital's industry. Financial Strength Index® (FSI), developed by Cleverley, is a tool designed, especially, for hospitals and bases on four dimensions: profitability, liquidity, leverage and the age of physical facilities (comp. Cleverley 1990; Cleverley and Harvey 1992; Cleverley 2002). Cleverley provides a relatively straightforward interpretation—*"the FSI implies that firms with large profits, great liquidity, low levels of debt, and new physical facilities are in excellent financial condition"* (Cleverley and Cleverley 2005). Coyne and Meadows (1991) also studied early warning signals for hospital industry and showed that a key indicator, from the point of view of financial difficulties' forecasting, was a quick ratio (QR). Price (2005) proved that seven indicators, which were important for financial distress forecasting, were Cleverley's FSI, Altman's modified Z-score, operating cash flow ratio, funds flow coverage ratio, cash interest coverage ratio, cash flow to total debt ratio and total free cash flow ratio. Koyuncugil and Ozgulbas (2012) found that warning signals can be generated by two parameters: the cost of services and the operating profit. Another question is whether models developed for different countries can effectively detect bankruptcy of companies operating in other countries. Mączyńska suggests that models developed using discrimination analysis tools may not be directly applicable in other countries, due to the fact that economic processes might have different characteristics (Mączyńska and Zawadzki 2006).

The aim of this research was to compare different bankruptcy forecasting models and their results, for hospitals from Poland, The Czech Republic and Slovakia. We have posed the following hypotheses:

H1: different bankruptcy forecasting models may give different signals;
H2: bankruptcy forecasting models elaborated for hospital industry gives more similar signals.

The H1 hypothesis suggest that different forecasting models can generate different, sometimes even contradictory, signals, which lower their usefulness and cause interpretational problems. In order to verify this hypothesis, we have chosen a selection of bankruptcy prediction's methods: IN model, model G INE PAN, FSI and M-Model.

The IN model, created by Inka and Ivan Neumaier, is based on the Z-function model (Altman 1968) with respect to Czech businesses. This model was constructed using a multiple discriminant analysis. Indicators were chosen on the basis of the financial statements and real market values were not employed. The first model—IN95, constructed in 1995, included six indicators, while the latest (IN05) represented the former insolvency of Czech businesses (Neumaierová and Neumaier 2002).

The G INE PAN model, created by M. Mączyxńska and M. Zawadzki, was estimated using the sample of 80 companies—among them 40 threatened by bankruptcy and 40 "healthy" enterprises, quoted on Warsaw Stock Exchange. This analysis included data for the years 1997–2001. Initially, 45 financial indicators were considered—the final model was built on a basis of 4 variables (Mączyńska and Zawadzki 2006).

The FSI model, constructed by Cleverley and Cleverley (2005) consisted of 4 financial indicators adapted from previous research which identified the financial ratios most correlated with long-term fiscal viability (Lynn and Wertheim 1993). The FSI model was dedicated especially to the hospital industry.

The M-Model is our authorial proposition, elaborated on a basis of the analyses of 333 hospitals from The Czech Republic, Poland and Slovakia. Using taxonomic methods (all models presented above were based on discriminant analysis) (Siedlecki 2013; Siedlecki 2014), we constructed 3 measures of hospital's financial condition (M1, M2 and M3) which allowed to predict the financial distress in hospital (Bem et al. 2015b). Two of them (M1 and M2) were qualified into further research. Then, using a training dataset (30 hospitals in poor financial condition) and testing dataset (77 hospitals) we estimated the cutting point values of M1 and M2 for hospitals characterized by poor, average and good financial condition (Siedlecki et al. 2015). This model was generally based on previous analysis of hospital financial condition' indicators (Bem et al. 2015a, b, c; Bem and Michalski 2016; Siedlecki et al. 2015).

The H2 hypothesis suggests that bankruptcy forecasting models, elaborated for hospitals industry, give more consistent results than tools constructed for productive or service enterprises. In order to prove this hypothesis, we have mutually compared results generated by analysed models using Gamma correlation coefficients.

In this study, we have employed data from 133 hospitals coming from The Czech Republic, Poland and Slovakia. Although in analysed countries hospitals can operate in different legal forms (public entities and companies), due to many similarities in organizational schemes and funding (mainly public funds) of the healthcare system, hospitals from studied countries can be considered as a homogeneous research sample (Bem et al. 2015a, b, c; Hajdíková et al. 2013, 2014; Bem 2013; Ucieklak-Jeż and Bem 2014; Soltes and Gavurová 2014a, b).

In order to verify our research assumptions, we have employed statistical tools, among all Gamma correlation coefficient. The analysis has been supported by Statistica 10 Package.

65.2 Methodology and Data

Research sample consisted of 133 hospitals from The Czech Republic, Poland and Slovakia. Financial data, covering the years 2012 and 2013, were collected, by hand, from Emerging Markets Database (EMIS). We initially investigated 368 hospitals. Some part of observation had to be rejected due to the lack of all required data. We have also rejected:

- all entities classified as "hospital activity" for whose hospital activity were not a primary source of revenue;
- hospitals having less than 3 hospital wards and hospitals without an emergency room; and
- psychiatric hospitals and rehabilitative hospitals.

Finally, the research sample consisted of 133 hospitals (72 from Poland, 39 from Czech and 22 from Slovakia).

In order to verify research hypotheses, we have employed several bankruptcy models—IN model, G INE PAN model, FSI model and M-Model.

The IN05 model:

$$IN05 = 0.1u_1 + 0.04u_2 + 3.97u_3 + 0.21u_4 + 0.09u_5$$

where

u_1 total assets/liabilities
u_2 earnings before interest and taxes (EBIT)/expense interest
u_3 earnings before interest and taxes (EBIT)/total assets
u_4 total revenues/total assets
u_5 current assets/current liabilities and short-term bank loans and overdrafts

G INE PAN model is constructed as follows:

$$W = 1.5X_1 + 0.08X_2 + 10.0X_3 + 5.0X_4 + 0.3X_5 + 0.1X_6$$

X_1 EBT + depreciation/liabilities
X_2 total assets/liabilities
X_3 EBIT/total assets
X_4 EAT/revenues
X_5 inventories/revenues
X_6 revenues/total assets

The FSI model:

$$FSI = \frac{\text{Excess Margin} - 0.04}{0.04} - \frac{\text{Days Cash on Hand} - 50}{50}$$
$$- \frac{\text{Debt Financing} - 0.50}{0.50} - \frac{\text{Accumulated Depreciation} - 0.50}{0.50}$$

where

Excess Margin (%)   Total operating revenues plus non-operating revenues minus total operating;

Days Cash on Hand (days)	Unrestricted cash and investments, divided by daily cash operating expenses (total operating expenses less depreciation/amortization expenses);
Debt Financing (%)	Total assets minus unrestricted net assets, divided by total assets;
Accumulated Depreciation (%)	Accumulated depreciation, divided by gross property, plant and equipment

The M-Model:
For M1 measure:

$$\alpha_{1i} = \left(\frac{X_1}{0.729254} - \frac{|X_2 - 1.2|}{9.21694} - \frac{X_3}{2.627635} + \frac{X_4}{5.334226} \right.$$
$$\left. - \frac{X_5}{0.514318} + \frac{X_6}{0.926257} + \frac{X_7}{0.897459} + 3.324571 \right) \Big/ 5$$

For M2 measure:

$$\alpha_{2i} = \left(\frac{X_1}{0.729254} - \frac{|X_2 - 1.2|}{9.21694} - \frac{X_3}{2.627635} + \frac{X_4}{5.334226} \right.$$
$$\left. - \frac{X_5}{0.514318} + 4.484300 \right) \Big/ 7$$

where

X_1 EBIT/sales
X_2 Current assets/current liabilities
X_3 Total debt/total assets
X_4 Sales/total assets
X_5 Employee benefit expenses/sales
X_6 (Net profit + depreciation)/total debt
X_7 (Net profit + depreciation)/total assets

Selected models have different cutting points. Two models—G INE PAN and FSI—introduce 4 instead of 3 ranges—in order to ensure comparability, we subsume a category "excellent" into "good" category (Table 65.1).

We have applied 5 analysed models. Results have been organized by assigning ranks, according to the following pattern (Table 65.1):

- "−1" for hospitals characterized by poor financial situation or bankrupted/insolvent—this result should be interpreted as a source of a strong warning signal;
- "0" for hospitals in weak/fair/unsatisfactory financial situation—this should generate a warning signal for managers;
- "1" for medical entities characterized by good/satisfactory/excellent financial condition.

Table 65.1 Comparison of bankruptcy prediction's models

Rank	IN05	G INE PAN	FSI	M1	M2
−1	<09 (bankrupt)	$W < 0$ (bankrupt)	<−2.0 (poor)	– if $\alpha_t < 0.71$—a strong warning signal, high probability of financial difficulties	– if $\alpha_t < 0.7$—a strong warning signal, high probability of financial difficulties
0	0.9–1.6 (unsatisfactory financial situation)	0.0–1.0 (weak/fair)	−2.0–0.0 (fair)	– if $0.71 < \alpha_t < 0.81$ —a warning signal, the average risk of financial difficulties	– if $0.7 < \alpha_t < 0.8$ —a warning signal, the average risk of financial difficulties
1	>1.6 (satisfactory financial situation)	1.0–2.0 (good) and > 2.0 (excellent)	0.0–3.0 (good) and > 3.0 (excellent)	– if $\alpha_t > 0.81$—lack of a clear warning signal—low probability of financial difficulties	– if $\alpha_t > 0.8$—lack of a clear warning signal—low probability of financial difficulties

Source Own study

In order to verify research hypotheses, we have used Goodman and Kruskal's Gamma as symmetric measure of rank's association. Gamma correlation measures the strength of association of the cross-tabulated data, when both variables are measured in the ordinal scale. *G* statistic is regarded as the maximum likelihood estimator for the theoretical quantity γ, where (Sirisha et al. 2016):

$$\gamma = \frac{P_s - P_d}{P_s + P_d}$$

and P_s and P_d are the probabilities that a randomly selected pair of observations will place in the same, or opposite order, when ranked by both models. Critical values for the gamma statistic are found by using an approximation to the Student's t-distribution, where

$$t \approx G \sqrt{\frac{N_s + N_d}{n(1 - G^2)}}$$

and *n* is the number of observations.

65.3   Results and Discussion

During the first part of the study, we have evaluated hospitals using five models of bankruptcy forecasting (IN05, G INE PAN, FSI, M1, M2). The highest number of "bankruptcies" has been identified by IN05—on average 59.4% of the hospitals are at the risk of bankruptcy, especially in Poland (42.3%), comparing to 25.4% in Slovakia. The lowest number of bankruptcies has been identified by models FSI and G INE PAN—respectively, 24.1 and 21.8%, again with the lowest percentage of entities in financial distress in the case of Slovak hospitals (Table 65.2). Our previous findings suggest that, from the point of view of bankruptcy forecasting, hospitals having "*an average/unsatisfactory*" financial situation, described by the rank "0", are the most important. This rank can be described as the "*grey area*", where hospitals in financial distress can be hidden, but not effectively detected by employed forecasting model. The highest number of medical entities of this type has been detected by the FSI model—on average 68.4% of hospitals (72.2% of Polish hospitals, 65.8% of Czech hospitals and 63.6% of Slovak ones). The lowest number of observations has been classified to the grey area by the IN05 model (23.3% of research sample) (Table 65.2).

During the next stage of research, we have employed Gamma correlation coefficient in order to measure the relationships between the results of financial health assessment obtained using respective models and described by ranks: $-1, 0, 1$.

The analysis for the year 2012 has shown a strong correlation between results for models: M1 and M2 (0.9585), FSI and G INE PAN (0.9479) and between IN05 and G INE PAN (0.8960). A little bit lower correlation coefficients can be observed for pairs: IN05 and FSI (0.5789) and between IN05 and M2 (0.5289). All correlations are statistically significant at the level of the $\alpha = 0.05$ (Table 65.3).

Table 65.2 Results generate by analysed models, by countries, in 2013

	IN05 (%)	G INE PAN (%)	FSI (%)	M1 (%)	M2 (%)
Czech Republic					
1	28.9	36.8	10.5	7.9	5.3
0	18.4	34.2	65.8	42.1	52.6
−1	55.3	31.6	26.3	52.6	44.7
Poland					
1	8.3	25.0	6.9	16.7	29.2
0	23.6	48.6	72.2	51.4	51.4
−1	68.1	25.0	20.8	31.9	19.4
Slovakia					
1	27.3	50.0	18.2	18.2	9.1
0	31.8	40.9	63.6	40.9	50.0
−1	40.9	9.1	18.2	40.9	40.9
Total					
1	**17.3**	**32.3**	**9.8**	**14.3**	**18.8**
0	**23.3**	**42.9**	**68.4**	**46.6**	**51.1**
−1	**59.4**	**24.1**	**21.8**	**39.1**	**30.1**

Source Own study

Table 65.3 Gamma correlation coefficients for analysed models, in 2012

	IN05	G INE PAN	FSI	M1	M2
IN05	1.000000	0.896077**	0.578903**	0.629505**	0.528943**
G INE PAN		1.000000	0.947931**	0.834483**	0.689018**
FSI			1.000000	0.834311**	0.750459**
M1				1.000000	0.958557**
M2					1.000000

*Significance level $\alpha = 0.1$, **significance level $\alpha = 0.05$ and ***significance level $\alpha = 0.01$
Source Own study

Table 65.4 Gamma correlation coefficients for analysed models, in 2013

	IN05	G INE PAN	FSI	M1	M2
IN05	1.000000	0.873512**	0.718276**	0.679953**	0.294561**
G INE PAN		1.000000	0.950791**	0.808992**	0.457151**
FSI			1.000000	0.722356**	0.467742**
M1				1.000000	0.886442**
M2					1.000000

*Significance level $\alpha = 0.1$, **significance level $\alpha = 0.05$ and ***significance level $\alpha = 0.01$
Source Own study

The analysis of data for the year 2013 has indicated slightly lower correlation coefficients, particularly in the case of the M2 measure. The strongest relationship have shown G INE PAN and FSI (0.9507) and G INE PAN and IN05 (0.8735) models. By far the lowest, but still considered as medium, correlation coefficients have related to the M2 model—for all models, except M1, 0.2945 for IN05, 0.4571 for G INE PAN and 0.4677 for FSI. All correlation coefficients are statistically significant at the level $\alpha = 0.05$. (Table 65.4).

According to the H1 hypothesis and based on the analysis presented above, we can conclude that studied models have led to the different results; however, the degree of this diversification is different for each of the pairs of models. *These observations allowed us for, at least partial, acceptance of the H1 hypothesis.*

In the H2 hypothesis, we have assumed that models designed especially for hospital industry (FSI, M1 and M2) should lead to similar conclusions, according to the financial distress forecasting. Our analyses have showed, however, that results for FSI model are relatively less correlated with results for M1 and M2. In contrast, they are characterized by the highest correlation with models developed for the business sector, especially with G INE PAN model. *On the basis of the above, we have been forced to reject the H2 hypothesis.*

65.4   Conclusions

When designing a research plan, we have assumed that models developed for hospital industry should lead to similar conclusions. In order to verify this assumption, we have compared FSI model, developed for American hospitals with our models, elaborated for Polish, Czech and Slovak hospitals—M1 and M2.

What is more, we have found that FSI gives far more consistent results in models developed for the business sector—IN05 and G INE PAN. The source of this difference may be the fact that American hospitals operate on commercial basis and profit constitutes their primary goal, what is accompanied by the dominant role of private funding in the health system.

It seems, however, that in the case of analysed countries, models dedicated to commercial businesses activity should not be directly applied to hospitals. Therefore, we can see a need to create new models or upgrade the existing ones, in order to create a tailor-made solutions. This also applies to the measures M1 and M2, which are relatively simple and their modification does not require sophisticated statistical tools (new indicators can be easily added or eliminated).

Certain weakness of this research is the short time of the analysis. Another problem is that the effectiveness of bankruptcy forecasting should be tested on a group of bankruptcies, which, in the case of hospitals in studied countries, is very difficult, because, in practice, hospitals do not go bankrupt—they generate debt and receive financial help from public authorities/owners. Further research should therefore include a construction of a group of hospitals in a very difficult financial situation (indebted, with a negative operating margin) that could be considered as "the bankrupt model".

References

Alexander JA, Weiner BJ, Griffith J (2006) Quality improvement and hospital financial performance. J Organ Behav 27(7):1003–1029

Altman E (1968) Financial ratios, discriminant analysis and the prediction of corporate bankruptcy. J Finance 4:589–609

Altman E (1983) Corporate financial distress. Wiley, New York

Altman E (1999) Bankruptcy & distressed restructurings. Analytical issues and investment opportunities. Beard Books, Washington

Bartak M, Gavurova B (2015) Economics and social aspects of long-term care in the context of the Czech republic and the Slovak republic EU membership. In: Proceedings of 12th international scientific conference: economic policy in the European Union member countries, p 35–44

Bazzoli G, Andes S (1995) Consequences of hospital financial distress. Hosp Health Serv Adm 4:472–495

Bem A (2013) Public Financing Of Healthcare Services. e-Finanse 9(2):1–23

Bem A, Michalski G (2016) Hospital profitability versus selected healthcare system indicators. In: CEFE 2015—Central European Conference in Finance and Economics. Technical University of Kosice, Kosice, p 52–61

Bem A, Prędkiewicz K, Prędkiewicz P, Ucieklak-Jeż P (2014a) Determinants of hospital's financial liquidity. Procedia Econ Finance 12:27–36

Bem A, Prędkiewicz K, Prędkiewicz P, Ucieklak-Jeż P (2014b) Hospital's size as the determinant of financial liquidity. In: Proceedings of the 11th international scientific conference European financial systems 2014, p 41–48

Bem A, Ucieklak-Jeż P, Prędkiewicz P (2014c) Income per bed as a determinant of hospital's financial liquidity. Prob Manage 21st century Sci Soc, UAB 2:124–131

Bem A, Prędkiewicz P, Ucieklak-Jeż P, Siedlecki R (2015a) Profitability versus debt in hospital industry. In: European financial systems 2015. Proceedings of the 12th international scientific conference, p 20–27

Bem A, Siedlecki R, Prędkiewicz P, Ucieklak-Jeż P, Hajdikova T (2015b) Hospital's financial health assessment. Gradient method's application. In: Enterprise and competitive environment. Conference proceedings, p 76–85

Bem A, Prędkiewicz P, Ucieklak-Jeż P, Siedlecki R (2015c) Impact of hospital's profitability on structure of its liabilities. In: Strategica 2015 proceedings, p 657–665

Beaver WH (1966) Financial ratios as predictors of failure. Journal of accounting research, p 71–111

Brozyna E, Michalski G, Soroczynska J (2015) E-commerce as a factor supporting the competitiveness of small and medium-sized manufacturing enterprises. In: Gavurová B, Šolté M (ed) Central European Conference in Finance and Economics (CEFE2015). Technical University of Košice, Košice p 80–90

Chen HF, Bazzoli GJ, Hsieh HM (2009) Hospital financial conditions and the provision of unprofitable services. Atlantic Econ J 37:259–277

Cleverley W (1990) Improving financial performance: a study of 50 hospitals. Hosp Health Serv Adm 2:173–187

Cleverley W (2002) Who is responsible for business failures? Healthc Financ Manage 56 (10):46–52

Cleverley WO, Cleverley JO (2005) Scorecards and dashboards: using financial metrics to improve performance. J Healthc Financ Manage Assoc 59(7):64–69

Cleverley WO, Harvey RK (1992) Does hospital financial performance measure up? Healthc Financ Manage 46(5):21–26

Coyne JS, Meadows DM (1991) California HMOs may provide national forecast. Healthcare financial management: journal of the Healthcare Financial Management Association 45(5): 34–36

Gavurova B, Soltes M (2016) System of day surgery in Slovakia: analysis of pediatric day surgery discrepancies in the regions and their importance in strategy of its development. E + M Ekonomie a Manage 19(1):74–92

Gurčík L (2002) G-index – metóda predikcie finančního stavu polnohospodářských podnikov. Agricultural economics, 48(8):373–378

Hajdíková T, Komárková L, Pirožek P (2013) Financial and operational performance of hospitals in the Czech Republic. In: Proceedings of the 10th international scientific conference, European financial systems, p 120–5

Hajdíková T, Komárková L, Pirožek P (2014) Komparace právních forem nemocnic působících v prostředí zdravotnických služeb v ČR. In: Jedlička P (ed) Hradecké ekonomické dny 2014 sborník recenzovaných příspěvků Díl I. Nakladatelství Gaudeamus UHK, Hradec Králové, pp 254–261

Harkey J, Vraciu R (1992) Quality of health care and financial performance: is there a link? Health Care Manage Rev 17(4):55–63

Holmes M, Pink GH (2013) Change in profitability and financial distress of critical access hospitals from loss of cost-based reimbursement. NC rural health research program

Jervis KJ, Younis MMZ, Forgione DA (2011) Hospital financial distress, recovery and closure: managerial incentives and political costs. J Public Budgeting Account Financ Manage 23(1):31

Kim TH (2010) Factors associated with financial distress of nonprofit hospitals. Health Care Manager 29(1):52–62

Koyuncugil AS, Ozgulbas N (2012) Early warning system for financially distressed hospitals via data mining application. J Med Syst 36(4):2271–2287

Landry AY (2009) Factors associated with hospital bankruptcies: a political and economic framework. J Healthc Manag 4:252–271

Langabeer J (2005) Predicting financial distress in teaching hospitals. J Health Care Finance 33 (2):84–92

Lynn M, Wertheim P (1993) Key financial ratios can foretell hospital closures. HFMA J 47 (11):66–70

Mączyńska E, Zawadzki M (2006) Dyskryminacyjne modele predykcji bankructwa przedsiębiorstw [Discriminant models of prediction of corporate bankruptcy], Ekonomista, 2

McCue M, Mark BA, Harless DW (2003) Nurse staffing, quality, and financial performance. J Health Care Finance 29(4):54–76

Michalski G. (2010) Planning optimal from the firm value creation perspective. levels of operating cash investments, Romanian J Econ Forecast 13(1):198–214

Michalski G (2015a) Full operating cycle and its influence on enterprise characteristics: V4 food and beverages processing firms case. In: Kapounek S, Kapounek S (ed) 18th international scientific conference "Enterprise and the competitive environment", March 5–6, 2015, Mendel University in Brno, Brno, Czech Republic, p 559–568

Michalski G (2015b) Relation between cash levels and debt in small and medium wood and furniture industry enterprises with full operating cycle. Procedia Econ Finan 34:469–476

Michalski G (2016) Risk pressure and inventories levels. Influence of risk sensitivity on working capital levels. Econ Comput Econ Cybern Stud Res 50(1):189–196

Michalski G, Brozyna E, Soroczynska J (2015) Cash levels and its role in full operating cycle enterprises: 2005–2013 Czech, Slovak, Hungarian and Polish Enterprises Case. In: European financial systems 2015. Proceedings of the 12th international scientific conference, Masaryk University, Brno, p 382–390

Noh M, Lee Y, Yun SC, Lee SI, Lee MS, Khang YH (2006) Determinants of hospital closure in South Korea: Use of a hierarchical generalized linear model. Soc Sci Med 63(9):2320–2329

Neumaierová I, Neumaier I (2002) Performance and Market Value of the Company (Výkonnost a tržní hodnota firmy). Grada

Pink G, Holmes G, D'Alpe C, Strunk L, McGee P, Slifkin R (2006) Financial indicators for critical access hospitals. J Rural Health; Official J Am Rural Health Assoc Nat Rural Health Care Assoc 3:229–236

Price CC (2005) Distress detectors: measures for predicting financial trouble in hospitals. J Healthc Financ Manage Assoc (8):74–76, 78–80

Price CC, Corbett A, Cameron AE, Price DL (2005) Distress detectors measures for predicting financial trouble in hospitals: early-warning systems that anticipate financial distress can provide management with powerful tools to help identify and rectify problems before they reach a crisis. Healthc Financ Manage Aug 2005: 74 +. Academic OneFile. Web. 25 Feb. 2016

Raisova M, Buleca J, Michalski G (2014) Food processing firms inventory levels in hard times. 2004–2012 Slovak, Czech and polish enterprises case. Procedia Econ Finance 12:557–564

Richards CA (2014) The effect of hospital financial distress on immediate breast reconstruction. Columbia University

Siedlecki R (2013) Prognozowanie trudności finansowych przedsiębiorstw z wykorzystaniem metody gradientowej. Finanse, Rynki Finansowe, Ubezpieczenia, Uniwersytet Szczeciński 62:677–687

Siedlecki R (2014) Forecasting company financial distress using the gradient measurement of development and S-curve. Procedia Econo Finan 12:597–606

Siedlecki R, Bem A, Prędkiewicz P, Ucieklak-Jeż P (2015) Measures of hospital's financial condition—empirical study. In: Strategica. Local versus global. International academic conference, p 666–675

Sirisha B, Babu MK, Gowthami V (2016) A study on impact of literacy of farmers during the purchase of agricultural inputs. Int Bus Manage 10(6,7):26–731

Soltes V, Gavurová B (2014a) The functionality comparison of the health care systems by the analytical hierarchy process method. E + M Ekonomie a Manage 17(3):100–117

Soltes V, Gavurová B (2014b) Slovak hospitals efficiency-application of the data envelopment analysis. In: SGEM2014 conference proceedings, September (2):773–784

Szczygieł N, Rutkowska-Podolska M, Michalski G (2015) Information and communication technologies in healthcare: still innovation or reality? Innovative and entrepreneurial value—creating approach in healthcare management. In: Nijkamp P, Kourtit K, Buček M, Hudec O (ed.) 5th central European conference in regional science conference proceedings. Technical University of Košice, p 1020–1029

Ucieklak-Jeż P, Bem A (2014) System ochrony zdrowia—finansowanie, efektywność, restruk-turyzacja. Wydawnictwo im. Stanisława Podobińskiego Akademii im, Jana Długosza w Częstochowie

Chapter 66
Determinants of Long-Term and Short-Term Debt Financing: Evidence from Poland

Bogna Kaźmierska-Jóźwiak, Jakub Marszałek and Paweł Sekuła

Abstract The study attempts to extend the knowledge with debt structure and its determinants in Poland. We compared the results we achieved with the results of studies conducted elsewhere in the world. The analysis covered a group of 111 companies listed on the Warsaw Stock Exchange over the period 2002–2012. The study demonstrates that tangibility is the strongest determinant of debt structure of companies included in the analysis. We found statistically significant, positive relation between tangibility and the propensity to raise long-term debt and statistically significant negative relation for short-term debt. The study gives the evidence of significant relationship between the size and propensity to raise debt as well. No statistically significant relation between the profitability of enterprises and debt was found, while it was confirmed in other studies available across the world. It can attest to the fact that the analysed companies use debt for tax purposes. We also demonstrated negative relationship between the variable that describes a firm's growth and short-term debt. We found that Polish companies make their economic decisions using similar grounds as in the countries of mature market economies. No emerging market specifics is primarily caused by the situation on the Polish debt market which is generally dominated by banks controlled by foreign investors.

Keywords Debt · Financial policy · Polish companies · Emerging market

B. Kaźmierska-Jóźwiak (✉) · J. Marszałek · P. Sekuła
Department of Finance and Strategic Management, University of Lodz,
22/26 Matejki Street, 90-237 Lodz, Poland
e-mail: bognakaj@uni.lodz.pl

J. Marszałek
e-mail: j.marszalek@epf.pl

P. Sekuła
e-mail: pasek@uni.lodz.pl

© Springer International Publishing AG 2017
D. Procházka (ed.), *New Trends in Finance and Accounting*,
Springer Proceedings in Business and Economics,
DOI 10.1007/978-3-319-49559-0_66

723

66.1   Introduction

The debate on capital structure started with the work of Modigliani and Miller (1958), who published a breakthrough paper, in which they put forward their capital structure irrelevance theorem built on the assumption of perfect capital market. In the subsequent decades, the issue of corporate capital structure was the subject of numerous studies and analyses, focused on developed markets, in particular on the USA. Recently, we can notice that there is a growing interest not only in developed countries, but also in developing countries (Frąckowiak et al. 2005), (Majumdar 2010), (Koksal et al. 2013). Despite some progress, capital structure of firms from developing markets apparently remains a highly questionable issue.

Besides, we need to bear in mind that studies concerned primarily on the relation between equity and liabilities paying relatively little attention to the structure of debt in the context of capital structure. In the previous research (Kaźmierska-Jóźwiak et al. 2015), we analysed determinants of debt-equity choice on the Polish capital market. Therefore, our current study attempts to extend the knowledge with debt structure and its determinants in Poland.

The authors intend to compare the results they achieved with the results of studies conducted elsewhere in the world. Studies on capital structure of firms in the UK, including determinants of short- and long-term debt, were conducted by Bevan and Danbolt (2002). Similar studies were conducted in India on manufacturing companies by Majumdar (2010) while Kuehnhasen and Stieber (2014) conducted studies on data from firms from Europe, Japan, and the USA.

This paper is organized as follows: Sect. 66.1 provides a literature review, Sect. 66.2 presents data description and the research methodology, results and analysis are provided in Sect. 66.3, and summary is presented in Sect. 66.4.

66.2   Literature Review

Bradley et al. (1984), Haris and Raviv (1991) followed by Rajan and Zingales (1995) observed that the following factors are crucial for the capital structure of a company: size, profitability, tangibility, and growth. The above variables are used in studies on determinants of capital structure conducted by Bevan and Danbolt (2002), Majumdar (2010), as well as Kuehnhasen and Stieber (2014). Hence, the authors decided to use the set of the same variables to study the determinants of long-term debt and short-term debt of Polish nonfinancial listed companies.

66.2.1 Size of a Company

The size of a company is listed among the key factors that determine capital structure of a firm. It should be pointed out that there is no clear theory that would help us anticipate the impact of the size of a company upon its leverage. The trade-off theory states that there is a positive relationship between company size and the level of leverage. On the other hand, the pecking order theory of corporate leverage states that such relationship is negative.

Empirical evidence regarding the relationship between corporate leverage and firm's size is rather mixed. Kester (1986) discovered an insignificant negative effect; Barclay et al. (1995) found that the correlation between size and gearing reverses polarity, dependent upon whether the estimate is a pooled OLS, or a fixed-effects panel regression. Rajan and Zingales (1995) found a significant positive correlation between company size and leverage degree. Similarly, Bevan and Danbolt (2002) observed that the relation between corporate leverage and company's size is specific and depends on the type of debt. For long-term debt, they demonstrated positive relation, for short-term debt—negative relation (Bevan and Danbolt 2002).

Significant relationship between the size of a company and short-term debt was confirmed by Majumdar (2010). Kuehnhausen and Stieber (2014) observed positive, but very weak relationship between the size and both types of debt: short-term and long-term debt (Kuehnhausen and Stieber 2014). Thus, it is hypothesized that long-term debt (short-term debt) is positively (negatively) related to company size (Hypothesis 1).

66.2.2 Profitability

In terms of the pecking order theory, companies prefer internal rather than external sources of finance. More profitable companies would be less likely to use debt, since they produce enough net profit that can be used as internal source of finance. These observations imply a negative relation between profitability and debt. It is confirmed by the studies of Titman and Wessels (1988), Rajan and Zingales (1995).

The analysis of studies that have taken account of the debt structure (long-term debt and short-term debt) demonstrates negative relationship between profitability and the propensity to raise long-term and short-term debt. The above relationship was confirmed by Bevan and Danbolt (2002), Majumdar (2010) and Kuehnhausen and Stieber (2014). Thus, the study hypothesizes that long-term (short-term) borrowing is negatively (positively) related to profitability (Hypothesis 2).

66.2.3 Tangibility

Due to the conflict of interest between lenders and shareholders (Jensen and Mekling 1976), debt providers may demand some security for the debt. Tangible assets are the best security for lenders. Therefore, tangibility can be considered as debt's determinant. Bradley et al. (1984), Titman and Wessels (1988) and Rajan and Zingales (1995) found a significant positive relationship between tangibility and total leverage. However, Chittenden et al. (1996) and Bevan and Danbolt (2002) indicated that the relationship between tangibility and leverage depends on the type of debt. While these studies revealed positive relation between tangibility and long-term debt, negative relation was found for short-term debt. Similar results were found by Kuehnhausen and Stieber (2014). The study of Majumdar (2010) revealed significant negative relationship between tangibility and short-term debt. The study hypothesizes that there is a positive (negative) relationship between long-term debt (short-term debt) and tangibility (Hypothesis 3).

66.2.4 Growth

Many researchers, inter alia (Myers 1977), (Barclay and Smith 1996, 1999), (Ozkan 2000), argue that the relationship between growth opportunities and debt may depend on the type of debt (short-term vs. long-term debt). Under the agency theory, the agency problem may be mitigated if the firm issues short-term rather than long-term debt. Consistently with these predictions, Titman and Wessels (1988), Chung (1993), Rajan and Zingales (1995), Barclay and Smith (1996) confirm a negative relationship between growth opportunities and the level of either long-term or total debt. Bevan and Danbolt (2002) found a negative correlation between growth opportunities and total debt and positive relation between short-term debt and growth opportunities.

With regard to growth, two indicators are used in this research. The percentage change in total assets will be used as the indicator of growth rate—growth in total assets can be viewed as growth in tangibility. Growth prospects will be measured by the ratio ((total assets − net book value + market value)/total assets). Growth prospects inform about investors' expectations when it comes to future growth of the company; relatively high ratio may suggest investors anticipate dynamic growth of a company in the future; hence, their inclination to high market valuation is compared to the book value of assets. Based on the growth rate, we can formulate the next hypothesis.

It is hypothesized that level of long-term borrowing (short-term borrowing) is negatively (positively) related to the level of growth opportunities measured by ((total assets − net book value + market value)/total assets) (Hypothesis 4).

This study incorporates another measure of growth—growth in total assets. Growth in total assets can be viewed as growth in tangibility. Assuming that tangibility and leverage are positively related, we hypothesize that growth in total assets is positively (negatively) related to the long-term (short-term) debt. The study of Majumdar (2010) revealed positive (negative) relationship between this measure of growth and long-term (short-term) debt. Thus, it is hypothesized that long-term borrowing (short-term borrowing) is positively (negatively) related to the growth rate.

66.3   Research Methodology

The analysis covered a group of 111 companies listed on the Warsaw Stock Exchange. These were nonfinancial companies listed throughout the entire period of the analysis, i.e. over the period 2002–2012. Financial companies, inter alia, banks, insurance companies, investment vehicles or entities without a history of listings over the entire period 2002–2012 were excluded from the study group. Data used to analyse the determinants of capital structure of studied companies originated from the EMIS database. Financial data of companies originated from their consolidated annual financial statements. If such statements were missing, we used individual statements. Data on market value were taken from the stock-trading quote of the Warsaw Stock Exchange.

Panel and balanced data of cross-sectional and time-based nature are used. In such a case, relations among variables can be studied using the classical ordinary least squares (OLS) method. However, we need to bear in mind that the condition of the absence of individual effect must be met. Hence, the research procedure included three stages. First, using the Breusch–Pagan test, we checked whether individual effects should be introduced. Where no grounds were found to reject the null hypothesis, we assumed that a given panel model can be estimated using the classical OLS. If test values were high (LM multiplier), we rejected the null hypothesis in favour of the alternative hypothesis and we added individual effects. In the next stage, we conducted Hausman test to choose between fixed effects and random effects. High value of H statistics of the Hausman test gave preference to fixed-effects model while low value of the statistics suggested random effects model. The last stage consisted in the estimation of variables based on the selected model: one way fixed model or one way random model.

Conducted study was designed to analyse the determinants of capital structure in the context of debt structure. That is why in the model we used debt ratios as dependent variables. Depending on the model, short-term debt to total assets and long-term debt to total assets were the dependent variables:

- STD/TA—short-term debt to total assets,
- LTD/TA—long-term debt to total assets.

In our study, we used five independent variables. Ratios were selected based on the previous research practice in this field. We used the same measures that were studied in most research works included in the literature review.

- Firm size—natural logarithm of total assets—ln(TA)
- Profitability—return rate on assets, measures companies' performance and return on assets (ROA)
- Assets tangibility—fixed assets divided by total assets, the ratio analyses the structure of assets that may determine decisions on assets financing (FA/TA)
- Growth opportunities—(growth rate) change of total assets—growth rate of total assets interpreted as a measure of the rate of growth of a company (GR)
- Growth prospects—is the ratio ((total assets − net book value + market value)/total assets); growth prospects inform about investors' expectations when it comes to the future growth of a company; relatively high ratio may mean that investors anticipate future dynamic growth of a company; hence, the tendency to high market valuations was compared to book value of assets (GP)

Taking into account earlier studies and analyses of determinants of capital structure, we used the panel regression model in the following options:

$$(\text{STB/TA})_{i,t} = \beta_0 + \beta_1 \ln(\text{TA})_{i,t} + \beta_2 \text{ROA}_{i,t} + \beta_3 (\text{FA/TA})_{i,t}$$
$$+ \beta_4 \text{GR}_{i,t} + \beta_5 \text{GP}_{i,t} + v_{i,t} \tag{66.1}$$

$$(\text{LTB/TA})_{i,t} = \beta_0 + \beta_1 \ln(\text{TA})_{i,t} + \beta_2 \text{ROA}_{i,t} + \beta_3 (\text{FA/TA})_{i,t}$$
$$+ \beta_4 \text{GR}_{i,t} + \beta_5 \text{GP}_{i,t} + v_{i,t} \tag{66.2}$$

All dependent variables are represented by selected parameters of i companies in t time units (years), where is a total random error.

66.4 Results—Analysis of Long-Term and Short-Term Debt Financing Determinants

Determinants of capital structure were analysed in three options for 1221 observations, i.e. 111 companies throughout the period of 11 years. First, we analysed which variables, and how, impact the relationship between corporate short-term debt and the balance total measured with the (STD/TA) ratio. Independent variables were estimated based on the fixed-effects model (Table 66.1). The selection was suggested by Breusch–Pagan and Hausman tests. The value of Breusch–Pagan test was 312.50 (probability 0.0000) and Hausman test value was 31.56 (probability 0.0000). Four independent variables had statistically significant impact upon STD/TA—ln(TA) (negative for $p < 0.01$), FA/TA (negative for $p < 0.01$), GR (negative for $p < 0.01$), and GP (positive impact for $p < 0.01$). The goodness of fit of the model measured with adjusted R-square amounted to 32.67 p.c.

Four independent variables turned out to be statistically significant for p lower than 1 p.c. in the estimation of a panel model. The only exception was ROE, for which no statistically significant impact on STD/TA was detected. Three

Table 66.1 Impact of selected determinants on (STD/TA)

Variable	Factor	Standard error	Student's t-test	p value
const	1.08095	0.17966	6.0166	<0.00001***
ln(TA)	−0.03986	0.01502	−2.6537	0.00808***
ROA	−0.08191	0.08159	−1.0039	0.31563
FA/TA	−0.52859	0.10560	−4.9868	<0.00001***
GR	−0.03593	0.00896	−4.0097	0.00006***
GP	0.03808	0.00564	6.7480	
R-squared = 0.39015				
Adjusted R-squared = 0.32668				
F statistics = (115.1105) = 6.14721 ($p < 0.00001$)				

Significant variable for *$p < 0.10$, **$p < 0.05$, ***$p < 0.01$
Source Authors' calculations

independent variables—ln(TA), FA/TA, GR—had negative impact upon the dependent variable, while the impact of GP was positive. The ability of the model to explain the STD/TA dependent variable was also quite limited.

In the second option of the test, we tested dependent variable LTD/TA by analysing determinants of long-term debt of companies. First, we analysed Breusch–Pagan and Hausman tests, which suggested the application of fixed-effects model similarly to the previous option of the study. Breusch–Pagan test value amounted to 1090.02 (probability 0.0000) and Hausman test value reached 17.53 (probability 0.0036). Estimated values of independent variables for LTD/TA variable data are included in Table 66.2. Results show that the constant and two variables had statistically significant impact upon the dependent variable—ln(TA) (positive for $p < 0.01$) and FA/TA (positive for $p < 0.01$). The goodness of fit of the model measured with adjusted R-square amounted to 53.34 p.c.

Results of studies revealed rather significant differences between determinants of short-term debt and long-term debt of companies. The impact of only two variables:

Table 66.2 Impact of selected determinants on (LTD/TA)

Variable	Factor	Standard error	Student's t-test	p value
const	−0.06292	0.03803	−1.6544	0.09833*
ln(TA)	0.00932	0.00318	2.9303	0.00346***
ROA	−0.02557	0.01727	−1.4804	0.13904
FA/TA	0.11019	0.02244	4.9111	<0.00001***
GR	0.00055	0.00190	0.2924	0.77005
GP	0.00086	0.00119	0.7177	0.47307
R-squared = 0.57735				
Adjusted R-squared = 0.53337				
F statistics = (115.1105) = 13.12586 ($p < 0.00001$)				

Significant variable for *$p < 0.10$, **$p < 0.05$, ***$p < 0.01$
Source Authors' calculations

ln(TA), which is a measure of company's size and FA/TA that describes the structure of assets turned out to be statistically significant. The direction of impact of variables was also different for the analysis of short-term debt. Independent variables had positive impact upon LTD/TA ratio. It meant we could assume that the bigger a company, the higher its long-term debt in relation to total assets. That could suggest that bigger entities are perceived as more safe and thus have got better access to long-term financing than smaller companies. In the case of FA/TA positive impact upon LTD/TA meant higher share of external long-term financing in enterprises where the share of total assets was considerable. It means the propensity to finance fixed assets with long-term capital and striving to avoid time mismatch between appropriate assets and liabilities.

Panel studies of the determinants of debt structure revealed differences among independent variables that impact debt in statistically significant way. Moreover, for two variables, which were significant for short-term debt and long-term debt the direction of their impact turned out to be opposite, meaning one of them exerted positive impact while the other had adverse effect upon the dependent variable.

66.5 Conclusions

Following Bevan and Danbolt (2002), the authors analysed the relation between debt structure and a proxy for the size of a company, profitability, tangibility, firm growth and firm and growth opportunity. We based our analysis on data from 111 Polish nonfinancial listed companies.

Results of studies revealed rather significant differences between determinants of corporate short-term and long-term debt. The study demonstrates that tangibility is the strongest determinant of capital structure of companies included in the survey. Nevertheless, we need to note that, similar to studies by Bevan and Danbolt (2002), Majumdar (2010), Kuhnhausen and Stieber (2014), the relation between the changing propensity to raise debt depends on the nature of debt. We confirmed statistically significant, positive relation between tangibility and the propensity to raise long-term debt and statistically significant negative relation for short-term debt. Therefore, the results support hypothesis H3.

The study documented significant relationship between the size and propensity to raise debt and, like in the case of tangibility, we confirmed positive relation between the size of a company and long-term debt (similarly to Bevan and Danbolt (2002), Kuhnhausen and Stieber (2014)) and negative for short-term debt (Majumdar (2010), Kuhnhausen and Stieber (2014)). The results support hypothesis H1.

No statistically significant relation between the profitability of enterprises and a long-term (short-term) debt was found, while it was confirmed in other studies available across the world. The results do not support hypothesis H2. No relationship significant statistically can attest to the fact that the surveyed companies use debt for tax purposes. Therefore, increasing profitability may determine higher debt level. The reason may significantly impair the model specified in the pecking order theory. For Polish enterprises, tax reason is extremely important. Unstable tax system makes entrepreneurs trying to exploit the possibilities to reduce the tax paid. They fear that tax reduction and exemptions may be lifted soon.

Similarly to studies by Bevan and Danbolt (2002), our analysis gives the evidence of the statistically significant positive relationship between the proxy for growth opportunity measured as MV/BV and short-term debt. Our results indicate negative relationship between the variable that describes a firm's growth and short-term debt (see also Majumdar 2010). The results support hypothesis H4.

The differences observed in the debt structure of Polish companies may indicate differences in their financial policy. This can be seen especially in the case of profitability and the debt propensity relationship. However, those differences seem to be unimportant. Polish companies make their economic decisions using similar grounds as in the countries of mature market economies. No emerging market specifics is primarily caused by the situation on the Polish debt market. It is generally dominated by banks. The bond market is less developed. Polish banking sector is dominated by banks controlled by foreign investors. They run their banking business using the same solutions as in their home countries. This applies particularly to required security in the credit agreement. Therefore, crediting policy used by banks determines the possibility of incurring debt. That is may be a reason why Polish companies affect the same stimuli and their behaviour resembles Western patterns.

References

Barclay MJ, Smith CW (1996) On financial architecture: leverage, maturity and priority. J Appl Corp Finance 8(4):4–17

Barclay MJ, Smith CW (1995) The maturity structure of corporate debt. J Finance 50(2):609–631

Barclay MJ, Smith CW (1999) The captial structure: another look at the evidence. Journal of Applied Corporate Finance, 12:8–20. doi:10.1111/j.1745-6622.1999.tb00655.x

Bevan AA, Danbolt J (2002) Capital structure and its determinants in the United Kingdom: a decompositional analysis. Appl Financ Econ 12(3):159–170

Bradley M, Jarrell G, Kim EH (1984) On the existence of an optimal capital structure: theory and evidence. J Finance 39:857–878

Chittenden F, Hall G, Hutchinson P (1996) Small firm growth, access to capital markets and financial structure: review of issues and an empirical investigation. Small Bus Econ 8(1):59–67

Chung KH (1993) Assets characteristics and corporate debt policy: an empirical investigation. J Bus Financ Acc 20(1):83–98

Frąckowiak W et al (2005) Polityka kształtowania struktury kapitału w polskich przedsiębiorstwach na tle wybranych krajów Unii Europejskiej. In: Ostaszewski J (ed) Finanse przedsiębiorstwa. Wydawnictwo SGH, Warsaw, pp 153–171

Harris M, Raviv A (1991) Capital structure and the informational role of debt. J Finance 45 (2):321–349

Jensen M, Meckling W (1976) Theory of the firm: managerial behavior, agency costs and ownership structure. J Financ Econ 3(4):305–360

Kaźmierska-Jóźwiak B, Marszałek J, Sekuła P (2015) Determinants of debt-equity choice—evidence from poland. Emerg Mark J 5(2):1–8

Kester CW (1986) Capital and ownership structure: a comparison of United States and Japanese manufacturing corporations. Financ Manage 15:5–16

Koksal B, Orman C, Oduncu A (2013) Determinants of capital structure: evidence from a major emerging market economy. MPRA paper 48415. http://mpra.ub.uni-muenchen.de/48415/. Accessed 19 Jul 2015

Kuhnhausen F, Stieber HW (2014) Determinants of capital structure in non-fianncial companies. Munich discussion paper 39. http://epub.ub.uni-muenchen.de/21167/. Accessed 19 Jul 2015

Majumdar R (2010) The determinants of corporate debt maturity: a study of indian firms. J Appl Finance 16(2):70–80

Modigliani F, Miller M (1958) The cost of capital, corporation finance and the theory of investment. Am Econ Rev 48:261–297

Myers SC (1977) Determinants of corporate borrowing. J Financ Econ 5:147–175

Ozkan A (2000) An empirical analysis of corporate debt maturity structure. Eur Financ Manage 6 (2):197–212

Rajan RG, Zingales L (1995) What do we know about capital structure? Some evidence from international data. J Finance 50(5):1421–1460

Titman S, Wessels R (1988) The determinants of capital structure choice. J Finance 43(1):1–19

Chapter 67
A Working Capital and Liquidity

Aleksandre Petriashvili

Abstract The measure of working capital and liquidity was accepted as a useful tool for financial analysis a long time ago. Yet a critical review of the structure of this concept, in the way it is currently applied, raises some very serious questions concerning its validity as a measure of current position. Concept of liquidity and working capital exposes evaluation, but still some authors have different opinion about the question. This paper examines two core problems: first, what is meant by liquidity and, second, what is meant by working capital.

Keywords Working capital · Liquidity · Current assets

67.1 Introduction

The measure of working capital and liquidity was accepted as a useful tool for financial analysis a long time ago. Yet a critical review of the structure of this concept, in the way it is currently applied, raises some very serious questions concerning its validity as a measure of current position. Concept of liquidity and working capital exposes evaluation, but still some authors have different opinion about the question. It is correct when people use liquidity in connection with working capital, even though it is by no means limited to this area. This paper examines two core problems: first, what is meant by liquidity and, second, what is meant by working capital.

A. Petriashvili (✉)
Department of Corporate Finance, University of Economics, Prague,
Nam. W. Churchilla 4, 130 67 Prague, Czech Republic
e-mail: xpeta28@vse.cz

© Springer International Publishing AG 2017   733
D. Procházka (ed.), *New Trends in Finance and Accounting*,
Springer Proceedings in Business and Economics,
DOI 10.1007/978-3-319-49559-0_67

67.2 Working Capital

The core of the working capital concept has been subjected to considerable change over the years. Some authors consider that working capital is "the amount of current liabilities; net current assets" (Kohler 1952). Working capital is frequently used to measure a firm's ability to meet current obligation. Working capital is also called net current assets, net working capital. Capital which we used for working capital is only "currently" capital. Working capital or net current asset is an accounting term denoting a firm's short-term current asset, which is turned over fairly quickly in the course of business. They include raw materials, work in progress and finished goods, stocks, debtors and cash, less short-term current liabilities. Figure 67.1 shows the major components of the working capital cycle.

American Institute of Accounting agrees with the next definition: "Working capital, sometimes called Net working capital is the excess of current assets over current liabilities" (Committee on Accounting Procedure 1947). We can see that indicated above: the excess of current assets over current liabilities is net current assets. There appears to be some agreement among accountants that working capital represents an equity concept, that is, net owed current assets.

- For some authors working capital is difference between the total of the current assets and total of the current liabilities. However, other authors define the working capital as the portion of corporate's equity in the form of current assets.

For John Stuart Mill the foregoing concept has been anathema. He said: "Of the capital engaged in the production of any commodity, there is a part which, after being used once exists no longer as capital…Capital which in this manner fulfills the whole of its office in the production in which it is engaged by a single use, is

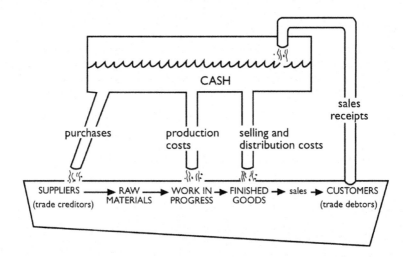

Fig. 67.1 Working capital cycle. *Source* Financial Dictionary: http://financial-dictionary.thefreedictionary.com/working+capital

called Circulating capital" (Mill 1936). Mill's "circulating capital" would be what is currently identified as current assets. According to J. S. Mill's we need to view not only emphasizing the net equity in current assets, also their nature and function. For Alfred Marshall and more part of neoclassicist authorities "working capital assets are composed of the raw materials, goods in process, finished products, accounts and note receivable, and free balances at the bank" (Marshal 1930). This is a schedule of the current assets on the balance sheet.

But Keynes introduces two major categories of capital: real capital and loan capital. The stock of real capital or material wealth existing at any time is embodied in one or other of three forms:

- Goods in use, which are only capable of giving up gradually their full yield of use or enjoyment;
- Goods in process, i.e., use course of preparation by cultivation or manufacture for use or consumption, or in transport, or with merchants' dealers and retailers, or awaiting the rotation of the seasons;
- Goods in stock, which are yielding nothing but capable of being used or consumed at any time.

We shall call goods in use fixed capital, goods in process working capital and goods in stock liquid capital (Keynes 1930). Working capital is necessary because some goods take time to produce. As we can see for Keynes working capital is only real goods and part of the real capital.

In the industrial process such assets or goods fall into two principal classifications: the fixed capital goods and not fixed capital goods. Now we need to understand what fixed and not fixed capital is. Fixed capital goods are those assets which have come into existence as a function of the savings—investment process as a means to reduce as well as multiply the exertions of man. The fixed capital goods can perform a specialized service indefinitely and we will get Mill's "circulating capital." The capital goods for which this specialized service is performed is the other broad classification of goods owned by industry, which is represented as current assets. We can see that we need to use fixed and circulating capital in conjunction.

All current assets stand on the same footing as that class of goods which is the recipient or the facilitating device for the profitable employment fixed capital, and this means all current assets we can use for term "working capital."

67.3   Liquidity

The second complicated problem is liquidity. There appears to be much more unanimity of understanding within the limits of definition, and the heart of the matter lies in two aspects: what is function of liquidity and relationship with corporate working capital.

Term liquidity becomes a form of business alike, from the depression of the early thirties. It is as much sought after and as little understood as social security, full employment or the insurance of bank deposits. Term liquidity is not a new term in the finance. As a measure of impetus was generated by the Temporary National Economic committee in the American economy, one monograph in particular paid special attention to the subject under review by devoting a chapter to "working capital" of American Manufacturing Corporations (Temporary National Economic Committee 1940). In this study the important difference between quantitative and qualitative factors is considered, and in terms of the latter it is stated that "turn-over is the circuit through which the typical working-capital dollar travels from cash to merchandise to receivables, back to cash.... however, the character of operations in different industries requires varying degrees of liquidity" (Temporary National Economic Committee 1940).

The concept of liquidity appears that two circumstances override all others: "that liquid or cash assets are those assets of any kind which may readily be converted into cash" (Special Committee on Terminology 1930) and there are degrees of liquidity respecting any asset at a particular time. It is said and we know too that cash and receivables are more liquid, than merchandise.

The concept that perfect liquidity is attained by the conversion of assets into cash, has some weak points. First, for a concept to become received doctrine, it must be true universally, and on several counts the advantages of holding "cash" may be undermined. For example, the debacle cash was the least preferable assets to hold in post-war Germany. In contract, cash was desirable during the Greenback period. Second weak is political area and that is the cyclical problem. When there is a depreciating currency within a country, the lower the proportion of current assets held in cash and the more profitable is the business. But when it is appreciating in contrary, the larger the proportion of current assets held in cash. We can see that those who hold to the concept that ownership of money or cash represents perfect liquidity cannot maintain their position with consistency.

Some authors, however, appear to have passed over this fundamental problem in their zeal to find a means to "measure" liquidity. In the notion of degrees of liquidity, it has been observed before that consider merchandise the least liquid and cash and receivables the most liquid. Some writers can put raw materials at the bottom of the list, then long-term receivables and then short-term, because long-term obligations are less liquid than short-term. This is a hierarchy resulting in liquidity preferences.

Now the concept that to "liquidate" an asset means to convert it into cash poses no problems different from those encountered in marketability. From this stand-point, consequently, little embarrassment is encountered. Goods have a value ranging all the way from a positive to a negative price. Second, the problem of liquidity through sale is approximately the same from the price problem of marketing. But the problem of price is itself only one of the biggest facets of global economy. If the presence goes unnoticed it means that each part functions properly. When any one part functions imperfectly, the whole is likely to failure. Additionally, the problem of converting current assets into cash is a limiting case of the main problem of the price mechanism and is by no means allied completely or simply to the problems of working capital. It seems that liquidity in this sense, is only a new name for a very old but very perplexing problem—price.

The liquidity of an asset is quality related to and measured by the ability to exchange the asset for money. It is not a physical property of the asset. But cash does not irrefutably represent perfect liquidity.

67.4   Conclusion

To summarize our results, we find that the term working capital should be used with current assets and the nature of an asset is not determined by name. It is determined by its function. Liquidity is the term used to describe how easy it is to convert assets to cash. The most liquid asset, and what everything else is compared to, is cash. This is because it can always be used easily and immediately. The term liquidity (price) makes more problems for marketing, than finance and accounting.

Acknowledgments The paper has been prepared within the research project "Theoretical approaches to optimize the capital structure" (supported by the internal grant system of University of Economics in Prague no. IGA F1/48/2016).

References

Committee on Accounting Procedure (1947) American Institute of Accountants. Res Bull 30, 248
Keynes JM (1930) A treatise on money. vol 2. Harcourt, Brace & Co., New York, p 128
Kohler EL (1952) A dictionary for accountants. Prentice Hall, Inc., New York (s.v. "Working Capital")
Marshal A (1930) Principles of political economy. Longmans, Green & Co., New York, p 75
Mill JS (1936) Principles of political economy. Longmans, Green & Co., New York, p 91
Special Committee on Terminology, American Institute of Accountants (1930) A preliminary report. Century Co., New York (s.v. "Current assets.")
Temporary National Economic Committee, Investigation of Concentration of Economic Power (1940) Financial characteristics of American manufacturing corporations. Washington, pp 67, 86–87

Chapter 68
Determinant Factors of Economic Value Added: Case of Ukrainian Wineries

Anastasiia Fialkovska

Abstract The paper investigates whether there is any significant relationship between EVA and the financial indicators, such as rate of return on invested capital, sales, operating expenses, share of borrowed capital, share of equity, taxes paid and assets. In the paper, the financial and accounting data of 12 wine-making enterprises provided by the Web site of Stock Market Infrastructure Development Agency of Ukraine in 2014 were used. Following the findings from literature overview, two main research hypotheses about the factors which have influence on the economic value-added dimension of the Ukrainian wineries were formulated. Our results show that only rate of return on invested capital has statistically significant cause–effect relationship with the EVA indicator among all chosen factors. Other determinant factors considered in the paper have no influence on EVA.

Keywords Economic value added · Factor · Wine enterprise · Financial performance

68.1 Introduction

In the current economic conditions, characterized by a high level of instability of the environment, the management of enterprise value concept becomes actual. This concept advises to abandon the inefficient accounting criteria for evaluating success of enterprise functioning and to take into account only one criterion, the most simple and clear for shareholders and investors—economic value added.

The analysis of foreign management practices shows that in recent years a top priority for financial managers is to ensure a stable increase in the enterprise's value, enabling owners and investors to be confident in the successful implementation of the strategy and the creation of business value added. If the enterprise is

A. Fialkovska (✉)
Department of Economic and Management of National Economy, Odessa National Economic University, Preobrazhenskaya Str. 8, Odessa 65082, Ukraine
e-mail: fian192@gmail.com

© Springer International Publishing AG 2017
D. Procházka (ed.), *New Trends in Finance and Accounting*,
Springer Proceedings in Business and Economics,
DOI 10.1007/978-3-319-49559-0_68

not able to generate sufficient economic income for a certain period of time, then its survival in market conditions is problematic. Managers, interested in meeting the interests of investors, should regulate costs and the enterprise's economic value at least to ensure a minimum level of profitability. All these facts confirm the need to improve the actual situation and the value-added creation, as opposed to financial data manipulation in order to obtain short-term benefits.

Since achieving the value creation depends on the efficiency with which resources involved in the business are used and generate a higher return on their cost, economic value added must be analyzed in correlation with the indicators which quantify the determinant factors of value.

The main objective of the paper is to analyze the intensity and direction of the link existing between economic value added and the indicators identified as drivers of the value creation.

The paper is organized as follows. After this introduction, the contemporary trends of the Ukrainian wineries' functioning were analyzed. In the next chapter, relevant literature dealing with the economic value added (methods of calculation, determinant factors, its uses and limitations, etc.) is reviewed. Following the findings from literature overview, two main research hypotheses about the factors which have influence on the economic value-added dimension of the Ukrainian wineries were formulated. The hypotheses are empirically tested on the wine enterprises listed on the Stock Market of Ukraine. The final chapter concludes; the main findings are summarized.

68.2 Wine-Making Industry in Ukraine

Wine-making is one of the important components of the food industry in Ukraine. Production volumes of the enterprises of the industry in the structure of the food industry are 6%. Currently, there are estimated 62 wine-making enterprises in Ukraine. The number of wineries has decrease significantly in 2014 (−38%) following the annexation of the Autonomous Republic of Crimea (ARC). The ARC took the second place by volumes of bulk wine and wine production in Ukraine.

The loss of the peninsula has led to a significant decrease in production and sales of wine in Ukraine (Fig. 68.1).

Over the last year, the production of wine was reduced by 38%: 11.7 million hl in 2013 to 7.2 million hl in 2014. The total volume of output is critically low, and in 2015 we can predict a slight drop in the percentage of 2014. More reduction cannot be, because the production is already at the minimum level. External trade also declined in 2014 (Fig. 68.2).

Thus, the state of the wine industry can be characterized as a crisis. In 2014, the wine industry was faced with a real anti-record. The activity of the wineries are also observed crises, manifested in losses (45.3% of the wineries have received a loss in 2014) and production cuts. However, the Ukrainian winemakers have considerable

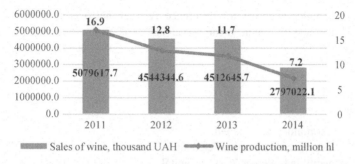

Fig. 68.1 Dynamics of production and sales of wine in Ukraine over the period 2011–2014. *Source* Own processing based on the data of the State Statistics Service of Ukraine

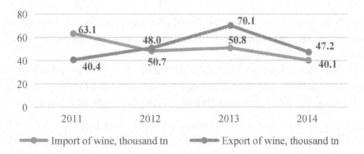

Fig. 68.2 Trends of import and export of wine over the period 2011–2014. *Source* Own processing based on the data of the State Statistics Service of Ukraine

potential, experience and other features to ensure the successful development of the industry.

68.2.1 *Literature Review and Hypotheses Development*

Economic value added (EVA) is a measure of financial performance of a company and represents a powerful business tool which, if used correctly, promises to improve company performance and produce greater returns to shareholders. EVA is not just another performance measure, but can be the main part of an integrated financial management system, leading to decentralized decision making. Thus, the adoption of EVA should indirectly bring changes in management, which in turn can enhance firm value (Morard and Balu 2009).

Economic value added is the difference between net operating profit after tax (NOPAT) and cost of capital. It can be calculated using the following formula (Ilic 2010):

$$EVA = NOPAT - WACC\% * IC \qquad (68.1)$$

where

EVA   economic value added,
NOPAT   net operating profit after tax,
WACC%   weighted average cost of capital,
IC   total business capital invested.

The reasoning that is underlying such indicator is quite simple: the own capital, seen as the loan capital, has a specific cost. In contradistinction to the loan capital cost, which occurs explicitly into the profit and loss account, the own capital cost is represented by the investors' remuneration and will be managed in a different accounting way (Şuşu 2013).

Except of the classical calculation formula of EVA, proposed by Stern & Stewart's office, there are also three other calculating methods of the EVA indicator, proposed in the economic literature (Nicoleta Guni and Munteanu 2014):

- In order to determine the EVA indicator, there must first be calculated the cost of the permanent capital of the company. The approach implies taking into account both the costs generated by paying bank interests for the borrowed capital, which are reflected in the profit and loss account, and the cost of its own equity, commonly known under the name of opportunity cost that is subject to a different accounting treatment. The calculating formula of this indicator is:

$$EVA = Nor - k \qquad (68.2)$$

where

Nor (Ren)   the net operating result,
k the cost of the permanent capitals.

- Another method implies treating the added economic value as residual income. This changes the calculation formula and not the result of the calculation:

$$EVA = CP \times (Rpr - k) \qquad (68.3)$$

where

Rpr   the profitability rate of the invested capital.

- The third method of determining the added economic value involves the integration of the operating expenses into a single monetary indicator of performance evaluation, according to which:

$$EVA = \text{The turnover} - \text{Operating expenses} - \text{The cost of permanent capital}$$

$$(68.4)$$

There is a positive correspondence between EVA and financial performance metrics (such as ROA and ROE). The results of relevant issues show higher-quality information content of EVA indicator as regards the ability to create shareholder wealth than the traditional performance measures (Chmelikova 2008).

Despite EVA's advantages, this measure has four limitations (Brewer and Chandra 1999):

1. Size differences. EVA does not control for size differences across enterprises. A larger enterprise will tend to have a higher EVA relative to its smaller counterparts.
2. Financial orientation. EVA is a computed number that relies on financial accounting methods of revenue realization and expense recognition. If motivated to do so, managers can manipulate these number by altering their decision-making process.
3. Short-term orientation. EVA overemphasizes the need to generate immediate results; therefore, it creates a disincentive for managers to invest in innovative product or process technologies.
4. Results orientation. EVA is accumulated at the end of an accounting period and do not help point toward the root causes of operational inefficiencies.

In relevant literature, a large amount of factors determined that EVA indicator is described (Ganea 2015; Porohnya and Los 2008). They are:

- rate of return on invested capital,
- sales,
- operating expenses,
- share of borrowed capital,
- share of equity,
- taxes paid,
- assets, etc.

Except of the financial indicators group, there are also group "Relationship with consumers," "Organization of enterprise's business-process" and "Staff, education and development." Due to lack of information, the relationship between EVA and financial indicators was analyzed in the paper.

Following the literature review, we built two hypotheses:

H1: There is a significant correlation between the EVA indicator and rate of return on invested capital, operating expenses, share of borrowed capital and share of equity.

H2: There is a nonsignificant correlation between the EVA indicator and sales, taxes paid and assets.

68.2.2 Results and Discussion

The empiric analysis of the interdependences established between the economic value added and its determining factors will be performed on a sample of 12 Ukrainian wineries, whose securities are traded on the Stock Market of Ukraine.

The study is based on the financial and accounting data provided by the Web site of Stock Market Infrastructure Development Agency of Ukraine for each of these enterprises in 2014, which were subsequently processed in Excel worksheets, with a view to determining both the dependent variable, EVA, and the independent variables—rate of return on invested capital, operating expenses, share of borrowed capital, share of equity, sales, taxes paid and assets.

The intensity of the relationship between the determining factors of the value creation and EVA will be identified by means of the correlation method, based on the estimation and interpretation of Pearson correlation coefficients.

The level of the indicators used in the correlation analysis for testing the first hypothesis is displayed in Table 68.1 for each studied enterprise.

The economic value added (EVA) has, as it can be seen in Table 68.2, both positive values (in 9 of the analyzed companies), denoting a higher wealth of the shareholders of this enterprise, and negative values (for 5 companies), which shows the destruction of value, pursuant to the performed activity.

The results obtained for the Pearson coefficient for the first hypothesis are included in Table 68.2.

The Pearson coefficient indicates a statistically significant cause–effect relationship between EVA and rate of return on invested capital. Other three indicators have no influence on the dimension of EVA. Thus, the first hypothesis was proved only partly.

The level of the indicators used in the correlation analysis for testing the second hypothesis is displayed in Table 68.3 for each studied enterprise.

The results obtained for the Pearson coefficient for the second hypothesis are included in Table 68.4.

The results obtained in Table 68.4 converge toward a statistically nonsignificant relationship. Sales, taxes paid and assets do not represent the determining factors for the economic value added. Thus, the second hypothesis was not confirmed.

Table 68.1 Indicators used for the correlation analysis for testing H1

No.	Enterprise	Economic value added, thousand UAH	Rate of return on invested capital, %	Operating expenses, thousand UAH	Share of borrowed capital, %	Share of equity, %
1	Tavriya OAO	−44,449	−5.57	173,311	67.5	32.5
2	Artemivsk Vayneri ZAO	−44,061	9.01	105,241	59.8	40.2
3	Koblevo OAO	121,475	14.52	44,540	63.9	36.1
4	Stolichniy Kiev Factory of Sparkling Wines Public JSC	37,616	7.04	56,737	41.7	58.3
5	Odesavinprom Private JSC At	120,915	5.67	54,557	100	0
6	Tsyurupinske OAO	102,365	33.49	16,503	86.5	13.5
7	Vidkrite Aktsionerne Tovaristvo Bolgradskiy Harchovik OAO	77,541	8.7	23,872	79.9	20.1
8	Odeskiy Zavod Shampanskih VIN ZAO	−62,376	−29.68	37,995	28.3	71.7
9	Zakrite Aktsionerne Tovaristvo Viktoriya ZAO	18,056	1.36	2933	74	26
10	Bolgradskiy Vinorobniy Zavod ZAO	6925	−7.97	11,356	100	0
11	Vinogradar ZAO	−5029	0.89	990	71	29
12	Agropromislove OB Ednannya Stariy Krim ZAO	−3680	1.06	413	80.7	19.3

Source Own processing based on the data published in the balance sheet and profit and loss account, 2014

Table 68.2 The correlation coefficients for testing H1

Independent variables	Pearson coefficient (r)	Level of significance (Sig. (2-tailed))	Statistical significance
Rate of return on invested capital, %	0.699	0.012	Significant
Operating expenses, thousand UAH	−0.308	0.33	Nonsignificant
Share of borrowed capital, %	0.48	0.114	Nonsignificant
Share of equity, %	−0.48	0.114	Nonsignificant

Source Own calculation

Table 68.3 Indicators used for the correlation analysis for testing H2

No.	Enterprise	Economic value added, thousand UAH	Sales, thousand UAH	Taxes paid, thousand UAH	Assets, thousand UAH
1	Tavriya OAO	−44,449	454,022	7622	1,000,458
2	Artemivsk Vayneri ZAO	−44,061	269,996	2744	649,532
3	Koblevo OAO	121,475	266,097	3579	289,141
4	Stolichniy Kiev Factory of Sparkling Wines Public JSC	37,616	220,356	1447	217,238
5	Odesavinprom Private JSC At	120,915	173,148	227	166,130
6	Tsyurupinske OAO	102,365	13,611	944	146,367
7	Vidkrite Aktsionerne Tovaristvo Bolgradskiy Harchovik OAO	77,541	121,012	810	115,249
8	Odeskiy Zavod Shampanskih VIN ZAO	−62,376	45,318	0	108,487
9	Zakrite Aktsionerne Tovaristvo Viktoriya ZAO	18,056	33,080	0	46,552
10	Bolgradskiy Vinorobniy Zavod ZAO	6925	18,091	11	97,134
11	Vinogradar ZAO	−5029	6406	49	38,425
12	Agropromislove OB Ednannya Stariy Krim ZAO	−3680	4422	45	39803

Source Own processing based on the data published in the balance sheet and profit and loss account, 2014

Table 68.4 The correlation coefficients for testing H2

Independent variables	Pearson coefficient (r)	Level of significance (Sig. (2-tailed))	Statistical significance
Sales, thousand UAH	0.034	0.917	Nonsignificant
Taxes paid, thousand UAH	−0.159	0.623	Nonsignificant
Assets, thousand UAH	−0.337	0.284	Nonsignificant

Source Own calculation

68.3 Conclusion

The paper discussed methods of the EVA calculation, strengths, limitations and its determining factors. A simple mathematical equation based on an enterprise's operating income after tax, investment in assets, and cost of capital will never provide any organization a sustainable advantage over its competitors. EVA can provide a valuable measure of wealth creation and can be used to help align managerial decision making with firm preferences; however, it is only one part of the performance measurement methodology and it must be used in conjunction with a balanced set of measures that provide a complete picture of performance.

References

Brewer PC, Chandra G (1999) Economic value added (EVA): its uses and limitations. SAM Adv Manage J (07497075) 64:4

Chmelikova G (2008) Economic value added versus traditional performance metrics in the Czech food-processing sector. Int Food Agribusiness Manage Rev 11:49–65

Ganea M (2015) Determinant factors of the economic value added in the case of romanian companies listed on the bucharest stock exchange. Audit Financiar 13:100–107

Ilic M (2010) Economic value added as a modern performance indicator. Perspect Innovations Econ Bus 6:94–97

Morard B, Balu F-O (2009) Developing a practical model for calculating the economic value added. Econ Comput Econ Cybern Stud Res 43:1–16

Nicoleta Guni C, Munteanu V (2014) The added economic value—an instrument for the performance measurement. Econ Manage Financ Markets 9:167–174

Porohnya VM, Los VO (2008) Design of the economic value added on enterprise. Bull Zaporizhzhya Nat Univ 1:107–114

Şuşu Ş (2013) The economic added value—major criterion on analyzing the financial performances on the level of high developed companies. USV Ann Econ Public Adm 13:149–156

Chapter 69
Dividend Policy of State-Owned Companies: Evidence from the Russian Federation

Olga Belomyttseva and Larisa Grinkevich

Abstract This paper analyzes the features of the dividend policy of companies in emerging capital markets. State ownership in the capital structure of large corporations is considered as one of the major features. The paper specifies the features of the dividend policy and provides a statistics analysis of dividend payout ratio and dividend yield of Russian state-owned joint stock companies. The recommendations presented in the study apply to government regulation of the dividend policy in Russian state-owned joint stock companies.

Keywords Dividend policy · State-owned companies

69.1   Introduction

Dividend policy is one of the most complex and controversial aspects of financial studies. Black (1976, p. 510) supported a similar view when stated that dividend picture "seems like a puzzle, with pieces that do not fit together." Brealey et al. (2010) described dividend policy as one of the top ten unsolved problems in finance.

Consequently, studies on dividend policy have produced a significant number of contradictory hypotheses, theories and ideas. The problem is that they mainly focus on developed markets and fail to provide enough knowledge on dividend policy in emerging markets and their segments. The scientists who conduct their research in the field of dividend policy in emerging markets are not numerous. Glen et al.

O. Belomyttseva (✉)
Department of Finance and Accounting, National Research Tomsk State University,
Pr. Lenina 36, 634036 Tomsk, Russia
e-mail: olbel@f123.ru

L. Grinkevich
Department of World Economy and Taxation, National Research Tomsk State University,
Pr. Lenina 36, 634036 Tomsk, Russia
e-mail: nasty_saturn@mail.ru

© Springer International Publishing AG 2017   749
D. Procházka (ed.), *New Trends in Finance and Accounting*,
Springer Proceedings in Business and Economics,
DOI 10.1007/978-3-319-49559-0_69

(1995) investigate dividend policy in different emerging markets; Gul (1999), dividend policy in Chinese enterprises; Aivazian et al. (2003), different emerging markets dividend policy in comparison with American firms; Naser et al. (2004), and Al-Kuwari (2004, 2009), the dividend policy of the countries of the Gulf Cooperation Council; Al-Malkawi (2007), the dividend policy of the Jordan companies; Sierpinska-Sawicz (2014), dividend policy of the Polish corporations; Wardhana and Nugroho (2014), dividend policy in Indonesian enterprises.

Apparently, dividend policy of companies in emerging markets has a number of distinctive features due to the factors determining its formulation, the active role of the state, efficiency, poor predictability, etc. With this in mind, the objective of our study is to investigate and determine the features specific to the dividend policy of Russian state-owned companies.

The structure of the paper is as follows. Chapter 2 presents a literature review on dividend policy of state-owned companies in emerging markets. Chapter 3 discusses specific features of emerging markets dividend policy. Dividend policy of Russian state-owned companies including dividend payout ratio standards and its background is addressed in Chap. 4. The conclusion and research prospects are outlined in the final chapter.

69.2 Literature Review

Studies on the dividend policy of state-owned companies in the emerging markets were first conducted in the 1990s. Among the economists who pioneered this area were Glen et al. (1995) with the published work "Dividend policy and behavior in emerging markets." They considered the mechanisms for investors' rights protection, which also covered minority shareholders, and the role of the state as a shareholder in this process. Gul (1999) studied the relations between state-owned shares and dividends based on the data from China. Particularly, he investigated the correlation between state ownership, fund raising and dividend payouts.

Naser et al. (2004) continued to investigate the exploitation of the minority shareholders within the banking sector in Gulf Cooperation Council countries. Similar findings concerning government ownership and large dividend payments were obtained by Al-Malkawi (2007) during the investigation of dividend policy in Jordan state corporations. He also revealed the existence of "a double principal-agent" conflict between the shareholders—individuals and the government representatives.

Boubakri et al. (2009) analyzed the evolution of strategic industries from public to private in 39 countries and adduced arguments in favor of privatization.

Sierpinska-Sawicz (2014) studied the dividend policy of state treasury shareholding companies and profit distribution to shareholders based on public corporations in Poland. Wardhana and Nugroho (2014) attempted to determine optimal dividend policy for several companies of Indonesia, both private and public.

It should be noted that studies on the dividend policy of state-owned companies are currently fragmentary and incomplete. Furthermore, they have been conducted only for a selection of countries with emerging capital markets.

69.3   Emerging Capital Markets Dividend Policy

Dividend policy of issuers in emerging capital markets is significantly different from that of issuers in developed markets. The author agrees with Glen et al. (1995, p. 9) that "dividend policy in those markets is often very different from the norms that have been accepted in developed countries." Aivazian et al. (2003, p. 387) holds a similar view, "emerging market firms are more sensitive to some of the variables, indicating the greater financial constraints under which they operate."

The prominent features of the dividend policy in developing capital markets are outlined below.

- The state as a majority shareholder in the capital structure of large corporations. This feature quite often implies irrational spending and inefficient investment policy. State ownership in enterprises results in a conflict of interests between the shareholder and the manager, both represented by the state. The state as a shareholder implements a fiscal function and is interested in maximizing dividends, while the state acting as a manager can take inefficient measures that affect dividend payment. Therefore, regulation of dividends level in the corporate governance of state-owned enterprises is a primary objective. Developing countries include a group of countries in transition from central planning to free market. These are primarily post-Soviet countries, which also comprise Russia. The participation of the state as a shareholder in these economies is extremely high. Dividends in this case can be treated as a disciplinary instrument. It should be emphasized that state ownership in the capital structure has some advantages over other investors, including minority shareholders. As a result, state-owned companies encounter fewer difficulties in raising funds. Consequently, they can afford higher dividend payments (Boubakri et al. 2009). The same view was expressed by Gul (1999) who specified that private companies find it more difficult to obtain debt financing and they are forced to rely on retained earnings for investments. The state can act as a safeguard for the minority shareholders by controlling insider shareholders and paying larger dividends (Glen et al. 1995), effectively improving company's reputation in the eyes of foreign investors (Naser et al. 2004).
- Concentration of stock ownership and weak corporate governance that lead to expropriation of the company's resources for the benefit of individual shareholders. According to this point, shareholders and other stakeholders may distort incentives in decision-making, which ultimately reduces corporate performance.
- Low and unstable dividend payments. In most cases, companies in emerging markets reinvest most of the profits. Dividend payments do not exceed 10% of

profit in the BRICS countries, with the exception of Brazil, where the dividend payments amount to 22.8% of net profit (Pirogov and Kravchuk 2011). Payments in the USA amount to 32.53% (Pirogov and Kravchuk 2011). Instability of dividend payments could be treated as volatility. As it was stated by Glen et al. (1995, p. 9), "dividend payments tend to be more volatile in emerging markets than in developed countries." Dividends in emerging markets are commonly paid at the end of the year, while developed markets mostly show interim dividends. Several studies demonstrate correlation between the dividend amounts and the size of a company in emerging markets. Therefore, according to Sierpinska-Sawicz (2014, p. 240), "the biggest companies transfer more of their generated net profit to shareholders." Al-Malkawi (2007) holds a similar opinion.

- Insufficient transparency and disclosure level. The transparency–disclosure index in developed countries is 74 out of 100, in developing countries—66 (Brockman and Unlu 2011). The researchers prove that greater transparency leads to higher dividend payments (Kowalewski et al. 2007).

69.3.1 Dividends in Emerging Markets on the Worldwide Scale

The share of total dividends in emerging markets companies is quite prominent—it constitutes up to 10–20% of the total dividends of the global economy based on statistics from 2011 (Table 69.1). The reports on dividends in emerging markets primarily refer to China, Russia, Brazil and India, with China holding the 10th position on the global dividend payout list of countries.

Dynamics of dividend payments in emerging markets is not consistent with similar dynamics in developed markets, which is clearly shown in Table 69.1. Moreover, in some cases, it shows multidirectional movement. These data are indicative of the significant role of developing capital markets in the development of global financial markets, as well as their high volatility.

69.3.2 The Dividend Policy of the Russian State-Owned Joint Stock Companies

The Russian approach to dividend payments based on shareholders' interests and the priorities of the company extends back over ten years. Currently, dividend policy in the largest Russian corporations is at the stage of development, and many issues, including the possibility of the dividend payments, have not yet been clarified both for corporations and for investors. Moreover, it should be noted that

Table 69.1 Annual dividends in emerging markets (in billion US dollars)

Year	Emerging markets dividends	Total dividends	Share of emerging markets in total dividends, %
2011	106.9	946.6	11.3
Percentage change	30	22	–
2012	116.1	1025.1	11.3
Percentage change	9	8	–
2013	130.2	1058	12.3
Percentage change	12	3	–
2014	116.5	1176.7	9.9
Percentage change	−11	11	–
Q314	59.3	290.3	20.4
Percentage change	2.8	4.6	–
Q315	46	297	15.5
Percentage change	−22.4	2.3	–

Source This table is compiled by the author based on Henderson Global Dividend Index, November 2015, Edition 8

Table 69.2 Share of the Russian Federation (RF) in joint stock companies of the MICEX blue chips index

Issuer	The RF's share, %	The share in the MICEX blue chips index, %
Gazprom	50.232	17.21
Sberbank	50 + 1	14.26
VTB	60.9348	5.13
Rosneft	69.5	5.08
Transneft	78.1	4.07
ALROSA	43.93	1.63
Total		47.38

Source Authorial computation and compilation based on the Moscow Exchange data

the nature of the dividend payment has scarcely been studied in the Russian financial science so far.

Shares of state-owned joint stock companies are among the top sellers in the Moscow Exchange. Six of the fifteen issuers in the MICEX (the main index of the Moscow Exchange) blue chips index are state-owned joint stock companies. The total share of state-owned companies in the MICEX blue chips index amounts to over 47% (Table 69.2). Hence, dividends of state corporations are a crucial factor in the market that attracts both investors and other issuers.

The dividend policy features of Russian state-owned joint stock companies can be defined as follows:

1. The policy of state-owned joint stock companies pursues low dividend payouts. Dividend yield usually ranges from 3 to 5%. A relatively high dividend yield is observed in OJSC "Rostelecom," which equals 7.18% per preference share in 2013 and 6.38% per preference share in 2014 (Table 69.3).

2. Considering the data of 2014, a significant part of state-owned joint stock companies followed the trend and increased dividends or maintained the same level against the general decline in profits. However, some of the largest dividend payers, namely OJSC "Rostelecom" (regarding dividends per preference share) and OJSC AHML (Agency for Housing Mortgage Lending), appeared to be exceptions to the trend. In fact, this trend led to a slight increase in the total dividends accrued by the major contributors to the federal budget at the end of 2014 (+2.73%) against the reduction of the total net profit of these issuers by 47.3% based on the Russian Accounting Standards (RAS). Although previously state-owned joint stock companies never showed any consistent pattern in dividend payment strategies, today the majority of state-owned joint stock companies adhere to the strategy of continuous

Table 69.3 Dividend payments and dividend yield of the largest contributors to the federal budget of the RF of 2013 and 2014

Issuer and type of shares	2013		2014	
	Dividend per share, rub.	Dividend yield, %	Dividend per share, rub.	Dividend yield, %
Gazprom ordinary shares	7.2	4.91	7.2	4.91
Rosneftegaz ordinary shares	1.57713	N/A	1.8	N/A
VTB ordinary shares	0.00116	2.75	0.00117	1.52
Transneft preference shares	724.21	0.96	757.87	0.55
ALROSA ordinary shares	1.47	3.06	1.47	2
Rostelecom ordinary shares	3.11596	3.43	3.34	3.7
Rostelecom preference shares	4.84856	7.18	4.05	6.38
RusHydro ordinary shares	0.01359	1.96	0.01562	2.88
Zarubezhneft ordinary shares	1188.12	N/A	1419.79	N/A
AHML ordinary shares	52.0975	N/A	40.5511	N/A

Source Authorial computation and compilation based on the companies' official data

Table 69.4 Net profit and total dividends on shares of the state-owned companies in the MICEX blue chips index in 2013 and 2014

Issuer	2013			2014		
	Net profit, bn rub	Total dividends, bn rub	Dividend payout ratio, %	Net profit, bn rub	Total dividends, bn rub	Dividend payout ratio, %
Gazprom	1139	170.4	15	159	170.4	107.2
Sberbank	362	72.4	20	290.3	10.2	3.5
VTB	100.5	15	14.9	0.8	18	2250
Rosneft	388	136.2	35.1	350	87	24.9
Transneft	158	7.9	5	59.5	2.9	5
ALROSA	31.8	10.8	34	−16.8	10.8	N/A

Source Authorial computation and compilation based on data extracted from the sites of issuers and various news portals. Net profit was accounted for all issuers based on IFRS in order to achieve comparability

dividend payout increase, which corresponds to the aggressive type of dividend policy (Antonyan and Belomyttseva 2014). Accordingly, a number of joint stock companies increased dividend payout ratio based on the net profit (Table 69.4).

3. The largest dividend payers among joint stock companies observe the standard of 25% of the net profit dividend payout and even exceed it (Table 69.4). This issue is considered in greater detail in section On the Standard Dividend Payout Ratio for Russian State-Owned Joint Stock Companies.

4. Dividend accounting is mainly performed based on the net profit in accordance with RAS. Six of the largest dividend payers out of nine perform dividend payments based on RAS. However, there are a growing number of issuers that account dividends on the basis of the International Financial Reporting Standards (IFRS).

5. The majority of state-owned joint stock companies estimates net profit for the calculation of dividend payments without regard to the consolidated financial statements of subsidiaries and affiliates.

6. State-owned joint stock companies rarely pay interim dividends. None of the state-owned companies among the largest payers make interim dividend payments.

7. State-owned joint stock companies generally observe the regulations regarding dividend policy, publish required information on the Web site and follow other requirements related to corporate governance and disclosure; however, in some cases it is mere formality and partly implemented.

In fact, the dividend policy of Russian state-owned joint stock companies generally corresponds to the common trends in emerging markets with uncertainty and volatility typical of them.

69.3.3 On the Standard Dividend Payout Ratio for Russian State-Owned Joint Stock Companies

The standard dividend payout ratio for state-owned joint stock companies of at least 25% of the net profit was first established in 2012 following the amendments to the Edict of the Government of the Russian Federation "On the Mechanism for Determining the Status of the Russian Federation as a Shareholder in Joint Stock Companies Whose Shares Are Owned by the Federal Government" of May 29, 2006 N 774-R. A similar standard (of at least 25% but limited to consolidated net profit of the company) is also specified in the "Guidelines on Dividend Policy Development in State-Owned Joint Stock Companies" approved in December 2014. However, these documents are advisory rather than mandatory.

This standard is observed and even over-fulfilled by some large companies following their unofficial arrangements with the Federal Agency for State Property Management. Obviously, not all state corporations observe the standard. Furthermore, none of the joint stock companies has been enabled by the government to lower their dividend payout ratio in the technical sense. Issuers can choose between RAS and IFRS and commonly follow the standard that ensures minimization of dividend payments. This matter has currently transferred into the field of morality and ethics.

The ratio of 25% of the net profit is definitely low, both for private companies and even more so for state-owned joint stock companies. An average dividend payout ratio in other countries ranges from 40 to 50% of the net profit, while for state-owned joint stock companies, this figure is set even higher.

69.3.4 The Background for the Development of the Dividend Policy of Russian Joint Stock Companies

Shareholder relations and corporate governance are current areas of reform in Russia. The reform of dividend payment policy, adoption of the new Corporate Governance Code, modifications to the dividend taxation rates, as well as privatization of shares in several large state-owned enterprises had had the most significant impact on the dividend policy development of the Russian state-owned joint stock companies during 2014–2016.

Amendments to the Federal Law "On Joint Stock Companies" with regard to the dividend payments procedure came into effect on January 1, 2014. Initially, there was one and the same date both for the closure of the register of shareholders participating in the general meeting and for the dividend payment. The former and the latter were then assigned separate dates following the changes introduced in 2014. This modification complies with the international norms and best practices of equity business and eliminates the contradiction, in which the list of parties entitled to receive dividends would be compiled prior to determining the amount of dividends. It also helped to reduce the terms of dividend payments. This innovation had a positive impact on the predictability of dividend payments to minority shareholders and enhanced the transparency of the Russian stock market.

Russia's new Corporate Governance Code was adopted in December 2014. It provides a number of recommendations with regard to the dividend policy of joint stock companies, including equal and fair participation in the profit for all the shareholders. The Corporate Governance Code is designed to protect dividend rights of current shareholders and prevent dilution of their shares in the commission of corporate actions. It also advises against any means of gaining profit at the expense of society and promotes dividend payments and liquidation value. While the Corporate Governance Code is advisory for private joint stock companies, it is in fact mandatory for state-owned companies, so it contributes to the improvement of corporate governance, including dividend payments.

Dividend taxation has undergone certain changes since January 1, 2015. The personal income tax or profit tax rate for dividends of investors that are tax residents of the Russian Federation equaled 9% in 2014. In 2015, this rate increased up to 13%. The new rate applies to all dividends paid in 2015 including those accrued at the end of 2014. This tax innovation (Belomyttseva 2015) reduces the actual investors' dividend yield by 4.4%; therefore, logically, investors expect to receive larger dividends in ruble terms.

Privatization of blocks of shares of major state-owned corporations will be held in 2016. The list of state-owned companies to be privatized has not been announced yet. However, it is clear that it will comprise "ALROSA," a blue-chip company, "Bashneft" and "Aeroflot" (both included in the "second tier"). The government is planning to gain revenue from privatization in 2016 in the amount of 1 trillion rubles (about 1.6 billion euro). Privatization implies a prohibition on the purchase of shares by nonresidents, as well as receiving loans for privatization transactions in the Russian state banks. The main objective of privatization under current volatility of the ruble and the decline of oil prices is to increase state income. However, with regard to corporate governance, privatization should contribute to the growth of economic efficiency; increase the number of shareholders; increase the free float; and enhance the development of domestic capital market. Privatized enterprises are likely to increase dividend payments based on the results of 2015 in an attempt to attract new shareholders. These measures will benefit the development of the stock market and support minority shareholders.

Thus, changes to the legislation with regard to dividend payment in 2014–2016 have diverse consequences on the dividend policy of Russian joint stock companies. The mechanism of dividend payment and protection of shareholders' rights has become more simplified, more logical and less prone to violations; development of stock market of privatized state corporations and introduction of aggressive dividend payment methods are likely to follow. It also includes increased tax burden from the perspective of an investor, which eliminates the impact of the dividend payment increase.

69.4 Conclusion

Today, it is obvious that measures must be taken to improve the quality control of the dividend policy in Russian state-owned joint stock companies. In practical terms, these measures should involve clarifying the legal regulation in the following focus areas:

1. Accounting for dividends based on the amount of net profit according to IFRS and accounting for net profit based on consolidated financial statements of subsidiaries and affiliates.
2. Interim dividend payments, which are common abroad, would be advantageous to shareholders, represented by both the state and other investors.
3. Differentiation of standard payout ratio depending on the size of the government stake. We find it reasonable to differentiate minority, blocking, controlling stakes and holding an entire interest and set different dividend policy requirements. It is also rational to differentiate the standard payout ratio depending on the industry, company's field of activity, date of establishment and other criteria. Introduction of some minimal-allowed dividend payments depending on the net profit is necessary.
4. The dividend policy of state-owned joint stock companies has a significant impact on both federal budget revenues, and growth of the investment attractiveness and market value of issuers' shares in a group they belong to. These measures will probably increase investment attractiveness of state-owned joint stock companies for minority shareholders, which is crucial, since a number of joint stock companies of this category demonstrate increased dispersal of ownership. For example, shareholders of OJSC "Sberbank of Russia" comprise 214 thousand individual shareholders, while in OJSC "Gazprom," this value exceeds 500 thousand individuals.

Further investigations are required to examine the effectiveness of the dividend policy of state-owned joint stock companies, as well as the effectiveness of corporate governance in these companies, including the assignment of ratings.

References

Aivazian V, Booth B, Cleary S (2003) Emerging market firms follow different dividend policies from U.S. firms? J Financ Res 26(3):371–387. doi:10.1111/1475-6803.00064

Al-Kuwary D (2009) Determinants of the dividend policy in emerging stock exchanges: the case of GCC countries. Global Econ Financ J 2(2):38–63

Al-Malkawi H-A (2007) Determinants of corporate dividend policy in Jordan: an application of the Tobit model. J Econ Admin Sci 23(2):44–70. doi:10.1108/10264116200700007

Antonyan DG, Belomyttseva OS (2014) The specifics of the dividend policy of Russian joint stock companies. Vestnik Tomskogo Gosudarstvennogo Universiteta. Ekonomika-Tomsk State University. J Econ 3(27):79–88

Belomyttseva OS (2015) A year of volatility and plentiful dividends. Rynok Tsennykh Bumag 8(455):40–43

Black F (1976) The dividend puzzle. J Portfolio Manag 2(2):5–8

Boubakri N, Cosset JC, Guedhami O (2009) From state to private ownership: issues from strategic industries. J Bank Financ 33(2):367–379. doi:10.1016/j.jbankfin.2008.08.012

Brealey R, Myers S, Allen F (2010) Principles of corporate finance. McGraw-Hill, Maidenhead, Berkshire

Brockman P, Unlu E (2011) Earned/contributed capital, dividend policy, and disclosure quality: an international study. J Bank Financ 35(7):1610–1625. doi:10.1016/j.jbankfin.2010.11.014

Glen JD, Karmokolias Y, Miller RR, Shah S (1995) Dividend policy and behaviour in emerging markets: to pay or not to pay. IFC Discussion paper, no 26. International Finance Corporation, World Bank Group, Washington

Gul F (1999) Government share ownership, investment opportunity set and corporate policy choices in China. Pacific-Basin Financ J 7(2):157–172. doi:10.1016/S0927-538X(99)00004-9

Kowalewski O, Stetsyuk I, Talavera O (2007) Does corporate governance affect dividend policy? Evidence from Poland. Available via International Finance Corporation. http://www.ifc.org/wps/wcm/connect/00d4140048a7e522a067e76060ad5911/Kowalewski.pdf?MOD=AJPERES

Naser K, Nuseibeh R, Al-Kuwari D (2004) Dividend policy of companies listed on emerging stock exchanges: evidence from banking sector of the Gulf Co-operation Council (GCC). Middle East Bus Econ Rev 16:1–14

Pirogov NK, Kravchuk DV (2011) Lintner's model: an example of emerging capital markets. Corporate Finance 4(20):5–11

Sierpinska-Sawicz A (2014) Dividend policy of state treasury shareholding companies. J Econ Manag 18:225–241

Wardhana AR, Nugroho AB (2014) Determining optimal dividend policy for state-owned company and private-owned company. In: Proceedings of 7th Asia-Pacific business research conference. Available via WBI conference proceedings. http://www.wbiworldconpro.com/. Accessed 26 Feb 2016

Chapter 70
Personal Bankruptcy in Královéhradecký and Pardubický Regions

Jan Hospodka, Jakub Maixner and Jiří Šimůnek

Abstract This paper focuses on an analysis of debtors who applied for debt relief between the January 1, 2012, and December 31, 2013, in the Czech regions of Královéhradecký and Pardubický. Debt relief, or personal bankruptcy, is a relatively new way of declaring bankruptcy by debtors unable to repay their debt, in action only since 2008. The main focus lies in the demographic structure—age, gender, monthly income—of debtors and their absolute extent of debt. The two regions were chosen as comparative studies due to their similarity in demographics and geography. Thus, deviations in the outcomes of the research on debtor structure would be unexpected and would validate further inquiry into this topic. However, the findings prove that the similarities of demographics among the debtors in the regions prevail. This paper constitutes only a narrow section of broader research, which aims to cover the demographic structure of debtors in all of the Czech Republic.

Keywords Insolvency · Personal bankruptcy · Creditor · Debtor · Czech Republic

70.1 Introduction

The research on which this paper is based analyzes the structure of debtors who were applying for a debt relief (so-called personal bankruptcy) in years 2012 and 2013. Personal bankruptcy is one of the new methods, brought by the new

J. Hospodka (✉) · J. Maixner · J. Šimůnek
Department of Financial Accounting and Auditing, University of Economics, Prague, Nam. W. Churchilla 4, 130 67 Prague, Czech Republic
e-mail: xhosj00@vse.cz

J. Maixner
e-mail: xmaij01@vse.cz

J. Šimůnek
e-mail: xsimj76@vse.cz

© Springer International Publishing AG 2017
D. Procházka (ed.), *New Trends in Finance and Accounting*,
Springer Proceedings in Business and Economics,
DOI 10.1007/978-3-319-49559-0_70

Insolvency Act in 2008, how to solve the situation of debtors who are heavily indebted and are not able to repay all of their debts. The amount of people applying for personal bankruptcy had been rising ever since. This paper analyzes two regions in particular—Královéhradecký and Pardubický Regions. These two regions were chosen mainly because of their demographic similarity. Debtors are analyzed in relation to their age, gender, income, the overall amount of their debt and the structure of their creditors.

70.2 Debt Relief

This research focuses only on individuals who do not have any debts from their business activities. An individual firstly has to verify whether there are more than two creditors and that the debts are more than thirty days overdue (Smrčka 2011). The decision, whether an individual can undergo a debt relief or not, is carried out by the courts to which individuals can apply with their proposals. Applicant has to prove to the judge that they can repay at least 30% of the overall amount of their debts. The process of debt relief—personal bankruptcy—starts with approval of a proposal by the local regional court fulfilling all the conditions. Each individual has only one opportunity to use this institute during his or her life without any exceptions. Legislation related to personal bankruptcy has been passed only a few years ago, and the Czech law is still getting used to it (Frelichová 2008).

Once successfully applied for, the debt relief protects the debtor from further sanctions by the creditors, e.g., fines, penalties or interests. Individual undergoing a personal bankruptcy is able to fulfill the debt obligations by two ways—to repay at least 30% of their debts using the repayment plan in the next 5 years following the successful debt relief application or by monetization of their assets. First method is the most frequently used and poses mandatory court supervision over the debtor for the whole time of the repayment plan. To have regular and sufficient income is primary condition to use this method. All of the income of the debtor is used to satisfy the creditors exempt from the so-called subsistence minimum determined by legislation. The second less used method of debt relief consists of monetization of assets and using the money to repay the debts. This method does not require 5-year supervision, and the debt can be fulfilled at once.

70.3 Methodology

This section describes the process needed to get all necessary information for this research. Core data were acquired from the Czech Insolvency Register (Ministry of Justice of the Czech Republic 2015a) which is available online from www.isir. justice.cz. This paper mentions only the debtors registered under the Regional Courts of the Hradec Králové and Pardubice, respectively. Unfortunately, there is no way how to simply gather all the relevant data automatically and it is therefore necessary to manually download scanned.pdf files about each debtor and obtain the data from these files. The collected data were afterward put together, and via imposing a few adjustments to the relevant information was obtained using the statistical methods—especially synthesis and induction.

In order to get unbiased information, the list of debtors was reduced of duplicated individuals, who applied for a personal bankruptcy more than once and were therefore multiple times in the list, and married couples were considered as two independent individuals. In the case of multiple applications, the last proposal of a particular debtor was used as the source of data. If the last proposal was older than August 31, 2014, the input data were taken from the proposal just before this date. This measure guarantees a higher comparison within the region and also between all remaining regions of the Czech Republic. Another problematic group of individuals were debtors that have the combination of personal and business debts. Only the personal are reflected in this research (i.e., business debts are abstracted debts). These adjustments were introduced in order to get the more accurate research and enable comparison between different regions.

The income of all debtors is divided into three groups—gross income, social contributions (including gifts) and net earnings. The gross income was adjusted onto a net income using the effective margin rate of taxation. All income units in the text below are displayed as a net income—adjusted gross income + social contributions + net income. The creditors are divided into three groups as the banking institutions, non-banking financial institutions and other (e.g., insurance companies, state institutions or individuals). As a method to sort the creditors into each group, the list of monetary financial institutions in the Czech Republic handled by the Czech National Bank (CNB 2015) was used.

The analyzed period starts from January 1, 2012, until the December 31, 2013. Because of the amount of debtors who applied for a personal bankruptcy in the analyzed period of time, the research was limited to 10% of all debtors, meaning every tenth debtor who applied for a debt relief.

70.4 Results

The primary aim of this research was to compare debtors in the Královéhradecký Region and Pardubický Region in relation to the number of inhabitants living in each of the regions. In order to successfully do this, a table presenting population numbers in both regions was needed. According to the Czech Statistical Office, the population of the examined regions was very similar in all age groups. Both regions have above 500 thousand people living in them with Královéhradecký Region having around 40 thousand more inhabitants than Pardubický Region. This fact was substantially important throughout the whole research. Table 70.1 shows the absolute demographic data of the regions and was used as a base for conclusions of this research.

Table 70.1 Demographic distribution of population

		Královéhradecký Region	Pardubický Region
Total population		547,916	511,627
Age group	0–14	79,127	75,093
	15–64	374,898	352,543
	65 and more	92,020	82,330
Gender	Males	268,967	252,310
	Females	278,949	259,317

Source Czech Statistical Office (2015)

Table 70.2 Successful proposals and unemployment rates in 2013

	Královéhradecký Region (%)	Pardubický Region (%)
The proportion of successful proposals	82.58	80.41
Unemployment rate	8.2	8.4

Source Ministry of Justice of the Czech Republic (2015a), Czech Statistical Office (2015)

Even though there are not significant differences between the populations' numbers in the two regions, for the purpose of this research relative numbers were considered more appropriate. Table 70.2 shows the percentage of successful proposals and unemployment rates in the two regions.

One can say that the proportion of (un)successful proposals will be positively correlated with the macroeconomic indicator of unemployment rate. That is not the case with bankruptcy proposals. Since the aforementioned law came into force in 2008, the number of proposals has been rising. On the other hand, unemployment rate was volatile throughout the same period and even in years with low unemployment rate, proposals for bankruptcy rose. It is necessary to mention that insolvency process for the individuals is not primarily intended for unemployed people. As it will be shown further, about half of debtors has net monthly income in the amount of 15–25 thousand CZK which is below the average wage in the Czech Republic. As mentioned above, there is no significant correlation between these two measurements and reasons for lower amount of approved proposals should be sought somewhere else. The cause which most often affects the approval of the debt relief is the lack of formal information that debtor must provide (Table 70.3).

Looking at the gender-based portion of insolvent population, again, the two regions seem very similar. Probably, the only significant difference is the portion of young debtors. While Královéhradecký Region has around 1% of males and females between the age of 15 and 24 years of all debtors, in Pardubický Region 3.4% of all male debtors are between 15 and 24 years old and more than 4% of female debtors in the same age group. The proportion of indebted men and women then proceeds to be almost the same in both regions with minor distinctions until the 45–54 age group. In Pardubický Region, more women in this age group are

Table 70.3 Age- and gender-based portion of insolvent population

		15–24 (%)	25–29 (%)	30–34 (%)	35–44 (%)	45–54 (%)	55+ (%)	Total (%)
Královéhradecký Region	Men	1.1	9.9	13.7	31.8	24.7	18.7	49.2
	Women	1	10.1	12.2	26.6	23.4	26.6	50.8
Pardubický Region	Men	3.4	11.1	13.7	33.3	25.6	12.8	50.9
	Women	4	12.4	12.4	18.6	29.2	23	49.1

Source Ministry of Justice of the Czech Republic (2015a)

indebted. On the other hand, in Královéhradecký Region more men are indebted. But if we compare our outputs with gender distribution in those regions according to the Czech Statistical Office, we come to the conclusion that debtors' distribution is the same for those who submit a proposal and whole population of the region.

Interesting fact is that women above 55 years tend to become debtors more than men in the same age category. This can be mildly influenced by the men's lower life expectancy. Additionally, it is much clearer that a person becomes more susceptible to fall under bankruptcy pressure when crossing the age of 35. Basically every group with age 35+ has double digits of the portion of the insolvent population. Considering age, most debtors are 35 years old or older. It is probably due to the fact that people younger than 35 years either did not have time to make a lot of debts or usually think that their financial situation is not as bad as it seems and believe to handle it in the future, maybe even by taking another loan.

As we observed the highest digits in the group of 35–44 years of age, we also tried to explain why this group becomes the most endangered by the necessity of proposing a debt relief. We can see an association with the increasing age of getting married. It can very much be the fact why troubles with debts hit the older group than we could assume (instead of group 25–34 years of age the group 35–44 gets hit). There are many ways how to measure an average age of getting married, but we should take into account that only first marriages make the difference, because if a person has already been through the divorce, then most likely will not have kids again and will not build a family again. This leads to the fact that mostly first-time marriages will produce children. Therefore, we come up with the need of going debt for these families. The pressure is even stronger when Czech Republic does not support new families adequately nowadays.

We can easily see the link between the most indebted age group and this relatively high age average of entering a marriage from the Czech Statistical Office reports. The average age reported is 32.3 years for men and 29.8 years for women. Whether they have children right after the marriage or not, the problems with repaying loans come to them usually few years later. This above-mentioned fact might be one of the driving forces why the age group of 35–44 is the most common that has problems with indebtedness. Looking at the total numbers, there is not a significant correlation between debtors' gender and declaring a bankruptcy since the gender allocation of debtors in both regions is almost the same.

It is also vital to mention that the ratio of debtors with a university degree tends to be insignificant when compared to the amount of debtors without a degree. This might be explained by better education in financial matters among these people and also by the fact that in the Czech Republic university education is free of charge. On the other hand, in countries such as the USA where student loans are considered quite common, the number of university graduates tends to be higher (Field and Bauman 2014).

Figure 70.1 shows the insolvent individuals related to their net monthly income. The debtors with income lower than 5 thousand CZK a month are not the most frequent ones among those who successfully submit a proposal. There are two possible explanations. First, with such low income, banks do not usually loan money and if you cannot borrow money, you cannot fall into insolvency. Second reason is that non-banking institutions which take advantage of people with very low income and offer them loans with higher interest rates often add additional cost of debts (fees, penalties). With such a low income, it is almost impossible to fulfill the necessary condition of repaying at least 30% of its debts.

On the other hand, people with income over 35 thousand CZK do not usually need a debt relief, because their income is big enough to handle extra expenses or even to pay the debts. People with higher income usually have better financial literacy as well. Most debtors who successfully submit proposals have income between 10 and 25 thousand CZK, which is below the average wage in the Czech Republic. There is no significant difference between the regions. Most of the people that ask for debt relief belong among the income groups of 10–15 thousand CZK and 15–25 thousand CZK. As with the previous tables, no significant differences between the regions can be found in Fig. 70.1.

The research then analyzed debtors according to their debts, and as with the income, the results of regions were very similar. There is less than 10% of those with debt below 200 thousand CZK in both regions. It is mainly caused by the need

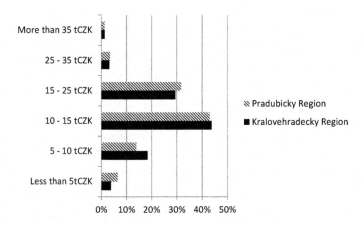

Fig. 70.1 Debtors according to their net monthly income. *Source* Ministry of Justice of the Czech Republic (2015a)

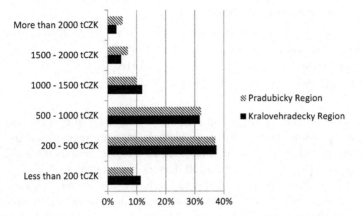

Fig. 70.2 Debtors according to the amount of their indebtedness e. *Source* Ministry of Justice of the Czech Republic (2015a)

for the debt relief itself. Most people are able to repay this debt and do not need to submit a proposal. On the other end of the scale, there are people with debts over a million CZK. It is also a small proportion of proposals for debt relief, but it is most probably due to the inability to repay at least 30% of debts (Fig. 70.2).

The average debt value of each approved debtor does not differ between the two regions. About 7 out of 10 debtors owe amounts between 200 and 1000 thousand CZK. Basically if lower than bottom bound the person does not need to ask for a debt relief. Furthermore, not many institutions are willing to loan more when a person is already heavily indebted. Our assumption was that higher income should allow a person to reach a higher value of taken debt. This is supported by the willingness of either banking institutions or non-banking institutions to loan more if a person earns more. In another words, the upper limit of total debt for a higher-income individuals is set higher comparing to lower-income individuals. Authors of this research realize that the bounds set up by them might be too wide to catch such a difference in total value of debt that would be caused by relatively small difference in incomes.

Finally, one of the most important conditions of the insolvency process is the plurality of the creditors. Every debtor must have at least two. Only very few have debts just to one type of creditor. Those are usually mortgages provided by banks in combination with consumer loans from different non-banking institutions. The debtors have mostly all three types of creditor groups. It is common to use loans provided by non-banking institutions to repay other debts—energy, rent, mortgage, etc.

Table 70.4 shows the percentage numbers in relation to the total number of debtors for each region and their indebtedness to different creditor groups. It is thus evident that not only vast majority of debtors owe to more than one creditor, but also to various types of creditors. As mentioned above the most common is a combination of consumer loans (in table mostly represented by the non-banking

Table 70.4 Indebtedness to different creditor groups

	Banking creditors (%)	Non-banking creditors (%)	Others
Královéhradecký Region	84.32	90.27	70
Pardubický Region	85.22	91.3	53.04

Source Ministry of Justice of the Czech Republic (2015a)

creditors group) and mortgages (in table mostly represented by the banking creditors group). More than 90% of all debtors in both regions are indebted to non-banking institutions. The least represented creditor group is the group, others, in Pardubický Region; only 53% of all debtors are indebted to this group.

According to the outcomes of this research, we can assume that there is often strong dependence on certain variables such as net income or total amount of debt. Comparing the two regions in the Czech Republic showed mostly very similar results in all categories for both of them. The success rate of a debt proposal is very high in both regions. Other results similar for both regions are the debtors' net incomes. The most indebted people are among those whose income is between 10 and 25 thousand CZK. Gender distribution among debtors in the regions showed one expected and one surprising result. The majority of debtors are people older than 35 years, and among the age group of people older than 55 years, women are more indebted than men.

The most common debtor in the regions announces bankruptcy before his or her total debt reaches one million CZK. On the other hand, most of all debts are higher than two hundred thousand CZK. Most debtors in both regions are indebted toward non-banking institutions, whereas the least represented creditor group is others. It is then to no surprise that in each of the examined regions more than half of the region's debtors are indebted toward all creditor groups.

70.5   Conclusion

In this paper, a comparison of individuals applying for a debt relief has been made between two regions in the Czech Republic. Both regions share rather similar economic characteristics, and it was therefore highly probable that the debtors in each region would not differ significantly when it comes to their age, gender, income and the overall amount of their debt. This hypothesis has proven to be correct. In both regions, the most common income group is between 12 and 25 thousand CZK per month and the amount of debt yet to be paid was between 200 thousand CZK and 1000 thousand CZK. A very interesting fact has come up during the research, and that is the fact that in the oldest age group 55+ women were more frequent among debtors than men, whereas in most of the younger groups, men were more frequent.

Acknowledgments This article has been prepared with the financial support of Internal Grant Agency of the University of Economics in Prague, which authors gratefully acknowledge.

References

Czech National Bank, Czech Republic (2015) Database ARAD. Available through: http://www.
cnb.cz/docs/ARADY/HTML/index.htm. Accessed 7 Nov 2015

Czech Statistical Office, Czech Republic (2015) Public database. Available through: http://vdb.
czso.cz/vdbvo/uvod.jsp. Accessed 20 Feb 2016

Field K, Bauman D (2014) The pitch: debt relief. The reality: borrowers may well pay more.
Chron High Edu 60(44):A4–A8. Academic Search Complete, EBSCOhost. Available through:
http://search.proquest.com.zdroje.vse.cz/docview/1553769735?pq-origsite=summon.
Accessed 29 Sept 2014

Frelichová K (2008) Oddlužení neboli osobní bankrot. In: Aplikované právo

Insolvency Act 2008. (law no. 182/2006 Sb.) Prague: MVCR

Ministry of Justice, Czech Republic (2015a) Insolvency register. Available through: https://isir.
justice.cz/. Accessed 25 Oct 2015

Smrčka L (2011) The relation between indebtedness of the government, public sector and
households in the Czech Republic. In E. Jircikova, E. Pastuszkova, & J. Svoboda (EDS.), 5th
International Scientific Conference on Finance and the Performance of Firms in Science,
Education, and Practice, Zlín, Czech Republic: Tomas Bata University in Zlín 433–446

Chapter 71
Existence of Size Premium: A Review of Literature and Suggestions for Future Research

Premysl Krch

Abstract The text provides a summary of previous research on the existence of size premium as a part of discount rate. The review shows that the studies provide very different findings. However, some common points may be identified. First, there are long periods with size premium being non-present in the markets. Second, the results of analyses show significant differences between the individual national markets. Third, the liquidity factor seems to play role in size factor.

Keywords Discount rate · Size premium · Fama–French · CAPM

71.1 Introduction

The valuation theory works with the concept of the value as a sum of future benefits given to the holder of the asset. This concept has changed gradually from the simple models of return period and future nominal gains to the models based on the present value of the future cash flows.

Assuming the market value as a proxy level of value for this report, the substance of opportunity costs is based on the assumption that the average market investor able to make diversified investments requires a return from the investment which is equal to the return that can be achieved from an alternative investment. This concept has also become a core of the weighted average cost of capital model (WACC) with the use of capital asset pricing model (CAPM). This model has become the worldwide most recognized and used approach to develop the discount rate and, although it has raised significant critical notes as well, it has proved as one of the most reliable models of discount rate and cost of equity development.

The classic CAPM model works with the following formula:

P. Krch (✉)
Department of Corporate Finance, University of Economics, Prague,
Nam. W. Churchilla 4, 130 67 Prague, Czech Republic
e-mail: pkrch@seznam.cz

© Springer International Publishing AG 2017 771
D. Procházka (ed.), *New Trends in Finance and Accounting*,
Springer Proceedings in Business and Economics,
DOI 10.1007/978-3-319-49559-0_71

$$C_e = R_f + \beta * \text{ERP} \tag{71.1}$$

where

C_e is the cost of equity
R_f is a risk-free rate, the reference rate of a minimum market risk which every
         market participant is exposed to
β is a beta coefficient, describing a volatility of a particular share compared to
         the capital market as a whole.
ERP   is a risk premium of the capital market as a whole.

This classic model was later broadened for other variables into its current form:

$$C_e = R_f + \beta * \text{ERP} + R_c + R_s + R_{cs} \tag{71.2}$$

where R_c is a risk premium of a particular national market compared to the reference country used as a proxy for R_f, beta and ERP variables.

R_{cs} is an adjustment for a risk of specific nature, which does not impact the market as a whole, but is relevant solely for the appraised company.

R_s stands for the risk premium for the size of the company. This premium is a subject of this text. Providing a summary of the relevant literature, I am aiming to define topics of interest for my further research which should be a core of my doctoral thesis work.

71.2   Current Knowledge and Findings

The reason, why the size premiums became relevant in corporate valuation practice, is according to Pratt et al. (2010 p. 40) mainly the fact that the empirical studies show that the returns reported by the small companies were regularly substantially higher than it would correspond to the original CAPM model. As the authors suggested, the growing return for small size of enterprises may be identified in the whole market from the original CAPM model. As the authors highlight, the growing return in relation to the decreasing size of the company can be visible in the whole market, but most notably in the segment of small companies. Also, they remind that the higher risk of small companies is not the only explanatory variable of the increased return in the CAPM model. It is a risk in excess to the simple variation interpreted using the beta coefficient. Furthermore, the relationship between the development of the large and small companies seems to correlate in the long term, which leads the authors to the hypothesis that the historical return data may provide a useful guidance for the future performance estimate as well.

Fama and French made their own research on the empirically different results of CAPM compared to the CAPM theory. In their own study, they confirmed that the size of the firm (measured with market capitalization) together with other factors explain the results which had been explained by beta so far. Based on their findings, they formulated own three-factor model, which can be explained with the following formula:

$$E_{ri} = R_f + (B_i \times ERP) + s_i \times SMB + h_i \times HML$$

where

R_f and ERP   are defined the same way as already described above
s_i is a factor of company's sensitivity on size variable
SMB   is a premium of small versus large companies
h_i is a factor of company sensitivity on the book to market value of equity variable,
HML   is premium reflecting the company ratio of the book and market value (value effect).

This model has been later verified and followed by various studies, which provided both confirming and denying own researches.

Griffin (2002), studied a question whether the time series of international equity returns are better explained using the global version of the three-factor model FF or using the national versions. The results showed that the models based on the national market data performed better than the models which used the aggregated global data.

Buus (2008) provided a research of academic studies on existence, origin and relevance of HML and SMB premiums. His compiled findings showed that the conclusions of individual studies substantially differed; however, the both factors were treated as a certain premium for risk which has to be undergone. On the one hand, the author highlights the fact that the question of mutual relationship between the equity index constructions, the size factor and the beta was not explained sufficiently.

In practice, the broadest recognition have been earned by the studies published by two companies—Morningstar/Ibbotson Associates and Duff and Phelps. The both studies are based on the empirical results of trading in the US markets. Let us provide a brief summary of both studies:

The Ibbotson SBBI Yearbook study (further referred to as "SBBI") was published by 2013. Since 2014, the study is not published anymore. The study analysed equity shares traded in the NYSE, AMEX and NASDAQ markets. The primary data used were the databases of the Center for Research in Security Prices, operated by the University of Chicago Booth School of Business (further referred to as CRSP). Data used for analyses represented a time series since 1926. The risk premiums were then classified according to the size deciles. For each decile, the authors then calculated

- beta,
- arithmetic average of return,
- current difference between the return and the risk-free rate,
- difference between the return according to the CAPM and the risk-free rate,

- the difference between the return and the result according to the CAPM. The difference was explained as the size premium (calculation was performed with an adjusted beta).

The resulting decile statistics of size premium with the use of adjusted beta has become a classic output of this analysis. Later issues provided more detailed segmentation of 10th decile first into 2 groups and later even to 4 groups. Such segmentation also showed that the growth in size premium for the larges companies of the 10th decile was relatively low compared to the 9th decile, whereas the smallest companies of the 10th decile showed substantially higher returns.

The criticism of SBBI analyses is usually based on the fact that the primary and in fact the only criterion is the market capitalization. For this reason, I would personally suggest using rather multi-criterion assessments.

The Duff and Phelps analyses started being issued since 1999 as a continuing edition of previous analyses by Roger Grabowski and his team. The size factor is considered, in the later issues, based on 8 criterions: market value of equity; book value of equity; average net profit over the last 5 years; market value of the invested capital; total assets; average EBITDA over last 5 years; total sales; number of employees.

The publicly traded companies were divided into 25 portfolios based on each criterion. Every year, the portfolio were revisited and rebalanced.

Apart from the 25 portfolio division, the study provides also a split to 10 deciles. In general, this study can be assessed as much more sophisticated than the previous SBBI studies.

Álvarez-Otero et al. (2006) worked out the study analysing the size effect on the firms entering the Madrid stock exchange based on 111 IPO over 1985–1997. The sample was divided into the group of small and large companies. The data showed that the undervaluation prior to the IPO compared to the later market valuation using the trading data was 15.34% for the large companies and 8.4% for the small companies. The results therefore showed opposite results than the US data. In the long term, 3 of 4 companies showed negative returns; however, any conclusions proving that the large companies performed better were statistically insignificant.

KPMG (2013) provided a study showing, among other factors, that approximately one-half of the Australian appraisers used the size premium. The value of such premium was by 5% for the companies below 250 MUSD of market value and declined with the growing market value. For the companies over 1 billion USD of market value the premium was zero. As the source, 38% used the SBBI data, 29% used own analyses, 24% used own estimates and 10% of respondents used other way of size premium development.

PriceWaterhouseCoopers (2014) study in Norway found that 83% of 188 respondents confirmed using of the size premium. The study also provided estimated value range for the premium—the smallest category for market value less than 100 million NOK showed the median value of 4–5% with substantial spread between the individual answers. For the value over 5 billion NOK, the premium was irrelevant. For comparison, the study also provided the information that the

Swedish companies with the market value below 100 million SEK were valued with 3.7% size risk premium.

Yermack (1996) studied the question of size indirectly. His findings collected over 1984–1991 showed that the value of the company is in opposite relationship to the number of its executive board members.

On the other hand, there is a quite broad group of opponents of the size premium use in valuation. Let us highlight some of these papers:

Horowitz et al. (2000) analysed the average monthly returns and using the cross-sectional regressions they studied the relation between the size and return. They identified difference between the annual returns of small and large companies to achieve 13% over 1963–1981. However, in the period beginning from 1982 the difference was negative −2%. Furthermore, eliminating the companies smaller than 5 million USD of market value from the sample, any statistically significant size effects on return disappeared. The conclusion was that the size should not be treated as a systematic variable of risk.

Graham et al. (2015) arrived at similar conclusion in their CFO Survey. The authors did not receive any signals from the gathered answers that would prove the existence of the size premium.

The approach based on the historical size premiums criticized also Damodaran (2015), who highlighted the fact that over the years 1981–2014, the average annual returns of small cap company shares were in average lower by 0.18% than the market as a whole.

One of the possible reasons may have been identified by Ibbotson (2013), who arrived at conclusion that the historical returns of the small companies differed significantly depending on the liquidity. If the returns according to the CAPM do not behave similarly between the groups with different liquidity, then the suggested conclusion was that a substantial portion of what was originally treated as a size premium is in fact the risk factor compensating the investors for holding the shares with worse liquidity.

Torchio et al. (2013), prepared a study based on an analysis of relationship between the size and liquidity. The premiums were split into deciles using the size and liquidity, working a similar way as the SBBI analyses. Finally, having used the split into the individual size deciles into the high a low liquidity groups they concluded that for the first 8 size deciles with the high liquidity, no size premium was present. For the 9th and 10th decile, the premium achieved level around 2–2.5%.

De Franco et al. (2012) studied the way how the analysts providing the investment recommendations choose the guideline comparable companies for their analyses. The authors confirmed that the analysts tend to choose the guideline companies with similar size, leverage, asset turnaround, industry and traded volumes. At the same paper, they, however, informed that many analysts tended to pick those companies with higher valuation. This may lead to overly optimistic estimated of target prices. From my point of view, it is not clear whether the size mattered in any other way than just as arbitrary criterion chose at the beginning of their research.

For emerging markets, a comprehensive review of previous researches was performed by Ross (2014). His reviews showed clearly that whereas the value effect (in the meaning of HML as used by Fama and French) can be clearly confirmed even with stronger effect than in the developed markets, the size effect resulted in unclear results and the new works even did not find any statistically significant difference between the companies with the small and large market capitalization.

The trend of the recent decades is the increasing interconnection among the national economies and markets. Hand in hand with this trend, new opportunities arise for investors in new regions. Such attempts may, however, face an informational barrier caused by national specifics and different accounting methods. For this reason, the national accounting standards undergo gradual unification in order to provide higher comparability and explanatory value of the accounting data, mainly in order to strengthen the protection of investors in the capital markets. The European Parliament and Council issued the Directive No. 1606/2002 on 19 July 2002 of implementation of the International Accounting Standards, which obliged all publicly traded companies in the European capital markets to keep their books in accordance with the IAS/IFRS standards.

In this context, the impacts of mandatory accounting according to the IAS/IFRS on improvement of comparable data have become a subject of various studies. As this question may have influence on the data used as a proxy for equity share research including my own research, I am taking opportunity to mention some of these studies, as they resolve mainly the question of underlying data comparability.

Yip et al. (2012) concluded that the situation was improving. For example, the obligatory IFRS reporting in European Union helped with the better comparability among the companies from different countries. The reason was not only the obligation to report in IFRS, but also higher quality of published information and overall improvement of corporate governance in the companies.

Chen et al. (2013) studied whether the IFRS introduction in Europe led also to the improvement in the reported profits. The conclusion was that although the quality of information had increased in general, there were differences among individual countries. The major improvements had been achieved by several countries in the Western Europe. Also, they find that the capital markets overreacted (with the exception of the UK) positively to the shift towards IFRS, than it would reasonably correspond to the growth in profit quality. Authors have therefore confirmed several previous studies reaching the same conclusion. From my personal perspective, this phenomenon may be explained with the higher demanded standard for the provided information, which leads the companies to the establishment of a sufficient analytic framework of operation. This seems to be very costly; on the one hand, however, such ability enables substantially higher quality of communication with the market investors, which makes the companies also more attractive for analysts and investors.

Compiling a dataset to be used for a research, a question of applicability of data from various national markets in one research comes into play. One can assume that if such markets are subject to similar market impacts, their development in time should be also similar. For our particular region of interest, I am assuming the

Czech Republic, its neighbouring countries and several other countries from the broader European region.

Dajčman et al. (2014) verified the degree of similarity in the development of the national capital markets in the Central Europe. For their study, they chose indexes of stock exchanges in the Czech Republic, Hungary and Slovenia as the less developed countries on the one side and of stock exchanges in Austria, France, Germany and the UK as the more developed countries on the other side. The found that the same movements of the different market indexes explained 68–81% of deviations. The indexes in the Czech Republic and Hungary showed a stronger mutual correlation as well as together compared to the developed countries' indexes, than the development of the Slovenian index. The strongest relationship of these two country indexes to the developed country indexes was observed for Austria, which the authors explained partly to the common historical groundings and also to the strong mutual economic relations. The results were in line with Dajčman's previous research (2012), in which he found that the correlation changes over time, growing temporarily in the periods of economic crises. The strongest correlation of the PX index was observed with the ATX, WIG20 and CAC40 indexes; the least correlated index was the LJSEX.

Avdulaj et al. (2013) studied the benefits of investment diversification on the comparison of the development of the Czech PX index to the German DAX index over 2008–2013. They found out that the benefits of a potential diversification were strongly volatile. That rejected the hypothesis that the benefits of diversification were reduced due to the crisis. The exception was that as a result of a strong mutual relation and assumed future acceptance of the EUR, although not decided when, the benefits of diversification should be gradually erased between these two markets.

A similar study was performed by Baruník et al. (2013), who extended their research from relation between PX and DAX also to the WIG and BUX indexes over the most intensive period of the financial crisis in 2008–2009. They concluded that the correlations and their intensity changes over time. Also they observed that the high-frequency trading provide a general low mutual correlation between the CEE countries. In opposite to other global regions, the CEE region does not seem to provide a remarkably strong relation between the leading regional economy and its peripheral economies.

Borys et al. (2009) worked a study testing the presence of value and size effects in the capital markets of the Visegrad Four countries—the Czech Republic, Slovakia, Poland and Hungary. Their research based on Fama–French model showed a lower size effect than was observable for the US companies; nevertheless, the effect was still observable.

Minović et al. (2014) performed a research based on the data from the Croatian stock exchange over 2005–2009, aiming on the overall market impact, the size impacts, the liquidity factor impacts on the required returns on the Croatian stock exchange. The results showed that the liquidity and size factors have significant impact on the price creation. Also they confirm the Fama–French model, adding that such factors may help to describe the more accurate description of the market imbalances.

In opposite, Zaremba et al. (2015) prepared a study of the impacts of a low liquidity and the transaction costs on the value premium the size premium and the momentum premium, based on the data gathered from the CEE countries including the Czech Republic over 2000–2013. The authors have also identified the significant value and size premium at the one side. However, the impacts of the low liquidity and transactional costs were fully decisive. After adjustment for them, both premiums were erased in fact.

Foye (2015) made a comparison whether it is better to use the inputs for more factor models for the individual countries or for the Europe as a whole. The results showed that the data for value premium and momentum premium were present all over the Europe. On the other hand, the premium for size had relation to the particular countries. Although the SMB premiums for the Europe as a whole were positive, the results were statistically insignificant. At least Italy, Netherlands, Sweden, Switzerland and UK showed, however, an existence of a strong size premium. The premium was observed also in other countries, among others Germany, Poland. The Czech Republic was not included in this research.

Looking into the Czech Republic, we can mention also the work by Prodělal (2012), who tried to transfer the results of the Morningstar SBBI studies to the Czech environment. Generally, this work was based on author's own suggested decile intervals to be applied instead of the decile intervals derived from the NYSE. From my point of view, this solution is rather an emergency solution. Furthermore, the work did not provide any guidance to the methodology which had led the author to exactly those intervals which he suggested.

Somewhat more useful was a survey performed by Kolouchová et al. (2010), who tried to describe practices used by the Czech appraisers. One of the topics was also the way of use and the parameters used in CAPM model. The collected responses showed that approximately 40% of the Czech appraisers use the size premium, in the range between 0.1 and 13% points and with 3 p.p. median value. About one-third used the SBBI study data, the remainder used mostly own expert estimates.

71.3   Conclusion

The above-mentioned overview shows that the question of existence of the size premium does not provide a clear answer neither in global scale, nor in Central Europe nor in the Czech Republic. Depending on the used data, period of observation, methodology and adjustment factors, if applied, the results of individual studies yield very different results. However, some findings may be identified repeatedly.

First, several studies showed that the size premium becomes often statistically insignificant for long time periods, the recent two decades being one such period as well. This leads many authors to the assumption that the concept of size premium is obsolete and disproved. In difference from the English-speaking markets, only few studies were performed to check this in the region of the Central Europe.

Second, some studies show that there are significant differences between individual countries in the question of size premium.

Third, the newer works mention the liquidity as a key variable in relation to the size factor. After adjustment for liquidity, the size premium often almost or fully disappears.

As a starting point for an anticipated future research, one can treat the following steps as useful:

First, work out own comprehensive research on existence of the size premium in the markets of the Central Europe, as the region which is economically, politically, legally and culturally the closest region to the Czech Republic. I suggest specifying this market using the following countries: Czech Republic, Slovakia, Poland, Hungary, Germany, Austria.

The second sphere that would be highly welcomed for closer research is an existence of differences between the individual national markets that made the whole data sample. From practical point, however, this approach would face the problems with limited number of publicly traded companies mainly in the Czech Republic and Slovakia. Therefore, I suggest an alternative solution, working with two groups of countries—one group comprising the Czech Republic, Slovakia, Poland and Hungary and the second group comprising the neighbouring developed markets of Germany and Austria.

The third question of liquidity is a crucial variable, which may significantly influence the interpretation of results achieved in the first two fields of interest. Nevertheless, with respect to the enormous scope of anticipated analyses in the first two points I consider this point rather as an open field for a subsequent research that may work with the results from analysis of the first two points as well.

Acknowledgments This is paper has been prepared as a part of and under financial support of the research scope of Faculty of Finance and Accounting of University of Economics in Prague No. IP 100040, which author gratefully acknowledges.

References

Álvarez-Otero S, Victor GMM (2006) The size effect of firms going public on the spanish capital market. In: Gregoriou GN (ed) Initial public offerings: an international perspective. Elsevier, Oxford vol 6. pp 65–79

Avdulaj K, Barunik J (2013) Can we still benefit from international diversification? the case of the Czech and German stock markets. Finance Úvěr-Czech J Econ Finance 63(5)

Baruník J, Vácha L (2013) Contagion among Central and Eastern European stock markets during the financial crisis. Finance Úvěr-Czech J Econ Sci 63(5)

Borys MM, Zemčík P (2009) Size and value effects in the Visegrad Countries. CERGE-EI. [Online] 09 2009. [Citace: 30. 11. 2015]. https://www.cerge-ei.cz/pdf/wp/Wp391.pdf

Buus T (2008) HML a SMB prémie v akademické literatuře - výše a podstata. Český finanční a účetní časopis. 2, 31–41

Chen Q, Jiang Y, Skeratt L (2013) Did the market overreact to the mandatory switch to IFRS in Europe? Brunel University London, London, July 2013. Working paper no. 13–26

Dajčman S (2012) The dynamics of return comovement and spillovers between the Czech and European stock markets in the period 1997–2010. Finance Úvěr-Czech J Econ Sci 62(4)

Dajčman S, Kavkler A (2014) Wavelet analysis of stock return energy decomposition and return comovement—a case of some Central European and developed european stock markets. Ekonomie Manage XVII(1)

Damodaran A (2015) The small cap premium: where is the beef? musings on markets. [Online] 04. 11. 2015. [Cited: 12. 30. 2015]. http://aswathdamodaran.blogspot.cz/2015/04/the-small-cap-premium-fact-fiction-and.html

De Franco G, Hope OK, Larocque S (2012) Analysts' choice of peer companies. August 08, 2012

Foye J (2015) A new perspective on the size, value, and momentum effects: broad sample evidence from Europe. [Online] 21. 06. 2015. [Citace: 21. 01. 2016]. https://www.google.cz/url?sa=t&rct=j&q=&esrc=s&source=web&cd=15&ved=0ahUKEwi24qSU9Z3LAhUijXIKHepc-DCs4ChAWCDswBA&url=http%3A%2F%2Fwww.iises.net%2Fproceedings%2F17th-international-academic-conference-vienna%2Ftable-of-content%3Fcid%3D26%26iid%3D27%26rid%3D4. ISBN 978-80-87927-10-6

Graham JR, Harvey CR (2015) The equity risk premium in 2015. University of Texas. [Online] 05. 29. 2015. [Cited: 12. 01. 2015]. http://faculty.mccombs.utexas.edu/keith.brown/AFPMaterial/GrahamHarvey-ERP%20Survey-5.15.pdf

Griffin JM (2002) Are the Fama and French factors global or country specific? John M Griffin—Professor of finance. [Online] 2002. [Cited: 01. 05. 2016]. http://www.jgriffin.info/Research/FFFactors.pdf

Horowitz JL, Loughran T, Savin G (2000) The disappearing size effect. Res Econ 54(1), 83–100

Ibbotson RG et al (2013) Liquidity as an investment style. Financ Anal J 69(3), 30–44

Kolouchová P, Novák J (2010) Cost of equity estimation techniques used by valuation experts. IES working paper, vol 8

KPMG (2013) Valuation practices survey 2013. KPMG Australia. [Online] 2013. [Cited: 10. 30. 2015]. https://www.kpmg.com/AU/en/IssuesAndInsights/ArticlesPublications/valuation-practices-survey/Documents/valuation-practices-survey-2013-v3.pdf

Minović J, Živković B (2014) CAPM augmented with liquidity and size premium in the Croatian stock market. Econ Res-Ekonomska Istraživanja

Pratt SP, Grabowski RJ (2010) Cost of capital in litigation: applications and examples. John Wiley & Sons, p 336 (4. vydání. s.l., 9780470944912)

PriceWaterhouseCoopers (2014) The norwegian market risk premium 2013 and 2014. [Online] 2014. [Cited: 11. 08. 2015]. https://www.pwc.no/no/publikasjoner/deals/risikopremie-undersokelse-2013-en.pdf

Prodělal F (2012) Přirážka za tržní kapitalizaci při stanovení nákladů na vlastní kapitál metodou CAPM . Znalecký portál. [Online] 17. 03. 2012. [Cit.: 05. 01. 2016]. http://www.znaleckyportal.cz/index.php?option=com_content&view=article&id=195:prirazka-za-trzni-kapitalizaci-pri-stanoveni-nakladu-na-vlastni-kapital-metodou-capm&catid=73:ekonomika-ceny-a-odhady&Itemid=113

Ross K (2014) The value and size effect in the emerging markets. Advisory research. [Online] 06 2014. [Cited: 12. 12. 2015]. http://www.advisoryresearch.com/wp-content/uploads/2014/06/Emerging-Markets-The-Value-and-Size-Effects-June-2014.pdf

Torchio F, Surana S (2013) Effect of liquidity on size premium and its implications for financial valuations. The forensic economics. [Online] 08 2013. [Cited: 12. 24. 2015.] pracovní draft. http://www.forensiceconomics.com/wp-content/uploads/2013/09/Effect-of-Liquidity-on-Size-Premium.pdf

Yermack D (1996) Higher market valuation of companies with a small board of directors. J Financ Econ 40, 185–211

Yip RWY, Young, D (2012) Does mandatory IFRS adoption improve information comparability? Acc Rev 87(5), 1767–1789

Zaremba A, Konieczka P (2015) Are value, size and momentum premiums in CEE emerging markets only illusionary? Finance úvěr-Czech J Econ Finance 65(1)

Chapter 72
Invested Capital, Its Importance, and Interpretability Within Income-Based Methods for Determining the Value of the Company

Tomáš Krabec and Romana Čižinská

Abstract The paper deals with the distortion of the economic reality in the accounting showing the volume and structure of invested capital. One of the main sources of deviations in the accounting value of assets from reality is the absence of certain assets, which the company owns but does not report them for certain reasons on its balance sheet. This is essentially the case of specific items of intangible assets, which can be divided into two categories: (1) identifiable and individually valuable intangible assets (e.g., databases, brand, domain names) and (2) primary goodwill or badwill, which occurs only when the return on invested capital (ROIC) is different from the level of WACC, i.e., the return demanded and expected by investors. We propose and name reasons for activation of identifiable intangible assets to ensure that the accounting figures reflect economic reality and are linked to the relevant opportunity costs.

Keywords Return on invested capital · Cost of capital

72.1 Introduction

Net asset value (value of invested capital) reported in the accounts compiled according to Czech accounting standards can be considered a completely irrelevant indicator for the use in valuation practice. Furthermore, in addition to it there is considerable methodological inconsistency in how the standard practice in

T. Krabec (✉)
Department of Financial Accounting and Auditing, University of Economics, Prague,
Nam. W. Churchilla 4, 130 67 Prague, Czech Republic
e-mail: krabect@vse.cz

R. Čižinská
Department of Economics, Faculty of Informatics and Management,
University of Hradec Králové, Rokitanského 62, 500 03 Hradec Králové, Czech Republic
e-mail: romana.cizinska@uhk.cz

D. Procházka (ed.), *New Trends in Finance and Accounting*,
Springer Proceedings in Business and Economics,
DOI 10.1007/978-3-319-49559-0_72

income-based valuation methods deals with the value of the capital invested. Separate category, which tends to be completely ignored by specialized Czech monographs, then is the sheer uselessness of the accounting value of the capital invested in evaluating the financial performance of the company and creation of value from the perspective of the owner.

Invested capital can be interpreted as the amount of capital tied up in assets that are necessary to ensure the operational activities of the company. It is therefore a principal set of assets necessary to operate the business. These assets which are known in the income valuation method using EVA as net operating assets (NOA) are represented by all property items, which the company uses, and which for a variety of reasons may not be reflected in the accounts. For the compilation of statutory statements according to Czech accounting standards, it is immaterial whether the enterprise has control over benefits of the asset, but what matters is the fact whether it holds ownership rights to the particular asset. In addition, however, there is an issue with the so-called identifiable intangible assets such as trademarks, patents, know-how, brand, reputation, and good relations with customers and suppliers. They embody obviously some potential future profit, but if they were not purchased, but made by the very existence and activities of the company, there is no valuation existing. Often it is not possible to determine the value of these assets with sufficient reliability—for example—because the potential future benefit does not occur with high probability.

The aim of this paper is to identify critical points within the income-based valuation methods such as discounted cash flow and economic value added, where there is a discrepancy of theoretical and economic concepts of a meaningful amount of the capital invested, respectively, in the net operating assets. The book value of assets of the company basically refers to the fact of how much was actually paid for the assets with regard to ongoing sustained reduction in purchase prices due to depreciation or a temporary reduction represented by value adjustments. The book value is thus a sort of indicative value which lacks any evidential value in the process of assessing performance and determining the value of the company (whether it be the result of any category of value). As reported by Mařík et al. (2011, p. 324): "*valuer or user of a valuation report [may] as additional information compare whether the observed valuation is higher or lower than the book value of equity and by how much. Significantly higher book value than the value based on the income may rise to the liquidation value to be found, because it shows signals that the income based value could be lower than liquidation value.*" In this case, any further operating of the business lacks sense, and the best financial result for the shareholder may be achieved by splitting, selling or liquidating of the assets of the company in some way.

All what has been said does not alter the fact that the result of the accounting valuation of assets, or equity, respectively, is a completely insignificant quantity. The price at which the asset was purchased (less an amount corresponding to its depreciation) does not match the real value of these assets—at this price, it is not normally possible neither to sell nor to repurchase the property. The second major source of deviations of the accounting value of assets from reality is then the absence of off-balance sheet commitments and especially of certain assets, which the company controls, but for certain reasons does not activate them on its balance sheet. These assets consist primarily of intangible assets, which for the purpose of this article can be divided into the following two categories:

- identifiable and individually measurable intangible assets (e.g., databases, brands, domain names);
- primary goodwill or badwill, which (as will be justified below) arises only when the return on invested capital (ROIC) is different from the level of WACC, i.e., the return demanded by investors.

72.2 The Volume of Capital Invested in Income-Based Valuation Methods

72.2.1 Discounted Free Cash Flow Method

Total income-based value of invested capital by using the discounted free cash flow can be determined by discounting cash flows from principal business operations. If we proceed from the assumption that the gross value is determined by the perpetuity, then applies that:

$$Hb = FCFF1/(WACC - g) \tag{72.1}$$

where

Hb	Gross value of the invested capital at the beginning of the year,
FCFF1	Free cash flow to the firm in the year 1,
WACC	Weighted average cost of capital,
g	Growth rate.

Free cash flow (FCFF) is quantified as the sum of operating profit after tax and depreciation after deducting gross investments in working capital and CAPEX. Gross investments less amortization represent net investment.

72.2.2 Economic Value-Added Method

Also the nature of this income-based valuation method shows that the accounting volume of invested capital is further irrelevant for the final gross value of the invested capital. The higher the capital invested, the lower the value of EVA in each year (and thus the value of MVA), but also the amount of invested capital as at the date of valuation is higher. If we proceed from the assumption that the gross value is determined by the perpetuity, then assuming zero growth rate (g) shall apply:

$$Hb = NOA0 + EVA0/WACC = NOA0 + (NOPAT0 - WACC * NOA0)/WACC$$
$$= NOPAT0/WACC \tag{72.2}$$

where

Hb	Gross value of invested capital at the beginning of the year,
NOA0	Gross value of invested capital at the beginning of the year,
EVA0	Economic value added in the year 0,
NOPAT0	Net operating profit after tax in the year 0,
WACC	Weighted average cost of capital.

If we assume the growth rate (g) different from zero, then the following applies:

$$Hb = NOA0 + EVA1/(WACC - g)$$
$$= NOA0 + (NOPAT0 * (1 + g) - WACC * NOA0)/(WACC - g), \tag{72.3}$$

$$Hb = (NOPAT0 * (1 + g) - g * NOA0)/(WACC - g)$$
$$= (NOPAT0 * (1 + g) - net\, investments)/(WACC - g) \tag{72.4}$$

where

Hb	Gross value of invested capital at the beginning of the year,
NOA0	Gross value of invested capital at the beginning of the year,
EVA1	Economic value added in the year 1,
NOPAT0	Net operating profit after tax in the year 0,
WACC	Weighted average cost of capital,
g	Growth rate.

72.2.3 The Importance of the Volume of Invested Capital in Terms of Economic Meaningfulness and Interpretability of Parameters and Valuation Results

The calculations show that for the gross final value of invested capital projected annual increase of invested capital (i.e., net investment) is thus essential rather than the absolute value of invested capital. This simplified view is obviously in the valuation theory and practice totally unacceptable. For the purpose of preparing the financial plan as part of an income-based valuation, it is absolutely necessary to perform thorough analyzes, forecasts, and justification of the individual sub-parameters, including consideration of their sectoral accessibility. By this, we mean the relative indicators of the financial plan as well: the investment rate, the net return on investment, and return on invested capital (ROIC).

If we start by preparing the financial plan forming the cornerstone of an income valuation by using standard financial statements (see Mařík et al. 2011, 2012), it will usually show a very high return on invested capital. It is because the amount of capital invested in the denominator of the calculation will be unrealistically low due to the absence of certain assets (especially identifiable intangible assets) on the balance sheet.

The result is then a methodological problem in the financial plan, consisting of a permanently higher return on invested capital, which, moreover, cannot even converge over time at the weighted average cost of capital. The problem of return on invested capital and the need for a convergence of the cost of capital is already sufficiently widely described and explained in the relevant literature (see below).

If the return on capital is not higher due to the proven and sustained existence of a strong competitive advantage, contributing to the creation of value, but only due to the fact that the financial statements do not reflect the economic reality of the company properly, then the whole process of income-based valuation is economically unjustifiable. Calculating with the assumption that the business will endlessly generate positive economic value added and profitability above the cost of capital generally really lacks economic rationale. Such a situation is known in economic theory as intramarginality of rent (see above, Marshall 1920), and is not sustainable in competitive industries over the long run.

Koller et al. (2006, p. 274) argue: *"The expected rate of return on new invested capital (RONIC) should be consistent with expected competitive conditions. Economic theory suggests that competition will eventually eliminate abnormal returns, so for many companies, set RONIC equal to WACC."* It is a well-known principle in economic theory since the late eighteenth century, the concept of competitive dynamics and the gradual elimination of the so-called economic profit and long-term availability of normal return which will reward the involvement of factors of production (see in context Stavenhagen (1969), Heuss (1965), Cox et al. (1981), Marshall (1920), Schumpeter (1986)).

Situation where return on invested capital does not converge to the level of WACC due to unjustifiably low levels of net operating assets, essentially assumes reinvestment of net cash flow at a rate of return equal to unrealistically high internal rate of return, because objectively there is not enough investment opportunities to enable such a high appreciation of funds. To address this, shortcoming economic theory has introduced a metric labeled as modified internal rate of return, which assumes reinvestment at the required rate of return (i.e., WACC).

The problem with unrealistically high return on capital due to underestimation of the volume of capital invested in the financial statements is not only at the level of interpretation. The volume of capital invested and its structure determines the level of capital costs, which must be based on its actual market structure. If the income-based valuation is not realized so that it calculates the correct absolute value of capital, it cannot be achieved that WACC will match the economically correct level. If the capital structure is determined iteratively, the actual market capital structure is obtained only by assuming that the relevant input parameters are selected properly—i.e., inter alia, the growth rate, and cash flow. To be able to quantify cash flow, it is obviously necessary to derive the level of net investment, which is the product of multiplying the growth rate (g) and the amount of capital invested.

72.3 Methodology of the Problem Solving in Relation to IFRS 3

To solve the above-mentioned problem with unrealistic volume of invested capital, we propose to activate the value of identifiable intangible assets in the financial statements of the enterprise being valued (see Čižinská and Krabec 2015a, b).

The inspiration for the design of this approach is the accounting standard IFRS 3. The accounting solution to business combinations builds simply speaking on the allocation of the purchase price on the fair value of the net assets, including real recognition and valuation of identifiable intangible assets (databases, brand, domain names, etc.). The rest of forming the difference between the fair value of the identifiable and individually valuable net assets and the purchase price consists of goodwill (see above). Goodwill reflects the value of residual unidentified (and individually not valuable) intangible assets.

When creating a financial plan, according to which a parameterization of inputs into income-based valuation model will be derived, one can also use this logic and activate all identifiable intangible assets. Even for valuation purposes, it is not required to value individual intangible assets separately (as would be required by the accounting treatment under IFRS 3), because sufficient is the information on their aggregate value. Identification of intangible assets and their separate valuation can be made subsequently with the fact that we already have a model (in calculation) confirmed information on how high is the sum of their individual values. For example, the VIM model can serve for individual valuation of identifiable intangible assets (see Čižinská, Krabec 2014).

72.4 Conclusion

The paper deals with the distortion of the economic reality in the accounting showing the volume and structure of the invested capital. One of the main sources of deviations from the accounting value of assets from reality is the absence of certain assets, which the company owns but does not report them for certain reasons on its balance sheet. This is essentially the case of specific items of intangible assets, which can be divided into two categories: (1) identifiable and individually valuable intangible assets (e.g., databases, brand, domain names) and (2) primary goodwill or badwill, which occurs only when the return on invested capital (ROIC) is different from the level of WACC, i.e., the return demanded by investors.

It is logical that the positive difference between ROIC and WACC (i.e., excess return) must be on an efficient market soon eliminated by competing investors and competitive pressure in the sector and is therefore unsustainable (competitors achieve a better payoff as they intensively invest in the creation of intangible assets).

So if return on invested capital does not exceed WACC due to verifiable and permanent existence of a strong competitive advantage, contributing to the creation of value, then the whole process of income-based valuation is economically unjustifiable. The problem of course is not only at the level of interpretation. The volume of capital invested and its structure determines the level of capital costs, which must be based on the actual market structure. If the income-based valuation is not realized so that it calculates the correct absolute value of capital, it cannot mean that the WACC and thus the cost of capital will respond to the economically correct level. Analogous in economic theory is the concept of a modified internal rate of return, which solves the problem of assuming reinvestment of net cash flow at a rate of return equal to unrealistically high internal rate of return.

Acknowledgments This paper has been prepared within the research project IP 100040 and the Project IG104026 which authors gratefully acknowledge.

References

Čižinská R, Krabec T (2014) Destroying and creating equity value through brand management: positive and negative brand impact assessment by using the VIM modelling approach. J Contemp Manag Issues 1:213–230

Čižinská R, Krabec T (2015a) Aktivace identifikovatelných nehmotných aktiv z hlediska důsledků pro výnosové ocenění podniku. Odhadce 2:44–55

Čižinská R, Krabec T (2015b) Income based valuation of IT companies: methodological issues related to invested capital [online]. In: 10th international scientific conference financial management of firms and financial institutions, pp 380–390 (7.-8. září 2015 [online]). http://www.ekf.vsb.cz/frpfi/en/conference_proceedings/

Cox H, Jens U, Markert K (1981) Handbuch des Wettbewerbs. Vahlen Verlag, München

Heuss E (1965) Allgemeine Markttheorie. Tübingen, Zürich

Koller T, Goedhart M, Wessels D (2006) Valuation. Measuring and managing the value of companies, 4th edn. Wiley, New Jersey

Mařík M et al (2011) Metody oceňování podniku - Process ocenění základní metody a postupy. Ekopress, Praha

Mařík M et al (2012) Metody oceňování podniku pro pokročilé. Hlubší pohled na vybrané problémy. Ekopress, Praha

Marshall A (1920) Principles of economics, 8th edn. Macmillan, London

Schumpeter JA (1986) History of economic analysis. Allen and Unwin, London

Stavenhagen G (1969) Geschichte der Wirtschaftstheorie. Vandenhoeck & Ruprecht, Göttingen

Chapter 73
Constructing Czech Risk-Free Yield Curve by Nelson-Siegel and Svensson Method and Their Comparison

Martin Hanzal

Abstract This article describes differentiation of risk-free interest rate which is part of discount rate within income methods of assets valuation. The main focus is on two methods—Nelson-Siegel and Svensson—and their application to Czech state bonds. The risk-free yield curve is then created on their basis, and results of these methods are mutually valuated.

Keywords Risk-free yield curve · Nelson-Siegel method · Svensson method

73.1 Introduction

According the analysis made by Podškubka (2012, p. 55), the most frequently used cost estimation of equity in Czech Republic is CAPM model. From this reason, we have to search for all of factors which affect it. Important part of this model is also risk-free interest rate.

There was a common habit in Czech and foreign praxis to use simplified risk-free rate in the meaning of united risk-free interest rate as flat yield curves. If we take a look at profitability of Czech, German or US bonds, it is obvious that this assumption is in conflict with the real situation on the market.

From this reason are today's theories such as Damodaran (2008) or Mařík (2011) closer to using differentiate risk-free interest rate for single year plans and second phase. The risk-free interest rate differentiation is recommended by Damodaran mainly for following reasons:

M. Hanzal (✉)
Department of Corporate Finance, University of Economics,
W. Churchill Sq. 4, 130 67 Prague, Czech Republic
e-mail: xhanm55@vse.cz

© Springer International Publishing AG 2017
D. Procházka (ed.), *New Trends in Finance and Accounting*,
Springer Proceedings in Business and Economics,
DOI 10.1007/978-3-319-49559-0_73

- Descending curve especially speaking of long-term risk-free rates being lower than short-term or
- When long-term rates are 4% higher than short-term rates. It means that there is a bigger difference between long and short-term rates and yield curve is steeply growing.

In other cases—according to Damodaran—the total error of using united risk-free interest rates is small. However, this opinion is not supported by any numbers and decision regarding statistical signification of the error brought into the valuation with the usage of flat yield curves is above the limit of this article.

To differentiate risk-free interest rate, it is necessary to create risk-free yield curve based on profit of risk-free assets. For this article, we consider domestic state bonds as the most suitable risk-free assets as stated in Schich (1997). Alternatively, we can even use swaps which are advised by Dvořák (2014a).

There were a lot of techniques developed to create risk-free yield curve out of bonds in case of insufficient number of zero bonds, e.g. Splines (McCulloch 1971), Polynoms of x-th grade, Smith-Wilson method (Smith and Wilson 2001), Nelson-Siegel method (Nelson and Siegel 1987), or Svensson method (Svensson 1994).

The main part of this article is also focused on creating risk-free yield curve targeting the Czech state bonds using Nelson-Siegel and Svensson methods and their information value comparison.

73.2 Usage of Nelson-Siegel and Svensson Methods in Foreign Praxis

Nelson-Siegel and Svensson methods are in foreign praxis used a lot especially for determination of inflation and interest rates estimation by central banks and models which are used to create yield curve are shown in BIS Papers No 25 (2005).

As Table 73.1 shows, the most used method of risk-free interest rate estimation is Svensson method. Model optimization is possible based on price of bonds (P) or their yield (Y). As we can see, central banks are split almost evenly regarding this question.

Table 73.1 List of central banks constructing risk-free yield curve

Central bank	Estimation method	Central bank	Estimation method
Belgium	Svensson/Nelson-Siegel (P)	Japan	Splines (P)
Canada	Splines (P)	Norway	Svensson (Y)
Finland	Nelson-Seigel (P)	Spain	Svensson (P)
France	Svensson/Nelson-Siegel (P)	Sweden	Splines/Svensson (Y)
Germany	Svensson (Y)	Switzerland	Svensson (Y)
Italy	Nelson-Siegel (P)	USA	Splines (P)

Source BIS Papers No 25 (2005)

Risk-free interest rate estimation methods Nelson-Siegel and Svensson were also researched by series of economists in different countries. Schich (1997) for Germany, Geyer-Mader (1999) for Austria, Germany, USA, Japan and GB, Aljinovič-Poklepovič-Katalinič (2012) for Croatia and Csajbók (1999), Bolder-Strelinsky (1999) or Diebold-Li (2006). We can also mention Czech authors Slavík (2001), Kladívko (2009) Hladíková-Radová (2012) and Dvořák (2014a, b).

Beginning December 2015 The European Insurance and Occupational Pensions Authority (EIOPA) has been publicizing risk-free yield curves for 52 states including Czech republic. Yield curves are being publicized on monthly basis to the last day of the month. Smith-Wilson method is used for their creation. In case of Czech republic, swap interest rates are used as risk-free assets where EIOPA methodology suggests adjustment due to the existence of credit risk of swap rates which is not necessary regarding bonds.

73.3   Theoretical Fundamentals of the Methods

73.3.1   Nelson-Siegel Method

The Nelson-Siegel method introducing parametrical model of spot and forward curves estimation was first described in 1987. The main advantage of this model is his flexibility allowing him to describe every basic shape of yield curves. Model is recommended for economics with lesser number of bonds (<30) where the risk of over-parameterizing is lower compared to method Svensson. Nelsen-Siegel model is based on forward rates estimation through solutions of differential equations of second grade with real identical roots and constant right side. Then, we can see following equation for forward rate.

$$r(m) = \beta_0 + \beta_1 * e^{(-m/\tau_1)} + \beta_2 * \left[\left(\frac{-m}{\tau_1} \right) * e^{(-m/\tau_1)} \right] \qquad (73.1)$$

where β_0, β_1 and β_2 are estimated parameters, τ_1 is estimated time constant, and m is due time.

By integrating the equation, we get an expression describing spot yield curve:

$$i(m; \beta_0; \beta_1; \beta_2; \tau_1) = \beta_0 + \beta_1 * \left(\frac{1 - e^{(-m/\tau)}}{m/\tau} \right) + \beta_2 * \left(\frac{1 - e^{(-m/\tau)}}{m/\tau} - e^{(-m/\tau)} \right) \qquad (73.2)$$

Creators of the model have been testing it on American short-term government obligations by assembling a yield curve for 37 different time periods from 22 January 1981 to 27 October 1983 with a median error of 7.81 BPS. Nelson-Siegel model shows slightly worse interlacing capability through the bonds maturity process but far better capabilities after maturity of last bond.

Biggest disadvantage of the model is bigger inclination to outliers errors (often bonds with longest period to maturity) because model automatically attaches greater scale to yield curve sections with more points being observed.

73.3.2   Svensson Method

Model Nelson-Seigel was followed by Lars E. O. Svensson (Svensson 1994) which pointed out that Nelson-Seigel model is suitable only for cases with one local extreme of yield curve. Nelson-Seigel method is not capable of modelling more complex shapes of yield curve. Due to this fact, Svensson has expanded his original model into two additional parameters which may cause additional curvature of yield curve. We can see following solution for forward rate as a result.

$$f(m) = \beta_0 + \beta_1 * e^{(-m/\tau_1)} + \beta_2^* \left[\left(\frac{-m}{\tau_1} \right) * e^{(-m/\tau_1)} \right] + \beta_3 * \left[\left(\frac{-m}{\tau_2} \right) * e^{(-m/\tau_2)} \right]$$

(73.3)

By integrating the equation, we get an expression describing spot yield curve:

$$i(m; \beta_0; \beta_1; \beta_2; \tau_1) = \beta_0 + \beta_1 * \left(\frac{1 - e^{(-m/\tau_1)}}{m/\tau_1} \right) + \beta_2 * \left(\frac{1 - e^{(-m/\tau_1)}}{m/\tau_1} - e^{(-m/\tau_1)} \right)$$
$$+ \beta_3 * \left(\frac{1 - e^{(-m/\tau_2)}}{m/\tau_2} - e^{(-m/\tau_2)} \right)$$

(73.4)

Empirical studies were made by Svensson on state bonds of Sweden, Germany, France, GB and USA when he wasn't dealing with interlacing capability of the model but with comparison of risk-free yield curves' development of these countries. Disadvantages of Svensson method are following:

- Higher number of parameters means bigger time demands for the calculation which confirms Bolder-Strelinski (1999) declaring 4 times longer calculation of parameters than Nelson-Siegel method.
- As by Nelson-Siegel, Svensson method has also problems with outliners. Geyer-Mader (1999) state that more parameters by Svensson method generally slightly better interlace shorter and middle part of yield curve. However, it shows more errors by distant outliners than Nelson-Siegel.

73.4 Construction Czech Risk-Free Yield Curve by Nelson-Siegel and Svensson Method

Construction of Czech risk-free yield curve by Nelson-Siegel and Svensson method will be made to one single day—29 January 2016. The results of both methods will be compared to each other and also to EIOPA risk-free yield curve from 31 January 2016.[1] Quality of the model will be verified by creating risk-free yield curves according to both models for every working day from 30 December 2015 to 29 January 2016 based on RMSE indicators (root mean square error)—determination coefficient, volatility of parameters β_0 and β_1 in time and time demands for calculation.

Czech state bonds are supposed to be input data. All relevant information about Czech state bonds is gained from the electronic trading platform MTS Czech Republic. According to Kladívko (2009) following bonds were excluded from calculations:

- Bonds with long time to maturity <12 months because of low trading frequency of these bonds and therefore economically unreal behaviour of given bonds and
- Bonds with variable returns.

When excluding bonds with long time to maturity <12 months, there is a problem with poorly defined very short part of yield curve, because shortest bond is due to April 2017. From this reason, we have to define short end of yield curve by other risk-free financial instruments. For this purpose, we will use state treasury bills (SPP), whose eminent is identical to state bonds eminent (Ministry of Finance):

- treasury bill emitted <3 months ago with shortest maturity date and
- treasury bill emitted <3 months ago with longest maturity date.

Following instruments are used to create risk-free interest rate to 29 January 2016.

Treasury bills rates represent spot rates which are not adjusted by any means. In case of state bonds, we calculate with average price of bond counted as the average between ASK and BID price. We also calculate yield until the maturity of bond through MID price.

73.4.1 Estimation Technique of Nelson-Siegel and Svensson Method

Table processor Microsoft Excel was used to calculate risk-free interest rate by Nelson-Siegel and Svensson method. For example, Matlab can be used as an

---

[1]EIOPA swap interest rates are published only on working days. 31st January is Sunday, so we can assume that EIOPA rates relates to 29th January 2016.

Table 73.2 List of using instruments

Instrument	Identification	Coupon (%)	Maturity	Shortcut
SPP	20403724	0.00	4.3.2016	SPP
SPP	22701727	0.00	27.1.2017	SPP
Gov. bond	CZ0001001903	4.00	11.4.2017	4.00/17
Gov. bond	CZ0001004592	0.00	9.11.2017	0.00/17
Gov. bond	CZ0001004709	0.00	22.1.2018	0.00/18
Gov. bond	CZ0001004246	0.85	17.3.2018	0.85/18
Gov. bond	CZ0001000822	4.60	18.8.2018	4.60/18
Gov. bond	CZ0001002471	5.00	11.4.2019	5.00/19
Gov. bond	CZ0001004717	0.00	17.7.2019	0.00/19
Gov. bond	CZ0001003834	1.50	29.10.2019	1.50/19
Gov. bond	CZ0001001317	3.75	12.9.2020	3.75/20
Gov. bond	CZ0001002851	3.85	29.9.2021	3.85/21
Gov. bond	CZ0001001945	4.70	12.9.2022	4.70/22
Gov. bond	CZ0001004600	0.45	25.10.2023	0.45/23
Gov. bond	CZ0001002547	5.70	25.5.2024	5.70/24
Gov. bond	CZ0001004253	2.40	17.9.2025	2.40/25
Gov. bond	CZ0001004469	1.00	26.6.2026	1.00/26
Gov. bond	CZ0001003859	2.50	25.8.2028	2.50/28
Gov. bond	CZ0001004477	0.95	15.5.2030	0.95/30
Gov. bond	CZ0001001796	4.20	4.12.2036	4.20/36
Gov. bond	CZ0001002059	4.85	26.11.2057	4.85/57

Source MTS Czech Republic, Czech National Bank

alternative. Every used bond defined in Table 73.2 is divided into repeating future bond payment and annuity payment with last coupon during bond maturity. There is a time interval m assigned to every payment which represents how far the future cash flow from present day is. By discounting of every future cash flow with discount factor where appropriate amount of interest rate is calculated by equation for Nelson-Siegel model and Svensson method and summing all of calculated present values of bond's future cash flows, is calculated the theoretical market price of the bond. At the same time, if we sum quoted price of MID bond and its aliquot interest yield, we get real market value of the bond. Optimization based on square yield deviation has been chosen for this model. It is suitable in particular case when the main target of yield curve is usage of its yields in different time moments. Optimization is made through Solver feature in MS Excel program.

There is a risk of finding only local minimum of square deviation instead of global minimum during optimization process. From this reason, there was more beginning points set using the Solver feature out of the basic set of 10,000 points. More beginning points, however, require setting of limiting conditions for each variable—such as interval where variables are located. During the setting of these limiting conditions, economic interpretations for each parameter were taken into

Table 73.3 Intervals for parameters

Parameters	Low interval	High interval
β_0 (%)	0.1	10
β_1 (%)	−50	50
β_2 (%)	−50	50
τ_1	0.001	10
β_3 (only for Svensson method) (%)	−50	50
τ_2 (only for Svensson method)	0.001	10

Source Own modification

account while intervals were chosen always the widest possible with certain reduction for lower time consumption of following calculation. Intervals for each parameter were chosen as shown in Table 73.3.

73.4.2 Estimation Results of Nelson-Siegel and Svensson Method

Czech risk-free yield curve is created as above stated by Nelson-Siegel and Svensson methods and is displayed together with mentioned EIOPA values in following graph (Table 73.4).

As Fig. 73.1 shows, the results of Nelson Siegel are very similar to Svensson method. Both examined models explain interlaced data with more than 99% as indicated by coefficient of determination (R). Speaking of interlacing capability, the most fundamental is RSME index where Svensson method shows slightly better results which is caused by additional parameters β_3 and τ_2.

Comparison of yield curve created with EIOPA values with Nelson-Siegel and Svensson model results is also interesting. EIOPA results compiled with swaps are far more different from bonds-based methods. As curves cross each other 2 times, we cannot really state which curve is better. The advantage of EIOPA curve is non-negative values of yield curve in short term which contradicts with standard economic theories regarding interest rates. But if we take a look at Czech or German state bonds profitability we can see that negative bonds interest rates are recently common for bonds with date of maturity shorter than one year.

Table 73.4 Values of parameters

	β_0 (%)	β_1 (%)	β_2 (%)	τ_1	β_3 (%)	τ_2	R^2 (%)	ø Error BPS
Nelson-Siegel	3.55	−3.59	−4.74	4.96	–	–	99.74	2.39
Svensson	3.47	−3.58	−4.79	4.69	0.36	0.657	99.80	1.80

Source Own modification

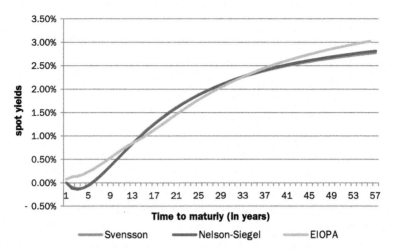

Fig. 73.1 Czech risk-free yield curve for to 29 January 2016. *Source* EIOPA (2016); MTS (2016) Czech Republic, Own modification

Differences in results of Nelson-Siegel and Svensson methods are evident, especially when examining interlacing capabilities of these models of risk-free instruments with very short-term maturity. This situation is shown by the next graph.

Figure 73.2 shows that Svensson method has better interlacing capability in short term because it includes two more parameters.

Svensson method therefore shows better interlacing capability and lower average error. Good results for one day do not have to mean anything. Interlacing capability and model stability is fundamental in long term which will be researched now.

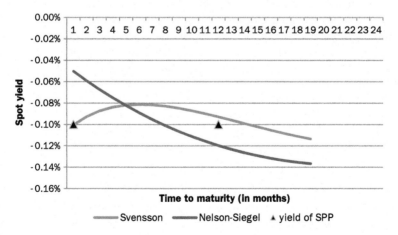

Fig. 73.2 Short end of yield curve. *Source* Own modification

Table 73.5 Results of capability and stability methods

	∅ Daily deviation β_0 (%)	∅ Daily deviation β_0 (% points)	∅ Daily deviation β_1 (%)	∅ Daily deviation β_1 (% points)	∅ R^2 (%)	∅ RMSE (BPS)
Nelson-Siegel	1.39	0.05	1.50	0.05	99.31	3.50
Svensson	2.24	0.08	4.38	0.17	99.62	2.61

Source Own modification

There was created risk-free yield curve by both models to determine interlacing capability and stability of every parameter in time for every working day from 30 December 2015 until 29 January 2016—meaning 21 consecutive working days (Table 73.5).

Both models show very good interlacing capability represented by R^2 index and more importantly RMSE index. Slightly better results of interlacing capability give Svensson method which has average RMSE od 2.61 BPS and the method also explains average 99.62% of interlacing data. In case of Nelson-Siegel method, we can see average RMSE 3.50 BPS and method explains 99.31% interlacing data.

Next monitored indicator was stability of β_0 and β_1 in time. In case of significant daily deviations, these models would be unstable and yield curves would change their shape significantly in short term which would lower the information capability of these models. In parameter stability comparison, Nelson-Siegel method shows slightly better results and has standard daily deviation of 1.39% β_0 index and 1.50% β_1 index which refers to average daily change of these coefficients by 0.05%. Svensson method shows average daily deviation of 2.24% β_0 index and 4.38% β_1 index which refers to average daily change of 0.08% in case of β_0 and 0.17% β_1.

The last criterion of models evaluation is calculation time consumption. Bolder–Strelinski (1999) state that Svensson model calculation is almost 4 times longer than Nelson-Siegel model. For this reason we measured time needed to calculate these models in MS Excel program (Table 73.6).

The average time of calculation and optimization of single parameters was 3 min and 30 s for Nelson-Siegen model and 6 min 30 s for Svensson method. Svensson model is in this particular case 1.86 times more time consuming than Nelson-Siegel. Therefore, time consumption is not that high as Bolder-Strelinski (1999) stated and should not be taken as a fundamental factor when choosing a method.

Table 73.6 Average time to calculation

Method	Average time to calculation
Nelson-Siegel	3 min 30 s
Svensson	6 min 30 s

Source Own modification

73.5 Conclusion

This article describes current problem of risk-free profitability differentiation for assets valuation especially using Nelson-Siegen and Svensson method. Above presented results show that both methods have very good interlacing capabilities and are suitable for yield curves construction. Both methods indicate their advantages and disadvantages compared to the other. The advantage of Nelson-Siegel model is its lower calculation time consumption and higher stability of parameters in time. On the other hand, the main advantage of Svensson method is considered to be its better interlacing capability of researched data. Therefore, we cannot clearly define which method would be primarily used in case of Czech state bonds. However, both methods proved by their results that they can be applied in assets valuation praxis.

Regarding to above stated facts, it is recommended to research following topics:

- Risk-free state bonds in comparison to swap interest rate
- Choosing risk-free instrument for identification of very short and very long end of yield curve (e.g. liquidity of these instruments) and
- Choosing the best model for Czech market (Nelson-Siegel method, Svensson method, Smith-Wilson method, etc.).

Acknowledgments Author gratefully acknowledges that this paper has been prepared under financial support of research project of Faculty of Finance and Accounting, University of Economics, Prague, which is realized within the institutional support VŠE IP100040.

References

Aljinovič Z, Poklepovič J, Katalinič K (2012) Best fit model for yield curve estimation. Croatian Oper Res Rev 3. ISSN 1848-9931

Bolder D, Stréliski D (1999) Yield curve modelling at the Bank of Canada. Bank of Canada, Ottawa. ISBN 0662276027

Csajbók A (1999) Zero-Coupon yield curve estimation from a central bank perspective. Working paper, National Bank of Hungary. ISBN 963-9057-19-3

Damodaran A (2015) Is the riskfree rate? A search for the basic building block. A. Stern School of Business, New York University. Dec 2008 [cit. 2015-03-20]. Dostupné z: http://people.stern. nyu.edu/adamodar/pdfiles/papers/riskfreerate.pdf

Diebold FX, Li C (2006) Forecasting the term structure of government bond yields. J Econometrics 337–364. ISSN 1872-6895

Dvořák M (2014a) Užití swapových sazeb pro stanovení bezrizikové míry se zřetelem na Českou republiku. Oceňování 7(1):3–26. ISNN 1803-0785

Dvořák M (2014b) Bezriziková úroková míra ze státních dluhopisů: přednosti a úskalí Svenssonovy metody. Oceňování 7(3):3–27. ISNN 1803-0785

EIOPA (2016) Risk-free interest rate term structure. Jan 2016 [cit. 2016-02-15]. https://eiopa. europa.eu/regulation-supervision/insurance/solvency-ii-technical-information/risk-free-interest-rate-term-structures

Geyer A, Mader R (1999) Estimation of the term structure of interest rates. A parametric approach, Working paper 37, Oesterreichische National Bank. ISSN neuvedeno

Hladíková H, Radová, J (2012) Term structure modelling by using Nelson-Siegel model. Eur Fin Acc J 7(2):36–55. ISSN 1805-4846

Kladívko K (2009) The Czech treasury yield curve from 1999 to the present. Czech J Econ Fin (Finance a úvěr) 60(4):307–335. ISSN 0015-1920

Mcculloch JH (1971) Measuring the term structure of interest rates. J Bus 44:19–31. ISSN 0021-9398

MTS (2016) Download section: ministry of finance of the Czech Republic [cit. 2016-02-15]. https://www.mtsdata.com/content/data/public/cze/fixing/download/

Mařík M (2011) Metody oceňování podniku pro pokročilé: hlubší pohled na vybrané problémy. Ekopress, Praha

Nelson CR, Siegel AF (1987). Parsimonious modeling of yield curves. J Bus 60:473–489

Podškubka T (2012) Náklady cizího kapitálu při výnosovém ocenění podniků v České republice, Praha. Disertační práce. Vysoká škola ekonomická. Vedoucí práce Petr Marek

Schich S (1997) The estimating the German term structure. Discussion paper 4/97. Franfurkt Am Main: Economic Research Group of the Deoutche Bundesbank. ISBN 3-932002-71-7

Slavík M (2001) Odhad časové struktury úrokových sazeb z cen domácích dluhopisů. Czech J Econ Fin (Finance a úvěr) 51:591–606. ISSN 0015-1920

Smith A, Wilson T (2001). Fitting yield curves with long term constraints. Bacon & Woodrow

Svensson LE (1994). Estimating and Interpreting Forward Interest Rates: Estimation and Interpretation. Discussion paper 19/96, Bank of Finland

Chapter 74
Discount Rate for Human Life-Related Decisions

Pavel Kuchyňa

Abstract The paper introduces legislation in Czech Republic relating to value of human life. It is compensation for pain and injury and compensation of people close to a departed person. There is one methodology provided by Czech court and also similar legislation in the UK followed by methodology. There are two general approaches and one of them requires a discount rate. The rate described there is based on government stock. This makes it close to risk free. After testing it on one particular lifelong decision and on one specific risk, the rates are reaching substantially higher values. The risk-free rate is not recommendable for the situation in Czech Republic. Using a flat rate for life is inaccurate.

Keywords Compensation · Discount rate · Human life

74.1 Introduction

The compensation for human life is a quite recent topic in Czech Republic especially after new legislation providing the necessary framework. Methodologies available for the purposes are still fairly limited, which may result in incorrect compensations. One of the topics that have been almost never discussed is a discount rate that could be used for the purpose.

It is very important to understand that any calculation leading to value of human life present in this paper is meant in relationship with compensation of loss of life according to the legislative framework. The danger is that some methods could be considered in more general sense. This could quite easily lead into some morally questionable conclusions and comparisons. Questions such as if it is rational to save

P. Kuchyňa (✉)
Department of Corporate Finance, University of Economics,
Prague, Nam. W. Churcilla 4, 130 67 Praha 3, Czech Republic
e-mail: pkuchyna@gmail.com

© Springer International Publishing AG 2017
D. Procházka (ed.), *New Trends in Finance and Accounting*,
Springer Proceedings in Business and Economics,
DOI 10.1007/978-3-319-49559-0_74

someone's life for a specific cost or comparing which life is more valuable. Trying to answer those requires additional assumptions and is subject to theoretical obstacles or more accurately requires deeper analysis to explain why it is not possible. Unfortunately, the format of this text does not allow discussion deep enough to cover all aspects of the topic.

The goal of this paper is to present multiple approaches of setting up the discount rate that could be used for setting up a compensation of loss of human life, additional goal is to indicate some specific rates to provide an idea of what would be reasonable values and illustrate an approach of its estimation.

Before being able to discuss the rates, it will be necessary to at least very briefly present related legislation and existing methodologies in Czech Republic and their equivalent from abroad. This paper will also cover two main methods that are used for the purpose of estimation of value of human life.

74.2 Legislation

The topic of value of human life is getting increasingly more important in last years. Civil code (Občansky zakonik 1964) valid between years 1964 and 2013 provided specific amount for loss of life of close person. The compensations were 240,000 CZK in most cases, and only siblings, parents, and children were eligible for receiving it. A different approach appeared at the end of the life cycle of the law, mainly in the last decade. The compensation was significantly increased in reference to other very general paragraphs stating that everyone has a right for fair a compensation of all losses including immaterial ones.

Since the first of January 2014, there is a new Civil code (Občansky zakonik 2012), which changed the approach to compensations of losses related to human life. This was in accordance with previous evolution of the law interpretation. There are four related areas.

74.2.1 Cost of Sustenance of Close Persons § 2966, § 2967, § 2968

Those costs represent the amount of money that the person who passed away provided to others. They can be either mandatory payments, for example, a father taking care of his child, or also voluntary payments that the departed person provided. The compensation can be handled as a regular payment or onetime payment if requested. This adjustment requires using an appropriate discount rate.

74.2.2 Compensation for Mental Harm § 2959

This is a financial compensation that should represent complete equivalent of psychical suffering that relatives or any other close person went through due to the loss of the deceased person. It seems that this paragraph has not been used yet, and what is more there is no methodology or accepted guideline available.

74.2.3 Costs of Funeral § 2961

Those costs represent any finances required for funeral of the deceased person. It is quite straightforward to determine it, and moreover, the specific amount may be known already when the compensation is decided.

74.2.4 Costs of Health Damage and Death § 2958

The area of focus of this paragraph is not loss of a close person. It covers the compensation for reduced health status for the person affected. It may seem unrelated to previous paragraphs of the law, but theoretical 100% significant injury, which would be equal to death, represents the upper limit of compensation to any relative. In other words, any close person is not eligible for receiving higher compensations according to previous paragraphs than the person would receive himself or herself if survived according to this paragraph.

74.2.5 Methodology of the Highest Court of Czech Republic

All paragraphs mentioned previously are very general and leaving enough space for many different interpretations. This is a reason why the Highest Court of Czech Republic published a specific methodology (Nejvyšší soud 2014). It is focused on costs of health damage and death § 2958. The main concern mentioned in the methodology is that the law allows the same number interpretations as many there are judges. This methodology should be a solution, which, however, is not mandatory. The idea is to split the compensation in two parts, compensation of pain providing a specific table listing all pains and the scoring system based on average salary and the other part is the permanent invalidity and exclusion from social life. The methodology provides a maximum compensation for 100% exclusion from life. This is in theory equal to death. The suggested compensation is 400 times higher than monthly average gross salary. Each incident should be evaluated based on expert opinion assessing the specific percentage.

It is important to point on the fact that the approach does not take into consideration the aspect of time and therefore it does not mention the term of discount rate at all.

74.2.6 Ogden Tables

There is a legislative guideline which is very similar to methodology of the Highest Court of Czech Republic valid in the UK. It is represented by Ogden tables (de Wilde 2011). The British methodology is supposed to be used for Cost of sustenance of close persons. It does not cover any other compensations existing in Czech legislation. The tables take into consideration following factors: age, life expectancy, income, gender, education, marital status and discount rate. The most important factor that is relevant for this text is the discount rate. The recommendation is to base it on yields on Index of Linked Government Stock. The Ogden tables refer to number 2.5%, but they also include a part providing the calculation guideline for discount rates varying from −2 to +3%.

74.3 Theoretical Approaches to Value of Human Life

There are two main approaches for setting up value of human life. They exist in many modifications. This paper contains a very brief introduction of the main variants. The reason is that they are not the primary focus of this text; however, awareness of their existence is important for understanding the purpose of discount rate.

74.3.1 Human Capital

This approach works with assumption that labor market represents perfect mechanism for valuation of human life. The more valuable the person is the more money would be needed to hire him or her. The problem is that there might be values that are not taken into account in setting up a wage. Landefeld and Seskin (1982) published Eq. (74.1) to calculate value of human life.

$$HC = \sum_{t=1}^{T} \frac{L_t}{(1+i)^t} \tag{74.1}$$

where

T remaining life time,
L_t labor income,
I discount rate.

It is evident that discount rate represents a key factor influencing the result of previous calculation. This approach is very easy to understand and interpret, and it seems to be perfectly fitting for one time compensation of sustenance for wife or children or anyone other person that is eligible.

74.3.2 Willingness to Pay

Willingness to pay represents an alternative approach. The value is based on the amount that individuals are ready to give up for reduction of a certain percentage of death. Robinson (1986) provides calculation (2) in his paper.

$$V = \frac{W_p}{\Delta p} \tag{74.2}$$

where

V value of human life,
W_p amount an individual is willing to pay to reduce risk,
Δp risk reduction.

The main problem of the approach is that people are not behaving rationally when making decisions that affect their lives. Death is a term that induces significant emotions in most individuals. This fact may lead to taking significant countermeasures and willing to pay inadequately high amounts and making the calculation result in very high value. On the other hand, the probabilities of most considered decisions are very low. For example, the chance that wearing a helmet would save someone's life when skiing is less than 0.0001%. The low likelihoods may result into underestimation of the risk and not taking appropriate countermeasures. The result of both contradictory factors is high volatility of the results obtained using this method. It is also not a relevant approach for this paper, because Eq. (74.2) shows that the discount rate is not one of the factors directly influencing the result.

74.4   Risk-Free Discount Rate

As already described previously, the discount rate may be based on risk-free interest rates in the country. This is a path followed in Ogden tables with recommended 2.5%. The equivalent in Czech Republic could be the yield to maturity of state bonds. Following table illustrates the local rates.

Most of the figures in Table 74.1 are significantly lower than the rate published in Ogden tables. The main reason is that the economic situation has changed since they were published, and the interest rates are lower than they were in most

Table 74.1 State Bonds

Name	Currency	YTM buy (%)	YTM sell (%)
ST. DLUHOP. 0.50/16	CZK	0.06	−0.50
ST. DLUHOP. 4.00/17	CZK	−0.17	−0.53
ST. DLUHOP. 4.60/18	CZK	−0.15	−0.32
ST. DLUHOP. 5.00/19	CZK	−0.11	−0.27
ST. DLUHOP. 3.75/20	CZK	−0.12	−0.20
ST. DLUHOP. 3.85/21	CZK	−0.04	−0.13
ST. DLUHOP. 4.70/22	CZK	0.04	−0.06
ST. DLUHOP. 0.45/23	CZK	0.34	0.12
ST. DLUHOP. 5.70/24	CZK	0.25	0.16
ST. DLUHOP. 2.40/25	CZK	0.43	0.34
ST. DLUHOP. 1.00/26	CZK	0.68	0.38
ST. DLUHOP. 2.50/28	CZK	0.70	0.64
ST. DLUHOP. 0.95/30	CZK	0.90	0.80
ST. DLUHOP. 4.20/36	CZK	1.26	1.22
ST. DLUHOP. 4.85/57	CZK	2.09	1.85

Source Patria Online (2016)

countries and most industries several years ago. In order to get the time symmetry, it should be preferred to use bonds with longer duration. According to the ST. DLUHOP. 4.8/57, the current discount rate for years between 2016 and 2057 would be about 2% based on the bond yield to maturity.

74.5 Indicative Calculation of Discount Rate

Determining discount rate that could be used for making a decision related to human life is an uneasy task. The previous chapter presented discount rate based on risk-free rates represented by state bonds. This chapter will provide one particular example of lifelong decision that represents a certain gain.

Many people are making a decision whether to start their career immediately after high school or if they should postpone their earnings and get a university degree first. A discount rate that an individual applies making such choice can be calculated as a difference between expected future income of the variant of starting their career after high school and the variant of getting a degree first and then searching for the first job later. An approach is to calculate internal rate of return using Eq. (74.3).

$$0 = \sum_{n=1}^{LE} \frac{CF_{Hn} - CF_{Un}}{IRR^n} \tag{74.3}$$

Table 74.2 High school and university income prediction

Year	High school variant	University variant	Difference
From 1 to 5	182,184	0	−182,184
From 6 to 50	182,184	306,774	124,590
From 51 to 55	149,496	166,812	17,316

Source Authorial computation, Cesky statisticky urad (2016a)

where

LE   life expectancy, remaining years,

CF_{Hn} expected cash flow in year *n*—high school variant,

CF_{Un} expected cash flow in year *n*—university variant,

IRR   internal rate of return.

Let us assume following, individual is at the age of 20 and is making a lifelong decision to study university. His life expectancy is 59 more years in year 2014. This means that he is expected to survive until the age of 89. Median of annual net salary of high school graduates is 182,184 CZK. Median of annual net salary of individuals who graduated university is 306,774 CZK. Expected retiring is at the age of 70 years. The expected pension in high school variant is 149,496 CZK and in university variant is 166,812 CZK.

We can use the figures from Table 74.2 as an input for Eq. (74.3) and get internal rate of return of 10.91%. This result is significantly higher than any risk-free rate. Moreover, it is reasonable to assume that the actual discount rate of this decision might be even higher as there are more benefits coming from getting the university degree except for increased expected income. The individual also gains knowledge that he or she may be able to apply in other areas that are not necessarily related to their careers and cannot be measured financially. Some people may study university for prestige of being able to use a university degree next to their name.

74.6 Discount Rate Based on Risk of Death

The third way of construction of discount rate that will be covered in this paper is using discount rate and adding a risk of death. Calculation (74.4) will be used for this purpose. It is a very much simplified approach because in reality there might be other reasons for loosing value of human life, especially when the subject of consideration is not own life but life of someone else.

$$DR_n = \frac{RF + p_n}{1 - p_n} \qquad (74.4)$$

Fig. 74.1 Discount rate for young age. *Source* Cesky statisticky urad (2016b), authorial computations

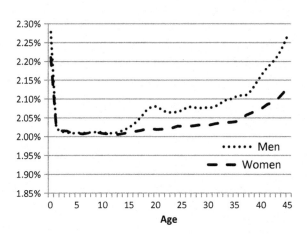

where

DR_n   discount rate in year *n*,
RF   risk-free discount rate,
p_n   likelihood of death in year *n*.

Following graphs illustrate what results can be calculated when we add likelihood of death to a risk-free discount rate 2% gained from Czech state bonds. The probability of death depends on gender and age (Figure 74.1).

The probability of death is very low in the beginning of life. It is slightly higher in the very first year, and then it drops to grow slowly afterward. The growth makes the risk of death more important and having relevant influence on the discount rate. The interesting fact is that men have increased chance of death during the first years of their adult age, and this does not seem to be the truth for women (Figure 74.2).

Fig. 74.2 Discount rate for medium age. *Source* Cesky statisticky urad (2016b), authorial computations

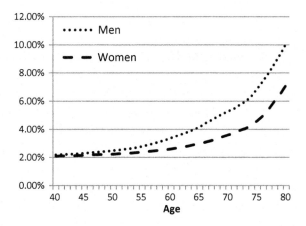

Fig. 74.3 Discount rate for elder persons. *Source* Cesky statisticky urad (2016b), authorial computations

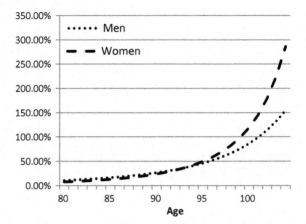

While aging the risk of death gets extremely influential for the discount rate making it about five times higher compared to risk-free rate of 2% at the age of 80 (Figure 74.3).

Toward the end of life, the risk of death affects the discount rate so significantly that it makes it almost impossible to get any value long term. The interesting fact is that although men have higher probability of passing away during most of their life, the probabilities change after the age of 90. This is exposing women to much higher death risk.

74.7   Discussion

The approach based on methodology according to legislation in the UK results in discount rate around 2%. This means that the rate applied would be similar to risk-free discount rate. The question is whether human life should really be considered as risk free. The human life lasts on average less than 100 years. The risk-free discount rates are typically based on bonds or stocks of developed countries. The USA was founded in 1776. The history of France or England can be traced back to medieval era. This is much more than any individual can possibly live.

The practical example demonstrated that the internal rate of return that would be applied for lifelong decision to get a university degree could be almost 11%, which is much more than risk-free rate.

The analysis of risk of death according to gender and age has shown that the risk of death gets very influential as individuals grow older. It may get very far from the neighborhood of risk-free rates as well. It also demonstrates the inaccuracy of using a single discount rate for the whole life.

On top of everything described previously, the risk of death is not the only risk to be considered. Between 45 and 50% of marriage end with divorce, this may have very similar impact as a mental harm according to § 2959 of Civil code described

Table 74.3 Duration of
divorced marriages

Duration years	Percentage of divorces (%)
0 years	0.8
from 1 to 4	18.0
from 5 to 9	20.6
from 10 to 14	16.8
15 and more	43.9

Source Cesky statisticky urad (2016c)

earlier. Table 74.3 segments divorces by duration of marriage. Data are based on
year 2012. It is self-explanatory that there is much higher risk of losing a partner by
divorce than by passing away.

74.8   Conclusion

There is legislation in Czech Republic that requires application of discount rate. The
compensation of loss of a close person is split in two main areas, mental suffering
and payments that the person passing away provided. The law specifically mentions
the option of the onetime payment in the second case. Unlike the British
methodology, the approach published in Czech Republic does not cover discount
rates. What is more, the local algorithm is focused only on losses on own live such
as disability. The 100% amount is purely theoretical.

The discount rate can be constructed based on risk-free discount rates. It seems
that there are some risks that should not be ignored as they relate to each specific
life. The one that cannot be avoided in any way is a risk of death which varies
throughout life. Another example is a chance of getting divorced.

This paper contained one calculation describing one particular lifelong decision.
The result was very far from risk-free rates. The conclusion of previous text is that
the risk-free discount rate is not appropriate for the purpose of the new Czech
legislation, and using a flat rate for the purpose is not accurate on top of that.

The next step will be to identify many more risks that could compose the
discount rate and moving from indicative values to specific results.

Acknowledgments The paper was elaborated as one of the outputs of the research project of the
Faculty of Finance and Accounting, University of Economics, Prague, which is realized in the
framework of the institutional support VŠE Praha č. IGA/48/2016 Teoreticke pristupy k opti-
malizaci kapitalove struktury.

References

Cesky statisticky urad (2016a) Percentage of employees, time paid and average monthly gross
    wages by education and by sex. Cesky statisticky urad, Praha [online]. 27 Feb 2016 https://vdb.

czso.cz/vdbvo2/faces/en/index.jsf?page=vystup-objekt&katalog=30852&zo=N&nahled=N&sp=
N&filtr=G ~ F_M ~ F_Z ~ F_R ~ F_P ~ _S ~ _null_null_&z=T&f=TABULKA&verze=-1&pvo=
MZD10&c=v44__RP2014

Cesky statisticky urad (2016b) Nadeje doziti a pravdepodobnost umrti. Cesky statisticky urad, Praha [online]. 27 Feb 2016 https://vdb.czso.cz/vdbvo2/faces/cs/index.jsf?page=vystup-objekt-vyhledavani&katalog=all&zo=N&skupId=1289&nahled=N&sp=N&filtr=G ~ F_M ~ F_Z ~ F_ R ~ F_P ~ _S ~ _null_null_&z=T&f=TABULKA&verze=-1&pvo=DEMD002&vyhltext=do %C5%BEit%C3%AD&pvo=DEMD002&c=v3__RP2014

Cesky statisticky urad (2016c) Nadeje doziti a pravdepodobnost umrti. Cesky statisticky urad, Praha [online]. 27 Feb 2016 https://www.czso.cz/documents/10180/25385875/16816074 +33157959.pdf/af958f6b-cd46-487e-83f5-2914f95c3f22?version=1.0

de Wilde R (2011) Actuarial tables: with explanatory notes for use in: personal injury and fatal accident cases. London, TSO, 2005

Landefeld S, Seskin E (1982) The economic value of life: linking theory to practice. Am J Public Health: JPH (New York) 72(6):12

Nejvyšši soud (2014) Metodika Nejvyššiho soudu k nahrade nemajetkove ujmy na zdravi: bolest a ztizeni spolecenskeho uplatneni podle § 2958 obcanskeho zakoniku. Nejvyšši soud CR [online] 27 Feb 2016 http://www.nsoud.cz/JudikaturaNS_new/ns_web.nsf/Metodika

Patria (2016) Dluhopisy online. Patria Online, a.s. [online]. 27 Feb 2016 http://www.patria.cz/ kurzy/online/govcz/dluhopisy.html

Robison J (1986) Philosophical origins of the economic valuation of life. Milbank Q 64(1):133–155

Zakon c. 40/1964 Sb., Obcansky zakonik

Zakon c. 89/2012 Sb., O Zakon c. 89/2012 Sb., obcansky zakonik

Chapter 75
Discount Rate in Business Damage Cases

Barbora Hamplová

Abstract This paper deals with the importance of determining the appropriate discount rate in business damage cases. The author examines the importance, both in terms of the requirements for discount rate in the business valuation, but also deals with the specific purpose of the computing—to compensate the plaintiff for economic loss.

Keywords Business damage · Discount rate · Business valuation · Lost profit

75.1 Introduction

This paper deals with the importance of determining the appropriate discount rate in business damage cases. The author examines the importance, both in terms of the requirements for discount rate in the business valuation, but also deals with the specific purpose of the computing—to compensate the plaintiff for economic loss.

The aim of this article is to identify the main parameters which can affect the determination of the discount rate.

The issue of quantification of the business damages is relevant de facto wherever it plays a role the business environment, or disruption of "a normal course of things" of this business environment. Within the execution of appraisers activities are appraisers often being appointed to quantify the amount of damages for the particular litigation for breach of contractual obligations. In connection with the valuation it can be stated that the procedures for quantifying lost profits are basically very similar to the procedures and principles used in creating financial plan and risk assessment in the valuation of companies.

Based on various examples of quantifying the damages from the practice of courts and Czech and foreign cases it is very difficult to link the legal assessment of

B. Hamplová (✉)
Faculty of Finance and Accounting, University of Economics,
Prague, Nam. W. Churchilla 4, 130 67 Prague, Czech Republic
e-mail: xhamb01@vse.cz

© Springer International Publishing AG 2017   815
D. Procházka (ed.), *New Trends in Finance and Accounting*,
Springer Proceedings in Business and Economics,
DOI 10.1007/978-3-319-49559-0_75

the damage and selection of the appropriate valuation method or the actual cash flow projections. The appraiser can often in terms of linking legal assessment of the damage and selection of the appropriate valuation methods get into the role of arbiter, as not always purely economic assessing is done, or decisions about setting parameters are from the perspective of economic theory and practice uncertain; however, it is essential to quantify the damage.

The main principle of the income approach is based on an estimate of cash flows from the future business activities of the company, and their transfer to the present value. The valuation process is as follows: First, it is necessary to define subject of valuation, as well as expert should estimate the likely cash flow of the company and its timing. The last step is to calculate the net present value of expected cash flow of the company.

The paper has following structure. Chapter 2 describes the two main approaches in computing the damage with identifying the differences which are important for the appropriate discount rate calculation. Chapter 3 identifies the main parameters in the process of the damage calculation which are determinative for the approach employed by the discount rate computing.

75.2   Basic Methodologies Used for Damage Calculation

As it is mentioned above, business damages are based on the as lost stream of economic income in the expected amount that otherwise would correspond to regular course of things. The appraiser usually determines the minimum amount in terms of the lost profits which the company would normally reached, and taking into account all the relevant expenses necessary to achieve the related income from entrepreneurial activities of the company.

With respect to that definition we could use two basic approaches for the damage calculation.

- So-called "business valuation" approach, which determines the lost business value based on the comparison of the value of the company (1) in case of "perfect condition" or "a normal course of things" which—unimpaired value based upon expected future performance as of the date of damage event and (2) the value of the impaired business based on the real or ascertainable data or real performance of the company for the period affected by damage event as of the date of injury.
- So-called "lost profit" approach, which computes the "but for" and real (impaired) streams of economic income based on the information known and available after the date of the legal wrongdoing.

Before identifying the main differences between those two methodologies it is necessary to take the damage events into account. As the appraiser should avoid assessing the damage causation, the determination of the damage by the plaintiff is decisive for the presumptions used for the valuation process. Business damages can arise from many of wrongdoings, for example:

- Breach of contract
- Intellectual property misappropriation
- Lost business opportunity
- Condemnation

As it is possible to describe many scenarios of the consequences of those wrongdoings, also the discount rate can vary based on the determination of the damage causation. The consequences could be:

- total loss of the business,
- loss of the part of the business for some period (at the level of particular department or activity or costumer),
- loss of the whole business for indefinite period.

With respect to the above mentioned, it is usually very important, what is the phase of the dispute. The first aspect for consideration is, whether the consequences of the alleged wrongdoing still persist as of the trial date and it is highly probable that they will persist for the next period. The second aspect for the consideration is, if there is the court decision about the damage causation.

According to the Harry (2011), if the damage valuation is released prior the trial date it is more appropriate to use business valuation methodology compare the situation after the trial date or after the court's decision, when the lost profit methodology is more appropriate.

As there is no mandatory procedure for business damage calculation according to the Pratt et al. (1998), Marboe (2009) and also Pratt and Grabowski (2014) based on the particular cases and court's resolution, the discounting and determining the appropriate discount rate is necessary for computing reasonably compensation.

75.3 Discounting in Business Damage Cases

The application of the discounting in the process of the damages calculation is regarding the basic principles of the above-mentioned methods a necessary process in order to convert the stream of the projected lost profits to the present value. In general the main argumentation for the discounting is reflecting the present value of an amount of money expected to be earned in the future period.

According to the financial principles of the discounting, the selection of the appropriate discount rate is crucial for the purpose to taking into account the time factor and the risk factor, as the entrepreneurial activities or the results are connected with risk and "a dollar today is more worth than a dollar tomorrow".

Future projected losses must be converted to present value. The reason is that if an award of damages is made a of a trial date, but the future losses would not be incurred for some period of time in the future, then the early receipt of such an award would overcompensate the plaintiff - such monies could be invested and would equal an even greater amount in the future. A lesser amount, the present value of future losses, needs to be computed. (Gaughan 2009, p. 267)

Since the determination of the discount rate within the process of the evaluation is one of the main issues in entire business valuation practice, let us consider two basic approaches, which are usually employed by experts, namely the "build up" model and the "Weighted Average Cost of Capital" model, which is established through the capital asset pricing model (CAPM).

In the first approach the expert "build up" the discount rate by using different identified risk components since the starting point is the "risk-free rate" which usually corresponds to a generally accepted risk-free investment such as government bonds.

The second approach is based on calculation of a cost of capital, while each category (cost of equity and cost of debt) of the capital is weighted. For the purpose of the determination of the cost of equity the capital assets pricing model (hereafter CAPM) is used, although only risk related to the market will be used and the required rate of return will not be considered. Therefore, this model is based on revenues of a risk-free investment, market risk premium, coefficient beta of the given industry (it expresses the risk level of a share relatively compared to the risk of the whole capital market).

This overview of international investment arbitrations shows that the discount rate in recent cases are much more reflected upon that in the earlier cases and frequently based on the valuation on the valuation methods explained above, namely the DCF method using WACC and CAPM. It is, therefore, not surprising that the discount rates selected by the parties are often not very far apart from each other. (Marboe 2009, p. 257)

Since above-mentioned approaches are appropriate for projected future stream of income and we could state that according to the practice in the area of business damage cases the discounting is one of the most important part of the business damage calculation which should be generally taking into account by submitting the evidence or expert opinion to the courts, another question arises—is there any need to discount the past losses?

To the extent that the historical losses estimation process already took the variation in the relevant risk factors into account, the past losses may already be risk - adjusted through the use of the information set that is available as of the date of the analysis. If the expert explicitly attempted to do this in the estimation process, then no further risk adjustment of past estimated losses is necessary. If not, then some accommodation for such uncertainty needs to be made. The risk adjustment process for past losses presents a fertile area for cross-examination when the expert has ignored this issue in estimating losses. (Gaughan 2009, p. 266)

Even though the discounting is primarily used for the conversion of the future income stream, the projection of the profits during the period which has already taken place in the past, there is some level of uncertainty within the process of the

Table 75.1 Common differences between the BV (ex ante) and LP (ex post) methodologies

Consideration	Business valuation	Lost profits analysis
Discount rate	Higher rate including subjective risk factor for unresolved uncertainties existing at the valuation date	Lower rate recognizing any risk resolution after the date of legal injury

Source Harry (2011)

projection. According to the above-mentioned citation and other opinions, for example: (Table 75.1).

It is very difficult to recommend an exact methodical procedure how in the above-mentioned models for determining the discount rate to reflect the knowledge of certain risk components in comparison with discounting by accepting principle of the decisive/valuation day, thus abstracting from any real data.

Besides, if the present value of the losses should be calculated, also those historical losses should be brought to the present value. This process includes the determination of the interest rate which is dependent on the country's legislation and courts'/arbitral practice.

In my opinion, the risk components may be different depending on the type of damage and also on the caused consequences as they are mentioned above. Let us have two different cases:

Case 1: The Company suffers the damage in the form of lost profits arose from breaching the contract by the supplier who did not deliver the material in defined period. The Company was not able to fulfill the terms of the contract with its client, while the subject of client's contract was to deliver the volume of products whose main component was undelivered material.

Case 2: The Company suffers the damage in the form of loss of the part of the business for indefinite time period, as the defendant misappropriated the intellectual property.

Let us presume the same trial date for both cases when the court determined that damages (1) had commenced three years prior the court's decision date and (2) had been projected for eight months after the judgment date in Case 1 (as the period was stated based on the terms of the contracts) and for indefinite period in Case 2.

If we focus on the damage prior the judgement date in both cases we could conclude the following: in Case 1 the volume of the production was stated by the contract with the client as well as the price and therefore the sales. For Case 2 we have to estimate the volume of the production and prices based on the real data from the relevant market and also expected market share based on the information about the competition and strengths and weaknesses of the Company. If we compare those two cases in terms of the certainty, according to my opinion, it should be considered, if in Case 1 is reasonable taking into account the risk of the relevant market as the demand is assured by the contract. Nevertheless, the discounting based on the risk-free rate is not fully recommended.

> Plaintiffs often argue that lost profits should be discounted at a risk-free rate of interest. This is incorrect. (Pratt and Grabowski 2014, p. 927)

> Naive experts often use a discount rate that is more closely associated with low-risk od even riskless income stream. For example, it is not unusual in a lost profits analysis to see an "expert" use a Treasury security as the source of the discount rate... Such an error results in an exaggerated loss estimate. (Gaughan 2009, p. 273).

Although the discounting of the ex post projection is not clearly explained in above-mentioned sources, for the discounting of the future income are the acceptable methods the subject of the compliance. In our two cases it is obvious that the certainty of the projected cash flows, even if the same approach is used, is significantly different. In those cases could be probably reasonable considering the application of the specific risk premium, even though it can lead to some subjective assessment of the expert.

75.4 Conclusion

According to the theory and practice of calculation of the business damages the discounting should be taken into account. When determining the appropriate discount rate should appraiser consider some basic characteristics and starting points of the cases which affect the risk assessment in the cash flow projection. Based on the studies on business damage calculation we can name following characteristics and starting points:

- Character of damage event and its consequences
- The phase of the dispute
- Methodology used for the calculation (business valuation or lost profits methodology)

It can be stated that the discounting of the future losses projection is generally recommendable, whereas it essentially follows from the nature of the methods that are used in determining the amount of the business damage. I can also conclude that there are generally accepted methods used for computing of the discount rate; nevertheless, in some cases is necessary to use the subjective assessment to reflect all parameters above-mentioned characteristics and starting points.

Acknowledgments This paper has been prepared under Institutional support of Faculty of Finance and Accounting, University of Economics, Prague (IP100040), which author gratefully acknowledges.

References

Gaughan Patrick A (2009) Measuring business interruption losses and other commercial damages, 2nd edn. Wiley, New Jersey

Harry PE (2011) Damages measurement and the business valuation report—challenges and pitfalls. Bus Valuat Rev 30(2):57–64

Marboe I (2009) Calculation of compensation and damages in international investment law. Oxford University Press Inc., New York

Pratt PS, Grabowski JR (2014) Cost of capital. Applications and examples, 5th edn, Wiley, New Jersey

Pratt PS, Reilly FR, Schweihs PR (1998) Valuing small businesses & professional practices, 3rd edn, The McGraw-Hill Companies, Inc., New York

Chapter 76
Medical Device Price and Valuation

Silvie Jerabkova

Abstract This paper deals with disunity in approaches towards what should be considered an adequate price of a medical device, what are its components and above all, how should a medical device be valued. Such a valuation is crucial for designing medical care reimbursement schemes, for health technology assessment (HTA) calculations and also for innovative medical device producers' investment decisions. The present paper analyses the components of medical device prices and presents some medical device valuation and pricing methods. Reimbursement and early-stage decisions involving the Bayesian prior are covered. Options valuation method and pay-for-performance are described. Specificities of the medical device market and industry are closely examined. Revenue-oriented method is put forward as a possible way of medical device valuation.

Keywords Medical device · Price · Valuation · Health technology assessment (HTA)

76.1 Introduction

The price of a medical device, despite a clear definition of each word, is rather a tricky concept. This paper deals with disunity in approaches towards what should be considered a "fair" price of a medical device, what are its components and above all, how should a medical device be valued. Such a valuation is crucial for designing medical care reimbursement schemes, for health technology assessment (HTA) calculations and also for innovative medical device producers' investment decisions. In the Czech Republic, the market price of a medical device does not give answers to those questions. The market price is often distorted by specific

S. Jerabkova (✉)
Department of Corporate Finance, University of Economics,
Nam. W. Churchilla 4, 130 67 Prague, Czech Republic
e-mail: silvie.jerabkova@gmail.com

© Springer International Publishing AG 2017　　　　　　　　　　　　823
D. Procházka (ed.), *New Trends in Finance and Accounting*,
Springer Proceedings in Business and Economics,
DOI 10.1007/978-3-319-49559-0_76

market attributes. The need for a clear methodology in determining medical device value, price and their interactions has led us to elaborate the present paper.

We are using elements from Bayesian statistics to both investment decision problems and to determine the reimbursement schemes. Options valuation methods are also discussed as a possible way to assess the revenues generated by using a medical device. Revenue drivers are thus defined. Pay-for-Performance method's applicability is examined in terms of assessing the quality of the health service rendered by the medical device in question.

Medical devices and their use in health care are considered as investment (in the sense of accounting), and they are therefore valued as such. Quality of the health care delivered or of the health problem treated plays the role of confirmation or rejection for the medical device being developed. Possible answers are offered to the question of "fairness" or "adequacy" of a medical device price given its components and market characteristics. Institutional aspect hence holds a strong importance.

Price and value of a medical device remain complex categories. According to different situations, different techniques might be employed. Our paper provides possible suggestions in this direction and pleads for wider use of revenue-oriented methods of medical device valuation.

76.2   Literature Review

Medical device prices do not reflect merely the value of the product itself, they usually consist of various additional components. They can reflect the concept of total cost of ownership; in this case, the prices would include services such as installation, financing conditions, utilities, upgrades, training and disposal (Hockel and Kintner 2014). Often though, these prices are bundled into a "purchasing price", which compromises any analytical efforts of disentangling particular components weight.

Prices of medical devices can also incorporate information systems and software, which accompanies them (De Backer and Van der Linden 2005). The price of a medical device also consists of its performance, the expected lifetime of the device, the reimbursement system in place in given country, competition among sellers (producers market share) and buyers (their price elasticity), regulatory environment, procurement structures (especially the existence or not of centralized purchasing organizations on given markets), physicians' clinical preferences (Hutchings 2010).

Medical device prices used in economic calculations are either list prices or contract prices, since sellers can either set their prices or bargain with the buyer. Manufacturers generally aim to recover the costs associated with the research and development process, cover the operating costs, which include fixed and variable costs associated with production, marketing, and sales departments, and obtain a profit margin (Santos and Tavares 2013).

Among the factors that influence medical device prices, we count clinical benefits that arise when using the device, health economic benefits such as the cost-effectiveness, social benefits, manufacturer investment in a particular country, procurement structure, investment in product research and development, patent and marketing exclusivity, comparator product price, innovation premiums, budget impact, equity, rarity and burden of the disease. Another important factors to be taken into account are the medical device brand identity or political and equitable considerations of the government.

76.3   Data, Results, and Discussion

Studies show that medical technology is one of the most relevant drivers of the increase in public expenditures on health. Thus, there is an increased need for health economic evaluations. Such valuations are crucial for designing medical care reimbursement schemes, for HTA calculations and also for innovative medical device producers' investment decisions.

76.3.1   Reimbursement and Early-Stage Development Decisions: Bayesian Approach

Current reimbursement schemes imply different incentives for healthcare organisations, among which there are the ones related to the medical technology, which represents one of the major drivers of costs (Le Pen and Berdeaux 2000). There exists a relation between the different reimbursement systems and the decisions of healthcare providers to adopt new technologies, i.e. the level of high technology medical equipment.

Thus, there is an impact of the main features of general reimbursement mechanisms (e.g. cost per case vs. fee for service) on the spread of medical devices and therefore their price. Regulatory, political and equitable considerations also play irreplaceable role in medical device pricing and often accounts for bias, such as market distortion and information asymmetry. In many major international medical markets, the government is actually both the ultimate purchaser of healthcare products and the arbiter of the markets in which they are traded (Hutchings 2010).

Recent history in the Czech Republic shows that under EU financed development projects, hospitals were involved in the "medical arms race", i.e. escalation of healthcare costs due to proliferation of expensive medical technology and devices. In a prospective payment system, such as the DRG one, hospitals are encouraged to keep their average cost below the payment rate in order to avoid making a loss and, thus, affecting technology adoption. On the other hand, DRG-based systems may also favour the purchase of innovative technologies if they can reduce admission costs. The impact of reimbursement mechanism on the medical device prices is thus ambiguous (see above).

Pricing of a medical device is a key element in go/no-go decisions in the medical device manufacturing development phase. Pricing a medical device from the vendor's point of view in the presence of uncertainty about what the reimbursement price threshold will be arises some methodological issues. When assuming a Bayesian prior distribution for this threshold (Girling et al. 2012), an economic modelling can be performed, anticipating thus the future distribution of prices.

76.3.2 Health Technology Assessment (HTA)

HTA is used to solve allocation tasks in health economics and their optimization. In most cases, HTA examines the clinical and cost-effectiveness. HTA is currently a widespread discipline, also thanks to the development of scientific assessment methods, which include clinical epidemiology and health economics. Although most of the devices last more than 1 year, standard costing methods for capital equipment are rarely used (Akpinar 2015).

The device costs are important components of total medical procedure costs. Decision-making in health care gains importance as opportunity costs of erroneous decisions are rising. Opportunity cost from a hospital perspective is a primary consideration. In the medical field, observed prices are often, in reality, regulated prices that diverge from the true opportunity cost of utilized resources (Le Pen and Berdeaux 2000).

The economic significance of the device price is underscored by the ratio of the price of the device to the total cost of all initial medical services that are associated with the device. There are difficulties in documenting unit prices for medical devices: prices are negotiated confidentially across different procurement authorities or are bundled with other devices that make it difficult to disaggregate.

76.3.3 Options Valuation and Pay-for-Performance

The real option method applies financial theory to value investment opportunities in real markets. The real options technique has been upheld as a superior technique to traditional methods of valuation such as net present value (NPV) and payback period in evaluations of new medical device projects (Johal et al. 2008). The option approach here would stand for the possibility to continue the innovative medical device development or to suspend it at previously defined phases.

Pay-for-performance gives financial incentives to clinicians for better health outcomes. The better the outcome is, the higher the reimbursement for the service rendered. This reimbursement model pushes medical device manufacturers to prove their products are worth the costs. The quality of the health service rendered by the medical device in question is being assessed.

Medical device manufacturers therefore have to respond to healthcare providers value-based purchasing initiatives by proving the costs spent on the purchase of their medical device are worth it. Transaction cost economics suggests that long-term relationship between hospitals and medical device vendors involving relationship-specific asset investments can potentially reduce costs and create value for hospitals (Tsen-Ho et al. 2010).

76.3.4 Specificities of the Medical Device Market

On medical device markets, different buyers pay different prices for the same product. This situation is described in economic theory as price discrimination. Healthcare providers (and thus medical device buyers) fight back by establishing "general purchasing organisations", which perform group purchases for several hospitals at once, exercising thus a pressure on medical device prices.

The bargaining power of medical device buyers is equally important. Seller's costs, buyer's willingness-to-pay and the competition level determine the framework of possible prices. It is crucial to know, to which extent the price difference is accountable to buyers different price elasticities, since different healthcare providers employ clinicians with different affinities towards particular medical device brands. Prices are thus influenced by factors such as competition, procurement structures and changing clinical preferences (Brown et al. 2008).

Medical device price trends are described by the experience curve (a relationship where the cost of value added decreases by a fixed percentage each time sales double). Medical devices tend to be vulnerable to confounding factors such as variations in clinical practice. A high value of the experience curve slope suggests that a market is likely to undergo a shake-out at some point in the future, that is, where price competition forces a sharp decline in prices (Brown et al. 2008).

Medical device industry uses a wide range of tactics to determine price, for example premium or prestige pricing, cost-based pricing, cost-plus pricing, demand-based pricing and competition-based pricing. Manufacturers need to consider how they will interact with purchasers and reimbursement organizations not just when setting prices, but throughout the lifetime of the device.

Medical materials are often traded at different prices worldwide; prices differ according to each country's marketplace (Ide et al. 2007). Generally, market prices are business secrets and they are often lower than the reimbursement prices. This is because physicians tend to have an incentive to select products with the largest spread between the reimbursed and purchasing price.

76.4   Conclusion

Experience indicates that many medical device manufacturers struggle to really understand the value of their products and capture a fair portion of the value through value-based pricing (Provines 2010). The most important is the value of better health—longer life as well as improved quality of life. The second benefit is the effect on the patient's financial situation and also on that of the caregivers.

Another definition of value in medical innovation is the costs and consequences of one treatment compared with the costs and consequences of alternative treatments. Value is usually quantifiable and is based on consequences or outcomes. Value is the worth in monetary terms of the economic, clinical, social and technical benefits provided to stakeholders in exchange for the price paid. Lastly, value is always relative to some alternative (Provines 2010).

One of the unique challenges of the medical device industry is the fact that the same innovation may create widely divergent value for each of the stakeholders involved in healthcare delivery. The perceived value of the innovation can, and often does, change. The value-based pricing is a straightforward way of incorporating cost-utility analysis into commercial product valuation for medical devices (Girling et al. 2010).

Acknowledgments This is paper has been prepared under financial support of IGS VŠE F1/7/2016, which the author gratefully acknowledges.

References

Akpinar I (2015) Medical device prices in economic evaluations. Int J Technol Assess Health Care 31(1/2):86–89

Brown A et al (2008) Application of the experience curve to price trends in medical devices: Implications for product development and marketing strategies. J Med Mark 8(3):241–255

De Backer Y, Van der Linden C (2005) Key account management: creating added value in European hospitals. J Med Mark 5(3):219–229

Girling A et al (2010) Early-stage valuation of medical devices: the role of developmental uncertainty. Value Health 13(5):585–591

Girling A, Lilford R, Young T (2012) Pricing of medical devices under coverage uncertainty—a modelling approach. Health Econ 21:1502–1507

Hockel D, Kintner M (2014) Total cost of ownership: the role of clinical engineering. Healthc Fin Manage

Hutchings A (2010) Rewarding innovation? An assessment of the factors that affect price and reimbursement status in Europe. J Med Mark 10(1):83–90

Ide H, Yasunaga H, Imamura T, Ohe K (2007) Price differences between Japan and the US for medical materials and how to reduce them. Health Policy 82:71–77

Johal S, Oliver P, Williams HC (2008) Better decision making for evaluating new medical device projects: a real options approach. J Med Mark 8(2):101–112

Le Pen C, Berdeaux G (2000) Diagnosis related group costs in a regulated environment. Pharmacoeconomics 17(2):115–120

Provines CD (2010) Overcoming organizational barriers to implementing value-based pricing in
    the medical devices & diagnostics industry. J Med Mark 10(1):37–44
Santos I, Tavares J (2013) Additional peculiarities of medical devices that should be considered in
    their development process. Expert Rev Med Devices 10(3):411–420
Tsen-Ho H, Hwan-Yann S, Pin-Pin L (2010) Enhancing value creation of device vendors in the
    medical service industry: a relationship perspective. Serv Ind J 30(11):1787–1801

Chapter 77
Specification of Net Operating Assets for Economic Value Added Calculation from Balance Sheets Reported According to IAS/IFRS

Štěpánka Křečková

Abstract This article deals with information validity of annual accounts of Czech companies compiled according to the principles of International Financial Reporting Standards (IFRS) with respect to specification of Net Operating Assets (NOA) of companies in order to calculate Economic Value Added (EVA). The article further shows results of an annual reports analysis of Czech companies, particularly the financial reports analyses of selected items of assets and liabilities (i.e. Investment Property, Non-current Assets Held for Sale, Leases and Goodwill) and the extent of their compatibility with the requirement of the respective standards IAS/IFRS.

Keywords Economic value added · Net operating assets · International financial reporting standards · Czech accounting standards

77.1 Introduction

Specification of net operating assets (further NOA) for economic value added (further EVA) calculation only from annual accounts published by companies may be very difficult for external analysts. This concerns mainly the internal information hidden to annual accounts external users (e.g. operational unnecessary assets), which is, without internal additional information, basically impossible to determine only on the basis of public financial figures. International financial reporting standards (further IFRS) offer partial solution of this problem, because they include some items of assets and liabilities not reported according to the Czech Accounting Standards (further CAS) at all (e.g. leased assets), or reported under a wider category of assets (e.g. assets held for sale). I performed an empirical research of annual reports

Š. Křečková (✉)
Department of Corporate Finance, University of Economics, Prague,
Nam. W. Churchilla 4, 130 67 Prague, Czech Republic
e-mail: xkres07@vse.cz

© Springer International Publishing AG 2017
D. Procházka (ed.), *New Trends in Finance and Accounting*,
Springer Proceedings in Business and Economics,
DOI 10.1007/978-3-319-49559-0_77

obligatory published by Czech issuers of listed securities, with the goal to check the information value of some specific categories of assets and liabilities reported in the annual reports of the Czech business companies according to the IFRS, with respect to determination of NOA from the prospective of an external financial figures' user. The results of this survey are presented in this article.

77.2 EVA and Net Operating Assets

EVA measure is an analytic tool used for business valuation and management, which was developed in the end of twentieth in consulting firm Stern, Stewart & Co. Positive EVA signalizes net operating profit generated by a core business of a company after covering of cost of total (own and loan) capital invested to the company. For company's shareholders and investors positive EVA means, their investment decision was correct. The higher the EVA, the higher value for shareholders was created.

Composition of EVA measure for period t is shown by the following formula[1]:

$$EVA_t = NOPAT_t - NOA_{t-1} * WACC_t \qquad (77.1)$$

Where NOPAT stands for Net Operating Profit After Taxes, NOA are Net Operating Assets and WACC stands for weighted Average Costs of Capital.

NOA are both long-term and short-term assets used by a company to its core business. Authors of EVA measure (Stern, Stewart and Co) created a complete list of particular accounting figures adjustments, this list is nevertheless their trade secret. Economic literature focused on business valuation and dealing with EVA model, recommend at least following adjustment of accounting data[2]:

- short term and long term non-operating assets, not related to a company's core business are excluded from the balance sheet
- non-interest bearing loan capital is excluded from the balance sheet, as there is a problem with its costs determination when estimating discount rate
- revaluation of assets expressed in their book value, so that the valuation express their real value, i.e. would take into consideration inflation and technical progress
- goodwill should be shown in its original non-amortized value
- costs with long term expected effects should be activated (e.g. marketing costs, costs of employees training, costs related to restructuring)
- financially leased assets include to NOA, in case the assets is uses in core business

[1]Mařík et al. (2007).
[2]Mařík et al. (2011).

Apart from accounting statements compiled according to CAS, the statements compiled according to IAS/IFRS can in some areas help the external users. It concerns the following items:

- Investment property—immovable used primarily as an investment instead for core business, should be excluded from NOA calculation. Whereas investment property are nor recognizable in financial statements according to CAS, they are reported separately according to the IAS/IFRS. Moreover the IAS/IFRS enable their reporting either in purchase cost or in fair value, in which case they are not further depreciated and depreciation therefore have no influence on NOPAT
- Non-current assets held for sale—should also be excluded from NOA, as they are expected to bring benefits when sold, rather than used in core business. They are also reported separately according to the IAS/IFRS, whereas according to the CAS not. Ones they are classified as assets held for sale according to the IAS/IFRS, they are not further depreciated and have therefore no impact on NOPAT
- Finance leases—operating and finance leases are not reported in balance sheet according to CAS, even if the leases assets are used for the company's core business. As opposite IAS/IFRS enables to show finance leases in the balance sheet of lessee. In fact, finance leases are treated according to the IAS/IFRS basically in accordance with EVA model (i.e. assets are shown in balance sheet in fair value with the related finance leases liabilities and the assets are depreciated) and therefore further adjustments of (finance) leases are not necessary.
- Goodwill—EVA concept recommend to include goodwill acquired through acquisition to NOA in its original non-depreciated value. According to the CAS is goodwill depreciated evenly for 5 years, whereas according to the IAS/IFRS goodwill is not depreciated and is only tested on impairment

Other items of financial figures (e.g. some costs activation) have to be adjusted upon NOA calculation regardless CAS of IAS/IFRS accounting statements are uses. These items are not dealt with in this article.

77.3 Annual Accounts of Business Companies' Survey Results

With respect to the items listed in the previous section (i.e. investment property, non-current assets held for sell, finance leases and goodwill) I conducted a research of annual accounts of Czech business companies, reporting according to the IAS/IFRS. Valuation methods used for long-term assets valuation was not part of this survey. Nevertheless it should be mentioned that the IAS/IFRS enable fair value revaluation also some assets that are not revaluated according to the CAS. Using annual accounts compiled according to the IAS/IFRS thus makes NOA

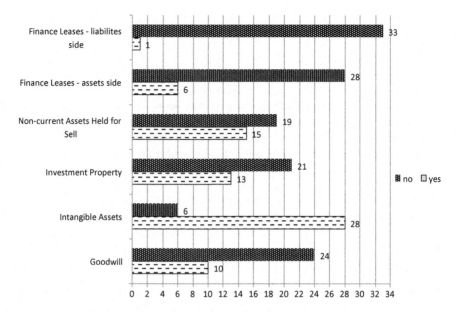

Fig. 77.1 Annual accounts survey results (Own creation based on data from The Central Storage of Regulated Information)

calculation easier when transferring accounting figures to "real/economic" figures upon NOA calculation.

For survey purpose I used The Central Storage of Regulated Information, the application provided by the Czech National Bank. There were **34 annual accounts** of production and trading companies (usually their annual reports) reported in years 2008–2011 included in the survey. The survey does not include banks and financial institutions. The survey is focused mainly on accordance of object items reporting and respective IAS/IFRS.

Frequency of monitored items reported in balance sheet in total sample of 34 companies is shown in the following graph (Fig. 77.1).

77.3.1   Investment Property

Investment property is handled in standard IAS 40.

According to the ISA 40 the accounting unit should choice one of the following models for investment property valuation:

- fair value valuation—investments are not depreciated (fair value reflects also potential value decrease) and possible changes in fair value are reported in profit and loss statement

- cost model—investments are depreciated and measured at depreciated costs less accumulated impairment losses (if any occur). Companies are obliged to public fair value of investment property in notes to the financial statements even when using cost model

Companies reporting investment properties according to the standard IAS 40 publish:

- criteria defined by companies for assets classification as investment property
- received rent from investment properties should be reported separately
- direct operational costs related to investment properties should be also reported separately

Companies using fair value model for investment properties publish also the following:

- net gain and losses from fair value changes
- changes in particular assets categories from investment properties and vice versa, i.e. properties used by companies (are handled in standard IAS 16) or inventories (handled in standard IAS 2)
- increase in investment property coming from acquisition through business combination

Companies using cost model for investment properties publish also the following:

- used depreciation method
- depreciation rates
- gross book value of assets
- accumulated depreciation and accumulated impairment losses at the beginning and end of the accounting period
- schedule of investment properties reported at the beginning and end of the accounting period
- investment property fair value
- should a company not be able to determine investment property fair value then should be relevant reasons explained and interval of possible fair value determined

13 companies out of 34 included in survey reported investment property in 2008–2011. Out of these 13 companies:

- all companies published criteria stated for investment property classification, in most cases by a statement the properties are not used either for core business or as administration premises for company's own use. Detailed property specification (property description, localisation etc.) was reported by one company only

- fair value valuation model was used by 7 (i.e. 54%) companies reporting investment properties, where only 3 stated using appraiser expert services for investment properties revaluation. The rest of companies did not specified the way of fair value determination
- received rent from investment properties was reported separately by 12 (i.e. 92%) companies, usually in notes to the financial statements where single revenues categories were described
- direct operational costs related to investment properties were separately reported only by 3 companies (i.e. 23%), where only 1 company that did not reported these costs separately, stated, the costs related to investment properties are insignificant and their quantification would be more costly than benefit from such information.

77.4 Companies Using Fair Value Model

Out of 7 companies using fair value model for investment properties valuation:

- all published gain and losses of fair value changes, alternatively stated information that difference from revaluation in reported in profit and loss statement
- one company only stated that changes in particular assets categories from investment properties and vice versa did not occurred.

77.5 Companies Using Cost Model

Out of 7 companies using cost model for investment properties valuation:

- all published used depreciation method, depreciation rates, gross book value of assets, accumulated depreciation, accumulated impairment losses and schedule of investment properties at the beginning and end of the accounting period
- only 5 companies (i.e. 8%) published fair value of investment property in notes to the financial statements. Out of companies not publishing fair value only one company stated the reason for that is future usage of this investment property for their core business. Nevertheless any interval of possible fair value was stated (Fig. 77.2).

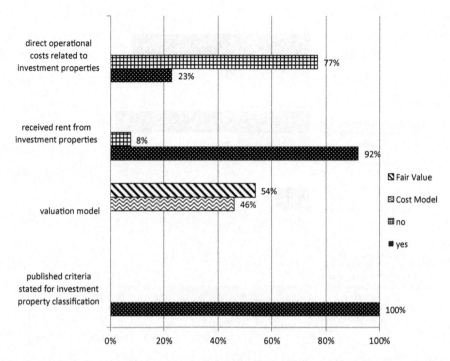

Fig. 77.2 Methods of investment property reporting according to the IAS 40—survey results (Own creation based on data from The Central Storage of Regulated Information)

77.5.1 Non-current Assets Held for Sale and Discontinued Operations

Non-current assets held for sale and discontinued operation are handled by IFRS 5.

Companies reporting non-current assets held for sale according to IFRS 5 should publish:

- description of non-current assets held for sale (of discontinued operation)
- impairment losses and reversals (if any occur) should be recognized in the statement of comprehensive income
- circumstances of sale of non-current assets or their removal from usage
- if applicable, the reportable segment in which the non-current asset is presented

15 companies out of 34 included in survey reported non-current assets held for sale in 2008–2011. No of them reported about discontinued operations. Out of these 15 companies:

- 13 companies (i.e. 87%) stated detailed description of non-current assets held for sale in their annual reports

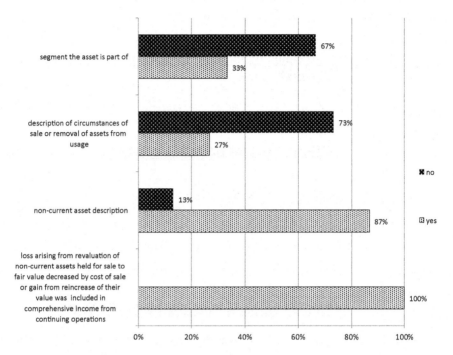

Fig. 77.3 Reporting of non-current assets held for sale according to IFRS 5—survey results (Own creation based on data from The Central Storage of Regulated Information)

- impairment losses and reversals were stated by all companies, nevertheless only in the form of general information within description of accounting methods, by stating these gains/losses are recognized in the statement of comprehensive income
- only 4 companies (i.e. 27%) stated circumstances of sale of non-current assets
- the reportable segment, in which the non-current asset is presented, was reported by 5 companies (i.e. 33%) (Fig. 77.3).

77.5.2 Finance Leases

Leasing is treated in IAS 17 and apart from CAS, according to which accounting units report liabilities from lease contracts only off-balance, regardless it concerns financial or operating leases, the IFRS report financial leases directly in the balance sheet of the lessee.

IAS 17 requires the following information in the financial statements of lessees:

- net book value of leased assets at balance sheet date
- reconciliation between minimum lease payments at balance sheet date and the present value thereof:

  - future payments for next year
  - future payments for 2–5 years
  - future payments above 5 years

- contingent rent to be recognised as an expense
- total future minimum sublease income under non-cancellable subleases
- description of significant leasing arrangements, i.e. contingent rent provisions, renewal or purchase options

11 companies out of 34 included in survey reported finance leases, where 6 out of them reported finance leases separately from other liabilities and 5 companies reported finance leases within other categories of liabilities (long-term and short-term). Only one company reported finance leases separately also on active side. 7 companies (i.e. 64%) out of 34 included in survey reported lease payments as separate item in cash flow statement.

Obligatory requirements on information publishing according to IAS 17 were fulfilled as follows:

- one of the companies included in survey did not publish the net book value of leased assets at balance sheet date
- reconciliation between total minimum lease payments at balance sheet date and their present value and classification of future payments for next year, up to 5 years and above 5 years was not presented in the notes to the financial statements by 1 company
- contingent rent recognised as an expense was not reported by no of the companies include in the survey as well as future minimum sublease income under non-cancellable subleases. Nevertheless 3 companies (i.e. 27%) only explicitly informed in the notes to the financial statements that they do not sublease any leased assets and therefore they do not report the respective items
- description of significant leasing arrangements reported 7 companies (i.e. 64%) (Fig. 77.4).

77.5.3 Goodwill

Issues connected to goodwill are handled in IFRS 3—Business Combinations and further in IAS 38—Intangible Assets that defines intangible assets as "non-monetary assets which are without physical substance and identifiable"[3]

---

[3]Dvořáková (2011).

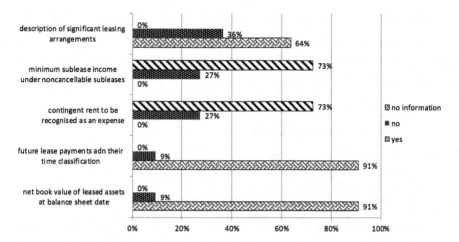

Fig. 77.4 Reporting of finance lease according to IAS 17—survey results (Own creation based on data from The Central Storage of Regulated Information)

As previously mentioned the NOA calculation should include only goodwill acquired within a business acquisition as an intangible asset. Internally generated goodwill should not be recognized as an asset and included in NOA, which is a recommendation in line with IAS 38 requirements that internally generated goodwill does not recognize as an asset as it is not separable and does not arise from contractual or other legal rights and it cannot be reliable measured in the cost.

10 companies out of 34 included in survey reported about goodwill in 2008–2011, out of which:

- 50% of companies evidenced goodwill as separate item of balance sheet. The second half of the companies reported total sum of intangible asset in their balance sheets, which was further categorized as a goodwill and other intangible assets in the notes to the financial statements
- all companies, apart from one, stated that this asset is not depreciated. One company only did not stated this information in the notes to the financial statements and it was not recognizable from the financial statements that this asset it not depreciated
- 8 companies (i.e. 80%) out of 10 reporting about goodwill, stated information in the notes to the financial statements explaining that goodwill is regularly tested for impairment. 2 companies did not published this information at all (Fig. 77.5).

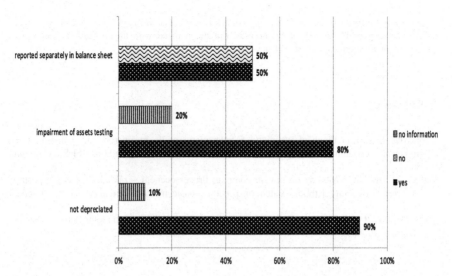

Fig. 77.5 Reporting of goodwill—survey results (Own creation based on data from The Central Storage of Regulated Information)

77.6 Conclusion

The survey results show that the Czech business companies are reporting the surveyed categories of assets in line with IFRS, nevertheless at the same time they do not always fulfil all requirements demanded by IAS/IFRS. This is rather surprising information considering the survey included annual reports audited by reputable auditing companies. On the other hand it should be emphasized there was minimum of business companies not fulfilling all IAS/IFRS requirements in each surveyed asset's category. For external users of financial statements is, in case of investment property and assets held for sell, positive, that in line with IAS/IFRS requirements are reported separately from other assets categories (e.g. reported according to IAS 16—Property, Plant and Equipment) and they are easily recognisable from balance sheets compiled according to the IAS/IFRS. Financially leased assets are basically not reported as a separate asset category, nevertheless are activated in line with the IAS/IFRS requirements and their value is separately published in the notes to the financial statements together with other material matters. Liabilities related to finance leas are often reported separately in liabilities side of balance sheet. Also goodwill in not always reported as a separate item and is included in intangible assets of the company. Particular value of goodwill is then further expressed in the notes to the financial statement in non-depreciated value.

Generally using financial statements complied in line with the IAS/IFRS can help valuers to identify net operating assets of a company, even though it is necessary to check the reliability and relevance of published data in additional information stated in the notes to the financial statements.

Acknowledgments This paper was prepared within the research projects of Faculty of Finance and Accounting of University of Economics, Prague, realized with the institutional support of University of Economics, No. IP100040.

References

Dvořáková D (2011) Finanční účetnictví a výkaznictví podle mezinárodních standardů IFRS (Financial accounting and reporting according to international standards IFRS), Computer Press

Mařík M et al (2007) Metody oceňování podniku: Proces ocenění – základní metody a postupy (Business valuation methods: Valuation process—basic methods and procedures. Ekopress, Praha

Mařík M et al (2011) Metody oceňování podniku pro pokročilé (Valuation methods for advanced). Ekopress, Praha

Chapter 78
Agricultural Land Valuation and Capitalization Ratio

Guler Yalcin

Abstract The valuation of agricultural land shall be based on the streams of income derived from the land according to Turkish law. Thus, valuation commissions and experts determine the values by using the income method. However, various difficulties are experienced in the implementation of the income method and it is not always possible to determine a realistic value. In this article, firstly basic valuation methods are mentioned and explained briefly. Then the principles for the implementation of the income method are examined, the difficulties and disputes are focused, and some suggestions are presented. When the land valuation problems are analyzed, the following titles can be listed: lack of practical experience of experts, the deficiencies and inconsistencies of institutional/organizational data, gaps and shortcomings in legal procedures. Also there is not any system which consists of all agricultural information or valuation information in Turkey. Such a system should be established, and this system should be configured in an institutional/organizational framework.

Keywords Agriculture · Economics · Valuation · Income approach

78.1 Introduction

Land administration plays an important role in the infrastructure for sustainable development. Sustainable development means that it effectively incorporates economic, social, political, conservation and resource management factors in decision making for development. The four land administration functions are different in their professional focus: land tenure (security and transferring land rights), land value (valuation and taxation of land), land use (planning and control of the use of

G. Yalcin (✉)
Faculty of Engineering, Department of Geomatic Engineering,
Korkut Ata University, 80000 Osmaniye, Turkey
e-mail: guleryalcin@osmaniye.edu.tr

© Springer International Publishing AG 2017
D. Procházka (ed.), *New Trends in Finance and Accounting*,
Springer Proceedings in Business and Economics,
DOI 10.1007/978-3-319-49559-0_78

land) and land development (implementing utilities, infrastructure and construction planning). The four functions interact with each other (Enemark 2012).

Land with its components named as "real estate" has some direct or indirect processes which concern private individuals/companies and public institutions in Turkey as in all over the world. Real estate values have a significant role on the basis of a sustainable land management. Value is defined as the total benefit, usage value and material amount that can be taken in return to the property. Real estates in the capital market are significant in terms of creating economic resources. Also, real estate value is one of the main issues in rural and urban land arrangements, urban renewal and expropriation applications (Candas and Yomralioglu 2014).

The finance and economic concept of the lands is one of three dimensions of sustainable development—economic, social and environmental. In this article, real estates are considered in the view of their economic value. Hence, basic three approaches to determine real estate value are explained briefly.

Real estate valuation is one of the subjects of economics for many years. One of the aims of many countries in twentieth century is to reflect the market, income and cost values to the tax, purchase–sale and other processes. Especially after 1929–1931 that is the term of economic crisis in the world, land valuation has become a professional occupation.

78.2   Basic Three Methods for Land Valuation

"Real estate appraisal," "property valuation" or "land valuation" arises from the opinion of the value for real property. Real estate transactions often require appraisals, and every property is unique with its specifications. In general real estate appraisal is the prediction of possible value on that day of real property appraisal, real property project or rights and benefits of the real property with the criteria of independence and objectiveness (Aclar and Cagdas 2002: 3). For appraisal process, there are three traditional methods such as *sales comparison approach method, cost approach method and income approach method* although many methods are used (Kokturk and Kokturk 2011: 723–862; Aclar and Cagdas 2002: 160; Hepsen 2014: 2; Linne et al. 2000; Gloudemans 1999; Kontrimas and Verikas 2011: 443).

According to sales comparison approach, the value is determined by comparing the object with the other objects sold in the market. For comparing the properties, the characteristics and attributes of two properties (the property which is chosen for comparing and the property which is to be valuated) must be the same. Dimensions of the parcel, the depth of the building, plan, urban functions, construction conditions, size, geology, topography, sociocultural reinforcements, transportation possibilities, all rights and restrictions that belong to it, type–style–design–size–age–actual situation of the buildings are features of the properties with building. If there are different characteristics or attributes between two compared properties, these differences are determined as monetary. Sales prices may be used to determine the values of the real estates via comparison method. Urban area and reconstruction (zoning) data are the main factors of the value. Therefore, if the comparison approach is selected to determine the land value, the similar lands and the lands which will be valuated must be in the same region with the same characters, and also the reconstruction data must be similar. The value is adjusted according to the differences, because the real estates have the differences (Aclar and Cagdas 2002: 161). This method is suitable for clear land. It has the advantages with quick and simple computations, reflection of the market price (Kontrimas and Verikas 2011).

The income approach is based on the value that is the present worth of future and suitable for objects generating income such as rental, service or production incomes. It is evaluated by discounting the cash flows generated by the object. Finally economic benefit from the real estate is estimated with this quite simple approach. The basic criterion is net income (revenue) (income from buildings, lands, products and services). In this valuation view, some interest rates are used such as capitalization ratio, debt coverage ratio and loan-to-value ratio. Also gross rent multiplier and discounted cash flow method are two other methods.

The cost approach method is generally used for hotel, factory, industrial sites, office buildings, administrative buildings, houses with gardens or lands with buildings. Main rule is based on approaching to the exact value. The exact value is cost amount on the valuation date of the real estate. It is composed of building value, outside facility value, private enterprises equipment and land value. In the cost approach, the value is determined by total cost value of land and others on it minus value-reducing effects of physical, functional and environmental factors. Briefly, the value of the object is determined by construction costs minus depreciation.

As a result, comparison method is used for building land, income method is for land, and cost method is for buildings.

78.3 Agricultural Land Valuation

Income approach is one of the most widely used methods for agricultural land valuation. This method is named as "the method for capitalization of income," "the method of usage value" and "analytical method" (Mulayim 2008). According to the income approach, a land value is determined by amassing all income that will be received in future from the land on the valuation date. In technical words, it has been put forward by the capitalization of the average land income with the interest rate in force (Rehber 1984). The basis for income approach is property income which is being evaluated. Therefore, it is necessary to have a steady income from the property which is being evaluated for the implementation of the method. Income approach method is used especially for the valuation of the lands. The income concerned is the net income of the soil or the net lease of the land (Gulten 2001). The following formula is generally used in the valuation of agricultural land with income method:

$$D = \frac{R}{f} \qquad (78.1)$$

where

D land value,
R net income of the land (land/soil annuity),
f capitalization ratio.

To apply this method as seen from the formula, the estimation of the income to be generated in the future of agricultural land which is being evaluated and the determination of an appropriate capitalization ratio are necessary.

The net income for the land is calculated by the subtraction of all cost factors (except land lease) from gross production value. The production costs are listed as soil preparation costs (e.g., sürüm), maintenance costs (e.g., fertilizing, hoeing, watering), harvesting–threshing costs, current expenditures (e.g., seed, fertilizer, pesticides, water), marketing expenses (e.g., bagging, shipping), capital interest (revolving funds or business capital interest) and administrative expenses (administration fee or general administrative expenses). However, the calculation of the net income varies whether the income is annual or periodic (Mulayim 2008; Engindeniz et al. 2015). Obtained income at the end of each year is called as "annual income." For example, if all annual income (for "n" years with "s" fixed income at the end of each year) is accumulated, the following formula is used:

$$S_0 = \frac{s}{f} \qquad (78.2)$$

This is "capitalization formula for annual fixed income that will be obtained in the coming years." It has been used in the valuation of a farm land having "s" income for each year.

The obtained income at the end of each "n" year (each period) is called as "periodical income." For example, if all periodical income at the end of "t" period is accumulated (t: period number, p: fixed income with equal amounts at the end of the period), "capitalization formula for periodical fixed income" is derived:

$$P_0 = p \cdot \frac{1}{(q_n - 1)} \qquad (78.3)$$

According to the income approach, the capitalization ratio is the interest rate of the capital invested on land. When sales prices of a sufficient number of land and their net income are known, capitalization ratio can be determined:

$$f = \frac{R_1 + R_2 + R_3 + \ldots + R_n}{D_1 + D_2 + D_3 + \ldots + D_n} \qquad (78.4)$$

f capitalization ratio
R net income
D sales prices

78.4 Problems on Determination of the Agricultural Land Values by Using Income Approach

Because the product type, the product alternation arrangement (münavebe) and capitalization ratio change for the irrigated or non-irrigated lands, the land (whether it is irrigable/non-irrigable) must be determined for agricultural land valuation. For irrigable lands, net income and land value are much higher. In this step the problem is on which conditions the land is acceptable as an irrigable land. Firstly it should be investigated whether there is a water supply (e.g., artesian, well) on the land. Apart from this, it should be examined whether the land is irrigated by cooperatives or by irrigation channels belonging to General Directorate of State Hydraulic Works (GDSHW). One of the most debated issues is in which certain situations the lands on the edge of the creek will be considered as irrigable lands. According to the Supreme Court decisions, experts put forth how much possibility for irrigated agriculture the land has, by considering the creek flow in summer/winter months. The other topic of discussion is: If an owner having a water supply irrigates his other land (this land does not have any water supply) with this supply, how this land having no water supply but irrigated by his owner will be evaluated. In fact GDSHW has the registration whose parcels have the artesian or well. However, investigations on the lands are needed because a large number of unregistered and illegal water supplies are used.

To determine the value according to the income approach, the first aim is to know which products are cultivated. Then annual average net income is determined. Information about products grown on irrigated/non-irrigated lands is primarily derived from Provincial/District Directorate of Agriculture. In addition, valuation commissions and experts make some determinations during the field inspection. For example; in non-irrigated conditions melons, chickpeas and tobacco products provide higher income than the wheat and barley do; in irrigated conditions, tomato, silage corn and pepper provide higher net income than cotton and wheat do. Therefore, it is observed that experts and commissions prefer the product patterns that are in local conditions and similar to the precedent land value. Here the other problem is which product will be used for the valuation if the land is not used for agricultural production and it is in the idle state.

Another issue to be considered is the product alternation arrangement. This information is firstly obtained from Provincial/District Directorate of Agriculture. In addition the experts and commissions get some determinations from the field. However, the approach in the determination of the alternation arrangement is in the direction based upon the order that results close to the precedent land value as the product selection. Also, it is observed that the information obtained from Directorate is occasionally inconsistent. The products which are legally limited or not produced in the region or greatly reduced in time can be presented as if they were common production form.

While calculating the net income production costs, the variable costs, land lease, interest provision of variable expenses and management provision (general administrative expenses) are added. Land lease has not been taken into account as a cost element because the provision of land use (or the annuity that can be derived from the land) is tried to be determined. These cost elements should be considered (Tanrıvermiş et al. 2008a, b).

The land value changes with capitalization ratio. Applying the same capitalization ratio in every region causes the different calculation of the land value from the real value. Therefore, objective results cannot be obtained.

Some Provincial/District Directorates of Agriculture do not have available data for that land valuation period. In application, experts often make calculations based on the previous year's data values, and then, they increase the value by using Wholesale Price Index (or Producer Price Index). However, instead of that, the valuation process should be calculated with the previous year's product and the calculated values of the products on the land should be added (Tanrıvermiş et al. 2011).

The commissions appraise the fruit orchards by using periodical income approach. Experts appraise them on annual net income based on the institutions' data according to the Supreme Court decisions. The Supreme Court says that land with trees is valuated and also the value of the tree is not added. In fact, when calculating the annual net income, the same value is determined for the fruit orchards at different ages. But it is expected that the orchards which have just begun to bear fruits or are nearly at the end of their economic life have lower value. On the other hand, for example, if net income of the annual products (e.g., cotton, wheat) is used to valuate, the result is the simple (bare) value of the land. For the annual net income for orchards, whether this value is for the simple land or land with tree is controversial.

If the orchard has different kinds of fruit trees, the valuation method is controversial again. Sometimes the tree type that makes up the majority is basic, and sometimes the simple land value is calculated and the trees' values are added to it.

Marketing of the fruits is also an important point. Some fruits have the extra features such as processing and the marketing. It provides an extra value. For instance, olive oil is obtained from olives, and grape and fig are dried. The approach here is that olive without processing, wet grapes and wet figs are bought and sold.

Windmills and greenhouses on the agricultural lands are the elements that are the subject of debate in terms of valuation.

Easement on the agricultural lands (e.g., for electric lines, natural gas, oil, water pipelines) causes depreciation of the land. According to the Supreme Court decisions, this depreciation is compensated up to maximum rate of 35%. The determination of the amount and the method of the depreciation is another discussion topic. In the application, firstly some experts divide the total area by the easement area and a ratio is obtained. This ratio is multiplied by the depreciation ratio. Then the total land value determined by income approach is proportioned with the ratio obtained by multiplication. Finally the value depreciation (price to be paid to land owner) is calculated (Engindeniz et al. 2015).

78.5 Conclusion

There is not a real estate valuation system in Turkey. However, various laws and related regulations exist in Turkey requiring the knowledge and monitoring of real estate values such as Expropriation Law, Real Estate Tax, Tax Procedure Law, Building Land Office, Courts, Cadastre Law and Capital Market Law. Also many different organizations/institutions (such as General Directorate of Land Registry and Cadastre, Capital Market Board, Governorates, Municipalities, Housing Development Administration, Special Provincial Administration, General Directorate of Highways and Revenue Administration) carry out validation studies.

When the land valuation problems are analyzed, the following titles can be listed: lack of practical experience of experts, the deficiencies and inconsistencies of institutional/organizational data, gaps and shortcomings in legal procedures. Also there is not any system which consists of all agricultural information or valuation information in Turkey. Such a system should be established, and this system should be configured in an institutional/organizational framework.

To perform the valuation correctly and to interpret the results healthily, it is necessary to know the purpose of the valuation. Valuation works are carried out for different purposes (nationalization, expropriation, insurance, taxation). Therefore, it must first set out valuation objectives.

In valuation process, commissions and experts have an important role. So, the people who know the region well, who have technical and economic agricultural information should be assigned as expert.

To make an accurate valuation, the determination of the capitalization ratio belonging to the region is important. However, the capitalization may change from region to region, even from land to land. Because of that reason, to determine this ratio with scientific studies will provide a significant contribution.

For net income approach, the information is obtained from Provincial/District Directorates of Agriculture. However, some valuations cannot be made because the agriculture companies do not have the registration for necessary data. So, the producers at agriculture companies should be encouraged to keep records deliberately. Indeed, Ministry of Food, Agriculture and Livestock has launched a variety of applications on this way.

To determine yield, price and cost data belonging to the products of the region correctly, special sub-units should be created, and trained staff and automation should be worked.

It seems to benefit from geographic information system (GIS) technology in the land valuation studies in different countries of the world. Valuation processes take place easily and quickly with valuation maps obtained by using GIS. On the other hand, it provides the possibility to obtain more objective and accurate results; the problem of the value differences in the same region can be resolved. Studies on the use of GIS in land valuation in Turkey are mostly done by Surveying/ Geomatics/Geodesy and Photogrammetry Engineers. Land valuation is one of the main working branches/areas/subjects of the Agricultural Economists. To achieve the correct results, Geomatics Engineers and Agricultural Economists should make common studies.

References

Aclar A, Cagdas V (2002) Taşınmaz (Gayrimenkul) Değerlemesi. TMMOB Harita Kadastro Mühendisleri Odası, Ankara

Candas E, Yomralioglu T (2014) Land valuation problems in Turkey. FIG Congress, Kuala Lumpur, Malaysia, 16–21 June 2014

Enemark S (2012) Sustainable land governance. FIG Working Week, Rome, Italy, 6–10 May 2012

Engindeniz S, Basaran C, Susam B (2015) Tarım Arazilerinin Kamulaştırma Bedellerinin Saptanmasında Gelir Yönteminin Uygulanmasıyla İlgili Anlaşmazlıklar. Ankara: TMMOB Harita ve Kadastro Mühendisleri Odası, 15. Türkiye Harita Bilimsel ve Teknik Kurultayı, 25–28 Mar 2015

Gloudemans RJ (1999) Mass appraisal of real property. International Association of Assessing Officers, Chicago

Gulten Ş (2001) Kıymet takdirinde gelir ve piyasa değeri yöntemleri (bilirkişilik). Atatürk Üniversitesi Ziraat Fakültesi Ders Notları Yayın No:77, Erzurum

Hepsen A (2014) Gayrimenkul Değerleme Esasları. Semaye Piyasası Lisanslama Sicil ve Eğitim Kuruluşu A.Ş. Online: http://www.spl.com.tr/Upload/files/1014.pdf, 18 Feb 2016

Kokturk E, Kokturk E (2011) Taşınmaz Değerlemesi. NETCOPY, Istanbul (Last press, Seckin Yayıncılık, NETCOPY Istanbul, 2015)

Kontrimas V, Verikas A (2011) The mass appraisal of the real estate by computational intelligence. Appl Soft Comput 11:443–448

Linne MR, Kane SM, Dell G (2000) A guide to appraisal valuation modeling. Appraisal Institute

Mulayim ZG (2008) Tarımsal Değer Biçme (Genel-Özel-Yasal). Yetkin yayınları, Ankara

Rehber E (1984) Tarımsal arazi kıymetlerinin takdiri üzerine bir araştırma. Ankara Üniversitesi Ziraat Fakültesi Yayın No:894, Ankara

Tanrıvermiş H, Akipek Ş, Bayramin İ, Gün AS, Aliefendioğlu Y (2008a) Ermenek Barajı ve Hidroelektrik Santrali Projesi Kamulaştırma Alanındaki arazilerin gelirleri, kapitalizasyon oranları ve birim arazi değerlerinin araştırılması. A.Ü. Fen Bilimleri Enstitüsü Taşınmaz Geliştirme Anabilim Dalı Yayın No:1, Ankara

Tanrıvermiş H, Akipek Ş, Bayramin İ, Gün AS, Aliefendioğlu Y (2008b) Bağbaşı Barajı ve Hidroelektrik Santrali ve Mavi Tünel Projesi kamulaştırma alanındaki arazilerin gelirleri, kapitalizasyon oranları ve birim arazi değerlerinin araştırılması. A.Ü. Fen Bilimleri Enstitüsü Taşınmaz Geliştirme Anabilim Dalı Yayın No:2, Ankara

Tanrıvermiş H, Aliefendioğlu Y, Demirci R, Arslan M (2011) Kandıra Gıda İhtisas Organize Sanayi Bölgesi kamulaştırma alanında arazi gelirleri, kapitalizasyon oranı, arazi değerleri ve kamulaştırma bedellerinin analizi. A.Ü. Fen Bilimleri Enstitüsü Taşınmaz Geliştirme Anabilim Dalı Yayın No:8, Ankara

CPSIA information can be obtained
at www.ICGtesting.com
Printed in the USA
LVOW02*0504240717
542326LV00001BA/3/P